HEALTH CARE ADMINISTRATION

Principles, Practices, Structure, and Delivery

Second Edition

Edited by
Lawrence F. Wolper, MBA
President
L. Wolper, Inc.
Great Neck, New York

AN ASPEN PUBLICATION®
Aspen Publishers, Inc.
Gaithersburg, Maryland
1995

Library of Congress Cataloging-in-Publication Data

Wolper, Lawrence F.
Health care administration : principles, practices, structure, and
delivery / Lawrence F. Wolper.—2nd ed.
p.   cm.
Earlier ed. has main entry under title.
Includes bibliographical references and index.
ISBN 0-8342-0598-X
1. Hospitals—Administration. 2. Health services administration.
I. Title.
RA971.H384   1994
362.1′068—dc20
94-22461
CIP

Aspen Publishers, Inc., grants permission for photocopying for limited personal
or internal use. This consent does not extend to other kinds of copying, such as
copying for general distribution, for advertising or promotional purposes, for
creating new collective works, or for resale. For information, address Aspen
Publishers, Inc., Permissions Department, 200 Orchard Ridge Drive, Suite 200,
Gaithersburg, Maryland 20878.

The dedication is quoted from *Camelot*, book and lyrics by Alan Jay Lerner,
music by Frederick Loewe, Random House, New York.

Editorial Resources: Jane Colilla
Library of Congress Catalog Card Number: 94-22461
ISBN: 0-8342-0598-X

Printed in the United States of America

2   3   4   5

To Emily and Lisa

The rain may never fall till after sundown.
By eight the morning fog must disappear.
In short, there's simply not
A more congenial spot
For happ'ly-ever-aftering than here
In Camelot.

Table of Contents

About the Author/Editor

LAWRENCE F. WOLPER, MBA, is President of L. Wolper, Inc., in Great Neck, New York, and Frosch/Wolper Health Care Consultants, Inc., in Fort Lauderdale, Florida. Both are full-service consulting firms specializing in strategic planning and marketing, managed care, the implementation of provider and integrated networks, and all aspects of physician group practice management. The firms have implemented multi-county provider networks and have negotiated managed care contracts on their behalf. In addition, L. Wolper, Inc., has extensive experience in managing large physician group practices and ambulatory surgery centers.

Mr. Wolper has over 15 years of consulting experience and represents major group practices, individual practice associations, management services organizations, integrated networks, national health care companies, and hospitals. Prior to founding his firm in 1987, he was a partner in KPMG Peat Marwick, with New York area and national responsibility for physician practice matters and ambulatory care. At that time, he was involved in the development of large group practices and provider networks, one of which, located in the Midwest, is one of the most successful vertically integrated systems in the country. Before his partnership in Peat Marwick, he was a consulting partner with Ingram, Weitzman, Mertens & Co., a large regional health care accounting and consulting firm.

Mr. Wolper is one of a number of consultants and health care attorneys to be accepted into the American Medical Association's Doctors Advisory Network™, a consortium of professionals with demonstrated expertise in practice management and managed care. He has published frequently on a variety of topics, including managed care, operational auditing, planning, cost containment, and practice management, in journals such as *Administrative Ophthalmology*, the *Journal of the Medical Group Management Association*, the *Journal of the Hospital Financial Management Association*, *Hospital Progress*, *Hospitals* (the journal of the American Hospital Association), and *Topics in Health Care Financing*. He is on the editorial review board of *Topics in Health Care Financing*.

Mr. Wolper received an MBA in Health Care Administration from Bernard Baruch College–Mount Sinai School of Medicine and a BA in Advertising/Marketing from Hofstra University. He was a Robert Wood Johnson Foundation Fellow in HMO Management at the Wharton School, University of Pennsylvania and an Association of University Programs in Hospital Administration Fellow studying the British national health system at the Kings Fund College of Hospital Management in London, England.

Contributors

William J. Aseltyne, JD
Assistant General Counsel
California Pacific Medical Center
San Francisco, California

Kevin W. Barr, MBA
Senior Vice President
Bon Secours—St. Mary's Health Corporation
Executive Director
Virginia HealthSource, Inc.
Richmond, Virginia

Karl G. Bartscht, MSE, FAAHC
Chief Executive Officer
The Chi Group, Inc.
Ann Arbor, Michigan

Sara Anne Beazley, MA
Staff Associate
American Hospital Association Resource Center
American Hospital Association
Chicago, Illinois

Lois J. Bittle, RN, MPA
President
Bittle and Associates, Inc.
Baltimore, Maryland

John D. Blair, PhD
Professor of Management and Director
The MBA Program in Health Organization Management
Texas Tech University
Lubbock, Texas

M. Lawrence Bonham, MD
Pediatric Associates
Los Gatos, California

Charles L. Breindel, PhD
Professor
Associate Chair and Director of Masters Program
Department of Health Administration
Virginia Commonwealth University
Medical College of Virginia Campus
Richmond, Virginia

Barbara J. Brown, RN, EdD, FAAN, FNAP, CNAA
Editor, Nursing Administration Quarterly
Consultant, Health Care Administration
Fraser, Colorado

Montague Brown, MBA, DrPH, JD
Chairman
Strategic Management Services, Inc.
Washington, DC

Paul J. Brzozowski, MPA
Vice President
Applied Management Systems, Inc.
Burlington, Massachusetts

Roberta N. Clarke, DBA
Associate Professor
Health Care Management Program
Boston University
Boston, Massachusetts

Russell C. Coile, Jr.
President
Health Forecasting Group
Santa Clarita, California

Mark A. Covaleski, PhD
Professor of Health Care Financial Management
University of Wisconsin—Madison
Madison, Wisconsin

Derek F. Covert, JD, CPA
Associate General Counsel
Catholic Healthcare West
San Francisco, California

Michael J. Dalton
KPMG Peat Marwick
White Plains, New York

Paul R. DeMuro, CPA, MBA, JD
Partner
Latham & Watkins
Los Angeles and San Francisco, California

Sheldon I. Dorenfest, MBA, CPA
President
Sheldon I. Dorenfest & Associates, Ltd.
Chicago, Illinois

J. D. Epstein, JD
Vinson & Elkins LLP
Houston, Texas

Eloise C. Foster, MLN
Director
American Hospital Association Resource Center
American Hospital Association
Chicago, Illinois

Myron D. Fottler, PhD
Professor and Director
PhD Program in Administration–Health Services
University of Alabama at Birmingham
Birmingham, Alabama

Anne Carbery Fox, MLS
Senior Staff Specialist
American Hospital Association Resource Center
American Hospital Association
National Library of Medicine
Bethesda, Maryland

Raleigh J. Hamilton, MBA
CEO and Administrator
MRI Center of Hampton Roads
Norfolk, Virginia

Susan Feigin Harris, JD
Vice President
Legal and Administration
Texas Medical Center
Houston, Texas

Beverly Henry, RN, PhD, FAAN
Professor and Head
Department of Administrative Studies in Nursing
College of Nursing
University of Illinois at Chicago
Chicago, Illinois

James E. Hosking, MBA, FAAHC
Partner
Coopers & Lybrand/Herman Smith Associates
Chicago, Illinois

Michael J. Kelley, MBA
Administrator
Retina Consultants of Southwest Florida
Fort Myers, Florida

Peter R. Kongstvedt, MD, FACP
Ernst & Young
Washington, DC

Anthony J. Kubica, MS, MBA
Senior Management Consultant
Superior Consultant Company, Inc.
Farmington Hills, Michigan

Janice M. Kurth, MBA

Frederick C. Lee, MHA

Joan Gratto Liebler, RRA, MPA
Professor and Chair
Department of Health Information Management
Temple University
Philadelphia, Pennsylvania

Charles D. Mahoney, MS, RPh
Director of Pharmacy
Rhode Island Hospital
Providence, Rhode Island

Donna Malvey, MHSA
PhD Candidate in Administration–Health Services
University of Alabama at Birmingham
Birmingham, Alabama

V. James McLarney, MHA
American Hospital Association
Chicago, Illinois

Norman Metzger, MEd
Edmond A. Guggenheim Professor Emeritus
Mount Sinai School of Medicine
New York, New York

Elizabeth W. Michael, MBA, RN
PhD Candidate
Area of Management
College of Business Administration
Texas Tech University
Lubbock, Texas

Ellen A. Moloney, MBA
Manager
Applied Management Systems, Inc.
Burlington, Massachusetts

Martin Paris, MD, MPH

James A. Patton, PhD
Professor of Radiology and Radiological Sciences
Administrator for Radiology Academic Affairs
Vanderbilt University
Nashville, Tennessee

Jesus J. Peña, MPA, JD

Gerald R. Peters, JD
Partner
Latham & Watkins
San Francisco, California

Ruby P. Puckett, MA, RD, LD
Director of Food and Nutrition Services
Shands Hospital at the University of Florida
Gainesville, Florida

Timothy M. Rotarius, MBA
PhD Candidate
Project Coordinator, Medical Group Strategy Research
     Network
Institute for Management and Leadership Research
Texas Tech University
Lubbock, Texas

Grant T. Savage, PhD
The MBA Program in Health Organization Management
Area of Management
College of Business Administration
Texas Tech University
Lubbock, Texas

William L. Scheyer, CPHM
City Administrator
City of Erlanger
Erlanger, Kentucky

Debra J. Schnebel, JD
Partner
Gardner, Carton, & Douglas
Chicago, Illinois, and Washington, D.C.

Loreen A. Schneider, JD
Garfunkel, Wild, and Travis
Great Neck, New York

Karolyn B. Shepherd, MBA(HOM)
Vice President of Development
King's Daughter Clinic
Temple, Texas

Geoffrey B. Shields, JD
Partner
Gardner, Carton, & Douglas
Chicago, Illinois, and Washington, D.C.

Sture V. Sigfred, Jr., MD
Vice Chairman of Diagnostic Radiology
Eastern Virginia Medical School
Norfolk, Virginia

I. Donald Snook, Jr.
President and CEO
Presbyterian Medical Center of Philadelphia
Philadelphia, Pennsylvania

Norton L. Travis, JD
Garfunkel, Wild, and Travis
Great Neck, New York

Robert A. Waterman, JD
Partner
Latham & Watkins
San Francisco, California

Carlton J. Whitehead, PhD
Professor and Coordinator
Area of Management
Texas Tech University
Lubbock, Texas

E. Gordon Whyte, MHA, PhD
Vice Chairman and Master Programs Director
Department of Health Systems Management
School of Public Health and Tropical Medicine
Tulane University Medical Center
New Orleans, Louisiana

John Woerly, RRA, MSA, AAM
Methodist Medical Center of Illinois
Peoria, Illinois

Lawrence F. Wolper, MBA
President
L. Wolper, Inc.
Great Neck, New York

Preface

The idea for the first edition of this book occurred to me when I was completing my master's degree in business and health care administration. I came across a text entitled *Hospital Organization and Management* by Dr. Malcolm Thomas MacEachern. A well-respected text, literally found on every administrator's bookshelf, it was, at that time, well out of touch with changes that had occurred in the industry since its first printing in 1935 and the couple of updates thereafter. At that time, I decided that I would like to produce a book that would encompass nearly all the relevant aspects of the health care industry.

Many years after I was graduated, the first edition of this text was published. The text included a section on departmental operations as well as one encompassing the functional/technical areas in the industry, such as information systems, management engineering, and marketing. I was pleased when, in 1993, Aspen Publishers asked if I would be interested in updating the text. By that time, as a result of major regulatory, delivery system, and technological changes, a number of chapters required updating. In addition, health care reform necessitated the inclusion of several entirely new chapters on topics such as managed care, ambulatory care, physician practice, and international health care systems. In light of the fact that many graduate programs in health care administration utilize the book, the revisions in this edition add more technical detail, giving the student a complete understanding of information systems, inpatient and outpatient Medicare reimbursement, physician practice, ambulatory care, and other topics. The book is organized into three parts as follows.

Part I, on the organization of the hospital, contains chapters that describe the major operating aspects of most key clinical and nonclinical hospital departments. The chapters are more detailed than those in the first edition with regard to processes and operating procedures in each departmental area. In addition, there are two detailed chapters on Medicare inpatient and outpatient reimbursement, neither of which were in the first edition.

Part II, on the operational and functional aspects of the health care industry, covers developments that have emerged in these areas over the past two decades. Unlike the topics of chapters in Part I, which are more hospital related, the topics in this section, while germane to hospitals, also apply generally to other provider organizations, such as nursing homes, ambulatory care centers, and physician practices. This section encompasses topics such as strategic planning, stakeholder management, human resources management, management accounting, marketing health services, and financing.

Part III, on health care provider and delivery systems, is an entirely new section devoted to topics that relate to delivery system issues. It is contemporary in that it includes chapters on cost containment, managed care, physician practice, and ambulatory care. However, it also is oriented to the past and future, including chapters on multiprovider systems, the legal structure of hospitals and delivery systems, business combinations, and a comprehensive review of international health care systems.

The book concludes with an epilogue containing six essays written by selected authors, the theme of which is, where will the industry be in the future?

This revised edition is more comprehensive and technical than the first, in many ways paralleling changes in the industry. Since MacEachern, there have been many changes in the financing and delivery of health care, but none that will be comparable to that which the industry is, and will be, experiencing. As stated in the first edition of this text several years ago, the success of health care reform in the long term will continue to be a function of expert and creative management. Exemplary of this will be a willingness to abandon old paradigms, a drive to be creative even when some goals will not materialize, and an ability to understand and manage the broader range of stakeholders in an integrating industry.

These goals may not be achievable in the next few years and may require a decade or more to realize benefits fully. It is my hope that, in our drive to reduce health care expenditures and restructure a vibrant industry, we do not move so far and fast along the continuum that the high quality of care always associated with our system will be subordinated to rationing and an overzealous pursuit of the lowest cost and highest profit. In addition to cost containment and universal insurance, we owe future generations the highest quality and most compassionate medicine possible.

Acknowledgments

There are many to thank for a book of this nature. To have found over 30 authors with a desire to write chapters for the first book had to be considered luck. Therefore, I am not certain how to describe how fortunate I have been in soliciting their interest in revising their chapters as well as in obtaining the participation of a number of new authors. What is certain is that I greatly appreciate their interest, cooperation, and timeliness in submitting outlines, and one or more chapter drafts, over the last year or so. Because of their stature, each of these professionals has been extremely busy as a result of industry reform, not to mention that many wrote on topics that have been changing rapidly. This notwithstanding, the overall quality of their research and writing underscores their knowledge and professionalism. I sincerely thank them for working with me through this long process. I also was fortunate to work with John Blair, PhD, and his colleagues in the Department of Health Organization Management at Texas Tech University. Dr. Blair, who also is the programs director, his colleagues, and Myron Fottler, PhD (University of Alabama Program in Administration–Health Services), have written excellent chapters on stakeholder management and multiprovider systems. They are responsible for my interest in and application of stakeholder management principles in my professional endeavors. I enjoyed working with them and look forward to future collaborations.

One author in this and the first book must be singled out and thanked not only for the excellence of his contribution to the text but for the impact that he has had on my career and professional life. A distinguished teacher and professor of mine while I was studying for my MBA, a prolific writer and speaker, and a very respected gentleman, Professor Norman Metzger has influenced me and my thinking throughout my career. From assisting in obtaining my first position in the industry to always being an available and knowledgeable professional and friend, Norman always has been an inspiration. He unquestionably is one of the most respected professionals in human resources management and labor relations in the health care industry, and after a dozen or so books and over 100 articles I have lost track of his contributions to industry literature. If one is lucky in his career, he can identify an individual who has been inspirational and has influenced his professional life. Norman has been that for me.

More than excellent authors are necessary for the completion of a book. I would like to thank my brother, Jim, for his consistent objectivity and support over the years, as well as his review of the first edition and the recommendations that he made for revising the text.

My wife, Maxine, has been supportive of this endeavor from its onset many years ago. She has been insightful in her reviews of, as well as a skilled editor for, many chapters in this book. Her understanding of the industry and her perspective on the manner in which medicine is practiced and health care is administered were invaluable through the planning of the book.

Lastly, I thank daughters Emily and Lisa because they have provided me with a great deal of the energy and enthusiasm required to conceive of, plan, and produce a comprehensive text such as *Health Care Administration*. As young adults, they and their generation hopefully will benefit from the industry changes that will occur in the coming years. The opinions about the industry that they offered during the development of the book provided me with a different level of understanding as to where our health care system has done well, and when it has performed poorly. That input did affect the content of the book. It is my hope that in some way this book will have a positive effect on the scope of change in the industry and the provision of health care services in the future. I suspect that with the magnitude of health care reform that is, and will be, occurring in the coming years, corrections will be necessary.

The challenge for the future that I make to my daughters and their contemporaries is to be vigilant in scrutinizing all aspects of the health care industry and life in general, and to be tenacious in seeking change when required.

Part I

Organization of the Hospital

Chapter 1

History of Hospitals

Lawrence F. Wolper and Jesus J. Peña

MEDICINE AND HOSPITALS AS POLITICAL FACTORS

Traditionally, medical historians and educators have often overlooked the relationship of medicine, in general, and hospitals, in particular, to political and economic affairs, prevailing social attitudes, and discoveries related to medicine.

Medicine and surgery date back to the beginning of civilization because diseases preceded humans on earth. Early medical treatment was always identified with religious services and ceremonies. Priests were also physicians or medicine men, ministering to spirit, mind, and body; priest/doctors were part of the ruling class, with great political influence, and the temple/hospital was also a meeting place.

The role of the priest/doctor and later the role of the temples as houses of refuge for the sick and infirm and as training schools for doctors are closely associated with the civilization's level of political development. The sophistication of the health care system has often been used for political propaganda to demonstrate the superiority of civilization. The pagan Greek temples served a political role, as was evidenced when the Chris-

tian Emperor Constantine closed the Aesculapia. The same political motivation can be seen in the spread of Moslem hospitals under Islamic rule in the 7th century and the efforts of the Soviet bloc health care system to manipulate health statistics to prove its claims of success in Cuba. For example, in a careful analysis of Cuban demographic data Kenneth Hill of the National Academy of Sciences found that "the consistency between the indirect and official incidence of infant mortality disappears. The indirect estimates indicate constant, or even rising child mortality, while the official figures show a continuous rapid decline."[1] This is a classic example of the use of the health care system for political purposes. The current movements toward health care reform in the United States, as well as in many European (Eastern and Western) countries and the former Soviet Union, are further and current examples of the interrelationships among politics, economics, and societal values.

MESOPOTAMIA

Medicine as an organized entity first appeared 4,000 years ago in the ancient region of Southwest Asia known as Mesopotamia. Between the

3

Tigris and Euphrates rivers, which have their origin in Asia Minor and merge to flow into the Persian Gulf, this fertile land has been called the cradle of civilization.

The first recorded doctor's prescription came from Sumer in ancient Babylon under the rule of the dynasty of Hammurabi (1728–1686 B.C.). Hammurabi's code of laws provides the first record of the regulation of doctors' practices, as well as the regulation of their fees. The Mesopotamian civilization made political, educational, and medical contributions to the later development of the Egyptian, Hebrew, Persian, and even Indian cultures.

GREEK HOSPITALS

For hundreds of years, the Greeks enjoyed the benefits of contact and cross-fertilization of ideas with numerous other ancient peoples, especially the Egyptians. Although patients were treated by magic rituals and cures were related to miracles and divine intervention, the Greeks recognized the natural causes of disease, and rational methods of healing were important. Additionally, what was known of human anatomy and physiology was more of a rational than a superstitious or religious nature.

Hippocrates is usually considered the personification of the rational nonreligious approach to medicine, and in 480 B.C., he started to use auscultation, perform surgical operations, and provide historians with detailed records of his patients and descriptions of diseases ranging from tuberculosis to ulcers. The temples of Saturn, Hygeia, and Aesculapius, the Greek god of medicine, all served as both medical schools for practitioners and resting places for patients under observation or treatment.

INDIAN HOSPITALS

Historical records show that efficient hospitals were constructed in India by 600 B.C. During the splendid reign of King Asoka (273–232 B.C.), Indian hospitals started to look like modern hospitals: They followed principles of sanitation, and cesarean sections were performed with close attention to technique in order to save both mother and infant. Physicians were appointed—one for every ten villages—to serve the health care needs of the population, and regional hospitals for the infirm and destitute were built by Buddha.

ROMAN HOSPITALS

The Roman talent for organization did not extend as readily to institutional care of the sick and injured. Although infirmaries for the sick slaves were established, it was only among the military legions that a system for hospitalization was developed. After the injured were cared for in field tents, the soldiers were moved to valetudinaries, a form of hospital erected in all garrisons along the frontiers. Apparently, those stone and wooden structures were carefully planned and were stocked with instruments, supplies, and medications.

The decree of Emperor Constantine in 335 A.D. closed the Aesculapia and stimulated the building of Christian hospitals. However, it was not until 369 A.D. that the wealthy Romans, converted to Christianity, started to build hospitals from Justinian to the benefactress, Fabiola, who built a hospital in 394.

ISLAMIC HOSPITALS

During the 7th century, the new evangelical religion of Islam began to preserve the classical learning still extant, which it later yielded to the European world.

The development of efficient hospitals was an outstanding contribution of Islamic civilization. The Roman military hospitals and the few Christian hospitals were no match for the number, organization, and excellence of the Arabic hospitals.

The Arabs' medical inspiration came largely from the Persian Hospital in Djoundisabour (sixth century, Turkey), at which many of them studied. Returning to their homes, they founded institutions that were remarkably well organized for the times. During the time of Mohammed, a real system of hospitals was developed. Asylums for the insane were founded ten centuries before they first appeared in Europe. In addition, Islamic physicians were responsible for the establishment of pharmacy and chemistry as sciences.

Some of the best known of the great hospitals in the Middle Ages were in Baghdad, Damascus, and Cairo. In particular, the hospital and medical school of Damascus had elegant rooms, an extensive library, and a great reputation for its cuisine.

In the Arabic hospitals, separate wards were set aside for different diseases, such as fever, eye conditions, diarrhea, wounds, and gynecological disorders. Convalescing patients were separated from sicker patients, and provisions were made for ambulatory patients. Clinical reports of cases were collected and used for teaching.

THE MIDDLE AGES

From the early Middle Ages in the fourth century to the late Middle Ages in the fifteenth century, trade was almost totally suppressed, and many city dwellers returned to the land. Religious communities assumed responsibility for care of the sick. The rational nonreligious approach that characterized Greek medicine during the era of Hippocrates was lost, as hospitals became ecclesiastical, not medical, institutions. Only the hopeless and homeless found their way to these hospitals, in which the system of separation of patients by diseases was eliminated, three to five patients were accommodated in each bed, and principles of sanitation were ignored. Surgery was avoided, with the exception of amputation, in order not to "disturb the body" and to avoid the shedding of blood per the church edict of 1163 that, in effect, forbade the clergy from performing operations. Religious orders emphasized nursing care; the first religious order devoted solely to nursing is considered to be the St. Augustine nuns, organized in approximately 1155.

Yet, hospital construction increased in Europe during the Middle Ages for two reasons. First, Pope Innocent III in 1198 urged wealthy Christians to build hospitals in every town, and second, increased revenues were available from the commerce with the Crusaders. The oldest hospitals still in existence are the Hotels-Dieu in Lyons and Paris, France. The term "Hotel-Dieu" indicates that it is a public hospital. The earliest mention of the Hotel-Dieu in Lyons is found in a manuscript of 580 A.D., in which its establishment by Childebert is recorded. The Hotel-Dieu of Paris was founded by Bishop Landry in 660, on the Ile de la Cite. In 1300, the hospital had an attending staff of physicians and surgeons caring for 800–900 patients, and its capacity was doubled in the fifteenth century. By the seventeenth century, it had been enlarged to two buildings, linked by the Pont au Double. In about 1880, these buildings were replaced on the island by the present Hotel-Dieu.

St. Bartholomew's Hospital, which was established in London in 1123, was attached to the Augustinian Priory of (Great) St. Bartholomew. Both church and hospital still exist, but the hospital was rebuilt between 1730–1759. The Hospital of Santo Spirito was built in Rome in 1204 by Pope Innocent III. By 1447, it housed 360 beds and utilized a system of stretcher-ambulances. The hospital survived on the same location until 1922, when it was destroyed by fire, but it was later rebuilt. The development of hospitals in Germany occurred largely in the thirteenth and fourteenth centuries through the activities of the Order of the Holy Ghost and the Order of the Lazarites. In Belgium, the still-active hospital of St. John in Bruges was established in the twelfth century.

In contrast, in Asia and Africa during the same period, construction of effective and efficient hospitals was spurred by Islamic rule and the Crusades. The two hospital systems enforced sanitary measures, performed surgery, and separated patients according to diseases: the Islamic hospitals because they were still following the Greek and early Roman traditions, and the hospitals created by the Crusaders because injuries sustained in combat necessitated surgery and the presence of pests and contagious diseases necessitated sanitary conditions and the strict separation of patients.

During the period of the Crusades (1096–1270), religious orders, which had as their chief duty the care of the sick, built a number of hospitals in the Mediterranean area. The most famous of these orders was the Knights of Saint John of Jerusalem. Because of the need to treat the casualties of combat, large hospitals with up to 2,000 beds were built. For years, those hospitals were the only active institutions following the advanced hospital practices other than the Islamic hospitals. For the first time, medical systems of the East and West vied for the supremacy of medical care.

HOSPITALS DURING THE RENAISSANCE

The Renaissance period lasted from the fourteenth to the sixteenth centuries. It received its name from the Italian "rinascita," meaning rebirth, because of a common belief that it embodied a return to the cultural priorities of ancient Rome and Greece. The healing arts were again characterized by a scientific, rational approach.

The academic world of northern Italy was tolerant of new cosmopolitan ideas. By the mid-fifteenth century, all major courts and cities of Europe sent their finest physicians to Italy for advanced training.

If the Middle Ages can be seen as the period of the great hospitals, the Renaissance was really the period of the great schools of medicine. Schools of medicine flourished in Germany and in central and eastern Europe. The scientific study of human anatomy as a science was facilitated by dissections of animals. In 1506, the Royal College of Surgeons was organized in England, followed by the organization of the Royal College of Physicians in 1528.

The major contribution of the Renaissance to the development of hospitals was in improved management of the hospital, the return to the segregation of patients by diseases, and the higher quality of medicine provided within the hospital. Clinical surgery took great strides during this period, not only in Italy but also in France, especially under Ambrose Pare, who reintroduced the ancient methods of stopping hemorrhage by using ligatures and abandoned the barbaric system of cauterizing irons.

Epidemic chorea, sweating sickness, and leprosy had almost ceased to exist, although syphilis continued to be common.

In the English Reformation from 1536–1539 hospitals affiliated with the Catholic church were plundered by King Henry VIII and were ordered to convert to secular uses or be destroyed. Many hospitals in the countryside of England were forced to close their doors and remained closed for two centuries. Only the powerful hospitals in London survived when the citizens petitioned the King to endow St. Bartholomew, St. Thomas, and St. Mary of Bethlehem hospitals. This was the first instance of secular support of hospitals.

HOSPITALS ON THE AMERICAN CONTINENT

The first hospitals of the New World were built in colonies of Spain, France, and England. Those built under the flags of Catholic Spain and France retained the ideals of the Jesuits, the Sisters of Charity, and the Augustinian Sisters and their hundreds of years of hospital knowledge. Hospitals built in the English colonies, however, reacted against English traditions.

The first hospital in the New World was constructed as part of a system for the occupation of overseas territories. Bartolome de las Casas, one of the priests who accompanied Columbus on his first voyage and a well-known historian, referred to the founding of the village of La Isabella in Hispaniola (today, Santo Domingo), in January of 1494: "Columbus made haste in constructing a house to keep supplies and the ammunition for the soldiers, a church and a hospital."[2] No further information survives to indicate whether the hospital was actually built. However, extant documents show that a hospital was built in St. Nicholas of Bari by mid-1494 and that, during the same year, it housed 40 Spaniards who were injured during an Indian revolt. Unfortunately, most of the hospital records were destroyed during the pillage of the city by Sir Francis Drake in 1586. The same hospital, in a different location, provided health care until 1883.

In Mexico, Hernan Cortes erected the Immaculate Conception Hospital in Mexico City in 1524, which is still an active hospital. In 1541, the Spanish crown passed a decree that required construction of a hospital in all Spanish and Indian towns of the New World.

In Quebec, Canada, in 1639, the French constructed the first hospital, the Hotel Dieu du Precieux Sanz, which was founded by the Duchess d'Aquilon. The Hotel Dieu de St. Joseph was founded in Montreal in 1644. In the English colonies, the oldest hospital was a small almshouse for the poor that was supported by a church in the city of New Amsterdam. This house and a tiny hospital established by the West Indian Company in 1658 eventually were combined and grew into the City Hospital of Bellevue in New York City.

The eighteenth-century American hospitals, except for the New Amsterdam Hospital and the one constructed in New Orleans by the Catholic church in 1720, departed from the charitable and religious spirit of the Old World hospitals. American institutions followed the model of the Pennsylvania Hospital, which was founded in 1751. According to an inscription on its wall, the institution intended to foster patients' self-respect and remove any stigma from a hospital visit by charging fees. Benjamin Franklin helped to design the hospital, which was built to provide a place for Philadelphia physicians to hospitalize their private patients. Franklin served as president from 1755 to 1757.

In another break with tradition the New York Hospital was founded in 1771 by private citizens who formed the Society of the New York Hospital and obtained a grant to build it. The hospital was characterized by a spirit of learning and research. As with other hospitals founded before the era of large fortunes, the New York Hospital was built on the contributions of small merchants and farmers.

Another innovation was the first hospital conducted only by women. The New York Infirmary for Women and Children was opened in 1853 by the first woman to earn a medical degree in the United States, Elizabeth Blackwell, and her sister. Again, this is another example of a privately owned hospital that was founded to accommodate physicians' needs.

The earliest federal involvement in hospital care was mandated by the 1798 United States Marine Hospital Service Act, which provided hospital care for disabled seamen. This Act was, in reality, a compulsory insurance plan, because wages were deducted for health care. As a result of the Act, the first Marine hospital was built in Norfolk, Virginia, in 1802, and in the same year, another was built in Boston, Massachusetts. In the following year, another Marine hospital was built in Newport, Rhode Island, and by 1861, there were 30 Marine hospitals. After the Civil War, the Marine hospitals admitted Army and Navy personnel and became the forerunner of the Veterans Administration Hospitals.

At the beginning of the twentieth century, nearly all of the U.S. hospitals were independent, either under voluntary or private auspices. However, after 1926, the number of tax-supported hospitals increased dramatically, and tax refunds were used to pay for many poor patients in voluntary hospitals.

The first psychiatric hospital in the United States was built in Williamsburg, Virginia, in 1773. This was the beginning of a large-scale construction of state psychiatric hospitals, which by 1950 reached a total of 557 hospitals with 628,300 beds. This movement came to a halt in 1955 with the discovery of psychotropic medication and the movement toward deinstitutionalization. In 1984, there were only 275 psychiatric hospitals, with 157,600 beds.

The European and Latin American tradition of charity hospitals, based on love of God and neighbors and the conviction that the government owed a responsibility to helpless citizens, was never part of U.S. hospital traditions. As a result, a more competitive system of hospitals developed, with fewer subsidies and less involvement of religious organizations in total health care. Massive government involvements in health care began in 1926 with the return of veterans from World War I. The possible bias in the system is indicated best by the fee schedule of 1870, in which delirium tremens cases were charged twice the normal fee. Yet, the positive element of the early system was that those who paid and those who did not slept side by side, but nonpaying patients were assigned housekeeping or simple nursing duties.

HOSPITALS IN THE SEVENTEENTH, EIGHTEENTH, AND NINETEENTH CENTURIES

The seventeenth century was the age of the scientific revolution, a major turning point in the history of hospitals and medicine. The mood of the century was not to find out why things happened, but how they happened. No longer was speculation accepted, but experimentation was the common denominator of scientific work. William Harvey's (1578–1657) proof of the continuous circulation of the blood within a contained system was the seventeenth century's most significant achievement in physiology and medicine. Experimentation led to the wide use of thermometry in clinical practice.

One of the most important inventions in the development of medicine and general science was the microscope. The two giants of seventeenth-century microscopy were Marcello Malpighi (1628–94) and Anthony van Leeuwenhoek (1632–1723).

In 1661, a book published in England, *Natural and Political Observations . . . Made Upon the Bill of Mortality* by John Gaunt, for the first time presented the idea that a large population was an asset to a country and that public health measures were a necessity. The book advocated measures to preserve and restore health, such as separate hospitals for plague victims, specialized maternity institutions, government concern

for the health of occupational groups, and the establishment of a central health council to organize public health. However, these measures were too far advanced for the seventeenth-century thinking and were ignored.

In the seventeenth century, new hospitals were only constructed in the new lands colonized in the Americas. The old hospitals in Europe were either slumbering under the maternal care of the Church, as in Italy, were passing into the control of national or municipal governments, as in France and Germany, or new hospitals were being founded by an enlightened crown, as in Denmark, Germany, and Austria.

During the eighteenth century there was a partial revival in the construction of hospitals in England. A movement was started to build a hospital in every parish by 1732. A total of 115 hospitals were already built by the parishioners, with the best known of them being St. Peters of Bristol. At the same time, philanthropists, such as Thomas Guy, founded hospitals for both charity and paying patients, including the Guy's Hospital in 1724, St. George's Hospital in 1733, and the Great London Hospital in 1740. The Quakers were very active in hospital construction as well, with William Tuke (1732–1822) founding the York Retreat for the Humane Care of the Mentally Ill.

The discovery of vaccination was the key medical achievement of the eighteenth century. Lady Mary Wortley Montagu (1689–1762) brought back to England the Asian technique of variolation, which she had observed in Turkey. In this procedure, serum extracted from the sore of a person with smallpox was injected into another person's skin to produce a resistance resulting from a mild case of the illness.

The eighteenth century was not merely a period of mass construction of new hospitals, but a period of consolidation and systematization. Physicians and hospitals, overwhelmed by the revolutionary discoveries of the previous century, struggled bravely to absorb and utilize the mass of new technology.

The nineteenth century is the keystone in the history of hospitals and is considered to be the beginning of modern medicine. Several events combined to produce the framework for the modern hospital.

The building of factories and the expansion of cities, with overcrowding of urban areas, occurred during the Industrial Revolution (1790–1825). The health of workers in the factories was important to their efficient functioning, and because the spread of epidemic disease was a danger to all segments of the population, the need for remedial measures was obvious. As a result, in every major city the construction of hospitals accelerated.

The assembling of large numbers of troops for the American Civil War (1861–1865) was accompanied by the inevitable outbreaks of communicable diseases. In the armies of both the North and South, little attention was paid to camp sanitation, and no provision was made for decent housing or food. Due to the lack of planning, the enormous numbers of casualties from the first few battles lay abandoned in the field for as long as two or three days.

Gradually, both armies evolved effective ambulance and hospital systems, procured adequate medical supplies, and developed well-trained surgeons. Yet, it was not until the battle of Gettysburg (July 1863) that the Union forces were able to remove their wounded from the field at the end of each day's fighting. It took two years of bloodshed to develop a good medical corps and an effective system of field hospitals. These advances in hospital management became part of the increasing development of the American hospital system and led to the creation of the Veterans Administration hospitals.

The legacy of Florence Nightingale may be the greatest contribution of the nineteenth century to the evolution of hospitals. The introduction of professional nursing services, which provided kindly treatment and emphasized a clean environment, was a giant step forward in institutional treatment.

Miss Nightingale began nursing training in Germany in 1836 and almost immediately wrote about the lack of hygiene in the German hospitals. Upon returning to England, she started implementing her ideas and acquired a reputation as an innovator. In 1854, the English government called her to improve the conditions of the sick and wounded soldiers during the Crimean War. She organized laundry services, kitchens, and a central supply department, and in 10 days reduced the death rate from 38 percent to an acceptable 2 percent.

Her capacity for organization and administration was endless. After returning to England, Nightingale founded the first school of nursing in 1860. In 1863, the school graduated the first group of 15 nurses, who later devoted their efforts to the promotion of nursing schools. Nightingale's writings were largely responsible for the transformation of nursing from a low, unpopular, and almost casual endeavor into a highly respected, essential part of the healing art.

Another important event in the history of hospitals was the discovery of bacteria as the causes of disease. Before that discovery, the principal focus of preventive medicine and elimination of infections in hospitals was sanitation: The provision of potable waters and the dispersal of foul odors remedied problems that were considered to be the important factors in causing epidemics.

It was Ignaz Semmelweis (1818–65), who, in keeping with the new statistical spirit of the nineteenth century, assembled and analyzed the clinical care data in the obstetrical wards of the Allgemines Krankenhaus Hospital in Vienna to prove the contagious nature of postpartum infections. The next step for Semmelweis was clear: to require physicians and students under his charge to scrub their hands with soap and water and soak them in a chlorinated lime solution before entering the clinic or ward and to repeat this after each examination. In 3 months, the obstetrical death rate declined from 18 to 1½ percent.

A few years later, Louis Pasteur (1822–95) proved that bacteria were produced by reproduction and were not spontaneous, as previously believed. He is considered the father of bacteriology. Joseph Lister (1827–1912) continued Pasteur's work. Lister noticed that broken bones over which the skin was intact usually healed without complication; when they were exposed, however, fractures developed the same type of infection that grew in amputations and other operations. He suggested that this finding provided additional evidence that some element circulating in the body was responsible for the infections. By 1870, the hospitals in Germany were paying strong attention to Lister's theories and sprayed carbolic solution in the operating room, drenching both surgeons and patients. As a result, it was possible to perform major surgery without fear of infection.

The discovery of anesthesia and steam sterilization modernized the practice of surgery and enabled it to be performed frequently. By 1831, all three basic anesthetic agents—ether, nitrous oxide gas, and chloroform—had been discovered, but no medical applications of their pain-relieving properties had been performed. It is believed that Dr. Clariford W. Long (1815–1878) of Georgia was the first to perform minor operations using sulfuric ether in 1842. The introduction of steam sterilization in 1886 was the beginning of surgical asepsis, in contrast with earlier, less effective antisepsis measures.

The three discoveries—bacteria as the cause of diseases, anesthesia, and steam sterilization—enabled the development of the modern hospital. By 1895, the foundation of the modern hospital was completed with the discovery of the X-ray by Wilhelm Konrad Roentgen (1845–1923). Hospitals were no longer a place where the sick and homeless found refuge and care, but rather a special place where treatment and more exact diagnosis were aided by technology. At the same time, the cost of hospital care increased dramatically, and hospitals were placed in direct competition with the private practitioner, who usually was unable to afford the costly equipment.

The American Medical Association was founded in 1847 under the leadership of Dr. Nathan Smith Davis (1817–1907). In 1864, 16 nations signed a treaty establishing the International Red Cross and specifying regulations for the treatment of wounded soldiers, including the provision that all hospitals—military and civilian—were to be neutral territory. Another landmark in the history of hospitals occurred in the nineteenth century when women were finally accepted as full-fledged medical practitioners, after a long struggle.

The next logical step in the development of medicine was specialization. By the end of the nineteenth and the beginning of the twentieth centuries, specialties and subspecialties developed to the extent that no general branch of medicine or surgery was without its subdivision of specialization.

As a result of all the above-mentioned discoveries and events, a great number of hospitals were constructed in the United States in a short period of time: for example, in Chicago—Mercy Hospital, 1852; Cook County, 1863; St. Luke, 1864; Chicago Hospital for Women, 1865; and the Jewish Hospital, 1868; in New York City—Roosevelt Hospital, 1871; Presbyterian Hospital, 1872; Polyclinic, 1881; and Cancer Hospital, 1886; and in Baltimore, Johns Hopkins Hospital, 1889.

By the end of that century, there were 149 hospitals in the United States with a bed capacity of 35,500. Less than 10 percent of all these hospitals were under government control of any kind.

THE MODERN HOSPITAL AND HEALTH SYSTEMS

The ideal modern hospital is a place both where ailing people seek and receive care and where clinical education is provided to medical students, nurses, and virtually the whole spectrum of health professionals. It provides continuing education for the practicing physicians and increasingly serves the function of an institution of higher learning for entire neighborhoods, communities, and regions. In addition to its educational role, the modern hospital conducts investigation studies and research in medical sciences both from clinical records and from its patients, as well as basic research in science, physics, and chemistry.

The construction of the modern hospital is regulated or influenced by federal laws, state health department regulations, city ordinances, the standards of the Joint Commission on Accreditation of Healthcare Organizations, and national and local codes (building, fire protection, sanitation, etc.). These requirements safeguard patients' privacy and the safety and well-being of patients and staff, and control cross-infections. The popular ward concept of the mid-nineteenth century is no longer permissible, and today hospitals have mainly semiprivate and private rooms. Although permissible in most states, four-bed rooms are seldom planned.

The changing emphasis from inpatient to outpatient service and rapid advances in medical technology have focused recent facility planning activities on medical ancillary expansion and freestanding outpatient centers. Developing separate or freestanding buildings has allowed hospitals to minimize the financial impact of restrictive hospital building codes and regulations.

However, the rapid expansion of nonhospital-based and independent ambulatory care facilities slowed substantially beginning in the late 1980s as a result of changes in reimbursement, deteriorating rates of reimbursement, and an overall decline in the economy. Hospital failures increased, as did bed closings. In addition, there was an increase in federal and state antikickback and safe harbor regulations that dampened the enthusiasm for joint ventures for nonhospital-based facilities.

The early 1990s and beyond place the hospital in the position of being only one component in the evolution toward vertically integrated hospital and other provider networks. Inpatient care will diminish with continued advances in medicine, and hospitals are likely to downsize. Simultaneously, ambulatory and doctors' office care will increase. The hospital, particularly compared with its earliest days, will play a very different role in the future as part of an integrated collection of providers and sites of care.

CLASSIFICATION OF HOSPITALS

The need has long been recognized for a system that would both integrate and differentiate terminology, definitions, and essential characteristics of health care institutions. The difficulties encountered in trying to relate and compare data obtained by different agencies using differing terminology and definitions have been apparent for many years. So also have been problems related to licensure, registration, accreditation, certification of institutions, and the financing of health care. The following discussion summarizes the most common systems of hospital classification now in use.

Public Access

One of the oldest and most useful systems of classification is used by the American Hospital Association (AHA) in its annual *Hospital Statistics* manual. That classification divides hospitals into community and noncommunity hospitals according to the degree of public access to the hospital.

Community hospitals include all nonfederal short-term general and other special hospitals, excluding hospital units of institutions, the facilities and services of which are available to the public.

Noncommunity hospitals include federal hospitals; long-term hospitals; hospital units of institutions, such as prison hospitals or college infirmaries; psychiatric hospitals; hospitals for tuberculosis and other respiratory diseases; chronic disease hospitals; institutions for the mentally retarded; and alcoholism and chemical dependency hospitals.

Ownership

Another type of classification is by ownership or control of the policies and operation of the hospital. Institutions are divided into four groupings under this classification: (1) government, nonfederal; (2) nongovernment, not for profit; (3) investor-owned, for profit; and (4) government, federal.

Government, nonfederal, includes all hospitals that are owned or operated by states, counties, or cities and are supported by state, county, or city appropriations. Although these appropriations are decreasing and are being replaced by reimbursements from third-party private payers, the political subdivision still retains the legal responsibility to cover deficits and to control policies and operations. Even though the administration of government, nonfederal hospitals has changed over the past decade, with most of these hospitals now being run by some type of a board of trustees, the power of the trustees is limited. The board oversees the quality of care rendered, but does not assume the combination of quality assurance and fiduciary responsibilities held by the boards of nongovernment, not-for-profit hospitals.

The largest group of the government nonfederal hospitals—the state psychiatric hospitals—has considerably decreased in number since 1955 because of the policies of deinstitutionalization of mentally ill patients and the availability of psychotropic medication.

Nongovernment, not-for-profit hospitals or voluntary institutions are owned and maintained by the organization represented in their incorporation certificate, which has no connection with any government subdivision. Their operating expenses are covered from patient fees, including third-party payments, donations, endowments, or assessments of its donors. In some localities, a city or state may agree to subsidize a not-for-profit hospital to enable it to provide services to nonpaying patients or to offer special services, but this is considered a subsidy with no control attached. The nonprofit, nongovernment hospitals comprise the largest group of hospitals, and their percentage of total beds has increased in the last three decades with the decreasing number and size of the state and local psychiatric centers. Yet, a new force in the hospital industry, the for-profit hospital, is becoming an increasingly strong competitor.

Control and ultimate responsibilities over nonprofit, nongovernment hospitals are vested with a board of trustees. The hospital is tax-exempt because of its charitable nature, but it is not dependent on government appropriations. The largest group among the not-for-profit hospitals

are the religious organization hospitals, which are usually incorporated under a church or under a separate charter.

Due to the increase in operating costs of the independent not-for-profit hospitals, a new entity has flourished during the last 20 years—the multihospital system. The for-profit sector has very successfully applied the principle of economy of scale in the ownership of several hospitals, and recently not-for-profit hospitals have joined together to enhance their ability to obtain capital, increase revenues through the greater number of beds, and generate purchasing savings through volume purchasing and management consolidation.

Actually, the multihospital concept originated in the year 1204, with the founding of the Hospital of Santo Spirito in Rome by the Pope. Hearing about the efficiency of the Hospital in Montpelier in France that was conducted by Guy de Montpelier, the Pope sent for him and entrusted him with the directorship of the Order of the Holy Ghost. Under Guy de Montpelier, the Order administered a tremendous number of hospitals throughout Europe, either starting them as new institutions or taking over the management of previously established hospitals. Almost 2,000 hospitals were founded in Germany and a great number were established in France under this Order.

Investor-owned hospitals are owned and maintained by individuals or corporations for the purpose of generating profits. The for-profit hospital has no source of funds other than those produced by the institution. The hospital is operated in a businesslike fashion. As a rule, the policy-making functions are carried out by the owners, but in the case of large for-profit institutions, a board of directors may be elected among the stockholders. It is a common practice for physicians working in the for-profit hospital to be shareholders in it as well. The most exclusive of the for-profit hospitals cater to self-paying patients, with the great majority relying on reimbursements from patients' insurance.

Government, federal is a narrow classification that includes hospitals owned and controlled by the federal government and supported by federal funds. The largest group is the Veterans Administration hospitals. The Veterans Administration hospitals are controlled directly by the federal government. Their physicians work on a full-time basis at the hospitals, and admissions are limited to disabilities connected with war or military service.

In addition to the Veterans Administration hospitals, a decreasing number of public health service hospitals serve the medical needs of merchant marines. There are now only six public health hospitals, which also care for federal employees and Native Americans living on reservations. In addition, the federal government owns and operates Army, Navy, and Air Force hospitals for each of the three branches of service. All these hospitals are federally funded and under the direct responsibility of the Surgeon General.

Length of Patient Stay

According to the average length of stay, hospitals are classified as either short- or long-term-stay hospitals. A short-term hospital stay is one that averages less than 30 days, with a national average under 7 days. A long-term institution has an average stay of over 30 days.

Number of Beds

Hospitals are also grouped by the number of beds: 6 to 24 beds, 25 to 49, 50 to 99, 100 to 199, 200 to 299, 300 to 399, 400 to 499, and 500 or more. This categorization is usually combined with other classifications, such as regional and teaching or nonteaching hospital, to provide an average cost per type of institution. For example, the cost per bed of operating a 50-bed nonteaching hospital in the Southwest is less than the cost per bed operation of a 400-bed teaching hospital in the Northeast.

Accreditation

Hospitals are also classified as accredited and nonaccredited, depending on whether they have been found to be in substantial compliance with the standards of the Joint Commission and/or the American Osteopathic Association.

For over 60 years, the health care industry has participated in a voluntary accreditation process that is designed to improve the quality of services provided in hospitals and health-related facilities. The term "voluntary" is misleading, because accreditation for hospitals has become so closely tied to the receipt of third-party payments that without the ability to make this claim, financial jeopardy constantly looms. Although accreditation is vitally important to hospitals for financial reasons, it also is a mark of distinction for the quality of patient care provided by hospitals and for the many nonhospital programs that are also eligible for it.

Teaching

Teaching or nonteaching is also a common classification in the hospital field. Teaching hospitals participate in the education of physicians through a residency program. Depending upon the type and number of residency programs offered, a hospital is either a major teaching or minor teaching institution. To be a full teaching hospital, the hospital should offer, at minimum, the following residencies: medicine, surgery, OB/GYN, and pediatrics. Many full teaching hospitals offer residencies in every subspecialty of medicine and surgery, in addition to pathology, anesthesiology, family practice, and many other programs. A partial teaching hospital usually has only two or three programs: medicine, surgery, pediatrics, OB/GYN, or any combination amounting to less than four.

Depending on the involvement and the participation of a university in its teaching programs, teaching hospitals are university hospitals, university-affiliated, or freestanding. Teaching costs are reimbursed under a complicated formula, but this is a subject of great controversy, with many state legislators advocating for an end to what is considered a subsidy to medical education.

Vertical Integration

Finally, hospitals can be classified according to vertical integration or the concept of regionalization. Under this system, hospitals are divided into primary care, secondary care, and tertiary care centers.

Primary care facilities, regardless of location or structure, offer services on a need/demand basis to the public. Those entities are designed, equipped, staffed, organized, and operated as an integral part of a comprehensive health care system and offer health services in an available,

personalized, and continuous fashion on an outpatient basis.

Secondary care facilities render care that requires a degree of sophistication and skills and that is usually associated with the confinement of the careseeker for a definite period of time. General acute hospitals or specialized outpatient facilities, such as ambulatory surgical centers, fall under this category.

Tertiary care facilities render highly specialized services requiring highly technical resources. This type of care is usually offered by university medical centers or specialty hospitals, such as burn centers.

NOTES

1. K. Hill, *Wall Street Journal*, December 10, 1984.

2. B. de las Casas, *History of Hispaniola* (1495).

SUGGESTED READINGS

Adams, F.R. 1891. *The genuine works of Hippocrates.* Translated from Greek, with preliminary discourse and annotations. New York: William Wood.

Albutt, T. 1921. *Greek medicine in Rome.* London: Macmillan & Co.

Ali, S.A. 1977. Europe's debt to Muslim scholars of medicine and science. *Studies in the History of Medicine* 1:36–48.

Aristotle. 1910. *Aristotle's works.* Translated by D'Arcy W. Thompson. Oxford: Clarenden Press.

Ashhurst, A.P.C. 1927. The centenary of Lister (1827–1927): A tale of sepsis and antisepsis. *Annals of Medical History* 9:205.

Baas, J.H. 1971. *History of medicine.* 2 vols. 1876. Translated by H.E. Anderson. Huntington, NY: R.E. Krieger Publishing Co.

Barrow, M.V. 1972. Portraits of Hippocrates. *Medical History:* 16.

Bell, E.M. 1953. *Storming the citadel: The rise of the woman doctor.* London: Constable & Co.

Blake, J.B., ed. 1968. *Education in the history of medicine.* New York: Hafner Publishing Co.

Boland, F.K. 1950. *The first anesthetic: The story of Crawford Long.* Athens, GA: University of Georgia Press.

Bowers, J.Z., and E.F. Purcell, eds. 1976. *Advances in American medicine: Essays at the bicentennial.* 2 vols. New York: Josiah Macy, Jr., Foundation and National Library of Medicine.

Brim, C.J. 1936. *Medicine in the Bible.* New York: Froben Press.

Brock, A.J. 1929. *Greek medicine: Extracts of medical writers from Hippocrates to Galen.* London: J.M. Dent & Sons.

Brockington, C.F. 1975. The history of public health. In *The theory and practice of public health*, 4th ed., ed. W. Hobson. London: Oxford University Press.

Browne, E.G. 1921. *Arabian medicine.* Cambridge: Cambridge University Press.

Campbell, D. 1926. *Arabian medicine and its influence on the middle ages.* London: Kegan Paul, Trench, Trubner & Co.

Clarke, E.G. et al. 1876. *Century of American medicine, 1776–1876.* Philadelphia: H.C. Lea.

Corlett, W.T. 1977. *The medicine-man of the American Indian and his cultural background.* 1935 reprint. New York: AMS Press.

Duffy, J. 1971. *Epidemics in colonial America.* Baton Rouge, LA: Louisiana State University Press.

Ebbel, B. 1939. *The papyrus ebers: The greatest Egyptian medical document.* With translation. Copenhagen: Ejnar Munksgard.

Edwards, C. 1921. *The Hammurabi code.* London: Watts & Co.

Frazer, J.G. 1963. *The golden bough: A study in magic and religion.* Abr. ed. New York: Macmillan & Co.

Hamarneh, S.K. 1975. *The genius of Arab civilization, sources of Renaissance*. New York: New York University Press.

Hanlon, J.J. 1974. *Public health: Administration and practice*, 6th ed. St. Louis: C.V. Mosby Co.

Harley, G.W. 1941. *Native African medicine*. Cambridge, MA: Harvard University Press.

The historical relations of medicine and surgery to the end of the sixteenth century. 1905. London: Macmillan & Co.

Hospitals, medical care, and social policy in the French revolution. 1956. *Bulletin of the History of Medicine* 30:124–149.

Hurd-Mead, K.C. 1973. *A history of women in medicine*. 1938 reprint. Boston: Milford House.

India's contribution to medieval Arabic medical Education and practice. 1977. *Studies in the History of Medicine* 1:5–35.

Jayne, W.A. 1925. *The healing gods of ancient civilizations*. New Haven: Yale University Press.

Kelly, E.C. 1905. *Medical classics*. Vol. 5. Baltimore: Williams & Wilkins Co.

Kump, W.L. 1973. Health care delivery system in ancient Greece and Rome. *Pharos:* 42–48.

A medical history of Persia and the Eastern Caliphate. 1951. Cambridge: Cambridge University Press.

Metchnikoff, E. 1971. *The founders of modern medicine: Pasteur-Koch-Lister*. 1939 reprint. Books for Libraries Press.

Moll, A.A. 1944. *Aesculapius in Latin America*. Philadelphia: W.B. Saunders Co.

Moodie, R.L. 1923. *The antiquity of disease*. Chicago: University of Chicago Press.

Moon, R.O. 1914. The influence of Pythagoras on Greek medicine. In *Proceedings of the seventeeth international congress of medicine, London*. London: H. Frowde.

Natural diseases and rational treatment in primitive medicine. 1946. *Bulletin of the History of Medicine* 19.

Osler, W. 1921. *The evolution of modern medicine*. New Haven: Yale University Press.

Phillips, S.D. 1973. *Aspects of Greek medicine*. New York: St. Martin's Press.

Piggott, S., ed. 1967. *The dawn of civilization*. New York: McGraw-Hill.

Riesman, D. 1936. *The story of medicine in the Middle Ages*. New York: Paul B. Hoeber.

Rosen, G. 1974. *From medical police to social medicine: Essays on the history of health*. New York: Neale Watson Academic Publications.

Taton, R., ed. 1963. *Ancient and medieval science from the beginnings to 1450*. New York: Basic Books.

Taton, R., ed. 1964. *The beginnings of modern science from 1450 to 1800*. New York: Basic Books.

Thorndike, L. 1923. *A history of magic and experimental science*. New York: Macmillan & Co.

Toole, H. 1963. Asclepius in history and legend. *Surgery* 53:387–419.

Underwood, E.A., ed. 1953. *Science, medicine, and history: Essays on the evolution of scientific thought and medical practice written in honour of Charles Singer*. London: Oxford University Press.

Vallery-Radot, R. 1906. *The life of Pasteur*. New York: McClure, Phillips.

Walton, A. 1894. *The cult of Asclepios*. Cornell Studies in Classical Philology. Boston: Ginn & Co.

Werner, D. 1941. *History of the Red Cross*. London: Cassell & Co.

Withington, E.T. 1894. *Medical history from the earliest times*. London: Scientific Press.

Wong, K.C., and L.T. Wu. 1976. *History of Chinese medicine*. 2 vols. New York: Gordon Press Publications.

Wylie, W.G. 1877. *Hospitals: Their history, organization, and construction*. New York: D. Appleton & Co.

Wynder, E.L. 1975. A corner of history: John Gaunt. 1620–1674, the father of demography. *Prev. Medicine* 4:85–88.

JESUS J. PEÑA, MPA, JD, currently practices law. He was a senior Vice President at Saint Michael's Medical Center, Newark, New Jersey. In this capacity, he was responsible for day-to-day operations and marketing. A member of the American Arbitration Association, he has studied hospital settlements that have affected the health industry and has served as a consultant to the World Health Organization (WHO) in several Latin American countries.

Mr. Peña worked with the Office of Technical Assistance of the United Nations, to improve the health care system in Latin America through the application of new managerial techniques by those committed to serving large numbers of indigent patients.

Among Mr. Peña's many publications are *Hospital Quality Assurance, Risk Management and Program Evaluation* and *Hospital Management: Winning Strategies for the 80's*, both published by Aspen Publishers, Inc.

Chapter 2

Hospital Organization and Management

I. Donald Snook, Jr.

HOW LARGE IS THE HOSPITAL INDUSTRY?

There are 5,200 community hospitals in the United States with a total capacity of 924,000 hospital beds. This represents a dramatic decline in the number of both hospitals and beds since 1981 (over 8 percent). As a measure of the hospital industry's output, these institutions handled some 30 million admissions and more than 322 million outpatient visits in 1991 alone. The hospital industry represents a mix of public and private sectors. This represents over a 59 percent increase in outpatient visits since 1981. Hospitals can be classified in several ways, among them community or noncommunity. Community hospitals include federal hospitals as well as certain specialty hospitals.

One key index used to measure or classify a community hospital is the institution's number of inpatient beds, often referred to as the hospital's bed size. Community hospitals may also be classified as investor-owned (propriety) or not-for-profit (voluntary) institutions. Although the number of investor-owned hospitals continues to increase, they represent only a small minority of community hospitals. Hospi-

tals may also be organized as either general hospitals or specialty hospitals. General hospitals see a wide variety of medical problems. Specialty hospitals (e.g., a children's hospital or a psychiatric hospital) limit their care to specific illnesses or patients. Hospitals can also be classified by religious affiliation. Catholic hospitals, represented by the Catholic Health Association (CHA), are a major segment of the religious hospital group.

GROWTH IN THE HOSPITAL INDUSTRY

During the past decade, hospitals have been forced to adapt to changes in the economy, technology, and delivery of health care services. As a result, the number of hospitals has declined since 1980. Some hospitals have closed, others have merged, and still others have become nursing homes or providers of other hospital services. There are fewer rural hospitals today than a decade ago, and there has been a decline in the number of hospital beds as well. The average length of stay for patients and the number of admissions have also declined. For the most part, these decreases are a reflection of improvements in medical technology and hospital reimbursement systems as well as of the need to improve economies of scale through mergers and acquisitions.

WHAT KIND OF SERVICES DOES THE HOSPITAL INDUSTRY PROVIDE?

Though there has been a decline in the nation's hospital bed capacity over the past decade, hospitals now provide increased services on an outpatient basis. The movement toward outpatient care is a result of extraordinary technological advancements and increased hospital efficiency in the delivery of patient care. In 1984, about 50 percent of community hospitals provided outpatient care, whereas today almost all community hospitals (over 86 percent) have outpatient departments. Many community hospitals (about 95 percent) also provide ambulatory surgery services. Nearly all community hospitals (93 percent) have 24-hour staffed emergency departments, though there has been a decrease in the number of hospitals offering trauma care centers, largely due to the high operating costs of such units.

ORGANIZATION

There are two fundamental ways to view a hospital organization. One may look at the broader overview, or may consider the more narrow departmental organization. Most hospitals in the United States tend to be traditionally organized; that is, they tend to follow the classical theory of organization. The traditional organization structure derives from the theory of bureaucracy described by the nineteenth-century German sociologist Max Weber (1864–1920). The reader is referred to Chapter 19 for a description of labor relations vis-à-vis organization structure.

Hospitals are mainly bureaucratic organizations and use bureaucratic principles. A principle of bureaucratic organization that applies effectively to hospitals is the grouping of individual positions and clusters of positions into a hierarchy or pyramid. Another effective principle of hospital organization is the consistent system of rules. Hospital rules are really guidelines of official boundaries for actions within the hospital. Examples of such rules include the set of personnel policies outlined in the personnel handbook and written nursing procedures for the care of patients in each nursing unit. Hospitals also use the principle of span of control very effectively. Under the concept of span of control, there is a limit to the number of persons a manager can effectively supervise. In a hospital a span of control of between five and ten people in a given functional area is normal to achieve operational effectiveness. This is especially true in classical functional areas such as housekeeping, dietary, and nursing. There is the division and specialization of labor in hospitals also. Specialization refers to the ways a hospital organizes to identify specific tasks and to assign a job description to each person. For example, a nurse's aide has specific tasks to perform that are different from those of a physician, a registered nurse, or a medical technologist. Notwithstanding the preceding, it is thought that the hospital of the future, perhaps as a member of an integrated network, will be required to be more flexible in its approach to organizational structuring. This remains among the major challenges of the future.

How Hospitals Are Organized

The most popular and traditional hospital structure is a pyramid or hierarchical form of organization. In this arrangement, individuals at the top of the pyramid (e.g., department heads) have a specified range of authority, and this authority is passed down to employees at the levels of the pyramid in a chain-of-command fashion (Figure 2–1). In this way, hospital authority is dispersed throughout the organization. Hospitals encourage a pyramid type structure, with supervisors delegating to two or three subordinates, who in turn delegate farther down the pyramid.

A second type of organizational scheme is a matrix organization. Matrix organization is oriented to solving problems or completing

Figure 2–1 Pyramid Organization

projects. It builds on the concept that representatives from a variety of hospital functional areas, including the medical staff, work together to solve problems. Under a matrix scheme, the authority within a given project does not rest with the employee's parent departmental manager or hospital administrator but with a project manager who has been charged specifically with accomplishing a very specific task. Under this arrangement the hospital organization operates more horizontally than vertically as input is given laterally within the organization. A typical matrix organization is shown in Figure 2–2.

Finally, there is a hybrid organizational arrangement known as product line management. Under this scheme, hospitals or divisions within hospitals are organized according to product line categories. These categories may be referred to as strategic business units. For example, a hospital might select to organize around its surgical or obstetrical services, called products, rather than around formal departments such as nursing.

Bureaucratic Principles

Division of Labor

Early scientific managers, such as Henri Fayol (1841–1925), pointed out that division of work or specialization in work is an excellent means of achieving greater productivity. Hospitals, which have scores of specialty tasks that need to be accomplished, have found that division of work has made it easier to accomplish these tasks. Written job descriptions and task lists are mandatory tools for the modern-day hospital personnel director. There are so many tasks to be performed in a hospital that each worker must know his or her precise limits and sphere of influence if the hospital is going to operate efficiently. Unlike history, however, vertically integrated systems will require that certain employee skills be less compartmentalized, allowing greater flexibility in staffing within one hospital or among the many hospitals in a multihospital system.

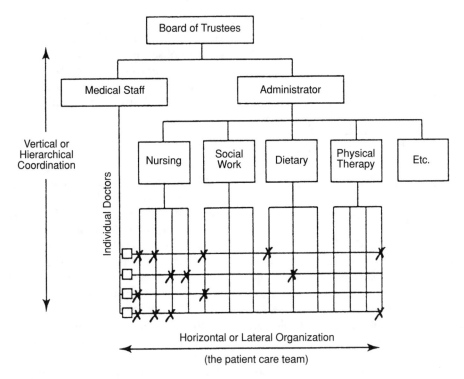

Figure 2–2 Matrix Organization. *Source:* Reprinted from D. Newhauser, The Hospital As a Matrix Organization, *Hospital Administration*, Vol. 17, No. 4, p. 20, with permission of the Foundation of the American College of Healthcare Executives, © 1972.

Pyramid Organization

Another key bureaucratic structure is a pyramid or hierarchical form of organization, in which positions in hospital departments are arranged in a hierarchical fashion (Figure 2–3). At the top of the pyramid is a department head, who has very clearly specified lines of authority. This authority is passed down to employees at lower levels in the hierarchy. These levels of authority create another principle: the chain of command.

A System of Rules

Hospitals operate according to a set of rules and regulations that outline the boundaries for employee actions within the institution. A hospital's personnel policies are described in a handbook that is distributed to employees. Written nursing procedures that outline how to care for patients are an example of an effective and

consistent system of hospital rules. The hospital support departments of housekeeping, dietary, and maintenance are run according to rules. The modern-day hospital could not operate without detailed organizational rules and regulations.

Unity of Command

Each employee in the hospital is responsible to one person: his or her boss. This traditional approach to having a single boss is part of the concept of the chain of command and authority. Violation of the unity of command principle by employees can lead to disciplinary action because it represents a violation of authority. The concept of unity of command is being challenged by a more contemporary form of hospital organization called matrix organization, in which members from more than one department are organized into teams for the purpose of completing ad hoc projects that require a range of

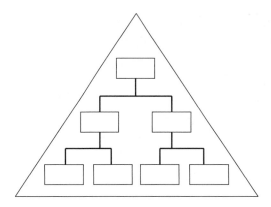

Figure 2–3 Hospital Pyramid Organization

skills. In addition, very formal unity of command runs a risk of dampening employee motivation and creativity, increasing unionization risk, and otherwise engendering an attitude of inflexibility. Few of these are favorable paradigms for the future.

Span of Control

According to classical organization principles, each supervisor can properly direct only a limited number of subordinates or functions. The exact number that a supervisor can properly supervise is debatable and may depend on the supervisor's or manager's level in the organization. The hospital's chief executive officer (CEO) has such broad responsibilities and functions that three or four subordinates (span of control) reporting to this individual might be quite appropriate, whereas managers at lower levels in the organization might be assigned twice that number of functions. Classical organizational theories hold that the more efficient organizations have a smaller span of control.

Delegation

The classical theorists agree that it is best for an organization to have decisions made at the lowest level possible that is reasonable and consistent with good management. Therefore, decisions of a relatively routine nature should be made by subordinates, and, when appropriate, top management can assign decision-making

power at lower levels in the organization. One of the complaints often heard from young, assertive managers seeking to grow in their position is, "My boss does not delegate." However, delegating authority does not release managers from their responsibility for control over the activity that is delegated.

Line and Staff

One easily seen bureaucratic principle is the differentiation between line and staff work in a hospital, which can be best understood by viewing it in terms of authority. Line authority denotes direct supervision over subordinates; for example, the head pharmacist is directly responsible for all the employees within the pharmacy under his or her supervision. In contrast, the staff function in the hospital is generally associated with advisory activities rather than direct supervision. The distinction between line and staff is dramatically seen within the hospital's nursing service department. In the nursing department, line authority is carried out by managers and supervisors, who may hold the position of nurse managers, head nurses, or nursing supervisors. The staff functions in nursing are frequently the responsibility of the trainers or educators. They conduct training called inservice; they are usually advisory to the managers and their line employees.

Coordination

With so many activities, departments, and functions in today's hospital, it is essential that they be coordinated effectively. Coordination is making sure in a conscious way that the different work efforts within the institution are synchronized and work together in harmony in order to achieve the hospital's objectives. Usually the hospital's staff are responsible for middle management ensuring coordination among departments. Unfortunately, departmental activities are not always coordinated. One of the main barriers to effective coordination is poor communication. Generally when a hospital has mastered communication among departments, coordination is much easier to accomplish.

A Team of Three

One of the reasons that hospitals are so complex lies in the relationship among the three major sources of power: the board, the CEO or management, and the hospital's medical staff. These relationships may be regarded as a kind of three-legged stool or a tripartite hospital governance concept. Just as the activities of the medical staff impact significantly on the management and governance of the institution, so do the board's actions impinge on the doctors. The main organizational units that enable the medical staff to relate formally to the board are the medical staff's executive committee and the board's joint conference committee. However, the more dynamic links between the board and the medical staff are in the informal day-to-day dealings between the two groups, both in the hospital setting and socially outside the institution. Also, many hospitals have found it beneficial to have one or perhaps two physicians serve as voting members on the board. Thus, there is a team approach to hospital organization.

The tripartite relationship is now challenged by the increasing pressure to provide high-quality, low-cost services that require a greater cohesiveness between the physicians and administrative staffs. More common goals and motivators must be sought as the industry moves toward the probability of fewer payees, bundled (hospital and physician) reimbursement, and capitation.

Corporate Restructuring in the Hospital

Corporate restructuring, or the segmentation of certain hospital assets and functions into separate corporations, was a popular strategy for hospitals in the 1980s, designed to assist them in adapting to changes in regulations and reimbursement. The most common form of corporate restructuring is when a hospital becomes a subsidiary of a parent holding company or foundation (Figure 2–4). Inpatient care usually remains as the primary function of the hospital corporation, and nonprovider functions may be transferred to other corporations related to the

hospital. The parent holding company and nonhospital subsidiaries are able to enter into less restrictive joint ventures with physician groups and other health care providers than are allowed by the traditional hospital structure. The traditional reasons for corporate restructuring include the optimization of third-party reimbursement, tax considerations, government regulation, flexibility, and diversification. In the early 1990s, corporate restructuring gave way to the creation of multiprovider networks, mergers and acquisitions, and the creation of vertically integrated and consolidated networks.

Multihospital Systems

An increasing number of freestanding hospitals are becoming part of a large multihospital system. A multihospital system is two or more hospitals that are managed, leased, or owned by a single institution. Some of the common advantages of multihospital systems include economies of scale with management, personnel, and purchasing; the ability to provide a wide spectrum of care; and increased access to capital markets.

Another development among nonprofit hospitals has been the creation of geographic alliances. An alliance is a formal arrangement among several hospitals and/or hospital systems that functions according to written rules. Unlike hospitals within a multihospital system, those in an alliance retain their autonomy. The advantage of an alliance is the development of a network of support among hospitals. For example, hospitals might join together in an alliance to gain purchasing power or to form a preferred provider organization to offer selected services to customers or patients at special rates.

How the Organization Works: Levels of Personnel

Below the assistant administrator level within the hospital is a large middle management group, the departmental management level. It is within the various departments of the hospital

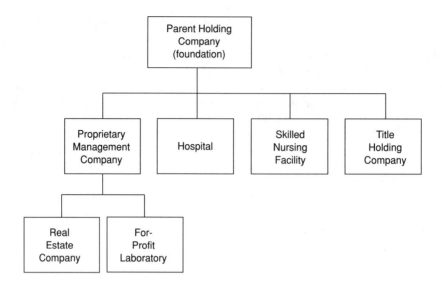

Figure 2–4 Hospital Restructuring. *Source:* Reprinted from *A Layman's Guide to Hospitals III: Hospital Corporate Reorganizations* by Coopers & Lybrand with permission of Coopers & Lybrand, 1981.

that the hospital's functions are carried out. There are five major functions within a hospital organization: (1) nursing, (2) fiscal or business, (3) ancillary services, (4) support services, and (5) medical staff responsibilities. Because the medical staff functions autonomously (is self-governing and is answerable to itself and the institution's board of trustees), the modern CEO has four major and distinct administrative (functional) groupings reporting to him or her as well as a liaison function with the hospital's medical staff.

A typical hospital organization chart is seen in Figure 2–5. However, an organization chart serves more than the purpose of identifying the CEO's function; it also is a guide for the hospital family and delineates the sphere of influence for the middle managers. It also serves as the basis from which to begin matrix management. One of the severe limitations of a hospital's formal organization chart is that it does not reflect the hospital's informal organization, a key element in any organization.

Committees of the medical staff and the board of trustees form a key organizational link between these two groups. The board's executive committee and joint conference committee are important communication vehicles; they provide an excellent forum for doctors to meet with administrators and the board to discuss problems. However, these are formal relationships. There is also a large informal communications network that functions on a day-to-day basis between the administration and the medical staff. Outside the hospital, informal relationships may exist between the hospital board and the hospital's medical staff.

Many hospitals find it beneficial to have one or two physicians serve as voting members of their board of trustees. Having physicians serve on the board embodies a team approach to hospital policy setting and hospital organization. If a hospital has decided against electing members from the medical staff to its board, it is common for the president of the medical staff, the medical director, or a representative from the medical staff to attend hospital board of trustees meetings. These representatives serve as excellent sounding boards for the trustees, and they can be a liaison between the board and the medical staff. However, sharing policy-making power with the medical staff does not in any way elimi-

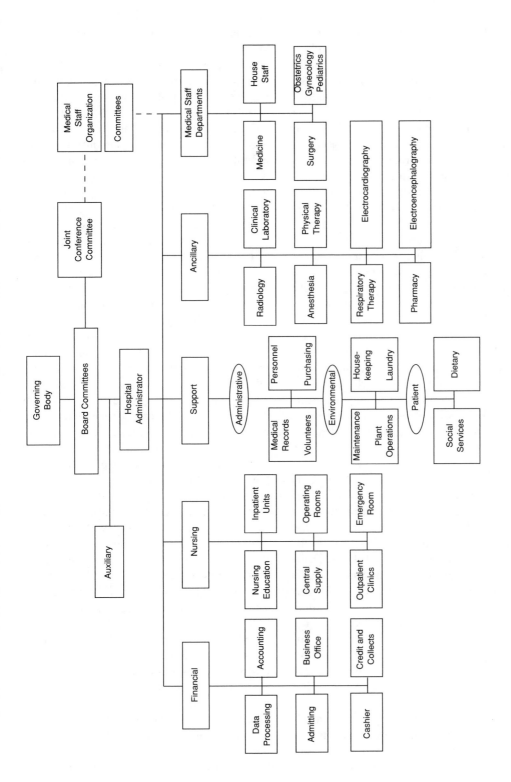

Figure 2–5 A Typical Hospital Organization Chart. *Source:* Reprinted from *Hospitals: What They Are and How They Work*, 2nd ed., by I.D. Snook, Jr., p. 22, Aspen Publishers, Inc., © 1992.

nate or mitigate the board of trustees' responsibility for the policy setting in the institution.

In the long run, no hospital will be successful without effective communication among the board of trustees, the CEO, and the medical staff. The best way to begin the communication process is for all three groups to understand clearly, and agree with, the hospital's objectives. Although the hospital's principal objective is to provide medical and health services, some hospitals have broader missions. Many hospitals serve as training sites for interns and residents. Some hospitals are major clinical research institutions. Whatever the objectives, however, the hospital's board of trustees, its CEO, and the medical staff must agree on them. An effective hospital organization must assign responsibility at all levels, and each of the three major players—the board, the medical staff, and the CEO—must thoroughly understand each other's responsibility and authority if the organization is to be successful. Finally, these three groups must agree on how the hospital will discharge its service obligation. Such agreement requires planning, which is best done among all three groups, not by one or two of the groups acting alone.

The CEO

Years ago, many CEOs, also referred to as hospital administrators, were often chosen from the ranks of the nursing department. In many church-related hospitals, it was common for the CEO to be selected from the ranks of the religious order or from among retired clergy. These administrators were hardworking and dedicated to patient care, but they also inherently followed the physicians' wishes. On the other hand, some administrators worked their way up from the business office or the chief financial officer position to become the hospital's CEO. It was also common in some hospitals to have a retired businessperson or physician assume the CEO position.

Such upward vertical mobility is not common today. CEOs are now more often products of a business school background. The first university course for hospital administrators started in the mid-1930s. As the field of hospital administration became more complex following World War II, the demand for trained hospital administrators increased. One of the greatest influences on the advancement of hospital administration was the formation of the American College of Health Care Executives (ACHE) in 1933. The college encourages high standards of education and ethics, and only those administrators who meet the college's requirements are admitted as members. Today, formal training of hospital administrators is provided by a number of universities in the United States and Canada. These universities offer graduate and undergraduate degrees in hospital or health care administration.

The master's degree is most widely accepted as the required academic preparation for health administration. Many programs offer a master's in business administration, while some offer the master's in public administration, public health. The former two degree programs are often more public policy than business and management oriented. The formal training program for hospital administrators covers three general areas: (1) administrative theory, (2) the study of various components of health care services and medical care, and (3) the study of hospital functions, including the organization and management within the hospital and the role of the hospital in the larger picture of health care delivery systems. The three basic types of skills developed in training are technical, social, and conceptual.

The hospital CEO of the 1930s and 1940s dealt primarily with the internal operations of the hospital. The administrator was concerned with matters that directly affected the patients treated at the hospital. This involved bargaining with employees, developing proper benefit packages, and determining the best methods and techniques to manage the institution. However, in the 1950s and into the 1960s and 1970s, increasingly strong labor unions, third-party payers, and governmental agencies all began to impact significantly on the hospital industry. During this period, the role of the administrator became a dual one, dealing with both inside and outside aspects of hospital management. More sophisticated and specialized management was required to operate a hospital effectively, and the

CEO became more involved in activities outside the hospital.

Today, the CEO has to strike the proper balance between internal and external activities. The main role of the CEO is to coordinate the facilities of the hospital with its resources so as to allow the medical care mission of the institution to be most efficiently and effectively carried out. Since hospitals are also businesses, their services are capable of being measured by business criteria. The CEO's responsibility is to handle and manage the assets of each, personnel, and materials. In the view of the ACHE, the responsibility of the governing body or the board of trustees is to function in a judgmental or deliberate fashion. According to the ACHE, the governing authority appoints a CEO, who is responsible for the performance of all the functions of the institution and is accountable to the governing authority. The CEO, as the head of the organization, is responsible for all functions, including a medical staff, nursing division, technical division, and general services division, that are necessary to ensure the quality of patient care.

Internal Activities of the CEO. Internal activities include duties such as the review and establishment of hospital procedures, supervision of hospital employees and operations (including fiscal activities), and the maintenance of internal relations. Traditionally, it has been the CEO's job to attend to those tasks in the hospital that directly affect the patients' well-being. For example, it is the responsibility of the CEO to see that the building and its facilities are in adequate order and that the personnel are qualified to fill their specific job requirements. Legally, the CEO must answer for the acts of employees under the principle of respondeat superior. Another traditional CEO function, which is even more important today, is to interact with the staff physicians. The administrator must keep both the physicians and the governing board informed about the hospital and its plans. Other important tasks involve the recruitment of new medical staff and the retention of existing staff.

Generally, CEOs attend board meetings in order to communicate ideas, thoughts, and policies that will help the hospital. They prepare and defend annual budgets to be approved by the board of trustees. This includes identifying new services that need to be offered as well as new major equipment that needs to be purchased. Negotiating reimbursement rates with third-party insurance plans (such as Blue Cross and Medicare) and preparing monthly financial statements and statistical data to present to the board are among the internal tasks performed by the CEO in concert with the chief financial officer.

Maintaining a positive relationship and effective communication with the hospital's governing body, medical staff, employees, and patients is very important. The official relationship between the CEO and the governing body is that of an employer and employee, but actually the CEO and the board function more as partners. The administrator is the representative of the board in the daily activities of the institution and must turn the board's power into administrative action. Indeed, the partnership relationship between the board and the administrator has been solidified now that the CEO is a voting member on many hospital governing boards. This is quite common in other industries, in which the CEO is also a member of the board of directors. Typically, when administrators are members of boards, they have the title of president of the institution working under the chair of the board. CEOs can become active, with voting privileges, or act as ex officio members on key board committees, including the nominating, bylaws, and planning committees. However, the CEO should not be chair of the board. The trustees on the board are stewards for the community, and the nature of this stewardship should not permit the administrator, an employee of the hospital, to be the chair.

The CEO should act in partnership not only with the board of trustees but also with the physicians and other health care personnel in the institution. Under the best circumstances, the administrator has a mutual understanding with, respect for, and trust in the members of the medical staff. One of the key responsibilities of the CEO is to communicate with the hospital's medical staff. It is the CEO's job to see that the physicians have the proper tools in the right place at the right time in order for them to carry out their role in the hospital.

Successful CEOs must be effective in keeping their medical staff informed about organizational changes, board policies, and decisions that affect them and their patients. Hospital medical staffs, though ultimately answerable to the board and its medical management, are also self-governing and have their own bylaws. The administrator should be sensitive to the medical staff's needs for self-governance and should support that need. From time to time, natural tensions will arise between the medical staff and the administration. Frequently the sources of this conflict can be attributed to poor communication. The CEO must communicate effectively with the medical staff if the hospital is to function efficiently. Consequently, the CEO must always be available to medical personnel.

The employee group provides many of the CEO's day-to-day challenges. The employees must look to the CEO as their work leader. It is the CEO's role to keep the employees informed of the critical role their services play in the successful operation of the hospital. This is easier to achieve with nurses and others who deliver direct patient care, but the CEO must continually be informing all employees of their mission and importance. In dealing with employees at all levels, it is critical that the CEO show objectivity, understanding, and fairness. The CEO must handle the authority to employ, direct, discipline, and dismiss employees with these important principles in mind.

Last, the CEO has a vital role in patient relations. The CEO must fulfill all legitimate patient requests for general comfort and care in order to assist their recovery. In dealing with patients, the CEO must also understand the needs of the patients' friends and relatives. Also, it is important that the CEO safeguard confidential patient information.

External Activities of the CEO. The outside activities of today's CEOs are numerous. They include relating to the community, understanding governmental relationships, and participating in educational and planning activities. One of the roles of the modern administrator is to educate the community about hospital operations and health care matters. This is usually done through various hospital publications and community lectures. It is the CEO's responsibility to present a positive image of the hospital. Public relations duties are considered key outside activities, and the CEO must promote public understanding of hospital programs through the mass media. One of the most valuable accomplishments of today's CEO is the negotiating of contracts with third-party payers (insurance companies). This is a time-consuming activity requiring a combination of management and negotiation skills. Today's CEO must stay on top of the latest government rules and regulations concerning funding, reimbursement, and planning issues. CEOs meet with governmental reimbursement agencies, planning bodies, and politicians in order to keep up-to-date and to lobby for hospital interests. CEOs may lobby on an individual basis, with area CEOs, or as part of regional or national groups through hospital associations.

Dealing with the public vendors and other health administrators and agencies is vital for the CEO. It is the CEO's job to remain in close contact with the community that sponsors the hospital or health care institution. The CEO must realize that the institution has a responsibility to the public and that the public has a right to be informed. The CEO has to maintain the highest ethical principles in dealing with vendors. It is the CEO who must remember impartiality and objectivity when representing the hospital in business dealings. Neither the institution nor the administrator can accept favors, commissions, unethical rebates, or gifts from vendors in return for doing business with a certain company.

The Physician Executive

Increasingly, and stimulated by trends toward managed care, physicians are taking a greater role in hospital management and the decision-making process because these affect their professional lives. Many physicians are assuming the top role of CEO. Other management roles for physicians are serving as the hospital's medical director, who is usually a full-time employee with senior administrative responsibilities, or as the chief of the medical staff. This latter position provides excellent training in supervision of personnel and resources and in coordination of activities. Many larger hospitals have full-time clinical department heads and a chief of medicine and a chief of surgery. All of these are excellent opportunities for physicians who wish to move up into the CEO ranks. It is likely that in the future more physicians will seek to assume executive management jobs.

Assistant Administrator or Vice President

One of the most important responsibilities of the CEO is to select and hire a competent administrative staff. It is the administrator's staff that is delegated the responsibility of seeing that the hospital is run smoothly and efficiently. The assistant administrator or vice president in charge of hospital operations, also referred to as the chief operating officer, assists the CEO in coordinating all hospital activities, such as support, ancillary, and fiscal services. Typically, there are assistant administrators or vice presidents in charge of all major functional areas in the hospital. The assistant administrator frequently is involved in staff functions and is a junior member of the hospital's administrative team. The assistant administrator plans and participates in studies and programs that help the CEO in the hospital. Frequently, the assistant administrator is a liaison between the hospital administrator and some of the other functioning hospital departments.

The Future for CEOs

Although hospitals are not growing in numbers, they have become much more complex and by doing so, have created a middle management level that did not exist 15 or 20 years ago. Other changes in the health care industry are also creating new jobs. With respect to female CEOs, the future looks bright. A review of the numbers of students who are entering graduate programs in hospital administration shows a growing number of women among the entrants. A review of the progress of recent women graduates shows that over 70 percent of them got the job of their first choice and that their starting salaries were comparable with those of their male counterparts.

THE MEDICAL STAFF

The hospital medical staff is an organized body of physicians, dentists, perhaps podiatrists, and in some instances allied health staff professionals who attend patients and participate in related clinical care duties. The medical staff has the greatest impact on the quality and quantity of care given in the hospital. The medical staff is the heart of the hospital. Members of the medical staff have been authorized by the board of trustees to attend patients in the hospital and are accountable to the governing authority. They are accountable to the hospital for high-quality patient care through the application of ethical, clinical, and scientific procedures and practices. Though the governing body has the ultimate legal and moral responsibility for the hospital, including the quality of medical care, the board of trustees cannot practice medicine and is dependent upon the members of the medical staff to admit patients and to provide quality patient care.

The medical staff is appointed by the board of trustees. The staff is then expected to formulate its own medical policies, rules, and regulations and to be responsible to the board for the quality of patient care. Though the medical profession is a highly disciplined, professional group, it is made up of highly individualistic members who have their own unique approaches to medicine and organizational relationships. Therefore, the task of coordinating the efforts of the medical staff with the board of trustees, the administrator, and the rest of the hospital can be a challenging one.

Medical Staff Organization

The internal organization of the medical staff varies from hospital to hospital. Complex university or teaching hospitals differ from the smaller community hospitals. Because of the efforts of the Joint Commission on Accreditation of Healthcare Organizations and its accreditation standards, the differences are fewer today than in the past. The standards stipulate that there is to be a single organized medical staff that has overall responsibility for the quality of the professional services provided by individuals with clinical privileges as well as the responsibility of accountability to the governing body.

Appointment to the medical staff is a formal process that is outlined in each hospital's medical staff bylaws, again with encouragement for standardization from the Joint Commission. A brief outline of the appointment process that a doctor must go through follows:

1. The applying physician completes a written application. The completed application is usually forwarded to the hospital CEO.
2. The application is reviewed for completeness and verification and then is sent for screening to the head of the specific department or specialty (e.g., medicine or surgery) to which the applicant is applying.
3. The application is then forwarded to the medical staff's credentials committee, which reviews the physician's qualifications and past professional performance. It is at this point that the credentials committee may request a meeting with the applicant.
4. The executive committee for the medical staff reviews and discusses the application. It sends its recommendation on to the hospital governing body.
5. The board of trustees as a whole or through one of its committees reviews the application. The board will accept, reject, or defer the application. If the application is questionable, requires more information, or needs discussion, it may be referred to the joint conference committee.
6. The physician is usually notified by the CEO that the appointment has been approved or rejected. Any limitations on privileges requested may also be noted in the letter sent to the physician. In receiving approval, a physician is granted certain clinical privileges (procedures the doctor is permitted to perform within the hospital). This is referred to as the individual's privileges delineation. The privilege delineation process is based on verifiable information made available to the credentials committee. A physician's demonstrated current competence in his or her discipline is the crucial determination of privileges. The privileges are listed on a form or placed on a record of some nature and kept on file in key places within the hospital, for example, within the operating room and the medical staff office.

The physician who has applied and been admitted to the staff is appointed in two separate categories of membership: (1) to a clinical department or section, and (2) with a status based on the extent of the physician's participation and privileges, referred to as a category. Staff membership status may be categorized as illustrated in Exhibit 2–1.

The organization of the hospital medical staff is divided into medical specialty departments and sections. For example, there may be departments of medicine, surgery, obstetrics and gynecology, and pediatrics. In larger hospitals these departments may be further subdivided into sections. Each clinical department has a physician designated as chief or director, who is the medical administrative head. This person is generally selected through a process outlined in the medical staff bylaws. Usually this is done either through election by departmental members or by appointment by the hospital board of trustees.

Closed and Open Medical Staffs

Historically, individual hospitals have controlled their own admissions to medical staff. However, in recent years hospital autonomy has eroded in this area. A closed medical staff is one that closely monitors and restricts any new applicants to the staff or to a department of the staff. This is generally done with the concur-

Exhibit 2–1 Categories of Medical Staff Membership

Attending Staff: Active staff members with full rights and privileges, voting prerogatives, and obligations to attend meetings, serve on committees, and handle emergency service responsibilities

Associate Staff: Staff members who have incomplete staff privileges and are in the transition from provisional active status

Provisional Staff: Staff members who were recently appointed and who have fewer privileges and responsibilities, such as the inability to vote

Courtesy Staff: Staff members who do not frequently admit patients and who do not have the full obligations of active staff membership

Consulting Staff: Staff members with areas of specialization who consult with other staff members and who do not have the privileges of treating and admitting patients

Temporary Staff: Staff members who are only given privileges for a designated period of time

rence of the hospital board of trustees. When a hospital does permit a closed medical staff, it is usually based upon considerations related to the quality of and need for patient care within the community. There may also be closed medical staffs within selected departments or sections in the hospital; the two most notable examples are the radiology and pathology departments. In these hospital-based departments, the hospital signs an agreement with a physician or a professional group to allow exclusive services in the department. The courts have generally found this to be a legal arrangement if such agreements are based upon significant medical, administrative, and, more recently, economic considerations. Closed medical staff issues are frequently addressed in the courts under the federal antitrust laws. Additionally, since the Federal Trade Commission has the power to promulgate rules and regulations defining unfair practices in this area, it is reasonable to assume that it will be the predominant enforcement agency relative to medical staff admissions in years to come. An open staff essentially admits all qualified physicians who meet the hospital's guidelines.

Medical Staff Committees

The Joint Commission standards dictate that the medical staff shall develop and adopt bylaws, rules, and regulations to establish a frame-

work of self-government and a means for accountability to the governing body. The bylaws outline the form of self-government of the medical staff. The medical staff conducts its business through committees. The committee chairpersons are either selected by members of the staff or appointed by the president of the staff.

One of the most important committees is the medical staff executive committee. It continues the medical staff business in the interim between general staff meetings. Generally, the executive committee is composed of the officers of the staff and a number of elected members from the staff. Typically, this committee meets monthly to conduct the business of the medical staff. The hospital CEO usually attends. The medical staff executive committee coordinates various committees and rules that affect the different clinical departments of the staff. The credentials committee, the medical records committee, the tissue committee, and the medical audit and quality committee are other key committees of the staff. The credentials committee has the responsibility to review the qualifications of new physicians applying for membership. This committee also reviews the credentials of medical staff members who must be reappointed. Reappointment is usually either once a year or every other year. The credentials committee could also be the committee to investigate breaches of ethics or misconduct among the members of the medical staff. This committee reports directly to the executive committee.

Since medical records have become the principal instrument for review of quality assurance in hospitals, the medical records committee has taken on a more important function in recent years. Initially the medical records committee was responsible for reviewing the forms that were used in the medical records. It now also reviews the quantity and quality of patient records as written by physicians, nurses, or other associated health professionals in the hospital. It also serves as a monitor of the physicians who may have delinquent medical records. This committee works closely with the hospital's medical records administrator.

An efficient medical audit committee and a well-functioning tissue committee traditionally have been key instruments in assessing quality. The tissue committee provides a vehicle to confirm the diagnosis for surgical cases and acts as a control on unnecessary surgery. Practicing surgeons plus a member of the hospital pathology department make up the membership. The tissue committee reviews all surgical cases to determine, based on the review of tissue taken from the patient, whether surgery was necessary. Tissue removed from an operation is forwarded to the pathology laboratory for postoperative diagnosis and review.

The medical audit committee, sometimes called the quality assurance committee, safeguards quality in the hospital. This committee is generally made up of physicians with some staff administrative support. It reviews the practice of medicine in all disciplines. Attention is given to clinical outcome and problem solving.

The Medical Director

Hospitals usually employ full-time medical directors. This is the most appropriate way to fulfill the hospital's responsibility for quality care in the institution. Some medical staffs see this trend as a threat to their self-governance and as an administrative encroachment into medical staff affairs. Generally, the medical director is a top-level management employee whose position may be full time or part time. If part time, the medical director may also see patients and therefore could be a member of the medical staff. The medical director's role is to evaluate clinical performance and to enforce hospital policy related to quality care. However, as in other management jobs, the role may be expanded to include other activities.

Allied Health Personnel

There continues to be an increasing number of nonphysicians and nondentists applying for clinical privileges within hospitals, including, but not limited to, podiatrists, chiropractors, physician assistants, nurse practitioners, nurse midwives, and psychologists. By applying for medical staff privileges, some of these groups have raised the question of how or if they fit into the medical staff.

Historically, reinforced by laws and regulations, hospitals have excluded these groups from practicing within the hospital. Generally, state regulations regarding nurse practitioners and physician assistants indicate that a physician must supervise their work. The American Medical Association basically agrees with the American Hospital Association on this issue and feels that full medical staff privileges should be granted only to physicians and dentists. The Joint Commission has been somewhat more liberal with regard to podiatrists and has delineated the scope of services that a podiatrist can provide within a hospital. The Joint Commission permits other duly licensed health care professionals to practice in hospitals under the supervision of a practitioner who has clinical privileges.

STRENGTHENING HOSPITAL AND PHYSICIAN TIES IN THE FUTURE: NEW PARTNERSHIPS

Working Closer Together

As changes come to the health care industry more frequently, and with greater impact than ever before, hospitals and their medical staffs are coming to the realization that they have much more in common. There is a general movement in the hospital industry for executives and boards to work more closely with their physicians. There is a common effort to improve relationships between the institution and its doctors.

Collaborating and working closely is not easy for the hospital managers or the practicing physicians. The training of physicians and managers has bred different mindsets. For example, physicians are trained to work independently, while managers work regularly in groups and value collaboration. History and past relationships have led both groups to focus on stereotypes in identifying each other.

The Physician-Hospital Organization

One of the important trends toward collaboration is represented by the current movement toward integrated medical delivery systems among hospitals, physicians, and insurers. The growth of managed care plans has led hospitals to use a new structure in working with their doctors, namely the physician-hospital organization (PHO). The PHO is designed to ease the burden for both groups in adjusting to increased managed care. Using the PHO, both parties can evaluate and negotiate managed care contracts. In the past, managed care firms either worked first with the hospital and then let the hospitals deal with the doctors or worked with the two separately. The traditional medical staff structure (which is highly democratic) has severe limitations in building an economic partnership. The need for greater synergy among hospitals, physicians, and insurers is becoming evident. More specifically, physicians are moving to be more involved in institutional decision making, while institutional managers are showing a willingness to share resources and control with their physicians. To be successful, both groups have to be willing to change the way they do business.

The first step toward integration is often when a hospital develops a PHO. It is the PHO that allows physician participation into the larger integrated system. It offers a mechanism for physicians and hospitals to act as partners. The PHO takes form as a formal organization and legal entity. PHOs are vehicles for hospitals and physicians to build an economic alliance. The new PHO partnership can contract with insurers and government purchasers. The PHO bonds the physicians and hospital together fiscally. As managed care expands, so does the PHO. Some see PHOs as being at the core of an integrated community health care system.

I. DONALD SNOOK, JR., is President of Presbyterian-University of Pennsylvania Medical Center in Philadelphia. He is also a faculty member in the graduate program in Health Care Administration at La Salle College in Philadelphia.

Mr. Snook has contributed numerous articles to health care management literature, has conducted seminars on physician recruitment and medical staff development, and is the author of *Hospitals: What They Are and How They Work, Building a Winning Medical Staff,* and *50 Effective Hospital Print Ads.* He is the originator of the "hotel-hospital" concept. He is the recipient of the American Healthcare Marketing Association's "CEO Marketer of the Year Award."

Mr. Snook holds a BBA in Marketing from the Wharton School of the University of Pennsylvania (cum laude) and an MBA in Hospital Administration from George Washington University. He has also completed the Health Management Systems Program at the Harvard Business School.

Chapter 3

The Medical Staff

Martin Paris

The U.S. health care system is today in the midst of radical reconfiguration. The relationships and prerogatives of the hospital's three major power centers (board of trustees, administration, and medical staff) therefore currently exist in a state of continuing and fundamental change. Power is increasingly becoming centralized within the board of trustees and the hospital administration; prerogatives that were previously jealously guarded by the medical staff are waning as a result of legal and economic changes. The emergence of independent practice associations (IPAs) is part of the realignment of power among the three power centers.

Paradoxically, however, as the autonomy of the medical staff erodes, maintaining good physician relationships is becoming an increasingly important part of the successful hospital administrator's job skills, and medical staff involvement in such nontraditional areas as resource allocation, strategic planning, and business development is becoming an increasingly critical determinant of the average hospital's future viability.

FUNCTIONS

Each hospital's medical staff has a single, preeminent responsibility: medical care quality as-

surance. The medical staff assures the quality of care received by the hospital's patients through the exercise of the following six powers:

1. defining and promulgating standards of medical care within the hospital
2. recommending candidates for appointment to the medical staff
3. granting specific practice privileges to individual members of the medical staff
4. monitoring and auditing the quality of medical care services provided by hospital departments and/or specific physicians
5. assuring the ongoing process of continuing medical education for the hospital's physicians
6. disciplining individual physicians whose practice patterns deviate from the norm

As the significance of clinical practice protocols increases as a result of managed care, the role of the medical director and medical staff will become more solidified.

HISTORICAL DEVELOPMENT

Although hospitals have existed for thousands of years, the modern hospital is a surprisingly recent innovation. The discovery of surgical an-esthetics and the popularization of techniques to ensure surgical antisepsis approximately 100 years ago transformed the hospital into a place to cure illness, rather than a place to comfort the dying.

The medical staff organization now characteristic of U.S. hospitals crystallized approximately 60 years ago as a byproduct of the last major revolution in U.S. health care practices. This revolution created our modern health care delivery system by imposing licensure, certification, and other professional standards on a health care system that until then had been remarkably unregulated.

Health care is currently one of the most heavily regulated enterprises in the country. At the turn of the century, the situation was quite different. The health care industry was characterized by (1) provider oversupply, (2) competition, and (3) freedom from regulation.

For example, in the late 1700s less than 10 percent of the country's "doctors" actually held degrees. One hundred years later, the situation had not changed substantially as physician licensure laws existed in only a handful of states. In the late 1850s, approximately 400—mostly commercial—medical schools existed. By 1930, this number had shrunk to 76 following publication of the Flexner Report and the imposition of its recommendations for the improvement of medical education. In the late 1800s, the typical community hospital permitted an "open staff" of virtually any and all community physicians to admit patients, exercising almost no oversight responsibility for their actions.

The national specialty board that today tightly control physician certification and credentialing were, at the turn of the century, still waiting to be born. The concepts of external monitoring, regulatory standard setting, and internal quality assurance auditing, now a routine activity in the hospital industry, were, at the turn of the century, still waiting to be accepted.

The organizations that were prominent in the wave of reform that created the modern hospital were the American College of Surgeons, the American Medical Association, and the Joint Commission on Accreditation of Healthcare Organizations.

The American College of Surgeons developed minimum standards for hospitals, which were adopted in 1919. The organization itself, now the major certification board of the surgical profession, was created in 1913. The major provisions of these minimum standards were as follows:

- Physicians who practice in a hospital must be organized as a definite medical staff with subgroups of active, courtesy, and associate members.

- Medical staff membership must be restricted to physicians competent in their field who practice according to ethical dictates.

- Formal rules and regulations must be adopted governing professional practice in the hospital.

- Reviews of the activities of the hospital's clinical departments must be conducted through monthly meetings of the medical staff.

- Complete medical records must be maintained for each patient to facilitate the process of clinical review.

- Adequate clinical laboratory facilities must be maintained.

Today, these standards would be considered extraordinarily basic. Nevertheless, of 692 hospitals surveyed in the first year the American College of Surgeons conducted its reviews, only 13 percent met these basic standards.

The requirements of the American College of Surgeons eventually were translated into minimum requirements for state licensure. However, in 1946, a full 27 years after the American College of Surgeons' first report, only 10 of the then-existing 48 states had passed state licensure laws. A condition of the Hill-Burton Act, the federal program that funded the postwar building boom of the U.S. hospital industry, was that all states receiving funds must adopt a hospital licensure law.

The American Medical Association, through its Council on Medical Education and Hospitals during the 1920s and 1930s, developed standards for hospital-based internship and residency programs. This standard-setting activity, coupled with the contemporaneous rise of strong national specialty board-certifying organizations, increased the momentum throughout the hospital industry for the development of effective and structured medical staff organizations.

Finally, the Joint Commission was formed in 1952 by a consortium of sponsors, including the American College of Surgeons, the American College of Physicians, the American Hospital Association, and the American Medical Association. The Joint Commission is now the single most influential accrediting organization in the hospital industry. Its standards, originally derived from those issued by the American College of Surgeons, have subsequently developed into an elaborate complex of guidelines that largely define our current expectations of the proper role, organization, and function of the hospital's medical staff.

The flurry of standard-setting and regulatory activity sparked by these three organizations resulted in an autonomous medical staff power center in the U.S. hospital where none had existed previously. Additionally, it cemented the division of the U.S. hospital into an administrative sphere controlled by the hospital's lay administration and a clinical sphere under the control of the medical staff.

The hospital reform movement in the United States, therefore, generated a corollary movement: medical staff autonomy. This is not surprising, because much of the energy driving the reform activity originated within the medical profession itself.

The end result of these reform activities was a hospital/medical staff relationship in the United States that is different from that of most other Western countries. In Europe, for example, hospital staffs are closed and are composed of full-time hospital-based physicians who are salaried employees of the institution or the state. Hospital-based practitioners provide specialty care on a referral basis. In contrast, office-based practitioners provide primary care and rarely treat hospitalized patients. In contrast, the typical U.S. hospital has voluntary staff of fee-for-service physicians engaged simultaneously in both hospital-based and office-based practice. Hospital staff physicians provide both primary and specialty care, and medical staff membership (in theory) is open to all community physicians able to meet professional requirements.

MEDICAL STAFF STRUCTURE

Medical staffs are organized along a continuum of almost infinite variability. The mores and politics of each hospital dictate how its medical staff will be organized.

At one extreme is the highly structured medical staff organization of the university teaching hospital, which is characterized by (1) full-time salaried chiefs of service, (2) a large proportion of full-time attending physicians, (3) division into major clinical and subspecialty departments, (4) an active ongoing schedule of medical staff conferences and educational activities, and (5) tight control of the staff credentialing process.

At the other extreme is the more loosely organized structure characteristic of the small, rural hospital in which the medical staff functions as a loose, unstructured federation of independently practicing physicians. This organization form is characterized by (1) an absence of clinical department subdivisions, (2) an absence of paid clinical chiefs of service, and (3) a less active schedule of staff conference and educational activities.

On the whole, the degree of organization of a medical staff can be ascertained by the answers to the following questions:

- How restrictive is the appointment process? Entry procedures range from an essentially open staff, with membership available to all licensed community physicians, to closed staffs, with virtually insurmountable barriers to entry, such as appointment to medical school teaching faculties and economic credentialing.

- How committed are the physicians to the hospital? Do most physicians admit to only one or to a multiplicity of hospitals? How many hours do they spend at the hospital? How onerous are the requirements for committee attendance and the other service obligations of medical staff membership?
- What percentage of the staff is on salary?
- Is the staff departmentalized into major and subspecialty clinical services? Are there full-time clinical directors for the major and subspecialty services? Are these chiefs paid or voluntary?
- What are the number of medical staff committees? How frequently do they meet?

Currently, and consistent with a vertically organizing industry, structures are emerging that incorporate hospital-based and non–hospital-based physicians in common or multiple entities that enter into equity ownership with a hospital in new entities such as physician-hospital organizations (PHOs) and managed care organizations (MCOs).

COMMITTEE STRUCTURE

The Joint Commission standards mandate the existence of only one committee: the executive committee. In practice, however, medical staff responsibilities are exercised through an elaborate committee structure. An outline of the principal committees and their functional interrelationships is presented in Figure 3–1.

The Joint Commission-mandated functions of the medical staff are administratively expressed in the following committees:

- *Medical records committee:* This committee reviews patient records to assure that complete medical records are maintained for all hospital patients. The committee additionally approves patient record forms and policies and procedures relating to the maintenance of medical records.
- *Tissue or surgical review committee:* This committee reviews the necessity for all surgical procedures performed at the hospital.

Its scope of review covers all procedures performed whether or not human tissue was removed. Broadly, it attempts to answer three questions: (1) was the procedure necessary? (2) was it performed in an appropriate manner? and (3) was the outcome satisfactory? Additionally, the committee is responsible for developing data about overall patterns of surgical care in the hospital.

- *Infection control committee:* This committee is responsible for assuring that the internal hospital environment minimizes the exposure of both patients and hospital personnel to infectious complications. It therefore develops policies and procedures relative to infection control and assures accurate reporting of infections occurring in the hospital.
- *Pharmacy and therapeutics committee:* This committee develops policies about the hospital's utilization and internal distribution of drugs. It approves the hospital's formulary, which lists those drugs authorized for storage in the hospital's pharmacy and for utilization by the medical staff. Additionally, it monitors patterns of drug utilization within the hospital, including aggregate expenditures and all adverse drug reactions. An increasingly important function of the committee is review of antibiotic usage, which is frequently organized in a separate committee or subcommittee of its own.
- *Utilization review committee:* This committee screens medical records for the inappropriate or unnecessary utilization of medical services. Its existence is mandated as a prerequisite for participation in the Medicare program.
- *Quality assurance committee:* This committee has broad oversight responsibility for monitoring patient care. It collects and analyzes data relevant to patient care outcomes, receives referrals from hospital personnel and/or other committees, and undertakes patient care evaluation studies as

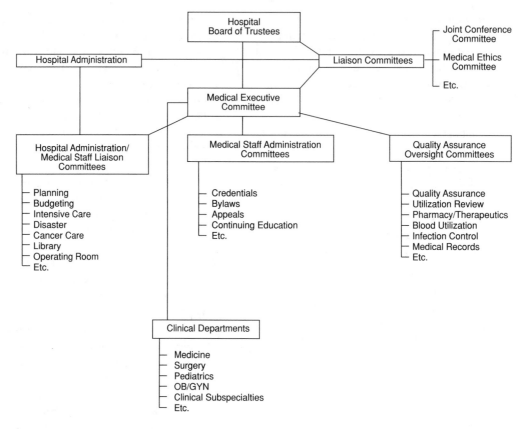

Figure 3–1 Illustrative Medical Staff Committee Structure

indicated. It is responsible for identifying problem areas, recommending changes as required, and monitoring the efficacy of corrective action.

- *Credentials committee:* This committee reviews all applicants for appointment to the medical staff, assures that all necessary documents are authenticated, reviews the past performance of all applicants in other hospital settings, and recommends candidates for appointment to the appropriate category of medical staff membership.
- *Blood utilization committee:* This committee collects and monitors data relevant to the utilization of blood and blood components within the hospital; evaluates the necessity of all transfusions given within the hospital; and ensures that policies and pro-

cedures relevant to storage, administration, and utilization of blood and blood components are appropriate.

- *Medical education committee:* This committee is responsible for monitoring the educational needs of the medical staff and for assuring that educational activities are consistent with these needs and with problems identified as a result of the staff's ongoing quality assurance activities.
- *Bylaws committee:* This committee develops the medical staff bylaws and recommends revisions to rules, regulations, and bylaws of the medical staff as required.

In addition to the above-listed core committees, many additional committees exist in most hospitals to meet specific needs. Examples of such committees include:

- *Joint conference committee:* This committee is designed to facilitate ongoing dialogue among the hospital's medical staff, its board of trustees, and its administration.
- *Ethics committee:* This committee develops guidelines and standards incorporating ethical considerations involved in the provision of health care services to the acutely ill.
- *Investigational review board:* This committee approves all experimental therapies rendered to hospital patients and assures that all necessary ethical, moral, and legal considerations are fulfilled in the conduct of such experimental activities. It additionally documents the patient outcomes of such experimental therapies.

Unique to each hospital are a variety of additional committees created to facilitate problem solving across administrative and medical departmental boundaries. These committees focus on specific issues usually relating to patient care or regulatory agency requirements. Examples include the following:

- operating room committee
- critical care/intensive care committee
- emergency department committee
- disaster committee
- dietary committee

MEDICAL STAFF DEPARTMENTS

Although not mandated by the Joint Commission, the hospital medical staff is typically divided into separate and distinct clinical departments, including medicine, surgery, pediatrics, OB/GYN, radiology, pathology, and anesthesiology. Each medical staff is free to select the number and type of clinical departments felt to be necessary for the proper conduct of the hospital's clinical activities.

Departments, once organized, must (1) be headed by a department chief, (2) have departmental rules and regulations to guide the collective efforts of its members, and (3) grant categories of membership paralleling the categories utilized by the medical staff as a whole. The Joint Commission mandates that major clinical departments meet once monthly to monitor patient care outcomes within the department and to propose corrective steps when necessary.

The activities of each department are guided by a department chief whose broad responsibilities include:

- accountability for professional activities of the members of the department
- ongoing surveillance of the professional activities of the members of the department
- recommending practice privileges for members of the department
- recommending standards used to grant practice privileges
- overseeing the continuing education activities of the department
- monitoring patient care outcomes for patients treated within the department

Department chairs may be paid or voluntary, full- or part-time, at the discretion of the medical staff and the concurrence of the hospital's board.

CATEGORIES OF MEDICAL STAFF MEMBERSHIP

Although not mandated by the Joint Commission, medical staff membership is typically categorized. Examples of such categories include:

- *Attending staff* who enjoy complete "citizenship" within the medical staff community. Active staff members are eligible to vote in medical staff elections, chair medical staff committees, serve as staff officers, supervise newly appointed staff members, chair clinical departments, and otherwise exercise the full prerogatives of medical staff membership.
- *Associate staff* who are in the process of advancement from provisional to active staff status. Such members hold incomplete staff privileges.
- *Provisional staff* who are newly appointed to the staff and are in the process of being

reviewed by senior members of the active staff. This review involves a process of observation during which the clinical competence of the provisional staff member can be assessed. Such staff members do not enjoy the full prerogatives of staff membership. Typically, they cannot hold office or vote on staff affairs.

- *Courtesy staff* who admit patients infrequently, but are given appropriate staff privileges to do so. Courtesy staff typically do not assume the full obligations of active staff membership.
- *Consulting staff* who, because of specific areas of specialization, are available for consultation to other staff members, but do not have independent privileges to treat and admit patients.
- *Temporary staff* who are given privileges for a defined period of time because of particular circumstances.

Obtaining medical staff membership is a complex and frequently onerous undertaking. A prospective candidate must first be appointed to a specific category of medical staff membership as described above. He or she must then obtain practice privileges on the staff. For example, a physician may be authorized only to admit and treat patients, but not to perform consultations; alternatively, he or she may be authorized to perform procedure A but not procedure B. A physician may be granted unrestricted privileges to perform procedure A, or he or she may be given restricted privileges, such as permission to perform procedure A only after obtaining prior authorization from the department chair or while under the direct supervision of a more senior staff member.

Before obtaining appointment and practice privileges, the applicant's request is typically separately reviewed and approved by a credentials review committee, a clinical department chair, the medical executive committee, and the hospital's board of trustees.

Once admitted to the staff, a physician who desires appointment to an additional department—usually a subspecialty—must go through this process once again and separately obtain a category of membership and specific practice privileges within the department.

LEGAL CONSIDERATIONS

The collective medical staff exercises substantial authority over the professional lives of its members by granting practice privileges, by monitoring practice patterns of individual physicians, and by appointing, as well as periodically reappointing, all members of the medical staff.

By exercising these powers the medical staff can determine which physicians will practice their profession and under what circumstances within the confines of the hospital. This power is consistent with the needs of public policy, which increasingly demands that physicians evaluate the care offered by other physicians and limit, as necessary, the practice rights of physicians who practice inappropriately.

Physicians, however, practice not only as colleagues but also as competitors. Decisions by the medical staff to limit, deny, or criticize clinical activities of specific physicians have substantial economic repercussions for the physician involved. Not surprisingly, therefore, there are correspondingly substantial legal consequences for those involved in promulgating such decisions.

A full discussion of medical staff/legal issues is beyond the scope of this chapter. However, some of the major issues that medical staff leaders must consider are:

- *Due process protection:* All medical staff actions must be taken in strict conformity with procedural guidelines incorporated within the medical staff bylaws. These bylaws, in turn, must incorporate a series of review and appeal procedures designed to protect individual physicians from arbitrarily or capriciously imposed sanctions.
- *Malpractice liability:* In most states, records of medical staff committees involved in quality of care assessment are subject to discovery proceedings in the event of malpractice litigation. Not surpris-

ingly this exercises a chilling effect on the zeal with which many committees exercise the all-important function of quality care assessment. Physicians are reluctant to criticize the actions of their colleagues if comments made as part of an educational and self-improvement process may potentially result in increased future malpractice liability.

- *Defamation liability:* A physician subject to medical staff sanctions may respond by initiating suit for slander, libel, or defamation against the individuals involved in the decision-making process. Again, the prospect of legal liability and extended litigation exercises a potentially negative impact on the zeal with which quality assurance monitoring is conducted.

- *Antitrust liability:* In 1975 the U.S. Supreme Court broadened the reach of the Sherman Anti-Trust Act, which banned anticompetitive and monopolistic activities, to include the health professions. A cascade of antitrust cases has been filed subsequently, frequently concerning the denial or limitation of hospital staff privileges. One of the more relevant is *Patrick v. Burget*, which resulted in a $2.2 million antitrust judgment against 11 physician members of a hospital peer review panel that was convened to consider revocation of a surgeon's operating privileges. The surgeon, who resigned from the hospital's staff prior to the committee's decision, charged that the panel, dominated by members of a group practice providing the bulk of the community's health care, was actually involved in an attempt to maintain monopolistic control of the region's health care system. The jury found for the physician. The U.S. District Court furthermore overturned an Oregon state law providing immunity for physician members of peer review panels, arguing that federal antitrust law preempted the applicable state law. *Patrick v. Burget* graphically illustrates the need to separate economic from professional considerations in medical staff quality assurance activities.

More recently, however, physicians have been denied privileges when they did not economically contribute, through admissions, to a hospital. Economic credentialing has become a more common criterion in the past few years as hospitals seek to limit medical staff size.

In a much different context, some hospitals have successfully used antitrust suits to seek protection against groups of physicians who have attempted to influence hospital policy through economic coercion: the threat of withholding admissions. Other antitrust issues are important and are considered in another chapter.

DYNAMICS OF MEDICAL STAFF/ HOSPITAL INTERACTIONS

The organization of the medical staff's committees, departments, and membership categories imposes a structure upon the hospital's internal decision-making process. However, the decisions made are defined by a more subtle amalgam of personality interactions, local political factors, economic considerations, personal rivalries, and the interplay among the medical staff, the hospital administration, and the board of trustees.

Each hospital must internally develop a process by which the long-term goals of the institution can be crystallized and implemented. This task is complicated by the fact that in many cases the hospital and its medical staff view each other's goals as mutually competitive. Accordingly, a mechanism must exist that allows priorities to be established and conflicts to be resolved.

The heart of this process is the hospital's internal committee structure. Indeed, the modern hospital's internal landscape resembles that of a complex legislative body. Business is conducted through an elaborate system of committees— board, administrative, medical staff, and mixed. These committees are organized on a standing and ad hoc basis.

The committee structure must foster two qualities between the hospital's administrative and professional leaders: **communication** and **trust**. Unfortunately, both commodities are frequently in short supply. Yet, the demands of an increasingly competitive and increasingly litigious health care environment make imperative a free flow of dialogue between the three major power centers of the hospital.

A hospital beset with medical staff dissension is invariably a hospital that has inappropriately organized medical staff and medical/administrative committees.

The five key questions concerning the medical staff/administrative committee system are as follows:

1. Who serves on medical staff committees and who chairs them?
2. How are these individuals appointed, and do they represent the interests of a broad spectrum of the staff?
3. Are the medical staff's opinion leaders represented in leadership positions on key committees?
4. Do the staff committees communicate effectively with each other and with the executive committee?
5. Are representatives of the hospital's board of trustees and/or administration members on medical staff committees?

Relationship with the Board of Trustees

The requirement for an open flow of information and dialogue has resulted in a trend to permit medical staff leaders to serve as voting members of hospital boards of trustees. These medical staff leaders serve either ex officio by virtue of their positions as medical staff officers or as elected representatives of the staff.

Board–medical staff interaction can be accomplished in several ways: direct medical staff participation on the hospital's board of trustees, appointment of board members to serve on medical staff committees, and creation of liaison and coordinating committees, such as the joint conference committee.

Indirect relationships, however, typically are an equally important mechanism of communica-tion. The social and economic status of senior members of most hospitals' medical staffs allows them access to social networks involving board members. As a result, such physicians often have an access to board members that rivals or exceeds that of the hospital's CEO.

Relationship with Administration

Medical staff/hospital administration relationships are predominantly bureaucratic, concentrated primarily in hospital committee interactions, and carried on through formal mechanisms of communication, such as newsletters, memoranda, and committee minutes.

Many hospitals' internal politics are characterized by tension between administration and medical staff. The relationship between the two can with some accuracy be compared to an uneasy armistice marked on both sides by wary vigilance, tension, and suspicion, with periodic eruptions of overt hostilities.

At most well-run hospitals this tension is minimized, but it is unrealistic to state that it ever completely disappears in any hospital. This tension is caused partly by the divergent economic agendas of the hospital and its affiliated practitioners and partly by the differing mindset of physicians and administrators. Most physicians value individual clinical autonomy; most administrators value team orientation and a corporate approach to health care delivery. Physicians are frequently oriented to short-term action because clinical decision-making as it relates to individual patient care mandates such an approach. In contrast, hospital administrators must focus on macro-institutional issues that frequently have a long-term and financial orientation. Because of the various constituency groups that the typical hospital administrator must satisfy, his or her focus must be more on bureaucratic process than on immediate action, the antithesis of the physician's preferred style.

These perceptual differences put a premium on understanding and mutual respect as a key element in hospital problem solving. Unfortunately these commodities, maintained on a sustained basis, are as rare in the hospital's political arena as they are in most other political arenas.

CHANGING TRENDS

The United States is currently in the midst of a radical reconfiguration of its health care delivery system. Not surprisingly, the structure of the hospital/medical staff relationship is undergoing a parallel reformulation. The historical prerogatives of the organized medical staff and the place of the individual physician within the hospital universe are being profoundly altered. The changes now occurring promise to be as far-reaching as the original wave of reform in the early 1900s that resulted in the creation of the present-day medical staff structure.

Major Factors

The principal factors currently changing the health care system are well known. They include the following:

- *Physician glut:* Since the mid-1970s, the number of physicians in the United States has grown far more rapidly than the population as a whole. In 1975 there were 158 physicians per 100,000 people; by 1990 there will be 228. Indeed between 1960 and 1977, the number of board-certified physicians has tripled. For physicians, therefore, it is no longer a seller's market. Indeed, it is now a buyer's market.

- *Competition:* The acceptance of entrepreneurialism in health care has made competition a preeminent fact of life for today's physicians. Indeed, today's physician faces competition everywhere: from prepaid systems, from for-profit companies, and increasingly from his or her own hospital. The competitive environment clearly gives an economic advantage to *systems* that can raise capital, hire managers, advertise for patients, and guarantee a totality of services—activities that are difficult, if not impossible, for isolated medical practitioners in office-based practice.

- *Vertical integration:* For-profit corporations, virtually nonexistent as recently as 1960, currently control almost 15 percent of the hospital beds in the United States. Networking and chain-building in the nonprofit sector are now growing as quickly. Estimates indicate that in the future approximately 90 percent of the hospital beds in the United States will be part of larger networks. This trend shifts the locus of hospital decision making from local to regional power centers and undermines the ability of physicians to influence the policies of hospitals they utilize.

- *Changing reimbursement policies:* Three factors are operative: (1) increased use of capitation payment, (2) the shift to prospective hospital reimbursement, and (3) the increasingly aggressive utilization review policies of third-party reimbursers. These have combined to create a "politics of scarcity" as the dominant feature of the health care environment.

Hospital managers must now devise strategies to manage with less and to preserve or expand their referral bases. Achieving this goal is impossible without active participation of medical staff members in the budgeting, planning, and marketing activities of the hospital—all historically new roles for the medical staff.

What will be the result?

The dominant trends now operative in the health care system are creating a somewhat paradoxical situation: a scenario for increasingly bitter competition and confrontation between hospitals and their medical staffs and a simultaneous incentive to link more closely and harmonize their activities.

The scenario for increased competition is clear. It is characterized by increasing competition in the ambulatory care arena and vertical integration.

The economic realities of the marketplace make it imperative for both physicians and hospitals to secure their own patient markets. To achieve this objective, both need to invade the "turf" historically considered to be the exclusive prerogative of the other: Hospitals are increasingly developing ambulatory care programs, such as primary and urgent care centers, that compete with physicians in office-based practice, and physicians trying to lock in more of the patient's available health care dollars are developing cooperatively owned ancillary service enterprises such as imaging, laboratory, and physical therapy centers, as well as outpatient surgical centers. For both physicians and hospitals, these activities are compelled as a matter of economic survival.

The health care systems of the future are being constructed to provide a totality of services, ranging from ambulatory to inpatient to convalescent, rehabilitation, and home care, under a single corporate umbrella. Increasingly, large employers or large union groups negotiate directly with large corporate providers for the medical care required by large populations of beneficiaries.

The pillar therefore upon which the separation of hospital and medical staff powers developed—the prohibition against the corporate practice of medicine—is steadily passing into obsolescence in fact, if not in theory. It is undeniable that, although the primacy of the patient-physician relation remains intact, an increasing percentage of patients in the future will not be brought to the hospital by physicians, but rather to the physician by the hospital, through the hospital's networking, advertising, outreach, or contracting activities.

To many physicians, therefore, the prospect of the hospital's emergence as either competitor or potential employer is a real and frequently unsettling prospect.

The scenario for increasing cooperation is equally clear. It is motivated by the following three facts:

1. The object of the health care delivery system is to render patient care.
2. Physicians cannot render satisfactory patient care without the hospital.
3. Hospitals cannot survive without affiliated medical staffs.

Although all trends currently operative in the health care system seem to be working to lessen the dominant position of physicians, in fact this loss of dominance extends to all traditional providers of health care, including hospitals. Indeed, hospital managers must cope with one sobering realization: the United States is considered an overbedded nation. Projections indicate that, over the next decade, as many as 10 percent of the nation's beds may be closed and with them a substantial portion of the nation's hospitals. For both the nation's hospitals and its affiliated physicians, the need to establish new relationships is a matter therefore of future economic viability.

Hospital/Medical Staff Relationships: The Key Issues

Hospitals and their medical staffs must redefine and reinvigorate their traditional partnership relationships, but how and in what form? The core set of issues with which hospitals and their affiliated medical staffs must grapple in the decade ahead include the following:

- The new health care environment has created an altered economic incentive system for health care providers. What organizational systems are best suited to develop a commonality of purpose and economic incentives between hospitals and physicians?

- The new health care environment has made the provision of cost-effective health care services an overwhelming priority. How can the hospital and the medical staff collaboratively develop strategies for the delivery of cost-effective health care?

- The new health care environment compels hospitals to take steps to secure their patient referral bases and reorganize as health delivery *systems*. These steps include, but are not limited to, recruiting and employing physicians, developing new programs, engaging in corporate restructuring, providing and aggressively marketing new services, and negotiating capitation and/or risk management contracts. How can hospitals ensure maximum medical staff involvement and minimal physician alienation as they go about these necessary but potentially threatening activities?

- How can quality of care best be monitored and assured in an era of competition, utilization review, and steadily diminishing resources?

- How can hospitals and their medical staffs best collaborate to secure their joint market share and equitably redistribute the resultant health care income?

- How can hospitals and their medical staffs best establish internal mechanisms to foster dialogue, trust, and communication?

New Organizational Forms

The medical staff organization of the future will clearly differ substantially from the model currently in existence. The outlines of the new structure are clear at present, although the specifics are not:

- Medical staffs will become more rigidly structured, more tightly organized, and more accountable to both the board and the CEO. The organizational structure of the future will favor a more corporate model than has heretofore existed in hospitals, with a greater centralization of both authority and accountability within the hospital's board and a greater delegation of power to the CEO. Hospitals, like other large and complex organizations, will continue to coordinate activities through elaborate systems of review, action, and liaison committees. However, the dichotomy that currently exists between the medical and administrative spheres of the hospital will cease to exist. A system of health care that emphasizes the delivery of health services as a commodity makes untenable the perpetuation of independent loci of power within the hospital.

- The core of full-time paid physicians who provide contract services to the hospital will grow.

- The cadre of full-time physician administrators hired by hospitals will grow.

- Physicians will increasingly tie their loyalty to one institution and not maintain credentials and privileges at multiple institutions.

- Nonphysicians will be permitted to join the staff in increasing numbers. Indeed, medical staff membership had previously been restricted to physicians and dentists. In 1985, for the first time, the Joint Commission permitted podiatrists to be appointed to the medical staff and changed its requirement to a stipulation that physicians and dentists must constitute a majority of the medical staff only. It is to be expected that multiple other nonphysician specialties, such as psychologists and chiropractors, will now accelerate their efforts to win hospital practice privileges and medical staff membership.

- Necessary interactions between the medical staff and the hospital will move beyond the hospital setting. Hospitals and physicians will increasingly become business partners in joint venture enterprises, including the gamut of activities encompassed by such alternative delivery systems as ambulatory, long-term, rehabilitative, home care, and above all prepaid health care.

Shortell has sketched three future scenarios for the structure of hospital/medical staff relations (Figure 3–2):

1. *Independent-corporate model:* In this model, the physicians separately incorporate and negotiate the basis of their relationship with the hospital. The basis of the negotiated relationship is contractually defined. The power of the traditional medical staff structure in this model is se-

Corporate Model

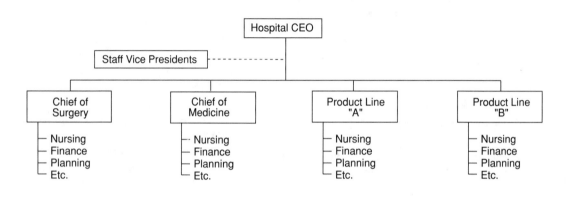

Divisional Product Line Model

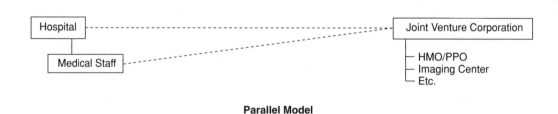

Parallel Model

Figure 3–2 Alternative Models for Hospital/Medical Staff Interface

verely curtailed and potentially obliter-ated. The new physician corporation, as the medical staff's negotiating agent, be-comes the dominant force connecting the staff with the hospital.

This model closely parallels the structure of the group model health maintenance organization (HMO), in which an inde-pendent, separately incorporated group of physicians negotiates an arms-length transaction with a separately incorporated prepaid health care plan.

In the hospital setting, this model substantially decreases the power of the independent fee-for-service physician within the medical staff hierarchy by forcing all physicians into a collective group setting. It is the group—a separately incorporated entity—that is responsible for negotiating the terms of its relationship with the hospital and the terms of its own relationship with its constituent physicians. The attractiveness of the arrangements negotiated by the physician group are, of course, a function of the health care market conditions existing in various communities at the time each contract is negotiated.

This model, to a limited extent, currently exists in the hospital industry in municipal hospital settings. In such settings municipalities have historically contracted with separate provider organizations, such as medical schools, hospitals, and/or physician groups, to provide professional staffing.

2. *Divisional model:* This model has been popularized by the experience of The Johns Hopkins Medical Center. In this model the hospital is organized along clinical departments. Each clinical department is made a separate revenue and cost center—almost a self-contained "minihospital"—with management accountability for performance vested in the physician chief of service. Support services, such as nursing, finance, and marketing, which have historically reported directly to the hospital administrator in a table of organization parallel to, but independent of, the hospital's clinical organization, are decentralized to the clinical divisions of the hospital. They no longer exist as separate hospital-wide support departments.

This model incorporates a radically new design for the hospital's internal management structure because it merges accountability for clinical and support services in "product line managers." The traditional hospital system separates caring and curing functions; this model merges them.

3. *Parallel model:* This model proposes the creation of separate organizations for the specific projects that are not well handled by the traditional medical staff/hospital organizational form. It acknowledges that the existing pattern of hospital/medical staff organization is inappropriate for the delivery models and incentive systems required by the new health care environment.

It responds to this challenge by creating new delivery models on an as-needed basis for specific situations. An example is the hospital/physician joint venture that can be created for any number of purposes and structured in any number of ways. New delivery models can be created on an ad hoc basis in response to specific needs.

The parallel model leaves the traditional structure of the hospital-medical staff relationship untouched. As required, new structures are created outside the traditional hospital environment.

This model is in fact the predominant mechanism by which hospitals and physicians are reacting to changes in the health care environment. Multiple studies have indicated that virtually all hospitals in the country are implementing or actively planning to implement such programs. Examples include separately incorporated joint ventures in which the hospital and its medical staff join for a specific purpose, i.e., establishing health care enterprises, such as imaging centers, laboratories, or prepaid health care plans. As a result of safe harbor and Medicare-Medicaid antikickback regulations of the 1990s, the form and ownership of joint ventures must be scrutinized very carefully.

SUGGESTED READINGS

Egdahl, R. 1985. Private medical practice: A critical factor in hospital-medical staff relationships. *Frontiers of Health Services Management* 1, no. 3:55

Ellwood, P. 1984. Ellwood's MeSH idea links physicians, hospitals in business partnership plan. *Review of the Federation of American Hospitals* 4, no. 36:38.

Fifer, W. 1984. The hospital medical staff of 1994. *The Hospital Medical Staff* 13, no. 6:2.

Heyssel, R. et al. 1984. Special report: Decentralized management in a teaching hospital. *New England Journal of Medicine* 310, no. 22:1477.

MacStravic, R. 1986. Hospital-physician relations: A marketing approach. *Health Care Management Review* 11, no. 3:69.

McCurdy, R. 1984. Changing physician-hospital relations. *Archives of Surgery* 119, no. 5:505.

McMahon, S. 1983. Prospective pricing ushers in new era in hospital/M.D. relations. *Hospital Medical Staff* 12, no. 8:2.

Morisey, M. 1985. Physician influence in hospitals: An update. *Hospitals* 59, no. 17:86.

Noie, W. 1983. A survey of hospital medical staffs. *Hospitals* 57, no. 27:80.

Ottensmeyer, D., and H.L. Smith. 1986. Patterns of medical practice in an era of change. *Frontiers of Health Services Management* 3, no. 1:3.

Punch, L. 1983. Payment changes pit M.D.'s vs. hospital. *Modern Healthcare* 13, no. 5:38.

Richards, G. 1984. How do joint ventures affect relations with physicians? *Hospitals* 58, no. 23:68.

Roemer, M. 1971. *Doctors in hospitals.* Baltimore: Johns Hopkins University Press.

Rosen, G. 1983. *The structure of American medical practice 1875–1941.* Philadelphia: University of Pennsylvania Press.

Shortell, S. 1982. The structural configuration of U.S. hospital medical staffs. *Medical Care* 19, no. 4:419–30.

Shortell, S. 1985. The medical staff of the future: Replanting the garden. *Frontiers of Health Services Management* 1, no. 3:3.

Spivey, B. 1984. The relation between hospital management and medical staff under a prospective-payment system. *New England Journal of Medicine* 310, no. 15:984.

Starr, P. 1982. *The social transformation of American medicine.* New York: Basic Books.

Thompson, R. 1984. *Physicians and hospitals: Easing adversary relationships.* Chicago: Pluribus Press.

Young, D., and R. Saltman. 1983. Prospective reimbursement and the hospital power equilibrium. *Inquiry* 20, no. 2:20.

MARTIN PARIS, MD, MPH, a board-certified internist, is the former Associate Health Commissioner of New York City and Vice-President for Medical and Professional Affairs for the New York City Health and Hospitals Corporation.

Dr. Paris has written and consulted extensively on issues related to hospital/medical staff relationships.

He received his MD from Yale in 1971. In addition, he received an MPH in health services administration from the Columbia University School of Public Health. He received his training in internal medicine at the Columbia-Presbyterian Medical Center in New York City.

Chapter 4

Nursing Administration: Practice, Education, and Research

Barbara J. Brown and Beverly Henry

Since the earliest days of civilization some type of nursing service has existed to provide care of the sick. This service was, of course, rendered without previous preparation; it was a spontaneous service of kindness to a member of the family or tribe or a service of compassion to a stranger. As civilization advanced and the sick were housed either in special shelters or in temples, the attendants nursing the sick could not escape acquiring certain practical experience that enabled them to give better care. Such attendants were probably priests or devotees who were motivated by religious compassion. The practical training acquired was incidental to the nursing care, rather than a product of planned procedure. Nursing services rendered by the early Christian deaconesses—usually widows of 45 years or older—and by later religious orders were similarly motivated by religious compassion, although some orders did make efforts to train their members in certain fundamentals of physiologic patient care. After the Reformation, when municipal hospitals were founded and nursing was in the hands of laypeople, some of them with criminal records and devoid of a spirit of self-sacrifice, nursing, as a career, sank to so low a level that respectable people refused to enter it.

DEVELOPMENT OF NURSING INTO A TRUE PROFESSION

One of the first notable efforts to train nurses was made in Paris in 1633 when the Community of the Sisters of Charity of St. Vincent de Paul was founded, and its members were taught the essentials of patient care by the nuns. This order was introduced into the United States by Mother Elizabeth Bayley Seton, who established the Sisters of Charity of St. Joseph in 1809. Other training efforts were made in the early nineteenth century in church orders in Ireland, and in Protestant England by nursing orders of the Church of England. On the Continent the most notable work in this respect was carried on by Theodor Fliedner, who in 1836 founded a deaconess home in Kaiserwerth, Germany, for the training of deaconess nurses. In subsequent years he founded numerous mother houses for deaconesses elsewhere in Europe and also in Asia and the United States. Although the emphasis of these organizations was still strongly on religious social service, a respectable amount of appropriate training for nurses was given. Florence Nightingale visited and later spent 3 months with the Fliedners at the mother house in Kaiserwerth.

Yet, by the mid-nineteenth century nursing was still not an independent profession. It was part of a career as a nun, or part of a career as a deaconess, or just a job for some layman or lay-woman, but it was not a profession in its own right.

The person who made nursing a profession was Florence Nightingale, commonly called the mother of modern nursing. Miss Nightingale's work in the Crimea brought public recognition of the role that good nursing by well-trained nurses could play in care of the sick. She was one of the first to advocate the need for a formal program of instruction in nursing. In recognition of her services in the British military hospitals in Scutari and in the Crimea, the British people contributed so generously to a public fund that the Nightingale Fund was created to enable Miss Nightingale to "establish and control an institute for the training, sustenance and protection of nurses paid and unpaid."[1] Thus was founded the Florence Nightingale School in connection with St. Thomas' Hospital in London in 1859.

In the United States sporadic efforts to train nurses had been made before the days of Florence Nightingale. For example, in 1798, Dr. Valentine Seaman of the New York Hospital gave regular lectures to nurses in anatomy, physiology, obstetrics, and pediatrics; he even published a synopsis of his lectures to serve as a textbook for nurses—probably the first of its kind. Somewhat later, about 1839, a regularly organized school of nursing was started under the auspices of the Nurse Society of Philadelphia by Dr. Joseph Warrington. The courses were rather elementary, but the school continued for many years. During the Civil War a further attempt to establish a school was made at the Women's Hospital of Philadelphia in 1861, with the course lasting 6 months. However, it was not until the early 1870s that schools of nursing embodying the principles of Kaiserwerth and the Florence Nightingale School in London were established in the United States. The first such school was in the New England Hospital for Women and Children in Boston (1872), which was patterned largely after Kaiserwerth; the second was the Bellevue Hospital School of Nursing in New York City (1873). A few months later, but also in 1873, schools of nursing were opened at New Haven, Connecticut, and at the Massachusetts General Hospital in Boston.

During the next 50 years the number of nursing schools increased to over 2,000. Without a doubt many were developed just to provide nursing service, for it was recognized that better-prepared nurses provided better patient care. As the supply of nurses increased and as hospital and medical care became more complex, it was logical that graduate nurses began to be employed to assume the major responsibility for nursing care. This provided a more stable nursing service and made it possible for the nursing students to receive a more carefully planned clinical experience.

In the meantime, new fields were opening for nurses. Perhaps the most rapidly developing field was that of public health. It soon became apparent that graduate nurses were in no way prepared to meet expanding opportunities in the prevention of disease and promotion of health, including maternal and child welfare, school and industrial health supervision, health teaching, and other activities. The report of the Committee for the Study of Nursing Education, published in 1923 under the title *Nursing and Nursing Education in the United States*, undertook to determine the type of education essential for public health nursing. The conclusions in the report emphasized the fact that specialization in nursing was built upon a foundation of sound basic nursing education and that, by and large, the nursing schools of the country were not preparing nurses to meet a changing role.

The nursing profession felt that grading of nursing schools would be one way to raise educational standards. The Committee on the Grading of Nursing Schools was organized with broad representation from the other health professions, from education, and from the general public. Funds were secured for "a study of ways and means for insuring an ample supply of nursing service of whatever type and quality is needed for adequate care of the patient at a price within his reach."[2] The committee, as stated in its own words, "was primarily interested in better education for nurses because better education for nurses means better care for patients."[3] The report was published in several volumes over an 8-year period. In its final report, *Nursing Schools Today and Tomorrow*, the committee stated frankly:

> We have no need of any more graduate nurses with mediocre training and background. There are altogether too many of them now. We have great need of nurses with training better than that which is given by the typical hospital school. We need trained nurses with a broader experience and better basic professional background. We need more really skillful, professionally-minded bedside nurses. We need nurses who have taken specialized training following the R.N. to fit them for special responsibilities. We need schools for professional training, on a par with the schools of other professions, which will produce a supply of graduate nurses to fill the positions which, in spite of overproduction, are not yet properly filled.[4]

These conclusions were repeated in different words in subsequent studies of far-reaching influence, as in *Nursing for the Future* ("The Brown Report"),[5] *A Program for the Nursing Profession* ("The Ginzberg Report"),[6] and *Nursing Schools at the Mid-Century*.[7]

During the first part of the twentieth century, medical care, and with it hospital and nursing services, were undergoing rapid change. There was growing acceptance of the concept that medical care encompasses prevention and rehabilitation, as well as the traditional diagnosis and treatment, and that the personal care of patients includes an emphasis on meeting their mental, social, and spiritual needs as well. As patients learned more about their own health needs, they demanded more information and a greater share in their own care. Thus the teaching role of nursing was established.

Soon the tremendous demand for nursing service became far greater than the supply of nurses. As a result, two new groups, practical nurses and nursing aides, began to be employed in hospitals in large numbers. Their presence added another role to professional nursing—teaching and supervising auxiliary personnel.

In 1952 a definition of what nursing had become was formulated by the Joint Commission for the Improvement of the Care of the Patient as follows:

> Comprehensive nursing should be designed to provide physical and emotional care for the patient; care of his immediate environment; carrying out the treatment prescribed by the physician; teaching the patient and his family the essentials of nursing that they must render; giving general health instruction and supervision of auxiliary workers.[8]

In a 1986 working document entitled *Essentials of College and University Education for Nursing*, the American Association of Colleges of Nursing described the practice and education for professional nursing in the following way:

> The practice of the professional nurse requires liberal and professional education, a value system, and cognitive and clinical skills that are applicable to a variety of settings; to various human responses; and to a wide continuum of ages, cultures, health beliefs, and individual expectations. The skilled practice of the professional nurse consists of clinical judgments and nursing interventions.
>
> Clinical judgment permeates the entire practice of the professional nurse in settings that are both structured and unstructured and in clinical situations with both predictable and unpredictable outcomes. Judgments in unstructured settings and decisions in situations with unpredictable outcomes are specific responsibilities of the professional nurse and, therefore, are distinguishing features of college and university education for nursing.

Clinical judgment distinguishes the practice of the professional nurse from others who may participate in nursing activities or carry out certain nursing procedures. The clinical judgment of the professional nurse focuses on the outcomes of nursing and health care. These outcomes include staying healthy, avoiding illness, decreasing symptoms of illness and discomfort, getting well, and coping with irreversible changes. Clinical judgments of the professional nurse are integrally related to the diagnostic and monitoring functions of professional practice. In addition, the nurse's liberal and professional knowledge, value system, and ability to provide skilled nursing interventions are fundamental to valid judgments and accurate decisions.

Skilled nursing practice is a type of knowledge, an application of knowledge, and a way of knowing. The application of knowledge in skilled practice requires judgment and innovation. Skilled practice is a combination of "knowing how," or practical knowledge, and "knowing that," or theoretical knowledge. New clinical knowledge may be formalized into theory as a result of systematically studying nursing practice.[9]

From the foregoing description it can be discerned that nursing functions today range from the very simple to the highly complex and that the differentiation of these is based on the level of judgment and the degree of skill demanded in meeting specific nursing situations. Or to state it another way, there are now several categories of nursing personnel who may contribute to the provision of nursing care for patients.

In the century that has elapsed since the Crimean War nursing has become a highly skilled and differentiated profession, keeping pace with the advance of medical science and demands for better and more complex care of patients.*

Hospital Nurses' Training and University Education

Registered nurses (RNs) make up the largest single professional group in the health care delivery system. In 1986 there were approximately 1.7 million RNs employed in the United States, two-thirds of whom worked in hospitals.[10] Registered nurses must be educated for a diverse array of positions in hospitals, nursing homes, community and public health agencies, physicians' offices, and health maintenance organizations (HMOs). Basic academic preparation for these positions takes place in three types of educational programs: diploma, associate, and baccalaureate.

Collegiate education for professional nursing has been a focus of concern in nursing throughout the past century beginning with the establishment in 1873 of the hospital-based Nightingale Training Schools in the United States. However, the movement of nursing into institutions of higher education where formal preparation for professional nursing, not merely training through apprenticeship, was possible was slowed by these factors: an emphasis in women's colleges on the liberal arts, restricted admissions for women in many of the country's major universities, and economic benefits that accrued to hospitals from the establishments of hospital-based nursing schools.[11]

In 1900 there were 4,000 hospitals in the United States. Of these, 432 had schools of nursing with 11,164 students, an increase from 35 schools and 1,552 students in 1890. In 1957, MacEachern stated:

Whether or not it is the function of the

---

*With the exception of the quote from *Essentials of College and University Education for Nursing*, the preceding material is reprinted from *Hospital Organization and Management* by M.T. MacEachern, pp. 509–512, with permission of Physicians' Record Company, © 1957.

hospital to carry the burden of nursing education, the fact must be accepted that, under conditions as found today, no other provision is made in most communities for this necessary activity. The situation will continue as at present until such time as financial aid is available through subsidies that will enable educational institutions to teach at least the theory of nursing in the same manner as provision has been made for advanced education in other professions and trades. The hospital will still be obliged to provide the clinical experience which gives practical application of the theory taught.[12]

Whereas in the middle 1950s about 25 percent of basic professional schools of nursing were conducted in universities and senior and junior colleges, by 1980, 33 percent of the nursing schools were located in universities or colleges, 19 percent in hospitals, and 48 percent in junior or community colleges.[13]

Essentials of University Education in Nursing, 1986

The American Association of Colleges of Nursing, in its 1986 document, outlined the elements of professional nursing education (Exhibit 4–1).

NURSING ADMINISTRATION EDUCATION, 1900–1980*

Nursing administration education in the university setting dates from 1899 when the forerunner of the National League for Nursing (NLN)—the American Society of Superintendents of Training Schools for Nursing—devel-

_____
*This section is adapted from E.H. Erickson, "The Historical Evolution of Nursing Administration Education," a paper presented at the annual meeting of the National Council on Graduate Education for Administration in Nursing, Philadelphia, Pennsylvania, May 1983.

oped courses that were taught at Teachers College, Columbia University, in New York.

At the turn of the century, 25 years after development of the first nurse training schools, the Society of Superintendents expressed concern about the lack of uniformity in the quality of instruction offered by the rapidly multiplying nursing school programs. The Society of Superintendents, which at the time had been in existence for 5 years, thought that the answer to the lack of uniformity was to improve training of nurse superintendents.

The Society arranged with Teachers College to offer a 2-semester program in administration. Courses that were required were psychology, ethics, psychology in teaching, physiology and hygiene, bacteriology, household chemistry, hospital and training school management, home sanitation and management, and social reform management.

The program was developed to prepare nurses for higher, responsible administrative positions in hospitals. The purpose of the program was not to supplement nurses' education, but to complete their basic nursing education. Another objective was to increase the supply of trained superintendents capable of taking charge of small hospitals and nurses' training schools.

In 1905 the course of study was extended to 2 years. Graduates were granted a diploma after completion of the second year. Lectures on the following topics were included: training school administration, hospital administration, hospital construction, hospital laundries, hospital planning, food production, and hospital economics.

The first basic nursing program in a university setting was begun in 1909 at the University of Minnesota. Other tax-supported universities followed the Minnesota model in which a diploma, not a degree, was awarded for a combination of academic and hospital activities. In 1916 Cincinnati established the first degree-granting nursing program, and in 1924 the first autonomous collegiate school was established at Yale. By 1920, 20 schools of nursing were under college control. At the same time, 180 diploma schools had some college affiliation.

Exhibit 4–1 Essentials of Professional Nursing Education

Liberal education of the professional nurse will ensure the ability to:

read, write and speak English clearly
think analytically and reason logically
understand a second language
understand other cultural traditions
use mathematical concepts, interpret quantitative data, and use computers
use concepts from the behavioral and biological sciences
understand the physical world
comprehend time and life from historical perspectives
gain a perspective on social, political, and economic issues
comprehend the meaning of human spirituality
appreciate the role of the fine and performing arts
understand the nature of human values

College and university education for professional nursing will foster the following seven essential values:

altruism
equality
esthetics
freedom
human dignity
justice
truth

AS PROVIDERS OF CARE, PROFESSIONAL NURSES WILL HAVE THE FOLLOWING:

KNOWLEDGE needed to determine health status and health needs based on the interpretation of health-related data.
    CLINICAL JUDGMENTS AND RELATED SKILLS needed to:
        select and obtain health data in collaboration with individuals, their families, and other health care professionals, and make nursing diagnoses based on health-related data.

KNOWLEDGE needed to formulate goals and a plan of care in collaboration with patients/clients and other health care professionals.
    CLINICAL JUDGMENTS AND RELATED SKILLS needed to:
        establish a plan of care based on the nursing diagnoses and patient/client preferences in collaboration with the patient/client and other health care providers.

KNOWLEDGE needed to implement the plan of care.
    CLINICAL JUDGMENTS AND RELATED SKILLS needed to:
        assist the individual to meet basic physiological needs in any state of health or setting,
        assist the individual and family to address psycho-social and spiritual concerns related to health care needs, for example, death and dying, stress, body image, self-esteem, and sexuality,
        assist other health care providers to carry out the health care plan,
        assist the individual and family to identify ethical and legal issues that affect health needs, such as right to die or refuse treatment, informed consent, and use of least restrictive restraints, and
        document patient/client information and communicate to other nurses and health care providers.

KNOWLEDGE needed to define learning needs of individuals and groups related to health.
    CLINICAL JUDGMENTS AND RELATED SKILLS needed to:
        educate individuals and small groups concerning the promotion, maintenance, and restoration of health.

KNOWLEDGE needed to evaluate patient/client responses to therapeutic interventions.
    CLINICAL JUDGMENTS AND RELATED SKILLS needed to:

continues

Exhibit 4–1 continued

evaluate the quality of care in terms of patient/client understanding and satisfaction, health and disease states, illness experiences, and cost effectiveness.

KNOWLEDGE needed to provide care for multiple* patients/clients.
CLINICAL JUDGMENTS AND RELATED SKILLS needed to:
provide direct care to multiple patients/clients in acute, long-term, and community settings.

KNOWLEDGE needed to use an analytical approach as the basis for decision-making in practice.
CLINICAL JUDGMENTS AND RELATED SKILLS needed to:
use clinical data and research findings as a basis for practice.

AS COORDINATORS OF CARE, PROFESSIONAL NURSES WILL HAVE THE FOLLOWING:

KNOWLEDGE needed to coordinate human and material resources for provision of care.
CLINICAL JUDGMENTS AND RELATED SKILLS needed to:
promote positive work group relationships that facilitate identification and attainment of nursing care goals,
guide and supervise nursing care, and
participate in evaluation of group members according to established protocol and using predetermined criteria.

KNOWLEDGE needed to collaborate with patients/clients, co-workers, and others for provision of care.
CLINICAL JUDGMENTS AND RELATED SKILLS needed to:
collaborate with patients/clients, co-workers, and others to improve health care for individuals, families, and groups.

KNOWLEDGE needed to refer individuals and their families to appropriate sources of assistance.
CLINICAL JUDGMENTS AND RELATED SKILLS needed to:
refer individuals and their families to appropriate resources when necessary to meet health needs.

KNOWLEDGE needed to function within the organizational structure of various health care settings.
CLINICAL JUDGMENTS AND RELATED SKILLS needed to:
facilitate changes in health care,
promote cost containment through appropriate use of human and material resources, and
promote a safe environment for patients/clients and health care providers.

AS MEMBERS OF A PROFESSION, PROFESSIONAL NURSES WILL HAVE THE FOLLOWING:

KNOWLEDGE needed to demonstrate accountability for own nusing practice.
PROFESSIONAL JUDGMENTS AND RELATED SKILLS needed to:
practice responsibly and accountably within legal, ethical, professional, and institutional parameters, and
recognize own learning needs and seek opportunities to meet them.

KNOWLEDGE needed to serve as a health care advocate in monitoring and ensuring the quality of health care practices.
PROFESSIONAL JUDGMENTS AND RELATED SKILLS needed to:
act as a health care advocate,
participate in evaluation of nursing practice through quality assurance programs, and
participate in monitoring nursing and health care services to ensure safe, legal, and ethical health care practices.

KNOWLEDGE needed to promote nursing as a profession.
PROFESSIONAL JUDGMENTS AND RELATED SKILLS needed to:
support activities of the profession that improve nursing and health care delivery and advance the discipline of nursing.

———
*Three or more.

Source: Adapted from *Essentials of College and University Education for Professional Nursing Final Report*, pp. 4–7 and 9–18, with permission of American Association of Colleges of Nursing, © 1986.

Master's degrees in nursing were granted for the first time in the 1920s. Between 1924 and 1925, 54 graduates of Teachers College received their baccalaureates and 8 received master's degrees. By 1935 there were 10 areas of study, which included supervision of schools of nursing, administration in hospitals, and administration in public health nursing.

During the 1920s and 1930s numerous studies of nursing education were done that focused on nursing administration education. One of the earliest undertakings was the Goldmark study in 1923. A recommendation of the Goldmark Report was that university-based nursing education at the baccalaureate level was appropriate preparation for teaching, administration, and public health.[14]

In 1934 the University of Chicago initiated the first educational program (other than that at teachers colleges) for hospital administration. It was a small, intensive program with 12 students. The second program in hospital administration was begun at Northwestern University's School of Commerce in 1943. This was a night school program under the direction of Malcolm MacEachern that offered both baccalaureate and master's degrees. One impact of the Chicago and Northwestern programs on nursing administration education was to increase the acceptance of formal study for nursing service administration.

In 1938 The National League for Nursing Education undertook accreditation of schools of nursing, and in 1941 the League published the first list of 1,200 accredited schools. In the 1940s, the issue of generic versus specialty education preparation at the baccalaureate level received attention. Until this period, baccalaureate education was primarily oriented to specialization in public health, nursing education, and nursing administration.

In 1946 the National League for Nursing Education's *Guide for Organization of Collegiate Schools of Nursing,* identified four advanced programs in nursing:

1. those leading to baccalaureate or higher degrees based upon diploma courses

2. those leading to higher degrees based upon a basic nursing baccalaureate

3. those leading to a certificate in an area of specialization built upon either a diploma or baccalaureate or any university degree

4. those that combined basic and advanced programs; for example, those that combined 2 years of college with 2 years of basic nursing.[15]

In 1950 with financial support from the W.K. Kellogg Foundation, under the leadership of Herman Finer, professor of political science at the University of Chicago, a group of deans, educators, and administrators was convened for a 6-month seminar to address the following questions: Is the science of administration needed in the conduct of nursing service? If so, how seriously is it needed? What inferences are to be drawn for the curriculum of schools of nursing and for the spread of knowledge of administration among nurses already on the job in various levels in nursing service departments? R.W. Tyler, consultant to the Kellogg Foundation, directed the project, which took as its task the examination and development of curricula for nursing administration. It recommended that curricula for nursing administration focus on the philosophy of nursing, health trends in nursing, theory of administration, interpersonal relationships, evaluation of nursing services, leadership, and research.

Subsequently 14 universities developed proposals for the educational preparation of nurses for nursing administration or supervision. Between 1951 and 1957, the Kellogg Foundation granted funds to 13 universities to develop multidisciplinary graduate programs to prepare administrators for hospital nursing services. Financial support was also made available for advanced educational preparation in nursing administration through the 1956 Health Amendments Act. In this period two important publications focused on nursing administration education. One was the 1952 publication, *Administration and the Nursing Services* by Herman Finer, in which Finer, as a consequence of the seminar discussions, defined nursing administration.[16] The other was that of Mary Kelly Mullane, *Education for Nursing Service Administration,* published in 1959, also by the Kellogg Foundation.[17]

In the 1960s one study that had an impact on nursing administration was the 1963 Surgeon General's Report, which contained the following recommendations:[18]

- Deans of collegiate programs, faculty of graduate programs, research investigators, and nursing administrators of large hospital systems and health agencies should have a doctorate.
- Directors and assistant directors of nurses in hospitals and health agencies should have master's degrees.
- Directors of nursing services in nursing homes giving skilled care should hold baccalaureate degrees.

Interest in graduate education for nursing increased markedly in the 1960s. It was apparent to nursing leaders that if nursing was ever to be a profession, not merely a vocation, education for professional practice would have to be housed in academic institutions and not in service agencies. Moreover, for nursing to legitimize itself as a profession, nurse scholars and researchers were needed who could delineate a body of clinical nursing knowledge. Whereas in past decades, graduate nursing education prepared nurses primarily for positions as administrators and educators, the goal of graduate education in the 1960s and early 1970s was to educate nurses for advanced clinical specialization in adult, mental, pediatric, and maternal health, for example. As recently as 1962, no accredited schools of nursing offered specialization in clinical nursing at the baccalaureate level.

The American Nurses' Association (ANA) and National League for Nursing (NLN) endorsed clinical specialization for graduate nursing education. In 1969, the ANA issued a *Statement on Graduate Education in Nursing* in which it was posited that the major purpose of

nursing graduate education was to be specialty preparation of nurse clinicians capable of improving nursing care and advancing nursing theory and nursing science.[19] The message was that advanced nursing was clinical nursing, which sustained and provided direct care to people in health and illness. Erickson claimed that the 1969 ANA Statement was developed because many individuals mistakenly believed that the traditional emphasis in graduate nursing education on preparation of teachers and administrators had devalued the direct care aspect of nursing practice.[20]

Despite the 1963 Surgeon General's Report that recommended advanced educational preparation for directors and assistant directors of nursing, enrollment in nursing administration and teaching programs and the number of such academic programs declined steadily between 1968 and 1977.[21] Another factor that contributed to a de-emphasis of nursing administration was the prevailing negative social attitude toward bureaucracy and administration in the anti-establishment era of the 1960s. In addition, the 1970 Lysaught Report, which was commissioned by the board of directors of the American Nurses' Foundation, recommended that nurse clinicians and educators be given priority in the competition for funding for graduate nursing education.[22] Whereas, in the early and mid-1960s, 21 percent of the nurses who enrolled in graduate study of nursing enrolled in nursing administration, the percentage between 1972 and 1973 dropped to 6 percent. During this same period, from the mid-1960s to the mid-1970s the overall number of students enrolled in graduate education in nursing increased markedly.

Declining enrollments and diminishing numbers of graduate-prepared nurse administrators occurred almost simultaneously with the explosive development of new medical technology and concomitant advancements in medical, surgical, and coronary intensive care. Fortunately, because of the trends in nursing education, clinical nurse specialists were available in some settings to provide direct patient care and instruct others in care of the acutely ill. Unfortunately, however, these same trends led to a widespread lack of well-educated nurse administrators capable of creating the sophisticated organizational systems that the new medical technologies warranted in the late 1960s and 1970s.

In 1977, a survey that was devised to construct a profile of nurse administrators, conducted by the American Society for Nursing Service Administrators and the American Hospital Association, found that 72 percent of the nurse administrators in 5,326 of the nation's hospitals did not have master's level education; of this 72 percent, 2 percent held associate degrees, 46 percent were graduates of hospital diploma programs, and 24 percent had baccalaureate degrees.[23] Only 0.5 percent of nursing administrators were doctorally prepared. Rapidly changing health care systems; high rates of turnover and attrition among nurses disillusioned with archaic, dysfunctional, and insensitive organizations; and widespread consumer and governmental concern with burgeoning health care costs—all of which characterized the period of the 1970s—heightened awareness throughout the country of the need for nurse administrators who were academically prepared to deal effectively with multiple and complex health system problems.

In the mid-1970s, consequently, the pendulum swung once again in favor of education for nursing administration. The 1979 report from the NLN's Perspectives Committee reaffirmed the need for graduate education that prepared nurse administrators, teachers, and leaders through concentrated academic pursuits, including application of research in the study of nursing's problems.[24] Davis, testifying on behalf of the NLN before the House Committee on Interstate and Foreign Commerce, Subcommittee on Health and the Environment, in 1980, described the shortage of nurses, stating that the most serious problem in nursing was the dearth of nurses in leadership positions and of well-educated nurse administrators.[25] Davis expressed concern, too, that the shortage of adequately educated nurse administrators would result in nonnurses managing nursing services.

NURSING ADMINISTRATION EDUCATION IN THE 1980S

With widespread national concern about (1) high rates of dissatisfaction, turnover, and attrition among nurses working in hospitals, (2) the possibility that nonnurses would assume responsibility for administering nursing services, and (3) escalating health care costs, three major studies were initiated in the early 1980s that subsequently had a significant impact on nursing administration education. These three studies were *Nursing and Nursing Education: Public Policies and Private Actions,* by the Division of Health Care Services, Institute of Medicine; the *Summary Report and Recommendations* of the National Commission on Nursing, sponsored by the AHA, The Hospital Research and Educational Trust, and American Hospital Supply Corporation; and the report of the American Academy of Nursing Task Force on Nursing Practice in Hospitals, *Magnet Hospitals: Attraction and Retention of Professional Nurses.*[26–28] The National Commission report made the following recommendations about nursing administration education:

> Nurse executives and nurse managers of patient care units should be qualified by education and experience to promote, develop, and maintain an organizational climate conducive to quality nursing practice and effective management of the nursing resource.
>
> Current trends in nursing toward pursuit of the baccalaureate degree as an achievable goal for nursing practice and toward advanced degrees for clinical specialization, administration, teaching, and research should be facilitated.
>
> High priority should be given to nursing research and preparation of nurse researchers.[29]

The Institute of Medicine study generated 21 recommendations. Recommendation 8 lent strong support to graduate education for nursing administration:

The federal government should expand its support of fellowships, loans, and programs at the graduate level to assist in increasing the rate of growth in the number of nurses with masters and doctoral degrees in nursing and relevant disciplines. More such nurses are needed to fill positions in administration and management of clinical services and of health care institutions, in academic nursing, and in clinical specialty areas.[30]

The response of educators and funding agencies to the recommendations in the three reports was strong. The number of graduate programs in nursing administration increased markedly after 1983. In the 1986 NLN publication of the Council of Baccalaureate and Higher Degree Programs, 129 programs in nursing were listed, along with a brief description of the curricula of each of the programs offered.[31] Of the 129 programs, 64 offered a major or minor component in nursing administration, management, or leadership. In 1985, the NLN also listed a total of 35 doctoral programs in nursing.[32] Of these, 15 described nursing administration as an area of study. Arndt, Blair, Brown, Cleland, Erickson, Fine, Marriner, Poulin, and Stevens played key roles nationally in the development of nursing administration curricula in the decade between 1975 and 1985.

A major issue in nursing administration education in the 1980s was how much clinical nursing knowledge—in the specialized areas of adult, mental, child, and maternal health, for example—should be integrated with management science in graduate programs for nursing administration. There was widespread agreement that nursing theory and research should be part of nursing administration curricula and that courses in health care finance, leadership, and policy should be taught, either in schools of nursing or in the related disciplines of public, business, or health administration. Multidisciplinary education was strongly advocated and supported by the W.K. Kellogg Foundation.

In Erickson's 1983 survey of 12 graduate nursing administration programs, 5 were multidisciplinary.[33]

A 1986 review of the literature on nursing administration education suggested that the following content areas be addressed in nursing administration education: consumerism, ethics, finance, health systems, nursing practice and systems, organizational behavior, personnel, policy, research methods, statistics, and theoretical functions.[34]

FUNCTIONS OF THE NURSE EXECUTIVE

In hospitals, nurses who are part of the executive management team and who are responsible for the management of the nursing organization qualify as nurse executives. In the not-too-distant past, nurses accountable for the department of nursing were typically called directors of nursing. As administration of health services has grown more complex, the term used to describe nurses in top-level executive positions has changed from nurse administrator to nurse executive, from director of nursing to vice-president of patient services. The purpose for this change in title is to convey more appropriately the scope of these nurses' responsibility.

According to "Guidelines on the Role and Functions of the Hospital Nurse Executive," developed jointly in 1985 by the AHA's Council on Nursing and the American Organization of Nurse Executives (AONE):

> The nurse executive provides leadership by setting and maintaining standards for the clinical practice of nursing, ensuring the fulfillment of the institutional goals and objectives of the nursing organization, and providing management expertise. In this role the nurse executive participates in assessing the environment, forecasting trends, transmitting values, communicating ideas, developing and imple-

menting policies, initiating programs and systems, and managing resources. The nurse executive is responsible for developing nursing staff. Such functions require executive management expertise and a comprehensive understanding of nursing practice issues. The nurse executive should be prepared by education and experience to effectively manage the functions, responsibilities, and accountabilities described in these guidelines. This preparation could include an appropriate graduate degree and progressive experience in clinical nursing and nursing management.[35]

The guidelines further state that the nurse executive performs these functions:

- assesses the influence of the health care environment on patient care and nursing practice in developing policies and programs for the nursing organization

- participates in initiating and supporting organizational mechanisms and systems that ensure the provision of effective patient care

- participates in the hospital's strategic planning activities

- is accountable for the clinical practice of nursing

- participates in the effective management of financial, human, material, and informational resources

- ensures that the nursing organization has an overall plan for the development and implementation of education and research programs.[36]

In the remainder of the chapter each of these functions is discussed in detail. Each discussion begins with a statement of philosophy to provide readers with a sense of what is believed and valued in nursing and ends with descriptions of practice-related applications.

Assessing Health Care Environments and Values for the Nursing Organization, Its Policies, and Programs*

A challenge for nurse administrators in the 1990s is to design health care organizations that are capable of effectively responding to rapid environmental change. According to Gawthrop, a primary task of management is developing an ethical perspective on administration that inspires innovation and facilitates integration of changing societal values into organizations' policies and programs.[37]

Therefore, a critical task for nurse executives is to develop democratic organizations that reflect the values, needs, and expectations of clients in the environments served by organizations. Nursing administration educational programs are increasingly based upon the premises that (1) there is an ethical component to every management decision, policy, and program and (2) nurse executives have the responsibility to develop a critical ontological consciousness—a sense of purpose, consequence, history, and order. The effort in nursing education is to harmonize knowledge of ethics with understanding of policy making and the design of complex institutions.

Reactive and Proactive Nursing Organizations

The health care environment of the 1990s is complex. Price-driven decisions challenge professional values and generate nearly innumerable complex ethical dilemmas. Organizational response to environmental turbulence can be reactive or proactive. In the reactive mode, response to change is reductionistic: Turbulent environments are perceived as excessively threatening to the smooth, efficient running of health care organizations. Consequently, environments and, most importantly, the people in those environments are reduced. What constitutes an organization's client population is nar-

*The authors acknowledge Gina Giovinco for her contribution to this section.

rowly delimited.[38] If a segment of society has little or no voice, if a group in need has expressed no opinions or voiced no expectations, reactive organizations minimize conflict by virtually eliminating and neglecting the needs of whole segments of the population in their policy-making deliberations.

Reactive administrators also minimize the disruption to the organizational status quo by enforcing classic methods of bureaucratic control. Vertical order in their agencies is tightened in the face of rapid-fire environmental change. Rules proliferate, chain of command is enforced, and reactive organizations grow taller, more centralized, and formal in an effort to control turbulence and maintain efficiency.

In the past, some health care organizations have been reactive. Nursing has guarded itself against demands for financial accountability, for example. Nurse administrators at times have been reluctant to be involved or to involve others in policy making relative to the budgetary process simply to avoid the conflict that necessarily is part of resource allocation. Historically, too, nurses have been hesitant about permitting access and participation in decision making to those who did not conform to the prevailing rules and values extant in health care organizations.

Increasingly, however, reaction has been replaced by proaction in health care generally and in nursing. In proactive organizations, nurse executives respond to environmental changes by viewing social change not as a phenomenon merely to be tolerated, but also as an opportunity to benefit patient care. Commitment to openness and criticism, sensitivity to the alleviation of client dissatisfaction and alienation, and sharing of professional power with consumers characterize forward-looking, proactive health care organizations. Proactive health care organizations, the converse of reactive organizations, serve the public. Sensitive to changing social values, their policies and programs are anticipative and innovative.[39]

In proactive organizations, nurse administrators welcome public participation and solicit in-

formation about needs and expectations from all constituencies. Whereas in reactive organizations the external environment is markedly reduced and guarded against, in proactive organizations the environment is expanded to include the broadest possible range of constituent groups. Moreover, in proactive organizations, administrators deliberately link individuals and groups in the external environment to their organizations' policy makers. Highly sensitive to public need and imbued with a strong sense of public purpose, proactive nurse executives assess changes in society to determine how their workplaces and policy processes will be designed. They design organizations and policy-generating mechanisms that replace traditional bureaucratic methods of control—rigid, vertical hierarchies—with mechanisms that permit consumers "to intrude into every corner of the business,"[40] in Peters and Waterman's words. In reactive health care organizations, consumer participation is viewed as dysfunctional. In proactive organizations the reverse is true: Bureaucracy and control solely by professionals are onerous, and participation in policy making and shared power are welcome.

Expanded notions of purpose, too, are the essence of a proactive orientation. Whereas in reactive organizations, organizational purpose is defined purely in terms of short-range, attainable objectives, administrators who operate proactively have a strong ethical sense of a larger, long-range public purpose and generate policies and programs that reflect that purpose.[41]

Nursing Administrative Responsibility

Two issues that are being increasingly addressed in the nursing profession are (1) how do nurse administrators develop an ethical perspective that inspires innovation and brings about an integration of social and organization values and (2) how do nurses enlarge their organizations' purpose and responsibility for constituents?

Delineating a World View. In contemporary nursing administration education, nursing students often start by delineating a world view and by developing what Gawthrop calls an ontological consciousness—a mature personal sense of purpose, consequence, history, and order.[42] The essence of maturity involves a principled level of critical thought and personal responsibility. Gawthrop suggests that the principled mature administrator infuses management with a clear sense of purpose.[43]

Nurses make conscious their world view, therefore, by asking questions related to their beliefs about purpose: How do humans seek purpose in their being? World view as defined by Hanlon[44] is the view of reality or what exists. The determination of what exists is key to developing planned change and enabling the activities of intention, planning, evaluation, and problem solving. Hanlon further defines "what ought to be" as the ideal pattern or values of the organization.

When nurse executives are able to define a visionary ideal pattern and develop a realistic long-range plan, which facilitates movement from what exists to what ought to be, then and only then does the nurse executive give purpose to the professional goals of the staff.

How do nurse administrators infuse organizations, their programs, and policies with a vivid, ethical purpose? As the well-known nurse leader, Margretta Styles, asked, how is the vitalizing sense of purpose that historically existed in nursing to be regained?[45]

Second, administrative nurses clarify their world view by asking questions about the consequences of change and decision making in complex systems. Are consequences viewed simply in terms of direct, simple, causal relationships? Or is there also awareness of the indirect effects of change? Are executives concerned only with finding direct relations between people, or do they also think holistically, seeking to understand complex networks in which many different perspectives are interrelated?[46]

Third, nurses examine their beliefs about history. Is the past viewed as separate from the present and future? Or is the past, present, and future viewed as an undivided, continuous meld in which the past "fits" with the present and in turn gives direction to the future?[47]

Finally, nurses consider their concept of order and ordered relationships and ask how their views affect the way they design organizational policy-making structures: hierarchically, from lower to higher or vertically, from simple to complex.[48]

Designing Organizations. Having raised their ontological consciousness by critically assessing their beliefs about people in organizations, executive nurses proceed next to analysis of alternative organizational designs. Administrative responsibility involves designing institutions that are capable of accurately gathering, sifting, and testing environmental information. As Pfeffer and Salancik posit, all organizations are inescapably bound up with the conditions in their environment and engage in activities to adjust to those environments.[49] Adjusting to environmental change involves designing organizations in ways that guarantee a close, productive linkage between institutions and the publics they serve. Styles, in her discussion of professionals, admonishes nurses against being "unresponsive to the needs of many classes of ultimate clients or users of services."[50] She advises nurses to build coalitions with citizen groups and reform the pyramidal structure of many of today's health agencies.[51]

According to Gawthrop, organizations with a strong sense of purpose but in which there are no longer the traditional elements of pyramidal, bureaucratic order are characterized "not by the absence of order but a redirection of order, not the absence of structure but a redesign of structure, and not the absence of control but a redefinition of control."[52] A key characteristic of proactive organizations is the creation of boundary-spanning agents to perform integrating tasks between organizations and environments.[53] Boundary spanners link organizations with their communities and in so doing ensure that even the toughest messages from the public are channeled into organizations' inner policy-making circles. Biller states that, in postindustrial society, organizational responsiveness is dependent upon development of environmental scanning devices and effective management of organizations' boundary transactions.[54] Designing organizations in which boundary-spanning agents play a featured role is an important way that nurse administrators can ensure that the environments of nursing organizations are effectively scanned.

Boundary-Spanning Agents: The Case of Clinical Nurse Specialists

Boundary-spanning agents are change agents who are deliberately designed into an organization and positioned at an organization's outer perimeter. The primary responsibility of boundary agents is to link an organization and its external environment by effectively transmitting the most essential data across the organization's external boundaries and into its policy-making core.

Gawthrop describes five characteristics of boundary spanners.[55] First, as representatives of organizations, boundary agents behave in ways consistent with the values of anticipatory and innovative organizations. They are committed to power sharing, openness, and change and are highly sensitive to public dissatisfaction. They have a sense of professional purpose. Second, boundary-spanning agents provide organizations with information gathered through intimate understanding of the interrelated environmental systems within which they operate. Boundary agents are capable of speaking the languages of constituent groups and of mingling with individuals from many walks of life. Third, boundary agents serve as problem solvers and as developers of citizens' problem-solving capability. Because they understand a wide range of individuals and groups, boundary agents are in an ideal position to aid clientele by suggesting innovations and pointing out new directions. Fourth, boundary agents are part of their organization's planning and policy processes, thereby ensuring that the needs, wants, and fears of clients are given organizational voice. As both spanners and policy makers, boundary agents extend the choices available to community groups and to organizations. Fifth, boundary agents are critical assessors of organizational policies and programs.

Immersed as they are in the environments where services are delivered, clinical nurse specialists serving as boundary spanners are in a position to evaluate the quality and success of their organizations' programs and to function as organization critics, providing both positive and negative self-correcting information. If a goal in health care is to create organizations that are sensitive to public need and environmental change, then access for administrators to both positive and negative data about program performance is necessary. An effort in nursing organizations, therefore, is ensuring that boundary spanners have direct access to top-level organization policy makers.

Boundary-spanning agents are in place in many health care systems. There are a number of ways that community needs are given voice. Board of trustee members, for example, represent select segments of the environment, and chief health care and nurse executives are often involved in voluntary, community-based business activities. An increasing number of nurses as well are members of community-sponsored committees, councils, and clubs. In that capacity they serve as informal boundary agents to the degree that they gather information about client needs, suggest solutions to health problems, and feed back the data they gather from the environment to their organizations.

In health care organizations, however, what are needed are full-fledged, formally designated boundary agents whose mission is related less to improving an organization's competitive marketing advantage and more to power sharing between organizations and clients. Marketing principles have long emphasized a close-to-the-customer philosophy to improve profit margins. The emphasis in health care should be predominantly on deliberate, well-planned community empowerment to improve health care.

Consequently, more and more nurse executives are advocating that, in hospitals, clinical specialists and nurses who plan and provide home health care services be formally designated as boundary agents. Highly educated and committed to community service, these intelligent and skilled nurses are a nursing organization's finest link with its external environment. The nurse executive's task is designing new organizational structures that ensure that nurses in key boundary positions have the time, materials, and autonomy to assess constituents in the environment, to determine how they perceive their needs, and to assist in developing their problem-solving capabilities. To perform these tasks effectively, nurses in boundary-spanning positions report directly to the chief nurse executive, thereby ensuring that relevant environmental information is acted upon in the shortest possible time. In some new health care organizations, nurses in boundary-spanning roles also disseminate information that they have gathered from the environment directly to health care administrators and to the board of trustees: Nurse executives, having deliberately linked clinical nurses to the environment, enable them to have direct access to top policy level decision makers.

Nurse educators as well have a responsibility for boundary spanning. In addition to educating future nurse administrators capable of designing new, proactive organizations where boundary activities are facilitated, faculty also prepare clinical nurse specialists for future boundary agent roles. Graduates of nursing graduate programs who are innovative, cooperative, and have a strong sense of purpose are sought after by hospitals, as are nurses with well-developed negotiation, evaluation, and organizational skills and a good deal of maturity. The accurate and sensitive transmission of the most essential data between organizations and clients requires gritty, persistent, intelligent nurses who understand clients and organizations and are capable of anticipating a future based upon the past and present, even in the most turbulent times.

Cleveland describes executives of the future as "brainy, low key, collegial, optimistic and . . . positively enjoying complexity and constant change."[56] Nurses with these characteristics are valued in the profession and are encouraged to achieve nursing's goal, which according to Rogers is promoting harmony between humans and their environment by gathering data about individuals and the world in which they live and using the knowledge gained to achieve the highest possible state of health.[57] To attain this goal, nurse executives recognize that they have an ethical obligation to integrate individual and organizational values, thereby increasing the likelihood that high health states will be achieved.

Peters and Waterman describe outstanding organizations as intensely customer oriented and unfailingly externally focused.[58] Customers are to private corporations as the American public is to health care organizations, whether those organizations are proprietary, for-profit institutions, or tax supported. Nurse executives should believe, as does Cleveland, that "no organization, whatever its formal ownership . . . [is] able to escape its public responsibility."[59] No organization is self-contained. Nurse executives in turbulent times take as their ethical responsibility the creation of organizational policies and programs sensitive to rapid environmental change and public need.

Initiating and Supporting Organizational Systems that Ensure Effective Patient Care

Colloton, in his discussion of nursing in rapidly changing environments, states that a challenge to nurse executives is to maintain and strengthen networks of professional relationships to ensure that the highest possible level of patient care is rendered with the resources available.[60] Nurse executives play a pivotal role in developing organizational systems that are responsive and responsible to customers. Excellence in nursing that is combined with outstanding medical care is the greatest contributor to a health care system's overall reputation. Excellence in nursing administration that ensures provision of high-quality care rests on the use of technical, conceptual, and human skills; on development of strong networks of professional relationships; on commitment to participation; and on the willingness to experiment with new organizational systems.

Technical, Conceptual, and Human Skills[61]

Technical skill is most critical at the beginning levels of nursing where in-depth specialized knowledge and analytical ability are prerequisites for effectiveness. In small hospitals nurses need a wide range of technical skills both in the varying health care specialties and in administration to ensure effective patient care. Nurse administrators in small hospitals, particularly those in remote rural areas, must be as skilled at handling emergencies, delivering babies, and monitoring intensive care as they are at managing infection control and medical records.

Nurse executives in large urban medical centers are accepting increased responsibilities for total patient care services, including nursing services and ancillary multidisciplinary services such as respiratory therapy, physical therapy, speech therapy, etc. Knowledge of advanced nursing practice is basic to providing comprehensive multidisciplinary leadership so that appropriate differentiation of practice and allocation of resources can be made. Additional financial knowledge, especially determining productivity units of measure for all disciplines, will enhance the nurse executive who becomes a health care executive.

Being a good conceptualizer involves the ability to see a total organization, the community within which an organization is embedded, and the relationships between the two. Also involved is the ability to label phenomena about which others may be only dimly aware and to see the implications of these for the care that patients receive in organizations. Graduate education in nursing emphasizes development of conceptual skills. In the finest graduate programs in the country strong emphasis is placed on nursing and organization theory that can be useful in assessing and improving organization systems.

Human or social skill in nursing entails the ability to work well with groups and build cooperative relationships with three key players: hospital administrators, physicians, and practicing staff nurses. Collaboration and cooperation within and between professional networks are essential for the future viability of hospitals and the provision of effective, humane patient care.

Network Building and Negotiating

In nursing, to heighten professional harmony, emphasis is placed on collaboration through the building of social networks. The most effective nurses spend considerable amounts of time building networks, cooperative relationships with individuals and groups who can provide them with the resources they need to accomplish goals.[62] Nurse administrators who ensure provision of the finest patient care build and maintain networks that are comprised of hundreds of individuals with varied backgrounds and interests in community, professional, business, and philanthropic groups. The strongest, most useful networks are typically built and maintained by nurses with a strong sense of their community and hospital's history, by nurses with the physical and intellectual stamina sufficient to persist in achieving objectives regardless of obstacles, and by those with a keen understanding of what is negotiable.

The topic of negotiation has received increasing attention in nursing during the last decade. In nursing, negotiation is addressed in the context of labor-management relations and bargained-for settlements that staff nurses reach with patients and nursing administrators reach with physicians and hospital executives. In such a field as nursing administration, where nursing practice and management are harmonized, there is equal concern with negotiation at the bedside, intraorganizational negotiations involving nursing managers, and interorganizational bargaining in policy-making arenas.

Four questions that typically undergird analysis of nursing negotiation are:

1. What are the contextual variables that affect the content and process of negotiations in nursing?

2. How do staff nurses and nursing administrators negotiate? What is their style of bargaining? What strategies do they use?

3. What are the issues most often negotiated?

4. What are the outcomes of nurses' negotiations?[63]

These nursing values underlie those four questions: Negotiation, as a give-and-take process between equals, is central to democratic relationships; clients are equal partners in their plan of care; development, implementation, and evaluation of plans of care should be collaborative activities; and decisions and plans made between people are most likely adhered to when they are negotiated, not dictated.

Humanistic values that assert devotion to a human being's dignity, worth, and capacity to achieve self-fulfillment through reason are the underpinnings of contemporary nursing. Negotiation, when it is viewed as a democratic process that involves freedom of discussion and commitment to the future and not necessarily equated with competition and conflict, is well aligned with the elemental humanism of nursing.

Collective Bargaining in Nursing

Concerns with the provision of effective patient care and the economic and general welfare of nurses providing that care in organizations have resulted in the changed views that nurses hold of negotiating and collective actions involving hospital management. The American Nurses Association (ANA) has played a central role in defining and interpreting nursing practice, the nursing care needs of patients, and the cost to hospitals of nurses providing care. The ANA, established in 1896, has evolved from a purely professional society to a collective bargaining unit that can represent registered nurses' job-related and professional problems. In the early part of the century, ANA opposed labor organizations and unions. In 1936, however, the ANA endorsed collective bargaining as "economic security." Since then leaders in ANA and its state affiliates have taken as an ethical imperative improvement of conditions of nursing practice.[64]

In 1966 the ANA Committee for Economic and General Welfare reported:

> The nursing profession has very little control over how salaries are set and administered and only limited control over the level of preparation an individual must have before she is employed to carry a certain level of nursing functions and responsibility.[65]

In the middle 1960s the average annual salary of the 621,000 registered nurses providing patient care was $4,700, as compared to the average salaries of $5,300 for secretaries and $6,700 for teachers. By 1967, starting salaries in federal hospitals had increased to $6,100; and by 1968, in New York City and San Francisco, $7,200 was the average salary.[66] In a 1977 survey it was found that salaries increased by nearly 30 percent over the previous 3 years, that nurses' salaries were highest in the northeastern seaboard states and on the West Coast, and that nurses who were union members earned, on average, 17 percent more than nurses who were not. By 1981, beginning staff nurses employed by the federal government earned between $11,500 and $16,700 annually; directors of nursing earned between $40,000 and $60,000; nurse anesthetists earned between $20,000 and $45,000.[67] In 1985, nurse administrators employed in multisystem hospitals of over 500 beds earned an average of $74,412 annually.[68]

By 1987, salaries for staff nurses ranged from $19,932 to $27,744 annually and in some areas such as San Francisco were over $40,000. Today nurse executive salaries in large urban settings and corporate multisystems frequently exceed $125,000 annually.

Although gains in economic and general welfare have been significant in nursing, they have not come easily. The decade of 1966 to 1976 was a time of turmoil and upheaval in many hospitals. In a number of these conflicts, nurse administrators resigned or were terminated by hospital executives, particularly in politically conservative, antiunion localities. As members of both their professional association—the ANA—and hospital management, nurse administrators in some cases were asked to choose between the two, knowing full well that refusal to rescind membership in ANA could cost them their jobs.

Today over 130,000 registered nurses work under state nursing association contracts. These nurses believe that through collective bargaining they have greater control over their practice and more say in the provision of effective patient care.

Other Contracts

Greater numbers of nurses are dissatisfied with the work environment and are being represented by labor unions such as AFL-CIO, SEICO, and others. Nurses are seeking opportunities for job mobility and increases in programs for professional growth. The career ladder is an important topic of discussion in many collective bargaining units.

How much can nurses be a part of the decision-making process? If nurses work closely on quality improvement and peer review to ensure that competency is recognized and clinical advancement is encouraged, is it possible for these same nurses to be represented by a union? Nurses who want to participate actively in the decision-making process to gain control over the work settings will find increasing conflict with the collective bargaining process, especially if they are members of general labor unions other than the ANA.

When the nurse executive enters collective bargaining negotiations, it is important to establish maximum and minimum ranges for settlements, and recognize that concessions are always necessary. Necessary skills include effectiveness in determining arguments, counterarguments, and uses of bargaining techniques in relation to the patient care services being represented. Bargaining power with the opponent is increased by focusing on common goals. It is important to test positions and strategies with colleagues.

A written agenda with opportunities for counteragenda should be drawn up. Both parties to the collective bargaining process must agree on the agenda. It is important during the negotiations process to determine the opponent's limits of authority, to study their position, and then to set aside areas of agreement and look toward problem resolution in the areas of disagreement. Recognize that there will always be unresolved issues. Choose the most capable individuals to be on the bargaining team and use effective bargaining techniques to reach agreement as soon as possible. Long-range planning with the financial officer must be done concerning the financial implications of collective bargaining for the institution.

Self-governance of nursing staffs, with staff participating actively in decision making in every step of the organization, may thwart development of unions in some settings. The role of the staff nurse in a professional practice environment may also be incompatible with collective bargaining.

Participation, Cooperation, and Professional Development

Where collective bargaining contracts do not exist, nurse executives search for ways of initiating and supporting organizational systems that ensure that nurses participate in making patient care decisions. A major nursing concern in the last decade has been how best to increase participation of nurses in decision making through development of decentralized and democratic organizations.

Corporate democracy, without unionization, has been slower to develop in American organizations, particularly health care institutions, than in European and Asian industries. Consequently, nurse educators and administrators often look to European and Japanese models of organizational participation to improve understanding of decentralization and self-management.

Nursing and hospital systems are comprised of a wide array of doctors and nurses with varying levels of education. Although the medical profession has been relatively slow to divide itself into stratified classes, hierarchic stratification characterizes nursing. There are three major categories of nursing personnel: registered nurses, licensed practical nurses, and nurse assistants.[69] The number of licensed practical nurses and nursing assistants has more than doubled in the decade following the end of World War II.

Within the registered nurse ranks there is the further classification of nurses by level of educational preparation. Although not as rigid, division into diploma, associate, and baccalaureate levels separates nurses considerably; hence, the emphasis in nursing on participation, cooperation, and professional development. Nurses recognize the importance of engendering the cooperation of many people and avoiding adversarial relationships with key individuals and groups whose cooperation they need.

More recently, a differentiated practice system designed to provide distinct levels of nursing practice based on defined competencies that are incorporated into job descriptions has been integrated into most practice settings. Current RN practice is set at a minimum level at which differentiation of RN competencies are established. Competencies are consistent with the minimum expectations for the associate degree (ADN) and baccalaureate degree (BSN) levels in the education sector. Client satisfaction improves because of the comprehensiveness and continuity of care. Nurse satisfaction improves, and therefore so does retention, due to placing the authority, responsibility, and accountability for the planning and the provision of high quality, cost-effective nursing at the staff level. Differentiated competencies are time- and setting-free and can be applicable in any practice setting. Differentiated levels of practice will, in the future, call for separate licensure laws and regulatory requirements. Proposals endorsing a regulation of advanced practice are currently before the National Council of State Boards of Nursing.

In the American Academy of Nursing *Magnet Hospital* report, organizational structures of "magnet" hospitals were decentralized, enabling nurses at all levels to formulate budgets for their units and experiment with innovative hiring, staffing, and scheduling patterns. In these hospitals, too, salaries and benefits were competitive or ahead of those in other hospitals in the respective localities. Hours of work and opportunities for promotion were also notably different; shift rotation was minimized or eliminated, an effort was made to reduce to a minimum the number of weekends that nurses had to work, and clinical career ladders were developed to provide nurses with opportunities for promotion and salary increases through development of ever-higher levels of clinical nursing skills. Personal growth and development of technical, conceptual, and human skills were also emphasized in these outstanding hospitals. The provision of effective patient care was ensured by carefully designed orientation programs and inservice training based on valid education needs assessment; and support for advanced education came through tuition reimbursement and flexible study time scheduling.[70]

Two of these magnet hospitals, Family Hospital and Virginia Mason Hospital, developed internship programs for new graduates intended to bridge the gap between nursing education and the reality of the practice setting. A constant struggle for maintaining clinical excellence in the practice setting has led to the need to establish comprehensive in-service and continuing education programs.

In-Service and Continuing Education

Educational programs that will effectively support an advancing profession have been developed. These programs, whether conducted for employees as part of the work setting or by continuing education (CE) divisions in schools of nursing, are based on the premise that the individual nurse clearly understands and fully accepts the direction and nature of proposed growth or change. Most nurses have learned goal setting and planning, and evaluating and problem solving as they relate to individual patient care. However, change within work settings and change in the community and political process relating to state, local, and federal legislation that affects the practice of nursing provides constant redirection to in-service and continuing education programs.

Orientation programs are required for all health care workers in Joint Commission-accredited settings. In addition, as new technology and procedures are introduced, specific courses are given to those employees affected. For example, all health care workers have to receive HIV/AIDS education annually and be familiarized with OSHA requirements. Health care system education departments are developed, which often include nursing and all other health care disciplines. In some settings nursing maintains a separate education department. This frequently depends on the size and structure of the organization. Opportunities are provided for staff to learn a new area of clinical or management practice in order to advance on the job.

New thought processes are tested and new ways of giving care to patients are provided in the learning process so that individuals may gain confidence and security before actually using these techniques in the direct patient care situation. To apply new learning to the work setting, the individual must be able to fit into the work setting. It is not enough to learn methodologies and processes for delivering patient care; students must be prepared to facilitate change in order to apply what they have learned in the work setting. The learning climate should support individuals through uncomfortable, awkward stages of advancement. Frequently, educational systems teach material that is not compatible with the realities of nursing. When new graduates attempt to apply such material, they become disenchanted and either fall back upon the old ways or reject them entirely and remove themselves from the practice setting.

Sixty million pages of new information are published each year on science and technology alone. Nurses must gain the equivalent of a new degree in the field every five years, for almost one out of every two facts learned in gaining a previous degree must be obsolescent if not obso-

lete within that period of time. Therefore, a nurse executive has a responsibility to provide an environment and a climate for the continuing education of all professional staff. The responsibility must also be shared by the setting in which the individual nurse practices. Budgets and time should be allocated to provide comprehensive continuing education programs for every nurse. Organizations should consider tuition reimbursement plans and scholarships in order to maintain professionally viable staff.

Changing Governance Structures:
Nursing Organization Bylaws

In addition to staff participation in the organization and development of the nursing services, self-management, comprehensive in-service, and continuing education programs, creative and innovative nurse leaders have established self-governing nursing staffs. Dr. Luther Christman was among the foremost nurse leaders to establish such a model at Rush-Presbyterian-St. Luke's in Chicago, Illinois, in the 1970s. Rose Medical Center in Denver, Colorado, under Lois Johnson, also gained national recognition as a self-governing model of nursing services. The elements of bylaws for a nursing organization are:[71]

- preamble
- delineation of role
- delineation of services
- membership of the nursing staff
- governance of the nursing staff
- discipline and appeals procedures
- coordination of the nursing organization
- bylaws revision
- rules, regulations, adoption, and amendment of the bylaws

Under shared governance structures the following councils are developed to govern the nursing organization, ensure effective patient care, and contribute to hospitals' strategic planning activities: councils for standards of nursing practice, nursing quality assurance, nursing education, nursing management, and a coordinating council.

Participation in Hospitals' Strategic Planning for the Future

As nurses develop expertise in managing organizations, governance of hospitals increasingly reflects the important role that nurses play in development of strategic plans. To have an impact on the plans of the organization as a whole, nurse administrators recognize that they must solidify their positions in organizations, understand the philosophy and long-term goals of their employing agencies, be knowledgeable about the technicalities of forecasting, and talk a language that others understand. Effective nurse executives develop coherent agendas of alternative strategies that are specific and address short-, medium-, and long-range issues and the methods for marshaling resources to address those issues.

Planning in turbulent times, as Drucker notes, is different than planning in periods where the continuation of trends can be predicted within a fairly narrow range, as was the case between 1950 and 1980. Today, and in the immediate future, strategic planning involves seeing new configurations, new unique markets, and new events and being prepared to take advantage of them. To think strategically is to be prepared to capitalize upon future opportunities.[72]

Futures Study in Nursing Administration

Understanding what the future may hold is increasingly important as nurse administrators recognize that participation in strategic planning in hospitals and health care systems calls for visionary leaders who are also technically competent forecasters.

Thinking strategically for the future, administrators are encouraged to have the following objectives:

- elucidating systems of values to identify social goals and make forecasts
- acquiring a sense of history of nursing, administration, and health care and the

changing structure of each in order to be able to predict changes likely in the future
- thinking strategically and solving highly complex problems in turbulent situations
- understanding, analyzing, and predicting past, present, and future alterations in the work force
- learning to humanize future organizations
- understanding development of the physical, biological, and social sciences; diffusion of technology; and decisions in organizations related to each.[73]

Coates maintains that alternative futures are possible, that it is useful to anticipate possible futures, that means can be found to chart a course among alternative futures, and that professionals are obligated to define, as nearly as possible, what lies ahead.[74] Nurse administrators concur. Engaging in strategic planning provides the basis for formulating accurate predictions about changes in society, the public's health, and the health care system. Nurses believe that thinking strategically despite uncertainty, delicately balancing scarce resources, solving problems quickly, and generating cooperation are responsible professional actions.

Nurse administrators use both exploratory and normative forecasting methods to think strategically about where nursing and their organizations are going and what they should be doing. Encouraging participation by representatives of all members of a nursing service, nurse executives develop decision-path analyses that identify sequences of events probable in reaching desired goals.[75] Other exploratory methods— brainstorming, Delphi, and scenario building— are used together with decision analysis to identify opportunities for future innovation. Brainstorming is used to generate concepts and identify components of future models of nursing and health care. Delphi surveys are used to obtain reliable data and consensus of opinion. Then using data from both brainstorming and Delphi exercises, nurses delineate probable alternative future practices, costs, consumers, and markets and the relationships of each to technological trends, changing legal statutes, regulations, and environments.[76]

Marketing of the Nursing Product*

Marketing has emerged in the 1980s as an essential aspect of strategic planning. Health care marketing, the aggregate of activities involved in transferring goods and services from the health care system to consumers, is a means by which hospitals fulfill their patient-centered mission. Marketing identifies aspects of the health care product important to actual and potential consumers of that product.[77] Because nursing care is a salient component of a hospital's health care product,[78] nurse executives, along with hospital administrators, are increasingly involved with marketing as a process whereby hospitals identify and respond to consumer needs via strategic planning.

Historically, marketing was more narrowly focused strictly as an economic activity. Today, the social aspect of marketing is recognized as well. Changes in government regulations related to advertising and more lenient professional codes governing advertising of hospital and medical services have increased the acceptance and use of marketing principles in health care. Rising costs of health services, reduction of levels of government reimbursement for care, increasing competitiveness among new types of health system agencies, and emphasis on wellness and health promotion also have increased use of marketing knowledge in health care organizations.[79]

In today's health care systems, delineating marketable products based on information about consumer needs and wants is a central activity. The health care product—commonly conceived of as service, physical plant, and personnel—is related to consumer satisfaction. Personnel, particularly nursing staff, are a major determinant of overall patient satisfaction. Doering's study, for example, found that when patients were asked about their satisfaction with hospitalization, one-fifth of all their comments mentioned some aspect of nursing care. Consequently, in nursing education and administration, marketing principles and techniques and their relationship to nursing care are increasingly emphasized.[80]

Principles of marketing are also being studied and applied by nurses in new roles. The National Alliance of Nurse Practitioners is undertaking a marketing effort that promotes utilization of nurse practitioners in a variety of health care practice settings. Nurse practitioners increasingly incorporate marketing strategies into their practices to assess potential clients and inform consumers and physicians about the kind and quality of services they provide and at what cost.[81]

Emphasis on Language

To participate intelligently as members of executive planning and marketing teams, nurses recognize the importance of linguistic skills. The most effective executives are fluent in the many languages spoken in today's organizations and in the communities served by those organizations. According to Daft and Wiginton, languages used in organizations range from the natural languages of general verbal expression and jargon to precise, special-purpose mathematical and computer languages.[82]

Studies of executive activities, by Mintzberg, Kotter, and Gronn most notably, describe administrative environments as highly verbal, in which managers spend at least three-quarters of their time talking and using language.[83,84,85] Pondy hypothesizes that leadership may be more than merely changing behavior: The most influential leaders, through their use of language, convey shared values, putting phenomena about which others are barely aware into words that give meaning to the work people do and that amplify their understanding.[86]

Language is emphasized in nursing because as Blair notes:

> The language of nursing and nursing knowledge and skills are no longer

*The authors acknowledge the assistance of A.R. Boyington with this section.

sufficient to interpret the goals, scope, and standards of nursing in the administrative, economic, and political arenas. . . . Nurse administrators along with administrators from other health disciplines must learn to speak a common administrative language.[87]

Health care organizations are highly complex and differentiated. A wide variety of languages are spoken by nurses, physicians, finance officers, and consumers. A goal of nurses is delineating the natural and special-purpose languages spoken by these key groups, locating the troublesome differences in the varying lexicons, and finding vocabularies that promote understanding. Close attention to language can go far toward improving the quality of relationships within organizations and with the public that are necessary if strategic plans are to be effective.

Public Relations*

The close relation of the department of nursing to patients, visitors, and doctors places it in a strategic position to achieve good public relations for the health care system and to detect signs of adverse relations when they appear. Nursing services are directly concerned with the reputation of the organization as one providing good patient care; with the reputation of the health care system as a good place for people to work; with the reputation of the nursing personnel as ethical in relation to the hospital, the medical staff, and other departments; with the reputation of the nurses for participation in the development of their profession and for their own growth as professional people; and with the reputation of the nursing staff as a group interested in better health for the community as a whole.

Progressive nurse administrators are eager to share responsibility for public relations, especially for the interpretation of nursing to allied groups, and to share in the improvement of the

*This section is adapted from *Hospital Organization and Management* by M.T. MacEachern, pp. 550–551, Physicians' Record Company, © 1957.

profession as a whole. Time and funds should be made available to permit them and members of their staff to attend conventions, professional meetings, and specialized institutes or workshops. When attending such outside activities, they must understand whether they are representing nursing service or, as is the case in some instances, the hospital as a whole. Participation on committees that represent overall community services is rightfully expected of nurse administrators and of members of their departments. This participation should be shared so that several members of the nursing staff may profit from this stimulating work. A health care system that encourages this kind of activity usually finds itself better understood by the community in which it is located, and it becomes known in professional circles as a forward-looking institution.

Closely allied to this area of public relations is the responsibility of the nursing department for contributing to the educational programs offered by the health care system to students in other disciplines, such as medicine, dietetics, physical therapy, and occupational therapy. Because no one department in the system operates in a vacuum, it is helpful to nurture the awareness of interdependence as soon as an individual begins to learn his or her specialty in the institution. Valuable assistance may be rendered by nursing services in interpreting the role of nursing and the need for utilization of many kinds of workers with varying degrees of skill. This is becoming increasingly important as the team concept of patient care is gaining acceptance and is being practiced in many hospitals and health care systems. Formalized programs for such participation should be planned by representatives from the various disciplines providing education to future practitioners.

Because nursing services have more continued contact with patients, doctors, and visitors than any other group of health care personnel, it is in a strategic position to influence the public and personnel relations of the hospital. The wise administrator therefore "tunes" his or her ear to nursing at frequent intervals.

Being Accountable for the Clinical Practice of Nursing

A primary concern of today's nurses is the quality of nursing practice and accountability for the effectiveness and cost of that practice. In a 1985 national study of nursing issues, in response to the question, "What are the major issues facing professional nurses today?" respondents—nurse administrators and nursing administration faculty—answered as follows:

* redefining organization-based nursing practice
* defining accountability
* defining quality in an era of costing nursing care
* identifying the nature of independent, community-based nursing
* increasing self-care, holistic health, and hospice care[88]

The clinical practice of nursing has changed dramatically in the last few decades. Lewis Thomas, in *The Youngest Science, Notes of A Medicine Watcher*, describes a first-hand, personal experience of nurses.[89] His description of nursing as it was, is, and will be, is poignant and worth reading.

> When my mother became a registered nurse at Roosevelt Hospital, in 1903, there was no question in anyone's mind about what nurses did as professionals. They did what the doctors ordered. The attending physician would arrive for his ward rounds in the early morning, and when he arrived at the ward office the head nurse would be waiting for him, ready to take his hat and coat, and his cane, and she would stand while he had his cup of tea before starting. Entering the ward, she would hold the door for him to go first, then his entourage of interns and medical students, then she followed. At each bedside, after he had conducted his examination and reviewed the patient's progress, he would tell the nurse what needed doing that day, and she would write it down on the part of the chart reserved for nursing notes. An hour or two later he would be gone from the ward, and the work of the rest of the day and night to follow was the nurse's frenetic occupation. . . .

> It was an exhausting business, but by my mother's accounts it was the most satisfying and rewarding kind of work. As a nurse she was a low person in the professional hierarchy, always running from place to place on orders from the doctors, subject as well to strict discipline from her own administrative superiors on the nursing staff, but none of this came through in her recollections. What she remembered was her usefulness.

> Whenever my father talked to me about nurses and their work, he spoke with high regard for them as professionals. Although it was clear in his view that the task of the nurses was to do what the doctor told them to, it was also clear that he admired them for being able to do a lot of things he couldn't possibly do, had never been trained to do. . . .

> I have spent all of my professional career in close association with, and close dependency on, nurses, and like many of my faculty colleagues, I've done a lot of worrying about the relationship between medicine and nursing. During most of this century the nursing profession has been having a hard time of it. It has been largely, although not entirely, an occupation of women, and sensitive issues of professional status, complicated by the special issue of the changing role of women in modern society, have led to a standoffish, often adversarial relationship between nurses and doctors.

Already swamped by an increasing load of routine duties, nurses have been obliged to take on more and more purely administrative tasks. . . .

Too late maybe, the nurses have begun to realize that they are gradually being excluded from the one duty which had previously been their most important reward but which had been so taken for granted that nobody mentioned it in listing the duties of a nurse: close personal contact with patients. . . .

. . . [Today] doctors worry that nurses are trying to move away from their historical responsibilities to medicine (meaning, really, to the doctors' orders). The nurses assert that they are their own profession, responsible for their own standards, coequal colleagues with physicians, and they do not wish to become mere ward administrators or technicians (although some of them, carrying the new and prestigious title of "nurse practitioner," are being trained within nursing schools to perform some of the most complex technological responsibilities in hospital emergency rooms and intensive care units). The doctors claim that what the nurses really want is to become substitute psychiatrists. The nurses reply that they have unavoidable responsibilities for the mental health and well-being of their patients, and that these are different from the doctor's tasks. Eventually the arguments will work themselves out, and some sort of agreement will be reached, but if it is to be settled intelligently, some way will have to be found to preserve and strengthen the traditional and highly personal nurse-patient relationship. . . .

I have had a fair amount of firsthand experience with the issue, having been an apprehensive patient myself off and on over a 3-year period on the wards of the hospital for which I work. . . .

One thing the nurses do is to hold the place together. It is an astonishment, which every patient feels from time to time, observing the affairs of a large, complex hospital from the vantage point of his bed, that the whole institution doesn't fly to pieces. A hospital operates by the constant interplay of powerful forces pulling away at each other in different directions, each force essential for getting necessary things done, but always at odds with each other. . . .

The nurses, the good ones anyway, make it their business to know everything that is going on. They spot errors before errors can be launched. They know everything written on the chart. Most important of all, they know their patients as unique human beings, and they soon get to know the close relatives and friends. Because of this knowledge, they are quick to sense apprehensions and act on them. . . .

If they infuriate the doctors by their claims to be equal professionals, if they ask for the moon, I am on their side.

Staffing of Nursing Services

Staffing is a very complex, multiple function responsibility of every nurse administrator. Broadly defined, staffing is the complete personnel function of creating the staff and maintaining favorable conditions in which the staff works at optimum. It includes selection, orientation, training, and development of nursing service personnel relevant to the delivery of quality patient care.

Staffing is the primary priority in creating a climate conducive to the professional practice of nursing. A nurse administrator can have nursing ideals intended to create a comprehensive delivery of nursing service as is evidenced in the primary nursing models. However, if in reality there are insufficient numbers of RNs to provide comprehensive nursing care, the comprehensive delivery of nursing services is not likely to occur. Several steps must transpire before staff may be successfully expanded and comprehensive nursing services delivered. Nursing administrators must create a climate and environment conducive to the professional practice of nursing.

The creation of the proper climate is defined by three elements:

1. *Optimum freedom:* the freedom of individual nurses to fully implement the nursing process on every patient to whom they are assigned

2. *Energy release:* leadership that enables individuals to maximize their potential in giving direction to decision making regarding the clinical practice of nursing

3. *Statesmanship:* the key that creates the linkage to other units within the system that facilitates the professional practice of nursing (e.g., collaborative practice with physicians)

Creating a suitable climate of operation is key to recruiting and retaining skilled nurses. This requires that all members of the group strive to achieve the objectives willingly, and in keeping with the administrative philosophy for the delivery of nursing services.

To accomplish this, one must be cognizant of the human element in all decision making, and strive toward a participatory management system, enabling all staff nurses to give control to the staffing and the budgetary functions that relate to meeting their needs as well as the individual patient's needs. This further requires that an assessment of individual employee needs be conducted, and an attempt made to satisfy these needs so that individuals can set their goals and feel comfortable about their accomplishments.

In staffing, concern is also given to the mutual interests of the total group, that is, the nursing staff on a particular unit as well as the entire work force of the health care organization. No individual works in isolation. Each person's goals are related to those of the group in which they work. Group satisfaction and acceptance is key to the staffing methodology that is used. Each person depends upon the other when one is striving for unity of goal, plan, and action.

There are a variety of staffing methodologies by which to achieve these principles. Each of these methodologies is interrelated, and no single one affords a total answer to the way in which staffing is or should be done. Methodologies include:

- *Descriptive:* Subjective judgment is employed, using a range of information, usually including such factors as census data, financial resources, comparative statistics, and so on.

- *Industrial engineering:* Assumptions are made that nursing is a composite of tasks or activities, including work distribution and work load factors as well as time and motion studies.

- *Management engineering:* Nursing care provided represents quality desired. Patient classification is valid and nursing service demands should be distributed. Standard time of procedures is also valid and reliable. This forces nursing administrators into a systems analysis approach, looking at staffing and defining the various components such as personnel data and statistics, age of patient, cost figures, personnel skill levels, supportive services, number of patients, categories of patients, and other variables. Current methodologies include application of nursing theory models to a system or a particular group of patients.

- *Operations research:* Studies and reports from industry utilizing mathematical allocation and situation models provide another methodology relating to classes of patients, task complexes, and cost values. The diagnosis-related group (DRG) is an outcome of such research.

Another major factor in staffing is recruitment. Recruiting mechanisms are key to creating an image conducive to selection of staff that are compatible with the organization's goals. Recruitment programs must be dynamic, creative, and innovative; must communicate the unique and distinctive role of nursing within an individual practice setting; and should project a conceptual image to the public of what nursing is really about. Selection of staff should involve the effort of many people: personnel department and nurse recruitment working hand-in-hand, with the nurse administrator having a final determination of who should join a staff that is committed to nursing excellence. In self-governance models, staff nurses interview and select fellow staff to join their ranks.

The movement toward an all-professional staff across the country in the 1970s and 1980s forced nurse administrators to review priorities in developing RN to non-RN staffing ratios. Nursing process was mandated to require that the direct caregiver be a nurse, not a nursing assistant. In addition, the severity and complexity of illness for hospitalized patients increased substantially with the initiation of the DRG reimbursement system. As salaries increased for RNs, increasing industrywide economic cutbacks imposed financial constraints, demand increased for RNs in non-hospital settings, and other creative ways of managing patient care evolved.

Patterns of Assignment. Four patterns of assignment are commonly used in organizing for patient care. These are the functional, case, nursing team, and primary nursing methods.

The *functional method* divides the different tasks among the personnel available to do them. For example, one person may take all the temperatures, blood-pressure readings, and so on, whereas another gives all of the medications. The advantages of this method are that one person becomes particularly skilled in performing the assigned tasks, the best utilization may be made of the person's aptitudes and preparation, less equipment is needed, and it usually is better cared for when it is used by only a few. The disadvantages of the functional method are that the

care of the patient is compartmentalized, the nurse knows little about the total medical care plan for any patient, and the patient tends to feel insecure, not knowing who is responsible for his or her care. There is little opportunity for staff development. This method of assignment is safe only when the head nurse can coordinate the activities of all members of the staff and make certain that nothing essential to patient care is overlooked or forgotten.

In *case management* and *managed care*, the case manager role is assumed by an RN. The case manager has definite areas of responsibility:

- coordinating care and services
- case finding and screening
- assessing client's goals, as well as physical, functional, psychological, social, environmental, and financial systems
- assessing client's informal and formal support systems
- analyzing and synthesizing all data for nursing diagnosis and interdisciplinary problem statements
- developing, implementing, and modifying plan of care (interdisciplinary)
- linking client with appropriate resources
- procuring services
- problem solving
- facilitating access
- providing direct patient care
- providing liaison services
- educating client, family, and community; facilitating self-care
- facilitating communication
- documentation
- monitoring client's progress
- monitoring plan to ensure quality, quantity, timeliness, and effectiveness of service
- monitoring activities to ensure that services are actually being delivered and that they meet client's needs
- evaluating client and program outcomes

In the *case method* of assignment each nurse is assigned the complete nursing care of one or more patients. The nurse participates in planning the medical care program, plans the nursing care, and is able to give the patient the physical and emotional support that is needed. The nurse is with the patient enough to understand what will make him or her comfortable. Patients invariably feel more secure when they realize that one person is thoroughly familiar with their needs and prescribed course of treatment. However, the general use of the case method assignment is unrealistic today. There are just not enough professional nurses to provide service through case assignment, nor is this method now thought to be essential for the average patient.

The *nursing team method* makes a professional nurse responsible for the complete nursing care of a group of patients, but with the help of practical nurses, nursing aides, and orderlies. As team leader professional nurses have a new kind of responsibility. They must still know how to give skilled nursing care themselves, but they must also be able to direct and supervise the work of the other members of the team. They therefore assume some of the responsibility that is given to the head nurse in the other methods of assignment. The team leaders consult with the physician and the head nurse about the prescribed course of medical treatment. With the members of their teams they develop a nursing care plan for each patient in their group. Activities are assigned according to the preparation and skills of the team members.*

In *primary nursing* the close personal contact between nurse and patient that Lewis Thomas describes is paramount. Quality of patient care and the quality of nurses' practice are overriding concerns. The ascendancy of education for nursing administration in the last decade has not lessened the major nursing purpose of clinical nursing care.

Primary nursing is a model of professional practice in which nurses accept ongoing 24-hour accountability for their patients. This model for organizing and delivering nursing care to patients has in some organizations supplemented or replaced other systems for delivery of care—team nursing, function assignment, and the case method, most notably.

In primary nursing, control of nursing practice is vested in a single nurse, who, with associate nurses, coordinates around-the-clock services rendered by physicians and other members of the health care team. Moreover, the primary nurse as a professional evaluates the care provided, makes recommendations for change, and implements new plans of care as the patient's health status alters.

Autonomy among professional nurses—defined as nurses with baccalaureate or higher levels of educational preparation—is valued, and the primary nursing practice model goes far toward giving nurses the freedom to make independent nursing judgments. It enables nurses to teach patients and their families about illness and healthful living and to plan regimens for improving or maintaining health.

Each of these assignment methods may require the same total number of personnel, but the ratio of professional to nonprofessional workers will differ. Probably the most realistic staffing pattern is a combination of a number of methods. For example, one professional nurse might be assigned to prepare and administer all of the medication orders; another might give total care to a critically ill patient or to one who needs an unusual amount of emotional support; and the greater number of patients would receive care from several different kinds of nursing personnel assigned in the most effective and economical manner, probably as a nursing team.*

Quality Improvement

Quality improvement in nursing is a planned, integrated, and coordinated activity used to assess, monitor, and improve the excellence of

---

*The preceding section is adapted from *Hospital Organization and Management* by M.T. MacEachern, pp. 522–525, with permission of Physicians' Record Company, © 1957.

*This paragraph is adapted from *Hospital Organization and Management* by M.T. MacEachern, p. 525, with permission of Physicians' Record Company, © 1957.

care provided to patients. Ensuring the quality of care provided to patients is the obligation of professional nurses. Self-regulation and peer review relative to quality of care are major components of nursing practice. Professional nurses are accountable for ensuring responsible performance in the conduct of their professional duties. Quality improvement activities undertaken by professional nurses address the efficiency and cost of care, as well as the effectiveness of care. Quality improvement in nursing is best facilitated through a system of peer review in which professional nurses support, evaluate, and counsel colleagues relative to the performance of their professional duties.

Quality improvement involves members of the nursing division and other disciplines in an ongoing program constructed and executed to promote excellence in nursing practice. The method employed systematically monitors and assesses the caliber, appropriateness, and cost of care based on current nursing standards and new and/or revised policies, procedures, and equipment. Additionally, the method evaluates the degree of compliance and/or improvement in health care delivery. The nursing quality improvement program provides direction for the development and implementation of change toward improved quality of care and efficient use of the health care system's resources.

An organized and comprehensive quality improvement program, including an effective utilization management program, is the health care system's response to various social, economic, and legal pressures. The program includes the assessment of quality, utilization review, and risk management components and, to be effective, is linked with the performance appraisal.

Collaboration in the Practice Environment

Most health care systems are undergoing rapid change and expansion, as are the educational programs related to health care. As a result of these changes, increased attention must be given to how the social organization affects all the persons who function within it, not just the patients. As medical centers grow in size and complexity, it is doubtful that today's practices are adequate to enable the centers to meet tomorrow's problems.

The shape and substance of the health care system of the future are directly dependent on the organizational environment in which health care is delivered. Health care systems may well follow some of the concepts of academic administration, as these concepts are intended to nurture educational research and service growth, which are so necessary. Whether a practice environment is educational in its thrust or is fully a service setting, there is a mandate to design a structure that provides efficient functioning while maintaining a climate of maximum freedom for the practicing professionals.

Rigid bureaucracy is not acceptable in health care delivery systems. There has been too much preoccupation with identifying unique roles for nurses, physicians, and others, which has resulted in rigid groups and a blurred overall design for health care. Nurses decry the confusion in educational programs. Physicians have recognized the need for new educational and administrative models. Nurses with advanced practice capabilities, such as nurse practitioners, nurse midwives, and clinical nurse specialists, have become true partners in practice with physicians in several areas and have achieved prescriptive authority in certain practice settings. Collaboration in the practice environment between all practitioners is essential.

The need for collaboration does not mean a need for a hierarchy of authority. Indeed, the tendency toward increased professionalization of health care providers requires less bureaucratization. Conflict can be lessened by integrating groups to form the communication processes that will nurture unification in the health care community. There is a need to eliminate competition among professionals and encourage collaboration. There always have been needs that could not be satisfied without interaction, and the technological advances taking place mean a need for increased interaction. Today's practice environments demand collaboration. All disciplines within the health care system will need to work together, sharing information and knowledge. A model for nurse/physician collaboration was begun in the 1970s between the ANA and the AMA under the auspices of The Joint Practice Commission. This model led to several project sites for implementing joint or collaborative practice structures in health care settings. Today it is more common to have interdisciplinary clinical committees review and discuss the total care of patients in a collaborative practice fashion. Settings in which this is happening have demonstrated a significant reduction in patient length of stay, improved patient satisfaction, and physician and nurse satisfaction, as well as other cost benefits.

Participating in Management of Financial, Human, Material, and Informational Resources

Nurses and nurse administrators are cognizant of resources and their measurement, availability, and allocation. Doing more with less has become a predominant theme in nursing organizations. Until recently whether there should be a financial management component in nursing administration education was widely argued, and frequently nurses and nurse executives were less than fully involved in financial management. Today that situation has changed. Sensitive to prices, costs, and competition, administrators and nurses realize that they are responsible for justifying the cost of resources relative to the severity of patients' illness and nursing care needs and that justification begins with careful, in-depth evaluation.

Evaluation of Nursing Resources

Evaluation of resources in nursing service is widely endorsed and implemented. Performance evaluation (by superiors, peers, and self) and evaluation of orientation and in-service education, patient care, and nursing programs are widely reported. Using a systems approach, Arndt and Huckabay suggest that, to evaluate a nursing service, the following factors must be considered: the basic philosophy, goals, and values of the nursing system and the congruence of nursing's goals with those of the total hospital of which it is an integral part.[90]

The nursing organization's environment as well must be evaluated before a determination about resources and performance can be made. At least four aspects of the nursing environment should be assessed: its educational, sociocultural, political, and economic aspects.

Next, resources available to the nursing organization that can assist or deter it in reaching its goals are determined. If, for example, a hospital is located in a remote rural community where the closest education institution is a community college that educates a small number of associate and licensed nurses, the ratio of professional to nonprofessional nurses will be far different than in communities where baccalaureate nursing programs proliferate. Finally, evaluation procedures also are used to define and assess the components, goals, activities, and performance of nursing subsystems, and their management. Even small nursing service organizations vary widely based on the educational level of nurses and the specialty services offered. Nurses who work in labor and delivery perform a significantly different work technology than do nurses who work in emergency or medical-surgical areas.[91]

The primary responsibility of all nurse administrators is ensuring the provision of quality patient care. For both administrators and staff nurses responsibility for the varying tasks that contribute to quality care varies according to the health care setting. In acute care hospitals nurse administrators have, as major responsibilities, budget and staff development, long-range planning, quality assurance, policy development, union-related activity, and indirect patient care. In contrast, in long-term care hospitals direct supervision, recruitment, staffing, and direct patient care are major responsibilities.[92]

Nursing Productivity

Hospitals in the not-for-profit sector and professionals are increasingly as sensitive to productivity and costs as are organizations in the for-profit sector of American business. Escalating health care costs, the focus on cost containment, and expansion of not-for-profit service industries to nearly one-fourth of the gross national product demand attention to productivity.[93] With the advent of prospective payment systems (PPOs) in which prices for care are predetermined, providers are highly motivated to provide care as efficiently and cost effectively as possible. Consequently productivity is of considerable importance to nursing management.

The concept of productivity—in the classic sense, the ratio of output to input—needs to be adjusted in health care settings because of the widespread variability of patient needs, expectations, resources, and illnesses. According to Levine, a logical productivity ratio that takes into consideration types of patients, types of nursing personnel, and quality of care, is as follows:[94]

$$\text{Productivity} = \frac{\text{Output of the nursing process as measured by the number of patients receiving care on the unit, weighted by their acuity level}}{\text{Input of the nursing process as measured by the equivalent number of registered nurse hours available, adjusted by the quality of care provided}}$$

To calculate productivity using this formulation, patient classification systems are used in most hospitals, and they depend heavily upon increasingly sophisticated management information systems.

*Nursing Information Systems**

The nurse administrator of the 1990s, faced with decreasing use of inpatient services, prospective reimbursement, changing product lines, and increasing competition, finds a clear understanding of computer technology and information management systems absolutely vital to the

---

*This section was developed by Kathy A. Counts, RN, BS, HIS Nurse Consultant, Shands Hospital, University of Florida, Gainesville, Florida.

accurate documentation of patient care and determination of staffing patterns.[95]

Stevens, in *The Nurse as Executive,* describes the nurse executive as participating in a system-wide assessment of management informational needs and in the development of appropriate data bases, including nursing data bases. Nurse executives support and facilitate integration of nursing information systems into institutions' overall information systems. In return, nurse executives and other members of administrative teams benefit from access to a comprehensive integrated management information system. Among the benefits realized are the capability to derive information on the type and amount of services rendered, to what clients, and with what outcomes.[96]

A variety of computer applications currently assist the nurse executive with everyday tasks of managing and planning nurse services. Among these applications are systems that collect abstracted data and format these data for reports, management information that takes a more active part in decision making, personnel scheduling systems of various kinds, and systems for quality control.[97]

Automated nurse scheduling constitutes the largest share of nursing computer applications. Existing systems range in complexity from simple to comprehensive ones that incorporate long-range patient acuity, personnel resource availability, and organizational and environmental factors.[98]

Monitoring the patients' physiologic changes is the oldest computer application in medicine and the one with which nurses have had the highest degree of interaction.[99] Patient monitoring systems observe and record events, enabling nurses to devote time to direct patient care.[100] Comprehensive data management systems found in hospitals' critical care units integrate data from all sources into a coherent picture. Benefits derived from these systems include the advantages of:

faster access to data, elimination of manual transcription with its unavoidable errors, printed detail and 24-hour summary records, complete charge capture for hospital and professional services, automatic collection of a rich data base for clinical research, and the flexibility to select various subsets of the data and view them in a variety of different ways, rather than forcing a single flowsheet format to serve myriad purposes.[101]

Additionally, a special advantage of computerized data management systems is the consistency and accuracy of the computer, regardless of the commotion occurring around it. According to Cuddeback:

An ironic fact of caring for critically ill patients is the inverse relationship between the completeness of manual records and their clinical importance. When all goes well, the records are extensive but superfluous; when problems arise, the records are scant and vague but crucial. The computer will help to smooth out these inconsistencies.[102]

Nursing information systems are also used to implement the nursing process, including the functions of planning, documenting, and evaluating.[103] More than a century ago, Florence Nightingale emphasized the importance of nursing observation and information.[104] The foundation of professional nursing is, in part, based on knowledge that comes largely from the traditional source of expert nurses passing on the wisdom of their experiences to novices.[105] As a result, nursing knowledge is often idiosyncratic and untested. Computers in hospitals provide nurses with a technology useful to define and validate nursing practice. Kelly notes the following:

Nursing has long struggled to define itself as a science with a theoretical base of knowledge and to thus unquestionably establish itself as a profession. . . . Inherent in this struggle has

been the problem of a wide diversity in nursing practice, not only in definition, but in quality as well. . . . The advent of computerized Hospital Information Systems offers an exciting challenge to nurses in clinical practice in hospitals and to the profession as a whole. It is the opportunity to make giant strides by defining and validating nursing practice and facilitating the application of standards of practice in the planning, delivery, and documentation of nursing care.[106]

Nursing data bases that are derived from observation can be built upon existing knowledge by selecting a conceptual model of nursing and deducing taxonomies for each step of the nursing process. By defining specific data items at each step and identifying the relationships of each item or combination of items, the ability to generate client-specific diagnoses and care plans from nursing assessment data will be forthcoming.

In the past, the delivery of nursing care has not been directly reimbursable. The current economic climate and legislative initiatives in health care focus increasing attention on the costs and effects of nursing care.[107] Nurse administrators need quantifiable data to determine accurately the cost of care that nurses provide. Computer literacy and usage skills are part of contemporary nurses' technical armamentariums.

Growth Management and Resource Reduction

Cutbacks, cost containment, and downsizing are all terms one hears in today's health care environment. Today, nurses understand their dependence upon resources, and theories of resource dependence are increasingly incorporated into nursing education programs.

Nurse theorists and researchers believe that nurses can make a unique contribution to understanding growth, less as endless expansion, but as devolution and decline. Nurses' knowledge and understanding of human growth as aging, decline, and death and nurse executives' experience with organizational decline and death—through closures, mergers, and consolidations, for example—suggest interesting avenues for future study and understanding in nursing of what Drucker calls "organized abandonment."[108]

Nursing Education and Nursing Practice

Improving resource management also involves developing and maintaining strong ties with academic institutions, particularly those that provide one of a nursing organization's most essential resources: nurses. As nursing education has moved out of hospitals and into colleges and universities a widespread concern has been voiced about the need to bridge nursing education and nursing service to ensure both that nursing education prepares nurses for the realities of the workplace, and, at the same time, that knowledge is transferred from the academic institution to the workplace.

Ensuring Education and Research Programs

The majority of nurse administrators in today's hospitals participate in the effort to join together nursing schools and nursing services. Administrators of nursing services typically serve on college advisory committees, deliberate with educators in decision making about clinical nursing experiences provided by hospitals and nursing organizations, and serve as preceptors to students to ensure effective education programs.

The research responsibility of nurse administrators is an equally important activity. Whereas historically nurses more typically participated in clinical research conducted by medical staff or in job analysis studies performed by industrial engineers, in the early 1970s, research took as its focus the phenomena unique to nursing practice and administration. With advancement of nursing as a profession and placement of nursing education in institutions of higher education, development of nursing as a scientific discipline has been a high priority for professional nurses.

Clinical Nursing Research

In 1975 Lindeman conducted a national Delphi survey to delineate clinical nursing research priorities. Recognizing that nurse specialists should be free to explore a wide range of promising ideas, Lindeman also realized that establishing research priorities in periods of constrained resources was an intelligent and logical approach to advancing the development of a scientific body of nursing knowledge.[109] The top-ranked research priorities defined in her study were as follows:

- determine valid and reliable indicators of quality nursing care
- determine means for greater utilization of research in practice
- determine and evaluate interventions by nurses that are most effective in reducing psychological stress of patients
- determine factors contributing to effective self-care education of patients with chronic disease
- determine effective means of communicating, evaluating, and implementing change in practice
- establish the relationship between clinical nursing research and quality care
- evaluate the effects of expanding the role of the nurse in patient care
- develop a set of physical and psychological assessment procedures that provide information necessary for nursing intervention and improved patient care
- develop valid, reliable nurse staffing patterns that adequately reflect patient needs and cost containment
- delimit and evaluate the functions and clinical parameters of the independent nurse practitioner

Between 1975 and 1985 additional Delphi studies were conducted by nurses in various specialties, such as mental health, critical care, and gerontology.[110, 111, 112] The research priorities depicted in Exhibit 4–2 are examples of top-rated research interests in nursing.

Exhibit 4–2 Nursing Research Priorities

Mental Health

Factors that contribute to repeated hospital admissions, interventions that reduce readmission of patients with chronic problems

Factors that contribute to continuity of care posthospitalization, emphasis on the role of the nurse

Criteria to assess patient compliance, interventions that enhance patients' response to health maintenance programs

Ways to deal with staff "burnout"

Gerontology

Prevention, formation, and treatment of decubiti

Coping mechanisms needed by the family and patient after discharge

Improvement of gerontologic preparation of ancillary and nursing students and staff

Strategies for attracting and retaining knowledgeable, interested staff

Critical Care

Effective ways of promoting optimum sleep rest patterns in the critically ill patient and preventing sleep deprivation

Measures to prevent or lessen burnout among critical care nurses

Effective orientation programs for critical care nurses: cost, safety, long-term retention

Effects of verbal and environmental stimuli on increased intracranial pressure in head-injured patients

---

Role of the Nurse Executive in Research

The nurse administrator's role in promoting research has been discussed by Abraham, Lindeman, Krueger, and Batey. Between 1975 and 1985 increasing attention in nursing focused on the responsibility of nurse administrators to generate, use, and disseminate research in service settings.[113]

Jacox in 1975 stated that nurse administrators should be able to read and evaluate research findings, support the research endeavors of clinical nursing staff, convey the legitimacy of nursing research to hospital administrators, actively acquire resources needed to conduct scientific investigations, and conduct research in nursing service administration.[114] To accomplish these goals, Jacox recommended unequivocally that there be a research component in nursing administration graduate education.

Padilla, in 1979, noted that a major aim of the nursing service organization should be integration of nursing research as a service responsibility.[115] To develop the scientific basis of clinical nursing practice Padilla suggested that nursing research become a standard of nursing practice.

Chance and Hinshaw in 1980 described the strategies used at the University of Arizona, University Hospital's Department of Nursing, to develop a successful nursing research program capable of producing data critical for clinical and administrative decisions.[116] In 1985 the AHA Council on Nursing and the American Organization of Nurse Executives, in their *Guidelines on the Role, Functions and Qualifications of the Nursing Service Administrator in Health Care Institutions,* stated, "The nurse executive ensures that the nursing organization has an overall plan for the development and implementation of . . . research."[117]

Nursing Administration Research

In 1978 Dimond and Slothower raised the question: What is nursing administration research?[118] *The National Nursing Administration Research Priorities Study,* a Delphi study, conducted in 1985, addressed this question.[119] In the Delphi survey, more than 600 priority research questions were submitted by national experts from nursing and health administration. Examples of priority research questions for nursing administration were:

- What are the philosophies, nursing care models, and administrative behaviors used by head nurses on units that deliver high quality care?
- What environmental, organizational, technological, and individual criteria are best used to evaluate the overall effectiveness of nursing departments?
- What organizational and individual factors support or impede interdisciplinary collaboration and coordination among nurse administrators, physicians, and other organizational members?
- What computer technologies are used in nursing, and what is the cost-benefit of these technologies for nursing practice and nursing administration?
- What impact will the increase in outpatient services have on nursing employment and management?
- In the next decade, what will nursing personnel supply and demand be?
- In the next decade, what will be the foremost ethical issues confronting nurse administrators?
- How are masters and doctorally prepared nurse specialists and practitioners effectively incorporated into health care organizations?
- How do in-service and patient education programs affect the quality of patient care, length of patients' hospital stay, need for health services, and health care costs?
- How do interdepartmental relationships hinder or enhance the productivity of nursing department employees?
- What education and skill mix of nurses provide the highest quality care and are the most cost effective in health care agencies of varying size, purpose, organization, and location?
- How can the efficiency of home health care be increased without decreasing effectiveness?

Exhibit 4–3 displays the categories, themes, and number of times a theme (or one similar to it) was the central idea of a research question.

NURSING IN THE FUTURE

Despite the unforeseen calamities that may occur over the next two decades, many people envision America as exhibiting a new generation of very privileged and highly educated people. We will have more material wealth and personal liberties than ever before. And we will have more time to allow creativity in our personal lives; more meaningful relationships within families and between people will exist. Health care environments will change considerably. Hospitals that are now going through diminishing inpatient care will become comprehensive systems selectively determining their health niche in a competitive product-line oriented patient market. Mission and roles will change from plurality of purpose to multidimensional purposes with many businesses, both hospital and nonhospital related. Hospitals will be intimately dependent on the external environment and will have high level control in the financial reimbursement and structure area with use of uniform payment for patient diagnosis and federally controlled lids on hospital costs.

Medical staff relationships will move into corporate grouping of physicians and hospitals with innovative partnership relationships among hospitals, physicians, and investors. Health planning will continue to be regulated at the federal level, and new technology will require high level selectivity with concerns that will bring ethical considerations into full bearing on every decision in allocation of resources. Freestanding hospitals will be an exception. Megasystems will be commonplace. The executive team will have new requirements of sophistication and specialized management expertise, with multidisciplinary integration being key to success. Integration of clinical, financial, and managerial decision making will be state-of-the-art. Most decisions will be assisted by the computer. So where does this put nursing administrators in terms of their future responsibilities?

Nursing will most likely establish a new level of professionalism between the nurse and the patient; a social contract of expectation as a provider with a direct relationship to the patient,

Exhibit 4–3 Categories and Themes in Nursing
Administration Research Questions

Cost containment, costing nursing	53
Prospective reimbursement, DRGs	46
Personnel mix	43
Evaluation of care, programs	38
Nursing care models, interventions	37
Staffing and scheduling	33
Nursing productivity and accountability	32
Environmental and organizational context	31
Nursing department structure	31
Nurse administrator characteristics	30
Job satisfaction, recruitment, retention	29
Nursing education, training	21
Nursing intensity, patient acuity, classification	20
Nursing administration education	19
Interorganizational and interdisciplinary relationships	17
Shared governance and decision making	15
Executive nurse administrators	13
In-service education	12
Nursing management: first, and middle levels	12
Career patterns, ladders, mobility	11
Computer technology	10
Home health and long-term care	10
Future directions in nursing	9
Nursing research	9
Ethics and values	8
Autonomous professional nursing	6
Nursing administration in multi-institutional systems	6
Policy and political involvement	6
Marketing	4
Unionization and collective bargaining	4
University hospitals	4
Consumer values, needs	3
Nurse manager selection	2

similar to the physician's social contract of today. The nursing image as a profession will be significantly improved and nursing's visibility will be acceptable as partnership in the provider world. Nursing service and nursing education will have come full circle into a renewed unification/collaboration model. This is evidenced by unification/collaboration models at Rush University, Chicago, Illinois; University of Rochester, New York; Case Western Reserve, Cleveland, Ohio; Yale University, New Haven, Connecticut; Rutgers University, New Brunswick, New Jersey; University of Califor-

nia, San Francisco; University of Southern California, Los Angeles; and University of Pennsylvania, Philadelphia.

Other nonuniversity or academic settings will increase the shared responsibilities of teaching and practicing with more of the education of the advanced practice of nursing taking place in high technology care, research referral, and multidimensional systems of patient care environments. This would include the high technology and home care. Nursing will emerge as a significant practice science with research becoming as common in each major practice environment as quality assurance is today.

Consumers will become increasingly aware of asking and looking for credentials of nurses, and will know the difference between a baccalaureate-prepared nurse, and a nurse who is prepared more technically. Consumers will demand the highest level of prepared practitioner available to meet their specific needs. The conflict between unionism and professionalism will emerge within the major employment settings having true shared and self-governance models, with chiefs of nursing services being elected by the nursing staff who are highly credentialed and equally prepared for leadership positions.

While there will be an increase in the shortage of nursing for the provision of services to the public, there will still be the preferential clinical expertise that would allow selection of staff into highly desirable positions based on a credentialing privileges review system similar to medical staff today. Certification in each area of nursing will be required. The field of nursing administration will clearly require advanced educational preparation, as well as certification through examination, to maintain positions of leadership. Today there are approximately 4,500 nurses with earned doctorates, according to American Nurses' Association data; in 20 years there should be twice that amount—over 10,000. The tertiary hospitals of today will become major critical care centers, which will lead to the need for entire nursing staffs to be critical care certified.

As life span increases, the choice to have smaller families may increase. This could place us in an era of increasingly complex needs for fewer people to provide those patient care resources. The ethical issues of life, death, allocation of resources, and quality of life will require major policy directions in the legislative scene. Every practitioner will need information processing capabilities and information systems.

The economic value of nursing will exceed comparable worth expectations, so that individuals will experience economic worth based on competency, expertise, and preparation. The entrepreneurial opportunities will expand tenfold with third-party reimbursement direct to nurses being available everywhere, including home care and care of the elderly.

At the forefront of all of these changes will be the corporate nurse and the corporate nursing role in ensuring that the consistency of quality care to patient and family and the nurturing part of nursing will continue into the future.

NOTES

1. C. Woodhaven-Smith, *Florence Nightingale* (New York: McGraw Hill, Inc.).

2. Committee on the Grading of Nursing Schools, *Nursing Schools Today and Tomorrow* (New York: Committee on the Grading of Nursing Schools, 1934), 16.

3. Ibid., 17.

4. Ibid., 42.

5. E.L. Brown, *Nursing for the Future* (New York: Russell Sage Foundation, 1948).

6. Committee on the Foundation of Nursing, *A Program for the Nursing Profession* (New York: The Macmillan Company, 1948).

7. M. West and C. Hawkins, *Nursing Schools at the Mid-Century* (New York: National Committee for the Improvement of Nursing Services, 1950).

8. *Report of the Joint Commission of the Patient, Board of Trustees of the American Medical Association and the Board of Directors of the American Nurses' Association and the National League for Nursing* (New York: National League for Nursing, 1953).

9. American Association of Colleges of Nursing (AACN), *Essentials of College and University Education for Nursing* (Washington, DC: AACN, 1986), 10.

10. Sigma Theta Tau, *Reflections*. 12, no. 1 (1986): 3.

11. V.L. Bullough and B. Bullough, *History Trends and Politics of Nursing* (Norwalk, CT: Appleton-Century-Crofts, 1984), 51–56.

12. M.T. MacEachern, *Hospital Organization and Management* (Berwyn, IL: Physicians' Record Company, 1957), 552–553.

13. American Nurses' Association, *Facts About Nursing, 82–83* (Kansas City, MO: American Nurses Association, 1983), 156.

14. J. Goldmark, *Nursing and Nursing Education in the United States* (New York: The Macmillan Company, 1923).

15. National League for Nursing Education, *Guide for Organization of Collegiate Schools of Nursing*, 1946.

16. H. Finer, *Administration and the Nursing Services* (New York: The Macmillan Company, 1952), 139–264.

17. M.K. Mullane, *Education for Nursing Service Administration* (Battlecreek, MI: W.K. Kellogg Foundation, 1959).

18. Report of the Surgeon General's Consultant Group on Nursing, *Toward Quality in Nursing—Needs and Goals.* (Washington, DC: Department of Health, Education, and Welfare, PHS Publication 992, 1963).

19. American Nurses' Association (ANA), Commission on Nursing Education, *Statement on Graduate Education in Nursing* (New York: ANA, 1969).

20. Ibid., 17.

21. Ibid., 16.

22. J. Lysaught, ed., *An Abstract for Action: National Commission for the Study of Nursing and Nursing Education* (New York: McGraw-Hill, 1971), 49–100.

23. R.B. Fine, The Supply and Demand of Nursing Administrators, *Nursing and Health Care* 4 (1983): 11.

24. National League for Nursing (NLN), *Master's Education in Nursing: Route to Opportunities in Contemporary Nursing* (New York: NLN, 1979), 2.

25. E.R. Lewis, The Purposes and Characteristics of Master's Education, in *Developing the Functional Role in Master's Education in Nursing* (New York: National League for Nursing), 1–12.

26. Institute of Medicine, *Nursing and Nursing Education: Public Policies and Private Actions* (Washington, DC: National Academy Press, 1983).

27. National Commission on Nursing, *Summary Report and Recommendations* (Chicago: American Hospital Association, The Hospital Research and Educational Trust, and American Hospital Supply Corporation, 1983).

28. American Academy of Nursing Task Force on Nursing Practice in Hospitals, *Magnet Hospitals: Attraction and*

Retention of Professional Nurses (Kansas City, MO: American Nurses' Association, 1983).

29. National Commission on Nursing, *Summary Report and Recommendations*, 9, 11, 15.

30. Institute of Medicine, *Nursing and Nursing Education*, 151.

31. Council of Baccalaureate and Higher Degree Programs, *Master's Education in Nursing: Route to Opportunities in Contemporary Nursing 1985–86* (New York: National League for Nursing, 1985).

32. Council of Baccalaureate and Higher Degree Programs, *Doctoral Programs in Nursing, 1984–1985* (New York: National League for Nursing, 1985).

33. E.H. Erickson, Historical Evolution.

34. L. Wagner, Nursing Administration Education: A Content Analysis of Select Nursing Publications, 1976–1985 (Master's thesis, University of Florida, College of Nursing, 1986).

35. American Hospital Association, Guidelines on the Role and Functions of the Hospital Nurse Executive, in *Guideline Document* (Chicago, IL: American Hospital Association, 1985), 1–3.

36. Ibid., 1, 2.

37. L.C. Gawthrop, *Public Sector Management Systems and Ethics* (Bloomington, IN: Indiana University Press, 1984), 78–162.

38. Ibid., 61–65.

39. Ibid., 66–68.

40. T.J. Peters and R.H. Waterman, *In Search of Excellence* (New York: Harper and Row, 1982), 156.

41. Gawthrop, *Public Sector Management Systems*, 55.

42. Ibid., 51.

43. Ibid., 55.

44. J. Hanlon, *Administration and Education Toward a Theory of Self-Actualization.* (Belmont, CA: Wadsworth Publishing Company, Inc., 1968), 134.

45. M. Styles, *On Nursing Toward a New Endowment* (St. Louis: The C.V. Mosby Co., 1982), 126.

46. Gawthrop, *Public Sector Management Systems*, 55.

47. Ibid., 55.

48. Ibid., 56.

49. J. Pfeffer and G.R. Salancik, *The External Control of Organizations* (New York: Harper and Row, 1978), 1–20.

50. Styles, *On Nursing*, 35.

51. Ibid., 141, 147.

52. Gawthrop, *Public Sector Management Systems*, 67.

53. Ibid., 70.

54. R.P. Biller, Converting Knowledge into Action: Toward a Post Industrial Society, in *Tomorrow's Organizations:*

Challenges and Strategies, ed. J.S. Jun and W.B. Storm (Glenview, IL: Scott, Foresman, 1978), 35–40.

55. Gawthrop, *Public Sector Management Systems*, 69–74.

56. H. Cleveland, *The Future Executive* (New York: Harper and Row, 1972), 89.

57. Styles, *On Nursing*, 94.

58. Peters and Waterman, *In Search of Excellence*, 157.

59. Cleveland, *The Future Executive*, 14.

60. J.W. Colloton, The Changing Environment, *Journal of Nursing Administration* 16, no. 4 (1986): 6.

61. R.L. Katz, Skills of an Effective Administration, *Harvard Business Review* 64, no. 2 (1986): 180.

62. J.P. Kotter and P.R. Lawrence, *Mayors in Action* (New York: Wiley, 1974), 65–104.

63. A. Cresswell and M. Murphy, *Teachers, Unions, and Collective Bargaining in Public Education* (Berkeley, CA: McCutchan, 1980). As adapted by J.W. Biasini in A Description of Negotiation Behaviors in Nurse-Patient Encounters in Hospitals (Master's thesis, University of Alabama in Birmingham, 1982).

64. L. Flanagan, *One Strong Voice: The ANA* (Missouri: Lowell Press, 1976), 167–175.

65. Ibid., 261.

66. Ibid., 261–262.

67. American Nurses' Assocation, *Facts About Nursing 82–83* (Kansas City, MO: American Nurses' Association, 1983), 256.

68. Multimanagement Yields Greatest Earning Power, *Hospitals* (March 20, 1986):42.

69. P. Starr, *The Social Transformation of American Medicine* (New York: Basic Books, 1982), 225.

70. *Magnet Hospitals*, 1–104.

71. T. Porter-O'Grady, Bylaws: An Expression of Self-Governance, in *Perspectives in Nursing—1983–1985* (New York: National League for Nursing, 1983), 122–127.

72. P. Drucker, *Managing in Turbulent Times* (New York: Harper and Row, 1980), 41–221.

73. J.N. Behrman and R.I. Levin, Are Business Schools Doing the Job?, *Harvard Business Review* 62, no. 1 (1984): 140–144.

74. J. Coates, Why Think About the Future: Some Administrative-Political Perspectives, *Public Administration Review* 36, no. 10 (1976): 580–585.

75. J. Martino, *Technological Forecasting for Decision-Making* (New York: American Elsevier Publishing Company, Inc., 1972), 357.

76. L. Moody and B. Henry, Futures Study in Nursing Leadership Education, *Nursing Economics* 4, no. 3 (1986): 134–137.

77. B. Kotter, *Marketing for Nonprofit Organizations*, 2nd ed. (Englewood Cliffs, NJ: Prentice Hall, 1982), 1–50.

78. A.R. Boyington, Characteristics of Hospital Marketing Programs (Unpublished manuscript, University of Florida, College of Nursing) 1985, 1–20.

79. D.D. Coddington et al., Strategies for Survival in the Hospital Industry, *Harvard Business Review* 63, no. 3 (1985): 129–138.

80. E.R. Doering, Factors Influencing Inpatient Satisfaction with Care, *Quality Review Bulletin* 9, no. 10 (1983): 291–299.

81. S. Shamansky, Marketing N.P. Services, *Nurse Practitioner* 6, no. 3 (1981): 42–51.

82. R.L. Daft and J.C. Wiginton, Language and Organization, *Academy of Management Review* 4, no. 2 (1979): 178–191.

83. H. Mintzberg, *The Nature of Managerial Work* (New York: Harper and Row, 1973).

84. J.P. Kotter, *The General Managers* (New York: The Free Press, 1982), 10–120.

85. P.C. Gronn, Talk as the Work: The Accomplishment of School Administration, *Administrative Science Quarterly* 28 (1983): 1–21.

86. L.J. Pondy, Leadership is a Language Game, in *Leadership, Where Else Can We Go?*, ed. M.W. McCall and M.M. Lombardo (Durham, NC: Duke University Press, 1978), 87–100.

87. E.M. Blair, Needed: Nursing Administration Leaders, *Nursing Outlook* 24, no. 9 (1976): 550–554.

88. A.L. Urquhart et al., Perspectives on Nursing Issues and Health Care Trends, *Journal of Nursing Administration* 16 (1986): 17–23.

89. L. Thomas, *The Youngest Science, Notes of a Medicine Watcher* (New York: The Viking Press, 1983), 61–67.

90. C. Arndt and L. Huckabay, *Nursing Administration* (St. Louis: C.V. Mosby, 1975), 136–151.

91. L. Litwak et al., *Evaluation in Nursing* (New York: National League for Nursing, 1985).

92. L.M. Simms et al., Nurse Executives: Functions and Priorities, *Nursing Economics* 3 (July–August 1985): 238–244.

93. E. Levine, Some Issues in Nursing Productivity, in *Costing Out Nursing: Pricing Our Product*, ed. Franklin Shaffer (New York: National League for Nursing, Pub. no. 20–1982), 237–253.

94. Ibid., 237–253.

95. V. Saba, Impact of Computers on Nursing Administration, in *Proceedings of the Fifth Annual Symposium on Computer Applications in Medical Care*, ed. H.G. Heffernan (Los Angeles: Computer Society Press, 1981), 712.

96. B. Stevens, *The Nurse as Executive*, 2nd ed. (Wakefield, MA: Nursing Resources, 1980), 352–355.

97. R. Zielstorff, Computers in Nursing Administration, in *Proceedings of the Fifth Annual Symposium on Computer Applications in Medical Care*, ed. H.G. Heffernan (Los Angeles: Computer Society Press, 1981), 717–721.

98. Ibid., 717–721.

99. S. Glantz, Computers in Clinical Medicine: A Critique, *Computer* 5 (1978): 68–77.

100. K. Andreoli and L. Musser, Computers in Nursing Care: The State of the Art, *Nursing Outlook* 33 (1985): 16–21.

101. J. Cuddeback, *Functional Description: Proposed ICU System* (Gainesville, FL: Author, 1985), 2.

102. Ibid., 1.

103. M. Kiley et al., Computerized Nursing Information Systems (NIS), *Nursing Management* 14, no. 7 (1983): 27–29.

104. F. Nightingale, *Notes on Nursing* (London: Brandon Systems Press), 59–71.

105. J. Ozbolt et al., A Proposed Expert System for Nursing Practice, *Journal of Medical Systems* 9 (1985): 57–68.

106. J. Kelly, Computers in Hospitals: Nursing Practice Defined and Validated, in *Proceedings of the Fifth Annual Symposium on Computer Applications in Medical Care*, ed. H.G. Heffernan (Los Angeles: Computer Society Press, 1981), 545–550.

107. R. Zielstorff, On the Need for Database Management Systems for Nursing, *Computers in Nursing* 3, no. 4 (1985): 22.

108. P. Drucker, 43–45.

109. C.A. Lindeman, Delphi Survey of Priorities in Clinical Nursing Research, *Nursing Research* 24, no. 6 (1975): 434–441.

110. M.R. Ventura and B. Waligora-Serafin, Study Priorities Identified by Nurses in Mental Health Settings, *International Journal of Nursing Studies* 18 (1981): 41–46.

111. L.A. Lewandowski and A.M. Kositsky, Research Priorities for Critical Care Nursing: A Study by the American Association of Critical Care Nurses, *Heart and Lung* 12 (1983): 35–44.

112. H.T. Brower, Research Priorities in Gerontological Nursing for Long Term Care, *Image: The Journal of Nursing Scholarship* 17 (1985): 22–27.

113. E. Hefferin et al., Promoting Research-Based Nursing: The Nurse Administrator's Role, *Journal of Nursing Administration* (May 1982): 34–41.

114. A. Jacox, The Research Component in the Nursing Service Administration Program, *Journal of Nursing Administration* 4, no. 2 (1974): 35–39.

115. G. Padilla, Incorporating Research in a Service Setting, *Journal of Nursing Administration* (January 1979):44–49.

116. H. Chance and A.S. Hinshaw, Strategies for Initiating a Research Program, *Journal of Nursing Administration* (March 1980):32–39.

117. American Hospital Association, Role and Functions of the Hospital Nurse Executive, in *Guideline Document* (Chicago, IL: American Hospital Association, 1985), 1–3.

118. M. Dimond and L. Slothower, Research in Nursing Administration: A Neglected Issue, *Nursing Administration Quarterly* (Summer, 1978): 1–8.

119. B. Henry et al., *National Nursing Administration Research Priorities Study, Report of Findings* (October 1984–September 1986), 1–2.

BARBARA J. BROWN, RN, EdD, FAAN, FNAP, CNAA, is a world-renowned nursing administration practitioner, teacher, writer, and consultant and is editor of *Nursing Administration Quarterly*. Dr. Brown was formerly Associate Executive Director, Nursing, at the King Faisal Specialist Hospital and Research Center in Riyadh, Saudi Arabia, where she served throughout the Gulf War. She was awarded the Jean MacVicar Outstanding Nurse Executive Award in 1993 by the National League for Nursing. Dr. Brown received her EdD (Educational Administration) from Marquette University, Milwaukee, Wisconsin, where she also received her BSN and MSN. She completed a residency in Hospital Administration at the Medical College of Wisconsin Teaching Hospital. She now makes her home in Fraser, Colorado, where she is engaged in writing, speaking, and consulting in health care administration.

Chapter 5

Radiology

Raleigh J. Hamilton, James A. Patton, and Sture V. Sigfred, Jr.

Today's radiology department is a multimillion dollar business that provides a wide range of highly specialized services. These are made available through the efforts of a highly trained labor force using expensive, complex, and often computer-based instrumentation. Many radiology departments are the pride of their hospitals. The high-technology diagnostic services are effective marketing tools in attracting physicians and patients, and the radiology procedures have been a tremendous source of revenue in the fee-for-procedure environment.

Radiology has shifted from being a revenue center toward being a cost center with the introduction of diagnosis-related groups (DRGs). DRGs pay a fixed amount per hospital stay for Medicare patients based on the disease(s) being treated and independent of the amount of resources required. In this environment, fewer resources translate into more profit and force the efficient management of treatment. The future brings with it a continuing shift toward capitation. With capitation (HMOs, state and federal

government plans, etc.), the radiology department will complete the shift from revenue center to cost center. In this environment, the high-tech equipment will be effective only if managed by involved radiologists who judiciously direct the use of services as justified by medical necessity. They must ensure that procedure algorithms result in a cost-effective process. Procedures must not be overly redundant or needlessly applied. The radiologist must educate referring physicians and must also monitor the use of procedures.

PHYSICAL FACILITIES

The physical facilities of the modern radiology department are constantly strained, not only by sheer volume, but also by continuous changes brought about by evolving technology and alterations in work flow patterns. The department must accommodate routine imaging equipment as well as specialized high-technology equipment, the work patterns of both general and specialized consulting radiologists, the efficient handling and disposition of both inpatients and outpatients (including injections of diagnostic drugs, performing sedations, and monitoring re-

The authors gratefully acknowledge the editorial assistance of Tom Ebers in the preparation of this chapter.

covery), and the processing of an almost insurmountable volume of records and information (including scheduling, film handling and filing, results reporting, coding, and billing).

The handling of information in the radiology department is generally accomplished by computerizing the department via the installation of a radiology information system (RIS). This system vastly simplifies scheduling, patient tracking, film handling and tracking, coding, results reporting, and billing. The handling of images also is becoming computerized via the development and implementation of picture archiving and communication systems (PACS). Although the costs are high, the resulting improvements in service are significant. Many imaging systems currently in use in the radiology department are already computer based and are compatible with PACS networks currently under development. All of these high-tech developments stress the physical plan because they are especially sensitive to temperature and electrical fluctuations. Special attention must be paid to air conditioning systems (HVAC) and power conditioning in order to meet the needs/specifications of this sophisticated equipment.

The primary charge of the hospital-based radiology department should be the provision of timely, efficient, and accurate consultation services to referring physicians for patients housed in the hospital. The need to reduce length-of-stay because of DRGs and managed care contracts places added emphasis on timeliness and efficiency. To meet these needs, many radiology departments have been designed around the concept of the diminishing rectangle (Figure 5–1).

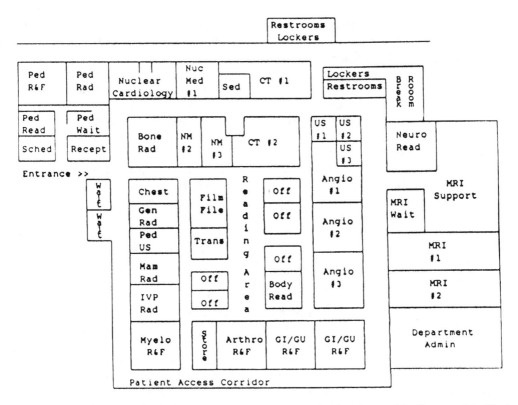

Figure 5–1 An Example of a Hospital-Based Radiology Department Designed around the Concept of the Diminishing Rectangle.

This approach positions imaging rooms on the outer boundaries of a rectangle, thereby making them easily accessible by a patient access corridor. The inner boundary of the rectangle is reserved for technical/staff support and physician work areas. The imaging rooms are accessed from this area by an inner corridor so that patients and staff are maintained in separate areas. An added advantage of this arrangement is that subspecialty areas (CT, MRI, nuclear medicine, ultrasound, vascular, pediatrics, and fluoroscopy) can be grouped together in order to efficiently utilize technical and support staff, including nurses trained in the subspecialties. Proper positioning of film processing equipment and supply closets containing specialty-specific materials also can be easily accomplished with this arrangement.

The strategic placement of imaging rooms is generally based on the concept of minimizing the movement of patients in the department. For example, the chest room and general radiography room should be positioned as closely as possible to the reception and waiting areas since they handle the greatest volume of patients. On the other hand, the rooms that handle the lowest volume of patients, such as vascular and MRI, can be located more centrally within the department. The central core of the department is reserved for image interpretation, transcription, and film handling. Reading areas are generally grouped by subspecialty or referring medical service in order to facilitate consultation with referring physicians. Current consultation patterns are now efficiently served in designated reading/consultation areas that are grouped by specialty and located at workstations where reports are dictated.

The department should be located in close proximity to the patient wards, operating rooms, and emergency department, in order to ensure fast response time and the ready availability of back-up staffing for acute service priorities. Other support services such as the film library and the nuclear pharmacy for nuclear medicine support also should be easily accessible from the main department. For example, the film library

supporting the department in Figure 5–1 is located on the floor directly below the department and is accessed by a dedicated film elevator from the film file room. Since most hospital-based departments serve both inpatients and outpatients, separate waiting areas should be established to segregate these two patient groups, with nursing care available to monitor inpatients.

Hospital-based radiographic facilities would appear to have an advantage in providing services in that there is a fixed referral base in place. Inpatients within the hospital who require radiographic procedures naturally are referred to the hospital-based facility. Outpatients requiring radiographic procedures prior to admission, or as follow-up after discharge, typically would be referred to the hospital-based facility. However, this is not always the case.

Hospital-based facilities are often not "outpatient friendly." These facilities must handle critically ill patients who often are not cooperative. In addition, pediatric patients or other patients requiring sedation typically are studied in these facilities. This patient population generally requires longer study times, resulting in reduced throughput and overall productivity. The schedule is occasionally disrupted by the demand for an emergency study. It is difficult for a hospital-based facility to mix the typical outpatient population, which places fewer demands on the operational structure, with inpatients. Subsequently, outpatients often experience delays in their procedures due to the special needs of the inpatients. Also, hospital-based facilities often are not "physician friendly." Referring physicians want quick turnaround in scheduling and reporting. Scheduling flexibility may be a problem for the hospital-based facility because of the inpatient workload. In addition, hospital reporting typically is handled in a fashion that results in delays in reports reaching the referring physician for outpatient procedures.

The number of outpatient facilities has significantly increased in recent years. Some of the reasons for this growth are the problems described previously for hospital-based facilities.

The outpatient imaging facility generally presents a very pleasing environment for the patient and is therefore very patient friendly. Parking is easily accessible, imaging schedules are maintained so that the patient does not experience delays, and throughput is optimized because set protocols generally can be utilized so that actual study time is minimized and predictable. These operations also are very physician friendly. Imaging slots are often reserved for physicians who refer to the facility. Reports and copies of films are delivered quickly by courier to the referring physician or reports are faxed. Staff skilled in marketing techniques often are utilized to cultivate a strong referral base, which has eroded the outpatient population in the hospital-based facility.

Outpatient procedures are important to the financial viability of the hospital-based radiology facility, and reductions in these referrals present significant problems in facilities management. It is therefore necessary for these facilities to compete directly with outpatient imaging centers. One approach being taken by a number of hospitals is to duplicate the outpatient facility within the medical center environment. Outpatient radiology centers are being included in the establishment of outpatient clinics in order to improve service to this population.

Hospital-based facilities that cannot establish separate outpatient centers must implement operational changes in order to place more emphasis on outpatient management. Service is the key, both to the patient and the referring physician. By efficiently managing the inpatient procedures through optimization of scheduling, efficient patient transportation, and effective patient care within the facility, it should be possible to establish an outpatient schedule overlaid on the inpatient schedule so that outpatient slots are identified and reserved for selected physicians who refer to the facility on a regular basis. Valet parking for outpatients is a value-added service that would reap significant dividends. Communication with the referring physician is also extremely important. Priority reporting and immediate faxing of reports or delivery via cou-

rier provides the physician with the service required. In other words, the development of a service-oriented, outpatient mentality is required to retain outpatient referrals to the hospital-based radiology facility. An example of a full-service outpatient radiology center is shown in Figure 5–2.

Radiology departments must shift their resources to match the direction of health care. Nearly 50 percent of health care is now in the outpatient sector, and the trend is to move even more to an outpatient basis. In the outpatient arena, market forces will demand competitively priced quality services that are provided in a convenient, comforting environment. The outpatient will not simply be "sent down to X-ray." The patient will make an informed decision as to where to go. The implications of operating in a market-driven sector are clear.

SUPPORT SYSTEMS

Priority of Examinations

Any busy X-ray department within a hospital will have examinations scheduled ranging from the purely elective study on an outpatient to absolute emergency procedures that need to be performed as quickly as practical. Departments, along with their radiologists and medical staff, must agree on the nomenclature and reasonable response times for various categories of examinations. Once established, these categories (such as stat, priority, urgent, same day, elective) should be made clear to the physicians and the nursing staff on the floors, within other departments of the hospital such as the operating room, and with local referring physician offices. It is ineffective for such a program to be in place when a requesting physician does not know the time parameters involved in each of the categories. This prioritization of examinations must strictly be adhered to to prevent "category shift" to ensure that an exam is done in an expeditious fashion. Once this system is established, monitoring of the appropriateness of the urgent categories is necessary to some degree to prevent

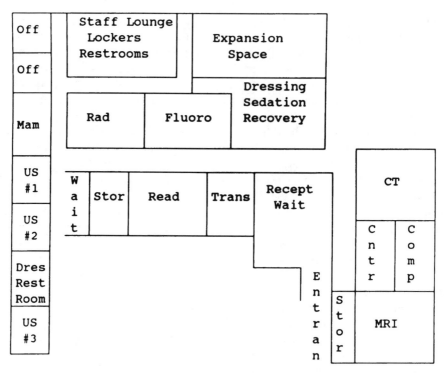

Figure 5–2 An Example of a Full-Service Outpatient Radiology Center

abuse and to ensure treatment of patients. Most departments have duplications in equipment and personnel such that elective examinations need not be markedly delayed due to in-hospital emergencies. This, of course, requires the cooperation of all involved to make a hospital department that functions as a smooth operation on many levels. A key factor in this process is keeping the patient informed when inevitable delays occur. Glitches in scheduling are always noticed by patients. The complaints may not reach management levels within an X-ray department, but they will usually reach the requesting physician. However, few patients will be intolerant of true emergencies requiring delays, if they receive an explanation of the reason for the delays.

The Dictation System

A modern state-of-the-art dictating system is essential for the smooth operation of any imag-

ing department. Such a system should be equipped to phone urgent results to the referring physician, should enable referring physicians to listen to the dictation as soon as it is completed, and should be capable of recalling earlier examinations by patient name. Modern dictating systems can be accessed by authorized personnel from outside the department and even outside the hospital system. The systems, while initially expensive, reward a department by lowering frustration levels of referring physicians as well as decreasing time spent generating reports on an urgent basis. Typed reports must be on their way to patient charts, or referring physicians' offices for outpatients, in a timely manner. Time-motion studies can be used to identify sources of delays so that they can be minimized. As a rule, the more expensive and high-tech the examination, the more urgently the result is needed. Prioritization of these dictations is a must. Courier delivery of typed reports (primarily for high-tech examinations such as MRIs) is becoming more the rule than the exception. Along with these reports, especially in neurosurgery and neurology referrals, selected images are usually delivered to the referring physician.

Notification of Results

The importance of notifying referring physicians of results goes beyond timely delivery of typed reports to offices and patient charts. Increasingly, radiologists and radiology departments are being held liable for the communication of important results to appropriate physicians. Legal actions have resulted from failure of the responsible physician to receive an important result. Each department must work with its radiologist and referring physicians on a mechanism for notification of urgent and emergent results. Once the medical staff have provided input into any given program, it tends to run more smoothly. Despite sophisticated call alert systems incorporated with dictation equipment, there is no substitute for physician-to-physician communication of life-threatening or potentially life-threatening findings.

Film Room

In a busy hospital, the radiology film room either can be a source of pride or embarrassment. It is felt by many that no other staff within a hospital are as underappreciated as competent film room personnel. Increasingly, sophisticated systems that track patient films and images are being developed. This area generally is one of many complaints and few compliments. Both radiologists and hospital administration must be aware of the stress placed upon film room personnel and be prepared to deal with it. As a hospital grows and the sophistication of its medical staff increases, the problems increase significantly. The presence of a teaching hospital can compound and add new layers of problems to an already staggering task. The entire imaging output of a department is capable of being stored in

a digitized fashion via PACS. Developments in this field will continue as costs of storage media decline and demands for improved access continue to grow.

Appointment Systems

There is a tendency in the radiology department toward a program of centralized scheduling. On the surface, this has a great deal of appeal. It reduces costs and allows a few individuals to develop strong relationships with referring physicians and their office staff. There are, however, areas within the imaging department (most notably angiography and interventional radiology) where central scheduling seems to work less well because of the need for physician-to-physician contact. Some areas may well benefit from being micromanaged. In addition to routine scheduling, specialty areas such as CT and MRI should have vacant slots that are available for urgent outpatient imaging studies. If these time slots are not filled, inpatients can generally be rescheduled to fill them so that downtime on expensive equipment and personnel is kept to a minimum. Again, referring physician involvement in developing the appointment system generally increases the chances of success.

SPECIALTY AREAS

General Radiology

Type of Service

The backbone of any hospital-based radiology practice is the general imaging section, which includes the routine plain films of extremities, chest, abdomen, as well as skull and spine. The mainstay of the fluoroscopic suites, which also are considered part of the general radiography section, are gastrointestinal tract studies (upper GIs, barium enemas, etc.). Also performed in this area are fluoroscopic manipulation of enteric tubes and the occasional contrast evaluation of the biliary and genitourinary systems, including intravenous pyelograms.

This area of the radiology department is generally staffed by board-certified radiologic technologists. As a rule, no training beyond this level is required.

Equipment Required

The general radiology area requires fluoroscopic suites and radiographic rooms capable of doing plain films of extremities, chest, and abdomen. Specialized equipment includes such items as panorex units, which perform tomographic examinations of the mandible. Routine linear and multidirectional tomography is also required in a good general imaging section. This section is also called upon to perform portable radiography in critical care units and operating rooms as well as to provide the bulk of imaging performed in a busy emergency department.

Future Direction of the Modality

The general radiology section always will be a backbone of any hospital department. By its very nature, it is not on the cutting edge of imaging, which presents its own set of unique problems. However, one significant advancement is the development of computed radiography systems that can provide digital images for PACS and can support the concept of filmless radiography. This technology can also eliminate "repeats," which typically are on the order of 3–5 percent.

Special Problems

General radiology has difficulty attracting and retaining high caliber technologists who, much like radiologists, gravitate toward the more subspecialized areas. Yet the imaging performed by the general radiology section often defines the level of pride and craftsmanship present throughout the department. Although not glamorous, the equipment required for a good general radiology section, including state-of-the-art processors as well as fluoroscopic and plain film units, is significant. General radiographic and fluoroscopic (R&F) rooms routinely cost in excess of $300,000. The addition of computer technology may force this cost up to $500,000. One of the major difficulties with a contracting budget is justifying replacement of R&F rooms that are no longer state-of-the-art and are barely adequate in performing routine duties. Cost-effectiveness rather than quality of images is often the primary consideration given when routine equipment is considered for replacement. In patient-focused hospital settings, it may be necessary to decentralize routine radiography. This is especially prominent in critical care areas and orthopedic wards as well as in the emergency department. This scattering of personnel and equipment significantly affects efficiency and cost effectiveness.

Ultrasound

Type of Service

Ultrasound, while for many decades the least represented in X-ray departments, underwent a renaissance and a period of rapid development in the 1970s, which has continued to the present. As ultrasound imaging has become more and more sophisticated, it has become the mainstay of imaging and diagnosis in the fields of obstetrics and gynecology as well as the gallbladder and biliary systems. Its use is increasing in genitourinary radiology, especially in diagnosing problems related to obstruction of the collecting structures of the kidneys. Interventional procedures, such as drainage of abscesses, decompression of infected gallbladders, and drainage of obstructed kidneys, are now being performed under ultrasound guidance. Initially, echocardiography was included under many ultrasound departments. This is now almost exclusively the province of cardiology units.

Personnel and Equipment Required

Ultrasound is a very technologist-dependent modality. A special one-year postgraduate training course is generally required prior to certification for ultrasound imaging. Ultrasound technologists are generally in short supply and high demand. Routine ultrasound imaging can be performed by systems costing less than $50,000.

However, color-flow Doppler units are now the norm, with price tags that approach $200,000.

Future Direction of the Modality

Ultrasound techniques have the distinct advantage of providing diagnostic imaging without using ionizing radiation. This is especially important in pediatric and obstetrical imaging. This advantage, coupled with increasingly sophisticated computer technology, especially in the realm of vascular assessment with Doppler color-flow capability, ensures a steady growth in ultrasonic imaging. Ultrasound also is used in the diagnosis of extracranial cerebral vascular disease as well as peripheral vascular disease, but these procedures are generally performed in a separate department away from the diagnostic radiology imaging area.

Special Problems

With a modality that is as operator-dependent as ultrasound, retention of highly trained technologists is a major problem. The ability of ultrasound to diagnose urgent medical conditions (e.g., acute gallbladder symptoms, ruptured ectopic pregnancies, and even acute appendicitis) makes it mandatory that around-the-clock ultrasound imaging be available. Ultrasound technologists are highly recruited for staffing the offices of private physicians who can offer improved working hours and salaries exceeding those paid by hospitals. Other problems in the area of ultrasound include the dilution of the practice base by obstetricians and gynecologists, who perform routine work within their offices during normal working hours but are unavailable to provide urgent and emergent ultrasound imaging after office hours.

Mammography

Type of Service

Increasingly, X-ray examination of the breast is being promoted and encouraged because of its ability to detect early carcinomas when they are presumably more curable with less disfiguring surgery. Over the last decade, this increasingly has become not only a medical but a political issue. Mammography patients are a "renewable resource" in that the American Cancer Society's guidelines suggest routine interval X-ray examination of the breasts. Patients who have had a positive experience in one mammography center will generally be receiving their repeat imaging in that same center. This, as well as the special nature of the examination and the attendant's anxieties, which accompany the patients to the mammography suite, have led to a very special treatment by most hospitals and outpatient mammography centers. There are mounting requirements by the American Cancer Society and the American College of Radiology, as well as hospital staffs, for assurance of high quality imaging and interpretation. Fellowships in mammography for radiologists who wish to subspecialize in this area of women's imaging are becoming increasingly popular. Continuing medical education requirements also are being instituted by third-party carriers to ensure adequacy of interpretation.

Breast carcinoma is the most common malignancy among women. This trend is expected to continue, and the mammography section of any imaging department will continue to have growth potential. There are generally two levels of mammographic services. One is generally hospital- or office-based and is a complete service, which includes physical examinations where appropriate, that is, actual mammographic examination of the breast, and, when required, ultrasound of the breast to assess whether abnormalities found on the mammograms are benign or in need of biopsy. Increasingly, prior to biopsy, localization of small lesions not detectable at surgery is being provided by mammography departments.

Personnel and Equipment Required

Sensitivity to patients and their anxieties is mandatory for mammographic technologists. In keeping with this, mammography suites are generally structured to provide a nonthreatening appearance and increasingly are separated from the mainstream of a busy X-ray department.

Routine mammography is performed using X-rays that, coupled with modern screens and X-ray film, result in what is referred to as a low dose examination. The risk of the low dose of radiation associated with the examination is generally felt to be far below the benefit ratio of identifying early breast carcinomas. This equipment is generally augmented with devices designed to help localize occult lesions prior to biopsy. Stereotactic equipment is often used for core biopsies, which increasingly are being performed within the X-ray suite. A mammographic suite also requires the availability of ultrasound, generally within the mammography section itself. Patients should receive all of the necessary imaging to appropriately identify any abnormality and make as accurate a diagnostic assessment as possible without the necessity of being returned for additional images and consultation. This generally requires a radiologist on site to assess the completion of each examination prior to the patient's departure.

Future Direction of the Modality

Mammography departments can expect, if they perform well, to have increasing growth throughout the perceivable future. There is growing awareness of early detection with its attendant superior prognosis and less disfiguring surgery. As stated earlier, patients who have a positive experience in a particular mammographic department will usually return to that center for their yearly mammograms. This repeat imaging allows a mammography section to experience a considerable steady and predictable growth. Breast screening programs also can be packaged as a marketable product in managed care services.

Special Problems

Particularly in the 1980s, physicians who are nonradiologists often have put mammography units in their own offices for imaging their own and other physicians' patients. The quality control was generally suboptimal and this did have negative volume impact on hospital-based mammography sections in the past. However, this effort has become less of a factor as conflict of interest laws, as well as quality assurance issues including licensure by the American Colleges of Radiology and Medicine, have been more universally accepted.

Radiation Therapy

Type of Service

Perhaps in no other hospital department is unity and family more important than in radiation therapy. Personnel, from transporters through physicians, typically become the patient's support system. A caring attitude is key, and personnel burnout is not uncommon. Radiation therapy departments are generally self-supporting and complete (medical records, transcription, transportation, etc.).

A well-run therapy department is an ideal focal point for the delivery of all cancer services. With the steady aging of our population and our continued abuse of tobacco, alcohol, and food, an increase in demand for radiation therapy services is expected.

Personnel and Equipment Required

The radiation therapy section is staffed by radiologic technologists who have received an additional year of formal training in radiation therapy technology. Burnout is also a problem with this work force, and radiation therapy technologists are typically at the high end of the technologist salary scale.

In addition to support equipment in clerical and nursing areas, radiation therapy departments require sophisticated and expensive equipment. The therapy equipment itself (the unit that produces radiation) is generally a linear accelerator, which has all but replaced cobalt units of past decades. Modern linear accelerators are able to produce different energy level radiation to tailor treatments to a specific patient's tumors. Specialized equipment known as simulators is also needed to assist in developing specific individualized therapy plans for each patient.

Future Direction of the Modality

Progress in radiation therapy directed toward improved cure and quality of life is to be expected at a steady rate. Department growth also is expected. The development of an efficient, caring, and compassionate department within a hospital system is a challenge that, once accomplished, can provide a focal point for all hospital-based cancer services. A close relationship between physicians (generally, exclusive contracts rather than open staff has been found to be most effective) and hospital administration is important in maintaining a well-respected and utilized radiation therapy department.

Computed Tomography

Type of Service

Computerized tomography (CT) was invented in Great Britain in the 1970s by Godfrey Hounsfield and immediately became an essential component of diagnostic imaging. The earliest CT scanners were units that only examined the brain but resulted in an immediate quantum leap forward in neuroradiology imaging. Subsequently, CT scanners have increased their scope to include the entire body. There has been steady improvement in CT scanners, especially in the quality of images and patient throughput due to reduced imaging times. Increasingly, interventional procedures such as biopsy and drainages are being performed under CT guidance, and the X-ray department and the radiologists are encroaching on what traditionally was the territory of general surgery. Interestingly, CT scanners were the first pieces of imaging equipment whose cost routinely approached and exceeded $1 million. This caused a tremendous focus upon CT scanning as an inefficient waste of money by third-party payors and by the government agencies. However, CT scanners have proven themselves to be vital in the management of routine as well as sophisticated diagnostic and even therapeutic areas. CT scanning is becoming a necessity on a 24-hour-a-day basis.

Personnel and Equipment Required

The CT area is generally staffed by technologists who have received on-the-job rather than formal training. Some departments provide combined training in CT and interventional radiology. This technology is vital to imaging and diagnosis in the 1990s and often becomes a very high stress area within the X-ray department with its attendant risks of personnel burnout. Even with its high costs, outpatient imaging centers have the ability to offer regular hours, improved life style, and excellent salaries, which compete for the services of hospital-based CT technologists. There has been steady growth of the technology since its introduction in the mid-1970s. A state-of-the-art CT scanner routinely costs between $700,000 and $1,000,000, with the higher cost systems being used in high-volume hospital-based departments and often located in trauma centers.

Future Direction of the Modality

Although nothing is threatening the diagnostic therapeutic areas currently served by CT, requests from nonradiologists for CT interpretation privileges (especially neurologists) offer a particular problem for hospital administrations who must balance the control quality of interpretation against the risk of alienating physicians who admit patients and use hospital facilities. Outpatient imaging centers compete for patients who are typically well-insured, while uninsured patients and those requiring care after hours generally utilize the hospital-based facility.

Magnetic Resonance Imaging

Type of Service

MRI became widely available clinically in the late 1980s. This complex imaging modality does not use standard radiation but rather depends upon the behavior of hydrogen atoms when exposed to radiofrequency waves in the presence of a strong magnetic field. MRI, in addition to its ability to image in multiple planes, gives remarkable resolution and detail. Since images depend largely on molecular composition, much physiologic and pathologic data can be learned. Various complex imaging sequences are necessary, and examinations are often tailored to the patient's specific problem. Exams are lengthy and, if properly performed, patient throughput is somewhat slow. The high magnetic fields present unique problems, not only with metallic surgical devices and foreign bodies but with monitoring and sedation. A significant number of patients experience claustrophobia while in the scanner, often requiring sedation and occasionally resulting in an inability to complete the examination. MRI provides superior evaluation of joints as well as of the brain and spinal cord.

Personnel and Equipment Required

Technologists are usually trained on-site. They generally have a background in CT. The MRI suite attracts bright technologists who are in demand not only in the hospital setting but in outpatient imaging centers, which offer stable hours, less stress, and often greater pay. The MRI areas tend to be stressful with great demand, often on emergent or urgent diagnostic problems. Technologist burnout is not unexpected. MRI's superior imaging capability makes around-the-clock availability necessary, at least on a call-back basis. This area of a radiology department is often physically separate from the main department (in that it has special room requirements that are best satisfied by building from scratch rather than modifying existing space). This presents challenges from transport, clerical, nursing, and film storage standpoints.

A variety of manufacturers offer MRI equipment. Magnetic field strengths vary widely, as does imaging capability and costs. Careful equipment selection with input from radiologists, technologists, administration, and referring physicians is necessary to select appropriate equipment. Costs are generally high, in excess of $1,000,000, for units appropriate for most hospital applications. Maintenance and supply expenses are quite high for MRI scanners.

Future Directions of the Modality

Much like CT, MRI has become indispensable to the diagnostic capability of a modern hospital. Its high initial and fixed operating costs result in considerable governmental and third-party payor criticism and complaints. Especially as radiology departments become cost rather than revenue centers, careful monitoring of referrals will be necessary. Again, considerable negative impact on hospital departments results from outpatient centers, which attract patients with insurance coverage, as well as from technologists leaving the hospital to provide around-the-clock coverage for a patient population with a significant uninsured or underinsured percentage.

MRI has the capability to image blood vessels (magnetic resonance angiography [MRA]). This capacity is being rapidly developed and will probably have an impact on invasive angiography, especially in select patient problems (screening for asymptomatic intracerebral aneurysms).

Angiography and Interventional Radiology

Type of Service

The fields of angiography and interventional radiology blossomed during the 1980s. This section of the radiology department not only includes diagnostic angiograms (detailed contrast evaluation of blood vessels) but increasingly is being called upon for therapeutic efforts, especially in the field of vascular diseases. Balloon angioplasty, as well as the opening of occluded blood vessels and grafts using potent medications that break up clots, is becoming the mainstay of angiography sections in the 1990s. Scheduling for these services often is extremely difficult and complicated in that these patients have acute problems requiring urgent or immediate attention. There is generally a moderate amount of trauma and after-hours service required. Procedures often are performed under general anesthesia or at least heavy sedation and require the services of critical care nurses for patient monitoring.

Personnel and Equipment Required

Special training is generally offered for technologists in angiography (often combined with CT scanning). This is a highly technical area of radiology requiring considerable hand-eye coordination as well as expert imaging capabilities. Departments are now digital, for the most part, and not as dependent upon expensive X-ray film as they were in the past. A trained nurse in the angiography section is required as well. Angiographic suites usually cost over $2,000,000. These sophisticated units are capable of acquiring not only standard X-ray film images but also sophisticated digital images that are computer generated.

Future Direction of the Modality

There is a continuous increase in the scope of the angiography and interventional radiology section. The approval of metallic stents to hold open blood vessels and other narrow structures has again resulted in a quantum increase in the level of use of this section. Interventional radiologists are increasingly becoming an active part of the medical treatment team, especially in the field of vascular disease. With the aging of our population, an increasing incidence of vascular disease and malignancies is an indicator of continuing growth in the area of angiography and interventional radiology.

Special Problems

The ability of minimally invasive therapy in the interventional section to return patients to a functional state earlier than is available with conventional bypass surgery has resulted in considerable problems in credentialing physicians to use the newer modalities. Eventually, third-party carriers probably will insist on increased use of balloon angioplasty rather than bypass surgery in those cases where the effectiveness of the two techniques is equal. The positive impact of interventional radiology techniques on length of stay and overall cost will certainly encourage future growth.

Disputes among nonradiologists (vascular surgeons and neurosurgeons) and radiologists in the interventional field can be expected to require administrative arbitration. Stringent requirements geared toward ensuring good outcomes of technical procedures should take precedence over the possible alienation of a referring physician.

Nuclear Medicine

Type of Service

Nuclear medicine imaging uses radioisotopes to tag physiological tracers (radiopharmaceuticals) to study organ function. Gamma radiation emitted by the tracers is imaged by position-sensitive detectors to provide pictures of the distribution in the patient. Nuclear medicine depends upon a steady supply of radiopharmaceuticals, which are generally no longer prepared in-house but rather are manufactured by radiopharmaceutical companies, and are dispensed by radiopharmacies that supply hospitals on a daily basis. Types of imaging available include bone scanning (a mainstay for detecting the spread of malignancies to bone), renal scanning (increasingly important in transplant assessment and follow-up), thyroid imaging (to assess degree of thyroid over- or underfunction), and lung scanning (for detection of pulmonary emboli, an especially common and potentially deadly complication among hospitalized patients), as well as less frequently performed studies such as gallium and labeled cell imaging to detect occult malignancies or infection.

Personnel and Equipment Required

Nuclear medicine imaging generally is provided by technologists who have had an additional year of training in nuclear medicine. Scintillation camera systems are typically coupled to computer systems to provide not just images but also functional data through the generation of time-activity curves. The cost of these imaging systems approaches $200,000, with computer systems adding another $75,000. The development of cross-sectional imaging systems (single photon emission computed tomography

[SPECT]) utilizing two to three detectors has now driven this cost to over $500,000. Portable scintillation cameras also are utilized to perform emergency studies on patients too ill to be transported to the department.

Future Direction of the Modality

Nuclear medicine imaging, like angiography and interventional radiology, is an area of dispute among radiologists and nuclear medicine specialists and cardiologists, especially for imaging of the heart. Oftentimes, combined interpretations are necessary to resolve the difficulty of keeping referring physicians and cardiologists content and providing quality assurance on imaging. Nevertheless, there has been steady growth and expansion of the capabilities of nuclear medicine departments. This trend is expected to continue.

Positron Emission Tomography

Type of Service

Positron emission tomography (PET) is a special branch of nuclear medicine that utilizes positron emitters as radioisotopes. These tracers are inherently tomographic in that they decay by the emission of two gamma rays at 180 degrees from each other. These can be imaged by rings of detectors positioned around the patient. These tracers also are physiologic in nature since isotopes of carbon, oxygen, and nitrogen are positron emitters that can be used to study organ physiology. An isotope of fluorine also can be used to tag glucose and study glucose metabolism.

PET procedures have proved useful in the study of brain function and the diagnosis and staging of brain tumors and dementia. In the heart, these procedures can be used to identify hibernating myocardial tissue that will respond to coronary artery bypass surgery. The technique also has demonstrated excellent sensitivity in the detection of tumors, especially in the lungs.

A significant problem with PET technology is that the radioisotopes have extremely short half-lives; therefore, an on-site production facility (cyclotron) is required to provide the necessary radiopharmaceuticals.

Personnel and Equipment

The PET facility is staffed by nuclear medicine technologists who have received on-the-job training in PET technology. Because of the low volume and small staff that are typical of most PET facilities, cross-training and rotational staffing of PET and nuclear medicine are attractive options for efficient operations. Radiochemists and/or radiopharmacists must also be available for radiopharmaceutical preparation and dispensing.

PET scanners and cyclotrons typically cost in excess of $2,000,000 each and must be supported by a radiochemistry laboratory. These requirements make PET a very expensive procedure and its use must be carefully tempered with medical benefits.

Future Direction of the Modality

PET technology has clear advantages as a research tool and should continue to be used in major medical centers. Routine clinical applications of the technology in the future will be determined by the outcome of pending review of reimbursement issues. At present, only a few applications have been approved by some private carriers and by Blue Cross/Blue Shield. Reimbursement for Medicare patients has not received approval at this time.

ORGANIZATION OF THE RADIOLOGY DEPARTMENT

The personnel needs of a radiology department require a significant amount of specialization, which reflects a cross-section of medical, technical, administrative, professional, and support skills. Specifically these labor requirements include general management, technical management, physicians, technologists, support functions, and special skills.

General Management

The general administration is handled by a physician serving as chair and medical director of the department as well as a departmental administrator and manager who usually has a degree in business administration and a background in radiology technology. These two administrators work together as a team to handle the management functions of the department, which often cannot clearly be separated into medical and nonmedical areas. Because of the complexity and diversity of the typical radiology department, operations management often is a team concept. The departmental administrator, technical supervisors, and supervisors of the film library, reception area, transcriptionists, and patient escorts comprise this team to develop, implement, and monitor operational plans for the department. In large departments, this management team often is joined by a professional services administrator and practice manager who assumes responsibility for professional billing and reimbursement, professional budgets, and professional operations.

In no other area within a hospital is change as apparent and as rapid as in the imaging department. This change is not only in the technical aspects of imaging but increasingly in the economic area. The management team that is made up of radiologists, hospital administrators, technical staff, and referring physicians can best respond to technical and economic pressures. Especially when new procedures or technologies are considered, the support of all members of this team is mandatory. A bad plan developed by a representative committee is often better accepted than a good plan that is mandated without input from all involved.

There is a natural antagonism that occasionally can develop between hospital administration and radiology departments. There probably is no other area within medicine where as many dollars can be spent as quickly as in the radiology department. Radiologists want to provide the best imaging technically possible; hospital administrators, on the other hand, are more bottom-line oriented and would like to generate as much income as possible from an existing imaging department. A typical example is an old fluoroscopic suite that turns out acceptable gastrointestinal contrast examinations. New imaging suites cost hundreds of thousands of dollars, yet third-party payors base pay on the basis of the examination, not on the cost of the equipment used or the quality of the examination. At some point, image quality and personnel safety mandate the replacement of a room. As a rule, a radiology department will wish to replace or add new equipment sooner than the hospital administration. A healthy balance, once achieved, benefits patient, hospital, referring physician, and radiologist. Once again, long-range planning that embraces the referring physician population, hospital administration, and the radiology group has the best chance of guiding an imaging department through uncertain times.

Technical Management

The technical management of the department is performed by the technical director and chief technologist, who must serve as an operations coordinator while working closely with the physicians and technical supervisors for the various subspecialty areas. The individual filling this position typically has many years of experience in radiologic technology and also may have administrative and business training, either through formal course work or on-the-job training. The day-to-day operations of the subspecialty areas (CT, ultrasound, angiography, MRI, etc.) are handled by technical supervisors reporting to the technical director due to specialization of service and technology differences in these areas. Nuclear medicine also is managed in the same way, but due to the significant differences of this technology, the technical director may report directly to the departmental administrator. For large departments, supervisors also may be designated for other sections such as GI/GU, pediatrics, trauma, etc.

Physicians

The specialized labor force in radiology includes physicians, who usually specialize by instrumentation and/or by body organ. The current trend is toward body organ specialization. This requires that the radiologist be proficient with the instrumentation that best images the organs in his or her specialty. An orthopedic radiologist would, under this model, be proficient in plain film, CT, MRI, and any new modality that relates to imaging of the skeletal areas.

Technologists

Technologists generally specialize by instrumentation. In recent history, the trend toward subspecialization of technologists has been consistent with that of radiologists due to increasing complexity of technologies and equipment. Technologists generally require two years of formal training to become certified in radiologic technology through a national board exam (American Registry of Radiologic Technologists [ARRT]). They may then specialize through on-the-job training in X-ray computed tomography, neuro- or abdominal angiography, GI/GU, fluoroscopy, pediatrics, trauma, mammography, operating room, etc. After an additional year of formal training, a technologist may become certified by national board exam in radiation oncology, ultrasound, or nuclear medicine. Formal training requirements for CT, MRI, angiography, and mammography may be established in the near future. One-year programs affiliated with academic institutions currently train bachelor degree technologists in radiologic technology, nuclear medicine, and radiation therapy. The trend toward specialization is now being tempered by the need to stress efficiency and reduce costs. Cross-training of technologists is now being utilized to reduce staff and increase efficiency. Areas where cross-training may be utilized are operating room/trauma, angiography/fluoroscopy, CT/MRI, and nuclear medicine/PET. As the demands continue for increased efficiency, it may be necessary to add other sections of radiology to the list for cross-section consideration.

Support Functions

A number of specialized staff are required to support the operations of the department. Nursing staff are critical to meeting the nursing care needs of patients within the department, especially in areas where interventional procedures and sedations are performed. Patient escorts, either from a central hospital pool or preferably stationed in the radiology department, are essential to the efficient operation of the department. Others include receptionists/schedulers, film library personnel, transciptionists, billing clerks, quality assurance/audit personnel, and clinical secretaries.

Special Skills

Because of the complex technologies present in the modern radiology department due to the implementation of magnetic resonance imaging, positron emission tomography, computer-based digital imaging equipment, and the use of sophisticated contrast media and radiopharmaceuticals, the need has grown for staff to provide basic science support within the department. These include physicists, computer scientists, pharmacists, and chemists to provide acceptance testing, quality assurance, routine monitoring, and scientific support for the sophisticated procedures utilizing these new and often prototype technologies. The use of RIS and PACS networks requires the presence of staff skilled in computer operations and maintenance in order to ensure the continuous availability of these critical tools. The high cost of service associated with the maintenance of radiology equipment by original equipment manufacturers has caused a number of departments to hire service engineers to develop in-house maintenance programs. Significant savings have been achieved by these changes.

The complex nature of the radiology department requires the coordination of a wide range of interlinking functions. The majority of tasks are performed in a serial fashion, and consequently the timely accomplishment of all tasks is essential in providing the timely distribution of the final report—the radiology report.

RECORDS AND REPORTS

For the purposes of meeting legal requirements and the creation of data bases required for management functions and audits, the radiology department must retain certain records.

The radiographic image (X-ray, CT, MRI, nuclear medicine or ultrasound image, etc.) is the legal property of the hospital. The hospital has a legal requirement to maintain the diagnostic radiographic image for a period of time that is stipulated by the individual state laws (often five to seven years). These state laws generally require that any radiographic image of a minor be retained by the hospital until one year after the minor is considered an adult in the particular state. The American College of Radiology has image retention recommendations that the radiology practice may choose to use as a standard of care.

Filing systems therefore must have a means by which to accommodate these requirements. Standards issued by the Joint Commission on Accreditation of Healthcare Organizations (Joint Commission) require the radiographic image report to be filed in the patient's chart. Generally the department files a backup copy of the report either in the patient's film folder or a separate file system. The use of an RIS permits the digital storage of these reports for future retrieval as needed. The retention of this extra copy is useful for the radiologist in reviewing previous studies. In addition, the extra copy is frequently used as a backup to the medical chart copy during an audit. Radiology departments not using word processing equipment for reports can benefit from having the request for service and the report on a combined form. The ability to document a signed request for service and to match this request with the final radiographic re-

port can be of great assistance during an audit.

Large departments that use word processors can benefit from using separate requests and report forms. A copy of the request form can be filed in the reception area for audit purposes. Separate report forms can be utilized by the transcription area to rapidly produce the final report. An example of request-for-radiology-service forms is shown in Figure 5–3. The use of an RIS for data management in the radiology department significantly improves all aspects of data handling and record keeping. Patients are scheduled via computer data entry; film jacket labels and procedure forms are printed via computer; patients are tracked in the department; exams performed and materials utilized are entered via computer; reports are transcribed and printed via computer; and billing is accomplished via computer. In addition, computer tracking is utilized in film filing and retrieval. Data entry is simplified by the use of printed bar codes on all documents associated with performed procedures, which can be easily read by the use of bar code reader or wand. Charge capture is significantly enhanced and audit data are readily available by the utilization of RIS. Budget projections data, Certificate of Need data, room utilization data, and staffing data also can easily be obtained from these systems.

Specialty areas should use log books to document patients and procedures regardless of whether an RIS is available. These documents serve as backup in case of RIS failure or as data to generate charge documents if an RIS is not available. An example of a specialty area log is shown in Figure 5–4.

Audits of reimbursement from third-party payors should also be performed on a regular basis. Each procedure must be billed using an acceptable CPT-4 code identifying the procedure. The bill must identify the requesting physician and the reporting/billing physician. The bill also must contain an ICD-9 code to identify the clinical reason for performing the study, and this code must meet medical necessity criteria established by the payor. Routine audits will identify errors in meeting these requirements so that they

FORM NO. 60-002-511 (REV. 10/92)

VANDERBILT UNIVERSITY

NASHVILLE, TENNESSEE 37232

Department of Radiology and Radiological Sciences

Request for Radiologic Consultation

PRESS FIRMLY, BE SURE ALL COPIES ARE LEGIBLE

Procedures Requested Only

date: / /

Pertinent Clinical Information Only

SYMPTOM/DIAG	ICD-9#:	DOCTOR NAME	DOCTOR NUMBER
	_ _ _ . _ _		

Location Code: ----------

Requesting Physician's Signature: ----------

Send Report To: ----------

Address: ----------

☐ IN PATIENT ☐ OUT PATIENT ☐ EMERGENCY ROOM

Mode of Transportation

☐ walk ☐ stretcher

☐ wheelchair ☐ portable

Nursing Remarks:

RN Init.

IS PATIENT PREGNANT? ☐ YES ☐ NO

ALLERGIES? ☐ YES ☐ NO

TO WHAT? ----------

Scheduling

SPECIFIC DATE: (if warranted) / /

A.M.

P.M.

Figure 5–3 An Example of a Request-for-Radiology-Service Form. Courtesy of Vanderbilt University Medical Center, Department of Radiology and Radiological Services, Nashville, Tennessee.

may be eliminated and reimbursement can be improved.

BILLINGS, COLLECTIONS, AND REIMBURSEMENT

Each specialty area of the radiology department should have a chart document that contains space for patient demographic information, pertinent clinical information, requesting physician, ICD-9 code (reason for performing the requesting study), and reporting physician. The document also should contain a list of procedures performed and materials used in that area along with identification codes for billing purposes. These codes generally are a part of the charge description master used by the hospital. For departments without RIS, these documents are transmitted to the billing office for data entry into the hospital billing system. For departments with RIS, the billing data are transmitted to the hospital billing system by direct data link or magnetic media after the report is finalized. An example of a specialty area charge document is shown in Figure 5–5.

Internal auditing of the billing process should be performed on a continual basis. This aspect is of such importance that a dedicated person should be available to perform this function. Comparison of final billing reports from the hospital billing system or the RIS, with charge documents and log books from specialty areas, typically identifies procedures and materials that have not been billed correctly. RIS printouts usually are available, indicating procedures that have been performed but not billed, and serve as excellent data for charge capture audits.

Correct charge capture is extremely important in the billing process. The final assignment of a code to a rendered service is done by the technologists in the specialty areas. The specialty charge sheets described earlier will facilitate this

Vanderbilt University Medical Center
RADIOLOGY

Date: Wednesday

APPOINTMENT SHEET

Time	MRA ROOM	Time	MRB ROOM	Time	MCN ROOM
8:00 am OP		8:00 am OP		8:00 am OP	
9:00 am Sed/OP		9:00 am OP		9:00 am OP	
10:00 am OP/IP		10:00 am OP		10:00 am OP	
11:00 am Sed/OP		11:00 am OP		11:00 am OP	
12:00 pm IP		12:00 pm OP		12:00 pm OP	
1:00 pm Sed/OP		1:00 pm OP		1:00 pm OP	
2:00 pm Sed/IP		2:00 pm OP		2:00 pm OP	
3:00 pm IP		3:00 pm OP		3:00 pm OP	
4:00 pm IP/OP		4:00 pm OP		4:00 pm OP	
5:00 pm OP		5:00 pm OP			
6:00 pm OP		6:00 pm OP			
7:00 pm OP/IP		7:00 pm OP/IP			
8:00 pm OP/IP		8:00 pm OP IP			
9:00 pm OP/IP		9:00 pm OP IP			
10:00 pm OP IP		10:00 pm OP IP			
11:00 pm IP		11:00 pm IP			

MC 3982 (8.93)

Figure 5–4 An Example of a Specialty Area Log Sheet. Courtesy of Vanderbilt University Medical Center, Department of Radiology and Radiological Services, Nashville, Tennessee.

process and minimize errors. The final part of the process is to receive payment for billed procedures. It is important to perform a regular analysis of net receipts to gross billings to evaluate the billing process. This analysis will provide indicators of narrowing margins and billing/collection problems. This review also should compare patient log book to gross billing to ensure that all services were billed properly. Having the involved radiologist assist in coding of complex

MC 2641 (9/84) USE BLACK BALL POINT PEN ONLY – PRESS HARD!!

Diagnostic Radiology Charges
ULTRASOUND

Charge Budget No.

Authorized By:

Is this visit accident related?
☐ YES ☐ NO

Is this sickness or accident employment-related?
1 ☐ YES ☐ NO

Is this sickness or accident covered by a contractual agency?
2 ☐ YES ☐ NO

D&H Account No.
\- - - - - - - - - - 9600

VANDERBILT UNIVERSITY
MEDICAL CENTER
NASHVILLE, TENNESSEE 37232

☐ Inpatient ☐ ER Location Code W800
☐ Outpt Rev 9400 ☐ Wkmn Cmp 9500
☐ CCS 9460 ☐ C/S/R 9420 ☐ Hemophilia 9560
☐ CRC 9440 ☐ Musc Dys 9580 ☐ Drug Studies 9480
☐ SCOR 9520 ☐ Neonatal 9540 ☐ ___ ___ ___

If answer to question 1 or 2 is yes or if D&H account give name of employer or agency

DIAGNOSIS

Location Code

ICD-9 ___ ___ ___ ___ ___ ___

REQUESTING PHYSICIAN

Quantity	34 - Code	Description
	60117-9	Amnio Tray
	70135-9	Emergency Charge
	60103-9	Ultrasound-Abdomen
	60116-1	Ultrasound-Amnio Guidance
	60111-2	Ultrasound-Aorta
	60121-1	Ultrasound-Biopsy Guidance
	60115-3	Ultrasound-Chest
	90406-0	US Bilateral Carotid
	60104-7	Ultrasound-Head
	60105-4	Ultrasound-OB
	60106-2	Ultrasound-OB-Repeat
	60113-8	Ultrasound-Pancreas
	60107-0	Ultrasound-Pelvic
	60101-3	Ultrasound-Portable
	60108-8	Ultrasound-Renal
	60119-5	Ultrasound-Renal TR
	60122-9	Ultrasound-Renal Trans Repeat
	60120-3	Renal Cyst Puncture US
	60110-4	Ultrasound Thyroid
	60124-5	Ultrasound-Aspiration
	60125-2	Ultrasound-Breast
	60126-0	Ultrasound-Gallbladd
	60127-8	Ultrasound-Lymph Nodes
	60128-6	Ultrasound-Pelvic Repeat
	40511-8	Other Exam Not Coded

Canary Copy - Department File / White Copy - Data Processing

Figure 5–5 An Example of a Specialty Area Charge Document. Courtesy of Vanderbilt University Medical Center, Department of Radiology and Radiological Services, Nashville, Tennessee.

procedures will probably result in fewer lost charges than having codes generated by clerical staff.

EQUIPMENT MAINTENANCE

Equipment maintenance is a very large annual expense in all radiology departments. The casual acceptance of these expenses as a cost of doing business is no longer viable. There are four major methods currently used to maintain equipment: service contracts, time and parts, insurance approach, and internal service.

Service contracts are generally provided by the original equipment manufacturers (OEM) at a cost ranging from 7 to 10 percent of purchase price. This contract includes parts/labor and preventive maintenance, guarantees up-time, and is generally the most costly of the four options. Because of the high costs, there are now many third-party service companies that provide the same service programs at significantly lower prices.

A service contact also can be written with the OEM or a third-party company for only labor, time, and parts. This is basically service on a pay-as-you-go basis. The significant risk with this option is the potential need for a replacement part that is very costly. Service also may be delayed until customers with full service contracts are served.

There are insurance companies that will write a full coverage policy for the maintenance of equipment at a price based on the age and condition of each item. The insurance company independently deals with the various service vendors to secure maintenance for the equipment. Third-party-supplied replacement parts may be used in the service process.

Many large departments now employ one or more full-time equipment engineers to provide internal service. The engineers will take first call on selected pieces of equipment, and call in the third-party service or OEM service as needed. Start-up costs may be high because of the necessity of acquiring test equipment and a replacement parts inventory. However, a good in-house service program is an important part of any large radiology department maintenance plan.

MARKETING

Marketing is extremely important, as many imaging services are moving into the outpatient sector. The lack of a significant marketing plan in an outpatient setting will be self-defeating.

The marketing efforts for inpatients will be directed at ensuring that the most cost-effective methods of diagnosis and treatment are applied. Educational efforts directed at referring physicians and monitoring of procedure requests will be required. Some departments, especially outpatient centers, now employ marketing personnel who actively solicit business from referring personnel. In some areas, these marketing practices are very competitive and result in loss of referrals of outpatients to hospital-based facilities.

TOTAL QUALITY MANAGEMENT

Total quality management (TQM) programs are now required by the Joint Commission. These programs examine the processes of providing services, identify the key components of the service, and monitor them against established benchmarks. TQM benefits by the inclusion of hands-on workers in the review of a process, and also includes input from all parties associated with a process. For example, TQM teams from the nursing department and the radiology department could work together to resolve problems that involve both departments and involve direct patient care.

MAJOR SUPPLY ITEMS

The major supply items used in the radiology department are contrast media and film/chemistry. Contrast agents are used in several sections of radiology to enhance the visualization of organ systems and to visualize blood flow. The ionic contrast agents used in the past sometimes caused allergic reactions, with even death a possibility in some patients. Although the risk of severe reactions was low, radiology departments quickly adopted the use of non-ionic contrast agents as they became available, because of a significant reduction in the potential for reactions with these agents. Unfortunately, the cost of this conversion is high, with non-ionics typically costing seven to ten times that of ionics. The result has been a significant increase in material costs for the department. Fortunately, criteria have been established for the use of non-ionic agents by the American College of Radiology, and adherence to these guidelines will help in controlling costs.

Film always has been an expensive supply item for radiology. Great strides are being made toward the utilization of digital storage and retrieval of images using PACS networks with a resulting reduction in film utilization. Nonetheless, most departments continue to be heavy film users. However, this is one potential area for significant savings in the future. In the past, film contracts have been very complicated, with multiple discounts and the inclusion of volume rebates as well as educational, training, and research options. The tendency is now toward the establishment of single vendor contracts with the final bottom line discount being the determining factor.

Chemistry traditionally has accounted for about 10 percent of the total film and chemistry bill. Chemistry will become more of a disposal problem in the future, as environmental rules tighten. Expended (silver-laden) solutions can be sold. Five hundred gallons of fixer solution will yield about $250, with silver at $4 per ounce. This amount will vary with the type of film being used. The film manufacturer's technical representatives can be helpful in estimating the silver yield from a specific film type.

RADIOLOGY IN THE TWENTY-FIRST CENTURY

With an accelerated shift in medicine toward managed care, radiology should experience a change from a revenue-generating center to one that generates considerable costs. Along with this developing change in radiology's economic position, there has been an expected shift in imaging service to the outpatient arena. This shift has occurred within hospital departments, which now cater to outpatient imaging and also has led to the development of outside outpatient imaging centers. Initially, these outside centers often were owned by nonradiologist physicians. Many of the outpatient diagnostic centers have changed ownership, with increasingly stringent regulations on physician ownership and self-referral.

In the future, hospital imaging centers will find it necessary to restrict or in some way control overutilization of imaging services. This change in attitude from accepting all examinations no matter how redundant to restricting examinations to those that are medically necessary will come at some cost. It will largely fall to the practicing radiologist to establish guidelines, especially for the use of high-tech equipment.

Expectedly, this control over imaging services probably will not be greeted warmly by practicing physicians, who traditionally have had no restrictions and, more importantly, no interference with the ordering or performance of diagnostic tests.

As hospitals and radiologists look toward the twenty-first century, strong alliances between physicians and hospitals will become more important. Assurance of quality care as well as cost effectiveness will require a delicate balance. Radiology residencies, which have long been supported by hospitals, are becoming threatened by the trend of third-party carriers not to accept the cost of postgraduate education for physicians. There will be less funding for diagnostic radiology residency positions from health care institutions. Even now, radiology residencies are occasionally unfunded, but the substantial economic burden on the individual physician will keep this from becoming a general trend. The likely outcome will be fewer diagnostic radiologists as well as the many subspecialties in diagnostic radiology. This overall trend could result in a decline in the progress made in radiology over the past decades. Again, the presence of well-trained diagnostic radiologists, and especially those radiologists with subspecialty training, enhances the image and capability of any given hospital. The presence of a radiology residency markedly improves the ability to attract top-quality radiologists. Care must be taken that imaging services, and thus patient care, do not suffer from the economic realities imposed by a shift in third-party payors away from postgraduate education.

Tertiary care hospitals have long been a mainstay in the supply of well-trained technologists for today's modern imaging facility. In an age of decreasing reimbursements, a threat exists with the closing of quality radiologic technology programs for purely economic reasons. The best and brightest students tend to gravitate toward the more high-tech (and most costly) subspecialty areas such as MRI, angiography and interventional radiology, and ultrasound. With X-ray-technology schools becoming less justifiable from a purely economic standpoint, one can foresee a shortage of highly trained technologists in the near future. This, of course, will carry with it a high price tag and possibly a decrease in the standards that we have come to expect from our imagers. In order to preserve the critical mass of technologists necessary for a health care delivery system, it would seem that governmental or some third-party support for training programs would become essential.

Historically, radiologists maintained a fairly passive role in practicing medicine. However, with the advent of CT scanning in the mid-1970s, radiology became the focus and hub of diagnosis in the health care delivery system. This gradually led to radiology becoming more of a "contact sport," which resulted in a change not only in radiology, but also in the type of physician attracted to the specialty. Throughout the 1970s and 1980s, radiology began to encroach more on other specialty areas. For example, the

ability to percutaneously biopsy (under CT guidance) distant and difficult to reach surgical lesions has made the diagnostic laparotomy almost a procedure of the past. Likewise, the interventional and vascular radiologist has encroached on the field of vascular surgery with balloon angioplasties, and, now, vascular stents. Currently, patients with biliary or urinary tract obstructions often are handled by an interventional radiologist.

With the changing economic phase of medicine, the next decade will be interesting. At best, and again with guidance from hospitals and health care providers, a more efficient system will result. The challenge always will be to provide high quality with shrinking resources. The sooner any given hospital is able to address these potential conflicts and develop a working team of administrators, radiologists, and referring physicians, the greater the survivability of quality health care will be at that institution.

RALEIGH J. HAMILTON, MBA, is the CEO and Administrator of five health care corporations in the Norfolk/Virginia Beach, Virginia, area. Each corporation is a shared venture between various hospitals in the area. He has served as Radiology Business Manager for both the University of North Carolina at Chapel Hill and Vanderbilt University Medical Center. He also has served as the Rate Structure Manager for the University of North Carolina at Chapel Hill and as Budget Officer at Duke University Medical Center. He has a dual major in Business Administration and Accounting from the University of North Carolina at Chapel Hill and holds an MBA from the Owen School of Management at Vanderbilt University. Mr. Hamilton is also a registered X-ray technologist.

JAMES A. PATTON, PHD, is Professor of Radiology and Radiological Sciences in the School of Medicine at Vanderbilt University Medical Center in Nashville, Tennessee, and is Administrator for Radiology Academic Affairs. He served for 6 years as Radiology Department Administrator at Vanderbilt and was responsible for clinical services, professional services, and academic affairs. He has a doctor of philosophy degree in physics and is the author of 70 articles, 75 book chapters, and 4 textbooks in nuclear medicine, magnetic resonance imaging, and radiology. In addition, Dr. Patton has served for 14 years as Program Director of the Nuclear Medicine Technology Program at Vanderbilt and has taught nuclear medicine physics and instrumentation to radiology residents for over 20 years.

STURE V. SIGFRED, JR., MD, is Vice Chairman of Diagnostic Radiology at the Eastern Virginia Medical School in Norfolk, Virginia. He specializes in interventional radiology and was a family practitioner prior to his radiology training.

Chapter 6

Laboratories

Paul J. Brzozowski and Ellen A. Moloney

Clinical laboratories are one of the most dynamic environments in health care today. The medical community is exerting pressure on laboratories to expand their scope of service at a time when changes in reimbursement regulations and population mix, the advent of alternative delivery systems, and competition from the private sector are forcing laboratories to become more competitive and operate under increasing fiscal constraints. In response to these pressures, laboratory professionals constantly must evaluate and integrate rapidly changing technology into their operations. Those responsible for laboratories must look beyond traditional management styles and marketing strategies to keep their laboratories viable.

To provide a better understanding of the laboratory operation and the changes in organization, roles, and technology necessary to manage the limited resources available to clinical laboratories, the following characteristics of clinical laboratories will be discussed:

- service levels
- organization
- staffing
- information systems
- physical plant and equipment
- laboratory regulation
- strategic planning

Such issues as skill mix, workstation configuration, workload, workflow, and customer service are examined in the context of these operational characteristics.

SERVICE LEVELS

Service levels can be defined as the variety of tests offered, and the turnaround time associated with that testing. In hospitals, service levels represent the laboratory's interpretation of the hospital's mission statement and perception of available resources. Properly defined service levels provide the basis for effective laboratory management because they affect decisions on staffing, skill mix, equipment configuration, facility design, and planning. Factors to consider in developing the range of testing performed by a hospital laboratory fall into one of these four categories:

1. medical needs
2. legal or professional requirements
3. technical and personnel capabilities
4. administrative considerations

Questions pertaining to the factors in each category were developed and incorporated into a questionnaire/worksheet format that has been used as a formal decision-making tool to help answer the question, "Should this test be performed in this hospital laboratory?" This approach was originally developed by the Centers for Disease Control and published in *Laboratory Management* in 1971.[1] The criteria have been updated and the format modified by Robert E. Hager and Paul J. Brzozowski.[2] Appendix 6–A provides a complete listing of these questions and explanations on how to interpret responses to these questions.

Defining 75 percent of a laboratory test menu is not as difficult as the remaining 25 percent. By reducing information into a well-defined, easy to use, structured format, this tool enables hospitals to use a multidisciplinary approach to define the remaining 25 percent of the laboratory service. Administrative, fiscal, clinical, and laboratory professionals are all encouraged to offer input into a final decision on whether a procedure will be performed in a particular laboratory. Once service levels are determined, a hospital can evaluate the other laboratory characteristics necessary to support the laboratory operation. Laboratory operations also exist in physician offices and as stand-alone commercial enterprises. Their mission and service levels will also vary based on the patient mix (physician offices) and client base (commercial laboratories) they serve. While the questions and focus may differ, the same approach can be used in these operations to determine service levels.

ORGANIZATION

Laboratories are usually divided into two major areas: anatomic and clinical pathology. Anatomic pathology is the division that processes surgical and gynecological specimens (Pap smears). Its subsections usually include surgical pathology and cytology. Occasionally in large teaching centers electron microscopy may be assigned to the anatomic division.

Clinical pathology is the division that processes the more familiar test requests, such as blood counts, coagulation studies, urinalysis, blood sugars, and throat cultures. Its subsections include chemistry, hematology, microbiology, urinalysis (microscopy), and blood bank. Again,

larger hospitals may expand these sections to include more defined units, such as a coagulation section (usually incorporated into hematology). Other subsections may include endocrinology, toxicology, serology, and tissue-typing lab. The number of formally designated subsections reflects the previously defined service levels. Appendix 6–B contains a representative list of tests performed in these sections.

To staff these areas, clinical laboratories employ a blend of medical, technical, and support staff. The number, titles, and job descriptions vary according to the size of the institution and scope of services provided. Most community general hospitals employ personnel in the following positions:

- pathologists
- laboratory scientists
- section supervisors
- technologists
- technicians
- phlebotomists
- clerks/medical secretaries

Because some variation in job description occurs, the following discussion presents the basic role of these positions and some of their commonly seen variations and challenges.

Pathologists are found in all institutions, from large teaching hospitals to small rural hospitals. Usually one pathologist is designated as the director. Large teaching and research facilities may appoint one director of anatomic pathology and another director of clinical pathology. The pathologist is a physician who has a specialty in pathology and is usually board certified in both anatomic and clinical pathology. Laboratory scientists may be employed to assist pathologists in operating the laboratory. These are individuals with advanced degrees, usually doctorates, in areas such as biochemistry, microbiology, or virology. They are usually found in large teaching centers, specialty hospitals, or commercial laboratories.

Laboratory managers—administrative technologists, laboratory coordinators—are usually medical technologists with administrative skills acquired through experience and/or formal education, such as an MBA. In very large institutions they may have only a business background and no clinical experience. If this is the case, usually one of two staffing patterns are found. An individual may be assigned the title of chief technologist: he or she is responsible for the technical aspects of managing the department, such as quality control, instrument maintenance, and the like. Alternatively, the section supervisors assume responsibility for technical supervision of each section of the laboratory. This alternative may present some organizational problems if section supervisors report to a business manager for administrative activities, and a medical director for clinical activities. Such a dual reporting relationship slows down the decision-making process, particularly when decisions affecting both administrative and clinical aspects of the department need to be made. Such is the case with equipment acquisition.

Section supervisors are usually assigned to one section of the laboratory, such as chemistry or hematology. Their time is usually split between bench work (performing test analysis) and supervision. In smaller hospitals one supervisor may cover several section areas. In larger institutions, where one section may employ from 30 to 40 staff technologists, section supervisors do very little, if any, bench work. Their roles are determined by the size and scope of the operation. They also may be assisted by people assigned as senior technologists in major subsections of the department. For example, in the chemistry department of a large laboratory, senior technologists may be assigned to subsections, such as radioimmunoassay, toxicology, or automated chemistry laboratory. Senior technologists may also be assigned functional rather than line management roles, such as responsibility for quality control or preventive maintenance. Technologists usually possess a bachelor of science degree in medical technology and have passed a registry exam given by one of several accrediting bodies, usually the American Society of Clinical Pathologists. There are sev-

eral recognized equivalency programs and specialties. These individuals perform all types of laboratory analyses and function independently.

Technicians possess less formal education, such as associate degrees. They require more supervision and function less independently. Along with technologists they provide the core of the laboratory staffing. Phlebotomists are individuals whose primary job is to procure blood specimens. They are usually trained on the job. Clerks/secretaries are used to process the information in the laboratory, sort patient reports, register outpatients, do general typing, and handle departmental mail. Secretaries have more formal training than clerks and may use word processing equipment, type pathology reports, and perform duties such as giving verbal reports, cross-indexing reports and slides, and assisting with tumor registry. Often smaller laboratories combine clerk/phlebotomist duties and secretary/receptionist functions. Other positions that may be found are education coordinator, quality control supervisor, or information supervisor. These people are usually found in large institutions with formal medical technology training programs, complex service levels, and sophisticated data processing systems.

New roles for the laboratory include marketing specialists and point-of-care-testing quality control coordinator. These roles reflect the changed mission of the laboratory. In smaller institutions several roles can be combined. For example, the information system supervisor may also be the account representative. Point-of-care testing may be maintained by chemistry since much of this testing is for chemistry (e.g., glucometers).

The goal of any institution should be to minimize the amount of bureaucracy and to have clearly defined reporting relationships. The key area where problems arise is in the laboratory manager role. Many times this person's loyalty is split between the medical director and an administrator, such as the chief operating officer or assistant administrator. Ideally the medical director should assume overall responsibility for the operation of the department and be encouraged to use the laboratory manager as a key support person. This statement does not imply that the laboratory manager is denied access to senior management. Quite the contrary. This access and a high degree of autonomy are crucial to the success of both the laboratory manager and medical director.

The recommendation that the medical director assume overall responsibility for the operation of the department is interpreted as follows. The medical director, through formal and informal feedback from the medical staff, determines the appropriate service levels; that is, the appropriate variety of testing available at the hospital, the turnaround times associated with that testing, and the tolerance limits (quality control and utilization) for services rendered. Once this information is communicated to the laboratory manager, the manager can identify the resources necessary to carry out these services. This includes addressing issues such as the physical plant, staffing/skill mix, information systems, and equipment needs. All of the above needs must be met within the financial and administrative constraints placed on the department by the board and senior management and must reflect the hospital mission statement. Another significant role of the medical director is providing feedback to the medical staff. The medical director must take an active role in effecting changes in physician practice patterns (e.g., ordering of microscopic urines and routine differentials, utilization of laboratory services in general). To be successful, the medical director needs a reliable database of physician utilization of laboratory services, and a thorough understanding of viable alternatives and constraints the laboratory operation presents. These factors have hospitals and clinical laboratories paying more attention to administrative duties, expectations, and compensation for these services in their contractual arrangements. Appendix 6–C contains a sample job description of a medical director of laboratories.

The time to prepare for and perform these duties requires a strong laboratory management team to keep the medical director informed, and able to deal with the day-to-day operation. In ad-

dition to the operational issues mentioned above, the responsibilities of the manager include:

- development of strategies that improve staff productivity
- cost reduction
- development and interpretation of management reports

The laboratory manager must be given responsibility for budget performance, maintaining service levels, personnel administration—recruitment, retention of personnel, performance evaluations, position control, etc.—and should have direct access to the people and information necessary to carry out this role. The medical director and manager roles indicate the need for a strong clinical and supervisory team to address the day-to-day technical issues, such as the ones mentioned previously.

Bureaucracy grows when the institution tries to reward employees with new, impressive titles and roles in lieu of proper recognition through promotion, pay raises, or similar incentives. In the long run, the organization suffers because reporting relationships become confused and territorial issues arise, causing deterioration in the quality of relationships. In summary, organizational structures should be as flat as possible, with a minimal number of titles; they should be based on the size and scope of the operation and the number of people employed. Further discussion of positions, titles, and related organizational topics is included in the skill mix/cross-training section.

STAFFING

Proper laboratory staffing is possibly one of the greatest challenges facing laboratory management today. In developing this topic the following subjects are addressed: workload and staff utilization, workstation configuration, and skill mix and cross-training. Focusing attention on these subjects helps ensure the maintenance of proper staffing levels.

Workload and Staff Utilization

Workload can be divided into two major categories: technical and nontechnical. Technical workload can be defined as the number of analyses (tests) requested of the laboratory. The hours needed to complete these analyses are linked primarily to the methodology employed and secondarily to turnaround time and staff proficiency. In the past, the College of American Pathologists (CAP) used time and motion studies to determine the amount of labor necessary to perform individual analyses.[3] Standards are expressed in terms of CAP units. One CAP unit is equal to one minute of supervisory, technical, clerical, and aide time necessary to perform an analysis. These time studies paid particular attention to degree of automation, often establishing unique labor standards for different manufacturers' analyzers. Applying these standards to both patient and nonpatient (quality control) test volumes identifies the required minutes to perform the technical portion of the workload. The technical workload usually consumes 60 to 70 percent of paid hours.

Nontechnical workload consists of activities such as ordering supplies, continuing education, and equipment evaluations. It is more difficult to assess. Hospital organization, mission statement, size, support systems, and physical facilities vary too much from institution to institution to allow the laboratory industry to develop industrywide standards for nontechnical activities. Also, allowances need to be made for downtime, personal time, fatigue, delay, and standby, such as on the night shift. Together, nontechnical workload and downtime consume 15 to 25 percent of paid hours. The remaining 10 to 15 percent of paid hours are consumed by benefit hours (vacation, sick, holiday). Actual payroll registers can be used to determine benefit hour requirements.

To properly assess the time requirements associated with nontechnical workload and downtime, some basic quantitative analyses are needed. Work sampling, frequency distributions, or time ladders (self-logging) techniques can be used. The hospital's management engineering department, consultant, or professional society can be used to assist laboratory personnel in completing these studies.

The studies should be comprehensive and should include all activities, including technical activities. Because even CAP units are based on averages, and are influenced by batch size and skill mix, they may not be appropriate in a laboratory in which these operational characteristics do not reflect industry averages (this is usually the case with both very large and very small laboratories). This approach will determine if the CAP units or other relative value units (RVUs) assigned to technical activities are a good fit for a particular laboratory; at the same time it identifies the nontechnical activities and downtime characteristics. Often, this complete approach results in work simplification and streamlining of the operation through better integration of all activities and skills. These studies have a more important value than in the past. This is because the CAP no longer updates its CAP units on a regular basis. Therefore, internal studies should be combined with benchmarking, available through various third parties such as professional societies and consulting firms. These efforts can be conducted as part of other studies as well. Cost accounting is one approach to quantifying units of measure and associating them with a cost.

As of June 1993, the CAP is no longer supporting its Workload Recording Method (CAP units). CAP is supporting the Laboratory Management Index Program (LMIP). LMIP includes a series of productivity modules that will use specific input data to allow assessment of individual laboratory sections. The input data will provide a central core of information to calculate productivity, utilization, and cost-effectiveness ratios. Peer group analysis will be structured into billable groups and complexity groups, and will take into account the variability between sections in laboratories.

Once these analyses are completed, workload can be compared to staffing levels to determine staff utilization. A simple definition for staff utilization is required hours divided by actual hours available, expressed as a percentage. In the laboratory, required hours are the product of CAP units times test volumes, plus nontechnical activities and the standards developed internally. Staff utilization should not be confused with productivity. Someone can be busy but not be productive (i.e., turn out one test result per shift). In the laboratory, productivity is the number of patient test results reported per unit of time.

Monitoring two ratios—CAP units (RVUs) per chargeable test and chargeable tests per venipunctures—helps avoid the pitfall of confusing staff utilization and productivity. For the sake of discussion, whenever units—both CAP or RVUs—are mentioned, it can be assumed that one unit equals one minute. These ratios also help assess batch size, number of stat requests, single test draws, number of nonpatient tests, and impact of equipment in terms of degree of automation. For example, a small laboratory with minimal automation and small batches will have a higher number of units per chargeable test than a large operation with large batches and highly automated procedures. An institution with a low number of stats and single test draws will have a higher number of chargeable tests per venipuncture, a desirable trait.

The manner in which tests are counted will affect these ratios. Basically, if a hospital counts groups or tests—such as a CBC or chemistry profile—as one chargeable test, it can expect to see 10–14 units (minutes) per chargeable test and 2.0–4.0 chargeable tests per venipuncture. The purpose of developing workload and staff utilization data is to allow managers the opportunity to improve the efficiency of their operations. The first step in this process is to establish workstations.

Workstation Configuration

Workstations are the basic functional unit in the laboratory. Tests performed at each workstation usually require the same skill level, equipment, and other resources to complete and often provide the same type of clinical information. For example, most laboratories have a coagulation workstation. Two common procedures performed at this workstation are prothrombin time and activated partial thromboplastin time. The results of this testing aid the physician in assessing a patient's clotting ability. Depending on volume these procedures are either semi-automated or automated. In either case they most likely require the same equipment and technical proficiency. Although a workstation is defined as a basic staffing unit, it may not be staffed for an entire shift. Properly configured workstations offer the manager the most flexibility in moving people from workstation to workstation as the day progresses to obtain maximum staff utilization and peak productivity. For example, after the morning batch of testing at the coagulation workstation is completed, the person assigned to that workstation usually moves to a different workstation in hematology. This flexibility leads to the best possible service at the lowest possible cost.

There are criteria that should be reached before staff is reassigned from one workstation to another. Usually, workload would need to decrease to the point at which two consecutive hours of personnel time can be identified before an individual is reassigned workstations. This decrease could reflect as much as 30 percent of the workload at a given workstation. Two hours is approximately the amount of time needed to set up and operate a second workstation. If less than two consecutive hours is available, the result is usually increased downtime—an operational characteristic that leads to lower productivity and increased costs. An alternative to reassigning staff is to increase the amount of testing performed at a workstation operating at less than capacity.

Large hospitals may have two or three people assigned to one workstation, each doing a very limited number of procedures. Smaller hospitals may assign one individual to several workstations throughout the shift. Such work assignments present challenges to managers and strategic planners, because they affect skill mix and cross-training, two operational characteristics linked directly to cost.

Skill Mix and Cross-Training

To understand skill mix, three ratios should be studied:

1. percentage of staff made up of support personnel (clerical/aide)
2. percentage of technologists that are registered
3. full-time to part-time staff ratio

A low percentage of support staff usually indicates either that technicians perform clerical functions, certain clerical activities are automated, or certain clerical activities are not being performed. A high percentage of registered medical technologists usually results in increased labor costs. Having too few part-time staff members reduces flexibility in terms of staff scheduling, and can lead to increased downtime by having personnel on the premises when they are not needed.

Small laboratories tend to have a higher percentage of registered medical technologists and a lower percentage of support staff or medical technicians. The staff technologists function more independently, exercise more judgment, do their own troubleshooting, are more extensively cross-trained, and use less automation. Similarly, these individuals may function as phlebotomists, clerks, and technologists when necessary to meet the workload fluctuations of the department. A technologist can fill downtime with clerical activities, but a clerk cannot perform testing. The skill level of a technologist is also more expensive, and is one major reason why smaller hospitals have higher unit costs. Therefore, although the amount of cross-training provides a good indicator of staff flexibility, as a rule, larger laboratories have less intersectional rotations than smaller laboratories. Skill mix and cross-training are closely related, particularly in the technical areas.

A great opportunity exists for cross-training among phlebotomy and clerical/computer op-

erator personnel. Staff that are cross-trained in these areas could support a central specimen processing area. To facilitate this process, the introduction of a laboratory assistant job classification is necessary. This category of employee would have four levels through which staff could be promoted. These include clerical, phlebotomy, send outs, and basic testing and planting of cultures. This strategy should have the following benefits:

- increased flexibility
- provision of relief to the technical staff
- reduced turnover
- inclusion of current clerk and phlebotomy positions

Cross-training may become more prevalent as the organizational structure and design of hospitals and ambulatory care centers turn toward patient-focused care. The phlebotomy responsibility, function, and related staffing may be assigned to the patient unit, not the laboratory. This function also could be part of nursing's responsibilities, particularly in critical care areas such as the emergency room, ICU, and remote sites such as clinics and ambulatory surgery.

INFORMATION SYSTEMS

The laboratory's product is information. The primary objective of any laboratory information system (LIS) is to present data in the most orderly, legible, and timely manner possible. Clinical laboratory information systems have become highly automated and sophisticated data handling systems. The benefits to the laboratory of this technology are more orderly and timely presentation of laboratory data and utilization of these data beyond traditional uses, such as effecting changes in physician ordering patterns, performing laboratory-pharmacy reviews, monitoring changes in antibiotic susceptibility patterns more completely, and conducting product line and DRG costing studies. Exhibit 6–1 presents a side-by-side comparison of the operational differences of an automated versus a

Exhibit 6–1 Workflow: Manual versus Automated System

Manual System	*Automated System*

Requisitioning

• MD orders laboratory test on physician order sheet	• No change
• Nursing personnel prepares requisition	• Order entry via hospital information system (HIS)
• Requisition transported to lab	• Activity eliminated

Specimen Procurement

• Requisition time stamped when received	• Activity automated
• Phlebotomist draws specimen	• Same (using computer label)
• Label tube	• Same (using computer label)
• Stamp or write time of collection	• Function automated, improved quality by forcing user response

Specimen Preparation

• Label pour-off tubes and sample cups	• Use preprinted aliquot labels
• Log in specimen	• Activity automated
• Assign accession numbers	• Activity automated
• Enter requests on worksheets	• Activity automated

Analysis & Data Handling

• Perform analysis	• No change
• Record results on worksheets	• No change for manual test, automated tests are run on-line
• Record results on logs	• Activity automated
• Data review by supervisor	• Process made easier due to on-line delta checks

Reporting

• Separate forms	• Activity eliminated
• Sort by nursing station	• Activity automated
• File/distribute	• Activity eliminated
• Write or tape results on summary sheets	• Activity eliminated
• Chart multiple documents	• Process simplified by handling only one document

Financial Data

• Sort charge tickets	• Activity eliminated
• Keypunch charges into HIS	• Activity eliminated (charges captured at time of order entry or by tape-to-tape interface)

Management Reporting

• Compile monthly statistics	• Activity eliminated

manual system, and Exhibit 6–2 shows the benefits of automation.

Vendor-supplied clinical systems have become well established as a regular part of the laboratory and are critical to its mission and management. Not only do they organize the work, accumulate data on specimens, generate clinical reports, maintain a longitudinal patient record, and post bills, they also keep audit trails, monitor quality control, log workload, and keep departmental policies and procedures on-line. Specialized systems often automate the blood bank and anatomic pathology. Most laboratories use minicomputers, but some rely on networked PCs. Improved communications and easy access to databases have been the key factors behind the numerous gains in productivity.[4]

Among the leading systems, the once distinctive differences between systems for reference laboratories and hospitals are now minimal. Many of the recent enhancements include:

- barcoding
- hand-held devices (particularly useful for the phlebotomy team or point-of-care testing)
- image scanning and storage
- limited voice recognition
- optical disk storage
- improvements in remote communication
- improvements in graphics
- limited electronic patient medical record.

Bar coding, once a novelty, is becoming a standard at many institutions. Many of the major laboratory analyzers have the capability to interpret bar code labels on the primary sampling tubes. Barcoding provides several advantages, including improved turnaround time, better specimen tracking and accountability, and fewer specimen identification errors.

The improvements in remote communication have allowed hospital-based laboratories to become competitive with the commercial laboratories. Hospital laboratories are increasingly marketing their services to physician offices, with one of the key components being access to pa-

tient results either through a terminal or printer located in the physician office.

In the late 1960s and early 1970s in-house development was a popular choice, primarily because of the limited availability of software systems in the marketplace. In the mid-1970s and mid-1980s, stand-alone turnkey systems became a popular strategy because of problems in the integration of the laboratory system onto the hospital mainframe.

The more recent trends of the early 1990s included the integrated system approach. There have been major improvements in the ease and cost of interfacing stand-alone systems with the hospital system. However, several major laboratory vendors have broadened their scope in developing hospitalwide clinical information systems. This integration provides many benefits from both a system administration and cost perspective. The level of integration includes off-site locations such as satellite labs, drawing stations, nursing home, and doctors' offices.

Inspection has become part of the laboratory information system operation. In response to what was perceived as neglect (improper monitoring, maintenance, and repair protocols), voluntary accrediting agencies—College of American Pathologists (CAP), American Association of Blood Banks (AABB)—, and federal regulatory agencies—Food and Drug Administration (FDA), Health Care Financing Administration (HCFA)—, have begun focusing attention to ensure that laboratory information systems are properly tested and monitored.

CAP has included questions on LISs on its accreditation checklist for many years. In 1989, AABB updated its guidelines to include more stringent documentation, testing, and standard operating procedures for blood bank computer systems. Since 1987, the FDA has made the inspection of the computer system a routine part of every blood bank inspection. HCFA, through its Clinical Laboratories Improvement Act (CLIA) regulations, has announced its intention to include LISs in its regular laboratory inspections.[5]

The laboratory manager, or the pathologist acting as a manager, oversees both bench tech-

Exhibit 6–2 System Improvement Because of Automation of Laboratory Information Systems

Benefits	*Reason*
Reduced errors in reporting results	• On-line delta checks • On-line instrument interfaces • Better presentation of data for supervisory review
Shorter turnaround time of patient results	• CRT inquiry as opposed to manual file searchers • On-line instrument interfaces with automatic send result features • More organized cumulative report format
Increased productivity	• Less transcription • Reduced filing • Less time spent charting, with telephone inquiries, and finding results • Automated statistics gathering
New features available with no increase in manpower	• Ability to update procedure manuals more often • DRG/case mix analysis
Reduced paper costs	• Use of stock computer paper rather than expensive multipart forms • Use of optical disk
Improved legibility	• Reports printed, not handwritten, and prepared in more orderly fashion
Automated statistics gathering	• Statistics computerized

nologists and the computer support group as they generate, process, store, and transmit information. In the past, these supervisory responsibilities consisted primarily of selecting, purchasing, and deploying LISs, analytical instruments, and test methods. In the future, the laboratory manager will work more closely with the daily information management component of the laboratory and hospital. Some of the elements of this collaboration are explained below.[6]

• As major capital expenditures, the LIS and other components of the information architecture are carefully scrutinized at higher organizational levels in hospitals for gains in quality and efficiency.

• The success of the laboratory increasingly will be measured in terms of the value added to the laboratory database.

• Competition is increasing within hospitals for control of the laboratory and other clinical databases, adding a political dimension to information management that requires the close attention of laboratory managers.

• Decisions involving information management tend to have a horizontal effect on all laboratories and are frequently mission-critical, thus requiring macro-management expertise.

• Information systems increasingly generate so-called information by-products, such as test turnaround times, that provide tools for enhancing the efficiency and quality of all laboratory operations.

PHYSICAL PLANT AND EQUIPMENT

After human resources, the physical facility is the most important element in providing laboratory services. In establishing criteria for laboratory design the previously discussed characteristics—service levels, workload, staffing, equipment, and workflow—should be considered. Service levels and workload dictate staffing and equipment configuration, which in turn dictate the amount of space. Workflow influences layout, and the size and type of hospital determine the location(s) of the laboratory within the hospital. In general, laboratory equipment is becoming smaller, more self-contained, and efficient to operate. As a result, less space is required for both equipment and staff, and fewer safety issues, such as toxic waste and noxious fumes, need to be considered. More tests are being performed in the patient care areas. This trend is likely to continue. These features make design of the laboratory easier.

Two very good sources for determining specific guidelines for actual space requirements are the CAP *Manual for Laboratory Planning and Design*[7] and the Ministry of Health (Ontario) *Hospital Planning Manual.*[8] The appendix of the CAP manual lists such indicators as net square feet or linear feet of bench space per bed, test, or FTE, which can be used to calculate the size of a laboratory. The Ontario Ministry of Health guidelines suggest modules with 160 net square feet per work area, with two people located in each module or 80 square feet per FTE. To compare this approach to the CAP findings it is necessary to allow additional space for specimen processing areas, computers, large freezers, patient waiting areas, and similar nontesting areas. All of these figures and ratios are meant to be used as guidelines and starting points, not absolute standards. In general, wide open rooms with movable cabinetry are preferable to small sectioned-off areas. Open space enables flexibility in altering layout in this dynamic environment and enhances productivity and staff utilization through improved workflow and people movement.

Exceptions to the open-space approach are work areas such as virology or histology. Because these sections handle virulent pathogens and toxic chemicals, they should be planned as more isolated areas. When possible, these areas should be located near outside walls to facilitate installation of exhaust hoods, and to meet more stringently controlled HVAC requirements.

Another factor influencing location is the functional relationship between the laboratory and user departments. It is highly desirable to locate laboratories near the intensive care unit, emergency room, operating rooms, and clinic areas. This approach minimizes the need for satellite laboratories and thus avoids any inefficiencies and expense they bring to an operation through smaller batch sizes, minimal staffing levels and corresponding downtime, and duplication of equipment. For some institutions, usually larger tertiary care facilities and health care networks, satellite laboratories may be necessary. However, these satellites reduce turnaround time for critical care and outpatient areas located great distances from the central laboratory, or for clinical departments that have a need for testing not performed in the central laboratory, such as endocrinology or genetic testing.

An approach for determining what laboratory procedures can be performed in the central laboratory versus what could be done in a satellite is explained below. The first step is to assess whether a satellite lab will do low-volume, complex special procedures not offered in the main laboratory. If it does, the satellite lab is functioning as a reference laboratory. The second step is to assess the service level demanded from the requisitioning departments. For example, in blood gas testing, time is an important consideration. If the specimen cannot be transported or analyzed fast enough in the central laboratory, then this would be a reason for performing an analysis elsewhere, usually in the operating room or intensive care unit. Many times, problems can be solved by use of tube systems connecting high volume areas (e.g., emergency room, surgical suite, and clinics) with the laboratory processing center. The third step is to review the duplication of equipment, skills, and staffing associated with more routine high-volume procedures. This type of duplication would add to labor costs by increasing staff downtime, equipment, and supply costs, such as more maintenance contracts and increased inventory levels. Such laboratories may provide convenience to clinical departments, but at a cost that may be prohibitive in today's environment. In addition to economic considerations, quality control issues need to be addressed. Satellite testing facilities utilize a variety of equipment, skill levels, and methodologies. Correlating patient results from various sources may be difficult. The same procedure may be performed in different places at different times of the day on different equipment.

Another factor to consider is the use of satellite ancillary services, a major concern in today's reimbursement environment. Decentralization makes monitoring and controlling utilization more difficult. For example, if blood gases were performed by the respiratory department, an increase in blood gases might occur. Not only are systems and equipment duplicated, but the output itself is different. Requisitions, reporting procedures, and charting policies may vary significantly from the central laboratory, causing confusion for clinicians.

LABORATORY REGULATION

In recent years, laboratories have come under more scrutiny and regulation from the federal government. At one time federal regulation applied only to laboratories that participated in the Medicare and Medicaid programs or engaged in interstate commerce. All of this has changed significantly since October 1988. After conducting extensive hearings on the quality of laboratories in the United States, Congress passed CLIA in 1988. This act superseded other regulations and brought all laboratories under its regulation. CLIA applies to all laboratories in the country that conduct testing on human specimens for health assessment or for the diagnosis, prevention, or treatment of disease. The final regulations were published on February 28, 1992. They set minimum standards for laboratory practice and quality, and specify requirements for proficiency testing, quality control, patient test management, personnel, quality assurance, certification, and inspections. Some requirements in proficiency testing, quality control, and

personnel are being phased in over varying periods of time; the remaining requirements became effective September 1, 1992.

The regulations are based on technical complexity in the testing process and risk of harm in reporting erroneous results. The previous regulations were based on location or type of operation. The same regulations apply to all testing sites, including physician office laboratories (POLs). There are three types of testing excluded from regulation by CLIA. These are:

1. testing for forensic purposes
2. research testing for which patient-specific results are not reported
3. drug testing performed by laboratories certified by the National Institute on Drug Abuse (NIDA)

CLIA has established three categories of testing based on the complexity of the test methodology. These categories are:

1. waived tests
2. tests of moderate complexity
3. tests of high complexity

For waived tests, the regulations do not specify quality control, quality assurance, personnel, or proficiency testing. Laboratories with a certificate of waiver will not be subject to routine inspections. Laboratories that perform moderate or high complexity testing, or both, must meet requirements for proficiency testing, patient test management, quality control, quality assurance, and personnel. The regulations for moderate and high complexity testing differ mainly in the standards for quality control and personnel.

With these regulations come cost. There is cost relating to participation in the proficiency testing program and to ensuring that a system exists for optimizing the integrity and identification of patient specimens throughout the testing process and accurate reporting of results. For some labs, particularly in remote areas, there is cost associated with the personnel standards. For all laboratories, there also will be the cost of inspections in order to maintain certification. Laboratories that perform unsatisfactorily on two consecutive or two out of three proficiency testing events risk sanctions for that specialty, subspecialty, or test. This may include suspension of the laboratory's certificate or cancellation of its Medicare approval.

Concern about the quality of cytology testing services, particularly Pap smears, also was an important issue prompting Congress to pass CLIA. Unlike the other laboratory subspecialties, the law contains specific standards for cytology. The cytology standards became effective in March 1990, in advance of the other components of CLIA. There are specific requirements for cytology proficiency testing, quality control, and personnel.

One of the most significant areas of impact for the cytology section is that the technical supervisor must establish and monitor the workload of each person who evaluates slides by a non-automated microscopic technique. Personnel can examine no more than 100 gynecological and nongynecological slides in no less than 8 hours, but no more than 24 hours. Personnel who have other duties or who work part-time must have their workload limit prorated by the number of hours spent examining slides. There are also specific requirements for the review of slides and the correlation with histopathology results. These regulations make an information system with these tracking abilities almost a necessity.

All laboratories that are subject to CLIA must obtain appropriate certification documents. Initially, laboratories must obtain either a certificate or waiver, or, if performing nonwaived testing, a registration certificate from the Health Care Financing Administration (HCFA). A certificate of waiver is valid for a maximum of two years. A registration certificate is valid for two years or until such time that an inspection to determine compliance can be conducted, whichever is shorter. A laboratory that meets the requirements of inspection will then be issued either a certificate (for laboratories complying with the Department of Health and Human Services [DHHS] program) or a certificate of accreditation (for laboratories complying with DHHS-approved private, nonprofit accreditation programs). Alternatively, a laboratory may acquire a state license in lieu of either certificate if it is a state with a federally approved licensure program. Laboratories that obtain state licenses will be required to comply with state rules and will be exempt from the CLIA program.

In addition to CLIA, laboratory management must deal with other regulatory agencies and their requirements. Many states have enacted regulations for clinical laboratories. Exhibit 6–3 provides a breakdown of state regulation of laboratories. The FDA regulates and inspects (unannounced) several thousand blood banks and facilities that manufacture or produce blood products. NIDA operates an inspection and approval program for laboratories that test blood and urine specimens obtained from federal employees for the presence of drugs of abuse. NIDA has comprehensive standards for its inspection program, which is separate from those under the direction of HCFA.

The laboratory also is subject to regulation regarding safety and infection control. The major agency involved in this area is the Occupational Safety and Health Administration (OSHA). Laboratories need stringent hazardous waste and universal precautions programs in order to meet the regulations and ensure a safe working environment for their employees. Both federal and state regulations include specific requirements for:

- written hazard communication programs
- labels and other forms of warning
- material safety data sheets (MSDSs)
- employee information and training

OSHA published its final rule for Occupational Exposure to Bloodborne Pathogens on December 6, 1991. The regulation requires an Exposure Control Program with the following components:

Exhibit 6–3 Summary of State Regulation of Laboratories

	Hospital Laboratories	Independent Laboratories	Physician Office Laboratories	Public Health Screening
Alabama	Y	Y	N	N
Alaska	Y	N	N	N
Arizona	Y	Y	Y*	Y
Arkansas	Y	N	N	N
California	Y	Y	Y	Y**
Colorado	Y	N	N	N
Connecticut	Y	Y	N	Y
Delaware	N	Y	N	Y
District of Columbia	Y	Y	Y*	N
Florida	Y	Y	Y	Y
Georgia	Y	Y	N	Y**
Hawaii	Y	Y	N	N
Idaho	Y	Y	Y	Y
Illinois	Y	Y	Y	Y**
Indiana	Y	N	N	Y**
Iowa	N	N	N	Y**
Kansas	Y	N	N	Y**
Kentucky	Y	Y	N	Y
Louisiana	N	N	N	Y*
Maine	Y	Y	Y	Y**
Maryland	Y	Y	Y	Y**
Massachusetts	Y	Y	Y	Y**
Michigan	Y	Y	Y	N
Minnesota	Y*	Y*	N	N
Mississippi	Y	Y	N	N
Missouri	N	N	N	N
Montana	Y	N	N	N
Nebraska	Y	Y	Y*	N
Nevada	Y	Y	Y	Y
New Hampshire	Y	Y	N	N
New Jersey	Y	Y	Y	Y
New Mexico	Y	N	N	N
New York	Y	Y	N	Y**
North Carolina	N	N	N	Y**
North Dakota	N	N	N	N
Ohio	N	N	N	N
Oklahoma	N	N	N	Y**
Oregon	Y	Y	Y	Y**
Pennsylvania	Y	Y	Y	Y**
Rhode Island	Y	Y	N	Y
South Carolina	N	N	N	N
South Dakota	Y	N	N	N
Tennessee	Y	Y	N	Y**
Texas	N	N	N	N
Utah	Y	N	N	N
Vermont	N	N	N	N
Virginia	N	N	N	Y**
Washington	Y	Y	Y	Y
West Virginia	Y*	Y*	Y*	N
Wisconsin	Y	Y	Y	N
Wyoming	Y	Y	Y	Y**

* Denotes passage of law with implementation of regulations in progress.

** Denotes specific tests only (e.g., cholesterol, HIV).

Source: ASCP News, March 1991, 4. Reprinted with permission of the American Society of Clinical Pathologists.

1. exposure determination for employee infection control
2. control methods including:
   - universal precautions
   - engineering controls
   - work practices controls
   - personal protective equipment
3. HBV vaccination
4. postexposure evaluation and follow-up
5. regulated waste disposal
6. labels and bags
7. housekeeping practices
8. laundry practices
9. training and education of employees
10. record keeping

Laboratory regulation is becoming an increasingly important area that requires laboratory management and staff time as well as coordination with other hospital departments.

STRATEGIC PLANNING

The clinical laboratory is one segment of the health care industry that has seen extensive regulation and competition for over two decades. This has forced hospital laboratories to develop alternative delivery systems and management tools to remain viable in an environment that the rest of the health care system is just now entering. In response to these pressures many hospital laboratories have designed and implemented ventures that allow them to enter new markets. Often a two-tiered approach is used. Initially hospitals market their services internally in the hospital community and secondly to external users outside the hospital. The traditional issues of price and service gain importance in this phase of marketing. Entering new markets results in volume increases that reduce unit costs and enable the expansion of service levels in-house by performing procedures that were not economically viable without this additional volume.

Current government cost-containment efforts include experimentation with regional competitive billing. This type of pressure is not new in laboratories. In the late 1970s the lowest-charge reimbursement regulations had a similar cost-containment objective. Some specific alternatives that hospital laboratories are considering to respond to these pressures include:

- entering into joint ventures with other hospitals to form regional laboratories
- sharing resources with other hospitals through cooperative ventures in which certain nonemergent procedures are performed in only one of the participating hospitals (e.g., microbiology at Hospital A and chemistry profiling at Hospital B)
- marketing excess capacity layout to both traditional users, physicians' office and group practices, and nontraditional users, such as other hospitals, industry, and veterinarians

The major goal of any of these ventures is to reduce unit costs, increase profitability, and generate nonpatient revenue while improving, or, at a minimum, maintaining quality and service.

The third alternative appears to be the most lucrative. Findings reported in the literature indicate that joint ventures consisting of four hospitals in a geographic area with a total of 750 beds and gross revenue of $7.5 million could reduce their workflows by 25–33 percent while reducing overhead and equipment need and gaining more sophisticated data processing systems.[9] Other alternatives have some savings associated with their strategies, but are less attractive than a joint venture regional laboratory.

In developing and evaluating these alternatives, laboratories have developed more sophisticated management information systems than other hospital departments. For example, the previously mentioned CAP workload reporting system was one of the first attempts to apply management engineering concepts in the hospital workplace. It has remained a model system that has constantly undergone review and revision as technology changes. This system can be incorporated into a costing system and used as a means to allocate labor costs per procedure. This is important in developing product-line costing systems.

Product-line costing has become an important topic in health care. Many laboratories have been developing costing systems to determine marginal and incremental costs for purposes of evaluating a variety of issues from equipment purchases to joint ventures. Those hospital laboratories that have not kept pace are finding that their laboratory services may be in jeopardy. Commercial laboratories and other hospitals are taking over in-house operations with the support of governmental regulations and policies that seem to foster this type of marketplace behavior.

CONCLUSION

Skill mix, workstation configuration, workload, and workflow determine the operational characteristics of clinical laboratories. Service levels determine workload and skill mix. Workload and skill mix affect organizational structure, staffing needs, information systems design, physical plant, and equipment needs. All of these operational characteristics provide the basis for determining what goals and objectives the planning process must develop and implement to keep the hospital laboratory a viable, state-of-the-art operation.

NOTES

1. J.H. Boutweil and C.E. Stewart, Jr., Service Levels in a Hospital Laboratory, *Laboratory Management* November (1971).

2. R.E. Hager and P.J. Brzozowski, Determination of Service Level Feasibility: Should We Buy and Staff This New Gizmo? (Center for Hospital Management Engineering Forum, Boston, Mass., June 13–14, 1983).

3. College of American Pathologists, *Manual for Laboratory Workload Recording* (Skokie, Ill.: CAP Workload Recording Committee, 1984).

4. T.L. Lincoln and D. Essin, Information Technology, Health Care, and the Future: What Are the Implications for the Clinical Laboratory? *Clinical Laboratory Management Review* 6, no. 1 (1992):95.

5. Raymond D. Aller, The Laboratory Information System As a Medical Device: Inspection and Accreditation Issues, *Clinical Laboratory Management Review* 6, no. 1 (1992):59.

6. B.A. Friedman and W.R. Dito, Managing the Information Product of Clinical Laboratories, *Clinical Laboratory Management Review* 6, no. 1 (1992):6.

7. College of American Pathologists, *Manual for Laboratory Planning and Design* (Danville, Ill.: CAP Subcommittee on Laboratory Resources, 1977).

8. Ministry of Health (Ontario), *Hospital Planning Manual.*

9. G.A. Fattal et al., Operational and Financial Outcomes of Shared Laboratory Services in a Consolidated Hospital System, *Journal of the American Medical Association* 253:2076–2079.

SUGGESTED READINGS

Centers for Disease Control. 1992. *Regulations for Implementing the Clinical Laboratory Improvement Amendments of 1988: A Summary.* Atlanta, Ga.: Centers for Disease Control, MMWR, no. RR-2.

Martin, B.G., ed. 1991. *The CLMA Guide to Managing a Clinical Laboratory.* Malvem, Penn.: Clinical Laboratory Management Association, Inc.

Appendix 6–A

Laboratory Service Levels Worksheet/Questionnaire

	TEST		
CRITERIA	**YES**	**NO**	**COMMENTS**
Medical Need			
1 Immediate Diagnosis and Treatment			
2 Diagnostic Confirmation			
3 Disease Prevalence in Area			
4 Epidemiologic Considerations			
5 Scope of Hospital Services			
6 Clinical Research			
Legal or Professional Requirement			
7 State or Local Requirement			
8 Professional Certification			
9 Thorough Diagnostic Coverage			
Technical and Personnel			
10 Available Comparable Tests			
11 Available Equipment and Reagents			
12 Safety Equipment and Facilities			
13 Available Experienced Staff			
14 Recurrent Experience Proficiency			
15 Total Scope of Workload			
16 Specimen Transportability			
17 Patient Transportability			
Managerial Considerations			
18 Available Acceptable Services			
19 Economic Efficiency			
20 Reduce Length of Stay			

RECOMMENDATION   DATE
    Eliminate
    In-Hospital
    Send-Out
    Other

Source: Adapted from *Laboratory Management*, with permission from Media Horizons, Inc., 1971.

LABORATORY SERVICE LEVELS WORKSHEET/QUESTIONNAIRE

Economic criteria are not the only criteria in the determination of service levels in the hospital laboratory. Other factors to consider in this decision include:

- medical needs
- legal or professional requirements
- technical and personnel capabilities
- administrative considerations

In order to include these criteria in a formal decision-making tool, a questionnaire was developed. The format of the worksheet is to answer the question, "Should this test be performed in this hospital laboratory?" for each of the criteria. These criteria were originally developed by the Centers for Disease Control and published in *Laboratory Management* ("Service Levels in a Hospital Laboratory," Dr. Joseph H. Boutweil and Carl E. Steward, Jr., November 1971.) The criteria have been updated and the format modified. A single-test format with line-item comment space was developed for documentation of unusual answers. Following an explanation of the criteria is the application of the tools to this group of tests.

CRITERIA

Each line item on the questionnaire was given a corresponding explanation of what information was sought in order to provide consistency in both the completion and discussion of these documents. This is a crucial factor given the various disciplines involved in the capital equipment decision-making process. These line item details, separated by category, are listed below.

MEDICAL NEED

1. Immediate Diagnosis and Treatment

   Is this test result required on an emergency basis?

   What is being evaluated here is the need to have a particular test result on a stat basis for the treatment of patients in life-threatening situations. A positive response would indicate that a stat service level is required.

2. Diagnostic Confirmation

   Is this test result used to confirm or rule out a previous diagnosis?

   This line item is used to determine if the primary role of a particular analysis is to confirm a diagnosis. A positive answer would indicate that this is the case and further imply that a 24- to 48-hour turnaround time is acceptable.

3. Disease Prevalence in an Area

   Is this test used to diagnose and/or monitor a disease characteristic to this particular area?

   Certain population mixes or environments dictate the need for specific types of diagnostic testing. Some examples are sickle cell testing in predominantly black populations or pulmonary function testing in mining areas. A positive response to this time indicates such a need.

4. Epidemiologic Considerations

   Is this test required to monitor the hospital environment?

Various environmental testing is required to determine the effectiveness of housekeeping and infection control procedures. This line item addresses the need to have a particular analysis available for this purpose. The need to complete such testing in-house should also be considered in responding to this question. Certain analyses, such as cultures, would be done in-house, whereas other more sophisticated environmental monitoring may need to be contracted out for a specific service or test samples sent out. A positive response would indicate the need to maintain specific environmental monitoring in-house. In today's environment, employee health services may generate a need for in-house testing not necessary just a few years ago.

5. Scope of Hospital Services

   Will this new procedure be consistent with the overall hospital services?

   A laboratory's service level must correlate with the hospital's overall service level. Tertiary care facilities would require more extensive laboratory service level due to the complexity of disease states that the patients referred to these centers present. Similarly, specialty hospitals, such as pediatric facilities and oncology centers, must possess test formularies that support their specialties. In this day of consumerism and marketing of services the answer to this question has taken on a new focus and may be more administrative than clinical. A positive response to this line item would indicate the need to perform a particular analysis for this reason.

6. Clinical Research

   Is the primary application of this test result to support research activities?

   Various services may be required to support research activities. A positive response to this line item would indicate that failure to provide such a service would jeopardize certain research activities. The response is not intended to assess the importance of the research activity; that should be addressed as a separate issue, with laboratory service being one factor in such an assessment.

LEGAL OR PROFESSIONAL REQUIREMENT

7. State or Local Requirement

   Will the failure to provide this service result in the loss of state or local licensure? Will adding this procedure require additional licensure?

   In order for certain laboratories to maintain their license to operate, they must maintain certain test formalities. Similarly, certain procedures, such as RIA, require additional (i.e., AEC, NRC) approval. A positive response to this question indicates that a licensure issue must be reviewed prior to making any decisions.

8. Professional Certification

   Will failure to provide this service result in the loss of any professional certification for either the institution or individuals?

   This item addresses both institutional and individual certification. Accrediting bodies, such as Joint Commission, may require that the hospital provide certain services in order to maintain accreditation. In a similar fashion, certifying bodies, such as ASCP or ASMT, may require that individuals maintain certain skills to meet certification requirements. Not complying with the above may result in loss of accreditation, certification, and related functions, such as training programs. Such losses may also affect reimbursement. A positive response here would indicate that failure to provide certain services would threaten continued accreditation or certification.

9. Thorough Diagnostic Coverage

Is this test required to provide an overall comprehensive laboratory service?

The hospital and its medical staff must be assured that all the tools needed to assess the variables routinely associated with the types of diagnosis and treatment normally encountered are available. A positive response to this item would indicate that the service being evaluated is required for this purpose. If this service is not provided, the hospital may need to consider referring certain types of patients to other facilities.

TECHNICAL AND PERSONNEL

10. Available Comparable Tests

Are other tests offering the same clinical information currently available?

A positive response to this line item indicates that the hospital provides other testing that offers the same clinical information. If the new service is not a replacement but an additional (duplicate) service, the feasibility of this addition must be questioned.

11. Available Equipment and Reagents

Are the equipment and reagents required to perform this procedure currently available in the laboratory?

A positive response here would indicate the laboratory currently possesses the equipment and supplies needed to perform the new procedure. The new procedure would not require a capital equipment expenditure. It also means that a new supplier for reagents need not be found, but only that an existing order be increased, possibly getting a volume discount.

12. Safety Equipment and Facilities

Are the current facility and safety equipment adequate to handle this additional procedure?

If a new analysis involves a totally new methodology, a significant cost in training the staff to perform the new analysis would be incurred. A positive response here would indicate that experienced staff members are available and are familiar with the new methodology. Therefore, a significant training expense would be avoided.

13. Available Experienced Staff

Are properly trained professionals available to the institution?

If the skills to perform certain testing, such as electron microscopy, are not available in the general workplace, the hospital should not consider performing this procedure because continuity of service and utilization of expensive equipment cannot be assured. Response to this question has taken on new implications with the introduction of point-of-care testing.

14. Recurrent Experience Proficiency

Will this procedure be done frequently enough to allow the staff to maintain proficiency?

If a particular analysis is performed only on rare occasions, the staff may not be able to maintain the appropriate level of proficiency. A positive answer to this question would indicate that the procedure would be performed frequently enough to maintain staff proficiency.

15. Total Scope of the Workload

Does this procedure fit into the current workflow?

A positive response to this question would indicate that this procedure fits into the philosophy of the overall test formulary. Further, the analysis can be logically assigned to an existing section or workstation, requiring minimal changes in the organizational structure.

16. Specimen Transportability

Can the specimen be transported?

If the specimen component being measured is unstable, requiring very specific environmental parameters, such requirements may prohibit transport of the specimen to a reference facility. Therefore, the analysis must be performed in-house, e.g., blood gases. A positive response indicates a specimen can be transported.

17. Patient Transportability

Can the patient be sent elsewhere for the same procedure?

If the component being measured is not stable, but the request is routinely done on an outpatient basis, perhaps the patient can be referred to a reference center. The specimen could be obtained at that time. A positive response to this question would indicate that this is the case.

MANAGERIAL CONSIDERATIONS

18. Available Acceptable Services

Is an alternative testing site available?

This is a particularly important issue in rural areas. The location and accreditation of referral centers may not be easily accessible or acceptable. A positive response to this question would indicate they are easily accessible and accredited.

19. Economic Efficiency

Is the test cost effective?

In today's reimbursement environment, cost feasibility is an important criterion. A positive response to this line item would mean that the hospital's reimbursement would not be negatively affected. Specifically, it could recoup the cost of providing the service.

20. Reduce Length of Stay

Will the introduction of this procedure reduce length of stay?

As with cost effectiveness, hospital utilization is an important criterion when evaluating new procedures. This issue is particularly important to facilities with high occupancy rates that are unable to obtain approval for additional beds. If a test can reduce or avoid hospitalization, it should be offered.

Sample of Test Type by Section

- Anatomic pathology
  1. gross and microscopic exam of surgical specimens
  2. histochemical special stains, e.g., immunoperoxidase
  3. cell blocks
  4. decalcification
- Cytology
  1. Pap smears
  2. fine needle aspirates
  3. body fluids (bronchial washings, pleural fluids, etc.) examinations
- Chemistry
  1. electrolytes (sodium, potassium chloride, CO_2)
  2. blood sugars
  3. drug levels
  4. enzymes (SGOT, CPK, LDH)
  5. electrophoresis studies (serum protein, hemoglobin)

- Hematology
  1. CBC
  2. white cell differential
  3. coagulation studies (prothrombin time, factor assays, etc.)
- Microbiology
  1. cultures (throat, sputum, wound—from any body source)
  2. Gram stains
  3. sensitivities (studies used to determine most effective antibiotic therapy)
- Microscopy
  1. urinalysis
  2. examination of other body fluids (synovial, or joint, fluid; spinal fluid) for cells, crystals, etc.
  3. Semen analysis
- Blood bank
  1. crossmatch (compatibility) testing
  2. ABO and Rh typing

Appendix 6–C

Job Analysis Checklist

Medical Director

Listed below are the specific duties and responsibilities associated with the general categories of activity included in most position descriptions.

1. *Clinical Service*

    a. The medical director must review annually or as changes occur, manuals (or their equivalent) for requesting laboratory services, specimen collection, patient preparation, reference values, and other pertinent information for utilizing laboratory services. This is to ensure that they are available, that they are up-to-date, and that their testing parameters are acceptable to users.

    *b. Test methodologies and procedure manuals must meet the approval of accrediting agencies.

    *c. The quality control program must be directed so that it is acceptable to accrediting agencies and the medical staff.

    d. A pathologist, qualified physician, or, when appropriate, a qualified doctoral scientist must be available to provide consulting services that include:

    • frozen section diagnosis in the surgical suite on both a stat and scheduled basis

    • requests by staff physicians for help in selecting and interpreting laboratory tests

    e. Frozen section diagnosis must be ready in a timely fashion and recorded on the patient's chart while the patient is in the operating room.

    f. Reports of laboratory findings and analyses must be completed and in the patient's chart in a timely fashion.

    *g. Appropriate outcome criteria must be established, monitored, and reported to the hospital quality assurance committee.

    h. Referral of slides, reports, and other appropriate materials must be sent to pathology specialists when so requested by the attending physician, or deemed necessary by the medical director.

    i. Work with the medical and surgical staff and transfusion committee must determine the adequacy of the inventory and utilization of blood products.

    *j. All departments must meet the standards of the Joint Commission, FDA, CAP, and other accrediting agencies (e.g., AABB) requested by the hospital.

    *k. The laboratory must conform to hospital standards for data and systems control, forms control, computer applications, and results delivery.

    l. Records must be maintained in accordance with hospital, government, and accrediting agency requirements.

    *m. New procedures must be introduced as appropriate for physicians, nursing service, laboratory staff, and patient needs.

    *n. Assistance must be provided to other clinicians when necessary to obtain specimens for analysis. Such assistance includes bone marrow aspirates and fine needle biopsies.

* Function often delegated to section chief.

2. *Human Resource Management*

   *a. The continuing education program must meet standards of accrediting agencies and the hospital. A minimum continuing education requirement must be established for each category of employees.

   b. Appropriate meetings of the laboratory department must be held for announcements and education. A record of such meetings will be included in monthly and annual laboratory reports.

   *c. Input must be provided as to the type of reference material to be maintained so as to meet standards of the hospital medical library. Appropriate technical books and manuals must be available at the work benches.

   *d. There must be participation in clinical department meetings.

   e. The continuing education requirements of the AMA, CAP, or equivalent must be met.

   *f. Appropriate CEU credits must be maintained.

   *g. There must be participation in the development of staff performance criteria and staff performance evaluations when appropriate. The medical director should provide input into the laboratory manager evaluation, and section chiefs should review the section supervisor evaluations as they pertain to technical ability.

3. *Administrative Responsibilities*

   a. Goals and objectives put forth by laboratory management and approved by the medical director must be compatible with those of the hospital as judged by the senior management of the hospital.

   b. Policies, rules, and regulations must be appropriate, understandable, and complete as judged by the senior management of the hospital. They must conform to those of the organization and not violate those of any government, accrediting, or regulatory agency.

   c. Physical plant and departments must be organized to provide maximum efficiency.

   *d. *Services* must be scheduled with full consideration of need, cost, and regulatory priorities to the satisfaction of clinicians and administrator.

   e. Must determine feasibility and maintain fiscal responsibility in introducing changes; therefore, requests for space, equipment, services, and personnel must be reasonable and justified with data. Purchases should be evaluated in light of cost effectiveness, quality, and service.

   f. There must be participation in plans to expand laboratory services in the hospital and in the community.

   g. Budgets (capital and operating) must be submitted on time and adhered to unless deviations are adequately justified and approved.

PAUL J. BRZOZOWSKI, MPA, is a Vice President with Applied Management Systems, Inc. (AMS), a health care consulting firm in Burlington, Massachusetts. He is responsible for the clinical and general consulting services of AMS. He is also experienced in mergers and consolidations. Prior to joining AMS, Mr. Brzozowski was the Executive Vice President of Addison Gilbert Hospital in Gloucester, Massachusetts. As Chief Operating Officer, he was responsible for the daily operation of the hospital. Prior to joining Addison Gilbert Hospital, he was a health care consultant for Peat, Marwick, and Mitchell, and the Massachusetts Hospital Association, with a primary focus on clinical laboratory operations.

Mr. Brzozowski has participated in many seminars, client in-service programs, and special lecture series, such as those sponsored by E.I. DuPont. He has over 23 years of health care experience.

He received a BS in medical technology from SUNY Upstate Medical Center, Syracuse, New York, and an MPA from Pennsylvania State University.

ELLEN A. MOLONEY, MBA, is a Manager with AMS. Ms. Moloney has been involved primarily in laboratory-related engagements. These engagements have included operational audits and support, needs assessment and acquisition of laboratory information systems, outreach marketing, and management support/training. She has also participated in engagements in diagnostic imaging, respiratory therapy, rehabilitation services, surgical suite, and information systems.

Prior to joining AMS, Ms. Moloney was the Laboratory Operations Coordinator at Salem Hospital. She has a thorough understanding of day-to-day laboratory operations, including personnel scheduling, test scheduling, and employee recruitment/retention issues.

She received an MBA from Bentley College, Waltham, Massachusetts; a Certificate from Salem Hospital School of Medical Technology, Salem, Massachusetts; and a BS from Rivier College, Nashua, New Hampshire.

She is a member of the American College of Health Care Executives, American Society of Clinical Pathologists, Massachusetts Association of Medical Technology, American Association of Clinical Chemistry, and the Clinical Laboratory Management Association.

Chapter 7

Patient Access Services (Admitting): Into, Through, and Out of the Health Care Process

John Woerly

Health care organizations have made a commitment to provide quality health care to the community they serve. Thus, health care organizations must be financially viable, cost effective, and sensitive to the needs of patients. Patient relations are influenced by employee attitudes, effective information gathering and processing systems, scheduling, and interdepartmental communications and coordination.

A health care admission/registration system (also referred to as patient access), like those of a hotel, university, or general business in its induction and intake procedures, is a system used to input information in an orderly manner to prevent overburdening the organization and its resources. The Patient Access Department plays an important part in developing and managing a planned strategy for patient flow. This patient flow, in many respects, dominates other admission/registration activities in that it regulates the frequency and speed with which all other health care services may be performed.

AREAS OF RESPONSIBILITIES

The Patient Access Department is responsible primarily for the timely, courteous, and accurate registration of patients. In this respect, the department supports quality assurance in the documentation of the patient's records. The registration function creates the patient records and the patient identification system for future record storage, and ensures the institution's data integrity as it relates to patient records. As such, the department creates the patient history for the Patient Accounts and Medical Records Departments. The patient information obtained in the registration process is entered into the institution's data system, either creating a new patient record or updating the current record. The Patient Access Department, in most cases, assigns the patient account number and/or medical record number that will be used by the institution for record-keeping and billing purposes. As such, the department serves as the foundation for medical records and billing/collections. Incomplete and/or inaccurate collection of information and disposition of the patient will adversely affect other departments and individuals. The advent of electronic billing is but one example in which the importance of data integrity can be observed. The process of submitting claims electronically demands complete and accurate collection of information by the Patient Access Department, in order to ensure timely, accurate billing. The Medical Records Department also must depend upon the Patient Access Department to properly assign medical record numbers in order to prevent potential duplication of patient records. This is vital to the Medical Records Department, as it is called upon to retrieve records for medical review in the delivery of health care. Additionally, the Medical Records Department uses demographic and clerical information obtained during registration in the abstracting of the medical records. In most cases, this transfer of information has been automated. Incomplete and inaccurate information will delay various processes and result in manual intervention (rework) by the Patient Accounts and Medical Records Departments.

Basic data gathered at the time of registration include: demographic, financial/legal, social, clerical, and clinical information. Primary data components may include:

- Demographic
  1. patient name
  2. patient address and phone number
  3. date of birth
  4. sex and race
  5. Social Security number
- Financial/Legal
  1. employer name, address, and phone number
  2. guarantor (person financially responsible for bill) name, address, and phone number
  3. guarantor's employer name, address, and phone number
  4. insurance name, address, phone number, policy number, preauthorization/precertification number, eligibility dates, injury information if liability or workmen's compensation case, subscriber information, billing priority if more than one insurance
  5. details of previous unpaid balances
  6. precertification and benefit information

7. completion of insurance forms and other third-party payor information
8. patient, guarantor, and/or responsible party signatures for release of information, consent for treatment, financial agreement/payment for services, release from liability, receipt of Medicare/Medicaid/CHAMPUS information, and receipt of advanced directives/living will information

- Social
  1. contacts in case of emergency—names, addresses, and phone numbers
  2. permission to receive visitors or notify the newspapers
  3. religion and church preference
- Clerical
  1. valuables taken for safekeeping
  2. registration date and time
  3. who provided and entered the information
  4. referral source, i.e., name of other hospital
  5. method of arrival, i.e., ambulance, walk-in, etc.
  6. room preference and assignment if an inpatient admission
  7. patient account number and/or medical record number
- Clinical
  1. diagnosis or chief medical complaint
  2. treatment plans, i.e., surgery
  3. physicians' names, addresses, and phone numbers
  4. physician orders

Additionally, the admission/registration department may go beyond the traditional role of the admission process. Today's health care environment has led to further expansion of job responsibilities in the admission department to include:

- patient scheduling
- patient placement

- preadmission, outpatient, clinic, physician office, nursing home, and emergency room registration
- financial screening and counseling
- acceptance of patient deposits
- patient information
- birth and death certificate preparation
- processing of consent forms for treatment, release of information, treatment, and living wills
- precertification
- preparation of daily census and other special reports
- maintaining patient identification system
- guest relations/patient representatives
- telecommunications
- patient transportation
- diagnostic testing
- marketing/liaison with physicians' offices
- other related areas, such as patient accounts management, utilization management, managed care contracting, discharge planning, and risk management

With the need to maintain cost effectiveness, organizations are restructuring lines of authority and responsibility. As such, the traditional Patient Registration Department's focus on direct customer service has evolved to encompass utilization and financial management. It is evident that the department's role will expand even further.

Depending upon job responsibilities, the traditional admission department may be referred to as Patient Registration or Patient Access Services. The latter reflects a wider spectrum of job functions and will be used as the model for this chapter. As defined by the National Association of Healthcare Access Management (NAHAM), "Patient Access Services provides quality services in registration and all of its support processes to patients, providers and payors into, through and out of their healthcare experiences."[1]

Considering the frequency and nature of this interaction, the department must be structured to maximize its effectiveness and efficiency through excellent management. The basic policies relating to patient admission generally stem from the governing board, based upon the recommendations from the administrator and medical staff. The role and function of the department may vary from institution to institution. Some are narrow in focus, whereas others encompass a broad scope of duties.

When a patient enters a health care institution for treatments or testing, the patient must be registered. One of the staff's goals is to create a smooth, pleasant transition for the patient from home to personal contact. Patients often get their first impression of the health care institution when they first speak to the person registering them. These feelings often remain with the patient and affect their attitude toward the institution, the staff, and their medical care. Patient Access staff can ensure that the institution's first impression is positive, by providing efficient, personable, and compassionate care.

DEPARTMENTAL FUNCTIONS

Inpatient admission services, the first of which also relate to outpatient registration, are[2] (see Figure 7–1):

- Intake
  1. reservations/appointment process
  2. registration/interviewing process
- Financial and utilization management
  1. verification of insurance eligibility and coverage
  2. precertification/authorization process
  3. early utilization management and discharge planning (i.e., social work, home care, preadmission testing)
  4. patient education regarding their insurance company's requirements, financial responsibility, and collection (i.e., deposits, payment contracts, etc.)

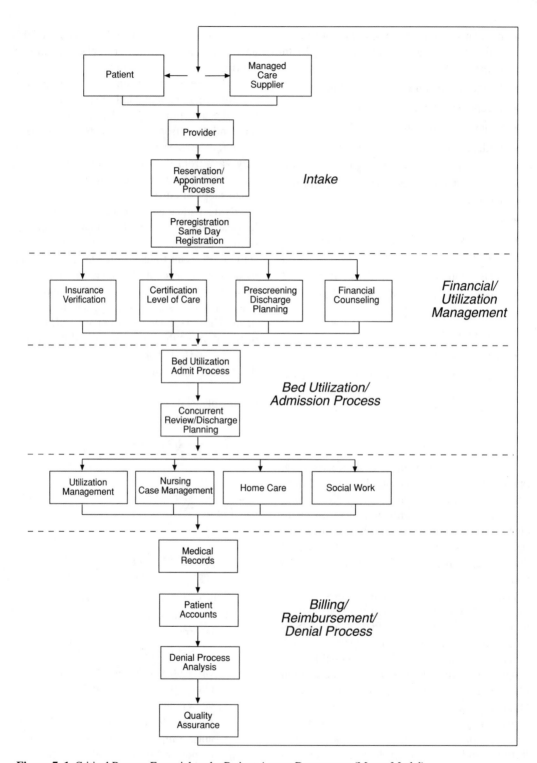

Figure 7–1 Critical Process Essential to the Patient Access Department (Macro Model)

- Bed utilization management
- Billing/reimbursement/denial analysis

Intake

Reservations/Appointment Process

The reservations/appointment process is an orderly way to prevent overburdening the organization and its resources. The first activity of such a control system may be described as a mechanism to cushion the complex internal hospital services from becoming overloaded. Therefore, it is critical in order to ensure positive patient relations and ensure stable utilization of resources to take patients into a general hospital using a planned strategy for patient flow. This patient flow, in many respects, dominates other access system activities in that it regulates the frequency and speed with which all other activities must be performed. In this respect, the controlling of input into the health care institution is a first and key function of a patient access system.

The second activity of a control system is primarily concerned with getting patients to where they need to be. In this activity, two additional functions are required: efficient initiation of the information flow (record keeping) and patient contact. In addition to a patient's personal apprehensions, problems or delays in the information flow, record-keeping functions, or in the input control function could project disorganization as viewed by the public.

The patient access system has a direct effect on other systems within the hospital. There is an immediate effect on staffing levels and resource utilization. One objective of a scheduling system is to optimize the available resources. There is a great need in the health care industry to balance capabilities and capacities with patient demand to ensure that the patient flow remains smooth.

Although still somewhat limited in its development, many health care providers are establishing a centralized patient scheduling system to better satisfy their customers. The primary objective of developing a centralized scheduling system is to provide an effective means for physicians and their staff to schedule patients for services by calling a centralized telephone number, instead of calling each diagnostic department. Additionally, the development of the scheduling system should allow the review and analysis of existing procedures to ensure that they are meeting the needs of our physicians, patients, and hospital staff in an effective manner.

Case Example: Workflow in Patient Scheduling. The sequence of events for the scheduling of an outpatient appointment (i.e., the initial step in the admission process) as developed at the Methodist Medical Center of Illinois exemplifies a typical centralized patient scheduling process. The following steps are utilized:

1. *Call made to schedule.* The physicians' office personnel wishing to schedule an appointment will call the Patient Scheduling Center.

2. *Scheduling personnel will check availability.* The scheduling personnel will check the department schedule for the day the physician desires the appointment to be scheduled. All times are scheduled on a first call, first served basis, with the exception of emergency situations.

3. *Scheduling personnel will schedule, enter data, and provide information.* The scheduling personnel will schedule a time and record needed identification information into the department's computer system. To book an appointment, the user selects the appropriate "book" and types in information to accurately identify the department/test and patient. If the patient is in the database, a list of candidate names matching the search criteria will be displayed. If the patient is not in the database, the patient can be registered into the system by entering basic information such as the name, date of birth, and Social Security number. Other demographic and scheduling information is then entered, including: physician(s),

principal diagnosis/chief complaint, and primary insurance coverage.

A search of appropriate times is then automatically generated by the system. Specific or general appointment criteria related to the desired appointment can then be selected. Available appointments can be retrieved by selecting any combination of the following search criteria:

- specific date
- appointment type
- appointment duration

After specifying the search criteria, the user can display available appointments. The appointment is reserved at the end of the browse mode, in order to make the appointment inaccessible to other users. The system prevents booking conflicts through conflict messaging. If any preparatory instructions are needed, the scheduling personnel will review the instructions with the calling party. If two or more tests are scheduled for the same day, the scheduling personnel will schedule the testing times as close to one another as possible, utilizing proper test sequencing techniques.

4. *Scheduling time confirmed.* Upon agreeing on an appointment time with the patient, the scheduling personnel will confirm the scheduled time with the physicians' office personnel.

5. *Physicians' office personnel complete required documentation.* The physicians' office personnel scheduling the test should complete the preprinted physicians' order form and the patient orders envelope and place the first two copies of the order form in the provided envelope. The remaining copy of the order form should be retained in the physicians' office for reference.

6. *Scheduling paper trail and reports.* Upon production of the patient flowsheet, the scheduling personnel will file the slip in chronological date order for future reference, preregistration, and patient check-in functions. The outpatient scheduling report will be distributed to the appropriate department(s) prior to the date of the patient's arrival.

Registration/Interviewing Process

Traditionally, preregistration is the means by which patients can be expedited through the intake process. When used to the maximum, preregistration also can be a good foundation on which to build a strong fiscal security. Additionally, interviewing patients at the time of admission or service can be difficult, because of their stress and anxiety. Thus, information may not be complete and/or accurate. The best time to verify the means of reimbursement is at the time the preregistration is completed. Pre-existing clauses, deductibles, and co-insurance coverage should be reviewed prior to the patient's service. Overall, preregistration is the building block that allows the patient and the institution to look at financial options prior to service to ensure complete and timely payment.

Financial and Utilization Management

The next step beyond preregistration is the concept of precertification and financial counseling. The act of registration places the health care giver at risk for the service delivered and the ensuing expenses. The two principal areas of financial risk are: the justification of the appropriateness of the service to assure that the third-party payor can be billed for the charges incurred by the patient, and compliance with third-party prior-approval programs.

Many employer groups and third-party payors have established prior approval programs for all elective admissions along with emergency admission reporting mechanisms. The policy benefits of the insured are usually keyed to the approval process. Typically, the patient is responsible for ensuring compliance. However, it usually reverts to the health care provider to follow up or risk financial loss. Patients who must meet or comply with these specific requirements prior to service must be identified. Thus, the ability to monitor both the employers and the insurance companies involved in these special requirements is essential.

A preregistration assessment of each patient scheduled for admission and outpatient testing will lower the financial risks of retrospective review prior to payment. A preregistration assessment program should include aspects of preregistration, utilization management, financial verification and counseling, discharge planning, and results reporting of preadmission tests.

The department also may be involved in other financial management processes, including managed care contracting, case mix analysis, billing and collections, charge entry functions, managing a patient transfer system, and managing the process for the Patient Self-Determination Act/Living Will. Managed care contracting may involve the review of the contractual agreement, establishing processes to ensure that the agreement provisions are followed, and providing basic utilization statistics.

The Congress of the United States has set a public policy into law, requiring under section 1867 of the Medicare Act that "all participating hospitals and their 'responsible physicians' provide a screening examination to any individual, regardless of ability to pay who comes into the emergency department . . . to determine if the individual has an 'emergency medical condition' or is in 'active labor.'" This public policy issue directly affects the Patient Access Department because the financial resources and payment ability of individuals who present to the Emergency Department and other entry points must be determined and documented by patient access staff. To further aid the health care provider, many institutions have developed a transfer center, which has the centralized authority to resolve clinical, financial, and political concerns in dealing with the acceptance of interhospital transfers. Although a transfer center can be viewed incorrectly as a "financial triage," it has an important mission of developing proper and timely referrals of medically appropriate trans-

fers. Historical information including the name of the hospital(s), the number of like procedure(s) or diagnosis, the length(s) of stay, total charges, and funding source(s) must be analyzed for continued fiscal viability.[3]

The Patient Self-Determination Act also has had a major impact on hospitals and health care providers because it establishes guidelines that require the maintenance of written policies and procedures governing patients' rights to make health care decisions, and the obligation of health care providers to communicate this information as well as other related information to their adult patients. This includes the patient's right to accept or refuse medical or surgical treatment, as well as the patient's right to make advance directives. The law defines an advance directive as a written instruction, such as a Living Will or a Durable Power of Attorney for health care, recognized under state law, relating to the provision of health care when the patient is incapacitated. Providers will also be required to provide adult patients with written policies respecting their patient rights.[4]

Future state and federal regulations will continue to demand the expertise of the Patient Access Department. As the department serves as a central source for patient database entry and point-of-entry communication with the patient, it is likely that the department will continue to serve a vital role in the carrying out of state and federal health care regulations.

Bed Utilization Management

Maximizing bed occupancy, while balancing patient care needs, nursing acuity levels, and external/internal utilization management restrictions relative to length of stay and coverage payment, is a critical element in the daily operations of a Patient Access Department. Ensuring that beds are used effectively is not only a function of the creative deployment of beds as they become available, but also requires effective communication with the physicians who admit these patients to the hospital. Additionally, successful access management requires the development and maintenance of effective relationships with other departments, primarily the nursing department and environmental services, to ensure the timely notification of discharging patients and the proper assignment of beds to meet both the needs of the patient and the nursing personnel. The high degree of interaction between these areas must be achieved to fully optimize patient placement and to reach expected levels of customer satisfaction. Additionally, the very issue of patient placement can affect patient outcome and length of stay, as well as the optimal utilization of staffing, equipment, and other facilities. The Patient Access Department also may be responsible for census maintenance, which would include facility, bed, and nursing unit statistics and room charges.

Departmental Information Standards

The importance of having accurate, up-to-date demographic and insurance information is essential. Equally important is the need to make the collection of this information as burdenless as possible to the patient. Various models for collecting and updating patient registration information exist today, ranging from a totally centralized approach to a virtually decentralized method. These approaches also may vary in regard to overall management responsibility, as well as the location of the transaction.

In May 1993 NAHAM conducted a study to determine average waiting times, registration times, and approach to registration. It was found that 63 percent of the survey participants had a centralized registration approach. The average waiting time for an outpatient registration was 8 minutes, while the average waiting time for an inpatient admission was 7.5 minutes. The average interview time for outpatient registrations was 7.88 minutes and 10.57 minutes for inpatient admissions. On a daily basis, a registrar averages 37 outpatient registrations and 17 inpatient admission registrations. Although these numbers may vary from institution to institution due to departmental procedures, processes, and the amount of data collected, these numbers may serve as a benchmark for registration activities.

Admission department standards were proposed in April 1992 by NAHAM to ensure high quality performance in the field of admissions. The standards state:

- The Admission Department is provided with adequate direction, staffing, and facilities to perform required functions.

   1. The Admission Department services are directed by a qualified admission administrator or director who possesses the administrative skills necessary to provide effective leadership and management of admission information systems.

   2. When employment of an accredited individual (AAM) is impossible, the hospital secures the consultative assistance of a qualified accredited access management administrator.

   3. Verification checks for accuracy, consistency, and uniformity of data recorded and used in quality assessment and improvement activities are a regular part of the admission process.

- The admission record contains sufficient information to identify the patient.

   1. Although the format and forms in use in admissions will vary, all admission records contain the following:

      (a) identification data

      (b) evidence of appropriate consent

      (c) the patient's name, address, date of birth, and next of kin

      (d) the chief complaint

- The Admission Department is guided by written policies and procedures.

   1. There are written policies and procedures concerning the scope and conduct of admission services.

   2. The director of the Admission Department is responsible for assuring that the development and implementation of the policies and procedures are carried out in collaboration with appropriate clinical and administrative representatives.

3. The policies and procedures are consistent with hospital and medical staff rules and regulations relating to patient care and medical records, and with legal requirements.

- The Admission Department policies and procedures relate to at least the following:

   1. the confidentiality of information

   2. the relationship of the department to other hospital services

   3. the role of the department in advising patients of their rights and responsibilities

   4. the role of the department in addressing advance directives

- The role of Admission Personnel in the hospital's overall program for the assessment and improvement of quality and in committee functions is defined.

- The role of the Admission Department in the utilization review program is defined.

   1. delineation of the responsibilities and authority of those involved in the performance of utilization review activities

   2. confidentiality policy applicable to all utilization review activities, including any findings and recommendations

   3. description of the method(s) for identifying utilization-related problems, including the appropriateness and medical necessity of admissions

The Patient Access Department also should have quality standards and a defined quality assurance program. Measurement of departmental functions should be monitored with performance compared to preset, agreed-upon standards. The frequency of monitoring performance should be dependent upon the relative importance of the function to the total departmental or institutional functions, history of error rates, and improvement opportunities identified.

The Quality Assurance Goal as established at the Methodist Medical Center of Illinois states: "Achievement of excellence in patient process-ing for the delivery of high quality patient care to the public we serve." Process effectiveness, efficiency, and economy are measured through critical success factors: customer satisfaction, accuracy, completeness, customer wait time, customer interactions, and service costs. As established in the department's Quality Assurance Policy, all information processed by the department will be of the highest accuracy possible, with a goal of 100 percent accuracy. Information will be processed and services provided on a timely basis, with turnaround time established in keeping with priority assignment and good practice. The area's manager is responsible for the ongoing review of the standards and for overseeing of the process to include evaluation and follow-up procedures. As such, the manager is responsible for consultation in the determination of the standards and for conducting monitoring and training processes when appropriate. All employees are expected to participate in the process to the greatest extent possible to include conducting their own monitoring and problem identification processes where feasible.

The process includes the measurement of accuracy, completeness, timeliness, and cost effectiveness through the monitoring of performance based upon established standards. Principles of Total Quality Management (TQM) will be incorporated, when possible, to enhance the measurement, analysis, and action process. The frequency of monitoring will be dependent upon the relative importance of the function, history of errors, and themes/improvement opportunities identified.

Standards have been established for various performance indicators, including:

- data accuracy
- utilization management/productivity
- efficiency/service time
- safety
- customer satisfaction

As an example, efficiency/service time is one of the primary indicators for the centralized patient scheduling areas, and is measured by the area's call handling activities, including:

- percentage of calls answered directly, sequentially answered, and abandoned
- percentage of time that staff are available/unavailable for calls
- percentage of calls and average time that calls are placed on hold
- average service time (time that staff member is speaking with customer)
- average call volume per time of day and day of week
- average call volume per staff member

Utilization management/productivity may be measured by the volume and type of appointments made. This will be based upon historical time studies and observation, and will vary from institution to institution. An average employee at the Medical Center should handle 40–55 appointments each day. A scale is utilized to measure achieved performance. Another example used in the analysis of services offered by the centralized patient scheduling area compares monthly statistics reflecting the number of scheduling calls received compared to the number of actual appointments scheduled, and the number of patients scheduled for service compared to the number of outpatient registrations. A breakdown of program utilization by physician, the number of tests scheduled in multiple ancillary departments, and the number of appointments scheduled more than 24 hours in advance of the testing date are also recorded for review.

MANAGEMENT RESPONSIBILITIES

Patient Access Services has a high degree of visibility and interaction with patients, the medical staff, and other organizational departments. The impact of advanced technology, judiciary decisions, and budgetary restraints requires an understanding of management principles. Information systems and networks affect staff efficiency, and set the tone of the customers' perception of the institution. Additionally, the department is a multifunctional service depart-

ment, operating 7 days a week, 24 hours a day, and 365 days a year.

The Patient Access Manager oversees the collection and coordination of necessary medical, financial, and demographic information needed for patient scheduling and registration to the institution. The manager affects the institution's financial stability through efficient registration and preadmission strategies, as well as through charge entry and test requisition input. As such, the manager must research, recommend, and implement improvements in the patient access systems, policies, and procedures to enhance services and optimize reimbursement. Additionally, the manager formulates the department's annual personnel, equipment, and supply budgets.

The manager should be business oriented, prioritizing departmental activities and those of the staff in terms of their relevance to achieving organizational goals. The manager must plan and cooperate with the medical team and the managers of other departments in meeting patient needs and information requirements. The manager also must ensure a systems orientation in the design and management of the department to best meet customer needs both in terms of quality service and financial savings to the patient, provider, and institution. Some specialized duties of the department manager include analyzing statistical data; planning, designing, and implementing new and upgraded information systems and networks; performing financial analyses on new and upgraded equipment; negotiating various types of contract and service arrangements with vendors; and analyzing business operations to identify applications for new technologies. The changing regulatory scene, whether the result of legislation or accrediting guidelines, requires that the manager keep abreast of the latest criteria that affect the department and the institution as a whole. Evaluation of the manager's performance includes consideration of (1) the department's credibility within the organization and with the medical staff, (2) the effectiveness of the manager's working relationships, and (3) the efficiency and quality of the department as demonstrated by time studies and accuracy feedback.

The position of manager requires the ability to comprehend and retain information that can be applied to work procedures. Excellent problem-solving skills are essential, as decisions and judgment utilized by the manager affect the operations and workflow of the institution and medical staff. Creativity and the ability to solve problems through fact finding, reasoning, intuition, and sound decision making are important attributes.

The position requires significant registration experience and/or advanced education in health care or business administration. The manager should have previous patient-related experience and a proven registration-related project track record. The attainment of the credentials of Accredited Access Managers (AAM) through NAHAM would be beneficial to this position. Continuing educational opportunities in Patient Access Services are available at local, regional, and national levels through NAHAM.

STAFF RESPONSIBILITIES

Department staff perform various clerical duties such as patient scheduling, patient transportation, preregistration and intake interviewing, patient placement, and insurance verification. Depending upon the complexity and organization of the institution, the staff member may be cross-trained in various job functions or, in the case of larger institutions, be more specialized. With the implementation of patient-focused care strategies, the traditional registrar may be cross-trained to perform clinical testing, as well as job functions beyond the traditional scope of registration.

The position's greatest challenges are ascertaining the informational, escort, and transport needs of the patients and visitors; ensuring timely registration/transportation service; accurately obtaining and processing patient registration and billing information; and promoting a pleasant and friendly environment for the great variety of persons coming to the institution. The staff member must have a thorough knowledge of various insurance documentation requirements, the institution's billing system, the proper registration type, and various data entry codes to ensure proper service documentation and billing of the patient's account from information obtained from the patient/family. Given the continual development of new programs, the staff member must assimilate new policies/procedures into their established work assignments.

Departmental personnel must be selected for their ability to handle a responsibility that requires thoroughness and accuracy, but also for specific personality traits. The registrar/interviewer must be patient, caring, and vivacious, asking the required questions as if they had never been asked before. Because of the sensitive information that may be gathered during the intake process, the staff members must follow strict patient confidentiality guidelines.

EMERGING TECHNOLOGIES AND TRENDS

New technologies and workflow designs will enhance the level of service delivered by the Patient Access Department. Automation, hand-held computers, bar-coding, and voice recognition systems are but a few of today's technologies that, if applied to Patient Access Services, could increase work productivity while enhancing customer satisfaction.

Today's health care delivery system is undergoing unparalleled change. Emerging health care reform, managed care, total quality improvement, the development of integrated health care delivery systems (alliances/networks/mergers), and organizational downsizing are but a few developments that are changing the delivery system on a macro and micro level. These efforts will have a drastic effect on patient access departments and their evolution. Although the services and functions offered by the department will remain fundamentally the same, the organizational structure may be modified. Opportunities to increase functional linkages to foster collaborative efforts among various health care disciplines will create uncertainty in the short-term, but will as an outcome develop a fully orchestrated access delivery system.

These changes must be anticipated and greeted with enthusiasm. Ultimately, it should be noted that the health care delivery system must contain the four critical macro processes described earlier. They most certainly will vary on the micro level and may ultimately be organized differently. What remains, however, is the need to process intake information in a timely, accurate, and professional manner, while positively affecting the fiscal integrity of the health care provider.

CONCLUSION

The profession's future will not rely on past history, but on the future commitment to be leaders in the development of a seamless intake and processing system. The successful health care provider will view the department as multidimensional and fully utilize the department's expertise to contribute to institutional goals. Looking at the intake process globally will prevent functional limitations due to organizational structure, and should lead to greater customer satisfaction.

NOTES

1. National Association of Healthcare Access Management (NAHAM), 1101 Connecticut Avenue, N.W., Suite 700, Washington, D.C. 20036. 202–857–1125.
2. Based upon Access to Accounts Receivable Model. D. Graham, Access to Accounts Receivable, *The NAHAM Management Journal* 20, no. 1 (1993): 7.
3. A. Freeman, Don't Use the 'D' Word, *The NAHAM Management Journal* 17, no. 4 (1992): 20–22.
4. M. Taubin and the Law Offices of Nixon, Hargrave, Devans, and Doyle, The Patient Self-Determination Act (Washington, D.C.: NAHAM, 1991).

JOHN WOERLY, RRA, MSA, AAM, has been the Director of Patient Registration/Telecommunications at the Methodist Medical Center since 1980. Under John's direction the department has implemented various patient amenity services, centralized scheduling, preadmission planning, physicians' answering service, and other customer-oriented programs. John is a Board Member of the National Association of Healthcare Access Management, serving as the Chairman of Accreditation and Education, and a member of the Editorial Advisory Board for both *Healthcare Access Management* and *Benchmarking*. He is a past recipient of the NAHAM Literary Award and the President's Award.

The Patient Registration Department is well-respected in the patient access services field, and has assisted other health care institutions in developing centralized scheduling and preadmission systems.

Chapter 8

Clinical Information Services

Joan Gratto Liebler

The medical records department has evolved to the clinical information department over the past decade in particular. It will continue to evolve substantially as integrated delivery systems create greater need for uniform and timely information. The department has changed from being the depository of medical information, to a vital source of data to support continuity of care, statistical information for reimbursement, utilization and peer review, legal issues, and similar clinical care and administrative demands. Manual processes in the department have been replaced in many cases by automated ones, such as computer-assisted diagnostic-related group (DRG) reimbursement calculations, chart tracking systems, and optical disc storage. A major shift in the method of entering and accessing the patient data is reflected in the rapid change from hard copy records to the computer-based patient record. The activity level of the department has grown substantially, and, consistent with the changed functioning of the department, the roles and functions of the clinical information specialists have evolved to encompass greater responsibility. The purpose of this chapter is to identify and discuss the significant aspects of a clinical information department. While the focus of the discussion is principally the hospital, most of the chapter is applicable to the clinical information needs of other provider entities, such as nursing homes and surgery centers.

CENTRALIZED CLINICAL INFORMATION SERVICE

It is desirable to place the functional responsibility for all aspects of clinical information processing in a central, comprehensive unit under the direct management authority of a specialist in health information management. In this way, continuity of care is more easily supported through continuous and coordinated documentation processes. This comprehensive, centralized service has as its usual functions these specific activities:

- patient/client identification and numbering system
- creation and monitoring of clinical information documentation
- quality assurance/clinical studies for continuous quality improvement

Special acknowledgment is made of the efforts and contributions of Elaine O. Patrikas, RRA, MA, Professor, Department of Health Information Management, Temple University, who was the original co-author of this chapter in the first edition of this work.

- utilization review studies
- risk management review and studies
- word processing/dictation-transcription system
- statistical abstracts and indexes
- special studies for medical, professional, and administrative staff reviews
- financial reimbursement support data, including diagnostic and procedural coding
- storage and retrieval system, including chart tracking system
- assistance in complying with legal and regulatory provisions and accrediting agency standards concerning health care data
- data security, privacy protection, and confidentiality provisions
- in-service education and training for professional and support staff
- educational programs for students under contractual and/or affiliation agreements
- assistance in research studies

ORGANIZATIONAL PLACEMENT AND INTERDEPARTMENTAL RELATIONSHIPS

As a support service, designed to assist those involved in direct delivery of patient care, the clinical information service is most properly assigned to the administrative division that includes closely related services. Because of the close relationship between timely and accurate documentation; chart completion and coding/DRG assignment; and the financial unit's processes of patient billing, financial audit, and correlation with documentation, it is desirable to place the clinical information service under the same vice presidential oversight as the finance/patient billing division. The close relationship with the institutionwide computer system/database should also be noted, with close coordination of clinical information database with this division.

STAFFING PATTERNS AND JOB TITLES

The director of the clinical information service is usually a manager trained in the specialty of health data management. The American Health Information Management Association (AHIMA), the national professional association of health data managers, provides a definition of the professional health information manager (see Exhibit 8–1).

Current credentialing requirements of the American Health Information Management Association are as follows:

> Registered Record Administrator (RRA): Candidate must be a graduate of an accredited health information management educational program at the baccalaureate level or above and pass the national certification examination of the American Health Information Management Association.

> Accredited Record Technician (ART): Candidate must be a graduate of an accredited program in health record technology and pass the national certification examination of the American Health Information Management Association. Most programs are at the associate degree level.

Various levels of technical and clerical support positions are created within the clinical information service. Job titles may include:

- data quality coordinator
- senior coder/abstractor
- research and statistics database manager
- data validation specialist
- concurrent review coordinator
- records processing specialist
- clinical reimbursement specialist
- data technician
- tumor registrar/cancer registrar
- oncology data coordinator
- quality improvement data specialist

Exhibit 8–1 AHIMA Professional Definition

The health information management professional collects, analyzes, and manages the information that steers the health care industry.

At the heart of the profession's information responsibilities are records, both computer-based and paper, of individuals' health care. The health information professional orchestrates the collection of many kinds of documentation from a variety of sources, monitors the integrity of the information, and ensures access to the individual record.

The professional also manages aggregate data based on the care of patients. The professional collects health care data by abstracting and encoding information, by using computer programs to interpret data, and by putting in place quality controls to ensure the data's validity. The professional designs and improves systems, both computerized and manual, to manage large amounts of health care data. And as with the individual patient record, the professional balances patients' privacy rights with legitimate uses of aggregate data.

The professional is qualified to manage individual records and aggregate data because of a unique combination of knowledge and skills in:

- health care databases and database systems
- medical classification systems
- flow of clinical information
- relationship of financial information to clinical data
- uses and users of health care information
- medicolegal issues and security systems

The professional is valuable because health information is valuable:

- for the patient's care, disease prevention, and health promotion
- for providers to evaluate the efficiency and effectiveness of care
- for reimbursement for health care services and analysis of alternative methods of coverage
- for developing public policy on health care, including regulation, legislation, accreditation, and health care reform
- for planning, research, decision support, and analysis

approved by AHIMA Board of Directors
December 6, 1991

Source: Reprinted with permission of the American Health Information Management Association.

- peer review organization liaison
- record completion analyst
- storage and retrieval file clerk
- word processing specialist
- senior medical record technician
- health record analyst
- release of information specialist

The Use of Contractual Services

Certain functions of the clinical information service may be carried out through contractual arrangements with specialty service groups. Depending on the availability of such service groups, and their relative cost effectiveness, contractual agencies offer assistance with word processing, both on- and off-site, records processing for microfilming, release of information, coding, and DRG validation. When such contractual services are utilized, the binding agreements always include strict provisions for adherence to the privacy and confidentiality aspects of patient data. Liability for any such breach should be identified as being that of the contractual service.

LEGAL, REGULATORY, ACCREDITING, AND PROFESSIONAL REQUIREMENTS

The content of the patient care documents and the various aspects of the clinical information systems are governed and shaped by a variety of constraints. These include:

- Licensure: refer to state licensing regulations for each level of care (e.g., inpatient acute, home care, emergency services); these are usually promulgated by the state department of health
- *Participation in Medicare/Medicaid: Conditions of Participation* Section 405.1011–1099 (Medicare Subpart J and following) CFR, Title 42
- Accreditation: current edition of the Joint Commission on Accreditation of Healthcare Organizations or similar accrediting body
- American Health Information Management Association's *Code of Ethics; Guidelines on Data Quality*, and *Professional Practice Standards* (latest editions)

Provisions of the medical and professional staff bylaws must also be taken into account so that there is consistency of expectation and practice throughout the organization.

THE PATIENT/CLIENT RECORD

Purposes

Underlying the myriad legal, regulatory, and accrediting agency requirements is the premise that there are compelling reasons to maintain the sophisticated and costly systems needed to comply with those requirements. The purposes of the patient record/clinical databases include:

- to foster continuity of care by maintaining a means of communication among the health care practitioners treating a patient now and in the future
- to provide information in support of insurance and reimbursement claims, proof of illness, and legal defense
- to provide a basis for quality improvement and educational reviews of care rendered by an individual practitioner as a member of the treatment team

- to provide proof of care rendered and legal defense for the health care provided (individual and institutional)
- to provide a means for cost-effectiveness studies, administrative planning, compliance with accrediting agencies, and provision of educational services to professionals in training
- to provide data for public health profiles, studies, vital statistics, and preventive medicine.

Ownership and Access

The medical record/client record is considered the property of the institution, which has the obligation to safeguard it from unauthorized use, access, loss, or destruction. The patient/client's legally recognized interest in the content of the record is honored by the development of appropriate access and release of information practices. Generally, material in the patient/client record is not accessed or released without the appropriate consent. Further, the documents are not removed from the premises except as required by court order or subpoena.

THE CONTENT AND SEQUENCE OF THE MEDICAL RECORD DOCUMENT

The content of the medical record reflects the various aspects of the care rendered. The legal, regulatory, and accrediting agencies provide specific requirements and guidelines for both the content and the time frames within which documentation should be completed. Because the medical record is both a clinical care document and a legal/business document, entries must be timely and accurate. Suggested guidelines are provided in Exhibit 8–2.

While the actual content of a given patient/client record will depend on the care rendered, there are standard and customary entries for each type of care. A summary of suggested content and sequence for acute inpatient, newborn, pediatric, and obstetric care is shown in Exhibit 8–3.

Exhibit 8–2 Guidelines for Medical Record Entries

Entries in the medical record shall be made to reflect each patient/client event of care. These entries shall be characterized by generally accepted documentation features, including the following:
- unique identification for each patient/client
  - name and identification number and date of birth on each page, front and reverse sides
  - no preprinted or pretyped ("canned") reports or entries
- original document in unit record
- factualness and objectivity
  - preliminary findings and observations noted as such
  - results of studies, tests and evaluations, and actions taken properly noted
  - freedom from negative comments about any individual, including patient or family member
- accuracy
  - legible handwriting; typed entries if possible
  - no misfiles
- creation in normal course of patient care
  - entries made according to standard content
  - entries made on approved forms
  - abbreviations limited to those listed on approved abbreviation list
- timeliness
  - documented as close to the time of the actual event as feasible
  - late entries and addenda so noted; reason for late entry or addenda given
  - identifiable and clearly noted date and time (month, day, year; A.M. or P.M.)
  - no charting ahead in anticipation of actually rendering the care
- freedom from inadvertent or intentional alterations and potential for such alteration
  - continuous entries, with no blank pages, lines, or spaces; line drawn to end of page when entries do not fill page
  - written in pen with permanent blue or black ink
  - error corrections done in a manner that does not obliterate original entry; error so marked; correction note indicated; date and signature of individual making correction entered
- authentication
  - signature (first and last name) on each entry
  - initials or title indicating professional credential
- internal consistency
  - data entries reflect similar observations of fact as recorded by different disciplines; when there is a difference of observation and/or interpretation, it is noted

Source: Reprinted from *Medical Records: Policies and Guidelines* by J.G. Liebler, p. 3:3, Aspen Publishers, Inc., © 1990.

The Computer-Based Patient Record

A major trend in health information management and in patient care documentation is the computer-based patient record. The Committee on Improving the Patient Record in Response to the Increasing Functional Requirements and Technological Advances of the Institute of Medicine defines the computer-based patient record as "an electronic patient record that resides in a system specially designed to support users through availability of complete and accurate data, practitioner reminders and alerts, clinical decision support systems, links to bodies of medical knowledge and other aids."[1]

The American Health Information Management Association, along with the Committee on Medical Informatics of the American Society for Testing and Materials, has developed a *Standard Guide for Description for Content and Structure of an Automated Primary Record of Care*. This set of guidelines defines the suggested content and logical structure for an automated medical record. In addition, it identifies the essential data

Exhibit 8–3 Summary of Suggested Content and Sequence of the Medical Record

I.   Identification/Demographic Information
    A. Admission/discharge sheet or fact sheet
    B. Registration form

II. Legal and Administrative Documents
    A. Notice of Patient Bill of Rights
    B. Consents:
        1. consent to treatment signed at admission
        2. updates to consent
        3. special consents (e.g., organ donation, blood transfusion, radiology, experimental drug or treatment, research subject, photograph or videotape, presentation/appearance at special teaching or clinical case conference session)
        4. operation and procedure consents
        5. anesthesia consent
        6. refusal of blood transfusion
        7. refusal of specified treatment
        8. waivers and releases
        9. departures against medical advice
        10. living will documents
    C. Power of attorney or conservatorship
    D. Psychiatric commitments/authorization to hold patient/client court orders
    E. Billing and insurance information data sheet
    F. Conditions/agreement for admission
    G. Medicare and Medicaid certifications
    H. Patient's/client's possessions at time of admission
    I. Patient's/client's possessions at time of discharge
    J. Release of information and requests for access to record consent/release/request forms, court orders, and subpoenas
    K. Listing of release of information and/or access to patient/client record; listing of material actually released

III. Discharge Data
    A. Discharge summary, including discharge instructions and after-care instructions
    B. Interagency referral forms sent to receiving facility
    C. Documentation associated with death of patient/client
        1. danger/critical list notice
        2. notification of family
        3. information compiled for completion of death certificate
        4. copy of death certificate if permitted by state regulations
        5. next-of-kin directives regarding mortuary services
        6. release of body/mortuary record
        7. autopsy consent
        8. autopsy report (preliminary report, provisional diagnoses, and full protocol)

IV. Physician Orders and Medication Records
    A. Allergic reaction notices
    B. Physician orders
    C. Pharmacist review of medication orders
    D. Record of medications given
    E. Anticoagulant record

V.   Clinical Assessment/Clinical Data Base
    A. Preadmission assessments and studies
    B. Interagency or physician referral form
    C. Emergency department form when patient/client sent directly to inpatient unit
    D. Ambulance/emergency transport summary

continues

Exhibit 8–3 continued

    E. Materials abstracted from hospital or clinic chart sent by referring agent or requested by practitioners

    F. History and physical examination

    G. Interval note/update of history and physical examination

    H. Consultations and special assessments

    I. Clinical laboratory studies

    J. Diagnostic tests and studies: requests and interpretations (e.g., radiology, electroencephalograms, electrocardiograms, nuclear medicine scans, pulmonary function studies, radioisotope studies, electromyograms)

    K. Biopsy reports, surgical pathology reports, and disposition of body parts

VI. Course of Treatment Documentation

    A. Patient/client care plan

    B. Discharge plan

    C. Physician notes

    D. Notes by health care disciplines except nursing (separate section)

        1. dietary/nutrition

        2. social service

        3. clinical psychology

        4. chaplaincy

        5. physical medicine and rehabilitation (e.g., physical therapy, occupational therapy, vocational rehabilitation, respiratory therapy, audiology and speech therapy)

        6. dentistry

    E. Additional material concerning specialized aspects of care

VII. Nursing Documentation

    A. Nursing assessment

    B. Nursing plan of care

    C. Tracking and flow sheets (e.g., intake/output, weight, bowel and bladder function, vital signs, critical care)

    D. Nurses' notes

    E. Interward transfer record

In addition to these documents, certain admissions shall have specialized forms reflecting particular aspects of the care:

- surgical care documentation
  - preanesthesia evaluations
  - anesthesia record
  - postanesthesia evaluation
  - operative report
  - blood transfusion record during surgery
  - intravenous infusion record during surgery
  - recovery room observations
  - tissue/pathology reports: any removal of body parts
- obstetrical care documentation
  - discharge summary: undelivered; complicated delivery
  - prenatal care summary
  - labor progress chart
  - labor and delivery summary with notation of outcome
  - analgesia and anesthesia evaluation
  - analgesia and anesthesia record
  - operation or procedure related to delivery
  - intravenous infusion record
  - postpartum record
  - toxemia monitoring
  - cross reference to newborn
  - pathology reports for tubal ligation or hysterectomy
  - consultations/physician review (e.g., Caesarean section, sterilization, abortion)
  - consents (e.g., sterilization, Caesarean section, abortion, disposal of stillborn, release for adoption)
  - fetal monitoring data

continues

Exhibit 8–3 continued

- court orders and special decrees (e.g., refusal of parent[s] to allow transfusions or certain treatments)
- newborns
  - footprint and identification verification
  - signed release for removal of infant by parent or designated agent of parent
  - birth certificate information (copy of certificate if permitted by state regulations)
  - cross reference to mother's chart including, as needed, prenatal care summary and fetal monitoring summary
  - discharge summary (e.g., complicated or premature births, neonate intensive care, prolonged stay)
  - summary of delivery
  - evaluation at birth
  - growth and development/pediatric assessment and/or low birth weight graphic chart
  - circumcision (e.g., consent, procedure summary)
  - neonate intensive care graphic records and notes
- pediatric chart
  - release of child to parent or designated agent of parent
  - clear notation of source of information/informant
  - history of childhood diseases
  - immunization record
  - growth and development comparative graphic records
  - court orders and special decrees (e.g., refusal of parent[s] to allow transfusions or certain treatments)
- emergency department (usually one composite form)
  - emergency department report
  - disposition note: discharged from emergency care, *or* admitted to inpatient care, *or* transferred to other health care facility
  - addendum notes (e.g., major trauma, infection, chest pain)
  - summary received from paramedics or emergency transport service personnel
- outpatient clinic
  - identification section
  - legal and administrative documents (e.g., consents for care; refusals of treatment; follow-up notes/attempts to reach patient/client who does not return for care, suture removal, or similar situations)
  - assessment, history, and physical examinations
  - treatment notes
  - concluding note showing disposition of patient/client and clear statement of end of episode of care
  - "fit for work" or health clearance forms
  - transfer forms (referral to other health care setting)

Source: Reprinted from *Medical Records: Policies and Guidelines* by J.G. Liebler, pp. 4:3–4, Aspen Publishers, Inc. © 1990.

elements that are necessary to develop computer-based clinical data systems.[2]

THE FUNCTIONS OF THE CLINICAL INFORMATION SYSTEM

The clinical information systems are developed and maintained to provide the timely and appropriate support services to identify, store, and retrieve the medical record as well as to provide assistance with the timely and accurate completion of the documentation. These support systems are described as follows.

Patient Identification

An essential aspect of the total health information system is an effective method of identifying each individual who receives an episode of care at the facility. Three reasons make it essential to have uniform registration forms and procedures:

1. Patients enter the system at a variety of points of service, e.g., emergency care unit, ambulatory care clinic, group practice, home care unit, inpatient admissions.

2. The intake process occurs at any time within a 24-hour, 7-day-a-week framework.

3. The personnel who carry out the intake process belong to different organizational units, each with its own jurisdiction within the overall institution.

A centralized registry for patient identification is usually maintained by the clinical information department, with coordination of information gathering with the various intake units. Because of the sheer volume of admissions/readmissions to the facility, a numbering system is the usual form of patient identification. By assigning one number, a *unique* identifier, used for every subsequent admission or episode of care for that patient, a unit number is developed and maintained. The patient identification thus becomes a combination of full legal name and unique identifying number. This combined identification is used on the record folder(s) for the patient and is entered on each document. Entering the identifying number is facilitated through the use of embossed identification plates.

Use of this unit number, in turn, allows for the creation of a unit record: one overall, continuous medical record file for that individual, reflecting the documentation of each inpatient stay and each outpatient service/episode of care. In order to avoid the assignment of the same number to more than one patient and, conversely, to avoid assigning more than one number to a patient, stringent number control systems are developed and coordinated by the clinical information department. The use of computerized processes can facilitate the maintenance of this identification system, especially when control edits are built into the number control program.

The use of a unique identifier for patient records is the norm. Alternatives to the unit number system include serial numbering and serial-unit numbering. In the serial numbering method, a new number is assigned to the patient for each admission; the medical records of a patient are consequently found under more than one number. To offset this problem of more than one record, serial-unit numbering is used: A new number is given for each admission or episode of care, but the medical records of all previous encounters are brought forward and merged as a unit record. This merged unit record is filed under the latest number assigned.

Creation of a Unit Record

The best interests of the patient are served when one record contains all the information about the individual's care. This concern for continuity of care is embodied in the regulatory and accrediting agency requirements and has implications for risk management. In the multi-component facility, a client/patient may receive care at more than one clinic or service, in addition to traditional inpatient care. The linkage of all the patient care information from these components is best accomplished through the maintenance of a unit record. Procedures are developed to foster integration and coordination of all information into one central patient file, made available in its totality for each episode of care. The numbering and filing systems and the record processing systems, along with modification of staffing patterns and hours of department service, are adjusted to meet this need in the multi-component facility.

Content and Flow of Documentation

The medical record documents are generated by each caregiver as the patient receives each service. Table 8–1 typifies several clinical transactions, the primary caregiver involved, and the document reflecting the care.

Format and Arrangement of the Medical Record

In concert with the medical and professional staff of the facility, the health information practitioner develops standardized formats for medical record entries. One of the three of the following formats is used:

1. *Source-oriented record:* Documents are arranged according to the origination of

Table 8–1 Documentation of Care

Clinical Transaction	Caregivers	Documents
Admission process	Admission and registration personnel, nursing personnel	Patient identification, consents
Initial assessment		
History and physical	Medical and nursing personnel	History and physical exam
Sociological	Social worker	Social service assessment
Clinical laboratory studies	Medical technologist, pathologist	Clinical laboratory reports
Radiologic reports	Radiologist, radiologic technician	Radiology reports
Consultations	Medical specialists, nutritionist, psychiatrist, psychologist	Consultant report
Orders for diagnosis and	Physician	Physician orders
treatment	Medical and surgical specialists,	(1) Operative reports, (2) progress
Ongoing treatment and progress	nurse anesthetists	note, (3) anesthetist reports
Nursing support and intervention	Nursing staff	Nurses' notes
Discharge	Physician	Final diagnosis, discharge summary
Autopsy	Pathologist	Autopsy report

the entry. Thus, nursing service notes, laboratory, radiology, social service, and physician services each are included in a separate section. Entries are filed chronologically within these distinct sections.

2. *Integrated record:* The emphasis in this pattern of documentation is on chronological entry. As each entry is made, it is placed in chronological order. Thus, a laboratory report might be followed by a social service note, followed by a physician order.

3. *Problem-oriented record:*[3] A problem list is developed that reflects current and past conditions, symptoms, and diagnoses for a given patient. Progress notes are keyed to the specific problem(s) using a consistent method of recording, the SOAP entry: an acronym meaning S—subjective information about the condition, provided by the patient or patient's designated informant; O—objective data, such as laboratory reports, radiology reports, and physical examination; A—assessment of the condition by the patient care provider; and P—plan of treatment or therapy.

DISCHARGE PROCESSING

Several activities make up the overall function of discharge processing. During the inpatient stay, the medical record is primarily used as the source of ongoing information about the patient's condition. At the time of discharge, the record is processed for permanent retention and subsequent use. These uses include development of an institutional statistical database, reimbursement process, medical and administrative committee use, and teaching/research use. These processes are described here in their general sequential relationship.

Record Assembly

Often, the sequence of documents in the record during the inpatient stay differs from the final order. For example, physician orders might be placed at the front of the record during inpatient stay, but are merged into an overall physician documentation section at discharge. After discharge, the documents are arranged in the proper order following a standardized sequence for the facility. A detailed review of each document is made at this time to ensure proper patient identification (name and number) and to prevent misfiles. Medical records are placed in heavy-duty folders that are usually preprinted with the proper identification number and color coded to correspond with the filing system. The patient name and the dates of admission/discharge may be entered on the outside folder for permanent reference.

Quantitative Analysis

An approved list of required medical record content is the basis for this review by clerical personnel who work under the supervision of trained medical record managers. Deficiencies and special problems are noted on a working list that is attached to the specific record. This record is then assigned to the appropriate physician or other practitioner for completion. The process is a detailed one because it is one of the first quality assurance/risk management review points in the system. Although it is the responsibility of each practitioner to make the necessary entries and sign them, the department has an overall responsibility to see that proper documentation is maintained. Thus, the system of quantitative analysis (record review) has developed. The time frames for completion of documentation are delineated in various regulatory and accrediting body standards.

Incomplete Record Control

A system of incomplete record control is developed to meet five major needs:

1. access by individual providers who are responsible for completion of data and/or signature entries
2. availability of the record for use in ongoing patient care during the immediate follow-up process, such as ambulatory care or home care services
3. availability of the record for filing of ongoing and late reports
4. monitoring and updating record deficiency status as entries are finalized and deficiencies are eliminated

5. maintaining the record in this temporary storage subsystem in a manner that safeguards it from unauthorized use and inadvertent destruction or loss

Suitable work space and dictation facilities are made available for the professional staff, usually adjacent to this incomplete record station. The assistance of trained medical record staff in this unit is customary. The workflow is related closely to that of the transcription/word processing function. Procedures are followed to log in the material received from the word processing unit and to make it available to the originator for signature.

MEDICAL DICTATION, TRANSCRIPTION, AND WORD PROCESSING

Machine-Generated Medical Documentation

Today, documentation is prepared using a variety of technologies, ranging from handwritten notes in ballpoint pen to computer-generated graphic displays of laboratory data. Although computer technology for direct conversion of the spoken word to printed form is under development, for all practical purposes hospitals today must still rely on human transcription of dictated material for production of machine-printed narrative reports. Systems of dictation, followed by transcription using word-processing equipment, are used by many hospital departments. Physicians generally favor the speed and ease of dictating reports over handwriting them, and machine-printed reports offer vastly improved legibility, as well as the option to easily produce multiple copies of a document in a single operation. However, these benefits do not come without cost, both for the initial capital equipment and for the ongoing costs of space and skilled personnel.

The continuing development of computer technology, with its inverse relationship of increasing storage capacity and processing speed to decreasing physical size and cost, will likely make the totally machine-maintained record a reality in the future. Until then, hospitals must still seek the most efficient and cost-effective systems to produce printed medical documentation using skilled medical transcriptionists.

Table 8–2 lists medical documentation that is commonly transcribed, with indication of the hospital department(s) typically carrying out this service.

Clinical Information Departmental Activities

As noted in Table 8–2, the clinical information department is typically responsible for the transcription of discharge summaries and operative reports; in addition, some departments also handle consultations and reports of medical history and physical examination.

Decisions regarding the extent of dictation/transcription service to be provided are ordinarily made by hospital administration in consultation with the director of the clinical information department and appropriate representative(s) of the medical staff. Three major decisions must be made:

1. To whom will the service be provided? (i.e., all physicians, attending physicians

only, selected clinical departments only, etc.)
2. What types of reports may be dictated/transcribed?
3. Will the service be provided on-site or through contract with an external service?

Dictation equipment is available in a variety of types and configurations from a multitude of vendors. The two major types of equipment in general use are those using the familiar audio-cassette (both standard and microsized) and those using continuous loop magnetic tapes in closed "tanks," which are less familiar to the general public. Some small facilities with a low volume of transcription may still find that individual desktop transcribing equipment and electric/electronic typewriters meet their needs. Dedicated word-processing equipment now appears to be the norm for larger hospitals with high-volume transcription services.

Although transcribed reports are authenticated by signature of the dictating physician, a system of quality control using random or other sampling techniques should be established. With authentication of the original report and its incorporation into the medical record comes the possibility that it will later be scrutinized in a legal proceeding, claim review, or future patient care; accuracy of transcription therefore becomes critical.

As compared with other clinical information department functions, transcription services can operate relatively independently; however, clear procedures must be established to maintain smooth relationships with these other units:

- with medical staff regarding incomplete, unclear, or "lost" dictation and distribution of report copies
- with clinical information department personnel involved with incomplete record control to ensure that completed dictation/transcription is properly credited
- with patient care units to ensure that completed transcription for still hospitalized patients is received at the appropriate location in a timely manner

---

Table 8–2 Transcribed Entries of the Medical Record

Document	Department
Discharge summary operative report history and physical exam report* consultation report*	Medical record department
X-ray reports, radioisotope scan interpretation	Radiology diagnostic imaging department
Tissue report, autopsy protocol	Pathology department
Interpretations of graphic data (EKG, EEG, EMG, etc.)	Associated clinical department

*These reports are also often handwritten or transcribed by secretarial staff of an attending physician's clinical department or private office.

- with the admitting department and operating room to ensure that needed control data (admission/discharge lists, operating room schedules) are accurate, complete, timely, and available
- within the transcription unit to ensure equitable workload distribution, productivity monitoring and quality control, consistency of report formats, and production of copies

External transcription services range from "cottage industry," with overflow dictation contracted out to one or more individuals working at home, to national corporations with local franchises that receive client hospital dictation via public telephone channels in a central facility.

The use of an external transcription service may offer some obvious advantages in relieving the hospital of responsibility for equipment acquisition and maintenance; space allocation; and personnel recruitment, training, and supervision; the obvious major disadvantage is the loss of direct control over the service, except through the option of nonrenewal of a contract.

Even when an external service is used, the monitoring of both quantity and quality continues to be critical. Control mechanisms should be established to ensure receipt of all dictated reports within the time periods specified by the contract. In addition, regular sampling of completed transcription for quality—accuracy of spelling, punctuation, format, completeness, etc.—and for comparison of invoice statements of work completed with actual work received is sound business practice.

RETENTION, STORAGE, AND RETRIEVAL FUNCTION

Record Retention

The health information manager develops a specific retention schedule that takes into account the following four variables that affect record usage:

1. continuity of care mandate
   - readmission rate to inpatient units

- ongoing care/follow-up within the facility's ambulatory programs, such as outpatient service, home care, or hospice care
- ongoing care in facilities and programs not under the immediate sponsorship of the hospital, such as long-term care and rehabilitation facilities to which patients have been transferred, independent/private practitioners, and other acute care centers. There is both a legal and ethical obligation to provide information to such facilities when direct transfer of the patient is arranged and/or when the patient requests the forwarding of such information

2. legal, regulatory, and accrediting requirements
   - specific federal and state laws and/or regulations
   - accrediting agency stipulations
   - statute of limitations for business record maintenance and for various legal actions
   - definitions under state law of legal adulthood and minor/child status

3. research activities
   - amount, type, and frequency of institutionally sponsored research
   - specific time frames, especially for longitudinal studies reflecting several years of follow-up care

4. educational programs
   - medical school sponsorship
   - nursing, pharmacy, dentistry, and allied health program sponsorship
   - affiliation agreements with other medical and professional schools and allied health training programs

The destruction of records at the end of the designated retention period is carried out under the supervision of the department manager. This process includes the proper filing of required information concerning such permissible destruction with appropriate administrative and governing board designees.

Storage and Retrieval System

Two basic objectives are met in the development of the storage and retrieval system in the clinical information department:

1. maintenance of records in a safe, restricted area, free from unauthorized use or unintentional destruction or loss
2. ease of location of records for patient care, research education, and administrative use

The specific system of storage and retrieval is either centralized or decentralized. In the centralized system, all information is filed in one location within the clinical information department. The major advantage of the centralized system is efficient, easy access to material because it is located in only one place. Adherence to various legal and accrediting mandates concerning record retention and availability is facilitated.

In the decentralized system, information about each patient is placed in a medical record that is maintained by the unit or service rendering the patient care. Although this system promotes speedy access to the information needed for a particular episode of care, the provision of the full clinical picture through a single, comprehensive record is made more difficult. A modified decentralized system is sometimes used in which record format and content and storage and retrieval system and equipment are uniform in all component units of the health care setting. This standardization eases retrieval of information because of the similarity of each subsystem. A linkage system is maintained so that records are requested from the designated primary location for use in other units for specific patient care transactions.

The satellite record system is another variation that can be useful in those clinical situations in which the follow-up care can be predicted in terms of frequency of return visits within a rela-

tively chronic or long-term time frame. Examples include obstetric care over several months, well-baby care, pain control clinic, or a substance abuse clinic. Because the primary, ongoing care is given in these specific units and the coordination of the care is done in the context of a major clinical episode, satellite record systems are useful. The record is charged out to and placed in a storage and retrieval unit at this designated satellite site. When the long-term episode of care concludes, the record is returned to the central clinical information storage area for routine retention and use.

Processing of Ongoing Reports

A major function of the storage and retrieval system personnel is the ongoing maintenance of medical record content. Provision is made for the systematic filing of reports that are processed after patient discharge or that are received after the customary record processes have been completed. In addition, those facilities that offer ongoing patient care through a variety of clinics and services have a situation of continuously generated patient data. The documents reflecting each episode of care are filed in the centralized patient record in a timely and efficient manner. Staffing patterns are developed to support this ongoing process of record maintenance so that the record is complete and up to date for each use.

Several adjunct processes work together with the basic storage and retrieval function to foster timely retrieval of specific records:

- an appointment system for planned ambulatory, home care, and similar follow-up encounters
- a known schedule for planned readmissions to the inpatient unit
- a staffing pattern in the work unit to accommodate walk-in and emergency service units, as well as unplanned readmissions
- a record request system for orderly retrieval of records for administrative and research use on a preplanned basis

- a temporary storage unit in a work area close to the central storage area where a large volume of medical records may be held for ongoing use by researchers and educators
- a charge-out system showing the name of the requestor, the location, the time and date of signout; in a low-volume usage facility, the system for charging out a record may be a simple one, such as a signout sheet with the specific information entered. The commercially made charge-out divider, placed in the permanent location of the medical record, is another common method. The volume of records charged out and the physical complexity of the institution's layout are major determinants for this subsystem.
- scheduled audit of the files for error detection and correction

These considerations are reflected in policy and procedure manuals for the unit; the health information manager develops such adjunct systems in accordance with the needs and requirements of the various patient care and administrative users of the health record.

Method of Storage

Storing the paper copy of the record in its entirety is a common method of storage when space and equipment and staff are available, record usage for immediate follow-up care is frequent and routine, and record usage after discharge is minimal. If any of these variables change, alternatives to hard copy storage are sought. Microfilm, microform, and computer output/microform systems offer a viable alternative when space and filing equipment are at a premium. A combination of hard copy and microform is yet another option. The complete inpatient record might be microfilmed, with the ongoing documents maintained in hard copy during the extended episode of follow-up care. To compare the total cost of hard copy retention to the microform method, it is necessary to consider the cost of floor space, filing equipment versus reader-printer equipment, cost of preparation and actual microfilming of the documents, and ease of use by the users of the record.

The use of commercial storage is possible, especially when there is relatively little record usage after discharge. As with the microform option, careful cost comparisons must be made. Finally, with either microform or commercial storage, consideration must be given to compliance with applicable regulations and statutes for record retention, provision for the safeguarding of the documents from unauthorized use or destruction, and access to the records in a timely manner should the need arise. The health information manager develops such contractual elements and carries out such assessments, taking all these factors into account.

Chart Tracking through Bar Coding

One specific application of modern technology to data storage and retrieval is that of chart tracking systems through bar coding. Bar code labels are attached to the medical record folders (both the temporary in-house folder and the permanent folder). The bar code is linked to the patient identification system, bearing the same identification number. Sign in/out terminals are placed throughout the patient care areas and in the clinical information unit. These locations are identified with appropriate bar codes. Authorized individuals may access the system (an online computer function) to determine the location of a particular record as well as review its past use. In addition to providing chart tracking, these systems are programmed to give various management reports to the clinical information managers. These reports typically reflect management issues such as:

- number of charts held by a borrower for more than the approved time limit (e.g., 30 days for research use)
- record movement: tracking consecutive usage, that is, the movement of the record from one point of use to another (e.g., use in one day in multiple clinics)

- patterns of STAT requests
- notification of records scheduled for archival retention or for destruction

Release of Information

Just as the clinical information department serves as the hub for patient data collection, gathering the diagnostic and therapeutic documentation created by hospital departments and practitioners to compile the patient medical record, so too does the department serve as a focal point for release of information from those patient records. Information from the medical record is requested by a variety of sources:

- insurance carriers and other third-party payors to substantiate claims for payment of care
- other caregivers to provide a sound basis for continuity of care
- attorneys for patient-related litigation
- insurers, employers, and other agencies for determination of benefits (disability, death, worker's compensation, etc.)
- law enforcement, public health, and other governmental agencies in carrying out their respective responsibilities

The volume of such requests varies with the size of the facility. Regardless of the volume, however, the response to such requests requires the involvement of personnel with knowledge of medical terminology, applicable federal and state laws and regulations, and hospital policy and procedure with regard to confidentiality of patient health information.

The following factors must be considered when handling each request:

- whether any data may be released: some federal and state laws/regulations prohibit release of certain types of information, e.g., data pertaining to alcohol/drug abuse
- whether special conditions must be met before information may be released: as with mental health data in some states, which requires special authorizations and concur-

rence of the physician or superintendent of a mental health facility
- whether a properly executed authorization from the patient, parent of a minor, legal guardian, or executor of an estate is required for release of requested data, is included with the request, or contains all required elements
- what information from the patient record is needed to satisfy the request
- whether a fee is charged for providing the requested data, with associated billing and bookkeeping procedures

Particular attention must be given to requests for diagnoses associated with drug or alcohol addiction, psychiatric condition, or HIV-related conditions. These conditions are surrounded by special restrictions on the release of information. Pertinent federal and state laws and regulations must be adhered to whenever such requests are processed.

In addition to the more routine types of requests/requestors noted above, requests may also be made by telephone, in the event of urgent patient care needs, or by subpoena or deposition when litigation reaches trial status.

Detailed procedures and trained personnel are needed to process all requests for information from patient medical records. In addition to developing procedures for assessing the authority of the requestor to obtain these data, procedures should be specified to:

- log requests received and filled
- maintain a record of information released for each patient
- maintain records of payments billed and/or received
- monitor volume and productivity
- assure return of records provided to the court by order of subpoena

Classification and Indexing

To facilitate retrieval of pertinent medical records for uses such as research, education, and quality assurance review, clinical data are numerically encoded and then indexed, using one of several recognized classification systems. Most acute care, general hospitals have adopted the *International Classification of Diseases, 9th Revision, Clinical Modification* (ICD-9-CM) for classifying and encoding diseases, clinical conditions, operations, procedures, and injuries. In addition to ICD-9-CM, other classification systems have been developed for specific clinical areas. The selection and implementation of the system(s) most appropriate for the facility are one of the major duties of the credentialed health information practitioner.

Abstracting for Statistical Reporting

The standardized collection of both detailed clinical and demographic data provides the institution with an in-depth database for a variety of uses, including research studies, statistical profiles, data for reports to regulatory and accrediting agencies, data for institutional planning, credentialing boards for practitioners, risk management, and professional staff committees such as utilization review and medical care evaluation/quality assurance.

Commonly maintained statistical profiles and indices include average length of stay, percentage of occupancy, daily census, mortality and morbidity rates, disease and operation indices, and physician indices. Special statistical profiles may be developed on an as-needed basis.

Ease of data collection is increased through the use of abstracting systems, whereby a statistical and clinical profile is developed for each patient at the time of discharge. The patient's identity is coded for protection of privacy. The cross-reference numbers make it possible to gain access to the detailed patient record should that become necessary and authorized as part of a specific study. For most studies and statistical reports, only impersonal data are needed. The usual information processed in the abstracting system includes detailed demographic data and specific clinical data, such as operations and procedures, blood transfusions, and similar information. The existence of several commercial companies that specialize in computerized abstracting systems facilitates these data-gathering processes. These companies range from regional to nationwide services, providing the facility with comparative data against which to analyze its own statistical profiles. The cost per abstract, the level of detailed information required and in turn made available for institutional use, the turnaround time, and quality controls are factors in the decision to select such a company. In facilities with an in-house computer system, internal abstracting services may be provided. The abstracting of patient data may be completed concurrent with the inpatient stay or at the time of discharge.

Registries, Indexes, and Vital Statistics

In addition to the statistical abstracts based on each patient's stay, several sources of data are developed in either registry or index form. These include:

- cancer/tumor registry
- trauma registry
- disease and operations index
- physician index
- organ transplant registry
- eye bank registry

Vital statistics and communicable disease reporting systems are included in this scope of work. These reports are carried out in accordance with city, state, and federal requirements and guidelines.

Reimbursement Processes

The present method of reimbursement by some third-party payors, especially federal and state agencies, has a direct relationship to record completion. The information necessary for the completion of such claims is drawn from the official medical record, which, in turn, must be complete and accurate.

A calculation of the number of incomplete records in relation to the amount of money collected from third-party payors can determine the financial impact of incomplete records. For example, a 500-bed teaching/research facility with 800 incomplete records and unfiled claims might have as much as $4 million in outstanding reimbursement. Timely record completion and rapid, accurate processing of the required reimbursement data have obvious implications for cash flow.

With the introduction of the federal prospective payment system (PPS) for reimbursement of inpatient care rendered to Medicare recipients, reimbursement is now also closely tied to the classification of clinical data according to ICD-9-CM. Diagnosis and operative procedure codes are the basic data required for assignment of a DRG, which, in turn, is used to determine the reimbursement to the hospital for that episode of care.

Coordination and cooperation with the billing/finance office of the facility are an imperative. Because of the importance of this function, a DRG coordinator, usually a credentialed health information practitioner, directs this unit.

With respect to outpatient billing, the procedure and diagnostic coding is according to CPT-4. This in turn is tied to the federally required Medicare Part B reimbursement scale: the resource-based relative value scale (RBRVS).

In developing new systems and modifying existing systems of coding for reimbursement, and the interrelationship of these two functions, attention must be given to the ongoing recommendations of the Department of Health and Human Services' work group: Workgroup for Electronic Data Interchange (WEDI), the Taskforce on Patient Information, and the Workgroup on Administrative Costs and Benefits. The recommendations, which include electronic billing and electronic health insurance cards, have a five-year phase-in plan (1992–1997).[4]

Quality Assurance and Medical Care Evaluation

Ongoing monitoring of the quality of medical care and the evaluation of patterns of utilization of health care resources constitute yet another activity of clinical information services. This activity involves two major processes:

1. utilization review, with emphasis on length of stay, discharge planning, and appropriate use of resources
2. medical care evaluation, with emphasis on monitoring and evaluating the quality of care provided. Medical staff committees have the primary responsibility for such reviews. Data analysis and display, preliminary reviews and abstracts, and the preparation of detailed audit profiles from selected medical records typify the supportive activities carried out by trained health information personnel.

These committees and review groups look to the clinical information service for the necessary data for such studies. Other review committees and groups for whom the clinical information service routinely prepares studies are these:

- Blood Usage Review
- Operating and Recovery Room Committee
- Pharmacy and Therapeutics Committee
- Radiation Safety Committee
- Risk Management
- Drug Usage Committee
- Credentials Committee
- Clinical Record Review Committee

CONCLUSION

A typical hospital and health facility clinical information department provides a wide range of services. These critical services fulfill the needs of patients, the institution, and society through both simple and sophisticated systems that continually balance the need for patient health data with patients' rights to confidentiality of these data. As the industry evolves more toward integrated delivery systems, the requirement for uniform, accurate, and timely information will increase.

NOTES

1. R.S. Dick and E.B. Stein, eds., *The Computer-Based Patient Record* (Washington, D.C.: National Academy Press, 1991).

2. American Society for Testing and Materials, *Standard Guide for Description for Content and Structure of an Automated Primary Record of Care,* Guide E 1384–91 (Philadelphia, 1991).

3. L. Weed, *The Problem Oriented Medical Record* (Cleveland: Case Western Reserve Press, 1969).

4. Department of Health and Human Services: Workgroup for Electronic Data Interchange (WEDI) (Washington, D.C.: 1992).

JOAN GRATTO LIEBLER, RRA, MPA, is Professor and Chair, Department of Health Information Management, College of Allied Health Professions, Temple University, in Philadelphia. Professor Liebler's expertise in health information management includes work in a variety of clinical settings, such as inpatient psychiatric hospitals, community mental health centers, neighborhood health centers, city and federal agency programs, and long-term care facilities.

In addition to management degrees, she has also completed advanced studies in the area of moral theology with an emphasis on medical ethics. Her major current research area is the legal, regulatory, and administrative impact of the Patient Self-Determination Act.

She has written extensively in the field of health information management. Her works include: *Managing Health Records, Principles of Management for Health Professionals,* and *Medical Records: Policies and Guidelines.* She was a founding member of *Topics in Health Record Management* and *Health Care Supervisor.*

Chapter 9

Inpatient Hospital Reimbursement

Michael J. Dalton

Most hospitals receive a substantial amount of their revenues from regulated payors such as Medicare, state Medicaid programs, and, in some areas of the United States, the Blue Cross and Blue Shield programs. Many of these payors use the reimbursement regulations that are published by the Medicare program. In addition, with the aging of the U.S. population, and the expanded coverage to people that are under 65 and disabled, over 50 percent of a hospital's revenue very often is received from the Medicare program. As a result, this chapter will focus on Medicare reimbursement, both past and present, which should give the reader an understanding of the methods by which hospitals receive payment for rendering services to their patients, and of the major functions of the Finance Department.

Since the inception of the Medicare program in 1966 and the Medicaid program in 1967, most inpatient hospital care was paid based on the cost per day to treat all patients, and outpatient care was paid on the average cost per outpatient visit. This payment system was based on the general principles of cost finding and, even though the Medicare inpatient system changed effective October 1, 1983, and the Medicare outpatient system changed effective 1986, the prin-

ciples of cost finding are still used by hospitals to report information to the various regulated payors.

COST FINDING

Cost finding is the apportionment or allocation of the costs of the nonrevenue-producing cost centers to each other, and to the revenue-producing centers based on statistical data that measure the amount of service rendered by each center to other centers. The purpose of general cost finding is to determine the full costs of operating the revenue-producing centers of the hospital. Generally, centers that provide the greatest amount of service to the greatest number of other centers, and receive the least in services from others, are apportioned in the first stages of the cost finding procedure; centers that provide service to fewer centers are apportioned in the later stages.

Cost finding, therefore, is the process of recasting or reclassifying the costs accumulated in the routine accounts maintained by the hospital for responsibility reporting purposes. The recasting produces information as to the full costs of operating the various revenue-producing organizational units or departments of the hospital. Cost finding is a procedure that is done apart from, but supplemental to, the regular accounting system. The results produced by cost finding are not recorded in the hospital's accounts or usual income statement. Instead, the results of cost finding are presented in a special cost-finding report.

The cost finding process was designed so that at the end of each fiscal year, a hospital would allocate the costs attributable to Medicare, Medicaid, and other cost-based payors. This method is referred to as step-down cost finding. The first step in this process is listing all costs of a provider in a trial balance format. Indirect costs—those not associated with direct care—are attributed to such cost centers as administration and general, depreciation, utilities, housekeeping, and dietary, among others. Direct costs include radiology, laboratory, operating rooms, emergency room, room and board, and routine care. Once this list is prepared, costs are further divided into salary and other expenses. An example of this trial balance format is shown in Table 9–1.

Adjustments to cost are then made according to numerous government regulations, in an attempt to arrive at patient-care-related costs. For example, cafeteria sales offset dietary costs because sales of meals in a cafeteria to visitors and/or staff are not considered allowable or necessary to patient care.

The next step is taking the adjusted trial balance and allocating indirect costs to direct costs using certain statistics. An example of this step-down process is shown in Table 9–2.

Other costs that are not included in Table 9–2, but would also be allocated, are listed below, with the most commonly used unit of measure to determine the appropriate allocation:

- laundry: pounds of laundry utilized
- nursing: hours spent in units
- house staff: time spent in units
- telephones: number of lines or usage
- data processing: usage of CPU
- patient accounting: volume of charges by department

After allocating (or stepping down) indirect costs to direct costs, the next step is allocating direct costs between inpatient and outpatient costs, most often on the basis of charges. The next step is to allocate program or Medicare costs based on charges, except for routine care, which is allocated based on days. This process is outlined in Table 9–3.

Charges also are the basis of the allocation of outpatient costs to Medicare, and the system works similarly with Blue Cross and Medicaid.

Table 9–1 Example of a Trial Balance Format

Description	Salaries	Other	Total	Adjustments	Adjusted Cost
Depreciation	—	100,000	100,000	20,000*	120,000
Administration and General	400,000	100,000	500,000	—	500,000
Utilities	—	150,000	150,000	—	150,000
Housekeeping	200,000	50,000	250,000	—	250,000
Dietary	100,000	75,000	175,000	(15,000)**	160,000
Radiology	500,000	50,000	550,000	—	550,000
Labs	300,000	200,000	500,000	—	500,000
Operating Room	150,000	200,000	350,000	—	350,000
Emergency Room	75,000	75,000	150,000	—	150,000
Routine Care	700,000	300,000	1,000,000	—	1,000,000
Total	$2,425,000	$1,300,000	$3,725,000	$5,000	$3,730,000

*Adding accelerated depreciation to straight-line depreciation
**Offsetting cafeteria costs because they would be recorded in dietary and are not allowable

Table 9–2 Step-Down Cost Finding

Description	Transfer from Trial Balance (Dollars)	Depreciation (Square Feet)	Administration and General (Total Costs)	Utilities (Metered Use)	Housekeeping (Square Feet)	Dietary (Meals Served)	Stepped-Down Costs (Dollars)
Depreciation	120,000	120,000					
Administration and General	500,000	10,000	510,000				
Utilities	150,000	5,000	24,500	179,500			
Housekeeping	250,000	5,000	40,800	10,000	305,800		
Dietary	160,000	7,500	26,500	30,000	24,000	248,000	
Radiology	550,000	6,000	88,000	25,000	18,000		687,000
Labs	500,000	6,000	80,000	12,000	18,000		616,000
Operating Room	350,000	3,000	55,900	12,000	9,000		429,900
Emergency Room	150,000	3,000	24,300	5,000	9,000		191,300
Routine Care	1,000,000	74,500	170,000	85,500	227,800	248,000	1,805,800
Total	$3,730,000	$120,000	$510,000	$179,500	$305,800	$248,000	$3,730,000

While the cost finding process has remained virtually unchanged since it was first developed, the hospital reimbursement system under the Medicare program underwent major changes during the 1980s with the implementation of the prospective payment system (PPS).

MEDICARE PROSPECTIVE PAYMENT SYSTEM

The Medicare PPS currently applies only to inpatient acute care services. The following types of hospitals, hospital units, and other types of providers are specifically excluded from system coverage:

- psychiatric hospitals
- rehabilitation hospitals
- distinct part psychiatric and rehabilitation units of acute care hospitals
- children's hospitals
- Christian Science sanitoria
- risk basis health maintenance organizations and competitive medical plans
- Veterans Administration hospitals
- hospitals in states that have a waiver from the PPS program

For most covered hospitals, the PPS became effective for their fiscal years beginning on or after October 1, 1983. Payment under PPS was based on a "blended" rate during a five-year transition period to national rates. One component of that blended rate was based on the Tax Equity and Fiscal Responsibility Act (TEFRA) target rate concept, using a hospital's base year cost-per-discharge, updated for inflation. This component represented the "hospital-specific" rate. The other component of the blended rate, the "federal" rate, was based on a combination of regional and national prices established by the Health Care Financing Administration (HCFA). These two payment components—the federal rate and the hospital-specific rate—were used in combination throughout the transition period to determine the payment rates for specific categories of illnesses or diagnostic-related groups (DRGs). Since the transition period ended, DRG payment rates are determined solely by the federal rate.

The DRG payment rates represent full payment to a hospital for all inpatient hospital costs, including the costs of inpatient routine care, ancillary services, and special care units, with the exception of the following cost components:

- capital-related costs
- direct medical education costs

Table 9–3 Cost Allocation to Program

	a	b	c	d	e	f	g	h
	Allocated Costs	Inpatient Charges	Outpatient Charges	Inpatient (%)	Inpatient Costs (d x a)	Medicare Inpatient Charges	Medicare Inpatient (%) (f ÷ b)	Medicare Costs (g x e)
Radiology	687,000	450,000	250,000	64	440,000	150,000	33.3	147,000
Labs	616,000	450,000	250,000	64	394,000	150,000	33.3	131,000
Operating Room	429,900	300,000	150,000	67	288,000	100,000	33.3	96,000
Emergency Room	191,300	60,000	200,000	23	44,000	20,000	33.3	15,000
Total Allocated Medicare Ancillary Costs								389,000

Total Routine Costs	1,805,800	
Total Routine Patient Days	60,000	
Average Per Diem	30.1	
Medicare Routine Days	20,000	
Medicare Routine Costs (days x per diem)		602,000
Total Medicare Reimbursable Inpatient Costs		$991,000

Hospitals may not bill Medicare patients for differences between PPS payments and actual charges. As in the past, those patients may be billed for the Medicare coinsurance and deductible amounts.

Costs that are excluded from the DRG payment rates are known as "pass through" costs. Pass through costs are reimbursed under the pre-PPS retrospective cost-based system, subject to certain limitations and reductions. Hospitals must file Medicare cost reports annually to be reimbursed for those costs. In addition, incremental payments are made under PPS for outlier cases and indirect medical education costs. Outliers are defined as cases involving atypical lengths of stay or atypical costs. Special payment provisions also apply when patients are transferred from one hospital to another as well as in other defined transfer situations.

Diagnostic-Related Groups

DRGs are the basis for payment to hospitals under the Medicare Prospective Payment System (PPS). Originally developed at Yale University, DRGs, as adapted for use by Medicare, are intended to represent groups of hospital inpatients that are clinically similar to one another

and relatively homogeneous with respect to use of resources.

The HCFA has established specific payment rates for each of 490 DRGs. The formula for calculating payment for a specific DRG is based on the PPS payment rate multiplied by the "cost weight" or "relative weight" of the DRG to which the case is assigned. Each DRG cost weight is intended to represent the average resources required to care for a case in that particular DRG, relative to the national average of resources consumed per case. For example, a case assigned to a DRG with a weight of 2.0 would, on average, require twice the amount of resources as the average case (i.e., a weight of 1.0). Periodic adjustments in DRG classifications and weighting factors are made by HCFA to reflect changes in resource consumption, treatment patterns, technology, and other factors that may affect the relative use of hospital resources. Generally, updates to the list of DRGs and cost weights are issued by HCFA in September of each year.

Each Medicare discharge is assigned to only one DRG regardless of the number of services furnished or the number of days of care provided. First, the physician records the patient's principal diagnosis, any additional diagnoses,

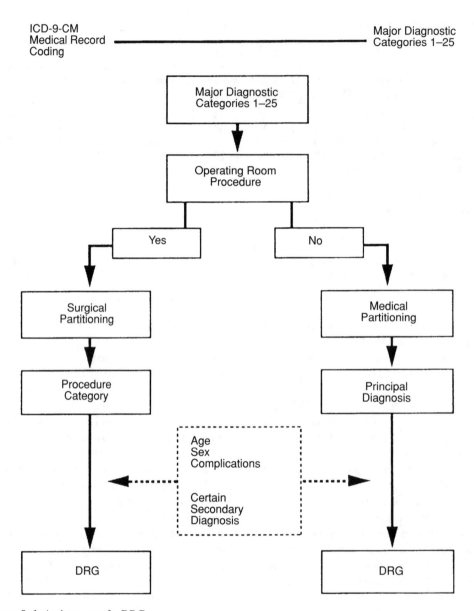

Figure 9–1 Assignment of a DRG

and procedures performed. The hospital expresses this information on the patient's bill using classifications and terminology consistent with the *International Classification of Diseases, 9th Revision, Clinical Modification* (ICD-9-CM). The principal diagnosis, up to four secondary diagnoses, the principal procedure, and

additional procedures are reported along with the patient's age, sex, and discharge status to the hospital's fiscal intermediary with the hospital's request for payment.

The fiscal intermediary enters this information into its claims system and subjects the data to a series of automated screens called the Medicare code editor (MCE). These screens identify cases that require further review before being classified into a DRG. Cases are then classified by a computer program (grouper) into the appropriate DRG. DRGs are organized into 25 major diagnostic categories (MDCs). The principle diagnosis (the medical condition ultimately determined to have caused the hospitalization) determines the MDC assignment. Patients in each MDC are subsequently assigned to a specific DRG, depending on certain variables. Within most MDCs, cases are divided into surgical DRGs (based on a hierarchy that orders individual procedures or groups of procedures by resource intensity) and medical DRGs. The medical DRGs are generally differentiated on the basis of the principal diagnosis. Both medical and surgical cases may be further differentiated based on age, sex, and the presence or absence of complications or comorbidities. With some exceptions, the grouper does not consider other procedures, such as nonsurgical procedures or minor procedures that generally do not require the use of an operating room. The typical DRG assignment process is shown in Figure 9–1.

Hospitals that are dissatisfied with the intermediary's decision regarding DRG assignment must request a review within 60 days after the date a claim is paid. The hospital may submit additional information as part of its request. The fiscal intermediary or the peer review organization (PRO) then reviews the case, and, if appropriate, changes the DRG classification.

Because of its extensive use of averages, a major shortcoming of the DRG payment mechanism is its failure to take into account the severity of a patient's illness. Current payment policies for both cost and day outliers do not adequately address the severity of illness issue. Congress has directed the HCFA to evaluate a variety of patient classification systems to address this shortcoming of the current system and to assist the HCFA in measuring and monitoring the quality of care. According to the HCFA, the process of evaluating various severity of illness methodologies, as well as refining DRG classifications, is still underway. Currently, there is no

deadline by which HCFA must select or recommend a particular severity of illness methodology (see Table 9–4).

Hospital Payment under PPS

The Medicare PPS generally applies to hospital fiscal years beginning on or after October 1, 1983. On the surface, the program initially appeared to simplify the process of reimbursing hospitals because it provided predetermined, fixed-price payments. However, PPS has proven to be much more complicated than was anticipated initially because of the lack of predictability of the payment rates; ongoing capital cost payment uncertainties; continued modifications to medical education payments; and a range of other regulatory actions motivated by federal deficit reduction initiatives.

When Congress approved the PPS, it initially established a three-year phase-in period to ease the transition from cost-based reimbursement to the fixed-price PPS. The phase-in period, which was subsequently extended to five years, is shown in the transition schedule in Table 9–5. During the phase-in period, Medicare payments were based on a blend of hospital-specific rates and regional and national DRG rates (federal rates). The base period for PPS was each hospital's fiscal year ended during the period from September 30, 1982, through September 29, 1983. The hospital-specific rate was established based on each hospital's allowable cost-per-case during the base period, trended forward for inflation. As shown in Tables 9–5 and 9–6, the federal rate was comprised of regional and national components during the transition period. Also, note that the hospital-specific portion of the blended rate changes was based on the cost reporting period of the hospital while, in general, the federal rate changes were based on the federal fiscal year.

The DRG payment rates are the essence of the PPS. They represent fixed payment amounts for each Medicare patient, regardless of the patient's length of stay or use of resources (with the exception of incremental payments for outli-

Table 9–4 Top Ten DRGs by Volume (Federal Fiscal Year 1989)

DRG	Description	Volume Ranking	Fiscal 1984 Cost Weights	Fiscal 1990 Cost Weights	Fiscal 1991 Cost Weights	Percent Change in Cost Weights 1984–1991
127	Heart Failure and Shock	1	1.0408	1.0169	1.0040	(3.5%)
140	Angina Pectoris	2	0.7548	0.6387	0.6296	(16.6%)
89	Simple Pneumonia and Pleurisy Age > 17 with C.C.	3	1.1029	1.2059	1.1878	7.7%
14	Spec Cerebrovascular Disorders Ex TIA	4	1.3527	1.2260	1.2212	(9.7%)
182	Esophagitis, Gastroent., and Misc. Digest. Dis. Age > 17 with C.C.	5	0.6185	0.7414	0.7497	21.2%
96	Bronchitis and Asthma Age > 17 with C.C.	6	0.7996	0.9734	0.9568	19.7%
209	Major Joint and Limb Reattachment Procedure	7	2.2912	2.3437	2.3689	3.4%
296	Nutritional and Misc. Metabolic Disorders Age > 17 with C.C.	8	0.8979	0.9404	0.9387	4.5%
138	Cardiac Arrhythmia and Conduction Disorders with C.C.	9	0.9297	0.8707	0.8331	(10.4%)
121	Circ.Disorders W AMI & CV Comp. Disch Alive	10	1.8648	1.6228	1.5772	(15.4%)

Weighted Average Change in Cost Weights—Based on 1989 Volumes   (1.5%)

Source: Health Care Financing Administration data

ers). These fixed prices vary depending on whether the hospital's location is urban or rural and are adjusted for differences in area wage levels.

During the transition period, the wage-adjusted federal rates were blended with the hospital-specific rate in accordance with the transition schedule (see Table 9–5) and multiplied by the relative weight factor for the particular DRG to which the patient had been assigned to determine the specific amount the hospital would be paid for that patient. Now that the transition to the federal rate is complete, only the federal rate is used in the calculation. Coinsurance and deductibles due from the patient are subtracted from this amount to arrive at the amount of Medicare payment to the hospital.

The federal rates are updated annually. Typically, preliminary federal payment rate schedules are published in June and final federal rates are published in early September of each year. In recent years, congressional "tinkering" and deficit reduction initiatives have delayed the annual determination of final federal rates to as late as November or December. Specific urban and rural federal payment rates are established for each of the nine census regions (regional rates) in addition to the national urban and rural payment rates. The federal rate is a blend of the regional and national rates during the transition period as shown in Table 9–6.

Calculating PPS Payment Rates

Described below is the method for calculating the adjusted *federal payment* rate for a PPS hospital:

1. Determine the appropriate regional and national payment rates, based on the hospital's geographic location.
2. Multiply the labor-related component of the payment rate(s) by the appropriate area wage index. Applicable area wage indices are published by HCFA in the *Federal Register*.
3. Add the respective labor-adjusted component to the nonlabor component for the applicable rate(s).

Table 9–5 Transition Schedule for Hospital-Specific and Federal Percentages

Cost Reporting Period Beginning On or After	Hospital-Specific Percentage	Federal Percentage*
October 1, 1983	75%	25%
October 1, 1984	50%	50%
October 1, 1985		
–The first seven months of the cost reporting period	50%	50%
–The remaining five months of the cost reporting period	45%	55%
October 1, 1986	25%	75%
October 1, 1987		
–The first 51 days of the cost reporting period	25%	75%
–The remaining days of the cost reporting period	0%	100%
October 1, 1988, and thereafter	0%	100%

*The regional and national components of the federal rate are shown in Table 9-6.

Exhibit 9–1 illustrates how a blended PPS payment rate is calculated.

The federal portion of the DRG base rates is supposed to be adjusted for inflation on an annual basis. Initially, the annual update factor was defined as the Hospital Market Basket Index plus one percent. Because of federal deficit reduction initiatives and allegations of "excess hospital profits" on Medicare business, the annual updating process has become highly political.

Patient Transfers

PPS payments are made on a per-discharge basis. Under PPS, a discharge is defined as occurring when a patient is formally released from the hospital, dies in the hospital, or is transferred to another hospital or unit that is excluded from participation in PPS. Accordingly, if the patient is transferred to another hospital that participates in PPS, a discharge, as defined under PPS, has not occurred. Because the prospective payment rates are designed to compensate hospitals for a patient's complete treatment, payment is adjusted when a hospital releases a patient without meeting the patient discharge requirements. Adjustments to PPS payments for transfer situations are handled as described below.

If a patient is transferred to another hospital that participates in PPS, the hospital transferring the patient is paid on a per diem rate basis, not to exceed that hospital's DRG-specific payment rate. The per diem rate is that hospital's DRG-specific rate, divided by the mean length of stay for the specific DRG to which the patient is assigned. The hospital from which the patient is ultimately discharged receives the full prospective payment rate.

Table 9–6 Regional and National Percentages Comprising the Federal Rate

Federal Fiscal Year Beginning	Regional Percentage	National Percentage
October 1, 1983	100%	0%
October 1, 1984	75%	25%
October 1, 1985	75%	25%
October 1, 1986	50%	50%
October 1, 1987		
–October 1, 1987 through November 20, 1987	50%	50%
–November 21, 1987 and subsequent periods	0%	100%

Exhibit 9–1 Sample Calculation: PPS Payment Rate (Excluding indirect medical education and disproportionate share adjustments)

Assumptions:
Patient discharged on April 30, 1990
DRG assigned: Simple Pneumonia and Pleurisy
        (DRG #89)
Hospital location: Nashville, Tennessee
Hospital fiscal year: June 30, 1990
Regional and national rates from *Federal Register*,
    April 20, 1990
Area wage index factor from Table 4a of *Federal
    Register*, September 1, 1989
Transition percentages from Table 9–6

Step 1 *Regional Portion*

	Regional Rate	Area Wage Factor	Adjusted Rate
Labor	$2,385.26	.8893	$2,121.21
Nonlabor	722.37	N/A	722.37
Regional Portion of			
Federal Payment Rate			$2,843.58 (A)

Step 2 *National Portion*

	Regional Rate	Area Wage Factor	Adjusted Rate
Labor	$2,467.88	.8893	$2,194.69
Nonlabor	874.11	N/A	874.11
National Portion of			
Federal Payment Rate			$3,068.80 (B)

Step 3 *Federal Portion Blending of Regional and National Rates*

		Blend Percentage from Table 9–6	Amount
Regional Portion (A)	$2,843.58	0%	$0.00
National Portion (B)	3,068.80	100%	3,068.80
Federal Payment Rate			$3,068.80

Step 4 *Calculation of DRG Payment*

		Transition Percentage from Table 9–5	Amount
Federal Payment Rate			
(Calculated Above)	$3,068.80	100%	$3,068.80
Blended Base DRG Payment Rate			3,068.80
DRG Cost Weight (DRG #89)			x 1.2059
Blended DRG Payment Rate—DRG #89			$3,700.67

Exhibit 9-2 gives examples that illustrate how to calculate payments to hospitals in transfer situations.

Outlier Payments

Under the PPS, additional payments are made for outlier cases; current legislation limits these payments to approximately five percent of total federal PPS payments. Since the inception of PPS, this target percentage has ranged from six percent in the initial year of the program to the current five percent level that has prevailed since fiscal year 1985. The criteria discussed below are used to identify outliers. If a case qualifies as both a day and a cost outlier, the claim is paid at the higher of the two amounts.

A discharge is considered to be a day outlier if the patient's length of stay (excluding days not covered by Medicare Part A) exceeds the geometric mean length of stay for discharges in that DRG by the lesser of 28 days or 3.0 standard deviations from the mean length of stay (day threshold). Final regulations for fiscal year 1991 increased the day outlier thresholds to the lesser of 29 days or 3.0 standard deviations. Hospitals receive an additional per diem payment for each covered day of care exceeding the day threshold. This amount is equal to 60 percent (marginal cost factor) of the average federal per diem rate for the applicable DRG. Burn cases are also paid based on a 60 percent marginal cost factor. The average per diem payment is derived by dividing the wage-adjusted federal payment rate for the

Exhibit 9–2 Sample Calculation: Payments to Hospitals in Transfer Situations (Excluding indirect medical education and disproportionate share adjustments)

Example A:

Hospital A (transferring hospital)—LOS 2 days, DRG Y
(Blended payment rate is $6,000.)
Hospital B (receiving and discharging hospital)—DRG Y
(Blended payment rate is $8,000.)
(Mean length of stay for DRG Y equals 10 days.)

Payment:

Hospital A—2 days x $6,000 / 10 days = $1,200

Hospital B—$8,000 when discharging = $8,000

Total Medicare payment for patient = $9,200

Example B:

Hospital A (transferring hospital)—LOS 4 days, DRG X
(Blended payment rate is $16,000 and the mean length of stay is 8 days.)
Hospital B (both receiving and subsequently transferring)—LOS 4 days, DRG Y
(Blended payment rate is $10,000; the mean length of stay is 10 days.)
Hospital C (receiving and discharging)—DRG Y
(Blended payment rate is $15,000.)

Payment:

Hospital A—4 days x $16,000 / 8 days = $8,000

Hospital B—4 days x $10,000 / 10 days = $4,000

Hospital C—$15,000 when discharging = $15,000

Total Medicare payment for patient = $27,000

DRG by its geometric mean length of stay.

The following example illustrates how the additional payment would be determined for a day outlier in federal fiscal year 1990.

> Hospital X is a teaching hospital located in Nashville, Tennessee. Hospital X has a ratio of interns and residents to beds of .1 and is eligible for a disproportionate share adjustment factor of five percent. Mrs. Smith was admitted to Hospital X on July 3, 1990, and was discharged on August 31, 1990.
>
> Mrs. Smith's stay was classified in DRG 89. Because Mrs. Smith's 59-day stay exceeds the 35-day length-of-stay outlier threshold for DRG 89, Hospital X is eligible for payment for 24 outlier days in addition to the otherwise applicable prospective payment. The amount of Hospital X's total DRG payment for this case, including the outlier payment, is calculated as illustrated in Exhibit 9–3.

A discharge that qualifies as a day outlier may also qualify as a high cost outlier if the cost of covered services exceeds the cost threshold established by HCFA. The hospital is paid the *greater of* the day outlier payment amount of the cost outlier payment amount. For federal fiscal year 1991 (October 1, 1990, through September 30, 1991), the cost threshold is the greater of two times the federal rate for the DRG or $35,000, both adjusted for area wage differences. For high cost outliers, hospitals receive an additional payment (marginal cost factor) equal to 75 percent (90 percent for burn cases) of the difference between the hospital's adjusted cost for the discharge and the cost threshold. (During the transition period, this amount was multiplied by the applicable federal blend percentage.) The adjusted cost of the discharge is determined by multiplying charges for covered services by the hospital's ratio of cost to charges for its most recently audited cost reporting period, and dividing by the indirect medical education adjustment factor and/or the disproportionate share adjustment factor, where applicable.

Pass Through Costs

The Medicare PPS DRG payment rates represent payment for all hospital inpatient costs ex-

Exhibit 9–3 Sample Calculation: Day Outlier Patient

Step 1
Computation of Federal Rate (Excludes Payment for Capital, Indirect Medical Education Costs, and Disproportionate Share Hospital Adjustments)
National Other Urban Standardized*

Amounts:

Blended Base DRG Payment Rate (from Exhibit 9–1)	$3,068.80
DRG Cost Weight	x 1.2059
Blended DRG Payment Rate (DRG #89)	$3,700.67

Step 2
Computation of Day Outlier Payments

Outlier days	59–35 = 24
DRG 89 geometric mean length of stay	7.2 days
Marginal cost factor	60%

Outlier payment (excludes adjustments for disproportionate share and indirect medical education costs) = Number of outlier days x (Total federal prospective payment ÷ Geometric mean length of stay for DRG) x Marginal cost factor = (24) x ($3,700.67 ÷ 7.2) x (.60) = $7,401.34

Total Day Outlier Payments =	$7,401.34

Step 3
Computation of Federal DRG Revenue

Regular federal payment	$3,700.67
Day outlier payment	7,401.34
Total federal DRG revenue	$11,102.01

Step 4
Computation of Indirect Medical Education Adjustment
Intern and resident/bed ratio = .1
Indirect medical education adjustment factor
$1.89[(1 + .1)^{.405} - 1] = .0744$ or 7.44%
Indirect medical education adjustment = Total federal DRG revenue x Indirect medical education adjustment factor = $11,102.01) x (.0744) = $825.99

Step 5
Computation of Disproportionate Share Payment
Disproportionate share adjustment factor = 5% or .05
Disproportionate share payment = Total federal DRG revenue x Disproportionate share adjustment factor = ($11,102.01) x (.05) = $555.10

Step 6
Computation of Total Federal DRG Payments

Total federal DRG revenue (including outlier payments)	$11,102.01
Indirect medical education adjustment	825.99
Disproportionate share payment	555.10
Total federal DRG payment	$12,483.10

*Region is not subject to the regional payment floor.

cept for those defined as pass through costs. Pass through costs are not subject to PPS, but continue to be reimbursed on a reasonable cost basis, subject to specific limits. Pass through costs include:

- capital costs
- graduate medical education costs

In addition, teaching hospitals receive an additional payment to defray the indirect costs of medical education. In a health reform environment, and to dissuade the education of specialists, these payments are threatened.

The data included in Table 9–7 illustrate the significance of pass through costs to PPS hospitals.

Capital Costs

When PPS was signed into law in April 1983, capital and related costs were to be excluded from it until October 1, 1986. On June 3, 1986, proposed rules to implement prospective payment for capital and related costs were published. However, on July 2, 1986, the Urgent

Supplemental Appropriations Act for fiscal year 1987 postponed the implementation of prospective payment for capital and related costs until October 1, 1987. The Omnibus Budget Reconciliation Act of 1987 further postponed prospective payment for capital and related costs until October 1, 1991. Until that time, capital and related costs continue to be paid on a reasonable cost basis, subject to certain payment reduction amounts discussed herein.

Since the inception of PPS, various prospective capital payment methodologies have been proposed by the Administration, the Prospective Payment Assessment Commission (ProPAC), Congress, and hospital industry groups. Determining whether capital costs can or should be included in DRG rates and establishing the appropriate amounts have been highly controversial issues. The federal government is likely to continue to take actions to minimize capital payments to hospitals as a means to reduce Medicare outlays.

Prospective capital payment rates will have diverse effects on hospitals depending on:

Table 9–7 Medicare Pass Through Payments As a Percentage of Total Medicare Inpatient Hospital Payments in the Fifth Year of PPS, by Hospital Group

Hospital Group	Capital Payments	Direct Medical Education Payments	Combined Total
All hospitals	10.1%	2.9%	13.0%
Urban	10.0	3.3	13.2
Rural	11.0	0.4	11.4
Large urban	9.8	4.2	14.0
Other urban	10.1	2.2	12.2
Rural referral	10.7	1.0	11.7
Sole community	11.0	0.2	11.2
Other rural	11.2	0.1	11.2
Major teaching	7.4	9.3	16.7
Other teaching	9.3	3.8	13.1
Nonteaching	11.5	0.2	11.7
Disproportionate share:			
Large urban	9.2	6.1	15.3
Other urban	9.9	2.4	12.3
Rural	11.0	0.8	11.8
Nondisproportionate share	10.4	2.0	12.4
Urban <100 beds	11.3	0.3	11.6
Urban 100–249 beds	11.7	1.1	12.8
Urban 250–404 beds	10.0	2.8	12.7
Urban 405–684 beds	8.9	4.7	13.6
Urban 685+ beds	8.0	7.5	15.5
Rural <50 beds	10.3	0.1	10.4
Rural 50–99 beds	11.6	0.1	11.7
Rural 100–169 beds	11.4	0.2	11.6
Rural 170+ beds	10.5	1.1	11.6
Voluntary	9.8	3.2	13.0
Proprietary	13.4	0.5	13.9
Urban government	8.4	3.8	12.2
Rural government	10.4	0.5	10.8

Note: Total pass through payments also include organ acquisition payments and other Medicare inpatient hospital payments not paid under PPS. Only capital and direct medical education payments are included in this table. Excludes hospitals in Maryland and New Jersey.

Source: ProPAC analysis of Medicare Cost Report data from the Health Care Financing Administration.

- the age or condition of the facility
- the level and cost of debt financing
- the amount of new technology previously acquired or needed in the future
- the hospital's Medicare and non-Medicare utilization levels

The variation of capital costs among hospital groups is illustrated in Table 9–8.

Medicare capital cost reimbursement principles have remained largely unchanged since the beginning of the Medicare program in 1966. Under the reasonable cost principles established at that time, providers are reimbursed for the Medicare portion of their capital-related costs.

Medicare regulations define capital costs to include:

- net depreciation expense, adjusted by gains and losses from the disposal of depreciable assets
- leases and rentals
- taxes on land and depreciable assets
- costs of betterments or improvements
- net capital interest expense, offset by a prorated amount of investment income on investments of unrestricted and borrowed funds

Table 9–8 Average Fifty-Year PPS Capital Costs, by Hospital Group

Hospital Group	Average Medicare Inpatient Capital Costs Per Case	Average Capital/ Operating Costs Ratio
All hospitals	$517	.123
Urban	565	.123
Rural	356	.123
Large urban	609	.121
Other urban	518	.126
Rural referral	425	.131
Sole community	353	.117
Other rural	324	.119
Major teaching	676	.102
Other teaching	542	.118
Nonteaching	480	.134
Disproportionate share:		
Large urban	649	.117
Other urban	528	.125
Rural	337	.123
Nondisproportionate share	495	.125
Urban <100 beds	506	.132
Urban 100–249 beds	583	.141
Urban 250–404 beds	548	.121
Urban 405–684 beds	565	.114
Urban 685+ beds	628	.109
Rural <50 beds	283	.107
Rural 50–99 beds	337	.121
Rural 100–169 beds	385	.131
Rural 170+ beds	403	.126
Voluntary	521	.122
Proprietary	596	.162
Urban government	492	.097
Rural government	318	.111

Source: ProPAC analysis of Medicare Cost Report data from the Health Care Financing Administration.

- costs of minor equipment, if depreciated over three years
- insurance on depreciable assets
- capital costs of related supplier organizations, subject to reasonableness
- capital costs of unrelated suppliers, only if:

  1. Capital equipment is leased or rented by the provider.
  2. The equipment is on the provider's premises.
  3. The charge for capital equipment is separately stated.

- return on equity for investor-owned providers (phased out)

The regulations define betterments and improvements as those that extend the estimated useful life of an asset at least two years beyond its original estimated useful life, or that significantly improve an asset's productivity. Betterments and improvements are depreciated over the remaining useful life of an asset.

The following costs are specifically excluded from capital costs:

- repair or maintenance expenses, including service agreements involving lease or rental arrangements
- interest expense on working capital loans
- general liability insurance
- taxes not assessed against property
- minor equipment expensed

It is in a hospital's best interest to capitalize equipment or other property that can legitimately be considered as capital items as defined in the regulations. In addition, because capital costs are, under present law, to be folded into the prospective DRG rates, it is advisable to depreciate assets as rapidly as possible within existing Medicare guidelines. Medicare generally follows the useful life guidelines set forth in the American Hospital Association's publication titled *AHA Guide to Depreciable Lives*.

Significant changes in capital cost reimbursement occurred as part of the Congressional budget balancing efforts of 1986 and 1987. The Omnibus Budget Reconciliation Act of 1986 (OBRA-86) began a process of defined reductions in Medicare's payment for capital costs until such time as a prospective payment system for capital could be implemented. Since OBRA-86, virtually all budget reconciliation amendments have included a continuation of the capital payment reductions. A summary of such reductions is shown in Table 9–9.

On August 30, 1991, HCFA released final rules for implementing a PPS for hospital inpatient capital costs. The final rule, effective for hospital cost reporting periods beginning on or after October 1, 1991, established a payment system that replaced the reasonable cost-based payment methodology with prospective payment for capital-related costs. When fully implemented, the new capital payment system will provide hospitals with a fixed payment amount (adjusted for each hospital's case mix) for each Medicare admission.

At inception, the PPS capital payment regulations utilized a standard federal rate for all capital-related inpatient hospital costs based on the estimated fiscal year 1992 national average Medicare cost per discharge for hospitals paid under PPS. The federal rate is updated each year based on HCFA's projected increase in capital costs, and is adjusted to account for each hospital's case mix, number of patient transfers, extraordinarily costly or lengthy cases (outliers), geographic location, and higher costs experienced by certain hospitals that treat a disproportionately high number of indigent cases or that have teaching programs. A hospital-specific capital payment rate was determined using the hospital's cost report covering the most recent 12-month cost reporting period that *ended* prior to December 31, 1990.

Under the PPS capital payment methodology, a hospital is paid using the following two methodologies:

1. If the hospital-specific rate is below the federal rate, then the hospital is paid under the fully prospective payment rate methodology.

Table 9–9 OBRA Reductions in Capital Cost Reimbursement

	Hospitals Subject to PPS	
Period Covered	Inpatient Services	Outpatient Services
Historical Information:		
October 1, 1987–November 20, 1987	3.50%	—
November 21, 1987–December 31, 1987	7.00%*	—
January 1, 1988–March 31, 1988	12.00%*	—
April 1, 1988–September 30, 1988	12.00%	—
October 1, 1988–September 30, 1989	15.00%	—
October 1, 1989–October 15, 1989	—	15.000%**
October 16, 1989–December 31, 1989		
OBRA Reduction Factor	—	15.000%
Plus Gramm-Rudman Reduction	2.092%	2.092%
Effective Capital Reduction Rate	2.092%	17.092%
January 1, 1990–September 30, 1990	15.00%	See below
January 1, 1990–March 31, 1990		
OBRA Reduction Factor		15.000%
Plus Gramm-Rudman Reduction		2.092%
Effective Capital Reduction Rate		17.092%
April 1, 1990–September 30, 1990		
OBRA Reduction Factor		15.000%
Plus Gramm-Rudman Reduction		1.400%
Effective Capital Reduction Rate		16.400%
October 1, 1990–September 30, 1991	15.00%	15.000%

*Further increased by 2.324 Gramm-Rudman reduction factor
**Because of a drafting error in the budget legislation, capital costs applicable to outpatient services were reduced to 85% of actual costs retroactively to October 1, 1989.

2. If the hospital-specific rate is above the federal rate, then the hospital is paid under the "hold-harmless" rate payment methodology.

A hospital paid under the fully prospective payment rate methodology receives a payment based on a blend of its hospital-specific rate and the federal rate based on the transition schedule shown in Table 9–10. (Under this option, the fiscal year 1994 rate would be based on a blend of 70 percent of the hospital-specific rate and 30 percent of the federal rate. Over the next 7 years, the federal portion of the payment will increase by 10 percentage points per year, while the hospital-specific rate will decrease by the same percentage. In the seventh year, hospitals will be paid 100 percent of the federal rate.) This transition schedule applies only to those hospitals that will receive higher payments under the fully prospective payment rate.

A hospital paid under the "hold-harmless" rate payment methodology receives a payment per discharge based on *the higher of:*

1. Eighty-five percent (90 percent in the proposed rule) of the reasonable costs associated with "old" capital (a "hold-harmless" payment) *plus* a payment for new capital based on the proportion of the new Medicare inpatient capital costs to total Medicare inpatient capital costs multiplied by the newly created federal rate. (Note: hold-harmless payments for old capital will be made at the rate of 100 percent for sole community hospitals); or

2. One-hundred percent of the federal rate.

The PPS capital rules provide a hospital with the opportunity to recalculate its hospital-specific rate in subsequent years to reflect changes in old capital costs as determined in a cost re-

Table 9–10 Fully Prospective Payment Rate Methodology Transition Schedule

Cost Reporting Period Beginning In	Hospital-Specific Blend Percentage	Federal Blend Percentage
Fiscal Year 1994	70.00%	30.00%
Fiscal Year 1995	60.00%	40.00%
Fiscal Year 1996	50.00%	50.00%
Fiscal Year 1997	40.00%	60.00%
Fiscal Year 1998	30.00%	70.00%
Fiscal Year 1999	20.00%	80.00%
Fiscal Year 2000	10.00%	90.00%
Fiscal Year 2001	0.00%	100.00%

porting period subsequent to the base year. "New" capital costs are excluded from the redetermination of the hospital-specific rate. Such requests for redeterminations may be requested for any cost reporting period subsequent to the base period but no later than the later of the hospital's cost reporting period beginning in fiscal year 1994 or the cost reporting period beginning after obligated capital that is recognized as old capital is put in use.

Because of the significant decrease in the federal rate included in the final rule for fiscal year 1994, HCFA has been directed to "redetermine" every hospital's payment methodology using their cost report for the cost reporting period beginning during fiscal year 1994.

"Old" capital costs are defined as allowable interest and depreciation expense related to capital assets that were put in use by December 31, 1990, or that were legally obligated through a "contractual agreement" entered into on or before December 31, 1990, and put in use for patient care before October 1, 1994. The regulations also include a number of other specific circumstances where assets may be treated as if they had been legally obligated at December 31, 1990, and accordingly recognized as old capital.

"New" capital costs are defined as allowable capital-related costs that are related to assets that were first put into use for patient care after December 31, 1990, and those allowable capital-related costs related to assets in use prior to December 31, 1990, that are excluded from the definition of "old" capital costs.

Graduate Medical Education (GME) Costs

The Medicare PPS provides for the reimbursement of defined medical education costs in addition to the prospective DRG payment rates. Medical education costs are excluded from the prospective DRG rates and have been addressed separately in order to recognize the direct and indirect costs associated with approved medical education programs. Reimbursement for medical education is segregated into direct and indirect medical education.

On September 29, 1989, the HCFA issued the long-awaited final regulations pertaining to Medicare's reimbursement of GME costs. These final regulations implement the direct medical education provisions of the Consolidated Omnibus Budget Reconciliation Act of 1985 (COBRA) and the Omnibus Budget Reconciliation Act of 1986 (OBRA-86). Prior to those acts, direct costs of GME programs were reimbursed on a reasonable cost basis under the initial PPS regulations. The final GME regulations provide for Medicare payment based on the following method:

1. Determine a fixed, base-year amount per intern/resident.

2. Update the base-year amount for inflation.

3. Multiply the updated amount by the number of allowable intern and resident full-time equivalents (FTEs) for the cost reporting period.

4. Determine Medicare's portion of allowable graduate medical education costs based on the ratio of Medicare patient days to total patient days multiplied by the product of step three above.

5. Allocate Medicare's portion of allowable graduate medical education costs derived in step four to Part A and Part B based on the ratio of Medicare's share of reasonable costs excluding GME attributable to Parts A and B.

Implementation of the final GME regulations has been applied retroactively to hospital cost reporting periods beginning on or after July 1, 1985. The implementation of these final regulations is expected to result in retroactive recoupment of approximately $400 million from teaching institutions.

The new reimbursement methodology determines a hospital-specific base year per intern/resident amount by dividing a hospital's allowable costs of direct GME by the number of its interns and residents. The base year is the cost reporting period beginning on or after October 1, 1983, and before October 1, 1984 (federal fiscal year 1984). In establishing the base year per intern/resident amount, HCFA has instructed Medicare intermediaries to reexamine or reaudit FY 1984 GME costs for nonallowable and misclassified costs. This is to occur even if the base year is beyond the normal three-year period for reopening a cost report.

In its audit instructions to intermediaries, HCFA has identified certain costs that are to be considered nonallowable GME costs. Those costs include GME costs allocated to the nursery, research activities, and other non-reimbursable cost centers. Some examples of misclassifications of operating costs as GME costs would be unrelated physicians' costs, administrative and general service costs, meal costs, travel costs, and medical library costs. GME costs incurred in distinct-part units or other PPS excluded units that participate in Medicare are included in allowable GME costs. Because the payment methodology sets future payments utilizing the FY 1984 base year as the initial starting point, it is critical that all allowable GME costs be identified. During the audit process, the hospital has an opportunity to present documentation of any factors that should be taken into account in the final determination of the base year per intern/resident amounts.

If during the audit process the intermediary determines that certain operating costs were inappropriately classified as GME in the 1984 base year, the intermediary will propose an adjustment to have them treated as normal operating costs and excluded from allowable GME costs. In this situation, the hospital can request its intermediary to reopen all PPS transition years and recalculate the hospital-specific portion of the PPS rates for those years. Hospitals not subject to PPS may also request to have their target rate recomputed to reflect adjustments for misclassified costs. The hospital must request this action of the intermediary. This request must be received no later than 180 days after the date of the notice by the intermediary of the hospital's average per intern/resident amount, and it must include sufficient documentation to demonstrate that the adjustment is warranted. If the hospital's PPS or TEFRA base-period cost report is not subject to reopening, the hospital's reopening request must explicitly state that the review is limited to the one issue, i.e., misclassified GME costs or misclassified operating costs that affect its average per intern/resident amount.

Intermediaries have been instructed not to increase 1984 base year GME costs for costs that were initially misclassified by the hospital as operating costs in the 1984 base period unless the hospital can demonstrate that the same misclassification occurred in its PPS/TEFRA base period. Hospitals will be notified by the Medicare intermediary as to their base year GME costs per intern/resident. From the date of notification, hospitals have 180 days to appeal the base year determinations, as well as to request an adjustment to the hospital-specific or TEFRA rate.

Base year GME costs are only one component of the formula in computing the base year per intern/resident amount; the other component is the base year number of interns/residents. The number of residents in the base year is generally equal to the total number of interns/residents working in the hospital complex; this includes hospital-based providers and subproviders. No matter how many hours an intern or resident works, he or she cannot be counted as more than one FTE. Interns/residents assigned to the nursery, to research activities, and to other nonallowable cost centers are to be included in the count. However, costs attributable to interns/residents in these areas will not be included in base year costs. This mismatching of costs and counts reduces the per intern/resident amount and likely will be challenged during the appeal process. Hospitals are required to document the number of interns/residents in the base year. The best documentation consists of time sheets or scheduled assignments. If auditable documentation is not available, the intermediaries have been instructed to contact HCFA for further instructions.

In addition to prospective DRG payments for inpatient hospital services, teaching hospitals receive a payment adjustment for the indirect costs of medical education, which is intended to compensate for the incremental, but not separately identified, patient care costs associated with approved intern and resident programs. Those costs may reflect factors such as an increase in the number of tests and procedures ordered by interns and residents relative to the number ordered by more experienced physicians or the need of hospitals with teaching programs to maintain more detailed medical records. In establishing the additional payment for indirect medical education costs, Congress emphasized its view that these teaching expenses are not to be subject to the same standards of efficiency implied under PPS, but rather that they are legitimate expenses involved in the postgraduate medical education of physicians which the Medicare program has historically recognized as worthy of support under the reimbursement system.

Because the indirect costs of medical education are defined in terms of increased operating costs, they are not separately identifiable on the cost report or in other financial or accounting records. Instead, these incremental costs have been statistically estimated as a function of teaching intensity. A proxy measure—the hospital's ratio of the number of interns and residents to the number of beds—has been used to measure teaching intensity. The coefficient describing this statistical relationship has been expressed as a percentage and applied as the indirect medical education factor.

To determine the payment estimated for indirect medical education, the formulas given in

---

Exhibit 9–4 Formulas for Computing Indirect Medical Education Adjustment Factors

Formula Effective for Discharges through April 30, 1986

$$.1159 \times \left(\frac{\text{Number of FTE Interns \& Residents}}{\text{Number of Beds}} \div .1 \right) =$$

Formula Effective for Discharges from May 1, 1986 through September 30, 1988

$$2 \times \left[\left(1 - \frac{\text{Number of FTE Interns \& Residents}}{\text{Number of Beds}} \right)^{.405} - 1 \right] =$$

Formula Effective for Discharges from October 1, 1988 through September 30, 1995

$$1.89 \times \left[\left(1 - \frac{\text{Number of FTE Interns \& Residents}}{\text{Number of Beds}} \right)^{.405} - 1 \right] =$$

Exhibit 9–4 are applied to the federal component of PPS payments (including outliers but excluding disproportionate share payments). The formulas were not applied to the hospital-specific component of PPS rates during the transition years because indirect medical education costs were included in the base-year costs that were used to establish that component.

CONCLUSION

The rapid changes in the industry and the assumed evolution to negotiated rates of payment motivated by managed care might appear to diminish the importance of the current methodologies for reimbursement. Whether capitated methods replace the current methodologies and their regulatory underpinnings may be moot because the PPS/DRGs are more than a reimbursement system.

This chapter, and Chapter 10, describe not only reimbursement methods, but approaches by which the consumption of hospital resources (human, equipment, etc.) can be measured and accounted for. This is even more true of the Medicare resource-based relative value scales for physician reimbursement. In a more competitive, revenue-restrained environment, the need for measures-of-resource use seems apparent. It may take years for the industry to evolve, but there also is a strong likelihood that PPS/DRGs will remain well into the future—perhaps, in the end, as an important means of financial and resource management rather than reimbursement.

MICHAEL J. DALTON has been a Consulting Partner in Health Care and Life Sciences at KPMG Peat Marwick for 7 years. He is also Practicing Director of Reimbursement and Financial Planning for the New York tri-state region. Mr. Dalton was also employed for 14 years as Vice President of the Provider Audit and Reimbursement Department at Empire Blue Cross Blue Shield. He received his Bachelor's degree in Business Administration from St. John's University and is a member of AICPA, NYSSCPA, and HFMA.

Chapter 10

Outpatient Hospital Reimbursement

Michael J. Dalton

Historically, a hospital's main purpose was to provide treatment in an inpatient setting that was usually accompanied by care in an emergency room and possibly in an outpatient clinic. During the past decade, however, the trend has been toward health care delivery in the outpatient setting, which has included not only emergency rooms and clinics, but private referred ambulatory services and ambulatory surgery. As a result, hospital outpatient service has increased steadily and currently accounts for approximately 30 percent of a hospital's total revenue.

Most health insurers provide coverage for services delivered in both the outpatient and inpatient settings. While most commercial insurance companies and the Blue Cross and Blue Shield plans reimburse hospitals for their care based on hospital charges, the Medicare program has developed its own methodology for reimbursement of outpatient hospital care. This chapter describes this payment methodology, as Medicare continues to be a growing source of revenue for hospitals.

The Omnibus Budget Reconciliation Acts of 1986 and 1987 contain a number of provisions that affect Medicare payments for outpatient services. The legislation required that, begin-

ning July 1, 1987, hospitals report claims for outpatient services using the HCFA's Common Procedure Coding System and that, by 1991, the Secretary of Health and Human Services develop designs and models for a prospective payment system for other hospital outpatient services.

Specifically, the acts required "bundling" of outpatient services rendered on or after July 1, 1987, outlined a new payment system for certain outpatient ambulatory surgical procedures performed by hospitals, and placed a cap on cost-based reimbursement for hospital outpatient radiology procedures equal to the prevailing charges for similar services provided in physician offices.

The Budget Reconciliation Act for fiscal year 1991 made several changes that affect payment for outpatient services. These changes include a 15 percent reduction of capital payments applicable to outpatient services for payments attributable to portions of cost reporting periods occurring during federal fiscal year 1991; reduction of capital payments by 10 percent for payments attributable to portions of cost reporting periods occurring during federal fiscal year 1992, 1993, 1994, or 1995; and a 5.8 percent payment reduction for outpatient hospital services that are reimbursed on a cost-related basis, for portions of cost reporting periods occurring during fiscal years 1991, 1992, 1993, 1994, or 1995. This 5.8 percent payment reduction also applies to the cost portions of blended payment limits for ambulatory surgery and radiology services.

BUNDLING OF OUTPATIENT SERVICES

Effective with services furnished on or after July 1, 1987, all hospitals must agree to furnish, directly or under arrangement, all items and nonphysician services received by Medicare patients that can be covered as hospital outpatient services when these services are furnished during an encounter with a patient registered by the hospital as an outpatient, or diagnostic procedures or tests (e.g., magnetic resonance imaging [MRI] procedures) furnished outside the hospital but ordered during or as a result of an encounter with an outpatient, if the results of the procedure or test must be returned to the hospital for evaluation.

Bundling is required not only for diagnostic and therapeutic services furnished during such an encounter, but also for prosthetic devices (e.g., intraocular lenses implanted or fitted during an encounter in the hospital). Ambulance service to or from a patient's residence is not subject to the bundling requirement. However, bundling is required for transportation of patients by ambulance or other vehicle regularly used between the hospital and diagnostic testing site for a test that is bundled.

The application of the above requirements requires considerable interpretation. Guidelines issued by Medicare to date have been limited. In a briefing to its members, the American Hospital Association provided the following guidelines to assist in evaluating the impact of bundling:

1. *Definition of an encounter:* An encounter is defined as a direct personal exchange in a hospital between a patient and a physician or other practitioner operating within hospital staff bylaws and state licensure law, for the purpose of seeking care and rendering health care services.

2. *Services provided under arrangement:* All services ordered during any patient/physician encounter that occurs in a hospital must be provided by the hospital either directly or under arrangement with another provider. The term *under arrangement* simply means that the hospital is purchasing the service from an outside provider, and that it assumes responsibility for those services. Under the bundling provisions, all services provided to hospital patients must be provided either directly or under arrangement. Thus, any service ordered during an encounter will be handled by Medicare as though it was provided under arrangement, whether or not the hospital in which the encounter occurred and the provider of the service actually have entered into a formal agreement. A hospital must have agreements with all providers of services ordered during an encounter occurring in the hospital; the fact that a hospital may not have an agreement with a particular provider does not change the responsibility of the hospital to purchase the services ordered on behalf of the patient.

3. *Definition of a bundle:* All services ordered during an encounter will be part of the bundle, whether provided by the hospital or a provider other than the hospital. If, however, the patient is referred to a second physician, only those services ordered during the encounter between the patient and the first or referring physician must be bundled by the hospital. The encounter between the patient and the second physician forms a second bundle. Presumably, follow-up visits between a patient and a physician will each form a separate bundle together with the services ordered during each follow-up visit.

4. *When bundling is required:* Bundling affects only services provided to hospital

patients. Physicians are not required to bundle their services in a hospital that are not otherwise bundled under Medicare physician billing guidelines. Nor is a hospital required to bundle individual services provided to patients referred to it by physicians or providers other than hospitals. Individual services provided to patients on referral from nonhospital providers form their own bundles. However, the general language cited above does require the bundling of services ordered during an encounter between a member of a hospital's medical staff and a patient if that encounter occurs in a hospital outpatient clinic, emergency department, ambulatory surgical center, or other outpatient treatment area, and if the results of the tests for service are returned to the hospital.

5. *Definition of hospital patients:* The requirements are based on a specific, but somewhat peculiar, definition of a hospital patient. When an encounter between a patient and a physician occurs in a hospital setting, the patient becomes the hospital's patient in the sense that the hospital is financially and otherwise responsible for the services ordered by the patient's physician.

6. *Billing requirements:* Hospitals are affected by the bundling requirements in two ways: as a purchaser of services from other hospitals or providers and as a provider or vendor of services to other hospitals.

7. *Purchaser role:* When a hospital provides services to a patient that were ordered during an encounter occurring outside of a hospital setting, the hospital will bill Medicare directly and collect required co-payments from Medicare beneficiaries. It is not necessary to bill the physician or provider making the referral.

8. *Vendor role:* When a hospital provides services to a patient of another hospital

(i.e., provides services that were ordered during an encounter between a patient and a physician that occurred in another hospital), the hospital is expected to bill the hospital in which the original encounter between the patient and physician occurred. The hospital in which the original encounter between the patient and physician occurred will pay the hospital providing the ordered service, include the charges for the service on its bill to Medicare, and collect required co-payments from the Medicare beneficiary as though it had provided the service directly.

9. *Payment determination:* Payments to vending hospitals will be determined according to billing and payment arrangements negotiated between them and the hospitals to whom they vend services. Payments to "purchasing" hospitals will be determined under current Medicare payment rules. These rules include a combination of Medicare defined costs and fixed fees.

NON-COST-BASED OUTPATIENT REIMBURSEMENT

Several outpatient services—namely, outpatient surgery and ambulatory surgical procedures, outpatient laboratory services, and outpatient radiology procedures—are no longer subject to full cost reimbursement and are instead reimbursed under the following payment mechanisms.

Outpatient Surgery and Ambulatory Surgical Procedures

As part of the Omnibus Budget Reconciliation Act of 1980 (OBRA-80), the Medicare program instituted payment for ambulatory surgical procedures performed in approved ambulatory surgical centers (ASCs). Approximately six years later, the Omnibus Budget Reconciliation Act of 1986 (OBRA-86) extended the ASC payment methodology to hospitals. Effective for cost reporting periods beginning on or after October 1, 1987, payment for covered outpatient ambulatory surgical procedures performed in a hospital is based, in part, on what the Medicare program pays for the same surgical procedures in an approved ASC.

The stated purpose of the new payment methodology for outpatient hospital ambulatory surgical procedures is to align Medicare payments for covered ASC surgical procedures performed in a hospital with payments to freestanding ASCs. HCFA believes that ASCs have lower fixed costs than hospitals, and is attempting to impose greater cost efficiencies on hospitals for outpatient ambulatory surgical procedures. To remain competitive, their charges must be similar to those of freestanding ASCs.

The Secretary of Health and Human Services determines which surgical procedures performed on an inpatient basis in a hospital also can be performed safely in an ASC or hospital outpatient department. The identification of covered and noncovered ASC surgical procedures is based on the following criteria:

- Procedures commonly performed on an inpatient basis but that may also, consistent with accepted medical practice, be safely performed in an ambulatory surgical facility should be included.
- Procedures included should be limited to those requiring a dedicated operating room and not requiring an overnight stay.
- Procedures commonly performed, or that may be safely performed, in physicians' offices should be excluded.
- Procedures not covered by Medicare should be excluded.

Generally, the two elements of the total charge for a surgical procedure are the physician's professional component and the facility services component. The ASC payment rates are for the facility services component only. Physicians continue to bill for their professional components separately and directly.

The ASC facility services component includes the following types of services: nursing, technician, and related services; use of ASC property and equipment; drugs, biologicals, and supplies directly related to the provision of surgical procedures; diagnostic or therapeutic services directly related to the provision of surgical procedures; administrative costs; materials for anesthesia; and blood.

The following items are excluded from the definitions of ASC facility services, and are separately billable under other Medicare provisions: laboratory, radiological, and diagnostic procedures other than those directly related to the performance of a surgical procedure; prosthetic devices, excluding intraocular lenses (IOLs); and durable medical equipment.

Payments to ASCs for facility services are based on prospectively set rates known as standard overhead amounts. All covered ASC surgical procedures are classified into one of eight standard overhead payment groups, each of which is associated with a prospective payment amount. ASC payment rates were originally set forth by Medicare in August 1982. These prospective payment rates, developed from 1979 and 1980 cost and charge information, were intended to reflect costs incurred by ASCs. HCFA classified procedures into groups using a charge-based index that is similar to the weighting process used for PPS. The published labor rates must be adjusted for area wage differences. The labor component of ASC prospective rates is established by HCFA as 34.45 percent of the published prospective rate. OBRA-86 mandated that, effective July 1, 1987, and annually thereafter, the Secretary must review and update ASC payment rates. Table 10–1 shows the calculation of an ASC payment rate.

Consistent with payments to freestanding ASCs, if more than one covered ambulatory surgical procedure is performed at a time, the ASC receives 100 percent payment for the procedure classified in the highest payment group, and 50 percent of the applicable group for each of the other procedures. Covered surgical procedures performed by a hospital on an outpatient basis

Table 10–1 Sample Calculation: ASC Payment Rate

Assumption:
Facility Location: Tampa, Florida
Date of Service: July 10, 1990

	Payment Group 1	Payment Group 8
Step 1		
Labor portion of rate:		
Aggregate Payment Rate for Group	$271.00	$ 871.00
Less IOL Allowance	—	– 200.00
Aggregate Payment Rate (Net of IOL)	271.00	671.00
Labor Component of Rate	x 0.3445	0.3445
HCFA Wage Index (Tampa, FL)	x 0.8996	0.8996
Adjusted Labor Component of Rate	= 83.99	207.95
Step 2		
Nonlabor portion of rate:		
Aggregate Payment Rate (Net of IOL)	$271.00	$ 671.00
Nonlabor Component of Rate	x 0.6555	0.6555
Adjusted Nonlabor Component of Rate	= 177.64	439.84
Step 3		
Labor-adjusted payment rate:		
Adjusted Labor Component of Rate	$ 83.99	$ 207.95
Nonlabor Component of Rate	+ 177.64	439.84
IOL Allowance	+ —	200.00
Labor-adjusted Payment Rate	$ 261.63	$ 847.79

that are not included in the current listing of ASC surgical procedures are reimbursed under other payment methodologies (i.e., reasonable cost, fee schedule, etc.).

The enactment of the OBRA-86 made significant changes in Medicare payment for ambulatory surgical procedures performed in hospital outpatient departments. The legislation mandated the development and implementation of a fully prospective payment system for outpatient hospital ambulatory surgical procedures effective for hospital fiscal years beginning on or after October 1, 1989. As of this date, a full transition to the ASC prospective payment methodology still has not been implemented by HCFA. The historical cost reimbursement method for these services was being phased out commencing with hospital cost reporting periods beginning on or after October 1, 1987. Payment for outpatient hospital facility services relating to ambulatory surgical procedures in the aggregate is now the lesser of:

1. The amount that would be paid for the services under the traditional lower of cost or charges reimbursement methodology, reduced by deductibles and coinsurance (the hospital-specific amount), or

2. A blended amount based on the hospital-specific amount as defined above and on the amount that would be paid to a freestanding ASC for the same procedure within the same geographic area, which is equal to 80 percent of the standard overhead amount net of deductibles (the ASC payment amount).

The blended amount is based on the transition schedule shown in Table 10–2.

For cost reporting periods beginning on or after October 1, 1987, but before October 1, 1988, the blended amount was determined by using 75 percent of the hospital-specific amount and 25 percent of the ASC payment amount attributable to the procedure. For cost reporting periods be-

Table 10–2 ASC Transition Schedule

Cost Reporting Period Beginning On or After	Hospital-Specific Amount	ASC Payment Amount
October 1, 1987	75%	25%
October 1, 1988	50%	50%
Portion of Cost Reporting for Periods		
Occurring on or after January 1, 1991	42%	58%

ginning on or after October 1, 1988, but before January 1, 1991, the blended amount is determined by using 50 percent of the hospital-specific amount and 50 percent of the ASC payment amount. For portions of cost reporting periods beginning on or after January 1, 1991, the blended amount is determined by using 42 percent of the hospital-specific amount and 58 percent of the ASC payment amount. The regulations have not specified when the transition to the full ASC payment amount will take effect.

OBRA-86 required a further disaggregation of costs and charges for cost reporting periods beginning on or after October 1, 1987. To implement the new payment methodology, all costs and charges related to ambulatory surgical procedures must be aggregated and treated separately from all other outpatient costs and charges. This allows for a separate lower of cost or charge calculation for covered ASC services. Reimbursement to providers (other than comprehensive outpatient rehabilitation facilities and hospices) for Medicare Part B services is subject to the lower of reasonable cost of services or customary charges for those services. Thus, if actual charges for Part B services are less than the related costs of those services, reimbursement is limited to actual Part B charges.

IOLs used in cataract surgery are subject to the outpatient bundling requirements and must be furnished directly by a hospital or under arrangements. Prior to March 12, 1990, an IOL furnished in connection with a covered ASC procedure was not considered to be a facility service and was instead reimbursed based on actual cost. Regulations issued in February 1990 eliminated the separate payment for IOLs and required that, as of March 12, 1990, payment for IOLs furnished in ASCs must be included in the

facility fee in an amount that is reasonable and related to the cost of acquiring the class of lens involved. All ASC procedures that involve the use of IOLs are grouped into payment group numbers six or eight. These two groups include an "add-on" amount of $200, which is intended to cover the cost of the IOLs. This provision is effective for both freestanding ASCs and hospital-based outpatient department programs. The IOL payment rate was frozen at the $200 level through December 31, 1992.

Outpatient Laboratory Services

Substantially all clinical diagnostic laboratory tests are paid based upon areawide fee schedules. Because Medicare payment is based on the lesser amount of the actual charge or Medicare's fee schedule, hospitals must ensure that actual charges for clinical laboratory services exceed fee schedule amounts in order to obtain full Medicare payment for clinical laboratory services. In addition, laboratory drawing services associated with clinical laboratory testing are billable separate from the clinical test itself.

Outpatient Radiology Procedures

As part of the Omnibus Budget Reconciliation Act of 1987 (OBRA-87), outpatient radiology services provided by hospitals on or after October 1, 1988, became subject to a blended payment limitation. This limit applies to aggregate payments for hospital outpatient radiology services, including diagnostic and therapeutic radiology, nuclear medicine, magnetic resonance imaging, ultrasound, and CAT procedures.

Under the provisions of OBRA-87, the amount of payments made for all or part of a cost reporting period beginning on or after October 1, 1988,

Exhibit 10–1 Formulas for Calculating Blended Payment Amount

**Services Provided
from October 1, 1988, through September 30, 1989**

Blended Payment Amount =
(.65 x lesser of cost or charges for outpatient radiology procedures) + (.35 x .62 x .80 Medicare prevailing charges)

**Services Provided
from October 1, 1989, through December 31, 1990**

Blended Payment Amount =
(.50 x lesser of cost or charges for outpatient radiology procedures) + (.50 x .62 x .80 Medicare prevailing charges)

**Services Provided
on or after January 1, 1991**

Blended Payment Amount =
(.42 x lesser of cost or charges for outpatient radiology procedures) + (.58 x .62 x .80 Medicare prevailing charges)

will be the lesser of the hospital's reasonable cost or charges (the lesser amount of the two) or a blended amount. Formulas for calculating the blended amount are shown in Exhibit 10–1.

For other outpatient departments, such as the emergency room and clinics, reimbursement is based on the cost of providing these services, which was more fully described in the previous chapter. However, Medicare is currently studying different methods of reimbursement, such as those described above, in order to avoid the continuation of cost reimbursement to hospitals. As in the past, this will typically result in less payment to hospitals for services rendered to the Medicare population.

THE FUTURE

Prior to the move toward managed care, other outpatient reimbursement methods were being developed. Ambulatory practice-related groupings (APGs), not dissimilar in intent from DRGs, were being considered as an outpatient reimbursement method. APGs, or similar methods, may have a place as common units of measure. The health care industry generally has lacked common units of measure. As such, even if they lose their use as reimbursement methods, DRGs, APGs, and resource-based relative value scales may retain their usefulness as a means to measure services.

Chapter 11

Pharmacy

Charles D. Mahoney and Anthony J. Kubica

Hospital and other institutional pharmacy services have changed dramatically in the past decade. These changes have paralleled those in the health care system. New classes of drugs have emerged, and innovative technology has transformed the manner in which drugs are dispensed, tracked, and administered. Pharmacy and hospital information systems assist the physician and pharmacist in drug selection, monitoring, and outcome evaluations. These changes have catalyzed pharmacy to a more proactive role in the health care delivery system. To remain viable in a rapidly changing environment, practitioners need to respond to both intrinsic and extrinsic forces, namely, emerging technology, and changing work force, and new customer expectations. Pharmacy is a good example of a profession changing in response to a new practice and reimbursement environment. The rise of large HMOs and other forms of managed care networks has created an era in which success, as measured by both internal and external customers, is achieved by offering services that provide significant economic as well as clinical value.

A new consensus has emerged regarding the clinical practice in pharmacy, and the role of the pharmacist has become increasingly more patient focused. This evolution led to the development of a more encompassing practice model, referred to as "pharmaceutical care." A widely recognized definition for this concept is proposed by Helper and Strand: "Pharmaceutical care is the responsible provision of drug therapy for the purpose of achieving definite outcomes that improve a patient's quality of life. These outcomes are (1) cure of a disease, (2) elimination or reduction of a patient's symptomatology, (3) arresting or slowing of a disease process, or (4) preventing a disease or symptomatology."[1]

Pharmaceutical care is viewed as a health care need, analogous to medical care or dental care. Provision of such care requires that pharmacists have a generalist, rather than specialist, orientation and be held responsible for the outcomes of drug therapy.[2] The scope of pharmaceutical care encompasses all treatment settings, emphasizing continuity of care from one setting to another. Its goal is to address the total pharmaceutical care needs of all patients.

The concept of total patient management is especially relevant in today's health care environment, which can be described as a more businesslike response to the competitive pressures and challenges facing the hospital industry. Under competitive prospective pricing systems, hospitals and/or managed care networks only can compete if they control costs, ensure appropriate utilization of resources, and demonstrate quality outcomes. Controlling pharmacy costs, however, has often been viewed narrowly as controlling drug acquisition costs. Controlling drug acquisition cost, or hospital formulary availability, is important, but it is only part of the total drug-therapy-related cost chain. Drug therapy is a key component in determining patient care outcomes; the impact of ineffective or inefficient drug use will have consequences beyond the acquisition cost of the product. The total cost of drug therapy includes, in addition to the acquisition cost, the number of times per day the drug is administered, the cost of preparing the drug for administration, the nursing and medical costs relating to medication administration and monitoring, the costs associated with side effects and adverse drug reactions, and the cost associated with therapeutic failures. The economic consequences of drug therapy should be evaluated on the above factors and how they relate to length of stay and total resource consumption. For example, reducing the total number of drugs included in a formulary, or overly aggressive restrictions on new pharmacological agents and delivery technologies, may provide short-term expense reductions, but may not decrease costs overall, and in some instances may increase expenses.

A contemporary pharmacy service requires individuals with high-level management, information processing, and clinical skills in order to provide the type of sophisticated services described in this chapter. The effective pharmacy manager establishes a drug use control system within the institution that not only ensures rational and economically sound drug therapy but also ensures that the right drug gets to the right patient at the right time to achieve the right effect.

DEPARTMENT OPERATIONS

Contemporary pharmaceutical services should be designed to provide for clinical activities, which by their nature are best performed by pharmacists present in patient care areas. Advances in technology have made it possible to monitor physician practice profiles and allow for comparisons among prescribers. Information systems that integrate the clinical and economic data on drug use, and provide feedback on the clinical and economic outcomes of drug therapy, are not being used to identify opportunities to improve care, and have resulted in the development of practice guidelines. Utilization patterns; patient outcomes; length of stay; and expense data by DRG, service, and physician have become essential tools in managing both the quality and financial aspects of care.

Drug Distribution

The primary mechanism for drug distribution in an institutional setting is the unit dose medication distribution system. The unit dose system was developed to provide a safe and effective drug distribution system. It has been endorsed by the Joint Commission on Accreditation of Healthcare Organizations (Joint Commission) and the U.S. General Accounting Office for its safety and economy and has become the standard for drug distribution in U.S. hospitals. A unit dose system is defined as one in which medications are contained in single unit packages and are dispensed in as ready-to-administer a form as possible; in addition, for most medications, no more than a 24-hour supply of doses is delivered or available in the patient-care area at any time.[3,4]

In this system, pharmacists receive a direct copy of the physician's order for review prior to dispensing needed medications. Medications to be administered to the patient in the next 24-hour period are contained in a bin specially designated for each patient. These individual bins are combined in a cassette and delivered to the patient-care area. Cassettes serve all the patients on the patient-care unit and are generally stored in a mobile cart on the unit. A duplicate set of patient-specific bins is maintained in the pharmacy and refilled with needed medications on a daily basis. Most pharmacy departments exchange medication cassettes once daily at a predetermined time. The disadvantage to the exchange system is that it is extremely labor intensive. One of the unit dose system's established benefits, which is currently revolutionizing the drug distribution system, is its adaptability to computerized and automated procedures as a result of being based upon patient-specific medications. Examples of automation used in hospital pharmacy practice include computerization, bar coding for inventory control, and drug ordering and robotics for centralized medication cassette filling.[5] One of the fastest growing technologies is that of automated dispensing systems. Currently, there are two types of automated dispensing systems, the point-of-use system and the automated medication bin filling system.

Point-of-Use

In the point-of-use system, medications are available for nurses to administer to their patients from microprocessor-controlled storage units located at the patient care units.[6] Utilizing technologies similar to those seen with banks' automated teller machines, the user gains access to the system via a confidential identification code and is prompted by touch screen through the necessary transactions for, in this case, patient-specific medication removal. All transactions are electronically recorded on a pharmacy-based computer system, which also integrates patient census (ADT) information, billing, and inventory control. This type of system is able to accommodate the manufacturer's unit dose packaging, and eliminates the labor-intensive medication cassette fill-and-exchange process in the pharmacy. While still in their developmental stages, these systems have the capability to store over 90 percent of a specific patient unit's medication with individualized inventories dependent on the unit's needs. The system is integrated with the pharmacy's computerized patient medication profile so that each medication order is reviewed and approved by a phar-

macist prior to administration to the patient. In order to meet immediate patient care needs there is the capability for nursing override to obtain select medications in emergency situations.

Automated Medication Bin

The automated medication bin filling system retains the cassette fill-and-exchange method of the unit dose drug distribution system, but eliminates much of the labor required in the process. This system utilizes robotic technologies, bar code readers, and microcomputers to automate the bin filling process.[7] All doses of medication are repackaged in a plastic bag, relabeled, and bar coded to identify the medication and expiration date, and are loaded into the pick station by the robot. The system then moves individual bins along an assembly line and, utilizing the pharmacy's computerized patient medication record, selects the appropriate medications for the individual patient by reading the imprinted bar code.

Automated dispensing system applications in hospital pharmacies are revolutionizing the drug distribution process. The systems are effective, efficient, and highly accurate, but are not without costs, as either capital expenditures or leases. Implementation of an automated system requires financial justification and a clear return on investment in terms of improving level of services and patient outcomes.

Centralized/Decentralized Operations

Drug product preparations (sterile and nonsterile compounding) and unit dose medication distribution functions are typically centralized in the main pharmacy area. Yet, in order to achieve the goal of optimal medication use in an institution, pharmacists are required to be accessible to the ultimate customers of the medication use system—the patient and the other health professionals who collaborate in patient-care decisions. Decentralization of pharmacy services or a combination of centralized and decentralized services have been utilized by pharmacy departments to improve the efficiency of drug distribution and accessibility of the pharmacist to the areas where patient care decisions are being made.

In some hospitals, pharmacists practice at the patient-care unit from satellite pharmacies where they can interact with the patients, physicians, nurses, and other health care providers. Immediate patient medication needs are serviced from the satellite location while the central pharmacy remains the core of the service, providing unit dose cassette fill and sterile product preparation functions. Pharmacists located in the satellites provide drug information, in-service education, patient medication education and drug therapy monitoring and evaluation services. Under this system, a minimal number of pharmacists practice from the central pharmacy primarily to supervise pharmacy technicians and other support personnel.

Another approach is a totally decentralized pharmacy system. Under this system, pharmacy satellites are established in strategic locations throughout the hospital at the patient care units. Complete pharmacy services are provided to the targeted patient care areas from the satellite pharmacy. Some institutions have used a mobile cart model for decentralized services. Pharmacy personnel utilize mobile carts from which they supply the patient-specific unit dose carts at the patient units. In addition to these three models, other combinations of systems can be used to respond to the specific needs of the institution. Automation of the drug distribution system will undoubtedly provide even more options in coming years.

Regardless of the drug distribution model used—whether centralized, decentralized, or a combination of the two—the critical factor is to ensure that the pharmacist is available at the patient-care area to participate in the medication use process. Decentralization of the pharmacist enhances the interaction between the pharmacist and the customers of the medication use system (patient, physician, nurse). This multidisciplinary collaboration facilitates the appropriate prescribing of medications, aids in the identification and resolution of medication use problems (i.e., medication errors, adverse drug reactions), and provides a ready source of drug information for patients and health care providers.

Sterile Products Preparation

Although the unit-dose system was a major advance over the earlier drug distribution systems, pharmacists continue to explore ways to improve drug distribution and administration. Another area that received attention was a pharmacy service for the preparation of sterile products such as intravenous (IV) admixtures (drug added to IV solutions), sterile preparations involving cytotoxic (used to treat cancer) and hazardous drugs, and parenteral nutrition solutions.

Drugs added to IV solutions have the potential to interact chemically with one another or with the solution, as well as to interact physically with the container. Ironically, although the pharmacist is the most knowledgeable about these interactions, the nurse actually prepares the medication. To close the gap between knowledge and preparation, and to free the nurse from these tasks, pharmacies have developed IV admixture programs. Pharmacy staff trained in aseptic techniques and sterile compounding prepare drugs for IV therapy in specially equipped areas for delivery to the patient care area. Since some admixtures are stable for only a few hours, timing of preparation and delivery is critical.

The pharmacist's role in parenteral preparation has been acknowledged by the Joint Commission in the following statement: "When any part of preparing, sterilizing, and labeling parenteral medications and solutions is performed within the hospital...the director of the pharmaceutical department is responsible...."[8] The American Society of Hospital Pharmacists' (ASHP) recommendations on quality assurance for pharmacy-prepared sterile products emphasize the pharmacist's responsibility for sterile product preparation.[9]

It is important that systems developed to prepare sterile products be safe, and the result of a multidisciplinary approach. Written policies and procedures should be developed for all aspects of the service, and it is vital that a quality assurance program be incorporated into the system. Many aspects of drug preparation can be delegated to properly trained support personnel. A well-designed system utilizing technical staff under the direct supervision of a pharmacist has been demonstrated to be cost effective and beneficial to patient care.

Increasingly, new methods and equipment are being introduced for compounding and providing drugs intended for IV administration. There has been an increase in the number of highly sophisticated computer-controlled compounding pumps that facilitate accurate and efficient preparation of complex sterile products such as parenteral nutrition solutions. Pharmacies on the leading edge of technology employ advanced computer programs to control and document functions such as product calculations, worksheet preparation, label production, and quality assurance for all pharmacy-prepared sterile products. Since all aspects of IV drug preparation and administration are undergoing radical change, an institution should continually evaluate its existing service.

To ensure that products are of high quality, the service should follow the recommendations set forth by the ASHP in their practice standards on quality assurance for pharmacy-prepared sterile products and on handling cytotoxic and hazardous drugs. These documents offer sound advice on topics such as policies and procedures; personnel education, training, and evaluation; storage and handling; facilities and equipment; aseptic technique; and quality assurance. Most important to a successful and safe sterile products service is the assurance of product integrity through the availability of suitable facilities and equipment that meet federal standards on airborne particulate cleanliness in clean rooms and clean zones. Current practice standards group pharmacy-prepared sterile products into three levels of potential risk to the patient. As the compounding complexity and the microbial growth potential of the finished product increase, the need for more elaborate facilities, equipment, and quality assurance procedures in-

creases in order to ensure product integrity and patient safety. While low-risk products may be produced satisfactorily in the environment of a certified Class 100 horizontal or vertical laminar airflow hood, current recommendations state that high-risk products should be made in a facility having a Class 10,000 clean room. Clean rooms are classified based on the maximum number of allowable particles 0.5 μm and larger per cubic foot of air. For example, the air particle count in a Class 10,000 clean room may not exceed a total of 10,000 of 0.5 μm and larger per cubic foot of air. Also essential is documented personnel education and training, encompassing a program of operator credentialing through regular process validation and end-product testing.

Computerization

Computerized pharmacy systems generally can be divided into two types: adjuncts to the hospital's information system (HIS) and dedicated departmental systems. The former typically use the hospital's mainframe. In its simplest—and least effective—form, data concerning pharmacy services are entered into the mainframe and reports are generated and distributed (usually monthly: on-demand reports are very difficult for HIS to accommodate). Of greater use to pharmacy directors are programs specifically written and tailored to pharmacy services. There are some distinct advantages to tailored systems because admission, discharge, and transfer (ADT) data are accessible and can be interfaced with the pharmacy system. Laboratory and medical record data can also be integrated. The second type of pharmacy system is a dedicated one using either mini- or microcomputers. Continuing advances in computer memory and speed have made some networked minis more powerful than many hospital mainframes. Pharmacy computer systems initially installed to support administrative and financial activities have evolved to provide the substantial support for clinical and therapeutic functions that the modern hospital pharmacy department must provide.

There are four major areas of computer capability that are required in the pharmacy:

1. Billing
   - charging for drugs dispensed and crediting unused/returned product
2. Clinical enhancements
   - real time detection and identification of potential drug-drug and drug-food interactions
   - ad hoc query capabilities
   - medication administration record (MAR) capabilities to synchronize nursing and pharmacy knowledge of the patient's drug status
3. Exchange real time data with other key hospital systems
   - with laboratory systems (permits rapid adjustment of therapeutic plans)
   - radiology (some clinical utility and substantial financial utility)
   - ADT integration with drug distribution
4. The ability to expand into other administrative and clinical areas as technology evolves
   - direct drug order entry by prescribers (with real time detection and flagging of troublesome drug orders)
   - interfacing with drug distribution systems (automated drug distribution systems; robotic systems)
   - full, real-time query client/server capabilities (capture of patient clinical and administrative data from a remote server)
   - interfacing to permit development and implementation of therapeutic management programs to ensure optimal pharmacoeconomic behavior

In addition to these rather specific applications, the pharmacy director should develop a departmental management information system. This makes possible the integration of key financial, clinical, and human resource data as a basis for the necessary planning, management, and control of department operations, currently and in the future. A few such examples would include

- financial and budget analysis and planning
- position and hours-worked control
- workload and productivity analysis
- drug therapy/DRG/case mix analysis
- trending analyses
- projection modeling

The information capabilities of the system should foster both accountability and clinical responsibility throughout the department, and should be focused on meeting the explicit needs of the department as well as the implicit needs of optimal patient care outcome through drug therapy. Another concern today is the ability of a single department or hospital system to be integrated in a health delivery network. Hospitals are rapidly consolidating inpatient long-term care facilities while establishing off-site primary treatment centers. Efficient information exchange is critical to health networks.

Patient Care Committees

The quality of patient care and medical staff practice patterns are directly related to the level of interdisciplinary collaboration and cooperation among the hospital's health professionals. Pharmacists are typically represented on the following patient-care or medical-staff standing committees: pharmacy and therapeutics, utilization review, quality assurance, infection control, safety, institutional review board (research involving human subjects), and material standards (value analysis for medical/surgical supplies and equipment). Of these, the two committees that are most important in ensuring optimal medication use in an institution are the pharmacy and therapeutics committee and the utilization review committee.

Pharmacy and Therapeutics Committee

The pharmacy and therapeutics committee is usually a standing (i.e., permanent) committee of the hospital's medical staff; it is an advisory group to the medical staff that develops, approves, and/or recommends policies and procedures that are concerned with the drug use process. Its actions often have a far-reaching therapeutic, clinical, and economic impact throughout the institution. The committee is the organizational link between the medical staff and the pharmacy department. In addition, the committee develops educational approaches on drug-related issues that should address the needs of the professional staff—physicians, nurses, and other health care practitioners.

Composition of this committee varies from hospital to hospital depending on tradition and political climate. Membership commonly consists of physicians, nurses, at least one hospital administrator, the director of pharmacy, and sufficient other pharmacists to adequately prepare and carry out the committee's work. The committee should meet at least quarterly, but preferably monthly; its minutes are maintained as a permanent record by the medical staff. The functions and scope of the committee have been described and are periodically updated by the ASHP. These functions are to:

1. serve in an advisory capacity to the medical staff and hospital administration in all matters pertaining to the use of drugs (including investigational drugs)

2. develop a formulary of drugs accepted for use in the hospital and provide for its continual revision; the selection of items to be included will be based on objective evaluation of their relative therapeutic merits and economic impact

3. establish programs and hospital procedures that help ensure cost-effective and safe drug therapy

4. establish or plan suitable educational programs for the hospital's professional staff on matters related to drug use

5. participate in quality assurance activities related to the prescribing, preparation, distribution, and use of medications

6. review adverse drug events occurring in the hospital

7. initiate and/or direct drug use evaluation studies

8. advise and give consent to the pharmacy in its implementation of effective drug distribution and control procedures

Developing an effective formulary is a significant committee responsibility. With the multiplicity of drugs available that have overlapping clinical indications, and with continually increasing cost, each institution must have a system in place to objectively evaluate the necessity for drug addition to the formulary. Because of the changing nature of health care delivery, the pharmacy and therapeutics committee can serve as an effective bridge between clinical preferences and the economic realities of modern drug therapy.

Utilization Review Committee

An effective ongoing program to monitor and affect drug use is needed to improve the quality of drug therapy and help assure appropriate, safe, and effective use of medications within the institution. This objective can be achieved by the pharmacist working through the pharmacy and therapeutics committee or hospital utilization review committee, and performing drug use evaluations. Drug use evaluations should focus on the major drug classes used in the organization and can be a part of the overall utilization review process, or can be a discrete component of the committee's efforts through establishment of a drug utilization review subcommittee.

Drug use evaluations are performed in order to collect and analyze drug use data, to identify trends and inappropriate drug usage, and to implement programs to rectify identified problems. These evaluations are designed to address all aspects of medication use, including the prescription, preparation, dispensing, and monitoring of drugs. The Joint Commission has stressed drug use evaluation as one medical staff quality assurance activity it expects to see in place and functioning during its accreditation surveys of hospitals. The Joint Commission has established a ten-step process for evaluating drug use.[10]

1. assign responsibility

2. delineate scope of care and service

3. identify important aspects of care and service

4. identify indicators related to the important aspects of care

5. establish thresholds for evaluation

6. collect and organize data

7. evaluate care

8. take action when opportunities for improvement or problems are identified

9. assess the effectiveness of the actions

10. communicate relevant information to the organizationwide quality assurance program

Ongoing monitoring and periodic evaluation of each selected drug should continue until it is shown to be consistently and appropriately used. Relevant drug use evaluation findings should be forwarded to the appropriate individuals, such as a physician chief of service, or departments, and may be used in granting or reassessing privileges and in conducting other performance evaluations.

ORGANIZATION

The pharmacy department should be organized in a manner that ensures an integrated approach and promotes the concept of drug use control. This requires establishing departmental and individual accountability for the safety, effectiveness, and economic consequences of drugs used in patient care. It also should be organized in a manner consistent with the standards promulgated by the Joint Commission, the ASHP, and federal and state laws and regulations.

The pharmacy department should be structured to ensure that the following services are provided:

- informational resources to support drug selection and use

- drug procurement

- drug storage and distribution

- drug preparation

- drug monitoring

- patient education

- drug use review

How the pharmacy is organized, as shown in its table of organization, depends on a number of factors, including the size of the institution, the drug distribution system, whether the hospital is a clinical training site for medical and pharmacy students, and the scope of medical and support services offered. The table of organization for pharmacy should ensure that the pharmacy program is responsive to the mission and strategic plan of the institution. The key divisions generally common to all pharmacy departments are clinical, drug distribution/preparation, and support services such as purchasing and computer systems. The level of service provided by the department is dependent on the empowerment of high quality front-line practitioners to initiate service quality enhancements. Use of contemporary human resource management techniques is key to pharmacy operations and optimal medication use hospitalwide. The pharmacy personnel complement typically includes pharmacists, pharmacy technicians, and clerical/secretarial staff.

At a minimum, all pharmacists must complete a five-year baccalaureate program in pharmacy accredited by the American Council on Pharmaceutical Education (ACPE) and be licensed by examination to practice pharmacy in the state in which the pharmacist is employed. In addition to the five-year bachelor of science degree, many colleges also confer the degree of Doctor of Pharmacy upon completion of one to two years of additional didactic instruction and clinical experience. In 1989 the ACPE pronounced a "Declaration of Intent" to establish new programmatic accreditation standards and foresaw "the time when the accreditation standards will focus upon a doctor of pharmacy program as the only professional degree program evaluated and accredited...as soon as the year 2000."[11]

Pharmacists have the opportunity to further enhance their education and experience through postgraduate residency and fellowship programs. A pharmacy practice residency is "an organized, directed, postgraduate training program that centers on development of the knowledge, attitudes, and skills needed to pursue rational drug therapy." Pharmacy residency programs are accredited by the ASHP. An ASHP fellowship is "a directed, highly individualized, postgraduate program designed to prepare the participant to become an independent researcher." In addition, many pharmacists, particularly those practicing in the hospital setting, advance their education via academic degree programs such as master's of science in pharmacy, master's of business administration, and the aforementioned doctor of pharmacy degree.

The traditional drug preparation and distributive aspects of pharmacy services are delegated to specially trained pharmacy technicians who work under the direct supervision of a pharmacist. Pharmacy technicians are typically high school graduates with one to two years of college education who have been trained either on-the-job in a hospital-based training program, or in one of the technical or junior college programs developing throughout the country. The training and effective use of technicians will be critical to the future impact of pharmaceutical care and improved medication use.

In addition to pharmacists and pharmacy technicians, other clerical and secretarial personnel support the activities and services of the pharmacy department. Such tasks as receiving, billing, provision of secretarial support, and physical transportation of products throughout the institution may be handled by these personnel. The primary objective of staffing a pharmacy department is to have a mix of personnel that optimizes the skill of each individual so as to provide an effective and efficient service in a cost-effective manner.

FINANCIAL MANAGEMENT

Drug expenditures currently account for approximately 5 percent of a hospital's total budget; by the year 2000 it is estimated that it could increase to 20 to 25 percent. In the typical pharmacy department, drug expenditures generally account for about 70 percent of the operating budget. Although medications are one of the most cost-effective methods of health care available, ensuring the rational, safe, and appropriate utilization of this treatment modality is a formidable challenge. Pharmacoeconomists are responsible for evaluating the total cost of therapy and helping the hospital make decisions about allocating resources in order to provide the most cost-effective care.[12]

The pharmacy department generates direct expense-based revenue for only a minority of third-party and private payors. Reimbursement for pharmacy services has been bundled with the overall hospital billing, which is related to a fixed or contracted payment for a specific treatment or admission type. The major impetus toward this type of system was the introduction of diagnostic-related groups (DRGs). Other prospective payment arrangements have continued to be implemented, including contractual agreements for provision of care for all members of health maintenance organizations (HMOs) and preferred provider organizations (PPOs). As a result of these developments, pharmacy has become more of a cost center. With these forces having an impact on the pharmacy department, it becomes critical that both labor and supply costs be monitored closely. Systems should be developed to utilize these resources in the most cost-effective manner. The goal of a pharmacy financial management program should be to develop mechanisms to identify costs, monitor financial performance, and develop appropriate strategies to correct unfavorable variances.

Costs and Productivity

To achieve these goals, the pharmacy manager can utilize a number of tools to assist in analyzing labor and supply parameters. The traditional assessment of actual expenses compared to budget does not give the pharmacy manager enough information to promote the most cost-effective use of supplies and services throughout the institution.

In a cost containment environment, staff utilization requires ongoing monitoring. Staffing not only will depend on the mix of pharmacists, technicians, and other support staff, but also on the ability of each team to get things done with the least number of steps, paperwork, and checkpoints, without sacrificing safety and quality. Staffing ratios as well as the functions of each category should be evaluated at least yearly. Staffing methodologies should be reconsidered to effect not only savings, but also to promote more productive and motivated staff.

Productivity measures should be established through a work measurement system, using standards established for different product and service categories (e.g., doses dispensed per adjusted discharge, clinical pharmacy service units per discharge). Since labor input will not always conform to volume patterns, productivity should be monitored frequently. Significant volume increases may signal the need for additional staffing in a given area. On the other hand, with decreases (unfavorable variances) the pharmacy manager may consider not replacing employees who resign, or replacing pharmacists with technicians for the more traditional distributive functions. The use of overtime may be appropriate in lieu of hiring additional staff. However, overtime expense can be limited by the use of part-time employees and per diem staff. Overtime is best used to cover peak work demands and to augment temporary increases in work volume.

Understanding the impact of changes in the type of products (e.g., oral dose forms, parenteral chemotherapy) being dispensed will also help to determine staffing requirements. This relates not merely to volume shifts, but also to products that are more labor and/or cost intensive. This may be caused by the type of patients being treated and the cause may not always be readily apparent. Analyses of cost per patient unit and changes in the drug volume per patient day on different units may help to assess the impact throughout the hospital.

By comparing a pharmacy department to those in other hospitals, areas of opportunity can be identified. Comparisons often relate a specific indicator or ratio (that applies to both organizations) that is then applied to industrywide ratios (i.e., patient days, discharges, etc.). Common indicators are doses dispensed, earned hours, FTEs, clinical units, IVs prepared, drug costs, total supply costs, salary costs, and total costs. The functional strengths and weaknesses among the comparison hospitals can be compared. The areas that provide highest value to the pharmacy manager can be explored further. The best in an area can be ascertained. By networking with other institutions, one may be able to identify excellent practices and low-cost providers.

Managing Drug Costs

Two strategies are applied in the continuous attempt to control drug costs: administrative and clinical. Administrative control is implemented through reductions in drug acquisition costs, inventory management, use of appropriate drug distribution systems, and computerization.

The goal of reducing drug acquisition costs is to provide quality drugs at the lowest possible cost. There are many chemically identical drug entities, known as generic equivalents, which are manufactured and distributed by many drug companies. The FDA requires that generic equivalents all act the same in the human body before they will grant a product license. Therefore, pharmacies can control drug acquisition costs by selecting the least expensive equivalent, whether through internal (hospital) bidding, through group purchasing, or negotiation with acceptable vendors. Once a drug goes "off patent," many versions of its equivalent will soon appear in the marketplace, and pharmacy managers should stay abreast of these imminent patent changes.

A more critical and emerging category of drugs that permit the pharmacist and the physician alternatives is referred to as "therapeutic equivalents." While not chemically identical, these drugs have similar therapeutic outcomes (for example, drugs to reduce the action of stomach acid on specific receptor areas). Therapeutic equivalents can also be candidates for group purchasing, internal bidding, or negotiation, but only after the pharmacy and therapeutics committee has approved the drug candidates as therapeutic equivalents.

Inventory management is another important management tool that can be used by the pharmacist to control costs. Avoiding redundant inventory increases working capital that can be used more productively in other areas of the hospital. Improving inventory turnover can be partially achieved by implementation of both generic and therapeutic equivalence policies (above). Numerous other inventory control techniques, such as ABC and economic order quantity (EOQ) should be incorporated into the management system.

ABC analysis is a method to ascertain the volume of products by expense (i.e., dollars) and by utilization (i.e., units). This allows the review of product use. The sorting parameter(s) can be single criteria to multiple criteria, providing the manager with the capability to analyze product use for various scenarios. This can be useful as a snapshot of product movement for a given period of time, as well as for identifying product shifts and utilization. The EOQ[13] is a mathematical method to determine the optimum product quantity to order. Its objective is to minimize the inventory costs associated with the product. The basic EOQ model takes into account the total costs associated with inventory—i.e., carrying costs and ordering costs. Carrying costs increase and ordering costs decline with higher inventories. The EOQ is defined as the level at which the total inventory cost is the lowest. This is at the point of an EOQ model line graph where the carrying cost and ordering lines intersect—the point where carrying costs and ordering costs are equal.

The type of drug distribution system used within the hospital can affect costs significantly. Most hospitals today use some variant of the unit-dose system of drug distribution. This system generally provides a 24-hour supply of drugs in ready-to-administer form in containers designated for individual patients. (This system is described in greater detail in the section on drug distribution.) Computerization is necessary to provide important data for decision making in many areas of pharmacy management, including cost control. Because of its importance this is discussed separately and at greater length elsewhere.

Clinical strategies for reducing drug costs offer opportunities for affecting patient outcome positively, while at the same time reducing institutional costs. Some of these strategies include formulary management, drug use review (which is mandated by the Joint Commission, so it is wise for the pharmacy manager to also get some direct utility out of the effort required), and clinical (or therapeutic) intervention at the time the physician is writing the drug order. A broad definition of a formulary is a list of drugs approved by the pharmacy and therapeutics committee that the pharmacy will routinely stock and always have available for patient care. Although the formulary is primarily a clinically oriented tool, it should also have a major impact on costs by reducing the number of drug entities that the pharmacy carries in its inventory. This is ideally achieved by continually reviewing opportunities to reduce the number of therapeutic and generic equivalents.

Drug use review (more commonly referred to as Drug—or Medication—Use Evaluation [DUE], to be consistent with current Joint Commission mandates) is the process by which the use of drugs throughout the hospital is continuously and formally reviewed. Not every drug can be reviewed frequently, but categories of drugs that tend to be (1) used in nearly every patient, (2) inherently pose a risk to the patients because of their potency, or (3) are newly approved drugs with which the hospital has little experience, all make good candidates for review. Antibiotics have traditionally been the most frequently reviewed drug class because (1) their use is widespread, (2) there is substantial therapeutic overlap among the drugs, (3) there are many generic and therapeutic equivalents, (4) establishing indications for why one drug can be used over another is relatively more simple than with other drug classes, and, finally, (5) newly introduced drugs tend to be very expensive.

Pharmacists practicing in patient care areas can greatly influence the choice of drug, its dosing, the best vehicle for administration, and the optimal monitoring requirements for the most cost-effective use of drug therapy. If, during the DUE process, a lower cost antibiotic is determined to be available in place of one that was ordered, the pharmacist intervenes to discuss therapeutic options available, and to explain why the options are being recommended.

Budget preparation and monitoring are other important financial management tools for the director of pharmacy, although an ongoing cost control system, using administrative and clinical strategies, is crucial to controlling overall drug-related costs. Budgets, theoretically, are a yardstick, a series of objectives that are to be met during the budget year. Patient care is a dynamic process, and a static, historically based budget cannot accurately reflect the impact of an ongoing cost containment system in such a dynamic environment. While many budgeting methods exist, all require active participation and intergroup cooperation from hospital administration and clinical department heads.

LEGAL REQUIREMENTS

Numerous legal statutes affect pharmacy operations in the hospital and other health facilities. Drugs are highly regulated by federal and state laws. The director of pharmacy is charged with assuring compliance with all applicable regulations developed by the state boards of pharmacy and departments of health; these vary widely from state to state. State laws often may be more stringent than comparable federal statutes. Among the most important of the federal laws are the Federal Food, Drug, and Cosmetic Act; Controlled Substances Act; Poison Prevention Packaging Act; and the alcohol tax laws. Controlled substances (e.g., morphine, Dilaudid, Vicodin, codeine, cocaine) are regulated by the Drug Enforcement Administration, and entail many bookkeeping requirements including registration, continuous inventory, reporting, and labeling.

Standards of pharmacy practice have been promulgated by the ASHP, and—if followed throughout—will approach ASHP's ideal of hospital pharmacy practice. The Joint Commission also mandates certain aspects of pharmacy practice. The two sets of "standards" for practice do not necessarily agree with one another in all matters.

CONCLUSION

In a rapidly changing health care environment, success will come to those who are creative, innovative, and expand their vision. The present drug use system in many hospitals does not identify an accountable individual, but delegates responsibility for all aspects of drug use in the institution. The pharmacy should be viewed as a clinical department that can serve as a bridge between the clinical and financial aspects of drug therapy.

NOTES

1. C.D. Helper and L.M. Strand, Opportunities and Responsibilities in Pharmaceutical Care, *American Journal of Hospital Pharmacy* 47(1990):533–543.

2. M.P. Lee and M.D. Ray, Planning for Pharmaceutical Care, *American Journal of Hospital Pharmacy* 50(1993):1153–1158.

3. Practice Standards of the American Society of Hospital Pharmacists 1991–1992, p. 10.

4. S.Y. Crawford and C.E. Myers, ASHP National Survey of Hospital-Based Pharmaceutical Services—1992, *American Journal of Hospital Pharmacy* 50(1993): 1371–1404.

5. C.E. Hynniman, Drug Product Distribution Systems and Departmental Operations, *American Journal of Hospital Pharmacy* 48, Supplement 1(1991):S24–35.

6. Pyxis Corporation Medstation Rx System, Product information brochure, 1993, San Diego, California.

7. Automated Healthcare Automated Pharmacy Station, Product information brochure, 1993, Pittsburgh, Pennsylvania.

8. Joint Commission on Accreditation of Healthcare Organizations, *Accreditation Manual for Hospitals, Volume I Standards. Pharmaceutical Services* (Chicago, 1993):111.

9. American Society of Hospital Pharmacists, Draft Technical Assistance Bulletin on Quality Assurance for Pharmacy-Prepared Sterile Products, *American Journal of Hospital Pharmacy* 50(1993):1448–1452.

10. Joint Commission on Accreditation of Healthcare Organizations, *Examples of Drug Use Evaluation* (Chicago, 1989):1–83.

11. Declaration of Intent: Revision of Accreditation Standards in 1990's in Keeping with Changes in Pharmacy Practice and Pharmaceutical Education. American Council on Pharmaceutical Education, Sept. 1989.

12. A.D. St. Jean and N.T. Landis, The Pharmacoeconomist—An Emerging Specialist in Health Care Institutions, *American Journal of Hospital Pharmacy* 50(1993):1062, 1066, 1068, 1073.

13. F.J. Weston and E.F. Brigham, eds., *Managerial Finance*, Seventh Edition (Hinsdale, Ill.: The Dryden Press, 1981):302–336.

CHARLES D. MAHONEY, MS, RPh, is Director of Pharmacy, Materials Management, and Central Transport with Rhode Island Hospital, a 719-bed academic medical center located in Providence, Rhode Island. He has worked in hospitals for over 25 years. Mr. Mahoney has published over 75 articles in the pharmaceutical and health care literature. He has made numerous presentations on pharmacy-related topics.

ANTHONY J. KUBICA, MS, MBA, is a Senior Management Consultant with Superior Consultant Company, Inc., a consulting firm based in Farmington Hills, Michigan. He has worked in the health care field for over 23 years and currently consults in the areas of operational and process improvement to a wide range of health care clients. Mr. Kubica has published extensively in health care literature, served on editorial boards of pharmacy journals, and has spoken widely on pharmacy-related topics.

Chapter 12

Health Care Facilities Food Service

Ruby P. Puckett

Health care organizations are changing because of an unstable economic climate, health care reforms, and the desire for social and cultural equality. These changes are seen in the ways that care has shifted from the hospital-based to outpatient departments, home health, and other outreach centers. As these changes in organization take place, the health professionals who deliver that care are also decreasing. Personnel are being cross-functionally trained through the provision of education and skills needed to perform more than one function. Dietetics, nutrition, and food service (DNFS) departments must find ways to meet these opportunities and changes.

DNFS is a major department in health care organizations. The department delivers services by employing professionals who practice the art and science of health, both for wellness and for improving the status of those who are ill. These professionals may be employed in hospitals, skilled nursing facilities (SNF), and intermediate care facilities (ICF); rehabilitative and residential care facilities, adult day care, child care, and mental health care facilities; home health agencies, hospice, ambulatory care, wellness/ prevention centers, and other off-site clinics.

All of these facilities are governed by policies, procedures, and standards as well as local, state, and federal regulations. Basically the standards and guidelines include the rights of the customer; quality of care that addresses nutrition, hydration, and special needs; standards for food service; therapeutic diets, dining, and other activities. Food service departments play a major role in the health and well-being of their customers.

DNFS departments are a part of the multidisciplinary team in all health care organizations. Departments are organized and managed differently depending on the complexity and size of the organization. All DNFS departments have two primary functions. First, they are manufacturing and distribution centers for meals to be served to all customers, whether patients or guests. Second, they provide a wide variety of clinical services that are generally unrelated to the meal production process. As such, the clinical staff serve as members of the overall facility multidisciplinary team providing input into the individual patient's nutrition needs, while providing nutrition care input into the critical pathway of care. The department as a whole participates in the continuous quality improvement (CQI) or total quality management (TQM) process that has been implemented within the organization. Personnel from the department may serve on internal CQI teams or represent the department on a multidepartmental hospitalwide team.

FOOD SERVICE SYSTEM

The procurement of supplies, the manufacturing of products, the distribution of the products, and the cleaning up process is known as the food service system. This system is present in all health care organizations. The system begins with the menu planning process, which is the key to the entire system. Once the menu is planned, recipes are developed, tested, and standardized. Procurement requirements are projected utilizing the forecasted number of meals and recipe needs. Orders for products are placed. Products are received, stored, and issued to a variety of units within the department and departments within the facility. Using recipes and based on the projected number of portions required, the food service system's production personnel prepare, cook, apportion, and transfer the finished product to all serving areas. After service, the soiled dishes are retrieved, washed, sanitized, and stored. The last step in the food service system includes trash removal, equipment sanitizing, and cleaning and sanitizing the work area.

CLINICAL NUTRITION SYSTEM

The clinical nutrition system increases in diversity depending on the classification of the health care organization, the types of services offered, the size, the ownership, the governing board, and medical staff bylaws. The service provided is at the request or in support of the medical practice and standards of care of the organization. Generally, the clinical nutrition personnel have as their goal the provision of individualized, direct, total nutrition care for all patients regardless of the type of diet order. The clinical nutrition personnel also serve as team members for the interdisciplinary approach of

care for preadmission, admission, discharge, and home care. These personnel also provide nutrition data for clinical pathways and positive outcomes of care. The clinical nutrition personnel may, through the provision of these services, identify secondary and complicating conditions and seek reimbursement for services. The clinical personnel have the responsibility for the nutritional assessment of the patients, the nutrition care plan, education of the patient and/or significant other, nutrition support for those patients requiring specialized products, data analysis, and charting. As members of the CQI process all members of the DNFS department are constantly seeking opportunities for improving, always keeping in mind the needs, wants, and perceptions of the patient.

The DNFS department uses approximately 6 to 9 percent of the direct expenses of the average hospital. In other health care facilities the percentage is usually lower. The department requires a large space and a variety of equipment to perform its task. The staff requirements vary depending on the size and complexity of the department or facility. Staffing needs in hospitals are usually greater than those in other health care organizations such as long-term care facilities. A high percentage of DNFS departments employ part-time staff. The number of full-time equivalents (FTEs) is most often the second or third largest, following nursing and environmental services, and occasionally maintenance and engineering or laboratory services. There is a broad spectrum of personnel from entry level dishwasher to multidegreed professional and clinical personnel. This chapter provides basic information concerning the operation of the DNFS department.

SYSTEMS APPROACH

The food service component of the department lends itself to a systems approach. Figure 12–1 illustrates this components system. Inputs into the system may come from outside regulatory agencies, such as the Joint Commission on Accreditation of Healthcare Organizations (Joint Commission) and the Health Care Financ-

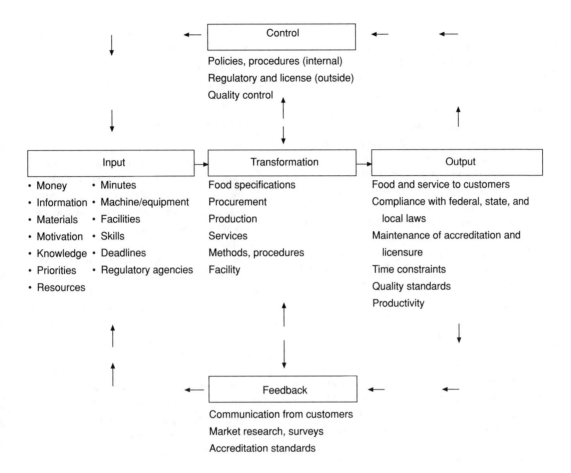

Figure 12–1 Components System

ing Administration (HCFA). Inputs may be physical, operational, and personnel. The action or transformation are actions by which the inputs are changed to outputs that must be acceptable to the total environment served, patients as well as other customers. The transformation process is controlled by the manager.

The control function includes management prerogatives for establishing policies, procedures, methods, space, layout, staffing, effective and efficient use of all resources, and standards for evaluating systems operations. The standard may be developed through the use of work sampling, work simplification, methods improvement, strategic planning, and workflow. Controls may be internal as well as external. Perhaps

the most important internal control is the menu. The menu then controls the labor and food cost, use of machines, purchase of equipment, layout, design, marketing, and the overall objectives of the department.

External controls are those laws and regulations that impose constraints on the organization. These controls may be federal (Omnibus Budget Reconciliation Act [OBRA], HCFA), state (laws and regulations as established by the legislature, licenses to operate), local (health department), Joint Commission standards, contracts that have been signed such as purchasing consortia, and housekeeping. The output of the system is the product and service that have been produced. These outputs may be routine, infrequent, or predictable. An example of each of these outputs for food service are: routine—preparation and service of three meals per day; predictable—the forecasting of the number of meals to be served in the cafeteria; and infrequent—a survey by the Joint Commission. The routine and predictable outputs are controlled by the manager through the use of proper management techniques. The infrequent output survey by the Joint Commission is predictable (time of survey) but infrequent (every three years). Unpredictable output would be a survey by the local health department. These surveys are unscheduled but the department must always maintain a sanitary and safe environment, utilizing the correct methodologies for preparing and serving food and meeting other established standards.

Time, quality, and work standards may be established to further define outputs. For example, patient meal service will begin at 7:30 A.M. and be completed by 9:00 A.M., meeting the temperature and quality standards as established by productivity measures. Some outputs may be unexpected, such as a disaster. However, policies and procedures should be in place to cover any unexpected event.

Feedback is an overriding component of the system. Feedback is the mechanism that provides data for adjustments and changes to inputs, outputs, and to some extent the transformation/action process. Feedback on the system must be evaluated for validity. No system is complete without records. Food service systems record keeping may be done in the office or a warehouse depending on state law requirement. However, with the introduction of many specialized food service software programs, record keeping for the system has been simplified.

SUBSYSTEMS

The food service is a system made up of a variety of interdependent subsystems. Subsystems are classified according to their function or purpose. The type of food service (cook-chill, convenience, and variety) will depend on the number of subsystems needed in an organization.

Most food service systems will have at least the following subsystems:

- menu planning
- procurement
- production
- distribution and service
- maintenance

These subsystems will be a function of all subsystems and will vary depending on the goals and missions of the organization. Safety, sanitation, and quality control are not considered subsystems within themselves, but are an integral part of the system as a whole.

Using the systems approach the food service director can focus on the entire department and view all the subsystems in relation to the whole. The systems approach is a conceptual approach to relationships within a department and emphasizes how effectively and efficiently subsystems interact and are integrated into the whole system for achieving the goals and missions of the department. Systems are objective and allow the food service to reduce bias concerning the system and to more objectively determine the management function and their interlocking or linking process within the system.

Menu Planning

The menu subsystem controls every input as well as every output. The menu determines the equipment needed, the amount of space required, type of storage, the number and skills of the personnel, scheduling methods, the cost of the operation, the type of production and service subsystems. Menus can be selective, nonselective, a combination of the two, or restaurant style. Menus are cyclic and vary from five-day to six-week. Long-term care facilities usually have four-to-six-week cycles.

The menu should take into consideration the perceptions and therapeutic needs of the patient, as well as the cultural diversity of the population. The menu should meet the 1989 Recommended Daily Allowance (RDA), the 1992 United States Department of Agriculture (USDA) Food Guide Pyramid, and the 1990

USDA and United States Department of Health and Human Service (DHHS) Guidelines for Americans.

In some health care organizations procurement of all organization supplies is the responsibility of the materials management department. In most health care organizations purchasing of food and supplies is the responsibility of the food service director, who develops the specifications for needed food and supply items and submits to the purchasing department for bidding. In large organizations a formal system is used. In small organizations informal purchasing is most often used. The food service director has final authority over what food is purchased. A variety of methods are used to purchase food and supplies.

Cost-effective bidding and efficient procedures can reduce costs. Weighing items, especially meats, checking product received versus specifications, and seeking discounts and rebates for large-volume purchases can save money for the department and organization and support the success of the department by ensuring that the required product was received for the intended use and at the minimum price and best quality.

Production

Most health care facilities utilize one or more production systems. The most common subsystem used are:

- cook-serve (conventional)
- cook-chill
- cook-freeze
- assemble and serve
- commissary system

There is a difference in each subsystem in the form the food is purchased, the amount of labor and equipment required, the time needed for preparation, and the skill of the personnel. All of the subsystems can produce a high quality of food depending on the skill of the employees, management control, and quality of product used in recipes. All subsystems employ a variety of personnel such as cooks, chefs, ingredient control assistants, salad makers, bakers, and other personnel.

The cook-serve subsystem is commonly referred to as conventional and/or "scratch" cooking. This system uses mostly fresh, canned, or frozen products according to the recipe. Few institutions utilize a butcher or butcher shop. Portion cuts have replaced the meat cuttery operation. Bakery products may still be prepared on site using frozen pastry shells, preportioned cookies, muffin mix, and prepared icing for cakes. This subsystem requires a higher inventory of supplies, as well as more staff, space, and equipment. It is a 7-day-a-week operation, usually 12 to 15 hours per day. Both skilled and unskilled personnel are used in the system. The system may have a lower unit of food cost because of greater control over menu items, and the use of seasonal products. Monitoring is important to avoid preparation of items too much in advance of service.

The cook-chill subsystem utilizes some of the aspects of conventional preparation, but rather than serving immediately, the food is chilled. When needed, the product is rethermalized. Not all foods can be prepared in this manner without modification to recipes and/or ingredients. Special thickening agents will be needed for some recipes, and food handling must meet strict sanitation codes. The Hazard Analysis Critical Control Point (HACCP) system, a safe and sanitary control system utilized by many USDA food processing plants, should be implemented and carefully monitored. The HACCP system is used to maximize food safety. It is a program of monitoring and adjusting procedures to protect food from becoming contaminated before it is served. The concept combines principles of food microbiology, quality control, and risk assessment to obtain as nearly as possible a fail-safe system. The public health officials in the United States as well as the 1995 Joint Commission standards encourage the implementation of this process. Some large facilities utilize laboratories to test food for a variety of bacteria, mold, and spores. Equipment must be meticulously cleaned, food rapidly chilled to at least 32 degrees and held in a temperature-monitored refrigerator at approximately 35 degrees or lower. Good personal hygiene for all production employees is a critical point in the preparation of the food. In some cook-chill operations highly skilled staff can be reduced to five days a week, eight hours per day, as food is prepared in advance and rethermalized by less skilled personnel.

The cook-freeze subsystem operates very much like the cook-chill subsystem, except that after cooking, items are frozen for storage. Rather than basing production according to short-term requirements, production personnel produce an inventory of foods, much as a manufacturer of convenience food would. The same precautions and advantages outlined in the cook-chill subsystem apply here. However, in this subsystem the temperature of the product should reach 0 degrees Fahrenheit in 90 minutes after initial cooking. The food should be stored at 0 degrees or lower, and must be packaged properly to prevent freezer burn. Cook-chill and cook-freeze subsystems are not recommended for health care facilities with fewer than 300 beds, and with a small number of staff/visitor meals, because there is a loss in economies of scale.

In the assemble-and-serve subsystem the food is obtained from a commercial source, usually in a frozen state, and rethermalized when ready to serve. Materials for salads may be ready to assemble, and bakery products ready to eat. Other products may be canned or packaged in individual ready-to-serve portions, such as juices and other beverages. This subsystem requires less space, high technological equipment, and fewer employees. Food costs are likely to be higher. Menus may not contain as much variety as in the other systems. Most facilities utilize a combination of these systems, unless facility size precludes the use of a particular approach.

Commissary food production, also called food factories, is a subsystem in which procurement and production of requested menu items is centralized, and items are prepared and delivered to a number of remote facilities for final preparation, rethermalization, and service. These remote facilities are frequently referred to as satellite service centers. In the commissary system, food is purchased in large quantities either raw, frozen, fresh, or canned and is stored properly until needed.

In summary, the food production system may be any of the previous systems discussed, or a combination of any of these. Foods are held either frozen, chilled, or heated for distribution to the satellites. Menu items may be in bulk or individual packages. The delivery of food to the facility will vary depending on the satellite storage capacity, operating hours, policies, and personnel available. Deliveries may be three times a day, once a day, three times a week, or weekly. In the cook-serve production subsystem food must be delivered prior to each meal. The delivery of this food must meet the local and state regulations, and consideration of distance, traffic delays, and method of preparation is vital to providing quality, safe food.

Since the early 1970s several facilities have embarked upon food factory concepts, applying cook-chill or cook-freeze technology to production. This entails the production of large quantities of food for delivery to multiple facilities from a central site. In addition, these off-site facilities typically promised returns based on sales of produced food to nonowned facilities, such as schools, other hospitals, and so forth. The capital investment for equipment was significant. The return on investment frequently failed to reach the goal, and the control of quality within the food factory required significantly different types of management than that found in most food service operations; the food factory concept required applications of manufacturing technology. The food factory concept, especially with the growth of multihospital systems, continues to find favor. Generally, the concept is sound, given adequate volumes of meals to support such a capital investment for manufacturing equipment and appropriate availability of management skills.

Distribution and Service

Service subsystems are methods that are used to transport prepared food, apportion it, and serve it to the customer, whether a patient or a cafeteria/catering customer. These subsystems may be centralized or decentralized. Centralized service subsystems are most often used in health care facilities. They require less equipment and labor, and offer greater control over quality, temperature, and portion size. Centralized food service is where patient meals are prepared, assembled in a central location in or near the main kitchen, and transported to patient units for service by food service and/or nursing; soiled trays are returned to a centralized location for sanitizing. In a decentralized system, the food is usually prepared in a central location and transported either in bulk or individualized portions to serving galleys on patient floors. The food may be placed in refrigerator/freezers for rethermalization at a later time, regardless of the area in which the finished patient tray is made up.

Patient service subsystems are based on either heat-retention or on rethermalization methods. The majority of hospitals serve meals to patients based on heat-retention methods. That is, the tray is prepared in a location and delivered to the nursing unit; the food was hot when it was placed on the tray, and methods such as unitized pellets, insulated trays, and so forth are used to maintain the temperature until the tray is delivered. Rethermalization methods add heat to the food at the point of service, or in a central location, but much later than when the tray was first assembled. They are used with cook-chill and cook-freeze production subsystems. The most common rethermalization method is microwaving; the second most common is heating in ovens in smaller units near patient areas. Rethermalization is especially appropriate when distances traveled with trays are significant, or when patients require feeding on nonroutine schedules. The most significant advantage of rethermalization is temperature acceptability; second is flexibility in service times. The most significant disadvantages relate to the menu constraints; many popular menu items do not rethermalize well, decreasing the variety possible for the patient menu. Further, when decentralized rethermalization occurs, logistical prob-

lems arise and quality control remains the responsibility of the person reheating the meal.

Tray-Line Configuration

The type of food production subsystem influences tray-line configuration and tray assembly. Tray-line configuration applies to the spatial relationship of the tray-line components such as the tray-line conveyor system, the carts, the workstations, space allocation, type of menu, number of personnel available, and the required number of trays per minute.

There are five basic tray-line configurations. They are:

1. one-sided with cart storage
2. one-sided with reach access
3. two-sided with perpendicular stations
4. two-sided with perpendicular and parallel stations
5. circular

The one-sided with cart storage tray line will fit into a long narrow space. The carts are easily stored, as there is not as much movement during actual tray assembly as in other front-of-the-server systems. The server does not have to twist and turn as much as in a traditional arrangement. The tray carts are queued on one side of the tray line feeding the loader end of the line. All workstations face the tray conveyor. This type of tray line may be expensive because of the electrical cost and belt repairs. Because the line is so long, mistakes are hard to correct. A reject table and runner would be needed, and a microphone to call for missed items.

The one-sided with reach across is most commonly used in a chilled assembly subsystem, in which most menu items have been preplated chilled before assembly, or as a part of assembly. In this configuration the menu rides on the conveyor facing the employee. Because the food items are located across the tray line, the workers are not interrupted by changing pans; the new pans are loaded by other employees independent of the actual assembly of trays. Therefore, the tray line has to stop fewer times for resupply of food. Since the food items are located across the tray line, there may be a requirement for more staff, as resupply of food is frequent.

The two-sided with perpendicular stations and the two-sided with perpendicular and parallel stations are frequently used in larger institutions. The linear space is not as long as in the one-sided; however, the width is greater. The complexity of the menu and the size of the institution will determine the number of serving stations needed.

The circular tray line may be oval or round. In this configuration some of the support system, such as refrigeration, freezer, plates, overhang shelves, and serving wells, is built into the tray line. This type of tray line requires less square footage to produce a given number of meals per minute, and less peripheral equipment is needed because many of the stations are built into the tray line. However, because of the build-in of stations, there is less flexibility in overall design.

Regardless of the configuration chosen, it is vital that the work of assembling trays be balanced. Balancing work means that no one employee has to do more twisting, bending, reaching, stooping, walking, and/or dipping and placing items on a tray than another employee. Both hands are used, minimizing hand-to-hand transfer. The less bending, twisting, or other such movements during the actual assembly of trays, the more effective the overall work environment, resulting in a more effective and less fatigued employee.

Temperature

There are five basic temperature maintenance systems. The system chosen will depend on the number of trays to be served, the time allocated for service, physical layout of the main kitchen, location of the nursing unit, and the distance to be traveled from preportion to service. The most common system is the unitized pellet. The pellet is encapsulated in a stainless steel base and may be metal- or wax-lined. The base is heated to approximately 250 degrees Fahrenheit. A heated plate containing apportioned food is placed on the unitized base and covered with a lid that may or may not contain another heated pellet. Cold foods are placed in serving dishes that may or may not be insulated. Tray assembly is completed in a centralized area. The tray is ready to serve when it is delivered to the patient units in unheated carts. Reusable china is usually used with this method. Insulated trays are thermal trays that have individual molded compartments for the placement of hot or cold foods. Food may be placed directly in the compartments, in disposable or in china dishes, and the entire tray is covered with an insulated lid. Trays are delivered directly to the patients' bedsides using open carts and/or noninsulated carts.

The hot/cold cart method contains separate tray slots adjacent to each other for hot food and for cold food. The cart is electrically heated and refrigerated. The cart may contain a freezing unit for frozen items, such as ice cream, and a coffee serving unit. The temperatures are electronically controlled. The carts are usually large and hard to push unless they are motorized, or follow a preplanned rail system. This cart has the advantage of proper temperature maintenance but is more difficult to clean and maintain. A similar system is called the split tray cart. This system has not been utilized as much in the last 20 years. Food may be plated cold and sent to a patient unit galley for storage until meal time. Hot food items may be rethermed on the floor at meal service by microwave, convection oven, and/or other rethermalization equipment.

Rethermalization carts are becoming more popular due to the introduction of the cook-chill, cook-freeze, and the assemble-and-serve subsystems. All foods are plated cold and placed in a cart that has been programmed to the menu item that will automatically heat the food to the appropriate temperature, while also maintaining the temperature of the cold foods.

*Tray Distribution, Service, and
   Presentation*

The distribution of trays to the patient's bedside may be the responsibility of nursing services, but is more often that of the food service department. When trays have been completely set up in a centralized area, the tray is ready to serve when it reaches the unit and can therefore be served to the patient more easily and quickly. This method of tray distribution requires fewer personnel, and there are usually fewer errors in service. If employees have to match trays or rethermalize trays in a galley, the possibility of error increases.

Tray distribution is the final step in providing the customer with what was ordered from the selective menu. The employee serving the tray should be well groomed, and wear a name tag and a uniform designating the department represented. The employee should always knock on the patient's door before entering, and greet the patient by courtesy title and last name. Employees who distribute trays to patients should be well trained in their task. They may be the only person from food service the patient sees while hospitalized, and they can either enhance or degrade the department by their actions.

Nursing, and in some instances the food service personnel, readies the patient for meal service by seeing that hands are washed, the overbed table is properly arranged, and the patient is positioned to eat. In some instances, once they have been trained in CPR and feeding methods, food service personnel may feed the patient. The distributor of trays should check the tray for spills and attractiveness, and ensure that all items are neatly arranged before serving the tray. The tray should be placed so the entree faces the patient, making it more convenient for the patient to eat. Courteous service on the part of the employee distributing and serving the patient makes for a more pleasant mealtime experience. In most hospitals tray delivery and pickup is performed by food service personnel. In long-term facilities tray delivery and pickup may be done by nursing personnel. In most hospitals, nursing personnel do not feel that passing and picking up trays is a high enough level skill to be included in their duties.

In-Between Meal Service

In addition to tray service, some patients require in-between meal feeding programs usually called nourishments, specialized programs such as enteral nutrition support, and menu processing. About 85 percent of the inpatient census requires tray service; the remaining patients are NPO or on enteral nutrition support. Of the patients receiving trays, 35 to 45 percent are on diets that are modified for consistency, minerals, sugar, etc. Modified diets do not usually include clear and full liquid diets, regular, or soft diets. Preparing modified diets requires more resources and a highly specialized cook who has the responsibility for the special preparation.

In-between meal feeding programs include three major categories:

1. floor stock
2. ad lib requests
3. scheduled special nourishments

Floor stock refers to food and beverage supplied to each nursing floor by the food service department; that floor stock is generally held within the nursing station, ready for use by a patient when a request is made. The most common items stocked are juices and soda. Cost varies depending on item, pack, and size. Floor stock is often misappropriated for personal use by staff, which increases the unit cost.

Ad lib requests are those items prepared and delivered based on a verbal request by a patient. For instance, a patient may request additional foods such as additional dessert and coffee. Typically, the patient requests the items from the nurse, who calls the order in to the DNFS department. The order is then filled and delivered. Frequently problems arise with this type of system because of the wide variety of items that might be requested by patients, the frequent breakdowns in communication, and the additional cost to the department. These problems have been solved in some facilities by implementing room service programs similar to those found in hotels. Some facilities charge for ad lib requests; others provide it as a service to all patients.

Scheduled nourishments are routinely provided based on a diet prescription generated either by the clinical dietitian or the physician. Most often, those patients receiving such foods or beverages either required frequent small feedings, increased quantities of nutrients, or a specific feeding schedule because of drug administration, such as a patient with diabetes mellitus. Scheduled nourishments are generally provided midmorning, midafternoon, and late evening. While not all patients require all three between-meal feedings, preparation of these type of products is very labor intensive, as are ad lib requests.

Specialized feeding programs include tube feedings (and other total enteral feeding systems) and total parenteral feeding (delivering nutrients directly into a major vein). Dietitians are greatly involved in determining products for these types of feeding programs. The costs of these feedings are most frequently billed to the patient through use of a pharmaceutical identification number; revenue potential is significant. An enteral products formulary, used by physicians and dietitians, simplifies the process and contains costs. Total parenteral feedings are usually based on individualized orders that alter basic solutions; solution mixing usually occurs in pharmacy departments due to the potential for sepsis.

OTHER SERVICE METHODS

In long-term care facilities patients may eat in a central dining room. Service in the dining room may be prepared-tray, family style, waitress, or cafeteria style. The method chosen will depend on the acuity of the patient, the philosophy of the facility, and the total dollars allocated for the provision of foodservice.

Nonpatient Meal Service: Cafeteria

The most common type of meal service for employees and visitors is cafeteria service. Cafeteria services can include coffee shops, specialized restaurants, sidewalk cafes, minifood courts, portable cafeterias, and more traditional employee-style cafeterias. In most facilities, the more traditional-style cafeteria exists. Historically, this type of cafeteria was provided for employee feeding, and revenue generation was not a serious consideration because the operating cost was written off as an employee benefit expense. In the 1990s, however, with changes in payment by government medical agencies, most hospitals now operate with revenue or net margin goals in mind.

Cafeteria pricing is always a sensitive issue. Pricing should reflect the operating philosophy of the health care facility. What is the objective: break-even, subsidy, or profit? Pricing should be compatible with that objective, permitting the management to reach its management strategies for resource control. For public relations purposes, prices should not all be changed at the same time. Rather, menu categories, or preferably a few items in each category, should be changed periodically in order to catch up on pricing requirements as needed. Changing prices at the same time results in reactions such as employee petitions, union difficulties, and even boycotts.

Because of employee expectations, and in order to meet revenue goals, cafeteria services generally include hot food and snack meal service throughout the work day. Most commonly, separate eating facilities are provided for medical staff. Late night cafeteria meals rarely provide enough revenue to offset costs, and, as a result, other alternatives are usually used to meet these demands, rather than operating a full-service cafeteria around the clock. In the South and Southwest, grill service for breakfast and for sandwiches is an expectation in almost every market segment. Marketing and promotion activities include special pricing, advertising to special interest groups (such as senior citizens living in the area), advertising, coupon systems, and frequent changes in menus and programming.

Cafeteria service systems are categorized either according to the type of service counter arrangement, or by the individuals actually apportioning the food. Service counters can be arranged in the following ways:

- scramble system
- sawtooth

- circular
- straight-line
- combination

Portioning systems can be either self-service or served.

A scramble system, also known as the shopping center or the serving square system, arranges a number of counters in a larger serving area, allowing access to the various counters independent of one another. For instance, there may be one counter for salads and one for desserts. The person who wants only a salad need not go to the dessert counter. This system improves traffic flow, but generally decreases impulse buying potential. Because the client must be familiar with the layout to really use the system effectively, this system is especially applicable for employee meal operations. Because of the number of counters, its labor costs are high.

The sawtooth system is an adaptation of the scramble system; it fits more easily in longer, narrower physical plants. The same concept of various counters is used, but instead of being scattered throughout a larger space, they are arranged at angles along a long, narrow corridor. With a wide aisle, this arrangement still permits improved traffic flow. A potential advantage of the sawtooth over the scramble system is that clients have to pass each counter, although they are not required to stop. This arrangement may improve the potential of impulse purchases, an important consideration when revenue generation is a concern.

The circular layout relies on a carousel-type piece of equipment. Food is apportioned in the kitchen and placed on the turning serving counter. The customer approaches the counter, waits at a station to see the selections, and selects preportioned food. The advantages of this system are the decreases in labor cost and the belief that waiting is decreased because patrons only wait until their individual selection is made (i.e., no one has to stand in line behind someone else, at least once he or she reaches the counter). The disadvantages are the impracticality of expanding such services with auxiliary equipment

if the market changes, the inability to merchandise the food at low peak periods (the small number of servings turning on the carousel look as if the last portions are being served), and the deterioration of the product that remains apportioned for long periods of time as it turns around the carousel. When the equipment malfunctions, the counter is inoperable.

The straight-line and its minor adaptations, such as the L-shaped system, are used in the vast majority of public and most institutionally based cafeterias. All items for sale are laid out along one counter that places various groupings of items, such as desserts, together in one display area, but all groupings are arranged so that the client must pass each display area. The major disadvantage of this system is the formation of long lines at peak times. Its major advantages are the decreased cost in equipment and labor, as well as the probable increase in revenue due to impulse buying resulting from the client going past every station on the service line. Combinations of these systems frequently exist. For instance, a salad bar may be added to a straight-line system. In served systems, which are most common, food service workers actually dish out the food as the client requests the items. In some systems, all menu items are dished upon request and in others some preportioning occurs. The advantage of preportioning is improved portion control and it also reduces labor cost when few persons are being served in the line. The disadvantages of preportioning are a potential decrease in quality and an overall increase in labor costs per portion if business is always brisk throughout the service period.

Self-service systems have gained popularity in recent years because of the advent of salad bars and other such self-service concepts. Some cafeterias are now totally self-service, especially if pricing is by weight, rather than by portion. Self-service is most appropriate when this type of pricing system overcomes the overportioning problems of self-service concepts. Originally thought to be a laborless system, self-service systems do require significant labor for replenishing food, cleaning up spills, and ensuring that food and serviceware are available and clients are assisted with problems.

Cafeterias and the Public

Many facilities have only one area for dining. Some employee groups complain about visitors eating in the same dining room or holding up lines in the cafeteria. Several approaches in design, such as sawtooth arrangement of counters, help resolve this problem. Some facilities restrict visitors from using the cafeteria services during certain hours. Other facilities offer separate serving or cashiering stations during peak service periods. Others suggest, through flyers placed in each patient room, that visitors use the cafeteria at less busy times. Often those flyers include positive wording, such as "avoid the long lines waiting for our fresh, delicious food." Some facilities permit visitors access at any time and ignore employee complaints, whereas others restrict visitors completely and forego the revenue and community relations potential of the cafeteria serving the public or at least patient visitors.

Branding

Branding has become an issue in commercial/cafeteria service. Many fast food organizations utilize a portion of the food service operation to offer familiar names and products, mostly to staff and visitors, but in some instances to patients. Depending on the wording of the contract, the company may or may not pay a small percentage of the overhead cost, but will furnish the equipment and staff to operate the service and provide a percentage of gross/net revenues to the facility. Contracts for implementing branding operations such as fast food operations must be explicit. The brand name is very prominently displayed. In some instances the price of the brand name may be more than if a nonbrand or in-house product was used. Other branding concepts may include the provision of a piece of equipment for advertising a product brand. Name-brand carbonated drinks and yogurt are examples. As cost continues to escalate there is a possibility of more branding in all health care facilities.

Catering Services

Depending on the policy and philosophical beliefs embraced by the facility, catering services include anything from a pot of coffee for a meeting with a medical director, to a nine-course meal for an outside community group, to an off-premise affair on a fee-for-service basis. Most commonly, however, catering services provide food and beverages to hospital and medical staff meetings, usually on-campus. The most frequent users of this service are administration and medical staff offices.

Having a standardized menu and requiring 24-hour advance notice almost always improves service and controls costs. Providing these services is highly labor intensive and often captures much of the department's management time, especially if adequate notice for functions is not received. However, no single activity within the department more significantly affects public opinion about its overall quality of service. If the physicians and administrative staff are satisfied and pleased with the catering services, that positive opinion affects the perception of the quality of service provided by the department in other areas as well. In some facilities, departmental management is unenthusiastic about catering, most often because of the labor problems it creates. However, the efforts required in catering go a very long way in creating positive public relations for the hospital and for the department.

Catering Costing and Transfers

Keeping the costs of catering in the food service's budget is appropriate if they are clearly segregated so that (1) management is aware of the real costs of providing the service, and (2) they are analyzed separately when comparisons are made to national median food costs per patient day. However, many hospitals encourage the practice of transferring the costs of catering to the user department, such as medical records or medical staff, so that the person requesting the function has an incentive to control the cost involved. Various methods of costing are used, including marked-up costs, raw food cost transfers only, and materials with labor costs only. The hospital's approach to cost accounting drives this costing system.

Vending Services

Vending in the vast majority of hospitals includes soda, snack, and sandwich or full meal vending. Most frequently, these services are subcontracted to a local company specializing in vending services. However, some hospitals elect to provide their own vending. Vending services are especially important for staff and visitors in the off-hours because they also ease the burden of an overcrowded cafeteria, and provide easy access to food as a result of the machines' usually diverse locations.

The major vending issues relate to contractual arrangements and responsibility for those contracts, sanitation and liability from hazards relating to food poisoning, and the public relations implication of what is actually sold in the machines.

Contractual arrangements vary widely. In some settings, the machines are owned by the hospital, serviced by the vendor, and maintained by the engineering department. In other settings, and probably most commonly, the vending company actually owns the equipment, stocks it with product, collects the money, keeps the equipment operating, and then pays the hospital a commission for the privilege of having machines on hospital property. The commission rate is usually a percentage of total sales less sales tax, and commission rates vary from 1 to 25 percent, depending on the type of product vended, the sales volume expected, the age of the equipment, and the local competitive environment among contractors. Commissions are not paid if the hospital management insists on locating equipment in low-sales-volume areas. Commissions also are often lower when a variety of machines are required by the hospital,

such as canned soda, ice cream, snack, sandwich, milk, hot canned food, and so forth, in an area that serves relatively few potential customers.

When facilities choose to own or lease their own vending equipment, the food service department buys all the product for the machines, makes other specialized product, fills the machines, collects the money, and takes all the risk in relation to location and equipment maintenance. There are significant advantages to this approach if volume is high enough and if locations are few enough to ensure a high dollar return for the investment in equipment. However, this type of activity is very labor intensive, especially if the number of foods prepared, such as packaged sandwiches, is very low, because under these circumstances manual rather than automated systems often are used. If the hospital bases human resources management on FTEs per bed, then there may be significant difficulty meeting the labor demands of the self-operated vending program, because those sales are relatively unrelated to number of in-house patients.

Vending machines often are maligned and frequently blamed for gastrointestinal upsets by consumers when in fact such machines are often much safer ways of dispensing food than most cafeteria lines. Modern machines are carefully monitored and their temperature is maintained. If the machine malfunctions, in most cases that malfunction precludes purchase of the product. The only real danger of food poisoning exists when the machine is loaded with spoiled or contaminated product, or when that product is not properly rotated. In a contractual arrangement, the hospital may wish to ensure that it is held harmless and indemnified from liability for claims of food poisoning or other accidents related to the vending equipment. The self-operated vending company must ensure that quality control mechanisms are in place, are continuously monitored, and consistently documented.

In the 1950s and 1960s, offering food through a vending machine was not a positive public relations activity, especially if the clientele demanded high levels of service. However, in this era, vending machines are considered a way of life by almost everyone, regardless of social or economic status. Equipment designs improved dramatically in the early 1980s, permitting operators to provide full meals, salads, and lighter yet very attractive fare.

Currently, the greater problem often faced by hospital management is the group of employees who are disgruntled with the variety of food in the vending machine. Often one of the easiest methods to overcome this dissatisfaction is to ensure that the department manager frequently meets with user groups to solicit their input. Residents, interns, and night personnel are traditionally the most vocal staff concerning the variety and quality of products in vending machines.

FINANCIAL CONTROLS

The financial controls on the food service system include budgeting methodologies and the allocation of cost. Some large facilities assign a cost center to each unit within the department, i.e., cafeteria, catering, patient food service, etc. Other facilities develop one budget for the entire department. Regardless of how the financial controls are set up, it is important that the financial objectives are met. The budgeting process usually is based on historical data, national cost per unit of service, and/or projected level of service for the next fiscal year, including all new programs. Some cost categories are sensitive to fluctuation in census or unit of service, others are not. Generally, food and supplies are census sensitive, while printing, advertising, and equipment maintenance are not related to census fluctuation, or fixed and variable costs. The most widely accepted method for budgeting combines inflationary adjustments of the historical unit of service costs; then that cost is adjusted for projected volume in units of service cost at projected volumes in unit of service. The monthly cost incurred should be measured against the budget, variances explored and justified, and, where possible, adjustments made.

Allocating cost to patient and nonpatient areas is difficult, but is a requirement of most third-party payors. When separate cost centers are set up for patients and nonpatients, the costs incurred in these areas can be charged back to the center for a more realistic cost for each area. The most common method used is based on the equivalent meal model that drives the productivity system. Total costs are allocated based on the percentage of equivalent meals per service area. For instance, if the patient meals comprise 65 percent of the total equivalent meals provided, then that patient meal cost center, in this model, would receive an allocation equal to 65 percent of the total costs for each expense category. The least common method is to cost account each cost based on actual usage. Although this approach in theory produces the most accurate cost picture, it is very labor intensive. A middle-of-the-road approach is to cost account a random sample of actual costs and compare the results to the equivalent meal model, adjusting it appropriately. Intermittently, that adjusted model is then evaluated based on other random samples.

Other control mechanisms include establishing standards and measuring outcome performance against the standards, and then benchmarking against other facilities within a specific group. Developing competencies to measure staff performance, instituting performance-based job description and evaluation, implementing CQI for improvement opportunities, and developing strategic plans and goals, also are applicable control mechanisms.

LAYOUT AND DESIGN

The final subsystem for food service systems is facilities planning, design, and equipment selection. The layout and design of food service must be functionally planned and efficient to operate. Most food service departments are in need of renovation because of the age of the equipment. New technologies, wasted space, insufficient storage space (especially refrigerator/freezer space), and the change in meal delivery are reasons for renovating DNFS.

The renovation process should be well planned to reflect interim service requirements, be compatible with interior design concepts used throughout the hospital, and be consistent with management's philosophies. The planning for a renovation should be a team approach. Administration and food service management must agree on menu pattern, production, service system, and the projection of growth in patient services as well as the nonpatient areas. The team members should be the food service management, representatives from hospital administration, architect, contractor, facility engineer, on-site manager for subcontractor, and, if needed, a food service consultant. A subcommittee of users, especially nursing, should be established for ongoing input.

A food service design consultant may be employed to assist with schematic layout and design, specifications for equipment, bid documents, estimating equipment cost, inspecting equipment for verification of specifications, and proper placement and installation before the area is turned over to the owner. The consultant should have food service experience and be independent of a food service equipment company. For large-scale renovations, the services of a food service consultant are required as the consultant's knowledge of systems and equipment can help to avoid costly mistakes. The most common mistake made during renovation planning is the delay in involving the director until plans are already drawn. The most cost-effective, efficient approach is to involve the food service director and other managers in the process before any drawings or other operational decisions are made.

CLINICAL NUTRITION SERVICES

The clinical nutrition service provided to both inpatients and outpatients in hospitals and residents in other health care facilities is performed under the direction of a registered and licensed dietitian. The goal is to individualize the nutritional care to meet the psycho-socio-economical cultural needs of the patient. Clinical nutrition service is composed of an internal team of registered dietitians (RDs), registered dietetic technicians (DTRs), certified dietary managers (CDMs), and other representatives as appropriate. Many of these professionals may also serve on interdisciplinary teams of care. Each member of the team has his or her own responsibility. RDs provide clinical expertise in nutrition-related complications and methods to determine their presence in particular patient groups. This is accomplished by nutritional assessment, including complex calculations and evaluations of laboratory values that provide these clinicians with information upon which to base recommendations for more effective care that can reduce length of stay and decrease morbidity and medical complications. RDs are also responsible for individualized nutritional counseling that includes behavior modification and education to the patient and/or significant other. Nutrition care plans, follow-up, and discharge planning in a multidisciplinary area are included in an RD's duties. Continuous quality improvement, seeking reimbursement for services rendered, and increasing marketing of service and entrepreneurial efforts have become vital elements of the successful clinical management operations.

DTRs and CDMs may be employed in large university teaching hospitals. They are most often employed in long-term care facilities and have total responsibility for the operation under the direction of an RD. Each team member has his or her own responsibility, yet each member plays a role in translating the physician's order into food that meets the individual's physical, rehabilitation, and restoration-of-health needs, as well as the social, emotional, religious, and psychological needs, wants, and perceptions of the patient. The RD (who may also be licensed in his or her individual state) is a graduate of an approved program in dietetics, having completed a coordinated undergraduate program and/or an internship, and passed a national examination administered by the Commission on Dietetic Registration. The RD must meet the continuing education requirements as established by the American Dietetic Association. RDs may be employed in outpatient settings and in specialty roles, such as nutrition support and wellness and prevention programs. Services provided in these settings are similar to services provided on an inpatient basis. RDs seek reimbursement for these services from third-party payors. RDs may also work in home health agencies; supplemental programs for women, infants, and children; programs for the elderly; weight loss clinics; consultants to physicians' offices; long-term care centers; and athletic training programs, as well as other entrepreneurial areas.

Dietetic technicians (DTs) have successfully completed a two-year degree program that has been approved by the American Dietetic Association. The degree may be in general management or nutritional care. The DT must pass a national examination administered by the Commission on Dietetic Registration to become a DTR. Continuing education is required to maintain registration. In hospitals the DTR who is proficient in nutrition works closely with the RD. The DTR screens patients for nutrition risk and refers results to the RD for further intervention; gathers data to be used in assessment and care plans; provides day-to-day nutrition care by calculating calorie counts, completing food recall diaries, assisting the patient in menu selection, and providing routine and general nutrition information to the patient and/or significant other; and assists in the development of educational materials. In some large facilities a DTR may oversee the operation of formula preparation. The DTR who is employed in long-term care may be a generalist and have responsibility for the entire operation. A consultant RD will provide advice and consultation to the DTR.

The CDM is an individual who has completed a Dietary Manager's Association approved course that consists of 120 hours of didactic learning and 190 hours of field experience, passing a certification examination and maintaining the required hours of continuing education. Size and complexity of a facility will dictate the need for all the practitioner/team members. In most long-term facilities, a CDM serves as the department manager with consultation of an RD to advise, observe, evaluate, instruct, and recommend. In large organizations the CDM is a day-to-day manager who supervises patient hosts, assistants, and aides for all phases of the food-service system.

The nutrition representative handles patient menus, diet-order changes, nourishment orders, and late-tray requests. When cross-functionally trained, the nutrition representative may prepare patients to receive their meal, feed the patients, record input and output, and perform other nursing assistant functions as assigned. The nutrition assistants work at a specific station at the trayline, placing various food items on trays; serving trays; retrieving trays; and sanitizing dishes, carts, and work area. The nutrition representatives and assistants may be supervised by a DTR or a CDM. All members of the nutrition team must possess and practice good guest-relation skills and sanitary and safety habits; promote a positive image of the department and facility; and at all times protect the confidentiality of the patient.

The team interacts with many other health care professionals, including physicians, nurses, pharmacists, therapists, and administration. Members of the team provide input into clinical pathways and critical paths. This approach is a multilevel, multidiscipline, multidimensional, long-term approach to care that flattens the organization, eliminates redundancy of bureaucratic functions, redesigns work, allows for creativity and empowerment of personnel, and gives the ability to take initiative to take risk. The administration must provide an environment of support for change.

DOCUMENTATION OF CARE

Documentation in the medical record is clearly defined in the Code of Federal Regulations for hospitals and skilled nursing facilities. The facility bylaws determine which professionals are credentialed to chart in the record, where to chart, and the method for charting. RDs, DTRs, and CDMs may all be credentialed to chart in the record. Some large hospitals do not always credential CDMs and may limit what the DTR may document.

CONTRACT MANAGEMENT VERSUS SELF-OPERATION

Contract management of departmental activities in U.S. hospitals is about 25 percent, for ICF and SNF the percentage is lower. That percentage has been relatively stable; however, recent trends show that the actual number of beds under control of contract management seems to be increasing. This means that although the total number of facilities under contract management control does not appear to be changing, the companies seem to be serving larger clients.

The questions of whether to have contract management in a food service department concern economics, relative scope, and difficulty of problems within the DNFS department. Contract management companies can often resolve major problems quickly, bringing management strategies into line. Their operating strategies include effective cost and human resources management. However, costs associated with contract management may exceed those of self-operation. The decision to use contract management must be analyzed based on need for change, effectiveness of management, and total cost. There are advantages to both self-operation and contract management. Each facility must decide what is best for that facility. Alternatives must be carefully considered and justified.

In choosing a management company, request for proposals (RFPs) should be sent to all companies determined eligible. The RFP should include the goals and objectives of the department; the menu, quality, and method of food purchasing; operating cost; responsibility of the management company to the facility; the role of the existing personnel (maintain facility employment and/or management company employees); union issues; rate of pay; benefits; financial provisions (cost per meal, cost per patient day); and any other data the institution may need. When evaluating the RFP, care should be taken to determine that like items are compared. If the decision is made to go with a management contract, the contract must be monitored. Problems, both economical and noneconomical; personnel issues; and quality concerns can arise.

CONCLUSION

The DNFS department provides a wide variety of services, which generally are labor intensive. Cost controls and effective management rely on the technology of various operating systems and careful resource control strategies. The food service operation usually accounts for less than 10 percent of the overall expense budget, but can dramatically affect the community opinion of quality of service provided by the hospital. It has the capacity to be a strong revenue producer and a strong community relations factor. Clientele can rarely assess quality of medical care, but the quality of food service provided quickly generates impressions that are lasting ones.

SUGGESTED READINGS

Darr, K., and J. Rakich. 1989. *Hospital organization and management text reading.* 4th ed. Owing Mills, Md.: National Health Publishing.

Finn, S.C., and G. Martin. 1991. The shifting balance of power: A new decade of decisions for dietitians. *Dietetic Currents* 18, no. 1:1–6.

Gilbert, J.A. 1990. *Productivity management: A step-by-step guide for health care professionals.* Chicago, Ill.: American Hospital Publishing, Inc.

Herz, M.L., et al. 1977. *Analysis of alternative patient tray delivery concept.* Natick, Massachusetts: US Army Natick Research and Development Command.

Huyck, N.I., and M.M. Rowe. 1990. *Managing clinical nutritional services.* Gaithersburg, Md.: Aspen Publishers, Inc., 28–32, 60–63.

International Association of Milk, Food and Environmental Sanitarians. 1991. *Procedures to implement the hazard analysis critical control point system.* Ames, Iowa.

Kaud, F.A., R.P. Miller, and R.F. Underwood. 1982. *Cafeteria management for hospitals.* Chicago, Ill.: American Hospital Publishing, Inc.

Puckett, R.P., and B.B. Miller. 1988. *Food service manual for healthcare facilities.* Chicago, Ill.: American Hospital Publishing, Inc.

Puckett, R.P., and J. Ninemeier. 1992. *Managing foodservice operations.* 2nd ed. Dubuque, Iowa: Kendall/Hunt Publishing Co.

Quinley, W.W. 1992. How hospitals get into trouble without trying. *Southern Hospitals* 58, no. 3: 12–32.

Rose, J.C. 1986. *Catering cost models.* Gaithersburg, Md.: Aspen Publishers, Inc.

Rose, J.C. 1985. Trayline configurations: The pros and cons. *Hospital Food and Nutrition Focus* 2, no. 2: 1–4.

RUBY P. PUCKETT, MA, RD, LD, is one of the country's leading dietitians and the Director of Food and Nutrition Services at Shands Hospital at the University of Florida. With an annual budget of $6.35 million, the department employs 168 full-time employees and serves over 140,000 meals each month to patients, employees, and visitors. The department completed Shands' largest comprehensive renovation project in 1991.

Puckett is the initiator of the award-winning *Dietary Managers Course Independent Study* and the author of the *Food Service Manual for Healthcare Facilities* (revised in 1992), an American Hospital Association best-seller. Author of over 250 articles, monograms, and abstracts, as well as 5 books, she recently completed the *Shands Hospital at the University of Florida Guide to Clinical Dietetics* (5th Edition) and co-authored *Foodservice Management: A Systems Approach for Healthcare and Institutions.*

Chapter 13

Materials Management

William L. Scheyer

It is commonly estimated that 30–50 percent of a hospital's budget is related to materials, equipment, and purchased services. Approximately half of this amount derives from the direct cost of acquiring materials and services, and the other half from the cost of managing them after acquisition. Labor expenses make up the largest portion of this second component.

Prior to 1970, the management of materials was often performed in a haphazard fashion, which was one of the contributing factors to the escalation of the cost of hospital care. In the 1970s, as these costs reached increasingly unacceptable levels, the concept of centralized materials management began to gain favor. As a result, methods of controlling expenses that had been used for many years in other industries began to be routinely applied in the health care industry.

During the 1980s, greater emphasis was placed on group purchasing programs, centralized management of total inventories, and increased reliance on vendors to provide additional services such as consignment buying, vendor management of in-house inventories, and "just-in-time" shipments. In fact, this shift to the practice of using the vendor to actually provide hospital support services has continued into the 1990s to such an extent that some people have difficulty defining the rightful place of a materials manager in the hospital.

As the national debate over health care cost control intensifies, so does the need to find ways to reduce the total cost of acquiring and managing materials and services. Regardless of how the job of materials manager is structured, the need to successfully perform the function of reducing cost will continue to be critical. While one would think that by now every hospital would have an effective materials management system in place, this is not the case. Therefore, it is still worthwhile for administrators to take a serious and critical look at how this function is being performed in their organizations. The shift to vertically integrated provider networks creates an ideal opportunity to consolidate the function of materials management and achieve exemplary economies of scale for all entities in a network.

The author wishes to thank Mr. Joseph Dattilo, President of Par Excellence Systems, Cincinnati, Ohio, and Mr. Richard Seim, Director of Materials Services at The Christ Hospital, Cincinnati, Ohio, for their assistance in reviewing the material contained in this chapter.

The classical definition of materials management in hospitals comes from Charles Hously, in his book, *Hospital Materiel Management*. He defines materials management as "the management and control of goods, services, and equipment from acquisition to disposition."[1] The essence of this definition is that there should be centralization of the purchasing, receiving, supply, storage, and distribution functions within the hospital. In addition, there should be centralized reprocessing of sterile, reusable supply items.

The two most critical elements in a materials management program are (1) a corporate strategy for ensuring that materials—goods, services, and equipment—are purchased at the lowest total cost and (2) a related strategy to ensure that inventories and their associated carrying costs are aggressively monitored and controlled.

SUPPLY CHAIN

The flow of materials can best be visualized as a closed loop. This supply chain is shown in Figure 13–1. Opportunities for significant cost reductions exist at each point within the chain.

Originating Department

The actual decision to acquire supplies and equipment almost always takes place in individual departments throughout the hospital. However, the materials manager can assist the head of the originating department in a number of ways, such as helping forecast needs for the coming year, providing information on sources of supply and prevailing market conditions, conducting negotiations with vendors, and designating effective systems for storing and maintaining materials until they are consumed.

Generally, hospital managers have been trained either in specific clinical disciplines or in general administration. Managers rarely have been trained in the techniques of materials management. As a result, the materials manager is a valuable resource for ensuring that supplies, equipment, and purchased services are used in a cost-effective manner throughout the organization.

The materials manager normally has direct responsibility for managing the functions of centralized purchasing, receiving, storage/distribution, and central sterile reprocessing. He or she

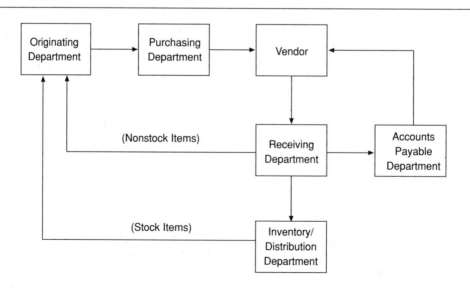

Figure 13–1 Supply Chain

has no direct relationship with the accounts payable department. However, it is vital that there be open lines of communication between accounts payable, purchasing, and receiving departments. These departments must work together effectively to process the high volume of purchase/receipt/payment transactions that occur every day.

Because there is generally no direct relationship between the materials management department and other departments within the hospital, there needs to be a corporate-level statement of policy concerning the execution of materials management functions. It is important that the materials manager establish a consulting-type relationship with all of the departments within the hospital in order to ensure that appropriate materials management practices are followed.

As hospitals utilize more special services from vendors, the originating departments have become more critical in assuring proper management of their supplies. For example, vendors may deliver orders directly to the originating department, as shown in Figure 13–2. Another variation is for the vendor to conduct PAR-Level inspections in the originating department and then deliver the needed materials directly to the department, as depicted in Figure 13–3.

In both of these cases, the actual receipt of the materials may not be controlled by the Receiving Department. It is important, therefore, for the originating department head to make sure that goods are actually received in the right quantities and reported correctly to the Accounts Payable Department. One risk is that the originating department personnel will not exercise sufficient care in accepting and documenting the delivery. A second risk, particularly in the PAR-Level situation, is that the vendor may overstock the department in order to increase sales. The materials manager must be involved in setting up and monitoring these special vendor services, so that the interests of the hospital are protected.

Purchasing Department

The primary contribution of the purchasing department is to lower the price of goods and services acquired by the hospital. The two main tools to be used in accomplishing this objective are competitive bidding and direct negotiation. By centralizing control of the purchasing function under the direction of the materials manager, it is possible to ensure that consistent and effective use is made of these tools throughout the organization.

In addition to negotiating lower prices, the purchasing agent can obtain favorable terms and conditions for the hospital, which are often not requested when the transaction is conducted by managers outside the purchasing department. Payment of freight charges, extended warranties, and other special services can frequently be obtained.

Another method of obtaining lower prices and additional services is through participation in formal group purchasing arrangements. Groups continue to gain in power and importance within the health care industry. They range from groups organized by local hospital associations to huge national groups with hundreds of participating

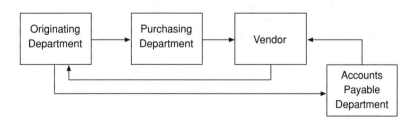

Figure 13–2 Supply Chain (Alternate 1)

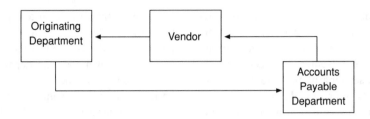

Figure 13–3 Supply Chain (Alternate 2)

organizations. Another variation is found in national hospital groups, both for profit and not for profit. All of these organizations have the same goal: pooling their purchases in order to obtain lower prices based on the high volume of the purchases. As the pressure to cut bottom line operating costs continues to intensify, the importance of joining the most effective purchasing groups increases.

The Vendor

Although vendors are not under the direct control of the materials manager, and their contributions to cost reduction are essentially extensions of the efforts of the purchasing agents, their role still deserves mention. Vendors have it within their power to provide the hospital with many cost-reduction opportunities, such as lower prices, favorable payment terms, local warehousing, consulting assistance, special usage reports, and in-service training.

It is important that the materials manager become skilled at establishing relationships with vendors that result in the hospital receiving as broad a range of benefits as possible. The hospital invests its business with the vendor, and the vendor invests those benefits and services that go beyond the normal selling price. It is important that both participants receive an adequate return on their investment. Consistent with the trend of shifting the functions of materials management to vendors, many organizations rely on a just-in-time approach to supply delivery. Accurate forecasting of departmental needs is re-

quired, along with accurate interaction between the computer systems of both hospital and vendor. In essence, the vendor makes more frequent deliveries of smaller quantities in order to ensure that the hospital department has the needed items just in time for use. This reduces on-hand inventories within the hospital, thus freeing up the funds related to maintaining inventories.

Some professionals in the industry feel so strongly about this approach that they believe hospitals should not even be in the materials management business. However, it is important to remember that the vendors would not provide these services if they did not add to their own profits. Administrators and materials managers should keep in mind that the basic work must be done; the question is whether it is more efficient and less costly for it to be done by the vendor or the hospital. Issues such as cost of labor and economies of scale must be weighed. Another factor is that the person who controls the details of the work usually controls the outcome of the process. Thus, if the hospital relinquishes too much control over the work to the vendor, it risks losing control over the final cost of the program.

Special vendor services are definitely of value, particularly when the vendor is willing to be creative and work with the hospital to customize programs that meet the special needs of the organization. Such programs are an increasingly common component of the management armamentarium of the modern hospital. However, as in any area of management, measurement and monitoring are the keys to success.

Receiving Department

The primary contribution of the receiving department is to ensure that the correct items, in proper condition, are officially received into the organization. Savings result from detection of vendor shipping errors, identification and correction of damaged goods, and timely notification of receipt to the accounting department in order to obtain all available discounts. The challenge to the receiving supervisor is to make sure that when goods bypass the receiving dock and go directly to the originating department, they are properly inspected and recorded into the inventory and payment records of the hospital.

This department's contribution to the hospital's bottom line rests largely on two key functions: (1) invoice matching, and (2) adjusting the timing of payments to vendors. It is essential that the vendor's invoice be accurately matched to the documents verifying receipt of the goods in the hospital. If this is not done consistently and accurately, there is a high risk of paying for goods not actually received.

In general, payments should be held for as long as possible up to the point that a discount will be lost. Excessive delays in making payments damage a hospital's business reputation and weaken its future negotiating power. However, excessive speed in making payments results in unnecessarily giving away the use of the hospital's money.

In order to successfully maintain an effective schedule of correct payments, there must be a smooth flow of communication between the purchasing, receiving, and accounts payable departments.

Inventory and Distribution Departments

In recent years, a great deal of attention has been paid to managing inventories within hospitals. Savings that result from reducing inventory levels include the release of money to be used for other purposes; the release of space to be used for other purposes; avoidance of the need to construct new space; lower expense as a result of reduced obsolescence, damage, and theft; and somewhat reduced labor needed to handle the lower level of supplies.

Most hospitals still spend the major part of their efforts on controlling official inventories, usually found in the central storeroom. However, the more aggressive hospitals are starting to concentrate on the unofficial inventories. This is particularly true of those that have adopted the special-vendor-services approach to the extent that they have eliminated their central inventories. Unofficial inventories are stocks of supplies that have already been entered as an expense in the accounting records. They should be considered inventories in that they are in storage and awaiting consumption. There is a particularly significant cost-reduction potential in supply-intensive departments, such as surgeries and cath-labs.

The selection of methods for distributing materials throughout the organization also can have an impact on the total cost of hospital operations. In general, the most effective systems are those that replenish supply levels to predetermined standards on a scheduled basis, without the end user having to initiate the request. Such automatic replenishment systems reduce the amount of time spent by relatively high-paid, clinically trained employees in ordering and handling supplies. In addition, such systems more accurately link the issuance of supplies to actual patterns of consumption. As a result, they tend to reduce overall inventory levels, thus resulting in the savings associated with inventory reduction. In addition, the maintenance of such systems provides another opportunity to monitor and promote product standardization, which further enhances the efficiency of the inventory system.

Computer Support

In the past, most materials management information systems were integrated with the hospital's financial information systems. As a result, enhancements to the materials management system often received lower priority. The proliferation of mini- and microcomputers has made it possible to acquire specialized hardware/software packages to support materials management functions at a relatively low cost. These programs are far more flexible and effective than in the past and can be operated as stand-alone systems or can be linked to the accounts payable system via specially written programs.

In order to maximize the benefits of a centralized materials management program, it is vital to have accurate and detailed information about the multitude of transactions that take place within the system every day. It is certainly not impossible to operate an effective system without computer support, particularly in smaller hospitals. The availability of relatively inexpensive personal computers with materials management software that can be used as stand-alones or linked in networks makes it easy for most hospitals to computerize this function. Larger hospitals almost have to computerize the materials management function in order to handle the large volume of transactional data generated each day. If the basic materials management functions are well designed, the additional advantages of computerized information support far outweigh the costs of the computer system.

MANAGING THE CORE FUNCTIONS

Purchasing

An effective purchasing department is the cornerstone of a successful materials management program. The keys to success in this area lie in (1) setting up well-designed systems for routinely processing large amounts of information both effectively and efficiently and in (2) establishing operational priorities that focus the most attention on those items that have the greatest impact on the organization.

The three purposes of the purchasing department are to:

1. assist all departments in obtaining products and services of appropriate quality from reputable and reliable vendors at the lowest total cost to the organization

2. ensure that appropriate and ethical business practices are applied throughout the organization

3. serve as a source of information for the rest of the hospital concerning available products, sources of supply, current and anticipated market conditions, and application of effective purchasing techniques

The first step in establishing a strong purchasing program is to obtain a written statement of support from the hospital's chief executive officer. This statement should be circulated to all departments, along with a description of how the purchasing system will work. This statement will clarify for everyone the fact that all purchasing transactions must be carried out using the centralized purchasing process. The best method for enforcing this requirement is to establish a numbered purchase order system and to refuse receipt of any item not covered by a hospital purchase order number.

The physical layout, procedures, and filing systems of the purchasing department can be organized in any number of ways as long as adequate provision is made for the following elements:

- use of a legally acceptable purchase order form that ensures terms and conditions favorable to the hospital

- a method for determining who is authorized to make purchases for the hospital

- a file of approved signatures for use in ensuring that purchases are made only by authorized people

- a clearly defined requisitioning process

- a list of approved vendors from whom purchases can be made

- clearly defined procedures for obtaining competitive bids from vendors

- a method for tracking and expediting open purchase orders

- a method for ensuring that proper credit is received for goods returned to the vendor

- a method for monitoring and documenting vendor performance
- a method for monitoring the timeliness and effectiveness of the performance of the purchasing department

It is important for the purchasing manager to develop and adhere to a strategic plan that focuses attention primarily on those items that have the greatest financial impact.

Application of a technique known as ABC analysis is helpful in developing this strategic plan. This technique is most frequently used in the area of inventory control, but can also be used in analyzing purchases. All expenditures are classified into major categories. The individual items within each category can then be rank-ordered according to dollar value. Approximately 80 percent of the dollars expended will come from approximately 20 percent of the items acquired. Generally, some items, such as X-ray film, certain classes of pharmaceuticals, and capital items represent a major portion of the budget. By concentrating attention on these items, time is spent most wisely and results can be maximized. Specific strategies for handling capital acquisitions, supplies, and purchased services should be developed. As mentioned previously, participation in purchasing groups has become one of the most important functions of the purchasing department. As more individual hospitals become members of larger corporate organizations or health care networks, purchasing groups play an increasingly important role.

Competitive Bids

Ideally, competition for the hospital's business will be sought in every case. It can be obtained through a number of approaches:

- requesting formal sealed bids to be opened publicly
- requesting written quotations to be evaluated in the purchasing department
- obtaining comparative prices over the telephone

- negotiating fixed contract prices for items or groups of items
- obtaining access to negotiated, competitive prices as a result of membership in a purchasing group

The method used to obtain competitive prices depends upon the nature of the items being purchased. Major capital items may require sealed public bids, whereas smaller routine items may require only telephone price checking. Items that are purchased repeatedly lend themselves to fixed contract pricing. No matter what method is used, it is good practice to document routinely the percentage of purchases made using competitive bidding of any sort. Sample bidding instructions are shown in Appendices 13–A and 13–B.[2]

The first step in initiating competition is to issue a request for proposal (RFP) or request for bid (RFB) to potential vendors. It should state very clearly what goods or services are being sought and should be sufficiently detailed to ensure that competing proposals or bids can be fairly evaluated. If additional negotiation will take place after the bids have been received, this should be stated in the initial request.[3]

It is important that all qualified vendors be given the opportunity to compete and that the purchasing agent not divulge the details of one vendor's proposal to another. Once all proposals have been received, they should be evaluated not only on the basis of price but also on total cost to the hospital. Such elements as price protection, warranties, freight charges, installation, and operating costs should be considered as part of the total cost. Once the final selection is made, sufficient time should be taken in preparing the purchase order so that all of the benefits obtained through the competitive process are protected in writing. Finally, all of the unsuccessful bidders should be notified of the selection. It is important that the hospital maintain a reputation for considerate and professional treatment of its suppliers in order to ensure active competition for future transactions.

Capital Equipment Purchasing

The process of acquiring capital equipment provides some of the greatest opportunities for cost savings. Whereas an entire supply inventory may account for $500,000, a single piece of high-technology clinical equipment can cost that much or more. As a result, reducing the cost of such items by even a few percentage points can lead to significant savings.

The initial step in managing capital acquisitions is the establishment of a program for financial justification. Ultimate approval of major requests must come from the CEO and the finance committee of the board of directors. However, the process begins with the head of the department from which the request originates. In order to promote uniform practice throughout the hospital and to enable the final decision makers to evaluate competing requests rationally, a standard system for developing financial justifications should be utilized. A worksheet for this purpose is shown in Exhibit 13–1.

Once a project has been approved, the purchasing manager should assist the requesting department head in the development of generic functional specifications. These should be written in terms of expected performance. Every effort should be made to make the specifications generic and to avoid writing them in a way that is specific to an individual company's equipment.

However, requesting department heads, as well as physicians involved in using the equipment, sometimes resist making the specifications generic. Traditionally, vendors have focused their marketing efforts upon the end users, who may be persuaded to write the requirements so that only one vendor's equipment is able to fulfill the specification. When this is done, the opportunity for competition is diminished, if not eliminated, and the hospital pays a higher than necessary price for the item.

Once specifications have been written, it is necessary to establish a method for determining whether the resultant bids actually meet the stated requirements. These standards of performance should be given to the competing vendors so that all bids are submitted in an acceptable format. In addition, once the equipment has been purchased and installed, these written standards should serve as the basis for ensuring that the equipment meets all requirements. The assistance of in-house technical support staff, or, if necessary, outside consultants, should be obtained to verify that the equipment is fully acceptable. Any deviations or problems should be identified and resolved quickly in order to ensure that the hospital receives full value for its money.

As in all purchases, capital acquisitions require that:

- a clear set of generic specifications be developed to serve as the basis for decision making
- as many reputable and reliable vendors as possible be allowed to submit bids for the order
- all quotations be fairly evaluated
- negotiations be coordinated through the purchasing department
- upon installation, all equipment be tested according to written standards and by qualified technical personnel to ensure that all requirements are satisfactorily met

Purchasing Techniques

Group Purchasing. Larger purchases generally result in lower prices. As a result, groups of buyers can, by pooling their buying power, gain even lower prices than any of the individuals acting alone. However, there are costs involved in belonging to a purchasing group. These include the direct cost of membership, usually expressed as an annual fee, and a certain loss of control in product selection. The members of the group must meet periodically to evaluate vendor proposals, products, and performance and to monitor how well the group itself is performing. There are also costs associated with participating in these meetings.

The question of whether a hospital should either join or maintain its membership in a group is purely an economic one. Will membership re-

Exhibit 13–1 Worksheet to Evaluate Purchasing Requests

I. Costs

A. Estimated cost of equipment (including shipping) $ _____   _____
                                                                       Dept. Manager
                                                                       Purchasing

B. Estimated cost of installation, building modifications (please attach details) $ _____   _____
                                                                       Dept. Manager
                                                                       Maintenance

C. Depreciable life of project   _____   _____
                                                      yrs.   Dept. Manager
                                                                      Accounting

D. Equipment to be replaced:

   1. Description _____
      _____
      _____

   2. Fixed asset number   _____

   3. Present age   _____

   4. Assigned useful life   _____

   5. Current book value $ _____   _____
                                                         Dept. Manager
                                                      Accounting

   6. Current market value $ _____   _____
                                                         Dept. Manager
                                                      Purchasing

E. Associated increase in expenses

	Year 1	Year 2	Year 3	Year 4	Year 5	Year 6	Year 7	Year 8	Year 9	Year 10
Training										
Labor										
Utilities										
Supplies										
Other										
Total increase in expenses										

II. Revenue and Decrease of Expenses

	Year 1	Year 2	Year 3	Year 4	Year 5	Year 6	Year 7	Year 8	Year 9	Year 10

A. Increases in revenue
  1. Revenue increases
     from additional
     inpatients
     a. Medicare										

b. Medicaid										
c. Others										

continues

Exhibit 13–1 continued

2. Revenue increases from additional list of current inpatients
    a. Medicare
    b. Medicaid
    c. Others
3. Revenue increases from additional outpatient testing
    a. Medicare
    b. Medicaid
    c. Others
B. Decreases in revenue
    1. Revenue decrease from reduced length of stay
        a. Medicare
        b. Medicaid
        c. Others
    2. Revenue decrease from reduced number of inpatients
        a. Medicare
        b. Medicaid
        c. Others
C. Net increase or decrease in revenue
D. Decrease of expenses
    1. Reduction in expenses from reduced length of stay
        a. labor
        b. supplies
        c. utilities
        d. other
    2. Reduction in expenses from reduced number of inpatients
        a. labor
        b. supplies
        c. utilities
        d. other
    3. Reduction in expenses from new technology
        a. labor
        b. supplies
        c. utilities
        d. other
    4. Total reduction in expenses

Source: Departmental document, reprinted with permission of St. Francis-St. George Hospital, Inc., Cincinnati, Ohio.

sult in lower total costs to the hospital? If so, membership is worthwhile. However, before committing to a particular group, some additional issues should be considered. The following are considerations to be studied involving the group itself:

- How well do group goals and objectives correlate with those of the institution?
- Is the group program well focused and mature or does the group still have to get its program fully organized?
- What are the administrative costs of the group? How efficiently does the group operate?
- How skilled is the group at negotiation? Is the group going to negotiate major contracts on the hospital's behalf; is the institution satisfied that the group can do that job well?
- How does the group handle product evaluation and standardization? Since product standardization is an essential element of group purchasing, is the hospital sure it can participate effectively in that process?
- How does the group track record overall compare with other groups—or with what the hospital can do on its own?

As for the vendors who hold agreements with the group, are the products, quality, and service they offer generally acceptable to the hospital? As for the other hospitals in the group:

- Are they larger or smaller than the hospital? Generally, smaller hospitals benefit most from being in groups with larger ones.
- What is the level of commitment of the member hospitals? More committed groups generally produce lower prices.
- How well managed are the other hospitals in the group? Are they institutions with which the hospital will be comfortable working closely?
- Has thought been given to the competitive position of the hospital vis-a-vis others in the group?

Other hospitals, including members, should be asked about the group. So, too, with other hospitals that might have belonged to the group but do not. Why not? And hospitals that once belonged to the group but left—Why did they?[4]

Almost every hospital now belongs to at least one purchasing group and many belong to more than one group. This presents a dilemma in that a group's effectiveness depends in part on its ability to deliver agreed upon blocks of purchases to its vendors. If members participate in more than one group, and each group provides contracts for the same items, which group's contract will the members utilize? The answer for the hospital is usually to use the contract that provides the lowest price, or that provides a preferred brand at a satisfactory price. However, in terms of being an honest and effective participant in the groups, the purchasing manager needs to think through the hospital's policy position on the issue of membership in multiple groups.

The keys to maximizing the benefits of group purchasing include:

- carefully selecting strong and effective groups to join
- establishing control over product standardization and support of the group within the hospital
- establishing a leadership position or, at least, a position of strength within the group
- consistently using the group contracts
- continually monitoring the price performance of the group to ensure that the hospital is getting best value

Prime Vendors. Another approach to obtaining lower prices and better service is to establish a relationship with a single vendor to which a major portion of the hospital's purchases are directed. In return, the vendor is expected to provide:

- lower prices
- extended price protection
- minimal back orders

- lower in-hospital inventory levels
- simplified paperwork in purchasing, receiving, and paying for items
- other special services

Potential disadvantages of using a prime vendor include the following:

- Economic competition may be reduced over a period of time.
- Inconsistent quality may exist across the vendor's complete line of products.
- The hospital may become overly dependent on the vendor, and a change in vendors may be disruptive to hospital routines.
- Prices may "creep" upward if inadequate controls are placed on the relationship.

Overall, a prime vendor relationship can provide significant economic and operational advantages to the hospital if it is well thought out, effectively negotiated, designed with adequate controls to protect the hospital, and carefully monitored. If any of these elements is missing, it can have a negative effect on the hospital.

Buying on Consignment. In consignment buying the hospital takes physical possession of items, but does not pay for them until they are actually consumed. Obviously, this method provides a cash flow advantage to the hospital. It also should cause the vendor to work more aggressively with the hospital to reduce inventory levels, because higher inventories mean more supplies for which payment has not yet been received.

As in any special arrangement, however, there are potential disadvantages, including the following:

- Proper inventory control practices are necessary to avoid payment for lost or damaged goods.
- Prices may rise more than a normal amount to cover the vendor's additional costs.
- The vendor may place too little stock in inventory.

- The vendor may place too much stock in order to obtain free warehouse space.
- If the vendor "buys out" existing supplies, it becomes difficult to terminate the relationship because a major one-time expense will be required to re-establish the hospital's inventory.

Consignment buying has traditionally been applied most often to expensive, specialized items that show relatively slow usage but to which the hospital must have immediate access. Examples include orthopedic hardware, intraocular lenses, and special types of sutures. However, a number of companies are now providing consignment programs for broad categories of medical/surgical supplies.

Stockless Purchasing. In this technique certain categories of supplies are removed from the hospital's inventory and are carried only in the vendor's warehouse. Hospital departments send requisitions for supplies directly to the vendor, instead of to the hospital storeroom. The vendor then prepares the orders for shipment directly to the individual departments.

The hospital's purchasing staff does not review orders, nor does the receiving department staff check them in. Consolidated invoices are reviewed by the accounts payable department only to verify that they are generally reasonable in size. The risk, of course, is that payment will be made for items that were not received. The control on these purchases must reside in the individual ordering departments, as they both check in orders when they are received and reconcile charges against their departmental budgets at the end of the month.

The advantages to the hospital in this system involve improved cash flow because of reduced inventories, and operating savings because of the simplified paperwork and reduced workload in purchasing, receiving, and, to some extent, accounts payable departments. Another advantage to the hospital is the ability to make use of the large-volume buying power of the vendor. For example, items that might be important, but of low volume to the hospital, would normally have a relatively high price. The vendor, because it buys for multiple accounts, can usually achieve a lower price. Part of this price reduction should be passed on to the hospital as a benefit of the program.

One disadvantage is that both the vendor and the individual ordering departments must be reliable in maintaining the accuracy of shipments and receipts. No emergency stock is maintained in a central on-site inventory, which makes accurate forecasting and ordering by the individual departments even more important. This can be somewhat mitigated by building a small reserve in the basic supply level of the ordering department. This should be done carefully, however, in order not to diminish the inventory reduction savings. As in consignment buying, the removal of supplies from the hospital's inventory has the effect of tying the hospital closely to the particular vendor. As a result, it can be difficult to terminate the relationship.

This technique can afford the hospital significant savings. However, it is vital that the vendor be carefully selected and that performance, in terms of prices, order fill rate, and stock picking/billing accuracy, be closely monitored. In addition, the hospital should identify a list of critical items that it cannot do without. The contract should identify this list and bind the vendors to never being out of stock on these items. Finally, the hospital should always maintain final authority over product selection. This should never be relinquished to the vendor.

Receiving

Another special vendor service is just-in-time (JIT) deliveries. This technique, which is common in manufacturing companies in Japan, is now used in many industries in the United States. The idea is to reduce the amount of on-hand inventory in the hospital and rely on the vendor to ship the supplies in smaller amounts, but more frequently, in order to garner inventory reduction savings for the hospital. In its purest

sense, the shipment arrives "just in time" for use, though hospitals usually set the quantities and frequencies so that they don't cut it quite that close.

This technique requires a high degree of accurate communication between the hospital and vendor, particularly in the transmission of electronic data. It also requires the vendor to establish a strong track record of complete and accurate fill rates and on-time deliveries. This system, as in stockless purchasing, also benefits from the negotiation of a critical items list.

The goal of the receiving department should be to make sure that all items ordered by the hospital are correctly counted and received into the hospital's accounting records and then delivered to the ordering departments. Every effort should be made to have receiving documents awaiting the arrival of shipments. These should be a duplicate of the purchase order, but without the expected quantities listed. This serves as a control to ensure that the receiving clerks actually count the items when they are received.

Separate areas within the receiving department should be designated for counting and completion of paperwork, holding items that are awaiting delivery, and holding items that are awaiting return to the vendor. Physical separation of shipments so that they do not become intermingled is important.

Once the initial counting and paperwork are completed, the receiving documents should be reviewed by a receiving control clerk. It is this person's job to compare the receiving documents to the log of open purchase orders and to reconcile any problems involving overshipments, undershipments, unit of measure errors, or counting errors.

Many of the special vendor programs involve shipments directly to the ordering departments. Whenever possible, it is still best to bring the shipments physically through the Receiving Department. A special challenge for the receiving supervisor will be to make sure these shipments are processed not only accurately but rapidly, as well. When shipments must go directly to the ordering department, it is worthwhile to try to assign a receiving clerk to work with the ordering department personnel to verify accurate receipt and posting. Even under new programs, it is worth the effort to follow tried and true materials management practices.

Inventory Control

The goal of inventory control is to hold the least possible number of supplies in the hospital, while not running out of critical items. Inventory in hospitals has usually been considered to be only that material stored in the official storeroom and carried as an asset in the accounting records. It is more appropriate, however, to also classify as inventory those supplies stored in the various operating departments of the hospital, even though they have been charged out as an expense to the departmental accounts. These so-called unofficial inventories can be worth up to three times the value of the official inventory.[5] Obviously, they provide a significant opportunity for total cost reduction.

The first step in reducing inventories is to conduct a physical count in each department of the hospital. Most areas do not use a perpetual inventory system; that is, one that keeps constant track as supplies are added to and deducted from storage. It is harder to calculate the inventory of these areas, because in addition to finding and listing each item, it is necessary to look up the most recent price of the items. By extending these prices against the quantities found to be on hand, a total value of inventory can be calculated for each storage location.

Once this is done, the figures should be compared to the value of supplies charged to the departments during the past year. A turnover rate can then be determined using the following formula:[6]

$$\text{Turnover} = \frac{\text{Annual dollar value of issues}}{\text{Average inventory value}}$$

Some department inventories turn over slowly, and some more quickly, because of their special nature. On average, however, the goal should be inventory turnover approximately 12 times per year.

Once the initial inventory values and turnover rates are determined, targets can be established for each department. The department head and the materials manager should work together to determine the goals and the strategies for achieving the goals. After the strategic plans have been established, periodic follow-up physical inventories should be taken to monitor progress.

The strategic plan should address (1) the identification of obsolete, expired, or slow-moving items and ways to dispose of them and (2) the identification of excess supplies of normally moving items and ways to bring the inventory levels back into line and keep them there.

Obsolete and slow-moving supplies may be disposed of through the following means:

- return to the vendor for credit (a restocking charge may be applied)
- find a user elsewhere in the hospital
- sell or trade to other hospitals
- sell to a salvage dealer

Normally moving items that have become overstocked can be brought into line by simply not reordering until a calculated reorder point has been reached. If the item is grossly overstocked, it can be reduced by returning the excess to the central inventory, finding a user elsewhere in the hospital, or returning it to the vendor for credit. The last option should be used only if there is a significant excess that will not be consumed for a long period of time and if there is little or no restocking charge.

A formal reorder point (ROP) can be calculated using the following formula:[7]

$$\text{ROP} = \text{usage per day} \times \text{lead time (in days)} + \text{safety factor}$$

Economic Order Quantity

Once reorder points have been established for items, the next question is how much to order. A standard method for determining order quantity in most other industries is use of the economic order quantity (EOQ) formula, which mathematically balances ordering cost and holding cost to determine the quantity that results in the lowest total cost.[8]

$$\text{Economic Order Quantity} = \sqrt{\frac{\text{Annual usage} \times 2 \times \text{Order cost}}{\text{Unit cost} \times \text{Holding cost } (\%/100)}}$$

The key elements of this formula include:

- *Ordering cost:* generally considered the cost to place an order, which includes labor, supplies, and overhead in the purchasing, receiving, and accounts payable departments

- *Holding cost:* generally considered the cost to handle and maintain the items once they are in the hospital's possession, which includes opportunity cost, labor, supplies, and overhead in the inventory departments

- *Unit cost:* generally considered the cost of a single unit of the item for which EOQ is being calculated

The EOQ formula sometimes can result in quantities that are impractical because the necessary storage space is unavailable. In those cases, the actual order quantity can be adjusted. However, as a general rule, the EOQ formula is a tool for identifying the most economically efficient quantity to order, and can serve as a foundation for adjusting final order quantities. The calculation is cumbersome unless it can be computer generated, which also causes many hospitals not to use it. Again, it is helpful to understand and to use it as a check system in setting final quantities.

Another approach to determining order quantity is to decide how many days of inventory you wish to keep on hand, or, alternatively, what turnover rate you wish to achieve, add required safety stock, and then calculate the required order quantity based upon the lead time of the particular vendor.

A sound strategy for reducing and effectively managing inventories, then, includes the following steps:

- Conduct physical inventories of each storage location.
- Calculate turnover rates for each location.
- Establish target turnover rates for each item and each location.
- Calculate reorder points and EOQs for each item.
- Conduct periodic follow-up physical inventories to assess progress toward the goals.
- Adjust goals, reorder points, and EOQs as appropriate, based upon changes within the system.

Distribution

The selection and design of systems for distributing materials throughout the hospital and for replenishing stocks of supplies in user departments are key variables in the ability to manage inventory levels effectively. There are four basic options for distributing material: (1) requisitions, (2) PAR-level systems, (3) point-of-use replenishment systems, and (4) exchange carts.

Any of these can be enhanced through the application of computer software programs, which can more accurately and more quickly handle the large volume and data generated by the multitude of daily transactions. However, computerization does not change the basic systems themselves.

Requisitions

This is the most traditional system and generally the least effective. Control of the process of deciding when and how much to order is retained by the personnel of individual departments. It is common either to find highly paid, clinically trained employees spending time performing this function or for this function to be delegated to lower-paid employees. In either case, it is often a low priority and does not receive adequate attention. As a result, the quality of the ordering process is inconsistent and random, which can lead to both unnecessarily high inventory levels and, at other times, unacceptably low levels. This system also has the effect of inflating the inventory in the central storeroom, as the storeroom supervisor builds an extra cushion to protect against random requests for large orders. A final result of this system is that it generates a large number of extra requisitions and telephone requests for additional supplies. These are time consuming and expensive for both the ordering department and the central storeroom.

The only advantages to this system are that it is simple; easy to understand, if not to do well; and requires minimal capital investment.

PAR-Level Systems

In this system a person from the central storeroom visits each ordering department on a scheduled basis, counts the supplies, writes an order, obtains supplies, returns them to the department, and brings the supplies up to a standard or PAR level. A variation of this system, utilizing computer support, analyzes data about past consumption and calculates a predicted order, and the storeroom employee delivers this order to the unit. Additional supplies that may be required are delivered on a later trip. In either case, this is a relatively labor-intensive system. In addition, it provides somewhat weaker control over the productivity of the employees who deliver the orders.

The advantages of this type of system are that it more effectively links the disbursement of supplies to actual usage. It places performance of the distribution function in the hands of employees who are lower paid than clinical employees and for whom the function is a high priority. Finally, it requires a relatively low capital investment.

A variation of the PAR-level system is point-of-use replenishment. Whenever a supply item is taken for use, it triggers a request for replenishment. This is usually supported by automatic computer generation of an order. However, it can be done by hand, though the total number of transactions makes this cumbersome and prone to errors of omission.

Replenishment orders can be filled from the hospital's central inventory or directly from the vendor's warehouse. In either case, the orders for single units of an item can be held for a period of time and consolidated into a reasonable size order to make more efficient use of the delivery system.

The materials management staff should consult with the ordering departments to set appropriate supply levels and delivery time requirements, and to periodically verify stock levels and fill rates. These systems can also be used to support cost accounting systems. When properly designed and managed, information on the total cost of supply usage for a patient with a particular diagnosis, or for particular procedures, can be obtained. This helps top management in making strategic marketing and operational decisions.

Exchange Carts

The fourth system is a variation of the PAR-level system. In this case, all or most of the supplies for a department are placed on a movable cart. The standard quantities can be adjusted dynamically through the application of a computer software program if desired. A second identical cart is also prepared. On a scheduled basis, the first cart, which has been depleted, is taken from the user department, and the second cart, filled, is exchanged with it.

The primary advantage of this system lies in having greater control over the productivity and performance quality of the employees who fill the carts. By replenishing all carts in a central area, the storeroom supervisor is better able to monitor performance. In addition, compared to the PAR-level system, travel time is reduced by replacing multiple trips between the ordering department and the storeroom with a single trip for delivering the cart. However, this advantage does not exist when comparing exchange carts with a computerized point-of-use replenishment system. In the latter case, orders are sent and consolidated by computer into a single order for delivery. The trend will continue to be more toward the installation of point-of-use systems whenever possible. However, the capital cost of the point-of-use installation will be a deterrent for some organizations. The disadvantages are that a large capital investment in carts is required, and space is needed for holding carts in both the user department and the storeroom.

A variation of this system for use in the surgery department is the surgical case cart system. In this system, carts are not exchanged, but are set up especially for each surgical case and then delivered to the surgery department. The disadvantages of space intensity and high capital investment are also present here. However, a special advantage is that space formerly set aside in the surgery suite, a particularly expensive location, can be released for more productive purposes. The carts can be prepared and stored in a separate, less expensive location.

In addition, the cart can be used as a back table during the surgical procedure and can then be used to transport all used or soiled supplies and instruments back to the central processing area. This is helpful from an infection control standpoint.

Selection of a System

Selection of a distribution system should take into consideration a number of factors, including:

- design of existing systems and how well they are working
- number of individual departments and storage locations
- quantity and mixture of supplies in each area
- existing storage and handling equipment
- available space
- physical relationship between departments
- traffic routes
- labor costs for each area
- cash flow considerations

Jamie Kowalski, a materials management consultant, has developed this 15-step planning model for selecting, designing, and implementing distribution systems.[9]

1. Determine on-hand inventory levels in each affected department. This calculation will be used as the basis for identifying appropriateness and costs of the current inventory level, as well as providing the foundation for establishing target inventory levels and turnover rates.

2. Identify supply/demand/usage for each user department for a 24-hour period. The need/demand can be determined by sampling actual consumption for a period of time; usually 31 days are adequate. High, low, and average daily demand figures for that sample should be noted. Numerical averages create a smoothing effect so the peak demands should be planned for. Finally, input should be obtained from the users by having them evaluate the data gathered. Frequently they can identify where a peak period is unrepresentative of routine activity and can help establish more appropriate levels of inventory.

3. Draft a list of all products to be used for each department. This list should include such information as (1) item number, (2) source, (3) description, (4) units of issue, (5) unit cost, (6) optimum inventory level, and (7) charge versus noncharge status. It can be prepared before taking physical counts and can serve as a master catalog/worksheet.

4. Determine frequency of supply replacement, which depends upon the type of system selected and the targets for on-hand inventory levels and turnover rates.

5. Identify the functional requirements and specifications required for all exchange carts if that system is used. Different size carts may be required for different areas, depending on the volume of products being maintained on the cart, as well as the frequency of restocking.

6. Determine the appropriate location for supplies at the user area. This should include a configuration for those supplies so that reordering and restocking, as well as on-demand item location, can be facilitated. It is important to include user department input in this vital process. Standardization layouts should be established as much as possible in order to enhance

the productivity in the ordering, restocking, and retrieval-for-use processes.

7. Determine the timing for inventory review, ordering, and restocking. Essential variables for making this decision include times of peak supply demand, corridor and elevator congestion, and staff availability.

8. Identify and determine the preferred methodology: individual order processing or batch or zone processing.

9. Establish the appropriate paperwork/record-keeping systems. This step includes designing forms, setting up automated data systems communications, and so on.

10. Adjust layout, configuration, and inventory levels at the supply source in order to accommodate the new system.

11. Conduct in-service education programs for all personnel involved and affected by the system.

12. Establish a mechanism for tracking nonroutine/random demand for supplies that occur outside the basic system to determine the continuing effectiveness of the system and the appropriateness of the product mix and inventory levels.

13. Establish a policy and procedure for making changes as appropriate. It is essential to ensure that inventory levels will be adjusted routinely to match changing demand.

14. Begin implementation on either a pilot project basis, batch or zone basis, or hospitalwide. Either way can be equally successful, depending on the degree of complexity and sophistication of the system selected and the extent of the impact of the change.

15. Schedule meetings for reviewing progress and making any necessary modifications.

Central Sterile Reprocessing

The essence of materials management is to be found in the processes of purchasing, receiving, storing, and distributing materials. However, a number of other functions that involve these processes have come to be associated with the materials management program. The most common of these is central service or central sterile reprocessing.

The central sterile reprocessing (CSR) department is responsible for the decontamination, inspection, packaging, and sterilization of reusable materials. In some hospitals, this department's responsibilities also include the collection and disposal of trash and the collection and decontamination of dishes and utensils for the food service department. In any case, the CSR department should be responsible for the reprocessing of all reusable materials for the medical and surgical departments.

This department has three primary objectives. The first is to ensure that a well-designed and documented program is in place to assess and adjust the quality of reprocessing functions throughout the organization. Such a program involves these activities: (1) establishing policies and procedures, (2) monitoring compliance with the policies and procedures, and (3) correcting deviations from policy and improving inadequate performance of procedures. The program should include elements such as the following:

- assignment of responsibility for the collection of soiled items
- definition of methods for containing soiled items during transport to the decontamination area
- procedures for decontamination
- procedures for inspecting items before repackaging
- definition of what constitutes acceptable packaging material
- procedures for properly setting up, packaging, and labeling reusable items
- procedures for operating and ensuring proper performance of sterilizing equipment

- procedures for storing, distributing, and handling sterile items throughout the hospital

- procedures for operating and ensuring proper performance of equipment used in decontamination

The second major objective is to ensure that all items leaving the CSR department have undergone a properly defined and executed sterilization process. The majority of items are sterilized—that is, made free of all living microorganisms—in a large-volume steam sterilizer. These are simply pressure vessels into which items to be sterilized are placed. All air is removed from the chamber, and then it is filled with saturated steam. It is vital that all air be removed because air acts as a buffer between the surface to be sterilized and the steam, which is the sterilizing agent. The steam must be of a defined temperature, and the contact with the steam must be maintained for a defined period of time. In order to state with confidence that sterilization has been achieved, it must be shown that the following steps have been taken:

- Items were properly packaged.

- Items were properly placed into the sterilizing chamber.

- All air was evacuated from the sterilizing chamber.

- The chamber was filled with saturated steam of the required temperature.

- The temperature and contact with the steam were maintained for the required period of time.

The only way to prove that an item is sterile is to open the package and perform laboratory analysis of the item. Obviously, this is not feasible because it destroys the item before it can be used. The most rigorous method available for testing the efficacy of the sterilization procedures and equipment is use of bacteriological monitors. In this method a package of live spores—the most difficult microorganisms to kill—of known strength are placed into the sterilizer. Upon completion of the sterilization process, the spores are analyzed in the hospital laboratory. If the spores are shown to have been killed, the assumption is that all other microorganisms in the sterilizer were also killed.

Bacteriological monitoring is relatively expensive. As a result, it is not commonly used in every sterilization cycle. At most, it is performed daily and in many cases on a weekly basis.

A program that includes (1) well-defined policies and procedures; (2) tests to ensure proper air evacuation, time, and temperature for every cycle; and (3) periodic use of bacteriological monitors should provide sufficient confidence that sterilization is being properly performed.

The third major objective of the CSR department is to perform the second most common type of sterilization in hospitals, which uses ethylene oxide (EtO) as a sterilant. Ethylene oxide is a toxic chemical, which can be hazardous to employee health. However, it is an extremely effective agent for sterilizing items that cannot withstand the rigors of steam sterilization. As a result, it must be used, but in a carefully controlled manner.

The Occupational Safety and Health Administration has established strict rules for the use of ethylene oxide. The current standard sets a limit for personal exposure of one part ethylene oxide per one million parts of air.[10] In order to ensure that this standard is met, a clearly defined ethylene oxide safety program must be established, which includes:

- policies and procedures for the use of EtO equipment

- proper design of the room containing EtO equipment

- proper ventilation of the room

- routine preventive maintenance and testing of the equipment and ventilation

- routine scheduled exposure testing of the work environment and the individual employees who operate the EtO equipment

Documentation must be maintained to prove compliance with all of these elements.

Other Related Functions

The hospital's materials manager almost always has direct management responsibility for the purchasing, receiving, central inventory, distribution, and central sterile reprocessing departments. In addition, this person is often given responsibility for other departments that are involved with the production and distribution of materials. The most common of these are (1) transportation services, (2) mail services, (3) print shop, and (4) laundry. In some cases, the pharmacy may be attached to the materials management division as well.

No matter what organizational arrangement is used, the most important fact is that materials comprise a major portion of the modern hospital's operating budget. Effective management of these materials is crucial to the survival of any hospital in the increasingly competitive environment of today's health care industry.

Materials Management Outside the Hospital

The health care industry continues to experience rapid change. More patient activity takes place in settings outside the hospital. In many cases, hospitals provide ownership and/or management support for these locations. Because the need for cost reduction is intense throughout the industry, effective materials management practices are vital in these other settings, as well.

Basic techniques are valid no matter where they are used. The challenge in offices, clinics, and outpatient centers is to apply the principle of materials management with smaller staff and space arrangements, and usually smaller volumes of material. The key is to stay focused on the basic principle and find ways to adapt it to the nonhospital setting. Hospital materials managers, as well as vendors, can be used as a resource in developing the nonhospital materials management control system.

Administrators should commit themselves to ensuring good materials management practice in all operating settings under their control.

NOTES

1. C.E. Hously, *Hospital Materiel Management* (Gaithersburg, Md.: Aspen Publishers, Inc., 1978), 2.

2. J.A. Dattilo and G. Meredith, Capital Equipment Purchasing, in *Handbook of Health Care Material Management,* ed. W.L. Scheyer (Gaithersburg, Md.: Aspen Publishers, Inc., 1985), 156–164.

3. R.E. Rourke, Streamlining the Purchasing Process, in *Handbook of Health Care Material Management,* ed. W.L. Scheyer (Gaithersburg, Md.: Aspen Publishers, Inc., 1985), 73.

4. Ibid., 101.

5. J.C. Kowalski, Supply Distribution Options—A New Perspective, in *Handbook of Health Care Material Management,* ed. W.L. Scheyer (Gaithersburg, Md.: Aspen Publishers, Inc., 1985).

6. J.W. Rayburn, Inventory Control, in *Handbook of Health Care Material Management,* ed. W.L. Scheyer (Gaithersburg, Md.: Aspen Publishers, Inc., 1985), 202.

7. Ibid., 190.

8. Ibid., 190.

9. J.C. Kowalski, Supply Distribution Options, 229–230.

10. R.L. Corn, Designing a Safety Program for EtO, in *Handbook of Health Care Material Management,* ed. W.L. Scheyer (Gaithersburg, Md.: Aspen Publishers, Inc., 1985), 260.

Bidding Instructions (Simple Format)

ITEMS BELOW APPLY TO AND BECOME A PART OF TERMS AND CONDITIONS OF BID. ANY EXCEPTIONS THERETO MUST BE IN WRITING.

1. Bidding Requirements:

    a. Late bids properly identified will be returned to bidder unopened. Late bids will not be considered under any circumstances.

    b. Bid prices must be firm for acceptance for thirty (30) days from bid opening date. Cash discount will not be considered in determining the low bid. All cash discounts offered will be taken if earned.

    c. Bids must give full firm name and address of bidder. Failure to manually sign bid should show title or authority to bind his firm in a contract. Firm name should appear on each page of a bid, in the space provided in the upper right-hand corner.

    d. Bid cannot be altered or amended after opening time. Any alterations made before opening time must be initiated by bidder or authorized agent. No bid can be withdrawn after opening time without approval by the Hospital, based on an acceptable written reason.

    e. Telegraphic response to any bid invitation must show: price bid, requisition number, opening date, description (brand, model, etc.) of product offered, and delivery promise. Confirmation on bid form should be postmarked on or before opening day and/or received within forty-eight (48) hours after opening day. Show regular information on envelope and add the word: "Confirmation." Telephone bids are not acceptable when in response to this invitation to bid.

    f. Engineering checklist must be completed and returned with this bid.

2. Specifications:

    a. All items bid shall be new, in first-class condition, including containers suitable for shipment and storage, unless otherwise indicated in invitation. Verbal agreements to the contract will not be recognized.

    b. Samples, when requested, must be furnished free of expense. If not destroyed in examination, they will be returned to the bidder, on request, at his expense. Each sample should be marked with bidder's name, address, and requisition number. Do not enclose in or attach bid to sample.

c. All quotations must be accompanied by descriptive literature giving full description of details as to type of material and equipment that is to be furnished under this contract. Samples, where required, shall be delivered to the purchasing department before the opening of quotations, unless otherwise stated in the specifications; failure of the bidder to either submit literature or supply samples may be considered sufficient reason for rejection of the quote. All deliveries under the contract shall conform in all respects with samples, catalog cuts, etc., as submitted and accepted as the basis for the award.

d. In addition to the requirements of paragraph C, all deviations from the specifications must be noted in detail by the bidder in writing at the time of submittal of the quote. The absence of a written list of specification deviations at the time of submittal of the quote will hold the bidders strictly accountable to the Hospital to the specifications as written. Any deviation from the specifications as written not previously submitted, as required by the above, will be grounds for rejection of the material and/or equipment when delivered.

3. Award:

Award of bid will be based on the information provided by the bidder. The award will be made consistent with PRUDENT BUYER POLICY of the Hospital. Considerations to this award will be:

1. Price 4. Delivery
2. Quality 5. Design
3. Service

(Not necessarily listed according to priority)

a. Cash discounts will not be taken into consideration in determining an award.

b. With regard to differences between unit prices and extensions, unit prices will

govern and extensions will be modified accordingly.

c. Freight charges may be a determining factor only when all price, quality, and service specifications are equal.

4. Delivery:

a. Failure to state delivery time obligates bidder to complete delivery in fourteen (14) calendar days. A five- (5)-day difference in delivery promise may break a tie bid. Unrealistically short or long delivery promises may cause bid to be disregarded. Consistent failure to meet delivery promises without valid reason may cause removal from bid list.

b. No substitutions or cancellations will be permitted without written approval of the Hospital.

c. Delivery shall be made during normal working hours only, 8:30 A.M. to 4 P.M., unless prior approval for late delivery has been obtained from Agency.

d. Any freight charges applicable to this quotation must appear on the quotation. All freight agreed to by the Hospital must be prepaid and added to the Hospital's invoice.

e. In all cases, seller will be responsible for filing damaged freight claims with the transporter of the merchandise.

5. Patents and Copyrights:

The contractor agrees to protect the Hospital from claims involving infringement of patents or copyrights.

TEFRA STATEMENT

Section 1861(v)(1) of the Social Security Act (42 U.S.C.Sec. 1395x) as amended, requires us, as Medicare providers, to obtain the agreement of persons who contract with us for services with a value or cost of $10,000 or more in any twelve-month period, that the books, documents, and records of such contractors must remain available for verification of cost by the Comptroller General for a period of four years following completion of the contract. Seller acknowledges and expressly agrees to this requirement, on its behalf and on behalf of any subcontractor who shall perform any part or all of this contract for Seller having a value or cost of $10,000 or more.

OSHA STATEMENT

Seller represents and warrants that all articles and services covered by this purchase order meet or exceed the safety standards established and promulgated under the Federal Occupational Safety and Health Law (Public Law 91-596) and its regulations in effect or proposed as of the date of this order. Seller will submit OSHA Form 20, material safety data sheet, upon request.

SUBMITTAL OR QUOTE CONSTITUTES ACKNOWLEDGEMENT AND ACCEPTANCE OF THE TERMS AND CONDITIONS AS OUTLINED ABOVE.

INQUIRIES PERTAINING TO BID INVITATIONS MUST BE DIRECTED TO DEPARTMENT MANAGER, PURCHASING.

Authorized Signature

Source: Departmental document, reprinted with permission of St. Francis-St. George Hosp., Cincinnati, Ohio.

Appendix 13–B

Bidding Instructions (Complex Format)

A. INSTRUCTIONS TO BIDDERS

In accordance with the contract documents set forth herein, proposals will be received by Hospital through __, 19__, at the (describe location).

1. *PROJECT SCHEDULE*

Schedule installation to be completed by __

2. *PREPARATION OF PROPOSALS*

a. The bidder shall submit his proposal on the attached proposal forms and specification sheets. No other forms will be accepted. A unit price and extended price shall be stated on the specification sheets for each item either typed or written in ink.

b. Each bidder is to bid on all items that he manufactures or supplies.

3. *SUBMISSION OF PROPOSALS*

a. All bidders shall submit __ proposals enclosed in a sealed envelope marked "Bid Document Equipment" on or before __, 19__.

b. The proposals with all literature and the Bond shall be delivered to: (address and designate)

c. Where proposals are sent by mail, the bidders shall be responsible for their delivery before the date set for the receipt of proposals. Late proposals will not be considered and will be returned unopened.

4. *WITHDRAWAL OF BIDS*

a. Bids may be withdrawn on written request received from bidders *prior to date fixed for opening bids.*

b. Negligence on the part of the bidder in preparing the bid confers no right for the withdrawal of the bid after it has been opened.

5. *COMPETENCY OF BIDDER*

a. A contract will not be awarded to any person, firm, or corporation that has failed to perform faithfully any previous contract with the Hospital.

6. *CONSIDERATION OF PROPOSALS*

    a. The Hospital reserves the right to reject any or all quotations or to waive any informalities or technicalities in any quotations in the interest of the Hospital.

7. *BID GUARANTEE*

    a. Each proposal shall be accompanied by a bid guarantee for five percent (5%) of the amount of the total bid. Bid guarantees shall be a Bond made on the Proposal Bond Form or a cashier's check.

    b. The Proposal Bond shall guarantee that the bidder will not withdraw, cancel or modify his bid for a period of sixty (60) days after the scheduled closing date for receipt of bids. The Proposal Bond shall further guarantee that, if his bid is accepted, the bidder will enter into a formal contract in accordance with the method of contracting hereinafter specified.

    c. In the event the bidder withdraws his bid within the sixty (60)-day period or fails to enter into a contract if his bid is accepted, he shall be liable to the Hospital for the full amount of the bid guarantee.

    d. The Proposal Bond shall be returned to all unsuccessful bidders after the successful bidder has executed the Performance Bond and the bid has been accepted by the Hospital.

    e. The Proposal Bond must be endorsed by surety or sureties, and names of endorsers must be typed immediately below signature.

8. *METHOD OF CONTRACTING*

    a. Award of contracts will be in the form of a Purchase Order made by the Hospital on the basis of the *best* bid from a qualified contractor.

    b. The successful bidder shall deliver to the Hospital a Performance Bond with sureties satisfactory to the Hospital in the amount of one hundred percent (100%) of the total accepted bid.

    c. The agent of the surety bonding company must be able to furnish on demand:

      a) Credentials showing power of attorney.

      b) Certificate showing the legal right of the company to do business in the state of the Hospital.

9. *INTERPRETATION OF CONTRACT DOCUMENTS*

    a. Discrepancies, omissions, or doubts as to the meaning of the specifications should be communicated in writing to the Hospital for interpretation. Bidders should act promptly and allow sufficient time for a reply to reach them before the submission of bids. Any interpretation made will be in the form of an addendum to the specifications, which will be forwarded to all bidders and its receipt by the bidder must be acknowledged on the Form of Proposal.

10. *RESPONSIBILITY OF THE BIDDERS*

    a. Bidders shall visit the site and note local pertinent field conditions such as availability of loading docks, elevators, and all other receiving and inspecting facilities.

    b. Bidders are responsible for the installation and start-up of their equipment including the following:

    c. Bidders are to include with this quotation complete information on the local service center including:

    d. Bidders are to include with this quotation all warranty information concerning the system components outlined in Bidder's Proposal.

    e. Bidders shall provide an annual price for manufacturer's recommended preventive maintenance program to be provided by factory-trained and qualified personnel, after the warranty period.

11. *SALES TAX*

    a. The Hospital is a tax-exempt institution.

    b. Copies of the exemption certificate will be furnished upon request.

12. *METHOD OF PAYMENT*

    a. Requests for payments (invoices) must include the following information for processing:

       1) Purchase order number
       2) Manufacturer name and catalog item number
       3) Dollar amount.

    b. Payment for equipment shall be made according to the following schedule:

       1) Ten percent (10%) of contract price as down payment shall be made within ten (10) days of acknowledgement of order.

       2) Eighty percent (80%) of contract price shall be due and payable within ten (10) days of delivery, installation (to include field assembly, interconnection, equipment calibration to manufacturer's specification, and checkout), and acceptance by the Hospital of all system components as outlined in Bidder's Proposal.

       3) Ten percent (10%) shall be payable six (6) days after acceptance by the Hospital.

    c. The Hospital reserves the right to refuse payment on an invoice due to damaged item(s), quantity variance, model variance, or any failure to comply with the contract documents.

B. FORM OF PROPOSAL

Submitted by: Date:

_____   _____

TO: HOSPITAL

We, the undersigned, have familiarized ourselves with the local conditions affecting the cost of the work, and with all contract documents for this work, including:

    INSTRUCTIONS TO BIDDERS   PROPOSAL BOND

    PROPOSAL FORM   BID SPECIFICATIONS

And also have received and incorporated into the makeup of the specifications the following addenda:

Addendum No. _____   Dated _____   Addendum No. _____   Dated _____

Hereby propose to furnish all labor, equipment, and transportation to delivery and install all materials, and to perform and supervise all work as required.

TIME OF COMPLETION: Installation must be complete by _____, 19_____.

EXECUTION OF CONTRACT: If written notice of acceptance of this bid is mailed, telegraphed, or delivered to the undersigned within sixty (60) days after date required for the receipt of the bid, or any time thereafter before this bid is withdrawn, the undersigned will, within ten (10) days after date of such notice, execute and deliver a Performance Bond.

NOTE A: Bids submitted by virtue of the proposal hereby acknowledged by the Hospital to be made under the assumption that the successful bidder will not be prevented, on account of strikes or other disruptions affecting sources of supply or affecting normal progress of the work, from obtaining the materials necessary to carry out this contract to complete the work covered thereby.

NOTE B: It is understood and agreed by the undersigned that the Hospital reserves the right to reject any or all bids, or to accept the bid that embraces such combination of proposal that will promote the best interest of the Hospital.

NOTE C: It is agreed that this proposal shall be irrevocable for a period of sixty (60) days after the date set for the receipt of proposals.

NOTE D: It is understood and agreed by the undersigned that they will cooperate and coordinate their work with the contractor who will be in the final stage of work at the Hospital.

The undersigned hereby designates the office to which such notice may be mailed, telegraphed, or delivered:

_____

_____

_____

Enter here the service information requested in 10-D of "INSTRUCTIONS TO BIDDERS":   _____

_____

_____

SIGNATURE OF BIDDER

SEAL (if a corporation)   Date _____

                                          Name of Firm _____

                                                              _____

                                                   By _____

                                                Title _____

                                   Business Address_____

                                                              _____

                                                              _____

                                   Telephone Number _____

                                State of Incorporation _____

NOTE 1:   If bidder is a corporation, write state of incorporation, and if a partnership, give full name of all partners.

NOTE 2: Any deviation from the specifications must be specifically stated. Include also an explanation where the bidder's project exceeds the above specifications.

NOTE 3: Alternatives, where presented in addition to the base bid, will be considered but must follow the instructions above, listing deviations to the specifications, and include complete descriptions and literature.

C. PROPOSAL BOND

KNOW ALL MEN BY THESE PRESENTS, THAT WE, _____
_____, (hereinafter called the Principal), as principal, and
_____, (hereinafter called the Surety), as surety, are
firmly bound unto the Hospital in the amount of _____
(amount not less than five percent (5%) of the accompanying bid plus the sum of all additive alternates) in lawful money of the United States for payment of which said Principal and Surety bind themselves, their heirs, executors, successors, administrators, and assigns, jointly and severally.

WHEREAS, said Principal has submitted to the Hospital a written proposal for certain work in connection with the (describe project), a copy of which is hereto attached.

NOW THEREFORE, the condition of this obligation is such that if said Proposal be accepted, the Principal shall, within ten (10) days of written notice thereof, enter into proper contract for the work covered by the Proposal, and shall furnish a Performance Bond satisfactory to said Hospital. If there is a difference between the amount of the Proposal and the amount accepted then, this obligation shall be reduced to five percent (5%) of the value of the Proposal accepted. This Proposal Bond shall be valid for a period of sixty (60) days from the date set for the receipt of the Proposal attached thereto.

Signed and sealed this _____ day of _____, 19_____

Witness: _____ (SEAL)

_____, _____

_____ Principal

Countersigned at _____ (SEAL)

By _____

D. SPECIFICATIONS

PART 1—GENERAL

1. *RELATED DOCUMENTS*

a. Contract Documents, including General and Supplementary conditions and General Requirement, and contract drawings for the Hospital, apply to the work specified in this section.

2. *DESCRIPTION OF WORK*

a. Successful bidder shall furnish, delivery F.O.B. jobsite, and install, all equipment specified herein, including all necessary attachment devices and all incidentals and accessories required for a complete and operable installation. Any omissions of the details in specifications does not relieve the bidder from furnishing a complete functioning installation of highest quality for all purposes intended.

b. The work shall be coordinated with the mechanical and electrical trades where services and connections are required for proper installation and operation of equipment.

c. It shall be noted that all interconnecting cabling throughout the installation shall be furnished by the bidder at no additional cost to the Hospital.

d. The Bidder is required to clean up, remove, and dispose of all debris resulting from work hereunder.

3. *QUALITY ASSURANCE*

a. Manufacturer's Qualifications:

1) Only manufacturers having a minimum of five (5) years experience in the manufacture and installation of the quality and type of the respective items of equipment specified herein shall be considered qualified.

2) Manufacturer shall be able to demonstrate to the Hospital's satisfaction, proximity of spare parts and availability of experienced, competent maintenance service.

3) Should the manufacturer find at any time during the progress of the work that, in his opinion, existing design or conditions require a modification of any particular part or assembly, he shall promptly report in writing such matter to the Hospital.

b. Substitutions

1) The following specifications are to establish a standard of quality and performance and are not intended to exclude any manufacturer or company from bidding quality equipment that can be proven to meet functional standards as set forth. The equipment to be furnished must meet the highest standards of the profession.

4. *CODE COMPLIANCE*

a. All equipment furnished and installed under this section shall comply with all requirements of local, state, and federal building, health, sanitary, and NFPA Codes.

5. *STANDARDS*

a. In addition to the above, the following standard shall apply to the extent referenced herein:

1) Underwriters Laboratories, Incorporated (UL): Listings and approvals as required.

2) Electrical components and wiring: Furnish and wire electrical components of equipment in this section to conform to NFPA 70 (National Fire Protection Association).

3) All new equipment must be HHS certified.

6. *SUBMITTALS*

a. Roughing-in Drawings:

1) The Bidder will provide rough-in drawings and will coordinate and verify the dimensions and required service with the architect.

2) Roughing-in drawings must be supplied within two weeks after receiving notice of the award, to provide information to other contractors performing the roughing-in.

b. Shop Drawings:

   1) Submit shop drawings and catalog cuts of standard manufactured items. Indicate in detail the methods of installation, connections, and all pertinent data relating to each item of equipment.

   2) Catalog cuts shall indicate the specified model and characteristics of the item being furnished.

c. Operating and Maintenance Instructions:

   1) The Bidder shall furnish the Hospital with four (4) bound copies of written instructions, giving detailed information as to how the equipment is to be operated and maintained. Maintenance manuals shall include appropriate parts list and the name of the service representative.

   2) In addition, a representative from the equipment manufacturer shall visit the project and instruct the Hospital personnel on the proper operation and maintenance of the equipment. The instruction period consists of not less than two (2) separate sessions, to be scheduled by the Hospital after occupancy.

d. Guarantee and Preventive Maintenance:

   1) Upon completion, and as a condition for acceptance of the work, the Bidder shall submit written guarantee(s) covering each item included in this section for a period one (1) year from date of beneficial use. The guarantee shall cover all workmanship and materials and the Bidder agrees to repair or replace all faulty work and defective materials and equipment, including labor.

   2) The Bidder shall be responsible for maintenance of the equipment for the first six (6) months, with all costs for parts, labor, and trips to and from the hospital covered by the warranty.

Source: Departmental document, reprinted with permission of St. Francis-St. George Hospital, Inc., Cincinnati, Ohio.

WILLIAM L. SCHEYER's 20-year career in the hospital industry culminated in his role as Assistant Vice President for Materials Management at Bethesda Hospital, Inc., in Cincinnati, Ohio. Bethesda, a multisite organization combining 2 acute care, 2 long-term care, and numerous ancillary facilities, is a leader in health care management. Mr. Scheyer is the editor of the *Handbook of Health Care Material Management,* taught this subject at the University of Cincinnati, and has served as President of the Greater Cincinnati Health Care Materials Management Association. Mr. Scheyer currently serves as City Administrator for the City of Erlanger, Kentucky, and is active in local government affairs in the northern Kentucky area.

Chapter 14

Facilities Management

V. James McLarney

Facilities management is a comprehensive program designed to ensure a safe and comfortable environment for patients, staff, and visitors. Typically, the engineering department assumes major responsibility for facilities management, but the importance of the contributions and co-operation of other functional areas, including environmental services and safety and security, must not be understated.

A comprehensive facilities management program includes the following functional areas:

- facilities engineering
- construction management
- building and equipment maintenance
- grounds maintenance
- security
- fire safety
- environmental safety
- general safety
- clinical engineering
- medical equipment management
- energy management
- telecommunications
- technology evaluation and acquisition
- space management
- renovation and remodeling
- facilities planning
- disaster preparedness
- compliance management

As hospitals and other health facilities continue to enter a more competitive environment characterized by free market forces and financial incentives to increase operating efficiencies, key decision makers in hospitals are applying management strategies that have traditionally been used in business and industry. Not the least of these strategies is keen attention to efficient operation of hospital facilities. Clearly, the single greatest capital investment for any organization is in its buildings and property. These costs, coupled with those of energy and other utilities, maintenance, renovation, code compliance, safety and security, represent a highly significant portion of the hospital's budget. Because of this, strict stewardship in maintaining the integrity and efficiencies of the building systems and equipment cannot be overemphasized. This chapter reviews the major components of a facilities management program and describes various management strategies.

MAINTENANCE

One of the most significant components of the engineering function is a preventive maintenance program. Simply stated, this means planning and scheduling maintenance of equipment and facilities to extend their life, reduce costly failures, and attain greater operating efficiencies. The importance of this program lies in two areas: safety and cost effectiveness.

Although it may seem somewhat obvious, the safety and well-being of patients, visitors, and staff can be largely dependent upon equipment and mechanical systems. A comprehensive, well-managed preventive maintenance program is the single most important factor in predicting failures and avoiding hazards related to the sudden loss of critical equipment.

An effective preventive maintenance program can serve as a powerful cost-containment tool. The useful life of a piece of equipment can be greatly extended through proper maintenance, resulting in less frequent capital expenditures for replacement equipment. Preventive maintenance also results in greater energy efficiencies.

ENVIRONMENTAL SAFETY

As stated earlier, the objective of facilities management is to provide a safe, comfortable environment for patients, staff, and visitors. By its very nature, a hospital uses materials and produces by-products that may present a threat to the safety of individuals. These materials and by-products fall into one of three categories: hazardous chemicals, infectious materials, and radioactive materials.

Hazardous Chemicals

Perhaps the largest category of potential hazards is that of hazardous chemicals. Strong acids and caustic materials, organic solvents, heavy metals including mercury, ethylene oxide (used extensively as a sterilant), nitrous oxide, and antineoplastic pharmaceuticals are typically used in hospitals. Most hazardous chemicals are found in the hospital's laboratory, although such other departments as engineering, housekeeping, and pharmacy also handle these materials.

A comprehensive management system should be employed when handling these materials. A comprehensive record-keeping and inventory program should be in place from the moment these chemicals enter the facility until they are safely disposed of. In many states, strict management programs are required by law and are enforced by state environmental protection agencies. Also required by many states are "right-to-know" programs whereby hospitals must advise all of their employees of the risks and hazards they are exposed to in the workplace.

There are three alternative means of disposing of these materials: dilution/sewage, incineration, and landfill. Caution should be exercised when choosing a disposal method to ensure that it is consistent with federal, state, and local codes and regulations. Because of the excessively high costs and environmental risks associated with disposing of any hazardous material in landfills, on-site incineration of these materials often is the safest and the most cost-effective management alternative. This method can be especially attractive if it is coupled with a heat recovery system that uses both hazardous wastes and the general waste stream as a fuel source.

Infectious Materials

Nosocomial (hospital-acquired) infections are an ever-present threat. Currently, the rate of nosocomial infection is far greater than necessary. Because of this, the importance of establishing sound procedures for handling infectious materials must be underscored.

It has long been thought that a primary means by which infections are spread is through ventilation systems. Therefore, hospitals and other facilities have been required to implement sophisticated ventilation systems that include positive and negative air relationships, laminar airflow systems, and very high air exchange rates: until recently the environment in operating suites was completely exchanged with fresh, outside air once every several minutes. Recently, however, leading experts in engineering and infection control have determined that the primary means by which infections are spread is by direct contact from one person to another, and by direct contact with contaminated materials.

Although one staff member must take the primary responsibility for developing an infection control program, the effort must transcend departmental lines. Key to a successful program is a comprehensive set of policies and procedures that provides guidance to all employees in handling infectious materials.

Three alternative means of disposing of infectious materials are sterilization, incineration, and landfill. The least attractive alternative is landfill. This method is expensive and presents unacceptable environmental risks and liabilities. Sterilization is an acceptable means of rendering infectious materials nonviable. However, depending upon the volume of materials this method may prove to be impractical. For facilities that have on-site incinerators, incineration will, in all likelihood, prove to be the most efficient and cost-effective manner in which to dispose of infectious wastes.

Radioactive Materials

Radiation control and safety practices are normally supervised by a designated radiation protection officer. This officer may be a physician trained in radiology or nuclear medicine. In smaller facilities the officer may be a consultant, and in very large hospitals he or she may be a health physicist.

Radiation sources are grouped in two categories: ionizing and nonionizing. Examples of ionizing radiation sources are X-rays and radioactive isotopes. Examples of nonionizing radiation sources are lasers and microwaves.

Radiation control measures are based on factors of time, distance, shielding, personnel protection devices, and ventilation. Radioactive waste disposal practices for both solid and liquid wastes are based on factors of decay, segrega-

tion, volume reduction, and dilution. In all cases, operating and disposal practices must conform to the regulations of the U.S. Department of Transportation and the Nuclear Regulatory Commission.

Asbestos

Nearly every building built before the mid-1970s contains asbestos. This fire-protection material has been identified as a hazard to health, causing lung cancer and asbestosis. If the presence of asbestos is identified, action must be taken to provide for the safety of employees and patients. The threat from asbestos may be correlated to exposure time and concentration. The group at highest risk are engineering and maintenance personnel because of their daily contact with insulated ducts, pipes, and building structures.

Asbestos management programs should include a thorough audit of the facilities. If asbestos is found it must be determined if it is friable, a dangerous deteriorating state in which the asbestos can be dispersed to the atmosphere. If the asbestos is friable, steps must be taken to eliminate any potential risks of exposure. Typically these would entail one of the three options—removal, encapsulation, or isolation. Regardless of which of the three methods is employed, consideration must be given to maintaining the fire safety qualities of the building. If the asbestos is not friable a program documenting its continued monitoring must be established.

Because of the current attitudes prevailing in the judicial system, building owners and operators who neglect their responsibilities in this area can place themselves in a position of high risk.

ENERGY MANAGEMENT

Hospitals and other large health facilities are the most intensive energy users of all commercial building types, consuming nearly 15 percent of all the energy used in the commercial sector. For every bed in a hospital, energy is consumed at a rate equal to the amount of energy used in two average American homes. In large hospitals annual utility costs can run into millions of dollars per year. Therefore, hospitals must aggressively seek to optimize their energy efficiencies. A report published in 1984 by the American College of Healthcare Executives (ACHE) indicated that energy conservation programs offered one of the greatest opportunities for cost-containment efforts in hospitals.

The greatest opportunity for energy savings comes from low-cost improvements to existing systems. A central component of such improvements is a comprehensive preventive maintenance program. Because nearly 60 percent of all the energy consumed in hospitals is used in the heating, ventilating, and air condition systems (HVAC), special consideration should be given to these systems.

When low-cost measures to reduce energy consumption have been fully implemented, a hospital may wish to investigate more capital-intensive projects. Two such projects that have been highly successful in hospitals are heat recovery from incineration systems and co-generation systems. However, a thorough engineering evaluation should be conducted before proceeding with any capital-intensive project.

A final area to which consideration should be given by hospital decision makers is energy interruption preparedness. Although hospitals are required to have emergency generators for short-term power supply interruption, hospitals may wish to secure additional fuel reserves for extended shortfalls.

FIRE SAFETY

Fires in health care facilities are more dangerous than fires in other types of buildings because rapid evacuation of patients is not possible. As the majority of patients are not capable of taking the necessary steps toward self-preservation, health care occupancies have been designed, constructed, or retrofitted with construction features that contain the spread of fire and its by-products—smoke, toxic gases, and heat. This philosophy is commonly referred to as "defend

in place." Due to this unique approach to fire safety it is essential that hospital managers and staff be fully aware of the fire strategies that apply to health care occupancies.

With health care occupants depending on staff to provide them with a safe environment, each hospital should maintain an up-to-date library of applicable codes, regulations, and manuals pertaining to fire safety and disaster planning. This library is an extremely valuable resource in preparing initial detailed fire safety programs and can serve as a ready reference for the continued re-evaluation of the hospital's ongoing fire safety programs. Two extremely valuable reference documents addressing fire and life safety are the *National Fire Codes,* published by the National Fire Protection Agency (NFPA) and the *Safety Guide for Health Care Institutions,* published by the American Hospital Association (AHA). Additional guidance may be found in the *Accreditation Manual for Hospitals* published by the Joint Commission on Accreditation of Healthcare Organizations (Joint Commission).

Planning for fire safety can be divided into three major steps: (1) eliminating the causes of fire occurrences, (2) controlling the spread—compliance with appropriate construction codes and standards, and (3) response—fire detection systems and staff training.

Cause

This is probably the easiest and least costly of the three steps to implement. Every facility should have a safety director and committee who have fire safety as one of their responsibilities. Through this committee fire plans and policies should be developed and reviewed at least annually. The development of hazard surveillance programs that are especially designed to review the physical plant on a scheduled basis should be another responsibility of the safety committee. The committee should develop policies that address smoking; the use of electrical appliances; staff training to recognize fire hazards; patient, staff, and visitor awareness programs; and the like. Other programs that are often used to reduce the causes of fire in health care facilities are preventive maintenance, electrical safety, and housekeeping.

Spread

Controlling the spread of fires is probably the most difficult and least cost effective of the three steps. Spread is prevented by fire containment—those measures taken to prevent fire and its by-products from spreading throughout the facility. Containment, or compartmentalization as it is typically called, provides the defense levels necessary to protect nonambulatory patients in place. The tool commonly used to evaluate and define this philosophy is the *Life Safety Code,* NFPA 101. The *Life Safety Code* suggests levels of construction for corridor walls, patient room doors, smokestop barriers, floor assemblies, vertical chutes, and shafts. Compliance with this standard, however, will not prevent a fire from occurring or provide for a rapid response if a fire does occur. Therefore, the other two factors, cause and response, are key elements of a total fire safety plan.

Response

The most modern and safest building is of little value if its staff are not trained in how to take advantage of its fire protection features. For this reason staff training is paramount and should take place during orientation, continuous in-service programs, and an intensive fire drill (internal disaster) program set up to provide staff with on-the-job training. Other devices or systems that assist staff are smoke detectors, a complete electronically monitored fire alarm system, automatic transmission of an alarm to the fire department, and a mechanical smoke evacuation system.

No fire safety program can be effective without discipline. It should be the responsibility of every employee to be aware of the hospital fire safety policies and protection features, to report all fire hazards, to observe smoking policies, and to know the location of fire alarms and extinguishing equipment.

TECHNOLOGY EVALUATION AND ACQUISITION

As facilities continue to acquire highly sophisticated equipment for diagnostic procedures, telecommunication, and management information services, care should be taken to ensure their cost effectiveness, system compatibility, and quality assurance. Ideally, an equipment review team should be established to evaluate alternative products before any purchase. This team should consist of potential users of the product, financial officers, administrators, and plant and clinical engineers. Engineering personnel can often give insight to technical issues that may have a bearing on which product is best. Certain products may need specific support systems that may significantly increase their operating and installation costs. For example, certain computers require extensive air conditioning and environmental control systems, and some imaging equipment requires additional structural support. Engineering personnel can also provide valuable information regarding state-of-the-art technology and the costs of maintenance, operations, and service contracts.

Finally, plant and clinical engineers can assist in the development of product specifications. Regardless of the cost of the equipment, complete and detailed specifications should be developed stating exactly which features must be included by the manufacturer. Failure to do this may result in the product being incompatible with existing systems or in noncompliance with standards and regulations.

SECURITY

Security is directly related to the welfare of patients, employees, and visitors. It is incumbent upon the board and administration to provide an appropriate level of security based on the conditions that surround the facility. Although the development of a security plan differs from one facility to the next, each institution should begin with an analysis of its own security vulnerability and risk, which is a function of its size, type, and location.

Potential risk may be divided into several general areas, including assaults on employees, patients, and visitors; disturbances; pilferage and theft; loss of patient and employee property; fire; accidents; malicious destruction of property; civil disturbances; natural disasters; and internal and external emergencies that might disrupt services.

The administration has the responsibility for determining the degree of security that must be established and maintained. Ensuring basic security begins in the design of the facility. It is at that point that security can be incorporated into all features of the structural and utility designs: exterior doors, traffic control, lighting, and so forth.

A security system may be structured several ways. Although many facilities have an in-house system, others use contract services. Both systems have distinct advantages and disadvantages. In-house services afford complete control over the selection and training of employees. Generally, these employees have a greater sensitivity to the unique needs of hospitals and more loyalty to the specific hospital that employs them. Conversely, the facility must accept full responsibility for effectively training these employees. In contrast, employees from contracted services generally have stronger training in security systems and philosophies. Companies offering security services usually have the capabilities of providing additional services on short notice.

TELECOMMUNICATIONS MANAGEMENT

As the services that are provided to their communities become more complex and sophisticated, the need to establish and manage sophisticated communications and information systems grows in direct proportion. Telecommunications systems have grown from switchboard operators and beepers to advanced computer-driven technology systems that encompass satellite transmission, data communications, telemetry, and computer-age telephone systems that play integral roles in the diagnosis and treatment of illness, as well as the performance of critical business communications. Currently, great amounts of money are being invested in communications and information systems, ranging from hundreds of thousands of dollars in smaller hospitals to millions of dollars in larger hospitals. There is little doubt that the dependency upon and investments in these systems will continue to grow at a higher than normal rate in the coming years. This trend shall be especially pronounced among multiprovider systems.

A telecommunications system may include:

- advanced telephone services
- data communications
- nurse call system
- paging
- physician registry
- television services
- telemetry
- satellite communications

Many facilities engage in telecommunications ventures that are highly successful in generating profitable revenues. Most prominent among these are the resale of WATS (wide area telecommunications services) and physician answering services.

GROUNDS MANAGEMENT AND SPECIAL ATTENTION TO THE FACILITY'S APPEARANCE

The appearance of a health care facility makes an important statement to the community at large, physicians, and the staff. The visual impression that a facility conveys represents a strong marketing tool: it is also one that is often neglected. A well-groomed exterior and clean interior can favorably influence potential customers—physicians and patients—and staff. Therefore, special consideration should be given to:

- appearance
- accessibility
- parking accommodations
- security
- lighting
- traffic control
- signage
- visitor opportunities, including private family rooms, chapel, gift shop, and cafeteria

BIOMEDICAL EQUIPMENT MANAGEMENT

Hospitals spend large sums of money on highly sophisticated equipment that is used for the diagnosis and treatment of various health disorders. Typically, this equipment includes such instruments as imaging devices, physiologic monitors, electrosurgical apparatus, spectrophotometers, defibrillators, respirators, and automated blood analyzers. Because the accuracy, precision, and reliability of this equipment are of critical importance, all hospitals have biomedical equipment management programs of one sort or another. In very small hospitals, this program may take the form of contract services with manufacturers, external medical equipment maintenance organization, or shared service organizations. In very large facilities, all but the most technically advanced imaging equipment may be maintained by internal staff. In medium-sized hospitals, in-house maintenance is becoming increasingly prevalent as the costs of service contracts continue to rise. It should be noted that hospitals are required to have comprehensive biomedical equipment management programs for accreditation by the Joint Commission.

Typically, a biomedical equipment management program has the following components:

- preventive maintenance program
- equipment evaluation and testing program

- standards compliance program
- staff training program (nonengineering)
- product recall management
- equipment inventory and control
- liaison with medical staff
- incoming equipment inspection

The required qualifications of biomedical equipment managers vary according to the scope and complexity of the management program. Solid training in electronics is a requisite for equipment technicians, and completion of graduate-level studies is highly desirable for managers of comprehensive programs in larger hospitals.

DISASTER PREPAREDNESS

Hospitals are required by the Joint Commission to have written plans to deal with internal and external disasters and to exercise these plans periodically to maintain their level of preparedness. Examples of internal disasters are fire, utility failure, and terrorism; external disasters may be hurricanes, common carrier accidents, and hazardous chemical leaks.

It is important that every staff member be familiar both with the hospital emergency policies and procedures and with their individual role in an emergency situation. Policies and procedures should be reviewed frequently to ensure that they are consistent with changes in the hospital and community environments. Typically, a disaster preparedness program contains the following components:

- *Disaster preparedness committee:* Because of the importance of disaster preparedness, the committee should be chaired by a person in a position of authority within the hospital's senior management staff. Other areas that should be represented include engineering, safety, nursing, medical staff, communications, environmental services, volunteers, laboratory, and other department heads who will play key roles in an emergency situation.

- *External liaison:* In nearly every emergency situation, hospitals must coordinate their efforts with members of external organizations. These organizations should be involved in the development and ongoing evaluation of emergency plans. Examples of such organizations include police and fire departments, units of local governments, ambulance services, clergy, state and local authorities (EPA, health departments, etc.), utility companies, and so forth.

- *Public relations:* In emergency situations members of the press and electronic media must be treated in a professional and businesslike manner. Information should be disseminated from a single authoritative source. Because the way in which a hospital responds to an emergency situation can leave a lasting impression on its community, the importance of this function cannot be understated.

- *Training and practice drills:* Staff training and practice are required by the Joint Commission and are necessary to ensure proper response in an actual emergency. A well-managed and diversified plan of education should be developed and administered with the endorsement and participation of senior management.

- *Central command center:* In an emergency situation, the hospital's plan must be executed from a single, centralized command center. It is important that this location be identified in advance and that it be equipped at all times with essential communication lines, critical documents and directories, and other materials that will be required in an emergency situation.

As in many other areas of hospital management it is important that senior administrators fully support emergency preparedness and that they clearly convey this support to the entire hospital staff.

STAFFING REQUIREMENTS

Staffing requirements in facilities management vary. This function is frequently understaffed and is often one of the first targets of staff reductions in times of financial hardship. It is understandable that senior managers might elect to sacrifice efficiencies in facilities management, rather than jeopardize the quality of medical services. However, it is important to realize that investment in facilities management can play an all-important role in helping protect a hospital from future financial hardship. Over time, the neglect of the physical plant and property can have devastating financial implications for any organization—a lesson learned the hard way by many large, urban hospitals, as well as by many of our nation's industrial concerns.

The qualifications and training requirements for facilities managers vary depending upon the size and type of hospital. Although a degree in an engineering discipline may not be required for the facilities manager in a small hospital, strong technical training or experience in mechanical and electrical systems is required to discharge properly the duties of this position in a hospital of any size. In larger hospitals, a degree in engineering is highly desirable, and in the largest of hospitals a degree in engineering with accompanying education in business or health administration is the most desirable preparation.

Perhaps as important as formal education is experience in health care engineering. Because the management of health care facilities presents unique challenges that do not exist in other industries, it is vitally important that the individual responsible for this function be cognizant of hospital-specific codes and standards, safety and fire protection philosophies, and environment considerations. Proficiency in this area requires at least 5 years of experience in a hospital setting.

Membership in the American Society for Hospital Engineering (ASHE) indicates that the individual is involved in continued professional development. Generally speaking, the most proficient hospital engineers have attained the Senior (SASHE) or Fellow (FASHE) level of membership within ASHE.

DIVERSIFICATION OF FACILITIES MANAGEMENT

Health facilities are moving quickly into an era of providing diversified services. They can no longer be stereotypically characterized as monolithic institutions that provide general acute care services. As hospitals continue to expand into vertical and horizontal health systems, the role of the facilities manager must change accordingly to meet newly created needs.

In a move to bring comprehensive health care services to their communities, hospitals are developing a range of properties beyond their walls. Examples of these properties include outpatient clinics, surgical centers, emergency treatment centers, long-term care centers, and substance abuse centers. As these new lines of business proliferate, facilities managers must assume additional responsibilities to ensure that they are properly managed and maintained. Satellite structures have new and unique building and operating codes and different compliance measures for accreditation than for hospitals. Telecommunications and management information systems will need to be interconnected among all facilities within the system. These changes will require the facilities engineer to become a multiproperty manager serving the needs of a variety of building types.

ENTREPRENEURIAL OPPORTUNITIES IN FACILITIES MANAGEMENT

As hospitals continue their evolution in a more competitive environment, the ways in which they conduct their business will also continue to change. Hospitals are seeking to identify new business lines that will enable them to serve their communities better. One way in which new services are being supported is through revenue that is generated by departments that traditionally have been considered strictly as cost centers. A growing number of hospitals are offering facilities management services to other hospitals and the community at large on a fee-for-service basis. Examples of these entrepreneurial activities follow.

- *Biomedical equipment management:* Larger hospitals are offering comprehensive biomedical equipment management services to smaller hospitals, clinics, and physicians at costs less than those normally offered through service contracts. The purchasers of these services receive high-quality workmanship from skilled professionals that ensures the reliability of their equipment and compliance with Joint Commission requirements. The providers of these services gain revenue that can be used to offset their operating costs.

- *Facilities management services:* Some hospitals are offering preventive maintenance and facilities engineering services to other organizations within their communities. Maintenance of heating and air conditioning systems of schools, libraries, and other organizations can be advantageous to both the hospital and its customers. Other hospitals are offering similar arrangements for the management of certain waste materials from other hospitals, doctors' offices, and school laboratories.

- *Telecommunications services:* Two types of telecommunications services—the resale of WATS (wide area telecommunications services) and physicians' answering services—have shown to be attractive revenue sources for hospitals. Because of the expansive size of the telecommunications systems in hospitals, frequently the largest in the community, they can often purchase WATS services at a cost significantly lower than that offered to the owner of a smaller system. If they purchase WATS capacity that is greater than their need, they may resell their unused capacity at a profit while setting a price that is still lower than the customer can get from the utility company. Providing physicians' answering services enables a hospital to offer a needed service to physicians within their communities and to generate welcomed revenue. An added advantage to this service is that it tends to establish a bond between the hospital and the physicians.

- *Food services:* Often, the food service department in a hospital is the most extensive and comprehensive within a community. Many hospitals have established food service programs with local schools and other community organizations. Some hospitals have even opened restaurants that offer special menus for people on restricted diets.

- *Laundry services:* Hospitals with in-house laundries have found that they can "take in wash" from other organizations and make a profit doing so. Among their primary customers are other hospitals, schools, and organizations providing uniforms to their staff.

The mission of all medical facilities is to provide high-quality health care services to their communities. Toward this end, facilities managers establish and maintain the environment and physical systems that permit the provision of this care. Although the objectives of the American health care system must continue to focus on the medical welfare of the people it serves, health administrators and managers must remain cognizant of contributions of facilities management and other support services in ensuring cost efficiencies and appropriate levels of safety and security to patients, staff, and the community at large.

Facilities management is, for the most part, a support function to medical services in health care facilities. However, when properly managed the facilities management function offers significant opportunities to minimize operating costs, generate limited revenues, ensure necessary levels of safety and security, and project a strong, favorable image to the community.

V. JAMES MCLARNEY, MHA, is the Executive Director for both the American Society for Hospital Engineering and the American Society for Healthcare Environmental Services of the American Hospital Association. In addition, Mr. McLarney directs the codes and standards advocacy program of the AHA and manages its disaster preparedness program. In this latter function, Mr. McLarney serves as liaison to the U.S. Department of Health and Human Services and to the Pentagon for the National Disaster Medical System. Moreover, several major research projects are under his direction.

Mr. McLarney received his bachelor's degree from Northern Illinois University and his master's degree in health administration from Governors State University.

Chapter 15

Environmental Services

Janice M. Kurth

Although not a revenue-producing department, poor housekeeping or environmental services performance can result in a loss of current patients, potential patients, and staff. The maintenance of a clean, safe, and esthetically pleasing environment is an important aspect of the provision of quality health care.

AREAS OF RESPONSIBILITY

Many of the responsibilities of the environmental services department are obvious and routine; some are not, and they will vary from institution to institution. Because of its broad spectrum of responsibilities, as identified below, many hospitals now refer to the housekeeping department as the environmental services department:

- cleaning and disinfecting of all areas of the facility
- discharge unit cleaning
- carpet and upholstery maintenance
- window cleaning or monitoring of contract
- pest control or monitoring of contract
- room set-ups in conference rooms and auditoriums
- furniture relocations

- interior design
- interior painting
- laundry
- plant care

As can be seen from the above list, several areas of specialized knowledge are required of any housekeeping department manager, including a basic knowledge of microbiology, hazardous and medical waste removal practices and laws, pest control methods, contract administration, fire and electrical safety, and a general knowledge of chemicals, specifically those used for cleaning and pest management. Many facilities require the department head to be familiar with plant maintenance, laundry operation, and interior design concepts as well. A thorough knowledge of management theory and practice is a primary requirement of the housekeeping department head, followed closely by financial management and budgeting skills. Specific areas of responsibility within the environmental services department are described below.

Microbiology

A primary function of the environmental services department is the provision of a clean, safe environment for patients, staff, and visitors. A safe environment is one in which the possibility of nosocomial infection is minimized or, ideally, eliminated, and one which is free of hazards such as slippery floors. The department head must know enough about microbiology to understand the types and transmission routes of various infective agents. The necessary knowledge can be obtained through college-level microbiology courses or through self-study. The Centers for Disease Control (CDC), the Association of Operating Room Nurses (AORN), Occupational Safety and Health Administration (OSHA), and other professional and government agencies make publications and guidelines available that contain a wealth of information on infection control practices. Professional organizations such as the American Society for Healthcare Environmental Services (ASHES) and the American Society for Hospital Engineering (ASHE) also are good sources of information. Today's environmental services staff are confronted with a complexity of disease entities and methods of treatment (e.g., multiple-drug-resistant tuberculosis, aerosolized pentamidine treatment, hepatitis B, HIV, to name only a few). It is imperative that the department head have a good base of information that is updated on a regular basis.

Waste Handling: Hazardous, Chemical, General

Waste removal falls under the jurisdiction of numerous agencies, including federal, state, and local departments concerned with protecting the environment. This plethora of regulators, each defining types of wastes in its own way, can complicate waste removal efforts. The categories of waste are defined by the area in which a facility is located, but are likely to include municipal or general waste, regulated medical waste (also known as infectious waste), hazardous and chemical waste, nuclear waste, and chemotherapeutic (also known as antineoplastic) waste. Each of these may be handled differently and regulated by one or more agencies. To avoid

problems—possibly in the form of substantial fines—flawless record keeping, including extensive policies and procedures development, is mandatory.

Municipal Waste

Municipal waste is unregulated and includes wastes from offices, coffee shops and cafeterias, public areas, and so on. It is usually compacted on-site and removed by either the city waste removal system or, more usually, a waste removal firm.

Regulated Medical Waste

This category accounts for the majority of the institution's waste removal expenditures. As a rule, it includes isolation, surgery, and laboratory waste. Definitions vary by area of the country and must be researched in depth by checking federal, state, and local regulations, including those issued by OSHA and the EPA.

Collection and storage methods within the institution vary, but, generally speaking, waste intended for the regulated medical waste stream is placed into red bags, collected by the housekeeping department, and taken to a processing area. Processing methods may include:

- incineration on-site
- autoclaving on-site
- microwaving on-site
- shredding and disinfecting on-site
- packaging for removal and destruction by vendor

A thorough cost/benefit analysis is necessary to determine which method is best for a given facility. Regardless of the method selected, the generator of the waste retains responsibility for the material from creation to ultimate disposal. Any potential liability for the material generated by a health care facility remains with the facility, even after the material is in the hands of a vendor. Thus, it is in the best interests of the facility to carefully select disposal methods, and if off-site destruction is the choice, then a thorough investigation of vendor options must be undertaken.

Hazardous and Chemical Waste

This category has been thoroughly defined by the EPA. Various federal and state laws and regulations list those materials that are considered hazardous and detail their handling and disposal. Most are not found in the health care setting, but some that are include mercury, toluene, xylene, and formaldehyde. The maintenance and engineering department also is a likely source of hazardous materials such as paint thinner or antifreeze. It is possible that asbestos is present as an insulating material in some buildings and, if so, it must be handled following very specific removal and disposal techniques. While there are extensive federal regulations regarding these materials, state regulations also must be consulted. Responsibility for this material remains with the generator, so it is imperative that a reliable vendor be chosen.

Nuclear Waste

Nuclear waste is usually generated in the lab as a result of certain kinds of testing, as well as in radiology or nuclear medicine. Facilities that conduct research also may generate nuclear waste. Storage and disposal is regulated by the Nuclear Regulatory Commission (NRC) and also may fall under the state and local codes and regulations. Responsibility often falls under the jurisdiction of the lab or radiology administrator. It is best that the storage and disposal be centralized to keep costs down and to ensure safe and consistent storage and handling practices. It is not unusual for the NRC to conduct an unannounced audit to review handling, storage, and disposal practices. They will devote particular attention to record keeping, tracking the material from its arrival at the facility to its use and disposal. Complete and accurate records are essential. The cost of disposal of nuclear waste is rising and many facilities that use nuclear materials in testing are looking for alternative test materials that may cost more initially but have no special disposal costs associated with their use.

Chemotherapeutic (Antineoplastic) Waste

This is another area that must be thoroughly researched before handling and disposal policies and procedures are developed. One must look at regulations, guidelines, as so on from federal, state, and local agencies. Some of the materials used in chemotherapy are on the hazardous materials list and nearly all of them are carcinogenic and require special handling. While not a universal practice, yellow bags are often used to segregate this waste. Housekeeping, nursing, and pharmacy need policies and procedures for the handling and disposal of these materials as well as spill clean-up procedures. A reliable, licensed vendor to remove them from the facility is mandatory.

As stated earlier, the importance of selecting a reliable vendor cannot be overstated. To avoid potential legal problems, it is wise to compare a number of factors before making a decision, and to include a number of departments in the decision-making process.

The environmental services department generally is responsible for managing the budget dollars for waste removal and for the handling of waste within the facility. Therefore, they should be a part of the decision-making process. Materials management or purchasing has the expertise to negotiate prices and terms and also should be included. Others that may need to be included will vary by the size, function, and structure of a particular facility.

Factors that need to be considered include cost, frequency of pickup, disposal method and location, reputation of the vendor, and reliability. Each of these should be investigated in a consistent and thorough way with each vendor. A detailed methodology is available in the 1992 ASHES publication entitled "Selecting a Waste Vendor."

Contract Management

Often the environmental services department monitors contracts for waste removal, window washing, pest control, upholstery and carpet cleaning, plants maintenance, professional dry cleaning services, and a variety of other related services. The monitoring responsibility is assigned to that department because of the specialized knowledge required to ensure adequate performance by the contractors. Although the materials management or purchasing department usually signs and/or approves contracts, the details of these contracts, and the schedule for performance and approval of the completed work, are usually specified by environmental services. However, the environmental services department head should use the expertise of the materials management department when negotiating contracts.

The decision whether to use a contractor or in-house staff depends on the nature of the services needed, the labor available within the facility, the facility itself, the knowledge and skills available, licensing requirements, equipment needs, cost of the service on the outside, and a variety of legal issues.

Consider window washing as an example. If the facility has only one story, it almost certainly is more cost effective to perform window cleaning using facility labor. To do so requires no special equipment, no expensive liability insurance, and no permits or licenses. If, however, the facility is a multistory complex, a significant investment in sophisticated equipment, special training for the employees, and perhaps licensing requirements may be necessary. Then it may well be more cost effective to contract for the service.

Pest control provides another excellent illustration of the variables in the decision-making process. It may appear on the surface that pest control can be handled by an in-house crew working under the supervision of the environmental services manager. Before making that decision, however, the administrator must be satisfied that whoever provides the services has the necessary knowledge and training. Pest management usually includes the use of chemicals that are poisonous to humans and animals. The seriousness of misusing such products cannot be overstated. Some state or local agencies may require permits or licenses by those performing pest control activities.

Chemicals

Nearly every aspect of environmental services includes the use of chemicals. Disinfectants, floor finishes, toilet bowl cleaners, and carpet cleaning products are used on a daily basis. Some products have greater potential for misuse than others. The effective department head must be aware of what chemicals are used, why they are used, how to use them properly, and what their potential side effects are. A basic knowledge of chemistry is necessary to prevent accidents that may occur from the combination of two or more chemicals. For example, when ammonia, which is found in many floor stripping compounds, and bleach are combined, a toxic gas is produced. The well-informed department head can provide training and education to the staff to avoid potentially dangerous situations. Material safety data sheets (MSDSs) must be on hand for all products used by the department.

Safety

Health care staff must be mindful not only of the safety of the patients in their care, but also of the safety of visitors and staff. Wet floors, frayed electrical cords, chemical agents, machinery, and worn carpeting are potential hazards to visitors, patients, and staff. That is why various government agencies have specified guidelines, rules, and, in some cases, laws that deal with safety issues. Each member of the management staff of a health care facility has an obligation to know and follow safety regulations that apply specifically to his or her department and those that apply to the facility in general. There also is an obligation to pass this information on to other department members. The Joint Commission on Accreditation of Healthcare Organizations (Joint Commission) recently has strengthened its guidelines regarding safety issues in its revised Plant Technology and Safety Management Section.

Safety issues specific to environmental services include correct chemical usage, including MSDSs for each product, use of wet floor signs, equipment repair and maintenance, correct machine operation, proper disposal of wastes, and safe procedures for cleaning public areas. General safety issues include use of fire control equipment, electrical safety, fire prevention, poison control, and patient safety in emergency situations. The department head should be familiar with regulatory agencies, such as the National Fire Protection Association, Occupational Safety and Health Administration, Centers for Disease Control, the Joint Commission, and other federal, state, and local agencies, and their publications.

Laundry*

Smaller health care facilities with in-house laundries and some large institutions may elect to combine the environmental services and laundry departments. The decision to combine the two departments should be thoroughly analyzed, or the result may be that the institution has two poorly run departments.

The skills and knowledge necessary to operate a commercial laundry efficiently and effectively are far different from those needed by the environmental services manager. Sophisticated laundries use complex automated machinery and chemicals, and the trend is toward even more mechanization. Therefore the laundry manager's job is less labor intensive and more equipment oriented than that of his or her counterpart in environmental services. The decision to combine the two departments largely depends on the size of the facility. Environmental services departments in larger facilities may have more than 100 employees, a sizable responsibility for any manager. It may not be realistic to expect one person to effectively manage two very large departments.

---

*The information for the section on laundry operations was furnished by Michael Catanzaro, Director of Environmental Services at South Nassau Community Hospital, Oceanside, New York.

Many facilities are turning to outside commercial laundries for their fabric care, especially as their laundry equipment begins to age and require replacement. Rather than expend extremely limited capital dollars on new equipment, the decision may be made to contract for the service. Another option is to invest in new equipment and to utilize any excess capacity to provide service on a fee basis to other institutions.

The laundry operation is similar to that of a small factory, with its own problems, operating within the larger framework of the facility. Its goals are similar to other ancillary departments within the facility, which, of course, are to provide uninterrupted, quality services to patients and staff, in an efficient and effective manner.

One of the first questions that must be addressed in laundry operations is the determination of the amount of linen needed within the facility to provide quality patient care. This determination requires the input of the nursing department. Factors such as census and patient acuity and length of stay all play major roles in determining each unit's par level. Par level refers to how many pieces of a particular linen item a unit or department receives on a daily basis.

Once the par levels for all units and departments in the facility have been determined, the sum is that facility's one-day par. This only determines the facility's one-day linen usage, not the total linen required to ensure adequate linen in the system.

If the laundry operates seven days per week, it will be necessary to carry par four of linen, which is determined as follows:

- one day's par in use
- one day's par processed and ready for delivery
- one day's par soiled
- one day's par in laundering process

Add an additional day's par for each day the laundry does not operate. Example: If the laundry is closed on weekends, increase the base par four by two days' par, to total a par level of six. If the facility's par for sheets is 3,600 sheets, the sheets needed in the system is 3,600 sheets. If at any time the inventory of sheets dips below 3,600, the laundry will not be able to provide adequate service to the nursing units. Additional linens must be added to replace linens that have been removed from the system due to wear, tear, staining, and pilferage.

There are many ways linens can be removed from the system. Each time linens are processed, cotton content is removed due to the action of the heat and chemicals needed to clean and disinfect them. Wash temperatures must be maintained at 160 degrees to ensure the proper disinfectant action. Fabric life is diminished by the heat from dryers and ironers. Loss also can occur because ambulance services often replenish the stocks of linen from emergency room supply closets. Housekeeping personnel have been known to use towels and other linens as cleaning cloths, cutting them and rendering them useless for their original purpose, and pilferage by patients, visitors, and staff can occur.

An item that suffers great potential for loss is scrub attire. The number of scrub suits that can be lost during the course of a year is significant. Many facilities have taken steps to try to curtail their losses. Many have emblazoned their name and/or logo all over the garments, which in some cases serves to enhance their value. One possible solution to this problem may be the use of a personalized locker exchange system. Each scrub suit is numbered to a corresponding locker, which is assigned to a physician, nurse, or other staff member. Scrubs are delivered to each locker with a master key. Soiled scrubs are delivered to a locked receptacle by the user, where they are retrieved and counted. These are the only scrubs in the system. The individual users are financially responsible for missing scrubs.

Production levels for laundries are extremely difficult to measure. There are no standards that can be applied universally to all operations. Modernization and automation levels of each plant must be considered independently. Site-specific time and motion studies are required to set production standards for a specific laundry.

A laundry manager whose sole responsibility is the provision of linen to the facility will ensure a product that meets high-quality standards, an acceptable labor cost, and an efficiently operating laundry. The manager's responsibilities include production, quality, infection control, scheduling, inventory control, purchasing, delivery, and safety.

Interior Design

Many aspects of the interior design function relate directly to the environmental services department. For example, the selected wall and floor coverings must be maintainable by the cleaning crew within the facility, and window treatments, cubicle curtains, and bedspreads must be cared for properly to retain a good appearance level. Historically, interior designers have not always been well informed about which floor covering is best suited to a particular area, or which wall covering can be cleaned without losing its fine appearance. An initial good appearance is not the only criterion that needs to be met when planning the interior design of a facility; maintainability, utility, durability, and cost are also key factors. It is reasonable to expect the environmental services department head to provide invaluable assistance in these areas. A high-pile carpet is not generally advisable for an area with computerized equipment because it generates a good deal of static electricity that can interfere with the equipment's operation. A wall covering without a protective coating is inadvisable in many areas of a facility because stains and people prints may be impossible to remove without damaging the material or reducing its appearance, or both. Certain window coverings must be dry cleaned, rather than laundered, resulting in longer downtime, a potential odor from dry cleaning solvent, and higher cleaning costs.

MANAGEMENT

The environmental services department head should possess a unique set of skills, a broad base of knowledge, and excellent management skills. Managerial ability is the single most important qualification for this position because of the labor-intensive nature of the department. Poor management practice results in an increase in overtime, higher absenteeism and tardiness, decreased productivity, and low morale.

Contract versus In-House Management

Under certain circumstances contract management of the department may be prudent. Several professional organizations provide referral services to the industry, including ASHES and the National Executive Housekeepers Association (NEHA). A call to their respective national offices and/or an advertisement in their publications are good places to begin.

It may be helpful to determine who runs the environmental services departments of neighboring facilities that are exceptionally well maintained, and ask them for referrals. They may have an assistant department head who is ready to move up, or they may know of qualified persons in another area. Authors of articles or books in housekeeping periodicals and publications also may know of potential candidates. Those who are active within the field know who is available and who is well qualified.

If contract management is feasible, a thorough review of the management company's proposal and contract is required. The contract generally spells out the exact services that the department will perform under the guidance of the contractor. Those services not specifically spelled out under the terms of the contract will be performed by some of the facility's other employees or by the environmental services department for an additional fee. It is therefore necessary to have a detailed listing of the services performed currently by the in-house staff, in order to compare it to that which is proposed. Does environmental services currently transport linen carts, wash walls, clean exterior window glass, move furniture, or delivery supplies? If these items are not included in the contract, but were previously performed by the department, a determination

about who will perform them once the contract is in effect should be made.

Often, the contract company supplies all cleaning agents and equipment at a cost to the facility, resulting in a significant initial investment for the institution. If the facility wishes to terminate the contract it will need to purchase its own equipment and supplies. A contract management firm supplies the management expertise with which to run the department, but the staff itself generally remain employees of the facility. It may be difficult to build genuine team spirit when the members are on different teams, and morale problems may result. Another potential morale problem centers around the term of the management contract. The contract company usually is free to change the department manager (i.e., their employee) as frequently as desired. Just as the facility develops a sound working relationship with one manager, that manager may be relocated. This can be difficult and unsettling for the department's line employees.

Another factor that must be taken into consideration before signing a management contract is whether department employees are unionized. A union is likely to be opposed to contract management because they know that cost cutting is the goal, and that the department budget consists of 80 to 90 percent labor costs. In a nonunion environment in which recent union activity has occurred, employees may be swayed toward unionization if a switch is made from in-house management to contract management.

HALLMARKS OF A WELL-RUN DEPARTMENT

A well-run environmental services department is observable from a view of the facility. Is the facility clean and pleasant smelling? Is there little or no valid complaining from patients, staff, and visitors? As you walk through the facility, are the employees busy? Are absenteeism, tardiness, and overtime within reasonable limits? Does the department operate within budget? If the answers to the above questions are affirmative, then chances are the department is being efficiently and effectively managed.

Policy and Procedure Manual

The Joint Commission mandates that the department have a policy and procedure manual. The first section of the manual should contain a table of organization, job descriptions, and job assignments for all the positions within the department. Among the procedures that must be included in the manual are cleaning in surgery, isolation, and other special and invasive procedure areas; care and use of equipment; waste removal practices; safety practices, including material safety data sheets on the products used by the department; general cleaning procedures, and cleaning frequencies. There also should be policies for notifying the department in case of illness or tardiness; uniform requirements and personal hygiene; vacation bidding procedures; disciplinary procedures; authorized break and lunch areas; and other policies that the custom and practice of the particular facility deem necessary.

Quality Assurance

An effective quality assurance program is another essential element of the well-run department. Such a program does not have to be sophisticated or complex to be effective. Criteria should be defined as simply and precisely as possible.

After criteria are defined, the next step is to develop an instrument to record the results of an inspection. Ideally, it should include the date of the inspection; name of the inspector; items being scrutinized; method of indication if a given item meets, exceeds, or falls below the standard; and a method to note correction of any deficiencies. The data from quality control inspections can be manipulated in a variety of ways, but the usefulness of the program is not dependent upon sophisticated statistical analysis. The level of complexity should remain at the discretion of the department manager.

The quality control program also should specify the number of inspections to be made in a given time period. Perhaps each supervisor may be required to inspect two patient rooms, one public bathroom, one stairwell, and one corridor per day, for example. Many software programs exist today to assist the department head in maintaining quality standards. Cost of equipment and software, as well as clerical time to input data, must be considered before a commitment is made to computerize.

Workload Analysis

Doing workload analysis is probably the most important part of the department manager's job. It also is difficult, time-consuming and potentially subjective. All of this should be kept in mind when reviewing any workload analysis. Workload analysis generally is undertaken either to establish adequate staffing levels, or to justify the staffing levels that exist. It categorizes the activities of every aspect of the department and the frequency with which they are performed. Many facilities have management engineers who assist the department managers in determining, among other things, staffing levels. Computer programs also are available that make staffing analysis faster, more accurate, and easier to adjust as changes in frequencies or layout of the facility occur.

A number of criteria have been used to calculate the number of employees that are required in an environmental services department. However, for several reasons these methods are not always accurate predictors. One method that often is used is based on the number of beds in the facility. The method is best described in an article that appeared in *Executive Housekeeping Today:* "Multiply the number of beds in your hospital by .15 to arrive at the number of FTEs required. A 300-bed hospital would have 45 housekeepers (including supervisors and excluding the executive housekeeper)."[1] This very simple, unsophisticated way to determine the number of employees fails to take many things into consideration, such as the changing health care environment, service mix, facility design and age, traffic patterns, and other factors.

For example, consider two facilities, each with 200,000 square feet to be cleaned; one is a mental health facility requiring routine, nonspecialized maintenance, whereas the other, an acute care hospital, specializes in open heart and hip replacement surgery. The surgery suites in the acute care facility require a more intensive level of attention, and follow-up care for surgery often takes place in an intensive care unit, another area requiring intensive labor efforts. Although each facility has the same number of square feet, the acute care hospital clearly requires the larger labor force.

Staffing levels analysis should be accomplished through a comprehensive analysis of the duties performed by the department; the frequency with which those duties should be performed to maintain the desired appearance level; the surfaces to be maintained, such as terrazzo, carpet, or tile; and the availability of labor-saving equipment.

In order to conduct such an analysis, the department manager will need accurate and up-to-date floor plans of the entire facility that can be used to devise a code for identifying the various areas of the hospital by function. Blueprints or floor plans also serve as a road map when interpreting the results of the study. When prints are not available, it is necessary to conduct a walking survey, during which each room, closet, office, corridor, stairwell, or elevator is noted in list form in some logical order. It is essential that this listing be as accurate as is humanly possible.

The second step is to determine, for each area listed in the survey, what cleaning tasks are to be performed and at what frequency. Frequencies for certain areas may be dictated by regulations of various agencies or governing bodies. One example might be the frequency with which a patient room designated as an isolation area would be cleaned. The CDC publishes guidelines that mandate daily cleaning of spaces that are likely to be subject to state and/or local health ordinances. Public areas, such as lobbies and waiting rooms, may require attention several times a day. The frequency of cleaning may need to be adjusted as technology and the needs of the facility change.

The third step is to determine standard times for the routine tasks performed by the department. There are a number of ways to do this, but only two are described here. The first and preferred method is to carry out time studies using actual employees of the department. The second method uses published data that detail approximate times for the performance of certain tasks; however, this is prone to errors of omission and does not take into account the institution's unique needs.

The determination of standard times for routine cleaning, such as cleaning patient rooms, discharge units, offices, and corridors, is less complicated and less subjective than the determination of standards for project work, such as floor maintenance, carpet care, and wall washing. The establishment of these standards depends on the square footage and age of the institution, its walls and floor coverings, the traffic level and patterns, and the desired appearance level in a given area. Time studies can be conducted to determine average time per square foot for each procedure; these times can then be multiplied by the desired annual frequencies to arrive at the amount of time needed on an annual basis.

An easily overlooked consideration in the determination of staffing levels is the inclusion of PF&D (personal, fatigue, and delay) time, and travel and preparation time; the omission of these factors will result in serious understaffing. An adjustment must also be made for vacation, holiday, and sick time based on each institution's personnel policies.

Although a workload analysis is a complex project, the department head equipped with the appropriate educational background and experience will have little difficulty in completing it. Every environmental services department should do such an analysis and review it periodically.

CONCLUSION

The environmental services department is a nonrevenue-producing service department in the health care institution, and, as such, it may be tempting to underestimate its role in the facility's successful operation. Yet, the department has a large labor force and budget that requires constant monitoring. A poorly run department results in dollars needlessly spent. A poorly maintained facility creates a negative impression on visitors, staff, and patients, which may affect their perception of the quality of care that is provided. The net effect may be that the public will choose to receive care elsewhere, and staff members may decide to provide care in a setting that they feel is more adequately maintained. In a competitive environment, neither is an acceptable alternative.

NOTE

1. G. Mullinnix, Contract Management: Is 50% of the Hospital Market within Reach?, *Executive Housekeeping Today* April (1983):19.

JANICE M. KURTH, MBA, is the author of two texts on housekeeping in health care facilities: *Essentials of Housekeeping in the Health Care Facilities* and *Environmental Services Policy and Procedure Manual*. She was President of the Environmental Management Association's Health Care Facilities subsidiary, from 1984 to 1985, as well as a founding member and first President of the American Society for Healthcare Environmental Services (ASHES).

Ms. Kurth received her bachelor's degree from DePaul University, Chicago, and her MBA from Loyola University of Chicago.

Chapter 16

The Health Sciences Library

Eloise C. Foster, Anne Carbery Fox, and Sara Anne Beazley

Information is a vital institutional asset. One attribute of a successful organization is its ability to manage information to ensure its availability for rapid decision making. As hospitals, ambulatory care organizations, long-term care facilities, and multi-institutional systems evolve into integrated delivery systems, they need and use information for many purposes, and the health sciences library plays an essential role in providing broad-based institutional support.

Many of the ideas and concepts in this chapter were drawn from *Hospital Library Management,* edited by Jane Bradley et al., and "The Hospital Health Sciences Library: Challenges and Future Direction," edited by Holly Shipp Buchanan. These publications are fully cited under Organization and Management in the Suggested Readings. The new authors gratefully acknowledge their contributions as well as those of the authors and reviewers of the first edition, and the following reviewers of this revised chapter: Christiane J. Jones, chief, Library Service, VA Medical Center, Biloxi; Becky J. Lyon, head, NN/LM Network Office, National Library of Medicine; Connie Poole, acting director, Medical Library, Southern Illinois University School of Medicine; Patricia J. Wakeley, librarian, and Kay E. Wellik, manager, Health Sciences Library, St. Joseph's Hospital and Medical Center, Phoenix.

Once primarily concerned with providing service for physicians involved in direct patient care, today's health sciences library provides an expanding range of information support to meet the informational, educational, and research-related needs of both clinical and administrative staffs of health care organizations, and health education needs of patients and consumers. Using multimedia and computer resources, as well as books and periodicals, the library may be characterized as an information access or transfer point, rather than a storehouse for the printed word. Its staff members are information organizers, handlers, and facilitators.

HISTORICAL PERSPECTIVE

The modern health sciences library has its antecedents in early collections of information intended for physicians practicing in hospitals and in facilities established to support curricular needs in hospital-based schools of nursing. The first medical library in the United States was established in 1762 in the Pennsylvania Hospital in Philadelphia.[1] As hospitals became increasingly involved in medical education, library facilities for physicians expanded. In the early 1900s, library services to patients became a focal point. Following World War II, libraries began a period of significant development, fueled by prosperity and major increases in research and volume of information produced. In the 1960s and 1970s, many nursing and medical libraries merged because of space and financial limitations, the need to support expanding continuing education programs, and the closing of many hospital schools of nursing.[2]

Passage of the Medical Library Assistance Act in 1965, establishment of the Medical Library Advisory Committee of the Joint Commission on Accreditation of Healthcare Organizations (Joint Commission) in 1967,[3] establishment of the National Library of Medicine's (NLM) Regional Medical Library program in 1967,[4] and publication by the American Hospital Association (AHA) of its *Statement on Role of the Health Science Library in the Hospital* in 1969 coincided with a period of considerable development in health sciences libraries and heralded a shift in emphasis from resource or collection building to service provision and resource sharing.[5]

The 1970s were a particularly fertile period for health sciences libraries. Both the 1975 version of the AHA's statement titled *Health Science Libraries in Hospitals* and the 1978 Joint Commission's standards for professional library services addressed the need to serve the entire hospital staff. The NLM's Regional Medical Library program provided training, fostered resource sharing and cooperation, and extended computerized information retrieval. Specialized services using new technologies were implemented to meet changing information needs in innovative ways.

In the 1980s, as hospitals and other health care organizations responded to industrywide changes and the move from a regulated to a competitive environment, there were significant challenges and opportunities in the area of information access and transfer. In addition to more traditional roles, health sciences libraries provided fee-based services to target audiences, provided administrators with information for decision making, contributed to the development of institutional information management programs, and presented an incentive in physician recruitment programs. Impetus for the form and function of health sciences libraries also came from a seminal 1982 report issued by the Association of American Medical Colleges.[6] The report supported the long-range development of integrated institutional information management networks and described how these could be achieved through the development of technologically sophisticated libraries.

In the 1990s, an examination of supporting roles and functions is under way as health sciences libraries, along with their parent institutions, seek to contribute to the provision of high-quality, cost-effective, and patient-focused comprehensive care in an environment that is shifting to an emphasis on provider cooperation, collaboration, and community outreach. This shift is in response to challenges posed by a changing health care delivery system as the United States moves to reform and restructure health care in order to ensure accessibility, control costs, and provide effective care. Accompanying these changes in the structure of health care delivery are rapid technological developments, such as the computerized medical record, integrated information management systems, and the electronic information superhighway. Health care institutions are also challenged to envision and utilize these technological developments in the provision of efficient, continuously improving patient care and in the assessment of health care processes and outcomes.

ORGANIZATIONAL POSITION

The position held by the health sciences library within the organizational structure of the institution reflects the size, functions, and structure of the parent organization. Many libraries are independent departments, whereas some are part of another unit such as an education or medical records department. Being part of another department is generally less desirable than reporting directly to an administrative officer with decision-making authority. However, it may be possible for the library to function effectively as an independent component of a larger department as long as the library retains direction over its programs and budgets. In general, the library should be in a similar organizational position to other units with institutionwide responsibilities.

Libraries in health care organizations that are part of academic medical centers may have a reporting relationship to the university's health sciences library. Multi-institutional systems may have a centralized library with satellite locations at member facilities. One organizational approach places other institutional information support functions such as education, community relations, audiovisual production, teleconferencing, or internal and external information and communication systems under the direction of the library to reflect its central information access and transfer function. Placement with institutional planning as part of an institutional information office is also feasible, as is placement directly under a chief information officer or within an information management group.

CLIENTELE

The primary clientele of the health sciences library is the entire staff of the health care organization. Many existing medical and nursing libraries are integrated to meet administrative and support services needs through one facility. Libraries in teaching facilities also need to support the work of students, as well as the special requirements of faculties and researchers. Organizations with which the health facility has a contractual relationship of some kind, such as affiliated hospitals in a multihospital system, joint ventures with physicians, managed care programs such as health maintenance organizations and preferred provider organizations, home care agencies, hospice programs, freestanding clinics, and independent practice associations, may also be service audiences for the health sciences library.

Patients—both inpatients and outpatients—are another potential service audience, either for health-related information or for general reading materials. Many health sciences libraries are exploring ways to provide or support community access to consumer health information. Some possibilities include supporting community wellness or outreach programs, working with public libraries to increase understanding of health information resources, and providing direct access to health information. Providing service to patients and the community may require review by the health care organization's legal counsel.

STANDARDS

Recognizing the importance of health sciences libraries, a number of voluntary health associations, government agencies, and library associations have supported their development. This support often has taken the form of developing guidelines and standards, terms that are sometimes used interchangeably. Guidelines usually define principles basic to the establishment and operation of a service, and compliance is generally voluntary. Standards, in contrast, define the minimum adequacy of facilities and services, and compliance is expected by the issuing body. National organizations or government agencies that presently have standards or guidelines for health sciences libraries include the American Hospital Association, American Medical Association, American Osteopathic Association, Canadian Council on Health Facilities Accreditation,[7] Canadian Health Libraries Association,[8] Joint Commission, Medical Library Association,[9] and United States Department of Veterans Affairs. Selected sources of standards and guidelines for health sciences libraries can be found at the end of the chapter.

For many health sciences libraries, the most significant standards are those of the Joint Commission. In the first set of Joint Commission standards published in 1953, the library was referred to as a desirable element, but not an absolute prerequisite for hospital accreditation.

Three major revisions have been made to the standards since 1953. In 1978, professional library services became a prerequisite for hospital accreditation. The 1986 *Accreditation Manual for Hospitals* introduced a new format and rating scale and minor language changes that remained in place from 1986 through 1993.[10] In 1994, the Joint Commission made sweeping changes to standards for professional library services, emphasizing an integrated approach to information management by setting standards that describe a vision of effective and continuously improving information management in health care organizations. These standards are contained in a new "Management of Information" chapter, which discusses organizationwide planning of information processes to meet the need for internal and external information, and the management of knowledge-based information (also referred to as the "literature").[11]

The Joint Commission stipulates that knowledge-based information systems, resources, and services are vital to the hospital's ability to design, manage, and improve patient-specific and organizational processes. In order to meet current Joint Commission standards, the health sciences library should (1) participate in institutionwide planning for information management; and (2) provide knowledge-based information systems, resources, and services based on assessment of organizational and user needs, taking into consideration access to authoritative, timely information, and linkages with both internal information systems and external databases and information networks to support patient care and organizational decision making.[12]

PLANNING AND EVALUATING LIBRARY FUNCTIONS

In defining the collection and services to be provided by the health sciences library, the mission and goals of the parent institution and the information needs and preferred information-gathering methods of the library's primary audiences are critical considerations. The library should be actively involved in institutionwide planning efforts to ensure continuously improving information management and should have a defined annual plan that is linked to the budget as well as to 3-year and 5-year plans. Formal needs assessments or surveys and formal and informal contact with users are useful in determining user needs. Organizational goals and user needs change over time and the library manager should be responsive to and, where possible, proactive in developing appropriate service modifications. Potential new audiences should be assessed and included in future planning. Factors to consider in planning new services or service modifications are need, fiscal and personnel resources required, ability to maintain the service as it grows, policy and procedural issues, promotion, and continuous quality improvement.

It is difficult to evaluate library services in a useful way without objectives and success criteria such as those established in a program of continuous quality improvement. The library should maintain relevant quantitative statistics and report them regularly. However, such operational audit statistical measures as volume of service, timeliness of service, or revenue received are meaningless unless they can be compared to an established benchmark. Therefore, each service should have identified performance standards and outcome-and-process criteria for successful operation. Along with the services themselves, these criteria may change over time and should be regularly evaluated for continuing relevance.

Another aspect of continuous quality improvement is the measurement of client or user satisfaction with services provided. Very brief questionnaires, either completed on an ongoing or scheduled basis, can measure user satisfaction. It is important to have outcome-and-process success criteria so that one knows whether the results of a survey are acceptable. A follow-up mechanism should be in place to resolve any complaints from dissatisfied users. Frequent users might also be polled for their responses to proposed modifications.

PERSONNEL

A high-quality staff is essential to the success of the library. The library should be under the direction of a qualified library manager who has a master's degree in library science from a school accredited by the American Library Association. An undergraduate background in the sciences may be helpful. Certification of competencies in health sciences library administration, technical services, and public services is also desirable. This is currently available through the Medical Library Association by meeting its criteria for membership in the Academy of Health Information Professionals. The library manager is responsible for planning and organizing resources and services to meet institutional goals.

The professional staff should possess both technical and administrative skills. An understanding of the principles of organization of knowledge and of information transfer and delivery, a strong service orientation, excellent interpersonal and communication skills, an ability to work with people at all levels, a high degree of flexibility, and time management skills are essential. Technical competencies in information organization and retrieval, including collection development, cataloging, reference services, and document delivery are necessary. Computer literacy, as well as knowledge about the application of computer processes to information organization and retrieval and to decision support techniques, is also essential. Professional staff membership in the Medical Library Association's Academy of Health Information Professionals is also desirable.

A support staff is needed to accomplish many of the daily activities of the library. The level of staffing required depends on the nature and extent of the library's services. Previous library experience is advantageous when dealing with technical processes, such as reference, document delivery, and cataloging. Communication skills, commitment to service, flexibility, and time management skills are important characteristics for the support staff.

The titles of the library manager and other staff members should reflect the organizational structure of the parent institution. Throughout this chapter, library manager is used as a generic term. Other examples of titles include director of the library, library administrator, chief of library services, health sciences librarian, or chief information officer.

Salaries should be commensurate with those of other institutional staff members in similar technical or administrative positions and with similar educational backgrounds. Salaries also should be competitive with other institutions of similar size and programs. Each library staff member should have a written job description and should participate in the institution's performance assessment and salary and benefits program. A number of options are available to extend the staffing complement, including use of contract services, consultants, shared staffing, or circuit-rider arrangements where a single individual serves more than one hospital. Library volunteers also may be used.

Both professional and support staff development should be encouraged. For health sciences librarians, this may be accomplished through membership in professional associations, such as the Medical Library Association or the Special Libraries Association, and participation in continuing education programs offered by these associations. Institutional in-service training programs also may be offered both by the library and by the institution as a whole. Professional library staff should be informed about their institution's services and programs in order to better serve their clientele. Staff development in new computer technologies and their applications should be particularly stressed.

FINANCIAL MANAGEMENT

Primary financial support for the health sciences library should come directly from the operating budget of the parent institution. Except in rare instances, libraries are cost or service centers and do not generate revenue in excess of expenses. The major expenses in the library's budget are personnel and resources for the collection. Other costs include equipment, supplies, vendor charges, document delivery fees, public relations, service contracts, and staff travel to and fees for professional meetings and professional development opportunities. Capital expenditures also should be identified and planned for in accordance with institutional policies. The library manager should be expected to prepare a detailed budget within institutional guidelines, to justify it, and to manage it once approved. The budget should support defined programs and expenses as identified in the library's annual and long-range plans.

Additional support can come from a variety of sources that vary from institution to institution. Funds may come from provision of fee-based services; through donations from the medical staff, the auxiliary, or a friends-of-the-library group; through development and sale of print products, software, media products, or training courses; through endowments and gifts; or through grant funding. The National Library of Medicine's Extramural Programs Division provides a variety of grants to support research and development activities leading to the better management, dissemination, and use of biomedical knowledge, including health sciences library resource grants to assist in improving information access and services for health professionals. Local foundations or corporations also may be potential sources of seed money or project support.

FACILITIES

The space, furnishings, and equipment for the library should support its goal of serving as an information resource for all identified service audiences. The library should be physically located to facilitate access by all users, including the disabled, and should meet architectural accessibility and ergonomic requirements enacted through the Americans with Disabilities Act. Placement in a remote location discourages library use. Because users may need access to the library at any time, it should not share space with a conference room or other facility that may make the library routinely unavailable.

The library space needs to be adequate to accommodate the collection, work areas for the library staff, and areas for users. Space and electrical systems also need to be capable of supporting electronic data processing and computer technologies, advanced multimedia technologies, and integrated information and communication systems. The total size of the library and the amount of space devoted to these functions vary.

Furniture should be comfortable, accessible, and designed to support study and reading. Convenient access to a photocopier is a requirement for both the library staff and users. Telefacsimile (fax) equipment is becoming increasingly important for fast document delivery. Computer terminals and modems are needed if the library's catalog is online or if users or the library staff are performing online bibliographic or factual database searches. Personal computers linked to internal local area networks and electronic mail (e-mail) systems and to external computer networks provide new capabilities and flexibility in information management and retrieval. CD-ROM (compact disk read-only memory) equipment provides an alternative to online systems in which data are stored on optical disks for retrieval or reading on personal computers. Television and videocassette equipment enables the viewing of alternate information formats.

Many health care organizations, including all acute care hospitals, operate 24-hours-a-day. Unless the libraries in these facilities are staffed around the clock, provisions are needed for limited access during closed times. Various security options are available including the use of restricted keys. Specialized security systems that protect library materials from theft through magnetic or radio-frequency mechanisms now are available to smaller libraries. Given the value of the collection and computer equipment and the potential dangers of not having these resources when they are needed, security systems may be a sound investment.

COLLECTION

The collection of materials appropriate for each institution depends on the clientele and services, clinical research and educational activities, and environmental factors, such as geographical proximity to other resource collections. The collection should meet the immediate day-to-day needs of the identified service audiences. Meeting these needs requires an increasingly wide range of formats, including electronic journals, full-text databases, bibliographic and factual databases, videocassettes and videodisks, as well as reference books and textbooks, printed journals, audiovisuals, teaching aids, and historical materials.

No library can expect to own everything its users may need. The scope and depth of materials collected should be based on known and projected user needs and should reflect the goals and programs of the institution. The outcome of an assessment of user needs and institutional goals is a collection development policy that governs not only what is acquired and in what format but also how long it is retained. Books, journals, multimedia materials, and databases are then selected or deselected by the library staff within the framework of the collection policy.

Collection development policy is changing from a "just in case" to a "just in time" concept, by relating selection to library and commercial document delivery options in order to supply timely access to items not owned by the library. Although each library needs different materials to meet the varying requirements of its parent institution, there are several lists of recommended titles in medicine, nursing, allied health, and health administration, which can provide a starting point for building collections in these areas. Citations for these lists can be found in the suggested readings. Library users should be encouraged to recommend books, journals, or other resources. Book reviews from journals in relevant fields are also a good source.

Ideally, cost-effective purchasing and inventory control are supported by a centralized budget for purchase of print and nonprint materials for the entire health care organization. If all such purchases are coordinated through the library, location of those materials can be recorded and unnecessary duplication avoided. Although most libraries are offered and accept gift materials, it is unwise to rely on gifts or secondhand subscriptions as the basis for the collection. The result is inconsistent coverage.

The acquisition of materials can follow standard purchasing procedures used by other institutional departments. Vendors that specialize in the provision of books and periodicals for libraries may be worth using in order to simplify the purchasing process. In general, the specific nature of materials purchased for library collections and the extended receiving time for subscription publications require that receipt of orders and claiming of unfilled orders be handled by the library rather than by the purchasing department.

Once materials are received, they should be organized for efficient identification and retrieval. Journal subscriptions require special control and organizations because of their continuing nature. Whether a manual or automated system is used, the receipt of each journal issue should be recorded, and issues that are not received need to be claimed. If necessary, selected titles may be housed in special locations or routed to staff. Regular receipt and processing of journal issues are especially important because of the timeliness of information they contain and the budgetary commitment they represent.

For nonperiodic publications, several national cataloging and classification schemes can be used in the health sciences library. Although a library also can develop its own system, this limits the library's ability to use bibliographic utilities and may become easily outdated as the collection grows and the field changes. The National Library of Medicine's classification scheme and thesaurus, *Medical Subject Headings* (MESH®), frequently are used. The Library of Congress classification scheme and subject headings are sometimes preferred.

Typically, access to materials in the collection has been provided through a card catalog file with entries under authors' names, titles, and subject headings. As automation has been applied to information handling, the traditional card catalog has begun to give way to online access, which sometimes is supplemented by a printed book catalog. As health care organizations expand the use of automation and new information technologies within their operations, the library should be included. Automated systems are available that work with a variety of hardware that already may be in place within the organization. The integration of library records with other automated information systems within the health care organization should be an institutional goal.

SERVICES

Services provided by a health sciences library should be tailored to the mission and programs of the health care organization and the needs of the clientele. However, every health sciences library should provide basic information to support patient care, education, and administration.

Access to the Collection

Providing access to materials contained in the library is the most basic service of a health sciences library. Therefore, books, journals, and other materials should be organized and placed where they can be easily located by users. Circulation services, in which books and sometimes journals are loaned for specified periods, commonly are available to selected users.

Reference Services

Reference services, in their broadest context, are the processes of providing information contained in the collection or outside it in response to requesters' needs. Without the capability to provide these services, the library does not exist—it is simply a reading room. Reference services can take many forms. Users may be assisted

to locate information in the collection through subject access in a card catalog or through printed indexes to journal literature, such as *Cumulative Index to Nursing and Allied Health Literature, Hospital Literature Index, Index Medicus, Abridged Index Medicus,* and *International Nursing Index.* A collection of reference materials may be used to provide quick factual answers, such as addresses, agency names, statistics, and definitions. Special files may be developed to contain answers to inquiries specific to the institution. In certain instances, referral to other organizations, institutions, or libraries may be used to respond to inquiries. In-depth research assistance may include selection of information sources, data compilation, or preparation of summaries.

Access to online CD-ROM bibliographic databases, such as the National Library of Medicine's MEDLARS® (Medical Literature Analysis and Retrieval System) databases, especially MEDLINE® and the Health Planning and Administration (HEALTH) database, which is produced cooperatively by the American Hospital Association and the National Library of Medicine, should be provided in order to extend the range of information available. Access to CD-ROM databases is available for fixed, annual subscription fees, while access to online databases generally is charged on a per usage amount.

Private-sector vendors, including companies such as BRS Information Technologies, The Bureau of National Affairs, Inc., CD-Plus, DIALOG Information Services, Inc., and Mead Data Central, Inc., also provide access to various bibliographic databases. Access to full-text and nonbibliographic databases should be provided. Several relevant examples include the following: LEXIS® Health Law Library, a full-text database covering U.S. federal and state laws and regulations, produced by Mead Data Central, Inc.; The Blue Sheet, a full-text database covering developments among governmental and private biomedical research institutions, produced by FDC Reports, Inc.; and Diagnostics Business-Matters, a full-text database of *Diagnos-*

tics-Business Matters, the industry newsletter on companies that develop and market medical diagnostic products, produced by Fortia Marketing Consultants Ltd. These are just a few examples of the large numbers of producers of electronic information resources and their databases that may help the health sciences library meet the information needs of its particular clientele. Other products and vendors may be found in the *Gale Directory of Databases* (cited in the suggested readings under Information Technologies), which provides a comprehensive, up-to-date listing and description of available databases in all subject fields.

While literature searches may be performed for users by the library staff, access to some online files is also available directly to the requester through user-friendly software that simplifies the search process, such as the National Library of Medicine's Grateful Med® microcomputer software package. When direct access by users to online databases is provided, the library staff members act as intermediaries by helping users select and access appropriate databases and providing training.

Special programs, such as clinical librarian services or Literature Attached To CHarts (LATCH), can be established for particular user groups. Clinical librarians participate in rounds with assigned teams, noting questions and providing appropriate literature for team members. LATCH programs provide information such as journal articles attached to charts for use by clinical staff.

Document Delivery

Document delivery services include delivery of documents from the library's collection and form other collections of document suppliers. Circulation, or loaning books and journals within the institution, is one method of document delivery. Interlibrary loan, or the loaning of books and journals from one library to another at a user's request, is another. One development in this area is the National Library of Medicine's DOCLINE®, which provides for automated interlibrary loan request and referral, thereby improving service to the health professional by rapidly routing interlibrary loan requests electronically throughout the National Network of Libraries of Medicine™ (formerly the Regional Medical Library Program). Another development is the National Library of Medicine's Loansome Doc®, a document-ordering feature that is designed to provide end users with quick and easy access to documents retrieved through Grateful Med.

Provision of photocopies is an essential service. Every library should provide self-service and staff-mediated photocopying. The library should ensure that all requirements of the copyright law are met by library and other hospital staff, when providing or requesting photocopies of documents, and should provide guidance to the rest of the institution concerning compliance with this law. A current awareness service is another kind of document delivery in which journal issues or photocopies of title pages are routed to users to keep them abreast of the most recent information published in their area of interest. Table of contents databases, such as CARL, UnCover, Faxon Finder and Faxon Express, and OCLC's ContentsFirst and ArticleFirst, also provide current awareness services with document delivery components that supplement local holdings. Interlibrary loan and purchases from other document suppliers are important means of providing access to materials not in the collection.

Public Relations

A key factor in the library's value to the institution is its use by identified clientele. Assuming that the library staff is qualified, the collection sound, and the services well designed and timely, public relations efforts may provide the edge to encourage increased use. A good place to start is with the new members of the health care organization staff. The library should be presented as one of the benefits available to potential employees during recruitment and to new employees during orientation. A library users' guide or manual should be distributed to all new staff members alerting them to available services.

The library can maintain visibility through displays, newsletters, promotional pieces (brochures, bookmarks), e-mail bulletin board notices, and outreach programs explaining specific services or programs. A very important aspect of visibility is the inclusion of the library manager in institutionwide or systemwide planning of information management as well as other activities and programs. This ensures that the library manager is knowledgeable about issues facing the institution and can plan services accordingly.

In addition to the internal support functions, the library may develop services or products that are of value to the community or other health care organizations or providers. Outreach services may be especially attractive to maintain referral patterns from individual practitioners or group practices. Product line management is necessary for these services in much the same way as for other health services or activities. Marketing activities should be planned and accommodated in the pricing structure for the product, if it is to be sold. The library staff can take advantage of the expertise of the institution's planning, marketing, and public relations staff in planning these types of community activities.

Innovative Service Approaches

With limitations on budget and personnel, no library can expect to meet every information need from its own resources. Health sciences libraries have historically cooperated with one another to extend resources and services. Cooperative arrangements may be as simple as an informal agreement between two libraries to share materials or as formal as a consortium with dues, bylaws, and formal resource-sharing agreements. As multi-institutional systems have grown, so have opportunities for health sciences libraries within the systems to share resources and centralize certain functions. While during the 1980s some of the more informal arrange-

ments changed as institutions within a given community became increasingly competitive, the new era of health care reform is emphasizing integration—cooperation and collaboration between health care organizations and their departments.

Several of the ways health care organizations can offer or extend information services include circuit-rider programs in which more than one facility share the services of a librarian, remote access telecommunication linkages, contracts with document suppliers or information brokers for services, centralization of library functions such as cataloging, and the development of coordinated selection and acquisitions programs for purchase of materials.

A revolutionary approach to information access and service delivery is the developing National Information Infrastructure. The Internet, a worldwide computer communication network and information highway, is the starting point for this infrastructure. Connection to the Internet allows users to send electronic messages to specific individuals, participate in discussion groups, browse distant library catalogs, and transfer and download entire files of information. The health sciences librarian is in a position to envision the opportunities to be gained by increased access to information and the possibilities for innovative, far-reaching communication to be gained by Internet connection, and to provide guidance to the health care organization in the realization of this valuable resource.

CONCLUSION

The health sciences library within the health care organization is a focal point for access to information through the collection, storage, dissemination, and transfer of information critical for patient care and administration. The library selects, acquires, organizes, and provides access to information to support the needs of its identified user groups. It also facilitates access to information outside its own collection. Fundamental to the effective functioning of the library are the selection of a well-qualified professional and support staff, participation of the library manager in the decision-making structure of the institution, and adequate budgetary support for program goals. As health care institutions are positioning themselves to respond to a changing environment, and to state and federal health care reform, health sciences libraries can facilitate institutional access to the information that health personnel require in order to make responsible and knowledgeable decisions concerning patient care and approaches to health care delivery in their communities. Rapid advances in information systems technology and innovative service approaches enable the health sciences library to respond in nontraditional ways as institutional information centers.

NOTES

1. L. M. Prime, Hospital Libraries, in *Hospital Organization and Management,* ed. M.T. MacEachern (Berwyn, Ill.: Physicians' Record Company, 1957), 836.

2. J. Bradley, et al., eds., *Hospital Library Management* (Chicago: Medical Library Association, 1983), ix.

3. The Joint Commission on Accreditation of Hospitals (JCAH) changed its name to the Joint Commission on Accreditation of Healthcare Organizations in 1989.

4. The Regional Medical Library (RML) program changed its name to the National Network of Libraries of Medicine™ (NN/LM™) in 1991.

5. P.A. Wolfgram, Hospital Libraries in the United States: Historical Antecedents, *Bulletin of the Medical Library Association* 73, no. 2 (1985):35.

6. N.W. Matheson and J.A.D. Cooper, Academic Information in the Academic Health Sciences Center: Roles for the Library in Information Management, *Journal of Medical Education* 57, no. 10, part 2 (1982): 1–93.

7. The Canadian Council on Health Facilities Accreditation is in the process of approving new standards, as of March 1994. Current standards were published in 1991, for implementation in 1992.

8. The Canadian Health Libraries Association is in the process of approving new standards for health sciences libraries, as of March 1994. Current standards were published in 1989.

9. The Medical Library Association is in the process of approving new standards for health sciences libraries, as of March 1994. Current standards were published in 1984.

10. Joint Commission on Accreditation of Healthcare Organizations, *Accreditation Manual for Hospitals, 1986* (Chicago: 1985), 201–204.

11. Joint Commission on Accreditation of Healthcare Organizations, *Accreditation Manual for Hospitals, 1994* (Chicago: 1993), 35–44.

12. Ibid., 43.

National, regional, state, and local organizations are available to provide resource materials and professional development opportunities for library staffs. Selected national library associations are listed here. Health care organizations may also provide information and guidance.

- American Library Association (ALA)
  50 East Huron Street
  Chicago, IL 60611
- Medical Library Association (MLA)
  Suite 300
  Six North Michigan Avenue
  Chicago, IL 60602
- Special Libraries Association (SLA)
  1700 18th Street, N.W.
  Washington, DC 20009

The National Network of Libraries of Medicine™ (NN/LM™) is funded by the National Library of Medicine through the Medical Library Assistance Act of 1965 and its extensions. The following description of the Network is derived from the *National Library of Medicine Fact Sheet: National Network of Libraries of Medicine*™ published in October 1993. The purpose of the Network is to provide health science practitioners, investigators, educators, and administrators in the United States with timely, convenient access to biomedical and health care information resources. Administered by the National Library of Medicine, it consists of 8 regional medical libraries (major institutions under contract with the National Library of Medicine), 136 resource libraries (primarily at medical schools), and some 3,800 primary access libraries (primarily at hospitals). The regional medical libraries administer and coordinate services in the Network's 8 geographical regions. Current Network programs focus on reaching health professionals in rural, inner-city, and other areas who do not have access to medical library resources to make them aware of the services that Network libraries can provide; they also focus on interlibrary lending, reference services, training and consultation, and online access to MEDLINE and other NLM databases. Three of the regional medical libraries are designated online centers, and they conduct National Library of Medicine online training classes and coordinate online services in several regions.

- National Network of Libraries of Medicine
  National Library of Medicine
  8600 Rockville Pike
  Building 38, Room B1-EO3
  Bethesda, MD 20894
  Telephone: 301-496-4777

SUGGESTED READINGS

Organization and Management

American Society for Healthcare Human Resources Administration of the American Hospital Association, and Wyatt Company. 1992. SubFamily: Library. In *Job description manual: ADA workbook*. Vol. 2. Chicago: American Hospital Association.

Bradley, J., et al., eds. 1983. *Hospital library management*. Chicago: Medical Library Association.

Buchanan, H.S., ed. 1985. The hospital health sciences library: Challenges and future directions. *Bulletin of the Medical Library Association* 73, no. 2:29–58.

Bunting, A., ed. 1994. *Current practice in health sciences librarianship series*. Metuchen, NJ: Scarecrow Press.

Byrd, G.D. (1991). The ethical implications of health sciences library economics. *Bulletin for the Medical Library Association* 79, no. 4:382–387.

Darling, L. et al., eds. 1988. *Handbook of medical library practice*. 4th ed. 3 vols. Chicago: Medical Library Association.

Foster, E.C., and P.J. Wakeley. 1991. *Survey of health sciences libraries in hospitals—1989. Executive summary*. Chicago: American Hospital Association.

Hafner, A.W. 1990. Medical information, health sciences librarians, and professional liability. *Special Libraries* 81, no. 4:305–307.

Herrin, N.J. 1991. The liability of the hospital librarian: Why you need a professional medical librarian. *Hospital Topics* 69, no. 3:26–29.

Holst, R. 1991. Hospital libraries in perspective. *Bulletin of the Medical Library Association* 79, no. 1:1–9.

Medical Library Association. 1989. *The copyright law and the health sciences librarian*. Rev. ed. Chicago.

Medical Library Association. 1992. *MLA 1992 salary survey*. Chicago.

Medical Library Association. 1992. *Platform for change: The educational policy statement of the Medical Library Association*. Chicago.

Medical Library Association and Association of Academic Health Sciences Library Directors. 1993. *Health care reform and the health sciences librarian*. Chicago.

Messerle, J. 1987. Health sciences libraries: Strategies in an era of changing economics. *Bulletin of the Medical Library Association* 75, no. 1:27–33.

Olson, S., et al., eds. 1991. *National guide to funding for libraries and information services*. New York: Foundation Center.

Roper, F.W., and M.K. Mayfield. 1993. Surveying knowledge and skills in the health sciences: Results and implications. *Bulletin of the Medical Library Association* 81, no. 4:396–407.

Special Libraries Association. 1993. *SLA biennial salary survey 1993*. Washington, DC.

Wakeley, P.J., and E.C. Foster. 1993. A survey of health sciences libraries in hospitals: Implications for the 1990s. *Bulletin of the Medical Library Association* 81, no. 2:123–128.

Wakeley, P.J., et al. 1985. Health science library and information services in the hospital. *Hospital & Health Services Administration* 30, no. 4:112–123.

Standards and Guidelines

Accreditation Council for Graduate Medical Education. 1993. General requirements of the essentials of accredited residencies in graduate medical education (effective July 1, 1992). In *Graduate Medical Education Directory: 1993–1994*. Chicago: American Medical Association.

American Hospital Association. 1990. *Library and information services*. (management advisory). Chicago.

American Osteopathic Association. 1992. Professional library services. In *AOA accreditation requirements for acute care hospitals*. Chicago.

Canadian Council on Health Facilities Accreditation. 1991. Library services. In *Acute care: Large community and teaching hospitals*. 1992 ed. Ottawa, Ontario.

Joint Commission on Accreditation of Healthcare Organizations. 1992. Libraries and information networks. In *1993 accreditation manual for mental health, chemical dependency, and mental retardation/developmental disabilities services*. Vol. 1—Standards. Oakbrook Terrace, IL.

Joint Commission on Accreditation of Healthcare Organizations. 1993. Professional library and health information services. In *1994 accreditation manual for hospitals*. Vol. 1—Standards. Oakbrook Terrace, IL.

Joint Task Force of the Association of the Academic Health Sciences Library Directors and the Medical Library Association. 1987. *Challenge to action: Planning and evaluation guidelines for academic health sciences libraries*. Chicago.

Medical Library Association. In preparation. Standards for hospital libraries. Chicago.

Task Force on Hospital Library Standards, Canadian Health Libraries Association. 1989. *Standards for Canadian health care facility libraries: Qualitative and quantitative guidelines for assessment, 1989*. Toronto, Ontario.

United States Veterans Administration. 1986. Chapter 400: Library service. In *Planning criteria for VA facilities*. Washington, DC.

Collection

American Hospital Association Resource Center. 1989. Health care administration: A core collection. *Hospital & Health Services Administration* 34, no. 4:559–576.

Arenales, D., et al. 1993. *Collection development manual of the National Library of Medicine.* 3rd ed. Bethesda, MD: National Library of Medicine.

Brandon, A.N., and D.R. Hill. 1993. Selected list of books and journals for the small medical library. *Bulletin of the Medical Library Association* 81, no. 2:141–168.

Brandon, A.N., and D.R. Hill. 1992. Selected list of books and journals in allied health. *Bulletin of the Medical Library Association* 80, no. 3:223–239.

Brandon, A.N., and D.R. Hill. 1992. Selected list of nursing books and journals. *Nursing & Health Care* 13, no. 3:139–150.

Cooper, E.R. 1990. Options for the disposal of unwanted donations. *Bulletin of the Medical Library Association* 78, no. 4:388–394.

Goldsmith, E.E., and B.A. Evitts. 1991. The creation and maintenance of a hospital archives. *Medical Reference Services Quarterly* 10, no. 1:35–48.

Interagency Council on Library Resources for Nursing. 1992. Essential nursing references. *American Journal of Nursing* 92, no. 9:83–90.

McCue, M.P., et al. 1989. Establishing hospital archives. *Hospital Topics* 67, no. 5:33–36.

Morse, D.H., and D.T. Richards, comps. 1992. *MLA DocKit #3: Collection development policies for health sciences libraries.* Chicago: Medical Library Association.

Perez, A., et al., eds. 1990. *Core collection in nursing and the allied health sciences: Books, journals, media.* Phoenix: Oryx Press.

Soehner, C.B., et al. 1992. The landmark citation method: Analysis of a citation pattern as a collection assessment method. *Bulletin of the Medical Library Association* 80, no. 4:361–366.

Services

Cimpl, K. 1985. Clinical medical librarianship: A review of the literature. *Bulletin of the Medical Library Association* 73, no. 1:21–28.

Davis, F.L., et al. 1992. The use of independent information brokers for document delivery service in hospital libraries. *Bulletin of the Medical Library Association* 80, no. 2:185–187.

Hafner, A.W., ed. 1994. Symposium: Medical libraries and patient information services. *Bulletin of the Medical Library Association* 82, no. 1:43–66.

Hardy, M.C., et al. 1985. Evaluating the impact of library services on the quality and cost of medical care. *Bulletin of the Medical Library Association* 73, no. 1:43–46.

Jajko, P. 1992. Beyond online: Primary research as a value-added service. *Medical Reference Services Quarterly* 11, no. 2:67–78.

Kernaghan, S.G., and B.E. Giloth. 1991. *Consumer health information: Managing hospital-based centers.* Chicago: American Hospital Association, Hospital Research and Educational Trust.

King, D.N. 1987. The contribution of hospital library information services to clinical care: A study in eight hospitals. *Bulletin of the Medical Library Association* 75, no. 4:291–301.

Kuller, A.B., et al. 1993. Quality filtering of the clinical literature by librarians and physicians. *Bulletin of the Medical Library Association* 81, no. 1:38–43. [Published erratum appears in *Bulletin of the Medical Library Association* 81, no. 2 (1993):233.]

Marshall, J.G. 1992. The impact of the hospital library on clinical decision making: The Rochester study. *Bulletin of the Medical Library Association* 80, no. 2:169–178.

McCorkel, J., and V. Cook. 1986. Computer-assisted instruction: A library service for the community teaching hospital. *Bulletin of the Medical Library Association* 74, no. 2:115–120.

Messerle, J. 1990. The changing continuing education role of health sciences libraries. *Bulletin of the Medical Library Association* 78, no. 2:180–187.

Palmer, R.A. 1991. The hospital library is crucial to quality healthcare. *Hospital Topics* 69, no. 3:20–25.

Rees, A.M., ed. 1991. *Managing consumer health information services.* Phoenix: Oryx Press.

Salisbury, L., et al. 1990. The effect of end-user searching on reference services: Experience with MEDLINE and current contents. *Bulletin of the Medical Library Association* 78, no. 2:188–191. [Published comment appears in *Bulletin of the Medical Library Association* 78, no. 4 (October 1990):411.]

Veenstra, R.J. 1992. Clinical medical librarian impact on patient care: A one-year analysis. *Bulletin of the Medical Library Association* 80, no. 1:19–22.

Wood, S., ed. 1994. *Reference and information services in health sciences libraries.* Metuchen, NJ: Scarecrow Press. [First volume of *Current Practice in Health Sciences Librarianship Series,* ed. Alison Bunting. Metuchen, NJ: Scarecrow Press.]

Quality Management

Baker, S.L., and F.W. Lancaster. 1991. *The measurement and evaluation of library services.* 2nd ed. Arlington, Va: Information Resources Press.

Fischer, W.W., and L.B. Reel. 1992. Total quality management (TQM) in a hospital library: Identifying service benchmarks. *Bulletin of the Medical Library Association* 80, no. 4:347–352.

Howell, P.B., and C.J. Jones. 1993. A focus on quality—the library's role in occurrence screening. *Medical Reference Services Quarterly* 12, no. 2:83–89.

Phillips, S.A. 1990. Productivity measurement in hospital libraries: A case report. *Bulletin of the Medical Library Association* 78, no. 2:146–153.

Rashid, H.F. 1990. Book availability as a performance measure of a library: An analysis of the effectiveness of a health sciences library. *Journal of the American Society for Information Science* 41, no. 7:501–507.

Robbins, K., and R. Holst. 1990. Hospital library evaluation using focus group interviews. *Bulletin of the Medical Library Association* 78, no. 3:311–313.

Taylor, M.H., and T. Wilson, eds. 1990. *Q.A. quality assurance in libraries: The health care sector.* Ottawa, Ontario: Canadian Library Association, Library Association Publishing Limited.

Information Technologies

Brandt, M. 1993. New Joint Commission standards: Management of information roles of health information management professionals. *Journal of AHIMA* 64, no. 11:81–84.

Braude, R.M. 1993. Impact of information technology on the role of health sciences librarians. *Bulletin of the Medical Library Association* 81, no. 4:408–413.

Cibbarelli, P.R., comp. and ed. 1993. *Directory of library automation software, systems, and services.* Medford, NJ: Learned Information, Inc.

Creth, S.D. The health information environment: A view of organizational and professional needs and priorities. *Bulletin of the Medical Library Association* 81, no. 4:414–420.

Gilbert, C.M. 1991. Challenges in health care information

transfer: The role of hospital libraries. *Bulletin of the Medical Library Association* 79, no. 4:405–408.

Jones, C.J. 1993. Charting a path for health sciences librarians in an integrated information environment. *Bulletin of the Medical Library Association* 81, no. 4:421–424.

Jurow, S., and S.B. Barnard, eds. 1993. *Integrating total quality management in a library setting.* Binghamton, NY: Haworth Press.

Klein, M.S. 1989. Adapting IAIMS to a hospital library level. *Bulletin of the Medical Library Association* 77, no. 4:357–365.

Marcaccio, K.Y., ed. 1994. *Gale directory of databases. Volume 1: Online databases. Volume 2: CD-ROM, diskette, magnetic tape, handheld, and batch access database products.* Detroit, Mich.: Gale Research, Inc.

Facilities

Doran, B.M. 1989. Planning a new medical library: A personal perspective and review of the literature. *Health Libraries Review* 6, no. 2:63–75.

Fraley, R.A., and C.L. Anderson. 1990. *Library space planning: A how-to-do-it manual for assessing, allocating and reorganizing collections, resources and facilities.* New York: Neal-Schuman Publishers, Inc.

Hannigan, G.G., and J.F. Brown. 1990. *Managing public access microcomputers in health sciences libraries.* Metuchen, NJ: Scarecrow Press.

Malkin, J. 1992. Teaching and research facilities. In *Hospital interior architecture: Creating healing environments for special patient populations.* New York: Van Nostrand Reinhold.

ELOISE C. FOSTER, MLN, is Director of the American Hospital Association Resource Center. She has written and contributed extensively to publications in the health administration and health sciences library fields.

ANNE CARBERY FOX, MLS, is Senior Staff Specialist in the American Hospital Association Resource Center. She is based at the National Library of Medicine, Bethesda, Maryland, and works on cooperative resources, the Health Planning Administration database, and the *Hospital Literature Index.*

SARA ANNE BEAZLEY, MA, is Staff Associate in the American Hospital Association Resource Center. She also contributes to cooperative resources, the Health Planning and Administration database, and the *Hospital Literature Index.*

Part II

Operational and Functional Aspects of the Health Care Industry

Chapter 17

Strategic Planning for Health Care Provider Organizations

E. Gordon Whyte and John D. Blair

STRATEGIC PLANNING REQUIRES STRATEGIC THINKING

The U.S. health care system has not resulted from a coordinated planning effort that carefully considered strategically developed alternatives. Rather, the system has grown out of a variety of responses to a range of market forces. Changes in direction for health care organizations have come as an outcome of their individual responses to specific interpretations of the organization's mission and their assessment of the opportunities that exist in their particular environment.

Health care provider organizations must assess the future in terms of their ability to meet the expectations of a better informed public and a more active diversified group of purchasers of care and services. Also, the fact that government is assigning itself a larger role in controlling the growth of the system calls for constant monitoring by providers. Finally, the relationship between hospitals and physicians, long considered the linchpin of the health care system, is changing as well. Physicians now perceive their preeminent role as the primary customers of hospitals, and as the driving force of the system as a whole, eroding through the growing influence of managed care organizations. This has resulted in a reduction in physicians' authority to direct the care of their patients within the system.

The way these factors have converged along with other changes in the current health care environment has caused health care provider organizations to more fully discern the necessity of addressing and understanding the environment in which they must interact and deliver their services. The forces in the environment are *compelling* the system to change rather than *allowing* the system to assess and change itself. In other words, the paradigm of the health care delivery system and the environment in which the system operates are being changed *for* the industry rather than *by* the industry.

Without an awareness of how their organization affects other organizations and is, in turn, affected by other organizations and other forces in the environment, health care managers run a risk of developing plans that are myopic and, thus, ineffective management tools. Many of the past plans have been a striking example of the failure of industry leaders to think and act in a manner that recognizes that their organizations are part of a large system.

Today, it is essential that health care managers conceptualize their organizations in systems terms. As they do this, they will begin to measure each decision they make in terms of its ramifications in and on the environment. This conceptualization is the basic component of strategic thinking.

BEGINNING THE STRATEGIC PLANNING PROCESS

Every health care provider organization has a purpose for existing. Because of the nature of the health care industry, it would seem that defining the purpose of a health care provider organization would be a simple undertaking. But a simplistic approach to defining purpose can often lead an organization to a false sense of directedness. The purpose of a hospital in the current environment is not what it once was, nor can it be assumed that all hospitals have the same purpose.

When an organization expresses its purpose in a clearly composed set of statements it creates its mission statement. In order to arrive at a comprehensive definition of the mission of a health care provider organization, it is necessary to consider the various needs and goals of the key stakeholders. Without input from these groups and individuals, it is possible for the organization to misstate the mission and thereby run the risk of misdirecting its efforts. Managing the relationships with those individuals and groups who have significant interests in, and are significantly affected by, the actions and decisions of the health care provider organization is accomplished through strategic stakeholder management.

Strategic stakeholder management transforms the complex relationships that exist in and between organizations and their external environments into logical, systematic frameworks that can be communicated and acted upon. This framework encourages proactive integration of the organization with the environment.[1]

Identifying organizational stakeholders, and developing strategies for managing the organization's relationships with them, are key components of strategic planning and ultimately of strategic management. Competitive strategy formulation and implementation is improved when managers are able to anticipate stakeholder actions and develop proactive strategies and action plans.[2]

Analysis of the turbulent environment in which health care provider organizations find themselves today reveals more complex stakeholder relationships and a growth in the number of active stakeholders. In the recent past, hospital administrators might have been able to comfortably describe their stakeholders as board members, medical staff members, patients, some payors, and a few key vendors. This is no longer the case. Today's stakeholder relationships will more likely be much more complex. Every stakeholder relationship must be accurately identified and assessed. Those stakeholder relationships identified as "key" must be managed by the organization in terms of the potential for that relationship to threaten or benefit the organization.

The identification, assessment, and diagnosis of stakeholder relationships, along with the development of strategies for managing the relationships, should be fully integrated into the organization's strategic planning process. Each strategy decision made during the planning process should be examined in terms of the anticipated reaction of the key stakeholders affected by that decision. By evaluating the needs and goals of the key stakeholders, the organization is better able to develop a clear definition of its mission and specific strategies for carrying out that mission through the management of the key stakeholder relationships.

To know its real mission, an organization must be able to answer the question, "What business are we in?" The answer to this question is different for virtually every health care provider organization in every setting and every community. Descriptions of the business of a hospital, physician group practice, nursing home, or home health agency can vary greatly depending on such things as ownership, location, competition, state of the economy, politics, availability of technology, ethics, and the values of the people in leadership positions within the organization. Often, persuading the leadership of an organization to define its mission is difficult. Mission often is taken for granted and dismissed as being obvious. Yet, when discussed in detail, differing opinions usually are expressed.

The mission statement will become the basis for all other planning that will be undertaken by the organization. It is the driving force of organizational planning at all levels. Mission must be the guiding light for health care provider organizations as they try to navigate today's stormy health care environment. The misguided tenet of the 1980s and early 1990s of "no margin, no mission" is now being replaced by "strong mission, strong margin." The key to successful planning and goal attainment is clear organizational direction based on a coherent mission that is rooted in a strong set of mutually held organizational values.

One of the most frequently cited examples of the success of a value-based, mission-driven organization is the Disney Corporation. The inculturation process required of new Disney employees is extensive and thorough. The key to Disney's success is not the process through which employees go, but the values and coherent mission of the organization. So, while the Disney process is replicative, it will succeed only over the long haul in an organization that adapts the process to its own values and mission.

Getting to the Strategic Level

Perhaps the most difficult phase of the strategic planning process is defining exactly what strategic planning is, why strategic thinking is required for success, and how accomplishing both can be successful only if implementation is instituted through strategic management.

Many health care executives believe that the survival of their organizations is enhanced as a result of the use of a strategic approach to operations, including strategic thinking, planning, and managing. Through the adoption of a strategic approach, linkages are created between philosophical underpinnings, organizational culture, operational direction, and financial decision making. This crucial connection opens a clear path to the ultimate success of the organization achieved through fulfillment of its mission and the attainment of its goals.

The strategic approach to operation can be implemented at all levels of an organization. At its base, the strategic approach requires each manager to have a thorough understanding of his or her particular unit and the specific environment in which the unit operates. In order to contribute to the good of the whole organization, the unit's relationship with its environment should be central to every action taken. By extension, senior managers must recognize and consider the association between the organization and its external environment, realizing that this relationship is fundamental to each action taken by the organization as a whole.

Failure to recognize the nature and particular characteristics of the operating environment of a particular institution can result in policy directives and program implementation that are doomed to failure. A simple example would be a chain of nursing homes using standardized monthly menus designed to provide adequate nutrition and reduce cost through the use of large national purchasing contracts. If the chain has a home in south Jersey and another in south Louisiana, each institution will quickly come to understand that while it may be more expedient and efficient to plan and purchase dietary items this way, the palates of the residents are very different, and either the residents of one of the homes will be dissatisfied or perhaps all of the residents in both homes will be dissatisfied.

At the organizational level, a directive to institute an Alzheimer's wing in each home may be just as shortsighted as the centralized menu planning, if the needs of the particular market (environment) and the stakeholders in that market are not considered.

Defining Strategy

There is a growing interest in, and use of, strategy in the health care sector today. In order to move a health care organization toward thinking, planning, and managing strategically, executives must first agree on what strategy means.

Strategy is an approach to thinking, planning, and decision making in a business situation that requires a manager to know, understand, accept, and support the mission of the organization, or unit within an organization, and to relate that mission to the environment in which decisions will be implemented. The driving force behind strategic thinking, planning, and managing, is mission.

All organizations have goals. The goals, articulated or not, act as a point of reference in thoughtful decision making. However, many goals are set to accommodate a short-term interest; to appease or please a superior; or to comply with organizational policy, procedure, or outside regulations. These constraints, when joined with personality, values, and management style, can cause a manager to make decisions and act in a manner that has been described by Lindbloom as "muddling through."[3] When the muddling-through approach is utilized, managers make decisions that are guided more by the specifics of a particular situation than by agreed-upon goals developed through a formalized planning process and previous strategy selection. Managers who muddle are not mission driven and are constrained by "how things are." A strategic approach forces a manager to know "how things are," and to make decisions in support of "how things could be" or "must be" in order to fulfill the organization's mission in its defined environment.

In using a strategic approach, a manager recognizes the constraints within the organization and its environment. As a result of ongoing monitoring, he or she has a thorough understanding of the internal and external environments and uses this collection of information to make decisions that will advance the organization toward mission fulfillment.

Information generated through the monitoring process is both quantitative and qualitative in nature. Both are needed in the decision-making process. Managers must make sound decisions that are based on feelings, impressions, and opinions, as well as on quantitative data. Throughout the process, decisions are made with consideration given to both environment and mission.

According to Shrivastava,[4] strategy is not simply a means of making an organization more financially successful. It is a way of making the organization more useful and productive to society, which in turn will enable it to prosper. Again, the importance and veracity of the new axiom for the 1990s—"strong mission, strong margin"—is exemplified.

THE STRATEGIC PLANNING PROCESS

Health care organizations frequently begin their planning processes, strategic or otherwise, by creating a set of desired goals. In the case of an organization struggling to survive, these goals are usually expressed in extreme terms. With this set of goals as the guiding light, managers proceed to "back into" the planning process. In other words, they ask the question, "What do we need to do to accomplish these goals?"

In a strategic approach to planning, the process begins with an in-depth assessment of the organization, its mission, and its environment. There is an attitude of openness and willingness to challenge conventional wisdom and the existing paradigms. Strategic thinking enables a manager to consider how to change the environment rather than simply reacting to it.

Changing the paradigm and/or adjusting to the environment requires time, effort, resources, creativity, and risk taking. This is the nature of strategic planning. It starts with information about the organization and its environment, evaluated in light of the organization's mission. It encourages the manager to ask, "How can we further our mission given this collection of information?" rather than "What do we have to do to reach these goals?" This approach challenges a manager to be proactive, think creatively, and set aggressive goals.

Step One: Planning the Process

The strategic planning process is a series of connected steps that result in an organization assessing its mission, internal strengths and weaknesses, and external opportunities and threats; identifying goals and objectives; developing alternative strategies for attaining those goals; selecting the best combination of strategies; and monitoring the organizational behavior and progress toward mission fulfillment through goal attainment. Several steps are outlined to define these activities. There is nothing fixed about the number of steps. Each organization will divide the process into a different number of steps, and each probably will change the process each time it is repeated, based on the current organizational structure and the environment in which the planning is being done.

The first step in any strategic planning process is developing a road map through the planning process itself. Often this is referred to as the "plan to plan." In this phase, those individuals responsible for directing and guiding the strategic planning process assist the leaders of the organization in deciding the following:

- the committee structure to be used in developing the planning data, assessing the resulting information, and making the selection of strategies to be implemented
- the methodology to be used in gathering data, e.g., primary or secondary collection
- the members of the planning team(s); i.e., which administrators, medical staff members, governing body representatives, and department heads will participate and at what level
- the frequency of the meetings to be held by each team and committee, a specific time frame for completion of each assigned task, and a schedule of the meeting times for each committee and team
- the expected duration of the entire planning process, remembering that speed is never a goal of strategic planning; the emphasis must always be on thoroughness and clarity

An example of a plan to plan is shown in Table 17–1. It is important to note that not only are the various steps clearly delineated but there is also an approximate time frame allotted to each step and a designated person(s) responsible for its completion.

Step Two: Developing and/or Assessing the Mission Statement

The value-based mission statement is the foundation on which the rest of the strategic planning process is built. As has been noted, the mission statement is developed in response to the organization's definition of the needs and interests of its stakeholders. In an era of health care reform, it will be more difficult to define and to assess the mission of health care provider organizations. This will be due primarily to the changing role of health care providers and changing expectations of the market. Since early in the history of this country, emphasis has been on the provision of the highest quality of care at virtually any price. Expectations of the marketplace were in large part set by the providers. Physicians and hospitals told the patients and, by extension, the community what they should expect in terms of outcomes and cost of medical services.

When stakeholder expectations were controlled by the provider organizations, it was a relatively simple task for the organization to define its mission to meet the expectations that were prescribed. In today's environment, the marketplace and organizational stakeholders are more informed and vocal. They set their own expectations.

Because the individuals who participate in the mission assessment process also are usually key stakeholders, it is more important than ever that they share a core set of values and purpose. Without these underpinnings, there is increased risk that each individual will respond to and act in reference to personal interests, which may not be consistent with the interests of the other group members and with the purpose of the organization.

Table 17–1 Planning the Planning Process

Planning Steps	Time Frame	Responsible Person(s)
1. Develop a planning procedure and gain agreement from key individuals.	Two meetings held within two weeks	Administrator, planning director, and planning consultant
2. Assess organization mission statement.	Two-day retreat	Administrator, board chair, and physician representative
3. Assess external environment.	Six weeks	Planning director, planning consultant, and planning staff
4. Assess internal environment.	Six weeks (simultaneous with external environment)	Planning director, planning consultant, and planning staff
5. Develop organizational goals.	Two weeks following circulation of internal and external assessment data	Administrator, board planning committee, planning director, and planning consultant
6. Formulate strategic options for accomplishing each goal.	One month after agreement on organizational goals	Administrator, planning director, planning consultant, board planning committee, and staff planning teams
7. Select and develop strategic options to be implemented.	One week after formulation of strategic options	Administrator, planning director, planning consultant, and board planning committee
8. Approve the strategic plan with specific options, costs, and estimated implementation dates supplied by the governing body.	First board meeting following final selection of strategic options	Governing body
9. Develop action plan and implementation schedule for each chosen strategic option.	Varies with the complexity of each option. However, no longer than one month will be allowed any option.	Administrator, planning director, and various department heads

Mission assessment usually is conducted by members of the governing body and upper management levels in the organization. In many instances, it is recommended that this step of the strategic planning process be conducted in a retreat format. This will allow for the greatest level of attention and participation by organization leadership. The end result is a shared sense of purpose that will facilitate the strategic decision making that will occur later in the planning process.

Step Three: Conducting the External Assessment

In order to accumulate the necessary information that will be required for strategic analysis and decision making, assessments of the external and internal environments must be carried out.

Assessing the external environment in today's turbulent times takes a high level of attention to detail and an ability to assimilate a large quantity of data that will have significant gaps in it. The goal of this assessment is to more fully understand the position of the organization in its environment. Duncan, Ginter, and Swayne have developed specific objectives for this phase of the process that will help to ensure that the best possible environmental description is developed. These objectives are as follows:[5]

1. to classify and order information flows generated by outside organizations

2. to identify and analyze current important issues that will affect the organization

3. to detect and analyze the weak signals of emerging issues that will affect the organization

4. to speculate on the likely future issues that will have a significant impact on the organization

5. to provide organized information for the development of the origination's purpose, mission, objectives, internal assessment, and strategy

6. to foster strategic thinking throughout the organization

External environmental assessment assists those involved in the strategic planning process to identify the potential threats and opportunities for the organization. The external environment can be systematically assessed using the following taxonomy as a guide:

1. *Macro-environment*: Includes major trends and events taking place outside of the specific environment in which the organization operates, e.g., the global economy, industry trends, national economic indicators.

2. *Regulatory environment:* Includes recent or expected changes in the myriad of regulations that directly affect the organization.

3. *Economic environment:* Includes trends, events, and economic indicators that are specific to the marketplace in which the organization operates; also included in this area is an assessment of the growth, strength, and impact of managed care arrangements on the delivery of health care services in the marketplace.

4. *Social environment:* Includes issues such as the public health status of the marketplace, health impacts of generalized social behaviors such as poor diet, sexually transmitted disease, smoking, and substance and alcohol abuse; also included in this area is an assessment of the demographic changes and trends in the marketplace.

5. *Political environment:* Includes factors such as recently enacted or pending legislation at the local, state, and federal levels.

6. *Competitive environment:* Includes defining and assessing the strengths and weaknesses of the organizations and individuals who are seeking to provide the same or similar services to the organization's targeted segments; also included in this area is an assessment of any recent or expected changes in strategic alliances among providers in the marketplace.

7. *Technological environment:* Includes assessments of recent advances in pharmaceuticals, genetics, and high-tech equipment, as well as the knowledge base, skills, and talents of the organization's workforce pools.

The external environmental assessment is intended to clarify those specific aspects of the environment that affect the organization today and in the foreseeable future. Therefore, it is necessary for the strategic planning teams to develop methodologies that are appropriate for forecasting significant events and trends.

No matter how thorough and sophisticated the forecasting techniques, they do not foretell the future. The best they can do is provide strategic decision makers with the best available information and the best strategic thinking of the individuals involved in the planning process.

Both the external and internal environmental assessments generally are conducted by internal staff under the guidance and supervision of the person charged with shepherding the strategic planning process. There are two overriding characteristics of successful external and internal assessments: thoroughness and usefulness. The search for the data to be used must be well thought out and exhaustive. Every important element of the environments must be investigated. Once the staff are confident that they have collected all available and relevant data that are necessary for strategic planning purposes, they should then configure those data into formats that make them understandable for the individuals who will be making decisions. In other words, the data must be converted into useful information.

In many cases, this will require several different presentation formats in order to ensure that every participant understands the assessments. Some individuals more readily grasp information presented in visual formats such as bar graphs and pie charts, while others prefer tables and lists. Still others want written detailed reports. It is the responsibility of the staff who have collected the data to report it in a way that is useful to each decision maker involved in the process.

Step Four: Conducting the Internal Assessment

Through conducting a structured internal assessment, a health care provider organization will become aware of its strengths and weaknesses. This step in the strategic planning process is sometimes given cursory attention. This is true for a couple of reasons. First, it can be organizationally and personally painful to make a detailed self-evaluation Second, as with the preconceived notions that were described surrounding the assessment of the mission statement, some health care executives feel that they already know the strengths and weaknesses of their organizations.

The internal assessment not only identifies organizational strengths and weaknesses, it also evaluates them in relation to the specific external opportunities and threats that have been identified. The matching of strengths and weaknesses with opportunities and threats exposes critical information that will be used in the development of the strategic alternatives in step six of the strategic planning process, described later in this chapter.

To facilitate this phase of the process the organization can be divided into ten operating components. Each component is first assessed on an individual basis. Then the component is evaluated relative to the other components in the organization.

The ten components evaluated in the internal assessment are:

1. *Management:* Includes evaluation of the number of levels; strength of each level as a whole and the individuals in that level; management skills; and formal delegation of decision-making authority.

2. *Human resources:* Includes evaluation of the skill levels in technical areas; availability of appropriately prepared personnel; recruitment and retention track record; and efficiency in scheduling.

3. *Finance:* Includes evaluation of the availability and use of capital funds; use of operating revenues; ratio analyses; budget variances; and internal control mechanisms.

4. *Marketing:* Includes analysis of the characteristics of current patients, such as payor source, acuity, demographics, origin, and destination; referral sources; review of the current level of usage of services or product lines offered; channels or mechanisms for service delivery; promotional techniques; and success rates of each.

5. *Clinical systems:* Includes evaluation of output measures of volume and quality; level of technology available; level of technology needed; and skills and knowledge base of clinicians.

6. *Organizational structure:* Includes analysis of the linkage of human resources, technologies, marketing, and management talent.

7. *Organization culture:* It is uncertain what the effect of culture is on the actual productivity of an organization. However, evaluation of culture as part of the internal assessment can aid an organization in developing a value system and behavioral expectations that support the mission.

8. *Physical plant:* Primary interest for planning purposes is whether the plant serves to constrain or facilitate future growth and change.

9. *Information systems:* Typically, this component has very high levels of dissatisfaction in health care provider organizations. This assessment should evaluate the

system's ability to link the financial, clinical, and marketing information systems.

10. *Leadership abilities:* Includes evaluation of the demonstrated leadership of the organization's senior and executive managers, the governing body, and department and section heads. This is a particularly sensitive area to evaluate and is, unfortunately, frequently left out of the process.

Most of the components listed above require the gathering and assessment of both quantitative and qualitative data. In the internal assessment phase, as in all other phases of the strategic planning process, the ability of the decision makers to exercise judgment in evaluating and prioritizing the information is as critical as the collection of the data itself.

In converting the internal and external data into information, the staff will want to compile a list of the organization's internal strengths and weaknesses, and the opportunities and threats that exist in the external environment. This listing and the analysis of the list is referred to as a SWOT (strength, weakness, opportunity, threat) analysis.

It is not uncommon to find the list of strengths and weaknesses to be much longer and in-depth than the list of external opportunities and threats. This frequently happens because most staff members are more familiar with their own organization than they are with the external environment, and the data are more readily available. Also, there are finely tuned, well-known formulas for analyzing and interpreting internal data. The same is not true for the external data. Health care executives are generally more comfortable interpreting balance sheets than they are interpreting political climates.

Step Five: Setting Goals and Objectives

Much of the management literature spends time differentiating between goals and objectives. For the purposes of strategic planning, as it is being discussed in this chapter, it is more important to select one or the other term and use it consistently throughout the entire process.

Goals (or objectives), in this context, are end points that the organization plans to reach in a specified period of time. They have three characteristics. First, goals are reachable. This is not meant to imply that goals should be easily reachable. They should be challenging in order to motivate staff and employees to work toward meeting them. Second, goals are verifiable. Verifiability may not always mean that the goals are discretely measurable or quantifiable. However, it is absolutely essential that at the end of the agreed upon time period, there be a clearly defined means for demonstrating whether or not the goal was reached. Third, goals have to be specific and explicit. They must establish specific outcomes that will contribute to the fulfillment of the organizational mission. Responsibility for their accomplishment must be explicitly assigned to individuals or groups within the organization.

Goals flow from the matching of organizational strengths and weaknesses with environmental opportunities and threats. The goals should reflect in reachable, verifiable, specific, and explicit terms the organization's efforts to maximize its strengths and avail itself of the opportunities, while minimizing its acknowledged weaknesses and defending itself against identified threats.

With regard to how many goals an organization should set, there is no agreed upon guideline. However, the organization should apply the same rationale here that it used in selecting reachable goals. Setting too many goals can have the effect of making some or all of them unreachable because they will suffer from a lack of attention and activity. Employees are motivated by their successes in reaching their goals and organizations flourish as a result of motivated employees accomplishing agreed upon goals.

Setting the strategic goals for the organization is the single most important step in the entire strategic planning process. Every step that has preceded goal selection has served as preparation for making these decisions. Every step that follows goals selection will be directed at moving the organization toward mission fulfillment through the accomplishment of the selected goals. The selection of the goals is a function of the thoroughness of the data collection and the conversion of the data into information. The successful accomplishment of the goals is a function of the strategic thinking abilities of the involved decision maker.

Selection of the individuals who will participate in this step of the strategic planning process will have direct impact on the future of the organization. These decision makers will review the mission statement; interpret the planning information; and analyze the strengths, weaknesses, opportunities, and threats. They will set the course and direction that the organization will follow for the foreseeable future.

The selection of these individuals to serve on what is generally called the Strategic Planning Committee is vital to the success of the process and by extension to the success and survival of the organization. It is rare that someone from outside the organization is selected for participation at this level, with the exception of a paid strategic planning consultant. Because of the importance of these individuals and the power that they will exercise over and within the organization, maneuvering or outright campaigning for a position on this committee is common among governing body members as well as executive staff.

This is another opportunity for the use of a stakeholder analysis. There will be individuals who, because of their positions, must be included (e.g., chair of the governing body, CEO, COO, CFO). However, every effort should be made to choose other individuals who have been identified as strategic thinkers in the organization. In all cases, the stakeholder assessment will assist the person selecting the planning committee members in evaluating the strengths, power bases, and values of the individuals selected.

Step Six: Formulating Strategic Options

Once the goals have been set, the organization develops the means for relating them to the environment. These means are the strategies. In this phase in the strategic planning process, the planning teams or planning committee may use techniques such as brainstorming and planning retreats, among others. In addition to statistical forecasting, Zentner suggests the use of scenarios in planning by health care provider organizations.[6] Through the construction of alternative scenarios, planners are able to assist decision makers in assessing the consequences of alternative decisions by combining selected environmental factors into a wide spectrum of possible situations.

The purpose of this step is to develop a list of realistic strategies that could lead to the accomplishment of each goal. In some instances the lists may be extensive and in others limited. If the planning team seems unable to generate more than one strategy for a given goal, this may signal that there is a predetermined decision about the strategy to be used to accomplish that particular goal. That predetermined strategy should not be accepted without serious discussion and evaluation.

Each proposed strategy not only should address itself to a specific goal, but it also should take into consideration specific stakeholders. For instance, if an urban hospital is going to consider a rural outreach strategy as a means of increasing inpatient referrals to its cardiology unit, it must simultaneously consider the willingness of its cardiology staff to accept referrals from that area, and the possible reactions of the physicians in the targeted rural community.

Alternative strategies can be categorized into three types:

1. *practical alternatives* that can receive immediate approval and that are easily implementable
2. *incremental alternatives* whose implementation in some sequence will lead to eventual accomplishment of the goals
3. *radical alternatives* that will require significant change in the organization but implementation of which will result in rapid movement toward goal attainment

Neither the number nor the type of alternative strategies is important. The fact that each suggested strategy is realistic, implementable, and stakeholder-based is very important.

Step Seven: Selecting and Developing the Strategies

It is important that the selection of the strategies to be implemented be seen as a separate step from the development of the alternative strategies. If strategy selection is seen as a part of the option development step, each option will be evaluated at the time it is suggested. This instantaneous evaluation retards the production of alternatives because team members become fearful of immediate rejection of their alternative ideas. By separating the two steps, each alternative is given its due consideration and participants are more likely to contribute to the process.

The selected strategies should make use of the information developed in the external and internal environmental assessments. The development of the specific procedures and actions required to implement the strategies should be heavily dependent on the assessment of the importance of the desired goals and the impacts of the selected strategies on the various stakeholders in the organization. Each stakeholder has expectations for the organization that are going to be affected by the goals and strategies. Managers in health care provider organizations have to anticipate the reactions of the stakeholders to the proposed goals and strategies and manage the various stakeholder relationships in a manner that capitalizes on stakeholder support and minimizes their opposition.

Peter Drucker warns planners of four common mistakes that can be made at this stage of the strategic planning process.[7] The most common mistake is failure to test the new strategy before full implementation. There are many techniques that can be used to test a strategy, including pilot projects, focus groups, delphi groups, and in-depth stakeholder interviews.

The next most common mistake cited by Drucker is one he labels "righteous arrogance." In almost every case, a strategy will have to be amended and modified in some way as the plan-

ning process progresses. Failure to make the necessary changes because that is not the way it was conceived or proposed can result in a potentially successful strategy failing to be selected for implementation. The accepted strategy needs to become "owned" by the planning committee, and the person who contributed the original proposal needs to relinquish personal ownership of the idea.

The third mistake is the failure to develop and propose radical strategies. The proposed strategies should not all be modifications of the way business is done at any particular moment. In other words, there comes a time when one has to design for the specific requirements of a job, rather than trying to improve what has always been done.

The fourth mistake is to assume that there is just one right strategy for each goal and that the role of the planning committee is to figure out which one it is. There may be several equally right strategies that can be selected for a given goal. The role of the committee is to select the one that will accomplish the goal in the most efficient and effective manner, taking into consideration the mission and the stakeholders involved.

Finally, Drucker offers these words of advice when selecting a new strategy for implementation: "If at first you don't succeed, try once more. Then do something else." He notes that often a new strategy will not work the first time it is tried. Before abandoning the entire strategy the organization should assess what went wrong and attempt to fix it. This assessment and willingness to modify strategy will intensify an organization's commitment to a selected strategy because the individuals involved will know that it is not simply a matter of making it work the first time. It is a matter of making it work in the end.

Step Eight: Developing the Implementation Plan

So often in the past the strategic planning process has faltered at this point. It is sometimes argued that once an organization moves to the implementation of the strategies, it has shifted from strategic activity to operational activity. This approach collapses in the wake of strategic management. Since all decisions and actions are seen with respect to their effect on mission fulfillment and goal attainment, then each action taken as part of the implementation of the strategic plan is strategic.

The implementation plan requires the organization to assign specific responsibility for each strategy to an individual or group within the organization. Each strategy is also assigned a time line and a completion date. The plan for implementation should be presented in a format that is similar to the "plan to plan" shown in Table 17–1 and discussed earlier.

In some cases, important checkpoints are established to measure movement during the process. In all cases, progress is monitored and evaluated. Likewise, the evaluation of the strategies has the effect of causing the organization to monitor and evaluate the environment as well. This kind of feedback allows the organization to continuously evaluate the effectiveness of its selected strategies and to make adjustments as deemed necessary. These adjustments may range from minor tinkering with the action plan or time lines to complete abandonment of the strategy and/or adoption of a new strategy in extreme cases.

THE ROLE OF THE PLANNING DIRECTOR AND DEPARTMENT

The planning director, whether that person is a member of the staff or a paid professional planning consultant, is not responsible for the plan. Further, it is not the responsibility of the planning department to produce an annual update of the strategic plan.

The role of the planning director is to facilitate and guide the process. A successful planning director does not feel psychological ownership of the planning document. Rather that person feels the "thrill of success" as a result of completing the process, and commitment by the key stakeholders in the organization to the successful implementation of the strategies.

The decision to use an outside consultant is one faced by almost all organizations at some point. In almost all cases, it is recommended that an outside consultant be used the first couple of times through the strategic planning process. This outsider will have the ability to be more objective about the work being done. Likewise, the consultant will be in a stronger position to ensure that deadlines are met and that everyone who is supposed to be involved continues to participate. In other words, sometimes outsiders can say things and do things that insiders would like to be able to say and do but are constrained because of internal conditions, relationships, and politics. Furthermore, the consultant will bring technical and professional expertise to the organization that often is not available in the early attempts at the process.

CONCLUSION

Health care provider organizations are struggling to survive in a dynamic and sometimes dangerous environment. This situation requires an approach to management of these organizations that goes beyond the institutional boundaries of the past. These organizations must realize that they are not only part of the health care delivery system but are also part of the larger ecosystem in the United States and thus are affected by national and international issues.

Strategic planning is one part of a new approach to running health care provider organizations in this environment, called strategic management. Through the use of strategic management and specifically strategic planning, an organization is able to develop a sensitivity to its internal and external environments. This environmental sensitivity allows organizations to evaluate their relationship with their individual stakeholders and develop plans to strategically manage those relationships.

At the base of strategic planning and management is an organzationwide dedication to fulfilling the mission of the organization. This shared dedication creates a cohesion that ensures consistent decision making directed toward the survival and success of the organization in today's turbulent environment.

NOTES

1. J.D. Blair and M.D. Fottler, *Challenges in Health Care Management: Strategic Perspectives for Managing Key Stakeholders* (San Francisco, Calif: Jossey-Bass Publishers, 1990), 2–3.

2. Ibid., 10–11.

3. C.E. Lindbloom, The Science of Muddling Through, *Public Administration Review* Spring (1959):79–88.

4. P. Shrivastava, *Strategic Management: Concepts and Practices*. (Cincinnati, Ohio: Southwestern Publishing Co., 1994), 6.

5. W.J. Duncan et al., *Strategic Management of Health Care Organizations* (Boston: PWS-Kent Publishing Co., 1992), 75.

6. R.D. Zentner, Scenarios: A Planning Tool for Health Care Organizations, *Hospital & Health Services Administration* Summer (1991): 211–222.

7. P.F. Drucker, *Managing the Non-Profit Organization: Principles and Practices* (New York: HarperBusiness, 1990), 69–71.

E. GORDON WHYTE, MHA, PhD, is Vice Chairman and Director of Master Programs, Department of Health Systems Management, in the School of Public Health and Tropical Medicine at Tulane University Medical Center. He also is President of Gordon Whyte and Associates, a health care planning and marketing consulting firm. Dr. Whyte has previously served as Vice President of Strategic Planning and Marketing at St. Mary of the Plains Hospital, Lubbock, Texas; and Administrator of HealthSouth Rehabilitation Center of New Orleans. He is a licensed nursing facility administrator and a member of the Education Committee of the National Association of Boards of Examiners for Nursing Home Administrators. He received his master's degree from Trinity University in 1975 and his PhD from the University of Mississippi in 1985.

Chapter 18

Strategic Stakeholder Management for Health Care Executives

*John D. Blair, Timothy M. Rotarius, Karolyn B. Shepherd,
Carlton J. Whitehead, and E. Gordon Whyte*

The health care environment is undergoing fundamental and somewhat revolutionary changes. A sweeping restructuring of the health care industry is currently taking place, even without proposed government changes. Reform *is* occurring. The effect of this reform—whether government-mandated or driven by private-sector initiatives such as in managed care or because of powerful buyer groups demanding more health care for less money—is unknown. However, it *will* affect the future of the industry by driving the development of increasingly complex, integrated organization networks.

One characteristic of these new networks is that leaders of health care organizations must manage relationships with a growing number of active, powerful, and sometimes competing

stakeholders—any individuals, groups, or organizations who have a stake in the decisions and actions of an organization and who attempt to influence those decisions and actions. These stakeholders exert an influence on every health care management issue and must be recognized and evaluated for their potential to support or threaten the organization and its competitive goals.

Much of the emerging health care literature champions the development of integrated health care networks and systems as the fundamental strategy for facing the uncertain future created by health care reform. Managers, seeking to position their organizations for optimal strategic responsiveness to a still poorly understood future, have turned to linkages with others who have often been competitors or adversaries. Thus, hospitals, physicians, and health plans are creating the kinds of vertically integrated networks and systems discussed by several authors.[1] These new networks and systems magnify the need for managers to engage in effective strategic stakeholder management.

Figure 18–1 illustrates how complicated health care relationships can become. The number and types of complex relationships that today's health care executives face routinely are inadequately presented by this simplified model

Significant portions of this chapter are adapted from Chapters 3 and 4 of *Challenges in Health Care Management: Strategic Perspectives for Managing Key Stakeholders* by J.D. Blair and M.D. Fottler, pp. 80–171, with permission of Jossey-Bass Publishers, © 1990. Readers are referred to this text for added detail and tool kits (aids in implementing and facilitating the stakeholder management process).

We acknowledge Myron Fottler and Grant Savage for their contributions here, and express appreciation to Larry Wolper for his insightful comments on earlier drafts.

of key relationships. However, this model does illustrate how complex health care relationships have become. It also suggests that today's strategic stakeholder management tools need to be sophisticated and powerful if executives are to effectively lead their health care organizations.

Figure 18–1 depicts a private, tertiary-care hospital (Hospital A) which is contemplating a strategic alliance with a multispecialty physician group (Group A). Strategic alliances of this sort often are formed to allow for the attainment of some overall competitive goal. Also identified in Figure 18–1 are a myriad of other relationships that come into play because of this contemplated strategic alliance. What initially would have been viewed as a simple, dyadic relationship has mushroomed into a large number of key relationships (notice that only *key* relationships are shown in this figure, not *all* the relationships), which need to be acknowledged, addressed, and managed.

Although this figure is shown only as a hypothetical illustration, it very easily could be reality for any urban tertiary-care hospital. Many hospitals already are forming or have formed one or more strategic alliances with physicians. Some hospitals have even formed alliances with both physicians and health plans in order to present a more fully integrated health care system.

Figure 18–1 shows many key relationships. Those relationships that are highlighted with question marks are used as examples throughout this chapter. These are relationships that need to be examined in light of a strategic alliance between Hospital A and Group A. As can easily be seen, there is an array of relationships between the hospital and the stakeholders that can be changed or called into question through the formalization of just one specific strategic alliance. The key relationships Hospital A has with its stakeholders represent a pattern of informal, but interconnected stakeholder relationships, which, if properly and strategically managed, can lead to a formal network structure.

This simplified model of key relationships has come about because of the turbulent health care environment. Many of these newly created relationships have forced organizations to match the ever-changing environment. Unique opportunities exist to explore the consequences of creating and managing relationships among key hospital, physician, and health plan stakeholders.

Few organizations have fully developed an integrated, articulated strategic approach for managing their key stakeholders. For most organizations, executives' stakeholder management perspectives are, at best, incomplete, and their approaches to stakeholder assessment and management are underdeveloped and haphazard. At worst, they display a total lack of explicit awareness of, and involvement in, a systematic and effective stakeholder management approach. Health care leaders require a detailed, overall approach, along with specific tools and techniques, in order to facilitate managing stakeholders strategically. The strategic approach to stakeholder management provides a means of properly identifying all the players, their roles, and their level of stake in the network.[2] In other words, it can help identify key contingencies that are likely to lead to significant opportunities for cooperation or risks of conflict among key network stakeholders.

This chapter identifies how health care executives can develop more productive relationships with the key people—employees, physicians, community leaders, hospitals, competitors, managed care organizations, and others—who hold a stake in the management decisions of health care organizations. The examples used throughout this chapter (and represented by question marks in Figure 18–1) are those varied and complex relationships that affect a specific type of health care organization—hospitals. The examples will view strategic stakeholder management through the perspective of hospital executives. We will identify how hospital executives must change from an organizational (i.e., hospital) perspective to a system or network perspective.

The steps in our approach to strategic stakeholder management include:

- Identify all relevant external, interface, and internal stakeholders.

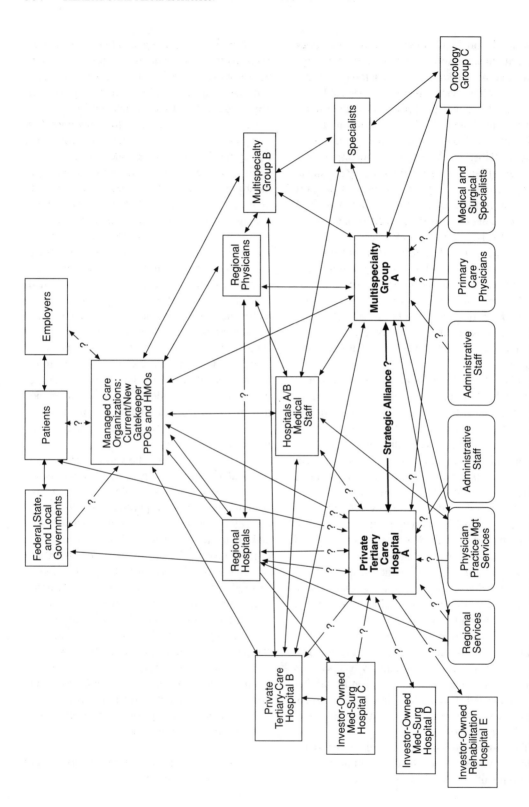

Figure 18–1 Key Stakeholders for a 1990s Urban Tertiary-Care Hospital: A Simplified Model

- Diagnose each stakeholder in terms of potential for threat and potential for cooperation.
- Ensure that the diagnosis for each stakeholder is relevant for the specific issue facing the organization (i.e., in this chapter, the emerging issue of increasing hospital-physician integration and the development of integrated delivery systems).
- Classify each stakeholder as supportive, mixed blessing, nonsupportive, or marginal.
- Formulate generic stakeholder management strategies: involve the supportive stakeholder; collaborate with the mixed-blessing stakeholder; defend against the nonsupportive stakeholder; and monitor the marginal stakeholder.
- Implement these generic strategies by developing specific implementation tactics and programs for each strategy-stakeholder combination.
- Evaluate managerial implications of effectively managing stakeholders from a strategic point of view.
- Identify which employees, as internal stakeholders, should be involved in the implementation process.

IDENTIFYING ORGANIZATIONAL STAKEHOLDERS

Exhibit 18–1 provides a listing of the typical stakeholders in a large U.S. hospital. The asterisks identify those stakeholders that appear on the illustrative stakeholder map (Figure 18–1). This table categorizes each stakeholder into one of three distinct stakeholder groups: external, interface, and internal.

The hospital must respond to a large number and a wide variety of external stakeholders including suppliers, competitors, related health organizations, government agencies, private accrediting associations, professional associations, labor unions, patients, third-party payors, the media, the financial community, special interest groups, and the local community. Whereas the internal and interface stakeholders are at least partly supportive of the hospital, many of the external stakeholders may be seen as neutral, nonsupportive, or even openly hostile.[3]

External stakeholders fall into three categories in their relationship to the health care organization. Some provide inputs into the organization, some compete with it, and some have a particular special interest in how the organization functions. The first category includes suppliers, patients, third-party payors, and the financial community. The relationship between the organization and these external stakeholders is a symbiotic one, since the organization depends on them for its very survival. These stakeholders, in turn, depend upon the organization to take their outputs. Without the organization or others like it, the stakeholders providing inputs could not survive. The degree of dependence of the organization on these stakeholders (and vice versa) depends on the number and relative attractiveness of alternative providers of similar services.

Consequently, the relationship between the organization and its stakeholders providing necessary inputs is one of mutual dependence. As such, the two parties cannot, or do not want to, do without one another. However, they may experience conflict as to how to cooperate. For example, a hospital and its patients may conflict over the price charted for certain services, but neither wishes to sever all relationships with the other.

The second category of external stakeholders (competitors) seeks to attract the focal organization's dependents. These competitors may be direct competitors for patients (i.e., other hospitals) or they may be competing for skilled personnel (i.e., related health organizations). Competitors do not necessarily need one another to survive. While cooperation between hospitals and their competitors has increased in recent years, so, too, has competition. Competitiveness, rather than cooperation, best defines the nature of the relationship, at least most of the time.

Exhibit 18–1 Stakeholders for Typical Large Hospital

A. **External Stakeholders**
   1. Competitors
      - Other hospitals*
         Private, not-for-profit*
         Public
         Investor-owned*
      - Physician practices (for outpatient services)
      - Other alternatives, e.g., freestanding
        outpatient surgery, diagnostic, or instant care
        centers
   2. Related Health Care Organizations
      - Other hospitals in region (noncompetitors)*
         Private, not-for-profit*
         Public*
         Investor-owned*
      - Physician practices*
         Solo*
         Single-specialty medical group*
         Multispecialty medical group*
      - Nursing homes
      - Pharmacies
      - Home health agencies
   3. Government Regulatory/Licensing Agencies*
      - Federal
      - State
      - Local
   4. Private Accreditation Associations
      - e.g., Joint Commission on Accreditation of
        Healthcare Organizations
   5. Professional Associations
      - e.g., for certification of hospital professionals
         National
         State
         Local
   6. Unions
      - National/international
      - Local
   7. Patients*
      - Private pay patients
      - Insured patients
         Direct contract with employer
         Through contract with managed care
           organization
         Pay through prospective payment
         Pay at full rate
         Pay at discounted rate
         Pay through capitation
      - Indigent patients
         Residents
         Nonresidents
      - Patient families

   8. Third-Party Payors
      - Governments
         Federal
         State
         Local
      - Regional employers
         Through indemnity insurance
         Through managed care contract
         Through direct contract
      - Business coalitions
      - Insurance companies
      - Managed care organizations (as purchasers of
        hospital services)
   9. Hospital Suppliers
   10. Media
      - Local
      - National
   11. Financial Community
      - Including joint venture investment partners
   12. Special Interest Groups
      - e.g., American Association of Retired
        Persons, veterans' organizations for VA
        hospitals, or Alcoholics Anonymous for
        psychiatric/substance abuse programs
   13. Religious Organizations
      - Denominational organizations, e.g., synods or
        dioceses
      - Local churches/synagogues
      - Pastors/priests/rabbis
   14. Local Community
B. **Interface Stakeholders**
   1. Nonmanagement Medical Staff*
      - On staff only at this hospital
      - Also on staff at other hospitals*
      - Partners in joint-venture with hospital
   2. Hospital Board
      - Trustees with policy authority
      - Advisory only
   3. Parent Companies/Organizations/Religious
      Orders
   4. Stockholders/Taxpayers/Contributors
   5. Related Health Care Organizations (e.g., as part
      of integrated delivery system)
      - Other hospitals in regional network*
         Private, not-for-profit
         Public
         Investor-owned
      - Physician practices as strategic partners in
        alliance*
         Solo
         Single-specialty medical group

continues

Exhibit 18–1 continued

Multispecialty medical group*
Group's own internal stakeholders as *indi-rect* stakeholders:
    Administrative staff
    Primary care physicians
    Medical specialists
    Surgical specialists

C. **Internal Stakeholders**
   1. Management
     • Top managers

- Physician managers/medical director
- Nonclinical managers (e.g., marketing, financial, regional services, practice management services)
- Clinical functional managers
- Clinical product line managers
2. Nonmanagement Employees
- Professional
- Paraprofessional
- Support personnel

*Specifically illustrated in earlier stakeholder map (Figure 18–1)

Source: Adapted from *Challenges in Health Care Management: Strategic Perspectives for Managing Key Stakeholders* by J.D. Blair and M.D. Fottler, pp. 81–83, with permission of Jossey-Bass Publishers, © 1990.

The third category of external stakeholders (special interest groups) includes any organization that is concerned with those aspects of the organization's operations that affect their interests. The major special interest groups affecting hospitals are government regulatory agencies, private accrediting associations, professional associations, labor unions, the media, the local community, and various political-action groups. Because of the nature of the special interest, conflict most often defines the nature of this relationship. The conflict is most often solved by compromise and, in some cases, overt collaboration.

In Figure 18–1, Patients; Managed Care Organizations; and Hospitals B, C, D, and E are all seen as external stakeholders for Hospital A.

Interface stakeholders are those who function both internal and external to the organization, that is, those who are on the interface between the organization and its environment. The major categories of interface stakeholders include the medical staff; the hospital board of trustees; the corporate office of the parent company; and stockholders, taxpayers, or other contributors. These tend to be among the most powerful stakeholders in health care organizations, but are easily misunderstood because they are thought of as "us" or "them" when they are both—and neither.

As in the case of internal stakeholders, the organization must offer each interface stakeholder sufficient inducements to continue to make appropriate contributions. However, the inducements can be even more complex than in the case of internal stakeholders because of the lack of such things as a structured human resource system or adequate management authority. Examples include such inducements as professional autonomy (medical staff), institutional prestige or political contacts (hospital board), good financial returns (corporate office), access (taxpayers), and special services or benefits (contributors). Specific examples of interface stakeholders for Hospital A on Figure 18–1 include: Groups A and C, Medical Staff for Hospitals A and B, and Regional Hospitals.

Finally, internal stakeholders are those that operate almost entirely within the generally accepted bounds of the organization and typically include management, professional, and nonprofessional staff. Management attempts to manage these internal stakeholders by providing sufficient inducements to gain continual contributions from them. The stakeholders determine whether the inducement is sufficient for the contribution they are required to make. This is partly determined by the alternative inducement—contribution offers received from competitive organizations.

Unless both the organization and the stakeholder believe such an agreement will be mutually beneficial and of fair value (relative to alternatives), agreement will not be reached and/or sustained. Under conditions of scarce resources, the exchange partners can be expected to attempt to obtain as high an inducement as possible while giving as low a contribution as possible. Restructuring the situation (i.e., a better compensation and benefit package) is the way the organization may induce or persuade employees to make the needed contribution. Alternatively, individuals in the organization also engage in manipulation, bargaining, and coalition activity in order to protect both their own interests and that of the coalition (also including external coalitions such as unions or professional associations) to which they belong. In Figure 18–1, internal stakeholders are identified by the rounded corners on the boxes. These stakeholders include: Regional Services; Physician Practice Management Services; Administrative Staff for Hospital A; and Administrative Staff, Primary-Care Physicians; and Medical and Surgical Specialists for Group A.

Once all the stakeholders have been classified into their respective categories, it becomes obvious that health care organizations do not face just one or a few stakeholders. Rather, health care executives must learn to manage a *portfolio* of stakeholders. It is vital that the leaders of health care organizations see the strategic implications of these stakeholder portfolios. No longer can specific functional managers be concerned with only those obvious stakeholders that fall within their functional responsibilities. Instead, these managers must be cognizant of all the other relationships that are influenced by their one-on-one specific stakeholder episodes. The challenge facing health care organization executives is the creation of consistency and effectiveness in all of these individual stakeholder episodes.

DIAGNOSING KEY STAKEHOLDERS IN TERMS OF POTENTIAL FOR THREAT AND POTENTIAL FOR COOPERATION

To manage stakeholders, health care managers must be involved in a continuous process of internal and external scanning when making strategic decisions. They must go beyond the traditional issues in strategic management, such as the likely actions of competitors or the attractiveness of different markets. They must also look for those external, interface, and internal stakeholders who are likely to influence the organization's decisions. As introduced earlier, managers must make two critical assessments about these stakeholders: (1) their potential to threaten the organization and (2) their potential to cooperate with it.[4]

Diagnosing the Stakeholder's Potential for Threat

Hostility or threat appears as a key variable in several formulations of organization-environment-strategy relationships.[5] Physicians, for example, are often explicitly identified as a group that does or could apply extensive pressure on hospitals, thereby having an impact on the hospital's effective strategic management.[6] Looking at the current anticipated threat inherent in the relationship with a particular stakeholder or group of stakeholders is similar to developing a worst-case scenario and protects managers from unpleasant surprises.

Stakeholder power and its relevance for any particular issue confronting the organization's managers determine the stakeholder's potential for threat. Power is primarily a function of the dependence of the organization on the stakeholder.[7] Generally, the more dependent the organization, the more powerful the stakeholder. For example, the power of staff physicians is a function of the hospital's dependence on those physicians for patients, alternative sources of patients, the use of hospital beds, and the provision of hospital services.

This is different than the normal exchange relationship focusing on potential for cooperation, since it also introduces a clear potential to threaten the organization by denying it needed resources and providing them to another, such as competitor. Health care organizations' relationships with physicians are often of this second kind and contain a potential for threat in an otherwise cooperative relationship.

Therefore the organization's managers need to systematically anticipate and evaluate the actual or potential threats in its relationships with stakeholders and, in some cases, evaluate threats that face their supportive stakeholders. These threats may be focused on obtaining inducements from the organization that may or may not be provided. These desired inducements include financial resources, participation in decision making, and enactment of certain organizational policies versus other possible policies. Alternatively, these threats may focus on undermining the fundamental viability of the organization.

Diagnosing the Stakeholder's Potential for Cooperation

Because stakeholder analyses emphasize the types and magnitude of threats that stakeholders pose for the organization, the second dimension of level of cooperation in the organization's relationship with its stakeholders is easily ignored. This dimension should be emphasized equally as managers attempt stakeholder diagnosis. This more clearly directs attention to potential stakeholder management strategies that go beyond the merely defensive or offensive in confronting stakeholder pressures. Diagnosing this dimension suggests the potential for using more cooperative strategies. These strategies focus on cooperation in stakeholder relationships in terms of the actual or potential contributions that are valued and needed by the organization. For example, two competitors who are facing a common threat of discontributions from a given stakeholder, such as a third competitor who has purchased a helicopter to aid in rural market penetration, may well be potential allies in counteracting such a move through a joint venture helicopter of their own with the cost being split between the two joint venture partners.

Another example of competitors joining together against a common enemy is occurring as hospitals merge to reduce the bargaining power of preferred provider organizations (PPOs).

PPOs have been able to demand price concessions from hospitals in markets where several hospitals compete for market share. However, with unprofitable hospitals falling by the wayside, the remaining hospitals can merge. The PPO is then left with only one dominant organization with which to negotiate, and is left in a very weak position since it cannot threaten to send its members elsewhere. However, stakeholder management does not end for hospital administrators planning to implement this strategy. While the Antitrust Division of the U.S. Department of Justice is carefully monitoring these types of mergers, there is an increasing awareness by both the public and regulators that in order to meet the three criteria of cost, quality, and access, these types of mergers may be necessary. Health care executives need to anticipate the likely reaction of regulators—who represent the public's stake—regarding prospective mergers.

Health care organizations today should find cooperative potential particularly relevant because it may allow them to join forces by creating networks and other health care systems with other stakeholders and better manage their respective environments. One may look at the cooperation or cooperative potential of a relationship in a parallel fashion to looking at actual or potential threat, except, in this case, one is looking at a best-case scenario, and, in so doing, one may discover new possibilities otherwise ignored because of fundamental assumptions and perspectives.

The stakeholder's dependence on the organization and its relevance for any particular issue facing the organization determine the stakeholder's cooperative potential. Generally, the more dependent the stakeholder on the organization, the higher the potential for cooperation. Often, however, the organization and the stakeholder may be very interdependent. For example, in a small town with a limited number of physicians and one hospital, the hospital and the physicians usually have high levels of mutual dependence. Although the hospital may encounter potential threats from some physicians who send patients to another hospital in a larger city, it may also have cooperation from most other physicians who want to keep the patients in the community.

Factors Affecting the Potentials for Threat and Cooperation

Besides power and dependence, other factors also affect the level of a stakeholder's potential for threat or cooperation. In Table 18–1, a list of stakeholder characteristics is provided that health care executives should examine when diagnosing the potential for threat or cooperation.

Table 18–1 focuses on four major factors: control of resources, relative power, likelihood and supportiveness of potential stakeholder action, and coalition formation. For each factor, there are two or three different basic situations possible. Lines in Table 18–1 separate the specific situations according to each major factor. Generally, only one situation from each of the four factors will apply to a given organization's

relationship with a particular stakeholder. The exceptions would be if the stakeholder is likely to take both supportive and nonsupportive actions or if the stakeholder is likely to form a coalition with both the organization and other stakeholders, potentially nonsupportive to the organization. It also is indicated whether the presence of a specific situation within each factor will probably increase, decrease, or either increase or decrease each type of potential. After one has looked at the probable impact of the relevant situation on overall cooperative or threatening potential, then it is a qualitative judgment on the part of a manager to weigh the relative importance of the four factors in making a final stakeholder diagnosis most appropriate for that organization at that time.

Exactly how a factor will affect the potential for a threat or cooperation depends on (1) the specific context and history of the organization's relations with that stakeholder and (2) the historical and contextual relations with other key stakeholders influencing the organization. For

Table 18–1 Factors Affecting Hospital Stakeholder's Potentials for Threat and Cooperation

	Increases or Decreases Stakeholder's Potential for Threat?	Increases or Decreases Stakeholder's Potential for Cooperation?
Stakeholder controls key resources (needed by hospital)	Increases	Increases
Stakeholder does not control key resources	Decreases	Either
Stakeholder more powerful than hospital	Increases	Either
Stakeholder as powerful as hospital	Either	Either
Stakeholder less powerful than hospital	Decreases	Increases
Stakeholder likely to take action (supportive of the hospital)	Decreases	Increases
Stakeholder likely to take nonsupportive action	Increases	Decreases
Stakeholder unlikely to take any action	Decreases	Decreases
Stakeholder likely to form coalition with other stakeholders	Increases	Either
Stakeholder likely to form coalition with hospital	Decreases	Increases
Stakeholder unlikely to form any coalition	Decreases	Decreases

Source: Reprinted from *Challenges in Health Care Management: Strategic Perspectives for Managing Key Stakeholders* by J.D. Blair and M.D. Fottler, p. 126, with permission of Jossey-Bass Publishers, © 1990.

example, a hospital manager may be able to assess the cooperative or threat potential of the medical staff only in the context of how competing institutions are managing their medical staffs and in the context of how the organization has treated its medical staff in the past. By carefully considering the factors in Table 18–1, executives can fine-tune their analyses and management of stakeholders.

As an example of the potentials for threat and/or cooperation, consider federal, state, and local governments. They can influence organizations in at least two different ways: through political actions and as regulators. Governments use political activities to alter the strategic decisions organizations make (e.g., antitrust issues vis-a-vis physician-hospital alliances). On the other hand, regulations cause organizations to change operational activities (e.g., Medicare forms and rules).

The next section of this chapter introduces several different levels of health care organization integration, ranging from the traditional system of independent health care providers, through the typical physician-hospital organizational (PHO) form, all the way to fully integrated health care delivery systems.

EMERGING LEVELS OF INTEGRATION IN HEALTH CARE DELIVERY

A wide range of possible organizational forms exists in today's turbulent health care environment. A model by Coddington, Moore, and Fischer[8] highlights nine different integration forms using only two key dimensions (with each dimension having three levels of integration—little or none, medium, and high); integration among physicians and integration between hospitals and physicians.

According to their model, integration among physicians ranges from solo practices and traditional medical staff relationships (little or no physician-physician integration) to physician coalitions (medium-level physician-physician integration) to large single- or multispecialty groups (potentially full physician-physician in-

tegration). Integration between hospitals and physicians ranges from traditional hospital organizations (little or no physician-hospital integration) to management service bureaus (medium-level of physician-hospital integration) to physician-hospital organizations (PHOs; potentially full integration on the hospital-physician continuum).

The two dimensions of integration (physician-physician and physician-hospital) are useful for classifying typical health care delivery systems in the United States. However, one other major player must be added to the integration puzzle in order to reach the fully integrated health care system. That third player is the health plan. Only when the health plan is integrated at a high level with the PHO-type organization will an organizational form be created that can assume all the health care needs of a given population.

As physicians become more integrated among themselves and as health plans begin to integrate with hospitals and/or physicians, the necessity of effective strategic stakeholder management becomes apparent. For example, what happens when physicians initiate their own physician-physician integration? Their power relative to the hospital becomes stronger and they become more of a threat to the hospital. Hospital management needs to understand this phenomenon fully in order to effectively manage their strategic issues.

Additionally, hospital executives need to understand how their direct competitors use these new organizational forms to their own best interests. For example, as competition becomes more and more integrated, all the organizational players need to have carefully thought-out and designed stakeholder management strategies in order to stay competitive.

Is any one distinct physician-hospital-health plan integration level better than any other? Absolutely, especially in today's volatile environment, when a hospital does not know from day to day whether tomorrow will be more demanding than yesterday. As each hospital moves closer toward the fully integrated health care system, the better prepared that hospital is, both strategically and opportunistically, to deal with the environment.

CLASSIFYING DIFFERENT TYPES OF STAKEHOLDERS

The two dimensions—potential for threat and potential for cooperation—map stakeholders into a diagnostic framework. As discussed previously, these two dimensions of classification serve as summary measures of stakeholder supportiveness or lack thereof and incorporate information from multiple factors. Using these two dimensions, four types of health care stakeholders, as shown in Figure 18–2, can be characterized.[9]

There is a dynamic process occurring at all times. Stakeholders initially categorized in one cell might be moved to another cell as a result of what the organization does or does not do, what stakeholders do or do not do, what new informa-

tion the organization has that would change the classification, and what issue currently faces the organization and its stakeholders.

Prior to discussing the four types of stakeholders, it should be made clear that one stakeholder can be both a direct and an indirect stakeholder. By direct, we mean that the stakeholder deals directly with the organization. An indirect stakeholder is still a stakeholder, but exerts influence through an intermediary. In Figure 18–1 there are several stakeholders who hold this double distinction. For example, Governments, Patients, and Group C are both direct and indirect stakeholders of Hospital A. The implications of these double distinction stakeholders will be discussed further in this chapter.

Type 1: The Mixed Blessing Stakeholder

The mixed blessing stakeholder plays a particularly key role. With mixed blessing stakeholders, the health care executive faces a situa-

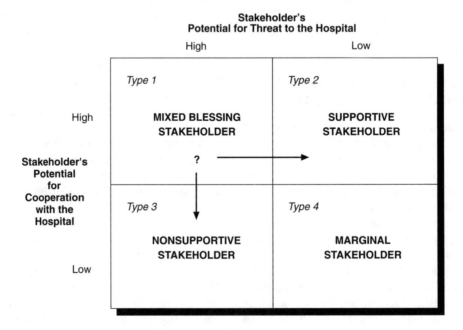

Figure 18–2 Diagnostic Typology of Hospital Stakeholders. *Source:* Reprinted from *Challenges in Health Care Management: Strategic Perspectives for Managing Key Stakeholders* by J.D. Blair and M.D. Fottler, p. 129, with permission of Jossey-Bass Publishers, © 1990.

tion in which the stakeholder is high on both types of potential: threat and cooperation. Normally, stakeholders of the mixed blessing type would generally include not only the medical staff but other physicians not on the staff, insurance companies, insured patients, and hospitals with complementary but not competing services. Physicians probably are the clearest example of this type of stakeholder. Although physicians can and do provide many services that benefit hospitals, physicians also can threaten hospitals because of their general control over admissions, the utilization and provision of different services, and the quality of care.

Some special interest groups also are a mixed blessing. For example, substance abuse programs at hospitals are influenced by groups such as Alcoholics Anonymous (AA). These groups have a significant stake in the hospital's program and its therapeutic approach. Such groups can either enhance referrals to the program or can undermine the program, thereby having great impact on its clinical and financial viability.

Figure 18–2 also shows a question mark under the mixed blessing stakeholder type with two arrows. One is directed toward the type 2, supportive stakeholder. The other is pointed at the type 3, nonsupportive stakeholder. These arrows imply that a mixed blessing stakeholder could become either more or less supportive. Later in this chapter, appropriate stakeholder management strategies for each type of stakeholder will be discussed.

Many of the relationships highlighted in Figure 18–1 (highlighting refers to those relationships that have a question mark) are those between Hospital A and mixed blessing stakeholders. In this example, Hospital A recognizes two different kinds of mixed blessing stakeholders: direct and indirect. For example, Groups A and C are classic examples of direct mixed blessing stakeholders for Hospital A. Even though Hospital A is contemplating a strategic alliance with Group A, the physicians are still of the mixed blessing variety of stakeholders.

Additionally, competing institutions such as regional hospitals also are classified as mixed blessing stakeholders. These regional hospitals represent the rural-type health care provider facilities in the region surrounding Hospital A. Because of the referral ties they have to Hospital A, these regional hospitals indicate potential for cooperation. However, because the regional hospitals also compete directly with Hospital A, they also are a potential for threat, even if the regional hospitals happen to be relatively minor competitors.

Governments and patients are indirect mixed blessing stakeholders. Since each of these stakeholders is classified as supportive in a direct sense (and will be discussed as such later), the introduction of the intermediary (i.e., the managed care organization, which is a nonsupportive stakeholder of Hospital A) obviously creates some potential for threat that does not exist when these stakeholders are dealing directly with Hospital A. This threat potential could come from the very nature of the intermediary, which, as mentioned above, is a nonsupportive stakeholder.

Type 2: The Supportive Stakeholder

The ideal stakeholder is one that supports the organization's goals and actions. Managers wish all their stakeholders were of this type. Such a stakeholder is low on potential threat but high on potential for cooperation. For example, in a well-managed hospital, its board of trustees, its managers, its staff employees, its parent company, the local community, and nursing homes will be of this type. In many large medical centers with multiple health care facilities, a common support facility such as a power plant, laundry, or parking consortium typify the concept of the supportive stakeholder.

In the continuing example of Hospital A attempting a strategic alliance with Group A, several supportive stakeholders surface. Assuming Hospital A does not own its own rehabilitation facility, Hospital E, which is a rehabilitation hospital, would be supportive because Hospital A feels little or no direct competitive threat from Hospital E. In fact, Hospital E has every reason to be a supportive stakeholder in Hospital A in the hopes of maintaining a good referral contact. However, if Hospital A did have a rehabilitation facility or was planning on adding one, then Hospital E would cease to be a supportive stakeholder and would likely become a nonsupportive one due to the competitive nature of their relationship.

As mentioned previously, governments and patients are supportive stakeholders when viewing their direct relationship with Hospital A (i.e., without managed care organizations being an intermediary). Both governments and patients desire to have available the services that Hospital A provides when they need them. Therefore, governments and patients tend to be supportive (at least until the cost-of-care issue surfaces) because they have everything to gain by being supportive. This example clearly shows that the same stakeholder can assume different stakeholder postures given the contextual or situation attributes of the stakeholder issue.

Type 3: The Nonsupportive Stakeholder

Stakeholders of this type are the most distressing for an organization and its managers. They are high on potential for threat but low on potential for cooperation. Typical nonsupportive stakeholders or hospitals include competing hospitals, freestanding alternatives such as urgi- or surgicenters, employee unions, the federal government, other government regulatory agencies, indigent patients, the news media, and employer coalitions. Special interest groups may often prove to be nonsupportive stakeholders, as in the case of pro-life demonstrations that have slowed or halted normal business, particularly for ambulatory women's centers.

Figure 18–1 shows two major nonsupportive stakeholders: managed care organizations and competing Hospital B. Both of these stakeholders share similar types of relationships with Hospital A. For example, they both try to manage the same key stakeholders as Hospital A, which sets up confrontational types of behaviors.

Interestingly, the managed care organizations, even though they are nonsupportive stakeholders to Hospital A, are one of the two necessary organizations required for Hospital A to form a fully integrated health care delivery system (the other one being some kind of physician group, represented in Figure 18–1 by Group A). This presents the major strategic issues facing today's health care executives: how to effectively manage nonsupportive stakeholders today so that in the future those same stakeholders will be less threatening and more cooperative. This issue will be explored later in this chapter.

Type 4: The Marginal Stakeholder

Marginal stakeholders are neither high on threat nor cooperative potential. Although they potentially have a stake in the organization and its decisions, they generally are not relevant for most issues. For a well-run hospital, typical stakeholders of this kind may include volunteer groups in the community, stockholders or taxpayers, and professional associations for employees. However, certain issues such as cost containment or access to care could activate one or more of these stakeholders, causing their potential for either threat or cooperation to increase.

Figure 18–1 identifies two marginal stockholders to Hospital A: Hospitals C and D. These investor-owned hospitals tend to be specialty-oriented and do not directly compete at the tertiary-care level with Hospital A. Therefore, they are not perceived as being either cooperative or threatening.

Issue-Specific Stakeholder Diagnosis

Not everyone will agree with the set of stakeholders that have been used as examples for each type. There is a very good reason to be uncomfortable with such global classifications of particular stakeholders. The most important issues facing organizations and their managers at a given time change constantly. Of all the possible stakeholders for a given health care organization, the ones who will be relevant to its managers depends on the corporate/competitive strategies being pursued as well as the particular issue. If the issue is cost containment, the stakeholders who are concerned will be different than if the issue is access to health care. The diagnosis of the relevant stakeholders in terms of the four stakeholder types will probably be different on these two issues as well.

As an example, the relationships between Hospital A and its internal stakeholder, regional services, will be explored. In this example, regional services performs important duties to maintain the vital links between the urban hospital (Hospital A) and the regional, or rural, hospitals. In this capacity, regional services is clearly a supportive type of stakeholder to Hospital A, as they attempt to ensure that the regional hospitals act as a referring hospital to Hospital A. However, given the issue-specific scenario shown in Figure 18–1 of Hospital A attempting a strategic alliance between itself and Group A, regional services now faces the introduction of Group A into its company's (Hospital A's) network. The introduction of these physicians from Group A has the potential to represent a threatening action to the smooth operations of regional services, since physicians have historically been a mixed blessing to regional services' major stakeholders, the regional hospitals.

In other words, the potential strategic alliance between Hospital A and Group A may challenge the traditional way regional services conducts business, as perceived by regional services. Therefore, they may react harshly and choose to become a mixed blessing stakeholder regarding this specific issue. This example of the inherent issue specificity in classifying stakeholders into a typology suggests that stakeholder diagnosis is an ongoing activity for health care managers. Managers cannot assume that a stakeholder that is supportive on one issue will be that way on every issue, nor that a stakeholder that is nonsupportive on one issue will be so on another. Both opportunity and danger await the organization from its stakeholders, especially from those of the mixed blessing type.

Moreover, whatever the classification of a particular stakeholder on a specific issue, managers should explicitly classify stakeholders to bring inadvertent managerial biases to the surface. For example, if a manager identifies all stakeholders for any particular issue as nonsupportive, then the manager should critically examine his or her assessment of the relationship between the organization and its stakeholders. If a particular stakeholder always is thought of as the same in terms of threat and cooperation, it suggests that the manager may be missing opportunities for capitalizing on potential for cooperation, but it may also be running the risk of being blindsided by underestimating the potential for threat on a specific issue.

FORMULATING GENERIC STRATEGIES FOR STAKEHOLDER MANAGEMENT

Stakeholder diagnosis of the type attempted in Figure 18–2 suggests some generic strategies for managing stakeholders with different levels of potential for threat and for cooperation. In Figure 18–3, we present a fourfold typology of such strategies. Each of these strategies can be either proactive or reactive. Since executives continually manage a wide variety of stakeholders (in terms of their potential for cooperation and threat), all executives need to use a combination of strategies at any one time.

Strategy 1: Collaborate with the Mixed Blessing Stakeholder

The mixed blessing stakeholder, high on both the dimensions of potential threat and potential cooperation, may best be managed through collaboration. The goal of this strategy is to turn mixed blessing stakeholders into supportive stakeholders. If executives seek to maximize their stakeholders' potential for cooperation, these potentially threatening stakeholders will find their supportive endeavors make it more difficult for them to oppose the organization.

**Stakeholder's
Potential for Threat to the Hospital**

	High	Low
High	*Strategy 1* **COLLABORATE** with the Mixed Blessing Stakeholder	*Strategy 2* **INVOLVE** the Supportive Stakeholder
Low	*Strategy 3* **DEFEND** against the Nonsupportive Stakeholder	*Strategy 4* **MONITOR** the Marginal Stakeholder

Stakeholder's Potential for Cooperation with the Hospital

Figure 18–3 Generic Stakeholder Management Strategies for Hospitals. *Source:* Reprinted from *Challenges in Health Care Management: Strategic Perspectives for Managing Key Stakeholders* by J.D. Blair and M.D. Fottler, p. 133, with permission of Jossey-Bass Publishers, © 1990.

For example, the proposed strategic alliance between Hospital A and Group A (see Figure 18–1) represents a collaborative strategy. If this alliance took the form of building a freestanding surgicenter or imaging center, such collaboration effectively stops the physicians, a mixed blessing stakeholder, from building a center themselves and thus competing with hospital-based surgery or diagnostic procedures. The hospital can contribute its name and capital resources while the physicians will presumably send their patients to the hospital when inpatient services are needed. Both the hospital and the physicians potentially will benefit.

Regional hospitals represent another mixed blessing stakeholder to Hospital A. If Hospital A can use creative contracting covenants to ensure some form of referral pattern from the regional hospitals, Hospital A has effectively utilized the collaborative strategy. However, these contractual covenants could be viewed as a defensive posture of the organization. The use of this kind

of collaborative strategy indicates the caution that must be undertaken when using this strategy.

This caution is warranted because of the inherent instability of mixed blessing stakeholders vis-a-vis the organization. Therefore, an effective collaboration strategy with them may well determine the long-term stakeholder-organization relationship. In other words, if this type of stakeholder is not properly managed through the use of a collaborative strategy, the unstableness of these types of stakeholders could lead to a mixed blessing stakeholder becoming a nonsupportive stakeholder.

Strategy 2: Involve the Supportive Stakeholder

By involving supportive stakeholders in relevant issues, health care executives can maximally capitalize on these stakeholders' cooperative potential. Because these stakeholders pose a low threat potential, they are likely to be ignored as a stakeholder to be managed and, therefore, their cooperative potential may be ignored as well.

Involvement differs from collaboration in two ways: (1) Involvement further activates or enhances the supportive capability of an already supportive stakeholder and (2) collaboration includes an element of caution due to the high potential for threat inherent in mixed blessing stakeholders. With the involvement strategy, the emphasis is not on reducing threat, since its potential is low. Instead, this strategy attempts to capitalize on the already existing potential for cooperation by converting even more of the potential into actual. Collaboration, on the other hand, involves much more of a give and take on the parts of the organization and the stakeholder. Collaboration may require the organization to give up or expend certain key resources or change important policies to gain stakeholder support either through lowering threat and/or by increasing cooperation. As mentioned earlier, collaboration strategies contain an element of caution that involvement strategies do not.

Managers can operationalize the involvement strategy by using participative management techniques, by decentralizing authority to clinical managers, or by engaging in other tactics to increase the decision-making participation of these stakeholders. For example, Hospital A management may invite clinical managers to participate in the analysis and planning for eliminating redundant programs. The clinical managers are more likely to become committed to achieving such an organizational objective than if they had not been involved in establishing it. A key requirement for the success of this type of strategy is the ability of the managers to enlarge their vision of ways to further involve supportive stakeholders in higher levels of cooperation.

Nonmanagerial professional and support employees represent another class of stakeholders who belong in this category and for whom an involving strategy might be effective.[10] Employees do not pose a great deal of direct threat to the organization, although union activism, the perception of poor third-shift conditions, or human resource shortages can make their continued service problematic under certain circumstances. Yet their cooperative potential may not have been fully tapped.

At this time, many group practices and hospitals are explicitly involving their supportive employees and in-house volunteer stakeholders by training them to manage mixed blessing stakeholders such as funded patients, patient's families, and physicians. They are doing this through guest or customer relations programs designed to enhance the management of one or more potentially threatening stakeholders by increasing the cooperative potential of a key internal stakeholder. Another involving stakeholder management technique is the "womb to tomb" marketing approach to caring for patients (see Chapter 26 in this book for specific details of this marketing approach).

Another utilization of involvement is explicitly strategic and focuses on systematically linking human resource management systems and practices to overall strategic management. It is called strategic human resource management (SHRM), and has only recently been introduced into the field of health care management.[11] It is very consistent with the strategic stakeholder management approach, since SHRM increases involvement of a generally supportive internal stakeholder (employees) in furthering the strategic goals of the organization through effective and strategically linked human resource management.

Regarding employee management strategies, hospital executives need to be aware of physician perceptions when entering into alliances with physicians. Physicians generally are considered to be mixed blessing stakeholders from a hospital perspective. However, hospital executives often use involvement strategies to manage them. This can strain the hospital–physician relationship. For example, assume a hospital buys a physician practice, thereby making all the physicians employees of the hospital. If hospital executives try to exert typical hierarchical authority and typical involvement strategies over the newly acquired physicians, the physicians will most likely rebel. Even if the physicians are employees of the hospital, they may still view themselves as partners in the venture. As such, the physicians would expect to be involved in strategic decision making at the highest levels. This example is a classic case of the hospital misdiagnosing the physicians as nonthreatening supportive stakeholders, when, in fact, the physicians are powerful mixed blessing stakeholders.

Strategy 3: Defend against the Nonsupportive Stakeholder

Stakeholders who pose high threat but whose potential for cooperation is low are best managed using a defensive strategy. The federal government and indigent patients are good examples of this nonsupportive stakeholder group for most health care organizations. In terms of Kotter's[12] framework on external dependence, the defense strategy tries to reduce the dependence that forms the basis for the stakeholders' interest in the organization. In stakeholder terms, a defensive strategy involves preventing the stakeholder from imposing costs—or other disincentives—on the organizations.

However, health care executives should *not* attempt to totally eliminate their dependence on nonsupportive stakeholders. Such efforts either are doomed to failure or may result in a negative image for the organization. For example, trying to sever all ties with the federal government is counterproductive if a hospital hopes to market to older patients. And a public hospital that tries to deny access to all indigent patients will almost surely be viewed negatively by the public and the local government.

Consider an example of this defensive strategy in action, using the federal government's regulatory agencies as the stakeholder. For example, given the regulations hospitals face, their most appropriate tactic is to explore ways of complying with the demands imposed by the federal government at the least possible cost.

Diagnostic-related groups (DRGs) that produce a surplus for the hospitals define their areas of distinctive competence. Hence, hospital executives might adopt a case-mix approach to the delivery of health care, modifying the services they offer based on cost and process accounting. Investing in more effective management information systems and specialized medical records "grouper" software, and recruiting and paying for more highly skilled medical records personnel are all part of this defensive strategy vis-a-vis a nonsupportive, demanding third-party payor and/or regulator.

This generic strategy also can take the form of driving out or reducing competition. For example, Hospital A (Figure 18–1) might be able to successfully drive out competition from Hospital B (another private tertiary-care hospital) by securing a monopoly over a particular market segment through PPO contracting. On the other hand, to reduce competition with urgi- or surgicenters, Hospital A could build new ambulatory facilities or restructure existing facilities. In these examples of the defense strategy, the connection of stakeholder management to broader strategic management is very clear, involving many traditional marketing and strategic notions for handling competitors.

Indigent patients often are thought of as nonsupportive of hospitals, especially county facilities. A defensive strategy that could be used on indigent nonsupportive stakeholders would be for the hospital to close its doors on these types of patients. This would effectively stop the indigents from using expensive emergency department facilities in the place of relatively less expensive primary care clinics. However, rather than resort to such drastic measures, perhaps if the county hospital opened up more primary care clinics in surrounding regions and informed the indigent population about the services provided at the clinics, the county hospital might change these nonsupportive stakeholders to mixed blessing stakeholders. While the stakeholders still would be high on threat potential, at least the stakeholders would now have some potential element for cooperation.

Strategy 4: Monitor the Marginal Stakeholder

Monitoring helps manage those marginal stakeholders whose potential for both threat or cooperation is low. For example, numerous special interest groups are opposed to certain procedures, such as abortion or artificial implants, or are concerned about certain patient groups such as the aged. Typically, these groups have only a marginal stake in the activities of the organization, affecting operations indirectly through advocating a moral or ethical viewpoint. Taxpayers and stockholders also represent marginal stakeholders. They are unlikely to be either of much help or much hindrance unless the organization takes actions that activate them. In essence these stakeholders are unstable when viewed by the organization. They can move into any one of the other three types of stakeholders if the issue is of enough importance to them.

Often patient families are considered as marginal stakeholders. Leaving this key marginal stakeholder unmonitored ignores the possibility of the development of a supportive stakeholder that can make a decisive difference in facilitating the course of patient care. On the other hand, dissatisfied patient families that go unnoticed potentially can wreak havoc on an organization. Assigning specific responsibility for monitoring this stakeholder to a member of the patient care team can avert disaster for the organization's management.

The underlying philosophy for managing these marginal stakeholders is proactively maintaining the status quo, but with finances and management time kept to a minimum. Executives address issues on an ad hoc basis. The general thrust of this approach is to "let sleeping dogs lie." Keeping them asleep, however, may require an organization to engage in ongoing public relations activities and be sensitive to issues that could activate these groups to become an actual threat.

Marginal stakeholders should—in general— be minimally satisfied. What it takes to keep a particular marginal stakeholder minimally satisfied may increase over time, thus necessitating greater involvement of managerial time and other organizational resources. Managers must monitor such expenditures of inducement or disinducements to determine whether they have become excessive or whether they are perhaps inadequate at this time because the marginal stakeholder has become a key stakeholder, in general or on a particular issue.

An Overarching Stakeholder Management Strategy

In addition to using the four strategies specifically tailored for stakeholders who are classified into one of the four diagnostic categories, health care executives also may employ an overarching strategy. This overarching strategy moves the stakeholders from a less favorable category to a more favorable one. Then, the stakeholder can be managed using the generic strategy most appropriate for that new diagnostic category.

For example, rather than simply defend against the news media as a nonsupportive stakeholder, a hospital could implement an aggressive program of external relations with openness to the media. If successful, the program would change the news media to a less threatening category as a marginal stakeholder, allowing it to be managed through a monitoring strategy. If the hospital is willing to invest more time, energy, skill, and money in the effort, the media might even become a supportive stakeholder.

In the continuing example of Hospital A (see Figure 18–1), contemplating a strategic alliance with a mixed blessing stakeholder (Group A) can present an opportunity for Hospital A. If Hospital A effectively manages Group A with a collaborative strategy such as building a surgicenter for the group of physicians, Hospital A also may have successfully turned a mixed blessing stakeholder into a less threatening supportive stakeholder.

However, it is important to recognize that even if mixed blessing stakeholders are collaboratively managed, they may not become supportive stakeholders. Every player in this new era of health care delivery is not voluntarily becoming involved and integrated. As such, stakeholders do not always react as the strategy suggests. Additionally, if long-term strategic goals are pursued without ensuring tactical success, stakeholder management will not work effectively. For example, organizations can create structural integration (i.e., strategic integration) fairly early. However, if social and cultural integration (i.e., tactical integration) is not achieved, then the new structure may not work.

Of course, stakeholders generally will not just sit still and be managed. Stakeholders who are powerful and, hence, threatening are as likely to try to manage organizations as vice versa. Many organizations and their stakeholders continuously engage in management and countermanagement strategies. To manage these stakeholders effectively, executives should continuously identify stakeholders and match their diagnosis with appropriate strategies. In other words, it is suggested that periodic repetition of the prior steps to ensure that key assumptions still apply is a prudent strategy.

STRATEGY IMPLEMENTATION AND OUTCOMES OF EFFECTIVE STRATEGIC STAKEHOLDER MANAGEMENT

Strategic stakeholder management represents a new way of thinking for health care executives. Given the importance of key stakeholders for an organization's overall business strategy, successful implementation of the stakeholder management concept should provide the organization with a competitive advantage. At best, hospital executives' stakeholder management perspectives are incomplete, and their approaches to stakeholder assessment are underdeveloped and haphazard. At worst, they display a total lack of explicit awareness of, and involvement in, a systematic and effective stakeholder management approach.[13]

This chapter has focused on further developing systematic and strategic stakeholder approaches—integrated with still broader strategic management issues. A key issue in all strategic action is the implementation of the planned and articulated strategy. As such, this chapter turns from conceptual planning to the outcomes of organized action.

Figure 18–4 is an illustration of what can occur with a consistent and conscientious stakeholder management implementation strategy. Notice that Figure 18–4 is basically the same as Figure 18–1, except for shading of some boxes. It shows the development of a quite fully integrated health care system. The three necessary components of these integrated delivery networks are present: a hospital, a large multispecialty physician group, and a health plan.

The shading of the boxes (as the legend shows) represents the hospital's different stakeholders and the nature of their relationships now that the strategic alliance between Hospital A and Group A has been consummated. Assuming all the various stakeholder relationships were effectively managed and formalized into this specific vertical integration, the original patterns of informal but interconnected stakeholder relationships now serve to structure network relationships and systems.

The new integrated delivery system (Figure 18–4) still has embedded within it many formal and informal networks. These integrated network systems are an outcome of strategic stakeholder management. However, even with the formal development of this integrated health care delivery system, sophisticated health care executives know the game is really just beginning. New stakeholder challenges will have been raised. Stronger competitors (by virtue of the network) and new and varied partners will have emerged. The health care delivery system will be more complex and complicated than ever before. The number of relationships will have grown geometrically. No longer will the old internally oriented human resources approach to solving production problems suffice.

Executives will not have the same level of hierarchical control and the hospital will no longer be independent as a result of developing alli-

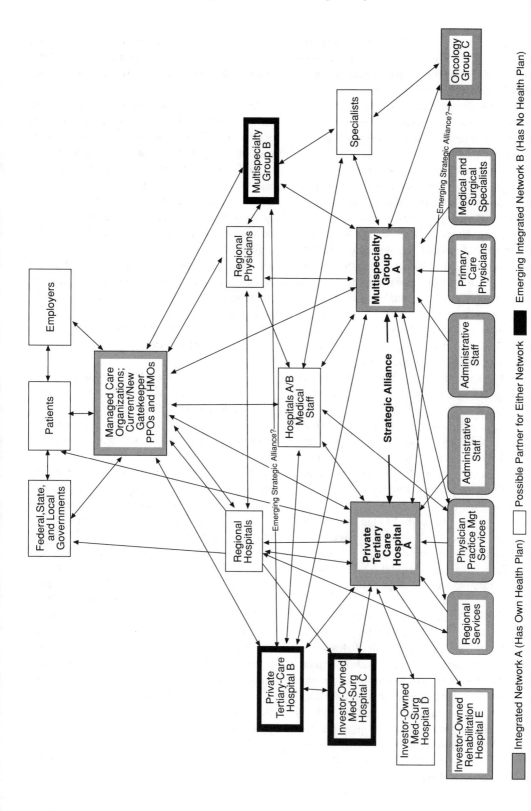

Figure 18–4 Competing Integrated Regional Networks

ances. The overall power of the hospital may increase, but at significant cost to independence and control. Executives must coordinate with and be acceptable to strategic partners. All of this requires further development of yet additional tactics and stakeholder management strategies to manage these new changing relationships.

Recall that in Figure 18–1, Hospital A was contemplating a strategic alliance with Group A. Recall also that both Hospital A and Group A each counted managed care organizations as key stakeholders. Hospital B, however, was acting independently from its key stakeholders. In fact, from Figure 18–1, it does not appear that Hospital B was even thinking about forming any kind of increasingly complex and integrated health care delivery network.

Attention now should be turned back to Figure 18–4. Notice that the strategic alliance between Hospital A and Group A has been finalized. This has effectively divided the entire health care delivery system for the area represented by the figure into three components: those organizations affiliated with Network A, those organizations affiliated with the emerging Network B, and those organizations that have yet to be included in either network, but that are possible partners for either network.

Although all the pertinent actions and reactions to get from Figure 18–1 to Figure 18–4 are shown on Figure 18–4, several changes must have taken place because of the successful strategic alliance between Hospital A and Group A. A representative sample of possible scenarios follows.

Hospital A, Group A, and a managed care organization have created a truly integrated health care delivery network. As a result of Hospital A effectively utilizing strategic stakeholder management, it has been able to change its internal mixed blessing stakeholder (regional services, as discussed in the stakeholder typology section) into a supportive stakeholder through the creation of a joint team composed of players from regional services and physician practice management services. Together, this joint team will effectively manage those regional hospitals and regional physicians in hopes of enticing both stakeholders into joining Hospital A's health care network.

Additionally, a joint strategy team has been created between the internal administrative staff of Hospital A and the internal administrative staff of Group A. This new team was developed to facilitate the smooth transition of Hospital A and Group A from thinking of each other as mixed blessing stakeholders to seeing each other as strongly supportive. A key component of this new joint strategy team would include the development of a joint information systems capability. This would be necessary to ensure that the real and important issues of both the hospital and the physicians are met. It is likely that neither information system currently in place at either the hospital or the group practice would provide the necessary information to the other party or to the alliance itself.

With the consummation of the strategic alliance, both administrative staffs are supportive stakeholders to the other and are now strategically involved in each other's organization. However, just because a strategic alliance becomes formalized does not mean that all the employees and managers of each respective organization will instantly function as supportive stakeholders. Rather, stakeholder management tactics such as joint strategic teams composed of players from both fields are necessary in order to begin the process of jointly moving together to face the new challenges in the environment.

Figure 18–4 also shows the disappearance of the relationship between Hospital A and Hospital D. It should be noted that Hospital D is not affiliated with any other stakeholder shown on the stakeholder map. For reasons such as geographic location, quality of medical staff, deteriorating physical plant, etc., Hospital D is no longer viewed as playing an important part of the strategic plans of any other organization depicted in Figure 18–4. This more than likely resulted from Hospital D's mismanagement of its stakeholders or its lack of unique strategic value as a partner.

Hospital B, a direct competitor and non-supportive stakeholder to Hospital A, is attempting to imitate the successful strategic alliance between Hospital A and Group A. Hospital B is involved in an emerging strategic alliance with Group B. However, Hospital A is not content with being the first to form a health care network. On the contrary, Hospital A hopes to maintain that lead in strategic alliance formation. Notice the potential new strategic alliance between Hospital A and Group C. With Hospital A's proven success at creating network partners through the accurate diagnosis, classification, and management of stakeholders, Hospital A undoubtedly will be able to continue expanding its network.

IDENTIFYING MANAGERIAL RESPONSIBILITY FOR DIFFERENT STAKEHOLDERS

While the previous sections have shown the variety of stakeholders who have an interest in today's health care organization (and, specifically, in today's hospitals and hospital systems), it would be a mistake to assume that the Chief Executive Officer (CEO) or any other single individual manages all of these diverse stakeholders. Instead, the evolution of some of these organizations has seen the development of management specialists whose major purpose is to manage particular stakeholders. For example, in some organizations a medical staff director, or Vice President for Medical Affairs (VPMA), has the major responsibility for managing the medical staff. Nonetheless, others, including the CEO, are also available to help handle non-routine problems.

In our continuing example, there are four executives who also typically devote much of their time to managing several key stakeholders. These roles were chosen as examples—but not the only ones—of managers who have responsibilities for several stakeholders.

The Director of Physician Practice Management Services (PPMS) is responsible for developing a physician/provider network capable of delivering health care to the insured patient base in an efficient, cost-effective manner. This person is also integrally involved in medical staff development and recruiting. The Director of Regional Services (RS) has been discussed previously (recall all of our earlier examples involving regional services). Here it is important to note that RS can work collaboratively with PPMS by creating joint RS/PPMS teams to provide service to regional physicians affiliated with rural hospitals in Hospital A's regional network.

The Chief Financial Officer (CFO) and the Vice President of Marketing (VPM) will work closely with Hospital A's new network partner, the health plan as managed-care organization. As a result of Hospital A forming this health care delivery network, the hospital has assumed a much greater portion of the financial risk than it previously had. For example, with capitation, the hospital agrees to treat all the patients in a given population for a preset amount of money. If the patient's medical bills exceed this preset amount, the health care providers absorb the excess cost. Due to this increased financial risk, the CFO is quite involved with the new network risk contracting functions. The VPM has direct responsibility for promoting Hospital A's interests (both individually and in the network). The "all-in-one" concept of health care delivery is still new to the purchasers of health care. A key responsibility of the VPM is to counter any actions by competing health care networks.

A required characteristic of each of these specific hospital executives is that each one of them must let go of the old hospital mentality of "filling beds" and "if we own it, we can control it." Instead, they must embrace the new health care network mentality of providing the highest quality, easiest access, most cost-effective health care for a given population. As previously mentioned, physicians are generally reluctant to be managed or controlled by hospital executives. As such, hospital executives need to develop a mentality that will allow for physicians to remain an important part of the strategic direction of the new health care delivery network, while also ensuring that the new system runs well.

Stakeholder maps that show the potential opportunities and responsibilities of each stakeholder manager can aid in managers' understanding of the strategic stakeholder process. This technique provides a way to go from a general stakeholder map developed during stakeholder assessment to incorporating stakeholder management into an executive's job description. This aids in clarifying and communicating unique and overlapping managerial roles and responsibilities. Obviously, development of these maps requires some agreement among the various managers concerning who (singular or plural) will manage which stakeholders on which issues. This process typically involves internal negotiations and the development of organizational policies and procedures. The advantage of the stakeholder map is to clarify relationships and responsibilities.

CONCLUSION

To survive the turbulent and revolutionary changes facing the health care industry, health care executives must better manage their external, interface, and internal stakeholders. Organizations have to rethink their strategies and operations as they face increasing and potentially conflicting demands for effectiveness and efficiency from these stakeholders. Executives must minimally satisfy the needs of marginal stakeholders while they maximally satisfy the needs of key stakeholders.

To satisfy key stakeholders, managers must make two critical assessments about these stakeholders: their potential to threaten the organization and their potential to cooperate with it. When determining the stakeholder's orientation, managers should account for factors such as control of resources, relative power, likelihood and supportiveness of potential stakeholder action, and coalition formation. These factors should be interpreted in light of the specific context and history of the organization's relations with it, and other key stakeholders influencing the organization as well as that stakeholder.

Incorrectly categorizing a stakeholder into the wrong classification type is, in itself, indicative of a lack of stakeholder management expertise. However, it leads to an even worse problem, for, if a stakeholder is incorrectly classified, the chosen strategy for managing that stakeholder will obviously be wrong also. Using the wrong strategic stakeholder management strategy can be very detrimental to an organization. Incorrectly classified stakeholders will be more likely to move from whichever type they are to a type that has a greater potential for threat coupled with even less potential for cooperation.

The stakeholder's orientation discloses whether it is supportive, marginal, nonsupportive, or a mixed blessing. As an overarching strategy, managers should try to change their organization's relationships with the stakeholder from a less favorable category to a more favorable one. Then, the stakeholder can be managed using the generic strategy most appropriate for that "new" diagnostic category. In other words, health care managers should involve supportive stakeholders, monitor marginal stakeholders, defend against nonsupportive stakeholders, and collaborate with mixed blessing stakeholders.

Executives need to do more than merely identify stakeholders or react to stakeholder demands. They must proactively develop or enhance their organization's capacity for strategic stakeholder management rather than concentrating only on effectively dealing with a particular stakeholder on a specific issue. This means they need to satisfy their key stakeholders by offering appropriate inducements in exchange for essential contributions. Executives also should monitor their marginal stakeholders so that they do not become key nonsupportive stakeholders and confront the organization with undesired discontributions.

In order to effectively manage stakeholders, health care executives must recognize that the implementation of strategic stakeholder management strategies requires a thorough understanding of negotiation strategies.[14]

To survive in the future, organizations should establish goals for their relationships with current and potential stakeholders as part of an effective strategic management process.[15] Such goal setting should include clear analyses and consideration of both the organization's and the stakeholder's goals.

Even with effective strategic stakeholder management activities, many challenges will exist for health care executives. The turbulent, unpredictable, and, yes, exciting times are not over for the health care industry. Government reforms will continue to be proffered. Employer coalitions will gain in strength and demand concessions from health care providers and administrators. Managed care will become a stronger force. The game is far from over. However, those health care organizations that take an active lead in managing their stakeholders and that consciously build stakeholder management into their strategic plans will increase the accuracy of their stakeholder diagnoses and will begin to gain from the effectiveness of their strategic stakeholder management strategies.

NOTES

1. Arthur Andersen and Co., Best Practices Report on Physician/Hospital Integration—An Overview, 1993; J.D. Blair, et al., Achieving Competitive Advantage through and within Integrated Health Care Networks: Synthesizing and Applying Firm Resource and Stakeholder Management Theory (Lubbock, Tex.: unpublished manuscript, area of management, Texas Tech University, January 1994); B. Borys and D.B. Jemison, Hybrid Arrangements as Strategic Alliances: Theoretical Issues in Organizational Combinations, *Academy of Management Review* 14, no. 2 (1989):234–249; L.R. Burns and D.R. Thorpe, Trends and Models in Physician-Hospital Organization, *Health Care Management Review* 18, no. 4 (1993):7–20; R. Gillies, et al., Conceptualizing and Measuring Integration: Findings from the Health Systems Integration Study, *Hospital & Health Services Administration* 38, no. 4 (1993): 467–489; S.M. Shortell, et al., Creating Organized Delivery Systems: The Barriers and Facilitators, *Hospital & Health Services Administration* 38, no. 4 (1993):447–466.

2. J.D. Blair and M.D. Fottler, *Challenges in Health Care Management: Strategic Perspectives for Managing Key Stakeholders* (San Francisco, CA: Jossey-Bass Publishers, 1990); J.D. Blair, et al., A Stakeholder Management Perspective on Military Health Care, *Armed Forces & Society,* no. 4 (1992):548–575; M.D. Fottler, et al., Assessing Key Stakeholders: Who Matters to Hospitals and Why? *Hospital & Health Services Administration* 34, no. 4 (1989):525–546; R.E. Freeman, *Strategic Management: A Stakeholder Approach* (Marshfield, Mass.: Pitman Publishing, 1994); R.O. Mason and J.J. Mitroff, *Challenging Strategic Planning Assumptions* (New York: John Wiley & Sons, Inc., 1981); G.T. Savage, et al., Strategies for Assessing and Managing Stakeholders, *Academy of Management Executive* 5, no. 2 (1991):61–75.

3. Blair and Fottler, *Challenges in Health Care Management.*

4. J.D. Blair and C.J. Whitehead, Too Many on the See-saw: Stakeholder Diagnosis and Management for Hospitals, *Hospitals and Health Services Management* 33, no. 2 (1988):152–156; Freeman, *Strategic Management;* C.J. Whitehead, et al., Stakeholder Supportiveness and Strategic Vulnerability: Implications for the HMO Industry's Competitive Strategy, *Health Care Management Review* 14, no. 3:65–76.

5. D. Miller and P.H. Friesen, Archetypes of Strategy Formulation, *Management Science* 24 (1978):921–933.

6. J.D. Blair and K.B. Boal, Strategy Formation Processes in Health Care Organizations: A Context-Specific Examination of Context-Free Strategy Issues, *Journal of Management* 17, no. 2 (1991):305–344; S.M. Shortell, *Strategic Choices for America's Hospitals: Managing Change in Turbulent Times* (San Francisco, Calif.: Jossey-Bass Publishers, 1990).

7. J. Pfeffer and G. Salancik, *The External Control of Organizations: A Resource Dependence Perspective* (New York: Harper and Row, 1978).

8. D.C. Coddington, et al., *Integrated Health Care: Reorganizing the Physician, Hospital and Health Plan Relationship* (Englewood, Colo.: MGMA, 1994); D.C. Coddington, et al., Integrated Health Care Systems: The Key Characteristics, *Medical Group Management Journal* November/December (1993):76–80.

9. Blair and Whitehead, Too Many on the Seesaw.

10. Blair and Fottler, *Challenges in Health Care Management.*

11. M.D. Fottler, et al., eds., *Strategic Management of Human Resources in Health Services Organizations* (New York: John Wiley & Sons, Inc., 1988); M.D. Fottler, et al., Achieving Competitive Advantage Through Strategic Human Resources Management, *Hospital & Health Services Administration* 35, no. 3 (1990):341–363.

12. J.P. Kotter, Managing External Dependence, *Academy of Management Review* 4, no. 1 (1979):87–92.

13. Blair and Fottler, *Challenges in Health Care Management.*

14. Blair and Fottler, *Challenges in Health Care Management,* Chapter 5; J.D. Blair, et al., A Strategic Approach for Negotiating with Hospital Stakeholders, *Health Care Management Review* 14, no. 1 (1989):13–23; G.T. Savage and J.D. Blair, The Importance of Relationships in Hospital Negotiation Strategies, *Hospitals & Health Service Administration* 34, no. 2 (1989):231–253.

15. Blair and Boal, Strategy Formation Processes in Health Care Organizations; M.E. Porter, *Competitive Advantage* (New York: Free Press, 1985); M.E. Porter, *Competitive Strategy* (New York: Free Press, 1980); Shortell, et al., *Strategic Choices for America's Hospitals.*

JOHN D. BLAIR, PhD, is Professor of Management; Director, the MBA Program in Health Organization Management (HOM) in the College of Business Administration; and Associate Chair of the Health Organization Management Department in the School of Medicine at Texas Tech University. He is also Director of Medical Group Strategy Research Network for the Institute for Management and Leadership Research and the past Chair of the Health Care Administration Division of the National Academy of Management. He is also Co-Principal Investigator of the *Facing the Uncertain Future* Delphi Study, a joint project between the Medical Group Management Association (MGMA) and Texas Tech University. His most recent books are *Challenges in Health Care Management: Strategic Perspectives on Managing Key Stakeholders* (1990) and *Challenges in Military Health Care* (1993). He received his PhD from the University of Michigan in 1975.

TIMOTHY M. ROTARIUS, MBA, is a PhD student in Strategic Management, and Project Coordinator for the Medical Group Strategy Research Network in the Institute for Management and Leadership Research in the College of Business Administration at Texas Tech University. He is also Co-Project Director of the *Facing the Uncertain Future* Delphi Study, a joint project between the Medical Group Management Association (MGMA) and Texas Tech University. He has previously held administrative and operational positions in a large multispecialty group practice. Additionally, he has been professionally involved in the development and implementation of major operational efficiency improvements, in labor and management relations, and in venture capital investment and divestiture analysis. He received his MBA from the University of New Mexico.

KAROLYN B. SHEPHERD, MBA (HOM), is Vice President of Development for King's Daughter Clinic, in Temple, Texas. Her responsibilities include building that multispecialty medical group's integrated delivery system. Previously, she was Director of Practice Management for the Lubbock Methodist Hospital System, the largest health network in Texas. She was responsible for the planning and implementation of the department that manages the hospital's most significant stakeholder, the physician. Also, as the principle of CBS Enterprises, she served for 14 years as a financial and management consultant to private industry. She received her MBA from Texas Tech University.

CARLTON J. WHITEHEAD, PhD, is Coordinator and Professor, Area of Management; Director, Research Program in Organizational Design and Strategic Management, Institute for Management and Leadership Research; Associate Director, Texas Center for Productivity and Quality of Work Life in the College of Business Administration, Texas Tech University; and Professor of Health Organization Management, School of Medicine, Texas Tech University Health Sciences Center. He has published extensively in scholarly journals and books, and participated actively in professional organizations. He received his PhD from Louisiana State University.

Chapter 19

Human Resources Management

Norman Metzger

Social forecaster John Naisbeth points to the biggest challenge of all for those who will be in human resources management in the last decade of this century and in the early part of the twenty-first century: it is the need to reconceptualize roles. Change will be the order of the day. New technology; robots; electronic workstations; and local, regional, and international communication networks will change the work arena. The most dramatic change of all will be the rapid decline in rigidly defined jobs. The concept of work in the twenty-first century will *not* be the same as that which was prevalent in the twentieth century. Organizational structures will be as unfamiliar to us as those in the twentieth century were to individuals familiar with nineteenth-century organizational patterns.

Naisbeth's predictions certainly are applicable to the rapidly evolving health care industry, in which few solo hospitals and physicians may exist in the future. Integrated health delivery systems, comprised of organizations (e.g., hospitals, physician groups, surgery centers) that historically may have had little to do with one another (and, in fact, may have been competitors) will challenge future generations of managers and human resource professionals.

HUMAN RESOURCES MANAGEMENT: HISTORICAL BACKGROUND

The earliest work relationships were based upon the principle of slavery. Masters owned and commanded as many workers as they financially could support. There was very little concern about inefficient use of labor, and slaves were available if one had the resources to feed them. Slave owners assumed many of the functions that one associates with modern personnel administration, e.g., recruitment (the cruel but efficient method of enslaving and transporting able-bodied workers), training, housing, catering, and industrial medicine. The one discipline that was conspicuously absent was collective bargaining.

The serf system developed in the agriculturally based society of the Middle Ages. Such workers were not chattel, but were attached to the land that they worked. It was not until the advent of the handicraft system, the true forerunner of modern industrial society, that a more sophisticated approach to training and management developed. This new approach was a system of craftsmen who took on younger men as apprentices and taught them a trade. Apprentices were paid little, if any, wages and lived with their masters. However, they could aspire to, and often reach, journeyman status. Indeed, if they could save money and purchase a few tools, they could start their own business. Craft guilds developed from this system. These associations regulated the quality of materials, wages paid, and terms and conditions of apprenticeship training. Personnel management in the handicraft system was the responsibility of the master craftsman.

During the Industrial Revolution, the status of the worker changed dramatically. The enormous expansion of markets, much more sophisticated and efficient transportation, and the continuous development and improvement of machines that replaced hand tools and steam power multiplied the efforts of individual workers. New social and economic classes emerged, and wage earners for the first time formed a distinct class. Slowly, but perceptibly, a changing attitude toward the worker evolved. A growing emphasis was placed on personal and individual values. Because workers could move to new areas where free land was available, for the first time employers realized that a dissatisfied employee could leave the job and become an independent landowner or farmer.

Personnel management did not become a distinct discipline until the development of large organizations, in which a great number of people came to work together. Paternalistic at first, the discipline was then geared to prevent or undermine unions; finally, it evolved into a professional approach to the managing of labor. It started slowly and was initially limited to specific employment departments. B.F. Goodrich developed the first employment department in 1900. A labor department was formed in 1902 at National Cash Register. In 1910 Plimpton Press had a full-fledged personnel department. The growing emergence of personnel departments in organizations was pointed out in a 1920 book by Ordway Tead and Henry C. Metcalf, *Personnel Administration: Its Principles and Practices:*

> . . . [T]he fundamental reason for the development of a separate administra-

tive division for the direction of the human relations is a growing recognition that people are endowed with characteristics different from those of machines or of raw materials. And if people are to be directed in ways which give best results, the direction must be specialized just as direction in the other major fields of management have been specialized.[1]

Tead and Metcalf were early observers of the growing importance of personnel administration as a management science. They certainly were precocious in their acknowledgment that:

> it is manifestly true that in the majority of corporations production is today affected adversely not so much because of technical inadequacies as because of the failure of managers to recognize that workers are human beings who demand the considerate treatment which only intelligence and insight regarding human nature can suggest.[2]

Two factors—welfarism and the scientific management school—contributed to the institution of a formal employment management department in U.S. industrial plants. Welfarism, more commonly termed "paternalism," was a movement active in both society at large and within the industrial world in the 1920s. It was aimed at improving the general tenor of American life and the living standards of the poor and unfortunate by ameliorating hard working conditions. Under this general rubric, managements made available various facilities, such as libraries and recreational activities; offered financial assistance for education; provided medical care; and instituted hygienic measures for their workers.[3] Personnel or employment departments had the responsibility of literally buying employee loyalty through the development and administration of a host of different types of welfare plans, most of them aimed at curbing union membership and keeping labor costs at a minimum. In addition, during the period of the 1920s many states passed workers' compensation laws, which became a prime force in causing employers to take positive steps to reduce and prevent work injuries and to organize company health programs.

The scientific management school was a product of many industrial engineers, but none more important than Frederick M. Taylor, who claimed that hidden waste in an organization and the resultant costs were caused by the inefficient use of labor. He introduced the concept of standardization of equipment and conditions, so that work could be more efficiently performed. Taylor believed that workers needed to be "won over" and "led" by management, and he was firmly committed to the legitimacy of management's unshared hegemony over the work process and workplace.

Taylor's theories had a great effect on the development of the field of professional personnel management. Although he could not be deemed the father of modern personnel administration, his insistence that management must pay attention to matters such as employee selection, training, and compensation programs was indeed a basic element from which modern human resources management developed. However, his quantitative approach to human relations has been greatly discredited by the labor industrial psychologists—the behavioral scientists—and his motives are still suspect.

Elton Mayo and F.J. Roethlisberger made an enormous contribution to the development of modern human resources management. Their research at the Hawthorne plant of the Western Electric Company recognized complex working relationships that had been previously overlooked. They found that workers tend to cluster together in informal groups in order to fill a void in their lives that results from the lack of attention paid by the modern industrial organization to their basic need for cooperation and comradeship. Many years later Rensis Likert and Daniel Katz[4] conducted research that supported the important role managers play in the success of an organization. Employee-centered supervisors—those that were cooperative, reasonable, and ex-

ercised a democratic management style—were more successful than production-centered supervisors who were more defensive and authoritarian. Frederick Herzberg[5] saw the human desire for achievement as a critical element in the efficient operation of any institution. He concluded that management's great deficiency is its failure to capitalize on this desire.

Finally, A.H. Maslow made significant contributions to the understanding of worker needs. His research indicated that, although the thwarting of unimportant desires produces no psychological results, thwarting of a basically important need does have a psychological effect. He established that there are at least five sets of goals or basic needs: physiological, safety, love, esteem, and self-actualization. These basic goals are related to each other and arranged in a hierarchy of importance. When a need is fairly well satisfied, the next higher need emerges. He therefore concluded that the human being is a perpetually wanting animal.[6] Building on Maslow's work, behavioral scientists in general see the worker as having personal and social as well as economic needs. In this view, the worker does not want to be paid for merely doing what he or she is told, but also wants to satisfy, through the work, a need for security, independence, participation, and growth. This perspective is the basis of human resources management as practiced successfully in many hospitals throughout the country.

The profession of personnel management involves the development, application, and evaluation of policies, procedures, methods, and, most importantly, programs—broad-based and continuing—relating to the individual in the organization. The field of human resources management is eclectic, drawing from many other disciplines, such as sociology, economics, psychology, and law.

FUNCTIONS AND RESPONSIBILITIES OF THE HUMAN RESOURCES DEPARTMENT

The health care field is both unique and complex. Over 300 distinct jobs or major job classifications can be identified in the hospital industry. The industry's work force is predominantly female; it is comparatively young, with a majority of workers under 35; it is highly fragmented, compartmentalized by function and occupation, with between 50 and 70 departments in most major short-term hospitals. It is slightly more organized by unions than general industries throughout the United States (unions still win more elections in the health care industry than they do in the general industry elections throughout the United States). In short, the hospital industry is huge and labor-intensive.

More than half of the U.S. work force now consists of minorities, recent immigrants, and women. White males are a statistical minority. White males would make up only 15 percent of the increase in the work force over the next 10 years. The fastest growing segment of the U.S. population is over 85 and the fastest growing segment of the work force is between the ages of 45 and 64. The changes in the makeup of the work force have affected the health care industry (see Table 19–1). With the presence of more women and minorities in management positions, the industry is experiencing a group with a fresh perspective of the workplace. These are employees who want to be involved in decision making about their jobs. Changes in employee perspectives must be juxtaposed with the downsizing

Table 19–1 The Work Force in 2005

Fastest-growing health care occupations, 1990–2005

| | Employment* | | |
Occupation	1990	2005	Percent Increase
Home health aides	287	550	91.7
Paralegals	90	167	85.2
Systems analysts	463	829	78.9
Personal/home care aides	103	183	76.7
Physical therapists	88	155	76.0
Medical assistants	165	287	73.9
Radiologic technologists	149	252	69.5
Medical secretaries	232	390	68.3
Physical therapy assts.	45	74	64.0
Surgical technologists	38	59	55.2
Medical records technicians	52	80	54.3
Respiratory therapists	60	91	52.1
Child care workers	725	1,078	48.8
Registered nurses	1,727	2,494	44.4
Nursing aides/orderlies	1,274	1,826	43.4
LPNs	644	913	41.9

*Numbers in thousands
Source: Bureau of Labor Statistics: *Monthly Labor Review*, November 1991, Vol. 114, No. 11.

Who's entering the work force?

Hispanics: a 75% increase
Asians and others: a 74% increase
Blacks: a 32% increase
Women: a 26% increase

Who's leaving the work force?

White, non-Hispanic males: 82% of those leaving

Source: Kutscher, Ronald E. "New BLS projections: findings and implications." *Monthly Labor Review*, November 1991, Vol. 114, No. 11.

that many health care organizations have experienced in the past decade. Many boards of trustees and CEOs have come to understand the need to restructure the work environment. Health care institutions are becoming leaner, flatter, and far more flexible. Notwithstanding the limited budgets now in effect in many health care institutions, there is a far greater investment in human resources than in the past. Incentive systems that are different from traditional compensation programs are prevalent. The need to build trust between management and its employees had come to the fore. With all these changes, the role of the human resources department has been transformed radically from guarding management prerogatives, to developing a caring and nurturing environment.

To manage this labor-intensive industry, a human resources department should fulfill many of the following functions:

1. Human Resources Planning
   - job analysis; job descriptions
   - planning of staffing levels
   - establishment of work force plans and policies: determination of work force objectives and inventory of current work force
   - job evaluation: establishing comparative worth of each job, wage surveys, and classification and pricing of jobs
   - wage and salary administration: designing records and information systems, control of the Table of Organization, designing and administering merit programs, and processing forms

2. Employment
   - identifying sources of supply: public and private agencies, search organizations, and specialized agencies (retired individuals and handicapped)
   - selection: design of forms
   - interviewing, testing, and reference checks
   - referral for pre-employment physicals
   - maintenance of records and turnover statistics

3. Induction and Orientation
   - design of staff orientation program
   - coordination of line orientation program
   - processing for benefits
   - follow-up: probationary period

4. Benefits Administration
   - processing of new employees
   - maintenance of records
   - design of plans
   - policing ERISA requirements
   - trusteeship of various plans

5. Personnel Training and Development
   - design and coordination of skills training and management development programs
   - assessment centers
   - administration of tuition refund program

6. Evaluation and Motivation of Work Force
   - design and administration of performance evaluation program
   - design and administration of incentive program
   - coordination of quality-of-work-life program
   - training of management in motivational skills
   - design and implementation of job enrichment program
   - design and coordination of employee communication programs
   - administration of employee newsletter

7. Labor Relations
   - collective bargaining
   - contract administration: discipline and discharge administration, grievance and arbitration procedures, and NLRB hearings
   - affirmative action programs and EEO provisions

8. Health and Safety Responsibility
   - physical examinations
   - safety and health education programs
   - OSHA requirements

9. Employee Recreation and Activities
   - employee housing, food service, and recreational programs
10. Personnel Policies
    - design and administration
    - implementation of recommended changes
11. Outplacement
    - retiree programs, including services for terminated employees and counseling services

Human Resources Planning

The need for scientific wage determination in hospitals is no longer in question. Dissatisfaction about wages has three separate causes: inequities among wage rates paid within classifications and among classifications that employees consider similar to their own, individual or group pressure for higher earning power, and inappropriate market positioning. Hospitals have come to accept that a sound method of establishing wages is through job evaluation. Job evaluation has three purposes: to determine the relative worth of the various jobs in the institution, to establish a wage scale that incorporates fair differentials among jobs, and to correct pay inequities where necessary. When defensible job rates are established on a quasi-scientific and logical basis, the issue of compensation is removed from the world of conjecture, arbitrariness, and subjectivity and personalized rates are abolished. By establishing a formal wage pattern that conforms to hospital wage rates in the area and in general with community wage rates, job evaluation is a key tool for the administration in meeting competition.

Job Analysis

Job analysis is the scientific determination of the actual nature of a specific job. Each of the tasks that make up the job is studied, as well as the skills, knowledge, abilities, and responsibilities required of the worker. Job analysis examines the job *as it is*—its duties, responsibilities, working conditions, and relationship to other jobs. There are three steps in the analysis of any job: identifying the job completely and accurately, describing the tasks of the job, and indicating the requirements for a successful performance.

Through a job analysis job facts are secured for the following purposes:

- *Job evaluation:* The facts assembled from a job analysis are used in the evaluation of jobs that will set the wages.
- *Selection and placement:* Job analysis results in job descriptions—specifications that are an orderly and effective guide for matching applicants to positions.
- *Performance evaluation:* Quantified job descriptions provide standards against which an employee may be rated.
- *Training:* Detailed information provided by job analysis can serve as a basis for a training department's curriculum.
- *Labor relations:* Job analysis provides specific breakdowns of duties, which can be used to answer grievances regarding the nature of the employees' responsibilities.
- *Wage and salary survey:* Job analysis provides a method of comparing rates of jobs in one institution with those in others.
- *Organizational analysis:* Job analysis can clarify lines of responsibility and authority by a detailed breakdown of each job and can indicate functional organizational positioning of jobs.

Three basic methods of obtaining information about jobs are (1) questionnaires sent to the job incumbents, which are then checked by the supervisor; (2) interviews conducted by job analysts; and (3) personal observation of the actual performance of a job by a job analyst.

Job Descriptions

Brandt states that "no single instrument is as important to effective wage and salary administration as the job description, yet there is evidence that it receives far less attention than it requires to assure either that it is properly prepared in the first place or that its uses are properly understood or directed."[7] This criticism has been addressed by modern wage and salary administration sections of hospitals' human resources departments throughout the country. Once all the requirements of a specific job are assembled, the job analyst reviews the questionnaire and notes from an interview or direct observation and organizes the information into a job description. Patten, Littlefield, and Self[8] offer these eight principles as a guide to writing effective job descriptions:

1. Arrange job duties in logical order. If a definite work cycle exists, duties may be described in chronological order. When the work cycles are irregular, more important duties must be listed first, followed by less important duties

2. State separate duties clearly and concisely without going into such detail that the description resembles a motion analysis.

3. Start each section with an active functional verb in the present tense.

4. Use quantitative words where possible.

5. Use specific words where possible.

6. Avoid proprietary names that might make the description obsolete when equipment changes occur.

7. Determine or estimate the percentage of time spent on each activity, and indicate whether the duties are regular or occasional.

8. Limit the use of the word "may" with regard to the performance of certain duties.

Job descriptions become indispensable to the process of classifying work into management components. In order to ensure maximum agreement between supervisors and subordinates, the administration must provide well-written and up-to-date job descriptions. These descriptions must be widely publicized, and the supervisor and incumbents in each position must be in complete agreement with their contents. The descriptions are a foundation upon which to build a formal job evaluation plan, an effective and objective guide for intelligent selection and placement, and a source of detailed information for inaugurating training programs. With proper quantification, the job descriptions can also be used as a standard by which employees may be rated.

Job Evaluation

The primary objective of job evaluation is to determine the relative worth of each job in the institution according to the basic determinant of each job's requirements. Once the relationship between jobs has been established, fair pay differentials can be designed, and any existing pay inequities can be corrected.

Because a job evaluation plan may ultimately affect every worker in the hospital and because critical policy decisions must be made, it is advisable to have a representative job evaluation committee guide the effort. In the average-size hospital an excellent committee would be made up of the human resources director, the director of nursing, the building service manager, the executive engineer, and an administrative representative of the laboratories. It is essential that members of the committee and the committee as a whole be as knowledgeable as possible about the largest number of job areas in the institution. Members must be impartial and analytical as well.

Because the job evaluation plan is the cornerstone of the compensation program of the hospital, it is essential that the following basic principles be agreed upon at the outset:

- Grant upward salary adjustments to currently underpaid employees to conform with the findings of the evaluation.

- Prohibit any downward salary adjustments to current employees as a result of the evaluation.

- Pay employees at rates equal to or better than the rates for positions requiring comparable skill, effort, and responsibility in the industry and the community.

- Establish and maintain fair wage differentials between jobs in all departments in terms of the value of each job to the institution.
- Pay all employees in accordance with all applicable federal and state legislation or regulations governing wages, hours, and other conditions of work.
- Follow the principle of equal pay for equal work assignments in the institution.
- Recognize and reward employees based upon their individual ability, outstanding performance, and length of service within the rate range established for the job occupied.
- Develop a plan that is objective, simple, and acceptable to the personnel affected.
- Develop a plan that is flexible and adaptable to the unique needs of the institution.

The two most commonly used types of job evaluation programs are the point method and the factor comparison method or variations thereof. Both are quantitative systems, and both consider each job one element at a time.

The point rating method measures specific features of a job using a predetermined rating scale. Job features that are most commonly measured in this method include education, experience, complexity of duties, monetary responsibility, contacts, working conditions, and, for supervisory jobs, type of supervision and the extent of supervision. Each feature has a range of degrees to which points are assigned. The sum of the points assigned to a given job indicates its relative standing among the jobs being rated. The job as a whole is not measured.

Factor comparison plans, in contrast, do not employ specific scales for jobs measurements. The essential ingredient of such plans is a job-to-job comparison, rather than a job to predetermined scale comparison. In this complex but flexible system, key jobs are compared to each other on the basis of several factors, including mental demands, skills, working conditions, responsibility, and physical demands. Most factor comparison plans do not exceed seven factors. This method's basic assumption is that these key jobs have correct salaries attached to them and thus represent a standard. Pooled judgments on the basis of repeated judgments of competent evaluators must be used in obtaining final figures.

Two other methods of job evaluation, which are used less frequently in hospitals, are the classification method and the ranking method. The ranking method considers each job as a whole and measures each job against every other. It attempts to establish an order of relative worth. Job descriptions are necessary, but the jobs are not subdivided into factors. To use such a plan, which is applicable in smaller institutions, it is necessary to select committee members who have sufficient familiarity with a wide range of jobs.

The classification method, also known as the predetermined grading method, has been widely used in evaluating jobs in the federal and state governments. The evaluation is accomplished by preparing a set of job grades, with definitions for each grade, and classifying individual jobs in relation to how well they match the job definitions. A list of benchmark jobs, which serve as illustrations of the types of jobs that fit into the specific grade, usually accompanies each grade description. Underlying the job classification method is the basic principle that within any given range of jobs there are differences in levels of duties, responsibilities, and skills required for performance.

Wage and Salary Administration

It is important that the hospital develop a clear policy covering wage and salary administration, including the responsibilities for implementing such policies. One institution, Mount Sinai Hospital in New York, outlined such responsibilities in 1970 as follows:

- It is the responsibility of the human resources director to establish wage objectives and approve wage and salary policies, coordinate the activities involved in handling of wage matters and evaluate performances against these objectives, prepare and update job descriptions, and perform job analyses and evaluations.

- The human resources director is the executive director's designated representative for the administration of the wage and salary policies. He or she is responsible for ensuring that the approved salary and wage administration policies, programs, and procedures are administered to meet the institution's requirements; recommending changes in wage and salary objectives and policies; after classifying all jobs into their appropriate job classifications and grades according to their function requirements, establishing and approving the rate of compensation that employees are to receive for the performance of work on either an hourly or salaried basis; approving all employee transfers, promotions, demotions, and merit increases; and establishing and performing periodic checks to ascertain and ensure that all employees are properly classified.

- The human resources department conducts periodic wage and salary surveys necessary for the maintenance of equitable ongoing rates for positions in the institution.

- The human resources department conducts periodic audits of the wage and salary administration program, wage objectives and policies, organizational structure for salary administration, merit rating plan, wage practices, and salary administration.

The design of appropriate forms is a key element in developing necessary controls over wages and salaries. Many hospitals have computerized such forms, of which the most common one is the requisition form. It is used to establish new positions, to ensure appropriate administrative approval of the legitimacy of the need, to aid in recruitment, and to initiate payroll action. It is also used for personnel replacements. The personnel action form is a document used to request changes in status, such as reclassification, transfer, salary increase, and termination. Personnel files, which may be set up either manually or be computerized, are essential to ensure that the employee's work lifespan with the institution is reflected in a permanent and protected form.

In addition to other responsibilities, the wage and salary division is responsible for control over the authorized Table of Organization. Other personnel reports emanating from the wage and salary division are turnover reports, seniority reports, average wage reports, and vacancy evaluation reports.

Screening and Selection: The Employment Process

As discussed in the earlier section on history of the human resources discipline, the first personnel departments, in the main, were solely concerned with the search for and selection of employees. Effective recruitment requires a determination of future needs, the clear definition and description of the types of people needed, and an evaluation and determination of methods to be used in each particular case. When the employment division within the human resources department receives a requisition, it must review the specific job requirements for this position, the profile of a successful applicant, the most productive source for finding such an applicant, and the market conditions. Most hospitals have accepted the need for centralized screening and decentralized hiring.

Recruitment

Recruitment is a proactive, positive mechanism. In order to be effective in this area the human resources director must be involved in the organizational planning function. It is not enough to know which positions are vacant; it is equally as important to anticipate the needs of the hospital in the changing health care environment.

Before establishing a sound recruitment program sources of personnel must be identified and developed. Modern employment departments carefully research the market. Sources of recruitment include present employees, employee referrals, walk-in applicants, applicants who send in written resumes, public employment agencies, private employment agencies, retired military personnel, other retired individuals, schools and colleges, and unions.

Very often hospitals have a written policy that requires the posting of all available positions. Posting provides present employees the opportunity to apply for such positions or to recommend others. An institution's present employees are an excellent source of referral of qualified applicants. Many hospitals offer bonuses to present employees for recommending successful applicants for difficult-to-recruit vacancies. The largest single group of candidates are those who apply to the institution's employment office without any formal solicitation by the institution. Private employment agencies are widely used, once again for difficult-to-recruit classifications. Successful recruitment of professional positions can be achieved by visits to college campuses.

The most widely used recruitment technique is that of placing classified ads. The employment manager is responsible for either writing such ads or working with companies that specialize in such services. Such companies usually do not charge the hospital any fee higher than the institution would pay directly to the newspaper or magazine.

The physical characteristics of the employment office are critical factors in the reception of applicants because an applicant's first impression of the institution is made in there. The ease of locating it, cleanliness, space for waiting, privacy afforded during the interview, and, indeed, the cordial reception by employees in the department are remembered by applicants long after their initial contact with the institution.

Selection: Design of Forms

Recruitment is a positive function, whereas selection is a negative one. Recruitment attempts to attract as many applicants as possible; selection is a sieve through which only the most able

applicants pass. The selection process has as its hallmark the effective appraisal of applicants' qualities that are indicative of job success. The process necessitates the making of a value judgment, a forecast as to which applicant will turn into a productive employee. To aid the employment department in fulfilling such responsibility, five tools are widely used: the application blank, interview, personnel tests, reference checks, and pre-employment physicals.

Employment managers must be fully aware of federal Equal Employment Opportunity laws when selecting employees. These laws require that employment decisions, including hiring, be made solely on the basis of the worker's job qualifications or other job-related criteria. They bar the employer from considering certain general characteristics, such as race, national origin, religion, gender, and, to a lesser extent, age.[9] Federal laws specifically prohibit certain questions from being used in the interviewing process and on application blanks.

The primary objective of the application blank is comparing the applicant's qualifications with the qualifications required for the available job. Therefore, only elements that can legitimately be considered in the hiring process should be contained on it. Most application blanks contain the following items: identifying information, such as name, address, and telephone number; education and training; work experience; and personal references. Many state and local governments also have laws prohibiting discrimination.

Interview

No other tool is more effective in the selection process than the face-to-face interview. Peskin describes the following functions and objectives of the employment interview:

> Employment interviewing is the open exchange of information between persons of acknowledged unequal status for a mutually agreed upon purpose, conducted in a manner that elicits, clarifies, organizes or synthesizes the

information to effect positively or negatively the attitudes, judgments, actions or opinions of the participants, thereby making possible an objective or rational evaluation of the appropriateness of an employee for a specific job.[10]

The interview has been described as a conversation with a purpose. It is intended to match people with jobs, elicit from the applicant data relevant to making a sound employment decision, provide the applicant with necessary information about the job, and, not the least, serve as a means of creating good feelings toward the institution.[11]

The employment section is usually responsible for preliminary screening, whereas final, in-depth interviewing is conducted by the line supervisor. The initial screening interview indicates whether the candidate is generally qualified for the job. The in-depth placement interview, conducted by the line supervisor, determines specifically whether the candidate meets the detailed requirements of the job and whether his or her work habits, attitudes, and personality are compatible with working in the institution. Job specifications and job descriptions are invaluable aids in the interview process.

An integral part of the process is the information stage in which the interviewer presents a picture of the institution and the job under discussion. It is important that the applicant fully understand the requirements of the job. Too often, employees start new jobs and find a marked difference between their initial understanding of the requirements and the actual on-the-job requirements. A study conducted on Superior-Subordinate Communications in management concluded that:

> If a single answer can be drawn from the detailed research study into superior-subordinate communication on the managerial level in business, it is this: If one is speaking of a subordinate's specific job—his duties, the

requirements he must fulfill in order to do his job well, his intelligent anticipation of future changes in his work, and the obstacles which prevent him from doing as good a job as possible— the answer is that he and his boss do not agree but differ more than they agree in almost every area.[12]

This common misunderstanding often starts at the original placement phase.

The rejection of an applicant on the basis of the screening interview should be done with as much compassion as possible. The employment function serves a public relations function as well.

Reference Checks

Reference checks are widely used in hospitals, and the responsibility for carrying out this function lies with the employment section. To ensure the accuracy and sincerity of such checks, privacy and confidentiality must be guaranteed. An often-used technique for obtaining such references is to send a form letter (form card) to former employers. However, more effective means of obtaining such information are face-to-face interviews or telephone calls to former employers. Many institutions contact the applicant's last employer by telephone, using the letter or card form for earlier employers. To ensure the validity of a reference, it is imperative to attempt to obtain such information from the applicant's former immediate supervisor. Personnel records usually reflect, in references, information noted on termination forms. Such information is guarded, which often reflects the concern of a former employer about lawsuits and charges of discrimination. Many former employers are reluctant to put in writing any derogatory information about an individual who has worked for them.

An equally important responsibility is the checking of credentials. It is essential to validate education and licensure credentials directly with the issuing institution. Some employment departments require that the applicant present photostatic copies of diplomas, degrees, and licenses. Because of hospitals' responsibility to protect patients, specifically in the area of ascertaining the qualifications and licensure of employees, it is critical that this process be assiduously carried out under strict controls.

Pre-Employment Physicals

The pre-employment physical should be given in advance of hire in order to eliminate the expense and embarrassment of terminating the candidate within the first few days of employment on the basis of a physical defect that might affect his or her ability to do the job. In order to be rejected on the basis of a physical disability, that disability must significantly restrict the applicant's ability to do the job. A handicap that does not affect performance may not be considered in making employment decisions. Whether a particular handicapped individual is qualified depends upon whether the handicap is job-related. Even after an employee is found by virtue of a pre-employment physical to have a job-related handicap, the employer still is obligated to make "reasonable accommodation without undue hardship" to the operation of the facility. The applicant turned down for physical reasons should be so informed.

Affirmative Action Programs

The human resources department is responsible for ensuring the institution's compliance with Equal Employment Opportunity laws. The courts have held that, in order to promote equal employment opportunity, positive affirmative action is required to eliminate the effects of past discrimination, along with result-oriented activities that go beyond the establishment of neutral, nondiscriminatory merit hiring. The implementation of affirmative action programs is usually the responsibility of the human resources department. The mechanism by which an affirmative action program is developed includes (1) work force analysis, the collection of availability statistics reflecting the available number of members of the protected class living in the organizations' relevant recruitment area; (2) utilization

analysis, which compares the institution's work force statistics with the availability statistics to determine which job positions reflect underutilization of protected class members; and (3) the hiring and promotion goals wherein the institution identifies job areas of underutilization and prepares an affirmative action plan.

Personnel Testing

Many hospitals find tests attractive because they appear to provide the quantitative evaluation of an applicant that does not seem to be obtained from an interview or a reference check. It is well to note that, although modern construction of tests has facilitated administration and scoring, tests are neither infallible nor universally precise. They should be combined with other selection methods and not used as the sole selection criterion.

The critical measure of tests and their application for a specific institution is their validity—whether they measure the elements tested and whether these elements relate to job performance. Testing of the test involves its application to present employees in one's institution. For example, if the test is designed to measure job output, its validity would be determined by the regularity and consistency with which it forecasts job output. Another measure of a test's effectiveness is its reliability—the consistency with which a test measures whatever it was designed to measure. If a test is to be reliable, it must give the same measurement (score) each time it is given to the same person. When selecting a test it is imperative that the employment department have a scientific appraisal of the test's validity and reliability to ensure fair opportunity for all those who apply.

Moreover, federal and state laws impose conditions on the use of tests in determining selection or promotion. The tests cannot be discriminatory in their construction, administration, or resultant action. The test selected to measure the qualifications of an applicant must be specifically related to the requirements of the job.

For many candidates the test is both a traumatic and important experience. It should be conducted in a professional setting. Although the institution may depend more on the interview and reference checks than on the results of tests, applicants are, in most cases, impressed with test results and feel them to be more decisive than other selection methods. Therefore, each candidate should be apprised of the role that test results play in the final selection. It is best to communicate the fact that, although test results can be an effective predictor of performance, they are not used as a substitute for good judgment. The test refines the judgment of the interviewer when added to the interview itself.

Induction and Orientation

A new employee forms permanent and, too often, irreversible attitudes toward the job, supervisor, and hospital much earlier than management believes. The management task of induction and orientation has been assigned to human resources departments, with special emphasis on the social adjustment to a new milieu. If an induction and orientation program is to succeed it must have clearly stated and publicized objectives, must be thoroughly understood, and must be carefully planned. Such a program has four general objectives: to reinforce the employee's confidence in his or her ability to cope with the new work assignment, to communicate complete and detailed conditions of the person's employment, to inform the person of rules and regulations governing his or her employment, and to instill in the employee a feeling of pride in the hospital.

Once the objectives of the hospital's induction and orientation program have been established, a clear statement of philosophy must be publicized. What follows is an example of a sound statement of a hospital's policy on induction and orientation:

> It is the policy of the hospital to imbue a sense of "belonging" in each new employee. To this end, the administration and supervision subscribe to the following statement of principle:

1. Human resources are a most precious asset and require our understanding and empathy.

2. Each new employee who joins our hospital staff must be convinced that he or she is, indeed, welcome and needed.

3. All information necessary to acquaint a new employee with his or her new job, the hospital, and his or her fellow employees must be presented at the onset of employment.

4. Total objectives of the hospital and the role the new employee plays in relation to the successful attainment of these goals must be shared with the new employee; sharing of goals does not cease with the end of the probationary period.

5. Responsibility for induction is clearly that of the line supervisor; it is a long process and may well mean the difference between average ongoing performance and exceptional performance.

The expense of a sound and effective formal induction and orientation program is infinitesimal when compared to the cost of employee turnover and inefficiency. Four principles—none of which can be compromised or neglected—underlie a successful induction program:

1. A new member of a group or an organization must go through an extensive process of adjustment, during which he or she must learn new rules and adapt old habits to the new group.

2. This adjustment can be facilitated by providing the new employee with facts relating directly to the job and to employment in the hospital as a whole.

3. The responsibility for induction and orientation must be delegated clearly to a capable member or members of the man-

agement team. Although the line employees are truly responsible for induction, the human resources department should be given a substantial part of this responsibility.

4. The process of induction does not end the first week or after the first month of employment. It must be recognized that induction and orientation is a rather long process and is, in the final analysis, the link between good selection and good job performance.

Dubin offers the following clear description of the basic task of orientation and induction:

> Orientation and indoctrination of a new member are essentially processes of acculturation. He has to learn ways of behaving, a set of standards and expectations, and a point of view largely foreign to him in their specific details, although he may be generally familiar with them in their broad outline. A great deal of the new employee's time may be spent during his early weeks and months of employment simply becoming adjusted to the organization.[13]

The important consideration in the entire induction and orientation program is to build up, as rapidly as possible in the mind of the new employee, an understanding of the hospital's operation and his or her part in these operations. The premise one builds upon is that an employee who is informed—who knows the what, why, how, and when of his or her role in the large organizational structure—is likely to be more efficient, motivated, and sympathetic to the total goals of the hospital than one who does not possess this knowledge.

Some useful techniques for imparting needed information are described below.

- *Notice of employment in writing with complete details:* Such notice should be received by the employee before he or she reports to work. It is a written statement of the actual job offer, including the title of the position, a brief description of the position, the supervisor's name, the pay rate, and the reporting time and place.
- *Institutional tours:* Many successful induction programs include institutional tours to key areas.
- *Employee handbooks:* In almost all successful induction programs an employee handbook is distributed. These handbooks are essentially a statement of policy, conditions of employment obligations, and benefits. Successful orientation programs include time for the employee to review with the supervisor the handbook's contents.
- *Sponsorship system*
- *Informational lectures and films:* At the formal staff orientation, either a film developed specifically for the hospital or one about hospitals in general can be presented.

The staff induction, usually performed by the human resources department, is a formal and integral part of the orientation process. It is not unusual for key department heads to present information about their services and the role they play in the total patient care delivery system to groups of new employees.

The line induction is performed by the supervisor. It starts on the first day of employment, when the supervisor should introduce the employee to some of his or her fellow workers and carefully explain, preferably in private or at the very least in a nonpressured atmosphere, the responsibilities of the job. The fellow employee or supervisor responsible for on-the-job training takes over the next phase of the induction and orientation program. Sponsorship is a useful mechanism for effective orientation. One of the more experienced employees in the department is asked to "sponsor" or be responsible for each newcomer. The experienced employee talks with the newly hired employee, joins him or her during the rest period, explains the customs and rules, and attempts to make him or her feel at home in the new work situation. The sponsor often joins the employee in his or her first lunch and escorts the employee to the time clock at the end of the workday. The sponsor should be a senior, loyal, well-motivated employee.

Many hospitals establish a probationary period, a time for testing out an employee. It permits the institution the right to terminate employment of a new employee during a 30-day, 60-day, 90-day, or 6-month probationary period. Certain benefits do not start until after the probationary period.

Turnover is costly. The highest percentage of turnover occurs with new employees during their probationary periods. The human resources department is responsible for ensuring the implementation of effective induction and orientation programs that are designed to lower the turnover rate. Good habits are developed from the very start, as are bad habits. An employee who displays poor work habits during the probationary period is a bad risk for productive and efficient employment.

Performance Evaluation

Performance appraisal is a most complex and controversial area of supervisor-subordinate relationships. The development of a sound performance appraisal program is the responsibility of the human resources department.

Merrihue describes effective performance evaluation as follows:

> The supervisor who obtains the best from his employees is the one who creates the best atmosphere or climate of approval within which his work group operates; he accomplishes this through the following methods:
>
> 1. He develops performance standards for his employees and sets them high to stretch employees.
>
> 2. He measures performance against these standards.
>
> 3. He consistently commands above-par performance.
>
> 4. He always lets employees know

when they have performed below-par.[14]

The primary purpose of performance evaluation is the improvement of job performance by these methods:

- communicating specific standards to employees, gaining acceptance of those standards, and using those standards to measure the employee's performance

- measuring the employee's performance against the agreed-upon standards

- jointly developing with the employee a plan of action to assist the employee to overcome obstacles to his or her development and to strengthen his or her capabilities

- offering constructive suggestions and tangible assistance to the employee toward his or her development

- encouraging reactions, facing and resolving differences, and reaching a mutual understanding of the implications of the review.

The end-product of the performance evaluation program is an understanding between the employee and his or her supervisor that includes the employee's understanding of what is expected of him or her, how the expectations are met, and ways to improve performance. Workers will be better motivated if they know precisely what is expected of them, if they have the opportunity to obtain assistance as needed, if they know exactly how a supervisor feels about their performance, and finally if they receive appropriate recognition when it is deserved. A successful performance evaluation program encourages employees' reactions to the evaluation and facilitates the identification of different perceptions about job performance. Evaluation provides a manager with the means of rating job performance on a more objective basis and identifying those employees who are qualified for positions with greater responsibility.

Human resources departments in hospitals are delegated the responsibility of developing performance evaluation programs that accomplish the difficult objectives described above. Goal-oriented job descriptions are most useful in such systems. Performance evaluation must be based on clear, well-defined, and fully communicated expectations of goals.

Performance evaluation forms seem to take as many shapes as the number of institutions using them, and there is no one best method. Some of the options are described below:

- *Rating scales:* This is probably the most commonly used form. Scales are developed in a graphic or multiple-step format, which requires the supervisor to make a choice of appropriate rating along the scale. Rating is often done on various traits, such as ambition, character, cooperation, responsibility, attendance, and punctuality.
- *Checklists:* These rate various traits, but instead of using a quantitative measurement (numbers, letters) as in a rating scale, each trait is evaluated according to descriptive statements.
- *Employee comparison systems:* These do not require the use of an absolute standard as found in rating scales and checklists. Instead, the supervisor who is doing the rating is asked to compare the employee being rated with other employees being evaluated.
- *Goal setting:* This is widely used and often referred to as management by objectives. The employee is rated according to the degree to which he or she attains predetermined job goals.

No matter which form the performance evaluation takes, the goal should be to reinforce performance by a systematic assessment of observable work achievements. Most employees, if communicated to properly and given the necessary assistance, will improve their performance.

Training and Development

There are three basic goals of any training program: the acquisition of knowledge, the development of skills, and the development or modification of attitudes. These goals must be clearly defined and communicated, possibly in a policy on training, adopted by the board of trustees and underwritten by the CEO. This policy statement should address how the training function will be carried out, who will be responsible for its administration, the types of training involved in the overall program, the relationship of line to managerial staff in the implementation of the program, and how the cost will be borne.

Training objectives are based upon specific desired outcomes, some of which follow:

- Break-in time for new employees can be reduced.
- Labor turnover can be reduced.
- Employees can be better prepared for higher positions and to assume responsibility.
- Employees can obtain heightened interest in the job and hospital, thereby increasing their job satisfaction.

Training and development is not a single-shot effort or a short-term program, but rather a continuing effort made up of a variety of programs that are developed with professional leadership and planning. The quality of patient care in an institution depends almost entirely on the knowledge, skill, and attitude of the staff delivering it. Training's potential for improving employee performance and operational effectiveness can be realized only when line managers view it as an integral part of their responsibilities, rather than a function or activity performed in a vacuum by an education or personnel department.[15] The increased participation of hospital administrators and department heads in the design and implementation of training programs has significantly refined the training needs assessment picture and greatly increased the number of such programs. The trend is toward training based on operation needs, almost to the exclusion of generalized learning programs.

The human resources department is responsible for determining training needs through a needs analysis. This analysis is geared to answering these questions:

- Where are existing staffing shortages or inadequate supplies of employees who are promotable?
- Where do specific skill shortages within the hospital exist?
- Where do specific skill shortages in the labor market exist?
- Which areas of service have been identified as deficient by patient complaints?
- Where is a department unable to function within the prescribed budgets?
- Where are poor morale levels?

Based on these identified needs, a reliable roster of actual skills must be assembled and a differentiation made between potential skills and actual skills.

The most prevalent form of training in hospitals is on-the-job training, which is conducted on a one-to-one basis and often informally. The planning of such training should be a joint effort between the human resources training division and line supervision. Conferences and lectures are widely used in hospitals to effect desired training results.

LaParo[16] warns that it is absolutely essential that hospital trainers systematically analyze and assess training needs. The disciplined use of a systems approach in designing programs is a key factor in ensuring that training becomes a solution of first choice only when the root cause of an operating problem can be traced directly to a lack of job knowledge and/or skill on the part of the employee(s).

Management Development

Management development is an:

> individual process involving the interaction of a man, his job, his manager, and total work environment . . . [which] results in the acquisition of new knowledge, skills, attitudes in a planned orderly manner to improve present job performance while accelerating preparation for advancement into more responsible positions.[17]

These topics are most frequently included in a management development program:

- leadership, human relations, working with people, behavioral science concepts, motivating people
- management theory and practice
- hospital policies, benefits, personnel procedures
- labor relations, labor laws and regulations, collective bargaining
- hospital organization, role of the line departments, role of the staff, staff services
- problem solving, decision making
- role of the supervisor
- safety, Occupational Safety and Health Act
- hospital administrative procedures
- goal setting, management by objectives

Management development programs, which are usually the responsibility of the human resources department's training and development section, should offer ongoing opportunities to supervisors to improve their knowledge and increase their skills in employee relations. A critical element in the success of such programs is the initial careful selection of individuals for managerial positions.

PLACEMENT OF THE HUMAN RESOURCES DEPARTMENT IN THE INSTITUTION'S ORGANIZATIONAL STRUCTURE

To fulfill their broad spectrum of responsibilities, human resources departments have grown in size and have attracted professionally trained executives for leadership positions. Human resources directors are key members of the top administrative group in many hospitals, and most report to the CEO, reflecting the industrial model. Placement at that top management level promotes better institutional decisions by encouraging all other administrators to give weight to human resources factors in their decision-making process. With this placement, members of the top administrative group of the institution perceive the human resources department director as having higher status than a department head or operating supervisor. In addition, with sufficiently high status the human resources administrator can effectively urge the establishment of new programs. Placed at the top of the organizational structure, human resources departments are more likely to be seen as creative and innovative, and more weight will be given to their ideas, suggestions, recommendations, and advice.

Human resources professionals are valuable resource people who assist, advise, and aid the administration in solving people problems. They provide surveys, analyses, information, directions, programs, and concerns all directed toward an effective utilization and motivation of the hospital work force.

Titles for the top human resources executives in hospitals vary considerably. In institutions with corporate structures, the individual who heads the human resources or personnel function may well be called vice president for human resources. Other titles are personnel manager, human resources manager, personnel administrator, director of human resources, director of industrial relations, director of personnel, chief of personnel, associate director for personnel, or assistant director for personnel.

Jobs that report directly to the top executive of the human resources department are employee relations manager, labor relations manager, wage and salary administrator, manager of training, employment manager, and benefits manager. Other positions in the department include managers of human resources research, safety, employee services, employee counseling, and housing. In other subsections of the department, one finds such positions as job analyst, employment interviewer, personnel statistician, personnel assistant, and personnel clerk. In some institutions, the health service department reports to the human resources administrator.

It is not sufficient that the vice-president for human resources direct his or her own thinking and activity toward a strategic planning process. The mindset and commitment must filter throughout the human resources staff. However, there is risk of romanticizing all this "fun" activity of influencing the leadership of the organization at the expense of good, basic personnel administration. Compensation, benefits, employment, contract and regulation compliance, and other ongoing programs must be well managed.

In helping human resources staff maintain their expertise in their specialized functions, yet still assume this new kind of leadership role, these strategies for their development are recommended.

- *Provide opportunities for external education and professional affiliation.* Many educational programs, both in specific areas of human resources and in business administration, are available at reasonable cost at universities, at junior colleges, and through professional seminars. Also, membership in professional societies, such as the American Society for Healthcare Human Resources Administration (ASHHRA) or the American Society for Personnel Administration (ASPA), or their local or state chapters, is not expensive and provides stimulating exchange among colleagues. A portion of the human resources budget devoted to the professional development of staff is money well spent.

- *Send human resources staff out into the hospital to do their work.* If they do all their work in their offices, expecting employees always to come to them when they need assistance, their function will never be perceived as proactive. "Road shows" are one effective way to expose human resources staff to the environment they need to know and understand. For example, an employee relations specialist might ask to speak at various departmental meetings on subjects such as the disciplinary policy or the grievance procedure. Or people from the employment or compensation areas might do an educational "road show" on promotions and transfers. By having human resources staff appear in other departments, such as the laundry or a nursing conference room, respect for those functions is conveyed. This also allows the human resources staff to get more in-depth knowledge of their customers' issues.

- *Create interdisciplinary work teams.* When projects are undertaken, involve staff from a variety of human resources areas as well as from departments. For example, if an exit interview program is being developed, line managers should participate with human resources people in devising the questionnaire and deciding how the data will be used. This process assures support for the program but, more importantly, results in a product that reflects issues important to the whole organization. Other opportunities for expanding staff members' knowledge of the organization can be created in the form of ongoing committees on topics such as employee health and safety and employee recognition programs. Also, internal experts could be invited to attend human resources staff functions. A physician speaking on the research going on in the organization, a development officer talking about the hospital's reliance on fund-raising, a facilities engineer describing how buildings are planned and maintained—all serve to open human resources staff's eyes to the broader scope and purposes of the organization.

- *When possible, expose human resources staff to top management and members of the board of trustees.* Hearing those who are ultimately accountable for the effectiveness of the organization reinforces the importance of its mission and the value of all employees in supporting it. If such opportunities do not exist, the human resources staff could initiate activities and

events to create a dialogue throughout the hospital.

- *Teaching and mentoring are important functions* in assuring that human resources staff rise to the level of competence needed to lead the organization. They can learn the principles and mechanisms of strategic planning, and they can follow the excellent examples set by top-flight human resources executives, both within their institution and in others.[18]

Assessment Centers

Assessment centers are used to identify candidates for managerial positions. These centers perform this function more effectively than the usual appraisal procedures, because all assessees (1) have an equal opportunity to display their talents, (2) are seen under similar conditions and situations designed to bring out the particular skills and abilities needed for the position or positions for which they are being considered, and (3) are evaluated by a team of trained assessors unbiased by past associations, who are intimately familiar with the position requirements.

In using assessment centers to select applicants for management positions, the institution is primarily interested in estimating managerial potential of its employees, but centers may also produce useful training and development recommendations. The program of the assessment center should meet, as a minimum, the following specifications:

- It must validly measure management potential. Decisions made on the potential development of the individual worker must be related to actual job performance factors.

- It must have high face validity and acceptability to both the health care institution and to the person being assessed.

- It must be administered as an integral part of the hospital's staff development program. The assessment program should serve as a partial individual needs analysis, because the output reports will include information about the individual's skills that may be improved through education and development of training programs.

- It must be flexible enough to permit assessment of managerial potential at various levels and functional areas of specialization.

- It must be comprehensive enough to tap a wide variety of potential managerial characteristics. The complexity and breadth of managerial functions require an elaborate battery of measuring devices for adequate coverage.

- It must have a high payoff value in relation to investment and the cost of administration.

- It must be feasible in terms of the realities of the hospital's particular organizational structure and climate, as well as be practically and theoretically sound.

As part of the assessment center method, a battery of psychological tests, including those for mental ability, numerical ability, logical thinking, and personality, is administered. A systematic pattern interview, which consists of a reservoir of preplanned questions, to be asked of all candidates, usually follows the testing. The interviewer evaluates the participant on the basis of his or her actions and words in the interview. This interview is usually followed by an "in-basket exercise." This semistructured exercise is designed to measure a number of variables that together make up a large part of what is called leadership ability. In the exercise, the persons being assessed sit around a table. Observers are in attendance, but do not participate. The group is briefed on the assigned topic for discussion, or a problem is posed to the group for solution. Each participant is asked to put him- or herself in the role of an administrator in that situation. He or she must then make judgments, delegate assignments, and indicate decisions. Each observer takes notes on an assigned number of participants, assessing variables such as leadership, interpersonal relations, flexibility, oral skills, and quality of participation.

Human Resources Strategic Planning. An effective human resources strategic plan is one that supports the overall strategic plan of the organization or integrated health delivery system. This overall business plan may be one of growth or consolidation, one introducing new services or improving current programs, one of specialization or diversification. In any event, the human resources strategy and management responses must complement and enhance the possibility of a successful outcome.

Second, the strategic plan must define the organization's benefits and values. Employees at all levels must be permitted to understand the culture and contribute to the common beliefs and expectations that employees have for each other and for how their jobs should be performed, from simple phone courtesy to the detailed training of surgical teams. The blending of multiple organizations into delivery networks makes this strategic goal imperative.

Finally, the plan must encourage the development of specific and measurable objectives to determine success and to allow individuals to see results and participate in shaping and influencing these outcomes. The leadership and work force values that emanate from the thoughtful consideration of these factors must reflect the organization's values of quality and service: how it relates to the patient; how it views itself as an organization; and how it will carry out its commitment to cost containment, service, and efficiency. The successful integration of these values in an organization requires the commitment of senior management. Management practices and attitudes need to ensure that the medical facility's labor force is seen not merely as a necessary expense, but also as a crucial asset requiring wise investment and sound management in order to realize significant return.

Before embarking on the development of a human resources strategic plan, the human resources director needs to assess the readiness of the organization to develop an effective plan. Questions that should be asked include the following:

- What are the key organization concerns or goals expressed by senior management?
- Which of these critical concerns or goals depend on human resources for success?
- How does your organization view its work force: as an asset? as an expense?
- How would you judge your own performance and the human resources department's level of performance?
- Are you part of the senior planning group? If not, why not?
- Have you thought hard about the long-term implications of a changing health care environment for the human resources aspects of your organization?
- Are you prepared to raise, and persist in the discussion of, difficult and complex human resources issues for which there appear to be no easy or convenient solutions?

Thus, the human resources director can only model the organization's commitment to a concept that treats human resources as a valuable organizational asset to be managed for an investment return, like any other asset. By adopting this philosophy, the human resources director will be required to oversee four important responsibilities essential to a human resources strategic plan.

1. *Install information systems to establish an employee database.* The human resources director must ensure that the information systems and data are available to enable the organization to understand how human resources can and should be measured. These data range from a comprehensive organizational employee attitude survey to turnover statistics, benefit utilization, and work force demographics. In short, the organization must be able to measure and understand the tremendous investment that it has in a labor-intensive

organization such as a hospital medical group or integrated delivery system.

2. *Train and educate management and staff concerning human resources management issues.* The human resources leadership must play a central role in training and developing employees and managers with regard to their approach to human resources management. This will require consultation and support from other departments, because the human resources function will be in the unique position of articulating the organizational values and principles regarding the human resources department.

3. *Participate in the development and redesign of human resources policies, procedures, and practices.* The human resources director will be required to oversee and/or participate in the development or modification of organizational policies, procedures, and practices regarding human resources. These operation revisions may include the discussion and consideration of staffing patterns and compensation policies, as well as employee training programs.

4. *Prioritize human resources responsibilities.* The human resources director must assess and prioritize the tasks of the human resources department and his or her own functional responsibilities. A department that is awash in paperwork compliance and consumed by urgent operational issues will not be effective in a strategic environment, which requires a director to give greater emphasis to broader organizational issues and the planning necessary to achieve the desired results.[19]

Encouraging Organizational Acceptance of the Human Resources Strategic Plan. Although there is no simple blueprint for assuring that a human resources strategic plan will be embraced by the organization, four steps are essential for a successful introduction.

1. The senior management of the organization must be involved sufficiently to develop "ownership" in the human resources strategic plan. They must have argued about, challenged, designed, and accepted a strategy of human resources principles that they feel are critical to the long-term success of the medical facility.

2. The human resources strategy must have a clarity and directness about it so that employees at all levels understand it. While a human resources strategy will be tough, of necessity, on numerous facets of the organization, the strategy must have a cohesiveness that provides a reference point for key human resources decisions and programs.

3. There must be an explicit commitment to preserve the adopted human resources principles during the communications and implementation phases. Recognizing the limitations and resistance that will exist in any organization, particularly one as diverse and complex as a health care delivery organization, it is important that management visibly demonstrate ownership of the human resources strategy. The recognition that the establishment of these key human resource principles is a multiyear effort will temper unrealistic expectations and minimize frustration.

4. The human resources function must have the credibility, influence, and expertise to allow the human resources strategy to be communicated effectively and instituted throughout the organization. Not only must the communication process allow information to flow regularly to employees, but also it must allow information from employees to reach the decision and policy makers of the organization. This results not only in the reinforcement of, and adherence to, key human resources principles, but also in the sharing of human resources values, standards, and key organizational principles.

Figure 19–1 illustrates the strategic role of the human resources department at Yale–New Haven Hospital. The vice president of human resources coordinated the hospital's human resources management and professional staff in developing and implementing this successful strategic plan.[20]

Labor Relations

Labor relations in the health care industry are subject to a complex body of statutory, administrative, and case law. All nongovernmental health care facilities are covered by the federal labor law, the National Labor Relations Act. Once a union is certified, all matters relating to wages, hours, and working conditions, which the nonunion hospital decided without outside interference so long as its policies were in compliance with state and federal laws, must be determined through the collective bargaining process. The contract that is finally signed is, in effect, a statement of mutually agreed-upon personnel policies. The function of labor relations is usually the responsibility of the human resources director. Four specific elements of labor relations deserve attention:

1. union organizational drives—how hospitals react to such drives
2. preventive labor relations
3. collective bargaining—negotiations
4. contract administration, including disciplinary, grievance, and arbitration procedures

Most hospital employees who join unions see them as a limited-purpose economic institution. They are searching for something that they perceive they cannot presently find in the institution. Unions are quite selective in their organizational targets because an organizational drive is costly both to the union and to the institution. Unions are less likely than in the past to mount an organizational drive based upon an invitation by a hospital's employees. Once determining on both a cost-effective and philosophical basis that

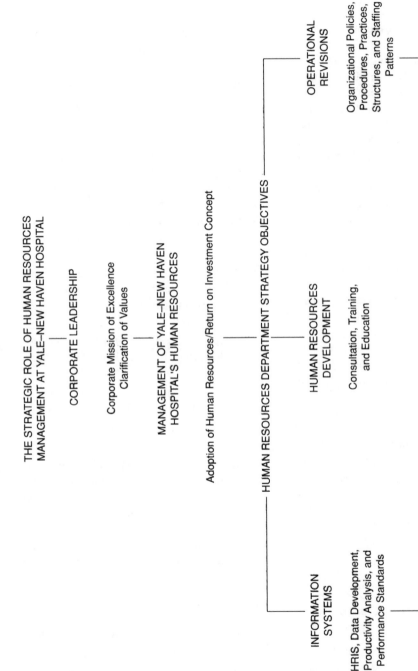

Figure 19–1 The Strategic Role of Human Resources Management at Yale–New Haven Hospital

a specific institution should be organized, the union attempts to rally employees to respond to some overt action taken by the hospital administration or professional staff, which may be perceived as unfair or unjust. The union organizer is selected either from within the institution or the union hierarchy on the basis of an ability to relate to the specific problems in that particular hospital. The organizer first attempts to establish a base within the hospital by selecting employees within the institution who can be the focal point of organizing activity. Once a hospital organizing committee has been established, the campaign moves forward. When the appropriate appeal or combination of appeals has been developed by a joint effort between the organizer and the organizing committee, handbills appear. Unions have effectively used handbills to communicate differences in benefits between the target of its effort and another institution that it had already organized. Thus, the union attempts to communicate its power by enumerating gains it has won at other institutions. Authorization cards are then solicited.

During an organizing campaign, actions of the hospital and the union are specifically governed by various decisions of the National Labor Relations Board (NLRB). The labor relations department of a hospital must be familiar with all provisions of the National Labor Relations Act and decisions of the NLRB, specifically in the area of solicitation and distribution. More often than not, the desire for unionization is created by management's actions, rather than by the union. The following list states permissible and impermissible actions on the part of a hospital.

Hospitals can take the following actions:

- Explain the meaning of union recognition and the procedure to be followed.

- Encourage each member of the bargaining unit to cast his or her ballot in the election.

- Communicate to employees that they are free to vote for or against the union, despite the fact that they signed the union authorization card.

- Communicate to all employees why the administration is opposed to recognition of the union.

- Review the compensation and benefits program, pointing out the record of the administration in the past.

- Point out to employees the statements made by the union that the administration believes to be untrue and communicate the administration's own position on each of these statements.

- Prevent solicitation of membership by the union during working hours if there is a general no-solicitation rule that has been implemented assiduously in the past.

- Continue to enforce all rules and regulations in effect before the union's request for recognition.

- Send letters to employees' homes stating the administration's position and record and the administration's knowledge of the union's position.

- Discuss the possibility of strikes when hospitals become unionized and the ramifications of such strikes.

- Discuss the impact of union dues and, in general, the cost of belonging to the union.

- Discuss the position of the institution with employees individually at their work areas.

- Respond to the union's promises during the pre-election period by pointing out to employees that if the hospital were to meet union demands it might be forced to lay off employees (this statement can be made as long as the administration points out that the layoff would be an involuntary action necessitated by the union's demands).

Hospitals cannot do the following:

- Promise benefits and threaten reprisals if employees vote for or against the union or have supervisors attend union meetings to determine whether employees are participating in union activities.

- Grant wage increases or special concessions during the election period, unless the timing coincides with well-established prior practices.
- Prevent employees from wearing union buttons, except in cases where buttons are provocative or extremely large.
- Bar employee union representatives from soliciting employee membership during nonworking hours, when the solicitation does not interfere with the work of others or with patient care.
- Summon an employee into an office for private discussion about the union and the upcoming election (this does not preclude an employee from coming in voluntarily to discuss these things).
- Question employees about union matters and meetings.
- Ask employees how they intend to vote.
- Threaten layoffs because of unionization or state that they will never negotiate with the union even if it is certified.
- Hold meetings of employees within the 24-hour period immediately preceding the election.

Discipline

Hospitals that have been organized by unions have found it necessary to establish formal labor relations divisions within their human resources departments, which are delegated the responsibility of overseeing the disciplinary, grievance, and arbitration procedures. "Management has the right to manage; employees have the right to grieve," is an old industrial relations maxim. It simply means that the power of decision is vested in management; management has the right to act. However, in acting, management must live by certain rules incorporated in the collective bargaining agreement. It has the unquestionable right to impose discipline, up to and including discharge, if it has sufficient and appropriate reasons. Yet, the burden of providing "good and just cause" for discipline rests on administration. Jules Justin, a prominent labor

arbitrator, lists some noteworthy principles of corrective discipline.[21]

- To be meaningful, discipline must be corrective, not punitive.
- When you discipline one, you discipline all.
- Corrective discipline satisfies the rule of equality of treatment by enforcing equally among all employees established rules, safety practices, and responsibility on the job.
- Just cause or any other comparable standard for justifying disciplinary action under the labor contract consists of three parts:
  1. Did the employee breach the rule or commit the offense charged against him or her?
  2. Did the employee's act or conduct warrant corrective action or punishment?
  3. Is the penalty just and appropriate to the act or offense as corrective punishment?
- The burden of proof rests upon the supervisor who must justify each of three parts listed above that make up the standard of just cause under the labor contract.

Discipline is usually meted out by oral reprimands, warning notices, suspensions, and terminations.

Too often, institutions develop rules and policies that run counter to the prevailing customs operative over the years in the workplace. It is important that the rules and regulations be perceived by employees as necessary. The hospital's cardinal responsibility in the disciplinary procedure is to attempt a restructuring of the employee's behavior, not to punish him or her.

The Bureau of National Affairs conducted a study of many successful policies controlling disciplinary actions; it found the following common elements:[22]

- Company rules are carefully explained to employees. Indoctrination courses, employee handbooks, bulletin notices, and many other methods of bringing rules to workers' attention are used.

- Accusations against employees are carefully considered to determine whether they are supported by facts. Witnesses are interviewed, their statements are recorded, and careful investigations are made to ensure that both sides of the story are available and are presented fairly. Circumstantial evidence is kept to a minimum in judging the facts. Personality factors and unfounded assumptions are eliminated.

- A regular warning procedure is established and applied. Sometimes all warnings are in writing, with the original handed to the employee and a copy filed in the worker's record in the personnel office. Sometimes first warnings are delivered orally, but a written record of that action is filed. Warnings are given for all except the most serious offenses: those that management has made clear to everyone mean immediate discharge.

- Some companies bring the union into the disciplinary case early in the procedure. They provide copies of warning notices and advance notice of other disciplinary actions that management has to take.

- The employee's motive and reasons for the violation of rules are investigated before disciplinary action is taken. Then the penalty is adjusted to the facts: whether the employee's action was in good faith, partially justified, or totally unjustified.

- The employee's past record is taken into consideration before disciplinary action is taken. A good work record and long seniority are factors in the employee's favor, particularly where a minor and first offense is involved. Previous offenses are not used against the employee, unless the individual is reprimanded at the time they occurred or warned that they would be used in any future disciplinary action.

- Companies make sure that all management

agents, particularly first-line supervisors, know the employer's disciplinary policies and procedures and observe them carefully. This is particularly important in the case of verbal warnings or informal reprimands.

- Disciplinary action short of discharge is used wherever possible.

Grievance Procedure: Resolving Employee Complaints

Many so-called grievances are informational in nature, resulting from a lack or breakdown in communication; for example, the employee misreads the rule, clause, or policy. Others result from a dissatisfaction with the rule, clause, or policy—they are gripes. However, whether they are gripes, complaints, or bona fide grievances, they must be addressed. A large majority of grievances result from a decision made and/or communicated by first-line supervisors. Therefore, if a theory of due process is to prevail, it becomes necessary to permit an employee to contest an immediate supervisor's decision and to have an avenue of recourse beyond that ruling.

The major purpose of the grievance procedure is to dispose of the grievance fairly and equitably and, where possible, reach an agreement. To do so facts must be obtained and evaluated objectively; fact finding is at the heart of the grievance procedure. The most effective grievance handling, which results in fair and equitable resolution of employee disputes, requires (1) energetic pursuit of all facts, (2) omission from the hearing procedures of preconceived ideas about the validity of the grievance, (3) a desire to dispose of the grievance by protecting the rights of the institution and of the employee, and (4) a willingness to admit that management is wrong, if that is the case.

The basic principles of grievance adjustment are as follows:

- Inherent in successful grievance adjustment is a commitment to adjusting the employee's complaint properly and on its merits.

- Because the majority of grievances derive from a decision by a first-line supervisor, there must be a direct avenue of appeal beyond that ruling.
- A grievance procedure that has as its terminal step a review inside the institution is not as effective as one that provides for an outside review (arbitration) by an impartial third party.
- There should be a strong desire to resolve dissatisfaction and conflicts before they become real problems.
- Supervisors should empathize with their employees, try to understand their problems, and be able and willing to listen in a nonjudgmental fashion.
- Supervisors should balance their personal commitment to the interest of the institution with a sense of fair play on behalf of the employees.
- Employees deserve a complete and empathetic hearing of all grievances.
- The most important job in handling of grievances is obtaining the facts. Therefore, supervisors must listen attentively and encourage full discussion and defer judgment.
- Supervisors must look for the hidden agenda, look beyond the selected incident, and judge the grievance in context.
- Hasty decisions often backfire. On the other hand, the employee deserves a speedy reply.
- Supervisors should try to separate fact from opinion or impressions while investigating a grievance, consult others when appropriate, and, most importantly, check with the personnel office.
- The supervisor, after coming to a decision, should communicate it to the employee promptly, giving the reasons for the ruling and informing the person of the right to appeal an adverse outcome.

- Decisions must be made and then "sold" to the employee. The decision is less effective if the individual does not understand its rationale.
- Common sense is an essential ingredient in arriving at a decision.
- Written records are most important. They serve as a review for the supervisor to ensure consistency of grievance handling.[23]

Management's responsibility in the administration and adjudication of grievances includes the following:

- hearing and discussing the grievance facts with the employee
- investigating the facts during and after the hearing
- formulating a decision based upon the facts
- answering the grievance

The typical grievance procedure contains four steps. In the first step the employee submits the grievance to the first-line supervisor. In many instances, the employee's representative is involved in this step. In the second step the employee and the union representative, where applicable, appeal the decision from step 1. The specific management representative at this point differs from institution to institution, but he or she should be superior of the first-line supervisor. In some hospitals the personnel department handles the second step. In step 3, the employee and the union representative, where applicable, appeal the decision to a labor relations' representative of the institution. In some facilities the third step, which is the last in-house appeal, is conducted by an associate director of the institution. Step 4 is the arbitration procedure.

Some institutions prefer an informal rather than a formal grievance procedure. A lower-level employee may find it difficult to express frustrations, fears, and needs to a person in a much higher position, who appears to be isolated from the everyday problems of the rank-and-file worker. Most high-level executives find the grievance procedure activity to be an imposition on their busy schedules.

Arbitration. Voluntary arbitration, the terminal step in the grievance procedure and a contract dispute, is judicial in nature. When the two parties—the union and the hospital—are unable to resolve a dispute by mutual agreement, they submit the particular issue to an impartial third party for resolution. The solution deriving from this procedure is final and binding on both parties.

Arbitrators are usually selected by agreement of both parties and more often than not are chosen from a national panel of arbitrators provided by the American Arbitration Association. The hospital's case is usually presented by a labor attorney. Some institutions delegate the responsibility for presenting their case to the labor relations director in the human resources department.

Participatory Management: Quality Circles

The development of programs that increase worker participation will be the single greatest challenge to human resources managers in the 1990s. Many studies show that when employees are given the opportunity to make more decisions about their work, they are more productive and satisfied, and their needs are fulfilled. Need fulfillment or frustration results directly in either constructive or defensive behavior. Dissatisfied employees do not provide the excellent level of care so desperately needed in hospitals. Such dissatisfaction leads to an ineffective work force, costly absenteeism, and labor confrontations.

Worker participation plans must develop a spirit of cooperation and teamwork as their end-product. The critical nature of shared decision making must be sold down the line to the organization.

In one study,[24] hospital management structures were analyzed to identify the features that led to alienation of nonsupervisory personnel. The study's hypothesis was that the degree of alienation is inversely related to the degree to which nonsupervisory nursing personnel are allowed to participate in management's decisions. The results bore out the hypothesis, indicating that alienation is greater when nonsupervisory staff are not allowed to participate in the decision-making process and that inflexible bureaucratic systems tend to increase frustrations and depersonalization in staff relations, causing a loss of initiative.

In addition, many studies in the area of democratic vis-a-vis authoritarian leadership styles have generated these findings:

- The greater number of competent judges, the greater the validity of their combined judgments.
- When there is worker participation, there is a tendency for the members to sharpen and refine an idea before it is given to the group, and the group in turn is able to reject and correct ideas that escape the notice of individuals when working alone.
- Tasks that were performed through cooperation rather than competition were more efficiently accomplished, with members exhibiting a higher degree of motivation and morale.
- Group discussion under the democratic approach is more likely to alter opinions, and conversely attitudes are less likely to change under authoritarian approaches.
- Participation increases the likelihood that a goal is set that is congruent with the group's perceived values.
- As a result of discussion of establishing goals, members are more likely to have adequate knowledge of the nature of the goal, its value to themselves, and its true attainability.

To increase worker participation, hospitals are investigating and, in some cases, implementing the quality circle process. Applying theories of behavioral scientists such as Maslow and Herzberg, Japanese industrialists introduced quality circles into manufacturing firms three decades ago and into areas where quality of service and the involvement of employees were essential. The preeminent exponent of the quality circles concept in Japan is Kaoru Ishikawa, who was a professor at the University of Tokyo. According to Ishikawa, the outcomes of quality circles include the following:

- developing oneself and others
- increasing quality awareness
- encouraging the brainpower of the work force
- improving worker morale
- developing managerial abilities of circle leaders
- implementing and managing accepted ideas

The benefits of participatory management are still being carefully monitored in factories throughout the United States.

The concept of participatory management and its positive effects on productivity were first espoused in the early work of Elton Mayo, a professor on the faculty of the Harvard Graduate School of Business Administration. Some 60 years ago, in one of his first major studies at a Philadelphia textile mill, he analyzed the excessive labor turnover rate in one of the mill's departments. When the workers were given an opportunity to schedule their own work and rest periods, dramatic results occurred: Morale improved, turnover fell, and productivity rose. Mayo concluded that these positive outcomes resulted mainly from allowing employees to participate in the managing of their own work. His seminal study at the Hawthorne Works of the Western Electric Company identified that increased productivity resulted when all employees in the experimental workroom were given a major voice in deciding the management of their own time. In addition, he pointed out that the opportunity to discuss their work problems with the interviewers gave these workers unprecedented freedom to ventilate their feelings, permitting them to view their situation more objectively and to develop positive solutions.

Six basic principles are operative in quality circles and can be applied whether an institution adopts them or not:[25]

1. Trust your employees. Expect that they will work to implement organizational goals if given a chance.

2. Build employee loyalty to the company. It will pay off.

3. Invest in training and treat employees as resources, who, if cultivated, will yield economic returns to the firm. This means developing employee skills. Long-term employee commitment to the organization is an objective.

4. Recognize employee accomplishments. Symbolic rewards mean more than you think.

5. Decentralize decision making.

6. Regard work as a cooperative effort with workers and managers doing the job together by implementing consensual decision-making processes.

Quality circles embody the principle of participatory management to its fullest. They are based on the theory that an organization's workers are closest to the problem and indeed may be part of the problem and that therefore they are best equipped to remedy it, thereby increasing their output and improving the caliber of work or service. A quality circle is a small group of 5–15 employees, usually from the same work area doing similar work, who meet together on a voluntary basis and discuss, with the assistance of a facilitator and leader, solutions to job-related problems. Quality circles give a broader base of employees the opportunity to speak up in an atmosphere where management is listening.

The Quality Control Institute in California, one of the several consulting organizations involved in promoting and assisting in the formation of quality circles, defines the quality circle process as follows:[26]

- *Problem identification:* Typically several problems are identified. Problem selection is a prerogative of the circle.
- *Problem analysis:* Formed by the circle with assistance, if needed, by appropriate circle experts.
- *Problem solutions or recommendations to management:* The circle makes them directly to its manager using a communication technique described as "the management presentation."

According to the Institute, circle suggestions either cost nothing or can be financed from normal department budgets. Moreover, the entire training of the circle members emphasizes that the best way to control problems is to avoid them.

Quality circle programs are organized along these lines:[27]

- A quality circle effort is initiated only upon the decision of senior management.
- Initial meetings for a quality circle are held with all union, management, and supervisory personnel.
- Participation in the circle is voluntary.
- The managers who decide to try a circle then make presentations to the hourly workers, at which participation of the hourly workers is voluntary.
- Participation of management in the circle is voluntary.

In the quality circle process, it is the individual who is important. Employee self-esteem is increased, and consequently employees are more open and do not fear a display of openness as they discuss, suggest, and set quality goals and methods for reaching these goals. An employee who participates in a quality circle is more likely to be concerned about the effectiveness of the recommendation springing from the activity and, therefore, would be more effective in monitoring the group's activities. The key to the success of a quality circle is top management's complete support and confidence in the concept.

Personnel Policies

The description of the hospital's or health system's personnel policies in a written manual is essential in obtaining understanding and commitment to those policies by the entire management team and by employees. The human resources department is responsible for the assembling of all such personnel policies into a manual. In collecting such information, careful attention to past practices must be paid, and the participation of department heads is essential. The policy manual, which must be precise, complete, and understandable, usually covers the following areas:

- *Benefits:* health benefits, workers' compensation, disability, Social Security benefits, pension plan
- *Compensation:* salary determination, salary increase policy, reclassifications, pay schedules, overtime pay, shift differential, on-call pay, uniform allowance, severance pay
- *Disciplinary action:* guidelines, warning notice policy
- *Employment:* employment standards, type of employment, probationary period
- *Grievance procedure*
- *Health, safety, and security*
- *Hours of work and time off:* work schedule, meal and rest periods, holidays, vacation, sick leave, leave of absence
- *Performance review*
- *Employee recognition program*
- *Seniority*
- *Services and activities:* blood protection program, gift shop, recreational activities
- *Termination:* retirement, resignation, discharge
- *Training and development*

Benefits Administration

A recent national survey by the American Hospital Association and Ernst & Young of employee benefits in hospitals found:

- On average, hospitals pay 68 percent of the cost of individual medical coverage.
- Vision coverage is offered to employees in 24 percent of all hospitals surveyed.
- Thirty-six percent (36 percent) of all hospitals offered short-term disability benefits to their employees
- A little over half (56 percent) of all hospitals offer an employee assistance program to their employees.

Employees view their total benefit plan as a means of reducing or offsetting entirely the financial loss that they can incur due to death, disability, medical expense, or retirement.

Employee benefits management is an integral part of the human resources department and requires intensive planning, close supervision and integrated direction. Expanded health protection benefits, including dental, drug, psychiatric, and optical plans, are being developed at a faster pace than ever before and may be required to attract and retain employees. The human resources manager must become more knowledgeable about such plans.

Pension Plan

The most fundamental decision in the design of pension plans is the choice of the basic formula. Most hospital plans contain either a career-average salary or final-average pay formula. The career-average pay plan generally bases its benefits on the earnings either during each year of service or on an average of the total salary earned during a career. This approach tends to produce a lesser, albeit less expensive, benefit in an inflationary economy. Generally, the final-average pay plan bases benefits on the earnings of the participant during the last 5 years of service. The theory underlying this method is that the benefit payable at retirement is automatically inflation-proof because it is related to the average wage just before retirement. Both these plans are defined benefit plans. In contrast, in defined contribution plans the employer establishes the amount of the contribution that the institution desires to make on behalf of each participant. There is no definition of a definitely determinable benefit. The contribution may be defined as a percentage of pay or a flat annual rate per salary range. The present law—the Employee Retirement Income Security Act (ERISA)—specifies rigid eligibility, participation, vesting, and funding requirements. The benefits administrator must be thoroughly familiar with all its provisions.

Social Security benefits may be integrated into the pension benefits formula, thereby reducing the amount of money that the institution contributes to pension benefits. Not-for-profit hospitals operating under Section 501(c)(3) of the Internal Revenue Code can sponsor tax-sheltered annuity programs. Under these programs, the employer can contribute either a percentage of salary or a flat dollar amount to the annuity. The money accumulates on a tax-free basis until the annuity income is received.[28]

Preretirement Planning Programs

Many hospitals provide programs to ease employees' transition to retirement. These programs are usually offered 5 years in advance of normal retirement and are intensified in the last year before retirement. Individual counseling and group seminars focus on the psychological adjustment to retirement, benefits and financial aspects of retirement, and health considerations. They serve a morale-building function in the latter part of an employee's career in an institution.

Disability Insurance

In addition to legislated short-term disability programs, many hospitals provide long-term disability. Such plans usually begin at around 26 weeks. They contain maximum benefit levels and a coordination of benefits with other plans to eliminate duplicated coverage. The benefit levels usually are set at less than full take-home pay.

Health Insurance Plans

Hospitals offer a broad spectrum of comprehensive health insurance plans, including hospital, medical, surgical, and major medical coverage. Some large hospitals have developed self-insurance plans as cost-saving devices. These are usually administered in conjunction with an umbrella policy, which covers claims in excess of a specific stop-loss and individual claim level. Plans may be administered in-house or through insurance companies. In addition to the financial advantage of administering plans in-house, the personal touch and the value of reimbursement being handled directly in the institution have enormous morale implications. Many hospitals now provide dental, optical, and pharmaceutical benefits. These are usually offered under third-party plans, but many institutions have found, as with other insurance plans, that self-insurance is a viable option.

Other Employee Benefits

Hospitals are providing a myriad of employee benefit programs in addition to traditional pension and health benefits. Programs such as educational assistance, purchase discount programs, credit unions, legal and automobile insurance, banking services, and housing are among the most widely provided programs under the general rubric of employee benefits. Educational assistance programs benefit both the individuals taking advantage of such aid and the institution, inasmuch as the employee is prepared for advancement. Purchase discount programs, including car rentals, motel and hotel discounts, restaurant and sports events discounts, are very popular. Credit unions have been found to be a useful means of serving employees' banking needs. They provide checking account services, loans, and other services that ease financial burdens of employees.

Flexible Benefit Plans

These are plans that allow employees to use specific dollars assigned to benefits, in the manner that best meets their personal needs. They involve employees and their families directly in the decisions on how much to select and spend for each benefit. They provide a means for employees to know the real cost/worth of their benefits.[29]

Flex allows employees to use specific dollars to purchase benefits, thereby tailoring the plan to their personal needs. For most people the choices to date are between an indemnity plan and a health maintenance organization (HMO) or preferred provider organization (PPO) option. But they probably have never taken a hard look at benefits within the benefit plan, and that certainly is what a flex plan does.

What Is Gain Sharing?

Gain sharing is an organizational program designed to improve productivity, enhance quality, and reduce cost. The benefits that accrue from these improvements are then shared in cash with the employees who produced them. Gain sharing is a group incentive program with the emphasis of teamwork. Furthermore, gain sharing is intended to capture the numerous small savings that collectively add up to substantial savings. Further, gain sharing creates an environment for sustained, continual improvements.

The concept of gain sharing is simple. First, the hospital calculates its historic rates of productivity (and, where measurable, quality). Then, new targets are set. If performance reaches the new targets, the hospital and its employees share the monetary gains. Because it involves money that the hospital otherwise would not have saved or earned, the program is self-funding. In this sense, it is a win-win program for both the hospital and its employees.[30]

FUTURE DIRECTION OF HUMAN RESOURCES MANAGEMENT

During the 1990s and the beginning of the twenty-first century human resources departments' challenges and responsibilities will change radically. The need to develop trust, which is a particularly difficult task, will be critical. The establishment of enduring trusting relationships depends on the creation of an overall climate of justice and fairness, which will be one of the responsibilities of human resources managers. Creation of that climate may require clear, representative decision-making structures, which involve those members of the staff with the relevant interest, expertise, and credibility appropriate to the given issue.[31]

Human resources directors will need to deal with a burgeoning robot population as well. Such a population will number close to 250,000 by the year 2025. Job training and retraining will be important because many jobs will be changed by advances in technology, changing reimbursement systems, and robot populations. In addition, in integrated delivery systems, economies-of-scale goals will require that certain employer categories be shared by all institutions within the system.

The human resources administrator will also occupy the position of keeper of the ethical standards of the organization. He or she must assume the role of mentor and advisor to the operating executives.

The role of physicians in hospitals will change radically. Doctors will become more dependent upon hospitals, in terms of increased competition for privileges. Women will constitute a growing percentage of physicians.

Retirement issues will radically change. Employees will be retiring earlier, with recreational options far in excess of what is available today.

The computer will allow an entirely new arrangement of work. Human resources managers of the future will be expert in the use of the computer; the computer will free such managers from the maintenance function of human relations: wage and salary administration, benefits administration, and even employment. With such freedom, they can direct their maximum efforts to the essential core of human relations: building trust, building a structure of participatory management, and creating flexible and ingenious reward systems.

The most compelling challenge facing health care human resources administrators over the next several years is to identify to the industry's leadership the inextricable link between humanized work and working conditions on the one hand, and the levels of productivity that survival requires on the other. Compassionate and efficiently rendered patient care is not possible without a humanized and democratically organized work environment. Organizational health and survival need to be linked with the empowerment of health care workers. If health care administrators cannot be expected to speak and understand the language of social justice within the work place, then they need to be spoken to in the idiom of institutional survival.

Exclusion from the essential features of patient care management and the absence of work autonomy are the two most consistently cited sources of dissatisfaction for health care workers. These factors must be seen as an instrumental part of the destructive process through which adversaries are made of our employees. Despite its historically low levels of productivity, the industry has failed to move beyond a classification structure based on fractionalized job functions that serve to routinize and de-skill job functions rather than expand them.

There are still opportunities, however, to advance the alternative model. Indeed, the failures of the present strategy may eventually make the alternatives more attractive to health care administrators, if only out of desperation. There already are several instances in which the requirements of the burgeoning marketing function have caused some health care institutions to probe the issue of job satisfaction. That this concern has emerged from a patient relations perspective rather than out of a concern for the working lives of health care workers need not deter us.

The present course is a prescription for industrial conflict and will almost certainly result in higher levels of successful union organizing, even as the proportion of unionized employees in other sectors of our economy continues to decline. More importantly, it is a prescription for failure, particularly in a more cost-competitive and integrated delivery system environment.[32]

THE GROWTH OF MERGERS, AFFILIATIONS, AND MULTIDIVISIONAL HEALTH CARE ORGANIZATIONS

It is clear that the government's drive toward universal health care coverage will be addressed by the industry in what may be called a "positioning phase." Large tertiary-care institutions are—and will continue to position themselves for the new world of health care providers by—acquiring, merging, or affiliating with institutions that will better meet the new realities. Some institutions will decrease their number of beds, look for "feeder" institutions that provide primary care, merge with other tertiary institutions in order to reduce duplication of services, and concomitantly reduce costs.

These new arrangements produce many challenges to the human resources executive. Consideration must be given to areas such as:

- compensation programs
- benefits programs
- personnel policies
- union representation/labor relations
- employment facilities
- training programs

Critical to the decision-making process in these areas of human resources, and the decisive element in such considerations, is whether the organization will centralize all or some of its human resources functions, or whether it will maintain a decentralized service.

There are clear benefits in opting for a centralized service in compensation, benefits, personnel policies, and training. Yet, regional differences can be defended. As to employment, centralization is preferred if the units are geographically close. A difficult problem may confront the new relationship in the area of union representation. Maintaining a merged multidivisional organization, where some units are unionized and similar units in another division are not, may bring a myriad of problems. In addition, a

union may attempt to organize the latter unit, or petition the NLRB on the basis of an accretion to the existing similar unit, which is organized.

It should be clear that a careful consideration to merging human resources services must include legal requirements, local standards, efficiency, and cost implications. Too often such decisions to affiliate, merge, or acquire omit the input of the human resources executive. This is a mistake, which often is hastily addressed after the fact.

CONCLUSION

Over the years, Robert Levering and Milton Moskowitz, separately and together, have studied workplaces in order to identify the characteristics of those that are considered—by employees and management—great places to work. In earlier studies hospitals were noticeable by the fact that they rarely appeared in the listing.

The critical element for inclusion in the list of the best places to work has been the essential factor of employee-employer relationships. There have been some very positive changes—not the least of which is the inclusion of three hospitals among the "100 Best"—since their first study in the early 1980s.

In Levering and Moskowitz's second edition of *The 100 Best Companies To Work for in America*, they note positive changes in five key areas:

1. *More employee participation:* This growing phenomenon often develops after layoffs. The reduction in management thrusts upon employees the need to participate in reorganization programs.

2. *More sensitivity to the problems of working mothers and fathers:* Many of the companies (including three hospitals) listed in this book provide child-care options and flexible work schedules.

3. *More sharing of the wealth:* Many of those listed have profit-sharing or gain sharing programs. Beth Israel Hospital in

Boston uses a version of the Scanlon Plan, a share-the-wealth scheme, wherein employees share directly in productivity gains.

4. *More fun:* Those companies and hospitals selected for inclusion in this book have employees who are enjoying themselves; the institution has a sense of humor that is *not* inconsistent with a serious, productive institution.

5. *More trust between management and employees:* Employees trust their supervisors and management; managers and supervisors trust their employees. Indications of such trust are the absence of time clocks; regular meetings where employ-

ees can discuss their concerns; job posting; and constant training.[33]

The three hospitals cited as exceptional places to work were Beth Israel Hospital of Boston (listed in the top ten!), Baptist Hospital of Miami, and Methodist Hospital of Houston. These institutions are the models for our industry. At a time when many health care institutions are attempting to position themselves for the coming changes inherent in health care reform legislation, we can look to these three (and many more not listed) for a clear direction of renewal and dedication toward the improvement of employee-employer relationships. A significant partner in developing and directing such a renewal will be the human resources professional.

NOTES

1. O. Tead and H.C. Metcalf, *Personnel Administration: Its Principles and Practices* (New York: McGraw-Hill Book Company, 1920), 51.

2. Ibid., 64.

3. H. Eilbert, Development of Personnel Management in the U.S., in *Management of the Personnel Function*, ed. Heckman and Hueneryager (Columbus, Ohio: Charles E. Merrill Books, Inc., 1962), 20.

4. R. Likert and D. Katz, *Motivation: The Core of Management* (New York: American Management Association, 1953), 3–25.

5. F. Herzberg, *Work and the Nature of Man* (New York: World Publishing Co., 1966).

6. A.H. Maslow, A Theory of Human Motivation, *Psychological Review* 50(1943):370–396.

7. A.R. Brandt, Describing Hourly Jobs, in *Handbook of Wage and Salary Administration*, ed. M.L. Rock (New York: McGraw-Hill Book Company, 1972), 1–11.

8. J.R. Patten, et al., *Job Evaluation: Text and Cases*, 3rd ed. (Homewood, Ill.: Richard D. Irwin, 1964), 93–94.

9. B. Essig and M.H. Singer, A Brief Look at the Federal Equal Employment Opportunity Laws, in *Handbook of Health Care Human Resources Management*, ed. N. Metzger (Gaithersburg, Md.: Aspen Publishers, Inc., 1981), 115.

10. D.B. Peskin, *Human Behavior in Employment Interviewing* (New York: American Management Association, 1971), 12.

11. M.M. Mandell, *Choosing the Right Man for the Job* (New York: American Management Association, 1964), 154.

12. N.R.F. Maier, et al., Superior-Subordinate Communication in Management, in *AMA Research Study 52* (New York: American Management Association, 1961), 9.

13. R. Dubin, *The World of Work* (Englewood Cliffs, NJ: Prentice-Hall, Inc., 1950), 337.

14. W.C. Merrihue, *Managing by Communication* (New York: McGraw-Hill Company, 1960), 122.

15. H.C. Laparo, Training, in *Handbook of Health Care Human Resources Management*, ed. N. Metzger (Gaithersburg, Md.: Aspen Publishers, Inc., 1981), 277.

16. Ibid.

17. R.L. Desatnick, *A Concise Guide to Management Development* (New York: American Management Association, 1970), 11.

18. L. Avakian, Human Resources Leadership—A Perspective from the Trenches, in *Handbook of Health Care Human Resources Management*, ed. N. Metzger (Gaithersburg, Md.: Aspen Publishers, Inc., 1990), 47–48.

19. E.J. Dowling and E.A. Kellman, A Case Study in Human Resources Strategic Planning, in *Handbook of Health Care Human Resources Management*, ed. N. Metzger (Gaithersburg, Md.: Aspen Publishers, Inc., 1990), 29–30.

20. Ibid., 30–31.

21. J.J. Justin, *How To Manage with the Union, Book 1*, (New York: New York Industrial Workshop Seminars, Inc., 1969), 294, 295, 301, 302.

22. *Grievance Guide*, 6th ed. (Washington, DC: The Bureau of National Affairs, Inc., 1982), 5–6.

23. N. Metzger and J. Ferentino, *The Arbitration and Grievance Process* (Gaithersburg, Md.: Aspen Publishers, Inc., 1983), 23–24.

24. J. LaPorte, Participatory Management—The Technique to Alleviate Alienation of Bureaucratic Organizations (Thesis, University of Ottawa, 1972).

25. R.E. Cole, *Work Mobility and Participation: Comparative Study of American and Japanese Industry* (University of California Press, Berkeley, Calif., 1979), 84.

26. Quality Control Institute, *Quality Circles* (Quality Circle Institute, Red Bluff, Calif., 1987).

27. E.P. Yager, Quality Circle: A Tool for the 80s, *Training and Development Journal*, August (1980):60.

28. G.R. Guralnik and J.F. Sapora, Employee Benefits Administration, in *Handbook of Health Care Human Resources Management* (Gaithersburg, Md.: Aspen Publishers, Inc., 1980), 455–472.

29. R.E. Johnson, Flexible Benefit Plans, in *Handbook of Health Care Human Resources Management*, ed. N. Metzger (Gaithersburg, Md.: Aspen Publishers, Inc., 1990), 311, 313.

30. K.E. Romanoff and J.B. Williams, Gainsharing, in *Handbook of Health Care Human Resources Management*, ed. N. Metzger (Gaithersburg, Md.: Aspen Publishers, Inc., 1990), 147.

31. S.M. Shortell, The Medical Staff of the Future: Replanting the Garden, in *Frontiers of Health Services Management* 1, no. 3 (1985): 3–48 passim.

32. B. Metzger, Human Resources Administration: An Alternative Model, in *Handbook of Health Care Human Resources Management*, ed. N. Metzger (Gaithersburg, Md.: Aspen Publishers, Inc., 1990), 14.

33. R. Levering and M. Moskowitz, *The Hundred Best Companies To Work for in America* (New York: Currency-Doubleday, 1993), xii–xiii.

NORMAN METZGER, MEd, is Edmond A. Guggenheim Professor Emeritus of Health Care Management of The Mount Sinai School of Medicine. He was for many years Vice President for Human Resources and Vice President for Labor Relations of The Mount Sinai Medical Center in New York City, where he is presently Executive Consultant for Human Resources and Labor Relations.

Professor Metzger is President of the Health Care Division of Adams, Nash & Haskell, Inc., a management advisory group. He is also a senior consultant for Martin H. Meisel Associates, an executive search company.

Professor Metzger was President of the League of Voluntary Hospitals and Homes of New York, and of the American Society for Healthcare Human Resources Administration (ASHHRA).

Professor Metzger is the author, co-author, and editor of 15 books, and has written over 100 articles on labor relations, personnel administration, and social behavior. In 1987, he became a recipient, for the sixth time, of the Annual Award for Literature, given by ASHHRA, in recognition for his outstanding contribution to hospital personnel administration literature.

Professor Metzger conducts management seminars and workshops on subjects such as empowerment, transformational leadership, interviewing skills, communications, labor relations, and motivational skills.

He is a founder and adjunct professor in the Graduate Program in Health Care Administration, jointly sponsored by Mount Sinai School of Medicine and Baruch College. He has been a visiting professor at over 20 universities.

Chapter 20

Planning Health Care Facilities and Managing the Development Process

James E. Hosking

BACKGROUND

The Hill-Burton Hospital Survey and Construction Act of 1946 encouraged construction of health care facilities by recognizing that voluntary hospitals needed capital support for renovation and expansion of hospital facilities. Consequently, many new hospitals and hospital expansion programs were completed during the 1950s and 1960s. Through a series of health planning laws, the emphasis within government programs shifted from supporting hospital construction to controlling it. With the enactment of Public Law 89-749 in 1966, construction and expansion began to be evaluated in terms of the entire area's needs, instead of viewing each development program in isolation. Subsequent laws refined this process of comprehensive health planning. P.L. 90-174 and P.L. 92-603 initiated 1122 Reviews, and P.L. 93-641 set up the Certificate of Need process.

In the 1980s, demands for greater convenience, an increased supply of physicians, new technologies, and continued cost pressures led to a major shift to ambulatory services and new competition for traditional hospitals. Solo physicians formed large, single, or multispecialty groups and added diagnostic services to the offices. Entrepreneurial groups formed partnerships to build and operate freestanding surgery and cancer centers in direct competition with the local hospital.

A major impetus for the ambulatory shift was the enactment of the Medicare prospective payment system (PPS) in 1983. Under this system, hospitals are paid a predetermined amount for Medicare inpatients based on diagnostic-related groups (DRGs) regardless of costs. Initially, capital costs continued to be cost reimbursed; however, in 1992, capital costs began being phased into the DRG payment over a 10-year period. Thus, by 2002, a fixed payment per DRG must be allocated to cover capital costs, as well as operating expenses, depreciation, and interest charges.

Similarly, various managed care initiatives by private carriers have forced inpatient utilization down and prompted health care providers to become more cost conscious. "Downsizing" became common in the early 1990s, and is likely to continue. New health care reform proposals promise to continue the cost pressures on hospitals as well as physicians, long-term care facilities, ambulatory surgery centers, and most other alternative providers. All these efforts to constrain capital outlays make careful planning and development of health care facilities increasingly important.

These growing cost pressures on health care providers strengthen the need for a strategic plan to guide the development plans of health care providers. A strategic plan outlines the goals and vision of the institution and highlights strengths, weaknesses, threats, and opportunities. It also establishes priorities for program development, which should be the basis of physical development.

Once the institution's strategic plan is approved, the physical facilities planning process can begin to address the facility requirements necessary to implement the plan in an orderly and progressive manner. Without approval and organizational "buy in" to the plan, the facility planning process may not be focused and could meander on tangential issues, lengthening the overall process.

The two major phases of the facility development process, design and construction, evolve through many separate but interrelated activities that can be grouped into two major categories— facilities planning and implementation planning. Facilities planning is the process of planning and building the physical facility. Implementation planning involves related activities, such as systems design, operations planning, equipment and furniture planning, and regulatory approvals, that are necessary for occupancy to proceed in a timely manner. Generically, this process applies to all types of health care facilities; however, the complexity, time frame, and regulatory approvals could vary significantly.

Figure 20–1 outlines a generic schedule of the facility development process for a hospital project with an appropriate time frame for each activity. The sequence and duration of each of these activities vary somewhat depending on project scope, complexity, and implementation strategy. The process outlined is applicable to any facility, physician group, etc.

Working with a qualified external planning team and following the guidelines of a reason- able schedule, the institution's role in the process is to review, comment, and make timely decisions on the recommendations of the external team that is made up of health care consultants, architects/engineers, construction managers, financial and legal consultants, and other consultants and advisors. This review-and-response interaction among the various parties may require administrative and board decisions before the next phase of activity can begin.

FACILITIES PLANNING AND DESIGN

There are seven major steps in the facilities planning process. The sequence of the few activities varies according to the development strategy employed.

Master Site and Facilities Planning

A master site and facilities plan defines a framework for addressing the organization's potential facility needs over an undefined period. With a sound master site and facility plan, the institution can respond to rapid growth or to the need to replace existing facilities in a phased and logical manner. The organization's master site and facility plan considers several key items, including the following:

- interdepartmental relationships
- flow of patients, visitors, staff, and supplies throughout the institution
- site development, including parking needs and traffic patterns
- other current and planned facilities on the campus, such as an ambulatory care center, physicians' office building, long-term care facility, parking structure, and specialty centers
- a functional and engineering evaluation of the immediate and long-range value of each structure
- property acquisition or disposal
- vertical and horizontal transportation systems
- future expansion of services and programs

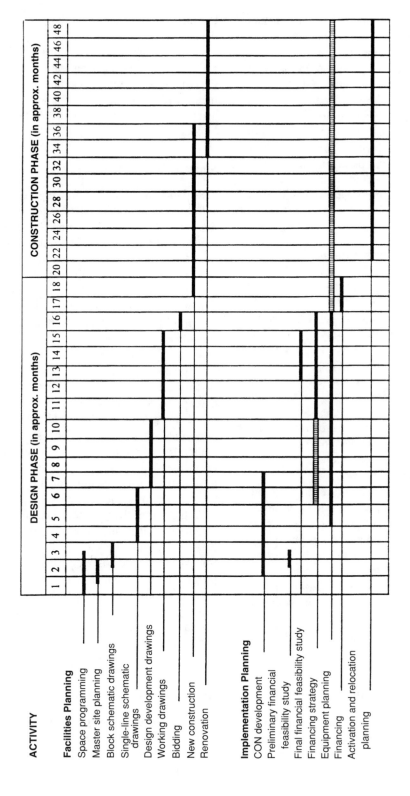

Figure 20–1 Stages in Facility Development Process. *Source:* Copyright © 1993, Herman Smith Associates, a Coopers & Lybrand Division, Chicago, Illinois.

During the master site and facility planning phase, the organization approves a fundamental long-term development concept, development priorities, and potential phasing of that development. Once reviewed and approved, the master site and facility plan is used in conjunction with the organization's program priorities and budget constraints to identify the scope of the initial phase of the proposed project. Program priorities that are defined in the organization's strategic plan should guide the facility development priorities illustrated in the master site and facility plan.

Functional Space Programming

Once the scope of the project is defined, the organization or, in many cases, a health care consultant, prepares a functional space program that describes in detail the space requirements for each department included in the proposed project. The functional space program describes present and future activities, outlines operational concepts, reviews historical and projects future utilization and staffing, outlines room-by-room space needs, identifies major proximity requirements and planning considerations, and conceptually illustrates departmental and intradepartmental organization of space.

During the functional space programming phase, the organization's role is to determine the departments to be included in the project; review the future program, utilization, operational systems, and staffing assumptions in the functional space program; and approve or amend the proposed departmental space allocations and the conceptual organization of intradepartmental space. A project budget must also be developed to guide the decisions regarding facilities' expansion priorities.

Block Schematic Drawings

Block schematic drawings are outlines of the individual departments indicating the proposed size and location of all the departments. The drawings also show major vertical and horizon-

tal traffic patterns and relationships among the departments.

During the block schematic phase, the organization—primarily management—approves the location of departments, deciding which departments will be located in the new construction and which will remain as is or expand in existing buildings.

Single-Line Schematic Drawings

Single-line schematic drawings further develop the departmental-block schematic drawings to show internal departmental layouts, relationships, and room sizes. The main emphasis in this stage of planning is to determine the location of the rooms within the departmental blocks. Single lines show wall or partition location without regard to wall thickness.

During the single-line schematic phase, the organization—in particular, the department managers—reviews and approves architectural floor plans (departmental layouts), preliminary exterior elevations, generic equipment lists, and other preliminary design concepts. At this point, the planning team should provide the organization with adequate square footage and cost information for the Certificate of Need and preliminary financial feasibility analysis so that the project scope can be adjusted as necessary to avoid problems in later stages of the project.

At the end of the schematic design stage, the health care consultant or architect prepares room data sheets outlining building systems criteria for the departmental areas included in the project. These documents cover the recommendations regarding communications, lighting, heating, ventilation, and air conditioning, medical gas, and equipment considerations, which will be defined in the design development process.

Design Development Drawings

Design development plans detail the single-line schematics to show wall thicknesses and locations of major built-in-equipment and casework, as well as mechanical, electrical, structural, and architectural systems required within the individual rooms in the project. Also at this time, the equipment consultant prepares equipment specifications and provides "cutsheets" for the architects and engineers.

During the design development phase, the organization—in particular, the department managers—reviews and approves room details, outline specifications, room finishes, and design refinements. Examples are the number and location of medical gas outlets; locations, width, and type of doors; types of heating, ventilating, and air conditioning systems; details of casework; and selection of windows and exterior materials.

Working Drawings

In the working drawing stage, mechanical, electrical, and plumbing systems are sized, and architectural details are refined to meet the requirements of the departments that were outlined in the design development drawings. During this phase, the organization reviews and approves working drawings and final specifications before they are released to potential contractors for bidding. Typically, this phase involves limited participation at the departmental level of the organization.

Construction

The last major phase of the facilities development process is the actual construction of the new and/or renovated facilities. The construction or renovation activities are scheduled to minimize interruption of normal operations, although some institutional functions may be restricted or inconvenienced.

During the construction phase, the organization needs to minimize change orders, both owner- and contractor-initiated, plan for occupancy of the new building, and procure medical equipment and furnishings.

IMPLEMENTATION PLANNING

Project implementation is a process that occurs simultaneously with facilities planning and design. The sequence of its four basic activities

varies, depending on the institution's facility development strategy, internal management capabilities, and external factors.

Certificate of Need Development

In most cases, particularly for licensed facilities, a Certificate of Need must be developed and submitted to the state and possibly to the regional review agencies for approval. The development of the application must be timed to permit the facilities development schedule to proceed without major interruptions. Generally, the application is submitted after the organization's approval of block schematic plans; however, some states require single-line schematic drawings.

The organization must develop a strategy to move the Certificate of Need through the review process with minimal delays and compromises. In some states, applications are batched and must be submitted according to a predetermined schedule. This could affect the overall project schedule and estimated costs and must be considered to ensure the project is not delayed.

Financial Feasibility Study and Financing Strategy

An evaluation of the organization's financial operations must be conducted to determine its debt capacity. Based on this evaluation, a strategy is developed to finance the project at a reasonable cost while providing flexibility to respond to future capital needs. In order to prepare the financial feasibility study, the organization, with the assistance of the external planning team, must develop an overall project budget identifying all project-related costs—professional fees, land acquisition, equipment, legal, financing, and construction.

The organization needs to determine how it will fund this facilities development project and other capital requirements of the master plan. A preliminary feasibility study should be performed early in the project based on major assumptions regarding construction costs, utilization, and interest rates so that the project scope can be adjusted as necessary with minimal loss of time and effort. The final feasibility study is performed after the receipt of construction bids and is based on actual interest rates at the time of financing. If bond financing is involved, additional consultants such as underwriters and bond counsel will be required to help sell the bonds.

Equipment Planning

Evaluating existing equipment and determining what can be relocated and what additional equipment will be needed for the new and/or renovated facilities is essential. Equipment planning activities should begin as early as possible so that the initial project budget and Certificate of Need application can accurately reflect equipment needs. Once defined, equipment requirements are communicated to the architects and engineers to ensure adequate room sizes, layouts, and utilities.

As technology becomes more sophisticated, medical equipment consumes a greater percentage of the overall capital budget. Appropriate planning may require external assistance to ensure objective determination of reuse, proper lead times for timely installation, adequate planning information, and competitive pricing.

Facility Activation and Occupancy Planning

Thorough planning is necessary for the smooth opening and activation of the new and/or renovated facilities. Development of operational systems, determination of staffing levels and staff recruitment plans, definition of relocation strategies, equipment installation schedules, and development of a building activation schedule all occur during this phase. Sound activation and occupancy planning facilitates full productivity of the new and/or renovated facilities once they are occupied.

GENERAL FACILITY PLANNING PRINCIPLES

Whether evaluating the adequacy of existing facilities or considering new construction, some functional facility planning considerations must be taken into account. Primary planning considerations include separating patient, service, and public traffic flow, maximizing operating efficiencies, providing for future expansion, and optimizing functional relationships. Although these basic considerations have been addressed by many innovative solutions over the years, most of these concepts have not withstood the test of time. The following concepts produce the best life-cycle return on capital dollars.

Nursing Units

Inpatient facilities should be developed around the primary unit, the patient bed. The patient bed should be integrated into complete nursing care services that are composed of effective and efficient nursing units in the range of 32 to 40 beds. Additionally, the private room versus the semiprivate (two-bed) room controversy must be resolved. An equal mix of private and semiprivate rooms is typically appropriate. However, the increasing acuity of inpatients and patient desire for privacy has shifted the mix toward all private designs for the 1990s.

Nursing units should be located in a patient tower served by a central elevator core. Ideally, two to three nursing units are located on one level to share some common support services. If one or more nursing units are provided on the same level, traffic should not have to pass through one nursing unit to reach the other unit.

Today many hospitals are implementing patient-centered care and redesigning patient care delivery systems. Under the patient-centered care concept, some medical and administrative ancillaries are typically decentralized on the nursing floors. Although this is the current trend for patient unit design, long-term flexibility must be considered to avoid costly errors.

Medical Ancillary Services

Medical ancillary facilities should be located in a multilevel base so that they can be expanded independently as necessary. Consideration must be given to the outpatient and inpatient mix served by each service. With the trend to ambulatory care, depending upon volume, separate inpatient and outpatient ancillary services may need to be considered, especially if many physicians are practicing in or adjacent to the hospital, and if the volume of service is high enough to justify duplicate staffing and equipment.

The medical ancillary services located in the multilevel base should be organized and designed in anticipation of future expansion. Major medical ancillary departments that are expensive to relocate, such as radiology, laboratory, surgery, emergency, dietary, and central reprocessing, should be located by exterior walls and next to "soft" areas—office areas—that could be converted inexpensively to other uses.

Elevators and Transportation System

Generally, patient, service, and visitor/personnel elevators should be centralized but segregated to maximize flexibility during peak load times. This is a very important consideration, particularly when elevators are out of service. If the elevators are centralized, a malfunctioning elevator will not greatly disrupt traffic patterns and service within the central transportation core. Another important aspect of elevator planning is flexibility in terms of size. All patient/service elevators should be large enough to carry a hospital bed with an orthopedic frame. Patient/service elevators should not be visible from the public areas.

Materials transportation systems, such as pneumatic tube, tote-box, or cart-type systems, should be considered. However, with the increased use of hospital information systems, the need for pneumatic tubes or dumbwaiters is decreasing. Similarly, efficient materials management and unit-dose pharmacy systems reduce the need for automated tote-box and cart-type systems. Although automated materials transportation systems are generally expensive to install and maintain, they should not be ruled out as impractical or too expensive until a full life-cycle cost analysis has been completed. In assessing materials transport alternatives, it is important to verify the existence of adequate floor-to-floor heights to accommodate the system.

Traffic Patterns

Ideally, travel through the facility, particularly patient travel, should be minimized to one elevator trip. Thus, it is desirable to locate all ancillary services so that they can be reached from any nursing unit by traveling in one elevator. This principle also holds true for outpatients, who should be able to come to one central point, and be easily referred to the appropriate service.

General horizontal circulation patterns should be planned to separate inpatient and outpatient/service and public traffic.

Travel Distance

Minimizing the distance that personnel travel from one department to another will reduce operating costs; therefore, if at all possible, all departments should relate to the central transport area. Generally, all facilities require a two- or three-level ancillary base with the bed towers located above to minimize these distances.

Some hospitals have separated medical ancillaries, bed towers, and support services into distinct buildings built to different building codes to reduce initial construction costs. Generally, the initial savings are not significant enough to outweigh the long-term flexibility limitations.

Relationships

Interdepartmental relationships should be considered in planning a major facilities expansion or replacement. Ideally all services should be centrally located and adjacent to the elevator core. However, some compromises must be made. Figure 20–2 identifies key interdepartmental relationships to consider in facility planning.

In order to reduce operating costs, hospitals should consider grouping smaller departments to share support areas such as reception and waiting, locker/lounge areas, and conference rooms.

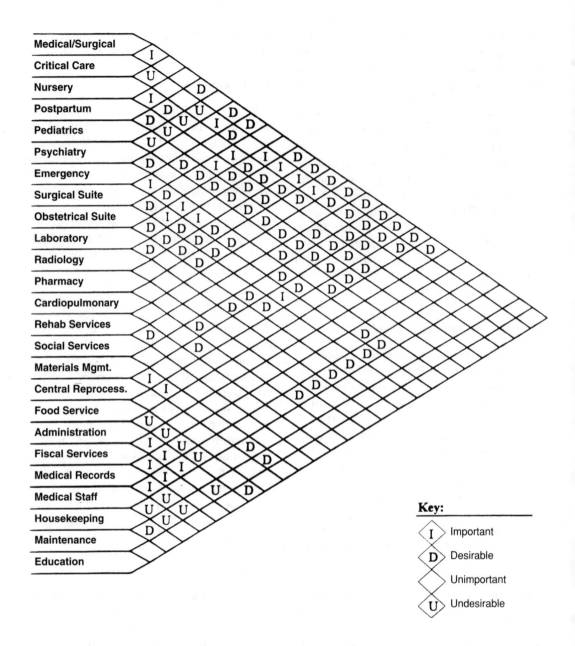

Figure 20–2 Desirable Interdepartmental Relationships. *Source:* Copyright © 1993, Herman Smith Associates, a Coopers & Lybrand Division, Chicago, Illinois.

Intradepartmental Design Principles

The internal design of departments should also meet similar criteria for service, patient, and staff traffic separation. Consider the following general principles:

- The patient reception and waiting area should be near the entrance of the department, but should not open directly into work areas of the department.

- Gowned waiting areas should be near the treatment spaces. Patients should not be required to walk through public areas after gowning.

- To maximize privacy, toilet rooms should open off the corridors and not open directly into waiting spaces.

- Staff lounges should not be adjacent to patient waiting areas or treatment areas.

- Storage and utility spaces should be designed to maximize flexibility and should have a minimal amount of built-in casework.

- Examination and treatment room doors should be hinged to maximize patient privacy as the door opens.

Entrances

Ideally there should be six distinct entrances—the main entrance for patients and visitors, employee entrance, physicians' entrance, emergency entrance, outpatient entrance, and receiving entrance—with appropriate parking readily available. These entrances should relate to the departments utilized by the groups and should direct the traffic into the appropriate elevator core and circulation system of the hospital.

Facility Replacement

To allow for an orderly progression of facility replacement, new construction should be related to the latest existing construction. In this way, the oldest buildings can be phased out without interrupting the functions housed in the newer buildings.

The planning principles enumerated in this section can be used to evaluate existing facilities and determine the long-term use of the organization's physical assets.

SPACE DETERMINATION

An important aspect of physical planning is the determination of space needed for the function being considered. Departmental space must be consistent with the scope of services to be provided; however, it should not be planned around the current scope of services, management concepts, or individual departmental desires without considering trends in the field. Any standard or published guidelines should be questioned and must be related to the organization and operation of the department. It is important to examine the source document of a published guideline to determine exactly what variables were included in the calculation.

Space guidelines for departments specifically should relate to the services, activities, and productivity of the department. Although these guidelines can be used to set gross square footage estimates, a detailed functional space program must then be developed based on the specific needs and demands of the department. All facilities have slightly different operating procedures that affect space needs.

In analyzing the space needs of a service, it is important to consider these major factors that influence utilization:

- scope of services—services that the department provides

- operations—hours of operation, policies of scheduling certain tests on certain days or special room designation in surgery

- equipment—use of automated versus manual equipment, dedicated versus multiuse equipment, potential new technology

- staffing—full-time versus part-time and maximum number of people on the primary shift, which influences the number of workstations required

- workload—projected inpatient/outpatient mix, procedure mix; projections must consider impact of clinical protocols, capitation, and other relevant factors.
- competition—likelihood of new providers or existing hospitals and physician groups increasing market share; in the new managed care market, hospitals are more likely to have significant market gains or losses as contracts shift.

If outpatient volume is large, it may be desirable to develop a freestanding outpatient service center, rather than attempt to accommodate both inpatients and outpatients in one facility. Outpatient volume will increase if outpatient activities can be consolidated in one location with convenient registration and parking independent of the traffic and complexities of the main building.

INTERNAL PLANNING TEAM

Hospitals have evolved from isolated, self-sustaining single-site institutions to multicampus corporations that provide an extremely complex variety of services in a highly competitive marketplace. The overwhelming proliferation of external influences on internal hospital programs and decision making has created new roles for management at every internal administrative level.

In facilities planning activities, the administrative decision-making process must provide a framework for an internal planning team's activities, which are focused toward an end product—a facility that is consistent with institutional objectives.

Most members of an internal planning team do not understand the facility planning process and are unaware of the decisions required at various stages in it. Moreover, the more articulate members of an organization may inappropriately influence the facilities planning process through personalized decisions, rather than an institutional perspective.

To focus the efforts of the internal facility planning team, it is necessary to do the following:

- Educate internal planning team members—board of trustees, medical staff, department managers, and in-house planners—about the facilities planning process.
- Define at what management level project decisions are to be made.
- Organize the facility planning team to facility decision making and implementation.
- Establish a communication mechanism to disseminate planning decisions to prevent the reintroduction of issues that were already resolved.

The organizational structure of the internal planning team changes as organizational complexities change. The team needed to plan and implement a facility project is ultimately determined by the scope and nature of the project. Power struggles are inevitable as managers attempt to direct more project resources to their departments at the expense of other departments. A well-managed institution should be able to maintain project control during such inevitable conflicts.

Members of the Internal Planning Team

The organization and, therefore, the decision-making process for facility planning should not differ from the decision-making process for daily operations. The secret of proper planning-team organization and subsequent control lies within an already existing organizational structure. Information gathering and consensus building provide a critical basis for final, administrative decision making. The information gathered is weighed and evaluated, but not every suggestion can or should be incorporated into the final facility plan; thus, the need for informed decision making.

The roles of the various internal team members in the physical facility planning process are described below:

1. *Governing board:* For all practical purposes, the board has full authority and responsibility at all stages in the physical facility planning process and is free to delegate all or portions of the decision-making responsibility to management of the organization. In the physical planning process, the board has these major responsibilities:
   - establishing the basic objectives of the functional space program through approval of the strategic plan and master site and facility plan
   - hiring an appropriate external planning team and ultimately auditing its performance and approving its actions
   - approving the capital program budget and overseeing its control
   - discharging or delegating the ability to sign contracts and approving change orders relating to the construction project.

2. *Chief executive officer:* The major responsibilities of the chief executive officer (CEO) in the facility planning process are no different than in the organization's operations. The CEO, by virtue of his or her responsibility for the organization's operations, must make or approve all plans for physical facility implementation as they affect the operating mode of the organization.

   Capital development programs affect the organization's operating costs significantly and should not be delegated to a lower organizational level. To ensure provision of the best input for critical decisions, the CEO should select an experienced and knowledgeable external planning team—health care consultant, financial advisor, financial feasibility consultant, fund-raiser, construction manager, architect/engineer, legal counsel, and underwriter. The external planning team provides the technical input required for proper administrative decision making.

3. *Medical staff:* Although physician influence in hospitals varies, the physician is usually an individual entrepreneur who has significant control over the utilization of a health care facility. As both the provider and consumer of health care services, the physician is a major force in initiating facility development programs. The medical staff is perceived to have significant authority in the facility planning decision-making process.

   In this process, the physician's main role is to provide appropriate technical input about the requirements of implementing a specific program or service. The most effective method of securing this input is through the use of the existing medical staff committee structure or, as appropriate, the establishment of a single ad hoc medical staff planning committee to advise management and the external planning team. The input and output of an ad hoc committee should be controlled within the context of the pre-established project implementation constraints.

4. *User groups:* User groups are typically comprised of key staff and physicians associated with a particular department. User groups can play an important advisory role in the facility planning process, providing input on specific department space and equipment needs and comment on design concepts. Although they can be given decision-making authority, in most cases the user groups should be advisory only, and the decision-making/control function should rest with the CEO or his or her designate. The establishment of specific facility-planning user groups depends on the scope and magnitude of a particular project.

5. *In-house planner:* Given the complexities of management, many organizations have a staff planning department to support the CEO. The in-house planner can be the prime source of the organization's input to the facility development process. This

individual can also be effectively used as the conveyor of input that ultimately will form the basis for rendering management decisions. Another invaluable role of the planner is to communicate management decisions pertinent to the project to the entire organization.

Educating the Internal Functional Planning Team—The Planning Process

Understanding the process of facility planning is the most important step in establishing a control mechanism for the internal functional planning team. At the point when an organization begins a facility development project, the following key elements in the facility planning process should be in place:

- strategic plan establishing organizational priorities and goals
- review of construction alternatives for providing the programs and services and for prioritizing the programs and services to be implemented (master site and facility plan)
- maximum financial expenditure (budget) for the development project that establishes the upper limit of the relative size or scope for the project
- reasonable time frame for facility project implementation
- approvals from local, regional, and institutional authorities, as well as accreditation, licensure, and reimbursement bodies

To a significant degree, these steps, which are precursors to physical facility planning and implementation, establish major project parameters for a specific facility planning process and thereby provide a framework for the institution's internal planning process.

Framework for Controlling Time and Input

The ultimate success of a physical facility plan depends on control of time, the functional space program, and design criteria.

The best method to help an organization's internal planning team understand its role, project time frames, and the facility activation process is the development of a critical path method (CPM). A properly developed CPM outlines the necessary tasks, the internal planning team's input, and the time frame necessary to complete a particular planning sequence. The CPM is a road map for project scheduling that educates the internal planning team members about the project sequence, team members' roles, the decision-making process, and current project status.

The functional space program preparation is another crucial element in project control. The functional space program identifies specific project elements approved by the organization and serves as the basis for architectural drawings for the facilities to be constructed. The approved functional space program should be utilized as a document to control project scope. Deviation from the scope outlined in the functional space program should be approved at the executive management level.

The design criteria document serves as a control mechanism for the internal planning team by predefining building systems for facility design and development. Design criteria should outline specific design constraints for each program element, such as building systems, mechanical and electrical parameters, and finish requirements, as identified and approved by management.

Appropriate input from the internal planning team members is required for developing control documents. Proper project direction from management, timing, and organization will stimulate the required internal planning team inputs and create a dynamic, positive planning attitude, thereby ensuring proper control and project direction.

Facility planning projects are a series of controlled compromises accomplished within the constraints of time, money, and strategic program planning. The perceived role and relative input to the decision-making process of its participants vary by individual perception and level within the organization. Ultimately, however, the CEO is responsible to the governing board for implementing the facility plan and must, with appropriate input from both the internal and external planning team members, manage and control the project.

EXTERNAL PLANNING TEAM

In most cases, a health care facility cannot rely on internal resources augmented by an architect/engineer to conceive, orchestrate, implement, and activate a major facility development program. A team of professional external resource people is generally needed to manage the project properly.

The need for an external planning team is best indicated by the vast quantity of details required by the external regulatory and approval processes. These regulatory demands have, in effect, mandated the development of an external team to minimize possible project delay and maximize the chance for project approval. Hospitals initiate a major building program every seven to ten years. Most administrators are involved in one to two projects in a career. In contrast, qualified external planning team members are involved in several similar projects each year and know the best approaches and options to streamline the process and minimize the organization's risks. In addition, time constraints associated with an external approval process mandate tight project control, and external professionals, being experienced in the process, are able to provide that control.

A comprehensive external team includes a facility planning consultant, equipment planning consultant, architect/engineer, financial advisor, financial feasibility consultant, fund-raiser, construction manager, legal counsel, and underwriter. The external team's composition is related directly to project complexity and the hospital's internal expertise and varies by project.

By its nature, a facility project has a defined goal, is a one-time effort, and has a specified completion point. Selecting and controlling the external team influences the project outcome and its cost. Necessary changes must be made

early in every project to avoid cost overruns. The outcome of a facility development plan is based on cumulative decisions, and the possibility of influencing a project is reduced as time progresses, as shown in Figure 20–3. A poorly run project can cost millions of dollars in construction delays, change orders, and operating costs over the life of a facility project. An inefficiently organized department or an over- or undersized department creates operating problems and increases personnel costs. A poorly engineered facility generates increased maintenance expenses and/or operating costs. An improperly located building or department may preclude future expansion opportunities. A poorly executed financing plan may limit future capital development opportunities.

Team Members and Their Responsibilities

A simple project may be implemented solely with an architect/engineering firm, whereas a complex project may require a comprehensive team. Health care expertise requirements, program complexity, the external planning environment, and project implementation requirements, to a large extent, determine the makeup of the external team. The relative roles, responsibilities, and tasks of team members must be clearly identified at project inception. Their particular expertise should be sought and controlled with respect to overall project direction.

- *Facility planning consultant:* The facility planning consultant's primary role is to define the required departmental space and inter- and intrarelationships necessary to optimize cost-effective operations (functional planning). He or she provides management skills relating to project implementation, thereby translating the institution's program objectives into space requirements and operationally effective designs, as well as providing operational and systems expertise through building activation. The consultant's recommendations are based on a review of the organization's strategic plan program plans

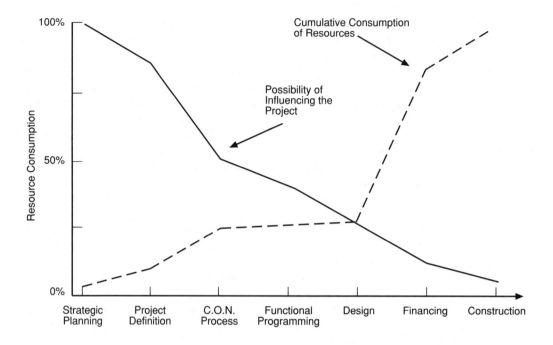

Project Implementation Phases

Figure 20–3 Conceptual Diagram of Resource Consumption. *Source:* Copyright © 1993, Herman Smith Associates, a Coopers & Lybrand Division, Chicago, Illinois.

and forecasts of departmental workloads, staffing, and operating and management systems.

In some cases, the facility planning consultant or an independent project manager coordinates the activities of all external professional team members, monitors the budget and schedule, and integrates internal and external planning team decisions from project definition to final facilities activation. In general, a qualified health care planning consultant understands the tasks necessary for project implementation and the outputs required of various external team members throughout the process.

The facility planning consultant may be independent or may represent a health care consulting firm that takes a broader health care planning role in assisting the institution in defining its overall project scope. During the external approval phase, a

health care consultant may make valuable recommendations in project strategy and in dealing with the planning agency. The health care consultant brings a working knowledge of the approval process, case histories of similar situations, and an understanding of the disciplines necessary to implement the project.

- *Equipment planning consultant:* Historically, equipment planning was handled by the organization's purchasing department in consultation with individual departments. However, the ever-increasing sophistication of technology, emphasis on cost containment, and required coordination of departmental needs demand that management assume the responsibility of inventorying and evaluating existing equipment, preparing and monitoring equipment lists and budgets, preparing specifications, and coordinating procurement and installation. This process usually demands time and expertise not available within the hospital organization.

- *Construction manager:* A qualified construction manager provides multiple levels of input to a facility project. During the external approval process, the construction manager is responsible for developing credible construction cost inputs for submittal documentation. This costing is based on the program definition provided by the organization, the facility planning consultant, and the architect/engineer. The construction manager provides construction input into cost-benefit analyses of alternative construction techniques and assists the project team in maximizing facility development within the limits of an approved project scope and budget. The construction manager may also be called on to render a guaranteed maximum price for financing purposes or a phased construction process and may act as an owner/agent in the construction process.

  During construction, the construction manager receives bids, schedules work, coordinates subcontractors, and manages the construction program to minimize construction time and provide the earliest possible occupancy.

- *Architect/engineer:* The architect is responsible for translating the functional space program into an operationally cost-effective design maximizing the reuse of existing physical resources as appropriate. The engineer develops the infrastructure (structural, mechanical, electrical, and plumbing systems) necessary to appropriately support the architect's design. In many cases, the architect and engineer are a single A/E firm; however, it is just as likely for the engineering services to be provided by independent single or multiple engineering firms.

  The regulatory process and innovative methods of project implementation have changed the traditional role of an architect/engineer. The regulatory approval process requires that major project decisions be made in early design because the organization will have to live within a maximum capital expenditure. Thus, decisions regarding the inclusion of pneumatic tube system or air conditioning of an old building will have to be decided during schematics. A phased construction approach has also changed the traditional role of an architect/engineer, requiring that certain design packages be developed and bid before all working drawings are complete.

  Many states require submission of single-line schematics for regulatory review, whereas others require only block schematic drawings. It is important to ascertain the requirements specific to your state so that the drawings can be developed to the minimum level of detail required. The level of detail on drawings submitted in the approval process should be minimized to reduce the institution's financial exposure at the "front end" when regulatory denial is possible. However, even though drawing detail may be minimal for the approval phase, the architectural/engineering firm must participate actively in defining project scope and design criteria for costing purposes.

- *Legal counsel:* In today's health care environment, legal counsel is necessary from the preliminary project definition phase through approval and activation. Legal counsel's role varies, depending upon the local environment, the political structure of the regulatory process, community acceptance of the project, and project complexity. Several types of legal counsel may be required, including lawyers in reimbursement, regulatory process (zoning variances, CON, etc.), and bond counsel specialties.

- *Fund-raiser:* A fund-raiser has several distinct roles. The first is to develop the feasibility study to estimate fund-raising potential. Because this study measures community support to some degree, it can be utilized as part of the external approval process. A fund-raiser would also be involved in managing the campaign if the hospital commits itself to a fund drive.

- *Financial advisor and/or financial feasibility:* Most major hospital projects require external financing advice. The financial consulting tasks begin with preparation of a preliminary financial capability study outlining the impacts of the proposed project on an organization's fiscal structure. The financial consultant assesses the debt capacity and debt limitations of the organization, the probable impact of refinancing existing debt, the impact of the project on the organization's operating costs, and an assessment of the likelihood of financing the project.

  The financial consultant's role varies in each project phase. During the CON approval process, the consultant tests demand figures, assists management in preparing operating budgets, and develops a preliminary capability study for submission with the application. During the implementation process, the consultant monitors overall hospital operations and, in order to secure permanent financing, prepares a financial feasibility study to be submitted with public offering documents.

- *Underwriter:* Underwriters sell money to an organization for a fee. In most major facility projects, an underwriter is involved for financing unless there is a possibility of private placement (e.g., a direct, negotiated sale). An underwriter's role generally does not begin until interim or permanent financing is sought, although, if required, he or she can assist the hospital in the regulatory process by assessing the hospital's financial status and bond rating probabilities and establishing an appropriate interest rate for budgetary purposes. The underwriter's major input, however, is required while developing the financing instrument and actual bond sale. Hospitals must exercise caution in developing the financing instrument to preserve flexibility for future capital development projects.

Selecting External Team Members

Regardless of the external team members selected to assist in project implementation, the selection process should not vary. A legitimate selection process is highly structured and uses objective evaluation criteria. Its purpose is to establish not only the firm's capabilities but also individual experience and capability pertinent to the institution's situation. A structured selection process should be accomplished in these phases with multiple, distinct, and objective evaluation criteria used to select firms with a demonstrated track record.

1. Phase I—preliminary selection and preinterview qualification
   - Identify type of external professionals required.
   - Preselect probable firms for qualifications.
   - Solicit preliminary information from identified firms.
   - Analyze and identify potentially qualified firms.
   - Conduct a preliminary reference check on qualified firms.
   - Identify qualified professional firms.
2. Phase II—selection process
   - Invite prequalified firms for a site visit.
   - Solicit proposals.
   - Following a definitive presentation, interview using a structured format.
   - Select the firm.
3. Phase III—contract development
   - Develop a definitive contract, including an outline task analysis by project phase.
   - Negotiate contracts and fees. (A well-qualified firm will not necessarily cost any more than a less-qualified firm.)
4. Phase IV—maximizing professional talents

- A clear definition of what is to be performed by the multidisciplinary team members, when it is to be performed, and who is to perform the tasks maximizes effective use of these external professionals.

After external team selection, a representative from each discipline on the external team must meet with the organization's representative and develop a project schedule that describes that profession's relative role and responsibilities for each phase of the project. This schedule will need to be updated on a monthly basis as the planning continues. Maximizing the external team members' talents depends totally on the professionals' ability to interact in a dynamic process and to respect other professionals' judgment with respect to the stage of project development and that professional's particular role. Simply put, each professional should be accorded the respect of the other team members and be permitted to take the lead on appropriate issues, thus maximizing the benefits of each individual's skills and expertise. When and if conflicts arise, team members must work together to discuss and solve the problem.

DESIGN AND CONSTRUCTION APPROACHES

Despite competition and cost constraint pressures, health care facilities will continue to be built, upgraded, and expanded. Demand for medical care programs is increasing in the outpatient and new technology sectors. Additionally, existing health care facilities will continue to be replaced to comply with codes, maintain accreditation, and gain a competitive advantage.

A variety of facility construction alternatives are available; each affects owner control, building quality, project duration, and, ultimately, project cost. The major facility implementation alternatives are as follows:

- traditional approach
- team approach
- design/build approach
- project management approach

Traditional Approach

In the traditional and most common method of building implementation, an owner, under separate contract, engages a facility planning consultant and architect/engineer to plan and design a building. The architect/engineer and the facility planning consultant prepare a functional space program and a set of working drawings and specifications. The project is then bid on a lump-sum basis to reach a fixed construction figure. The owner, in soliciting competitive bids, typically awards the contract for construction to the lowest bidder. The sequential process allows for the establishment of a fixed construction figure before committing to the building implementation.

Team Approach

In the team approach, as in the traditional process, the owner contracts with a facility planning consultant, architect/engineering, and construction manager to develop and implement a building program. However, the construction is completed in the shortest possible time. This process could be organized by the following methods:

- all contracts coordinated and managed by the owner
- joint venture of various professionals
- project management approach, in which a project manager by contract is responsible directly to the owner for team coordination and ensuring that the project meets the owner's requirements

Design and construction phases are typically overlapped, rather than done in sequence as in the traditional approach. Also, the construction manager might guarantee a fixed cost—guaranteed maximum price—for the project early in the development process if the scope of the project is clearly defined.

A significant advantage of the team approach is that it minimizes planning and construction times. In a team approach (with a construction manager), construction can begin before the completion of all working drawings. A bid package consisting of logical groupings of building elements is prepared at various stages of the project. For example, excavation, off-site utilities, and foundations might be developed in a complete bid package and be bid and awarded before completion of the total design of the project. Depending on project requirements, each of these bid packages might be competitively bid or negotiated.

In addition to the initial consulting service, the construction manager may guarantee the project construction cost early in the design process. Most often, this occurs at the end of the design development phase when the major elements have been identified; i.e., the building area is fixed, mechanical systems have been defined, and the relative building quality is established.

Design/Build Approach

A simple description of the design/build or "turnkey" construction approach is that a developer or single party undertakes the entire responsibility for delivering a project to the owner. The developer or single party acquires or is provided the land, designs and builds the project under one financial transaction, and delivers a final product to the owner. The vendor is responsible for the total effort, and the owner is relieved of all management and coordination responsibility. There are many variations of this approach.

This process is typically less time consuming than the traditional approach. Generally, the vendor negotiates contracts with local suppliers, eliminating the need for competitive bids. The vendor must stay within a pre-established budget and thus must make cost-effective design decisions in order to develop the building within the originally guaranteed cost.

However, if this budget has been set before completion of design and construction documents, the owner has little or no control over cost-cutting measures or construction standards because there typically is limited enforceable documentation describing the end-product or building. The owner knows what the project is going to cost but not what the end result will be. Although short-run capital costs may be lower, long-term operating costs could be greater.

Project Management

Project management is not strictly an alternative approach to facility implementation, but rather a process of implementing a building program. Because of the complexity of today's facility planning projects, many experts believe that the traditional approach for developing, planning, and financing health care construction is no longer effective or responsive to the current health care environment. This belief has led to the development of the project management approach.

A project management process in facility implementation requires the assembling of an appropriate group of professionals to implement a project. A single spokesperson is responsible to the organization for project implementation. This new specialist—the project manager—is under contract to the organization for coordinating and managing the professional disciplines involved, acting as the organization's advocate, reporting to its governing body, and developing cooperatively the strategy and accountability of every planning and implementation function. A project manager provides an understanding of each professional's contribution to the project, a knowledge of concurrent task scheduling, management communication skills, and an ability to interpret and solve problems. The project manager or project management process is a contracted extension of institution management. This process, although typically used in a team approach, can also be used in a traditional approach.

Review of Alternatives

From the owner's perspective, each of these alternatives has different effects on the organization, and no single alternative is best for all projects. The alternatives can be evaluated objectively and subjectively according to the following criteria:

- owner's authority
- project fees
- project costs
- project duration
- building quality
- checks and balances
- owner coordination
- owner control
- owner liability

For projects costing less than $5 million, a traditional approach or a design/build approach provides an advantage to the owner, assuming that proper controls can be levied against the contract bidder.

In a major building program—one costing $10 million or more—or a complicated renovation project requiring phased construction, the team approach is typically the most cost-effective approach for the institution. The team approach can either be organized through separate contracts with an owner or through a project manager. The concept has been used for years in industry. Its application to the health care field is intensified by the many cost constraints in the health care industry today.

FUTURE FACILITY PLANNING TRENDS

During the 1970s, utilization review programs pressured hospitals to reduce lengths of stay and thereby cut costs. Yet, since reimbursement was cost based, there was no incentive to reduce costs directly, the number of admissions remained high, and use rates for most beds and services continued to increase. During this era, capital costs, including those for construction, were passed on to third-party payor or consumer in the form of increased rates.

The implementation of the government PPS established flat rates for reimbursement based on specific DRGs for inpatient care, and use rates dropped dramatically. Hospitals are faced with the need to deliver services within stringent cost constraints and with a smaller inpatient base. Under managed care, there is more of a need to distribute physical resources to multiple delivery sites convenient to subscribers.

An obvious response to these cost constraints has been increased attention to modernizing, rather than replacing, facilities. In addition, many organizations, responding both to reimbursement limits and increasing consumer demands, have changed their emphasis from inpatient care to ambulatory care. In many facilities, inpatient areas have been retrofitted for ambulatory and other alternative uses. Generally, the trend toward inpatient downsizing and outpatient care will continue. Additionally, hospital and alternative providers will continue to expand home care programs and preventive care, particularly if capitation is expanded as a payment mechanism.

Many hospitals that have delayed or reduced building programs in the 1980s will either face major construction programs in the future or be forced to continue to operate obsolete facilities through the late 1990s. It is likely that the amount of money available for major capital projects will be limited. Because of the shrinking inpatient market and proposals for health care reform, the number of independent hospitals is decreasing rapidly as providers join forces in networks and in many cases merge assets. Thus, a major facilities planning focus for the late 1990s will be reallocating the existing physical resources of independent facilities into a cost-effective integrated system with multiple campuses. Downsizing and redesign will continue to be a major role in the 1990s.

Facility Design

Continuing change in the health care environment will affect facilities development for the late 1990s as follows:

- *Private patient rooms:* To attain cost-effective occupancy levels while continuing to meet the needs of more acutely ill patients, as well as segregate patients according to sex, disease, smoking, age, or other variables, hospitals are increasing the proportion of private rooms. A larger percentage will be monitored and designed for critical care.
- *Technological advances:* Flexibility will continue to gain importance in facility planning. In the 1960s, hospitals had to accommodate nuclear medicine; in the 1970s, CT scanners; and in the 1980s, magnetic resonance imaging. In the 1990s, new technological advances will continue to make new demands on facilities. These advances have focused on enhancements of current technology and bedside testing. The primary impetus for the enhancements has been information technology. Information technology will continue to be a major factor in the future with filmless radiology departments, integrated hospital computerized medical records, noninvasive surgery, telediagnostics, and other developments. To accommodate new technology, facilities must be planned to maximize remodeling flexibility and expansion capability.
- *Life-cycle costing:* In addition to initial costs, operating costs must be considered in the selection of mechanical and electrical systems and in the design of nursing units and ancillary services. Life-cycle costing presents many opportunities for reducing operating costs and conserving scarce resources, and it must be considered in any future facility project.
- *Departmental consolidation:* Over the years, health care has become more specialized; small clinical and nonclinical services have developed throughout institutions. Similarly, organizations have created additional layers of management. With downsizing and redesign activities, it is likely that many of the small hospital departments of today will be consolidated or eliminated to reduce the duplication of support staff and facilities. Facilities planning should focus on grouping reception, waiting, and staff areas for multiple departments. Similarly, the number of department managers will be reduced and become working supervisors.
- *Outsourcing:* Hospitals have historically maintained an on-site warehouse, laundry, kitchen, central supply, and pharmacy. Over the years, some hospitals have closed in-house laundries and many hospitals have begun to implement just-in-time warehouse policies. These trends will intensify. Hospitals will also look for ways to further reduce costs in these areas by outsourcing. Hospitals will contract with off-site central reprocessing vendors, utilize prepared meals, or depend on shared production kitchens and implement just-in-time pharmacy systems potentially run by the hospital system. Similarly, hospitals could outsource records management or business office functions (to the extent they may be needed).
- *Square footage per bed:* A trend that developed in the 1970s was an increase in the required number of square feet allotted per bed as hospitals added new services and programs. Traditionally, this square-foot-per-bed figure was computed by dividing the total square feet of the hospital by the number of beds. Never a truly representative figure, the concept has become outmoded as more services are provided on an outpatient basis and as an increasing number of services are developed and delivered off-site. Increasingly, ambulatory and outreach services will be separated from acute care programs and be established in free-standing facilities and even malls. Thus, it is more accurate to look at square footage in terms of service utilization, seeking the most efficient use of space for technology and treatment purposes.

Freestanding Facilities

For the 1990s, major facility development issues will involve not only the retrofitting of inpatient facilities but also the development of freestanding alternative health care delivery centers, such as urgent care centers, primary care centers, ambulatory surgery centers, birthing centers, and wellness centers. These alternative delivery centers are designed for ambulatory, non-life-threatening conditions that need not be treated in a hospital. The centers represent the health care industry's response to the population's growing health care consumerism, managed care, concern about high hospital costs, and interest in convenience and greater participation in the care of family members.

Changing Delivery Approaches

Another factor in the development of alternative delivery centers has been significant hospital/physician competition in metropolitan areas. Physicians are seeking alternative ways to maintain or create a patient base. Under managed care more independent physicians will merge into large group practices. In order to maintain cur-rent income, physicians will need to review operations and make better use of their physical facilities. Additionally, physicians will continue to compete with hospitals and other physicians for profitable ambulatory services by catering to consumer desires for evening and weekend hours, house calls, or out-of-hospital deliveries.

As physicians and hospitals become more integrated through PHOs/MSOs and clinical parameters are implemented, significant changes in medical ancillary services utilization could occur. Similarly, physicians may be more willing to extend operating hours and improve equipment utilization. Thus, some undersized facilities could quickly become adequate or even oversized.

These major factors—managed care, physician/hospital relationships, hospital competition, changes in the reimbursement system, and the consumer movement—are creating permanent changes in health care delivery. Health delivery organizations must retool and adjust to these changes through a continuous reexamination of opportunities and their weaknesses. To be successful, CEOs will need to monitor new developments and strategic options and take decisive action to stay ahead of the competition.

JAMES E. HOSKING, MBA, FAAHC, is a partner with the Herman Smith Associates division of Coopers & Lybrand in Chicago, Illinois. As director of the health care facilities and equipment planning group, Mr. Hosking is responsible for project management, quality review, and product development for all facilities planning activities. Those activities include needs assessment, site selection, master site and facility planning, functional space programming, functional planning, and medical planning for over 500 health care clients.

Mr. Hosking has served on the faculty of several seminars on facility planning sponsored by the American Association of Health Care Consultants, and the American College of Health Care Executives and has published numerous articles on facility planning topics.

Mr. Hosking holds an MBA in health care administration from the University of Chicago and a BS in industrial engineering from the University of Michigan. Mr. Hosking is a fellow in the American Association of Health Care Consultants, a fellow in the Health Care Information and Management Systems Society, and a Diplomate in the American College of Health Care Executives.

Chapter 21

The Shifting Nature of Management Accounting Practices in the Health Sector

Mark A. Covaleski

The development of management accounting practices and information is related to the broader changes experienced by the health care industry over the past 30 years. In turn, these changes in the industry are a direct consequence of changes in societal expectations. During the period of the 1960s through the early 1970s, the expansion of health services delivery was the focus of concern. Societal expectations were that health care was a right of the population. The result was legislation that almost exclusively focused on expansion of health services, with little regard to costs. Control of resources was left to the various providers, such as hospitals, clinics, physicians, and private insurance companies, as they collectively passed the rising health care costs on to society. Accounting practices and information developed in this period served almost exclusively to maximize reimbursement revenues with little regard to containing costs.

The 1970s was a period of recognition of a national crisis in the health care industry in terms of the dramatic increase in expenditures for health care. This perceived crisis contributed to a shift in focus to health care cost containment. The federal and state governments intervened in a more aggressive manner in such regulatory processes as capital expenditure control and rate-setting programs. Government efforts included such requirements as the establishment of uniform hospital accounting systems, the description of financial operations and costs incurred by each hospital participating in these capital expenditure and rate-setting programs, and the provision of accounting information for a formal budgetary review of each participating hospital. This period also brought about some initial efforts to develop budgeting and cost accounting systems as traditionally used in manufacturing industries.

A common element of these two periods, the post-Medicare/Medicaid era of the 1960s and the cost-containment era of the 1970s, was that accounting systems and information were not necessarily developed for meaningful managerial purposes. In fact, these forms of accounting were essentially divorced from the critical administrative, managerial, and clinical logics that guided institutions through these two periods. At the financial accounting level the emphasis was on stewardship as evident in the use of fund accounting for financial reporting purposes. The recent AICPA Audit Guide has provided guidance to make health care financial reporting

more consistent with the corporate world by il-
lustrating single-fund reporting (i.e., the various
restricted funds are collapsed into one set of financial statements). This single-fund format
makes the financial statements more readable to
the capital markets that are concerned with the
overall economic viability of the organization,
and de-emphasizes the role of financial reporting in terms of providing stewardship information about particular parts of the organization,
such as various restricted funds.

Regarding managerial accounting systems,
the revenue-maximization systems of the post-
Medicare/Medicaid era were buffered from the
critical managerial and clinical processes and
were handled by financial specialists isolated
from operations. The various forms of accounting information produced in the cost-containment era were also, for all practical purposes,
buffered from any critical managerial and clinical processes. More accounting information was
produced and more accountants were hired as
they tended to these environmental disturbances
in the form of increasing regulatory pressure, but
little, if any, of the information was seriously
believed or considered in the management of a
health institution.

Thus, for the most part, there was no meaningful managerial accounting information developed in health care institutions in these two eras.
It was not until a third era—the 1980s and early
1990s, in which private sector rationality was
dominant—that accounting information has prevailed in the managerial and clinical logics of
health institutions. The purpose of this chapter is
to address the nature and roles of managerial accounting information in this era of private sector
rationality. The first part describes the characteristics of this contemporary era of private sector
rationality and the emerging roles of management accounting information. The second part
places these potential roles of management accounting information in a specific framework.
The third and final part of the chapter integrates
the contemporary issues and the proposed
framework into a closing discussion.

ACCOUNTING AND PRIVATE SECTOR RATIONALITY

Two major forces that have contributed to the
contemporary era of health services delivery are
related to the pricing of health services: (1) the
development of diagnostic-related groups
(DRGs) and related capitated payment schemes
and (2) the opening of competitive pressures
within the industry, which have enhanced major
structural changes such as managed care. A
commonality of these two forces is their primary
reliance on prepayment for health services, i.e.,
prepayment by DRG categories and prepayment
for population served (capitation) as often seen
in managed care. Furthermore, both these forces
have affected, and are affected by, the development of managerial accounting information in
health care institutions. These two forces, in
turn, have promoted two types of concerns about
the management of health institutions—efficiency and the selection of services.

The efficiency issue is promoted by DRGs
because of the standard base that they provide
for clinical assessment and financial exchanges.
This issue is also promoted by competition in the
traditional sense as institutions attempt to keep
costs down in order to sell their services and live
within capitated amounts. Thus, both payment
mechanisms such as DRGs and capitation, as
well as structural changes such as competition,
promote a concern for efficiency of operations.
Importantly, the concern for efficiency has been
the historical management logic that created and
cultivated managerial accounting in other industries.

The second major concern about the management of health institutions that has been promoted by payment and structural changes is the
definition and selection of services that an institution will offer. DRGs provide a "product definition" from which an institution charges for its
services. Because an institution sells a significant portion of its services in this manner, it is
challenged to consider managing them accordingly. Competitive forces reinforce the same

challenge, as it is in the interest of the health care provider to manage the population from which the provider received a fixed dollar amount. This concern for selection of service is resulting in the unbundling and purchasing of distinct services, thus challenging institutions to manage in this manner. Although these payment and structural forces are promoting a selection of services logic, management accounting does not have the historical precedent—as it does with the efficiency logic—from which to consider these issues. Therefore, although this managerial concern—the definition and selection of services—is possibly the more significant issue in terms of the institution's future or economic viability, traditional managerial accounting models are dysfunctionally fixated on the first concern of efficiency.

Impact of Payment and Structural Changes

The critical regulatory efforts in the early 1980s to contain health care costs pertained to the change in reimbursement mechanisms by the federal government for Medicare patients. Through efforts and pressures from the General Accounting Office, Congress, and the Department of Health and Human Services, the rate-setting effort to contain costs resulted in price-per-case reimbursement as defined by DRGs. Reflecting a management science approach to health administration, case-mix reimbursement systems provide incentives for cost control and efficiency. More specifically, these systems link the diagnosis and resources by combining medical records with financial data, thereby matching the costs and outcomes by providing health services.

The DRG approach is a cost-containment approach widely espoused in both the traditional management accounting and management sciences literature. Physicians are encouraged to use hospital and other resources efficiently. Tighter internal accounting control systems are instituted around patient treatment processes. The significant contribution of case-mix reimbursement is that it establishes a framework to define and collect costs on a "multiproduct" basis. The product lines are the patients served, who are placed in common groups (DRGs) based upon similar amounts and types of services received. Thus, the stated goal of a case-mix reimbursement and accounting system is to provide a financial framework and the definition of standard costs of treating specific types or groups of patients. At this point the case-mix accounting system has provided the government and hospital administration with some form of accountability as well as measurements of production and efficiency. This sort of information is valuable in aiding physicians in their attempts to limit unnecessary resources and utilization.

Case-mix reimbursement represents a wage contract between purchasers and providers of health services around DRG categories. Essentially the accounting data challenge physician discretion in coordinating the activities of the health industry and allocating its resources. More specifically, the forms of management accounting developed around DRG categories include standard costing, pricing, and budgets. Through DRG contracts, the government gains some control over the labor productivity by establishing a centralized organization and administering the tasks of providers. By assuming some control of labor productivity, the government and hospital administration govern their self-interests in this internal nonmarket domain. Management accounting information concerning conversion costs within DRG categories then becomes the mechanism of raising productivity and driving slack out of the production process.

Competitive forces and the resulting development of managed care purchasing through capitated contracts have been developing in the late 1980s and early 1990s. This form of health care delivery and related prepayment structure has also eliminated the obfuscation of institutions' services resulting from the internal cost shifting and the cross-subsidization of services. This unbundling of services becomes necessary as institutions seek to understand the discrete services that will be provided as well as their cost. This merger of actuarial and management accounting information serves the health care provider in a competitive capitated environment in at least two ways: (1) enhanced cost/price knowledge as institutions compete to sell health services; and (2) control of costs as institutions attempt to live within the capitated amount. The increasing scarcity of public funding strengthens the need for institutions to identify such services and manage them accordingly in their efforts to expand or even maintain capacity. Significant changes in provider structure should result from this redefinition of traditional service boundaries.

Competitive forces have also arisen as the various payors for health services have attempted to achieve efficiencies by defining health benefits in terms of newer, less costly alternatives. The increasing existence of prepaid medical insurance plans has resulted in payors controlling the flow of patients to hospitals. Insurers bargain for rates and services with multiple providers. Because of these competitive forces health care providers will no longer necessarily be paid what the provider considers to be their reasonable costs of care, regardless of the definition of services provided. The bargaining process will force providers to focus on negotiating for blocks of marginal hospital utilization as defined by distinct packages of services that the provider has to offer. As larger portions of the hospital's revenues are determined through negotiated contracts for packages of services and smaller portions are determined through traditional cost reimbursement mechanisms such as fee-for-service, institutions will be forced to define their cost commitments in the form of assets, expenditures, and related price setting. Otherwise, institutions will find themselves committed to serving patient populations that consume more resources than generated.

In essence these competitive forces introduce new uncertainties that will challenge health care managers to redefine the hospitals' business. As these institutions seek market niche in the growth sectors of the health care business, they will have to define their asset commitments and related costs and price-setting mechanisms accordingly. Health care providers can redefine their services in terms of consumer needs and mobilize their accounting information to deal with the demand for health services. These competitive forces result in bidding for groups of enrolled patients, thus challenging accountants to analyze anticipated costs while committing the hospital to specific rates for particular groups of patients. This price competition forces the provider to define its structure in terms of a flexible mix of clinical and related services.

Managerial Accounting and the Pursuit of Efficiency

The focus on efficiency facilitates the development of management accounting information for several reasons. The first reason is the historical precedent; these accounting systems were developed to some extent during the cost-containment era of the 1970s. They varied significantly in the extent to which they were developed by organizations or how seriously the accounting information was taken, but, nonetheless, the basic issue of attaching responsibility to resources and output was at least surfacing in the 1970s. Second, the unbundling of services to define distinct categories for purposes of DRG and capitated pricing provides more concrete categories from which to gather and consider accounting information and influence physicians who previously were not subject to efficiency logic defined by accounting measures. Third, as suggested previously, competition results in health care providers being limited in their ability to pass on inefficiencies of services in the form of cross-subsidies in pricing. Each service needs to justify its costs within severe price constraints. Perhaps the most significant reason why this emerging managerial concern for efficiency facilitates the development of managerial accounting information is that it is consistent with why and how managerial accounting developed in other industries. The health industry is just borrowing what has already existed in other industries for several decades.

The emphasis on the unbundling of health care services and establishing cost/price relationships at the lowest unit of analysis has emphasized the importance of meaningful cost allocation systems. In contrast to cost allocation systems of the 1960s and 1970s, which focused upon revenue maximization, the emphasis in today's environment is upon being able to establish meaningful cost definitions such that the health care provider can engage in informed strategic and operational pricing strategies. For example, as many hospitals attempt to expand their outpatient services, such as hospital-based ambulatory care, they discover that they cannot compete cost-wise with freestanding ambulatory care providers, largely due to the hospital's inpatient costs being allocated to its ambulatory care center. Knowing this cost information from a detailed and meaningful cost allocation system is a starting point from which to make an operational decision, e.g., price at something less than a full-cost basis to compete with the freestanding center.

Another example of the seriousness with which health care providers are taking cost allocation systems is reflected in the accounting system of one large Midwestern clinic. In this clinic several departments form an overhead cost pool. Historically one major definition of service provided was established for each department, which, in turn, provided the basis (or cost driver) for the allocation of the costs in this department to the various physician practices. For example, executive administration was one of the departments in this cost pool; the logic of its service definition and resultant cost driver is as follows: service = governance; cost driver = revenue; justification = revenue. This formula is indicative of the size of individual physician practices and, in turn, the size of the various departments is highly correlated with the use of the governance time of executive administration. The remaining departments in this cost pool and their respective service and cost driver definitions are as follows: ambulatory care services (service = clinical op-

erations; cost driver = FTEs); medical records (service = medical records management; cost driver = visits); accounting (service = payables/reporting/budgeting; cost driver = revenue); human resources (service = personnel management; cost driver = FTEs); marketing (service = marketing; cost driver = revenue); registration (service = registration management; cost driver = visits); and professional billing (service = fee management; cost driver = revenue).

It was felt by the physician practice areas that this allocation approach was too general to assign costs in a meaningful way, thus undermining cost/price strategies, belief in the income distribution system, cost control, etc. The first step to enrich this cost allocation system was to better define the work being done in each of the eight overhead departments. This is something that can be done by the departments themselves with the help of industrial engineers. This further refinement of work definitions in overhead areas is also at the heart of total quality management (TQM) efforts such that this TQM information can be merged into the cost accounting effort. For example, the function of the human resources department (HR) was no longer defined as just personnel management, but refined more specifically to three major work efforts or services that it provides the clinic: (1) personnel management; (2) staff/physician coordination; and (3) staff benefits regulations. In turn, the cost driver from which physician practices would be assigned costs from HR was no longer based upon proportion of full-time equivalents (FTEs) they had in the clinic but, instead, upon three cost drivers: (1) number of FTEs allocated HR time and related costs devoted to personnel management; (2) number of physicians allocated HR time and related costs devoted to staff/physician coordination; and (3) staff expenses allocated HR time and related costs devoted to staff/benefit regulation. This more detailed allocation of HR costs served several purposes, including more accurate cost definitions in the physician practice areas, which, in turn, enhanced management decisions such as pricing strategies, cost control, and income distribution.

This improved cost allocation methodology also makes the overhead departments more accountable to their customers (i.e., the physician practices), which should result in more cost control with these overhead departments.

Cost allocation is critical to current efforts to provide more accurate and equitable income distribution formulas in group practices. Income distribution formulas have evolved from very simple methods such as dividing the group practice net income by equal shares or volume (number of visits or gross receipts). The flaw in terms of economic accuracy of these relatively simple methods of distribution is that all the costs of doing business such as discounts, direct expenses of the individual practices, and the clinic's overhead expenses are not being charged directly to the practice but, instead, are being pooled and shared equally or on some volume definition. This is questionable not only in terms of accuracy but, more importantly, in terms of incentives for the physician practices to keep these costs of doing business down as, essentially, these costs become subsidized across the individual practices. Most group practices have gone the next step and have modified their income distribution formula from gross billings to gross receipts, thus essentially serving the purpose of capturing discounts by each individual practice such that these costs are no longer subsidized across practices. The next step beyond this method is basing the income distribution formula on net receipts such that the direct cost of each practice is charged to the respective practice. These direct costs are now also removed from the pool of costs subsidized by all practices. The final set of costs of business that now need to be addressed are the clinic's overhead costs. Once these are assigned in some relatively meaningful way, each physician practice will have a relatively accurate individual income statement that can serve as the basis for income distribution. This last step—the allocation of overhead cost—cannot be done with the certainty and accuracy of tracking discount or direct expenses, but is a major improvement over a system that might just track as far as gross

billings and lets all of the costs of doing business be collected in a pool and assigned in some rather arbitrary manner.

Management accounting is commonly defined as serving three major purposes: (1) planning and controlling routine operations, (2) inventory valuation, and (3) aiding nonroutine management decisions. Management accounting has its historical roots in the scientific management perspectives of turn-of-the-century manufacturing. Many of the individuals who made significant contributions to the development of mass production were also the pioneers of cost accounting and scientific management. It was this combination of engineers and cost accountants who became intimately familiar with the problems of factory and mass production. These manufacturing firms could typically be defined as operating routine technologies, such as assembly lines, in fairly predictable markets and engaging in centralized decision making. In order to gain compliance with the central decisions, procedures were specified by formalizing, standardizing, and developing rules for role performance. Middle and lower managers, therefore, had little discretion and power.

Planning and control information was straightforward, with management accounting systems focusing on efficiency measures such as standard costs and variance reports. Thus the routineness of the operations and market and the long duration of work process as defined by the assembly line emphasized the development of the first two purposes of managerial accounting—planning and control of routine operations and inventory valuation. The third purpose— nonroutine decisions—was by design a less significant issue.

An important issue, therefore, becomes one of questioning the wholesale adoption of management accounting measures and logics for health institutions. Should the rush toward efficiency as defined by accounting systems and information be a top priority? In their concern for efficiency, these accounting systems and related information are based on assumptions and ideologies that may not be appropriate nor in the best interests of health care providers in today's environment.

What about the nonroutine services and the development of new programs and services by health care providers as they seek new and more revenue sources? Managerial accounting's historical and fundamental concern for efficiency is being questioned in other industries that do not adhere to the underlying assumptions of managerial accounting. For example, traditional cost accounting has been limited in high-technology firms because the manufacturing environment is different than that traditionally assumed in management accounting. High-tech organizations are oriented toward continuous technological change, growth, and fast reaction time. Similarly, high-tech products and services have a basic applied science characterized by complexity and rapid change. The time span in the production of these products and services is greatly reduced. Thus two of the three purposes of management accounting—planning and controlling routine operations, and inventory valuation—are significantly restricted in a high-tech environment. Nonroutine decisions become more important.

There also is considerable pressure on high-tech firms to move into the market as early as possible in order to capture a large share of that market. This market pressure is clearly being felt in the health industry as well. High-tech products are primarily start-up and growth-stage-oriented, and pass through the mature and decline stages comparatively rapidly. However, the nonroutine nature of the start-up and growth stages of products has not been the typical domain of management accounting. Rather, it is premised on the mature and declining stages of products, with their characteristics of stability, long production runs, and cost-control emphasis.

The greatest impact on management accounting arises from marketing preceding production of high-tech products. The sell-produce sequence, as compared to the design-produce-sell sequence of traditional manufacturing, forces cost estimates and projections, not actual cost experience, to be the basis for critical pricing decisions. Another effect of the sell-produce sequence is that inventory levels are quite low; thus inventory control and costing become less important. Finally, the long production runs and long lead times for product and service development that permit the separation of production and development in traditional manufacturing settings do not exist in high-tech firms. Therefore, it becomes difficult to gather the body of data necessary for setting standards. Standard costing with all of its control and performance evaluation features becomes irrelevant.

Marketing, research and development, and strategic planning are typically defined as adaptive management activities and are frequently recognized as critical managerial functions for organizations greatly involved in set-up and growth-stage services. By contrast, integrative activities, such as production and accounting, are recognized as critical to the mature stage of the product life cycle. Accounting practices and information have to take start-up and growth stage services seriously to be recognized as important in adaptive management strategies. Reimbursement and cost-containment efforts, if taken too seriously, can result in accounting systems misperceiving the health care organization exclusively in terms of a mature product orientation, while ignoring many of the pressures and characteristics of the competitive environment.

The essential issue that needs to be considered when defining and analyzing management accounting roles in health institutions is that some organizations choose to compete not exclusively by efficiently providing mature services that have general consumer acceptance, but rather by introducing a constant stream of new services. Indeed, health care providers have improved substantially over the past decade in controlling their routine services. The traditional tool for cost control has been the budget process, which has evolved significantly by moving from static budgets, to flexible budgeting, to acuity-based budgets. The improvement has allowed health care managers a better understanding of their costs and related cost variances such that they can improve their control efforts as well as their planning in the future. While static budgets serve planning purposes by having the management team identify and commit themselves to expected expenses for the upcoming period, these budgets are difficult to use for control purposes (variance analysis) because of their inability to distinguish between volume driven variances versus managerial efficiencies and inefficiencies. Flexible budgets allow for the budget to be utilized in a meaningful way in variance analysis because of their ability to parcel out volume impacts, thus serving to identify managerial efficiencies and inefficiencies. However, acuity factors may still be buried in what the flexible budget has identified as a management variance. Organizations have started to merge acuity data with the flexible budget such that acuity factors can also be parceled out, leaving a cleaner designation of what is identified as management variances. In short, as the health care organization evolves from utilizing static budgets to flexible budgets to acuity-based flexible budgets, it evolves from depicting all cost variance as management variance, to breaking out the volume impact on management variance, to breaking out the volume and acuity impact on management variance.

However, an increasing number of innovative health care organizations' portfolios of product offerings contain services that compete based upon the value of their unique characteristics, not because the services are cheaper than those of competitors. The success of innovating organizations depends upon quality and unique services. Undue emphasis on cost minimization and efficiency can be counterproductive. Managerial accounting systems, however, do not recognize services that compete on the basis of unique characteristics valued by consumers. Present management accounting systems are improving exclusively on tracking cost efficiencies of routine services. While this is a positive trend, the nature of competition today in many industries, including health care, demands internal information that recognizes the shifting nature of technologies, services, and markets. It is the

nonroutine decisions that take on significance. Routine planning and control may no longer be the exclusive keys to success for modern organizations.

Managerial Accounting and Adaptive Management Activities

The economic foundation of health care institutions is the portfolio of assets defined by the programs and services provided by the institution. Its economic viability is a function of its asset utilization and program activity, which provides the economic returns sufficient to preserve the underlying capital base. The preservation of capital is fundamental to health care providers. Such preservation efforts involve not only matters of internal efficiency in the spending of capital but also, and perhaps more importantly, the commitment of assets to providing programs that will enhance the economic value of their capital. These provider-level financing decisions involve the commitment of funds in investment or divestment decisions.

Health care accounting information needs to become more closely associated with adaptive management activities, such as strategic planning, as health care organizations move away from an emphasis on facilities planning to a more market-oriented approach. It is important, in this strategic planning effort, for hospitals to define a set of programs or activities for which the organization will commit resources. In essence this is the selection of services discussed earlier. Doing so necessitates the development of an accounting system capable of providing data on cost, revenue, and investment along program lines. This portfolio of services or programs provides the basic structure of a strategic perspective. Therefore accounting information needs to be developed on a basis consistent with the strategic plan.

Traditionally, however, the development of accounting information in the manufacturing industry—which, in turn, was adapted by the health care industry—has been oriented toward measuring the efficiencies within responsibility centers or departmental lines. With the advent of DRG payment and expansion of capitated payment, however, the health care industry has been making major advancements in the accumulation of financial data by DRG categories or patient populations, thus providing some early efforts to define major programs or product lines in a hospital as consisting of a defined set of DRGs and/or populations. Return on assets committed to these programs should be an important criterion in program selection, which again requires that accounting data be available along program lines. Return on these portfolios of assets should be used as part of an overall system of program evaluation and selection.

In summary, as portrayed in Exhibit 21–1, the distinction between traditional management accounting and health care high-technology organizations provides a basis for redefinition of managerial accounting roles in the health care industry. At the traditional end of the continuum are organizations that tend to deal with routine processes—work, markets, and decision making—while providing products or services that can be defined as mature or declining. These organizations have the luxury of carefully designing the product; setting explicit detail, standards of production, and costs of products; and then selling the product accordingly. They are dominated by production and accounting logics, whereas the marketing of these products and services is less important as the products are fairly well established or guaranteed. The concern for efficiency over service selection seems to make sense.

At the nontraditional end of the continuum are organizations that tend to deal with nonroutine processes—work, markets, and decision making—while providing products or services that can be defined as start-up and growth oriented. These firms often sell the service before they have had an opportunity to design carefully, measure, and standardize operations and costs. They are dominated by marketing logics as they strategically shift their assets commitments to various programs and services while the efficiencies of production become less relevant.

Exhibit 21–1 Organizations of Management Accounting

Efficiency	Service Selection
Routine as to	Nonroutine as to
work	work
markets	markets
decisions	decisions
Mature product orientation	Start-up and growth orientation
Logics = design/sell/produce	Logics = sell/produce
Historical and educational basis for managerial accounting systems	

Here, the concern for service selection over efficiency seems to make sense.

This model has several implications for health care organizations. First, these organizations should identify where they lie on this continuum and define their corresponding needs for accounting information. It would be futile or simplistic to place any organization on only one spot on this continuum. There are probably some parts of the health care organization where the routine end of the continuum and related focus of accounting is appropriate. There are likely to be many other services that can be thought of from a marketing orientation. If such an analysis is not made, the development of accounting information will not find a neutral spot on the continuum, but rather will focus on efficiency. The cost-containment logics of the 1970s pointed health care organizations in this direction. The development of DRGs and capitated populations has painted a routineness about health services from which standards can be developed. Competitive pressures tend to provoke a concern for providing services more efficiently so they can be sold at a lower price. The most important reason that accounting will be focused on efficiency, however, is because that is where managerial accounting has historically developed. Until the focus of accounting is challenged to move, as has been done in at least a few high-technology firms (only after years of finding out that the traditional orientation was not serving critical managerial decisions), it will focus on the routine.

To illustrate the issues raised thus far, the following section describes a concrete example of where the shift in the nature of managerial accounting might occur. This example illustrates a strategic profit model that aggregates accounting information in terms of returns generated on assets invested. It is argued that the traditional predominant focus of managerial accounting on efficiency is only one component of the overall strategic profit model that seeks to maximize return on asset commitments.

STRATEGIC PROFIT MODEL

The strategic profit model identifies two profit paths available to an institution. A hospital can improve its rate of return on its assets by increasing its (1) profit margin or its (2) rate of asset turnover (Figure 21–1). Thus, this model provides a basis for programming the performance of the entire organization, as well as its major profit centers and investment centers.

Margin Management

The management of the first profit path—profit margin—is referred to as *margin management;* it deals with the traditional managerial concern for efficiency of operations. The statement of revenues and expenses is the basis for margin management. As illustrated in Figure 21–1, the profit margin is generated from the percentage of net income relative to the entire net revenue. The issue becomes how much money the health care organization earns (net income) relative to the net operating revenues it takes in. The objective of increasing the profit margin is achieved by increasing the numerator, which is the net income.

Net income, in turn, consists of net operating revenues less expenses plus nonoperating revenues. Thus, the increase in profit margin is achieved by increasing net operating revenue, decreasing operating expenses, or increasing nonoperating revenue. Note that these are separate management responsibilities. The attempt to increase nonoperating revenues needs to be

managed by efforts such as increasing investment income or increasing fund-raising efforts at cost containment—keeping costs down. This focus, in turn, is the basis for most of management accounting development in the form of budgets, standards, variance analyses, and the like. Finally, increasing net operating revenues is managed by at least three separate efforts. The increase in patient activity, typically a marketing responsibility, contributes to the increase in net operating revenue. Lowering deductibles— charity, bad debts, and contractual allowances— is, in turn, part of separate management domains and responsibilities. Finally, increasing other operating revenues, such as through the sale of management advisory services, laboratory services, or engineering services, has become a critical area for the organization's financial viability.

The first major path of the strategic profit model, margin management, is broken down into several management domains. The advantage of this model is that it can isolate for purposes of analysis and planning the areas of responsibility. For example, in Figure 21–1, net operating revenues can be increased by either expanding patient service revenues, lowering deductibles, or increasing other operating revenues. These various domains—efforts to raise outside charitable funding, financial investment strategies to generate investment income, cost-containment efforts, marketing and clinical service provision strategies, various efforts to deal with deductibles, and finally the other activities that hospitals do to raise funds—can all be placed in the flow of responsibilities identified in the strategic profit model.

Asset Management

Asset management is the second major critical path of the strategic profit model; it involves the emerging managerial concern for the selection of services. This critical path is concerned with the activity (net operating revenue) related to the structure (total assets) of the hospital. As shown in Figure 21–1, the objective is to increase asset

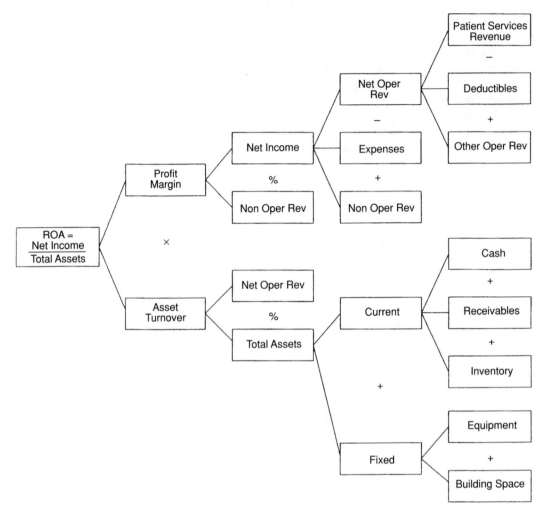

Figure 21–1 Return on Assets

turnover, suggesting a need to define and utilize the assets that a hospital has on hand. Asset turnover is defined by the net operating revenue divided by the total assets of the institution. Where margin management dealt with the efficiency of this activity by contrasting the amounts of money that remained (net income) to the activity (net operating revenue), the major concern of this path is strictly the activity generated for the amount of assets invested.

The objective of increasing the asset turnover number can be achieved in one of two ways.

First, the numerator can be increased; in other words, the health care organization can expand its activity using its existing assets through increasing patient services revenues, decreasing allowances, or expanding other operating revenues. More importantly, however, health institutions are turning to the denominator—asset commitments. The asset turnover number can be increased if the investment in assets is decreased for the same amount of net operating revenue. This is merely suggesting that organizations are pruning their asset commitments in an effort to maintain their services. Or stated another way, hospitals are entering more carefully into asset commitments that will expand the numerator, the net operating revenue, such that the overall asset turnover is increasing. This path of asset management is an accountant's depiction of current efforts of project or service management. This model serves to reward the services that are generating the activity (net operating revenue) with further commitments and purge the services that cannot generate the activity to justify the asset commitments.

The analysis of asset commitments deals with two major asset categories—current and fixed. Current assets, such as inventory and accounts receivable, offer no activity potential; they are generally managed with lowest commitments while maintaining a buffer for liquidity. Efforts to lower the current assets will, in turn, lower the total assets against which to consider net operating revenues. This will increase asset turnover, reflecting a more efficient utilization of the organization's assets. The primary strategy for current assets, therefore, is one of disinvestment to the extent of a safe liquidity buffer.

Fixed assets, however, are more selectively managed. Because the fixed assets represent the space and equipment that provide the base for operating revenues, there cannot be a general strategy to purge their existence because doing so would also destroy the ability to generate revenues. Thus, the notion of selective investment and disinvestment becomes relevant. The assets related to projects and services that are generating operating revenues will be rewarded with further investment. Those assets that are not related to operating revenues will not receive further commitment. Stated in terms of the asset turnover equation, those assets related to services that do little for the numerator (net operating revenue) are purged from the denominator (total assets) to allow for an improvement in asset turnover. This treatment of these "dead" fixed assets is much like the treatment of current assets; the denominator must be minimized because they contribute little or nothing to the numerator.

However, there are some projects and services that contribute extensively to the net operating revenue. Thus, the commitments to the assets (the denominator) are justified by the more-than-offsetting increase in net operating revenue (the numerator). This results in an overall increase in asset turnover, thus reflecting good asset management. Finally, the best of all worlds is to improve on the activity of the services that are already there. This improvement can be achieved through marketing or clinical strategies; the denominator (the assets) remains constant while the numerator (net operating revenue) increases, thus improving asset turnover. As a result, a financial winner can become an even more attractive service, or an unprofitable service can become more viable.

Return on Assets

Return on assets (ROA) embraces both the margin management path and the asset management path. The combination of these two paths provides a meaningful basis for evaluating and programming the performance of a health care organization and its profit centers and investment centers. As illustrated in Figure 21–1, the ROA really is a merger of the profit margin (net income divided by net operating revenue) multiplied by the asset turnover (net operating revenue divided by total assets). Algebraically, the net operating revenue drops out of both terms, leaving net income over total assets—the definition of ROA. Conceptually, though, it is important to maintain the two separate paths. These separate paths suggest that ROA can be improved in one of two ways: (1) profit margin (efficiency), which in turn initiates all the management domains discussed earlier to improve this number; and (2) asset turnover (activity), which initiates the various management efforts to justify selective investment and disinvestment opportunities and efforts. Thus the notion of ROA should not be considered an accounting computation disassociated from management efforts but, instead, a management tool to analyze various management strategies.

The critical issue raised by this presentation of the strategic model is that the integration of margin management and asset management through these accounting numbers encompasses many critical management decisions. It lends insights both to issues of efficiency and service selection. In a normative sense the organization would obviously like to analyze its programs and services according to both issues. However, the focus of management accounting information has been primarily on one path—the profit margin—and on one component within the path—control of expenses. As suggested earlier, health care organizations are just discovering the other path of asset management as they are unbundling and evaluating their portfolio of assets in terms of profitability, and managing them accordingly. Asset management, identifying or projecting revenues related to asset or service commitments, may be a more appropriate focus than the issue of the efficiency of the commitments made.

CONCLUSION

This chapter is concerned with the entrenchment of rational, calculative accountability formulations—characteristics of reimbursement payment mechanisms—and the potential influence of these techniques on meaningful strategic and managerial decisions in health care institutions. Health care organizations should not overreact to the pressures of reimbursement and cost containment by adapting structural perspectives of control that are facilitated by rational accountability formulations, tenets, and assumptions of which remain basically unquestioned in organizational and accounting literature.

Health care organization administrators are faced with both constraints and expectations from society. They are expected to strive actively for containing costs, ostensibly by adhering to the tenets of rationality in decision making. Cost containment can allegedly be achieved by strengthening old and implementing new management control practices, such as budgeting. The need for budgeting to support rational-

ity seems to be self-evident, and the merits of accounting go unquestioned. The traditional budgeting and control literature and related educational and consulting institutions have also been quite effective in selling themselves and the related business technique to hospital management. Health care organization administrators, and, to some extent, clinicians, are putting forth a good-faith effort to account for resources, accepting their own shortcomings.

In the meantime, it seems that the demands for cost containment and efficiency through rationality and centralized decision making predominate over the demands related to the increasing complexity of service definitions and related cost and revenue determinations. The traditional accounting emphasis on efficiency is deflecting attention away from emerging critical managerial functions. Accounting and its related issues, processes, and agent should not be taken for granted. The rationality of budgeting and control systems may hinder, rather than help, the performance of full-ranging managerial functions. These systems may inappropriately create rationality where it does not exist. Decision making becomes centralized, controls are added to compensate for problems resulting from the removal of discretion, and communications move up and down the rational hierarchy. The consequence of such an organizational posture is an inordinate reliance on formal accounting to determine efficiency, with a failure to use other monitoring and management processes. The danger for health institutions is that these rational models of control and related accounting information systems may tie up the institution, making it more rigid, rather than more flexible. The implicit world views of these accounting models frequently serve as consensus forces and delay institutional adaptation to changing markets. Administrators in these dramatically changing environments need to spend less time serving pervasive accounting information systems and, instead, develop more skills and engage in bargaining, strategic planning, and negotiating—all of which should be served by accounting information.

Mark A. Covaleski, PhD, is a Professor of Health Care Financial Management at the University of Wisconsin—Madison. Dr. Covaleski has become a nationally known speaker and educator on management development in the health care setting. His major focus is to develop the critical skills and knowledge base related to financial management and teach them to non-financial managers. His programs have been oriented to a variety of professionals (physician managers, physician board members, nurse managers, department heads, clinic managers, administrators) for a variety of health care provider organizations including hospitals, group practices, health maintenance organizations, independent practice associations, and governmental agencies. He has also provided programs for professional associations as well as executive education for the School of Medicine and the Graduate School of Business at the University of Wisconsin—Madison.

Dr. Covaleski is a three-time recipient of the Teacher of the Year Award by the Health Services Administration Student Association where he teaches students from programs in Health Services Management, Physician Administration, Nursing Administration, and Pharmacy Administration. Dr. Covaleski is a licensed CPA in the State of Wisconsin. He received his PhD from the Pennsylvania State University, an MBA from the University of Utah, and his BS from Gannon College. He has also taught at the Copenhagen School of Business and Economics. He has been the recipient of the Robert A. Jerred Distinguished Service Award by the School of Business for his involvement as a board member with nonprofit organizations.

Dr. Covaleski has published extensively on issues pertaining to health care financial management and has been cited as among the most prolific authors (top 3 percent) of accounting professors by the *International Journal of Accounting*. He is on the Editorial Board of *Health Care Management Review* and the *Journal of Accounting and Public Policy*. His involvement with research grants has included issues such as heart disease prevention, critical care nursing, mental health services delivery, evaluation of flight emergency services, and capital reimbursement policies for the nursing home industry. Dr. Covaleski has served as an advisor to the Department of Health and Social Services in the State of Wisconsin, and has served as an expert witness in rate setting cases for several health care providers.

Chapter 22

Financing of Health Care Facilities

Geoffrey B. Shields and Debra J. Schnebel

From the late 1960s until the mid-1980s, tax-exempt financing accounted for the great bulk of health care financing for hospitals, nursing homes, life-care facilities, and HMOs. That began to change with the Tax Reform Act of 1984, which placed a limitation on the use of industrial development bonds for profit-making business corporations. In addition to further restricting the use of industrial development bonds, the Tax Reform Act of 1986 placed limits on the use of tax-exempt financing for health care facilities other than acute-care hospital facilities. Furthermore, there are frequent discussions taking place in Congress about imposing a volume limitation on the use of the tax-exempt bonds to finance nonprofit hospitals. With the vertical integration of nonprofit health care delivery systems, innovative techniques are developing for financing physician office buildings and equipment used for outpatient care with taxable and tax-exempt bonds.

It is becoming increasingly necessary for health care institutions and their chief financial officers to consider an assortment of financing techniques. Techniques that must be examined include taxable and tax-exempt bond financing,

public offerings and private placements of taxable debt, limited partnerships, joint ventures, and sales of streams of business to unrelated institutions. In addition, it seems likely that equity financing for large for-profit corporations will continue to be a major source of financing.

Table 22–1 identifies the amount of money raised for nonprofit hospitals and other health care providers through various types of bonds offerings. As can be seen, most financing has been through the issuance of tax-exempt bonds.

The amount of equity capital raised through partnerships, joint ventures, and stock offerings during the last few years has been significant. The rate of initial public offerings of stock is an indication of new business development. As presented in Table 22–2, initial public offerings of stock issued by health care companies have raised significant equity capital, but the amount is small compared to debt offerings during the same period.

This chapter addresses securities and financing issues of importance to all entities that are interested in raising capital, including hospitals, nursing homes, physician–hospital organizations (PHOs), independent practice associations

Table 22–1 Health Care Bond Financing Volume 1988–1992

	1988		1989		1990		1991		1992	
TOTAL	$12,864,200	(599)	$15,409,400	(707)	$14,143,600	(645)	$18,442,600	(826)	$23,274,100	(924)
First quarter	3,581,300	(137)	2,415,400	(134)	2,558,100	(126)	2,423,000	(126)	4,489,900	(192)
Second quarter	3,147,600	(139)	3,575,300	(177)	3,592,500	(160)	4,981,300	(217)	6,319,200	(250)
Third quarter	2,981,200	(164)	3,895,000	(175)	3,599,800	(162)	6,628,900	(266)	5,564,100	(208)
Fourth quarter	3,154,100	(159)	5,523,700	(221)	4,393,200	(197)	4,409,400	(217)	6,900,900	(274)
Acute-care	9,663,000	(360)	11,743,200	(447)	10,845,100	(414)	14,947,200	(536)	19,281,200	(649)
Single-specialty	629,700	(28)	897,100	(39)	654,000	(33)	900,600	(33)	805,600	(32)
Children's	365,100	(12)	371,000	(11)	289,400	(9)	422,900	(15)	731,000	(17)
Equipment loans	345,900	(13)	511,800	(19)	528,700	(19)	629,800	(28)	238,800	(16)
Miscellaneous	382,000	(42)	384,800	(21)	237,200	(4)	0	(0)	0	(0)
Nursing homes	498,000	(68)	505,800	(82)	535,900	(76)	697,600	(114)	856,900	(105)
Life care	980,600	(76)	995,700	(88)	1,053,300	(90)	844,300	(100)	1,360,500	(106)
Tax-exempt	12,791,900	(574)	14,979,200	(679)	13,983,800	(605)	18,259,000	(794)	22,969,700	(868)
Minimum-tax	37,300	(8)	307,900	(13)	42,300	(4)	55,700	(5)	38,800	(6)
Taxable	35,000	(17)	122,300	(15)	117,500	(36)	127,900	(27)	265,600	(50)
New-money	7,271,000	(369)	10,085,800	(509)	10,365,900	(513)	13,511,600	(600)	11,699,000	(547)
Refunding	5,593,200	(230)	5,323,600	(198)	3,777,700	(132)	4,931,000	(226)	11,575,100	(377)
Negotiated	12,350,100	(546)	14,435,400	(620)	13,615,700	(566)	17,483,800	(738)	22,433,800	(821)
Competitive	167,700	(23)	586,700	(40)	314,700	(41)	632,700	(47)	424,500	(59)
Private placements	346,400	(30)	387,300	(47)	213,200	(38)	326,100	(41)	415,800	(44)
Revenue	12,662,700	(560)	15,162,100	(649)	13,967,400	(596)	18,094,200	(755)	22,743,300	(848)
General obligation	201,500	(39)	247,300	(58)	176,200	(49)	348,400	(71)	530,800	(76)
Fixed-rate	10,901,700	(520)	13,550,700	(635)	12,463,600	(578)	16,452,400	(744)	21,201,900	(844)
Variable-rate	1,962,500	(79)	1,858,700	(72)	1,680,000	(67)	1,990,200	(82)	2,072,200	(80)
Bond insurance	4,449,100	(169)	5,300,400	(156)	5,457,700	(153)	8,510,700	(254)	10,416,700	(272)
Letters of credit	2,027,200	(89)	1,668,500	(77)	1,731,800	(77)	1,691,800	(86)	830,300	(57)
Insured mortgages	1,011,300	(24)	978,800	(18)	353,500	(16)	327,500	(20)	0	(0)
State governments	45,800	(3)	148,200	(5)	54,100	(3)	59,000	(4)	250,400	(7)
State agencies	5,520,500	(175)	7,637,500	(215)	7,023,200	(218)	7,682,700	(243)	10,558,500	(297)
Municipalities	2,923,200	(201)	2,987,900	(248)	2,930,900	(218)	4,150,300	(287)	4,672,100	(287)
Local authorities	4,367,400	(219)	4,435,800	(235)	3,844,600	(197)	6,475,700	(288)	7,548,700	(328)
Public colleges	7,400	(1)	200,100	(4)	290,800	(9)	74,600	(4)	244,300	(5)

Dollar amounts are in thousands of dollars. Number of issues sold are in parentheses.

Source: Securities Data Company, Inc.

(IPAs), health maintenance organizations (HMOs), clinics, home health care companies, and the myriad of other entities that provide health care services.

TAX-EXEMPT FINANCINGS

In recent years nonprofit hospitals have gained access to the capital markets primarily

Table 22–2 Initial Public Offerings (IPOs) of Health Care Company Securities

Date Range	Proceeds (millions)	No. of Issues
1982	21.5	2
1983	434.6	31
1984	133.2	18
1985	210.0	15
1986	227.0	19
1987	186.4	14
1988	56.9	5
1989	179.9	8
1990	127.9	9
1991	1,760.3	38
1992	1,263.7	38
1/93–11/23/93	590.5	11
Industry Totals	5,191.8	208

Source: Securities Data Company, Inc.

through tax-exempt financing. Health care institutions, qualifying as organizations described in Section 501(c)(3) of the Internal Revenue Code of 1986, as amended (IRC), and exempt from tax under Section 501(a) of the IRC, may borrow on a tax-exempt basis—i.e., the interest on the bonds will not be includable in the gross income of the owners thereof for federal income tax purposes. Although tax-exempt financing for hospitals remains available, the Tax Reform Act of 1986 limits the use of tax-exempt financing for health care facilities other than hospitals. Tax-exempt bonds for health care facilities other than hospitals, such as nursing homes, day-care centers, and ambulatory care facilities, are subject to a $150 million limit per institution (or group of institutions under common management or control).

The IRC permits municipalities and other local governmental units to issue tax-exempt securities and to loan the proceeds of such issues to 501(c)(3) organizations for qualifying uses. The tax-exempt bonds must be issued by a state, municipality, or other local governmental unit (the issuer). The issuer loans the proceeds of the bonds to the hospital. The hospital's payments to the issuer on such a loan are used by the issuer to pay the principal of and interest on the bonds.

The bonds are so-called revenue bonds; that is, the bonds are payable solely from the revenues received by the issuer from the hospital and are not a general obligation of the issuer.

As a general rule, tax-exempt financing is available to a hospital for capital expenditures in connection with its charitable activities. Generally, bond proceeds may be used with respect to activities carried on by the hospital that do not constitute unrelated trades or businesses. No more than 5 percent of the proceeds of the bond issue may be used for (1) facilities in an unrelated trade or business, (2) facilities used by a nonexempt person, and (3) costs of issuing the bonds.

In addition, the state law that authorizes the issuance of the bonds by the state municipality also circumscribes the permissible uses of the bond proceeds. As a general rule, a not-for-profit institution can apply the proceeds of tax-exempt bonds to pay, or to reimburse itself, for capital expenditures relating to a hospital, nursing home, or other health care facility. Under recent IRC regulations, an institution may seek reimbursement for expenditures incurred within 18 months before the date of issuance of the bonds, if and up to 3 years after the date of issuance of the bonds, provided that such expenditures have not been previously financed and the issuer or the hospital has prior to the incurrence of any such expenditure declared its intent, in a resolution of its Board, to finance such expenditures.

In addition, tax-exempt bonds can be used to refund existing debt, taxable or tax-exempt, the proceeds of which had been applied toward eligible uses. A refunding occurs when the proceeds of the new issue are applied to the payment of the existing debt. The refunding of the existing debt releases the institution from the covenants in the existing debt's documents and permits it to renegotiate the structure and the covenants with respect to the new issue. In addition, if there have been changes in the capital markets, such as lower interest rates, the institution may further achieve debt service savings.

Typically, tax-exempt bonds that bear a fixed rate of interest provide for a *no-call* period during which the bonds cannot be prepaid. On a typical 30-year bond issue, the no-call period would generally be 10 years. Such instruments also generally provide that the bonds may be *advance refunded*. In an advance refunding, the proceeds of the new debt are deposited in an escrow account and invested in a portfolio of government securities. The cash flow of principal and interest from the escrow portfolio is designed to match the debt service requirement on the existing, or refunded, debt. Thus, although the refunded bonds remain outstanding, the payments on the refunded bonds are provided through the escrow account, and the institution is released from the obligations with respect thereto. In order to achieve a legal defeasance—a discharge from the obligations—of the documents in connection with the refunding of the existing debt, those documents must specifically provide for such. The Tax Reform Act of 1986, however, imposed restrictions on advance refundings. Generally, bonds issued before 1986 may be advance refunded only twice; however, any pre-1986 bonds may be advance refunded at least once after March 14, 1986. Bonds issued after 1985 may be advance refunded only once.

Finance Team

When a health care institution decides to raise capital externally, it should begin assembling its finance team. First, the hospital should identify who on its staff will be responsible for the day-to-day activity relating to the financing. Typically, that person is the chief financial officer (CFO). In order for the financing to reflect the needs and desires of the institution, it is important that the CFO play an active role in the financing process as spokesperson for the hospital. The financing process will take a great deal of that person's time, but will also require input from other persons and departments. The chief executive officer (CEO) and the board of directors are ultimately responsible for approving the finance plan. In identifying, describing, and costing the project to be financed, planning personnel must be involved. Also, in preparing the

information on the hospital to be disclosed in the offering document, persons must be enlisted to collect and digest a significant amount of data and documentation regarding diverse aspects of the institution.

A key member of the finance team is the investment banker. Often, the investment banker is chosen by a panel of management and board members to whom a select group of bankers have made written and oral presentations. The hospital should look for an investment banker with experience in health care finance. A banker familiar with the health care industry, the legal restrictions on hospitals and tax-exempt financings, and the market for the hospital revenue bonds can provide valuable input into the structuring of the financing and will facilitate the financing process. Most important, however, the banker must be someone with whom the key hospital participants feel comfortable and have confidence. He or she should have shown a particular interest in the institution and its financing needs because the finance plan should be tailored to its specific needs. In a public offering, the investment banker acts as underwriter, or purchaser, of the bonds, ensuring that the bonds are sold and the financing consummated. Although each of the major firms can successfully underwrite most hospital issues, the hospital should request and review each banker's experience with financings for similar institutions, comparing the respective interest costs and fees.

The underwriter is represented by its counsel. The role of underwriter's counsel is to ensure that the offering and sale of the bonds comply with federal and state securities laws. Thus, underwriter's counsel is responsible for preparing the offering document that provides full disclosure of the transactions, the bonds, the issuer, and the hospital. The hospital is also represented by counsel, either the hospital's general counsel or special counsel experienced in tax-exempt finance. Hospital counsel must provide assurances to the other participants regarding the tax-exempt status of the institution, the validity of certain corporate actions, and the adequacy of disclosure of the hospital's operations.

Hospital's counsel also represents the hospital in negotiations regarding the structure of the financing and the covenants to be contained in the documents.

A critical player in the process is the issuer. A state, municipality, or other governmental unit must issue the bonds in order for them to be tax exempt. In any given jurisdiction, there may be one or more eligible issuers. Several states have created state financing authorities to issue bonds on behalf of qualifying health care institutions. In other cases, a municipality or a local governmental unit is authorized to issue bonds on behalf of such institutions. The authority and powers granted to issuers, the experience of issuers, and the extent of involvement of the issuers vary widely. When a choice of issuers is available, hospital counsel and the investment banker can explain the disadvantages and advantages of using each issuer and aid the institution in selecting the issuer. The issuer retains a bond counsel who is responsible for drafting the legal documents. In addition, bond counsel renders the opinion that bonds are legally and validly issued and that the interest on the bonds is exempt from federal income taxation and any state taxation, where applicable.

The hospital's auditors must also be involved in this process. They assist in the preparation of certain financial information to be included in the offering document and consent to the use of the audited financial statements, accompanied by the auditor's letter, in such an offering document. In addition, the auditors must give "comfort" with respect to changes in the hospital's financial condition up to the date of the issuance of the bonds.

In certain cases, it may also be necessary to obtain a feasibility study that sets forth projections of the operational and financial performance of the hospital. A feasibility study may be necessary if (1) the hospital is undertaking a major project that is anticipated to have a substantial impact on its operations or financial performance, (2) some other change occurs in the marketplace, such as the addition of a new hospital to the service area, that is anticipated to have a substantial impact on the operations or financial performance of the hospital, or (3) the continuing financial viability of the hospital and its ability to pay on the debt are otherwise questioned. In general, projected operational and financial data, whether in terms of a study or internal projections, must be prepared for review by the rating agencies, investors, and/or credit issuers. In many cases where a study is not necessary, an independent evaluation can be beneficial. Whether to prepare a feasibility study is a judgment call based upon the strength of the institution and the nature of any changes occurring within the institution or in its marketplace.

Financing Process

Once the finance team is assembled, the financing process typically takes 2 to 3 months. During this period, the finance team undertakes a *due diligence* review. The due diligence process includes substantive review of all significant matters affecting the hospital. First, the various lawyers will review numerous documents, including corporate documents, material contracts (for example, loan documents, leases, union contracts, insurance policies, etc.), physician contracts, supply contracts, management contracts, and more. In addition, the finance team will conduct interviews of key hospital personnel, including the CEO, the CFO, a member of the Board, and a member of the medical staff. The purpose of this extensive review process is to assure that the disclosure in the offering document is accurate in all material respects and does not omit to state a material fact.

Concurrently, the documentation for the financing will progress. Drafts of bond documents will be prepared by bond counsel to reflect the structure of the issue and any particular needs or concerns of the hospital. Generally, several drafts of the documents will be generated and reviewed to assure the needs and desires of the hospital are properly reflected in the legal documentation. Also, underwriter's counsel will prepare the offering document. Diverse members of hospital management will be called upon to assemble the information—for example, history of the hospital, governance, hospital services, medical staff, affiliations, demographics of the service area, market share data, utilization statistics, and other miscellaneous information—to be disclosed in the offering document. This information must be carefully reviewed to ensure its accuracy and completeness.

The hospital will also be required to prepare documentation, including historical financial information, utilization statistics, and financial projections, for presentation to and analysis by the rating agencies and/or prospective issuers of credit enhancement (bond insurers and/or banks issuing letters of credit). Generally, an oral presentation by the key management personnel, a member of the Board, and a member of the medical staff will also be arranged for each rating agency and/or credit enhancer, during which hospital personnel highlight the strengths of the institution and respond to any questions or concerns of the rating agency and/or credit enhancer. Although the rating agencies and credit enhancers put significant emphasis on the quantifiable criteria, subjective impressions are also considered in determining a rating.

Structuring the Issue

When a hospital considers a financing, a number of questions arise. How much debt should be incurred? What is the project being financed? Should any existing debt be refinanced? What should the maturity of the debt be? Should the interest be at a fixed rate or variable rate? What is the credit or security for the debt? Should credit enhancement be obtained? Choosing the appropriate financing vehicle for an institution requires a careful review of the hospital's current capital needs, its operational and financial strengths and weaknesses, and its future plans. The finance team, and particularly the investment banker, can provide hospital's management and board with the objective factors to consider in selecting a finance plan. In addition, the risks and rewards of alternative financing plans can be analyzed in relation to the hospital's par-

ticular needs and goals, and a recommendation can then be presented. It is important that the hospital management have input in this process to ensure full consideration of the hospital's current and future plans, to evaluate the potential impact of the finance plans on the hospital, and to ensure that the finance plan coincides with the hospital's needs and desires.

Financing Methods

Tax-exempt financing has traditionally offered hospitals a ready source of long-term, relatively low-cost capital. Several years ago virtually all tax-exempt hospital issues were fixed-rate financings, with a term of approximately 30 years. Also at that time, a major portion of those dollars represented the hard construction costs of major renovations and expansion, additional nursing towers, and satellite hospital facilities. The long-term, fixed rate financing assisted the hospital in its financial planning by "fixing" its cost of capital. This approach also enabled the hospitals to conform to the old accounting adage that the term of the financing should match the life of the assets.

More recently, many hospitals have issued variable rate demand bonds in order to take advantage of the low interest rates available in the short-term market. The nominal maturity of the variable rate demand bond (VRDB) is long-term, frequently 30 years. The interest rate on the bonds, however, is based on the short-term market, fluctuating in accordance with the designated adjustment period and index selected. In order to attract investors to these short-term rates, the investor is given the right to tender the bond for purchase at a designated period, either 1 day, 7 days, 1 month, 3 months, 6 months, a year, or several years. Typically, the put period coincides with the pricing period. Typically, any bonds tendered would be remarketed to and purchased by other investors.

With VRDBs, the investor requires assurance that funds will be available to pay the purchase price of the tendered bonds if they cannot be remarketed. In order to ensure this liquidity, most hospitals are required to provide some form of liquidity/credit enhancement, such as an irrevocable letter of credit providing liquidity and credit enhancement or a line of credit for liquidity with an insurance policy to provide credit enhancement. The term of the liquidity facility is generally limited to 3 to 5 years.

The hospital accepts certain risks in using VRDBs. These bonds are subject to the fluctuation in short-term tax-exempt rates. If there is an aberration in the capital markets so that bonds cannot be remarketed, tendered bonds will be purchased from a draw on the liquidity facility. Repayment to the liquidity issuer will generally result in higher interest costs—typically, the bank's prime rate—and a shorter amortization period, which may be on demand or over a period of several years. Such an event can substantially increase the hospital's annual debt service costs. Although the VRDB issue is rated on the basis of the credit/liquidity facility, the rating agencies analyze the hospital's ability to repay the debt in this worst case scenario in evaluating outstanding ratings on existing debt or in rating any subsequent debt issued on the hospital's credit.

Upon the expiration of the liquidity facility, the VRDBs no longer can be marketed at short-term rates unless a replacement liquidity facility is obtained. Generally VRDB issues are structured to provide for conversion to a fixed interest rate at the option of the hospital upon obtaining an opinion that such conversion will not affect the tax-exempt status of the bonds. Because of these inherent risks in variable rate financing and the impact on the hospital's credit ratings, VRDBs are generally recommended only for stronger credits—at least A-rated—with substantial liquid assets.

Investment bankers continue to develop new financing techniques and structures. The devices and structures take on many different forms, to address the investment requirements of specific classes of investors and thereby provide lower overall interest costs to the hospital. The new financing devices are in some cases only available to the stronger credits undertaking larger

financings (i.e., $50,000,000 or more) and invariably result in more complex documentation. A hospital's patience in undertaking the more complex financings, when properly structured, however, can be rewarded by quantifiable dollar savings.

Some of the financing products require the hospital to hedge any variability in interest rates with an interest rate swap with the underwriter, or other third party. Where swap agreements are employed, the hospital must determine what, if any, additional risks the hospital may bear. Is the swap a perfect hedge for the bonds? In other words, are the payments on the swap based upon the same market index and at the same intervals as the bonds, under all contingencies? Is the hospital taking the credit risk of the counterparty on the swap agreement? In other words, if there is a default by the other party on the swap agreement, is the hospital still liable on the bonds? If so, is the hospital comfortable with assuming the credit risk of the counterparty? Do the cost savings outweigh this potential additional risk?

It is imperative that a hospital and its counsel fully understand the structure and the additional risks, if any, which the structure presents, so that it may properly evaluate the alternative financing methods and make the appropriate selection for its needs and circumstances.

Security

The obligation of the hospital to repay the loan from the issuer may be secured by property of the hospital. The property may be real estate, equipment, securities, or revenues of the hospital. Entities with stronger credit may be able to issue unsecured debt, which is not secured by any property or revenues of the institution. In the event of bankruptcy, the holder of such an obligation is a general creditor of the hospital, subordinate to any secured party. Such unsecured debt is generally accompanied by fairly restrictive negative pledge provisions, which restrict the hospital's ability to grant a prior security interest in its assets to other creditors. The negative pledge should not be drafted as an absolute prohibition against prior liens, but rather as a limitation—for example, a provision that the hospital may encumber not more than 10 percent of its assets. Such a restriction provides protection to the investor and yet allows the hospital some flexibility in its future capital financing.

Security may be provided in the form of a pledge of the gross revenues of the corporation, coupled with a negative pledge. As a practical matter, the revenues pledge does not affect the operations of the hospital so long as it is not in default or in bankruptcy. Many documents provide, however, for a lockbox such that in the event of a default or of bankruptcy, the trustee may direct that the revenues of the hospital be deposited with the trustee. By controlling the hospital's cash flow, the trustee effectively gains control of the hospital's operations. Although it is preferable to avoid the lockbox requirement, if such a requirement cannot be avoided, its application should be specifically limited to events of payment default and/or bankruptcy.

For health care entities with weaker credit or specific legal requirements, debt may have to be secured by a mortgage on the property of the entity. The security interest includes all or part of the real property and existing and after-acquired buildings and equipment. If a mortgage is required, the property to be pledged should be narrowly defined. If possible, it is in the hospital's interest to exclude property that is not integral to the operation of the hospital, such as office buildings, vacant lots, and parking garages, to preserve flexibility and to facilitate future borrowings or corporate restructurings. The mortgage should also contain provisions that allow for the release of obsolete and/or unsuitable equipment and the substitution of alternate collateral.

Master Trust Indenture

A *master indenture* is a financing instrument that provides a mechanism for consolidating the credit of the participating corporations and for developing a legal framework for the future borrowings of each such participant. The master indenture structure is most useful for multihospital systems, restructured hospitals, and hospitals planning to restructure. It provides a network of cross-guarantees among the participating corporations that permit a pooling of the credit while maintaining the legally distinct corporations.

As such, the master indenture provides a common framework for multiple borrowings by several entities; a mechanism for incurring various types of debt, whether taxable or tax exempt; and a uniform set of covenants applicable to all participants. Ideally, all participants and all debt would conform to the standards of the master indenture. Often, however, investors and credit issuers in specific financings will demand specific covenants in addition to the provisions of the master indenture.

The master indenture may impose operating requirements and restrictions on each of the participants in the group. Because the hospitals have traditionally been the stronger credits among the participating corporations, the covenants in the master indenture have been in large part designed to address the operations and financial conditions of hospitals. Such restrictions and limitations may not be appropriate for corporations engaged in other businesses, whether or not they are health-care related.

Credit Enhancement

The ratings awarded to hospitals by the rating agencies have been declining. The advent of the prospective payment system (PPS) for Medicare, alternate delivery systems, and the resulting increased competition among hospitals for a declining number of patient days have made investors and rating agencies wary. In addition, the uncertainty of the health care market as a result of the possibility of health care reform has made investors increasingly cautious.

Credit enhancement of bonds is designed to provide the bondholder with security in addition to the credit of the hospital. For a specified fee, the credit issuer promises to pay the bondholder upon a payment default by the health care borrower. Typically, such credit facility has been in the form of a letter of credit from an AA or AAA-rated bank or a municipal bond insurance policy issued by an AAA-rated insurance company. The credit facility raises the creditworthiness and the rating on the bonds. A higher rating enables the bonds to be sold at a lower interest cost in the marketplace and provides a broader market for them.

The market for VRDBs demands strong credits. Thus, most hospitals that have variable rate financing must obtain credit enhancement. The cost of the credit support is one of the costs of the transaction that enables the hospital to take advantage of short-term interest rates. These costs of credit support must be factored in when determining what financing structure to pursue.

The decision to provide credit enhancement for a fixed rate, long-term bond issue, however, is primarily an economic one. Does the interest rate savings caused by the higher credit rating more than compensate for the credit issuer's fees? For most hospitals with AA or lower rating, the answer to this question has been yes.

Restrictive Covenants

In the debt documents, the hospital is required to agree to comply with various restrictions upon its operations. In general, covenants found in hospital financings are fairly standard. The covenants, however, have evolved to reflect changes in the health care industry. Also, the provision in a document can be tailored to some extent to meet the specific circumstances of the hospital. It should be noted, however, that the covenants provide the rating agencies, credit issuers, and/or investors with assurance that the hospital's credit quality will be maintained. To the extent that the covenants are significantly weakened, the market's perception of the credit will decline, and a higher interest rate will be demanded. Thus, the negotiation of covenants requires a balancing of the hospital's desire for flexibility and the market's demand for credit protection.

The restrictions are designed to ensure the continuation of the hospital's ability to generate revenues and preserve assets. Some of the key provisions are briefly reviewed below.

Additional Indebtedness

In order to protect the creditor's access to revenues and assets, the hospital's ability to incur additional debt is limited. Debt is typically defined to include capitalized leases and guaranties of the obligations of other persons. Standard requirements for additional debt measure the ability of the hospital to generate sufficient revenues to pay debt service on a historical and/or a projected debt service basis. In addition, the documents may provide for a *basket*, i.e., a minimum level of debt that can be incurred without the necessity of meeting any financial performance tests. Specific provisions may also be included regarding variable rate indebtedness, refunding indebtedness, completion indebtedness, and short-term indebtedness.

Transfer of Assets

In light of the many corporate reorganizations undertaken in response to the changing health care environment, hospitals have desired the ability to transfer assets to provide seed capital to affiliates or to capitalize joint ventures. However, in order to preserve the assets available to repay the debt, the documents specifically restrict the ability of the hospital to transfer such assets. Transfer of assets frequently includes investments in or loans to affiliates.

The typical provision permits transfer of up to a specified percentage (for example, 5 percent) of its assets in any 12-month period. In addition, transfers may be made if specified debt service coverage tests are met or if the transfer is for fair consideration. Also, an exception can be made for specific transfers of cash or assets that are contemplated at the time of the financing. Under a master indenture, transfers among participants can be made without limit.

Mergers

The standard provisions permit mergers only if certain financial tests relating to the net worth and debt service coverage of the surviving entity are met and if after the consummation of the merger there would exist no event of default. In addition, an opinion of bond counsel that the merger would not adversely affect the exemption from federal income taxation of interest payable on the bonds may be required. Under a master indenture, mergers among participants are not restricted.

Rate Covenant

The rate covenant is a maintenance test whereby the hospital agrees to set its rates so as to generate sufficient revenues to pay the debt service on the bonds. In addition, the hospital agrees that if its debt service coverage drops below a specified level, typically in the range of 1.10 to 1.25, the hospital will retain an independent consultant to make recommendations regarding the operations of the hospital so as to achieve such coverage. The hospital further agrees to follow such recommendations to the extent feasible. This requirement to retain a consultant may be waived upon a finding that laws or regulations, such as rate review, prevent the hospital from maintaining the specified coverage.

Insurance

In order to protect investors' interests in the ongoing operations and viability of the hospital, the documents set forth specific requirements for insurance coverage of its property and the operation thereof against casualties, contingencies, and risks, including public and professional liability. It is in the hospital's interest to avoid the setting of specific dollar limitations on this coverage. One such approach provides that the hospital maintain insurance in such forms and in such amounts as is customary in the case of corporations engaged in the same or similar activities and similarly situated and as is adequate to protect its property and operations. The hospital may be required to obtain on an annual basis a report certifying adequate insurance coverage or an insurance consultant servicing the hospital's insurance program. Self-insurance should also be permitted. A typical covenant provides for self-insurance if an insurance consultant determines that self-insurance is prudent under the circumstances.

POOLED FINANCING

A number of statewide and county health facilities financing authorities have established pooled financing programs. The authorities issue bonds, the proceeds of which are held as a pool of funds available to loan to hospitals for eligible purposes. The pooled programs offer the hospital the opportunity to participate in an existing issue and to avoid the lengthy financing process of its own.

With the 1986 Tax Act, the availability of pooled financing was severely restricted by the prohibition on "blind pools"; i.e., pools of money borrowed prior to indemnification of and commitment by each of the ultimate borrowers from the pool. However, many of the pre-1986 pools provide for recycling the principal of the loans taken from the pools, so blind pool money remains available in many instances and should be pursued as an alternative to other types of financing.

The typical pool bond issue provides for loans at a variable interest rate with maturities up to 7 years. The loan proceeds must be used for the purchase of equipment and, in some cases, for other capital expenditures. These debt instruments impose the same risks as a single hospital issue of variable rate debt with respect to the fluctuation of interest rates and the marketability to tendered bonds. In addition, the hospital must consider the impact of repaying the debt over 7 years. When any substantial amount of money is borrowed, the relatively high annual debt service may effectively restrict the hospital's ability to incur any additional debt in the future. As with a variable rate issue by a single hospital, the bond issue must be supported by a liquidity/credit facility. The issuer of the liquidity/credit facility has the power to accept or reject the hospitals that want to participate. In some cases, a hospital may be required to obtain a letter of credit in order to participate.

The clear advantage of the pooled program to a participating hospital is its simplicity. The hospital can participate in a financing that has already been structured. The documentation has, in large part, been developed before the hospital's participation. The financing time and effort can thereby be minimized. This, however, can also be a disadvantage because it virtually eliminates the ability of the hospital to structure the financing to meet its particular circumstances. In some cases, a hospital may negotiate specific covenants with the credit facility issuer, but generally not to the same extent as in a single hospital financing.

The pooled financing can also accomplish significant economies of scale by the sharing of issuance expenses with other participating hospitals. These savings, however, can be minimized or eliminated if the hospital is required to obtain a letter of credit in order to participate. In addition, under certain circumstances, the hospital's share of expenses may be disproportionately high if the bond proceeds are not loaned out in a timely manner.

The terms of the pooling of the financing structure must be reviewed carefully. To what extent is the hospital liable if another borrower defaults in its debt service payments? Generally, pools are structured so that a hospital has no direct liability for a nonpayment by another borrower. However, all earnings on the funds held by the trustee administering the pool may be available to make up a nonpayment by any borrower. Typically, each hospital would receive a credit against its debt service payments for its pro rata share of any such earnings. If such earnings are instead applied to make payments for a defaulting borrower, a hospital will suffer an economic loss.

Each hospital must review the specific provisions of the pool(s) available to it and the appropriateness of the pool to meet its capital needs. In addition, the hospital should review any existing debt documents to make sure that the participation in the pooled program is permitted and that such participation will not unduly restrict its future flexibility.

TAXABLE BONDS

As described above, tax-exempt financing has accounted for the great bulk of health care financing for hospitals. However, a number of hospitals that did not wish to borrow money through a governmental entity have chosen to borrow on a taxable basis. The volume limitation on tax-exempt financing for nonhospital health care facilities or other restrictions imposed by the Tax Reform Act of 1986 should result in an increase in hospitals' use of taxable financing. The obvious difference between taxable and tax-exempt financing is the difference in the interest rates. Because the interest on tax-exempt bonds is exempt from federal income taxes and, in some cases, state income taxes as well, that interest rate can be correspondingly lower than the interest rate on taxable bonds.

However, other differences between the markets for taxable bonds and those for tax-exempt bonds should be noted. Taxable hospital bonds have been, for the most part, privately placed with institutional investors, including insurance companies, pension funds, and banks. The terms of the financing have been tailored to meet the demands of these investors. Typically, therefore, the maturities of taxable hospital bonds have been limited to 15–20 years as compared to 30-year maturities for tax-exempt bonds. The amortization of the principal over this shorter period substantially increases the annual debt service requirements.

In a private placement, the covenants of the debt instruments are negotiated directly between the borrower and the investor. The type of covenants in tax-exempt and taxable financings are very similar, except that the covenants in taxable bonds are generally more restrictive and may include certain asset-based covenants, such as a debt-to-total capital ratio and liquidity ratio. In some cases a mortgage may be required. However, with a limited number of bondholders, it also becomes possible to obtain amendments to the debt instruments through bondholder consents. Institutional investors are selective in their investments and have limited their investments to the better credits (at least A ratings). Thus, many of the hospitals that have sold tax-exempt bonds in the public market may not be well received by the institutional investors.

Federal and state laws and regulations do not restrict the use of proceeds of taxable bonds. Legally, these proceeds can be used for any creditworthy purpose. Thus, taxable bonds provide a source of money for activities and/or entities that cannot be funded through tax-exempt financing. For example, taxable debt may be the only source of financing for office buildings and venture opportunities. However, investors in ventures often seek a participation or equity position in the venture.

EQUITY FINANCING AS A CAPITAL-RAISING TECHNIQUE

Joint ventures among two or more institutions have become a common way of efficiently raising capital and expertise to enter into health care ventures. Generally, the participants in the joint venture bring a combination of expertise, capital, and market access to the joint venture. Joint ventures normally take the form of either a business corporation or a partnership. Equity offerings of stock or partnership interests can also be used to broadly raise capital from passive investors. In a business corporation stock is issued to the various investors, and control of the corporation is exercised through the vote of the shareowners, who elect members to a board of directors. Structuring a venture as a corporation has the advantage of limiting the liability of the shareholders to the value of their shares of stock and permits the accumulation of capital at the corporate level. However, a major disadvantage is that the earnings of the corporation are taxed at the corporate level and again to the shareholders when they receive dividends.

In a partnership, as opposed to the corporate forum, there is no federal income tax at the partnership level, and profits and losses are deemed to be received by the partners in the year earned. Control of the management of the partnership is generally exercised by a general partner, desig-

nated as such by the partnership agreement, who assumes responsibility for management; in a general partnership with more than one general partner, control of management may be exercised through a partnership committee that generally selects the managers of the partnership and meets periodically with management.

Advantages of Equity Financing

The following advantages are often cited for raising money through a partnership or stock offering, rather than through the issuance of debt:

- *Ability to raise capital at a low cost:* If the enterprise is attractive and there is a good chance for future capital gains, then capital can be raised at a fairly high multiple of expected earnings.
- *No interest debt burden:* No fixed interest payments are required on partnership or stock interests in the firm. This feature frees a venture from the burden of paying interest during its start-up years when there is often a loss.
- *Leverage:* By improving the net worth and debt-to-equity ratio through the offering of equity, a company enhances its ability to raise additional capital through debt.
- *Acquisitions:* In a stock company, stock can be used to acquire assets, partnership interests, or stock in another venture. Thus, the need to raise cash is held to a minimum.
- *Personal incentive:* Stock and partnership interests and options can be structured to provide incentive for management. This can be a valuable tool in attracting and holding top-flight management.

Disadvantages of Using Partnership Interests or Stock To Raise Capital

Perhaps the major disadvantage of using equity to raise capital is the dilution of ownership interest that occurs as a result. In a successful venture the percentage of earnings that must go to the investing equity partner would be substantially higher than the percentage of earnings that would be necessary to pay off indebtedness. Dilution of ownership also means that minority owners may insist on having some say in the management of the business. This can raise problems for management, particularly if business is not going well.

JOINT VENTURE STRUCTURES

Hospital/Hospital Joint Ventures

Joint ventures among hospitals are a particularly effective means of sharing services between two or more hospitals so that there is a minimum of overlap and capital can be expended most wisely. They are also effective in starting up new ventures that require a larger purchasing base or market area. When several hospitals participate in the joint venture, the hospitals themselves can provide not only the seed capital but also the initial market for the joint venture products or services.

Hospital/Physician Joint Ventures

Most commonly, in hospital/physician joint ventures, the physicians are included to provide capital and also often to encourage their use of the hospital as their primary referral center. Often the trick in these joint ventures is to obtain for the physicians the tax deductions available to the partnership form. To do this it is often most advantageous to organize the joint venture between a for-profit affiliate of the hospital and the physicians to avoid the limitation of tax benefits where nonprofit corporations are involved.

PHOs have become a very common joint venture mechanism for vertical integration of health care services. Typically, physicians and hospitals use PHOs to jointly market their services to managed care companies and large employers. PHOs generally are structured as business corporations with the physicians either individually or, more often, through a professional corporation, holding 50 percent of the stock and the hospitals involved holding the other 50 percent of the stock.

Hospital/Other Provider Joint Ventures

This type of joint venture is particularly popular now with HMOs, ambulatory surgery centers, and specialized hospitals, such as psychiatric and drug abuse hospitals. In these joint ventures, the nonhospital entity often brings particular expertise to the transaction, and the hospital provides its service area reputation, staff, and sometimes, space within the hospital facility. Usually both participants make capital contributions. Discussed in other chapters in this text, there is a range of structures for these. Issues of control and ability to share stock to new participants are particularly important.

Tax-Exempt Hospital/Proprietary Hospital Chain Joint Ventures

This type of joint venture, which often includes a management contract to the proprietary chain, is a way in which proprietary chains can gain access at a minimal cost to a new service area. Generally the proprietary chain contributes its expertise and cash, and the hospital provides market access and facilities. Often, establishment of the joint venture is a multistep process. First, the institutions enter into a contract for management to be provided by the proprietary hospital. This is followed by a joint venture and finally by purchase of the facility by the proprietary hospital.

However, IRS Rev. Proc. 93-19 specifically limits the duration and compensation for management contracts in which a for-profit company manages tax-exempt bond-financed property. Careful attention should be given to this revenue procedure when negotiating management contracts.

LEGAL ISSUES: CONTROL AND LIABILITY EXPOSURE

Partnership Form

The Uniform Partnership Act, adopted in all 50 states, and the Uniform Limited Partnership

Act, adopted in a majority of states, give all general partners in a general or limited partnership the right to direct involvement in the partnership's day-to-day business affairs. However, both acts allow joint ventures to vary their statutory rights and responsibilities in written partnership agreements. Therefore, if there is more than one general partner, partners can, through contract, decide which responsibilities will go to which partner. The partnership agreement generally requires that all general partners must vote on certain major partnership decisions. General partners have unlimited obligation for partnership liabilities.

Corporate Form

The business corporation acts of most states typically grant shareholders of corporations the right to approve major changes proposed by the corporation's board of directors, such as amendments to articles of incorporation, mergers, consolidation, and sale of all, or substantially all, of the corporation's assets. On such other matters as an election of directors, state corporation laws commonly permit corporations to vary shareholders' voting rights. Therefore, the bylaws of the joint venture corporation might define each joint venture/shareholder's voting rights with respect to election of directors. For example, each joint venturer might be given the right to elect a certain number of directors; the number of directors that each joint venturer is entitled to elect may or may not be in proportion to each joint venturer's percentage of ownership of the corporation.

Subject to the provisions of the relevant state's corporation law, the shareholders of the joint venture corporation also may establish, in written shareholder and stock subscription agreements, certain restrictions on the shareholders' ability to transfer the corporation's stock and their obligation to make additional capital contributions and to pay assessments on the stock.

FEDERAL INCOME TAXATION OF A BUSINESS CORPORATION

Unless a corporation qualifies as a 501(c)(3) corporation, a professional corporation, or as a Subchapter-S (small business) corporation, it is taxed twice—once at the corporate level and once at the shareholder level when dividends are passed out to the shareholders.

If the corporation is a for-profit business corporation, 501(c)(3) institutions should not be concerned about the impact of a joint venture corporation so long as the joint venture is operated as a separate and distinct corporation and the exempt organization's participation in the profits of the joint venture corporation is in proportion to its capital contributions to the corporation.

Dividends paid to a 501(c)(3) tax-exempt organization by its taxable subsidiary are not taxed as unrelated business income as long as the subsidiary is not considered by the IRS to be a mere instrumentality of the exempt parent. If its participation in a taxable joint venture corporation is properly structured, a tax-exempt organization can avoid federal income taxation of dividends paid to it by the joint venture corporation.

The IRS does scrutinize a taxable joint venture corporation to determine whether the tax-exempt shareholder receives a return from the corporation's net profits that is proportionate to its capital contribution to the corporation. If, for example, the IRS finds that the tax-exempt shareholder purchases 50 percent of the corporation's stock but receives only 40 percent of the corporation's dividends, it will consider the tax-exempt shareholder's capital contribution to be, in part, the transfer of tax-exempt assets to a taxable entity (the taxable shareholder) in violation of the prohibition in Section 501(c)(3) against private inurement. This problem can also arise when the taxable joint venturer receives a disproportionate share of the corporation's income through payment schemes other than stock dividends. Unreasonable bonus plans for a taxable shareholder who is also an employee of or contractor to the corporation can also create private inurement problems. The tax-exempt shareholder must be certain that the joint venture corporation is organized so that each participant's share of return from equity is proportionate to equity contributed and that no other payment mechanisms exist in the organization that unfairly distribute income to taxable participants. The IRS's principal concern with respect to the involvement of an exempt organization in any for-profit venture with private individuals or taxable entities is whether earnings rightfully due the exempt organization will inure to the benefit of a private investor. Therefore, to avoid an inurement violation, an exempt organization should require that the profits of the corporation be distributed to it in proportion to its capital contribution to the corporation.

FEDERAL INCOME TAXATION OF A PARTNERSHIP

As discussed above, a partnership is not a taxable entity under the Internal Revenue Code. Instead, profits and losses are passed on to each of the partners. The nonexempt partners thus may benefit directly from the partnership's losses, deductions, and credits without incurring a tax at the partnership level.

These advantages of a partnership have certain limitations. First, partners are taxed on their allocable share of partnership income, regardless of whether it is actually distributed. Second, a partner may deduct its share of partnership losses only to the extent of the basis of its partnership interest. Generally, a partner's basis is equal to the amount of cash and the cost of any other property contributed to the partnership, as well as its share of partnership liability for which it is "at risk." A partner's basis is increased by the partner's share of undistributed income and decreased when cash or property is distributed or losses incurred. However, unused losses may be carried forward indefinitely by the partners for as long as they own a partnership interest.

Private inurement rules of Section 501(c)(3) also require that an exempt general partner receive distributions of partnership income in proportion to its capital contribution to the partnership. Therefore, for example, if the exempt general partner contributes 50 percent of the total initial capital of the general partnership, it must receive 50 percent of the partnership income distributions. The exempt general partner must receive a credit toward its capital contribution equal to the fair market value of any property other than cash that it contributes to the partnership. Also, if a nonexempt general partner is appointed the managing general partner of the partnership, the management fee must be reasonable compensation for the services performed. An inflated management fee would artificially reduce the income and funds available for distribution to the general partner or partners and thereby effectively result in a disproportionate share in favor of the nonexempt partner. If the business conducted by a general partner is considered related to the 501(c)(3) purposes of an exempt general partner, partnership income distributed to an exempt general partner is not taxable as unrelated business income.

Otherwise, an exempt general partner must include its share of the gross income of the partnership—whether or not it is distributed—and its share of the partnership deductions directly connected with such gross income in computing its total unrelated business taxable income. The exempt general partner must also carefully monitor the amount of unrelated business taxable income it generates from participation in one or more joint ventures to ensure that such income does not outweigh the income generated from its charitable activities and thereby threaten its 501(c)(3) exemption.

In both limited and general partnerships, the partnership must be structured to provide sufficient attributes of partnership so that it will not be taxed as a corporation. The Internal Revenue Service focuses on four attributes of a corporation: continuity of life, limited liability, centralized management, and free transferability of interest. The presence of absence of these four corporate attributes determines whether a partnership is taxed as a partnership, rather than as a corporation.

A limited partnership in which a corporation serves as sole general partner has difficulty demonstrating that it lacks the corporate characteristic of limited liability. The principal concern of the IRS with such an arrangement is that the sole corporate general partner may be "thinly capitalized." If the sole corporate general partner does not have "substantial assets" (other than its partnership interest) that can be reached by the partnership's creditors or it is merely a "dummy" or "shell" acting as an agent of the limited partners, it is not considered to have unlimited liability.

The IRS has issued rulings that set forth various tests that should be satisfied. One of the more difficult of these tests requires a sole corporate general partner's net worth as the general partner at all times to equal certain specified fair market values. These values are (1) the lesser of 15 percent of the partnership's total capital contributions or $250,000 if the total capital contributions to the partnership are less than $52.5 million or (2) at least 10 percent of the partnership's capital if the total contribution of the partnership exceeds $2.5 million.

The value of the general partner's interest in the partnership may not be counted toward these minimum net worth levels. These minimum net worth requirements often cause difficulties when the sole corporate general partner is a corporation formed by two or more joint venturers for the sole purpose of acting as the sole general partner of the limited partnership.

SALE AS A CAPITAL-RAISING TECHNIQUE

Although much is written about selling part of a venture to raise capital—whether through a joint venture, a stock sale, or a partnership sale—little is written about sale of an entire venture so that capital can be better used for another venture. Redeployment of assets through the sale of one or more of a multihospital system's hospitals or one of a restructured system's companies may be the best means available for raising capital for the corporation's remaining businesses.

Before making a sale, a careful appraisal should be made of the value of the asset to be sold. Investment banking firms use a wide variety of market value tests to determine this value. These include price earnings multiples enjoyed by publicly held companies engaged in the business of the enterprise to be sold, confidential information of the price paid in similar transactions, and real estate appraisals. Often these firms provide advice on how the enterprise to be sold could be restructured to enhance its value when sold.

CONVERSION

Perhaps the most dramatic type of restructuring is conversion from nonprofit to for-profit form.[1] California and Wisconsin have special conversion statutes that permit nonprofit institutions to convert to for-profit upon payment of the going concern value of the enterprise to the state or to a nonprofit charitable institution. In other states, conversion is accomplished through a leveraged buy-out mechanism. This technique involves creation of a shell business corporation that then buys the assets of the nonprofit corporation.

In conversions the major concern of the parties is that a sufficient price is paid for the assets of the nonprofit institution so that the attorney general of the state will not challenge the transaction as a violation of the charitable trust doctrine or *cy press*. Normally, preclearance is sought from the attorney general's office, and in the case of conversions of HMOs the approval of the state department of insurance is also sought.

For enterprises that can entertain high price-earning multiples upon conversion, a conversion to for-profit form can be a very effective way to gain access to capital at a minimum price because once the enterprise is in for-profit business corporation form it can issue stock.

PRIVATE PLACEMENTS AND PUBLIC OFFERINGS OF SECURITIES

Issuance of securities, whether through partnership participations, shares of stock, warrants, or bonds, is heavily regulated by both state and federal law.

State securities laws are often referred to as "blue sky" laws and were enacted for the most part earlier this century to protect the public from the sale of "lots in the blue sky." The primary concerns of state securities laws are the registration of securities, securities brokers, and investment advisers and the prohibition of fraud. Most state securities laws do, however, provide for exemption from registration of certain types of securities and certain transactions. The debt securities of 501(c)(3) organizations and tax-exempt bonds are generally exempt from registrations under state securities laws. A Uniform Securities Act has been adopted in over 35 states.

The Federal Securities Act of 1933 governs the primary and secondary distribution of securities. Ownership interest in joint ventures and syndications are regarded as securities within the meaning of Section 5 of the 1933 Act, as are stock and bond issues.

The 1933 Act was enacted in response to the stock market crash of 1929. Congressional inquiries into the events surrounding Black Tuesday uncovered the widespread practice of distributing securities to investors without any disclosure of information that could aid the investor in his or her decision making. The 1933 Act was therefore enacted to "...provide full and fair disclosure of the character of securities sold in interstate and foreign commerce and through the mails and to prevent frauds in the sale thereof."

In drafting the provisions of the 1933 Act, Congress recognized the burdens that its regulation requirements might place on certain distributions of securities. Accordingly it provided registration exemptions for certain securities *and* certain types of transactions. Among the transactions exempted from registration were issuance of securities by 501(c)(3) organizations, tax-exempt bonds, and those securities included in the private placement exemption of Section 4(2) of the 1933 Act. Over the years both the courts and commentators found Section 4(2) lacking in specificity, and in 1982 the SEC enacted Regulation D, providing new, specific private offering guidelines. Section 4(2) and Regulation D provide exemptions from registration for certain sales to wealthy, sophisticated individuals and institutions, for very small offerings, and for intrastate offerings.

Before issuing securities it is necessary to retain expert securities counsel to determine whether the offering can be made on an exempt basis so that the very expensive process of federal registration can be avoided. Securities counsel should also be asked to advise the institution about compliance with state blue sky laws. An issue that is exempt from federal registration may not be exempt from state registration.

Securities counsel and the institution's investment banker should also be requested to provide advice on the advantages of a publicly registered offering of securities. Securities that can be freely traded provide management with certain substantial advantages in their employee incentive plans, their ability to acquire other companies, and their ability to raise large amounts of capital. On the other hand, public registration under the 1933 Act subjects a company to cumbersome and expensive ongoing public disclosure requirements.[2]

CONCLUSION

As with many other aspects of the health care industry, health care finance is in a period of rapid change. During the last decade, tax-exempt bonds have been the main type of security used by health care institutions to raise capital. That is rapidly changing. As of 1986, severe restrictions were imposed on Industrial Development Bond financing for business corporations, including the proprietary health care companies.

Less severe, but still detrimental, restrictions have been placed on tax-exempt bonds for 501(c)(3) corporations, and Congress is again considering imposing additional limitations.

Thus, the health care industry and its investment bankers are turning to other methods for raising capital, including joint ventures, sales of assets, real estate partnerships, conversions from nonprofit to for-profit form, and stock offerings. It seems that health care companies will utilize an increasing variety of mechanisms to raise capital.

NOTES

1. For a detailed description of conversion from nonprofit to for-profit form, see K.C. Dunn et al., The Dynamics of Leverage Buy-Outs, Conversion, and Corporate Reorganizations of Not-For-Profit Health Care Institutions, *Topics in Health Care Financing* 12, no. 3 (1986): 19–35.

2. For a detailed discussion of private and public offering of securities, see *Topics in Health Care Financing* 12, no. 3 (1986).

GEOFFREY B. SHIELDS, JD, is a Partner and Chairman of the Governmental Organization and Tax-Exempt Finance Practice at Gardner, Carton, & Douglas in Chicago, Illinois. His practice is in health care and 501(c)(3) finance, including all aspects of tax-exempt bond financing, and mergers and acquisitions. Mr. Shields has worked on a wide range of mergers, acquisitions, and corporate reorganizations for educational institutions, health care and elderly housing companies, including the antitrust aspects of those transactions.

Mr. Shields has been an editor and contributing author on many books and articles on financing, mergers, and acquisitions for health care institutions. He received his JD from Yale Law School and his BA from Harvard University.

DEBRA J. SCHNEBEL, JD, is a Partner at Gardner, Carton, & Douglas in Chicago, Illinois. She practices in the area of corporate and securities law and represents a number of financial institutions in commercial loan and private placement transactions, including secured and unsecured loans, structured and asset-backed financings, and restructurings of such loan transactions. She also represents foreign issuers in connection with Euro-bond offerings and domestically-placed securities.

Ms. Schnebel previously was Vice President of Capital Markets in the Health Care Group at PaineWebber Inc. She received her JD from Northwestern University School of Law and her BA from Allegheny College.

Chapter 23

Health Care Information Systems

Sheldon I. Dorenfest

INTRODUCTION

Concerns over access, cost, and quality in our health care system have created a dramatic demand for complete transformation of almost every aspect of health care delivery. With this environment, there now exists an opportunity to improve the quality of health care while reducing costs through better health care information systems (HCIS). Present health care enterprise information systems are primarily manual and are characterized by a high degree of redundancy, high error potential, lack of timeliness in the processing and filling of orders, high cost, and organizational complexity. Past efforts to automate these information systems barely have begun to highlight the substantial opportunities for improvement that exist. In fact, sometimes automation efforts have had the opposite result by increasing costs and duplicating efforts.

The HCIS industry includes automation within an acute-care community hospital setting, physician offices and clinics, less-acute-care hospitals, other providers (drug and alcohol re-

habilitation and psychiatric hospitals, nursing homes, freestanding ambulatory clinics, etc.), and federal government and associated programs (hospitals and Medicare/Medicaid). As shown in Table 23–1, the market share for acute-care hospitals and their associated inpatient and ambulatory services is going to decrease as a percentage of the total market while the rest of the providers' market share as a percentage of the total will increase. These different types of providers also are beginning to form integrated health care delivery systems with software requirements that will have to serve the needs of all of them in one setting. This integration within the community will require that patient data for all episodes of care throughout the delivery system be accessible at the provider location where the patient is being treated.

Not only is the industry redefining the way care is delivered, but also the way it is reimbursed. Providers will no longer be able to rely on fee for service. Instead, they will be competing with other providers to gain contracts in a managed care environment. As these health care institutions seek to compete for contracts and cope with the increasing pressure of cost controls, outcomes management, increased compe-

Table 23–1 The Health Care Information Systems Industry Market

Market Segments	1993		Forecast 1996		
	% (in Billions)	% of Total	% (in Billions)	% of Total	% Growth
Acute-care hospitals and their associated inpatient and ambulatory services	$4.9	65.3%	$6.7	60.9%	36.7%
Physician offices/clinics	$.8	10.7%	$1.3	11.9%	62.5%
Less-acute-care hospitals and other providers	$.8	10.7%	$1.5	13.6%	87.5%
Federal government and associated programs (hospitals and Medicare/Medicaid)	$1.0	13.3%	$1.5	13.6%	50.0%
TOTAL	$7.5	100.0%	$11.0	100.0%	46.7%

Source: Copyright © 1994, Sheldon I. Dorenfest & Associates, Ltd., Chicago, Illinois.

tition, and quality service delivery, one thing is certain: improved information systems will be a much greater priority and therefore will warrant larger investments than ever before.

New technological advances and demands for connectivity in the health care enterprise are providing opportunities in the health care information systems industry. Information technology will be the critical enabler to many enterprisewide solutions, including multiple registration points, decentralized ordering from ambulatory centers, access to patient records at multiple points, and use of data by both owned and nonowned facilities. Many strategies aimed at achieving such goals are currently being developed and implemented all over the United States. As shown in Figure 23–1, the health care information systems market falls into many segments, but hospitals are becoming even more of a driving force in which all other providers will need to share their information.

All successful providers will need to be able to use information from every part of the care process to:

- capture clinical and demographic information accurately at its source as a by-product of delivering patient care while maintaining proper confidentiality

- present the necessary information elements at the right time in the care process to facilitate case management
- share clinical information with those inside and outside the enterprise with confidence that the information accurately represents the truth
- analyze information given to others and accurately predict the conclusions
- use information effectively to better match health care facilities and personnel with population, conserve resources, and stabilize or lower the cost of health care delivery

Although health care reform has produced new information system needs, long-term central information system issues have remained unsolved. Lack of implementation and management skills along with inadequate software account for the majority of limitations that have, to date, impeded successful use of information systems. In order to keep up with the changing industry, health care executives will spend a larger percentage of their operating budgets on automation, but only if better products become available, installations are managed better, and more benefits are realized.

The coming years represent an unparalleled opportunity for health care executives and clini-

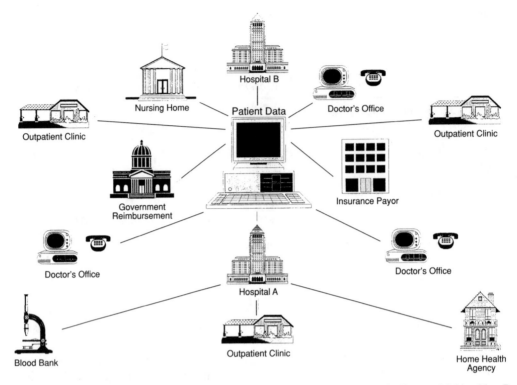

Figure 23–1 Integrated Health Care Systems and Community Health Care Networks Emerge Making New Demands on Computer Systems. *Source:* Copyright © 1994, Sheldon I. Dorenfest & Associates, Ltd., Chicago, Illinois.

cians to transform information systems into a meaningful guide to cost containment and quality improvement. In order to achieve this, however, timely information must be widely available to those who need it throughout the entire health care enterprise. Collaboration rather than competition among health care providers will be the protocol for success throughout the rest of the century and perhaps beyond.

This chapter begins first by discussing automation in an acute-care community hospital environment because this should continue to be where the majority of capital and resources will be allocated. Topics will include the historical development and current status of hospital computerization of "core systems," the rapidly growing area of departmental systems, and major issues having an impact on automation. The discussion will then shift to the role of informa-

tion systems in other components of the health care information systems market, including physician offices/clinics, less-acute-care hospitals and other providers, and federal government-associated segments (hospitals and Medicare/Medicaid).

The final portion of this chapter will cover various governmental and nongovernmental health care reform initiatives directed toward achieving the necessary information requirements needed in this new health care enterprise environment.

ACUTE-CARE COMMUNITY HOSPITAL ENVIRONMENT

As shown in Figure 23–2, hospitals spent $4.6 billion or 1.9% of their total operating budgets on automation in 1992. The most heavily com-

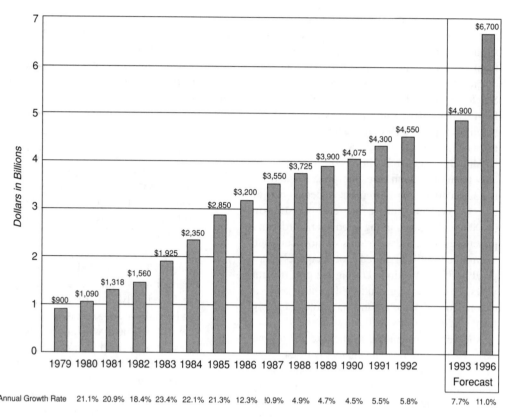

Figure 23–2 Growth Trends in the Acute-Care Market. *Source:* Copyright © 1994, Sheldon I. Dorenfest & Associates, Ltd., Chicago, Illinois.

puterized function in today's hospital is the patient accounting area with 97.7% of all community hospitals automated. Patient care applications follow with 43.6% automated. The patient accounting application automates inpatient billing, outpatient billing (optional), and discharged accounts receivable. Patient care applications include, at a minimum, the automation of patient care orders at the nursing station and the communication of those orders to ancillary services departments (laboratory, pharmacy, radiology, etc.). Most patient care systems include limited results reporting from ancillary departments to the nursing station. Comprehensive systems now include patient charting, extensive results reporting from the ancillaries, nurse care planning, nurse staffing, and patient acuity. In 1992, sales of ancillary department systems such as

laboratory, pharmacy, radiology, and materials management systems grew 20 to 40% over 1990 levels.

CONCEPT OF CORE AND DEPARTMENTAL SYSTEMS

In the past, most hospitals felt it was ideal to purchase as much software and support from one supplier as possible; however, the concept of core systems emerged to reflect a group of applications an enterprise will typically purchase to provide the foundation of all business needs. Since all other departmental applications supplement and build on information already in the core system, it is crucial that it remain consistent and be accurate before it is incorporated into different applications throughout the whole enterprise. Hospitals vary in the number of departmental systems they purchase from specialty vendors; some purchase almost all applications from a single vendor while others take the best-of-breed approach for almost every application. Single vendor solutions are most often chosen for the benefit of integration, while best-of-breed solutions are chosen to achieve the highest level of functionality in every department.

Although the definition of core systems will vary from one health care enterprise to the next, the applications most often associated as part of a core system include patient registration (ADT), patient accounting, medical records, and patient care. Specialty systems vendors continue to emerge to fill niche needs not adequately supplied by HCIS vendors. During the past several years, hospitals have continued to purchase additional niche systems and have moved away from single vendor solutions.

Ancillary departments in the late 1960s and early 1970s were revenue centers with the laboratory being the largest, followed by pharmacy and radiology. Because of its size, the laboratory was the first department to introduce automation through the use of automated instruments. With the advent of minicomputers in the early 1970s, affordable and justifiable products for larger laboratories became available. By the end of the 1970s, minicomputer prices had fallen and products were being developed for all large ancillaries. The 1980s fueled significant growth in all departmental automation segments with the introduction of the microprocessor. Today, market value of all departmental segments surpasses that of patient accounting and patient care, and market value of the four largest ancillary segments is roughly equal to that of patient accounting and patient care.

MAJOR HEALTH CARE ISSUES HAVING AN IMPACT ON ACUTE-CARE HOSPITAL AUTOMATION

Unlike a business environment, acute-care hospitals historically have not been subjected to rigid financial scrutiny by either the government or consumers. As a result, both financial and clinical issues concerning quality and fairness have emerged. In order to dispel such doubts in a managed care environment where providers will be competing with each other to gain contracts, there are a series of issues hospitals need to address if they are going to remain competitive, including:

1. *Making current systems work better:* Frequently, when newly automated systems are implemented, activities that could be eliminated in the manual system continue to be performed, resulting in duplication of effort and confusion.

2. *Reengineering the enterprise:* Even when the newly automated system replaces manual activities, the labor savings can be found only in parts of people's jobs, and health care organizations have lacked the courage and wisdom to restructure these jobs in order to take full advantage of the newly automated systems. On the other hand, hospitals embarking on patient-focused care or related operational change initiatives need better systems to support these new ways of operating.

3. *Quality initiatives:* Automation will be a crucial tool used to generate statistical information to help focus on problem areas and initiate improvements in both billing and patient care. In the quality process, it is top management's role to control the culture of the organization so the improvements proposed will be implemented. Lower and middle management normally have implemented these changes.

4. *Computer-based patient record (CPR) automation strategies:* In most hospitals in 1993, the patient's medical record is still composed of many pieces of paper that are prepared manually and look remarkably similar to the paper record of the 1960s that might be found in the hospital's archives. However, the 1993 record has more pieces of paper because

of clinical and technological advances of the last 30 years, as well as more regulations requiring specific documentation. With an early interest in automating the patient's medical record, and significant efforts toward that goal over the past 25 years, why has the industry not been more successful? Some key problems have impeded successful implementation of the ideal health care information system by both developers and hospitals, including the ones listed below:

- Many developers have oversimplified users' needs and the requirements of new systems. They lacked understanding of manual systems being automated and created the new automated system as if the manual system did not exist. They also based the new system on inadequate direction from hospitals' management.

- Developers needed to bring products to market before they were ready because of the large investment required to succeed.

- Developers have not always learned from past experience and tend to repeat the same mistakes by underestimating the capital required and by setting overly optimistic time schedules.

- Development projects have been undertaken with large blind spots. By not knowing what they did not know, developers were impeded from meeting their targets.

- Developers moved into programming of the systems without adequate overall design of architectural and functional requirements. As a result, many projects have been doomed from their inception.

- Awkward breaks and gaps in the automated systems have resulted in improper person-to-machine interfaces, which do not work as well as the previous entirely manual system.

- Automated systems are described in foreign terms to users instead of terms with which manual system users have familiarity. Therefore, communication between developers and users is less effective.

- When present systems finally become operational, they add instead of eliminate work, and the result for many new systems is duplication of effort and lower productivity.

Today's HCIS market is still plagued by many problems. The greatest limitation the industry faces is that comprehensive patient care systems that effectively automate the medical record are not ready for implementation.

5. *Systems integration and connectivity:* Over the last several years, hospitals have selected and implemented a variety of stand-alone systems to satisfy niche needs, since no single vendor can satisfy everyone's requirements. The increase in the number of software vendors used has resulted in problems accessing data in disparate system environments. Therefore, interfacing and integrating have become a must-have, even for small hospitals, in order to prepare for the changes health care reform will mandate. Connecting foreign software systems has not worked well. Although hardware connectivity exists and technically works well, software connectivity has not. Although there is a high degree of data access, there is limited information for actual decision making. Furthermore, integration and information-sharing issues, such as the need for standardized data elements and statistics, have not been adequately addressed. As seen in Figure 23–3, most vendors use similar terminology, such as *interface engines*, *repositories*, etc., to describe their approach toward networking and connectivity. Areas in which networking/connectivity is becoming critical are:

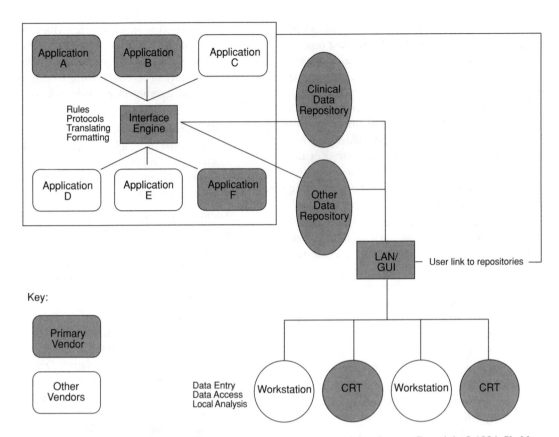

Figure 23–3 Everybody's Approach Toward Networking and Connectivity. *Source:* Copyright © 1994, Sheldon I. Dorenfest & Associates, Ltd., Chicago, Illinois.

- departmental networking
- enterprisewide networking
- postmerger integration and consolidation
- multihospital organizations
- ambulatory care services
- home health care services
- physician links
- community health care networks
- regional health information networks

In each of these areas of opportunity, networking media and network management tools will be crucial to the security and maintenance of data in order to protect patient confidentiality. Integration within a vendor's own product line is available through the use of common databases in which data are entered once and made available to all systems and users who need access. Methods of interfacing data from other systems and integrating data into a repository are being developed using three forms:

- scanned or faxed data that require heavy manual input
- text from dictation, usually from ASCII storage in word processors
- fully coded or structured data as by-products of automated ancillary department processes

Access to the repository is provided by a compatible network with an effective user interface. Whether this will lead to the CPR of the future is still unknown.

6. *Downsizing:* Less expensive midrange computers now have the same capabilities that were once limited to mainframes. Midrange computing also requires fewer data processing staff than is required for a mainframe environment. This is why downsizing has become such a big trend. Client server environments and open-systems architecture are quickly becoming an economical alternative to mainframe computing.

Our discussion thus far has concentrated on the portion that comprises 65% of the HCIS market. Though it is a smaller share, the remaining 35% of the market, which includes physician offices and clinics, less-acute-care hospitals and other providers, and federal government and associated programs (hospital and Medicare/Medicaid), is growing steadily.

OTHER COMPONENTS OF THE HEALTH CARE INFORMATION SYSTEMS MARKET

Physician Offices and Clinics

The large volumes of paperwork, growth in managed care, growing documentation needs, complexity of government reimbursement, and shifting characteristics of physician practices and clinics have fueled the need for information systems in this segment of the market. The physician office and clinic information system market accounted for $.8 billion or approximately 11% of the total health care information system market and is expected to rise to $1.3 billion or 12% of the total HCIS market in 1996.

Whether physicians have their own practices or are in practices owned by hospitals, there is an increasing demand for interfaces to hospital information systems in order to obtain accurate demographic and insurance information, place orders for patients, and retrieve test results. The continued growth of managed care contracting

has resulted in an increasing demand for systems that help with contract management. There also is a need for software that tracks services from different providers, provides better clinical tools to measure outcomes and costs, and enhances access to information in other systems, particularly the hospital's. Furthermore, regulatory complexities also will increase the need for physician practices to have better and more efficient information systems. Since practices of all sizes are becoming more sophisticated users of information systems, this has caused an increase in replacement of older systems currently in use.

Less-Acute-Care Hospitals and Other Providers

Approximately 11% or $.8 billion of the total HCIS market was spent on the less-acute-care hospitals (drug and alcohol rehabilitation, psychiatric, etc.) and other providers in 1993. This market is expected to increase 14% or $1.5 billion of the total HCIS market in 1996. Included in this segment of the market are nursing homes, freestanding ambulatory services, home health care, behavioral health, and other specialty inpatient services.

Federal Government-Associated Segments (Hospitals and Medicare/Medicaid)

After acute-care hospitals and their associated inpatient and ambulatory services, federal government-associated segments (hospitals and Medicare/Medicaid) accounted for the biggest portion of HCIS dollars spent, with $1 billion (13%) of the HCIS market in 1993. This is forecasted to increase to about $1.5 billion or 14% in 1996. Included in this market segment are military hospitals, The Department of Veterans Affairs (VA), and information systems for Medicare/Medicaid claims processing.

The Department of Veterans Affairs (VA) is the largest operator of health care systems in the federal sector and operates the largest centrally directed health care system in the United States through 171 VA medical centers (VAMCs), 362 outpatient clinics, 129 nursing homes, and 35 domiciliaries. Automation efforts for VAMCs started in the mid-1960s. Prior to 1982, only a few VA facilities were supported by automation. Currently, the VA is implementing on a national scale software that supports film/chart tracking, dietetics, radiology, mental health, medical center procurements, surgery, nursing, order entry/ results reporting, patient-based cost accounting, quality management, and VAMC payroll administration.

Information systems for Medicare/Medicaid claims processing is an important part of this market. The number of hospitals now filing claims electronically is rapidly increasing. Compared to paper claims, electronic claims submission is a more accurate and efficient method that greatly expedites government reimbursement. The savings to be realized through full use of electronic claims submission ultimately will contribute to an overall reduction in the administrative costs of health care delivery.

GOVERNMENT AND NONGOVERNMENT HEALTH CARE REFORM INITIATIVES

Even before the Clinton administration unveiled its plan, there already were a series of significant parallel thrusts that had been spawned by the pressures for health care reform. Several of these thrusts have already begun to have a significant impact on health care information systems. Aside from efforts to achieve the CPR, additional efforts include: managed care, community care networks, the Joint Commission on Accreditation of Healthcare Organizations (Joint Commission), and outcomes measurement.

Computer-Based Patient Record Initiatives

While many of today's patient care systems originally were conceived to automate the medical record, most of them in use today contain very limited functionality. Recent government initiatives calling for a CPR, however, have

heightened interest in and the desire for an automated medical record. In April 1991, the Institute of Medicine (IOM) of the National Academy of Sciences completed an 18-month study for improving patient records in response to the need for better information management and increasing technological advances. The IOM Committee defined the CPR and its attributes by stating that:

- The CPR should contain a problem list, health status, and functional level, as well as clinician rationale for patient care decisions.

- CPRs should be linked with other clinical records to provide a longitudinal patient record.

- The CPR system itself must protect patient confidentiality.

- CPRs must provide convenient access to authorized users at all times, support direct data entry by practitioners, and allow for custom-tailored views of data.

- CPR systems should be linked to knowledge, literature, and bibliographic databases.

- The systems must be flexible and expandable to support the evolving needs of users.

The committee concluded that the CPR is an essential technology for health care because the uses and demands of patient data are increasing; more data are being generated, making it more difficult to track the data; and information management capabilities are required in order to improve the quality of health care while managing the costs associated with care. Additional recommendations called for the public and private sectors to set up a Computer-Based Patient Record Institute (CPRI), which was accomplished in 1992. The role of the CPRI is to initiate and encourage the development of health care information systems (toward the goal of a comprehensive longitudinal patient record).

The Healthcare Open Systems Trials (HOST), formerly Healthcare Information Trial System (HITS), was established in 1992. It is a for-profit consortium and a subsidiary of Microelectronic Computer Consortium (MCC), a for-profit cooperative research and development consortium. As a joint venture with CPRI, HOST will serve to implement the goal of a fully-integrated, open health care information system with a longitudinal patient record as a by-product, and provide benchmarks to justify providers' investments in information systems.

While these government and nongovernment initiatives could be a positive force in moving toward the needed solution, there also is a risk of repeating mistakes of the past. Pushing too quickly for solutions to problems that are not well understood could result in another series of failures. The computer-based patient record is not the only project under way that is part of the solution to health care reform. Many other government and nongovernment initiatives have surfaced making the role of information systems critical to the success of reducing the cost of health care.

Managed Care

Many areas in the country already have a significant portion of health care purchased through a managed care relationship. The management of patient care has become a critical factor in maintaining a health care organization's financial health. In order for providers to remain competitive in a changing environment, information management has become critical and information needs more specific. Information must now be available to provide essential management tools to:

- monitor the profitability of contracts based on actual costs
- monitor resource consumption
- predict and track resource needs based on patient diagnoses
- access historical patient clinical data throughout a continuum of care
- document quality outcome measures to meet Joint Commission requirements and specifications

- allow physician access to clinical data for risk management and efficient resource management
- provide communication links between group practices and patient care facilities for consolidation of clinical data
- provide multidisciplinary access to patient orders, test results, progress notes, etc., during hospitalization

Although case management systems are not readily available, most of the data required for effective resource management are captured in existing financial and clinical applications such as order entry, medical record abstracting, patient accounting, and ADT. Such data often are difficult to consolidate because of the need for various system interfaces, and much of the longitudinal information needed for continuum-of-care management is not being stored on any system. Capabilities many organizations lack include:

- critical pathways and variances between actual and expected services
- care plans and/or case management plans
- nursing diagnosis or problem lists
- progress notes and multidisciplinary charting
- measurable quality outcomes
- referral tracking
- patient history and physical data
- full complement of test results

Outcomes Measurement

In the managed health care environment, emphasis will be on health care outcomes, thus requiring the capability:

- to curb inappropriate utilization
- to use data for comparative purposes
- to provide knowledge to the consumer facilitating informed purchasing decisions
- to provide information to medical decision makers at the point of service

Community Care Networks

In order to facilitate patient referrals in the mid-1980s, hospitals linked physicians' office computer systems to the hospital's information system to provide doctors with access to patient information. The changing health care enterprise makes linking physicians to a single hospital insufficient. Instead, it is necessary to link providers to wherever patient care is delivered (hospital, clinic, office, lab, imaging center, etc.) via a communitywide or regional health information network. Terms commonly associated with such a concept are: community health information networks (CHINs), community health management information systems (CHMISs), and regional health information networks (RHINs).

The exact structure of the network, the role hospitals will play, and the set of basic health care benefits have not yet been determined, and will be dependent upon the needs of each community. Hospitals, physicians, and private insurers could own and operate networks, co-own the networks with other providers, or could serve as providers of services under contract within a network. The set of services covered under the public program would be the minimum that must be covered in the private sector. The AHA's proposal has called for an independent, national commission that would determine a comprehensive set of basic health care benefits.

Healthcare information networks (HINs) are complementary enablers for the AHA's model, linking community providers, employers, payors, and patients. It is important to remember that the information network is simply a communication infrastructure for delivering services at the point of contact with customers. Some HINs are planning a central repository that captures information as transactions pass through the network. The repository is not necessary to obtain many of the communication benefits; however, it is quite useful for analyzing and reporting disparate data.

Some issues regarding HINs still need to be addressed:

- Management will need to make a paradigm shift away from the traditional resistance to sharing patient information.
- Confidentiality of information will need to be protected.
- Costs to initiate an information network will have to be determined.

In many cities, the John A. Hartford Foundation, the Microelectronic Computer Consortium (MCC/HOST), the Workgroup for Electronic Data Interchange (WEDI), and the National Institutes of Health (NIH) are supporting some of these networks initiatives. Vendors such as IMS, Wellmark, Ameritech, Med Power, SMS, and others have developed and are marketing products to establish information networks as well.

The Joint Commission on Accreditation of Healthcare Organizations (Joint Commission)

The Joint Commission evaluates and accredits more than 5,200 hospitals and more than 3,000 other health care organizations. In anticipation of the evolution toward a new performance measurement mandate in health care, the Joint Commission launched its agenda for change in 1987. Three major initiatives are involved:

1. reformation of the Joint Commission's standards to emphasize actual organizational performance and impose standards for information management
2. redesign of the survey process to provide more interactive on-site evaluation and education
3. development of the indicator monitoring system (IMS), a national database resource to support performance improvement in hospitals and other patient care settings

The IMS was implemented on a voluntary basis in 1994. In 1996, participation by accredited hospitals will become mandatory and IMS will become a fully integrated component of the accreditation process, reaching its peak capacity of 30 indicators. In order for IMS to serve as a useful reference database and as a benchmarking source, it is important that the same indicator data be collected from all organizations to which they apply. Even more important, when performance data are to be factored into the accreditation decision, the same data must be used consistently among all organizations.

Summary of Health Care Reform Initiatives

The obvious key to successful health care reform is information. Everyone needs information and no one has the means to obtain the appropriate information easily. The federal and state governments need information as a basis for regulation to set targets and rates, to review health plans, to assert new technology, and to inform consumers. All providers need information for patient monitoring, assessment, triage, outcomes management, medical decision making, physicians' profiling, billing, procedure-specific cost findings, planning, budgeting, and better partnership building. Insurers need information to assess their risks and their plans' effectiveness. Finally, purchasing groups need information to compare prices and their plans' effectiveness. The value of information will skyrocket as health care reform unfolds.

Since the health care information system enterprise cannot easily perform any of the criteria required for success today, the challenge will be to reach the goal in planned and measurable stages. The major initiatives mentioned in this chapter will play a role in stimulating awareness and will help prepare the industry for change. Of the activities currently in progress, two will have short-term implications. The Joint Commission's agenda for change will have the most immediate impact on hospitals by focusing their attention on the monitoring of indicators and the information needed to support it. The Joint Commission, through the accreditation process, will raise awareness by imposing information standards.

Health care reform surely will press for administrative simplification, which will cause providers to change the way they interact with payors. The other ongoing efforts will produce funding that will help the industry learn how to overcome the obstacles in its path. The inescapable conclusion is that the industry's greatest handicap in managing information is not the absence of technology but the absence of skills and experience. The most effective response to prepare for the future will be based on an accurate self-assessment of a health care organization's current situation and then development of both short-term and long-term strategies. In the short-term, health care organizations must improve use of currently automated systems and purchase new systems based on an accurate understanding of what can and cannot be done.

WHAT IS NEEDED FOR SUCCESS?

The Process of Creating Strategies for Successful Automation

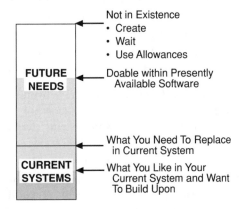

In the near-term, health care organizations must ask:

- Given their current situation, where are they satisfied, what works? Where are they dissatisfied, what does not work?
- Is it the systems or the way systems are used that needs to be changed?

- What priority does the enterprise place on producing timely and accurate information?
- How effectively is information shared among departments, physicians, and other providers?
- How much of the patient care process is automated?
- Given the organization's current situation, which new system's needs can be accomplished, which cannot, and how does the organization move from where it is now to where it wants to go?
- How much time should the process take and how much will it cost in capital and resources?

Once the assessment has been completed, the health care organization can begin to develop its short-term and long-term strategies.

In developing long-term strategies, health care organizations should:

- make short-term investments judiciously so that suppliers are encouraged to invest in products that meet long-term needs
- work toward an industry consensus
- communicate these needs to suppliers
- ensure that CEOs make this issue a priority

The models for community care networks and integrated health delivery systems are well known, but the information systems' require-ments to support these models have been grossly oversimplified. Many contend that success will be dependent upon a combination of the CPR and an electronic superhighway, yet the actuality of these solutions is many years into the future.

Until this system is created, hospitals must:

- develop automation strategies based on an accurate understanding of what can and cannot be done
- concentrate on improving currently auto-mated systems and manual systems and make investments in suppliers' systems ju-diciously
- select a system that best fits their needs, and effectively implement the system to achieve maximum desired results
- choose suppliers who are investing in prod-ucts that will meet long-term needs
- invest time in building an industry consen-sus and in communicating options to the vendors

Achieving the successful system of the 1990s requires strong leadership. The health care institution's CEO must understand and influ-ence this effort. With proper application of that influence, an integrated system with a fully auto-mated medical record could be achieved by the end of the decade. Without such influence, hos-pitals will still be waiting for this system at the end of the century.

SHELDON I. DORENFEST, MBA, CPA, has been involved in the health care industry for over 25 years. He formed and is President of Sheldon I. Dorenfest & Associates, Ltd., a health care consulting firm, in 1976. He has experience in strategic business planning and hospital data processing planning and implementation for the health care industry. For over a decade, Sheldon I. Dorenfest & Associates, Ltd. has been monitoring the hospital computing market and Mr. Dorenfest has personally directed the research involved in compiling The Dorenfest 3000+ Database™, an information source that accu-rately depicts the state of the art in hospital automation, and the firm's educational seminars and publications. Prior to his formation of the firm, he was the Founder, President, and Chief Executive Officer of Compucare, and Director of Corporate Business Consulting Services for Abbott Laborato-ries. He is a frequent speaker at ECHO, HIMSS, AHA, VHA, and HISSG meetings. Mr. Dorenfest has been widely published in industry publications such as *Computers in Healthcare*, *Healthcare Execu-tives*, *Healthcare Informatics*, *Healthweek*, *Hospitals*, *Modern Healthcare*, and *National Report on Computers*.

Chapter 24

Quality Assurance to Quality Improvement: The Transition

Lois J. Bittle

Defining quality in health care has been problematic, primarily because it has many different components. Quality can be viewed as clinical effectiveness, or, in a broader sense, as those characteristics of the medical care process that the patient values. Generically, quality is a word, and combined with health care is a parity statement. That is, it suggests that health care received by a particular provider or hospital is as good as that which would be received by any other provider. However, this is an incorrect supposition.

The word *quality* relates to a subjective opinion where meaning is given to the word by the participant. In health care, the definition varies based on the individual or group providing the response. Each participant, provider, purchaser, and/or payor defines quality in operational terms based on its respective interests, priorities, objectives, and interpretation. The organization that defines this multidimensional concept of quality also determines the tools for measurement. For example, quality to a patient in the health care system is access and timeliness of service; to physicians, it is achieving desirable outcomes; to hospitals, it is financial viability and satisfied customers; to payors, it is the rec-ognition that good quality equates to lower cost and customer satisfaction.

Finally, any definition of quality is highly dependent on the leadership of an organization or government bureaucracy creating an environment that sends powerful messages throughout the organization. This message communicates a set of core values and commitment that influence the work force to continuously improve the organization's performance. Clearly, quality in health care is a complex and relative issue. Notwithstanding, this operational definition is more clearly stated by today's mentors on quality, most notably Philip Crosby, W. Edward Deming, J.M. Juran, and, more recently, Peter Senge.

INDUSTRIAL INFLUENCES ON DEFINING QUALITY

Though many view the quality revolution to be foreign, many of the roots of the current influences for quality management and improvement originated with Dr. W. Edward Deming, an American statistician whose teaching in postwar Japan led to the development of leadership principles. According to the quality experts, there is a philosophy and approach to continuous improvement of products and service. Generically, managing and improving quality requires a systematic approach to guarantee that organized activities happen the way they are planned, the success of which is highly dependent on the philosophy of the organization. Current labels applied to quality measurement and improvement include Total Quality Management (TQM) and Continuous Quality Improvement (CQI).

Crosby defines quality as "conformance to requirements." He argues that where requirements are clearly stated, measurements can be taken to determine conformance to those requirements. Nonconformance, then, is the absence of quality.

Crosby's 14-step quality improvement begins with the commitment of leadership and management to recognize that senior leadership must participate in any quality improvement program; the bringing together of representatives of select areas to form teams in an effort to determine the status of quality, the cost of quality, and to raise the level of quality awareness among employees. Further emphasis is placed on "zero defect" where doing things right the first time fulfills the quality mission to regularly meet and/or exceed the specified goal. In this context Crosby asserts that "quality is free" and points out "what costs money are the unquality things—all the actions that involve not doing the job right the first time." He sees quality management as a systematic way of guaranteeing that organized activities happen the way they were planned. However, the degree of success or failure of QM efforts depends on the level of awareness of what constitutes quality and the commitment at the leadership level.

Deming's philosophy encompasses a holistic approach to management in which the organization is viewed as an integrated entity. Deming argues that quality is not productivity assessment, zero defect programs, or employee suggestion programs. He views quality improvement as a philosophy, not a program—the driving force of the organization where learning and living the management style fosters a cycle of never ending improvement in design/redesign, conformance, and performance. He defines quality as the never ending improvement of the "extended process." Emphasis is placed on those components that make up the internal system and process and those processes that incorporate the external consumer; the ultimate goal is customer satisfaction.

Juran defines quality as fitness for use, and requires that product features respond to customers' needs and be free from deficiencies. He argues a planning, control, and improvement approach and places strong emphasis on the ability and foresight to plan for quality improvement. He seeks a foundation for total quality management through leadership and likens quality to finance, in which planning, control, and improvement are critical. This "Juran Trilogy" centers on effective leadership; well-established goals; an infrastructure that emphasizes education and training; customer and supplier relationships; mechanisms for measurement; and processes to support quality planning, quality control, and quality improvement.

For Peter Senge, author of *The Fifth Discipline*, the real message of the quality movement is to build learning organizations. For learning organizations, learning is linked to quality. His emphasis is on improving the thinking process (just as you would improve other processes); the move toward "systems" thinking (viewing the whole versus the parts); the availability of a guiding vision and clarity of intent noted in vision and mission statements; and personal mastery—the adequacy of an individual's knowledge base and management change skills.

THE IMPACT OF THE CURRENT ENVIRONMENT

The federal government's aggressive effort to change the current health care delivery system places mounting external pressure on the health care industry. Demands for quality come from federal agencies controlling the health care dollar, from regulatory agencies that control licensing and accreditation, and from the legal system, in which case law sets precedents based on less than the "standard" of care provided.

In addition, competitive pressures and consumer demands weigh heavily on health care institutions to provide services at lower costs. Major pressure comes from:

- intense scrutiny by the health care community, by purchasers, payors, regulators, and the public
- budget cuts, benefit redesign, and increasing numbers of people who are not insured
- limited success of current quality assurance (QA) efforts required by the Joint Commission on Accreditation of Healthcare Organizations (Joint Commission) and federally mandated utilization requirements
- increasing sophistication in technology, equipment, and application
- the thrust toward organizational transformation and new tools and methods.

Health care organizations will be challenged to improve the quality of care and service provided, and will need to adopt new ways to measure and demonstrate quality to their respective publics. New frameworks for the delivery of health care will continue to emerge and test the ability of existing organizations to survive.

THE REGULATORY ENVIRONMENT

With emphasis on cost and access remaining a priority, existing government-financed health care programs and proponents of health care reform will continue to focus on services that are "reasonable" and "necessary" and mandate review of the quality of care delivered. In 1972, Congress established professional standards review organizations (PSROs) charged with the responsibility of overseeing costs and the quality of health care provided by federally funded programs such as Medicare, Medicaid, and Maternal and Child Health. In 1982, the Health Care Financing Administration (HCFA) established policy for medical review through the Peer Review Improvement Act, P.L. 97-248. The Tax Equity and Fiscal Responsibility Act of 1982

created Title XI, Part B, of the Social Security Act and replaced PSROs with new systems of utilization and quality control known as peer review organizations (PROs). Additionally, HCFA modified Medicare conditions of participation for non-Joint Commission-accredited hospitals, and utilized state-level Departments of Health to assess the quality of care through development of standards comparable to the Joint Commission guidelines.

Quality of care efforts continue to be initiated by an array of organizations including federal and state governed, private purchasers, and accrediting and hospital-sponsored organizations. Exhibit 24–1 is a summary of some areas from which quality of care initiatives have and will continue to be promulgated.

The proposed direction of health care reform seeks to combine elements of managed competition and single payor concepts. The intent is to provide every American with a basic standard benefits package under group purchasing cooperatives called health alliances that contract on a risk-adjusted capitated basis with private health care plans in order to give alliance members a choice among health maintenance organization (HMO), PPO, and fee-for-service plans.

MANAGED COMPETITION AND SINGLE PAYOR DEFINED

The basic element of managed competition is the creation of sponsors who act as collective purchasing agents for large groups of individuals, allowing individuals to choose among health plans on the basis of cost and quality. The function of the sponsors is to negotiate with insurers and/or health plans in an effort to create a menu of choices among the different plans available to their subscribers. A single payor system is a state-run insurance program that operates within a global health care spending budget. These budgets limit the number of dollars spent for premiums to health alliances.

Under managed competition, insurers would be required to accept any individuals who purchase coverage through the sponsor. This pre-

Exhibit 24–1 Sources of Quality of Care Initiatives

Executive Branch

- The Health Care Reform Plan with emphasis on systems for reporting and measuring quality
- The Health Care Financing Administration: focused initiatives on Medicare and Medicaid quality, hospital, ambulatory, and managed care settings; produce Medicare mortality data; focused, diagnosis-specific studies
- The Clinical Laboratory Improvement Act of 1992
- Public Health Service, Agency for Health Care Policy and Research (Public Law 92-410), technology assessment, practice guidelines development, and outcomes research
- Health Resources and Services Administration: supervises The National Practitioner Data Bank; research and outcome data on Organ Transplantation
- Inspector General, Department of Health and Human Services: oversees PRO sanctions of physicians or hospitals in violation of Medicare obligations; monitors adherence to Medicare and Medicaid provider exclusions; initiates projects focused on volume, type, cost, and quality of procedures performed in physicians' offices
- Department of Veterans Affairs: quality improvement checklist program utilizing 31 indicators of performance
- The Civilian Health and Medical Program of the Uniformed Services (CHAMPUS): regionalized peer review, demonstration projects on ambulatory surgery, hospice care

Legislative Branches

- General Accounting Office's report on malpractice payments relative to the National Practitioner Data Bank
- Prospective Payment Assessment Commission's focus on outpatient settings, care provided to Medicare beneficiaries, effectiveness of Medicare's peer review organizations
- Physician Payment Review Commission's focus on the issue of cost and quality in Health Care Reform
- Other passed and pending legislation: Public Law 92-539, The Mammography Quality Standards Act, imposes new federal standards for mammography (1992); repeal of preprocedure review and second opinion requirements; others

The Private Sector

- The Institute of Medicine, a series of quality-focused studies
- Joint Commission: Agenda for Change and Indicator Monitoring System; emphasis on organizational performance
- Medical professional organizations: American Medical Association's recommended creation of the National Advisory Council on Health Care Value; the dissemination of materials related to practice guidelines
- Hospitals: The American Hospital Association developed a guidebook on the use of practice guidelines
- The National Association of Children's Hospitals and Related Institutions has created a quality of care project and initiated a demonstration project, the National Pediatric Intensive Care Quality Monitoring and Assessment Project

State Level Activity

- Many states are adopting legislation on a number of quality-related issues, particularly in the area of dissemination of quality-related data and the use of practice guidelines in affirmative defense in malpractice suits

---

cludes insurers from avoiding poor risks and fosters the need to define ways to control the costs of care. While the goal of health care reform may be cost containment, the plan seeks to enhance health through prevention (immunizations, prenatal care, etc. for the poor and uninsured) and fosters key reform tools such as report cards. Under managed competition, health plans will be encouraged to define performance criteria for employers who contract for their services in an effort to guide purchasing decisions.

Absent other mechanisms and a national database to provide fair and comparable analysis of each health plan's service, the respective plans will focus on basic qualitative indicators such as access and satisfaction. Other, less consumer-interpretable information (up to 50 national measures, e.g., C-section and mammography rates) would be produced and updated regularly to reflect quality improvement goals in quantitative terms.

Elements of health care reform focus on benefits to all, managed competition, insurance reform, and global budgets, among others, and create new pressures for health care organizations to prepare for new price structures, business partners, organizational structures, competition, and information management approaches previously not viewed as priorities. Questions regarding quality arise when it becomes unclear how distribution of care and services will be measured; what quality standards, state or regional, alliances or oversight organizations will be held to; who will measure the performance of the respective plans; and what the outcomes of care will be.

At the health care provider level, of importance in this evolving environment is leadership's ability to respond by reassessing the organization's purpose and defining a competitive strategy based on current knowledge of costs, and the organization's level of quality and performance.

The Joint Commission

The Joint Commission, a nonfederal regulatory agency, continues to define standards of performance for health care organizations. Organized in the early 1950s, its purpose was to certify the safety and quality of hospital performance. In 1975, the Joint Commission began to examine the systems hospitals used to measure effectiveness and aligned itself with the Social Security Amendment, which spoke to payment for unnecessary services. In the early 1980s, the QA standard evolved partially in concert with the medical malpractice crisis. Emphasis was placed on the governing body's responsibility for establishing mechanisms for addressing quality, such as credentialing and privileging of the medical staff, peer review and application of findings to measure practitioner performance, and systems aimed at solving problems that had significant impact on patient care outcomes.

In the late 1980s the Agenda for Change was established as a Joint Commission attempt to refocus quality process from determining the capability of an organization to provide quality of care to broadening the scope of an organi-

zation's current activities to encompass refinement of the system, management philosophy, and ultimately to adapt a means for measuring performance. This shift from individual focus to organizational focus and the transition to performance measurement (with resulting data), will become the basis for accreditation in the future. This approach fits into the proposed national performance database scenario. The Joint Commission views 1997 as the transition point for establishing data elements to become a value-added adjunct to the accreditation process. Health care organizations incorporating TQM/CQI concepts into their quality review process will need to ensure that those medical staff-required functions referenced in the medical staff standards continue to be addressed either through traditional QA review mechanisms, or through newly applied performance measurement methodologies.

Other accrediting agencies similar to the Joint Commission exist and serve to establish standards for managed care organizations, among them the National Committee for Quality Assurance (NCQA), whose standards for quality generally follow those of the Joint Commission. In many states, licensing is linked to accreditation status.

THE LEGAL ENVIRONMENT

Case law continues to establish precedent for the health care industry regarding quality issues. The shift from inpatient to outpatient care delivery will carry with it new areas of potential liability. *Darling v. Charleston* is the landmark case that held hospitals liable for corporate negligence. The Court concluded that the hospital had an independent duty to oversee the care provided to its patients in accordance with applicable licensing regulations, accreditation standards, and its own bylaws.

In the most widely reported case regarding managed care organizations (MCOs), *Harrell v. Total Health Care*, the Court concluded that the HMO had failed to conduct reasonable investigation, creating a foreseeable risk of harm to members. While some states provide immunity for nonprofit HMOs, Harrell's case speaks to the failure to appropriately credential and supervise participating providers. The legal theory of *respondeat superior*, an employer's liability for the conduct of its employees, applies to MCOs just as it does in hospitals.

Tort reform is viewed as a critical part of the health care reform package. While changes are contemplated, the nature and scope of tort reform are unclear. Major emphasis should occur in areas of noneconomic damages for pain and suffering, a limit on the percentage of awards that plaintiffs' attorneys can collect in contingency fees, the elimination of joint and several liability, the tightening of the statute of limitations for filing medical malpractice lawsuits, and a reduction in the bureaucracy and paperwork that impede efficient care delivery.

It should be noted that many observers remain hopeful that substantive reforms will be included in health care reform with at least one alternative being highly considered: enterprise liability. Unlike other incremental reforms, enterprise liability would remove physicians from the system entirely and shift the liability burden to larger entities that provide care. Any move toward tort reform serves to highlight the need for continuous improvement in how organizations deliver patient care. The greater the efforts in quality management and improvement, the lesser the threat for claims of medical malpractice. The very technique of process improvement serves as a risk prevention tool.

TQM/CQI CONCEPTS APPLIED TO THE HEALTH CARE INDUSTRY

Creating a quality strategy requires an understanding of the concepts underlying the improvement process and a determination of how these concepts can be applied consistent with the culture and values of the organization. Attention to how the organization thinks, the current knowledge it possesses both professionally and organizationally, and the creation of a simple, logical approach to what has to be accomplished, are among the priorities for effective application.

Knowing what methods exist to support quality improvement (QI) is paramount but inadequate if the methods are not tailored to the specific needs of the organization. Key to successful application is to adapt the process to the organization, as opposed to fitting the organization to the process. The following operational definitions are provided in an effort to establish a common ground.

- TQM—An *operational style* that enables the precise definition of opportunities to improve the efficiency, effectiveness, and value of care and service provided to both internal and external customers.
- CQI—A *series of mechanisms* used to identify and act on opportunities to improve the efficiency, effectiveness, and value of services provided.

Tailoring a quality improvement process to the organization is not as simple as purchasing a ready-made product. However, doing so will build commitment and an awareness of the need to dismantle long-standing barriers to effective performance. Other major core issues health care organizations must address to support effective TQM/CQI application include:

- the willingness to change
- the desire and ability to create an environment for change
- the willingness to prepare and educate leadership, managers, and all employees; to acquire new knowledge
- the development of a plan with well-defined goals and objectives
- a budget for change
- a willingness to voice major changes needed to remain competitive

Absent wanting to assess and modify current behaviors, any approach to improving the quality of care and service provided will result in misguided activity.

TRADITIONAL APPROACHES

Emphasis on traditional quality assurance followed mandates and standards set forth by licensing and accrediting agencies, state departments of health and the Joint Commission primarily, as well as federal agencies, predominant among them HCFA, which oversees the Medicare, Medicaid, and Maternal and Child Health Insurance programs. However, the quality environment is rapidly changing. Increasing public awareness places pressure on providers to demonstrate quality through cost effectiveness, outcomes, and customer satisfaction.

Today's approach to quality improvement is noted in contrast to traditional QA in Exhibit 24–2.

The increasing demand for quality, a concept not yet fully understood, by employees, insurers, accrediting and licensing agencies, and the public poses a challenge to the health care provider to demonstrate an ability to focus on community, plan services rationally, deliver consistent quality care/service, and meet or exceed customer expectations.

Given the complexity of the health care environment and the variety of providers and settings, there is no one best approach to quality improvement. Documented success from industrial organizations including Ford, Florida Power & Light, Hewlett Packard, and others came from incorporating a combination of approaches from Deming, Juran, Crosby, and others. The cornerstone of success is to carefully assess the personality of the organization in terms of leadership and management styles, the current climate, and what works for you.

THE FRAMEWORK FOR A TQM/CQI SYSTEM IN A HEALTH CARE ORGANIZATION

An organization that consciously moves toward quality improvement faces the challenge of creating an environment supportive of change in attitude, behavior, and processes in order to consistently create a quality product. While TQM and CQI concepts have been endorsed and applied by the health care community to some degree, applications vary from organization to organization based on:

1. commitment and intent
   - board mandate
   - mission statement
   - realigned strategic plan
   - structured training
2. design, organization, and direction
   - traditional QA/peer review structure or separate leadership steering committee/QI Council
   - reporting requirements
     –to the CEO
     –to the medical director
   - operational vs. clinical
3. process
   - the type of issues, processes, and/or functions selected for review
   - the degree of evaluation
   - determining root cause
   - measuring statistical significance
4. linkage to traditional QA
   - part of or separate from the current QA process
5. measurement of effectiveness

ELEMENTS OF A CQI PROCESS

In health care organizations, select critical components are necessary to provide the framework for day-to-day functions in keeping with the concept of CQI and current external agency requirements. There are several components important to successful application.

An Established Leadership Philosophy

It is well recognized that the leadership of an organization creates the expectations and establishes the attitude of that organization. Today's approach to CQI emphasizes quality leadership,

Exhibit 24–2 Contemporary Approach to Quality Improvement

QI	QA
• internally driven	• externally driven
• emphasis: process	• emphasis: people
• performed by all	• delegated to some
• variation accepted	• variation not in conformity
(common and/or special cause)	(someone did it wrong)
• realign processes	• fix problems; action before measure
• reduce variation	• establish thresholds
• organize teams	• assign responsibility
• plan, do check, act	• take actions to improve "problems"

recognizing that building an organization's culture is a function of leadership. Guiding principles established by leaders are conveyed through organizational policy in order to create the environment important to a shared sense of purpose. The transformation to quality leadership takes significant commitment from key leaders in the health care organization, the board of trustees, the CEO, the medical staff, and nursing. New skills are required, among them building shared vision and systems thinking. These new skills will soon distinguish the traditionalist from the innovator.

In application, this quality leadership principle formulates an environment for improving the methods for *how* products and services are produced in addition to *what* is done. Where management focused on profit and loss, quality leaders emphasize meeting or exceeding the customer's needs both *externally* (the purchaser or user of the product or service) and *internally* (the individual whose work depends on the quality of the preceding individual's work). This approach lends credence to the significant value of contributions made by those performing the service or generating the product. While the words may suggest a fad, the underlying concept remains. That is, in order to improve, health care organizations will have to master and demonstrate their ability to:

- lead by incorporating policy with values important to the providers of care
- conform to standards (e.g., deliver the product or service as advertised)

- meet or exceed customer needs
- continually improve processes and systems
- improve the quality of thinking and interacting in the organization

A Definition of Quality for the Organization

As previously stated, one question facing the health care organization is what quality is and how it is measured. While the definition may not be clear, each organization must agree on a definition suitable to its purpose in order to proceed. Given the definitions by the industrial sector, the American Medical Association (AMA) characterizes quality as that "which consistently contributes to the maintenance or improvement of health and well being." However, the definition varies depending on the constituency. For example, quality as defined for hospital trustees is the continuing surety that the medical care rendered in their institution meets acceptable standards and that patient safety and interest take highest priority at all times. Without a unifying concept of quality, efforts toward improving it will remain as fragmented, isolated initiatives.

Key elements to support a unified approach to quality improvement are:

- an operational definition of quality compatible with the organization's purpose, strategic plan, and current climate
- defined mechanisms to support quality measurement

A Defined Structure To Ensure Accountability for Continuous Improvement

Critical to the process of quality improvement is the guideline for establishing direction, priority, and resources. The plan must be clear, and someone must be in charge of guiding the process, being accountable for continuity, coordination, and implementation of the learning process and improvement methodologies.

Key elements to support accountability are:

- specificity of intent in clearly defined vision, mission, and strategic plan documents, corporate and medical staff bylaws, and QI plans
- a defined structure that encompasses board oversight and senior management/medical staff coordinating teams; key involvement of other select medical and administrative leadership staff, quality, risk, and utilization management professionals; and other front line employees in the form of task forces and committees (as applicable) to support TQM/CQI application and oversight
- a process for real time education and training of all personnel
- specifications for quality goals at each level of the organization

Mechanisms for Effective, Consistent Communications/Reporting

Whether emphasis is on the "vital few" or the "trivial many," mechanisms must be in place to support documentation and communication of the strategies used to define and eliminate sources of problems.

Key elements to ensure consistent documentation and communication include:

- defined requirements for reporting and communication
- standardized, concise reporting formats to support other methodologies for quality assessment, in addition to incidents and other adverse events
- adequate tools to support process description, data collection, and data analysis
- trend analysis to define variations and follow-up to ensure that performance is improved and gains are held
- defined requirements for feedback of information for educational purposes, to reward success

A Measurement System To Evaluate Quality at All Levels in the Organization

An important milestone toward improvement is knowing where variations in conformance and performance exist. This requires a means to track and measure performance and customer satisfaction.

Key elements include:

- a structured, disciplined process to support systems quality
- defined key functions and an interdisciplinary approach to process review and problem definition
- a plan for ongoing systematic review and evaluation of major processes and aspects of clinical care delivered; periodic review of standards and requirements to ensure consistency of application
- an established set of core quality and risk indicators defined to measure quality, risk, and utilization; cost indicators to measure resource consumption
- identification of existing data sources to support definition of variations in performance and measurement of outcomes
- the reuse of existing data to define the current state-of-the-art
- the creation of usable databases specific to the organization's needs

Mechanisms for Peer Review

Regardless of the process used for quality review and measurement, peer review will remain a constant in assessing the appropriateness of clinical performance.

Key elements include:

- emphasis on CQI through clinical process review and analysis of trends, patterns, and outcomes
- the development and use of measurement tools including practice guidelines, protocols of care, critical pathways and standards
- utilizing peer review for significant issues and clinical QI, both qualitative and quantitative
- emphasis on education to improve performance

A Well-Defined Process for Ongoing Feedback/Education

Knowledge dissemination is a by-product of quality improvement. Therefore, to support continuous improvement of products and services requires the creation of a cycle of learning supported by feedback and education.

Key elements include:

- participation in the process
- documented requirements for communication with prescribed timelines
- the use of tools to motivate personnel (e.g., newsletters, bulletin boards, etc.)
- availability of "how-to" assistance
- creative use of recognition programs targeted at service improvement efforts

THE STRUCTURED USE OF DATA AND INFORMATION

To effect quality requires the use of statistics to study characteristics of the service being performed (process), in order to cause the process to behave consistently and reliably (control).

Although the health care industry has existed in its current form since the 1700s, health care information systems are in their infancy for hos-

pitals and other providers. Currently the health care industry is data rich and information poor. Hospital information systems (finance and health records) contain volumes of data on performance that support third-party payor and external agency requirements, and conformance to federal government programs (Medicare, Medicaid). In reality, however, the health care organizations do not use their own data to create information about the processes of care provided within their institutions. These existing data have the capability of demonstrating variations in resource consumption, performance, outcomes, and costs, albeit flawed. However, given that external agencies utilize the same data to define the organization's performance, it is appropriate for organizations to begin reviewing these data as valuable resources. Some examples include the use of financial data to support drug utilization review and the use of the medical records database to define variations in outcomes for a given diagnosis, diagnostic-related groupings (DRGs) or procedures, or to define patterns of individual performance.

Potential existing internal sources of data include:

- billing data (charges by item, by cost center)
- case mix and medical record abstraction
- DRG grouper/assignment
- order entry and results reporting
- laboratory systems
- pharmacy systems
- infection control data
- scheduling systems
- employee health and accident
- staffing mix/levels
- other manual prepared quality, risk, utilization data based on Joint Commission, federal, or third-party payor requirements

Other external sources of data exist to support comparisons. These data can provide specific or general comparisons based on the organization's need.

The medical informatics and information management industry is expanding rapidly. Sophisticated information technology exists using natural language processing, expert systems, and transaction processing systems. A potential barrier to widespread use of systems dedicated to quality is the ability to support confidentiality and security of the patient-specific data as the industry seeks to link multiple databases. More research is required before systems can truly provide a view of the continuum of care provided to patients and outcomes, both clinical and organizational. However, more simplistic applications currently exist to support definition of performance within the respective institution.

The thrust for data and information, stimulated by the health care reform initiatives, will continue to grow, with many groups having their own vision of definitive "report cards." Health care organizations will need to build a base of performance to determine their own dimensions of performance based on logic in order to remain competitive and accredited.

THE COST/QUALITY EQUATION

Business and industry's search for price and value spawn the economic criteria that play a significant role in the health care delivery process. In managed care arrangements, efficient use of resources is a determinant for physician compensation, a tool for competition to influence third-party payor contractual relationships, a mechanism to define over (and under) utilization of resources. In hospitals, there is no similar incentive for the orchestrators of care. Hence the hospital strategies for quality improvement are heavily dependent on the strength of the leadership to bring about change.

While the AMA is moving toward definition of outcome measures and clinical practice guidelines, the actual oversight for quality may occur at a state rather than a national level. As previously stated, in health care reform, managed competition is intended to foster competition among health providers on the basis of cost and quality. However, quality-driven competi-

tion will require the creation of a uniform database in order to effectively portray the cost of care and related outcomes.

THE IMPACT OF POOR QUALITY

There is little industry outcome data to demonstrate effectiveness and cost/quality performance. As yet, only sporadic attempts have been made to learn about the true, long-term outcome of medical interventions. Some hard examples of substandard care, however, tend to be measured in cost reductions. Examples of reduced days waiting for alternate levels of care from 2.46 to 1.26 saved one hospital $987,000 over a two-year period; monitoring antibiotic use created an annual savings of $400,000 at yet another hospital. More global studies focused on unnecessary surgery (RAND Corporation of Santa Monica, California), where approximately 14 percent were found to be inappropriate (53,200 of 380,000 bypass surgeries), where the cost differences between surgery and alternative forms of treatment provide an estimate of lost health care dollars.

Finally, a report published in the *New England Journal of Medicine* documented a dramatic reduction in postsurgical wound infections where CQI methodologies were applied to the administration of antibiotics within a specified time prior to surgery. Experts estimate a nationwide cost savings of $1 billion per year where an estimated 1,000,000 of 23,000,000 surgeries produce such infections.

ECONOMIC AND PRODUCTIVITY MONITORING

In the interim, and at the organizational level, it is not difficult to determine the cost of quality given Crosby's definition of the price for nonconformance with standards. Applied to health care, this might include the cost of producing certain laboratory test results, or the cost of diagnosing and treating DRG 209, Major Joint Procedures. Another approach to defining the impact of poor quality can begin by evaluating the efficiency and effectiveness of services provided. This three-pronged approach calls for:

1. *A productivity analysis* utilizing existing data and considering numbers of tests and treatments to support performance measurement, budgeting, staffing, etc.
2. *An economic analysis* or the bottom-line view that addresses the financial viability of the organization in general and/or specific services and may include such items as actual costs/charges to reimbursement, average charges across providers, charges by DRG, etc.
3. *A comparative analysis* based on the literature and/or market-basket comparisons for specific procedures (coronary artery bypass, C-sections) and diagnoses (myocardial infarction); internal analysis based on diagnoses, procedure, and protocols of care; and demonstration of both organizational and practitioner performance bearing in mind that the focus is on improving quality of service, outcomes, and customer satisfaction.

It should be noted that several states—California and Florida as examples—have statutory requirements that instruct hospital boards to provide for the control and use of the physical and financial resources of the hospital and support the use of economic factors in medical staff credentials decisions.

CUSTOMER SATISFACTION

Significant to any cost/quality equation is customer satisfaction. From the patient's perspective (as the customer), value is viewed as the relationship between the quality and the price of the service, with the definition of quality based on the individual's own perception. Determining what constitutes value and, most importantly, the awareness that the patient ultimately judges the quality and the value of the care provided is critical to successful TQM/CQI application. As society is becoming more aware of value, measurement of patient satisfaction is utilized more frequently, but in varying levels of sophistication throughout the health care industry.

The concept of customer satisfaction has far-reaching significance in a model TQM/CQI environment. Customers are viewed as anyone receiving a service throughout the organization. To continuously improve quality, each customer's needs must be identified in order to create the requirements for performance, and be met in order to produce customer satisfaction and, ultimately, a quality product. In health care organizations, the customers are all employees and physicians, and the product can be viewed as the treated and discharged patient.

BASIC STEPS IN ESTABLISHING A CQI PROCESS

There are many variations to establishing a CQI process ranging from the sophisticated to the very simple. The following is a synthesized version of these approaches to highlight essential guideposts; it assumes leadership commitment and understanding of the concepts of CQI.

Planning for quality is initiated at the leadership level with appropriately structured documents beginning with the organization's Mission Statement, which outlines the intent of the organization in serving its community. Additional expanded description should be found in the organization's Strategic Plan displaying how elements of the CQI process will be applied within the given time frame and as it applies to the growth of the organization. Generally, a CQI "road map" is defined in an annual plan describing goals, objectives, timelines, and accountability.

The CQI process is educated into being through a broad range of mechanisms but, most importantly, through real time application. Key individuals are primed to facilitate the CQI process application throughout the organization.

Next, a structure for CQI is required. This may begin at the Board level depending on the size of the organization. Generally the next level is an oversight council formed to support process application, identify projects, establish goals and priorities for improvement, and communicate results, in which change agents are identified and given the authority to facility change.

Cross-functional quality improvement project teams are formed to:

- address specific clinical or nonclinical processes of care, and define and isolate problems or processes in need of measurement or improvement
- collect data to support problem definition and analysis
- identify potential solutions, barriers to resolution, and costs
- test proposed solutions
- implement change and measure results
- provide feedback to the council

The roll-out phase occurs as select individuals become proficient in training, education, and facilitation and can effectively convey the philosophy and strategic objectives of CQI as well as apply and teach the tools of CQI to individuals, teams, and departments in the organization.

The Logic of CQI

- *F*ind an opportunity to improve.
- *O*rganize a multidisciplinary team that knows the process; assign a facilitator.
- *C*larify the problem; isolate breakdowns in the process.
- *U*nderstand the cause of variation.
- *S*elect an intervention.

then

- *P*lan interventions to improve the process using one or two major variations.
- *T*est the intervention on a small scale.
- *C*heck the effects the intervention has had on the process.
- *A*ct on the process if the intervention works.

Critical Factors to Successful CQI Process Application

- Active leadership—including board members, physicians, administrators, and nurses
- Continuous education and involvement for all employees
- Emphasis on customer focus with periodic solicitation of customers' views on how accepted standards are being met
- A collaborative approach among those who orchestrate and administer the service/function under assessment
- The use of new methodologies to review process and outcomes
- An environment that promotes proactive, how-can-we-do-it-better thinking, one that encourages and supports
- Continuous education and reinforcement

Alternatively, key steps for establishing a basic, transitional quality improvement process requires an organized approach to measurement and improvement and can be initiated in the following way, assuming key leadership is leading the process:

1. Define quality; specify what quality is being measured.

2. Establish objectives, define your services (what do you do). List and rank.

3. Focus review activities based on existing data.
   - Define focus—high volume, high risk, cost, outcome, etc.
   - Create a task force to brainstorm and achieve consensus
   - Define parameters of review; 100 percent or sample

4. Determine what you want to measure.
   - Long-standing issues
   - Length of stay by diagnosis and procedure
   - Resource consumption
   - Meeting established requirements (protocols, clinical guidelines)

5. Utilize basic methodologies for measuring quality.
   - Understand the process (describe it)
   - Define variations in the process, achieve consensus
   - Select cause of variation
   - Collect data to validate cause

- Display data
6. Choose the type of review.
   - Joint Commission approach (aspect of care, indicator, criteria)
   - Protocol review (meeting the requirements)
   - Process review: define process as it exists, measure against requirements
   - Variation-based, utilizing existing databases
7. Apply appropriate techniques to the review process.
   - Indicator development, protocols, clinical guidelines
   - Flow charts
   - Cause and effect diagrams
   - Control charts, statistical significance, etc.
8. Plan change.
   - What or who needs to change
   - How change is budgeted
   - When change should occur
   - Who is accountable

APPLICATION TO MANAGED CARE

More individuals are receiving medical care through HMOs, the flagships of MCOs, or other similar health care systems that oversee and manage the delivery of health care services and monitor prescribed treatment for subscribers. This form of health care delivery and financing is expanding and may well dominate the industry in the near future, even though "report cards" that speak to managed care performance have only recently been established. For the majority of MCOs, little data exist to determine the quality and/or effectiveness of care.

Given the attributes of managed care delivery systems, there is wide variation in the application of quality assessment techniques. There is consistency of application in some instances due to federal and state regulatory requirements. However, state requirements and enforcement mechanisms are not evenly applied; HMOs do not need to meet federal requirements; there are few regulatory requirements for other forms of managed care, such as PPOs.

There are a variety of approaches to managing and improving quality in managed care plans. Traditional quality assurance methodologies can be applied to encompass structure, process, and outcome. Some examples include structure (governance, medical staff credentials process, communications flow); process (audits, focused studies, peer review); and outcome (admissions to hospitals, mortality, rates of breast cancer/mammograms in a given population, measles/immunization rates in given age groups, hospitalizations in given diagnoses, resource utilization, medical malpractice claims, etc.).

Newer directions based on the concept of TQM/CQI focus on systems and the performance of the entire organization beginning with vision and mission statements, strategic plans and goals. TQM/CQI methodologies applied to managed care focus on monitoring key elements of the managed care process, predominantly access to care and services (preventive and/or restorative), timeliness of service, outcomes of care, customer satisfaction, and patient-centered case management. Not unlike hospitals, emphasis is on review of processes of care, conformance to requirements in the form of well-established policies and procedures and contracts for service, protocols of care, application of clinical guidelines, and, of course, actual practitioner and organizational performance. To some degree, more quality control potential exists in the MCOs due to the specificity that can occur in contracting with providers of care.

More importantly, MCOs have computerized databases capable of driving a quality improvement process by defining performance that warrants further assessment; that defines outcomes of care; and that defines resource consumption. Further, the processes of care in MCOs lend themselves to the tools of TQM and CQI, for example, flow charting an administrative process (structure), movement of patients through the system or clinical care processes (process), and early detection of breast cancer (outcome).

Exhibit 24–3 lists baseline indicators to support quality measurement.

In summary, measuring and improving quality is a survival mechanism for MCOs. Once a foundation has been established, assessing the level of quality, managing, and/or improving quality is a logical style of operation that emphasizes continuous learning as a way of organizational life.

ANALYTICAL TOOLS TO SUPPORT PROCESS ANALYSIS/IMPROVEMENT

The ability to clearly define and measure performance and to search out the true cause of recurring problems has been a weakness in health care. For years the industry vacillated between endorsing structure, process, and/or outcome review, missing out on the use of logical tools applied to what organizations do. Confusion still exists over the value of performance measurement versus true research; the value of simply knowing where and when to improve. In clinical quality, research methodologies have long been available and have been used strategically and selectively but not considered in the day-to-day applications of health care delivery. The following are examples of the more commonly used industry models that have proved effective in measuring, managing, and displaying variations in performance.

The Pareto Principle

The use of the Pareto Principle emphasizes problem-solving efficiency. Emphasis is placed on the "vital few and the trivial many," demonstrating that the vital few account for most of the total effect. This principle gives rise to the 80/20 rule—80 percent of the problems stem from 20 percent of the causes. A Pareto chart is simply a bar chart that demonstrates causes to support prioritization. Some hypothetical examples of the Pareto principle are:

- In reviewing a 25-step billing process, 5 of the procedures accounted for 65 percent of the inaccurate bills.

Exhibit 24–3 Baseline Indicators To Support Quality Measurement

Licensure, education
- Credentials process
- Recertification
- Work history
- Contract inclusions

Actual individual performance
- Patient satisfaction
- Utilization patterns
- Member complaints
- Documentation standards
- Adverse event monitoring
- Performance against practice guidelines

Office practice standards
- Safety
- Access
- Privacy

Accreditation standards
- National Committee Quality Assurance (NCQA)
- American Accreditation Program (AAPI)
- Utilization Review Accreditation Commission (URAC)
- Other

Case law
- Medical management programs
- Benefits application vs. medical care

- Of the 20 or more steps in an admissions process, 4 of the steps account for 80 percent of the customer complaints.

Brainstorming

Defining processes, procedures, and medical management of specific diagnoses in need of improvement is the first step. Many techniques can be employed but one most commonly used in an effort to orchestrate group thinking is brainstorming. This idea generation/evaluation mechanism fosters creative, uninhibited discussion and consensus building.

Prioritization serves to rank the ideas in order of importance, build consensus, gain an understanding of the group's perception, and efficiently channel the improvement efforts.

Fishbone Diagram

Cause and effect (fishbone) analysis is used to translate the priorities determined from brainstorming into a work model to delineate the possible causes of the defined problem or process in need of improvement (effect), forcing the question "why" to ensure the real (root) cause is adequately defined. Generally, areas most likely to serve as a factor in the cause include people, policy/procedures, provisions (supplies), and place.

The root cause is that which causes the event or outcome directly or indirectly, is controllable, and if removed would eliminate or reduce the problem.

Other Forms of Variation Data Display

Histograms are geographic summaries of variation in a set of data that define frequency of occurrence and the spread between the highest and lowest value. Histograms provide a concise picture and summarize large amounts of data to define patterns. The variation is displayed in a pattern where clues are provided to the causes of problems and obvious abnormalities can be seen at a glance.

Run charts are used to visually represent data. They are used to monitor a process to see whether or not the long-range average is changing. Run charts are the simplest tool to construct and are used to identify meaningful trends or shifts in the average.

A *control chart* is a run chart with statistically determined upper control limits and lower control limits that serve to determine when the process is said to be "in control." These limits are calculated by running a process untouched, taking samples, and plotting the sample averages onto a chart to determine patterns. Where the points fall outside the established limits, the process is said to be out of control. The fluctuations of the points within the limits result from common causes or variations built into the process and serve to demonstrate there is variability in every process. These can be affected only by changing the system. However, points outside the limits come from special causes and must be eliminated in order to consider the process in control. Properly used, a control chart is a continuous guide to constant improvement.

Caveats: What Works and What Doesn't Work

Introducing the use of statistical methods is difficult and critical. Management's sensitivity to the need for training and education, the availability of a statistician, and the integration of applied statistical methods must be part of, not in addition to, day-to-day functioning.

The movement toward quality measurement and improvement applications is still not well understood in the health care industry. The applications in health care organizations range from testing the water with one finger to total body immersion, on many occasions, as a reaction versus an action. More specifically, there is confusion over the meaning of continuous improvement. These terms alone promote a resistance by being interpreted as not good enough. On the other hand lies the confusion over standards, clinical guidelines, protocols of care, etc., interpreted as rigidity, "cookbook," loss of freedom. For organizations operating in a learning mode the interpretation is different. Herein lies the problem, for changing an organization's culture and belief system takes time.

The logic behind continuous improvement is adequate to warrant exploration of TQM/CQI concepts. The cost/quality examples noted earlier demonstrate this point. There CQI methodologies were applied to review of key processes (e.g., the use of antibiotic prophylaxis: wide variations in infection rates were noted based on when the antibiotic was administered. It was noted that a 3.3 percent rate was reduced to 0.6 percent when the antibiotic was administered appropriately). Doing things right the first time, and doing the right things, imply dollars, time, and energy are wasted when organizations perform otherwise.

TQM/CQI works best when:

- There is a recognition of the time it takes to change an organization's behavior.

- The process is implemented for the right reason (e.g., always seeking to improve what we do).

- Consideration is given to who comprises the organization's customers.

- Leadership recognizes and promotes its value.

However, TQM/CQI doesn't work when:

- The organization is not ready to accept this long-term commitment.

- Top management is not prepared to lead; staff are not trained.

- Emphasis is mainly on cost reduction versus customer satisfaction and process improvement.

- The entire organization is not mobilized; systems thinking does not exist.

- The voice of the customer is not heard.

TQM/CQI must be viewed as a philosophy and a methodology that encompass specific approaches to problem definition, analysis, correction, and implementation. The transition from traditional QA to a TQM/CQI modality can be accomplished efficiently and effectively by initiating the process with an assessment of the current system. This begins with defining the attitude of the organization toward quality in general and toward change; toward current documented commitment; and toward the structure, process, and outcomes of existing quality improvement activities to establish the baseline for system refinement or reorganization.

CONCLUSION

Soaring health care costs have prompted an aggressive federal effort to support change in the system of health care delivery. As health care leaders face these mounting external pressures,

internal pressure to improve will be heightened. Moving forward to meet the challenges will require careful planning, control, and execution and, of utmost importance, points to a compelling need for current skills in systems thinking and the demanding realities of true improvement.

The process begins in knowing why the organization exists. The mission of the organization is central to the principles of organization effectiveness and speaks to the commitment to continuously improve the quality of patient care and services. This commitment, noted throughout the organization's documents in the form of mission and vision statements and strategic plans provides the infrastructure for improvement. The mission statement clearly defines the organization's purpose; the vision statement establishes where the organization wants to go; the strategic plan provides the road map with specific goals, objectives, and budgets. This planning for quality forms the basis for leadership.

Next, improvement requires knowledge; knowledge of systems, variations, and the psychology of change. In health care, integration of system components (departments, functions) is challenged in the continuous improvement environment. Health care organizations traditionally focused on the individual component versus the system. Critical to the process of improvement is recognizing variations as not good or bad but as always present. Failure to recognize that each type of variation requires a different response causes health care organizations to spend an inordinate amount of time and money reacting to common causes in stable systems, thereby achieving no gain. Additionally, organizations will need to revisit their policies, practices, traditions, and habits. Understanding what motivates performance and how people respond to change is essential to fostering a sense of purpose in this process of continuous improvement.

Finally, the timetable for establishing a CQI environment is dependent on the organizational model chosen, the resources committed, and dedicated education and training. Implementation is the key challenge to be successful. TQM and CQI begin with active leadership involvement and education (real time) as to the process and benefits. Concepts and methodologies must be flexible and adapted (not adopted) to the organization's needs. Support throughout the organization grows when start-up activities are manageable and measurable results are achieved.

REFERENCES

Al-Assaf, A., et al. 1993. Perceptions of VA chiefs of staff on total quality management implementation. *American Journal of Medical Quality* 8, no. 3:123–127.

American Hospital Association. 1993. *Initial summary and analysis of President Clinton's health care reform proposal.* Chicago.

Benchmarking: A new tool for quality improvement in healthcare. 1992. *The Quality Letter* April 9.

Benchmarking: Beating the best. 1992. *QRC Advisor* July.

Bergman, R. 1993. Quantifying quality: Experts wonder what's behind numbers. *Hospitals & Health Networks* June 20:56.

Boland, P. 1993. Quality management. *Managed Care Quarterly* 1, no. 2

A Clinton reform preview. 1993. *American Medical News* April 26.

Coffey, R., et al. 1992. TQM brings financial benefit to the University of Michigan Medical Center. *The Quality Letter* June.

Crosby, P. 1980. *Quality is free.* New York: NAL Penguin, Inc.

Gitlow, H. and S. Gitlow. 1987. *The Deming guide to quality and competitive position.* Englewood Cliffs, NJ: Prentice-Hall, Inc.

Johnson, N., and D. Nash. 1993. Key factors in the implementation of a clinical quality improvement project: Successes and challenges. *American Journal of Medical Quality* 8, no. 3:118–122.

Joint Commission on Accreditation of Healthcare Organizations. 1993. Defining performance of organizations. *Journal on Quality Improvement* 19, no. 7:215–221.

Joseph, E., et al. 1992. *Practical guide to CQI.* Chicago: Care Communications.

Juran, J. 1991. Managing for quality in the health industry. Summary of a presentation at the Mid-Atlantic Society for Health Systems Spring Conference. Baltimore, Maryland, April 9.

Koska, M. 1992. Using CQI methods to lower postsurgical wound infection rate. *Hospitals* May 5:62–64.

Lewis, A. 1993. Too many managers: Major threat to CQI in hospitals. *Quality Review Bulletin* 19, no. 3:95–101.

The partnership strategy: Can major purchasers and providers collaborate to improve value? 1992. *The Quality Letter* March.

Rice, W. 1993. Motivation: The most basic process in TQM/CQI. *Journal for Healthcare Quality* 15, no. 3:38–42.

Senge, P. 1992. Building learning organizations. *Journal for Quality and Participation* March.

Senge, P. 1990. *The fifth discipline: The art and practice of the learning organization.* New York: Doubleday/Currency.

Senge, P. 1990. The leader's new work: Building learning organizations. *Sloan Management Review* Fall: 7–23.

Tracing the cost of quality isn't hard, two hospitals show. 1992. *QI/TQM* November.

Walton, M. 1986. *The Deming management method.* New York: Putnam Publishing Group.

LOIS J. BITTLE, RN, MPA, is a nationally known consultant, educator, and author with over 20 years' experience in health care systems design, development, and implementation for quality management/improvement, risk management, and utilization management.

She is a featured speaker, task force, and committee member to numerous national and international health care organizations; has been published in professional journals; has authored and co-authored several publications on quality assurance and risk management. Ms. Bittle currently serves as a Board member for a Washington, D.C.-based hospital, the National Association of Children's Hospitals and Related Institutions, Inc., the Leonard Cheshire Center, U.S.A., and the Health Services for Children with Special Needs, a Washington, D.C.-based managed care organization.

Before founding her own firm, Ms. Bittle was Director of the statewide QA/RM Project for the Maryland Hospital Association's Education Institute and prior to that was Program Administrator of the Professional Liability Program at the Johns Hopkins Hospital.

Chapter 25

Management Engineering: Role in Increasing Productivity

Karl G. Bartscht

Management engineering is the practice of industrial engineering in the health care field. The name of the discipline is changed not only to encourage acceptance by health care professionals but also to indicate its application to management.

The health care delivery system will undergo significant changes in the 1990s because of pressures for health care reform. The major change, increased managed care, leading toward primarily a capitated system, will require health care providers to ensure high value (and in some cases, low cost) services. Management engineering tools and techniques, with particular emphasis on increased productivity, will be invaluable in achieving high value/low cost services.

The discipline of engineering is defined by the Accreditation Board for Engineering and Technology (ABET), formerly Engineers Council for Professional Development (ECPD), as the "profession in which a knowledge of the mathematical and natural sciences gained by study, experience and practice is applied with judgment to develop ways to utilize economically the materials and forces of nature for the benefit of mankind."[1] The key words in this definition are:

- mathematical and natural sciences, particularly with emphasis on a *quantitative approach*
- applied with *judgment*, implying that not everything can be quantified
- economically, implying a *concern with costs*

According to the American Institute of Industrial Engineers (AIIE), the special field of industrial engineering is concerned with:

the design, improvement and installation of integrated systems of people, materials, equipment and energy. It draws upon specialized knowledge and skill in the mathematical, physical and social sciences together with the principles and methods of engineering analysis and design to specify, predict and evaluate the results to be obtained from such systems. The element that is unique to industrial engineering . . . is the explicit reference to people and to the social sciences in addition to the natural sciences.[2]

The key words in this definition are:

- design/improvement and installation, implying that whether one starts from scratch or with an existing system, installation is also a part of the job
- systems of people, materials, equipment, and energy, hereafter referred to as a resource system or systems
- specify, predict, and evaluate, implying that not only is the system defined but also its expected outcomes or performance are defined and evaluation of systems operations is a part of the process

The *Handbook of Industrial Engineering*[3] has defined these 12 areas of industrial engineering specialization:

1. organization and job design
2. methods engineering
3. performance measurement and control of operations
4. evaluation, appraisal, and management of human resources
5. ergonomics/human factors
6. manufacturing engineering
7. quality assurance
8. engineering economy
9. facilities design
10. planning and control
11. computers and information systems
12. quantitative methods and optimization

With the exception of manufacturing engineering, all of these areas of specialization are applicable to health care/hospital operations. Several of them are covered in other chapters of this book, including human resource management, management information systems, quality assurance, strategic planning, materials management, and facilities planning. Quantitative management engineering methodologies and techniques are used in each of those areas.

Quality assurance, as expanded by Deming to include total quality management (TQM) and subsequently continuous quality improvement (CQI), is a most basic application of management engineering, which has been described as the design, improvement, and installation of integrated systems of people, materials, equipment, and energy.

After briefly describing the history of the application of management engineering to the health care field, this chapter focuses on cost containment and productivity management and then briefly describes some other areas of management engineering specialization.

HISTORY

In their book, *Hospital Management Engineering: A Guide to the Improvement of Hospital Management Systems*,[4] Smalley and Freeman provide a very complete history of the use of management engineering in hospitals. They trace the history from the motion study of a surgical procedure by Frank B. Gilbreth at the turn of the century, through the dearth of hospital activity in the 1920s and 1930s, and the post–World War II period to the present. Some events of interest are the employment of the first (recorded) full-time hospital management engineer in 1952, the development of university programs for education and service in the 1950s and 1960s, and the founding of the Hospital Management Systems Society (HMSS) in 1961.

HMSS's membership has expanded from the original group of management engineers, who were primarily hospital-based or university faculty, to include administrators and consultants. Over 700 hospitals have organized management engineering departments, and an equal number secure management engineering services from either multihospital system programs or consulting firms.

The 1960s and 1970s

In simplest terms, management engineering is directed at increasing the utilization of system resources, either through reducing costs or increasing productivity, including throughput. As the health care environment has changed, so has the utilization of management engineering.

The first significant use and expansion of management engineering services occurred during the 1960s and 1970s. However, because hospitals were generally reimbursed on a cost basis, there was little incentive to reduce costs. Hospital management engineering efforts were directed at improving operations in problem departments utilizing engineering techniques. Examples of such efforts were improving the patient admission process and supply systems and developing employee scheduling systems. It was rare that real economies were achieved, except in cases where accounts receivable or inventory holding costs were reduced.

As hospitals initiated more sophisticated budgeting processes, it became clear that a more objective system for determining personnel requirements than the one of "needing more personnel than we have now" was necessary. Early work at the University of Michigan in the 1960s resulted in the development of staffing methodologies:[5] quantitative, detailed, step-by-step procedures for determining personnel requirements. They were subsequently refined and modified by hospital association-sponsored efforts in order to make them easier to apply. These staffing methodologies were then applied through educational programs, booklet format, and shared data collection systems.

However, the need for quantitative methodologies was still not appreciated. In general, the incentive to reduce costs was not there, except where hospital management recognized the need to contain costs by managing more effectively.

During the 1960s and 1970s the other use of management engineering that evolved was its application in planning new facilities. In particular, as hospitals increasingly utilized debt financing for replacement and expansion of facilities, ways to reduce operating costs were sought in order to pay debt service. Berg[6] reports on such an analysis that projected an annual operating savings of $4.5 million generated by the operation of more efficiently designed facilities.

The 1980s

The advent of the federal prospective payment system (PPS), combined with state Medicare and statewide/regional Blue Cross plans, changed the incentive system for hospital payment in the 1980s. The emphasis was on reducing acute hospitalization, particularly lengths of stay. Not only did lengths of stay drop during the decade—admissions fell, too. Admissions dropped because of several outside influences, including physician peer review organizations and the shift of care to other settings, such as outpatient and nursing homes, and through technological advances and the increased availability of alternative settings.

The result was a drop in occupancy, which resulted in excess personnel (the nursing shortage of the 1970s became a surplus in the late 1980s and early 1990s). Management engineering provides an objective approach to staffing issues that ensures that reductions occur where the change in workload is actually warranted and in a way that is sensitive to the disposition of employees.

However, hospitals were able to work the system to maximize reimbursement, with minor personnel reductions. Once personnel costs, such as drugs, supplies, and food, were reduced, shifts to outpatient services resulted in increased revenues and cost shifting to the fee-for-service payors. This resulted in financial health for hospitals at the end of the 1980s.

The 1990s

Maximizing the PPS system was short-lived, when pressures to reduce health care costs became a primary issue with employers (particularly as they incurred the cost shifting arising from the perceived federal and state underpayments). In the late 1980s and the early 1990s, this resulted in the new reimbursement demon "managed care."

Early managed care insurers sought pure discounts in exchange for guaranteed volumes and rapid payment. But the real objective was the reduction in utilization. While PPS primarily influenced length of stay reductions, the managed care insurer has prompted further length of stay reductions, plus forced inpatient services to the outpatient setting and to the physician's office. This has been enhanced by technological advances that facilitate relocation of important services to facilities specializing in skilled nursing, home care, subacute care, and rehabilitation—all of which provide alternatives to long inpatient stays.

These changes in service settings have resulted in resource and information management problems. Resources of people, equipment, and facilities are underutilized in the inpatient setting. However, they are in short supply in the ambulatory and postacute settings. Information systems that provide effective resource management are still embryonic in the inpatient setting, and nearly nonexistent for alternative settings. The full application of management engineering tools and techniques will be needed to solve these resource problems in the coming years.

The Future

In many ways, the real benefits of management engineering are yet to be achieved in health care operations. Benefits will be achieved through supporting pricing strategies, effective information systems, and efficient facility design. The major objective, in the author's opinion, of the PPS is to create a price-competitive health care environment by enabling purchasers of health care to solicit bids from health care providers to provide specific disease category services or total hospital care for specific population groups. Management engineering can be used to do the following:

- reduce costs of present operations, be it for a department or a disease entity
- provide a resource standard as a basis for a cost-accounting system to facilitate effective pricing
- provide a productivity management system to monitor and control utilization of resources

Management engineering can increase the effectiveness of information systems by applying systems design and analysis techniques for analyzing manual systems being replaced by the computer. Such techniques:

- measure the existing systems: labor, costs, response times, storage space, etc.
- identify improvements in the manual system that could be achieved without computerization
- provide design criteria that ensure that all necessary procedures are provided and all unnecessary procedures are deleted
- monitor implementation to ensure that replaced functions are eliminated
- monitor operations to ensure that goals are met

The use of management engineering in the planning of new facilities is directed at ensuring that:

- the space plan reflects the actual amount of the space required based on projected workloads and systems
- workstations and departments are located to minimize travel
- movement, communication, and information systems satisfy current requirements and have the ability to expand to meet future needs.

The application of management engineering to health care operations is a necessity for survival in the 1990s.

COST CONTAINMENT

The change in reimbursement systems from a cost base to a PPS, drop in inpatient occupancy, and the emergence of price competition place cost containment as a top priority for all hospital managers. Cost containment implies that either (1) total operating costs are reduced, (2) labor costs, the largest cost item, are reduced, (3) costs per unit produced are reduced or at least maintained, or (4) more service is provided for the same cost.

As defined earlier, management engineering is primarily concerned with containing or reducing operating costs. And, in the author's opinion, the cost of providing management engineering services *has to be justified by a reduction in operating costs.*

Labor Cost Containment Has the Largest Payoff*

Labor costs are only one part of the cost containment equation. What is important is the output that results from a labor expenditure. The ratio between output and resources expended to obtain a desired output is also called *productivity.* Therefore, one approach to labor cost containment is to increase productivity.

Productivity always implies a given level of quality for any output. Increased quality for the same amount of input (labor) may result in cost containment. Low quality may result in the reprocessing or redoing of the work.

Further, cost containment can be achieved only if one takes the broad view or total systems approach to the health care delivery systems under study. One may be able to maximize productivity of one department, but if doing so has adverse effects on other departments, its benefits may be outweighed by the disadvantages.

Another method of labor cost containment is to replace labor, with either personnel with lesser skills or nonlabor expenditures. For example, a practical nurse may replace a registered nurse. This question—can someone at less cost do the same job?—is asked too infrequently. Automated systems—simple examples are utensil washers and floor cleaning machines—can also reduce labor costs. The computer to date has not yet fulfilled its labor-reduction potential. Computerization seems to reduce costs in the ac-

counting/patient billing area, but when looking at the total systems cost—the fixed cost of computer programming, operating, and leasing equipment—it is not clear that there has been cost containment, particularly labor savings. However, purchasing outside electronic data processing services by the output—patient bills, general ledger, etc.—has produced labor savings. Labor costs have also been reduced through other types of expenditures, such as use of disposable products. Many disposable products have not only reduced labor due to the elimination of reprocessing but have also enabled the use of better health care techniques. But again, one must look at the total system cost. Disposables increase storage and disposal requirements, and, in some cases, environmental pollution.

A more significant goal in containment of labor costs is to reduce the demand for service, and in turn labor, in the first place. Is it feasible? Yes! Outpatients can be scheduled for more efficient service, preadmission procedures and outpatient surgery can eliminate certain inpatient care tasks, and proper inventory levels can eliminate handling requests. In fact, rather than a last step, the first step in any cost-containment effort should be answering the question: Do we have to do this job at all?

Finally, effective cost containment must have a long-term effect. Two key ingredients—the involvement and commitment of management and a monitoring system to provide management with continuing, updated reports on productivity and quality—are required to sustain cost savings.

Deterrents to Labor Cost Containment

The cost-based reimbursement system is a deterrent to labor cost containment. Limitations on reimbursement conflict with the continuous demand for new and additional services by patients and physicians. When they are sick, patients feel that care at any cost is not too much, yet upon recovery and receipt of the bill, they may feel that the price is rarely worth the care. The physi-

---

*The remainder of this chapter (except where noted) is adapted from *Topics in Health Care Financing*, Vol. 3, No. 3, pp. 39–62, with permission of Aspen Publishers, Inc., © 1977.

cian, as manager of the care required and delivered, often ignores economic factors in pursuit of this care by misusing inpatient facilities or demanding exotic equipment and services that are provided elsewhere.

In the middle stands the hospital manager. In the past, as long as a hospital's cost increases were equal to those of its neighbors, there was no problem and the hospital manager could keep the physicians happy and stay financially viable. However, with PPS, the hospital manager is feeling the pressure of holding costs on a daily basis. But what can be done?

Direction for Achievement

Clearly, equipment purchases can be delayed, and nonessential outside services dropped, but for how long? More and more hospitals are faced with fixed debt service requirements and other new expenses, such as increasing malpractice insurance premiums. There are three possible directions for containing costs:

1. increase total revenue without raising rates: do more business with the same resources

2. decrease supply costs through more effective purchasing

3. increase labor productivity

The first direction is achieved through *decreasing length of stay and increasing the throughput of outpatients*—more outpatients treated per hour, extended outpatient hours, Saturday and Sunday utilization, etc. As a result, fixed assets—plant and equipment—are maximized, but this direction still requires some labor. The second direction—*decreased supply costs*—can be achieved through group purchasing and application of value analysis techniques. The key is to ensure that supplies do not result in increased labor costs due to greater processing or handling requirements.

The third direction is through *increasing labor productivity*. Although much effort has been expended in this direction, the net effect has un-

fortunately not always been significant, primarily due to limited applications in restricted areas. For example, a study of the housekeeping department may achieve significant reductions in its labor costs, but these improvements may be small relative to overall staffing. Gray and Steffy, in their book *Hospital Cost Containment*,[7] describe a series of cost-containment systems that show how to:

- measure, analyze, and monitor productivity

- conduct a value analysis

- organize hospital functions into a top-efficiency operation

- improve and evaluate worker performance

- institute a quality control system

- use space as efficiently as possible

- share services

- manage equipment

- audit all hospital operations

- schedule patients

- plan and control budgets

- determine the benefits of capital investments

PRODUCTIVITY MANAGEMENT

Productivity management provides the techniques that can make the greatest contribution to cost containment. Unfortunately, even with the pressures for cost containment, it is not obvious at this time that such techniques are considered standard management tools of today's health care manager, as opposed to marketing, strategic, or planning techniques.

The lack of importance placed on productivity management is a major problem. Many hospitals have a policy that any expenditure over $500 (or $5,000) must be approved by the board. However, no approval is necessary to hire one new employee, who may cost $10,000 to $15,000 per year and may be there for 10 years. This is actually a $100,000 to $150,000 decision. The expenditure for labor must be placed in the proper perspective.

As the American Hospital Association stated in 1973:

> Many hospital administrative personnel have been reluctant to attack the task of managing their employees' productivity. They often are unaware of (1) the approaches and tools available to them in the trade literature, and (2) the basic techniques and steps that provide the needed foundation for effective use of the more sophisticated techniques.[8]

This reluctance was further substantiated in an Arthur Andersen study.[9] Not only are many managers not trained in productivity concepts but also their perception of their employees is as loyal and hard working. Until recent years, employee salaries have been low, and their hours were long. This is no longer the case. In fact, in many areas of the country, the hospital pays the highest wages of any employer. There are also certain human characteristics that contribute to this reluctance to explore productivity management. It is always difficult to suspend or lay off employees, and there is always fear of upsetting the employees. Concerns of union activities are always present. Besides, whenever management is observing, all employees are busy. The real questions are: is this always the case, and what are they busy doing? We have reached a point in hospital productivity management at which we can no longer live with the status quo.

Cost containment achieved through improvement of productivity of ongoing operations should strive for a minimal goal of savings of 5 percent, an expected goal of 10 percent, and in many instances, a realizable goal of 15 percent in any year. This is not a one-time cost or savings but an annual savings.

The approach for improving productivity has seven steps (Figure 25–1):

1. management orientation

2. overview studies
3. productivity reporting
4. quality control
5. in-depth studies
6. performance/reward systems
7. monitoring, review, and change

Management Orientation

First, a philosophical framework must be established, which in turn should establish why productivity improvements are necessary and what benefits are expected. As Figure 25–1 suggests, the management orientation includes at least two levels—the individual department manager or supervisor and the manager's superior (and top management).

A set of objectives must next be stated. These objectives should be related to expected benefits within a certain period of time. For example:

- *Objective 1:* All departments will be analyzed as to existing manpower productivity levels within an 18-month period.
- *Objective 2:* Changes resulting in a $400,000 annual saving should be initiated within 12 months.
- *Objective 3:* Productivity for all departments will be reported on a monthly basis.

The objectives must also state the responsibility of top and middle management and commitment and support they will contribute. Finally, the costs of increasing productivity must be a consideration, so return on investment should be included in the objectives. Obviously, one would not want to expend more dollars on a cost-containment program than it could return in additional service and in reduced costs.

Top management's major input focuses on four areas:

1. establishment of objectives
2. creation of an environment that allows managers to effect change, and the provision of technical assistance where needed
3. control of individual productivity in-

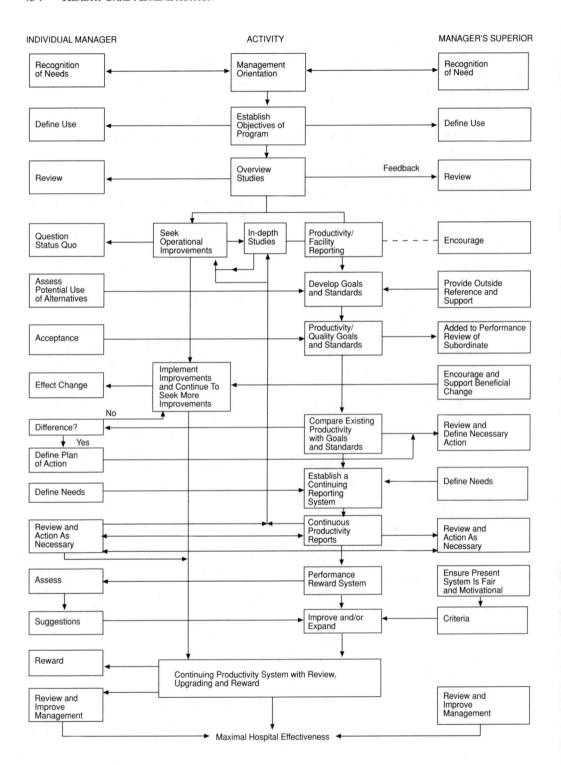

Figure 25–1 Productivity Improvement Steps. *Source:* Courtesy of Chi Systems, Inc., Ann Arbor, Michigan.

creases so that they are not made at the expense of the overall organization or the quality of service

4. utilization of productivity measures to assess personnel performance evaluation and long-range planning of facilities and labor

The achievement and maintenance of cost containment goals can take place only if the department manager and/or supervisor is committed and involved. They can make improvements work or make sure they do not. The first step in obtaining their involvement and commitment is to explain to them why cost containment is necessary. The second step is to review goals and secure agreement on (or negotiate) specific goals for each department. The usual problem is that the establishment of a cost-containment program in a department implies that department members are not performing as expected. It is therefore important to emphasize that cost containment is a new management direction in which all managers are to be involved. Likewise, it should be emphasized that to the agreed-upon cost-containment goals will be added their performance measures as part of their periodic evaluation by top management. The establishment of departmental cost-containment goals must be accompanied by provision of adequate staff support to achieve these goals.

Overview Study

An overview study has two purposes.

First, at a relatively low cost, it provides data that enable management to decide whether an in-depth analysis will prove economically justifiable. Second, it enables the engineer or analyst to direct his or her efforts to specific problem areas during an in-depth analysis, thus minimizing the cost of the more detailed study.[10]

In addition, the overview provides a profile of labor productivity and the initial baseline for a productivity reporting system.

An overview study should be directed by a person trained in the use of such a technique. If a staff person with these qualifications is not available, consultants from shared management engineering programs[11] or management consulting firms should be retained. This initial study can then be the basis for future work by existing staff (if available).

The overview study should provide three outputs: staffing analysis, quality survey, and systems and management review. The *staffing analysis* utilizes gross workload data and predetermined productivity standards to determine total staffing needs in comparison with existing staff. The *quality survey* measures performance relative to quality. This is particularly crucial to ensure that increased productivity does not have a negative impact on quality. Quality surveys are conducted by random sampling, involving observations and work counts. The *systems and management review* identifies and analyzes problems involving the management structure of the department and the systems, methods, and procedures for performing work. The management structure analysis looks at organization, skills, and work assignments. Systems analysis looks for duplication of effort, unnecessary steps, and imbalance of workstations.

As a result of the overview study, four directions can be pursued (Figure 25–2).

Productivity and Quality Reporting

A productivity reporting system is one part of a resource utilization management information system that measures labor productivity. The other part is the quality control system, which measures the quality of services.

An effective productivity reporting system should generate a continuous—at least monthly—timely report on productivity of each department and a comparison of productivity over time to show trends; for example, this month compared to last month, this month compared to same month last year, or year to date compared

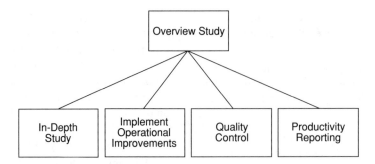

Figure 25–2 Directions Stemming from an Overview Study. *Source:* Reprinted from *Topics in Health Care Financing*, Vol. 3, No. 3, p. 44, with permission of Aspen Publishers, Inc., © 1977.

to last year to date. In addition, this system should provide the following information.

Measurement of Actual Productivity in Person-Hours Per Output

Actual productivity can be measured in person-hours per output or output per person-hour; these outputs are specific for each department. See the radiology example in Table 25–1. Increased labor productivity may result from:[12]

- a decrease in person-hours invested with no change in output; staffing is reduced, decreasing both direct and indirect salary costs for the hospital
- an increase in output with no change in staff; additional services are provided with increased efficiency, avoiding additional salary costs by not having to hire more staff.

Actual Productivity Compared to a Performance Goal

Actual productivity (person-hours per output) can be compared to a performance goal of person-hours per actual output.

*The reason for analyzing productivity is to determine if the existing productivity level is acceptable. One of several methods to establish a comparative value must be selected to make this judgment. A comparison of

current productivity to historical performance, comparison to other institutions or groups of institutions, guidelines developed by professional societies, and measured (engineered) time standards are used most frequently.

Most comparatives provide meaningful information which can be translated into improvement objectives, and comparisons with predetermined measured, or engineered, standards appear to be the most meaningful form of evaluation. The standards assumedly represent an objective, unbiased per occurrence representation of labor requirements necessary to produce a single unit of output. They are unadulterated by any existing nonproductive labor practices or inefficient work methods.

Measured productivity time standards can be viewed in a number of different ways. Several elemental work tasks must be performed in a department regardless of the workload unit volumes produced. Conversely, other tasks will be performed in direct proportion to the workload unit vol-

*This extracted material is reprinted from *Health Care Strategic Management*, with permission of Chi Systems, Inc., © January 1984.

Table 25–1 Workload Unit Recording Systems: Productivity Measurement Results for Radiology—Input = Person-Hours

Method/Component	Person-Hours Invested (Input)	Workload Units Produced (Output)	Person-Hours Per Unit
Aggregate:			
Total procedures	930	1,820	0.51
Totals	930	1,820	0.51
Service specific:			
Radiography	600	1,400	0.43
Fluoroscopy	250	400	0.63
Specials	80	20	4.00
Totals	930	1,820	0.51
Procedure specific:			
Radiography			
Chest—PA & lat.	50	250	0.20
Chest—PA	30	180	0.17
•	•	•	•
•	•	•	•
•	•	•	•
Subtotal for radiography	600	1,400	0.43
Fluoroscopy			
Barium enema	20	20	1.00
Gallbladder	10	20	0.50
•	•	•	•
•	•	•	•
•	•	•	•
Subtotal for fluoroscopy	250	400	0.63
Specials			
Head angiography	30	10	3.00
•	•	•	•
•	•	•	•
•	•	•	•
Subtotal for specials	80	20	4.00
Totals	930	1,820	0.51

ume. Consider that the activities of a department manager require one full-time position, and staffing will not vary according to the number of procedures, tests, etc. performed. On the other hand, the number of person-hours necessary to perform procedures will depend upon the number of procedures performed. The position-hours associated with managing the department becomes a fixed task, and the processing of procedures a variable task.

Fixed tasks can be viewed as components of the cost of doing business. In addition to routine department management supervision, other fixed tasks include preparation of departmental statistics, administrative clerical services, daily activation and quality control of diagnostic devices, routine supplies inventory and replenishment, departmental/hospital meetings, and giving or receiving inservice educational sessions. Similarly, variable work tasks, such as scheduling appointments, prepping patients, and filing new reports, contribute directly to the production of each processed workload unit. The time required to perform each variable task may either be the same or different for each specific procedure.

Engineered productivity time standards are frequently established by developing a fixed and a variable component. The fixed component represents the labor requirements necessary to perform all fixed work tasks; the variable component, the additional resources required for each processed workload unit. All departments will have at least one fixed component. The number of variable components will relate to the level of detail reflected in the workload unit recording system. Mathematically, this relationship is expressed as follows:

Standard time = fixed component
+ (variable standard component
× workload unit volume)

These time standards can be used to determine the required person-hours for processing the observed workload unit volumes over a specified period of time. The predetermined time interval between reporting cycles, the reporting period, is typically defined to coincide with the availability of data concerning inputs or outputs.

In the radiology example, if an aggregate measure of workload (total procedures) is used, one variable component appears in the equation. If the workload unit recording system uses service-specific information (radiography, fluoroscopy, and special procedures), three variable components are required. If the workload unit recording system is procedure specific, the productivity standard equation will include as many variable components as there are specific procedures. The required person-hours for the three-alternative workload unit recording systems for a 4-week period is illustrated in Table 25–2.

To determine how effectively departmental labor resources were utilized during the reporting period, required person-hours determined by using the productivity standards can be compared to the actual person-hours used. This measure of labor utilization, the department's productivity index, is expressed as a percentage of required person-hours divided by actual person-hours. If 4,200 person-hours were utilized the productivity index for the radiology department example presented in Table 25–2 would be calculated as:

$$\text{Productivity Index} = \frac{3,500}{4,200} \times 100$$

$$= 83.3\%$$

At this point, the value of a service- or procedure-specific workload unit recording system becomes apparent. The detailed information produced can be compared to existing staffing patterns for each major facet of departmental operations. Often, such comparisons provide the basis for staff reallocation or schedule adjustments.

The key to the development and utilization of time standards is their acceptance by the department manager. Because the measurement of work is, in most instances, a new concept to department managers, gaining this acceptance is not always an easy task. In particular, managers

Table 25–2 Workload Unit Recording Systems: Total Required Person-Hours for Radiology Procedures—Period = 4 Weeks

Method/Component	Workload Unit × Volume (Procedures)	Productivity Standard (Hours/ Procedure)	= Required Person-Hours
Aggregate:			
Total procedures	7,640	0.41	3,122.00
Totals			3,500.00*
Service specific:			
Radiography	5,200	0.33	1,716.00
Fluoroscopy	2,378	0.50	1,189.00
Specials	62	3.50	217.00
Total required person-hours			3,500.00*
Procedure specific:			
Radiography			
Chest—PA & lateral	600	0.16	96.00
Chest—PA	520	0.13	67.60
•	•	•	•
•	•	•	•
•	•	•	•
Subtotal for radiography	5,200	0.33	1,716.00
Fluoroscopy			
Barium enema	65	0.83	53.95
Gallbladder	60	0.35	21.00
•	•	•	•
•	•	•	•
•	•	•	•
Subtotal for fluoroscopy	2,378	0.50	1,189.00
Specials			
Head angiography	22	2.60	57.20
•	•	•	•
•	•	•	•
Subtotal for specials	62	3.50	217.00
Total required person-hours			3,500.00*

*Totals include a standard time of 378 hours for fixed work tasks over a 4-week period.

have realistic concerns such as the difference in patients served (age, diagnosis, cooperativeness) and the random demands for services placed on most departments. To overcome these concerns, it must be recognized that, in reality, all department managers actually are measuring work when they establish labor budgets and work schedules. From there, one proceeds to define major work activities. Time standards are applied to these major work activities. These are then modified to take into account fluctuations in workloads as caused by patients with different degrees of illness, peak and valley demands, delays, and approved time off of staff members.

In some cases, the department managers may not accept the predetermined time standards.

Because the first objective is to establish a productivity reporting system, an interim time standard may be established as an initial goal. This "negotiated" time standard would then be used at the initial reporting phase.

It has been the experience of the author, as well as colleagues in the field, that the establishment of a system to report productivity is beneficial in itself. It provides a regular vehicle by which the department manager can review the performance of his or her department. As a result of this report, the department manager may initiate further studies and changes to increase productivity. Most good managers want to do a better job, and the report provides them a way of measuring improvement.

Written Reports to All Management Levels

The productivity report should be shared with all management levels: hospital, divisions within the hospital, departments within each division, and sections within each department. Figure 25–3 illustrates this concept. The report should cover the level of detail necessary at each level for effective management control.

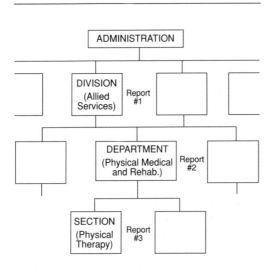

Figure 25–3 System Organization. *Source:* Reprinted from *Topics in Health Care Financing*, Vol. 3, No. 3, p. 46, with permission of Aspen Publishers, Inc., © 1977.

Exhibits 25–1 and 25–2 illustrate monthly reports produced under the CHIMIS[13] productivity reporting system, for two different levels within the sample organization.

Productivity must be continuously updated because the procedures being performed (the output) change over time, new ones are added, and others are deleted. Second, as more data are developed for each department, more refined time standards can be derived by dividing certain comprehensive procedures into more specific procedures. In addition, negotiated time standards, set as initial goals, should be reviewed and revised as necessary.

QUALITY CONTROL PROGRAM

The myth that increasing productivity reduces the quality of care has limited efforts to increase productivity. Not only is this generally not true but there is also significant evidence that increased quality can be consistent with increased productivity. Common sense tells us that, if something is done correctly the first time, there is no need to repeat the effort.

The primary objectives of a quality control program are to provide:

- a quantitative measure that indicates the level of quality on a continuing basis
- positive feedback that allows corrective action to be taken
- quality assurance upon implementation of new systems, equipment, or workload revisions

Quality

The ultimate measure of the quality of the health care system is the health status of the community. Determination of quality of health in an area can be derived from indices of unnecessary disease, unnecessary disability, and unnecessary untimely death.[14] However, the relationships of such measures of quality to the services provided by specific physicians or hospital departments are undefined. Therefore, one

Exhibit 25–1 Sample of Hospital Report

CHI SYSTEMS	21-Apr-76	22:35	REPHOS.L38	PAGE 1

HOSPITAL

```
                                    ******* CHIMIS *******
                                    ** HOSPITAL REPORT**
                                    **** MARCH 1976 *****
```

	EARNED	PAID	
DIVISION	MAN-HOURS	MAN-HOURS	% PROD
HOSP ADMINISTRATION	519.000	528.000	98.3
EMPLOYEE SERVICES	14746.417	13528.000	109.0
ALLIED SERVICES	21135.314	21784.000	97.0
FISCAL SERVICES	21410.943	21834.000	98.1
SUPPORTIVE SERVICES	35482.832	32818.000	108.1
NURSING SERVICES	66734.731	68158.000	97.9
DEVELOPMENT	173.000	177.000	97.7
PLANNING	519.000	531.000	97.7
TOTALS	160721.238	159358.000	100.9

- - - HISTORICAL - - -   *INDICATES CURRENT MONTH

JAN	FEB	MAR	APR	MAY	JUN	JUL	AUG	SEP	OCT	NOV	DEC

PERCENT PRODUCTIVITY

90.5	102.7	100.9*	0.0	0.0	0.0	86.2	86.0	91.9	92.0	92.3	85.6

THIS MONTH EARNED FTE   929.0
THIS MONTH PAID FTE   921.1

PAST 12 MONTHS PRODUCTIVITY   91.9

Source: CHIMIS, A Management Information System, Chi Systems Inc., Ann Arbor, Michigan.

should use measures that are more specific to the services being provided by the respective physicians or departments.

A comprehensive definition of quality is difficult to develop due to its many components and the need to determine the relative values of "good" and "bad" quality. Rather than attempt a synthesized definition of quality, existing definitions and concepts are examined to specify the dimensions of quality relevant to a quality productivity program.

Random House Dictionary defines quality as "character with respect to fineness or grade of excellence."[15] Gavett's definition of quality related to production is that "the quality of a product or service is expressed in terms of a given set of attributes that are required to meet the . . . needs for which the product or service is created."[16]

Many definitions of quality refer to quality control, which can be defined as "the sending of messages which effectively change the behavior of the recipient."[17] A more useful definition of control is "that function of the system which provides direction in conformance to plan, or in other words, the maintenance of variations from system objectives within allowable limits."[18] Components of a control system include:

- a monitored characteristic or operational variable
- a monitoring device or method

Exhibit 25–2 Sample of Section Report

```
CHI SYSTEMS              21-Apr-76              22:34              REPSEC.L38              PAGE 7

HOSPITAL      —                                            ******* CHIMIS *******
DIVISION      —ALLIED SERVICES                             ***SECTION REPORT ***
DEPARTMENT    —P.M. & R.                                   *****MARCH 1976 *****

SECTION       — PHYSICAL THERAPY
```

		M-H/PROC	EARNED	PAID	
WORKLOAD UNIT	VOLUME	STANDARD	MAN-HOURS	MAN-HOURS	% PROD
THERAPEUTIC EXERCISE	780	0.601	468.780		
GAIT TRAINING	569	0.694	394.886		
HOT PACKS	340	0.432	146.880		
ULTRA SOUND	281	0.555	155.955		
ROOM VISIT	503	0.324	162.972		
TRACTION	128	0.447	57.216		
HUBBARD-UNASSISTED	4	0.863	3.452		
HUBBARD-W/THERAPIST	7	1.202	8.414		
WHIRLPOOL-ALL	76	0.478	36.328		
EXERCISE-OTHERS	267	0.554	147.918		
MASSAGE-ALL	314	0.516	162.024		
DIATHERMY-ALL	119	0.468	55.692		
P.T. LEVELS-ALL	11	0.678	7.458		
OTHER MODALITIES	66	0.615	40.590		
FIXED			221.000		
EPI			0.000		
SECTION TOTALS			2069.565	1799.000	115.0

```
- - - HISTORICAL - - -        *INDICATES CURRENT MONTH

  JAN    FEB    MAR    APR    MAY    JUN    JUL    AUG    SEP    OCT    NOV    DEC
 —  —  —  —  —  —  —  —  —  —  —  —  —  —  —  —  —  —  —  —  —  —  —  —

PERCENT PRODUCTIVITY
  95.5   116.8  115.0*  0.0    0.0    0.0    95.6   95.5   106.1  153.3  112.8  94.8

THIS MONTH EARNED FTE    12.0
THIS MONTH PAID FTE      10.4

PAST 12 MONTHS PRODUCTIVITY        108.7
```

Source: CHIMIS, A Management Information System, Chi Systems Inc., Ann Arbor, Michigan.

- a standard of performance for each monitored characteristic
- a comparison of actual to predetermined standard performance
- an activator that can effect change

In a quality control system, therefore, the rating of operational variables is done by comparison to standards or, at least, predetermined values of quality. The purpose of a quality control system is to give some assurance that the standards of services are maintained.

Quality control systems exist, and can be developed, for both medical care provided by physicians and for services provided by hospital departments. Some departments, such as nuclear medicine and tissue pathology, have strong medical components. Quality of medical care is monitored by the hospital's utilization review and medical audit programs. Medical record abstracting services provide information for use by the medical review committees of the hospital.

Quality of services can be measured from three perspectives: input, process, and output. A comprehensive system measures quality from all three perspectives, with an emphasis on output measures.

Input measurement involves the quality of inputs—labor, facilities, equipment, and supplies—used to provide departmental services. Input quality measurements include staff educational requirements, types of linen purchased, type of lighting installed in the operating room, and the physical characteristics of the building.

Process measurement involves the quality of the organization and the methods it uses to provide services. Assessment of process answers the question: Is the process proper or performed correctly? Methods are compared with standard procedures, and when standards do not exist or are not applicable, relative values are determined. Examples of process quality measurements include written procedures for the care of isolation patients, identification procedures for patients going to surgery, staffing schedules, sterile technique maintained in the operating room, and appropriate tagging of contaminated linen.

Output measurement involves the quality of the services provided by a department. Examples include timely delivery of drugs by the pharmacy, cleanliness of a patient's room after discharge cleaning, timely and courteous answering of telephones, and achievement of nursing care objectives.

A distinction between absolute and relative measures of quality should be made. An absolute quality measure requires no interpretation, whereas relative quality measures require interpretation and rating. The question—does the surgical light work—is an absolute quality measure; the light either works or not. However, the question—is the ambient room temperature sufficient—is relative to the activity being done and the judgment of the observer.

Measurement Variables and Standards

Measurement variables are activities on which judgment or decision can be based. Both qualitative and quantitative measurement variables can be used, but quantitative variables are less subjective. Examples of measurement variables are sterility of instrument trays, accuracy of accounting records, cleanliness of patient rooms, and person-minutes per pack.

Standards are specific values of measurement variables. Each quality and productivity measurement variable can have specific levels or standards established as acceptable or unacceptable. Examples of standards are 95 percent acceptably cleaned rooms or 5 instrument trays packed per hour.

Measurements To Develop Standards

Continuous measurement of quality is often prohibitively expensive. Therefore, quality and productivity are usually measured by sampling the measurement variable.[19] Problems to be avoided in sampling include concentrating on only one of the many quality and productivity variables, sampling only problem situations, and taking nonrepresentative samples. Three methods of avoiding these problems are to randomize the samples, take a large enough sample to be representative, and include all relevant variables in the sample.

In measuring quality and productivity, the concepts of reliability, validity, and bias must be considered. *Reliability* refers to the ability of two or more persons to make similar judgments on the measurement variables or for the data to be judged similarly on multiple occasions. *Validity* refers to the ability of the observation to measure what it is supposed to measure. *Bias* occurs when one judge or observer of the data systematically rates the variable differently than others.

In addition, quality and productivity measurement needs to be applicable to repetitive measurement over time, as opposed to a one-time evaluation. Measurements should also be responsive to changes in input or process during the sample interval (commonly 1 month). The quality question for a maintenance department, does the department have a preventive maintenance program—would always be answered "yes" if such a program existed, regardless of the performance of the program. The question—has a minimum acceptable number of items been preventively maintained during the sampling period—would measure departmental performance during the period.

Interaction among Departments

In the development of measures of quality and productivity for the services provided by the various functional units or departments within the hospital, the point is eventually reached where the performance of a given element of service is dependent upon some other element previously performed by another department or functional unit. Before the laboratory can be expected to run a battery of tests on a sample of blood, it must first receive a requisition for this service from nursing or from a physician. Most of the time, responsibilities for required prior services can be assigned to either one of the two units directly involved. However, there are some instances in which a third party or element enters the picture. These are the "network" systems. Consider the situation in which an X-ray examination is requested for an inpatient. All forms have been properly processed. Before the examination can occur, however, the patient must be transported from his or her bed to the X-ray department, a function that belongs neither to nursing, the X-ray department, nor to the physician. The network system here is patient transportation, which is likely handled by a patient transport or messenger service, and its own quality of performance can be measured as an individual functioning unit. Other network systems include communications (verbal and physical—hard copy, electronic, recorded), material supply (procurement, reprocessing, storage, distribu-

tion), education, and equipment and facility maintenance. The responsibility for the operation of each network system can, in fact, be assigned to some functioning unit or individual, and the performance of that responsibility can be measured.

When interaction among departments does not involve a third party, the concern becomes the accurate definition of the department's interface with another department and the determination of where one department's responsibility ends and that of the other begins. The quality and productivity measurement variables must then be defined consistently with the interface definition so that monitoring and reporting will be appropriate.

Relationship of Quality and Productivity

The relationship of quality and productivity is neither easily determined nor consistent; it varies with the levels of quality and productivity and the procedures used by the hospital.

Beginning with the current quality level and current productivity, both can usually be increased to some point. At that point, they cannot be simultaneously increased, but other alternatives are (1) increasing quality at the same productivity level, (2) increasing productivity at the same quality level, (3) increasing productivity while decreasing quality, and (4) decreasing both quality and productivity. The difficulty is knowing at what quality and productivity level the hospital is currently functioning and monitoring where it is on future dates.

Providing this information is a major reason for a quality-productivity program that simultaneously measures and integrates quality and productivity. Then, as changes in either level are planned, the impact on the other can be determined.

The following examples demonstrate increases in both productivity (decreasing cost) and quality. Most of these involve several departments, emphasizing the importance of interdepartmental effects on quality and productivity.

Pharmacy Ordering

In some hospitals, physicians write pharmacy orders on the patients' charts. These orders are then transcribed by a ward clerk, checked by the head nurse, and sent to the pharmacy to be filled. Changing the system so that a carbon copy of the physician's order is sent directly to the pharmacy decreases errors of interpretation of the physician's order, thereby increasing quality, and reduces staff time needed to transcribe and verify the physician's order, which can increase productivity or decrease cost.

Early Admission Testing

Traditionally hospitals have admitted patients to their rooms, orders for admission tests are written by the physicians, and then the patient receives the admission tests. Earlier admission testing both reduces cost and improves quality. Earlier testing is done one of two ways: on the day of admission before the patient reaches his or her bed (early testing—ET) or before the day of admission (preadmission testing—PAT). ET and PAT often improve quality because physicians receive test results earlier, reducing the probability of surgery or other action being taken before test results are available. Costs are also decreased by reducing the length of stay of patients[20,21] and reducing the amount of time needed to escort patients from patient floors to testing areas.

Paging System

Although widely used, many institutions still do not take advantage of paging systems for their communication needs. Quality is improved by reducing response time of services required by patients. Physicians, nurses, and others can be reached in emergencies or other situations. Productivity is improved by reducing walking time and delays.

Coordinated Admission and Surgery Scheduling

Close coordination of admission scheduling and surgery scheduling is very important for sur-

gery patients. This can be done several different ways, but the advantages are similar. Quality is improved when fewer schedule changes and cancellations result in less patient and physician disruption. Productivity is improved by reducing the personnel time needed to schedule and reschedule both admissions and surgery. The probability of unused surgical time due to last-minute cancellations is also reduced.

In-Depth Studies

The in-depth study is a detailed study of a function or department directed at either the entire operation or a specific problem identified by the overview study or the productivity-quality reporting system. An in-depth study is warranted when the following occurs:

- significant differences between existing and required staffing levels
- significant quality control problems creating safety, health, and/or public relations problems
- ineffective interaction with other departments and functions that creates problems for those other departments

In-depth studies are far more expensive than the overview study, often costing between 10 to 15 times that of the overview study. Therefore, the expected benefits must at least exceed this amount by a minimum of two or three times. One must be cautioned that some difference in staffing levels could be due to the scope of work and activities in the department, not improper staffing. The in-depth study accounts for these activities and establishes time standards for the work required to perform them.

The in-depth study is usually directed at a specific problem, such as organization, scheduling, employees, patients, information flow and handling, methods improvement, patient/materials movement, and layout and equipment. Many references are available on identification of problems and problem-solving approaches.[22,23] A few comments on each of these problems follow.

Organization

Organization studies are directed at achieving the correct balance between span of control and delegation of responsibility with related authority. Too large a span of control may result in poor supervision and, in turn, low productivity. Determining the appropriate number of persons to be supervised by each supervisor is further complicated by their location of work. In a hospital, staff members may work on different floors and in different departments; for example, housekeeping personnel. Conversely, too small a span of control may result in additional levels of hierarchy. Such levels may be established to provide opportunities for promotions within departments. In a nursing department, there may be several levels of supervision before one finds a nurse totally committed to patient care; these levels may include a nursing director, associate nursing director, assistant nursing director, nursing supervisor, head nurse, assistant head nurse, team leader, or nurse. But are they all necessary?

Scheduling

The installation of effective *scheduling systems* can yield a big payoff in terms of achieving cost containment and improvement in productivity. This very broad area involves patients, employees, and available facilities. Facilities is a limiting factor—that is, not enough rooms available—although an artificial one in many ways, if one thinks of 24-hour, 7-day/week operations.

Scheduling of patients may be difficult because of the random arrival of certain types of patients. However, statistically arrivals do follow certain patterns, and upon further analysis, one finds that a majority of inpatients and outpatients can be scheduled. The biggest fault in scheduling is the peak load syndrome. In too many cases, patients are scheduled "en masse" for a block of time. Examples are 8:00 A.M. surgery, admissions from 1:00 P.M. to 3:00 P.M., and the noon meal from 11:00 A.M. to 12:00 P.M. When one realizes that the processing of 10 patients in 1 hour takes twice as many personnel as 5 patients per hour for 2 hours, the peak load scheduling problem should be obvious. The

usual case is that the number of required employees is determined by the peak load, with the rest of their 8 hours being used with fill-in operations. Usually, reduction of the peak load requirements—spreading out the patient schedule—results in reduction of staff.

A larger inefficiency in scheduling employees is in the 7-day operations—nursing, dietary, housekeeping—that involve the majority of employees. Because most employees work only 5 days, coverage is required for the other 2. The actual requirement for a 7-day position is 1.4 full-time equivalents (FTEs). It is not uncommon to see scheduling of 3 employees for every 2 positions, which results in an excess of 0.2 FTEs for every 3.0 FTEs. In a 300-bed hospital with 450 nursing, 90 housekeeping, and 75 dietary personnel, this coverage represents over 40 extra personnel.

The difficulty of scheduling work for hospital personnel is due to the lack of repetition of tasks during an 8-hour shift. The key to effective scheduling of tasks is to ensure that personnel understand all tasks that must be performed, why they are necessary, when they must be done (not necessarily *at* which time, but *by* what time they must be completed), and what the priorities are. Peak load requirements must be smoothed as much as possible, and traditional hours—that is, 7:00 A.M. to 3:30 P.M., 8 A.M. to 5:00 P.M.—must be examined to determine whether they are the times appropriate to the necessary tasks. In past studies, the author has found that a midnight nursing shift (11:00 P.M. to 7:30 A.M.) was primarily staffed to provide personnel for the early morning activities for patients (6:00 A.M. to 7:30 A.M.).[24] A change in the daily shift hours resulted in reducing the midnight shift requirements by almost 50 percent. Scheduling studies and analyses really are just the application of common sense. *Why* must a task be performed, for *whom* by *what* skill, by what *time*.

Information Flow

Information flow is not only concerned with how effectively information flows from one organization level to another, as well as from department to department, but just as importantly *what information does not flow*.

Management cannot function without a proper flow of information, both historical reporting and projecting for the future. Departments cannot effectively interact with and serve other departments without the timely receipt of adequate information indicating the others' needs. Some studies have suggested that up to 25 percent of all activities in a hospital are involved with information handling. Therefore, a reduction in this activity must lead to improved productivity. The major problem in achieving real cost containment is that most of the information handling effort is spread over all employees. Therefore, an improvement in information handling may decrease an employee's workload by 30 minutes, but he or she still has 7½ hours of work to do. To realize this 30-minute savings may require extensive reorganization of tasks.

Several improvements in information flow and handling result in cost-containment benefits. Improvement in record keeping in many hospitals has resulted in increased revenue and greater knowledge of resources expended. Planning ahead can enable services and supplies to be requested on a scheduled "batched" basis, eliminating "stat" requests and processing of single requests, rather than in a batched or bulk basis. However, a deterrent to achieving cost containment through the substitution of automated information processing equipment may be the increased cost of hardware rental and skilled computer programming staff.

Methods Improvement

Methods improvement is the study of how work is performed, and its objective is to reduce human motion (walking, handling, reaching). In the global sense, everything mentioned in this section is methods improvement. There is always a better way to perform a task, and there is never a "best" way, only a "least worst" way. Improvement is always possible.

Patients and Materials Movement

Patients and materials movement studies apply methods improvement and information han-

dling analysis. This is the key to effective interaction among departments. Too often one hears from a department manager that department members are doing the best they can but that they never have the patients or materials on time. It is rare to find a hospital staff that does not complain about its messenger service or its patient escort system; they are easy scapegoats for all problems. The important step in this analysis is the recognition that movement problems cannot be solved by individual departments because they involve all those departments that must interact with each other. It is difficult to project the potential cost savings from an effective patient and material movement system because there are usually new costs associated with the system. System benefits come from smoothing the workload in the individual departments.

A related activity is material management studies—the analysis of the purchase, storage, handling, movement, and use of supplies and other purchased materials. Greater benefits are being derived from these studies because of both the increased use of such items and the inflationary price spiral. Labor considerations become important when one analyzes handling and movement requirements.

Layout and Equipment

Layout and equipment studies should be geared to reduction of walking distances and total labor input. For existing operations, layout of equipment and workstations is usually limited by the space within existing walls and the cost of moving permanent fixtures. The management engineer is usually frustrated by this analysis because many mistakes could have been avoided by more effective facility planning. It is rare that significant labor savings can be achieved through layout changes. The major benefit is usually a more effective use of space that results in the availability of more space, which in most hospitals is a real benefit. One must recognize that this benefit is still limited by total existing space.

Labor savings are being achieved through automation, such as in the dietary department (automated dishwashing and tray preparation) and in housekeeping (floor washers). The clinical laboratory also benefits from highly automated processing of procedures, as does the radiology department. A major question is whether the labor replacement results in real cost reduction. In the clinical laboratory, if one is seeing an increased volume and number of procedures, is it clear that productivity is increasing? Is this increase proportionate to the capital investment in equipment? Even more serious is the question that medical professionals are asking: Is this increase in laboratory procedures really necessary?

When an analysis of the cost benefits of an equipment investment is made, the objectives of using the new equipment must be clearly understood. For example, is the objective of the investment to increase service, reduce labor, or both? If the objective is labor reduction, a labor savings must be realized; saving one hour per day for each of eight persons is not a cost reduction unless work can be reassigned to achieve a reduction in one staff position. Another weakness in equipment studies lies in the basis for comparison. Most comparisons are with the existing operations. Despite the many reports that have justified a large investment in automated material handling systems, one is hard pressed to justify such systems when looking at how the existing system can be improved without (or with very little) capital investment. In other words, justification for equipment should be made based on comparison with the most effective manual system.

Implementation of Productivity and Quality Control Programs

The development of recommendations and new systems is academic if it is not followed by implementation.

A variety of quality and productivity systems have been developed over the last 20 years and are in use today in various institutions. Key problems encountered with the implementation

and use of these productivity and quality control programs have been:

- complexity and subsequent difficulty in implementation that have resulted in only partial use
- reports produced that are neither used at all nor integrated into the management process or review of managers' performance
- systems that have not been comprehensive or specific enough, resulting in the common and easy practice of blaming lack of productivity and/or quality on another department
- lack of attention paid to interactive effects among departments

The process of implementation requires that the responsible operating manager fully understand and concur with it. The manager must understand the basis for the recommendations, how the new systems and procedures are to work, and what the expected benefits are. Many times, all of the recommendations may not be acceptable to the manager. This situation may result in partial implementation, with further development by the analyst and the manager of the remaining recommendations.

The next step in implementation is to establish with the manager a timetable of activities and expected results. This should then be followed by an orientation of all employees involved in any changes. They in turn must be informed of the desired goals and the timetable of the implementation. If a change in procedures, methods, or use of equipment is proposed, instructions must be formalized and training must take place. If new schedules are developed, then assignment of tasks must be developed to be consistent with new schedules.

The actual change to new schedules and/or procedures necessitates close monitoring and continuous support in the form of directions and encouragement. As the new recommendations become more and more routine, this monitoring and support can be decreased. Included in the implementation plan must be a periodic review, such as monthly, to ensure that everything is going as expected.

In implementing changes we are asking people to change their routine way of doing things. This is never easy!

Performance Reward Systems

Underlying the entire process of managing productivity gains is the realization that some reward should ultimately result from the improved performance. The nature and extent of the reward mechanism are certainly dependent upon the level of employee considered. The range, however, should encompass cost-reduction cash bonuses, incentives, perquisites, improved reimbursement formulas with third-party payors, alternative uses of funds, and compensatory time off. In no case can it be expected or warranted that improved results will be obtained without some form of recognition of an individual's contribution to these results.

Monitoring, Review, and Change

Cost containment for ongoing operations must be a continuous activity. Productivity and quality control reporting systems provide regular feedback that must be monitored on an exception basis; that is, to detect when productivity and quality deviate from an expected range, including both high and low deviations. When productivity and/or quality is below performance expectations, it should be investigated. Above-expected performance, which should be examined as well, may be due to the use of new procedures, services, or equipment. This would then require updating the productivity and/or quality control program.

This continuous reporting system has several by-products. Evaluation of new equipment purchases may be based on their effect on productivity. Personnel budgets can be developed based on existing utilization of personnel. The justification for new positions should have a very reliable basis. Performance objectives for management can target increased productivity

or quality level goals that can be quantified. Performance reward systems must also be reviewed and updated. When a hospital has gone through the above cost-containment steps, it should be able to compare itself favorably with any well-managed business.

MANAGEMENT ENGINEERING FOR FUTURE OPERATIONS

Management engineering should be as useful in long-range planning as it is in ongoing operations. Many planning decisions have major effects on the cost of operating any facility. Initial decisions establishing demand projections are used to establish staffing budgets. Facility layout and design affect movement distances, and equipment decisions influence labor utilization.

The first step in long-range planning is to determine *who* the institution is serving with *what* services. Next, projected changes in service areas and services to be provided are made. Management engineering can provide mathematical forecasting models. Too often the effects of these changes are assumed without question. For example, if the projected service area is doubling in size, the planner assumes that a proportionate change will take place in the institution. Likewise, the planner assumes that all new technology must be provided by the institution. It is rare to have the planner say, "Wait a minute, we can't be all things to all people!" This happens only after some sort of financial study is performed and infeasibility is indicated, which occurs usually after a large amount of time, dollars, and effort has already been expended.

Early in the planning stages, the resource implications of programmatic decisions must be assessed. The two major resources of a hospital are facilities and labor. The early question to be answered is: Who is going to pay for the new service? A part of any early long-range planning efforts must be a preliminary financial feasibility or debt load study to determine how much money is required. Another realistic concern is the availability of sophisticated skills to operate new services.

The technology of the management engineer must be utilized in the planning effort. Labor forecasting, itself a skill, should not be based on what is now done, but on what should be done and what can be done if the constraints of existing sites, buildings, and equipment are removed.

The projected volume of service *workload* will dictate the amount of space required. There is a direct relationship between workload, labor, and space. Most space programmers now determine space based on workstations, the major centers of activity within a department. These workstations either are a function of labor or dictate labor. Inaccurate or nonprecise projections of workload may have a negative effect on the utilization of manpower.

Facility design can affect labor utilization in at least two ways. Layouts of departments and workstations would be based on the function that is to be performed and should incorporate ways in which labor utilization can be reduced, such as reductions of walking distances, elimination of reaching at workstations, or provision of sufficient and easily accessible storage. It is rare that the management engineer and users are brought into the facility design process.

The other effect on labor utilization is lack of sufficient facilities. Seldom does a health facilities planner consider life-cycle costs, the total costs of acquiring and operating a facility over the life of the facility. Ongoing operating costs and initial capital costs are equated utilizing present value or present worth techniques.[25] Too often, the capital budget is exceeded and must be reduced, resulting in smaller spaces, less elevators, and less automation, all of which increase labor requirements. Because the operating costs of any health institution exceed the initial capital costs in two to four years, they should be the deciding factor in the establishment of the initial capital budget.

Most Certificate of Need regulations and investment bankers now require financial feasibility studies and labor budgets. These studies establish a base for developing a productivity reporting system and illustrate the relationship between operating costs and capital investment costs. The author has recently been involved in 2 building programs ($20,000,000 plus and $60,000,000 plus) in which projected labor savings due to increased productivity provided the basis for pursuing the project. In one case, a 1-year cost containment program reduced the payroll in excess of $4 million. The effect on the profit and loss and balance sheets was sufficient to handle the additional debt financing required for the project. In the second case, projected labor savings due to more efficient facility organization, layout, and equipment was accepted by planning authorities for the issuance of a Certificate of Need.

New facilities can be designed, planned, and operated in many ways to increase productivity and achieve cost-containment goals. One such way is to eliminate a centralized nursing station in nursing unit design. The "no-nursing station" concept decentralized many nursing duties, transfers nonnursing administrative duties to nonnursing personnel, provides sophisticated communication and message handling systems, and enables storage of all supplies in the patient room. A study in one hospital, which was subsequently confirmed in several others, showed that although the number of nonnursing personnel increased, the same quality of patient care had been provided with a 14 percent reduction in total labor.[26]

Management engineering provides a significant set of management tools; the future of health care management will require their application.

NOTES

1. G. Salvendy, *Handbook of Industrial Engineering* (New York: John Wiley & Sons, Inc., 1982).

2. Ibid.

3. Ibid.

4. H.E. Smalley and J.R. Freeman, *Hospital Management Engineering: A Guide to the Improvement of Hospital*

Management Systems (Englewood Cliffs, NJ: Prentice-Hall, Inc., 1982).

5. K.G. Barscht, et al., *Hospital Staffing Methodology Manuals* (Ann Arbor, MI: Community Systems Foundation, rev. ed., 1968).

6. N.H. Berg, Medical Center Applies Financial Strategies to Renovation Project, *Hospitals* 53, February (1979).

7. S.P. Gray and W. Steffy, *Hospital Cost Containment through Productivity Management* (New York: Van Nostrand Reinhold Co., 1983).

8. American Hospital Association, *Management of Hospital Employee Productivity: An Introductory Handbook* (Chicago: American Hospital Association, 1973), 1.

9. Arthur Andersen & Co. and the American College of Hospital Administrators, *Health Care in the 1990s: Trends and Strategies* (1984).

10. K.G. Bartscht, Productivity Management: Integral Element in the Management Process, *Health Care Systems* (Newsletter of The Hospital Management Systems Society) 15, May-June (1976): 3.

11. American Hospital Association, *Management Engineering for Hospitals* (Chicago: American Hospital Association, 1970), 13.

12. Chi Systems, Inc., *CHIMIS, A Management Information System* (Ann Arbor, MI: Chi Systems, Inc.).

13. Ibid.

14. D.D. Rutstein, *Blueprint for Medical Care* (Cambridge: MIT Press, 1974).

15. L. Urdang, ed., *Random House Dictionary of the English Language, College Edition* (New York: Random House, 1968), 1080.

16. W.J. Gavett, *Production and Operations Management* (New York: Harcourt, Brace & World, Inc., 1968).

17. H. Weiner, *The Human Use of Human Beings* (Boston: Houghton Mifflin Co., 1950).

18. R.A. Johnson, F.E. Kast, and J.E. Rosenzweig, *Theory and Management of Systems* (New York: McGraw-Hill, 1963).

19. Chi Systems, Inc., *A Proposal to Develop and Implement an Innovative Quality-Productivity Management Program to Blue Cross of Greater Philadelphia, Pennsylvania for Graduate Hospital of The University of Pennsylvania, Philadelphia, Pennsylvania* (Ann Arbor, Mich.: Chi Systems, Inc., 1976), 11.

20. R.J. Coffey, Preadmission Testing of Hospitalized Patients and Its Relationship to Length of Stay (Ph.D. diss., University of Michigan, 1975).

21. D.M. Warner, Preliminary Analysis of Benefits of Preadmission Tested (PAT) Patients (Unpublished paper, University of Michigan, September 26, 1972).

22. E.L. Grant, and G.W. Ireson, *Principles of Engineering Economy*, 5th ed. (New York: The Ronald Press Co., 1970).

23. Comptroller General of the United States, *Study of Health Facilities Construction Cost, Report to Congress* (Washington, DC: U.S. Government Printing Office, November 20, 1972).

24. K.G. Bartscht, An Analytic Approach to Nursing Scheduling, *Hospital Topics* September (1963).

25. D.D. Rutstein, *Blueprint for Medical Care*.

26. Comptroller General, *Study of Health Facilities*.

KARL G. BARTSCHT, MSE (IE), FAAHC, has planned, designed, and managed health systems since 1961. He is presently CEO of The Chi Group, Inc., and its affiliated companies: Chi Systems Inc., Michigan Health Systems, and International Health Care Management, Inc.

At Chi Systems, Mr. Bartscht has directed the development of long-range strategic plans and implementation strategies for numerous health care institutions. His expertise includes strategies for minimizing institutional life-cycle costs through evaluation of the trade-offs between capital investment and reduced operating costs.

Mr. Bartscht also serves as chief executive officer of Michigan Health Systems, Inc. (MHS), a for-profit organization formed by Chi Systems and a number of Michigan not-for-profit hospitals. MHS has developed networks for the sharing of services among cooperating institutions, distribution of MHS products, and establishment of competitive strategies to improve market position and revenue generation for network participants. International Health Care Management, Inc., is a management company for 18 nursing homes with 2,700 beds.

Consulting assistance has been provided by Mr. Bartscht for some of the nation's largest health care organizations, as well as for the U.S. and Canadian governments.

In addition, Mr. Bartscht has been extremely active in research and development efforts, including the development of computerized financial planning models; the design of planning/marketing databases; development, design, construction, and operation of a prototype nursing station; design of burn care units; design of patient scheduling systems; development of hospital staffing methodologies; and development of methodologies for planning and evaluating departmental space requirements.

Mr. Bartscht is publisher of two monthly professional journals: *Health Care Strategic Management*, which deals with the full range of strategic planning issues facing today's health care organizations, and *Hospital Materials Management*, a journal of health care materials management.

Chapter 26

Marketing Health Care Services

Roberta N. Clarke

The future role of marketing in health care is in question. Some experts believe that marketing, as it has been practiced in the past, with a heavy consumer focus, will disappear. In its place, there may be an emphasis on industrial marketing.[1,2] In contrast, some predict an even greater effort will be directed toward consumer marketing.[3] This is predicated upon the expectation that previously nonexistent provider information, detailing patient satisfaction and clinical outcome results, will become available to consumers, allowing them even greater and more informed choice than before.

Then again, a common and possibly not unfounded fear voiced by the public, by clinicians, and by the business community following the nation's first attempt at health reform, is that consumers will suffer from significantly lessened rather than greater choice with regard to their health care. Fears of poorer access, of restricted competition, and ultimately of the development of a single payor system in the United States lead many to believe that consumers will slowly see their ability to choose their provider organization, their physicians, and their benefit package dissipate.

MARKETING MISSION AND OBJECTIVES

It is no wonder that the function of health care marketing in the future is difficult to define. With the possible move toward a predominantly managed care environment, the traditional mission and objectives for marketing have been turned upside down. While the majority of health care marketing efforts historically have attempted to increase the volume and usage of hospitals, medical practices, nursing homes, and other medical providers, the future objectives of most health care providers will sometimes be directed toward minimizing volume or use and, as a result, cost.

Success may no longer be defined by high occupancy rates and a high volume of procedures, but by keeping the cost of "covered lives" low. As managed care organizations transfer the capitated risk for patients onto the providers with whom they contract, these providers will be asked to assume a "womb to tomb" approach to caring for patients. For these contracted providers, marketing can then be applied to a variety of tasks, from marketing patient compliant behav-

473

ior (encouraging patients to follow through with all their physicians' instructions with regard to medications, exercise, life style, and so on) to educating patients regarding when they should forego seeing the physician and just live with their symptoms.

Volume will continue to be an objective for health care marketers. Managed care organizations will continue to look to increase the size of their memberships. Hospitals will, after downsizing if necessary, aim to maintain a high occupancy level, in order to cover their fixed costs. In order to maintain an acceptable level of quality in performing certain surgical and other procedures, providers will seek to attract a sufficient quantity of patients. However, anyone thinking that the marketing objectives of a health care organization can be defined as simply seeking to increase volume will find that they have underestimated the complexity of the new health care marketplace.

One of the tasks, then, of the marketing function is to carefully define the full range of objectives toward which it must work. A health maintenance organization (HMO) must simultaneously seek a high volume of membership while encouraging a low volume of usage. Even this is simplistic, however. High volume in preventive care and early disease diagnosis must be encouraged while certain nonacute symptomatic visits are likely to be discouraged. Each of these objectives may require a different marketing strategy.

DEFINING THE COMPETITION

The same complexity that leads to multiple marketing missions and objectives also requires a more systematic and sophisticated approach to defining the competition. Previously, a hospital could define other hospitals as its competitors; nursing homes competed with other nursing homes. There was some overlap between types of providers: an inpatient psychiatric unit of an acute care hospital might have competed with a freestanding psychiatric hospital; physical therapists, chiropractors, and orthopedic surgeons

might all have competed for the same patient with chronic acute low back pain.

However, the near future holds the promise of far more confusion in identifying the competition. The vertical integration of a variety of health care organizations into systems can result in one's customer becoming one's competitor. For example, an HMO with which your hospital used to contract now contracts in the same service area instead with a competing hospital; the organization you used to consider to be a friend, or, more appropriately, a customer, is now a foe and competitor. Yet to launch a marketing offensive against that HMO might not be wise because it might once again contract with your hospital in the future, since few health care vertical integration relationships specify exclusivity; i.e., the relationship of the HMO with the competing hospital does not prevent it from once again developing a relationship with your hospital as well.

Alternatively, organizations that were once ardent competitors may become part of the same system and thus expected to complement each other rather than compete. Even more extreme a competitive change is the merging of two or more former competitors; examples of these mergers abound as health care providers conclude, at least for the time being, that size, geographic coverage, and service coverage make them more marketable. In the long term this may not hold true, particularly if enough hospitals and providers in a network are not high in quality, and thus, potential customers elect other networks. Many networks may be trading away long-term marketability for short-term assumed economies of scale. The wisdom of this assumption also remains to be proven. The economies of scale that a number of merged health care organizations have expected have not always materialized in the basic services they provide. The heavy cross-functional dependence of medical specialties and services, for example, prevented two hospitals that had formally merged from eliminating these specialties from one hospital and placing them solely in the other. Both hospitals needed infectious disease, nephrology, endocrinology, psychiatric and substance abuse, ENT, and other consults and related diagnostic and treatment capabilities in-house for their in-patients. The inconvenience, cost, and possible clinical repercussions of having to move a pa-tient from one hospital to the other for a specific test for which the diagnostic equipment was not available in the first prevented the hospitals from eliminating the services as they had initially planned. This scenario has been repeated around the country.

The more common result of hospital mergers has been to essentially eliminate one of the hos-pitals as an acute care hospital, transitioning them into substance abuse centers, rehabilitation providers, walk-in facilities, chronic care cen-ters, congregate living quarters for the elderly, housing centers for needy women and infants, etc. These are valuable services, for which there may be more demand than for the acute care ser-vices that the hospital facility used to provide. However, this must be recognized not so much as merging with the competition as it is eliminat-ing the competition. It is the weakest hospitals that have been transitioned into other nonacute uses, while the stronger hospitals with which they merged remain in the acute care business. The mergers of hospitals with more equal status is less likely to result in one of them closing; the issue yet to be proven is that there are significant economies of scale to be achieved when these hospitals both continue to operate as acute care facilities.

Mergers outside of the health care industry may give us a glimpse of the future. The high flying mergers and acquisitions period, which characterized the 1980s in the general commer-cial sector, within a decade led to a less than ex-citing and sometimes traumatic period of dives-titures and fraudulent conveyances.[4] Businesses that had merged later found that the expected gains from the mergers were not to be found. No one yet knows if the health care industry will exhibit the same cycle of merger followed by di-vestiture as did the commercial sector. The rush of health care organizations to merge, network, integrate, or somehow become part of a system

has distracted them for the moment from fully assessing the benefit of such arrangements. One thing is already clear: these arrangements do not necessarily guarantee an increased flow of pa-tients and/or members. There are still excess beds, in specific areas excess physicians, and, as a result, organizations will still have to compete for patients and members.

Until provider networks become more stable, the naming of one's competitors may be possible only on a short-term basis. A competitor may be defined as any organization that lessens the like-lihood of your organization achieving its desired marketing exchange. The formation of inte-grated systems expands those included in this definition as competitors. Moreover, the uncer-tainty of future membership in these systems makes it unclear who may be a current competi-tor but a future collaborator. This makes it diffi-cult to invest in competitive positioning strate-gies or to develop strengths and competencies based on one's competitors' strengths and weak-nesses.

INDUSTRIAL MARKETING

The need to market to businesses and organi-zations, referred to as industrial or business-to-business marketing, will remain as strong as or stronger than it was before. Whether the target market consists of employers, the government, insurers, alliances, or managed care organiza-tions, the nature of industrial marketing remains the same: marketers will have to be skilled in or-ganizational analysis in order to understand to whom to sell and what to sell. Failing to identify the decision-making unit or buying center, as it is often referred to in an industrial marketing set-ting, is likely to result in unsuccessful marketing efforts. This means knowing who within the or-ganization plays the roles of initiator, influencer, decider, purchaser, and user.

For example, historically, pharmaceutical companies hired detail salespeople to sell exist-ing and new drugs to physicians, who would then prescribe or recommend them to their pa-tients. In this scenario, the physician was the decider and the patient was the user (and often the purchaser as well). Increasingly, however, organizational health care providers such as hospitals and managed care organizations have created formularies that determine which drugs their physicians may prescribe, based on their determination of cost and efficacy. The individuals who select drugs for the formularies (consisting of infectious disease physicians, pharmacists, quality assurance nurses, and so on) are now the initial deciders. The practicing physician can decide only within the limited set of formulary-approved drugs. A pharmaceutical company that continued to sell only to physicians and did not attempt to address the formularies would stand a good chance of unnecessarily losing significant business. Such activity would reflect a failure to comprehend the changing nature of this particular buying center or decision-making unit.

Organizational buyers are fewer in number than are consumers (individual buyers) but represent larger overall volumes of purchases; e.g., a physician can sell more strep test services to an HMO than to an individual consumer or family within one year. Therefore, because of the smaller numbers of industrial buyers, the investment in analyzing their buying center behavior may be less while resulting in greater payoff because these buyers have the potential for greater purchase volumes. This analysis may come in at least two forms. One is to perform "snowball" research within the target organization; this entails speaking to the individuals within the organization thought to be involved in the purchase and asking them to identify all others within the organization who might also influence the particular purchase. The analysis proceeds by following up on all names given, determining the role each individual plays, and soliciting more names and identification of roles until no new names are given. The sum of this type of information usually allows the marketer to conclude who plays what roles in the decision-making unit/buying center.

The other most common source of information that may help in organizational analysis is focus group research. This would usually be done across a number of similar organizations as opposed to within merely one organization. For example, a medical software company that had traditionally sold to the hospital market was planning in 1994 to enter the managed care market with a new piece of software. Within the hospital market, the company knew that the decider was most often the planner. However, within the managed care market, they were uncertain to whom they should target their promotion and personal selling, given that the title "planner" was not a common one in most HMOs and preferred provider organizations (PPOs). Therefore, the company held six focus groups with a variety of people in different jobs at a number of managed care organizations in order to assess who would be the likeliest deciders and influencers in the purchase of this new product.

One interesting trend to note is the expansion of the marketing of certain health care products beyond traditional organizational buyers to include consumers. The reclassification of certain previously ethical drugs (those that consumers could buy only with a prescription from a physician) to OTC (over-the-counter or available without a prescription) status is one example. Others can be found in mail order catalogues such as *Comfortably Yours* or *Self-Care*, which carry products, such as special chairs for arthritic patients, to be sold directly to the consumer, which used to be available only through specialty retailers or other organizational sellers. This calls for some marketers whose expertise had in the past been limited only to organizational selling to now learn how to market directly to consumers.

DERIVED DEMAND

The belief on the part of many marketers that consumer marketing will not require much attention in the coming years does not take into account derived demand. As an example, consider a hospital that is trying to convince the management of an HMO new to the area that it should be the HMO's primary hospital for inpatient and outpatient admissions. The HMO will be influenced by the hospital's willingness to negotiate on price, by the extent to which it can provide care for the full range of medical problems that HMO members will have, and so on. However, one key consideration is the desirability of the hospital to potential HMO members. If the hospital as the HMO's primary hospital is considered unacceptable by potential HMO members, then the HMO itself will be considered a less attractive health plan and will have difficulty enrolling members. The HMO derives its demand in part from the attractiveness of the hospital(s) to which it admits, as well as from the physicians who are on its panel.

The essence of derived demand is a two-stage marketing process. The marketer must develop a set of products and services to appeal not merely to the immediate customer but to the customer of the immediate customer. A large medical group practice could make itself attractive to a managed care organization by agreeing to significant discounts. To achieve the low costs necessary to give these discounts, however, the medical group might deny quick access to all but the sickest patients. While the discounts initially may be appealing to the managed care organization, the lack of access, which would soon become apparent to the patients, would make the medical practice unattractive to them and would steer them away from this practice in future enrollment periods. As a result, the managed care organization would derive little long-term demand from consumers through contracting with this practice. Ultimately, with little derived demand, this practice would become unattractive to the managed care organization.

From a marketer's perspective, with the right information available, derived demand offers an opportunity to influence industrial buyer behavior. Any health care provider (of significant size) that can produce credible market research establishing consumer preference for its services within its target market area is in a good position to negotiate with managed care organizations; the stated consumer preference establishes that the provider can bring to the managed care organization derived demand for its services. Similarly, managed care organizations (at least those that are well managed) do their own consumer preference research to establish which providers are sufficiently attractive to consumers that their presence on the managed care provider list overwhelms the need for a significant discount from them.

The key again to utilizing derived demand is information: market research on consumer preferences. However, the relatively unsophisticated market research that has characterized health care marketing efforts will not uncover derived demand very well. Asking consumers if they would prefer hospital A to hospital B may establish a preference for one over the other but does not assess the trade-off that consumers might be willing to make, accepting the less preferred provider for a specified dollar lower premium or more convenient location. To capture this level of information, one probably would wish to do trade-off analysis. As a market research methodology, this is commonly called *conjoint measurement*. The methodology requires the identification of those variables that appear most likely to affect a buyer's purchase decision (in a specific, not generic, type of purchase situation). These are likely to include variables wherein the attractiveness to the consumer can be measured at different levels, such as a $3.00 vs. $5.00 vs. $10.00 co-pay per visit. Each of the variables, at different levels, is combined with other variables and is presented as a package to the consumer interviewee, who is asked to assess the attractiveness of the overall package. For example, a shortened version of two packages for an HMO might be:

Option A	*Option B*
$3.00 co-pay	$10.00 co-pay
primary care visits with nurse-practitioner	primary care visits with a physician
acute illness appointments available within 48 hours	acute illness appointments available within 24 hours
admits to most preferred hospital in the area	admits to moderately preferred hospital in the area

The consumer is asked to rate the preferability of a large number of these packages. Using an algorithm, conjoint analysis can then determine which variables at which levels prove to be most attractive to the consumer and when they are willing to trade off one desirable variable for another. While most health care organizations will not have the capability to carry out this type of market research in-house, qualified market research firms should be able to perform this. Over time, this may become one of the tools that health care marketers will add to their expected set of skills.

Some network managers have failed to take derived demand into account. The natural tendency among some has been to put together the lowest cost hospitals and practices; this may mean that no tertiary care facilities are on the provider list, nor the highly popular local women's health center, nor a specialty children's hospital, and so on. The network managers' assumptions underlying this choice of providers is that low cost will outweigh all other considerations and, for some, as a conjoint analysis could probably show, it will. However, for many potential members, cost is secondary to access to preferred providers. Moreover, even for those for whom cost is the primary concern, if they find, once in the network, that they are unhappy with quality, as they perceive it, they are likely at the next enrollment period to search out another network or managed care organization, even at a slightly greater cost. Failure to consider derived demand may work in the short run but is likely to create higher turnover of customers in the long run.

CONSUMER CHOICE AND PURCHASE BEHAVIOR

Consumer choice and purchase behavior can be expected to change based on the following:

The Promise of Increased Information Availability

Government-based health reform proposals have included in them provisions for a National Health Board collecting and presumably distributing, to the public, information on the providers in their area. Even prior to government reform, employers were beginning to collect information that they could share with their employees. For example, a *Wall Street Journal* article of October 8, 1993[5] reported that three large employers (GTE, Digital Equipment, and Xerox) were surveying a sizable sample of their employees regarding their satisfaction with their health care providers, including managed care organizations, and were going to report back the results to all geographically relevant employees. This "report card" on health care providers and managed care organizations would then presumably allow employees to compare these organizations intelligently and make informed choices.

From a marketing and consumer behavior perspective, the implications are enormous. Most annual health care enrollment or purchase behavior historically has been characterized by the dissonance attribution model of consumer behavior. Under this model, consumers make a high involvement (i.e., very important) decision with very little information. To assure themselves that they are not making the wrong decision, they often choose what they perceive to be the safe choice: the most well-known organization or the organization recommended by the benefits clerk (the most immediately available expert when one might be enrolling in a health plan at work), or the organization in which they have already been enrolled, where the feeling of safety is based on personal experience. Rarely have consumers incorporated valid, objective, and comprehensive provider and insurance carrier information into the consumer decision-making process,[6] in no small part because the information was not available.

However, the advent of the new promised information on health care providers and carriers suggests that a far larger portion of the population will behave, or at least try to behave, according to the learning model. This consumer behavior model fits far better with the scenarios laid out by the classic economists, who assume that all purchase behavior is information based, and allow consumers to compare and contrast purchase alternatives, form intelligent opinions regarding which alternatives are preferable, and purchase based on these informed opinions. For those individuals capable of analyzing somewhat complex information, the option to behave according to the learning model may now be available. Marketers should be sensitive to their desire for data, and should constantly be attuned to what the data say about the quality of the organization's health services and related services. For the marketer, the data should be a welcome addition (if it does not already exist) to the tools used for continuous quality improvement. For learning model buyers (assuming they trust the quality and coverage of the data), the data will speak for itself.

However, much depends, not only upon the availability of the data, but upon its integrity and validity. It is not clear that some of the attributes important to the consumer can be easily measured. The denial of access to a specialist when it is necessary is difficult to measure, for example. If consumer self-reports are relied upon, it is to be expected that some of the reports of needing to see a specialist may be inflated; patients may think they need a specialist when in fact it is not necessary. The reporting organization, on the other hand, has the incentive to downplay the number of reports of denied access to specialists. The task of measuring a void, of measuring what did not happen, is usually more difficult than measuring what did happen.

The integrity of the data also may be challenged by inappropriately aggregating it. For example, services of variable quality are provided by health care providers of all kinds. An aggregation or collapsing of the data to simplify or make it easier for everyone to use (i.e., some of the consumers will report excellent experiences while others will report terrible experiences, which could average out to mediocre experiences, without noting the extremes) could easily mislead those who wish to and are capable of utilizing the data. A bimodal distribution of satisfaction ratings could hide the high level of dissatisfaction on the low end through the reporting of means or medians. In health care reform, particularly with state purchasing cooperative board members that may know little about health care, the ability to promulgate objective information may be difficult.

Moreover, some marketers might find themselves under pressure to portray their health care organization in the best possible light using the data, even if that portrayal is misleading. It is not unreasonable to expect a scenario in which the marketer takes the single best rating or set of ratings and positions the organization on that one rating or set while ignoring the remaining ratings. For example, a hospital might receive very high ratings on nursing care while receiving average or below ratings on physical plant, having up-to-date diagnostic equipment, having a wide array of specialists, and on providing coordinated care. The hospital management, in the interests of best representing the hospital, might (not unreasonably) then advertise that their hospital provides some of the best nursing care in the area.

The danger, from a policy perspective, is that many consumers will rely upon the advertisements, which appear to represent predigested information, rather than upon the full body of information available. However, few advertisements are likely to provide the information that negatively portrays the organization; the job of advertising is generally construed to be to sell the organization, not to demarket it. Therefore, we can expect a biased presentation of the data by health care organizations; the subjugation of available and/or required data from informing the consumer to selling the consumer has been a common practice in other industries and can be expected in ours as the government, employers, or other outside bodies require the collection of an outcome and satisfaction database. And while the consumer may wish to act by the learning model and use the collected data, the act of analyzing data is foreign to most people. The natural tendency is to substitute the predigested data, as presented in advertising form, and to feel as if one were acting by learning model, when in fact one is being misled to consider only the most positive data about the organization.

Moreover, it is not yet reasonable to assume that the relevant data will be available. One of the big problems in reporting customer quality perceptions and satisfaction data is the failure of senior management to budget for the measurement of the data.[7] New standards by the government, by alliances, or by employers may require that such data be produced, thereby forcing health care organizations to budget for the collection of the data. Even then, because this is relatively new for most health care organizations, it is not clear that the data measures will be standardized from organization to organization. What one hospital labels as a condition leading to high consumer satisfaction (let us say, a one-hour wait in the emergency room) might be labeled as unacceptable by another hospital. This will make it even more difficult for the consumer capable of analyzing data to intelligently compare and contract health care organizations.

As a result, the dissonance attribution model is likely to remain the predominant model of consumer behavior as it is in many other industries, because most people either do not have the capacity or the desire to wade through the data and turn it into usable information or they do not trust the integrity of the data. (The people who are inclined and capable of doing so are the same type of people who read *Consumer Reports* and seek out data provided by the National Highway Traffic Safety Administration when buying a car. However, the health care industry does not yet have an independent unbiased agency that can collect the data, objectively analyze it, and present it in a trustworthy predigested format.)

Dissonance attribution buyers still will look for the safe choice. Again, however, the availability of the new data will provide marketers with new ways to portray their organizations as safe or high quality. We can expect to see, as we have in other industries, a health care organization latch onto the one piece of data that suggests that this organization is best at what it does. An HMO that is rated in publicly available information as providing the quickest access to physician appointments will no doubt find it to its advantage to promote this fact, hoping that the consumer will generalize this best-of-service

rating to other service aspects of the HMO. What the HMO will not say, of course, is that it received low ratings on its cliniclike atmosphere and on its resistance to refer members to specialty physicians. Unfortunately, dissonance attribution buyers are unlikely to wade through the data that might tell them that the HMO excels in only one area while falling deficient in others.

Universal Coverage

Formerly, many consumers felt locked into their health insurance or managed care organization for fear that a pre-existing condition might preclude them from switching to a different provider organization. The promise of universal coverage is that consumers will be able to switch at will, from one re-enrollment period to the next, without fear of being denied access to health coverage. As a result, some consumers who have previously appeared to be highly brand loyal, staying enrolled with the same organization for many years, may in the future take on the appearance of novelty seekers, switching to new providers on an annual basis. At the very least, we can expect to see more switching in consumer purchase behavior because what had appeared to be loyalty to and satisfaction with a health care provider or plan may merely have been fear of leaving. The ability of consumers to switch from one plan to another without penalty would seem to provide health plans with an additional incentive to keep their members satisfied and their marketers with an additional task to maintain a high enrollment level. This also will produce more adverse selection as consumers with specific illnesses switch to other plans if they learn that their plan does not have the best specialist, for example, for their illness.

Historically, the marketing efforts of health care providers, health insurance, and health maintenance plans have appeared more intent on attracting patients, customers, and members than on retaining them. Hospitals, and medical group practices that have formally engaged in marketing, have relied heavily on tactics such as promotion and advertising, to the detriment of the more strategic functions of marketing. Insurers and health maintenance plans have done the same, with an additionally heavy use of sales forces to sell the product. However, the increasing ability of consumers to switch health plans and providers will challenge health care organizations to find new ways to retain patients and members. No amount of advertising, promotion, and selling can retain a customer who is unhappy with a service; promoting great nursing care or short waits, when the patient's experience suggests that basic medical care is nonempathetic and abruptly delivered, will not counteract the patient's own experience. The focus of marketing efforts, if retention is the goal, shifts to providing visibly good service quality.

Service marketers and academics in the last ten years have been trying to measure and quantify service quality. Parasuraman et al. devised a now well-accepted model of service quality,[8] which has been applied to health care settings with mixed results.[9,10] While this model, called the SERVQUAL instrument, may not apply fully to health care settings as it was developed, over time it is likely to be modified to better fit health care consumer behavior. It measures constructs such as reliability, responsibility, tangibles, assurance, and empathy. Once its measures are better related to health care consumers' satisfaction, we can expect marketers to rely on it and on other validated measures of customer-defined quality in their search for ways to retain customers.

Greater Number of Health Plans from Which To Choose

If health reform takes the format initially suggested, consumers may be able to choose from among all the health plans approved by their regional health alliance. This could number in the tens of health plans. In contrast, many employers have in the past limited the number of options they made available to their employees. Few employees had the luxury of choosing between ten or more health plans. The increased number of choices may have the same initial effect on consumers that universal coverage is expected to have: consumers who engage in higher levels of

switching behavior. Because previous behavior that may have been attributed to brand loyalty and satisfaction may merely have been due to limited choice, if a wider array of choices are available, consumers may engage in greater trial behavior in order to try out their new choices. However, since the choice of health plan is a high involvement decision, the consumer will have to be convinced, through advertising, personal selling, word of mouth, or some other form of promotion, that newly available health plans are safe choices.

Increasingly Standardized Benefit Packages

If the government mandates relatively standardized benefits packages for approved health plans, then consumers seeking to find the points of differentiation between plans will have to rely more heavily on satisfaction and service attributes, location of physicians and facilities, and other factors that the government cannot standardize. Again, the implications for marketers are that they must attend to those areas where they can effectively differentiate themselves.

One of the easiest areas of differentiation conceptually is in pricing. It is fairly simple to differentiate one's plan as the lowest priced plan. Extensive advertising, promotion, and education are not necessary to demonstrate a lower, i.e., more attractive, price. However, the ability to maintain a competitively low price is dependent upon having a low cost structure. And if a low cost structure is due not to significant re-engineering of the service process so as to continue to deliver a consumer-perceived high quality of service, but rather is due to denial of access to services, long waits, and so on, differentiation on that basis will prove to be advantageous only in the short run as members dissatisfied with the level and quality of service opt to join a competing plan in the next re-enrollment period.

However, even price differentiation may be more difficult in the future. While Alain Enthoven[11] and the Jackson Hole Group[12] (whose recommendations were the basis for the initial health reforms) fully support price competition, although challenging the value of service and product differentiation, it appears that there is a momentum growing to install price controls that would limit the ability of organizations to differentiate on the basis of price. The use of price controls has met with resistance by the many professionals (including Alain Enthoven) that have constructed managed care behavior on the ability of market forces to work.

The initial draft of the health reform plan stated that providers may not charge or collect more than the fees approved by the regional health alliance. In addition, the alliances can choose not to offer any plan whose premium exceeds the average plan premium by more than 20 percent. For all intents and purposes, this appears to be price setting, an action that makes differentiation on the basis of price difficult if not impossible. In addition, from a marketing standpoint, the inability to differentiate on price means that price sensitive segments are denied the choice of buying less service for less money; conversely, price insensitive segments are denied the choice of buying more and paying more for the choice. Also, true innovation entailing differing prices is hampered; the result is that the ability of organizations to differentiate themselves is lessened and consumer choice is lessened.

This one-product-serves-all approach is anathema to the concept of customer-responsive marketing. It denies the organization the ability to segment the market, develop a product, package, or set of services that meets particularly well the needs and wants of a specific segment, and to differentiate itself from its competitors. While it is not clear that this is what the health reform policy makers envision or want, the attempt to standardize the benefit package and the price does in fact leave health care providers at risk of assuming the same mentality that public utilities traditionally manifested, the here-it-is-take-it-or-leave-it attitude toward the marketplace.

Given the possibility that the same efforts to standardize the benefits package and price will be applied to promotion, as the initial discussions of health reform suggest, health plans will find the arena within which they must compete limited to areas such as customer service, location, and distribution/access issues. Location is the most obvious of the issues to address; physician practices, hospitals, outpatient facilities, etc. have known addresses. Choices have been or will be made regarding geographic coverage relative to where the served market works and lives. Acquisition of other providers and plans has become a fast-growing mode of expanding geographically within the health care market in the recent past. Convenience of location is clearly one of the key decision factors that people use in selecting their health care providers and in the decision to stay with those providers.

RETENTION

The consumer decision to stay with a provider is most often unexamined and undervalued by those in health care marketing. When marketing is still defined too heavily as advertising, promotion, personal selling, and other efforts designed to encourage trial, as stated before, strategies to encourage retention receive little attention. Yet a well known American Management Association study, since replicated by many others, points to the conclusion that it costs five times as much to capture a new customer as to keep an existing one. Unfortunately, most health care organizations still define marketing as encouraging trial (capturing new patients or members) rather than retention. This is not a wise choice fiscally, given the higher cost of attracting a new customer, nor in light of the standardization of health benefit package, price, and possibly promotion that is anticipated, which will make it all the more expensive to find ways to differentiate one's offering to patients unfamiliar with one's organization.

Customer service and distribution/access strategies do address the retention needs of an organization. Customer service—and a variety of services marketing issues, such as managing the service process experience so that the customer can project a positive outcome based on a positive process experience—has become a major focus of total quality management (TQM) efforts. Most larger health care organizations have instituted TQM, CQI, or some other form of patient/member-based re-engineering process management that is designed to deliver a seamless service and, if introduced to the organization correctly, to devote its efforts to building long-term relationships with its customers rather than a series of one-time transactions. The ubiquitous presence of TQM discussions in the health care field suggests that any further discussion here would be primarily repetition.

Distribution and access issues, on the other hand, are only beginning to be recognized as one of the battlefields where the fight to retain customers will be fought. The concept of access always has been a sensitive one to consumers of health care. Time access is a constant and consistent source of irritation, if not anger, in health care market research: waiting to get an appointment; waiting in the clinician's reception area for a visit, procedure, or test; and waiting to hear the results of one's tests all have caused great customer dissatisfaction and have conveyed a sense of poor service.

Given an expected movement of most of the marketplace into managed care, where one of the primary cost saving measures is based on denial of access—denial of access to one's choice of provider, denial of access to any provider of a subspecialty if the gatekeeper believes it is not necessary, denial of tests deemed to be too expensive for 98 percent of the cases with your set of symptoms, even though you may be in the 2 percent who truly needs that test in order to diagnose the clinical problem correctly—health care organizations can expect to see much higher levels of dissatisfaction stemming from perceived (or real) access problems.

Physicians too have become increasingly sensitive and vocal about denial of access. In greater numbers they are noting, to their patients and the press, the barriers presented by the managed care gatekeepers whose job it is to assess the necessity of physician-recommended tests, procedures, and care supposedly in the interests of the patients. The physicians often view the gatekeepers more as denying patients needed care in the fiscal interests of the organization. In fact, the underlying philosophy of denying access may be based upon a legitimate recognition of unnecessary tests and care being delivered, driving up health care costs. However, anecdotally, the dissatisfaction with denied access stems from real fears of improper denial of access. In market research, consumers say things such as "What if an X-ray can't show the problem and I really do need an MRI? What if my physician is right and I really do need this surgery? What if my physician gives up too easily and doesn't fight for the surgery I need?" When gatekeepers are young, inexperienced, and possibly not well-trained in specialty areas, denial of access becomes not merely a marketing and retention problem, but also an ethical and clinical problem that cuts to the very heart of the health care business. If patients seek their own alternative opinions from nonnetwork doctors who disagree with the initial conclusions drawn by the patient's plan, conflict and potential liability may be produced.

With a wider range of health plan choices, with no fear of losing health coverage due to pre-existing conditions, and with the proposed availability of patient/member satisfaction ratings by health plan, consumers are far more likely than they were in the past to express their dissatisfaction with both customer service and access problems by leaving for another provider or plan. Particularly with regard to denial of access, the marketing task when addressing retention is to explain denials of access to consumers and physicians in such a way that they can appreciate and agree with the decision to deny; alternatively, it is to examine the denial process to ascertain that denials are not being made inappropriately. Where this is not done, dissatisfaction may be manifested not merely through increasing retention problems, but, at the extreme, through the filing of medical malpractice suits. Either way, the health care organization places itself in long-term fiscal jeopardy if its retention rates climb dramatically.

DATA-DRIVEN MARKETING

Marketing, correctly performed, always has been data driven (except when applied to true innovations when true believers are needed, because no data yet exist to support their contentions that they are championing a winning product, service, or idea.) Marketing strategy should emanate from analyses of the market, target segments, competition, environment, technological, regulatory, and political changes. These analyses are possible only when the appropriate data have been collected to analyze. This seems obvious, but many health care marketing functions are handicapped by having insufficient data capabilities. Employers recently have demanded, and the government in some form apparently will demand, patient satisfaction data. Efforts are already being made to collect clinical outcome data from providers and insurers. The inability to report the data to industrial buyers and to the public will greatly hamper an organization's ability to market itself.

In addition, the ability to produce data tracking your own patients or members gives your organization an advantage in segmenting your users, in identifying sources of dissatisfaction, and in identifying member trends. For example, internally produced data demonstrated for one small HMO that members who were assigned to three specific primary care physicians left the HMO at a much higher rate than the average member. Because the HMO was growing so quickly, these three physicians were always busy in spite of the fact that their service delivery style offended patients enough to cause them to leave the HMO. From a marketing perspective, it is important to identify service provider problems such as these. Member satisfaction surveys might have identified these three physicians as problems, but since their patients left the HMO, the patients might not have even been around long enough to be included in a membership study.

A marketing function that is fully supported will be given the tools with which to do its job. Insufficient data support, whether for internal data capture and analysis; for market research; or for market, competitive, and other external data analysis, cuts at the very heart of the marketing function. Health care organizations that hope to thrive in the future must expect to position marketing as not merely a creative function but as a data-driven, analytical, and strategic function.

NOTES

1. E. Berkowitz and M. Guthrie, The New Health Care Paradigm, *The Academy Bulletin* October (1993): 1–2.

2. J. Burns, Reform Seen Cutting Marketing's Role, *Modern Healthcare* 27 (1993): 33–34.

3. R. Cohen, Healthcare Reform and What It Means for Marketers, *Healthcare Marketing Report* 11 (1993): 1–4.

4. A. Michel and I. Shaked, *Takeover Madness: Corporate America Fights Back* (New York: John Wiley & Sons, Inc., 1986).

5. R. Winslow, Three Big Firms Survey Workers To Evaluate, Improve Health Care, *Wall Street Journal* October 8 (1993): B3.

6. H. Smith and R. Rogers, Factors Influencing Consumers' Selection of Health Insurance Carriers, *Journal of Health Care Marketing* December (1986): 86–98.

7. A. Woodside, What is Quality and How Much Does It Really Matter? *Journal of Health Care Marketing* 11, no. 4 (1991): 61–67.

8. A. Parasuraman et al., A Conceptual Model of Service Quality and Its Implications for Future Research, *Journal of Marketing* 49, no. 2 (1985): 41–50.

9. R. Shewchuk et al., In Search of Service Quality Measures: Some Questions Regarding Psychometric Properties, *Health Services Management Research* 4, no. 1 (1991): 65–75.

10. D. Headley and S. Miller, Measuring Service Quality and Its Relationship to Future Consumer Behavior, *Journal of Health Care Marketing* 13, no. 4 (1993): 32–41.

11. A.C. Enthoven, Why Managed Care Has Failed to Contain Health Costs, *Health Affairs* (Fall 1993): 27–43.

12. P.M. Ellwood, et al., The Jackson Hole Initiatives for a Twenty-First Century American Health Care System, *Health Economics* (October 1992): 149–168.

ROBERTA N. CLARKE, DBA, Associate Professor and former Chairman of the Department of Marketing at Boston University's School of Management, is one of the leading experts in the field of health care marketing. She is the past President of the Society for Healthcare Planning and Marketing, a professional society of nearly 4,000 members affiliated with the American Hospital Association. She won the Health Care Marketer of the Year Award from the American College of Health Care Marketing in 1985, the first year it was awarded. With Philip Kotler, she co-authored *Marketing for Health Care Organizations*, considered to be the leading text in the field of health care marketing.

Professor Clarke received her MBA and Doctorate from the Harvard Graduate School of Business Administration. She is a recipient of the Boston University School of Management Broderick Prize for Excellence in Teaching. Her executive and graduate student audiences range from health care and nonprofit to high technology, communications and service industries. She has been teaching health care marketing courses at Boston University's Health Care Management Program since January 1974, which has clearly positioned her as one of the first to specialize in the field. Dr. Clarke has served on the editorial review board of the *Journal of Healthcare Marketing* since its inception and is on the editorial boards of many other health care publications.

Professor Clarke is a nationally known speaker and writer in the health care and social service fields as well as in the area of service management. She has worked extensively with hospitals, medical groups practices, HMOs, PPOs, home health agencies, physician professional associations, and many other types of health-related organizations in the U.S. and developing countries.

Part III

Health Care Provider and Delivery Systems

Chapter 27

Multiprovider Systems

Myron D. Fottler and Donna Malvey

No health care system in the world has undergone as much structural change as has that of the United States over the past three decades. It has been suggested that the extent and swiftness of structural change in U.S. hospitals are unprecedented in postindustrial society.[1] Nowhere is this change more evident than in the transition to multiprovider systems. The previous cottage industry of individual, freestanding hospitals has become a complex web of systems, alliances, and networks.

The development of hospital systems in the United States initially encompassed horizontal integration of facilities and resulted in the creation of multihospital systems that provided similar acute care services in multiple locations. More recently, expansion of system capability has occurred by way of vertical integration and diversification into activities that may or may not be related to the hospital's inpatient acute care business. This system development reflects the transformation of multiprovider systems from providers of acute care to providers that are capable of addressing a continuum of health care needs.

Given this evolution, multihospital systems have been redefined as multiprovider health care systems to incorporate structural changes in organizational arrangements and to reflect the provision of a wide range of services beyond acute hospital care. The American Hospital Association (AHA) describes a multihospital health care system as "two or more hospitals owned, leased, sponsored or contract managed by a central organization."[2] In this chapter, multiprovider health care systems (referred to as "systems") will include multihospital systems as defined according to AHA criteria, but will also cover the broader consequences of system development, including vertical integration and other diversification activities.

This chapter examines the following questions and issues:

1. How and why have multihospital health care systems evolved and changed over time?

2. How does the performance of systems compare to the performance of independent, freestanding institutions?

3. How do systems compare to nonsystem institutions in terms of specific functions such as governance, human resources, and information systems?

4. What has been the impact of horizontal and vertical integration?

5. What are the legal constraints faced by systems?

6. What managerial recommendations concerning systems can be made?

HEALTH CARE SYSTEM DEVELOPMENT

Overview

A variety of environmental forces have been identified as shaping the delivery of health care services and motivating variations in the development of hospital systems. Preeminent among these forces has been the shift from an industry providing hospital services to one that furnishes health care services. An aging population, the increasing demand for chronic care, and new technologies that support alternative delivery systems have focused attention on a broader spectrum of health care services.[3,4] Subsequent to this shift has been the recent recognition that health care is a local business and that the market for health services is local and not national in nature.[5,6] Indeed, industry performance has indicated that patients tend to feel allegiance to local hospitals and not to national hospital chains.[7] Thus, the influence of consumer choice at the local and regional level has emerged as a powerful influence in the delivery of health services.

The expansion of system capacity through horizontal integration has been declining, and this decline has been attributed primarily to economic forces. Specifically, rising health care costs, the shift to a risk-based payment system such as the prospective payment system (PPS), and other cost containment efforts and regulations have negatively influenced the horizontal growth of hospital systems. Moreover, these forces have precipitated a trend toward economic concentration, consolidation, and vertical integration.[8]

Although the economic concentration of hospitals is not a new trend and has its origins in the 1970s with the growth of investor-owned hospi-

tal systems, what is radically different is the shift toward a local and regional orientation. Risk-based payment has compelled systems to consolidate, downsize, and divest because an inventory of hospitals is no longer profitable.[9] Furthermore, government policies that, until recently, essentially subsidized hospital acquisitions through reimbursement of much of the cost of acquisition now discourage horizontal integration by limiting reimbursement of capital expenditures for investments in facilities.[10] While there has been concern that industry trends seem to be unduly influenced by financial gain, there is some optimism that emphasis on vertically integrated regional strategies will refocus attention on patients and quality of care issues.[11] What is conspicuously absent has been the goal of improving the quality or access to health services for local community residents. Yet this will be a primary focus of the U.S. health care system over the next decade. Systems may need to realign their goals to this underlying reality.

There are a diversity of arrangements that represent the configuration of U.S. hospitals, including alliances, joint ventures, federations, consortiums, networks, and systems. All of these arrangements involve partnerships and shared activities. It is expected that the system arrangement, however, will continue to predominate and ultimately represent 80 percent of all U.S. hospitals.[12]

Shortell has argued that most systems have formed as a defense against an increasingly uncertain, complex, and hostile environment.[13] The primary motivations have been to maintain or gain market share by becoming more competitive, to increase access to needed capital, to gain exposure to new ideas, and to further career development opportunities for system personnel. The primary force behind industry consolidation has been the search for economies of scale and economic gain.

Evolution of Health Care Systems

To understand the evolution of the health care systems, it is necessary to examine both the external and internal environments of hospitals.

Exhibit 27–1 summarizes the economic, political, and social variables that have influenced hospitals since the inception of Medicaid and Medicare. Beginning in the mid-1960s, a dramatic increase began to occur in the number of systems and in all ownership categories.[14] By 1980, the number of systems in all ownership categories had grown to a total of 267 systems containing 30.7 percent of all nonfederal community hospitals and 35 percent of their beds. The success and rapid expansion of horizontally integrated multihospital systems were motivated by a cost-based payment system and a price insensitive environment that encouraged and rewarded system growth. Medicare reimbursement essentially provided coverage of costs and a reasonable return on investments. Consequently, systems could purchase high-cost, inefficient hospitals in diverse locations with little risk of failure.[15,16] In addition, investor-owned systems gained access to capital markets by their ability to issue stock and used this financial resource to underwrite their acquisitions.[17]

While both investor-owned and not-for-profit systems pursued horizontal integration, their levels of economic concentration were distinct. Not-for-profit systems accumulated fewer hospitals per system and were less geographically dispersed while their investor-owned counterparts tended to be larger, more geographically dispersed, and dominated by a few large systems.[18]

Horizontally integrated systems were expected to offer hospitals the following advantages:

- increased access to capital markets
- reduction in duplication of services
- economies of scale
- improved productivity and operating efficiencies
- access to management expertise
- increased personnel benefits, including career mobility, recruitment, and retention
- improved patient access through geographical integration of various levels of care

- improvement in quality through increased volume of services for specialized personnel
- increased political power to deal with planning, regulation, and reimbursement issues

As it turns out, the only advantage that system hospitals have demonstrated is an increase in labor productivity through more efficient use of personnel, and investor-owned systems appear to maximize labor productivity more than not-for-profit systems. Because cost-based reimbursement offered few incentives to systems to operate efficiently, there were no rewards for reducing costs.[19,20,21] Instead, systems found that they were able to enhance their performance by ". . . using size and scale to drive certain economies or to respond to certain opportunities such as competitive contracting."[22] In addition, it is now thought that many of the proposed benefits of economies of scale in systems may actually be limited. Moreover, certain diseconomies of scale have been associated with extremely high corporate overhead expenditures.[23,24,25]

According to health care analysts, hospital systems, for the most part, have failed to fully integrate and have been unable to perform as systems rather than as collections of facilities.[26] It has been suggested that both vertical and horizontal integration are required for systems to truly behave as systems. Horizontal integration only represents the integration of hospital administrative services. In order for a system to be fully and functionally integrated, clinical services must be vertically integrated within the system.[27]

The absence of shared or common institutional interests may contribute to a system's inability to completely integrate. While not-for-profit systems have been more likely to select members based on commonality of missions, investor-owned systems have tended to be more influenced by existing market conditions, the local economy, and payor mix.[28,29] Furthermore, there is evidence that many hospitals have formed or joined systems to obtain access to expertise on regulatory matters and to enjoy advantages in the political environment. Affiliated

Exhibit 27–1 Environmental Factors Affecting Health Care Industry and Resulting Strategic Responses of Hospitals, by Time Period

External Economic, Political, and Social Environment	Internal Environment of Hospitals	Resulting Strategic Responses
Pre-1965		
Favorable reimbursement	Rapid growth	Expansion/growth of autonomous,
Lack of competition	Expanding technology	freestanding hospitals
Plentiful philanthropic support	Increasing personnel specialization	
Favorable political environment	Rising costs	
Minimal government regulation	Treatment of medical disease	
Public support		
1965–1983		
Substantial increase in the number of physicians	Slowing of individual growth	Consolidation of autonomous hospital systems
Increased competition	Duplication of technology	Growth of systems for the sake of growth
Decline in philanthropic support	Outdated facilities	Debt financing of acquisitions
Less favorable political environment	Increase in debt financing	Diversification
Government provides reimbursement under Medicare and Medicaid	Decline of political influence	
Increased government regulation	Excess capacity	
Aging population	Increased rate of rising costs	
Post-1983		
Continuous hostile political environment	Lower profits	Greater differentiation of system strategies
Less favorable reimbursement environment	Downsizing	Organizational restructuring
Increased business and consumer concern with health costs	Job redesign	Vertical integration
Increased price competition	Excess capacity	Local and regional system orientation
Aging population	Shift from inpatient to outpatient care	Divestiture of unwanted facilities
	Decentralized decision making	Development of continuum of care at regional/local level

hospitals have the ability to establish a political presence through name recognition, a coordinated message, and the financial ability to retain political advisors.[30,31]

The pursuit of horizontal integration by hospitals has been attributed in part to hospitals' attempts to deal with an increasingly complex and often hostile environment that created intense financial pressures and risks that threatened institutional survival.[32] System affiliation offered hospitals opportunities to reduce or diversify certain facility-specific risks. Hospitals could gain management expertise, access to capital,

and improve their overall financial status through affiliations with well-managed, financially sound institutions. However, system affiliation cannot be expected to reduce risks related to general economic conditions or the overall health care industry.[33] In terms of overall performance, system hospitals have not demonstrated any advantage over nonsystem hospitals in terms of ability to respond to changes in health care industry such as PPS.[34]

PPS has combined with rapidly rising costs and increasing price sensitivity by consumers, employers, and insurers to provide the impetus for diversification. By shifting to the hospital the financial consequences of the medical care provided in the institution, PPS has created a powerful incentive for systems to control costs and to establish interdependencies among hospitals and their physicians and a variety of other service providers and payors.[35] Because system hospital costs tended to be higher than those of nonsystem hospitals under cost-based reimbursement, systems have experienced intense financial pressures under PPS to reduce costs if they are to remain competitive. Investor-owned systems have been especially challenged because their costs were typically higher pre-PPS than either those of not-for-profit systems or freestanding hospitals.[36]

Investor-owned systems initially pursued vertical integration on a national scale, but these attempts were not very successful. Thus, these systems have shifted their vertical integration efforts to a smaller scale that includes regional and local approaches.[37] In addition, investor-owned systems have pursued strategies involving downsizing, divestiture, and consolidation. In 1987, the largest investor-owned system, Hospital Corporation of America, spun off approximately 25 percent of its hospitals and the second largest investor-owned system, Humana, reported a less than 1 percent increase in number of operating beds. Almost all investor-owned systems have sold off their European hospitals.[38,39] Some industry analysts believe that not-for-profit systems are better positioned to achieve vertical integration because, unlike their investor-owned counterparts, they are smaller in scale and less geographically dispersed.[40]

It was expected that most hospitals would be system affiliated by 1990. While that expectation has not been realized, systems continue to grow moderately and in directions other than those involving horizontal integration. Tables 27–1 and 27–2 provide descriptive information on systems during 1992. The number of systems has increased approximately 19 percent from 250 in 1985 to 309 in 1992. During 1992, there were 2,873 hospitals affiliated with systems, representing a 23 percent increase from 1985. Moreover, when comparing the number of hos-

pital beds in systems, 1992 represents a 27 percent increase over 1985. The not-for-profit systems currently represent 80 percent of systems and control almost half of all system hospitals and close to 60 percent of hospital beds in systems.

Table 27–1 shows the number of systems by source of control. Nonprofit systems continue to predominate in terms of numbers. Approximately 80 percent of systems are nonprofit (249 of 309), as compared to 18 percent that are investor-owned and 2 percent that are government-owned. Within the nonprofit category, most systems have no religious affiliation.

Table 27–2 provides a breakdown of the number of systems that own, lease, sponsor, or contract management hospitals and other providers within each of the categories identified above. Only about 20 percent of systems own, lease, sponsor, *and* contract manage (62 out of 309). The other 80 percent either own, lease, or sponsor (77 percent) *or* they only contract manage (3 percent). A comparison across the three major subcategories of systems shows 25 percent of investor-owned systems (14 of 55) manage, own, lease, and sponsor hospitals and other providers as compared to only 19 percent of not-for-profit systems (48 of 249) and none of the federal government systems. To the extent that a full range of services may be advantageous in the future, investor-owned systems may have an edge. The nonprofit systems without any religious affiliation are *least* likely to provide comprehensive services for member institutions.

Since vertical integration of multihospital systems is a relatively recent phenomenon, there is no descriptive evidence available on the extent to which systems have vertically integrated. There is also little descriptive evidence related to other diversification activities of system hospitals. Because this information is unavailable, it is impossible to assess the impact of vertical integration and diversification on system performance. Consequently, any attempts to report on performance of multihospital health care systems will be subject to these limitations.

Modern Healthcare reports that during 1992, systems enjoyed a 28 percent increase in prof-

Table 27–1 Multihospital Health Care Systems, in 1992, by Type of Organizational Control

Type of Control	Code	Number of Systems	Percent of Systems
Catholic (Roman) church-related	CC	71	23.0
Other church-related	CO	15	4.9
Other not-for-profit	NP	163	52.7
Investor-owned	IO	55	17.8
Federal government	FG	5	1.6
		309	100.0

Source: Reprinted from *The AHA Guide to the Health Care Field,* 1992 Edition, p. B3, with permission of the American Health Association, © 1992.

its.[41] What is particularly significant in their findings is that not-for-profit systems (excluding public systems) demonstrated a 39 percent increase in operating profits compared with a 2.2 percent increase for investor-owned systems.

The sharp decline in operating margins experienced by investor-owned systems is narrowing the performance gap between them and their not-for-profit counterparts. Not-for-profit systems attributed their enhanced performance to decreasing expenses, layoffs, and downsizing strategies, and increases in their investment or nonoperating income. Investor-owned systems claimed similar strategies underlying their profitability, and in addition reported achieving efficiencies through restructuring of debt, divestitures, and consolidation. In particular, these systems reported divesting health maintenance organizations (HMOs), primary care centers, insurance programs, medical supply businesses, and businesses unrelated to health care.

While the not-for-profit systems showed higher percentage increases in profits, the investor-owned systems averaged operating profits of $79.9 million compared with average profits of $44 million for nonpublic, not-for-profit systems. *Modern Healthcare* associates the difference in dollar profits with size, since the investor-owned systems participating in their survey averaged 32.2 hospitals per system compared with the not-for-profit systems averaging 6.7 hospitals per system. On a per-hospital basis, profits were higher in the nonprofit systems.[42]

In addition, *Modern Healthcare* revealed some emerging trends among systems. Increasingly, systems are becoming owners and managers of physician group practices and are purchasing rehabilitation centers. Public systems continue their downward trend, reporting losses in 1992 of $826.8 million, which is a 16.4 percent increase over losses posted for 1991. These losses appear to be attributable mainly to the poor financial performance for public systems in New York City and Los Angeles.[43]

Comprehensive Health Systems

A rapidly changing environment and the legacy of the diagnostic-related group (DRG) system and other risk-based payment methods have motivated both hospitals and physicians away from joint ventures and toward the development of fully integrated vertical networks representing comprehensive health systems. In the 1980s, hospitals and physicians formed joint ventures that typically allowed for medical care and services to be provided outside of the hospital's facility as well as outside of the traditional medical staff structure. While many of these joint ventures succeeded, there were also many notable failures.

In the 1990s, few joint ventures are being formed because they have become especially risky and expensive, and create regulatory and legal problems for providers.[44] In addition, joint

Table 27–2 Multihospital Health Care Systems in 1992, by Type of Ownership and Control

Type of Ownership	Catholic Church-Related (CC)		Other Church-Related (CO)		Total Church-Related (CC + CO)		Other Not-for-Profit (NP)		Total Not-for-Profit (CC, CO, + NP)		Investor-Owned (IO)		Federal Government		All Systems	
	No.	%	No.	%	No.	%	No.	%	No.	%	No.	%	No.	%	No.	%
Systems that only own, lease, or sponsor	56	78.9	10	66.7	66	76.7	128	78.5	194	77.9	39	70.9	5	100.0	238	77.0
Systems that only contract-manage	1	1.4	0	0.0	1	1.2	6	3.7	7	2.8	2	3.6	0	0.0	9	2.9
Systems that manage, own, lease, and sponsor	14	19.7	5	33.3	19	22.1	29	17.8	48	19.3	14	25.5	0	0.0	62	20.1
Total	71	100.0	15	100.0	86	100.0	163	100.0	249	100.0	55	100.0	5	100.0	309	100.0

Source: Reprinted from *The AHA Guide to the Health Care Field*, 1992 Edition, p. B3, with permission of the American Health Association, © 1992.

ventures are now being described as transitional organizational arrangements or intermediate steps in the process toward complete vertical integration. Pressures from changes in reimbursement and cost controls have intensified pressure on the hospitals to gain vertical control and influence over physician practice patterns.[45] Meanwhile, physicians' declining incomes and access to capital have precluded their aggressive pursuit of physician joint ventures.[46] Physicians' joint ventures also are on the wane because the economic motivations of physicians are increasingly diverging from one another as a result of changes in reimbursement, which are affecting different specialists differently.[47]

Managed care appears to be driving providers more and more toward vertical integration. It has been reported that in heavily managed care markets, providers are pursuing complete vertical integration more rapidly in order to compete effectively.[48] Managed care has eroded the patient care market for both physicians and hospitals. In addition, managed care represents intervention in day-to-day medical treatment. Physicians view this intervention as threatening to their autonomy and incomes.[49] Many independent practitioners are approaching hospitals and medical centers asking to be acquired or given employment contracts. Physicians are increasingly joining integrated health networks because they recognize that the health services market is becoming increasingly oriented toward managed care.[50] Physicians believe that hospital ownership of medical practice is a more favorable alternative to managed care because hospital ownership of medical practices can be organized under structures that allow the physician to retain some control over medical practice.[51] In many circumstances, managed care is driving physicians and hospitals to fully integrate into single structures such as physician–hospital organizations (PHOs) or foundations that can gain leverage in negotiating with managed care contracts or can achieve the ability to contract directly with employers to provide medical services. Today's hospitals and physicians are looking for more permanent and enduring vertically integrated structures to accommodate their relationships, needs, and joint activities.

Many hospital systems have been quickly moving to develop delivery systems that are capable of providing health services to a large number of people on a capitated basis. Systems have purchased medical clinics, other hospitals, and even prepaid managed care organizations. Some systems are aligning themselves with insurers in order to expand their markets. However, many systems have little experience in capitated contract arrangements.[52] In addition, investor-owned systems are seeking alliances with nonprofit systems in order to respond to the trend toward managed care. Investor-owned systems have found that they lack many of the costly services and departments, such as emergency room and obstetrics, that are needed to make them full-service organizations capable of competing for managed care contracts. Thus, they hope to acquire these costly services through affiliation with nonprofit systems. Nonprofit systems, meanwhile, are reluctant to form alliances with investor-owned systems because investor-owned systems have an image of high-cost providers and as such could negatively affect nonprofit systems in their efforts to obtain managed care contracts or in their negotiations with third-party payors. While the gap in charges is narrowing between nonprofit and investor-owned systems, the perception appears to be present among consumers, employers, and insurers that investor-owned systems are high-cost providers.[53]

While physicians are seeking integration with hospitals, most hospitals, with the exception of larger ones, have not aggressively pursued acquisition of group practices. Two-thirds of hospitals have not developed any formal affiliations with group practices. When hospitals do enter into formal affiliation arrangements with physician group practices, it is typically through an employment arrangement and not contractual.[54]

Nevertheless, it is obvious that comprehensive managed care at the local and regional levels is the wave of the future. Systems that can provide such comprehensive services and can demonstrate high quality and cost-effectiveness will be winners in the emerging health-care environment. Systems or individual providers who are unable or unwilling to move in this direction may well be among the losers over the next decade.

As noted in Exhibit 27–1, Phase 1 (pre-1965) predated the development of systems. Phase 2 (1965–1983) was a period of development and unbridled expansion of systems. Phase 3 (post-1983) began with the implementation of prospective payment, declining system profits, downsizing, and restructuring. The latter part of Phase 3 (the 1990s) is a period of reconfiguration, rebuilding, and redesign of systems. Chaos and creativity are the norms as traditional boundaries disappear and competition gives way to collaboration. The focus is now on the provision of comprehensive health services at the regional and local levels.

SYSTEM PERFORMANCE

While systems have demonstrated a continuing ability to financially outperform their nonsystem counterparts, many health care analysts believe that, other than efficiencies in labor productivity related primarily to fewer full-time equivalent employees and lower turnover, system hospitals have not demonstrated comparative advantages over nonsystem hospitals.[55,56] Furthermore, while system hospitals have greater opportunities to reduce their costs through sharing administrative services such as legal, data processing, accounting, and staffing services, the overhead costs involved in managing these and other activities have been extremely high.[57,58]

Specific financial advantages, defined by higher returns on equity, have been found to be related to system affiliation.[59] Despite the fact that system hospitals appear to be better off financially than their nonsystem counterparts, there is no evidence that system hospitals provide more services to the community or more charity care than nonsystem hospitals.[60] *Modern Healthcare* found that during 1992, investor-

owned systems reported average community benefits as 1.9 percent of their net patient revenues and average charity care expenses as 1.4 percent of their net patient revenues. Secular not-for-profit systems reported 2.6 percent of net patient revenues for average community benefits and 2 percent for average charity-care expenses. While investor-owned systems are contributing less community and charity care than secular not-for-profit systems, their contributions have actually increased over 1991 while those of the secular not-for-profit systems have remained unchanged. Unprofitable public systems continue to be the predominant underwriters of charity-care and community benefits.[61] There appears to be a negative correlation between provision of community benefits and profitability in all systems.

Investor-owned systems were clearly at a disadvantage when PPS introduced price competition because, as mentioned previously, their prices and costs of producing services were high. While investor-owned systems were more profitable pre-PPS, their profitability subsequently declined with their inability to charge higher prices.[62] One advantage investor-owned systems have not lost is a more profitable payor mix. Medicaid and Medicare represent a lower percentage of their payor mix compared with not-for-profits or nonsystem hospitals.[63] However, as the population ages, and hospitals become more dependent on Medicare, this advantage may disappear.[64]

Although certain cost-saving benefits may be derived within a system, primarily in the areas of purchasing and reduction of duplicative services, the creation and expansion of a system can also lead to increased costs. As a system increases or anticipates increasing in size, a significant amount of the system executives' time is focused on planning, policy enforcement, and related activities. There is less time available to devote to day-to-day conduct of the system's business affairs or the delivery of health services. Then the executives either try to do too much in terms of present activities and future planning or they hire new administrators to whom they delegate day-to-day operations. Quality of management may suffer and/or costs may rise. The better-performing systems keep a very tight rein on corporate staff costs.[65]

The sharing of services among system member institutions geographically situated in proximity to one another may reduce costs by avoiding or eliminating the duplication of necessary but marginally profitable (or unprofitable) services.[66] Examples include legal services, data processing, and hospital staffing services. In one study it was noted that hospital staffing costs in systems were reduced by 25 percent through the sharing of services.[67]

Table 27–3 shows median hospital profit margin by system status and bed size. Smaller hospitals are less profitable than their larger counterparts. Large, investor-owned system hospitals are the most profitable. The main factors explaining the higher profits in investor-owned system hospitals are higher prices, lower staffing levels, and lower wages.[68,69] System hospitals in general tend to be more profitable because they have a more proactive strategic orientation than do independent hospitals.[70]

In sum, there is little support for most of the alleged advantages of systems relative to their nonsystem counterparts. While systems are more profitable, they appear to provide little added value in terms of increased economic or community service benefits. Most systems have been unable to transform their objectives into reality. A large part of this may be because most systems have not behaved as systems.[71] They have not achieved their potential or demonstrated a strong competitive advantage.

DISTINGUISHING CHARACTERISTICS OF SYSTEMS

Corporate Structure

The existence of a corporate structure has been described as the most obvious characteristic distinguishing a system hospital from a freestanding institution. Systems will use an organizational structure that consists of a corporate or systemwide component and a field component of facility managers. At the institutional level, reporting relationships will differ depending on system ownership. Within investor-owned systems, the facility's chief executive officer will usually report to a corporate officer. In not-for-profit systems, the facility's chief executive officer may report to a hospital board of trustees, a corporate board of directors, or less typically to a system corporate executive.[72] With the move toward vertical integration, system organizational structure becomes even more complicated as the linkages become incorporated into the organization's structure.

As systems began to form, there were no textbook models to follow. Although the investor-owned systems had already developed a corporate structure, it was based on ownership of the majority of hospitals in the system. The not-for-profit systems created structures largely by learning as they went along.[73] As systems grew, they experienced problems with expanding corporate staffs, bureaucracy, and conflicts of interest between the corporate and field components. The potential for conflict generation in a system is enormous because the complexity of the system makes it more open to disruption. "When

---

Table 27–3 Median Hospital Operating Margin, by Bed Size and System Status, 1991

System Status	Bed Size			
	0–99	100–299	300–499	500 +
Independent hospitals	0.55	2.36	2.88	3.46
Investor-owned chain hospitals	1.46	3.09	7.16	7.40
Nonprofit chain hospitals	0.74	2.60	2.98	4.59

Source: Reprinted from *Wyeth-Ayerst Compendium of Hospital Economics* by R. Essner, p. 24, with permission of Health Learning Systems, © 1993.

you add institutions in a multi, the conflict generated is not arithmetic, it is logarithmic."[74] One study of nursing home administrators found that those who were part of systems and reported to corporate offices experienced more stress and role conflict than did their counterparts in free-standing facilities.[75] Systems require managers to have superior mediation skills in order to respond to these challenges.[76]

Governance

Governance of hospitals remains basically unchanged despite the unprecedented, rapid, and dramatic upheaval in the health care industry. For systems, the lack of development in governance is particularly problematic, since governance must occur at a variety of levels in order to meet both systemwide and institutional needs. However, the presence of multiple boards to address multiple needs often causes additional conflict, bureaucracy, and power struggles. It has been suggested that systems should recognize governance on two levels. The first is the organizational or strategic level of governance, where systemwide decisions and policies are considered. The second level refers to operational governance, which addresses local operations of institutions and should be advisory to institutional management. Since the work of system facilities depends on the degree of success achieved through operational governance, this level should be subsumed under systemwide governance.[77]

Systems have tended to rely on three models of governance. The most popular, the parent holding company model, is also the most decentralized. This model represents a systemwide governing board in addition to separate governing boards for each institution. The second model is a modified parent holding company model where there is one systemwide governing board with advisory boards substituted for those at the institutional level. These two models tend to be used by systems that represent large numbers of hospitals. The parent holding company model is more closely associated with systems

affiliated with religious organizations, while the modified parent holding company model tends to be found in investor-owned systems. The third model is the corporate model, which consists of one systemwide board with no other boards at any other level. The major advantage of this governance structure is its simplicity and clear lines of authority. This model tends to be used by systems with smaller numbers of hospitals in the system and is usually associated with not-for-profit and public systems.[78]

The type of governance model used by a system has not been found to influence strategic decision making, for which systemwide boards assume responsibility. However, in decision making at the institutional level, the type of governance model appears to be influential. The parent holding company model tends to leave hospital-level decisions to the hospital governing boards, while the modified parent holding company model seems to give all boards equal involvement in most hospital-level decisions. Meanwhile the corporate model demonstrates greater involvement by the systemwide board in hospital decisions.[79]

System governance has been recognized for its complexity by the Joint Commission on Accreditation of Healthcare Organizations (Joint Commission) primarily through changes in standards for governing boards. In 1986, the standards were upgraded to reflect the complex responsibilities that result from an increase in numbers of boards and the dynamic relationships that exist between these boards and all levels of the organization. Specifically, if there are multilevels of governance, there must be mechanisms to ensure communication and participation at all levels. In particular, there must be mechanisms to assure that medical staff will have the ability to communicate and participate at all levels of governance in matters involving patient care.[80]

Human Resources Management

Human resources management may be among the greatest challenges in multihospital health care systems. Because these systems are exceedingly complex and diverse organizational arrangements, they require significant numbers of highly skilled and specialized personnel at a variety of levels. Systems also offer opportunities not found in nonsystem hospitals. They can develop staff-sharing programs between hospitals, which contribute to reduced personnel expenses as well as provide the potential for quality improvements. In addition, access to and retention of personnel may be enhanced in systems. Name recognition often facilitates recruitment of personnel. A comprehensive personnel data bank can be compiled providing system members with a pool of qualified applicants. Systems also represent variety, mobility, and job security for employees who can move to different jobs within the system.

The ability to attract and retain personnel can be enhanced through the development of career ladders within the system. Promotions and transfers can occur without the employee exiting the system. A corporate office can also provide individual facilities with human resources expertise they would not be able to afford on an individual basis. Finally, representing large numbers of employees can assist in the development of more comprehensive and less expensive benefits packages that are attractive to both employees and the system's budget.[81]

Modern Healthcare reported that during 1992, system downsizing contributed to the increased profitability of both investor-owned and not-for-profit systems. It has been suggested that downsizing may be easier to manage in a system hospital compared with a freestanding facility because systems have more ability to move staff around within the system and better protect employees' economic security. Stability of employment at one facility within the system can provide job openings for employees displaced by staff reductions at another system facility.[82]

Employees in systems, however, do face the stress of being exposed to the effects of vertical and horizontal integration. There has been almost no research on the impact of mergers, acquisitions, and other strategies on employees, nor is there a human resources model to deal effectively with the effects of system development

on employees. Human resources managers must deal with system changes and assure that employees are recognized as assets within the system.[83]

The complexity and responsibility of managing a system are reflected in compensation for system executives. In 1989, multihospital system executives earned more than their counterparts in freestanding hospitals. Salary increases for system executives were reported to be 30 percent over the previous year, while freestanding hospitals showed only a 5 percent salary increase.[84] Systems also find advantages in reduced CEO turnover. CEOs are involved in high-risk relationships with medical staff and boards and often lose their jobs because of failing relationships. In a system, the CEO can move to another facility, and the system does not lose an important management resource.[85]

One of the major challenges for a system is aligning the interests of physicians with those of the system and promoting physician participation.[86] It has been suggested that physicians in systems may have the greatest opportunities to influence standards of care. Investor-owned systems, in particular, have been identified as promoting physician participation in governance.[87] Yet, it has also been noted that physician loyalties often are associated with the individual facility and not with the larger system. Solutions for improving physician loyalty include increasing the numbers of physician administrators within the system, increasing the numbers of physicians on corporate boards, and improving communication with physicians.[88]

However, systems may find more benefit in encouraging the development of physician multihospital organizations (PMHOs). A PMHO is a formal structure that specifies decision rights and role responsibilities of physicians within the organization. This structure guarantees to physicians a role in decision making at both the hospital and the system level. The challenge for systems then becomes how to coordinate physician and hospital decision making on system-level issues.[89]

From 1980 to 1990, the growth in system costs was dramatic, and many systems are decentralizing operations and shifting functions back to the institutional level where they appear to be less expensive. Staffing costs for systems include salaries, benefits, and purchased services for administrative employees at the system's corporate, regional, hospital, and other unit levels. Estimated staffing costs for systems for 1992 show that approximately 63 percent of expenses will be spent at the corporate and regional level. The remaining 37 percent will be spent at the local or institutional level.

Of particular interest is the finding that the biggest impact on staffing costs appears to be type of integration. Vertically integrated systems appear to be more expensive to operate in terms of staffing costs, perhaps due to the diversity of operations and the challenge of integrating these diverse functions. System staffing costs were 5.3 percent of net revenues for horizontally structured systems compared with vertically integrated systems, which are estimated to expend 6.7 percent of net revenues on systemwide staffing costs. While vertically integrated systems initially have higher staffing costs, these costs are anticipated to decline within 3 to 5 years when the benefits of vertical integration are realized.[90] Whether they do or not remains to be seen.

Type of ownership appears to have no influence on systemwide staff costs and average staff costs appear to be similar for all types of systems. The most profitable and efficient systems appear to operate with fewer people on their management staffs and pay higher than average salaries to their employees. Financially successful systems have reported spending about one-third more on human resources, planning, marketing, and public relations compared with their lower performing counterparts.[91]

In theory, these advantages should exist for all systems. In practice, many systems restrict themselves to only certain subcategories of personnel. For example, some religious-associated systems require or prefer their executives to be practicing members of the religious organization. This obviously restricts the talent pool as does the practice of paying below the market in religious systems.

In addition, the development and enforcement of appropriate standards of professional qualifications and job performance are crucial to the success of systems. The development and operation of a system is extremely complex and requires significant numbers of highly skilled and specialized personnel. The system needs to set and enforce appropriate standards of qualifications and performance and then recruit individuals who can meet these standards. If this is not done, the anticipated advantages of systems will not be achieved.

Financial Management

System hospitals vary in terms of the financial responsibilities of CEOs for capital management. CEOs of individual institutions in investor-owned systems typically have a reduced role in creating capital, since that function normally resides with corporate officers. Both investor-owned and not-for-profit systems routinely require corporate approval to make expenditures that extend beyond yearly budgets. The capital approval process may also differ according to system ownership. Investor-owned hospitals tend to rely on authorization from the corporate office and not-for-profit systems usually require approval from both the hospital level and systemwide governing boards.[92] How successfully capital is managed within the system influences the cost and pricing structure and ultimately the ability of the facility to be competitive within its own defined market segment.[93] Thus, capital allocation assumes a prominent position in system management.

Traditional capital allocation approaches that focus on discounted cash flow, net present value, and internal rate of return may be inappropriate for multihospital health care systems. For systems, shaping capital structure involves systemwide vision and integrating both local and corporate needs that will extend beyond the normal capital budget process.[94] The system confronts different facilities having different needs and facing different risks. Several facilities can be located in very distinct markets with different financial performance trends and different future potentials as well as widely diverse facility, management, and medical staff characteristics.[95] A multifactored model that incorporates varying needs and risks, and that is based on the capital asset pricing model (CAPM), can be derived to allocate capital among a variety of member institutions.[96]

Of particular importance to systems is the concept of a system-level mission fund. A member institution that is significantly subsidized by the system may be considered a mission activity in which the system allocates part of its overall system finances to continue the mission of this particular institution. It is expected that the institution would not be able to survive without this funding. As in a single institution, systems can establish allocations to mission activities based on either ongoing cash flow subsidy or on the endowment model. Often a combination approach can be employed.[97]

Perhaps the most distinctive and important economic advantage of a system in terms of its capital allocation strategy is the system's ability to minimize the amount of aggregate safety stock that is required without jeopardizing the benefits and intended purpose for maintaining this system safety stock. For systems, safety stock represents a powerful advantage that reflects a system's ability to reduce or even eliminate specific risks to facilities through diversification of risk across multiple facilities. Thus, as the number of facilities in the system increases, the importance of a single facility's performance declines, and the contribution to safety stock can also be reduced. For systems, this reduction in safety stock requirements frees up capital for allocation at other levels within the system and represents a substantial economic benefit.[98]

Systems should also focus on hospital growth pools that are similar in conceptualization to growth pools at the individual level, but include both system-level and hospital-level risk pools. After all allocations have been made, remaining capital should be assigned to this pool to provide funding for system level initiatives that may include vertical integration and other diversification activities.[99]

Because the capital allocation process in a system involves both corporate and facility participation, the process must be supported by a strong system culture; communication among all participants to the process; an incentive system that associates hospital management's compensation with both the overall performance of the system and the individual performance of the facility; appropriate management and financial systems; an effective budgeting process; and an implementation plan.[100]

Bankruptcy presents special problems for systems and their members. "When dealing with a financially troubled hospital that is part of a multihospital system, the problems seem to multiply geometrically."[101(p50)] Legal and practical problems arise from multiple boards and overlapping memberships on these boards. Fiduciary obligations of board members can conflict, especially when what is appropriate action for one institution may not be beneficial to the system. Board members with multiple loyalties can be disruptive. Furthermore, statutes and case law of a particular state may support the community or individual hospital interests over system interests.[102]

Bond rating is another important consideration for systems. Systems have earned higher bond ratings than freestanding institutions and have shown stability in ratings over time. This performance has been attributed to their ability to diversify risk and size. Rating agencies tend to measure successful systems performance by centralized operations and mechanisms for monitoring planning, budgeting, and capital expenditures of system members.[103]

Systems also have access to pooled financing that permits a hospital to use financial resources that would be otherwise unavailable. However, there can be disadvantages of this type of financing since member institutions may be required to submit their assets as collateral, and the system, overall, may find that it is subordinating long-term financial goals to strengthen the financial position of weaker member institutions.[104]

Systems have the potential to increase interest earnings through a cash sweep, which is a technique that is designed to eliminate the time lag between receiving and investing funds. It involves a daily electronic withdrawal of funds from all hospital operating accounts, and these funds are then placed into one central account where the interest begins accruing immediately. This technique allows the system to eliminate the problem of idle cash in local banks.[105]

The financial markets have appeared to favor systems as sounder risks than independent free-standing facilities. Empirical evidence indicates that systems have generally received higher credit ratings than most independent hospitals.[106] Thus, membership in a system may increase access to financial resources for its individual member institutions.

However, the advantage may prove disadvantageous to the system's more financially healthy member institutions if their assets are depleted to support the needs or excesses of the system's weaker or less responsible members. To the extent that financing is available from outside sources, the stronger facilities still may be forced to pledge or otherwise encumber their assets to support the debt-financed operations and activities of the system. The separate long-range plans and goals of stronger member institutions may be subordinated and harmed to shore up other system institutions and to honor pledges and guarantees.[107]

Financially weaker institutions within the system may incur even greater detriment if the system functions inefficiently or becomes over-leveraged. High interest, debt service costs, and fees for system corporate services may negatively affect the survival prospects of weaker institutions to a greater degree than the more stable units.

Management Innovation

The upheaval in the health care environment has created a variety of pressures for managers. Managers are expected to contain costs without jeopardizing quality of care; downsize while simultaneously increasing productivity, and maintain good relationships with medical staffs who have grown increasingly wary of management interference in patient care issues. As expecta-

tions for what managers can accomplish increase, so does the demand for managerial innovation. Given the growth of systems and the complexity of these organizations, it is imperative that these systems promote managerial innovation.

Systems have the organizational resources to encourage managerial innovation. While free-standing hospitals are connected only through ad hoc relationships, systems have the benefit of group norms and more formal relations that can assist in implementing innovation. Moreover, systems have routinized communication channels that enhance the diffusion of innovation. Mature systems, in particular, have greater chances for assuring managerial innovation. As a system matures, it recognizes the importance and value of communications and works to build channels and mechanisms that encourage the sharing of information. Mature systems also usually have a larger resource base from which to implement new programs.[108]

Technology Assessment

With the rapid increases in technology development and pressures to contain costs without decreasing quality of health services, institutions are focusing attention on evaluating new technologies. Unlike single facilities, systems must address the needs of multiple facilities that are frequently in multiple locations. Thus, making decisions on which technologies to adapt can occur at the interregional level and involve broader standards of assessment. When the organization extends beyond the local community, community standards may not be appropriate.[109]

The dilemma for systems depends on the extent of decentralization within the organization. A highly centralized system can assist individual hospitals in technology assessment, but the resulting guidelines for adopting or implementing the new technology may be inconsistent with community standards. A decentralized system, on the other hand, can allow local facilities to assess technology within the context of the facility's environment. The limitation of this approach is that it can lead to expensive duplication.

Risk Management

Systems are positioned to take advantage of new laws that regulate financing mechanisms for insurance. Increasingly, systems are obtaining liability and other insurance coverages through alternative methods of financing. In particular, risk retention groups, a financing mechanism authorized by the Federal Risk Retention Act of 1986, present systems with unique opportunities for a reliable and stable source of liability protection. These groups are essentially insurance companies formed by institutions with similar interests, such as hospitals, to provide any casualty coverage except workers' compensation. There is a requirement that all policyholders must also be stockholders. Unlike traditional insurance that must conform to regulations of each state in which it operates, risk retention groups are able to operate nationwide once licensed in one state. Another alternative to traditional insurance is captive insurance companies. These companies are organized to write coverage for only one employer or one group of employers. Seven states have currently created tax laws that would allow systems to take advantage of this arrangement.[110]

Marketing

While little is known about the practice of marketing in systems, a recent study of marketing in systems revealed minimal differences between investor-owned systems and not-for-profit systems. Differences were identified in size of marketing staff, with larger staffs found in investor-owned systems where marketing responsibilities are more likely to be specified within the formal organizational chart. The larger staffs tended to be associated with a decentralized approach to marketing. Thus not-for-profit systems, which reported smaller marketing staffs, were found to employ a more centralized reporting structure for the marketing function. Overall, however, investor-owned and not-for-profit systems demonstrated remarkable similarities in patterns of influence over marketing mix, the status of marketing information systems, and attitudes toward marketing. Explanations for these similarities include the move by not-for-profit systems to a more aggressive and bottom-line orientation, thereby making the two types of systems less distinctive.[111]

What has become evident in marketing is the recognition that most hospital markets remain local or regional in nature. Local and regional systems have demonstrated higher levels of market control in distinct areas than larger, more geographically dispersed investor-owned systems.[112] The trend toward system strategies that focus on regional and vertical integration will be expected to influence marketing efforts in systems.

Information Systems

Increasingly, systems are facing new information requirements to accommodate strategies involving downsizing, reorganization, restructuring, and divestitures as well as demands by payors for information on costs of health services. Management of information within systems must facilitate communication between a diversity of operations and across a variety of facilities.[113] In systems, the trend is toward centralizing information systems, with information systems managers reporting to either the CEO or to executive officers in charge of operations or finance. Furthermore, these managers typically face expanded responsibilities that include telephone systems, management engineering, and data communications. In addition, information systems management has increasingly become involved in the implementation of alternative delivery systems. The growth of information systems management within hospital systems reflects the growing requirements and information needs of diversification and integration strategies.[114]

Health care systems linking hospitals, physicians, insurers, employers, and others form the foundation of most health reform proposals. Shared information on health outcomes and costs of care will help to identify and encourage the most efficient forms of care. This requires the development of health information networks.[115] Such an information network would help to direct patients to the most appropriate settings and reduce redundancies.

HORIZONTAL AND VERTICAL INTEGRATION

Horizontal integration strategies dominated system development during the late 1960s through the mid-1980s and have diminished in significance with the implementation of PPS and cost reduction programs of other payors. It is expected that there will be fewer systems purchasing hospitals because of the financial disincentives and increased risk.[116] In addition, recent evidence suggests that there may actually be a saturation point for system horizontal integration and that hospital acquisition is selective. Selection factors have been shown to include market characteristics, mission compatibility, and facility management. Thus, the potential for horizontal integration as a strategy will be limited by financing mechanisms and selective acquisitions.[117]

Major trends in strategy formulation have been identified to include extensive vertical integration and diversification as well as a trend toward regionalization. Explanations for these strategies include a diffusion of risks, environmental pressures, and promotion of organizational growth in mature systems. Furthermore, it has been recognized that system strategies will be influenced by differences in size, ownership, and geographic dispersion.[118]

Pre-PPS, investor-owned systems were described in terms of their similarities. It was shown that these systems offered similar strategies, and did not differ significantly in their management of facilities or in measures of efficiency such as length of stay, bed size, and case mix.[119] However, post-PPS there has been a remarkable distinction in strategies among investor-owned systems, particularly with respect to diversification activities. They have been diversifying into a variety of businesses both related and unrelated to the hospital and appear to be deriving an increasingly large share of revenue from these activities.[120,121]

Diversification through integration of clinical services transforms a horizontally integrated system into a vertically integrated one. Vertical integration involves incorporating within the organization either stages of production (backward integration) or distribution channels (forward integration), that were formerly handled through arm's length transactions with other organizations.[122]

A vertically integrated system is described as offering ". . . a broad range of patient care and support services operated in a functionally unified manner. The range of services offered may include preacute, acute, and postacute care organized around an acute hospital. Alternatively, a delivery system might specialize in offering a range of services related solely to long-term care, mental health care, or some other specialized area."[123] The intended purpose of vertical integration is to increase the comprehensiveness and continuity of care while simultaneously controlling the channels or demand for health services. Thus, vertical integration emphasizes connecting patient services with different stages in the health services delivery process.[124]

Vertical integration can occur through a variety of arrangements. Some of these arrangements include:

- internal development of new services
- acquisition of another organization or service
- merger
- lease or sale
- franchise
- joint venture
- contractual agreements
- informal agreements or affiliations
- insurance programs[125]

While hospital systems increasingly are becoming vertically integrated, the experience is mixed.[126] Factors inhibiting vertical integration involve government scrutiny by the Federal Trade Commission (FTC) to ensure that integration does not lead to monopolistic or noncompetitive arrangements. In addition, physicians may resist vertical integration since it allows the system to channel referrals among physicians and facilities[127] and gives the system control over demand.[128] Finally, vertical integration may be complicated by the problems involved in moving sick people through a dispersed system of care. Vertical integration does not imply that all services will be offered at one site.[129]

Management implications for vertically integrated systems are as complex and diverse as the arrangements themselves. Initially, managers must ensure that the integration strategy is consistent with the mission of the system and its priorities, and that the communications structure supports the organizational changes. Capital requirements and financing must be examined for all system components with particular consideration given to financial incentives and economic benefits for these components. Furthermore, managers must realistically determine whether expertise and other resources are available to establish and maintain vertically integrated arrangements. If the system lacks the resources to achieve successful vertical integration, it may prove to be a better strategy for the system to collaborate with other organizations where risks and costs can be shared.[130]

Diversification strategies in the 1990s represent a significant departure from those of the 1980s. During the 1980s diversification occurred primarily in nonacute care services and were intended to compensate hospitals who were losing revenues under PPS by generating revenue through new sources. In many instances hospitals diversified into a wide range of businesses that were completely unrelated to health care such as dude ranches and travel agencies. Many diversification efforts failed during this decade in part because management was unprepared to manage services unrelated to the hospital's core business of acute care. In the 1990s the purpose of diversification shifted from generating revenues to offering health services that reduce hospital costs.[131]

Diversification strategies in the health care industry have mirrored the turbulence and uncertainty in the environment and have involved introducing new services, and deleting others on a trial and error basis. Some efforts have been more successful than others.[132] What has become apparent is that diversification activities related to the hospital's core business tend to be more profitable than diversification activities that are partially or totally unrelated to acute care.[133] During both the 1980s and the 1990s, ambulatory care and physician joint ventures were the most profitable diversification strategies. Furthermore, after over a decade of experience with diversification, experts now recommend that the diversification activity should be expected to generate, at a minimum, at least 10 percent of total revenues to be considered a worthwhile investment.[134] While hospitals were pursuing diversification prior to the implementation of PPS, it has been noted that there only has been a modest increase in these activities post-PPS. It has been suggested that lack of capital has retarded diversification efforts.[135] Some experts believe that the failed diversification activities of the 1980s have made managers more cautious.[136] Many of the national chains have been diverting individual activities to clean up their balance sheets and move out of markets in which they have perceived weakness.

While approximately one-third of rural hospitals are affiliated with systems either through ownership, lease, or contract management arrangements,[137] recent evidence suggests that the strategic value of system affiliation for rural hospitals has changed as a result of PPS. Specifically, affiliation with a system does not increase a rural hospital's chances for survival. Investor-owned rural hospitals that affiliate with investor-owned systems are less likely to close, but investor-owned rural hospitals that affiliate with not-for-profit systems increase their risk of closure. Thus, investor-owned system affiliation may be a reasonable strategy, but only for a rather limited group of rural hospitals that includes small, investor-owned facilities.[138]

The trend toward regionalization recognizes that 99 percent of health care services delivered in the United States will take place within the region where the patient resides. System strategies are shifting their focus to establish predominance in local and regional markets rather than national ones.[139] The national companies learned that uniform corporate policies were not always sensitive to state and local market and reimbursement differences. Recent experience indicates that the role of larger investor-owned systems is declining and that system growth for the proprietary sector is occurring in small local and regional investor-owned systems, many of which are newly established systems.[140] Vertical integration is consistent with the trend toward regionalization because it concentrates resources in local markets in order to establish a dominant presence in these markets.

As a result of all these factors, an industry that was once moving toward rapid consolidation through national chain ownership, appears to be moving now toward regionally based operators with strong local ties.[141] This is reflected in the acquisition activities of nonprofit organizations, hospitals, and small regional operators. Many in the field now believe that vertically integrated regional delivery systems that emphasize primary care and preventive medicine will prove to be the best approach to providing health care services. The focus will be on development of a continuum of care that incorporates a range of services from preventive to long-term care.

ANTITRUST CONCERNS

There are many legal considerations inherent in the development of multiprovider systems including antitrust, corporate practice of medicine, fraud and abuse, state anti-kickback rules, and others. Legal considerations are covered in depth in other chapters of this book. However, a brief summary of antitrust concerns is worthy of note in this chapter because it is directly related to the previous discussion.

Most system arrangements ordinarily increase a system's antitrust exposure. Although health care was once considered immune from antitrust laws, in recent years the Supreme Court has applied the antitrust laws to the activities of hospitals and other health care providers.

The basic goal of antitrust enforcement is to protect the free enterprise economic system by preserving vigorous and fair competition. The antitrust laws are enforced by the Antitrust Division of the U.S. Department of Justice and the FTC. Additionally, any private party allegedly injured by anticompetitive conduct can bring a civil action in federal court to recover damages. Because the amount of damages is tripled if liability is found and a finding of liability to one plaintiff may impose liability with respect to all parties with similar complaints, the risk of private antitrust claims is probably the most threatening.

The threat of this kind of litigation must not be overlooked. Antitrust litigation can be long and costly. The responsible officers and directors may be subject to civil or criminal liability as a result of a corporation's anticompetitive activities. The prevailing party may be awarded attorney's fees and the amount of the actual damages is tripled in settlements under antitrust laws. Moreover, any member of a multi-institutional arrangement could be sued and required to pay all damages, not just its share. The failure to consider antitrust in the formative stages of competitive strategy can result in embarrassing, expensive, and economically disastrous consequences.

Antitrust Violations

Activities that tend to lessen the freedom to compete in the marketplace are most likely to be scrutinized under the laws. Because every contract restrains trade in some way, the legal rule of thumb that has developed is that only "unreasonable" restraints on competition are illegal.

Nevertheless, the antitrust rules do prohibit certain kinds of agreements that are viewed as outright (*per se*) illegal. These include:[142]

- *price fixing:* an agreement among competitors to establish prices, other price-related terms of trade, or quantity of production
- *division of markets:* an agreement between competitors that allocates customers, terri-

tories, or services for the purpose or effect of reducing or eliminating competition

- *group boycotts:* an agreement between competitors not to do business with a supplier, customer, or another competitor

These are the kinds of agreements that could subject perpetrators to criminal penalties, in addition to the triple damages usually awarded successful antitrust plaintiffs.

Generally speaking, activities other than those in the *per se* category are evaluated under a "rule of reason" antitrust standard. A common trend is that the antitrust plaintiff has to prove either actual anticompetitive effect in the marketplace or that the activities under scrutiny may substantially lessen competition.

Examples of cases where systems are vulnerable under the "rule of reason" standard include the following:[143]

- The merger of hospitals that "substantially lessens competition or creates a monopoly"—that is, hospitals in close geographic proximity—may be in violation of Section VII of the Clayton Act.
- The sharing of budgets and discussions of price by hospitals under separate corporate ownership may constitute price fixing, which is prohibited under the Sherman Act.
- Cooperative attempts by hospitals to divide markets through allocation of customers— attempts to reduce duplication of services—could be illegal under the Sherman Act.

It has been noted that the antitrust laws are not neutral regarding organizational structure.[144] Systems with centralized management control are more vulnerable to legal challenge than systems that decentralize management control. Systems in close proximity are more vulnerable than systems in different geographic areas.

Relevant Market

Under either the *per se* rule or the "rule of reason" standard, the initial determination of which

"relevant markets" are affected is critical to evaluating the potential antitrust consequences of most strategies. The relevant market is that segment of the economy—viewed in terms of both product and geography—where the activity under scrutiny appreciably affects competition. What determines whether two products or services are in the same relevant market is the reasonable interchangeability of use between the product or service itself and the substitutes for it. If two products are close substitutes for each other, they are viewed as being in the same relevant product market for antitrust purposes.

The geographical component of the relevant market is often equated with the source, geographically speaking, of patients. Studies of patient origin and medical office locations of physicians often serve as good indicators of the geographic boundaries of a hospital product market.

Systems can gauge their antitrust vulnerability associated with various collaborative activities by using the "30-percent rule." Specifically, a provider could be courting danger if it holds 30 percent or more of the relevant market share in a particular line of business. The identification of markets and competitors is often the key to both providing and defending against antitrust allegations.

A Preventive Audit

Because the risks of antitrust scrutiny and liability are very real and very substantial today, preventive care is essential. Such an approach involves at least six affirmative elements:[145,146]

1. identification of potential antitrust problem areas
2. development of a formal statement of policy and procedures for antitrust compliance
3. access to corporate antitrust counsel
4. management training and sensitization with respect to antitrust compliance matters

5. periodic antitrust compliance audits
6. obtaining advanced approvals for strategic organizational changes before implementing such changes

Potential problem areas include any agreement, understanding, or communications with competitors regarding prices, services to be offered, areas where they will compete, or any other matter affecting the price or availability of hospital services. The mere exchange of information may be unlawful if the purpose or effect is to set or stabilize prices, divide service markets, or facilitate other parallel conduct. Although exclusive contracts between hospitals and other medical care providers, such as radiologists, can be justified on a number of grounds, their use should be reviewed as part of the antitrust compliance program. Tying arrangements, in which a hospital that controls the availability of one service refuses to sell that service to anyone not also purchasing a second service, can be a significant potential problem unless the two services are interdependent. Likewise, price discrimination and joint efforts by hospitals and physicians to resist competition by excluding potential competitors can create significant antitrust exposure.

A simple antitrust evaluation of proposed competitive strategy consists of a few straightforward questions.[147] Who are the potential plaintiffs? What are the relevant markets affected? Is the agreement or activity under scrutiny subject to the rule of reason standard or could it be a *per se* antitrust violation? If the rule of reason standard is applicable, do the anticompetitive effects outweigh procompetitive results?

Hospital management should have ready access to antitrust counsel. Some hospitals have an experienced in-house antitrust lawyer, whereas others use private law firms. Training seminars bringing together management personnel and antitrust counsel can also be helpful. The objectives of such sessions include demonstrating to all management personnel the organization's commitment to antitrust compliance, explaining the preventive program, and developing management sensitivity to antitrust issues.

Finally, obtaining advanced approvals before implementation of an organizational change can be advantageous. If a system obtains an advanced approval (Certificate of Need) for acquisitions from its state's planning agencies, it is arguable that the merger or acquisition is immune from antitrust scrutiny. A U.S. District Court in North Carolina recently dismissed an antitrust challenge to an acquisition in finding that the state agency's consideration of the acquisition's anticompetitive effect before granting the Certificate of Need immunized the acquisition.[148]

Likewise, a system may obtain an advanced business review of its proposed multi-institutional arrangement from the Justice Department. This procedure is the best available prearrangement indicator of legality because it indicates the department's "present intent" regarding the proposed conduct. The Justice Department issues a positive response only when it is persuaded that the proposed change is clearly permissible.

Critics charge that increased collaboration among providers will lead to monopolistic business practices like price-fixing. However, partnerships focused on community needs may actually have the effect of increasing access and lowering costs. The object is not to exclude competition or maximize income. Antitrust constraints should not be a problem. Systems will likely avoid federal antitrust scrutiny if they have data to convince regulators that the collaboration will benefit the community.

Little evidence exists supporting the view that antitrust laws have blocked or "chilled" collaboration. In fact, internal AHA data indicate hospital collaborative ventures have been thriving.[149] These documents identify nearly 300 collaborative ventures entered into recently by hospitals as well as nearly 200 hospital mergers that occurred between 1980 and 1991. In sum, it appears that collaborative activity that lowers costs and prices; increases quality, access, or output; and/or has other benefits to the community should pass antitrust scrutiny.

Implications

All types of multihospital systems raise the risk of antitrust violations and their associated penalties. Horizontal mergers obviously have a higher risk than do either vertical integration or various nonmerger activities. Such risk is greater in areas that already exhibit a high market concentration, such as rural areas.

Health care executives need to consider the antitrust implications of a multi-institutional activity early in the planning process before such an activity is implemented. Indicators of potential problems include a high HHI index or a postmerger control of more than 30 percent of the relevant market. Prevention is the best strategy. In addition to the continuous preventive antitrust audit described earlier, submitting proposals to the relevant health planning agency for a Certificate of Need and securing an advanced business review from the Justice Department will minimize potential future problems.

CONCLUSION

The growth and development of multihospital health care systems in the United States has been characterized by integration of services and economic concentration and consolidation of resources. The transition to multihospital systems reflected the horizontal integration of facilities that began with investor-owned acquisitions in the late 1960s. Investor-owned systems entered into multihospital system arrangements because they had access to capital markets and because federal reimbursement encouraged and rewarded growth. Not-for-profit hospitals began to horizontally integrate in the mid-1970s in response to competition from investor-owned chains and the regulatory effects of state Certificate of Need legislation and rate review programs.[150] Until the mid-1980s, the primary difference between investor-owned and not-for-profit systems was one of magnitude. Investor-owned systems concentrated on national markets and evolving into large national multihospital systems whereas the not-for-profit systems focused on local and regional markets.

The implementation of PPS, the shift to DRGs or risk-based payment systems, and the increasing price sensitivity of both consumers and employers precipitated the transformation of multihospital systems to multiprovider health care systems. Today's systems are characterized by trends toward vertical integration, regionalization, and related diversification. These new systems represent more than a collection of hospitals. Instead, they offer a continuum of health care services that extends beyond acute patient care.

Of particular significance is that the differences between investor-owned and not-for-profit systems are being increasingly replaced by similarities. Not-for-profit systems are behaving more like investor-owned systems in terms of increasing focus on profitability, the external environment, and competitive strategies. Not-for-profit hospitals have established for-profit subsidiaries and are engaged in selling services to other hospitals for a profit. In general, not-for-profit systems are exhibiting many of the attributes that once exclusively identified investor-owned systems. Today's not-for-profit multihospital health care system is a healthy competitor and is narrowing the profitability gap with investor-owned systems.[151]

Meanwhile, the role of the large investor-owned system has been declining. With the recognition that health care is a local business and that survival depends on dominance in local and regional markets, the investor-owned systems no longer concentrate on competing in national markets. Investor-owned systems are gravitating toward growth in smaller local and regional markets and are moving out of markets where they are poor competitors. These systems have streamlined, reorganized, refinanced, and divested themselves of unprofitable and, for the most part, unrelated activities.

The future of health care systems is highly speculative given initiatives for health reform. As the government's role in health care expands, these systems are more vulnerable to shifts in government policy as witnessed by the significant and far-reaching impact of PPS on these systems. Furthermore, there remains the question of public systems and their repeated record of poor financial performance. Can these systems benefit from the experiences that have led to success for both investor-owned and not-for-profit systems, or are these public systems the casualties of success of these other systems? Are public systems the new dumping grounds for unprofitable patients? Finally, there is the matter of systemness. Shortell criticized multihospital systems for their inability to perform as systems.[152] Will the focus on vertical integration, diversification, and regionalization increase the ability of multihospital health care systems to function as true systems? We believe most multihospital health care systems will emerge successfully from their growing pains and continue to solidify their position in the health care market.

Risk has identified several key trends relevant to systems that exist in most areas of the United States.[153] First, health care will be purchased primarily on a local or regional basis. Quality and value will be increasingly important to purchasers. Second, managed care will encompass a significant majority of the population. Third, fewer resources will be available to deliver care and the delivery of health care will continue to shift from acute-care to ambulatory settings.

RECOMMENDATIONS

1. Health care executives in multiprovider health care systems need to provide flexibility for member institutions to respond to specific local markets.

2. System leaders must face the formidable task of proving to the member institutions that the system adds value, its leaders are competent, and that they are capable of achieving the anticipated system advantages and resultant long-term benefits for the local unit.

3. Each system should develop a detailed mission statement and set of behavioral norms (i.e., culture) shared by each facility within the system in order to enhance cohesiveness.

4. Each system should develop a formal strategic plan for the system with input and a high degree of interaction among the corporate office and system institutions in all geographic regions.

5. Each system should develop a strategic human resource plan including staffing, training and development, performance appraisal, and compensation.

6. Each system should develop a system-wide management information system, quality assurance plan, market research, guidelines for new products and services, and bulk purchases that are utilized by each hospital; beyond these corporate services, the emphasis should be on autonomy and individualization of member institutions.

7. Each system should develop and implement explicit measures for quality of care, patient satisfaction, efficiency, and community benefit.

8. Each system should strive to achieve sufficient local market penetration, market share, and vertical integration along a continuum of care on a local or regional basis.

9. Each system should develop effective physician bonding strategies at the local, regional, and corporate levels with incentives for physicians to make cost-effective decisions with the best long-term impact on the patients.

10. Each system should emphasize developing health care in a managed-care mode rather than simply managing hospitals or acute care delivery.

11. Each system should develop an organizational structure that is simple, lean, flat, responsive, customer-driven, risk-taking, and focused.

12. Governance at the corporate level should be strategic in nature whereas governance at the institutional level should be operational in nature and focused on local community/region needs and concerns.

13. Systems should move toward consolidation of management layers by combining corporate functions and decentralizing decision making where possible.

14. Systems should move toward a single organized medical staff throughout with shared values and a common culture.

15. Systems should identify one or more discrete geographically defined service areas with large enough populations to support the provision of a full range of services and delivery settings.

16. Systems should rigorously test clinical protocols and methodologies to determine the most cost-efficient and effective ways of providing care.

17. Systems should centralize registration and medical record functions to make their networks more user-friendly and cut down on unnecessary duplication of tests.

18. Leadership is required to get the individual units of a system to think in terms of overall system performance rather than just in terms of the particular unit's performance.

19. Systems should integrate their medical staffs into all phases of system planning and management.

20. Only institutions that fit a particular culture and strategy should be invited to join or remain a member of the system.

21. Collaborative ventures that make sense in terms of economic returns and community benefits should not be inhibited by antitrust concerns.

NOTES

1. S.M. Shortell, The Evolution of Hospital Systems: Unfulfilled Promises and Self-Fulfilling Prophesies, *Medical Care Review* 45, no. 20 (1988):177–214.

2. American Hospital Association, *Guide to the Health Care Field* (Chicago: 1992), B2.

3. S.D. Smith and P.M. Virgil, Multihospital Systems: Applying Corporate Structures and Strategies, in *A Future of Consequence: The Manager's Role in Health Services*, ed. G.L. Filerman (Princeton, NJ: Princeton University Press, 1989), 54–75.

4. D.A. Conrad and W.L. Dowling, Vertical Integration in Health Services: Theory and Managerial Implications, *Health Care Management Review* 15, no. 4 (1990):9–22.

5. L.R. Kaiser, The Future of Multihospital Systems, *Topics in Health Care Financing* 18, no. 4 (1992):32–45.

6. R.R. Risk, Multihospital Systems: The Turning Point, *Topics in Health Care Financing* 18, no. 3 (1992):46–53.

7. D.M. Kinzer, Twelve Laws of Hospital Interaction, *Health Care Management Review* 15, no. 2 (1990):15–19.

8. W.D. White, The Corporatization of U.S. Hospitals: What We Can Learn from the Nineteenth Century Industrial Experience, *International Journal of Health Services* 20, no. 1 (1990):85–113.

9. J. Nemes, For-Profit Chains Look Beyond the Bottom Line, *Modern Healthcare* 20, no. 10 (March 12, 1990):27–36.

10. M.J. McCue et al., An Assessment of Hospital Acquisition Prices, *Inquiry* 25 (1988):290–296.

11. Shortell, The Evolution of Multihospital Systems, 179.

12. Ibid., 192.

13. Ibid., 177–214.

14. White, The Corporatization of U.S. Hospitals, 102.

15. Risk, Multihospital Systems: The Turning Point, 46–47.

16. Kaiser, The Future of Multihospital Systems, 35.

17. Smith and Virgil, Multihospital Systems, 54–55.

18. White, The Corporatization of U.S. Hospitals, 102.

19. A.M. Sear, Comparison of Efficiency and Profitability of Investor-Owned Multihospital Systems with Not-for-Profit Hospitals, *Health Care Management Review* 16, no. 2 (1991):31–37.

20. Shortell, The Evolution of Multihospital Systems, 183.

21. T.L. Ramirez, Introduction to Multihospital Systems, *Topics in Health Care Financing* 18, no. 4 (1992):1–23.

22. Risk, Multihospital Systems: The Turning Point, 47.

23. W.O. Cleverly, Financial and Operating Performance of Systems: Voluntary versus Investor-Owned, *Topics in Health Care Financing* 18, no. 4 (1992):63–73.

24. Ramirez, Introduction to Multihospital Systems, 9–10.

25. Shortell, The Evolution of Multihospital Systems, 181.

26. Ibid., 177–178, 180.

27. R.E. Toomey and R.K. Toomey, The Role of Governing Boards in Multihospital Systems, *Health Care Management Review* 18, no. 1 (1993):21–30.

28. McCue et al., Assessment of Hospital Acquisition Prices, 294–295.

29. Shortell, The Evolution of Multihospital Systems, 178.

30. White, The Corporatization of U.S. Hospitals, 105.

31. Ramirez, Introduction to Multihospital Systems, 7.

32. Shortell, the Evolution of Multihospital Systems, 180.

33. R.D. Federa and T.R. Miller, Capital Allocation Techniques, *Topics in Health Care Financing* 19, no. 1 (1992):68–78.

34. Risk, Multihospital Systems: The Turning Point, 47.

35. Conrad and Dowling, Vertical Integration in Health Services, 12–13.

36. Cleverly, Financial and Operating Performance of Systems, 67–69.

37. White, The Corporatization of U.S. Hospitals, 105.

38. Ibid.

39. J. Nemes, U.S. Hospital Chains Retreat from Europe, *Modern Healthcare* 21, no. 36 (1991):39–40.

40. White, The Corporatization of U.S. Hospitals, 103.

41. J. Greene and J. Nemes, Not-for-Profits Lead Rise in Income Growth, *Modern Healthcare* 23, no. 21 (1993):27–53.

42. Ibid.

43. Ibid.

44. G. Borzo, Closer Ties with Physicians Skirt Safe Harbors Fears, *Health Care Strategic Management* 10, no. 11 (1992):19–22.

45. C.K. Jacobson, A Conceptual Framework for Evaluating Joint Venture Opportunities between Hospitals and Physicians, *Health Services Management Research* 2 (1989):204–212.

46. J. Johnson, Dynamic Diversification: Hospitals Pursue Physician Alliances, "Seamless" Care, *Hospitals* 66, no. 3 (1992):20–26.

47. D.A. Rublee and R. Rosenfield, Organizational Aspects of Physician Joint Ventures, *The American Journal of Medicine* 82 (1987):518–524.

48. Borzo, Closer Ties with Physicians, 19–22.

49. Jacobson, A Conceptual Framework, 204–212.

50. J. Montague, Straight Talk: Doctor-Driven Systems Tell How They've Gained Physician Allies, *Hospitals & Health Networks* 67, no. 13 (1993):22–27.

51. J. Unland, Group Practices and Hospital Affiliation of Medical Practices, *Health Care Strategic Management* 11, no. 3 (1993):15–19.

52. P.J. Kenkel, Filling Up Beds No Longer the Name of the System Game, *Modern Healthcare* 23, no. 37 (1993):39–48.

53. J. Nemes, For-Profit Hospitals Waving Goodbye to Era of High Prices, *Modern Healthcare* 23, no. 12 (1993):33–34, 37.

54. D. Burda, Most Hospitals Slow To Join with Group Practices, *Modern Healthcare* 23, no. 34 (1993):33.

55. L.R. Tucker and R.A. Zaremba, Organizational Control and the Status of Marketing in Multihospital Systems, *Health Care Management Review* 16, no. 1 (1991):41–56.

56. Shortell, The Evolution of Multihospital Systems, 183.

57. Ramirez, Introduction to Multihospital Systems, 5.

58. Cleverly, Financial and Operating Performance of Systems, 68.

59. Ibid., 65–66.

60. Shortell, The Evolution of Multihospital Systems, 182.

61. Greene and Nemes, Not-for-Profit Lead, 27–53.

62. Cleverly, Financial and Operating Performance of Systems, 66–69.

63. Ibid., 69.

64. Conrad and Dowling, Vertical Integration in Health Services, 13.

65. J. Greene, Healthcare Systems' Newest Balancing Act: Doing More with Less, *Modern Healthcare* 22, no. 39 (1992):52, 54, 56–58.

66. Ramirez, Introduction to Multihospital Systems, 1–23.

67. J. Williams, Successful Multis Keep Staff Costs to a Minimum, *Hospitals* 60, no. 10 (1986):38–40.

68. Cleverly, Financial and Operating Performance of Systems, 63–73.

69. Sear, Comparison of Efficiency and Profitability, 31–37.

70. G.O. Ginn, Organizational and Environmental Determinants of Hospital Strategy, *Hospital and Health Services Administration* 37, no. 3 (1992):291–302.

71. Shortell, The Evolution of Multihospital Systems, 177–214.

72. Smith and Virgil, Multihospital Systems, 59–61.

73. Kaiser, The Future of Multihospital Systems, 36.

74. Ibid., 43.

75. G.M. McGee et al., The Impact of Corporatization of Administrator Stress in Nursing Homes, *Health Services Management Research* 5, no. 1 (1992):54–65.

76. Kaiser, The Future of Multihospital Systems, 43.

77. Toomey and Toomey, The Role of Governing Boards, 23–24.

78. L.L. Morlock and J.A. Alexander, Models of Governance in Multihospital Systems: Implications for Hospitals and System-Level Decision-Making, *Medical Care* 24, no. 12 (1986):1118–1135.

79. Ibid., 1122–1123, 1125–1129.

80. Ibid., 1134.

81. Ramirez, Introduction to Multihospital Systems, 5–6, 11.

82. T. McLaughlin, Finding Jobs for 1200 Laid-Off Employees: Health One's Goal, *Hospitals* 66, no. 1 (1992):43–44.

83. G.H. Kaye, Multis, Mergers, Acquisitions, and the Healthcare Provider, *Nursing Management* 20, no. 4 (1989):54–62.

84. T. Droste, Multihospital Executives Continue To Earn More, *Hospitals* 63, no. 15 (1989):74.

85. Smith and Virgil, Multihospital Systems, 66–69.

86. D. Gregory, Strategic Alliances between Physicians and Hospitals in Multihospital Systems, *Hospital and Health Services Administration* 37, no. 2 (1992):247–258.

87. L. Burns et al., The Impact of Corporate Structures on Physician Inclusion and Participation, *Medical Care* 27, no. 10 (1989):967–982.

88. M.T. Koska, Systems Fight Uphill Battle To Gain Physician Loyalty, *Hospitals* 64, no. 6 (1990):60, 62.

89. Gregory, Strategic Alliances between Physicians and Hospitals, 250–251.

90. Greene, Healthcare Systems' Newest Balancing Act, 54.

91. Ibid., 56, 58.

92. Smith and Virgil, Multihospital Systems, 64.

93. G.F. Schwartz and C.T. Stone, Strategic Acquisitions by Academic Medical Centers: The Jefferson Experience As Operational Paradigm, *Health Care Management Review* 16, no. 2 (1991):39–47.

94. R.M. Albertina and T.F. Bakewell, Allocating Capital Systemwide, *Health Progress* 70, no. 4 (1989):26–32.

95. Federa and Miller, Capital Allocation Techniques, 72.

96. Albertina and Bakewell, Allocating Capital Systemwide, 26, 31.

97. Federa and Miller, Capital Allocation Techniques, 68–69, 73–74.

98. Ibid., 74–75.

99. Ibid., 75.

100. Ibid., 77–78.

101. L. Gerber and F.I. Feinstein, When the System Can't Save the Hospital: A Practical Overview of Workouts and Bankruptcy Alternatives, *Topics in Health Care Financing* 18, no. 4 (1992):46–62.

102. Ibid., 50–51.

103. H.J. Anderson, Sizing Up Systems: Researchers To Test Performance Measures, *Hospitals* 65, no. 20 (1991):33–34.

104. Ramirez, Introduction to Multihospital Systems, 6–7.

105. A.T. Solovy, Multis Sweep Cash, Boost Investment Income, *Hospitals* 62, no. 5 (1988):74–75.

106. Ramirez, Introduction to Multihospital Systems, 6.

107. Ibid., 12.

108. M.M. McKinney et al., Paths and Pacemakers: Innovation Diffusion Networks in Multihospital Systems and Alliances, *Health Care Management Review* 16, no. 1 (1991):17–23.

109. P. McGuire, Kaiser Permanente's New Technologies Committee: An Approach To Assessing Technology, *Quality Review Bulletin* 16, no. 6 (1990):240–242.

110. S. Taravella, Risk Management. Frustrated Healthcare Systems Seek Alternatives to Traditional Insurance, *Modern Healthcare* 18, no. 20 (1988):30–32, 36, 41.

111. Tucker and Zaremba, Organizational Control and Status of Marketing, 47, 53–54.

112. White, The Corporatization of U.S. Hospitals, 103.

113. T.L. Werner, A New Approach to Decision Support at Adventist Hospital System/Sunbelt, *Computers in Healthcare* 11, no. 3 (1990):49–50.

114. M. Hurwitz, Multis Move To Centralize IS Decisions, *Hospitals* 62, no. 5 (1988):75.

115. K. Lumsdon, Holding Networks Together. Shared Information Will Be Glue for Reformed Health System, *Hospitals* 7, no. 4 (1993):26–27.

116. McCue et al., Assessment of Hospital Acquisition Prices, 295.

117. J.A. Alexander and M.A. Morrisey, Hospital Selection into Multihospital Systems: The Effect of Market, Management, and Mission, *Medical Care* 26, no. 2 (1988):159–176.

118. J.A. Alexander, Diversification Behavior of Multihospital Systems: Patterns of Change, 1983–1985, *Hospital and Health Services Administration* 35, no. 1 (1990):83–102.

119. Sear, Comparison of Efficiency and Profitability, 35.

120. Nemes, For-Profit Chains Look Beyond Bottomline, 28.

121. A.M. Sear, Operating Characteristics and Comparative Performance of Investor-Owned Multihospital Systems, *Hospital and Health Services Administration* 37, no. 3 (1992):403–415.

122. Shortell, The Evolution of Multihospital Systems, 207.

123. Conrad and Dowling, Vertical Integration in Health Services, 10.

124. Ibid.

125. Ibid., 11.

126. M. Brown and B.P. McCool, Health Care Systems: Predictions for the Future, *Health Care Management Review* 15, no. 3 (1990):87–94.

127. F.K. Ackerman, The Movement toward Vertically Integrated Regional Health Systems, *Health Care Management Review* 17, no. 3 (1992):81–88.

128. Conrad and Dowling, Vertical Integration of Health Services, 12–14.

129. Ackerman, Movement toward Vertically Integrated Regional Systems, 85.

130. Conrad and Dowling, Vertical Integration of Health Services, 22.

131. J. Greene, Diversification, Take Two, *Modern Healthcare* 23, no. 28 (1993):28–30.

132. Alexander, Diversification Behavior of Multihospital Systems, 100.

133. S.M. Shortell, Diversification Strategy Benefits Innovative Leader, *Modern Healthcare* 20, no. 10 (1990):38.

134. Greene, Diversification Take Two, 28–29.

135. Alexander, Diversification Behavior of Multihospital Systems, 97–98.

136. Greene, Diversification Take Two, 28–29.

137. G.T. Savage et al., Urban-Rural Hospital Affiliations: Assessing Control, Fit and Stakeholder Issues Strategically, *Health Care Management Review* 17, no. 1 (1992):35–49.

138. M.T. Halpern et al., Multihospital System Affiliation As a Survival Strategy for Rural Hospitals under the Prospective Payment System, *Journal of Rural Health* 8, no. 2 (1992):93–105.

139. Brown and McCool, Health Care Systems: Predictions, 89–90.

140. White, The Corporatization of U.S. Hospitals, 102–103.

141. J.K. Piper and H.G. Collier, Multifacilities Move toward Regional Orientation, *Provider* 16, no. 6 (1990):18, 20–21.

142. R.J. Enders, Understanding Antitrust: Focus on the Relevant Market, *Healthcare Financial Management* 6 (February 1986):25–32.

143. R.A. Vraicu and H.S. Zuckerman, Legal and Financial Constraints on the Development and Growth of Multiple Hospital Arrangements, *Health Care Management Review* 4 (Winter 1979):39–47.

144. Ibid.

145. P.J. Nickles and M. Brown, Hospital Care Confronts Antitrust: A Preventive Care Audit Approach to Antitrust Compliance, *Health Care Management Review* 8 Winter (1983):46–48.

146. W.G. Kopit et al., Hospitals Must Consider Antitrust Implications of Multi-Institutional Arrangements, *Hospitals* 56 (March 1, 1982):82–84.

147. Enders, Understanding Antitrust, 30.

148. Kopit et al., Hospitals Must Consider Antitrust Implications, 84.

149. D. Burda, Mergers Thrive Despite Wailing about Diversity, *Modern Healthcare* 22, no. 41 (1992):26–28, 30, 32.

150. Shortell, The Evolution of Multihospital Systems, 178.

151. M.D. Hiller, Ethics and Health Care Administration: Issues in Education and Practice, *The Journal of Health Administration Education* 2, no. 2 (1984):147–192.

152. Shortell, The Evolution of Multihospital Systems, 177–214.

153. Risk, Multihospital Systems: The Turning Point, 46–53.

MYRON D. FOTTLER, PhD, is currently Professor of Management and Director of the PhD Program in Administration–Health Services, with a joint appointment in the Graduate School of Management and the School of Health Related Professions, University of Alabama at Birmingham.

In addition to teaching courses in human resources management, he has written more than 100 publications in the areas of health care cost containment, human resources management problems in health care, multi-institutional systems, and stakeholder management.

Dr. Fottler received his PhD in business from Columbia University.

DONNA MALVEY, MHSA, received her master's degree in health services administration from George Washington University and is currently a PhD candidate in Administration–Health Services at the University of Alabama at Birmingham. Her area of specialization is strategic management of health services organizations. She has co-authored articles on negotiation and the administration of the labor relations contract and on the development of comprehensive state level databases to assure adequacy of health professionals. Past experience includes teaching courses in labor relations and health care organization and management. In addition, she has served as the executive director of a national trade association representing health professionals and as a congressional aide.

Chapter 28

Integrated Delivery Systems

This chapter consists of selected readings and case studies from *Topics in Health Care Financing*. The selections encompass discussions about management services organizations (MSOs), not-for-profit foundations, and tax exemption and integrated delivery systems. In addition to the two case studies, the readings provide an excellent supplement to many related chapters in the book because of their balance between the structural and practical aspects of industry change.

MANAGEMENT SERVICES ORGANIZATIONS*

Paul R. DeMuro

A management services organization (MSO) is typically an organization that provides services to physicians and physician groups. However, it may also provide services to a hospital. An MSO that only provides services to physicians and physician groups may be known as a medical services organization.

GOALS AND OBJECTIVES FOR THE CREATION OF AN MSO

The goals and objectives of a hospital in participating in the development of an MSO are generally to compete in the managed care arena, strengthen relationships with physicians, and en-

sure the continued survival of the hospital. MSOs may be particularly helpful for hospitals that are not aligned with large, integrated, multispecialty medical groups.

Physicians might desire to be involved in the development of and to contract with an MSO to obtain greater access to more managed care contracts and to reduce their practice costs and the complexity of managing a physician's practice.

Points to consider during the MSO development process are presented in Exhibit 28–1 and discussed in this chapter.

ADVANTAGES AND DISADVANTAGES OF AN MSO

Advantages

The advantages of an MSO can be numerous. An MSO is useful in physician recruitment be-

*Source: This section is reprinted from P.R. DeMuro, Management Services Organizations, in *Topics in Health Care Financing*, Vol. 20, No. 3, pp. 19–27, Aspen Publishers, Inc., © 1994.

Exhibit 28–1 Developing an MSO

When developing an MSO, there are a number of questions that should be asked:

1. Is the business plan credible?
2. Is the MSO properly capitalized?
3. Who really controls or governs the MSO?
4. Are there any competent individuals to operate the MSO?
5. How much can the MSO pay for the physician's assets?
6. What are the assets?
7. How is the MSO operated and what does it propose to do?
8. How are the MSO's fees set?
9. What happens if the MSO fee is not set properly?
10. What are the Medicare fraud and abuse risks?
11. What are the antitrust risks?
12. What are the pension and benefit problems?
13. Could a private letter ruling be obtained from the IRS?
14. What can the physicians bill Medicare for if technicians and other professionals are employed by the MSO?
15. Will physicians not contracting with the MSO cause problems?

---

cause physicians can contract with the MSO to run their practice. The costs of opening and operating a medical practice can be made more certain. In addition, a contract with an MSO can be part of a physician recruitment package, thus minimizing the uncertainty for a newly recruited physician.

The development of an MSO can be a form of joint practice acquisition because the MSO can purchase certain assets of physician practices. It also can provide services to a number of newly recruited independent physicians in a central location.

An MSO also can be a first step toward an integrated delivery system. Initially, the MSO can provide limited services to a few physicians or a group of physicians. Over time, the range of MSO services and the size of the physician group may increase. The physicians may desire to incorporate into a medical group or the group may desire to expand into a multispecialty group. The multispecialty group may evolve into a medical foundation for capital formation and recruitment purposes. The hospital and the medical foundation can more closely align into an integrated delivery system.

With the continued shift to the delivery of health care services in an outpatient setting, an MSO might be used in the development of outpatient centers. Hospitals generally have not been efficient in providing outpatient services and have faced fierce competition from physicians and entrepreneurs. Physicians can participate in the delivery of care with the MSO managing their practices.

One of the major reasons for the development of an MSO is access to managed care plans. Many individual physicians or small physician groups cannot access the managed care plans. An MSO can aggregate physician participation for managed care contracting. In addition, it can include the hospital component as part of the contracts it negotiates. Furthermore, the MSO can seek to assist in the development of certain practice efficiencies by conducting aggressive utilization review.

A number of physician practice efficiencies can be achieved with an MSO. These include access to better information systems and lower per-physician costs, access to greater technical and management expertise, and better discounts on supplies and inventory.

MSOs afford physicians some medical practice autonomy. The physician retains his or her practice and some assets. The physician only has a contract with an MSO, as compared to other more integrated models.

Disadvantages

The disadvantages of an MSO include a number of legal concerns, including Medicare and Medicaid fraud and abuse, tax exemption, antitrust, and corporate practice of medicine. These legal issues are discussed in greater detail later in this chapter.

A potential disadvantage associated with an MSO is its financial risk. It must be operated as a business and generate enough revenue to continue to operate.

Inasmuch as physician practices are still owned by the physicians in an MSO model, from a hospital's perspective, the hospital may have little control. The contract with the MSO can be terminated by the physicians. However, if enough of the assets of the physicians' practice are owned by the MSO, it may make it more difficult for the physicians to place their practices in a new setting. However, many other health care delivery systems may be willing to take on or hire such physicians.

An MSO may only be a temporary solution to the necessity for developing a regional health care delivery system. The MSO contracts can be terminated, and they may not be of long-term duration.

NECESSITY OF A BUSINESS PLAN

As part of a decision to develop an MSO, the parties should prepare a business plan. This plan should be prepared by the principals and reviewed by experts. Its assumptions should be realistic and its data should be based on likely events. If a government agency enforcing the Medicare and Medicaid fraud and abuse laws, or the Internal Revenue Service (IRS), questions the development of a particular MSO, it is of paramount importance to be able to establish that the organization was a true business.

The business plan should include viable financial projections for revenues and expenses. If the MSO intends to charge the physicians a lesser amount for their overhead costs than they were previously incurring, there should be assumptions and information documenting that lower costs per physician will be incurred.

ORGANIZATION FORMS

For-Profit Entity

Typically, MSOs are established as for-profit corporations or as divisions of existing for-profit corporations. They may be owned by a hospital or group of hospitals, physicians or groups of physicians, outside investors, or combination of the above.

If a nonprofit hospital establishes a for-profit MSO, it typically will purchase stock in the new corporation. The hospital should have charitable purposes for the purchase of its interest in the MSO or be able to justify this investment as a good one.

Physicians may be investors in an MSO, but typically the development of such an organization takes a large amount of capital, which is unavailable to the physicians unless they transfer assets to the MSO in exchange for part of the value of their stock.

Nonprofit Entity

Occasionally, the parties will seek to establish the MSO as a nonprofit corporation or as a division of a nonprofit corporation. The MSO will likely have difficulty obtaining tax-exempt status from the IRS because it is generally considered more of a for-profit type business. If it wants to attempt to obtain tax-exempt status, it will have to make strong showings about its charitable purposes. If it is established as a division of an already existing nonprofit corporation, its income may be considered to be unrelated business income and thus subject to taxation. Depending upon the scope, nature, and purpose of the MSO, it might have an adverse effect on the tax-exempt status of the nonprofit entity.

An MSO may be established as a nonprofit corporation that does not seek tax-exempt status, and thus it would be a taxable nonprofit corporation.

MSO ACTIVITIES

The activities of an MSO can range from a minor scope of operation to turnkey operations.

Managed Care Contracting

Generally, when parties establish an MSO, they are interested in having a vehicle that will assist in managed care contracting. An MSO may be able to contract on behalf of a group of primary care physicians with health maintenance organizations (HMOs) on a capitated basis. Inasmuch as each of the physicians will be at risk, given the capitated nature of the contracts, the antitrust risk is reduced.

If the physicians are not part of an integrated group, the MSO may contract with managed care plans on a fee-for-service basis, but generally it should use the messenger concept. That is, the MSO should act as a messenger for each of the physicians in executing a contract on behalf of each physician, and there should not be collusion among the physicians.

Billing and Information Systems Management

An MSO might operate a billing service to perform billing for the physicians receiving services from the MSO. Ideally, the more physicians for whom the billing service provides services, the less expensive will be the service on a per-unit basis. In addition, the management expertise involved in billing and collections can be shared by the physicians receiving these services through the MSO. In addition, an MSO can provide an information systems management function.

Utilization Management and Review

An MSO also might provide utilization management and review services for the physicians receiving the MSO services. It can review physician practice patterns, methods of treatment, and assist in the establishment of protocols.

Supplies

An MSO may purchase supplies on behalf of the physicians. However, they may not be able to take advantage of a hospital's purchasing power because of certain legal restrictions and provisions in hospital purchasing contracts. However, the number of physicians receiving services from the MSO can increase the MSO's purchasing power.

Medical Office Space

An MSO might acquire medical office space on behalf of its physicians. Initially, physicians might assign their leases to the MSO, or the MSO might contract for space for newly recruited physicians. Over time, if the physicians desire to be more fully integrated, they might consolidate their space, with the MSO responsible for it, and achieving additional economies of scale.

Equipment

An MSO might acquire certain equipment on behalf of the physicians. This sharing of equipment could include technical equipment, office equipment, management information systems, and other specialized equipment.

Staff

The MSO might employ the nonprofessional staff for the physicians. This would enable the physicians to have access to better employees because it would likely be easier to pay a professional office manager more money if 10 to 15 or more physicians were sharing this person's expertise. In addition, there should be less duplication.

With respect to professional staff, it also would be easier for the MSO to attract better employees. There also should be less duplication of services. The physicians must be careful, however, because of the Medicare "incident to" regulations that prohibit a physician from billing the Medicare or Medicaid program for a service rendered by the physician's professional staff unless the physician actually rendered the service personally or employed and supervised the individual who was rendering the service.

Turnkey

An MSO might also be operated on a turnkey basis. Thus it could provide to the physicians all management services, space and equipment needs, employees, supplies, and other services necessary to operate the physicians' practices for a fee.

MSO FEES

Percentage Fee

Often, MSOs provide services to physicians for a percentage fee. This fee may be a percentage of the physician's gross or net revenues, or a percentage of the amounts received under certain managed care contracts (e.g., a percentage of the capitation payment). The percentage is usually difficult to calculate because the MSO may be a startup, the participants may have no or limited experience in this area, and the success of the MSO operations is unknown.

In setting this percentage, the MSO has a number of legal traps. For example, if a hospital owns the MSO, and the MSO charges the physicians less than the cost of the MSO's services to the hospital MSO, there may be allegations that there is a violation of the Medicare fraud and abuse antikickback regulations and violations of the prohibition against inurement of benefit if the hospital is nonprofit. These allegations might be made because the government may take the position that the only reason the hospital MSO set the percentage so low was to provide the physicians with a disguised payment for the referral of their patients to the hospital. The IRS might take the position that this use of the charitable assets which the hospital transferred to the MSO is a payment to the physicians that is not consistent with the hospital's charitable purposes.

Flat Fee

As a result, it is generally better to establish the MSO's fees for its services on a flat-fee basis. However, this is difficult to administer although easier to calculate. That is, a newly recruited physician receiving MSO services and starting a practice will not generate as much revenue as a mature practice. Therefore, the newly recruited physician would rather pay for MSO services on a percentage basis, rather than a flat-fee basis.

Although a flat-fee form of compensation can create less legal risk from the perspective of the Medicare fraud and abuse laws, both percentage and flat-fee contract rates can be set in advance. In any event, such fees should be set at fair market value, which may be determined in a variety of ways.

Hybrid Compensation

Some hybrid forms of compensation have been employed by MSOs. These forms might include a flat fee for certain space and equipment rental or a cost pass-through, and a percentage fee for other management services, such as billing. The reasoning is that the physicians are using the same space and equipment notwithstanding the number of patients whom they see; however, the amount of billing and other management services that they are using will directly vary with the number of patients they treat. It should be noted, however, that there is no Medicare fraud and abuse safe harbor protection for such arrangements.

ORGANIZATIONAL STRUCTURES

MSOs can take a variety of forms. A freestanding MSO might be an MSO that was developed by a group of private individuals, some of whom might include physicians and other investors. Figure 28–1 sets forth a copy of that model.

A hospital-affiliated MSO might be an MSO that the hospital owns as a for-profit subsidiary. An example of such an MSO is set forth in Figure 28–2.

A physician-affiliated MSO might be an MSO owned by a group of physicians. An example of that model is set forth in Figure 28–3.

A joint-venture MSO might be an MSO that is owned partially by a hospital or hospitals and physicians or physician groups. An example of that model is set forth in Figure 28–4.

An HMO-affiliated MSO might be an MSO that is owned by an HMO. An example of that MSO is set forth in Figure 28–5.

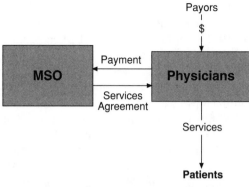

Figure 28–1 An Example of a Freestanding MSO

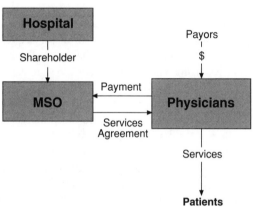

Figure 28–2 An Example of a Hospital-Affiliated MSO

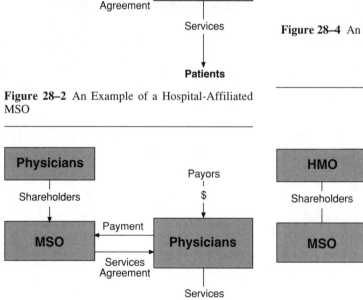

Figure 28–3 An Example of a Physician-Affiliated MSO

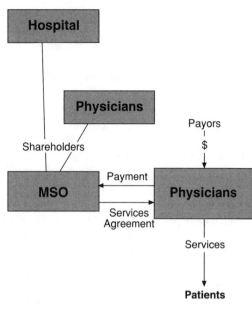

Figure 28–4 An Example of a Joint-Venture MSO

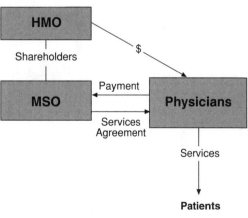

Figure 28–5 An Example of an HMO-Affiliated MSO

LEGAL ISSUES

There are many legal issues that affect MSOs. The major legal issues include Medicare and Medicaid fraud and abuse laws, tax, antitrust, corporate practice of medicine, and self-referral considerations.

The Medicare fraud and abuse antikickback laws can apply whenever the compensation paid by the physicians receiving MSO services is less than the actual cost of providing that service or fair value of same if a purpose for this low payment is for physician referrals. The false claims laws apply where the MSO might be given improper information by the physicians for billing purposes, or a physician bills for a service of which a large part was done by a technician, and the service violates the incident to regulations.

A nonprofit hospital participating in the development of an MSO should ensure that there are charitable purposes for the development of the MSO so as not to adversely affect the hospital's tax-exempt status. A hospital might consider obtaining a private letter ruling from the IRS.

If the hospital uses its monies to buy stock in a subsidiary MSO, and the MSO does not charge the physicians' fair value for the services provided, there will likely be allegations that the difference between the fair market value (what the MSO should have charged) and what it did charge was not within the scope of the hospital's charitable purposes, was private inurement, or was of private benefit to the physicians. Further-more, if there is any violation of the Medicare and Medicaid fraud and abuse laws, a November 1, 1991, IRS General Counsel Memorandum and recent IRS determinations for nonprofit medical foundations suggest that such violations can also affect the tax-exempt status of the non-profit entity.

With regard to antitrust, an MSO may be involved in joint contract decision making. If the nature of the contracts that the MSO will administer are capitation contracts, the antitrust risks are minimized. If the MSO is providing services for an integrated medical group, once again the antitrust risks are low. However, if the MSO is providing services to individual physicians or groups of physicians who are not fully integrated, and for contracts on a fee-for-service basis, it is necessary for the MSO to provide such services using a messenger model so as to minimize any antitrust risk.

The MSO must also be careful not to violate any prohibitions on the corporate practice of medicine. As the MSO moves toward a turnkey operation, and it owns many of the assets of a physician's practice, the space and equipment leases, and manages the physician's practice, there may be allegations that such a situation violates a state corporate practice of medicine prohibition, because although the physician is leasing his or her space through the MSO and operating his or her practice through a management contract, it begins to look as if the MSO is practicing medicine.

NONPROFIT MEDICAL CARE FOUNDATIONS*

Robert A. Waterman

A nonprofit medical care foundation (foundation) is a nonprofit corporation that generally

Source: This section is reprinted from R.A. Waterman, Nonprofit Medical Care Foundations, in *Topics in Health Care Financing,* Vol. 20, No. 3, pp. 13–18, Aspen Publishers, Inc., © 1994.

seeks exemption from federal income tax under section 501(c)(3) of the Internal Revenue Code. It typically renders medical care through a contract with physicians or a medical group or it employs physicians to render such care. It also may own or operate a hospital and render hospital care. The foundation may be called a nonprofit medical care foundation, nonprofit foundation, tax-exempt hospital-physician foundation, or a host of other names.

WHY FORM A FOUNDATION?

Physicians and hospitals each have their own reasons for establishing a foundation. Many of their major reasons are set forth as follows.

Physicians

Growth

Many physicians have decided that integrated groups—and in particular larger integrated groups—have a substantial edge in today's competitive marketplace for managed care contracts. Larger groups tend to be more attractive to the payors from a marketing and administrative point of view. In addition, size allows the physician group to be able to afford medical directors, strong managers, and the staffing to put into place and enforce rigorous utilization management guidelines. This in turn allows the group to price its services more competitively, and therefore gain even more managed care contracts, which allows further growth.

A nonprofit medical foundation type of organization allows the group to grow by giving it access to needed capital. That additional capital is available from two sources: the tax-exempt markets and the hospital. The tax-exempt markets will be available to the extent the combined financial strength of the group and the hospital will allow it. In addition, most hospitals have substantially more capital resources than physicians, and this form of organization allows the hospital to legally contribute to the foundation substantial funds, which would be used for guaranties of fair market salaries to physicians, research and charitable activities, and development of facilities.

Physician Recruitment

Many integrated physician groups are structured in such a way that physicians beginning practice must "buy in" to the group. New physicians are required to purchase both the right as a principal (shareholder or partner) to share in the profits (or losses) of the group and an ownership interest in the assets of the group. In some cases, the purchase price may be $100,000 or more. This buy-in puts the group at a substantial competitive disadvantage in attempting to recruit new physicians. This is especially true of physicians who have just completed training, who may already have incurred substantial debt. Since the assets of the group after the foundation is formed belong to the foundation, there is no reason in the foundation structure for anything other than a nominal buy-in to the group. The foundation structure therefore allows more competitive physician recruitment.

Guarantee of Market Incomes

Under the tax-exempt foundation model, the foundation can guarantee the physicians in the group fair market incomes. The group itself may not be able to afford these guarantees. Accordingly, in a volatile health care marketplace, these guarantees are appealing to many physicians.

Sale of Assets

To establish the foundation, the foundation will acquire the assets, including good will, of the group. This allows the physician owners of the group a one-time, and usually sizable, gain on the sale of their assets. These gains can be used either to retire debt the group incurred (which is often personally guaranteed by the physician owners) or for distributions to the physician owners.

No Taxes

The foundation model allows the organization not to pay property taxes and income taxes. Lower taxes mean more income available to physicians.

Donations

The foundation model allows donors to make tax-deductible donations. Some large foundations receive donations of millions of dollars per year. These donations can be used to fund operations or other activities, such as research, charity care, and facilities and program development.

Less Administration

Groups are hard to administer, and that administration often causes tension among the physicians. In the foundation model, the foundation takes care of all personnel, equipment, supply, billing and other paperwork, leasing, management, and other time-consuming issues. This leaves the physicians free to simply practice medicine.

Stability

Groups can be unstable. Tensions develop between the owners, and there can be spinoffs or even dissolutions. The foundation model increases the long-term stability of the organization. This is because the foundation is a nonprofit organization, and also because it owns all of the assets, including the managed care contracts. It is also because the contracting physicians have fewer issues to wrestle with—they only need to provide medical services.

Contracts

In the hospital–physician foundation model, the physician group may gain access to the hospital's contracts and often to its leverage with payors. In addition, the foundation model facilitates joint contracting between the hospital and the physician group with payors.

Hospitals

Managed Care Strategy

Many hospitals in the United States are in an intensely competitive situation. Much of that competition focuses on obtaining or keeping managed care contracts. A hospital with a medical foundation is often able to compete more effectively for managed care contracts. This is because a foundation is more appealing to payors—because of its size, its stability, and usually its increased visibility in the community.

Ownership of Contracts

Under the foundation model, the foundation has purchased and therefore owns the payor contracts. This means that even if some members of the group leave, the foundation is able to retain the contracts and therefore much of the business.

Research

The nonprofit foundation usually performs research and charitable activities. This contributes to the charitable mission of the tax-exempt hospital.

Cooperation

The foundation model allows the physicians in the group and the hospital to work cooperatively together.

Physician Recruitment

The availability of an affiliated organization with guaranteed employment possibilities makes physician recruitment easier. This is especially important with respect to primary care physicians.

STEPS TO FORMING A FOUNDATION

Identify or Form the Integrated Group

A nonprofit foundation normally provides services through a group practice. Thus, the first step is to either identify an appropriate group or form one. State law should be examined—California, for example, requires a group with at least 40 physicians, two-thirds of whom are full time. In addition, a decision in some areas has to be made as to whether it is cost efficient for a group to be formed where the physicians are in many different locations—the so-called clinics without walls. For states without a prohibition on the corporate practice of medicine, the foundation may be able to employ the physicians, avoiding the need to provide services through a contracted group.

Appraise the Value of the Group

At last one appraisal of the group or physicians' individual practices should be performed by an independent appraiser (some attorneys are now recommending two appraisals, to increase the credibility of the valuation with the IRS). The appraisers should discuss their methodologies with counsel before proceeding, since the IRS has established new criteria for such appraisals. Such appraisals should ensure that no value is assigned to the referral of any patients to a hospital.

Prepare a Business Plan

Before consummating the acquisition of the group, boards of directors of the hospital and group, as well as the IRS, will want to review a business plan, including *pro formas* prepared by an independent party. Such *pro formas* should show break-even within the first three years.

Agree on a Board and Committee Structure

The composition of the board and its standing committees (e.g., number of physicians, number of hospital representatives) is usually a major issue for both the hospital and the group, and should be worked out early in the process. If the foundation will seek tax-exempt debt, IRS bond rules may restrict the number of physicians from the group on the board.

In addition, the IRS now appears to be requiring that new tax-exempt foundations not have more than 20 percent of the board be members of an affiliated medical group (it is unclear whether this will be applied to foundations that already have their tax-exempt status). State law restrictions on board membership should also be reviewed.

As to committees, foundations should consider whether to form the following committees:

executive, finance, research and education, utilization review, contracts, compensation, and credentialing.

Determine Who Are the Members and the Rights of Membership

The parties should determine whether the hospital is to be the sole corporate member, and what its membership rights will be (e.g., will it have reserved rights as to sales of assets, merger, etc.). If the hospital is not the sole corporate member, the hospital will need to assess whether any contribution of funds to the foundation will affect its tax-exempt status.

Appraise Physician Compensation

An independent appraisal must be performed of the proposed foundation's compensation to physicians. This appraisal will be important to an IRS approval of the foundation's tax-exempt status.

Prepare Articles and Bylaws

Articles and bylaws of the foundation should be prepared. The articles will state the name of the foundation (usually a subject of much discussion) and its basic purposes. The bylaws will describe, among other things, the board, board committee structure and the qualifications of board members, how vacancies on the board are filled, terms and removal of directors, qualifications and selection of officers, indemnity rights of directors and officers, inspection rights, and the amendment procedure to the bylaws.

Prepare Professional Services Agreement

The parties should next prepare the professional services agreement or employment agreements. The professional services agreement contains the agreement between the foundation and the group as to services to be performed by the group and compensation of the group by the foundation. There are two basic methods of compensation that have been used to date: a percentage of revenues or a flat fee. Whichever method is used, the goal of the parties is usually to ensure that the group receive an amount sufficient to pay its physicians' fair market salaries. Most groups also provide for some sort of incentive compensation, rewarding quality, productivity, and cost-efficient practice of medicine. There are also usually provisions for sharing of the risk pool distributions from the health plans.

If the foundation employs the physicians there will be employment agreements between the foundation and the physicians. The employment agreement should provide for fair market value compensation. The use of an incentive compensation system between the foundation and the employed physicians has been called into question by the Office of the Inspector General.

Prepare Asset Purchase Agreement

The parties should next prepare the asset purchase agreement, by which the foundation will purchase the assets, including good will, of the group or physicians, for the appraised value of the group or physicians (or less than the appraised value, if it is to be a "bargain sale"). Issues addressed in this agreement include the following: liabilities to be assumed by the foundation, warranties and indemnities to be given by the group, the precise assets to be acquired and their tax allocations, and the method of payment to the group (e.g., cash, note, or assumption of debt). Since one federal official has recently argued that payment for the good will of a group could constitute a violation of the federal prohibitions on payments for referrals, counsel should be consulted in connection with the purchase of good will.

Perform Due Diligence

A thorough due diligence on the assets to be acquired should be performed. The due diligence includes a physical inspection (e.g., environmental; structural; soils; equipment; and heating, ventilating, and air conditioning systems [HVAC]) and a thorough review of contracts, leases, medical, and personnel records. If the cultures of the two organizations are different, the resolution of that culture difference should be thoroughly discussed. The pension plans and other benefit plans of the two organizations should also be reviewed, to determine whether affiliation or other rules apply and what the new pension and benefit structure ought to be. The following issues also are likely to surface: union agreements, different compensation arrangements for personnel, bond and loan agreement compliance issues, and assignability of certain contracts and leases.

Define Financing Options

If the acquisition of the group or physicians and the assets are to be financed, the financing mechanism and documents should be addressed before closing. Since a tax-exempt financing can sometimes take two to six months to arrange, this should be addressed with significant time before the closing. If the hospital is to contribute funds at the closing to capitalize the foundation, this too should be worked out prior to the closing. To preserve the hospital's tax-exempt status, the hospital may want to characterize funds it contributes as a loan until the foundation obtains its tax-exempt status.

Form the Corporation

The foundation's articles should be filed with the secretary of state in the state in which the foundation is located (foreign incorporation will be of little benefit to a nonprofit corporation).

Apply for Tax-Exempt Status

When the parties have completed the charter documents (articles and bylaws), acquisition documents (asset purchase agreement and exhibits, financing agreements), and operating documents (professional services agreement and business plan), they should apply for tax-exempt status for the foundation. IRS Form 1023 is the application with the IRS; each state will have its own form for income and property tax exemption.

Apply for a Provider Number

The Medicare provider number for the foundation should be applied for at the same time the tax-exempt status is applied for.

Notify the Payors

Payors should be notified of the conversion to a foundation and should be asked to consent in writing (where there are a substantial number of managed care lives, this step may be crucial to the hospital's willingness to go forward with the deal).

Closing

The final step to form the foundation is the closing of the asset purchase agreement. At the closing, the foundation will acquire the assets of the group, assume certain liabilities, enter into the professional services agreement, and retain all the nonphysician employees. Immediately after the closing, the foundation can begin operating as a medical corporation.

TAX EXEMPTION AND INTEGRATED DELIVERY SYSTEMS*

William J. Aseltyne and Gerald R. Peters

In forming an organization that will be used as a means for hospital–physician integration, one of the many threshold questions is whether the organization should be proprietary or nonprofit. The differences are more than cosmetic, running to the very purpose or mission of the organization. A proprietary organization is intended to provide its owners with a profit, while a nonprofit's assets must be used for public, rather than private, purposes.

If a nonprofit structure is chosen, a second question is whether the organization will seek to qualify for federal tax-exempt status under the Internal Revenue Code. Tax-exempt status has many benefits: the organization is not subject to the federal corporate income tax (35 percent as of this writing), or certain excise and unemployment taxes; it may gain access to low-cost capital through the use of tax-exempt bond proceeds;

and it may receive deductible contributions. In addition, certain other benefits may flow from federal exemption, including exemption from state income taxes and local property taxes.

This article describes the requirements that an integrated delivery system must meet in most circumstances in order to obtain federal tax-exempt status. This article also briefly describes the process for applying for tax-exempt status.

REQUIREMENTS FOR EXEMPTION

The Internal Revenue Code (the "Code") provides that an organization may be exempt from federal taxation if it meets certain criteria set forth in Section 501 of the Code. For an organization that provides health care services, the applicable criteria are found in Section 501(c)(3): the organization must be organized and operated exclusively—which has been interpreted to mean primarily[1]—for charitable purposes; no part of its net earnings may inure to the benefit of any private shareholder or individual; and no substantial part of its activities may involve in-

Source: This section is reprinted from W.J. Aseltyne and G.R. Peters, Tax Exemption and Integrated Delivery Systems, in *Topics in Health Care Financing*, Vol. 20, No. 3, pp. 46–53, Aspen Publishers, Inc., © 1994.

fluencing legislation. These criteria have generated several "tests" that are discussed below. These tests have been applicable primarily to hospitals, since they have been the traditional tax-exempt organizations in the health care arena; however, the IRS appears ready to adapt these tests to integrated delivery systems.

Charitable Purposes Test

Organization and Operation

Since an organization must be organized and operated primarily for charitable purposes, its governing documents (e.g., charter or articles of incorporation) must set forth the specific charitable purposes for which the organization has been created. The documents also must limit the organization to activities that generally further those purposes.

Community Benefit

The definition of the charitable purposes served by hospitals has evolved over time. For many years, the IRS required hospitals to provide some "relief of the poor" (i.e., charity care) in order to be deemed charitable, and thus tax exempt.[2] In 1969, however, the IRS established a new standard for hospitals seeking tax-exempt status, stating that the "promotion of health" was charitable if it benefited the community.[3] The IRS found that a hospital provided such "community benefit," even though it did not offer uncompensated inpatient care, if the hospital did the following:

- operated an emergency room open to all persons, regardless of ability to pay
- provided inpatient care to persons able to pay the cost of such care either directly or through third-party reimbursement
- was governed by a board of directors comprising independent community leaders
- had a medical staff open to all qualified physicians

Since 1969, the IRS has, with few exceptions, required these factors for hospitals to qualify as tax exempt. More recently, the IRS appears to have added a fifth requirement: the activities of the hospital must not violate federal laws such as the patient transfer law or the Medicare antifraud and abuse law.[4]

Several state and local authorities have taken a more aggressive approach to community benefit than the IRS, particularly since the mid-1980s, seeking to condition state or local tax exemptions on the provision of charity care.[5] In addition, legislation has been introduced in Congress (although no such legislation is pending as of this writing) that would have mandated certain levels of charity care in order for hospitals to retain their federal tax exemptions.[6] Such efforts are likely to continue unless Congress enacts a health care reform plan that provides universal access to health care.

Private Inurement Test

Section 501(c)(3) provides that the net earnings of an exempt organization may not inure to a private individual or shareholder. "The inurement prohibition serves to prevent anyone in a position to do so from siphoning off any of a charity's income or assets for personal use."[7]

The prohibition on inurement is absolute—that is, any inurement is sufficient to disqualify an organization from tax exemption. The prohibition, however, only applies to arrangements with "insiders." An insider is a person who is in a position to control or influence the activities of the organization. In the IRS's view, hospital insiders include all physicians on the medical staff, as well as directors and top management.[8]

The prohibition on inurement does not foreclose every financial arrangement between an exempt organization and insiders, although it does subject any such arrangements to increased scrutiny. Therefore, to avoid inurement, all arrangements with insiders should be negotiated at arm's length (i.e., as two unrelated parties would negotiate), and any compensation or other benefit should be commercially reasonable (i.e., payment of fair market value in exchange for goods or services).

Private Benefit Test

The private benefit test requires that any private benefit that results from the activities of an exempt organization must be incidental to the public benefit achieved by its activities.[9] Thus, any private benefit must be insubstantial in amount, and it must occur only as an unavoidable result of the organization's activities. While the prohibition on inurement applies only to insiders, the private benefit test applies to any benefit provided to nonexempt persons or organizations.

Political Activities Test

This test provides that an exempt organization cannot participate in any political campaign on behalf of a candidate for public office. An exempt organization may engage in activities that influence legislation, as long as such activities are an "insubstantial" part of the organization's operations.

APPLICATION TO INTEGRATED DELIVERY SYSTEMS

Until 1993, the IRS had offered little guidance as to how it would apply the above tests to an integrated delivery system that provides both hospital and physician services. The IRS has, however, approved the tax-exempt applications of two integrated systems in California: Friendly Hills HealthCare Network and Facey Medical Foundation. In addition, the IRS has published guidelines for its technical staff to use when considering exemption applications for newly created integrated delivery systems.[10] The IRS's rulings on the two arrangements and its guidelines indicate how it is inclined to treat the exemption of newly formed integrated delivery systems.[11]

Structure of Friendly Hills and Facey Transactions

The Friendly Hills transaction involved an integrated delivery system structured as a "medical foundation."[12] The Friendly Hills Foundation planned to purchase a 274-bed general acute care hospital, 10 clinic facilities and related real estate, equipment, inventory, medical records, and certain intangible assets (e.g., covenants not to compete, capitated payor contracts, trade names, etc.) from a multispecialty medical group comprised of approximately 160 physicians. The medical group's assets were valued at $125 million, although the purchase price would be set at $110 million, with the remaining $15 million to be treated as a charitable donation by the medical group members.

After the asset acquisition, the Friendly Hills Foundation would enter into a contract with the medical group, which would be reorganized and no longer own any assets, to provide health care services to Foundation patients. Compensation to the medical group would be paid primarily on a capitated basis.

The Facey Foundation was created as a part of UniHealth America, a multihospital health care system, in order to further the system's goal of providing "access to quality health care services at an affordable price."[13] A wholly owned taxable subsidiary of UniHealth planned to purchase the stock of Facey Medical Group, Inc., a multispecialty medical group, for a purchase price of $8,833,000. The medical group comprised 24 physician shareholders, with approximately 24 other physician-employees, and it delivered services at five clinic locations. The medical group owned the personal property and other assets at the clinics, but it leased the clinic office space. The purchase price included the medical group's intangible assets (e.g., trade name, patient records, software, workforce, payor contracts, covenants-not-to-compete, and good will).

After the purchase, the assets would be transferred (by some unspecified means) from the taxable subsidiary to the Facey Foundation. The Foundation, in turn, would enter into a services agreement with a newly formed medical group pursuant to which the group would provide health care services to Foundation "enrollees," and the Foundation would provide management services and nonphysician support personnel to the group. Compensation to the medical group would be based on a "reasonable percentage of adjusted gross revenue" for the first two years of the agreement, and thereafter would be based on arm's-length negotiations, reflecting competitive rates and not exceeding reasonable compensation.

The IRS's Analysis

The IRS's rulings in Facey and Friendly Hills do not offer much explanation of how the tax-exemption criteria might be applied generally to integrated delivery systems.[14] One difficulty with the rulings is that they do not single out which criteria are essential for tax exemption, and which others are favorable but optional. Nevertheless, the facts on which the IRS based its rulings are likely to become standards that an integrated organization must meet in order to receive a favorable ruling from the IRS. This is reflected in the IRS's recently issued training guidelines. Although an organization that does not meet certain specific criteria may still qualify for tax-exempt status, the process for doing so is likely to be more arduous.[15]

Charitable Purpose and Community Benefit

An integrated delivery system, like a hospital, must show that its organization and operations are designed to provide community benefit, thus furthering charitable purposes. The IRS, however, appears to have imposed more stringent requirements for an integrated delivery system to demonstrate such community benefit.

Emergency and Urgent Care Services

In both Facey and Friendly Hills, the IRS continued to require the provision of emergency services to patients regardless of their ability to pay. In Facey, the IRS looked to the acute care hospitals that were part of the system operated by Facey's parent corporation, rather than to Facey itself, which did not own or operate an acute care facility. In both rulings, the IRS also extended this requirement to physician clinics, requiring them to provide services to "anyone in immediate need of care" without regard to ability to pay.[16]

Charity Care

Facey and Friendly Hills each agreed to provide a certain amount of charity care in order to receive a favorable ruling from the IRS. Facey agreed to provide a specific amount of charity care (a minimum of $400,000 per year), while Friendly Hills offered to provide inpatient and outpatient services to "indigent emergency room patients" who required such services. This suggests that, for integrated delivery systems, the IRS may be resurrecting its pre-1969 hospital standard requiring charity care and applying it to outpatient, as well as inpatient, services.

Medicare and Medicaid

The rulings suggest that integrated delivery systems will have to meet a requirement similar to that applicable to hospitals—they must participate in the Medicare and Medicaid programs at both hospital and clinic sites without discriminating against program beneficiaries.

Open Medical Staff

Here, too, integrated delivery systems must meet the same requirement applicable to hospitals—their acute care hospitals must have medical staffs open to any qualified physicians. Some commentators have argued that this requirement will impede an integrated organization's ability to realize the benefits of managed care, which require an emphasis on primary care physicians.[17]

Research and Education

In both Facey and Friendly Hills, the IRS noted that the foundations provided significant programs in clinical research and public health education. In California, many integrated delivery systems are being organized under a provision of state licensure law that requires such programs. Whether the IRS intended to incorporate this into its standard for tax exemption is not clear. Of course, providing such programs provides a community benefit and therefore should be viewed favorably by the IRS even if it is not a requirement for tax exemption.

Governance

One of the most controversial aspects of the two rulings has been the IRS's statements regarding the governance of the integrated organizations. Both the Facey Foundation and the Friendly Hills Foundation would be governed by a 10-member board of directors. No more than two directors would represent the related medical groups, and no more than two directors would have financial interests in the operations of the foundations. In the Facey ruling, the IRS noted that board committees "also must be independent and broadly representative of the community," not including committees dealing with clinical matters, which "may contain unlimited physician participation."[18]

This "20 percent test"[19] has been criticized as too strict, forcing an integrated organization to forgo the expertise afforded by more significant physician participation.[20] One alternative would be to permit greater physician participation on the board and in committees, without giving control of the organization to physicians. This might involve a board comprised of 49 percent physicians and 51 percent community leaders, limited use of supermajority votes, and a conflict-of-interest policy that prohibits directors from voting on matters in which they have a financial interest (which, in many states, is already required under nonprofit corporation laws). The IRS's position on governance may be a "deal killer" for many potential participants—particularly physicians—in an integrated organization.

Compliance with Other Federal Laws

If the 20 percent test is the most criticized aspect of the IRS's two recent rulings, the lack of guidance on how the Medicare fraud and abuse law affects integration has raised the most questions. In both Facey and Friendly Hills, the IRS conditioned its rulings on compliance with the antikickback statute, which the IRS has usually left to the Office of the Inspector General (OIG) at the Department of Health and Human Services to enforce.[21]

Some of the confusion comes from a letter written in December 1992 by D. McCarty Thornton, Associate General Counsel at the OIG, to T.J. Sullivan, Technical Assistant for Health Care Industries at the IRS.[22] Thornton's letter states that it was written in response to the IRS's request for "informal" advice on the OIG's position with respect to the acquisition of physician practices. The letter states that such acquisitions, when made by hospitals or other nonphysician organizations, "raise grave questions of compliance with the antikickback statute"[23] because the arrangements might influence physicians' referral decisions.

The content and tone of the letter come close to suggesting that such acquisitions are a *per se* violation of the antikickback statute, in which event no organization could meet the compliance requirement for tax exemption. Thornton has since said that health care attorneys have overreacted to his letter, indicating that the letter was solely intended to highlight the potential for abuse in determining the purchase price for physician assets, and how physicians are compensated once they provide services to the new organization.[24] The IRS's recently issued training manual provides some guidance on valuation,[25] but the OIG, not the IRS, is charged with enforcing the antikickback statute, and so some confusion remains as to whether the IRS's position on valuation will comport with the OIG's.

Inurement and Private Benefit

The prohibition against inurement and private benefit will continue to apply to organizations seeking exemption. These tests, however, have played second fiddle to the IRS's pronouncements that integrated organizations must comply with the fraud and abuse law because the two most likely areas for inurement or private benefit are the acquisition of physician assets and physician compensation, both of which were addressed in Thornton's letter.

In the Facey and Friendly Hills determination letters, the IRS notes that the parties have represented that the physician assets (both tangible and intangible) were acquired at or below fair market value as determined by independent appraisals and arm's-length negotiations.

Physician compensation in both organizations will be determined by arm's-length negotiations, and such compensation will reflect competitive rates and will not exceed reasonable compensation. In addition, the Facey Foundation will have a committee, which does not include any physicians, to oversee physician compensation.

The IRS's tacit approval of the valuation of assets and physician compensation in Facey and Friendly Hills suggests that the inurement and private benefit tests were met, but such valuation and compensation are still subject to the OIG's standards. Again, until the OIG (rather than the IRS) provides more detailed guidance on acceptable methods of valuation and physician compensation, confusion on these standards will remain.

PROCESS FOR OBTAINING TAX-EXEMPT STATUS

What To File

In order for an organization to obtain federal tax-exempt status as a charitable organization, it must submit a Form 1023 application. The 1023 application requires an organization to describe in detail all material facts relevant to its operations, including basic factual information about the organization, a description of the activities the organization will undertake, and a budget or other financial information. The organization also must explain how it will be governed, and it must submit organizational documents such as articles of incorporation and bylaws.

When To File

An integrated organization should be "ready to go" before submitting a 1023 application; enough of the organization's operations should be finalized so that the IRS will be able to determine whether such operations meet the requirements for a tax-exempt organization. If too little information is provided, the IRS will seek additional information, which may delay consideration of the application. Thus, the organization may want to consider applying for exemption after negotiations have produced "final" documents, showing how physician practice assets will be acquired and how the newly created system will operate, but before integration takes place or the organization becomes operational (although the organization first may be incorporated under state law).

Alternatively, integration could proceed and the organization could become operational prior to obtaining tax-exempt status, with the condition that the arrangement would be unwound or restructured in order to meet any objections raised by the IRS. Therefore, whether tax exemption is sought before or after integration, the "final" documents should be subject to amendment, or at least to further negotiations, for purposes of obtaining the IRS's approval of the tax-exempt application.

An organization that applies for tax-exempt status within 15 months of the month in which it was formed will be treated as tax exempt retroactively to the date of its formation.

The Determination Letter or Ruling

The IRS issues a "determination letter" or "ruling" when it rules favorably on a 1023 application. A favorable ruling may be relied upon by the organization as long as there are no substantial changes in the organization's charter, purpose, or operations.

Determination letters are usually issued from the district offices of the IRS. Certain applications, however, are referred to the IRS's national office when they involve exemptions for which there is no precedent, or they involve more diffi-

cult questions of compliance with tax-exemption criteria. The Friendly Hills and Facey applications were both reviewed at the IRS's national office, and other applications involving integrated delivery systems may continue to be forwarded to the national office, although the IRS's issuance of guidelines for its staff suggests that it recognizes that exemption applications from integrated delivery systems may become routine.

MERCY MEDICAL FOUNDATION OF SACRAMENTO: A CASE STUDY*

Derek F. Covert

Mercy Medical Foundation of Sacramento was formed in September 1990, as the culmination of an 18-month negotiation process conducted between Mercy Healthcare Sacramento and the Medical Clinic of Sacramento, Inc. The goal of the process was to identify the ideal affiliation model between the hospital and medical group under existing state and federal laws and regulations. Mercy Medical Foundation represented the first true hospital-affiliated medical foundation in California; its formation coincided with the commencement of a frenzy of hospital/medical group affiliation discussions, increased regulatory scrutiny, and heightened national focus on "integrated delivery systems." Although it cannot be said that Mercy Medical Foundation represented the first hospital-oriented, multispecialty medical group practice in the country, its timing correlates directly to the development of the definition of integrated delivery systems, and the principles behind its structure and formation are echoed in the strategic plans of any hospital or health system with an eye toward the future.

Source: This section is reprinted from D.F. Covert, Mercy Medical Foundation of Sacramento: A Case Study, in *Topics in Health Care Financing*, Vol. 20, No. 3, pp. 70–79, Aspen Publishers, Inc., © 1994.

BACKGROUND

The Medical Clinic of Sacramento, Inc. (MCS), founded in 1948, is a multispecialty integrated group practice functioning in the Sacramento, California, area. At the time of the affiliation, MCS employed 57 physicians, including 27 shareholders. Primary care physicians represented approximately half of its staff, and just under half of its patient base represented managed care capitation arrangements.

In 1987, MCS occupied a newly constructed clinic facility in downtown Sacramento, under a long-term lease; a predecessor to Mercy Healthcare Sacramento was a 50 percent partner in the partnership that owned that facility. Additionally, five satellite facilities were operated by MCS in neighboring residential areas.

Mercy Healthcare Sacramento is a subsidiary of Catholic Healthcare West, a San Francisco-based, multifacility health care system operating 17 hospitals in California, Arizona, and Nevada, as well as numerous related health care activities. Catholic Healthcare West is cosponsored by three Catholic religious congregations: the Sisters of Mercy of Auburn, California; the Sisters of Mercy of Burlingame, California; and the Adrian Dominican Sisters of Adrian, Michigan. Mercy Healthcare Sacramento represents the

Sacramento region of Catholic Healthcare West, owning and operating five hospitals in and near Sacramento, California.

Mercy Healthcare Sacramento has grown from three to five hospitals in the last three years, primarily due to a consolidation of health care providers in the Sacramento region. Its relationship with MCS was related primarily to its role as a partner in the clinic facility leased and occupied by MCS described above. Additionally, Mercy Healthcare Sacramento and MCS were the primary providers under contract with TakeCare, an HMO with over 25,000 enrollees in the Sacramento area.

Sacramento was well into a consolidation process where hospitals and related providers were evolving into two hospital-oriented nonprofit systems organizations, including Mercy Healthcare Sacramento, plus a University of California-affiliated teaching hospital. Also, approximately one-third of the insured population is enrolled in the Kaiser Health closed-staff system. Additionally, a large "group without walls" practice was very active in the managed care arena.

Sacramento was suffering from a significant shortage of primary care physicians, and the few primary care physicians graduating from medical education programs were being funneled into the Kaiser Health System. As a tax-exempt organization, Mercy Healthcare Sacramento's ability to support the recruitment and retention of primary care physicians in the community was constrained by the inurement proscriptions of federal tax law, and the Inspector General's office of the Department of Health and Human Services was beginning to flex its muscles in the area of Medicare fraud and abuse, raising additional legal hurdles.

FACTORS LEADING TO AFFILIATION DISCUSSIONS

A variety of environmental pressures, combined with some unfortunate investment decisions by prior management, led to significant financial constraints on MCS. The cost of the long-term lease on the new clinic facility proved to be a significant dedication of capital, and the revenue increases anticipated from the new facility were not sufficient to offset the increased costs. Additionally, at a time when the medical group was shifting into a managed care environment, with related downward pressures on revenue, physician compensation was not adequately controlled.

As a result, MCS found itself with a large bank loan coming due, while experiencing a current deficit. The bank loan was extended and the deficit financed, at the expense of obtaining personal guarantees from the shareholder physicians, accounts receivable, and additional personal guarantees to secure a partial debt guarantee from Mercy Healthcare Sacramento. In order to adequately serve the debt, and avoid future deficits, physician compensation was gradually reduced by approximately 20 percent. As a result of the reduced physician compensation, MCS found it almost impossible to recruit additional physicians, particularly much-needed primary care physicians in the very competitive Sacramento environment.

By early 1989, MCS was immobilized by the juxtaposition of its two key problems: excess capacity and an inability to recruit. Although MCS probably could have maintained the status quo for some period, its leadership identified an immediate need to obtain access to additional capital in order to position itself for growth in the rapidly expanding managed care environment in Sacramento. Additionally, concerns arose regarding the ability to retain its existing medical staff as employment contracts expired.

Mercy Healthcare Sacramento had survived an earlier unsuccessful attempt at developing a so-called "group without walls" under a practice management company structure (now known as management services organizations, or MSOs). The experience created tension between the hospitals and medical staffs, as well as division among the medical staffs.

Other than a handful of relatively straightforward joint ventures, Mercy Healthcare Sacramento's primary foray in the physician affiliation arena was limited to the development of a regionwide independent practice association (IPA). As a typical IPA, its activities were essentially limited to independent physicians, and the vast majority of its physician members were specialists. Although the IPA had some success in obtaining managed care contracts, by definition it was unable to integrate physician practices and implement effective utilization and quality programs.

The substance of Mercy Healthcare Sacramento's relationship with the IPA was management services provided pursuant to a management services agreement. Mercy Healthcare Sacramento was ready and willing to evaluate other options for hospital-physician affiliations, provided that a higher chance of success than the MSO model was identified, accommodating a structure that would permit integration and effective utilization and quality programs.

More importantly, MCS and Mercy Healthcare Sacramento, through working together on joint managed care contracts, the clinic facility development and lease, and debt restructuring, had developed a relationship and identified basic congruence of values, goals, objectives, and a vision of the future. Through their experience in the managed care environment, both had identified a need to modify their structures to accommodate the changes in behavior and processes that would be necessary to succeed in a managed care environment. Although northern California had not yet entered into the Medicare managed risk business, southern California was dabbling, and both parties believed it was only a matter of time. It was clear to Mercy Healthcare Sacramento that although a motivating factor in the affiliation discussions for MSC was its financial problems, there were significant long-term benefits to both parties if an affiliation could be fashioned in an appropriate manner.

EVALUATION OF MODELS

The primary impediment to achieving the common objectives of Mercy Healthcare Sacramento and MCS was identifying a model that complied with federal and state legal parameters and accommodated the needs of the organizations to structure themselves as an integrated hospital–medical group organization. The traditional affiliation model in California was the MSO, and initial discussions were centered on that model; however, the handicaps of the MSO model loomed large in the memories of Mercy Healthcare Sacramento and Catholic Healthcare West.

Since California has a strong statutory prohibition against the corporate practice of medicine, the role of an MSO is limited to performing administrative and management functions on behalf of a medical group. Under this structure, it is very difficult to develop common financial incentives and goals, since the medical group retains complete control over payor contracting and physician hiring, and retains ownership of all revenues, subject to the payment of management fees to the MSO.

While it is possible under the MSO model for the MSO to control expenditures for space, equipment, and support staff, it is not possible for the MSO to acquire the intangible assets of the medical group, such as good will, medical records, and trade names. Under California state law, unless an organization acquires the good will of a predecessor, a covenant not to compete is not enforceable. Since an MSO is unable to acquire intangible assets of a medical group, the purchase price of assets acquired from the medical group is limited to the fair market value of its tangible assets, such as equipment, furniture, and any real property.

In the case of MCS, the acquisition of its tangible property by Mercy Healthcare Sacramento would not have provided sufficient funds to eliminate its debt, and it would be unable to realize any financial benefit from transferring its primary asset, namely the going-concern value of a multispecialty group practice, with managed care contracts, almost 70 physicians, and over 300 support staff, trained, in place, and functioning. MCS's trade name, "MedClinic," had significant recognition in the Sacramento community, and the medical group operated an ambulatory surgery center and clinical laboratory.

Of significant concern to Mercy Healthcare Sacramento in evaluating the MSO model for an affiliation with MCS, was the knowledge that to develop MCS's medical practice in accordance with its vision would require significant investment and incur significant operating losses during the turnaround/development period. As a tax-exempt organization, Mercy Healthcare Sacramento would need to avoid a situation that the IRS could characterize as prohibited inurement. It was felt that the likelihood of obtaining a private letter ruling from the IRS under the MSO scenario was unlikely, and a transaction that significantly jeopardized Mercy Healthcare Sacramento's tax-exempt status was not a possibility.

In a search for alternative structures, a licensing exemption in California state law was identified, which permitted nonprofit, tax-exempt organizations to operate clinics, so long as the organization had under contract at least 40 physicians, covering 10 board-certified specialties, two-thirds of whom worked full time performing services for the organization, and the organization performed health services education and research. The statute in question, Section 1206(l) of the California Health and Safety Code, had been adopted in 1980, under the co-sponsorship of legislators representing the districts where two large multispecialty group practices were located. Those group practices, the Palo Alto Medical Clinic, and the Santa Barbara Medical Clinic, had sought the exemption in connection with their earlier conversion to nonprofit status. As with most special interest legislation, the statute, perhaps unintentionally, provided an opportunity for other qualifying organizations to fit within the exemption.

Neither the Palo Alto Medical Foundation nor the Santa Barbara Medical Foundation, nor two subsequent foundations formed in the late 1980s, were affiliated with hospitals or other nonprofit health care providers. Although the Rees-Stealy Medical Group of San Diego had affiliated with the Sharp health system earlier, its structure was a modified MSO, which, upon analysis, did not appear to meet the needs of

Mercy Healthcare Sacramento and MCS.

In investigating the statute, including interviews with individuals involved in the conversions of the Palo Alto Medical Foundation and Santa Barbara Medical Foundation, it was determined that there was no reason that a hospital organization could not sponsor an organization qualifying under Section 1206(l), and the parties embarked on an evaluation of the foundation model. After joint visits to the Virginia Mason Clinic in Seattle, Washington, and the Palo Alto Medical Foundation, negotiations for the formation of Mercy Medical Foundation of Sacramento commenced. The structures of the existing California foundations were studied, but it was determined that the involvement of a hospital organization created a new set of dynamics that had not been a consideration in the organizations studied.

DEVELOPMENT OF ORGANIZATIONAL STRUCTURE

Identification of the foundation model and the structure of the affiliation was a quantum leap in meeting the common goals and objectives of the parties, as well as working through the legal issues. While it cannot be said that the medical foundation model is a legal panacea, and the model has a number of legal complications of its own, it proved to be much more manageable from a legal, financial, and organizational governance perspective.

Organizational and Governance Issues

The structure that was identified involved a new nonprofit subsidiary of Mercy Healthcare Sacramento, which would be named Mercy Medical Foundation of Sacramento. Mercy Medical Foundation would structure its affiliation with MCS in a manner that complied with Section 1206(l), qualifying it for exemption from California's licensing requirements. Although Mercy Medical Foundation would not be permitted to employ physicians, it could operate the clinics in a fashion that permitted it to purchase the intangible assets of MCS, and operate the group practice in its own name, on its own behalf, pursuant to a professional services agreement with MCS, whereby MCS's employed physicians would provide professional medical services to the patients of Mercy Medical Foundation.

Since Mercy Medical Foundation could legally acquire the intangible assets of MCS, including its trade name, payor contracts, medical records, and good will, a purchase price was negotiated (subject to independent appraisal) that allowed MCS to retire substantially all of its existing debt. Using capital obtained through a line of credit from Mercy Healthcare Sacramento, Mercy Medical Foundation was able to invest further in the infrastructure, the recruitment of primary care physicians, and the development of additional facilities of the group practice.

As the owner of the group practice, including its revenues, Mercy Medical Foundation had much more flexibility. While many legal issues remained, the inurement issue was reduced to determining whether the acquisition price was fair market value, and whether the compensation paid to MCS for professional medical services was reasonable. Mercy Medical Foundation would employ the support staff, assume real property leases, acquire virtually all the tangible property, and assume the payor contracts of MCS.

Since Mercy Healthcare Sacramento would serve as the sole corporate member of Mercy Medical Foundation, it would appoint the board of directors and the chief executive officer, approve budgets and capital expenditures, and influence the strategic direction of the group practice (see Figure 28–6). Additionally, Mercy Medical Foundation would be considered a Catholic health care provider under Canon Law, obligating the group practice to be operated in conformance with the ethical and religious directives governing Catholic health care facilities. While this requirement necessitated considerable discussion, and consultation with the local bishop's representatives, it was not a significant impediment in the affiliation.

Compliance with IRS guidelines for organizations that issue tax-exempt debt was necessary, since it was anticipated that Mercy Medical Foundation would attempt to acquire the clinic facility in order to reduce its occupancy costs. Pursuant to Revenue Procedure 82-15, the governing board of Mercy Medical Foundation would be limited to 20 percent representation from MCS. Again, while causing considerable discussion, this was not a significant impediment to the affiliation. MCS agreed to perform certain charity functions, and educational and research activities were identified that would continue.

Operational Issues

Once the organizational and governance issues were identified and resolved, attention was focused on the operational issues. The operational issues were more complicated, given the lack of a precedential model in California, the concerns of the MCS physicians in losing the autonomy necessary to practice effective quality medicine, and Mercy's lack of experience in managing group practices. A number of items were identified that would be handled on an evolutionary basis, based on trust and cooperation between the parties. These matters included the credentialing of existing and new physicians, quality assurance, and utilization review.

MCS would remain in existence, and its board of directors would retain a significant role in matters relating to the functioning of the medical group. Scheduling of physicians, the establishment of physician compensation systems, hiring and firing of physicians, out-of-group referrals, and similar matters remained under the control of MCS. A compensated medical director position was identified, and although it functioned as a liaison to the management of Mercy Medical Foundation, it reported to the MCS board of directors. Responsibilities were shared for physician recruitment and payor contracting strategies. Over time, the relationship has become somewhat collaborative, and more sharing of responsibilities has evolved. The division of re-

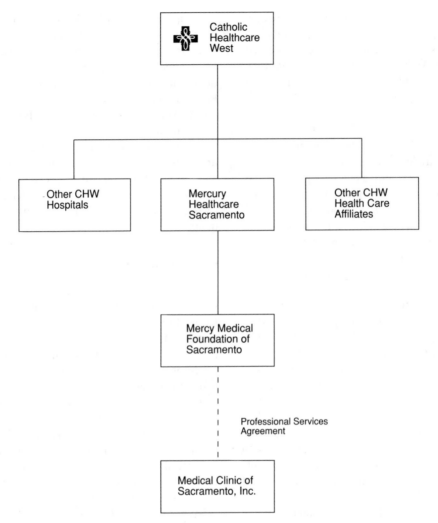

Figure 28–6 Organizational Structure Diagram Depicting the Affiliation between Mercy Medical Foundation and MCS

sponsibilities for primary functions is presented in Exhibit 28–2.

Of critical importance to Mercy Healthcare Sacramento was the communication of the arrangement to the medical community. Predictably, word that Mercy Healthcare Sacramento was "giving" a large amount of money to the MCS member physicians spread before a formal communication was conducted. Stormy medical staff meetings were held at which Mercy Healthcare Sacramento's "pluralistic" approach to medical staff development was described.

Mercy Healthcare Sacramento would continue to support the activities of the IPA, would continue its focus on specialty "centers of excellence," and the foundation model would remain available to other medical groups interested in pursuing MCS's strategy.

The most difficult allegation to confront was the charge that Mercy Healthcare Sacramento was entering into direct competition with its medical staffs. The shortage of primary care physicians provided some comfort to independent primary care physicians, but nonaligned

Exhibit 28–2 Primary Operational Functions

Mercy Medical Foundation
Payor contracting
Facilities and equipment
Support staff
Capital
Medical Clinic of Sacramento, Inc.
Professional medical services
Credentialing
Quality assurance
Utilization management

specialists correctly perceived the indirect threat, and if anything probably underestimated the long-term implications.

By the time the affiliation was implemented, most outside parties assumed it was already in place. A simple press interview was conducted, and other forms of publicity were avoided. Regulatory attention was quickly generated as a result of necessary filings, but outside attention was considered undesirable.

It took several months to work out the Medicare provider issues, due to the inflexibility of existing regulations. Approval for the tax exemption of Mercy Medical Foundation from the IRS National Office was easily obtained, but requests for copies of the exemption application from outside parties under federal disclosure laws were numerous, since there was a great deal of interest on the part of the health care legal industry in analyzing its revolutionary structure.

THE NEW WORLD

One thing all the parties to the affiliation would no doubt agree upon is that the dust has never settled. The evolution of the group practice occurred much more rapidly than anticipated, and opportunities for Mercy Medical Foundation to expand and enhance its purpose have exceeded its ability to respond. In a conscious effort not to overextend its resources, Mercy Medical Foundation has proceeded with due consideration, developing and maintaining consensus between the leadership of Mercy

Healthcare Sacramento and MCS; thoroughly analyzing new payor contracts, acquisitions, and the establishment of new satellite facilities; as well as the divestiture of the ambulatory surgery center, physical therapy service, and clinical laboratory. Supported by the economics and medical staff politics, some ancillary activities were consolidated with those of the Mercy Healthcare Sacramento hospitals.

Under the terms of the professional services agreement between Mercy Medical Foundation and MCS, MCS remained responsible for the payment to outside medical services. Given the obvious financial incentive to control those expenditures, MCS has instituted initiatives to subcapitate outside services where possible, negotiate reduced prices where possible, and minimize its use of outside services while maintaining a quality perspective. Having grown to over 100 doctors since the affiliation, MCS is continually re-evaluating the buy versus build analysis for the provision of specialty or ancillary services. Almost all of its growth has been in primary care physicians, though occupational medicine and urgent care services have been expended.

Mercy Medical Foundation has adopted a multiple-payor approach and has entered into managed care contracts with several new HMOs. Negotiations for provider contracts between the hospitals and the group practice have been coordinated, and at least two HMOs have terminated exclusive arrangements with other hospitals in return for the ability to contract with Mercy Medical Foundation and Mercy Healthcare Sacramento. The ensuring experiences, and the ability to conduct joint planning, have enabled the parties to perform a thorough comprehensive analysis of potential payor arrangements, culminating in a decision to commence Medicare risk contracting. The decision to contract for Medicare risk was deferred until the parties were comfortable, particularly since it became apparent that the HMOs would not initiate significant enrollment without Mercy Medical Foundation's participation.

The management structure of Mercy Medical Foundation initially consisted of the previous

MCS management, but substantial changes have been made, adding sophistication in operating systems, financial accounting, contract analysis and negotiation, and utilization review. Upgrades in management information systems have been made, but the long-term goal is to integrate the financial and clinical information systems with those of Mercy Healthcare Sacramento. Employee benefits have been improved, and support staff morale has increased. Quality improvement and mission awareness systems of Mercy Healthcare Sacramento have been adapted for Mercy Medical Foundation, but more thorough integration has been identified as a need.

A recent joint planning retreat between MCS, Mercy Medical Foundation, and Mercy Healthcare Sacramento very effectively identified substantial congruence in vision, but also isolated areas of disagreement. The rapid rate of growth, retention of physician autonomy and competitive compensation, the development of managed care systems, and a voice in the strategic direction of Mercy Healthcare Sacramento and Catholic Healthcare West were identified as concerns of MCS member physicians. A shared sense of dedication to the health of the community, the need to control costs and growth, and common visions of the evolution of managed care were agreed upon.

Acceptance of the group practice/medical foundation model in the Sacramento area has increased somewhat. The only other integrated group practice in the Sacramento region, the "group without walls" referred to above, entered into a hospital-sponsored foundation model with the other major Sacramento health care system in May 1992, although it has recently taken steps to shift its focus to primary care physicians. As primary care physicians in the community join MCS/Mercy Medical Foundation, some independent specialists have experienced volume reductions, and Mercy Healthcare Sacramento has experienced repercussions. Nevertheless, most skeptics now appreciate the effectiveness of the organization, though many seek to avoid its effects.

IMPLICATIONS FOR CATHOLIC HEALTHCARE WEST

The formation of Mercy Medical Foundation provided an impetus for Catholic Healthcare West in the development of integrated delivery systems. Although only one other foundation model has been established in the Catholic Healthcare West system, discussions are currently under way in four additional communities regarding foundation model medical group practices. Due in part to its experience with the integration with MCS, Catholic Healthcare West has developed expertise in medical group management and has been approached by unaffiliated, physician-owned medical group practices for affiliation discussions. Hospitals unaffiliated with Catholic Healthcare West are also attracted to the possibility of becoming affiliated with its group practice models, and mechanisms have been developed to pursue such opportunities.

Catholic Healthcare West has identified as a major strategic goal the integration of physician group practices with its hospital activities. Recognizing that hospital services will become a cost center under true managed care, Catholic Healthcare West has identified the need to devote resources and management expertise to the formation of medical group practices, and their integration into the health care network. In furtherance thereof, Mercy Medical Foundation was renamed CHW Medical Foundation, and its corporate membership transferred to Catholic Healthcare West, effective January 1, 1994.

While significant progress has been made in converting the Sacramento region into an integrated delivery system, much work remains to be done to truly align the goals, objectives, and financial incentives for all parties involved in the delivery of health care services to the community. However, if the dust ever settles, it is a safe bet that the formation of Mercy Medical Foundation of Sacramento will be viewed as the turning point for Mercy Healthcare Sacramento and Catholic Healthcare West in their conversion to an integrated delivery system.

CASE STUDY: THE INTEGRATION OF A MEDICAL FOUNDATION AND AN INDEPENDENT PRACTICE ASSOCIATION*

Robert A. Waterman and M. Lawrence Bonham

In December 1991, the board of directors of Health Dimensions Incorporated (HDI) faced one of the most important decisions in its history. The four-hospital system, based in San Jose, California, had to decide whether to form a medical foundation. HDI was being asked not only to form the foundation, but also to fund the acquisition by the foundation of the Good Samaritan Medical Group (the Group), an integrated group which at that time had 23 full-time physicians and about 27,000 managed care lives.

BACKGROUND

The HDI board was presented with several reasons for forming a foundation. The primary reasons were market-driven—HDI's once-dominant market share in Santa Clara County was under attack from well-funded competitors. In that environment, capturing and retaining the fast-growing managed care business was essential to HDI's survival. Retaining that managed care business meant working together with physicians in an integrated delivery system approach.

The HDI system studied various ways to work with physicians in an integrated delivery system approach, including a management services organization and a physician–hospital organization, among others. The foundation model was chosen because it was the most attractive to

those payors who paid by capitation. The foundation model also allowed HDI legally to fund the organization, since the foundation, like HDI, would be a nonprofit, 501(c)(3) tax-exempt entity.

Under Section 1026(l) of California's Health and Safety Code, in order for HDI to enter into a medical foundation, it needed to contract with at least 40 physicians, and two-thirds (or at last 27) were required to be full time with the foundation. Thus, a medical foundation required a full-time integrated group. Given this, the Group was the logical choice—it would have the required 27 full-time physicians experienced with managed care, had worked with the HDI system for years, and was willing to enter into the transactions necessary to effect the foundation.

On the other hand, there were substantial arguments put forth by the opponents of the foundation model. The most powerful argument was this: the foundation was to be funded by HDI, but only included a small fraction of its medical staff. Wasn't there some way to include these other physicians?

FORMING THE FOUNDATION

The HDI board, in December 1991, was persuaded by both of these arguments: that is, it saw the formation of a foundation as in the best interests of the system, yet wanted other physicians on the medical staffs to be able to participate. The board's solution was to include, as part of the foundation, a large existing independent practice association (IPA) affiliated with HDI's medical staff—the IPA of Santa Clara Valley (see Figure 28–7). Formed in 1986, the IPA had

Source: This section is reprinted from R.A. Waterman and M.L. Bonham, Case Study: The Integration of a Medical Foundation and an Independent Practice Association, in *Topics in Health Care Financing*, Vol. 20, No. 3, pp. 80–85, Aspen Publishers, Inc., © 1994.

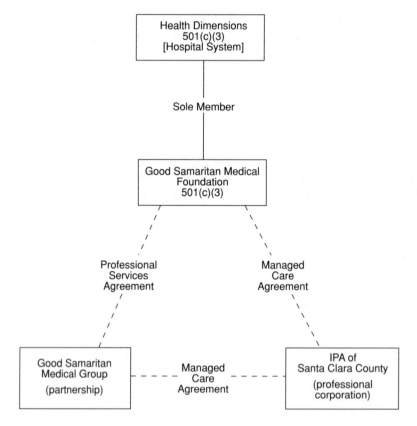

Figure 28–7 Organizational Diagram Depicting the Structure of the Good Samaritan Medical Foundation

approximately 300 physician shareholders, about 90 of whom were primary care physicians.

Problems

Including the IPA, however, meant overcoming numerous hurdles. Failure to overcome any of them could have meant the loss of the Group, the loss of a foundation, and perhaps could have endangered HDI's long-term viability.

No Precedent

There were no obvious precedents to a formal IPA-group-medical foundation integrated governance structure.

Different Cultures

Some said that mixing an integrated group and an IPA hadn't been done because it couldn't

be done. The ethos of the two organizations was too different, the argument went. The Group physicians were employees, the IPA physicians independents. The Group's practice was largely capitated medicine; the IPA physicians, on the other hand, had only a small percentage of their practices capitated. Finally, the Group physicians' entire practice was with the Group; the IPA physicians, on the other hand, often had less than 1 percent of their practices with the IPA. All these factual differences created enormous potential differences in outlook and attitude toward forming a medical foundation together.

Lack of Trust

At the beginning, the Group and the IPA had little trust for each other. Many IPA physicians believed that the Group might want to simply acquire the IPA and then dissolve it, and would be unwilling to treat the IPA as a true partner. Some physicians in the Group, on the other hand, believed that the IPA was seeking to share in the Group's much greater number of capitated patients but still maintain control, and that the IPA physicians, inexperienced with managed care compared to the Group, could bankrupt the new foundation.

Statutory Issues

Section 1206(l) of the California Health and Safety Code provides that a medical foundation must provide health care to its patients "through a group of 40 or more physicians and surgeons, who are independent contractors representing not less than 10 board-certified specialties, and not less than two-thirds of whom practice on a full-time basis at the clinic."[26] Since the approximately 300 physicians in the IPA would be part-time with the foundation, if the IPA and Group were to contract with the foundation, the foundation would not meet the "two-thirds full-time" requirement of Section 1206(l). This problem had to be solved before any foundation could be formed.

Governance

The group believed that since it brought to the foundation 27,000 managed care lives, over five times what the IPA brought, and substantially all the foundation's personnel and assets, it should be entitled to more governance control of the foundation than the IPA. The IPA, on the other hand, believed that it offered the foundation a substantial network of high-quality physicians, and that the Group was being paid for bringing its assets to the foundation. Accordingly, the IPA wanted equality with the Group as to board and committee control.

Exclusivity

The IPA wanted to be the exclusive network to the foundation. The Group desired to maintain its existing referral relationships. Although there was substantial overlap between the IPA and the specialist physician network of the Group, the Group feared disrupting its existing referral relationships.

Inclusion of IPA Physicians

The IPA wanted all its physicians eligible to be providers to the foundation on the day the foundation commenced operations. The Group, however, thought there were too many IPA specialists in certain areas to manage care effectively. The Group also was concerned that including all of IPA's primary care physicians— and allowing enrollees to choose either an IPA primary care physician or a Group primary care physician—would take patients away from the Group, and ultimately might lead to the destruction of the Group.

Solutions

To solve the problems set forth above, HDI, the IPA, and the Group established a task force to seek solutions. In the numerous task force meetings held over a three-month period, the parties grappled with the issues and got to know each other's point of view.

The potential synergies of the transaction kept the parties at the negotiating table. The Group, for example, began to see the IPA not only as a way to get a deal done with HDI, but also saw the marketing advantages of having the IPA as part of its organization. The IPA, which included about 90 primary care and about 210 specialist physicians, was geographically dispersed throughout the county and covered virtually all specialties. In addition, the Group saw that the IPA understood, as an organization, the necessity for managing care in a capitated environment.

The IPA, on the other hand, began to see the foundation model as a bold step for its future as an organization, and as a way to capture far more of the capitated business in the county for its member physicians. It also saw that being on the inside of the foundation would allow the IPA to help control the direction of one of the most important managed care forces in the country.

As the parties gained trust over time, the more detailed issues, such as governance and exclusivity, could now be addressed. The parties negotiated those issues in the context of two documents: the bylaws of the new foundation; and a managed care agreement among the Group, the IPA, and the foundation.

BYLAWS

The major Group–IPA integration issue addressed in the bylaws was governance, both on the board of directors of the foundation and on its committees.

Board of Directors

The Group initially insisted that it have one more seat on the foundation's board than the IPA; the IPA wanted an equal number of board seats. The Group eventually agreed to the IPA's position, largely because it could, as described below, initially have *ex-officio* representatives who would have the deciding votes on some key committees.

Committees

The parties discussed four different committees, whose authority and membership were extensively negotiated. The Manpower Committee would determine the criteria for adding part-time and full-time physicians. The Credentialing Committee would determine credentialing procedures and standards for the foundation. The Contracts Committee would negotiate all capitated contracts for the foundation. The Utilization Review Committee would develop and implement policies and procedures for utilization management and quality assurance for foundation patients.

All the committees had an equal number of Group and IPA representatives; however, the chairperson of each committee could break ties. The chairperson of the Manpower and Utilization Review Committees was the medical director (who was initially from the Group). The chairperson of the Contracts Committee was the chief executive officer of the foundation. The chairperson of the Credentialing Committee was the president of the foundation (who initially was also from the Group).

Officers

In order to distribute the officer positions between the IPA and the Group in an equal manner, the chairperson of the foundation was to be from the IPA, and the president of the foundation from the Group.

MANAGED CARE AGREEMENT

The major issues addressed by the parties in the Managed Care Agreement among the IPA, the Group, and HDI were exclusivity, phase-in, new group physicians, and compensation.

Exclusivity

The IPA asked for exclusivity for its physicians on all referrals. The final agreement states that the foundation must provide services *only* through the Group and the IPA, subject only to (a) certain grandfather provisions for existing referral relationships of the Group, and (b) the right of the foundation to add other groups or networks if there is a supermajority vote of the foundation's board and certain measures for the IPA are taken.

Phase-in

The Group asked that some of the IPA physicians not be "providers" to the foundation initially. Its concern was that there would be too many physicians, given the foundation's initial size. The agreement establishes objective standards as to when the growth of the foundation would be sufficient to justify adding additional IPA physicians as providers. (After the agreement was signed, the foundation accelerated that phase-in, and all of the primary care physicians and most of the specialists became providers to the foundation.)

New Group Physicians

The IPA was concerned that the Group would add specialists to its full-time membership.

Their solution: the agreement requires any new hires for the Group be reviewed first by the Manpower Committee.

Compensation

The Group is required to pay the IPA physicians a certain compensation rate for services—in some cases, capitation, in others, fee-for-service. Because the Group is liable for this payment, the IPA is technically a subcontractor to the Group, and therefore has no direct relationship to the foundation. This means that the foundation, as required under Section 1206(l) of the Health and Safety Code, is still only contracting through a group of physicians, two-thirds of whom are full time.

The managed care agreement was signed by all the parties on June 16, 1992—about six months after the board of directors of HDI authorized negotiations to begin between the IPA and the Group.

The foundation has since grown dramatically—in one year, almost doubling to over 40 full-time physicians and increasing the number of capitated lives over 50 percent, to over 40,000. The IPA and Group now work together on a daily basis, in numerous committees, to manage that growth, and to jointly gain market share for the foundation in Santa Clara County.

NOTES

1. IRC § 501(c)(3).

2. Rev. Ruling 56-185. (A hospital is charitable only if "operated to the extent of its financial ability for those not able to pay for services rendered and not exclusively for those able and expected to pay.")

3. Rev. Rul. 69-545.

4. *See* Internal Revenue Service Audit Guidelines for Hospitals, Contained in Manual Transmittal 7(10)69-38 for Exempt Organizations Examination Guidelines Handbook, Dated March 27, 1992 § 333.1; *cf.* Gen. Couns. Mem. 39862 (22 Nov. 1991).

5. *See*, e.g., *Utah County v. Intermountain Health Care, Inc.*, 709 P.2d 265 (Ut. 1985) (upholding tax assessment against two nonprofit hospitals primarily on the basis that the hospitals provided insufficient charity care); "Charity Health Bill Signed By Richard," *Houston Chron.*, 3 June 1993 (describing enactment of first state law to require hospitals to provide charity care in order to receive state and local tax breaks).

6. *See* H.R. 1374, 102d Cong., 1st Sess. (1991) (introduced by Congressman Donnelly); H.R. 790, 102d Cong., 1st Sess. (1991) (introduced by Congressman Roybal).

7. Gen. Couns. Mem. 39862, 8-9 (22 Nov. 1991).

8. Gen. Couns. Mem. 39498 (28 Jan. 1986).

9. Treas. Reg. § 1.501(c)(3)-1(d)(1).

10. Internal Revenue Service, 1993 Exempt Organizations Continuing Professional Education Technical Instruction Program Textbook.

11. To date, the IRS appears to be taking a more cautious approach with newly created integrated systems than it has with long-established integrated systems such as the Mayo Clinic.

12. IRS Doc. No. 93-1926 (29 Jan. 1993), *reprinted in* 7 Exempt Org. Tax Rev. 490 (March 1993). For a discussion of the different structures of integrated delivery system, see chapter 1.

13. IRS Doc. No. 93-4212 (31 March 1993), *reprinted in* 7 Exempt. Org. Tax Rev. 828 (May 1993).

14. Rulings and determination letters on tax-exempt status are generally not used by the IRS to expound tax policy, and such rulings and determination letters have no precedential value other than offering a glimpse of the IRS's mindframe on a certain matter.

15. Some commentators have suggested that the IRS, if challenged, could not enforce the standards set forth in the two rulings. *See*, e.g., Peters, *A Practical Examination of the IRS and OIG Rules for Integrated Delivery Systems*, 7 Exempt Org. Tax Rev. 765 (1993). Any such challenge, however, could be expensive and time consuming for the organization bringing it.

16. The IRS did not define what it meant by "immediate need of care." Presumably, the IRS was contemplating something broader than the definitions in the Patient Transfer Law, which only apply to acute care services. 42 U.S.C. § 1395dd.

17. Grant, Hanlon, and Margulis, "National Office of the Internal Revenue Service Approves Tax-Exemption for Medical Group Practices in Integrated Delivery System Context." Memorandum, 10 February 1993.

18. IRS Doc. No. 93-4212.

19. The IRS now also imposes a "20 percent test" on health care facilities that are the recipients of the proceeds from tax-exempt bond financings. *See* Rev. Proc. 93-19, 1993-11 I.R.B. 52.

20. *See* Peters, *supra* note 15.

21. 42 U.S.C. § 1320a-7b.

22. Letter from D. McCarty Thornton to T.J. Sullivan (22 Dec. 1992), *reprinted in* 2 Health L. Rep. (BNA) 244 (25 March 1993).

23. Ibid.

24. *HHS Official Tempers Agency Hardline On Acquisition of Physician Practices*, 2 Health L. Rep. (BNA) 389 (1 April 1993).

25. Internal Revenue Service, 1993 Exempt Organizations.

26. California Health and Safety Code § 1206(l).

William J. Aseltyne, JD, is Assistant General Counsel at California Pacific Medical Center in San Francisco and also teaches health law at the University of San Francisco School of Law. He received his law degree from the University of Michigan Law School, where he was on the editorial board of the *Michigan Law Review*.

M. Lawrence Bonham, MD, is a pediatrician with Pediatric Associates of Los Gatos, California. He received his bachelor's degree from William Marsh Rice University in Houston, Texas, and his medical degree at Tulane University in New Orleans, Louisiana. His pediatric residency was at Stanford University. He is a clinical instructor at Stanford University School of Medicine and medical director of the Independent Practice Medical Association of San Francisco, San Mateo, and Santa Clara Counties.

Derek F. Covert, JD, CPA, is the Associate General Counsel at Catholic Healthcare West in San Francisco, California. He is responsible for physician integration matters as well as tax exemption for the 19-hospital health care system. He received his bachelor's degree in accounting from the University of Akron and his law degree from the McDowell School of Law, University of Akron.

Paul R. DeMuro, CPA, MBA, JD, is a partner with Latham & Watkins in Los Angeles and San Francisco, California. He is a leading authority in managed care issues; Medicare reimbursement, fraud, and abuse; and integrated delivery system development. He received his bachelor's degree in economics from the University of Maryland at College Park; his law degree from Washington University, where he served on the board of editors of the law review; and his master's in business administration in finance from the University of California at Berkeley. He is vice-chairman of the Healthcare Financial Management Association Principles and Practices Board.

Gerald R. Peters, JD, is a partner with Latham & Watkins in San Francisco, California. He is a leading authority in health care business transactions, integrated delivery systems, and nonprofit taxation. He graduated from the University of California at Berkeley and received his law degree from Hastings College of the Law, University of California.

Robert A. Waterman, JD, is a partner with Latham & Watkins in San Francisco, California. He received his undergraduate degree at California State University at Long Beach and his law degree from the University of California at Berkeley, where he was a member of the board of editors of the *California Law Review*. His expertise includes integrated delivery systems; managed care; hospital, medical group, and health plan mergers and acquisitions; and day-to-day hospital issues.

Chapter 29

Ambulatory Care

Kevin W. Barr and Charles L. Breindel

Prompted by the reimbursement incentives of the 1980s, and facilitated by advances in medical technology, surgery, and anesthesia throughout the 1980s and 1990s, the delivery of health care is shifting from traditional hospital-based inpatient care to ambulatory and non-hospital-based settings. Some hospitals have experienced an erosion of their share of the ambulatory care market as physician, independent, corporate, and payor-sponsored facilities entered the marketplace in search of revenue diversification and/or cost management benefits. The migration from inpatient-based care to ambulatory care has been further fueled by increasing pressure from managed care organizations, national corporations, local businesses, and the federal government to curb the unbridled growth of health care expenditures.

Simply defined, ambulatory care includes those diagnostic and therapeutic procedures and treatments provided to patients in a setting that does not require an extended overnight stay in a hospital. Ambulatory care service settings include medical groups and group practice plans, home health programs, community health clinics, industrial clinics, ambulatory surgery centers, outpatient diagnostic centers, urgent-care

facilities, oncology centers, rehabilitation centers, and hospital-based ambulatory care facilities. Numerous managed care organizations and payors are beginning to define outpatient or ambulatory care as any treatment episode that does not exceed 24 hours in length regardless of whether the protocol includes an overnight stay in an inpatient or recovery care bed.

The most common hospital-based and non-hospital-based ambulatory care services include:

- urgent care or emergency care
- outpatient diagnostics (including diagnostic radiology, ultrasound, CT, mammography, electrocardiograms, endoscopy/colonoscopy/arthroscopy and MRI)
- home care
- outpatient surgery
- physician practice

Many of these services fall into the category of high-volume procedures that industry experts believe are most likely to be performed predominantly outside the traditional hospital-facility setting in the future. These services represent the core of most hospital-based outpatient revenues today.

The range of ambulatory care services and providers in today's health care marketplace is large and entire texts have been dedicated to this topic. Accordingly, this chapter focuses on that portion of the service spectrum most closely aligned with traditional hospital-based and emerging freestanding ambulatory care services. This includes those outpatient treatments and/or procedures that do not require an overnight stay in an inpatient facility, and includes care provided by hospital and non-hospital-sponsored facilities alike. The chapter also includes a discussion on home care and the routine cognitive and diagnostic ambulatory care services provided by physicians in a traditional medical office setting.

AMBULATORY CARE SERVICES— PAST AND PRESENT

Providers in the 1980s and 1990s

The provision of ambulatory care services has evolved dramatically during the mid- to late 1980s and early 1990s. Traditionally, the vast majority of outpatient care (excluding cognitive and basic diagnostic care provided in physician offices) has been provided in hospital-based facilities and, in most cases, on the campuses of such hospitals. However, in recent years, there has been explosive growth in the type and ownership of facilities in which ambulatory care is offered, blurring the definitions of what historically has been defined as hospital-based outpatient care and other ambulatory care services (Exhibit 29–1).

Until the late 1980s, competition for ambulatory care services was limited to a few traditional health care providers, including hospitals, independent physician groups, and other community health providers. Hospitals, once the dominant players in the outpatient market, now face aggressive competitors with significant capital resources. In certain markets, the competition for ambulatory care has evolved to include a range of traditional and nontraditional providers and owners, including corporate employers,

managed care organizations (i.e., health maintenance organizations [HMOs] and other insurers), corporate physician chains, and national diversified health care corporations (see Exhibit 29–2). Such competition largely has occurred in areas of abundance where financial access to care, population base, and supply of clinical subspecialists facilitate provider entrance. Geographically, these areas of abundance have translated into urban–suburban markets populated by employer-insured residents and Medicare recipients. Conversely, in other areas of limited abundance (e.g., rural and inner-city markets) and for certain populations (e.g., the poor, uninsured, and elderly), access to ambulatory care and breadth of providers is still limited. Hospitals, once the dominant outpatient provider in areas of abundance, now face aggressive competitors with significant capital resources and agility. In rural areas, hospitals often still are the dominant providers of ambulatory care.

A 1992 survey of outpatient care providers ranked Kaiser Permanente, a staff model HMO, as the second largest provider of freestanding ambulatory care in terms of number of operational facilities in the United States. Independent physicians, national ambulatory care corporations, and HMOs represent a source of continued competition for the traditional hospital organization.[1] This is particularly true in those markets that may be characterized as areas of abundance. The ambulatory care market of the 1990s has evolved to include numerous owner organizations, for example:

- outpatient chains
- imaging companies
- managed care organizations
- health care systems
- physician chains/franchises
- diversified health care companies

Changing Clinical Technology and Reimbursement

The rapid growth of ambulatory services and movement to freestanding and independently

Exhibit 29–1 Ambulatory Care Service Settings

Past	*Present*
• Hospital outpatient departments	• Chemotherapy and radiation therapy centers
• Physician offices	• Dialysis centers
• Home health agencies	• Diagnostic imaging centers
• Outpatient surgery centers	• Mobile imaging centers
• Hospital emergency rooms	• Fitness/wellness centers
	• Occupational health
	• Psychiatric outpatient/partial hospitalization
	• Rehabilitation centers
	• Freestanding ambulatory surgery centers
	• Sports medicine clinics
	• Urgent/primary care centers
	• Women's health clinics
	• Wound care centers

Exhibit 29–2 Ambulatory Care Providers/Owners

Past	*Present*
• Hospitals	• Corporate employers
• Independent physician practitioners	• Insurance companies/managed care organizations
• Community health providers/agencies	• Hospitals
• Home health agencies	• Independent physician practitioners
	• Independent corporate chains
	• National physician chains
	• Community health providers/agencies
	• Home health companies
	• National diversified health care companies

owned facilities has been driven primarily by three factors:

1. payor pressure to check rising health care costs associated with inpatient care
2. increased availability of reimbursement for ambulatory care procedures and providers
3. technological advances in ambulatory care occurring at an unprecedented pace

An additional factor contributing to the rapid growth (in some states) is the deregulation of Certificate of Need (CON) legislation. CON laws have traditionally restricted the expansion of new health services and providers.

Dramatic breakthroughs in diagnostic imaging, pharmaceuticals, therapeutics, biotherapeutics, anesthesia, analgesics, and optical and laser surgical instrumentation have resulted in significant reductions in inpatient stays, sharp growth of same day surgical procedures, and empty postsurgical beds. The development of new and advanced technologies and instrumentation, occurring at this historically unprecedented rate, will continue to affect the growth of ambulatory care beyond the turn of the century.

One example of this unprecedented change is the rapid acceptance of endoscopic surgical instrumentation. As reported by Biomedical Business International of Santa Ana, California, within two years after the introduction of the laparoscopic cholecystectomy procedure (by 1992), this surgical method accounted for nearly 20 percent of the gallbladder removals in the United States. Industry experts suggest that, by 1995, endoscopic surgery will account for 70 to 90 percent of the most common high volume surgeries performed in hospitals, specifically cholecystectomies, kidney removals, appendectomies, hysterectomies, and hernia repairs. Others predict that 80 percent of all abdominal and thoracic surgery will be performed laparoscopically before the year 2000.[2]

Figure 29–1 illustrates the dramatic impact of technological advances and reimbursement pressures on hospital-based surgery. In 1991, slightly more than 50 percent of total community hospital surgical procedures were performed on an outpatient basis.

Such changes accent a myriad of management and medical staff challenges for health care ex-ecutives, including careful selection and acquisition of new technologies, physician privileging criteria for new procedures, training of surgical support staff, and continuing medical education for medical staff.

Hospital-Based Services

In recent years, hospital administrators have realized that establishing a firm position in the ambulatory care market is critical to the continued survival of their organizations. The Health Care Advisory Board (a national health care research and advisory group based in Washington, D.C.) has emphasized that "the shift to ambulatory care is not simply another trend in healthcare; it is the future of the hospital. Outpatient [care] is . . . the only part of the hospital business that is booming."[3]

Between 1986 and 1991, community hospital outpatient visits in the United States increased at

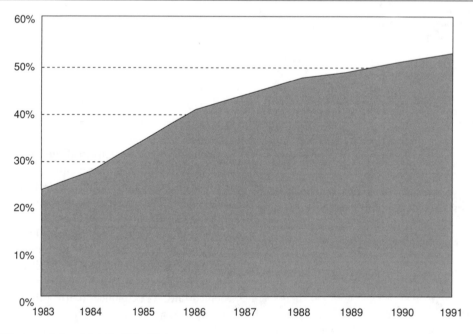

*All community hospitals in the United States.

Figure 29–1 Percent of Surgeries Performed on Outpatient Basis. *Source: Hospital Statistics, 1991–1992 Edition*, American Hospital Association, Chicago, Illinois.

an annual growth rate of 8.5 percent, growing from 155.3 million visits in 1986 to 233.5 million visits by 1991. During this same five-year period, community hospital inpatient admissions and inpatient days dropped approximately 4.1 percent (from 32.4 to 31.1 million admissions) and 2.9 percent (from 229.5 to 222.9 million days), respectively. Figure 29–2 shows the shifting trend in hospital-based outpatient visits and inpatient days.[4]

As the percentage of community hospital gross revenue generated by ambulatory care services advances to 50 percent by the year 2000, hospitals are expected to evolve into high-acuity service sites with significant ambulatory care components rather than the full-continuum inpatient facilities of the late 1980s and early 1990s. This transformation will produce new challenges for health care executives in the way they structure, organize, manage, staff, and market their organizations. It is important that hospital executives view ambulatory care as an essential portion of their overall health care business rather than a supplemental product-line of an inpatient facility. This change in the culture of management thinking comes at a time when the hospital industry's share of the ambulatory care market is declining. Hospital share of the ambulatory care market declined from 85 percent in 1986 to 77 percent in 1990 (Figure 29–3).[5]

Prior to 1985, outpatient care constituted less than 15 percent of total gross patient revenue for all community hospitals in the United States. The shift in treatments and procedures to the outpatient setting has been dramatic, with a typical community hospital capturing 25 or more percent of its total gross patient revenue from outpatient care by 1990. Most industry planners believe that by the year 2000, ambulatory care will account for 50 percent or more of the total

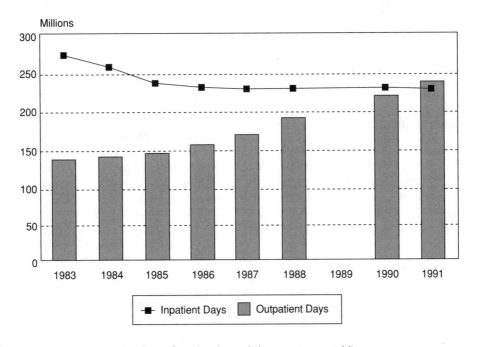

*All community hospitals in the United States. Outpatient data exclude emergency room visits.

Figure 29–2 Shifting Trends in Hospital Utilization. *Source: Hospital Statistics, 1991–1992 Edition*, American Hospital Association, Chicago, Illinois.

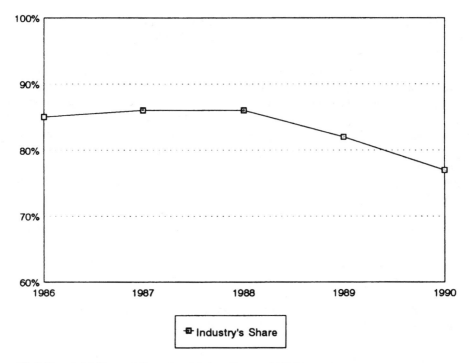

Figure 29–3 Hospitals' Share of Outpatient Market. *Source: 1991 National Consumer Study*, professional Research Consultants, Omaha, Nebraska.

gross patient revenue of a community hospital (Figure 29–4).

Freestanding Ambulatory Care Services

Freestanding ambulatory care centers can provide a variety of diagnostic and therapeutic services, including rehabilitation, diagnostic radiology, mammography, radiation therapy, chemotherapy, urgent care, and outpatient surgery. The most common types of freestanding centers are:

- diagnostic imaging centers
- urgent-care centers
- outpatient surgery centers

Diagnostic imaging centers typically have capabilities such as basic radiographic and fluoroscopic radiology, ultrasound, mammography, and often computerized tomography (CT). Highly competitive and mature markets tend to have other types of freestanding ambulatory care

services complementary to these conventional facilities, including women's imaging centers, women's health centers, mobile imaging units, rehabilitation centers, and sports medicine centers. Similar services often are available in independent physician and medical group practices as well, particularly obstetric/gynecologic physician groups likely to offer mammography and ultrasound testing.

Forces influencing the evolution of ambulatory care services from traditional hospital-based settings to freestanding facilities include:

- tightened reimbursement, particularly for high volume Medicare procedures (e.g., cataracts and cardiac catheterization)
- emerging technology supportive of freestanding facilities
- dramatic growth of proceduralists and the lucrative reimbursement thereof for outpatient procedures
- easing of Certificate of Need laws

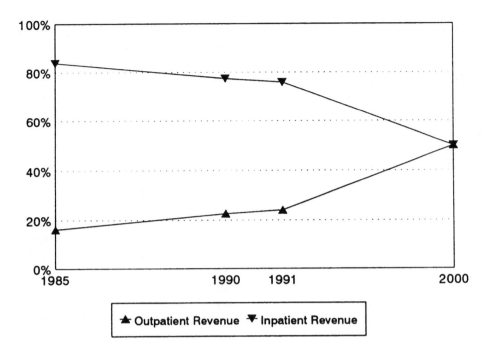

Figure 29–4 Percent Inpatient and Outpatient Gross Revenue. *Source: Hospital Statistics, 1991–1992 Edition*, American Hospital Association, Chicago, Illinois.

• physician interest in increasing efficiency resultant from one-stop location

The growth of independently owned and freestanding ambulatory care centers is forcing hospitals to become more responsive to customers' needs and preferences, including factors such as convenience, easy access, and limited waiting time. Freestanding ambulatory care centers are consuming an ever-larger portion of the market for outpatient procedures. In the 1980s, hospital emergency rooms were challenged competitively by a significant growth in minor emergency and urgent care centers, which focused on the minor injury and simple urgent care needs of the population. These facilities successfully skimmed off higher margin business from the traditional hospital emergency room and filled a void for consumers without an established family physician relationship.

Another example, the freestanding ambulatory surgery center market, is heavily dominated by independents and physicians. SMG Marketing Group, Inc., reports that in 1990, 80 percent of freestanding surgery centers were owned by entities independent of a hospital.[6] The most active specialty group to enter the freestanding ASC market was ophthalmology. As Medicare pushed for more cataract operations to be performed on an outpatient basis, and implemented its ASC Payment Groups, a dramatic increase in physician interest and ownership of freestanding surgical facilities occurred. Other specialties that became involved in building independent surgery centers include orthopedics and urology. The list of procedures routinely performed on an outpatient basis has grown steadily, to include cataract surgery, breast biopsies, arthroscopic knee surgery, hernia repair, removal of lesions, and gynecological procedures such as dilatation and curettage. During the five-year period 1988 to 1992, the number of freestanding surgery centers increased in excess of 75 percent from 964 facilities in 1988 to 1,696 facilities in 1991 (see Figure 29–5).

Four factors account for the rapid success of freestanding surgery centers:

1. rising consumer demand for same-day surgery
2. market penetration of managed-care plans and pressure from third-party payors to control costs
3. additions to the Medicare-approved list of ambulatory procedures covered for outpatient reimbursement
4. technological advances in surgical techniques

The federal government is expected to continue to expand its list of surgical procedures approved for Medicare reimbursement in freestanding and hospital-based ambulatory surgery centers. Managed care plans will follow suit and continue to be an important ingredient in the growth of freestanding surgery centers, particularly as their market penetration increases.

Freestanding surgery centers have experienced extraordinary growth in procedure volume as well. Between 1985 and 1991, the number of procedures performed in freestanding facilities increased approximately 230 percent, while hospital-based outpatient surgical procedures increased only 68 percent (see Figure 29–6).

Although the transition of inpatient procedures to the outpatient setting is certain to continue as medical technology advances, certain new technologies will be dependent on access to advanced hospital-based services in cases where inpatient back-up or conversion may be required. This will buffer somewhat the erosion of the hospital industry's share of the ambulatory surgery market. However, innovative freestanding center

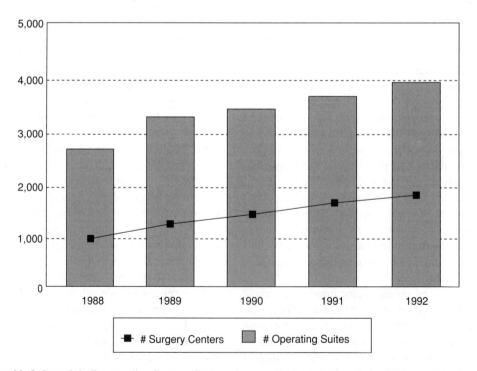

Figure 29–5 Growth in Freestanding Surgery Centers. *Source:* SMG Marketing Group, Chicago, Illinois.

Million Procedures

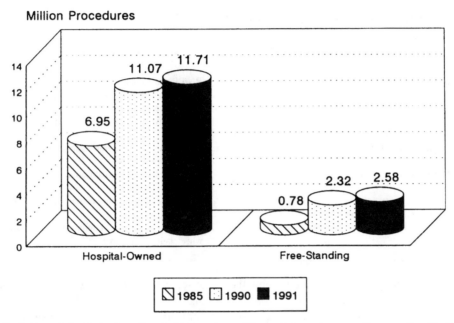

Figure 29–6 Growth in Outpatient Surgical Procedures (Hospital-Owned versus Freestanding Facilities). *Sources: Hospital Statistics, 1991–1992 Edition*, American Hospital Association, Chicago, Illinois. SMG Marketing Group, Chicago, Illinois.

executives already are beginning to adjust by establishing accommodations for overnight or extended stays. This is taking the form of extended recovery capabilities, including 23 recovery care and nurse-attended overnight stay facilities.[7]

Home Care Services

Broadly defined, home care service providers include certified and noncertified skilled nursing agencies, private duty nursing agencies, home infusion therapy companies, home respiratory therapy providers, and durable medical equipment (DME) suppliers. Most providers have a dominant core service complemented by ancillary service offerings rather than a full spectrum of home care services/products. Consequently, home care providers have generally followed a market niche strategy with many agencies maintaining a very narrow service offering (See Exhibit 29–3).

Proprietary home care agencies dominate the industry, accounting for nearly 50 percent of

home care providers in the United States. Not-for-profit and Visiting Nurse Association (VNA) organizations follow, claiming nearly 21 percent of the industry. Hospital-based agencies represent approximately 15 percent of industry providers. The number of home care agencies increased 88.9 percent during the six-year period 1986 to 1992, expanding from 5,283 to 9,982 providers (See Figure 29–7).

The most common home care service is skilled nursing care (See Figure 29–8). Historically, hospital-based agencies have focused primarily on skilled nursing care while proprietary agencies have been more aggressive in developing home infusion, chemotherapy, and assisted living services and DME products. Home infusion and nutrition therapies are becoming more prevalent offerings as a result of pharmacological breakthroughs, home chemotherapy treatment, and a growing trend for home-based rather than institutional treatment approaches for these care needs. Skilled nursing care and physical therapy services continue to grow, fulfilling a

Exhibit 29–3 Typical Home Care Providers and Services Offered

Provider Types	Core Services
• Skilled nursing (certified and noncertified) • Private duty nursing • Home infusion therapy • Home respiratory therapy • Durable medical equipment	• RN/LPN nursing care • Physical/occupational/speech therapies • Personal care (homemakers/aides) • Assisted living activities (housekeeping/shopping/transportation) • Intravenous pharmaceuticals/antibiotics • Home chemotherapy • Respiratory treatments/education • Oxygen • Rental/sale of respiratory equipment • Sale of medical supplies • Rental/sale of medical equipment (e.g., hospital beds, wheelchairs, IV pumps)

critical role in the postsurgical care for ambulatory and inpatient surgical patients.

Home care services have been one of the fastest-growing segments of the ambulatory care marketplace for the past decade due to clinical and treatment advances, emphasis on noninstitutional approaches to care, aging of the population, and advanced life span for Americans. Accordingly, home care agencies continue to see increases in the number of patients suffering from Alzheimer's disease, other forms of dementia, AIDS, and other types of chronic illnesses (See Figure 29–9).

Physician-Based Services

Independent and group medical practices account for a significant portion of ambulatory

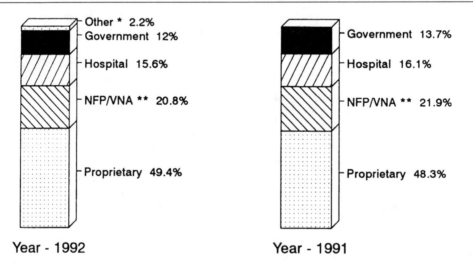

Year - 1992

Other * 2.2%
Government 12%
Hospital 15.6%
NFP/VNA ** 20.8%
Proprietary 49.4%

Year - 1991

Government 13.7%
Hospital 16.1%
NFP/VNA ** 21.9%
Proprietary 48.3%

*"Other" includes rehabilitation facility-based or nursing home care agencies.
**Represents not-for-profit and Visiting Nurse Association agencies.

Figure 29–7 Ownership of Home Health Agencies. *Source:* SMG Marketing Group, Chicago, Illinois.

Type of Service

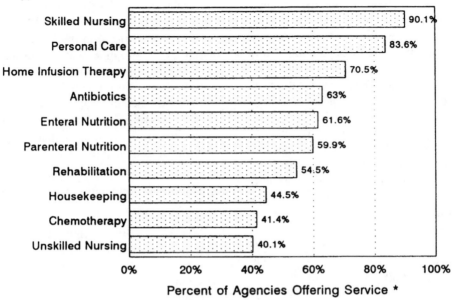

*Represents weighted average for all agency types and ownership.

Figure 29–8 Most Common Home Care Services. *Source:* SMG Marketing Group, Chicago, Illinois.

Condition of Patient Treated

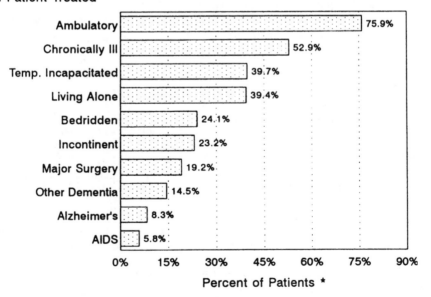

*Represents weighted average for all agency types and ownership.
Total not equal to 100 percent because categories are not mutually exclusive.

Figure 29–9 Common Conditions of Home Care Patients. *Source:* SMG Marketing Group, Chicago, Illinois.

care treatment activity in the United States. Per capita physician office utilization has remained relatively steady over the last decade, ranging from 2.6 visits per person in 1981 to 2.9 visits per person in 1990. The National Ambulatory Medical Care Survey reported an average of 2.7 physician visits per person per year in the United States in 1991, as shown in Table 29–1.

Faced with a trend toward tightened hospital and physician reimbursement throughout the 1980s and 1990s and growth of outpatient care alternatives, a significant number of entrepreneurial physicians and for-profit corporate chains have evolved within the ambulatory care market. These new entrants have focused on the more profitable business segments thereof. Physicians represent perhaps the most aggressive source of competition, one that essentially controls all outpatient referrals. In many communities, physicians represent a significant challenge to hospital executives, as they have established independent outpatient service capabilities.

In the face of declining reimbursement, physicians have found diversification into conventional hospital-based outpatient service areas to be an enticing and lucrative source of additional revenue and income. Factors accelerating this progression and its financial attractiveness include:

- introduction of Medicare's Physician Payment Reform and payor conversion to resource-based relative value scale (RBRVS) payment methodologies, causing compression of physician revenues
- inflation of medical practice overhead expenses, resulting in increased attention on future practice profitability

- growth of large group practices creating sizable patient bases, an immediate source of referrals for outpatient services
- growth of national medical practice franchises (organizations with significant capital and management resources) making physician-only ventures increasingly feasible, for example PhyCor, Pacific Physician Services, and Caremark International
- decreasing price of technologies, making equipment more affordable

Nontraditional Ambulatory Care Services

During the late 1980s, some hospitals followed a path of diversification into nontraditional ambulatory care services as a means to expand beyond traditional hospital-based services and augment current sources of revenue. Hospitals following this strategy largely were in pursuit of new sources of revenue to offset declining inpatient volume and income. Examples of some of the more frequently developed programs and services include:

- medical malls
- wellness and fitness centers
- weight management programs
- urgent care centers
- occupational health and industrial medicine programs

Such service diversifications were successful for some hospitals, but many did not capture the financial returns sought. In retrospect, some of these "early adopters" recognized the shifting delivery of health care from traditional inpatient settings to new and ambulatory service settings.

ORGANIZATION AND MANAGEMENT OF AMBULATORY CARE SERVICES

Types of Ownership

Before discussing the various organizational and management structures for ambulatory care service providers, it is useful to briefly define

Table 29–1 Physician Office Visits in U.S.

	1989	1990	1991
Number of office visits	692,702	704,604	669,689
Visits per 1,000 persons	284.4	286.3	269.3
Visits per capita	2.8	2.9	2.7

Source: National Ambulatory Medical Care Survey 1989, 1990, and 1991, National Center for Health Statistics.

several common classifications of ambulatory facility ownership, specifically, hospital-based, hospital-owned, joint venture, and freestanding.

Hospital-based ambulatory care facilities are solely owned by and are a central part of the physical plant of a hospital organization, whether the hospital organization is a taxable or not-for-profit corporation. Hospital-owned ambulatory care facilities are owned (in full or jointly) by the hospital organization, but usually are not part of the core physical plant of the hospital. A hospital-owned facility may be located on the hospital's campus or off-campus, whether wholly or jointly owned. Joint venture ownership is defined as a legal entity controlled by two or more parties organized under a contract or lease agreement, corporation, general partnership, or limited partnership. Freestanding ambulatory care facilities are not owned by a hospital. Common freestanding facility owners include independent physicians, physician partnerships, for-profit corporations, and insurance companies.

Organization and Management

Various organizational and management structures are found within the ownership arrangements identified above. Hospital-based ambulatory care services are usually organized under a traditional pyramid-style management design with various portions of the overall ambulatory care services reporting to multiple managers or administrators on the hospital's management team. The distinguishing characteristics of this form of organizational structure are the lack of a separate manager with distinct line authority for all outpatient services and the resulting hierarchical process for decision making (See Figure 29–10). Under the hospital-based organizational structure, the provision of ambulatory services is typically fragmented and viewed as an ancillary component to the more dominant inpatient service lines. Some hospital systems have established more progressive management structures for ambulatory care, organiz-

ing all outpatient functions (including patient registration) into an integrated business line under a single member of the hospital's senior management team.

Joint venture and freestanding ambulatory care facilities frequently have more streamlined organizational and management structures. These facilities are commonly organized under the direction of a policy board or management committee with a senior manager or administrator responsible for day-to-day operations and management. Representation on the policy board or management committee is determined by the degree of ownership and status of the shareholder corporation(s), or the general and/or limited partners.

The vast majority of hospital-based ambulatory services are located on-campus and thereby are affected by the constraints of the site, inpatient-oriented units, and other physical limitations of the hospital plant. Typically, this contributes to a lack of convenience and accessibility to the patient—service deficiencies of significant importance to routine, frequently performed outpatient procedures such as radiology, ultrasound, rehabilitation, and oncology. Frequently performed low-end procedures are those where convenience and accessibility are critical to customer satisfaction. Such attributes of service quality are less serious, yet not inconsequential, to the more intermittent ambulatory procedures and tests, for example, magnetic resonance imaging (MRI), ambulatory surgery, and cardiac catheterization.

While the percentage of hospital revenue attributable to ambulatory care continues to expand, a recent American Hospital Association survey of hospital CEOs revealed that only 21 percent of U.S. hospitals have a separate manager with distinct line authority for total outpatient activity and that this structure has changed little compared to preceding years.[8]

Physician Practice Structures

Physician practices can be organized under various designs and structures, including inde-

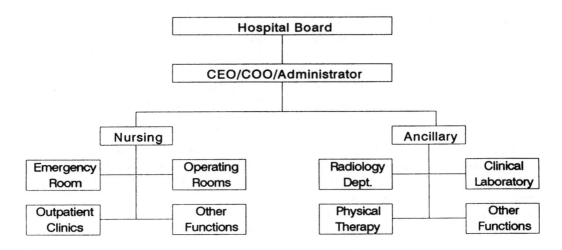

Figure 29–10 Typical Hospital-Based Structure

pendent practice, group practice (single specialty and multispecialty), hospital-based, hospital-affiliated, faculty practice plan, or group and staff model HMO practices. Common physician ownership configurations include sole proprietor, professional corporation, and partnership arrangements.

Hospital-affiliated physician practices include solo and group medical practices linked to a hospital (or hospital system) contractually through a management services organization (MSO) or employment by the hospital or a subsidiary hospital corporation or physician organization. A faculty practice plan is a multispecialty physician group practice based at a medical teaching university. This type of physician practice, while typically independent of university or medical school ownership, is an integral part of its medical education and residency programs. Group model HMO practices are prepaid group practices, commonly multispecialty groups, under contract to provide health care to members enrolled in the HMO plan. Group model physicians are not employees of the HMO. Staff model physician groups fulfill a similar function but are employed by the HMO plan.

There is a distinct trend for physicians to seek out group practice opportunities as they face

growing economic and efficiency challenges. The growth of managed care and flattening reimbursement are the two single greatest forces prompting physicians to seek out group practice opportunities. The American Medical Association reports that the number of physicians in groups (defined to be three or more physicians) increased 2.7 percent annually between 1984 and 1988. Thirty percent of all nonfederal physicians were organized under a group practice arrangement in 1988.[9] A panel of physicians who participated in a 1991 Delphi study conducted by Arthur Andersen and the American College of Healthcare Executives concluded that the percentage of physicians organized under a group practice will reach 40 percent by 1996.[10] Many physicians have found the group practice setting to be a more secure environment providing additional leverage in negotiating with managed care plans as well as an alluring method for controlling practice overhead expenses and realizing economies of scale benefits.

The consolidation of physicians into group practice organizations is taking shape under several approaches, including:

- mergers of individual physicians and groups into single-specialty and multispecialty groups

- formation of group practices without walls (a hybrid group practice model whereby independent office locations and some autonomy are maintained)
- growth of national medical practice franchises
- formation of hospital-affiliated group practices

Other less formal group networking initiatives include physician contracting networks and physician–hospital organizations (PHOs). These initiatives typically take the form of an alliance or coalition of independent practitioners joined with a hospital for direct contracting with self-insured employers and other payor groups.

Evolution of Hospital-Affiliated Medical Groups

The benefits driving physicians and hospitals to physician–hospital networks include the opportunity to:

- facilitate managed care and self-insured employer contracts
- enhance contract negotiating leverage
- offset increased administrative overhead
- share skilled expertise and staff required to handle the increased business complexity of medical practice
- improve recruitment and retention of physicians

In recent years, a definite trend for hospital organizations to acquire physicians' practices has emerged. This has been motivated by hospital executives' desire to protect market share, preserve historical referral sources, enhance payor contract negotiating leverage, and support the formation of vertically integrated delivery systems. The most popular acquisition target is primary care. Specialty practice acquisitions are occurring at a relatively infrequent pace. Rather, hospital-based and specialty physician relationships are forming around affiliations and alliances versus ownership.

The growth of hospital-affiliated and hospital-owned medical practices is demonstrative of a transformation in the way many health care executives are thinking about and approaching the marketing strategies for their organizations. In the 1980s, promotional-based marketing (specifically, consumer-focused advertising) dominated the marketing strategies of most hospitals. This approach, while still effective for very focused objectives and target audiences, is now outdated. A new direction, marketing distribution channel strategies, has already begun to emerge as the dominant strategy for the 1990s and is the foundation of many of today's successful integrated health care systems. This will continue through the turn of the century.

The development of hospital-affiliated group practices—whether they be through ownership, organizational affiliation, merger, or new corporate entities like a PHO—is representative of this shift and a means for hospitals to protect their position in the ambulatory care market. Ironically, most hospitals may have introduced hospital-owned and affiliated medical group actions as an inpatient strategy rather than an outpatient approach. Two other compelling, yet often less recognized, factors driving the formation of hospital-affiliated medical groups are the need to improve the efficiency in the delivery of care and to support the transition to bundled and capitated payment methodologies, a near-future reality for hospitals nationwide.

REIMBURSEMENT

Reimbursement for ambulatory care varies by the ownership structure of the facility providing the service, the nature of the service provided, and the payor responsible for payment. With the exception of Medicare, most payors reimburse providers of outpatient services on a percent-of-charge basis for general diagnostic and therapeutic services. Some HMO/PPO payors have carved out certain high-cost procedures such as cardiac catheterization and MRI with payment for such services prospectively set at a fixed fee per procedure.

With outpatient services consuming a larger portion of the Medicare budget, legislation to control payments for outpatient services has been introduced through the Omnibus Budget Reconciliation Act of 1986, 1987, and 1990. The result of this legislation has been to convert the payment of outpatient services (specifically laboratory, radiology, and outpatient surgery services) from full-cost reimbursement to various prospectively set payment methodologies. Further, with hospitals aggressively developing outpatient services and shifting costs as a means to offset declining inpatient income, other payors are focusing on the conversion from per-cent-of-charge-based reimbursement to fixed-fee payments.

Outpatient Service Reimbursement Under Medicare

Prior to 1986, Medicare reimbursed hospitals for outpatient services on a "reasonable-cost" basis, paying the lower of reasonable cost or customary charges. The Omnibus Budget Reconciliation Act of 1986 (OBRA-86) instituted several fundamental changes in the payment methodology for outpatient services provided by hospitals and freestanding ambulatory surgery centers (ASCs). The most significant of these changes include:

- a Congressional mandate for the Health Care Financing Administration (HCFA) to develop a prospective payment system (PPS) for outpatient services by 1991
- the qualification of hospital-based ASCs for Medicare reimbursement according to a prospectively set schedule of fixed, per-procedure payment rates
- a "blended" payment methodology for hospital-based ASC surgical procedures based upon a combination of the traditional reasonable-cost approach and the prospective rates for ASCs
- a limit on hospital-based radiology service payments as determined by the lesser of the traditional reasonable-cost approach or a

blended payment based upon a combination of reasonable cost and the Medicare prevailing charge.

The Omnibus Budget Reconciliation Act of 1990 (OBRA-90) required that Medicare expenditures for outpatient service be reduced by 5.8 percent between fiscal years 1991 and 1995. Current Medicare payment methodologies for hospital-based and freestanding providers are discussed below. To receive reimbursement from Medicare for the provision of services to Medicare recipients, ambulatory service providers must be a Medicare-certified facility.

Freestanding Ambulatory Surgery Centers

Payment for services provided in freestanding ASCs is based upon a prospectively set schedule of rates as determined by the HCFA. Freestanding ASCs did not quality for Medicare reimbursement prior to September 1982 when the ASC benefit was first implemented. Since that time, the number of covered procedures has expanded from 54 to over 2,400. Surgical procedures eligible for Medicare reimbursement in ASCs are classified into eight ASC-approved procedure groups. Each of the eight groups has a corresponding prospective payment rate, which is updated annually, to cover the "facility fee" portion of the ambulatory surgical procedure.

The Group 6 and Group 8 rates correlate to ophthalmic surgical procedures, which currently include a $200 add-on allowance to cover the cost of an intraocular lens prosthesis (IOL). The facility fee rates are intended to cover the standard overhead expenses incurred in providing ambulatory surgical services, including nursing services, supplies, equipment, and use of the ASC facility. Physician professional fees are reimbursed independent of the ASC methodology directly to the physician.

ASC facility fee payments include two components—a labor-related portion and nonlabor-related portion. This provision allows for the variation in worker compensation across geographic markets. The labor-related portion represents 34.45 percent of the total ASC payment amount and is determined according to regional wage indices as established by HCFA (HCFA Wage Index) published annually in the *Federal Register*. Table 29–2 shows the calculation of the payment rates (ophthalmic and non-ophthalmic) for a freestanding ASC located in Richmond, Virginia.

In cases where multiple ambulatory surgical procedures are performed concurrently, the ASC receives 100 percent of the payment for the procedure falling into the highest payment group and 50 percent of the applicable payment for all other procedures performed.

Hospital-Based Ambulatory Surgery

Medicare's reimbursement methodology for hospital-based ambulatory surgery specifies that hospital providers be paid the lesser of the hospital-specific reasonable cost or actual charge; or a 42/58 percent blended payment based upon the hospital-specific cost or charge and the ASC payment rate.

For the period October 1987 to October 1988, the blended payment was based upon a ratio of 75 percent hospital-specific cost and 25 percent of the ASC payment rate. Similarly, for the period October 1988 to October 1989, the blended

Table 29–2 Example Calculation—ASC Payment Rates (Richmond, Virginia)

		Group 4 Procedure	Group 8 Procedure
Step 1:	*Wage-Adjusted Labor Component*		
	ASC payment rate	$558	$730
	multiplied by		
	Labor-related percent	.3445	.3445
	multiplied by		
	Wage Index Value*	.9413	.9413
	equals		
	Wage-adjusted labor component	$180.95	$236.72
Step 2:	*Nonlabor Component*		
	ASC payment rate	$558	$730
	multiplied by		
	Nonlabor-related percent	.6555	.6555
	equals		
	Non-labor component	$365.77	$478.52
Step 3:	*Adjusted ASC Payment Rate*		
	Wage-adjusted labor component	$180.95	$236.72
	plus		
	Nonlabor component	365.77	478.52
	equals		
	Adjusted ASC payment rate	$546.72	$715.24
Step 4:	*Composite Adjusted ASC Payment Rate** *		
	Adjusted ASC payment rate		$715.24
	plus		
	IOL allowance		$200.00
	equals		
	Composite adjusted payment rate		$915.24

*Wage index for Richmond-Petersburg, Virginia MSA. Each MSA or non-MSA is assigned an index to reflect differing wage levels of the specific locality or area. Wage indices are established by HCFA and published annually in the *Federal Register*.

**Since the IOL allowance is not subject to the labor adjustment, the $200 allowance must be subtracted from the standard ASC payment rate before the wage index adjustment is applied.

Source: Federal Register, October 1, 1992.

payment was based upon a ratio of 50 percent hospital-specific cost and 50 percent of the ASC payment rate. The 42/58 percent blend became effective January 1991. Blended payments for services rendered after January 1, 1991 are based upon the following formula:

$$\text{(Lower of Hospital Cost or Charge} \times .42) + (\text{ASC Payment Rate} \times .58)$$

The blended payment applies only to those surgical procedures identified by Medicare as ASC-approved procedures. For those outpatient surgical procedures not classified as Medicare-approved ASC procedures, hospitals are reimbursed on a reasonable-cost basis. Section 1833(i)(2)(A) of the Social Security Act (as amended by OBRA-86) requires that the ASC payment rates be reviewed and updated annually and that the list of ASC-approved procedures be reviewed and updated every two years.

Hospital-Based Radiology Services

Under OBRA-86, payment for hospital-based diagnostic and therapeutic radiology services is based upon the lesser of the provider's reasonable cost or actual charge; or a blended payment of the lower of the provider's cost or actual charge times the Medicare prevailing charge for the specific procedure performed.

Blended payments for services rendered after January 1, 1991, are based upon the following calculation:

$$\text{(Lower of Hospital Cost or Charge} \times .42) + (\text{Medicare Prevailing} \times .80 \times .62 \times .58)$$

The prevailing charge is the amount paid to nonhospital providers for similar radiology procedures performed in physician offices as specified by the Medicare prevailing charge (i.e., fee schedule) for radiology services. Reimbursement under the above methodology applies to diagnostic and therapeutic radiology, nuclear medicine, ultrasound, MRI, and CT procedures.

Commercial/HMO/PPO Reimbursement

Commercial and managed care payors traditionally have paid for outpatient services on a percent-of-charge basis, discounting a provider's actual charge by 15 to 30 percent (or more) depending on the aggressiveness of the provider's pricing. In an effort to control rapidly rising outpatient expenditures, such payors have begun instituting prospectively set and fixed-fee payment methodologies for ambulatory surgery and other high-cost and high-volume outpatient testing (e.g., cardiac catheterization, CT, and MRI).

Payment of ambulatory surgery based upon Medicare's ASC payment groups or a single fixed rate for all procedures (i.e., a single average payment rate) is replacing discount from charge methodologies as commercial and managed care payors renegotiate provider contracts. Some payor contracts have taken further measures to control outpatient surgical costs by combining the facility fee and professional fee components into prospectively set global payment rates. This payment approach is facilitated by physician ownership of ASC facilities where the physician collects both the facility and professional fee components.

Similar prospective and global payment methodologies are evolving for other outpatient services mentioned, including payment schedules based upon relative value systems (e.g., the McGraw-Hill relative value system for radiology procedures).

Home Care Reimbursement

Reimbursement for home health agency services varies by the ownership structure of the agency providing the service and the payor responsible for payment. Agencies are reimbursed by Medicare primarily on a cost-per-visit basis. Medicaid reimbursement is similarly based on a fee-per-visit arrangement. Other payor reimbursement methodologies are based upon either a per-visit-fee schedule or a percentage of the provider's actual charge. Medicare is by far the largest payor for home health services, representing upward of 75 percent of the total volume of a typical hospital-based home health agency (See Figure 29–11). Accordingly, Medicare reimbursement is the focus of this section.

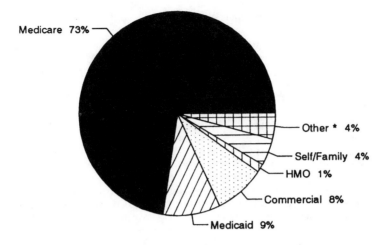

Hospital Agency

*"Other" includes charity, Veterans Affairs, and workers' compensation cases.

Figure 29–11 Payor Mix Profile. *Source:* SMG Marketing Group, Chicago, Illinois.

The Medicare program reimburses home health agencies at the lesser of per visit cost limits (as established by HCFA); per visit charges (actual provider charges); or per visit actual costs (actual aggregate costs incurred by a provider).

Since most, if not all, agencies price their charges above the Medicare cost limits in order to avoid lost reimbursement, charges rarely determine the level of reimbursement received from the Medicare program. Consequently, reimbursement from Medicare is based on either actual costs or cost limits (commonly referred to as "caps").

Standard Per Visit Cost Limits

As provided for in the Social Security Act, Section 1861(v)(1), HCFA is authorized to establish limits on allowable costs incurred by home health providers for payment of services rendered to Medicare recipients. Such limits on home health agency per visit costs have been maintained by HCFA since 1979 and are organized by six care modalities:

1. skilled nursing care
2. physical therapy

3. speech pathology
4. occupational therapy
5. medical social services
6. home health aide

These per visit limits are published annually in the *Federal Register*. The limits are applied to direct and indirect costs of the agency, including the cost of medical supplies routinely furnished in conjunction with patient care. Durable medical equipment, orthotics, prosthetics, and other medical supplies directly identifiable to an individual patient are excluded from the per visit costs and are paid on a cost basis without regard to the established limits. A cost report must be filed by each home health agency in order to receive Medicare reimbursement. Table 29–3 illustrates the standard per visit limits for freestanding home health agencies.

Wage-Adjusted Cost Limits

In order to normalize for differences in wage levels across different geographic markets, the Medicare program provides for adjustment of the standard limits using regional wage indices applicable to the locality of the provider agency. Table 29–4 shows the calculation of the cost

Table 29–3 Standard per Visit Limits for Home Health Agencies

Type of Visit	MSA (NECMA) Locations		Non-MSA Locations	
	Labor Portion	Nonlabor Portion	Labor Portion	Nonlabor Portion
Skilled nursing care	$74.40	$16.04	$84.39	$14.69
Physical therapy	76.86	16.53	89.92	15.65
Speech pathology	77.84	16.84	93.98	16.45
Occupational therapy	76.27	16.68	90.40	16.08
Medical social services	106.41	23.15	140.98	24.62
Home health aide	37.35	8.09	39.21	6.83

Note: MSA denotes Metropolitan Statistical Area. NECMA denotes New England County Metropolitan Area. Per visit limits shown above are effective for cost reporting periods beginning on or after July 1, 1993. Nonlabor portion limits for home health agencies located in Alaska, Hawaii, Puerto Rico, and the Virgin Islands are increased by additional cost of living adjustment factors. See *Federal Register.*

Source: Federal Register, July 8, 1993.

limit for skilled nursing care adjusted by the appropriate wage index for Richmond, Virginia.

Adjustment for Reporting Year

In addition to adjusting the standard per visit limits for market-specific wage differences, the adjusted per visit limits are subject to an additional modification to account for a provider's individual Medicare cost reporting year. The standard per visit limits set by HCFA are based upon a common cost reporting year beginning July 1 and ending June 30. If a home health agency has a cost reporting period beginning on or after August 1, an adjustment factor corresponding to the month and year in which the provider's cost reporting period begins is applied.

The factor represents the compounded rate of monthly increase derived from the projected annual increase in the market basket index (as determined by HCFA). The purpose of this adjustment is to account for the inflation in a provider's costs that occurs after the effective date of the common cost reporting period. As with the other provisions of Medicare reimbursement for home health agencies, the cost reporting year adjustment factor is updated annually and reported in the *Federal Register*.

Add-On Payment for Hospital-Based Agencies

Historically, hospital-based home health agencies received an "add on" payment equal to approximately 11 to 12 percent of the standard per visit limits for freestanding agencies. This hospital-based provider adjustment was suspended for all hospital-based agencies for cost reporting periods beginning after October 1, 1993. Consequently, hospital-based and freestanding home health agencies are subject to the same Medicare cost limits prospectively.

Year-end Settlement

Interim payments made to a home health agency throughout the year are based on the prior year's cost report settlement amount for the agency, adjusted for anticipated inflation. At year-end, the agency prepares and files (with the local Medicare intermediary) a cost report in order to reconcile actual reimbursement due to the agency. This process is commonly referred to as the year-end settlement.

The cost report is based upon aggregate actual costs versus aggregate per visit cost limits. As indicated above, Medicare will reimburse the agency for the lesser of the per visit cost limits or

Table 29–4 Example Calculation, Adjusted per Visit Cost Limits (Richmond, Virginia)

		Skilled Nursing Care	Home Health Aide
Step 1:	*Adjusted Labor Component*		
	Labor portion	$74.40	$37.35
	multiplied by		
	Wage Index Value*	.9379	.9379
	equals		
	Wage-adjusted labor component	$69.78	$35.03
	multiplied by		
	Special adjustment for budget neutrality**	1.027	1.027
	equals		
	Adjusted labor component	$71.66	$35.98
Step 2:	*Nonlabor Component*		
	Nonlabor component	$16.04	$8.09
	OSHA Adjustment***	.18	.18
Step 3:	*Adjusted Cost Limit*		
	Adjusted labor component	$71.66	$35.98
	plus		
	Nonlabor component	16.22	8.27
	equals		
	Adjusted cost limit	$87.88	$44.25

*Wage index for Richmond-Petersburg, Virginia MSA. Each MSA or non-MSA is assigned an index to reflect differing wage levels of the specific locality or area. Wage indices are established by HCFA and published annually in the *Federal Register*.

**Special adjustment to account for transition of the base year of the wage index applied to home health agency cost limits. For additional explanation, see *Federal Register*.

***Special adjustment to account for additional costs associated with meeting the "universal precaution requirements" of the Occupational Safety and Health Administration (OSHA) as established by OSHA in the *Federal Register* on December 6, 1991. Use of provider cost databases for subsequent years for setting home health agency cost limits eventually will preclude the need for this add-on adjustment.

Source: Federal Register, July 8, 1993.

the actual costs. This is determined on an aggregate basis for all types of visits rather than each individual care modality. As an example, if actual costs are above the costs limits in one visit modality—skilled nursing, for instance—the agency would still be reimbursed the actual aggregate cost. This would occur only if the cost levels for other visit modalities are less than their respective limits a sufficient amount to offset the skilled nursing care coverage. Table 29–5 shows an illustration of this year-end settlement process.

In this example, the agency receives cost reimbursement of $790,000, even though the actual costs for skilled nursing care exceed the aggregate per visit limit by $40,600. The agency is reimbursed the $790,000, as this is the lesser of the aggregate cost limit and actual cost amounts.

Ambulatory Patient Groupings

As noted above, OBRA-86 mandated that HCFA develop a prospective payment methodology for other hospital-based outpatient services. This methodology, while not yet finalized by HCFA, is known as the Ambulatory Patient Groupings (APGs) prospective payment system. The two main components of the APG method-

Table 29–5 Example Year-end Settlement (Richmond, Virginia)

Type of Visit	# of Visits	Adjusted Limit	Aggregate Limit	Aggregate Actual Cost
Skilled nursing care	5,000	$87.88	$439,400	$480,000
Physical therapy	2,000	$90.74	181,480	165,000
Home health aide	4,000	$44.25	177,000	145,000
Total	9,000		$797,880	$790,000

ology include a patient classification system and a prospectively set payment schedule similar to that established by the DRG (diagnostic-related group) methodology initiated for Medicare reimbursement in 1984. The APG methodology applies to payment for facility fees only, not professional fees.

The methodology classifies each outpatient visit into one of 297 APG diagnostic categories according to similar clinical characteristics and the associated clinical and administrative resources required to provide the care. A patient can be assigned to multiple APGs depending on the care setting (e.g., emergency room versus outpatient surgery) and the reason for the provision of the service (e.g., trauma versus well-care).

The basic unit of payment for the APG is an outpatient visit rather than the historical approach based upon each individual procedure or test performed. This variation provides an incentive for providers to control the cost of each visit through management of the services rendered and choice of the most effective clinical procedures and tests. As such, the APG payment rates include a portion to cover all routine services associated with the specific outpatient diagnosis, which determines the APG to which the patient visit is assigned.

If a patient is assigned to more than one APG or receives multiple ancillary tests during a single visit, payment would be based upon one of the prevailing discounted payment or procedure consolidation rules. Discounting or procedure consolidation would occur under one of the following conditions:

- significant-related-procedure consolidation
- ancillary service packaging
- multiple unrelated-significant-procedure consolidation and ancillary service discounting

Significant related procedure consolidation would result in situations where a patient undergoes multiple related procedures during a single visit if the additional procedure(s) involves minimal incremental time and resources. Ancillary service packaging relates to the inclusion of routine ancillary tests in the base APG payment. This would include ancillary tests, which are relatively low-cost services and typically performed in conjunction with a wide range of outpatient procedures and visits.

Multiple unrelated significant procedure consolidation and ancillary service discounting would result in situations where the patient undergoes multiple procedures or ancillary tests unrelated to the primary APG to which the patient is assigned. In these situations, payment for the additional procedures and ancillary tests would be based upon a discounted percentage of the standard APG payment rate under the theory that the cost of performing the multiple procedures concurrently is less than that of providing them under separate visits.

The APG system has not yet been proposed as legislation to Congress. The degree to which hospital providers will be affected by the APG payment methodology is dependent upon:

- the percentage of the hospital's net revenue captured from outpatient services

- Medicare patient revenues as a percentage of total outpatient patient revenue
- efficiency of outpatient department operations
- capabilities of the hospital's existing information systems to capture outpatient data in visit episodes

FUTURE CONSIDERATIONS

The future prospects for ambulatory care are limitless. Some elements of the future are clear; others are less clear and some have yet to be imagined. What is clear is that the future of ambulatory care will be significantly affected by clinical trends, regulation, and reimbursement.

Clinical Trends

Advances in technology will continue to affect ambulatory care through the turn of the century and beyond. Industry experts predict that genetic medicine and drug therapy may eradicate various major diseases over the next 20 to 40 years, the result of emerging technologies such as gene transplants, antisense viruses and vaccines, advanced drug therapy, and genetically engineered vaccines tailor-made for the patient requiring the treatment.

Continued advances in diagnostic and surgical instrumentation and treatment techniques will provide opportunities to increase the range of treatments furnished on an outpatient basis. These advances will include improved laser technology, bloodless surgery, programmable home infusion pumps, equipment miniaturization, advanced computerization of test results and transmission via ISPN telephone networks, and advances in fiber optics. These new technologies and treatment approaches will shift the focus of hospital-based ambulatory providers off-campus and into the home. As patients are discharged from inpatient treatment settings earlier and more are directed to ambulatory surgery, managers and clinicians will need to enhance their educational programming and home care

services to ensure that patients get proper, thorough, and timely education and follow-up.

Regulation

Many physicians fear that the enactment of stricter restrictions on physician ownership in ambulatory centers is inevitable. Countless new regulations already have been considered and proposed. Passage of safe harbor legislation will have a significant impact on physician ownership of ASCs because most prevailing ASCs employ some form of physician ownership. There is a shifting mindset among physicians about the long-term viability of ambulatory facility ownership. Physician actions to divest or alter existing ownership positions in ambulatory care centers will affect hospital strategies and relations with medical staffs. This already is seen in mature markets where physician ownership has been transferred to national nonhospital ambulatory care chains.

Reimbursement

Hospital-based and freestanding ambulatory care providers will face challenges associated with changing reimbursement, including Medicare's APG methodology. The introduction of APGs will create significant management and information systems challenges for hospital-based providers, as hospital outpatient statistics have not evolved to the extent that their inpatient counterparts have, and are often fragmented through individual department collection efforts. Further, the volume of data transactions is significantly greater.

Management Considerations

Future prospects for ambulatory care raise numerous management and medical staff challenges for health care executives, including careful selection and acquisition of new technologies, physician privileging criteria for new procedures, training of surgical support staff, and continuing medical education for medical staff. A thorough understanding of ambulatory care trends is critical to maintaining a strong position in this segment of the health care market. For many hospitals, developing a focused approach to ambulatory services has been handicapped by:

- fragmented measures of volume and costs
- a long-standing perspective of such services as supplementary to their inpatient counterpart
- an inability to focus planning efforts due to the diverse nature of outpatient care

In developing strategies for ambulatory care, health care executives must pursue new relationships with physicians, nontraditional management structures, and heightened attention to standards for and measurement of service quality. Many health care organizations are applying continuous quality improvement (CQI) principles to outpatient service areas with the goal of improving customer satisfaction and service quality. As a result, some organizations have seen dramatic results in improving key process variables such as patient registration time, reducing the overall patient waiting and registration time from 25 or more minutes to less than 10 minutes.

Organizing outpatient service areas as a separate operational division, or developing discrete ambulatory care centers, is another example of a fundamental change in the management culture. The characteristics of the effective ambulatory care manager will include superior service and customer-oriented qualities with solid marketing skills, an acute attention to customer satisfaction, and a passion for superior service quality.

Reimbursement and health care reform changes visible on the horizon are prompting hospitals to develop new relationships with physicians and other institutional providers in order to expand care delivery vehicles and develop a comprehensive ambulatory care network. Greater integration in the provision of care will require new treatment and service protocols, systems to measure outcomes, quality report cards, and investment in hospital information systems.

Service Excellence

With outpatient services making up an increasingly more significant portion of the health care industry, providing quality, customer-oriented service is a paramount concern. Most health care managers have tested the total quality management (TQM) waters of the 1980s; some presumably found TQM to be calming and others more faddish. TQM essentially involves attention to process, commitment to customer, involvement of employees, and benchmarking of best practices.[11]

The two primary customer groups for outpatient services are the referring physician and the patient. Key service quality indicators important to the physician as customer include:

- convenient location
- timeliness of service, specifically the speed in processing tests and/or treatments and reporting results
- rapid scheduling, specifically the ability to schedule a procedure or test within days (versus weeks) of identifying a need

Speed and timeliness of service are the most important criteria to this customer group. Universally, physicians characterize a superior outpatient provider as one with early appointment dates, coordinated registration of multiple tests, and minimal turnaround time for results reporting.

Key service quality indicators important to patients as customers include:

- convenient location and easy access
- speedy service, specifically registration and waiting time
- low anxiety atmosphere

As with physicians, patients rate outpatient service providers according to the speed and timeliness of service, characterizing a superior provider as one with minimal waiting time, smooth registration procedures, and limited interdepartment transfers. Nearby parking and a pleasant atmosphere where outpatients are not co-mingled with sicker inpatients are also important attributes.

With the exception of ambulatory surgery, service sites should be located such that patient convenience and access are maximized. Ambulatory surgery facilities should be placed in a location that surgeons find convenient and easy to use. For the hospital-based provider, this may mean the provision of services proximal to each other yet separate from inpatient areas that an outpatient may find unpleasant.

For many hospital-based providers, a focus on outpatient customer preferences and satisfaction has not been an acute priority. Until recent years outpatients typically have been treated as second-class citizens in a setting dominated by inpatients, a setting that favors the more acutely ill patient, who receives more immediate attention and treatment. In short, the "well" outpatient with lower acuity received lower priority. Further, most inpatient service facilities and support systems (modified to handle outpatients) were not designed to meet the specific service needs of the ambulatory patient. As a result, many hospital-based providers have aggressively worked to improve service quality for outpatients through implementation of numerous customer-friendly programs, such as valet parking, controlled-access outpatient parking, escort service, rapid results, express testing protocols, and elec-tronic transmission of results reporting to physician offices. The overriding goal of these efforts has been to win customers by providing unparalleled convenience.

CONCLUSION

The framework for which a health care organization defines itself in the future will be dependent upon how it envisions its role in the provision of ambulatory care. Many industry experts have argued that hospital-based providers have been slow to respond to the changing consumer and payor demands for different care delivery options. Further yet, these experts argue that the very foundation of a hospital-based provider in the way it operates, manages itself, and is embodied through its physical plant, are barriers to superior success in the ambulatory care market. All of these premises are true to some degree. More important, however, to the future of health care providers in the ambulatory care market, is the organization's ability to recognize the changes in the industry and conceive the possibilities (i.e., vision) of providing health care outside of the typical inpatient setting and treatment protocols.

NOTES

1. Outpatient-Care Providers Notch Another Year of Robust Growth; Rehab, Dialysis among Top Gainers, *Modern Healthcare* May 24 (1993):76, 78, 80.

2. New Surgical Technologies Reshape Hospital Strategies, *Hospitals* May 5 (1992).

3. *Maximizing Outpatient Revenues—Existing Hospital Strategies and Tactics* (Washington, D.C.: Healthcare Advisory Board [The Advisory Board Company], 1991), xv.

4. *Hospital Statistics, 1991–92 Edition* (Chicago: American Hospital Association).

5. *1991 National Consumer Study*, Professional Research Consultants, Omaha, Nebraska. *Maximizing Outpatient Revenues—Existing Hospital Strategies and Tactics*, 7.

6. SMG Marketing Group, Inc., Chicago, Illinois. 1991.

Maximizing Outpatient Revenues—Existing Hospital Strategies and Tactics, 8.

7. J. Henderson, Hospitals Seek Bigger Cut of Outpatient Surgeries, *Modern Healthcare* June 28 (1993):82–85.

8. CEOs Outline Outpatient Management Strategies, *Hospitals* March 20 (1992):1.

9. P.L. Havlicek, *Medical Groups in the U.S.: A Survey of Practice Characteristics* (Chicago, Ill.: American Medical Association, Division of Survey and Data Resources, Department of Professional Activities, 1990).

10. Arthur Andersen & Co. and American College of Healthcare Executives, *The Future of Health Care: Physician and Hospital Relations* (Chicago, Ill.: American College of Healthcare Executives, 1991).

11. TQM—More Than a Dying Fad?, *Fortune* October 18 (1993):66–72.

SUGGESTED READINGS

Balicki, B.J. et al. 1991. Guidelines for managing ambulatory surgery programs in the 1990s. *Journal of Ambulatory Care Management* January.

Bryant, M. 1991. The benefits of alternative care. *Business & Health* December.

Department of Health and Human Services. 1993. Medicare program: Schedule of limits on home health agency costs per visit for cost reporting periods beginning on or after July 1, 1993. *Federal Register* 58, no. 129:36748.

Department of Health and Human Services. 1992. Medicare program: Update of ambulatory surgical center payment rates. *Federal Register* 57, no. 191:45544.

Department of Health and Human Services. 1987. Medicare program: Payment for facility services related to ambulatory surgical procedures performed in hospitals on an outpatient basis. *Federal Register* 52, no. 190:36765; 52, no. 105:20623.

Department of Health and Human Services. 1987. Medicare program: List of covered surgical procedures for ambulatory surgical centers. *Federal Register* 52, no. 76:13176.

Henderson, J. 1993. Hospital seeks bigger cut of outpatient surgeries. *Modern Healthcare* June 28.

Henderson, J.A. 1992. Surgicenters cut further into market. *Modern Healthcare* May 19.

Henderson, J.A. 1991. Surgery centers continue pattern of growth. *Modern Healthcare* June 3.

Hoyler, G.M. 1992. Preparing for ambulatory patient groups. *Health Progress* March.

Kenkel, P.J. 1993. Delivering corporate healthcare services. *Modern Healthcare* June 7.

Marion Merrell Dow, Incorporated. 1993. *Managed Care Digest—Long-Term Care Edition 1993*. Kansas City, Missouri.

McDonald's methods come to medicine as chains acquire physicians' practices. 1993. *The Wall Street Journal* August 24: B1.

Outpatient acceleration—1992 survey traces continued ambulatory care growth. 1993. *Hospitals* May 5.

Pasternak, D.P. et al. 1991. Critical issues surrounding the evolution of ambulatory surgery. *Journal of Ambulatory Care Management* January.

Rizk, K.H. 1992. The billing process: Improving efficiency and effectiveness. *Journal of Ambulatory Care Management* April.

Tracking the long-term growth in outpatient care. 1991. *Hospitals* December 5.

Zuckerman, A.M. 1993. Meeting outpatient care challenges. *Trustee* April.

Zuckerman, A.M. 1993. Have focused strategy for ambulatory care. *Modern Healthcare* January 25.

KEVIN W. BARR, MBA, is Senior Vice President with Bon Secours—St. Mary's Health Corporation located in Richmond, Virginia. He also serves as the Executive Director of Bon Secours—Virginia HealthSource, Inc., the Corporation's subsidiary organization for hospital-affiliated physician activities and various community and home care services. Prior to joining Bon Secours—St. Mary's Health Corporation in 1991, Mr. Barr worked with the Northeast Healthcare Consulting Practice of Ernst & Young serving hospital and physician clients.

His career experience includes financial feasibility studies, strategic planning, certificate of need, assessment of health care service needs, valuation of medical practices, medical practice management, physician–hospital networks, managed care, and integrated delivery systems. He has contributed various articles to health care management literature and is a member of the affiliate faculty for the Department of Health Services Administration at the Medical College of Virginia.

Mr. Barr holds a BS in health care management and administration from the Medical College of Virginia and an MBA from Virginia Commonwealth University. In addition, he has an AAS degree in radiologic technology and worked in hospitals in a clinical capacity for several years.

CHARLES L. BREINDEL, PhD, is Professor and Director of the Graduate Program in Health Services Administration at the Medical College of Virginia campus of Virginia Commonwealth University, Richmond, Virginia. Prior to joining the University, he was a Senior Manager in the Mid-Atlantic Healthcare Consulting Practice of Arthur Young & Company (later Ernst & Young) where he directed strategic planning services.

Dr. Breindel has extensive experience in assisting public and private organizations in strategic, program, and market planning for health and hospital services. He has published numerous articles, book chapters, and monographs and done consulting in the United States and internationally for hospitals, governments, and private organizations with health care interests.

In addition to his doctorate from the Pennsylvania State University in health planning and administration, he hold three degrees in areas of mathematics. He has been a professor of health planning and marketing, and has held executive positions in hospital, nursing home, and health systems management.

Chapter 30

Physician Practice

Michael J. Kelley

Traditionally, the curricula of health administration programs, as well as medical schools, had little emphasis on the business and financial aspects of physician practice. Yet, over 20 percent of the national health care budget is spent on direct physicians' services. While significantly less than the portion of the budget devoted to hospital expenses, the size and impact of physician practices on the health care industry are even greater than its number would indicate. It is estimated that an additional 50 to 60 percent of health care costs are directed by physicians.[1] Indeed, physicians are responsible not only for the provision of services, but the ordering of hospital services and admissions.

While the physician and physician group sectors of the industry always have been considered highly fragmented and vertically isolated in nature, they are undergoing radical changes consistent with, and often in concert with, other sectors of the industry. In this chapter the role physicians play in traditional and alternative health care delivery models and the outlook for the physician segment of the health care industry will be covered.

FORMS OF PHYSICIAN PRACTICE

There are three major forms of physician practice: individual or solo physician practice,

single specialty group practice consisting of two or more physicians, and multispecialty group practice. Any of the forms may be either hospital based or independent. According to the American Medical Association (AMA), 33 percent of the U.S. total of 492,711 nonfederally employed active physicians practice in a group setting of three or more physicians. The number of physicians who practice in group settings is higher than the numbers indicate, in that the AMA defines group practice as three or more physicians. An additional 32 percent of physicians provide patient care in a setting other than group practice, solo, or two-physician practice. Included in this category are physicians employed by health maintenance organizations (HMOs), hospitals, medical schools, and state governments, among others. Only 34 percent of the physicians identify themselves as being in a solo or two-physician practice.[2]

Solo Practice

Solo practice is the choice of few individuals currently embarking on a medical career. Only 5.5 percent of physicians under the age of 35 are reported in solo or two-physician practices.[3] Physicians in solo practices often cite the freedom and self-determination made possible by independence as one of the major benefits. With no other physicians involved in the practice, a solo practitioner can practice medicine without the need to consult associates. The practice is able to directly meet the personal needs of the practitioner, in terms of scheduling, working style, and professional interests.

A solo practitioner may function as a self-employed individual or as an employee of the corporation that the physician wholly owns, whether a subchapter S or subchapter C corporation. Selection of the specific form of practice should be determined in conjunction with legal and tax planning advice. Each form has its own specific tax planning issues, including the deductibility of certain expenses, retirement plan options, and taxation of fringe benefits. In addition, there are legal consequences, including, among other things, the degree to which the practitioner's estate is protected from certain liabilities.

Single-Specialty Group Practice

Single-specialty group practices are a common form, with approximately half of physicians' group members affiliating in this manner.[4] In a single-specialty group practice, all the physicians practice in the same field of medicine. This does not mean, however, that the practices need to be identical. For example, an ophthalmic single-specialty group might incorporate subspecialties of the eye, such as retina, cornea, oculoplastic, and anterior segment subspecialists.

Physicians in group practice can enjoy a number of benefits. Historically, compensation for group practicing physicians, whether single or multispecialty, is higher than that of solo practitioners. This difference in compensation levels amounts to over $29,000 for the average physician.[5] While often cited as a reason for group success, there is little evidence that economies of scale are created. In fact, group physicians have a higher expense ratio than nongroup physicians. However, group practices often are able to make larger capital investments. Additionally, these practices often are able to employ more highly trained support staffs. This may

help explain both the higher expense ratios and higher incomes of physicians in group practice, a setting in which physicians generally see more patients per week while working a comparable number of hours.[6] The physician in group practice also can achieve life style benefits from reduced call schedules and cross coverage during times of vacation, illness, or disability.

Offsetting these advantages is a real need to develop consensus among physicians regarding practice philosophies and administrative policies. The difficulty of this task, combined with the inherent interpersonal relationships, causes a large number of group practices to end in dissolution, with estimated failure rates approaching 50 percent.[7] This often can be traced to failures in the recruiting process. During the recruiting process, physicians often spend insufficient time gaining an understanding of each other as individuals, determining the compatibility of personality traits, leadership styles, and expectations. More often, an inordinate amount of time is focused on the medical procedures and scholastic achievements of the candidate. The costs associated with the need to disassociate, both personal and financial, can be extremely high. Physicians should carefully investigate group practice opportunities and not overlook the personal and business relationships entailed in group practice.

Group practices also can be formed under different legal entities. A partnership is an unincorporated form of practice that can be established as a vehicle for group practice. Group members own and distribute practice income based upon the partnership agreement. There are clear disadvantages to partnerships with regard to liability issues. Each partner may be held individually responsible for the acts of any other partner related to the operation of the partnership.

Group practices are more often incorporated as either subchapter S or C corporations, with the same advantages and disadvantages as previously discussed. The group physicians act as employees of the corporation. The governance of the group is carried out under the articles of incorporation and bylaws of the corporation. Not all group physicians need be shareholders and officers of the corporation. Indeed, it is common for new physicians to work for some period of time before they are offered the opportunity to purchase stock in the corporation.

Multispecialty Group Practice

A multispecialty group practice shares many of the characteristics of single-specialty group practice, but will cross lines of specialization. Such groups might include primary, secondary, and tertiary care. Often these types of groups will exist in a managed care or academic environment. Many advantages can be cited for this model of practice. Multispecialty group practices tend to be, by their nature, larger than single-specialty groups. Many patients will have more than one significant medical problem, thereby creating opportunities for cross referral to physicians within the group practice. The size of the enterprise also can produce opportunities whereby each individual practitioner can benefit from the professionally developed corporate administrative systems and cross-marketing plans. Multispecialty group practices often can posture themselves as regional centers, drawing both self- and physician-referred patients from a larger geographic area than they would otherwise enjoy.

Offsetting these cited advantages are a number of problems associated with running a large enterprise. The number of physicians in a multispecialty group can make governance a difficult issue. In the typical single-specialty group practice, each physician may play a role in the joint governance of the enterprise. In the typical multispecialty environment, governance is accomplished through an executive committee with a chief medical and administrative officer. Income and resource allocation often is a difficult subject. Primary care and surgical specialties are often at odds. Primary care physicians often seek to be subsidized by the higher revenue-producing specialists and subspecialists, for whom primary care generates referrals and patient volume.

Notwithstanding the negative issues associated with group practice, many physicians believe the support services generated by the group, the presence of ancillary services, as well as the freedom from administrative and managerial tasks can offset the disadvantages. Group practice, whether subspecialty or multispecialty, is a growing force in the health care industry. Mergers and affiliations are becoming more common given the changes in the health care marketplace. Many health care experts predict the trend toward group practice medicine will accelerate and become an increasingly attractive choice for physicians beginning medical careers, as well as an alternative to be considered by solo and small group members. The trend to consolidation often is viewed as a natural economic result of increased competition for health care resources.

ALTERNATIVE HEALTH CARE DELIVERY SYSTEMS AND PHYSICIAN ORGANIZATION

Faced with high cost or the inability to obtain traditional medical insurance, organizations began to experiment with alternative delivery systems in the 1920s and 1930s.[8,9] In 1965, a survey conducted by the Department of Health, Education, and Welfare identified 582 prepaid medical plans.[10] But for the overwhelming majority of Americans, traditional fee-for-service medicine was the only available option. Not until the 1970s and 1980s did a significant growth in managed care plans begin. Nearly half of all employees covered by employer-sponsored group health plans are enrolled in managed care plans, according to a report based on 1991 data. The report noted that 25 percent were enrolled in HMOs, 22 percent were in preferred provider organizations (PPOs), and 5 percent were in point-of-service plans.[11]

Managed Care

Managed care is a widely touted phrase, but one that is not necessarily easily defined. Strictly speaking, managed care could be defined as medical care being directed and paid for by a third party, generally an insurance company. Under strict interpretation, this would define virtually any insurance policy or government program as a managed care program. Few policies or programs contain no restrictions on the services an insured can obtain. Virtually all have limits on overall spending, types of services covered, and number of services provided. Managed care plans can be sponsored by a profit or nonprofit organization and may reimburse physicians on a capitated or discounted fee-for-service basis. Services can be provided by salaried health care providers or by contract with independent physicians. They may have large open or closed panels of providers. They can function by directly providing medical services, or through the indemnification or reimbursement of incurred costs. On the basis of just these 5 characteristics, 32 permutations are theoretically possible. On a more general basis, though, managed care is generally defined as care that offers comprehensive benefits delivered by selected providers and financial incentives for members to use providers who are members of the plan.

HMOs

HMOs are medical care organizations that are responsible "for the provision and delivery of a predetermined set of comprehensive health maintenance and treatment services to a voluntarily enrolled group for prenegotiated and fixed periodic capitation payment."[12] Cowan defines five common characteristics shared by such plans:

1. a defined population of enrolled members
2. payment by the members determined in advance for a specific period of time and made periodically
3. medical services provided on a direct service basis rather than on an indemnity basis
4. services provided to patients by HMO physicians for essentially all medical needs with referrals to outside physicians being controlled by HMO physicians
5. voluntary enrollment by each family or member[13]

In an HMO, a primary care physician is responsible for determining what services are necessary and who will provide the services for enrolled patients. In the event the patient seeks care on a nonemergency basis from any health care provider not authorized by the HMO physician, payment is denied for the services. The effect of this health care delivery model is that it limits the services received by the patient to those deemed medically necessary by the primary care provider and attempts to eliminate duplicative or unnecessary costs. A frequently cited problem of traditional fee-for-service medicine is that the provider receives a direct financial benefit from ordering additional tests and procedures. Under the HMO model, the provider receives no financial benefit from the tests and referrals initiated. In fact, in the event that utilization targets are exceeded, the primary care physician may be penalized for health care costs incurred by the patients for whom he has accepted responsibility.

There are three models for organizing physicians in an HMO: the staff model, group model, or independent practice association (IPA) model. In the staff model HMO, physicians are salaried employees of the HMO. They furnish care exclusively to members of the HMO, with the HMO responsible for all nonclinical management. In some cases, these physicians are given incentives to control costs through bonus mechanisms that reward the physician for controlling costs.

In a group model HMO, the physicians may be organized as a multispecialty group. These groups often have their own separate legal entity and contract with the HMO to provide services to its members. The group receives a direct capitation payment from the HMO, which has been predetermined by negotiation, and may be entitled to supplemental payments based on the profitability of the HMO. The group then compensates individual physicians based on either a salary, productivity or utilization basis, or combination of all three.

The group model HMO can result in significant risk shifting to the group practice. Inasmuch as the physicians often are owners of the group practice, their net income can be directly affected by services provided to HMO members. Incentives to hold down overall health costs can take two forms: there may be prenegotiated accruals, or withholds, payable in the event costs are under budget and higher profits generated internally within the group through the lower costs associated with the provision of fewer services. The physician group often provides services to patients independent of the HMO, and may operate a component of the group practice on a traditional fee-for-service basis.

IPAs

An IPA is a legal entity composed of physicians and physician groups, each of which function as separate and independent practices. In practice, these function as networks of physicians who form together to contract for managed care while retaining a high degree of independence. Under an IPA-model HMO, large panels of physicians contract with the HMO to provide health services within a defined geographic area. Traditionally, physicians have been paid on a fee-for-service basis, but at a rate that discounts their customary charges. In many cases, the fee schedule is set by discounting the Medicare fee schedule. A portion of the discounts, referred to as withholds, often are paid to physicians if a surplus exists after payment of hospital, external, and administrative costs.

Faced with the desire of insurers to decrease their claims risk, some IPAs are developing capitated payment agreements. Under such an agreement, the IPA contracts to provide specified services at a fixed cost per beneficiary per month. The IPA then controls utilization issues within its organization and compensates individual practitioners for care on either a discounted fee for service or a capitated basis.

IPA physicians often have a large percentage of their practice income derived from traditional fee-for-services patients. One of the cost control weaknesses of this model is that the overwhelming majority of the physician income is still generated on a fee-for-service basis with the smaller remainder being dependent upon the entire group's cost behavior. Physicians continue to receive the bulk of their income from the number of procedures and tests they perform.

PPOs

PPOs are similar to IPAs in that physicians function on a fee-for-service basis. Unlike the HMO model, in which there usually is a primary-care gatekeeper who controls the services provided to enrollees, PPO-enrolled patients are free to make their own choice of providers. PPO physicians enter into an arrangement with the sponsoring organization, often an insurance company, and agree to a discounted fee for service. By offering the discount, the physicians hope to stabilize or increase the size of the patient population they service.

Subscribers typically are free to seek the care of physicians outside of the PPO panel, but are penalized by receiving a lower rate of reimbursement, resulting in higher cost to the beneficiary. PPOs often incorporate low co-payments and deductibles in order to create an incentive for patients to obtain discounted care and remain within the PPO panel. The patients may opt out of the panel and seek care elsewhere if they feel value is generated equal to the higher cost. PPO physicians do not share in any withhold pool and receive no direct incentive to hold costs down. The physician practices medicine on a discounted fee-for-service basis; income is directly related to the value and volume of services rendered.

All of these managed care models share a common goal—the reduction of health care costs. They vary substantially in the method and degree of control they exert on the individual practitioners. Not surprisingly, lowest physician costs are typically found where control upon physician activity is highest. Indemnity insurance, the traditional program insurance in which patients are free to choose any physician for any health care problem, have the highest costs. PPOs, which are the least restrictive on physician behavior of the managed care models, are also the most expensive. HMOs, with the highest levels of physician control, are generally the lowest cost model.

OPERATIONAL ASPECTS OF PHYSICIAN PRACTICE

Resource Management

Operations management in a physician setting is similar to that of any other organization. The goal is to maximize net revenue through the efficient utilization of resources. Resources include plant and equipment, physicians, ancillary staff, and time.

A number of resource costs are fixed, including rent and many other occupancy expenses. Other expenses, such as supplies, are variable in that they rise and fall in direct relation to the volume of procedures. Some expenses, such as staffing costs, are semivariable in that they can only be changed in incremental fashion, with a minimum level of cost that is essentially fixed. For example, a receptionist is necessary whether the physician sees two or five patients per hour.

Operations management seeks to provide services at the lowest possible cost. Inasmuch as the physician is usually the highest cost resource, effective utilization of this resource requires that the physician's activity be concentrated in areas where he or she is uniquely qualified: the practice of medicine. There are scientific measurement aspects of medicine, such as the range of motion of a joint or the weight and height of an individual. The "art" of medicine is the cognitive function, the evaluation of quantitative and subjective data followed by the definition of a management plan.

As a general rule, measurement activities can be provided at a lower cost by well-trained clinical assistants or physician extenders. Measurement activities take time, and time is a scarce resource for many physicians. When an activity is performed by physician extenders, the physician may increase the number of patients served as a result of the time savings.

Appointment Scheduling

It is for this reason that the appointment scheduling process is one of the key variables in physician productivity. The goal of the process is to have the physician rendering medical care as continuously as possible during scheduled hours.

There are two basic types of appointment scheduling: standard segment and wave. Under a standard segment system the number of patients the physician sees per hour is divided by 60 minutes and scheduled in equal segments. If a physician sees 6 patients per hour on average, an appointment is scheduled every 10 minutes. The problem with this scheduling system is that patients require varying amounts of time per visit. If it is assumed in this example that visits actually range from 5 to 15 minutes, the physician can encounter substantial periods of time when no patient is available to be seen.

Wave scheduling attempts to correct this natural variability by establishing a queue of patients. Under the same assumptions as above, a wave schedule would have 3 patients scheduled at the top of the hour and 3 scheduled at the half-past-the-hour time slot. Thus, if the first patient takes 5 minutes to be seen, the physician can move to the next patient who is already available to be seen.

A hybrid solution, called the modified wave, combines aspects of segment and wave scheduling. If a physician sees 6 patients per hour and the minimum visit is 5 minutes, appointments would be scheduled from the top of the hour in 5-minute intervals until half past the hour. This assures that the physician is always busy, but can lead to longer patient wait time.

Another alternative scheduling method is based on time units. Typically, the 5-minute exam has distinct characteristics from the 15-

minute exam. The 5-minute exam might be a routine postoperative exam and represents 1 unit of time, while the 15-minute exam would be an initial new patient visit using 3 units of time. By determining the type of exam, the number of units of time it will take can be determined. This can help to minimize patient wait times, which are stressful on both physician and patient, while reducing or eliminating periods of physician inactivity.

Defining the Medical Service for Billing

CPT Coding

In order for both physicians and their patients to be properly reimbursed for services by insurers, the identification of the procedure or procedures performed must occur. Medicare, as well as most insurance companies, utilize the American Medical Association's Physician Current Procedural Terminology (CPT) to describe the services provided to the patient. This process of reviewing the service and categorizing it is referred to as coding. The CPT book (updated every year) contains some basic coding information, as well as thousands of defined services or procedures. Each of the described procedures is defined by a specific 5-digit code. Under some circumstances, a code must be reported with one or more additional 2-digit modifiers that identify relevant additional information needed to determine the amount or type of service performed. For example, modifier 50 identifies that a bilateral procedure was performed during the same operative session. Modifier 54 identifies that the surgical care was provided by the billing physician and that another physician provided the preoperative and postoperative components of the surgical procedure. There are 25 surgical modifiers commonly used for surgical procedures and an additional 6 that refer to the evaluation and management sections of the CPT code.[14]

Some physician activities require the use of Health Care Financing Administration (HCFA) Common Procedural Coding System descriptors, HCPCS (pronounced "hic-pics"). Level 2 codes are a series of national codes that describe supplies, injectable drugs, physician, and other health care provider services not described in the CPT (HCPCS Level 1), as well as dental services.[15] A third level of descriptors, HCPCS Level 3, are local codes used by the Medicare carrier to describe services and activities for which national coverage has not been determined. The number of local codes is decreasing as Medicare moves toward a uniform national payment policy.

Care must be taken when coding, not only to ensure that the service was provided as described, but to avoid the unbundling of charges. Unbundling occurs when a procedure is broken down into discrete components rather than being identified by the procedure code that defines the entire service. The reason that unbundling represents an incorrect coding method relates to the way that the value of procedures is determined. The value of the work performed by improperly componentizing the procedure would be significantly greater than the work value that would derive from the global or bundled procedure. In other words, the sum is greater than the whole.

As an example, during the repair of a retinal detachment, a physician may inject medication, use a laser to seal the tear, and drain subretinal fluid. Each of those three procedures has its own discrete CPT code. When taken as a whole, they are regarded as components of CPT code 67105; repair of retinal detachment. See Exhibit 30–1.

Diagnosis Coding

The International Classification of Disease (ICD) is used to specifically code a diagnosis or diagnoses applicable to the service rendered. Published by the World Health Organization, the current version is the ICD9 Manual. The U.S. Public Health Service and the HCFA mandate the use of the ICD9 Manual for its programs. Approximately 1300 pages in length, the manual lists tens of thousands of diagnoses. Each diagnosis is given a unique 3-digit code, which can be further subclassified with an additional 2 digits, if necessary. The ICD9 coding of disorders resulting from impaired renal function, 588, is shown in Exhibit 30–2.[16]

Exhibit 30–1 Example of Bundled Codes

BILLED CODE

67105—Repair of retinal detachment, one or more sessions; photocoagulation (laser or xenon arc) with or without drainage of subretinal fluid

BUNDLED CODES

67015 – Aspiration or release of vitreous, subretinal, or choroidal fluid, pars plana approach (posterior sclerotomy)

67101 – Repair of retinal detachment, one or more sessions; cryotherapy or diathermy, drainage of subretinal fluid

67141 – Prophylaxis of retinal detachment with or without (e.g., retinal break) drainage, one or more sessions; cryotherapy, diathermy

67145 – Prophylaxis of retinal detachment (e.g., lattice degeneration) with or without drainage, one or more sessions; photocoagulation

67208 – Destruction of localized lesion of retina one or more sessions; cryotherapy, diathermy (e.g., small tumors)

67210 – Destruction of localized lesion of retina; photocoagulation (laser or xenon arc)

67227 – Destruction of extensive or progressive retinopathy, one or more sessions, cryotherapy, diathermy (e.g., diabetic retinopathy)

67228 – Destruction of extensive or progressive retinopathy, one or more sessions; photocoagulation

67500 – Retrobulbar injection; medication (separate procedure—does not include supply of medication)

92504 – Binocular microscopy (separate diagnostic procedure)

Source: CPT codes are copyright © 1993, American Medical Association.

Exhibit 30–2 ICD9 Codes for Disorders Resulting from Impaired Renal Function

---

588   Disorders resulting from impaired renal function

588.0 Renal osteodystrophy
   Azotemic osteodystrophy
   Phosphate-losing tubular disorders
   Renal:
      dwarfism
      infantilism
      rickets

588.1 Nephrogenic diabetes insipidus
   Excludes: diabetes insipidus NOS (253.5)

588.8 Other specified disorders resulting from impaired renal function
   Hypokalemic nephropathy
   Secondary hyperparathyroidism (of renal origin)
   Excludes: secondary hypertension (405.0–405.9)

588.9 Unspecified disorder resulting from impaired renal function

Source: ICD•9•CM Practice Management Information Corporation

Physician Reimbursement Methods

UCR System of Physician Reimbursement

Many indemnity insurers use what is referred to as a usual, customary, and reasonable (UCR) methodology, or close variant thereof. Under this method, the insurer collects a database of charges for each service submitted by all similar physicians in a geographic area. The insurer then sorts these from the lowest charge to the highest and limits payment to a determined percentile. Some commercial carriers will pay at the 50th percentile of the charge array, while some others may pay as much as the 90th percentile charge. This is referred to as the "customary charge." The fee that the physician normally charges for the procedure is the "usual charge." The third fee that the insurer considers is a "reasonable fee." This fee allowance could be lower or higher based upon documented special circumstances of the case. The insurer will pay the lower of the usual or customary charge, unless a reasonable-fee adjustment is warranted. An example of a UCR system is shown in Exhibit 30–3.

Relative Value Systems and RBRVS

As early as the mid-1950s, payors began investigating a relative-value-based method of physician payment. Under relative value payment methodologies, the economic cost of providing a service is the basis under which it is reimbursed. Physician time, training, and the

Exhibit 30–3 Determination of Allowable Fee under UCR Method

Table of Historical Charge Data			Examples—Insurer pays 90th percentile
Physician	*$*		• Dr. Smith submits charge for $75. Insurer allows $60. Charge exceeds 90th percentile UCR.
Dr. Smith	75		
Dr. Gomez	60	← 90th Percentile	
Dr. Casper	55		• Dr. Felix submits charge for $50. Insurer allows $50, the usual fee for Dr. Felix.
Dr. Felix	50		
Dr. Felix	50	← 50th Percentile	
Dr. Singer	47		• Dr. Alex submits charge for $75. Insurer allows $45 based upon his historical charges.
Dr. Alex	45		
Dr. Alex	45		
Dr. Jones	40		

intensity of the service, as well as practice and malpractice expense components, are all factors in the economic costs of providing a service. Rather than being a reimbursement system based upon historic charges, a relative value system quantifies the resources necessary to perform a service.

Relative value systems, when properly constructed, will have increasing value as a management tool. They offer the opportunity for an organization to measure the resources necessary to deliver services, and to compare them to an independently derived value. An organizational efficiency measurement can then be derived. Services can be measured in terms of both cost and revenue on an individual basis.

Relative value systems also provide organizations with a method to quantify the number of units of service provided. This method provides a common denominator that is unaffected by changing case mix and fee schedules. Many practices track, as part of their financial management systems, the number of patient encounters. Relative-value-system-based management recognizes that some encounters and services are worth more than others. For example, Medicare has established that a level 5 consultation with a physician expends 4.86 units of resources and a level 5 established patient visit expends 2.37 units.

Relative value systems also are useful in the measurement of the costs involved in providing care under capitated systems. The organization can track the number of units of service it provides and the capitated payment to computer the reimbursement per unit of service. By comparing the payor's reimbursement per unit of service to the organization's cost to provide a unit of service, management can make informed decisions about the profitability of managed care contracts.

The most significant relative value system in terms of impact on the industry was adopted in 1992 by Medicare, the Resource Based Relative Value Scales (RBRVS). The RBRVS system came into effect because of the belief that the historical Medicare payment structure favored subspecialty and surgical procedures rather than primary care and cognitive medical activities. Many felt there was a serious inequity when primary care physicians such as family practitioners were earning significantly less than subspecialty surgeons. For example, the median compensation of family practitioners in group practices was $112,585 in 1992. During that same year, the median compensation for orthopedic surgeons in group practices was $289,323.[17]

Determination of Relative Values

A team of Harvard researchers commonly referred to as the Hsiao Team, after its principal researcher, surveyed a cross section of physicians in multiple specialties to determine the amount of physician work involved in a number of described encounters. Physician work took into account the amount of time, intensity of effort, and technical skill required to provide the service. The physicians evaluated the work components relative to other defined encounters, indicating their perception of the amount of work involved in the task. These work values were then cross linked against all of the procedures surveyed. The intent of the study was to have a uniform scale under which all physician activities could be evaluated. The HCFA adopted and expanded upon the work done by Hsaio to develop a schedule of work values for all covered Medicare procedures.

Beginning January 1, 1992, the Medicare approved fee for any service could be defined by calculating the following formula:

PAYMENT = (WORK + PRACTICE EXPENSE + MALPRACTICE) × CF

$$[(RVUw_s \times GPCIw_a) + (RVUpe_s \times GPCIpe_a) + (RVUm_s \times GPCIm_a)] \times CF$$

where:

$RVUw_s$ = Physician work relative value units for the service

$RVUpe_s$ = Practice expense relative value units for the service

$RVUm_s$ = Malpractice expense relative value units for the service

$GPCIw_a$ = GPCI value reflecting one-fourth of geographic variation in physician work applicable in the fee schedule area

$GPCIpe_a$ = GPCI value for practice expense applicable in the fee schedule area

$GPCIm_a$ = GPCI value for malpractice expense applicable in the fee schedule area

CF = Conversion factor (dollar denominated)

Once the work components had been valued, two additional values had to be determined: practice expense and malpractice expense. The practice expense component reflects the overhead costs associated with providing the service. Practice expense and malpractice expense com-

ponents were calculated by reviewing their historical costs. These costs were based on specialty-specific overhead ratios. The practice and malpractice expense ratios for a particular service were calculated to reflect a weighted average based upon all the specialties performing the services. During the debate on the OBRA 89 legislation, debate arose over the need for adjustments to the fee schedule to account for variations and geographic costs. Geographic practice cost indices (GPCIs—pronounced "gypsies") were developed to make geographic adjustments against each of the fee schedule components. The practice-expense GPCI is intended to account for variations of office rents, employee wages, and other operating expenses. The malpractice GPCI was used to adjust the malpractice component of the cost in order to reflect the varying costs of malpractice liability insurance in different localities. The third factor, the physician-work-component GPCI, was the most controversial. Rural physicians complained that it was unfair to reward urban physicians with higher incomes simply because they practiced in areas with higher costs. They persuasively argued that a physician cost of living was directly linked to the attractiveness of the location. Compromise was reached where only one-quarter of the geographic variations of physician GPCI would be used to adjust the payments.

Once the work, practice expense, and malpractice components are determined, after adjustment for geographic costs, the sum is multiplied by the conversion factor. The conversion factor is a monetary multiplier and is used nationally to compute the reimbursement level. The conversion factors can be adjusted annually to meet the budgetary goals of the Congress.

Transition to the Full RBRVS Schedule

As part of the change in the Medicare reimbursement method, a phase-in period was incorporated into the law. Beginning January 1, 1992, and ending on January 1, 1996, under a series of formulas enacted in 1989 and modified in 1993, the impact of downward revisions in the fee schedule was buffered by an annual limitation on the amount of adjustment. The intent was to create breathing room for the practices, primarily surgical, that were most negatively affected by the changing reimbursement formula, to adapt their practices to the changing economics.

The Billing and Collection Process

Once the task of defining the service and linking it to its appropriate diagnosis is completed, the billing and collection phase of the physician reimbursement process is actuated. Each physician or group needs to create a billing and collection policy, a written set of procedures under which patients are expected to pay for the services they receive. A number of factors need to be considered when determining the payment policy. Does the group expect payment at the time of service (PATOS)? The advantages of this payment system—one of which is a rapid payment cycle with a low level of accounts receivable outstanding at any point in time—have to be weighed against the potential loss of patients, who resent the unwillingness of the provider to bill the insurance companies for their appropriate balances. Patients may choose to obtain their services at competitors who offer more liberal pricing policies. The group or physician also needs to decide whether it will become a Medicare-participating provider. Under this reimbursement option, the physician agrees to undertake the responsibility of collecting 80 percent of the approved charge directly from the Medicare carrier, making the patient responsible only for the 20 percent co-payment and deductibles. Again, the socioeconomic characteristics of the target market need to be considered.

Insurance Submission

After the CPT and ICD9 codes have been selected for the encounter, claims are submitted to insurance companies for payment. Claims can be submitted on paper, often on universal billing forms, or electronically if the practice is automated. Greater numbers of practices utilize automated billing, as payment often is made faster and important management information can be produced. The payor will apply its own rules when processing the claim. It may reject a charge based on inappropriate use, such as billing a follow-up visit as a new patient encounter. The insurer may also apply a fee screen. The fee screen will approve payment only for charges with specific diagnoses related to the services rendered. For example, Medicare will not pay for a fundus photograph (a photograph of the retina) when the diagnosis is cataract (cloudiness of the lens). Nor will Medicare pay for a Pap smear performed upon a male. The rationale behind these fee screens is that tests and procedures are only valid for a limited range of diagnoses and appropriate patient types.

Insurance companies also will often reject unbundled codes. As previously covered, unbundled charges represent multiple components of a global service. The insurance companies often adopt their own proprietary screens, which are not distributed. These screens may also incorporate frequency-of-use limitations.

The Accounting Process

In order to evaluate the efficiency of the billing process, the physician should establish an accounting system that collects all the pertinent information. One of the commonly used systems is the chart of accounts developed by the Center for Research in Ambulatory Health Care Administration (CRAHCA).[18]

Gross charges are defined as the full value of medical services provided before any adjustment. Gross charges are then reduced by the following items:

- charity adjustments
- contractually agreed-upon reimbursement discounts (i.e., the difference between the charge and what the insurer allows on an assigned claim)
- courtesy adjustments (such as for other physicians)
- employee discounts

The result is the adjusted (net) gross charges, or the maximum amount of payment that could be collected if all payors (insurers and patients paying co-insurance and deductibles) met their obligations. The next step in the collection process is to record all cash payments collected from patients or the amount paid on their behalf by insurance companies and other payors. Noncash adjustments are referred to as payment allowances. These noncash adjustments are comprised of bad debts, settlements, and provision for bad debts. Any remaining balance after the deduction of these items would represent a change in the accounts receivable.

The importance of timely and careful evaluation of the collection process cannot be overemphasized. Disruptions of cash flow have major negative impacts. First, if fees are not collected in an efficient manner, the practice could suffer a liquidity crisis and be unable to meet its ongoing obligations. Second, and perhaps more important, the older a receivable is, the less likely it is to be collected. Once a payor determines that the collection of fees is not being conducted in a businesslike fashion, any debt owed to the physician may be placed on a low or no-pay priority. As the time period between the rendering of the service and demand for payment increases, patients will rationalize reasons why the fee was too high or they didn't receive what was expected. There is a greater perceived value to the service at the time the service is rendered.

Collection Systems

A physician practice has a number of options, manual and computerized, under which it can manage the collection process. There are effective manual accounting systems, adequate for smaller practices, that operate under a payment-at-time-of-service collection policy. The two common manual accounting systems used are the double entry system and the pegboard system.

A double entry system uses a charge and payment journal and individual records for each patient that list the individual's charges and payments, referred to as a ledger card. When a charge is incurred, a charge is entered into the charge and payment journal as well as the ledger card. Thus, there is a double entry for each account activity.

The pegboard system improves upon the double entry system by relying on a single entry system. The ledger card is aligned in such a way that activity recorded in it also is recorded on a day sheet (listing all the day's transactions) by the use of carbon or duplicating paper. It also simultaneously creates the bill. Such systems, however, rely heavily on manual clerical functions for the billing and aging of receivables.

The trend for collection systems is toward computerized systems for a number of reasons. Most computerized collection systems are able to generate standard health claim policies efficiently. The overwhelming majority are capable of electronically transmitting these claims to Medicare carriers and other insurance companies. The net result is faster and more accurate turnaround of claims payments. Computer systems also can be programmed to efficiently generate bills to patients without interrupting normal office procedures.

Of particular importance is the ability to generate an aged accounts receivable, and other analyses. This report categorizes how old a receivable is; the age is calculated by number of days since the service was rendered. This is an extremely important number to track because of the previously described loss of collectibility. Such a system also can be set up to force the write-off or placement with collection agencies of uncollected debts.

Computerized collection systems also help reduce labor costs associated with manual systems. Submission of insurance claims on behalf of Medicare patients, now required by law, requires the repetitive entry of demographic and policy information. Many individuals also will expect the practice to generate commercial insurance claim forms, which helps to expedite the payment of physician services. Basic computer and software packages capable of handling small practices are available for under $5,000.

The need for information about the practice also makes computerization valuable, particularly in a managed care environment. The data entered in the course of recording account activity can give important insights into the demographics, case mix, and referral patterns in the practice. The ability to identify changes and extrapolate trends allows the physician to react proactively.

Computerized collections systems need not be owned by the practice. The practice can contract with an independent billing organization referred to as a service bureau. A service bureau functions solely to collect payments owed to physicians and other health care providers. By providing a collection function for a number of physicians, economies of scale and attention to the collection process can be achieved that may not occur within the physician's practice. Service bureaus typically are paid on a percentage-of-collection basis, and this motivates them to collect efficiently and promptly. This is not to disparage in any way the ability of a physician's own employees to effectively collect patient accounts. Many can and do achieve results comparable or better than service bureaus. Management oversight, training, and system design always is the key to a successful collection procedure, whether the activity takes place within the physician's office or through a service bureau. The efficiency of the collection function can be compared to collection data compiled by independent sources. A number of organizations, such as the Medical Group Management Association (MGMA), collect median data indicating gross and adjusted collection rates, as well as accounts receivable aging data.[19]

INSURANCE SOURCES

Medicare

Medicare, established in 1965, insures the elderly and long-term disabled for their medical costs. Medicare Part A primarily reimburses hospitals for the costs incurred by its beneficiaries. Medicare Part B covers services provided by physicians. Medicare has sought to control costs both for the program and its beneficiaries

since its inception. Reimbursement rates typically were lower than those paid by commercial insurance companies and private pay patients. The Deficit Reduction Act of 1984 established the participating physician program. Doctors enrolled as participating physicians would receive 80 percent of the allowed fee directly from Medicare after the patient had met a small deductible. The patient would then be responsible only for the 20 percent co-insurance. Nonparticipating physicians were free to charge and collect any fee they chose directly from the patient.

In 1987, Medicare began limiting the fees that could be charged to Medicare beneficiaries by nonparticipating doctors under the maximum allowable charge limits (see Exhibit 30–4). Further beneficiary cost limits were enacted in 1991, when Medicare beneficiary liability was limited to 125% of the nonparticipating fee schedule. This nonparticipating fee schedule was set at 95% of the participating-physician fee schedule. Since 1991, this payment differential has reduced to 115%, and some states have enacted even tighter payment regulation. Since there is a 5 percent penalty for nonparticipation, the actual premium a nonparticipating physician may collect is only 9.25 percent. As the payment differential narrowed between what a participating physician could collect and what a nonparticipating physician could collect, increasing numbers of physicians began to participate in the program. Patient education and Medicare publications have encouraged the establishment of relationships with participating providers in order to reduce beneficiary costs.

Other Significant Federal Programs

Medicaid was created in 1965 to fund the health care needs of the poor. States have the responsibility of administering the program, with some financial assistance from the federal government. Unlike most Medicare-covered services, beneficiaries often have utilization restrictions, such as the number of visits to a doctor they may make. Each state has the ability to enact its own fee schedule and utilization rules un-

Exhibit 30–4 Comparison of Medicare Fee Structures

Physician's normal charge	$150.00
Medicare Participating Fee Schedule Allowable	$100.00
Example 1 – Physician Participates	
Medicare pays physician 80% of allowable	$80.00
Physician attempts to collect from patient	<u>$20.00</u>
Total Reimbursement	$100.00
Example 2 – Physician Does Not Participate, Accepts Assignment	
Medicare pays physician 80% of 95% fee schedule allowable	$76.00
Physician attempts to collect 20% from patient	<u>$19.00</u>
Total Reimbursement	$95.00
Example 3 – Nonparticipating Physician, Does Not Accept Assignment	
Physician charge limited to 115% of 95% of fee schedule	$109.25
Medicare pays patient 80% of 95% fee schedule	<u>$76.00</u>
Physician attempts to collect directly from patient	$109.25

der the guidance and approval of the federal government. Many physicians will not accept Medicaid patients because of their typically lower reimbursement rates and often complex and confusing payment rules.

CHAMPUS is the health care system of reimbursement for government and military retirees and dependents of active and retired service personnel. Like Medicare, it pays on a fee-for-service basis, but can have significantly different reimbursement rates and coverages. Many physicians may elect to become participating providers under this system with the benefit of direct payment, as well as reduced out-of-pocket expenses for beneficiaries.

Commercial Insurers

As described in the earlier section on UCR (fee for service), there are many commercial insurance companies or indemnity insurers that provide coverage for physician services. The impetus to managed care, and community rating of premiums, has significantly reduced the number of commercial insurers that provide UCR payment. Most have introduced point-of-service coverage (a hybrid between UCR payment for nonpanel physicians, and reduced payment for panel physicians), and other forms of managed care. The UCR method of payment is the most rapidly changing aspect of commercial insurance coverage; there has been speculation that it will be the smallest source of physician insurance in the future.

THE FUTURE

The physician practice is undergoing a period of rapid evolution. Cost pressures applied by payors as well as increasingly competitive markets are causing the creation of new organizational structures and affiliations. The physician will continue to play a key role in the health delivery system. The nature of that role will be defined by both the political process and by economic forces.

NOTES

1. D. Coddington et al., *The Crisis in Healthcare* (San Francisco: Jossey-Bass, Inc., 1990), 38.

2. P. Havlicek and M. Eiler, eds., *Physicians in Medical Groups: A Comparative Analysis* (Chicago: American

Medical Association, 1993), 5–17.

3. Ibid., 7.

4. Ibid., 28.

5. Ibid., 16.

6. Ibid., 14.

7. American Health Consultants, *Physicians' Marketing and Management* 5, no. 10 (1992):5.

8. H. Hyman, *Health Planning: A Systematic Approach* (Gaithersburg, Md: Aspen Publishers, Inc., 1975), 10–13.

9. Health Insurance Association of America, *Source Book of Health Insurance Data* (Washington, DC, 1992), 2, 116–117.

10. Hyman, *Health Planning: A Systematic Approach*, 13.

11. Health Insurance Association of America, *Source Book of Health Insurance Data*, 17.

12. R. Shouldice and K. Shouldice, *Medical Group Practice and Health Maintenance Organizations* (Washington, DC: Information Resources Press, 1978), 10.

13. D. Cowan, *Preferred Provider Organizations: Planning, Structure and Operation* (Gaithersburg, Md.: Aspen Publishers, Inc., 1984), 5.

14. American Medical Association, *Physicians' Current Procedural Terminology* (Chicago: 1993).

15. J. Brittenhom ed., *1991 HCFA Common Procedure Coding System* (Los Angeles: Practice Management Information Corporation, 1991), 1.

16. *ICD.9.CM* (Los Angeles: Practice Management Information Corporation, 1993), 270.

17. *Physician Compensation and Production Survey: 1993 Report Based on 1992 Data* (Englewood, Colo.: Medical Group Management Association, 1993), 33.

18. E. Schafer et al., eds., *Management Accounting for Fee-for-Service/Prepaid Medical Groups* (Englewood, Colo.: Center for Research in Ambulatory Health Care Administration, 1989).

19. *1993 Cost and Production Survey Report Based upon 1992 Data.* (Englewood, Colo.: Medical Group Management Association, 1993).

SUGGESTED READINGS

Fox, P. et al. 1984. *Health care cost management.* Ann Arbor, Mich.: Health Administration Press.

The guide: A handbook to billing and maintaining a successful ophthalmic practice. 1990. San Francisco: American Academy of Ophthalmology.

McMurrian, H. et al. 1993. *Guide to physician and other health care providers.* Fort Worth, Tx.: Practitioners Publishing Company.

The Medicare 1992 handbook. 1992. Baltimore: U.S. Department of Health and Human Services.

Ophthalmic reimbursement manual. 2nd ed. 1992. Fairfax, Va.: American Society of Ophthalmic Administrators.

Wold, C. 1993. *Managing your medical practice.* New York: Mathew Bender.

MICHAEL J. KELLEY, MBA, is the Administrator of Retina Consultants of Southwest Florida, a tertiary care ophthalmic group practice offering comprehensive medical, surgical, and rehabilitation services, with locations in Cape Coral, Fort Myers, Naples, and Port Charlotte, Florida. Mr. Kelley began his health care career in 1980 as an administrator of an ophthalmic primary care group practice. He has participated as a lecturer in numerous professional educational programs, with a focus on financial management and employee motivation. He received a BS in biology as a Faculty Scholar at Florida Atlantic University and continued on to receive an MBA with an emphasis in marketing and management.

Chapter 31

Legal Structure of Health Care Delivery Systems

J.D. Epstein and Susan Feigin Harris

COMPETITION AND STRUCTURAL CHANGES WITHIN THE INDUSTRY

Collaboration between independent health care providers in effecting the delivery of health care is not new. Health maintenance organizations (HMOs) have been entities active in the health industry for many years and grew rapidly as a concept, originally, under the laissez faire rationale of the Reagan administration. HMOs, which vary considerably in structure and organization, may be described generally as organized systems of comprehensive health services provided to an enrolled population for a fixed, prepaid, per capita expenditure. Because specified services must be provided to HMO members in such a manner that the organization remains within a fixed budget, both for-profit and not-for-profit HMOs create incentives for health care providers to control the costs of medical care.

HMOs and capitation, however, were not immediately embraced as the panacea to the growing health care crisis in the late 1980s and early 1990s. Rather, other forms of managed care, like the preferred provider organizations (PPOs), developed and prospered as a preferred method of managed care due to the perception that such programs offered greater choice. HMOs and capitation as a form of payment, however, have rebounded dramatically and are viewed by many as the most cost-effective means of delivering health care. This renewed interest has resulted from greater pressures being placed upon providers by insurers to accept greater risk in the diagnosis and treatment of patients and the acknowledgment by physicians that managed care, in some form, has been widely accepted as the preferred method of insurance by employers, by state governments, and, finally, by the federal government. Many physicians have confessed that, if faced with managed care, they prefer capitation as the mode of payment, since such a payment mechanism affords the physicians, rather than another third party, the greatest rights and freedom to treat their patients as they see fit, and accept full risk and responsibility.

Hospitals and physicians are rapidly scrambling to accept today's challenges and, in doing so, have created new combinations and permutations of entities as well as a new vocabulary of health industry acronyms. Hospitals are combining with physicians through physician–hospital organizations (PHOs). Physicians are combining to form independent practice associations (IPAs) or clinical practice organizations (CPOs). Management companies have been created, called management services organizations (MSOs), and the list goes on.

Although hospitals and other health care providers have made significant progress in meeting the challenges of today's rapidly changing environment, some of their efforts at innovation are thwarted by other components of the health care industry. Many of the legal and organizational structures that evolved with hospitals have been much slower to recognize and adapt to the current changes in the industry, and this resistance to change poses considerable barriers to hospitals' ability to meet the competition in the coming years. This chapter examines some of the recent trends within the health care industry and reviews the legal and structural problems faced by hospitals as they struggle to survive in a highly competitive arena.

Vertical integration of health care service modalities and providers is the primary thrust of today's health care marketplace. Placing insurance and marketing services, professional medical services, hospital services, extended care services, and home health services under common management allows the vertically integrated system to compete more aggressively in today's cost-conscious, managed care environment. Patient populations are defined and provider resources can be balanced to minimize the cost of care. Numbers of physicians, allied professionals, support staff, hospital beds, home health aides, nursing beds, etc., all can be matched to patient needs, thereby reducing the economic burden of excess capacity.

The integrated health care delivery systems being created today are strategic alliances between hospitals and physicians (and possibly insurers) who share risk through common ownership, governance, revenue/capital, planning, and/or management, through a variety of vehicles (MSOs, medical foundations, PHOs, joint ventures, etc.). Ultimately, those providers that organize into partial or fully integrated delivery systems will be better positioned to compete with their fragmented peers.

NEW ALTERNATIVES IN HEALTH CARE DELIVERY

Current Examples of Integration

Historically, hospitals, physicians, and other health care providers have maintained primarily a symbiotic relationship, allowing for an enormous amount of independence from one another. In part, this autonomy was reflective of the independent professional status of the physician, as well as the perception that significant potential existed for economic conflicts of interest if physicians controlled (or owned), or were controlled or employed by, hospitals.

A number of health care institutions, however, have flourished outside of this norm, having developed an economically integrated approach toward health care delivery. These health care institutions are touted as examples for the future. Such collaborative efforts are, in fact, decades old. These older, well-developed systems fall generally into two categories—either they were developed through the driving force and power of the hospital or they developed under the aegis of a strong physician group. For example, Detroit's Henry Ford Health System has developed into a primarily hospital-driven, fully integrated system in which physicians are employed by the hospital.[1] The hospital, a major acute care center with a number of large ambulatory care clinics, also operates a successful HMO/managed care network and has done so for a number of years. Therefore, the Henry Ford Health System appears to have achieved full economic integration in which the physicians, the acute care and ancillary facilities, and the insured product components all exist under one corporate umbrella.

Conversely, systems such as the Geisinger system in Pennsylvania and the Ochsner medical institutions in New Orleans are primarily physician-generated-and-driven integrated models. Both have evolved from large multispecialty clinics into their current, more integrated form. The Ochsner system began with a group practice, the Ochsner Clinic, in 1942, and two years later formed a not-for-profit corporation called

Alton Ochsner Medical Foundation, which bought an old Army hospital.[2] In 1954, the Ochsner Foundation Hospital, which now operates 532 beds, replaced the Army hospital. The clinic employs over 300 physicians, and in conjunction with the foundation formed an HMO called the Ochsner Health Plan, which currently has 90,000 enrollees.[3] The Geisinger Foundation also formed a subsidiary HMO, Geisinger Health Plan, which has 120,000 enrollees.

The similarities among these systems, however, are difficult to discuss, since each system evolved in response to their various environmental needs, depending upon market forces, patient needs, and physician and institutional needs and desires. The common theme, however, that links the older, more established systems with the new wave of network development is the concept of seamless care; a health care conglomerate that offers, essentially, one-stop shopping.[4] The philosophy underlying the creation of these seamless networks is that an integrated system will not squander money or resources and will be better positioned to negotiate with third-party payors or other purchasers for health care delivery packages.

As noted above, many of the communities in which these integrated networks have formed also have been operating outside the norm for many years, and now find themselves in a position of being at the forefront of this revolution in health care delivery. One such community is Albuquerque, New Mexico. The genesis of integrated care in Albuquerque over the past 20 years is illustrative of what other communities are now facing. After managed care made its inroad in the 1970s, its market share quickly grew from 10 percent in 1982 to 25 or 30 percent in 1992. The city went from having a small managed care penetration to a higher percentage that was also integrated, with physicians working more closely with hospitals, eventually aligning with a single facility. Lovelace integrated delivery system is a product of this movement. Since March, 1991, Lovelace has been a wholly owned for-profit subsidiary of CIGNA Corporation.[5] The Lovelace system includes the Lovelace Medical Center, Lovelace Health Plan, the

Lovelace Physicians Group (which employs over 350 physicians), and satellite clinics. Lovelace originated in 1947 when Lovelace Clinic Physicians formed the not-for-profit foundation, which in 1969 acquired its acute care hospital. Albuquerque's providers, epitomized by Lovelace, have experienced a consolidation over the years, and now only three health care systems exist in the city. This parallels what is expected to happen nationwide.[6]

Brave New World

As cost-containment efforts and competition have influenced all levels of the health care industry, physicians and hospitals have recognized their growing interdependence. In the wake of increased use of outpatient and ambulatory care, good hospital–medical staff relationships have become increasingly important to hospitals' financial well-being, because it is still the physician who admits patients to the facilities. Physicians, meanwhile, receive fewer referrals from traditional sources and have sought entrepreneurial relationships over the years to supplement their overall decline in annual income. Hospitals and physicians are learning the financial and professional benefits of combining their resources, and are organizing their cooperative efforts into numerous joint arrangements focused upon greater integration.

The basic components of an integrated health care delivery system vary, but typically include the following:

- physician primary care and specialty care
- outpatient diagnostic and ancillary providers, such as freestanding imaging centers and freestanding cardiac catheterization centers
- alternative treatment centers, such as ambulatory surgery centers (ASCs) and freestanding radiation therapy centers
- acute care hospitals
- postacute-care providers, such as comprehensive outpatient rehabilitation facilities (CORFs), nursing homes, home health agencies, durable medical equipment

(DME) suppliers, and home IV therapy providers

- insurance, HMO, or managed care products

See Figure 31–1 for an illustration of an integrated health care delivery system.

The process of beginning to form an integrated system is a complex endeavor. Institutions and physicians must set aside prior stigmas, prejudices, and political desires to meet conceptually on an equal level before progressing down the path toward integration. The transition may be very gradual and must begin with the identification of mutual objectives, leading into the development of strategic plans to implement such objectives and culminating with the

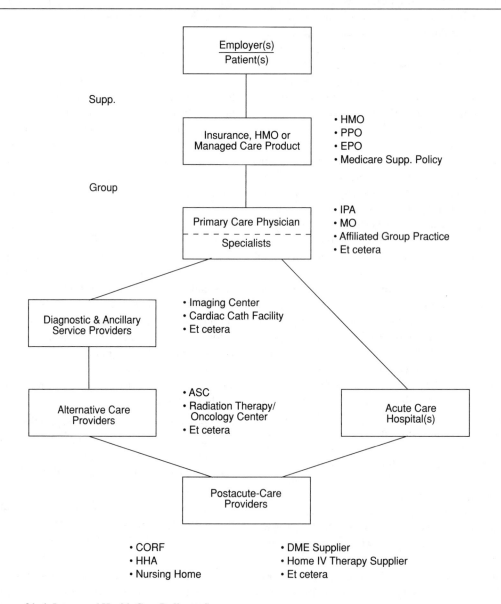

Figure 31–1 Integrated Health Care Delivery System

choice of legal structure and eventual implementation of the identified goals. This process will result in the identification of the type of legal entity or entities that should be created to obtain the objectives.

The PHO is the joint economic unit that frequently is formed when the parties seeking to collaborate are hospitals and physicians (see Figure 31–2). The PHO usually is an organization developed for the creation of cooperative relationships between independent parties, while allowing for significant flexibility, both in terms of organizational structure and in terms of its capability for a variety of activities and for future growth. Importantly, however, the PHO is only a concept and when applied to different environments and market areas it takes on different forms. Therefore, no one PHO is exactly like another.

A PHO can have as many or as few activities as the parties determine and they can be added or terminated from time to time. Typically a PHO provides: (1) a unified entity through which hospitals and physicians may negotiate contracts with various third-party payors; (2) a structure through which to jointly market the services of hospitals and physicians to the community and, more specifically, to purchasers and third-party payors; (3) management of risk by housing the performance of utilization review and quality control; (4) incentives for controlling costs; and (5) assistance in increasing operational efficiency of the hospital and physician practices to enable the parties to maximize revenues under third-party payor payment contracts.[7]

The centerpiece of the PHO is the entity created as PHO Central. This is a new business entity created by its basic partners, the hospital(s) and the physicians. PHO Central performs at least three fundamental functions: (1) It provides a forum to establish joint policy and strategic plans; (2) it identifies, evaluates, and develops specific ventures of mutual benefit to the parties; and (3) it develops and provides to the PHO partners those management and administrative tools that are necessary for success, but are too costly to be duplicated in each venture.

PHO Central could be a partnership, business corporation, nonprofit corporation, or whatever legal entity best fits the parties' objectives. The governing board of the PHO would be comprised of equal numbers of hospital and physician representatives.

Several options exist for the physician component of the PHO. The physicians can individually join the PHO, or they can form their own corporate entity, such as an IPA, to represent them in the PHO (see Figures 31–3 and 31–4). IPAs also can be a good way to bring primary care physicians into the network, an essential aspect of the creation of the network for managed care purposes. While IPAs are usually not organized to engage in the practice of medicine, the IPA also is flexible enough as an entity to be converted into an economically integrated unit for the purpose of accepting capitation payments, if the PHO is not legally qualified to accept such risk. As noted in Figure 31–3, in the IPA-model PHO, the physicians in their individual capacity are not members of the PHO. The physician members of the IPA participate in the PHO through contractual agreements. Physician members execute provider participation agreements with the IPA, binding such physicians to provide professional services in accordance with IPA-negotiated contractual agree-

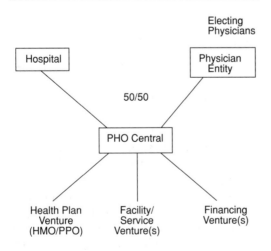

Figure 31–2 Physician–Hospital Organization (PHO)

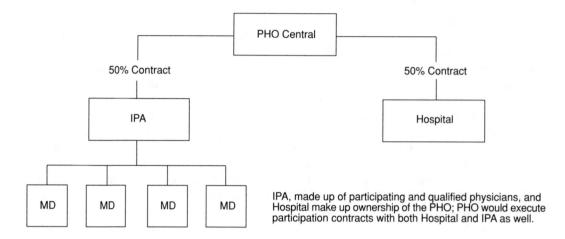

Figure 31–3 IPA—Flexibility Concerning Structure of PHO

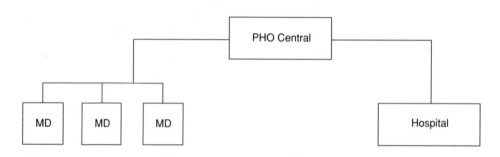

Figure 31–4 Individual Physician Model

ments. The IPA, in turn, executes a provider participation contract with the PHO, agreeing that its physician providers will provide physician professional services in accordance with PHO-negotiated contractual arrangements.

Figure 31–4 denotes a PHO in which individual physicians become members of the PHO and execute provider participation agreements individually with the PHO to provide professional services in accordance with PHO-negotiated contracts.

The typical PHO is made up of at least two provider components: the hospital and the par-

ticipating physicians. PHOs may vary concerning physician participation in the PHO. For example, some PHOs limit participation and membership to those PHO member physicians who are also members of the participating hospital's medical staff. Others open up participation, on a contractual basis, to non-medical-staff-member physicians. Moreover, some PHOs even limit physician participation further by limiting physician providers to certain participating hospital medical staff members. The extent of participation is governed, in large part, by political considerations, as well as the extent that primary care physicians are represented in the membership pool.

While the PHO is a flexible entity that has been utilized recently to bring hospitals and physicians together successfully in co-equal joint partnerships, other options for collaboration exist. The MSO is another option for physicians, hospitals, or even for PHOs. An MSO is an entity that is legally separate from the hospital or physician entity and, in some circumstances, from the PHO. The MSO may function simply as a practice management entity or as an owner of facilities, equipment, and supplies that employs nonphysician personnel. MSOs are versatile structures that can be formed and utilized to address a variety of circumstances. MSOs can be freestanding, hospital-affiliated, PHO-affiliated, or HMO-affiliated (see Figures 31–5 through 31–7).

Generally, the MSO provides a physician entity with fully equipped practice sites, including supplies, personnel, and administrative services. The nature of services provided by the MSO may be comprehensive. Although the MSO provides certain advantages concerning physician practice autonomy, greater access to managed care plans, and a form of joint practice acquisition, the MSO is perceived widely as a temporary solution—a mere step toward full integration. While the MSO model is, most often, the palatable option to physicians, its lack of struc-

ture can be a liability. MSOs could be subject to greater scrutiny under self-referral legislation or fraud and abuse provisions, if not structured carefully, since the MSO is connected to physicians through an administrative services contract in support of the delivery of professional medical services.

Another type of legal entity that has been created and that appears to afford physicians great flexibility in attempting partial integration is the clinic without walls concept. Physicians who form this kind of entity do not wish to merge their independent practices, but rather merely seek to obtain the same efficiencies of scale that other large practices enjoy. This expanded group of physicians also is attractive to payor groups.

The main feature of the clinic without walls is the central administrative services operation generally developed. Physicians retain their existing offices and the clinic without walls forms a central office that provides a full complement of services, including billing, accounting, group purchasing, claims processing, and managed care contracting. The clinic without walls may own and jointly operate several ancillary service laboratories or clinics, as well (see Figure 31–8).

While the clinic without walls concept is a step toward greater integration, several disincentives may be associated with this option. The Office of Inspector General has indicated recently its intent to focus upon clinics without

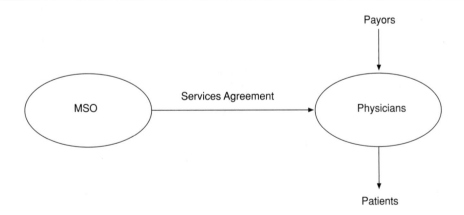

Figure 31–5 Freestanding Management Services Organization

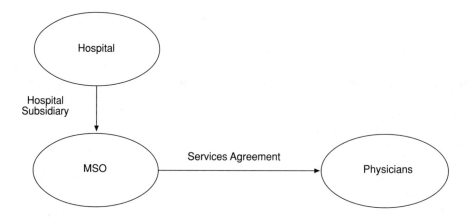

Figure 31–6 Hospital-Affiliated Management Services Organization

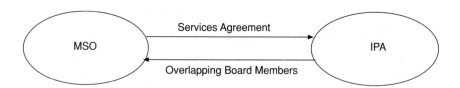

Figure 31–7 Physician-Affiliated Management Services Organization

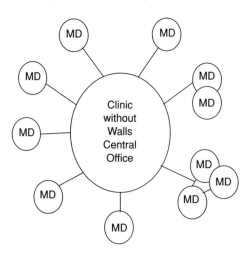

Figure 31–8 Clinic without Walls

walls, under the assumption that such arrangements may consist of sham operations intended to circumvent the self-referral laws by enabling physician members to receive payment for referrals by allowing the doctors to share in ancillary service revenue.

Other integration models, such as the affiliated group practice and the medical foundation are examples of integration and practice acquisition that may be utilized in conjunction with, or as a substitution for, collaboration between health care facilities and physicians. Greater integration of health care delivery is achieved by the medical foundation or affiliated group practice alternatives.

The medical foundation, as it is discussed in the industry, is primarily a creature of California law. California has a state prohibition against the corporate practice of medicine, preventing the employment of physicians. The law, however, contains an exception for a foundation that can accept payment for physician services. The medical foundation is a nonprofit corporation organized as an affiliate of the hospital, through a common parent organization or as a subsidiary of the hospital. To obtain tax-exempt status, the foundation must be organized and must operate for the benefit of the community. The medical foundation owns and operates a group practice, including the practice facilities, equipment, and supplies. The medical foundation employs all nonphysician personnel, contracts directly with patients and third-party payors, and may bill them in the name of the medical foundation itself.

Generally, a physician entity that is wholly owned by participating physicians affiliates with the medical foundation. This physician entity employs the individual physicians. The physician entity then contracts with the foundation to provide professional medical coverage for all practice sites operated by the foundation. The physician entity is generally compensated on a fixed-fee, budget, or percentage arrangement.

Physicians who participate in the foundation model may not feel that they have enough control, since their participation on its governing board may be limited. The IRS recently indicated that only 20 percent of the board of directors of a foundation can consist of physicians practicing in the network. Consequently, the physician component of the foundation may balk at this aspect of the model, and it may prove to be an obstacle that must be overcome.

For those states that do not contain the legal creature of the foundation, affiliated group practice arrangements can be a successful means of bringing the hospital and physician components of integration together. The physician group, if not already formed, is established by utilizing the traditional professional association (PA) or a certified nonprofit organization. This physician group then affiliates with a hospital or a PHO. The hospital or PHO would control the group practice through various direct or indirect mechanisms. The physician shareholders or board members, as the case may be, must meet certain qualifications. For example, the physician owner of the PA might be contractually bound to serve the sponsoring organization (the hospital or PHO) in an administrative capacity, most often as medical director. If the physician ceases to serve the sponsoring entity in the administrative capacity contemplated, the physician would be contractually obligated to transfer his or her interest in the physician entity to his or her successor. This relinquishment requirement would be duplicated in the various other corporate documents that make up this affiliation. The sponsoring entity also would enter into a management services agreement with the physician entity to provide comprehensive management and administrative services for the physician group. In the certified nonprofit organization model, the Hospital could be the sole corporate member with certain reserved rights, including the right to appoint the Board, thereby controlling the organization through that mechanism.

CONCLUSION

Change has begun to permeate every aspect of the health care industry and hospital leaders realize that reorganization and the development of innovative approaches toward health care delivery are important tools that must be utilized to ensure their survival. Eager to meet the challenges of greater competition and marketing demands, increased financial risks, and numerous governmental and employer pressures to control costs, many of today's hospitals are trading their independence to become part of vertically and horizontally integrated structures and alternative health care delivery systems. Whereas in the past, the health care industry was characterized by the proliferation of reorganizations, hospital mergers, joint ventures, investor-owned national hospital companies, and general decentralization, the industry now is reshaped at an ever-increasing rate by consolidation, mergers, acquisitions, and the overall move toward integration. The thrust toward greater integration of health care delivery is fueled, in part, by the knowledge that health care reform, as it is debated and discussed, includes the reliance on integrated networks of providers and managed care as the primary mode for the delivery of health care to all Americans.

As noted throughout this chapter, the options available to physicians and providers of care to integrate and consolidate are as varied as one's imagination. Groups may employ one or more of the above-noted models to accomplish their individual and joint objectives, depending upon the political and market forces in their health care delivery environment.

Hospital governing bodies must begin to shift their focus to address the needs of the future. In addressing the many varied needs of the brave new world of health care, providers must recognize the cultural and economic forces driving change, as hospitals, physicians, and insurers move to combine into a system for the purpose of taking care of the wellness of the entire community. This shift in the general mindset will result in providers of care being viewed as cost centers, rather than as revenue enhancers. Of paramount concern will be the overall community benefits provided by the system or network, rather than the financial success of each individual institution that makes up that system.

NOTES

1. This approach is not as simple in those states in which a corporate practice of medicine prohibition exists. The corporate practice of medicine prohibition, generally, prohibits an individual or entity that is not licensed to practice medicine from employing a physician and receiving fees for the physician's professional services.

2. D. Burda, Seamless Delivery, *Modern Healthcare* October 19 (1992).

3. Ibid.

4. Ibid.

5. Ibid.

6. J. Montague, Straight Talk, *Hospitals & Health Networks* July 5 (1993).

7. Drawn from an exposure draft of the American Academy of Hospital Attorneys' Practice Guide, *Formation and Operation of Hospital-Affiliated Providers, Network Organizations and Integrated Delivery Systems.*

J.D. EPSTEIN, JD, is Partner and Co-Chairman of the Health Industry Group at Vinson & Elkins LLP. In 1974, Mr. Epstein helped create the law firm of Wood, Lucksinger & Epstein, and became the managing partner of that firm in 1983. In 1991, he joined the law firm of Vinson & Elkins LLP. He represents thousands of hospitals, nursing homes, home health agencies, HMOs, prepaid group practices, medical staffs, and various vendors to the industry, as well as non–health care industry corporations with health care benefit concerns. He has appeared before administrative appeals boards, such as the Provider Reimbursement Review Board and the Blue Cross Association Medicare Provider Appeals Committee, represented clients in the federal courts, and negotiated and settled disputes relating to Blue Cross contracts. He has also consulted with clients in many areas such as third-party reimbursement, certificates of need, Hill-Burton matters, utilization review, corporate organization, acquisitions, mergers, consolidations, HMOs, PPOs, PHOs, integrated delivery systems, managed care network formation and contracting, and physician, paramedical, and vendor contracts.

Mr. Epstein has co-authored two books, entitled *Medicare Reimbursement Controversies* and *Appeals and the Provider Reimbursement Review Board*, and has authored numerous articles on subjects ranging from fraud and abuse to capital financing. He received his BS and JD degrees from the University of Illinois.

SUSAN FEIGIN HARRIS, JD, is the Vice President, Legal and Administration, of the Texas Medical Center. She recently moved to the Texas Medical Center from Vinson & Elkins LLP, where she was an associate in the Houston office Health Industry Group since 1991. Prior to her tenure at Vinson & Elkins LLP, Susan was an associate at the law firm of Wood, Lucksinger & Epstein.

Ms. Harris's practice has always focused upon the provision of legal services to health industry clients. She has particular experience in Medicare and Medicaid reimbursement and administrative appeals before the Provider Reimbursement Review Board. She also has experience in providing health care fraud and abuse risk assessments for proposed joint ventures, and defending clients in health care fraud and abuse investigations by the Office of Inspector General. In the area of managed care, she has particular experience evaluating and drafting provider participation agreements and has been active in the development of integration strategies with health care entities.

Ms. Harris received her BA from Duke University and her JD from the University of Houston Law Center.

Chapter 32

Business Combinations in the Health Care Field: Legal Implications

Norton L. Travis and Loreen A. Schneider

The current uncertain environment in the health care industry—caused by factors such as the advent of managed care, health care reform, declining inpatient admissions, federal payment limitations, and rising costs—has led many hospitals and other health care providers to seek to increase their market share by diversifying the scope of health care services that they are capable of delivering. One mechanism frequently utilized by hospitals and other health care providers to achieve these goals is to coalesce with other providers for the purpose of offering integrated health care services to patients. The provision of such integrated services usually is accomplished by health care providers entering into a business combination, such as a joint venture, merger, or other type of affiliation. These types of arrangements, however, almost always raise concerns under the federal and state fraud and abuse laws, as well as under the antitrust and tax laws. As a result, business combinations in the health care field must be carefully structured to avoid the significant adverse consequences of violating these laws.

The goals of this chapter are to present a brief overview of the laws that must be considered when structuring and operating a health care

business combination and to apply such laws in the context of the hypothetical set forth in this chapter. In each section of the chapter, the applicable laws first will be summarized. After the mechanics of the laws are described, their impact on structuring a business combination will be considered. There also will be a discussion of whether any safe harbor or exemption from such laws is available to those involved in structuring and operating the business combination. Finally, the laws will be applied to the facts set forth in the hypothetical.

HYPOTHETICAL

Doctors Black, White, and Green (the Physician-Partners) are cardiologists in private practice and have been granted privileges at Memorial Hospital (Memorial), a not-for-profit hospital. The Physician-Partners entered into an exclusive-contract arrangement with Memorial whereby they agreed to provide, on an exclusive basis, all of the cardiology services required by Memorial. In return for such services, each Physician-Partner receives a fixed salary from Memorial. In addition, each Physician-Partner is entitled to a bonus of 25 percent of the revenues generated by Memorial as a result of patients referred to Memorial by such Physician-Partner.

The Physician-Partners also are partners in a joint venture that owns and operates an imaging center (Scans-R-Us). Each Physician-Partner owns a 25 percent interest in Scans-R-Us. There is a fourth partner who holds the remaining 25 percent interest in Scans-R-Us, but she is not involved in the health-care field.

Because it is the closest imaging center to their practice, the Physician-Partners almost always refer patients requiring imaging services to Scans-R-Us. In fact, over 50 percent of the revenue generated by Scans-R-Us is attributable to patients referred by the Physician-Partners.

Dr. Brown is an employee of Scans-R-Us. He is paid a fixed salary, plus a 10 percent bonus of the revenue generated by Scans-R-Us as a result of patients referred by Dr. Brown.

Scans-R-Us is considering acquiring another imaging center. Because Scans-R-Us and the acquired imaging center are the only imaging centers providing certain specialized imaging services within a 100-mile radius, the Physician-Partners are quite anxious to go forward with the acquisition, expecting that they will be able to control the market with respect to these services.

While reviewing this chapter, consider if the previously described facts present a problem with respect to the Physician-Partners, Scans-R-Us, Memorial, or Dr. Brown.

FEDERAL MEDICARE/MEDICAID FRAUD AND ABUSE AND ANTIKICKBACK REGULATIONS

The federal Medicare/Medicaid fraud and abuse laws prohibit both the submission of false claims and the payment of a kickback in exchange for the referral of patients.[1] It is fairly easy to define the meaning of submitting a false claim. Basically, if a healthcare provider submits a claim for reimbursement under the Medicare/Medicaid programs and states that services were performed when they were not, or if a provider misrepresents the nature or quantity of the services performed, then the provider has committed a fraud by making a false claim. A violation of the false claims law constitutes a felony and may subject the offender to a $25,000 fine and imprisonment for up to five years.[2] Those convicted of violating the Medicare/Medicaid false claims law also may be subject to the penalties and sanctions that are contained in other state and federal statutes that are applicable to fraud cases generally. These statutes include mail and wire fraud statutes, the RICO statute and money laundering statutes.

While the meaning of submitting a false claim is fairly straightforward, it generally is more difficult to determine when an illegal payment or kickback has been made in conjunction with the provision of services to Medicare/Medicaid beneficiaries. The antikickback laws prohibit any direct or indirect offer, payment, solicitation, or receipt of remuneration to induce the referral of Medicare/Medicaid patients or to induce the purchase, lease, ordering, or arranging for any good, facility, service, or item paid for by the Medicare/Medicaid programs. If an individual is found to have violated the antikickback laws, he or she may be guilty of a felony and subject to imprisonment for up to five years and a fine of up to $25,000.[3]

In 1987, Congress enacted the Medicare and Medicaid Patient and Program Protection Act of 1987[4] (the Patient Protection Act). This law grants the Office of Inspector General (OIG), the prosecutorial branch of the Department of Health and Human Services, the authority to impose civil sanctions for a violation of the antikickback laws. Under the Patient Protection Act, the OIG may exclude any individual from participation in the Medicare/Medicaid programs for a minimum of five years if such individual has been convicted of a criminal offense relating to delivery of an item or service in the Medicare/Medicaid programs. During this five-year period, no payment will be made by Medicare/Medicaid for any services rendered, ordered, or prescribed by the excluded individual.[5] In addition to this mandatory exclusion, the OIG also has the authority to permissibly exclude a practitioner from participation in the Medicare/

Medicaid programs upon the occurrence of certain events, such as upon the conviction of fraud or financial misconduct, upon the revocation of the practitioner's professional license, or upon the practitioner's failure to grant the OIG access to his or her records and documents.[6]

With respect to the hypothetical set forth at the beginning of the chapter, both Memorial and the Physician-Partners could be liable for a violation of the antikickback laws. As previously explained, the antikickback laws prohibit any payment made for the purpose of inducing referrals of Medicare/Medicaid patients. While it is permissible for Memorial to pay the Physician-Partners a fixed fair-market-value salary, and even a bonus, for the cardiology services that the Physician-Partners provide, Memorial may not in any way base such compensation on the volume of referrals made by the Physician-Partners. As a result, because the 25 percent bonus paid by Memorial to each of the Physician-Partners is directly related to that physician's volume of referrals to Memorial, both Memorial and the Physician-Partners are potentially liable under the antikickback laws.

The Greber Case

Probably the most famous, and certainly the most controversial, case interpreting the antikickback laws is *United States v. Greber*.[7] Dr. Greber, a board-certified cardiologist, was the president and owner of Cardio-Med, a company that supplied a device capable of monitoring a patient's cardiac activity. In connection with the use of this device by Medicare patients, Dr. Greber made payments to referring cardiologists, supposedly for their interpretation of the tape that the medical device produced. In fact, Dr. Greber, not the referring cardiologists, interpreted the tapes. As a result, the court concluded that the payments to the cardiologists were for the purpose of inducing their referrals. On appeal, the federal circuit court concluded that even if the purpose of Cardio-Med's payments to the cardiologists was to compensate them for professional services, if one purpose of such payments was to also induce referrals, the antikickback laws were violated.[8]

Because of this one-purpose rule and other cases similar to *Greber,* every financial arrangement between those in a position to refer business and those providing items or services eligible for reimbursement under the Medicare/Medicaid programs must be carefully scrutinized. If *any* purpose for which a payment is made is to induce referrals, the payment may be unlawful under the antikickback laws. This means that even if the primary purpose for which a payment is made is permissible (such as the provision of necessary medical services), but the payment is also found to have the incidental purpose of inducing referrals, the individuals making and receiving such payment are subject to prosecution under the antikickback laws.

The Safe Harbor Regulations

If a health care provider is directly paid for a referral, this violates the antikickback laws. The 25 percent bonus by Memorial to the Physician-Partners falls under this general prohibition. It is less clear, however, whether a physician may refer a patient to an entity or other provider in which he or she has an ownership interest or other financial relationship, thus indirectly benefitting from the referral. Because the antikickback laws are broadly drafted (by including both direct and indirect payments), it is often difficult to determine when a particular arrangement is prohibited.

As a result, the health care industry sought guidelines within which to evaluate proposed transactions to determine if such transactions violate the antikickback laws. The Patient Protection Act mandated that the OIG promulgate regulations specifying safe harbors (i.e., when a business combination is permissible under the antikickback laws).[9] In formulating the safe harbor regulations, the federal government realized that many joint ventures and other arrangements among health care providers and suppliers are legitimate enterprises that provide needed health care services. The government was concerned, however, that these arrangements often allow the parties involved to induce or pay for referrals. As a result, the antikickback law, together with the safe harbor regulations, are not an outright prohibition on business combinations in the health care field; however, they significantly limit how a venture may be structured.

If the structure of a proposed health care business combination transaction adheres to safe harbor guidelines, the parties to the transactions are exempt from civil and criminal prosecution under the antikickback laws. If the transaction does not conform to the safe harbor guidelines, the transaction is not necessarily illegal, but the parties thereto are not assured that they will be immune from prosecution and the civil and criminal sanctions described above.

The safe harbor regulations cover the following areas: investment interests, space rental, equipment rental, personal service and management contracts, sale of practice, referral services, warranties and discounts, employment relationships, group purchasing organizations, and waiver of certain insurance benefits. A brief discussion of the investment-interests safe harbor is warranted as this is the safe harbor most frequently relied upon by those structuring health care business combinations.

The investment-interests safe harbor provides protection for investments in both public and private companies, provided that certain conditions are met. If an investment is in a public company, safe harbor protection exists if: (1) the company has undepreciated net tangible health-care assets of at least $50 million; (2) the investment represents the purchase of securities registered with the Securities and Exchange Commission on terms equally available to the public through trading on a national security exchange; (3) marketing of items or services to investors is the same as to noninvestors; (4) the investment is not achieved through a loan or guarantee by the entity in which the investment is made; and (5) the return on the investment is proportional to the amount invested.[10]

Not surprisingly, most health care joint ventures do not involve publicly traded companies, but, instead, private organizations. If an investment is in a private company or entity, it must meet all of the following guidelines to fall within the private company safe harbor: (1) no more than 40 percent of any class of investment in the entity maybe held by individuals or other entities in a position to refer Medicare/Medicaid patients or provide goods or services to the entity; (2) no more than 40 percent of the gross revenues of the entity may be derived from referrals, items, or services provided by investors in the entity; (3) the entity may not loan the investor the funds to make the investment or guarantee the investment; (4) the return from the investment must be proportional to the amount of the investment (and *not* tied to patient referrals); (5) the entity may not market its services more vigorously to investors than to the public in general; (6) the investment must be available on the same terms to those who are in a position to refer patients and those who are not; and (7) the investment terms cannot relate in any way to referrals.[11]

The first two tests—commonly referred to as the 60/40 tests—are clearly the most problematic. If more than 40 percent of the investors of any class either refer patients or provide any services to the entity, safe harbor protection is not available. Similarly, if more than 40 percent of the total revenue is derived from the investors in the entity—either individually or as a whole—the transaction is not protected by a safe harbor.

A venture is not necessarily in violation of the antikickback laws because it fails to meet the requirements of a safe harbor. The parties to such a venture, however, cannot be assured that they are immune from civil or criminal prosecution or penalties. As a result, if a particular business combination between health care providers does not fall within one of the safe harbors, those involved should first determine if the structure of the combination can be altered to achieve such compliance. If restructuring is not possible, those involved should consider if the benefits of the combination outweigh the considerable risks that they must assume in going forward without the protection of a safe harbor. As in any antikickback analysis, the key issue is whether any purpose of the venture is to induce referrals.

With respect to the hypothetical at the beginning of the chapter, the Physician-Partners probably could *not* legally refer Medicare/Medicaid patients to Scans-R-Us. The Physician-Partners' investment in Scans-R-Us would fail both 60/40 tests because: (1) more than 40 percent of the Scans-R-Us investors are in a position to refer patients to Scans-R-Us; and (2) more than 40 percent of the Scans-R-Us revenue is derived from referrals by investors in Scans-R-Us.

PHYSICIAN SELF-REFERRAL—THE STARK LAW

In 1989, Congress enacted the Ethics in the Patient Referrals Act of 1989,[12] more commonly known as the Stark Law. This law prohibits physicians from referring Medicare/Medicaid patients for certain designated health services to entities in which the physician (or the physician's immediate family) has a financial interest. Unlike the antikickback regulations, which apply to health care providers in general, this law applies only to physicians. Congress enacted the Stark Law because it was concerned that if physicians were permitted to self-refer, they might refer a patient to a facility in which they had an ownership interest, rather than to a facility capable of providing the best care to the patient. Congress also believed that self-referrals could lead to physicians ordering medical services not warranted by the patient's medical condition because of the physician's interest in the profitability of the diagnostic/therapeutic facility.

The Stark Law attempts to provide physicians with a "bright line" rule so that they will know in advance what types of business arrangements are prohibited. A financial relationship is defined under the Stark Law as: (1) an ownership or investment interest in an entity that may be through equity, debt, or other means, and includes an interest in an entity that holds an ownership or investment interest in any entity providing the designated health service; or (2) a compensation arrangement, which is any arrangement involving any remuneration between a physician (or an immediate family member of the physician) and an entity.[13] "Referrals" is de-

fined as the request by a physician for an item or service payable under the Medicare/Medicaid program and the request by a physician for a consultation with another physician and any test or procedure ordered or performed by or under the supervision of that other physician.[14] Referral also includes the request or establishment of a plan of care by a physician that includes the provision of designated health service.

The types of designated health services that are covered under the Stark Law are: clinical laboratory services, physical therapy services, occupational therapy services, radiology or other diagnostic services, radiation therapy services, durable medical equipment, parenteral and enteral nutrients, equipment and supplies, prosthetics, orthotics and prosthetic devices, home health services, outpatient prescription drugs, and inpatient and outpatient hospital services.[15]

Clearly, the prohibitions against referrals set forth in the Stark Law have a significant impact on the structuring of business arrangements with physicians. Most importantly, by including a prohibition against referrals for inpatient and outpatient hospital services, virtually any physician-hospital business arrangement could potentially violate the Stark Law. This is true because many physicians have a financial relationship in the nature of a compensation arrangement with the health care entities to which they refer patients.

The Stark Law does, however, contain several exceptions to its prohibition against referrals. A referral is not considered to be in violation of the Stark Law if such referral is to another physician in the same group practice as the referring physician, if the referral is for the provision of certain in-office ancillary services other than durable medical equipment, or if the referral is to a prepaid plan as defined in the Stark Law.[16]

In addition, there are also specific exceptions relating to the ownership/investment interest and compensation/lease arrangement prohibitions. With respect to ownership/investment interests, there is an exception for referrals to companies with publicly traded securities, referrals to hospitals in Puerto Rico, rural providers (as defined in the Stark Law), and referrals to a hospital where the referring physician has privileges and the ownership or investment interest is in the hospital itself, rather than a subdivision of the hospital.[17]

With respect to the exceptions relating to compensation/lease arrangements, referrals are not prohibited if the referring physician has entered into a lease agreement for the rental of office space or equipment on a fair-market-value basis with rent that in no way relates to the volume of referrals between the parties. Referrals also are permitted if a bona fide employment relationship exists between the parties, so long as the compensation is not tied to the volume of referrals. There also are exceptions relating to remuneration provided by a hospital that is unrelated to the provision of designated health services, physician incentive plan arrangements, isolated transactions (such as a one-time sale of property or practice), group practice arrangements under which designated services are provided by the group but billed by the hospital, and payments made by a physician for items and services.[18]

Penalties under the Stark Law include denial of payment, a forced refunding of any amounts collected in violation of the prohibition of referrals, a civil money penalty of up to $15,000 for each claim or payment for services rendered pursuant to a prohibited referral, and a civil money penalty of up to $100,000 for each unlawful arrangement or scheme.[19]

Enforcement

Both federal and state authorities have the jurisdiction to investigate and impose sanctions for Medicare/Medicaid fraud. At the federal level, the Department of Justice has the authority to prosecute health care fraud under a number of criminal statutes. Also, as explained above, the United States Department of Health and Human Services through the OIG has the authority to assess civil monetary penalties, and to exclude from the Medicare/Medicaid programs, any person or entity convicted of a criminal offense relating to Medicare/Medicaid fraud or found to have committed other specified acts.

In addition, state licensing boards have the authority to suspend or revoke the licenses of physicians and other health care providers upon a conviction of fraud or a similar offense. Furthermore, many states have enacted statutes similar to the Stark Law to prohibit certain physician self-referrals. For example, in New York, a physician may not refer patients to an entity with which he or she has a financial relationship for any of the following: clinical laboratory services, X-ray and imaging services, or pharmacy services. Unlike the federal Stark Law, the New York law prohibits referrals for the above services regardless of the patient's source of payment.[20]

With respect to the Physician-Partners, the Stark Law effectively will prohibit their investment in Scans-R-Us as of January 1, 1995, because, as explained above, this law prohibits a physician from referring any Medicare/Medicaid patient for certain specified health services to an entity in which the physician has a financial interest. Prior to January 1, 1995, such referrals are prohibited only with respect to clinical laboratory services—after such date, the prohibition will also apply to imaging services, as well as to the other services listed above. As a result, as of January 1, 1995, the Physician-Partners will have to refrain from referring Medicare/Medicaid patients to Scans-R-Us. Simply refraining from referring Medicare/Medicaid patients to Scans-R-Us, however, will not be permitted in those states with a state Stark Law (such as New York's law) that prohibits this type of referral whether or not the patient is a Medicare/Medicaid recipient. Consequently, the Physician-Partners will probably be forced to divest themselves of their interests in Scans-R-Us.

In the case of Dr. Brown, the Scans-R-Us employee, it would at first appear that he could refer patients to Scans-R-Us, even though he has a compensation arrangement with Scans-R-Us. As explained above, an individual may refer hospitals to a health-care entity with which he or she has a compensation arrangement if a bona fide employment relationship exists between the parties. This is true with respect to Dr. Brown and Scans-R-Us. A portion of his compensation, however, is a 10 percent bonus, which is tied to the volume of Dr. Brown's referrals to Scans-R-Us. As a result, this arrangement could subject Dr. Brown and Scans-R-Us to liability under the Stark Law.

ANTITRUST IN THE HEALTH CARE INDUSTRY

The purpose of the antitrust laws is to protect and promote competition. As explained at the beginning of this chapter, many providers are responding to changes in the health care system by merging or consolidating with other providers. Because many of these mergers are between competitors, there is the possibility that competition may be adversely affected, thereby triggering the antitrust laws.[21]

Previously, a merger between two not-for-profit hospitals was thought to be immune from prosecution under the antitrust laws. This is no longer true, however, and with the increasing number of such mergers taking place, scrutiny by the Federal Trade Commission and the Department of Justice is likely to increase in the future.

For antitrust purposes, the definition of mergers is quite broad. Basically, any time a business combination has occurred that results in common control by a single entity or group, a merger has occurred. For example, even the formation of a new group practice among formerly independent physicians would constitute a merger under this definition. Basically, mergers have three economic effects that are of concern in an antitrust analysis. First, a merger consolidates market power. That is, with fewer competitors, there is an increased ability to raise the price above or decrease the quality below a competitive level without losing customers (or patients). Second, a merger increases concentration in the market; if there are fewer competitors, it becomes easier to collude in such matters as price fixing. Third, the merger may have some positive effects, such as creating economies of scale and scope that permit greater output with less resources. Obviously, in any antitrust analysis, the negative, anticompetitive effects of the merger must be balanced against the positive, procompetitive effects of the merger in assessing the legality of the transaction.

The Relevant Federal Antitrust Statutes

Mergers in the health care industry may be challenged under Section 7 of the Clayton Act or Section 1 of the Sherman Act. Section 7 of the Clayton Act specifically addresses business consolidations and prohibits an acquisition whose effects "may be substantially to lessen competition or to tend to create a monopoly."[22] In order to prove a Section 7 claim, the plaintiff must define the specific product or service that is the subject of the claim as well as the geographic market where the anticompetitive activity is taking place. Consequently, if a merger is between parties who either do not provide the same goods or services, or who do not supply such goods or services to the same market, competition will not be adversely affected by a merger of such parties, and there will be no antitrust violation. If the plaintiff can establish that a business consolidation will consolidate market power within the geographic market to such an extent that those providing the specified product may raise prices, reduce output, or reduce quality, and that even after such actions customers are unable to easily substitute another product or supplier of the product, then a Section 7 claim may be established.

Section 1 of the Sherman Act prohibits "every contract, combination...or conspiracy, in restraint of trade or commerce among the several states."[23] A person who is alleging a violation of Section 1 of the Sherman Act must establish the following: (1) an agreement, conspiracy, or combination among two or more persons or distinct business entities; (2) which is intended to harm or unreasonably restrain competition; and (3) which actually causes injury to competition beyond its impact on the plaintiff, within a field of commerce in which the plaintiff is engaged.

The first element, proof of conspiracy, requires concerted action among two or more independent entities. That is, for a conspiracy to exist, there must be an agreement between at least two independent parties. In addition, courts generally hold that officers, employees and agents of a corporation, and wholly owned subsidiaries of a corporation are legally incapable of conspiring with each other.[24] Therefore, there is no Sherman Act liability for intracorporate agreements.

The second element of a Sherman Act claim is that the purpose of the conspiracy must be illegal or anticompetitive. To show this element, an individual must demonstrate that the competitors intended to adhere to an agreement that was designed to achieve an unlawful, anticompetitive objective. Finally, the person arguing that an antitrust violation has occurred must show that the conspiracy actually produced an anticompetitive effect. Anticompetitive effect generally is established by identifying the relevant geographic and product markets and proving the effect of the restraint within these markets, or by showing actual detrimental effects on competition, such as output decreases or price increases occurring after the formation of the conspiracy.

As explained in the beginning of this section, the primary purpose of the antitrust laws is to protect competition, not individual competitors. As a result, the fact that a particular merger or other business arrangement harms an individual competitor will not give rise to antitrust liability unless such merger or other arrangement also has an adverse effect on competition in general.

Hart-Scott-Rodino Reporting Requirements

Hart-Scott-Rodino Act[25] requires that certain mergers and consolidations be reported to the Federal Trade Commission before the transaction is consummated. The purpose of this law is to give the Federal Trade Commission the opportunity to investigate a business consolidation if the agency believes that such investigation is warranted. Not all mergers or other consolidations must be reported under this law. A business consolidation need only be reported if: (1) the

acquiring person has total assets or annual net sales of at least $100,000,000 and the acquired person has total assets of at least $10,000,000 or the acquiring person has total assets or annual net sales of at least $10,000,000 and the acquired has total assets or annual net sales of at least $100,000,000; and (2) the acquiring person is acquiring 15 percent or more of the acquired party's assets of voting securities; or (3) the purchase price or fair market value of assets to be acquired is $15,000,000 or more.[26] As many mergers in the health care field would not meet these tests, they would not have to be reported under the Hart-Scott-Rodino law. A significant number of hospital mergers, however, must comply with Hart-Scott-Rodino filing requirements.

Antitrust Safety Zones

On September 15, 1993, the United States Department of Justice and the Federal Trade Commission issued a joint statement outlining their new antitrust enforcement policies concerning business consolidations and mergers in the health care area. With respect to hospital mergers and other business arrangements between hospitals and other individuals and entities in the health care field, these two federal agencies created antitrust safety zones similar in concept to the safe harbors promulgated in connection with the Medicare/Medicaid fraud and abuse regulations. Therefore, if a particular arrangement or transaction is able to meet the requirements and falls within one of these safety zones, the agencies will not challenge such arrangement as violative of the antitrust laws absent "extraordinary circumstances." As with the fraud and abuse safe harbors, an arrangement falling outside the safety zones does not necessarily violate the antitrust law. Those involved in the transaction, however, cannot be assured that they will not be prosecuted.

With respect to the hospital merger safety zone, the Department of Justice and the Federal Trade Commission will not challenge any merger between two general acute care hospitals where one of the hospitals: (1) has an average of fewer than 100 licensed beds over the 3 most recent years; (2) has an average of daily inpatient census of fewer than 40 patients over the 3 most recent years; and (3) is more than 5 years old. As stated previously, mergers that do not fall within the safety zone are not necessarily anti-competitive. In fact, the joint statement explains that arrangements that: (1) do not increase the likelihood of the exercise of market power either because of the existence of strong competitors postmerger or because the merging hospitals were sufficiently differentiated; (2) allow the hospitals to realize significant cost savings that would not otherwise be realized; or (3) eliminate a hospital that would likely fail with its assets exiting the market, are not likely to be considered troublesome.

The other safety zones created by the joint statement are: hospital joint ventures involving high technology or other expensive medical equipment, physician's provision of information to purchasers of health care services, hospital participation and exchanges of price and cost information, joint purchasing arrangements among health care providers, and physician network joint ventures.

The Scans-R-Us acquisition of a neighboring imaging center could raise concerns under the antitrust laws. The Physician-Partners are interested in this acquisition because it will enable them to control the market with respect to certain imaging services. The federal reviewing agencies could conclude that this market consolidation would allow the Physician-Partners to raise prices on these services at will because, if the acquisition is consummated, there will be no competing imaging center within a 100-mile radius. As a result, individuals requiring these specific imaging services could not easily turn to a competing imaging center, even if Scans-R-Us tripled its prices or dramatically increased its turnaround time for imaging services.

TAX EXEMPTION ISSUES

Under IRS regulations, a tax-exempt entity must be organized and operated to provide a public benefit to the community and not a private benefit to those operating or affiliated with the entity. Specifically, the IRS private-inurement prohibition mandates that no part of the net earnings of a tax-exempt entity may inure to the benefit of a private individual.[27] The IRS private-benefit prohibition states that a tax-exempt entity may not serve a private rather than a public interest.[28] If a hospital, or any other tax-exempt entity, violates either the private inurement or the private benefit prohibition, it could lose its tax-exempt status.[29]

Previously, in examining hospital/physician relationships, the IRS found that as long as the relationship was conducted on an arm's-length basis and the hospital and physician received fair value for services rendered, such relationships would not affect a hospital's tax-exempt status. In 1991, however, the IRS stated in a General Counsel Memorandum[30] that if such relationships appear to violate the fraud and abuse/antikickback regulations, they may also be violating the private-inurement or private-benefit prohibitions under the tax regulations.

As a result, if a particular arrangement confers benefits on a private individual that are so substantial and excessive that the arrangement inures to the benefit of such individual rather than to the benefit of the tax-exempt entity, a private-inurement violation would exist. Similarly, if such an arrangement is interpreted as serving only a private interest rather than a public interest (with only an incidental private benefit), a private-benefit violation would exist. In either such case, the tax-exempt entity runs the risk of forfeiting its tax-exempt status.

With respect to the exclusive contract for cardiology services between Memorial and the Physician-Partners, the financial terms of the arrangement would have to be analyzed carefully in order to ensure that the arrangement was not so favorable to the Physician-Partners that it could be interpreted to inure to their benefit rather than to the benefit of Memorial. Otherwise, Memorial could risk forfeiting its tax-exempt status.

In defending such relationships, a hospital must be able to demonstrate that the arrangement serves the community through the hospital and that any private benefit is incidental to the community benefit. As it is increasingly likely that if a physician/hospital relationship presents a fraud and abuse/antikickback problem, that it could also subject the hospital to the loss of its tax-exempt status, hospitals should closely examine such relationships with both the fraud and abuse and the community benefit standards in mind.

OTHER LEGAL CONSIDERATIONS

In addition to the issues already discussed, there are many other factors that must be considered while a health care business combination is still in the planning stages. For example, the parties must determine if a certificate of need (CON) is required. Generally, although the law varies from state to state, a CON is required before a health care facility may commence new construction or renovation of an existing structure. A CON usually must be in place before a health care facility makes a significant capital expenditure.

Also, the tax consequences of the transactions must be discussed throughout the planning and implementation of a business combination. If the business combination will result in the creation of a new entity, the parties must determine if the entity will be for-profit or not-for-profit, and must consider the tax consequences of this determination to both the entity itself and the parties involved in the transaction. If the entity is to be not-for-profit, the appropriate federal, state, and local exemptions must be obtained. As obtaining these exemptions often takes a significant amount of time, the process should be commenced as soon as the decision to seek tax-exempt status is made. Finally, the private-inurement and private-benefit prohibitions discussed above must be considered both prior to structuring a transaction and during the operation of the tax-exempt entity.

Another regulatory issue that must be addressed before a business combination is consummated is whether any securities will be issued, and, if so, whether registration will be required under the federal or state securities laws. The definition of security under the federal securities laws is very broad and includes not only stock and partnership interests, but "participation in any profit sharing arrangement."[31] Because this definition is so broad, and because every issuance of securities either must be registered with the Securities Exchange Commission (SEC) or be issued pursuant to an exemption from registration, the parties to any business combination must ensure that either such registration takes place or that some exemption from registration is available.[32] As registration is a very expensive and time consuming process, it is wise to rely on an exemption from registration whenever possible. The most frequently relied upon exemption in health care business combinations is the private-offering exemption.

As with the fraud and abuse regulations, the SEC promulgated safe harbors (Regulation D of the Securities Act of 1933)[33] to aid in determining whether an offering of securities is private or not. If all of the elements of a Regulation D Safe Harbor are met, the offering is private and need not be registered. As with the fraud and abuse safe harbors, however, the fact that an issuance of securities does not meet the requirements of a safe harbor does not mean that the issuance is not private, only that the parties responsible for the issuance are not shielded from prosecution from securities law violations.

Finally, the parties to a health care business combination should consider if the transaction will violate any state corporate practice of medicine laws. These laws prohibit the practice of medicine by an unlicensed entity. For example, in New York, a business corporation may not provide physicians' services without CON approval.[34]

CONCLUSION

The parties to a business combination in the health care field must constantly keep in mind that the goals of the venture can be achieved only within the regulatory framework governing such ventures, including the Medicare/Medicaid false claim, antikickback and self-referral laws, antitrust laws, tax considerations, and the other regulations discussed in this chapter.

NOTES

1. Social Security Act § 1128B(b), 42 U.S.C. § 1320a-7 (1991).
2. *Id.* at § 1320a-7b(b).
3. *Id.* at § 1320a-7b(b).
4. Pub.L.No. 100-93 (1987).
5. The consequences of exclusion are far reaching. For example, an excluded physician generally would not be permitted to admit Medicare/Medicaid patients to a hospital, because the hospital would not be entitled to payment under the Medicare/Medicaid programs for any services ordered by the excluded physician.
6. Pub.L.No. 100-93 (1987).
7. 760 F.2d 68 (3rd Cir. 1985), *cert. denied,* 474 U.S. 988 (1985).
8. *Id.* at 72.
9. 42 C.F.R. § 1001.950 *et. seq.* (1992).
10. *Id.* at § 1001.952(a).
11. *Id.*
12. Social Security Act § 1877, 42 U.S.C. § 1395nn (1992), as amended by Pub.L.No. 103-66 (1993).
13. *Id.* at § 1395nn(a).
14. *Id.* at § 1395nn(h). Prior to January 1, 1995, the Stark Law applies only to the referral of Medicare patients. After such date, the Stark Law applies to referrals of both Medicare and Medicaid patients.
15. *Id.* at § 1395nn(a). Prior to January 1, 1995, only referrals for clinical laboratory services are prohibited. After such date, referrals for the other health care services listed are also prohibited.
16. *Id.* at § 1395nn(b).
17. *Id.* at § 1395nn(d).
18. *Id.* at § 1395nn(e).
19. *Id.* at § 1395nn(g).
20. New York State Public Health Law § 238-a (McKinney Supp. 1993), as amended by 1993 N.Y. Laws 443.
21. *See, e.g., United States v. Rockford Memorial Corp.,* 898 F.2d 1278 (7th Cir. 1990) (holding that Section 7 of the Clayton Act applies to not-for-profit corporations).
22. Clayton Act § 7, 15 U.S.C. § 18 (1973 and Supp. 1993).
23. Sherman Act § 1, 15 U.S.C. § 1 (1973 and Supp. 1993).
24. *Copperweld Corporation v. Independence Tube Corporation,* 467 U.S. 752 (1984).
25. Hart-Scott-Rodino Antitrust Improvement Act of 1976, 15 U.S.C. § 18a (Supp. 1993).
26. *Id.*
27. Treasury Regulation, 26 C.F.R. § 1.501(c)(3)-1(c)(2) (1993).
28. Treasury Regulation, 26 C.F.R. § 1.501(c)(3)-1(d)(1)(ii) (1993).
29. Internal Revenue Code § 501(c)(3) (1988).
30. General Counsel Memorandum 39,862 (November 21, 1991).
31. Securities Act of 1933, 15 U.S.C. § 77a(1) (1981).
32. *Id.* at § 77c.
33. Regulation D, 17 C.F.R. § 230.501 *et. seq.* (1993).
34. New York State Education Law § 6531 (McKinney 1985 and Supp. 1993).

NORTON L. TRAVIS, JD, is a graduate of the University of Massachusetts and Hofstra University School of Law, where he served as a member of the Law Review. Mr. Travis is a member of the American Society of Hospital Attorneys, the National Health Lawyers Association, the American Bar Association, Antitrust and Litigation Sections, as well as the ABA Forum Committee on Health Law. Mr. Travis is also a member of the New York State Bar Association (Antitrust and Health Law Divisions). He is the author of several articles of medical–legal import and is a frequent lecturer on various medical–legal subjects.

Mr. Travis oversees Garfunkel, Wild, and Travis's litigation practice and also devotes his efforts to the general representation of numerous hospitals, physician groups, physician associations, and other health-care-related business organizations.

LOREEN A. SCHNEIDER, JD, graduated from the State University of New York at Stony Brook and from the Washington College of Law at American University, where she served as a member of the American University Law Review. Prior to joining Garfunkel, Wild, and Travis, Ms. Schneider was a member of the corporate finance department at Skadden, Arps, Slate, Meagher, and Flom. Ms. Schneider specializes in the representation of health care providers.

Chapter 33

Corporate Cost Containment

Frederick C. Lee

As we approach the year 2000, a fundamental restructuring of the health care system continues to take place. One of the most notable features of the evolving health care system is the role played by business. An invigorated corporate voice in the operations and policies of health care has had an enormous impact on the largest revenue raiser of the health care system, the hospital. The overwhelming transformation of corporate interactions with hospitals from partner to adversary, from ally to questioning critic, has demonstrably influenced hospital strategic planning. As companies expand their cost-containment initiatives and strive for a more cost-efficient health care product, pressures to reduce costs in the 5,000 hospitals nationwide will continue to increase.

The impact of business's impact on hospital operations has been demonstrable only in the 1980s and early 1990s. Moreover, there is every indication that employers will expand their involvement and intensify their presence, bringing to bear economic clout and market power in future dealings with hospitals and the expanding health care system in general. A number of financial, societal, and cultural changes have di-rectly influenced the restructuring of relations between business and health care providers.

INCREASE IN COSTS

Historically, the health insurance portion of a company benefit package was considered a loss leader, the cost of doing business. In the 1970s and early 1980s, health costs doubled every 3 to 5 years, and this trend continues in the 1990s.

It was not uncommon for a company to experience increases of 20 to 30 percent each year. Having used their insurance benefit packages as magnets to attract the best and the brightest employees, corporations had committed the unpardonable sin of "giving away the ranch." First-dollar coverage, in fact, had not existed for a long time. The United Auto Workers' fight for comprehensive coverage with no cost-sharing ended in 1961 when an agreement with General Motors eliminated a contributory plan in which workers paid part of the insurance premium. By the 1970s, few constraints or checks remained in insurance policies, guaranteeing employees first-dollar coverage for hospital and physician charges. Surveys that charted the infusion of cost-management techniques into an employer's armamentarium did not even historically exist.

THIRD-PARTY REIMBURSEMENT

Employers providing group health insurance have been perceived as the purchaser of hospital care for their employee, retiree, and dependent patients. However, insurance companies have traditionally assumed the role of payor. They, in turn, have pursued objectives that were not always sought by their corporate clients. Inherent inflation and lack of restraint embedded in a charge-plus reimbursement practice fueled the rapid growth of insurance premiums. Because payment for insurance service was commonly structured as a percentage of claims basis, insurers lacked incentives to check burgeoning costs aggressively. Increases in total claims meant additional insurance profits. When discounts were negotiated with hospitals, with few exceptions, the savings were captured by third-party insurers, not corporate purchasers.

The growing concern about health costs was primarily focused on hospitals, which accounted for as much as 60 percent of an employer's outlays. As employers' health costs grew to exceed net profit margins, companies finally began to take note and to contemplate ways of mitigating that exponential growth. In fact, the combined shareholders' equity in the 55 top Fortune 500 firms would have only matched the total health care outlays in the United States in 1982.[1] General Motors alone spent $2.2 billion on health care in 1984. The precipitous increase in health costs compelled business to act.

By the late 1970s, large, astute public and private sector employers realized the folly of paying insurance companies to administer their employees' medical claims. Self-insurance also exempted employers from the growing proliferation of state-mandated benefits. A rapid move to self-funding by Fortune 500 corporations dramatically altered the all-powerful role of insurance companies. Deprived by multimillion dollar premium "floats" from which to pay claims,

insurers' roles were reduced to that of claims administrators, with service fees rendered by their large corporate clients for the processing and payment of each medical insurance claim.

Companies enriched by the savings generated by self-funding gained greater awareness of the value of investing in health cost management. The shift to self-funding also alerted companies to other weaknesses in the third-party system. In assuming a more typical business role, that of managing input costs, employers became more assertive, demanding accountability. As with other inputs, managers scrutinized prices and the quality of the product purchased. New requirements emerged for more information on the purchased health care goods and greater responsiveness on the part of suppliers to corporate concerns.

In part, private sector initiatives gained momentum only when senior management became involved. A 1984 survey of chief executive offers (CEOs) revealed that 387 of 397 of these Fortune 500 heads were personally involved in their company's cost-management efforts.[2] Three years before, only one in ten CEOs had shown concern about health care costs. The success of local business groups or health care coalitions has also been closely associated with the level of commitment from senior management.

By the mid-1980s, few large employers remained fully insured. Self-insured companies proliferated, exacting more responsiveness to their requests. When a large commercial insurer confessed to being unable to provide the information being sought by Hewlett Packard, it was fired and replaced by an aggressive third-party administrator. Blue Cross plans nationwide were found wanting by disenchanted employers and consequently experienced a substantial loss of market share. Smaller and smaller firms elected self-insurance as a preferable mode for group health insurance benefits.

For hospitals, the growing shift in authority from insurers to purchasers has resurrected awareness as to who is the true client. The AMA's much-heralded Corporate Visitation Program underscores the degree to which providers have intensified efforts on working with the purchasers of health care. New hospital ventures, such as wellness and occupational health programs that were developed to sustain or increase market share, are directly targeted to the business community.

THE HOSPITAL CONSUMER

Another characteristic of an earlier era of health care was the importance invested in appeasing physicians. Every hospital appreciated the value of a content medical staff. Often business and its patients were entirely ignored or taken for granted. Philanthropy thrived, and corporate representatives on hospital boards acted as rubber stamps for the growth and expansion plans of hospital administrators.

Hospital strategic planning, as a rule, focused on the concerns of the medical staff, not of large purchasers. However, the true consumer of hospital care—the patient who pays the bill—has enjoyed increased importance due to recent employer initiatives. Equipment purchases, expansions, or renovations rarely proceed without market research surveys. The demands of the finer physicians in the community, although still important, are sharing priority status with consumer preferences. Conventional market characteristics, in fact, where consumer demand stimulates provider responses, are finally having an impact on the hospital industry. New programs in sports medicine, subspecialty surgery, and cancer research, for example, now must promise positive revenue streams to enlist the support of increasingly wary financial officers. Tax-exempt financing is no longer risk-free, and hospital administrators are required to justify future expansion on the basis of potential profitability rather than the plenitude of low-cost financing.

Patients were ignored for an obvious reason. Until the last decade, they ostensibly had little or no financial stake in the care they received. Under the third-party reimbursement system, patients had no incentive to know the costs of their treatment. The critical consumer question was not "how much?," but "is it covered?" Now,

more often than not, patients pay co-payments and deductibles for the care they receive. Public and private sector employers have encouraged—through financial incentives—the use of outpatient surgery and second opinions. Patient cost sharing is now pervasive in group insurance plans.

LIMITLESS RESOURCES

For hospitals, the period from the 1960s to the 1980s were boom years. Hill-Burton capital construction funds from the federal government promoted rehabilitation or replacement of aging facilities. The introduction of Medicare and Medicaid established a guaranteed reimbursement stream for care that had often been provided with no compensation. Cost-based and charge-based reimbursement allowed hospitals to recoup expenses regardless of treatment regimen. Costs rarely entered into medical decisions; physicians merely prescribed treatment with the full expectation that all procedures would be reimbursed.

Not only was medical intervention pursued without regard for cost but also unit prices of all ancillary products were not deemed important. Physicians had no schooling in the costs of any prescribed procedures, devices, or drugs, nor were they educated on the cost differences between substitutable medications or other therapies. "Spare no expense" seemed to be the prevailing philosophy of medical staffs as they pursued their careers prior to the 1980s. Hospitals, closely allied to the physician, naturally adhered to the same modus operandi.

With insurers in control, the detached business community lacked awareness of medical costs. Labor negotiations concentrated on guaranteeing as much access to health care as possible at no expense to the employee. Freedom of choice in provider selection reigned supreme.

TRUST AND FAITH

In many respects, physicians retained a cloak of omniscience in the medical social structure.

Patients never questioned the treatment plans of their physicians, and employers permitted an attitude of price insensitivity. Advertising, the prime modality of marketing, was unheard of and, in fact, illegal in most segments of the health care industry. When *Goldfarb v. Virginia State Bar* in 1975 made professionals accountable for restraint of trade offenses, it did little to diminish the nefarious image of self-serving greed that characterized physicians willing to break the mold by "hawking their goods." Despite antitrust implications, physicians and dentists resisted the intrusion of advertising into their professions.

Increases in malpractice cases and a growing self-care movement that eschewed the medical profession all served to erode the godly image of doctors. Moreover, employer cost sensitivity led to attacks on weekend admissions and other preoperation days, conventional practices tailored to physician convenience rather than medical efficacy. Finally, young doctors out of medical school with thousands of dollars of educational debt were willing to transgress the time-honored practices and prohibitions created by the profession.

BUSINESS OF HEALTH CARE

The hospital industry has truly undergone a metamorphosis. Hospital administrators now have considerable academic financial training before joining a hospital's administrative team. Businesspeople, once relied on to contribute financial acumen to a hospital board's deliberations, have begun to articulate the concerns of their companies. With one in every six hospitals being for-profit and the great majority of nonprofit institutions emulating their proprietary peers, hospital care has assumed a decidedly more business orientation.

Although the surfeit was not evenly distributed, employers recognized that a more business-attuned hospital industry required more oversight. Dr. Stanley Wohl, a New York internist, corroborated that concern:

> Medicine concerns the inalienable right of each individual to enjoy the

healthiest, most disease-free body that state-of-the-art knowledge allows. In its commitment to that right, the practice of medicine has stood apart from the values of the marketplace. I fear that the unfettered corporate practice of medicine may well destroy that commitment.[3]

DATA AS LEVERAGE FOR EMPLOYERS

In the early 1980s, employers realized that their perception of health care cost escalation was entirely based on total dollars expended and percentage of increase from the previous year. They lacked knowledge, however, on where the dollars were going and how to target cost-management strategies. Thus for most employers, the first order of business was to collect a more comprehensive set of information from which to make management decisions.

Initially, corporations seeking data requested more information than they could comprehend or process. Insurers were besieged by employers demanding access to "all the data." Unprepared for such requests, insurers and third-party administrators generally charged exorbitant fees for the labor-intensive reports prepared for their clients. Another response was to produce a series of overwhelming computer printouts—incomprehensible to the layperson—that, more often than not, went unscrutinized and unutilized. The quality of the data initially also compromised efforts to gain a full understanding of community utilization and cost patterns. A premature release of mortality data by the Health Care Financing Administration (HCFA) in 1986 best exemplifies the problem. A hospice in Las Vegas, Nevada, was cited for the highest mortality rate of any hospital. Although government officials experienced embarrassment in fending off the obvious and unwarranted criticisms of the unrefined mortality data, a necessary dialogue was stimulated that is sure to lead to more precise and insightful statistics on quality of care in the future.

The health care data movement in its infancy suffered from a lack of standardization and reporting procedures. Insurers processed claims differently and often relied on narrative reports, rather than standard diagnostic and procedural codes. For employers with more than one carrier, the cost of integrating the diverse utilization and charge reports was often prohibitive, and the effort was unrewarding.

The creation of the uniform hospital bill, UB-82, by payors, insurers, physician groups, and hospital administrators advanced the state-of-the-art collection considerably. UB-82 is a standard form onto which more than 100 data elements are collected. Medicare adopted the UB-82 form for all hospital admissions and enforced the used of the *International Code of Diagnoses (ICD)*, 9th edition, for standardized five-digit diagnostic coding. Many states also adopted the UB-82 form for all payors, setting in place the reporting form that revolutionized data sets.

In 1977, Maryland began the first significant hospital data collection effort. By 1983, the state's hospital review commission was publishing purchaser guides for the private sector to employ in the selection of cost-effective hospitals. In 1987, the state took price guides one step further when it published physicians' charges for routine procedures, allowing consumers to compare the varying customary charges adopted by individual physicians. Iowa also has been a leader in medical data disclosure, starting in 1983 when the Iowa legislature overwhelmingly endorsed the creation of a state data commission to provide information to make the purchasing of hospital care more price sensitive.

Over the next 3 years, 20 states followed the lead of Maryland, Iowa, and the California Health Facilities Commission in collecting and publishing hospital data. Employers who had been deterred by the complexity and cost of company-specific data were aided by the development of comprehensive state data sets that reported provider-specific financial and charge information.

Local efforts in hospital data collection complemented state efforts. In Columbus, Ohio, a group of employers banded together with the local Blue Cross to lead a movement for the vol-untary collection and disclosure of average charge data on the 25 most common diagnoses for each of the community's hospitals. The second edition of the Columbus guide came out as a buyer's guide in 1985 and included helpful consumer tips on selecting physicians, questions to ask physicians, how to read a hospital bill, the value of outpatient versus inpatient surgery, and the advisability of second opinions for certain procedures. Efforts in Topeka, Toledo, Miami, Houston, Minneapolis, and the Piedmont region of South Carolina accomplished similar goals in collecting and reporting localized hospital specific charge data.

By 1983, a new industry of data collection and analysis was springing up to assist employers in interpreting their company-specific claims data. The health care data field grew to a billion dollar industry in 2 years due to the insatiable demands of ill-informed purchasers. Although horror stories of fruitless and costly data collection efforts emerged at the time of the data industry expansion, the knowledge and sophistication that employers gained with respect to the utilization patterns and charges of their communities made them far less intimidated in their dealings with hospitals.

For example, an analysis of St. Louis hospitals' financial conditions between 1982 and 1984 empowered employers in that community to adopt a much more harsh posture when approached for annual philanthropic contributions. Noting the 40.2 percent increase in profits despite a 10 percent reduction in occupancy over 4 years, certain employers refused to sustain their tradition of giving to hospitals that they perceived to be too well endowed.

The ultimate test of successful data gathering came in negotiated arrangements with providers. In California, South Florida, Cleveland, and Houston, employers used data to negotiate fixed diagnostic prices and per diem rates with hospitals. By the mid-1980s, however, preferred provider arrangements (PPAs) had failed to achieve the pervasive impact anticipated when they first appeared on the scene. Nevertheless, the information, which was sorely lacking in the previous decade, had become common enough to embolden benefit managers to deal on an equal basis with providers while justifying cost-management strategies to senior management. In fact, many corporations created new management positions solely responsible for health care.

HOSPITAL COST MANAGEMENT BY BUSINESS

In the mid-1970s, while searching for strategies to diminish the increase in annual health care costs, business representatives directed their energies at hospital cost management, where 60–65 percent of their benefit dollars were expended. Among the adopted strategies were hospital deductibles and co-payments, concurrent utilization review, case management, preadmission testing, encouragement of outpatient surgery, second opinions, reductions in emergency room usage and weekend hospital stays, preadmission authorization, and hospital bill audits.

Cost Sharing

In 1981, preliminary results from the RAND Corporation's 10-year study on health insurance demonstrated convincingly the cost effectiveness of co-payments and deductibles. The authors reported that persons covered in full for medical services spend up to 60 percent more than persons who have co-insurance (Table 33–1).

Business was already well positioned for implementing cost sharing in benefit packages. Buffeted by a nationwide recession in 1982, companies had little difficulty in making a case for jobs versus benefit cutbacks. Most employers instituted cost sharing across the board, whereas some employers, confronted by intractable unions, only modified the plans for their salaried workforce.

By 1985, the *Equitable Healthcare Survey III: Corporate Initiatives and Employee Attitudes on Cost Containment* revealed a dramatic acceptance of cost sharing, with 74 percent of the 1700 management executives interviewed

Table 33–1 RAND Insurance Study Results: Actual Annual Total and Ambulatory Expenditure Per Person by Plan

Plan	Total Expenditure	Ambulatory Expenditure
Free care	$401 ± 52	$186 ± 9
25% co-insurance	346 ± 58	149 ± 10
50% co-insurance	328 ± 149	120 ± 12
95% co-insurance	254 ± 37	114 ± 10
Individual deductible 95% co-insurance*	333 ± 74	140 ± 11

*Co-insurance in this plan applies to outpatient care only; inpatient care is free.

Source: Reprinted from *New England Journal of Medicine*, Vol. 305, pp. 1501–1507, with permission of Massachusetts Medical Society, © 1981.

introducing or increasing deductibles since 1982. A *Business Roundtable* survey in 1984 reported that 98.4 percent of the 122 respondents required a co-payment (Table 33–2).

More importantly, companies recognized the value of creating a financial incentive to entice employee involvement in the care they received. Through benefit redesign, cost sharing took on a new twist. Preferred sites, providers, and review mechanisms were encouraged by lessening patient co-payments. Cost-sharing modifications created financial incentives for outpatient surgeries, second opinions, and preadmission notification.

Not every corporation found it easy to introduce cost sharing. In fact, the flexible spending account (FSA) was a concept conceived by business to mollify its employees. Essentially FSAs were individual, pretax funds available to employees for the purpose of spending on co-payments, deductibles, and noncovered health care services. Quaker Oats established one of the first FSAs as the cornerstone of its Health Care Incentives programs. By giving employees a monetary incentive not to use care, Quaker reported a 20 percent reduction in admissions and a 34 percent cut in days of inpatient care in 1984. Xerox introduced a $400 FSA with a pay-related

Table 33–2 Co-payments at Business Roundtable Companies

(1)	(2)	(3)	(4)	(5)
Type of Service Subject to Co-payment	Number of Firms with Co-payment	Most Frequent Co-payment (Mode)	Percent of Firms with Co-payment Equal to Mode Salaried	Hourly
		(percentage)		
Physician office visits	117	20	74.4	51.3
Physician visits in hospital	98	20	65.3	40.8
Ambulatory surgery fees	55	20	65.5	40.0
Inpatient surgical fees	85	20	63.5	40.0
Inpatient psychiatric fees	86	20	65.1	40.7
Outpatient psychiatric fees	113	50	42.5	29.2
Emergency room fees	70	20	65.7	37.1
Hospital room and board	57	20	57.9	35.1
Other in-hospital charges	61	20	62.3	39.3
Dentist office visits	69	20	43.5	30.4
Laboratory services	80	20	73.8	48.8

Source: Reprinted from *BRT Task Force on Health Survey,* with permission of Eli Lilly & Company, © 1984.

(1 percent of income) deductible for its 56,000 employees in 1984 and observed dramatic cutbacks in utilization (Table 33–3). LTV, Alcoa, Goodyear, and other major manufacturers followed suit until the FSA was discontinued by an IRS ruling in 1984.

Utilization Review

In recognition of the physician's central role in the health cost equation, utilization review

Table 33–3 Health Care Utilization at Xerox

Type of Health Care	Percentage Decrease
Utilization (overall)	–22
Hospital admissions for elective or ambulatory surgery	–46
Hospital admission for surgery (all types)	–35
Hospital outpatient services (all)	–20
Hospital outpatient services (under $500)	–30
Inpatient psychiatric (adult only)	–21

Source: Reprinted with permission of Xerox Corporation.

(UR) has emerged as a key feature of cost management. Utilization review is the process of assessing medical care to assure its quality, medical necessity, and appropriateness in terms of level of care and treatment setting. Historically, UR was a self-policing mechanism used by licensure boards and hospital medical staffs and in the hospital accreditation process. Third-party administrators performed some UR as a claims auditing function, but neither the providers nor the insurers fortified their UR process with clout.

When Congress established the Professional Standards Review Organizations (PSROs) in 1972, its goal was to advance quality assurance while making the medical delivery system more accountable. Yet PSROs lacked enforcement authority. It was, in fact, the introduction of business into the UR field that led to greater scrutiny and more accountability, so much so that UR has become a thriving offshoot industry that is integral to the promotion of a more market-driven health care system. Utilization review became imperative for many corporations when data revealed that one in five admissions was unnecessary and one-third of all hospital days were inappropriate.[4]

The Washington Business Group on Health, a national association of large employers eager to be included in federal health policy formulation, approached Senator David Durenberger in 1981 with a recommendation for making the PSRO program more responsive. A program of performance-based contracting, centralized at the state level and based on physician peer review, emerged as the Peer Review Improvement Act of 1983. Peer review organizations succeeded PSROs in November 1984 and were empowered to pursue private sector contracts to complement their Medicare review authority.

Deere & Co. and Caterpillar, the two farm machinery giants located in Illinois, were instrumental in transforming their region's attitude and commitment to UR. Deere developed a Comprehensive Insurance Claims Handling (CINCH) system that allowed it to track each corporate claim. By merging CINCH with efforts of the Mid-State and Iowa Foundation for Medical Care, Deere drastically cut hospital days per thousand by 36 percent from 1978 to 1982. Caterpillar's efforts with the Mid-State Foundation for Medical Care achieved an 18.4 percent reduction in hospital days from 1977 to 1979. More importantly, the majority of other companies in Illinois and Iowa, prompted by the high priority given by the Midwest Business Group on Health to UR, followed the lead of Deere and Caterpillar.

Utilization review takes many forms. In an effort to manage medical cost increases better, companies have developed preadmission review, which enables intervention prior to admission. If admission is approved, concurrent review with early discharge planning can ensure appropriate hospital utilization for the duration of the inpatient stay.

Another form of utilization review is case management review, which targets specific high-cost hospital cases. Its goal is to move patients' care to more appropriate and less expensive settings than hospitals. Home health services are instigated by case managers overseeing hospital care. Benefit limitations, such as the type of provider covered, are often waived in case management programs to expand options and maximize cost effectiveness. In a pilot effort in 1983, Aetna saved $3 million by managing the care of 60 chronically ill patients. The case management approach has gained particular credence in disability cases in which companies attempt to redirect the resources for short- and long-term disabled workers. Worker disabilities cost the U.S. economy $56 billion in 1983, and those costs have been growing geometrically. Case management has also become specialized to certain sectors of the health care delivery system. Employers have lauded the savings achieved through specialty psychiatric case management reviews by firms such as Preferred Health Care and dental case management by U.S. Administrators.

Managing Surgery Caseloads

Corporate America has embraced second opinion programs aimed at discouraging or delaying invasive procedures. Efforts also have been focused on moving surgery from the inpatient to the outpatient setting.

Whether to make second opinions voluntary or mandatory was debated by companies throughout the 1970s. Compelling research from a 12-year study at Cornell Medical Center completed in 1983 helped settle the issue. Conclusive results revealed that mandatory opinions for 16 procedures saved $2.63 for every dollar spent; voluntary opinions yielded no savings. United Airlines' $20.97 and Singer Corporation's $19.67 in savings per dollar spent confirmed the value of mandatory second opinion programs.

Although the most effective second opinion programs rarely eliminate more than 15 percent of proposed surgery, they provide a beneficial oversight mechanism referred to as the "sentinel effect." By altering physicians and hospitals to this oversight, a degree of accountability is put into the health care system that offsets any additional administrative costs.

The American Hospital Association (AHA) estimated that outpatient surgery increased by

77 percent between 1979 and 1983 and has continued to increase into the 1990s. As an example, United Technologies (UTC) in Hartford attached incentives to a $150,000 gift to Manchester Memorial Hospital. UTC offered to double the gift to $300,000 if the hospital could raise its outpatient surgery from 20 percent of all hospital surgery to 25 percent of all surgery in 1 year. The hospital raised outpatient surgery to 27 percent, the community saved $66,000, and Hartford employers learned of a technique that was worth replicating for all areawide hospitals.

Employers have realized significant cost savings from moving the site of surgery to outpatient settings. A 1977 HCFA study acknowledged that the costs for surgical procedures are up to 55 percent less when performed in a freestanding surgery center and 15 percent less in a hospital outpatient setting. Convenience, less exposure to hospital infections, and avoidance of hospital recuperation further increase the value of outpatient surgery.

The Piedmont Region Business Group on Health went so far as to create a list of over 300 procedures that should be performed in an outpatient setting. Outpatient surgery as a percentage of total surgery has risen in that region from 8.3 percent in 1979 to 29.4 percent in 1984. Many employers have adopted shorter versions than the Piedmont list of 300 preferred outpatient treatments and have built in less co-payment as an incentive to move the care to the outpatient setting.

Discouragement of Unnecessary Hospital Use

Employers have used a variety of cost-management strategies that allow them to control more effectively the flow of patients into hospitals, in addition to the previously mentioned strategies of utilization review. In fact, many employers have specifically avoided constraining admissions and elected to divert their energies to reducing inappropriately long durations of inpatient treatment. In part, these efforts have been bolstered by a spate of new research studies

revealing marginal value gained for each additional day.

Cholecystectomies, which once averaged 12 days of inpatient treatment, have become 3–4 day hospital visits for a majority of hospitalized patients. Laparoscopic cholecystectomies have made this procedure a common ambulatory surgery event. Normal deliveries have been reduced from both the preoperative and postoperative ends. As an employer's most costly service, deliveries represent an area for great cost savings. They are also ideal for hospital negotiations in that they are generally discrete and predictable hospitalizations. The state of Utah has set a fixed global fee, including tests, medical personnel, and ancillary charges, for normal deliveries, cholecystectomies, and other discrete procedures (see Figure 33–1).

In Columbus, Ohio, certain hospitals have seized the competitive initiative by offering all-inclusive prices for 2-day deliveries. The hospitals even provide at-home nursing service.

Equitable Assurance Society reported 35 percent savings in psychiatric inpatient costs after implementing a stringent concurrent review program managed by Preferred Health. Provident Life, John Hancock, and a number of large, self-funded employers in the Northeast have adhered to the same approach, knowing that psychiatrists' practice patterns will begin to change with the introduction of an aggressive utilization monitoring program.

Zenith reported savings of nearly $250,000 in 1983 generated by its successful Medical Services Advisory Program. The program required employees to go through the company's screening program before admission for any nonemergent hospitalizations. Owens-Illinois experienced similar success with its preadmission counseling programs. By establishing an informed resource for employees, the company sought to make its workforce more educated while saving on unnecessary or inappropriate utilization. In 1983 the Owens-Illinois program saved $300,000, a 4:1 rate of return on its patient counseling and second opinion educational program.

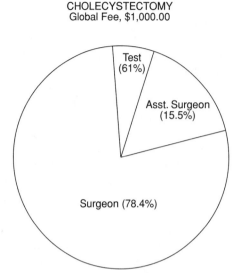

CHOLECYSTECTOMY
Global Fee, $1,000.00

Test (61%)

Asst. Surgeon (15.5%)

Surgeon (78.4%)

Figure 33–1 Utah Global Fee Reimbursements. *Source:* Reprinted with permission from Utah Public Employee Health Programs, Utah State Retirement Board.

Some preadmission programs are mandatory and exact painful penalties from those employees who fail to heed the protocol. LTV Corporation makes employees pay the full hospital charge if they circumvent its certification program. In 1983, the program's effective constraints on hospitalization reduced hospital admission by 31 percent, for a $1.8 million savings to the company. Chrysler targeted its preadmission authorization on back surgery where significant abuse was noted in 1983. It found that 2,264 of 2,679 days of care provided for medical back treatment were inappropriate. Similar abuse occurred due to generous podiatry benefits offered by General Motors. A preadmission screening program saved General Motors $3.8 million in 1984 on podiatry costs.

Many employers have sought to extract savings from more cost-effective use of diagnostic tests and services. For Goodyear, performing blood tests at its Lawton, Oklahoma, plant's $180,000 worksite clinic saves $36 per test. Continental Bank in Chicago provides an in-bank medical laboratory service to its 9,000 Illinois employees, which saved $66,000 in its first year of operation in 1983. Continental shaved $200 to $350 off each hospital's battery of tests by providing them to patients before admission.

Oversight of Hospital Bills

A study of Equifax, a hospital bill audit service based in Atlanta, in 1983 revealed that 98 percent of all hospital bills contained errors. Employers found the study disturbing and developed bill audit programs to reduce the number of errors. Business created incentives for employees to study hospital bills diligently by offering rewards for the successful detection of an error. Ryder Systems, one of the corporate pioneers in audit programs, saved $210 per hospital case in 1983 by sharing with employees 25 percent of the difference between the charge on the bill and the correct charges. Ryder capped payments to employees at $500 per bill. Equifax saved $3.16 for every dollar expended auditing hospital care for the Upholstery Union in 1984. CIGNA collected over $1 million in undocumented charges in the first 8 months of 1984 on $48 million in hospital charges. Employers undertook hospital bill audit programs as another tool for making employees more conscious of hospital costs while putting medical records and billing departments on notice of increased scrutiny of their practices.

ALTERNATIVE DELIVERY SYSTEMS

Health Maintenance Organizations (HMOs)

One of the first proactive measures adopted by employers to reduce medical cost inflation was the promotion of HMO enrollment. Employers recognized the value of shifting the financial risk of providing care to providers. They further welcomed the predictability of costs associated with fixed prospective monthly capitation rates. Working closely with the Office of HMOs and the National HMO Industry Council, business had an enormous impact on the growth in HMO enrollment.

Lockheed developed a corporate policy requiring all new employees to enroll in an HMO as a mechanism to expand its HMO penetration. Employers in several communities provided funds for feasibility studies to attract HMOs. Burlington Industries reported a 36 percent penetration rate on its first offering after an aggressive in-house marketing campaign. Ford Motor Company, an early proponent of HMOs, reported savings of $5 million from the $8^{1}/_{2}$ percent of its workforce enrolled in HMOs in 1982.

However, by the mid-1980s, some large employers began to question the cost effectiveness and purported savings of HMOs. Only 42 percent of companies participating in a 1986 Johnson and Higgins benefits survey recognized HMOs as effective in controlling costs. This questioning promoted a call for greater accountability and more comprehensive utilization data. HMOs had argued that because they do not experience-rate their premiums, there is no reason to collect precise utilization data. Some employers maintained that the savings reported by HMOs were attributed to preferred risk selection, rather than cost-effective managed care. In fact, J.C. Penney, Digital Equipment, American Airlines, Honeywell, Chrysler, General Motors, FMC, and Illinois Bell collected corporation data that supported their contention. Moreover, the companies accused HMOs of "shadow pricing," of setting HMO premiums based on a company's indemnity or average monthly costs. Because the experience-rated corporate premiums were established without the benefit of the modest costs attributed to large numbers of young, healthy employees who had enrolled in HMOs, company indemnity premiums had risen dramatically. This cycle of adverse selection, in which the older, less firm retain the employers' indemnity plan, is a common by-product of choice in health plans. The disenchantment with not being able to adjust HMO premiums for their younger enrollees led to an employer backlash and eventually a proposed change in the HMO regulations in 1987 regarding the method in

which an employer sets the HMO premium contribution. Moreover, a joint effort by a committee comprised of representatives from The Washington Business Group on Health and The Group Health Association—trade groups for HMOs—culminated in the creation of a standard data set for HMOs to meet the requests of employers.

Despite the small but vocal group of employers who strove to change HMO premium–pricing practices, a 1985 Lou Harris poll reported that most of the business community supported HMOs. Increasingly, employers advocated the concept of provider financial risk sharing and predictable, fixed prepaid costs. These very features formed the cornerstone of managed care programs that emerged in the mid-1980s.

Preferred Provider Organizations (PPOs)

With the dawning of active employer health cost management, opportunities for using purchasers' market power became self-evident. Purchasers discussed the value of contracting with preferred providers in order to gain unit price discounts for doctor visits and hospital stays. A spate of PPOs appeared on the scene in 1981–1982, but they were for the most part marketing arrangements initiated by providers, not purchasers. In fact, the first developmental stage of the PPO movement was characterized by considerable rhetoric, with only a handful of employers signing PPO deals. Moreover, analysis of some of the first arrangements demonstrated that the highest-cost hospitals were indeed offering discounts, as noted in Denver, but despite the discounts those institutions still were not preferred by knowledgeable customers.

Hewlett Packard and Stouffers Corporation have been credited as being the first companies to establish legitimate PPOs in which savings actually were generated to the employers. Both companies advanced the state-of-the-art in PPO negotiations by entering the discussions equipped with sufficient hospital data to act as informed purchasers. They also insisted on tight utilization controls to ensure that the savings captured through preferable unit price agreements were not offset by unchecked utilization.

The Medi-Cal bid program of 1983 administered by a governmental commission in California instigated a more aggressive and pervasive use by purchasers of negotiated agreements. The bid process used so effectively to garner bargain-basement hospital per diem rates for Medi-Cal became a model effectively adopted by Hughes Aircraft, Eastern Airlines, and a number of Taft-Hartley Trust Funds in California.

By 1985, the PPO movement had matured dramatically. Over 300 PPOs, of which more than 15 percent had been created by purchasers, were in existence. Dental care and, to a lesser extent, mental health had been carved out of employer indemnity plans to facilitate attractive unit price arrangements. In addition, some hospital companies, such as Humana, had succeeded in penetrating the employer marketplace to establish preferred arrangements. Innovative twists and better management of the caseload typified the corporate-initiated PPOs. The rhetoric of the early 1980s had blossomed into a movement involving more prudent and well-informed purchasers, and out of this rhetoric arose the term *managed care*.

Managed Care

The evolution of employers from ignorant and unconcerned payors to aggressive and insightful purchasers took a decade. The very term "cost management" is significant in and of itself. At the outset, employers were cautioned against containing an irrepressible force. In an aging society, with systemic inflation and predictably high-cost technological infusion, one could argue that the cost of medicine could never be contained. But employers are the best teachers when it comes to educating users to the health care system on ways to manage costs. Managing input prices represents the epitome of the private sector business mission. Thus, when employers came to realize that managing medical costs was not dissimilar to all the other management tasks applied by MBAs and their "school-of-hard-

knocks" counterparts, they welcomed the challenge and became obvious leaders for the managed care concept.

To an employer managed care is a comprehensive program. Key to stemming the rate of increase in medical costs is an approach that targets the health care triad: utilization, price, and capacity. Failure to address all three factors simultaneously can undercut the success of a managed care program. For instance, decreasing hospital days does not ensure a reduction in total hospital costs. Left unchecked, hospitals with very real fixed cost obligations can unbundle services or raise unit prices, even when confronted by stringent UR controls.

The next generation of negotiated preferred arrangements will embody the virtues of preadmission and concurrent UR, hospital bill audits, targeted data collection and analysis, and incentives for prudent employee utilization in appropriate settings. Capitation and other forms of financial risk sharing for providers will be integral to effective managed care systems.

Throughout the 1990s, many organizations developed what are hybrids of the HMO and PPO. Some, known as point-of-service (POS) plans, offer the consumer the ability to use "panel" providers by paying only a co-payment, and to select nonpanel providers at greater cost to the consumer. Regardless of the success of HMOs, they are not the prime choice of many individuals, and have not been proven cost-effective mechanisms with large heterogeneous populations. Point-of-service and other hybrid plans have become rapid growth alternatives in the 1990s.

Coalitions

A health care coalition is an incorporated confederation of parties involved with health care. The coalition movement in the United States has become a vital component of a multifaceted medical cost-management thrust initiated by corporate America. The first coalitions emerged in the mid-1970s, and the movement gained considerable momentum in the early 1980s. Over half of the coalitions in existence were started before 1983. By 1985, there were 155 local coalitions in the country, of which approximately half were strictly comprised of employers. Coalitions are as diverse in agenda and composition as the communities from which they emanate.

Coalitions by their very design can be more powerful than an individual company. By amassing the corporate clout of an entire community and gaining senior management support, coalitions can gain considerable credibility and market power.

Coalitions also became an appropriate locus for debate among all involved parties in the medical cost equation. Whereas many coalitions, concerned about costs, limited the role of providers to an advisory input role, few coalitions ignored the opportunities for dialogue. Coalitions hosted forums in which purchasers and providers examined viable solutions to the medical cost problem. Moreover, they provided a setting for exploring a community's long-range goals for its health care delivery system.

A number of coalitions had little to boast of other than the educational forum they established in their community. Yet although nominal in its impact on health costs, the dialogue generated by coalitions did lead to some change in the health care system. Seattle employers invested heavily in publishing a guide to health care understanding that significantly raised the level of consciousness in the community. The guide essentially taught employers how to manage health care costs. The coalition followed up their work in the primer with a guide to assessing utilization review firms, published in 1986. Seattle's employers have benefitted greatly from the educational guides generated by their coalition.

The 36 employers in the Richmond Area Business Group on Health produced a 250-page report entitled *Health Care Plan Design* that contributed greatly to private sector initiatives that have transformed Richmond into a hotbed of free-market alternatives. The New York Business Group on Health's newsletter consistently overflows with pertinent and timely information for a national readership. On the other hand, the very presence of a coalition, in and of itself, can have a salutary effect on inflationary factors in the local medical delivery system through the sentinel effect.

Educational forums notwithstanding, the good coalitions in the country have tackled far more ambitious objectives. From collection of data to feasibility studies, from program development to legislative lobbying, the more effective coalitions have had a great impact in their communities. Fortified by corporate support, financial security, and a commitment to effect change, Houston, South Florida, St. Louis, Memphis, and San Diego coalitions have established enviable track records and model agendas for other coalitions to emulate.

A number of coalitions, including St. Louis, South Florida, Penjerdel, Columbia, Houston, Utah, and Boston, engineered successful data-oriented projects. The collection of provider-specific price and utilization data allowed the South Florida Health Action Coalition to create a database for the selection of preferred providers. Six of the coalition's employers acted on the information by creating PPOs. One of the first PPOs set up by the Dade County School System reported savings of an estimated $2 million in its first year of existence.

The San Diego Employers Health Cost Coalition pursued a data collection effort that disclosed cost and quality information to its members. In setting up a coalitionwide PPO, the employers group required peer review organization (PRO) quality data from every physician desiring to participate. One-fourth of the area physicians were unwilling to submit to such scrutiny.

Coalitions in Maryland, Columbus, Minneapolis, Wichita, Seattle, and Dayton have all had success with price disclosure and buyers guides. The Iowa coalition worked diligently with the HSA to divulge physician practice pattern variations, another data tool for effecting change. By examining utilization of services that deviated dramatically from the norm, the coalition drew attention to procedures and medical specialties that were a community problem. Through education of doctors, excessive utilization was moderated. Generally, hysterectomies, back surgery, tonsillectomies, cardiac bypass, and prostatectomies have been identified as problem areas by these data collection efforts. This form of small area analysis was first pioneered by Jack Wennberg of Dartmouth Medical School and has subsequently been adopted by coalitions in Vermont, Maine, West Virginia, New Hampshire, Boston, and North Carolina.

For many coalitions, the prohibitive cost and lack of conformity in claims data argue for pursuing other, more manageable tasks. An assignment taken on by some coalitions has been the development of alternative delivery systems. These managed health care systems, most notably HMOs and PPOs, have received solid support from coalition supporters.

In Des Moines, Raleigh/Durham, Pittsburgh, and Hartford, where prepaid health care was an anathema until recently, coalitions helped finance feasibility analyses that demonstrated the potential viability of HMOs. The coalition efforts were rewarded by subsequent HMO penetration and the development of a more competitive marketplace in each locale.

By establishing a forum for the discussion of emerging issues, coalitions are well-suited for the efficient resolution of a delivery system problem. The Toledo employers played an instrumental role in 1982 in stopping the construction of a new neonatal intensive care unit (NICU) in their city. Coalition leaders argued effectively that the one existing facility adequately met the demand in the community. By assisting in the facilitation of an accord that permitted area neonatologists to have access to the only existing NICU, the coalition successfully warded off a $5 million construction project that would have added $1 million in additional annual operating costs to the community.

The Columbus coalition recognized the same logic of sharing limited resources when it brought its urologists together to negotiate access successfully to the community's sole lithotryptor. By discouraging competition for duplicative technologies and services, these two Ohio cities have limited the unnecessary and costly infusion of new technologies into their communities.

In dealing with capacity and new technology issues, coalitions will continue to have numerous opportunities to ameliorate a potentially damaging development. Because these efforts require a good working relationship with local providers, they represent one of the better opportunities of all-party cooperative coalition initiatives.

Although few coalitions have chosen to focus their energies on their state legislatures, the impact of such efforts can be substantial. The Colorado coalition in its first year of existence successfully lobbied for five bills in the spring legislative session of 1985. Included in the coalition's accomplishments was the passage of a data bill that shifts the costs and responsibility of data collection from the coalition to the state government. Several Illinois coalitions spearheaded by the regional Midwest Business Group on Health accomplished the same end in Illinois. In Connecticut, the Hartford coalition concentrated on a state rate-setting legislative package that passed in 1984. Similar attempts by the 1200-member Arizona coalition failed in a messy and costly, highly visible political confrontation with its hospital industry. The San Francisco Bay Area Purchasers Group devoted much of its time and agenda in 1984 to salvaging the state's data collection process that hospitals tried to eliminate. The San Francisco coalition has also received accolades for its responsible effort in setting standards for the retention of AIDS-afflicted employees in their workplaces. By involving physicians and specialists in infectious disease, the coalition arrived at a rational and compassionate program for the treatment of AIDS patients employed by coalition members.

The 14 Texas coalitions made indigent care legislative solutions a high priority. Similar coalition initiatives were pursued in other states.

The same kind of attention has been focused on medical malpractice, an issue that attracted the involvement of coalitions in Florida, New York, Delaware, Pennsylvania, and Missouri.

Coalitions have developed an impressive track record. They have proven that, when well managed and appropriately directed, they can have a significant impact on their local medical delivery systems. With a limitless array of new issues and problems emerging in the medical delivery system's evolution, their survival seems likely. Coalitions clearly are a formidable tool allowing corporations the opportunity to shape a more efficient and efficacious health care delivery system.

Corporate Medical Departments

With the escalation in medical costs came an increasing awareness among employers that providing medical care at the worksite would be more cost effective and convenient and would cause less downtime. The growing trend of expanding corporate medical departments has, in part, occurred due to the proliferation of worksite wellness programs. A hypertension screening program that detects elevated blood pressure has often incorporated monitoring of the disease into its duties. Some corporations have resisted the expansion of traditional occupational medicine departments focused on worksite injuries to the broader purview of medical treatment of disease. Yet, as worksites become more adapted to the needs of workers and as employers realize the value of providing medical services, particularly primary care at the worksite, the trend is likely to increase.

When Goodyear planned construction of a plant in Lawton, Oklahoma, the benefits and corporate medical departments strategically planned for a greater clinic capacity. In fact, serious consideration was given to providing all but tertiary care, including same-day surgery, at the plant. The tire company backed away from such an ambitious project, but does provide extensive medical services, including diagnostic laboratory tests. American Express has found value in contracting with a gynecologist to visit corporate headquarters one day a week in order to meet the gynecological needs of its female workforce.

Across the nation employee assistance programs (EAPs) have emerged as an additional interface between employees and the medical delivery system. Historically EAPs were staffed by recovered alcoholics and provided counseling and referral services to employees with drinking problems. They have evolved considerably, however, and now are often staffed by health care professionals able to counsel, treat, or refer employees not only for drug dependency but also for marital, psychological, and financial problems. Hughes, United Technologies, Lockheed, and Digital Equipment have established highly regarded in-house EAPs that address all emotional needs.

One of the most successful and extensive corporate medical departments is found at Gates Rubber Company in Denver. The clinic, which has been in operation for over 20 years, meets the medical needs of 13,500 Gates employees, as well as many other companies in the surrounding region. Over 200 medical personnel work full- or part-time providing primary and specialty care to clinic patients. The Gates Medical Center has also stocked a full pharmaceutical dispensary that, through high volume, makes prescription drugs available, convenient, and cost effective. The opportunity to manage medications and cut costs by making pharmaceuticals available at the worksite has also been successfully introduced by Uniroyal and Rockwell Industries.

Hospital usage has only been minimally affected by the expansion of corporate medical departments at the worksite. The number of physician visits, on the other hand, can be greatly reduced when a company's medical staff succeeds in promoting to employees an image of proficiency, expertise, and trust to accompany convenience and cost savings. Potentially, these more sophisticated primary care centers will reduce acute days of hospital care by improving the management of chronic disease and by detecting and intervening early to prevent serious acute illness.

CONCLUSION: FUTURE OF BUSINESS INVOLVEMENT

Business was slow to respond to burgeoning medical cost increases. When the phenomenon of escalating costs became apparent, it took employers 3 to 5 years to become fully aware of the vagaries of the medical care system. The learning period was necessary, for it allowed business representatives to achieve comfort in an alien world where a different language is spoken. Hospitals and physicians had considerable intimidation power when they initially confronted employers. That edge has since eroded. Hospital representatives have manifested an ever-vigilant mindfulness of the almighty dollar controlled by business. Even in situations where the intimidation power is retained, the fact that business is paying the bill cannot be ignored.

Employers have also come to recognize the need for concerted action at the local, state, and federal levels. By ceding a seat at the negotiating table when pertinent health care legislation is discussed, employers run the risk of foregoing one sphere of influence to concentrate on issues closer to home. That error in judgment has occurred often enough in the past. The likelihood of it recurring regularly is remote.

With the marketplace gaining greater standing, purchasers have leveled the playing field. Many of the perversities inherent in Medicare's cost-based reimbursement system have been eradicated.

A more interested and intelligent employer can offer considerable talent in formulating health policy and reshaping the delivery system. The health care dollar has finally come to mean something to business, and it is this attention to the billions of dollars spent yearly that will make employers integral to a redefinition of medical insurance benefits and utilization.

NOTES

1. G.S. Whitted, Research Report 84-3, IFEBP, June (1984).
2. *Industry Week* July 22 (1985):27.
3. S. Wohl, *The Medical Industry Complex* (New York: Harmony Books, 1984).
4. P.M. Gertman and J.H. Restuccia, *Medical Care,* August (1971), 855-871.

FREDERICK C. LEE, MHA, was Senior Vice President of Marketing for Preferred Health Care, a firm specializing in psychiatric utilization management. Formerly Vice President of Policy for the Washington Business Group on Health, he tracked all federal health legislative developments for the 200 large corporations that comprise the WBGH membership. He is also a featured columnist in *Business and Health*, the WBGH's topical monthly health publication.

He is a graduate of Harvard College and the University of Washington's Health Services Administration graduate program.

Chapter 34

Managed Health Care

Peter R. Kongstvedt

INTRODUCTION

There are many who believe that unrestrained fee-for-service medicine has led to inappropriately high utilization and is therefore the root cause of our health care cost crisis. While there is merit in the argument, it is simplistic. Health care costs are escalating at an alarming rate for many reasons, not just fee-for-service medicine. These other reasons include rapidly developing (and usually expensive) technology; cost shifting by providers to pay for care rendered to patients who either cannot pay or are covered by systems that do not pay the full cost of care; shifting demographics as our population ages; appropriately high expectations for a long and healthy life; the current legal environment leading to defensive medicine; administrative costs related to the care that is delivered; wide variations in efficiencies and quality of care that is rendered by all types of providers (professional and institutional); serious inequities and variations in incomes between all types of providers (regardless of efficiency or quality); and a myriad of other reasons. There are no easy answers to these problems, but neither are they insurmountable. This chapter will provide an overview of many of the major components of managed health care.

DEFINITION OF MANAGED HEALTH CARE

Managed health care, or managed care, is an approach to managing both the quality and the cost of medical care. Having said that, in the current environment there really is no single definition of managed health care; it is a term applied to a wide variety of systems. In general, there are at least two elements common to managed health care systems: some type of authorization mechanism and some level of restriction on a member's choice of providers. The authorization component may be minimal, such as a simple hospital precertification requirement; or it may be comprehensive, such as a primary care physician (PCP) "gatekeeper" model. The restriction in choice of provider may be minimal, such as a minor increase in co-insurance to see an out-of-network provider in a preferred provider organization (PPO); or it may be strict, such as a highly restrictive health maintenance organization (HMO).

Managed care may be thought of as a continuum of models. These models, which will be discussed later, are generally classified as follows:

1. indemnity with precertification, mandatory second opinion, and large-case management
2. service plan with precertification, mandatory second opinion, and large-case management
3. PPO
4. point-of-service (POS)
5. HMO
   - open panel
     –individual practice association (IPA)
     –direct contract
   - network model
   - closed panel HMO
     –group model
     –staff model

As the models move from indemnity with precertification, mandatory second opinion, and large-case management to closed-panel HMO, certain changes occur. These changes include:

- Elements of control over health care delivery become tighter.
- New elements of control are added.
- More direct interaction with providers occurs between the plan and provider.
- Overhead cost and complexity increases in the health plan.
- Greater control of utilization occurs.
- Net reduction in rate of rise of medical costs takes place.

While it would be comforting to classify all of managed care into one of these categories, in fact the U.S. health care system has been mixing and matching these elements to a great degree and many hybrids exist. Thus, the reader must recognize that managed care is nothing if not malleable.

With the current debate over health care reform, one new concept in health plans has been introduced: the accountable health plan (AHP). An AHP, which has not been fully defined, is a health plan that meets certain criteria regarding underwriting practices, guaranteed policy issues, premium rates and pricing, reporting requirements, and so forth. The point of an AHP, however, will be to provide consumer choice of health plans and provide access to care, and to do so in a fair and equitable manner. If major health system reform is enacted, how AHPs, purchasing cooperatives, or alliances (another concept under debate), and other elements of proposed health reform will affect managed care remains unknown, but it is very likely that the elements described in this chapter will be generally unaffected. The reason is that with or without major reform, the industry has been evolving toward managed care methodologies since the early 1980s.

TYPES OF HEALTH PLANS

Government Programs

In the United States in 1993, over 40 percent of health care was actually provided or financed by the federal and state governments. These programs include Medicare for the elderly and disabled, Medicaid for the poor, military programs (both direct care by military providers as well as the Civilian Health and Medical Program of the Uniformed Services [CHAMPUS]), the Federal Employee Health Benefits Program (FEHBP), the Veterans Administration, the U.S. Public Health Service, and some other programs. These programs may incorporate few to all managed care features, but they are not the focus of this chapter.

Traditional Insurance

Traditional insurance (which is rapidly becoming nontraditional) is basically made up of two types: indemnity insurance and service plans.

Indemnity Insurance

Indemnity insurance indemnifies the insured against financial losses from medical expenses. The only restriction is in the schedule of benefits covered by the plan. There are generally no practice restrictions placed by the plan on licensed providers. The insurance company reimburses the subscriber directly, or may pay the provider directly, but has no actual obligation other than to pay the subscriber. Professional reimbursement (i.e., payment to physicians and other professional providers) is subject to usual, customary, or reasonable (UCR) fee screens, while institutional reimbursement is generally based on charges.

Benefits are generally subject to deductibles (a flat dollar amount paid by the subscriber before any benefit is paid by the insurance company) and co-insurance (a percentage of the covered charge that is paid by the subscriber—for example, 20 percent). Any charges by the provider that are not paid by the insurance company are strictly the responsibility of the subscriber.

Most indemnity plans require precertification of elective hospital admissions, and may apply a financial penalty to the subscriber for failure to precertify. The plan may also perform some additional utilization management on hospital cases, but generally this is done over the telephone by plan-employed nurses located elsewhere. Large-case management may also be used to help control the cost of catastrophic cases. Mandatory second opinion programs may also be present for certain elective procedures (e.g., cardiac bypass surgery).

Costs for this type of health care coverage have been escalating faster than any other type of health plan. As those costs rise, more people move into managed care.

Service Plan

This term applies primarily though not exclusively to Blue Cross and Blue Shield Plans. In service plans, there are generally few restrictions on licensed providers who agree to sign a contract with the plan. The provider contract contains certain key elements: the plan agrees to reimburse the provider directly (eliminating collection problems with patients); the provider agrees to accept the plan's fee schedule as payment in full and not balance-bill the subscriber for any payment not made by the plan (other than normal deductible or co-insurance); and the provider agrees to allow the plan to audit the provider's records. Precertification, large-case management, and mandatory second opinion may be present and operate as they do for indemnity insurance.

The principle advantage of a service plan over indemnity insurance is the presence of the provider contracts and the reimbursement models that the contracts support. Professional fees are paid under a schedule of allowances that may in effect provide a discount to the plan. More importantly, the plan usually has significant discounts at hospitals that give it a competitive advantage. The hospitals grant these discounts for a variety of reasons, including ensuring a large volume of business, rapid payment, ease of collection, and occasionally advance deposits. The actual reimbursement to the hospital may be based on charges, per diems, diagnostic-related groups (DRGs), "cost plus," or some variation; these reimbursement methods are discussed later in this chapter. The reimbursement to provider physicians may be based on a discount to the Medicare fee schedule, or other uniform fee allowance schedule.

Preferred Provider Organization

PPOs are similar to service plans with some important differences. The total panel of providers is reduced to some degree, often substantially (e.g., only 20 percent of the total available providers). While the PPO may limit the number of providers in the network, there are two broad approaches: any willing provider versus criteria-based selection. In the former, any provider who wishes to participate and who agrees to the terms and conditions of the PPO's contract, must be offered a contract, at least until the PPO believes it has adequate numbers of providers. In the latter category, the PPO uses some objective criteria (e.g., credentials, practice pattern analysis, and so forth) which a provider must meet before a contract will be offered.

While reimbursement mechanisms to providers may fall along the lines mentioned under service plans, in general the discounts are greater. It should be noted that many service plans require providers to give them "favored nation" pricing; in other words, a provider may not provide a better discount to a competitor than it does to the service plan. Favored nation pricing is under great scrutiny for a variety of reasons. As a rule, PPOs do not place the providers at risk for medical costs; the concept of risk-sharing with providers is discussed later in this chapter.

Precertification, large-case management, and possibly mandatory second opinion are almost always present. The main difference is that failure to comply with these programs results in a financial penalty to the provider, not the subscriber. As under service plans, a contracting provider may not balance-bill the subscriber for any payment not made by the PPO, except for normal deductibles and co-insurance. In the event a subscriber chooses to seek care from a nonparticipating provider, the responsibility then falls to the subscriber, and the subscriber is at risk for any financial penalties or charges not paid by the PPO.

A hallmark of PPOs is a benefits differential if a member sees a provider who is not in the PPO network. A common benefits differential is 20 percent. For example, if a member sees a network provider, coverage is provided at 90 percent of allowed charges; if a member sees a provider not in the network, the coverage may be at the 70 percent level.

A distinction between two types of PPOs is worthwhile: that of risk bearing versus non-risk bearing. A risk-bearing PPO combines both the insurance or payment function with the management of the network of providers. A non-risk-bearing PPO refers solely to the network, and not to the insurance function. For example, a commercial insurer may create a network and sell coverage to clients; this would be an example of a risk-bearing PPO. Alternatively, a group of providers may come together as a legal

entity, establish fee allowances, credentialing criteria, utilization review, and so forth, and contract with independent insurers to provide medical services to those insurers' customers; this would be an example of a non-risk-bearing PPO.

Health Maintenance Organization

HMOs are fundamentally different from the health plans previously described. Although there are a few exceptions known as open-access HMOs that are similar in benefits design to PPOs, the vast majority of HMOs operate in such a manner as to further manage utilization and quality. It should be noted that HMOs often form the in-network portion of a POS plan, which is described later. Benefits to members in an HMO are restricted (with some exceptions) to those provided by HMO providers, and in compliance with the HMO authorization procedures. Benefits obtained through the HMO may be richer than those found in traditional insurance or in PPOs. Except for true emergencies or unless specifically authorized, services received from non-HMO providers are the responsibility of the subscriber, not the HMO. Services rendered by contracting providers who fail to obtain proper authorization are the responsibility of the provider, who may not balance-bill the member.

HMOs currently fall into two broad categories: open panel and closed panel. A third category, the network model, is not common except in certain parts of the country, but is likely to become more common in the future. Some HMOs mix model types in the same market. The principal differences are as follows.

Open Panel Plans

Open panel HMOs contract with private physicians and other professional providers to see members in the provider's own office. The provider is an independent contractor, and may contract with more than one competing health plan, as well as having fee-for-service patients. The provider may be reimbursed through a variety of mechanisms. The total number of providers in an open panel plan is larger than that of a closed panel plan, but usually fewer than in a PPO. Members must choose a single provider to be their PCP, sometimes referred to as a gatekeeper, who must authorize any other services. A member may change PCPs at designated times if necessary.

Open panel plans fall into two broad categories: independent practice associations (IPAs) and direct contract models. While the terms are often used synonymously, they are technically distinct.

In an IPA, the HMO contracts with a legal entity known as an IPA, and pays the IPA a negotiated capitation amount. The IPA in turn contracts with private physicians. The IPA may reimburse the physicians through capitation, or may use another mechanism such as fee-for-service. The providers are at risk under this model in that if medical costs exceed the capitation amount, the IPA receives no additional funds from the HMO and must accordingly adjust the reimbursement to the providers.

In direct contract models, the HMO contracts directly with the providers; there is no intervening entity such as an IPA. The HMO reimburses the providers directly, and performs all related management tasks. Direct contract models are currently the most common form of HMO.

Closed Panel Plans

Closed panel plans differ from open panel plans in that the closed panel plan uses physicians whose practice is confined to the HMO. The physicians practice in facilities that are likewise dedicated to or owned by the HMO. The total number of providers in the plan is by far the smallest of any model type. Members usually do not have to choose a single PCP, but may see any PCP in the HMO (although they may be asked to choose a primary facility in order to provide continuity). Closed panel plans fall into two broad categories: group model and staff model.

In group model plans, the HMO contracts with a medical group to provide services to members. The HMO pays the group a negotiated capitation, and the group in turn reimburses the physicians through a combination of salary and risk/reward incentives. The group is responsible for its own governance, and physicians are either partners in the group or associates. The group or the HMO provides the dedicated practice facilities and support staff, but most commonly it is the HMO's responsibility. The group is at risk in that if the costs of the group exceed the capitation amount, the reimbursement to the providers is lowered, although the HMO generally provides stop-loss insurance coverage to the group to protect the group from catastrophic cost overruns. Some groups exist primarily on paper, and actually operate strictly as cost pass-through vehicles for the HMO, thus resembling staff model plans.

In staff model plans, the HMO contracts with the providers directly, and the providers are employees of the HMO. Physicians are reimbursed by salary, with an incentive plan of some sort. The HMO has full responsibility for management of all activities.

Network Model

The last major category of HMO is usually referred to as a network model. The term *network model* is occasionally used to refer to an open panel plan, but this section will discuss only the "true" network model. In this model, the HMO contracts with several large multispecialty medical groups for medical services. The groups are paid under capitation, and they in turn reimburse the physicians using a range of mechanisms. The groups operate relatively independently. The HMO contracts with more than one group, but the number is usually limited.

Mixed Model

Nothing is pure and simple, and health plans are no exception. Many HMOs have adopted several model types, even in the same market, in order to capture additional market share. The most common form of mixed model involves grafting a direct contract model to either a closed panel or a network model. The HMO may also need to expand its medical service area, and may choose to contract with private physicians rather than make the expenditures required for a facility. In mixed model plans, the models often operate independently of each other.

Point of Service

POS plans combine features of HMOs and traditional insurance. An archaic but still technically valid use of the term refers to a simple PPO arrangement.* In a POS plan, the members may choose which system to use at the point they obtain the service. For example, if the member uses the PCP and otherwise complies with the HMO authorization system, the benefits for services may be more comprehensive, and require the member to pay only a minor co-payment; if the member chooses the self-refer or otherwise not use the HMO system to receive services, the plan still provides insurance coverage, but at a much lower level, such as requiring a deductible and co-insurance. The difference between in-network and out-of-network coverage for services generally ranges from 20 percent to 40 percent.

POS plans have been developed to meet the conflicting issues of cost control and total freedom of choice of providers. By bringing the issue of cost differential directly to the members at the point they seek medical services, the members become more active participants in the process.

PROVIDER REIMBURSEMENT

The topic of reimbursement is varied and intricate. In fact, a common problem in managed care is that managers devise new and unique methods of reimbursement that theoretically will yield a positive result, only to find that the health plan has no systems capability to support it. In addition, the cost of programming to support the new reimbursement methodology may far outweigh any advantage that it may have had.

---

*The federal government appears to be the only entity of any size that uses the term in such a manner.

Hospital Reimbursement

As illustrated in Exhibit 34–1, there are a variety of methods for reimbursing hospitals in managed care. A very brief description of these methodologies follows.

Straight Charges

As with any other payment mechanism in health care, the easiest method is straight charges. It is also the most expensive and the least desirable, and market forces dictate that it is not frequently used.

Discount on Charges

A common arrangement is a straight percentage discount on charges. In this case, the hospital submits its claim in full and the plan discounts it by the agreed-to percentage. The hospital accepts this payment as payment in full and does not balance-bill the member for the difference, except for allowed deductibles and co-insurance as appropriate.

The presence of co-insurance in the setting of a discount has led to a serious dispute in a number of plans. The issue is what the co-insurance applies to: the full charges or the discounted amount. Unless the benefits contract clearly states that co-insurance is to be applied to full charges regardless of what the plan ultimately pays, an argument can be made that the co-insurance should apply only to the discounted payment, since co-insurance is a percentage of the total payment.

Sliding Scale Discount on Charges

More common than straight discount are sliding scale discounts. With a sliding scale, the percentage discount is reflective of total volume of admissions and outpatient procedures.

How the plan tracks the level of discount needs to be established. Some may wish to vary the discount on a month-to-month basis, but more common is quarterly or semiannually, or even yearly. One may track total bed days or number of admissions. Whatever is finally agreed to, it must be a clearly defined and measurable objective.

Exhibit 34–1 Models for Reimbursing Hospitals

1. Straight charges
2. Discount on charges
3. Sliding scales for discounts
4. Per diem charges
5. Sliding scale per diem
6. Differential by day in hospital
7. Diagnostic-related groups (DRGs)
8. Differential by service type
9. Case rates
   - Institutional only
   - Bundled
10. Bed leasing
11. Capitation or percent of revenue
12. Penalties and withholds
13. Outpatient care

Per Diem Charges

Unlike straight charges, a negotiated per diem is a single charge for a day in the hospital, regardless of any actual charges or costs incurred. In this very common type of arrangement, the plan negotiates a per diem rate with the hospital and pays that rate without adjustments.

Hospital administrators are sometimes reluctant to add days in the intensive care unit or obstetrics to the arrangement unless there is a sufficient volume of regular medical or surgical cases to make the ultimate cost predictable. In a small plan, or one that is not limiting the number of participating hospitals, the hospital administrator is concerned that the hospital will be used for expensive cases at a low per diem, while competitors will be used for less costly cases. In such cases, one approach is to negotiate multiple sets of per diem charges based on service type (e.g., medical/surgical, obstetrics, intensive care unit, neonatal intensive care, rehabilitation, etc.), or a combination of per diem and flat case rate for obstetrics. A related topic is the occasional high cost medical device that becomes widely available after the per diem has been established; in such cases, it is possible to negotiate an outlier payment that equates to the cost to the hospital for that new device.

The key to making a negotiated per diem work is predictability. If you can accurately predict the number and mix of cases, you can accurately calculate a per diem. The per diem is simply an estimate of the charges (or costs) for an average day in that hospital, minus the amount of discount the parties agree to.

Sliding Scale Per Diem

Like the sliding scale discount on charges discussed above, the sliding scale per diem is also based on total volume. In this case, one negotiates an interim per diem; depending on the total number of bed days in the year, the plan either pays a lump sum settlement at the end of the year or withholds an amount from the final payment to the hospital for the year to adjust for an additional reduction in the per diem from an increase in total bed days. Adjustments are made on a quarterly or semiannual basis so as to reduce any disparities caused by unexpected changes in utilization patterns.

Differential by Day in Hospital

This simply refers to the fact that most hospitalizations are more expensive on the first day. For example, the first day for surgical cases includes operating suite costs, the operating surgical team costs (nurses, recovery, etc.), and so forth. This type of reimbursement method is generally combined with a per diem approach, but the first day is paid at a higher rate. This is not common, primarily because it is complicated, difficult to support on must claims systems, and should not be necessary if standard per diems have been calculated properly.

Diagnostic-Related Groups (DRGs)

Similar to Medicare, plans may use DRGs to pay for inpatient care. There are publications of DRG categories, criteria, outliers, and trim points (i.e., the cost or length of stay that causes the DRG payment to be supplemented or supplanted by another payment mechanism) to enable parties to negotiate a payment mechanism for DRGs based on either Medicare rates, or, in some cases, state-regulated rates. DRGs are perhaps better suited to plans with loose controls rather than plans that tightly manage utilization, since DRGs put the risk and reward solely on the hospital, rather than the health plan.

Differential by Service Type

Although similar to DRGs, service-related case rates are more crude. In this reimbursement mechanism, various service types are defined (e.g., medical, surgical, intensive care, neonatal intensive care, psychiatry, obstetrics, etc.) and the hospital receives a flat per-admission reimbursement for whatever type of service the patient is admitted to. If services are mixed, a prorated payment may be made (e.g., 50 percent of surgical and 50 percent intensive care).

Case Rates

Whatever mechanism is used for hospital reimbursement, a plan frequently finds it necessary to address certain categories of procedures and negotiate special rates. The most common of these is obstetrics. It is common to negotiate a flat rate for a normal vaginal delivery and one for a Caesarean section, or a blended rate for both.

Another common application of flat rates is in specialty procedures at tertiary hospitals, for example, negotiating a flat rate for coronary artery bypass surgery or for heart transplants. These procedures, while relatively infrequent, are tremendously costly.

A broader but increasingly common and important variation is the bundled case rate, which refers to an all-inclusive rate paid for both institutional and professional services. The plan negotiates a flat rate for a procedure (e.g., bypass surgery) and that rate is used to pay all parties who provide services connected with that procedure. Bundled case rates required a certain measure of cooperation and trust between a hospital and its medical staff.

Bed Leasing

A very uncommon reimbursement mechanism is bed leasing. This refers to a plan actually leasing beds from an institution, regardless of whether those beds are used or not. This assures revenue flow to the hospital, assures access to beds (at least some) to the plan, and is budgetable. It is perhaps best used in those situations where a plan is assured of a steady number of bed days, with little or no seasonality. The problem with bed leasing is that there is no real savings from reducing utilization, unless contract terms allow the plan to lease back the beds to the hospital if they are not being used.

Capitation or Percentage of Revenue

Capitation refers to reimbursing the hospital on a fixed per member per month (PMPM) basis to cover all institutional costs for a defined population of members. Percentage of revenue refers to a fixed percentage of premium revenue (i.e., a percentage of the collected premium rate) being paid to the hospital, again to cover all institutional services. The differences between percentage of revenue and capitation is that percentage of revenue may vary with the premium rate charged and the actual revenue yield. In both cases, the hospital absorbs the entire risk for institutional services for the defined membership base; if the hospital cannot provide the services itself, the cost for such care is deducted from the capitation payment.

In order for this type of arrangement to work, a hospital must know that it will serve a clearly defined segment of a plan's enrollment, and that it can provide most or all of the necessary services to those members. In these cases, the primary care physician is clearly associated with just one hospital, or group of hospitals that are in a common network.

Hospitals and physicians may come together through physician–hospital organizations (PHOs) to accept a full capitation contract with a managed care plan. While that may be attractive to a plan, the PHO must be careful to understand how the proceeds of the capitation will be distributed. It is common for the two parties in a PHO to feel that the other party deserves less of the capitation than they are receiving, and disputes can arise.

Point-of-service (POS) plans with an out-of-network benefit make capitation methods difficult to use, since capitation in POS may mean having to pay twice for a service; once under capitation and again if the member seeks service outside of the network. In areas where there are no real alternatives to a specific hospital (e.g., a rural area, or an area in which a hospital enjoys a dominant market share), this problem may not be material. Capitation tied to the percentage of admissions to that hospital may also attenuate this problem.

The other issue of which to be aware in this arrangement is that some state insurance departments may consider full risk capitation unacceptable. It may be reasoned that if the health plan is not actually assuming the risk for services, then it is not really a health plan, but only a marketing organization. In such a case, there may be a question as to which party should hold the Certificate of Authority, or license to operate the health plan.

Penalties and Withholds

As with physician services, occasionally penalties or withholds are used in hospital reimbursement methods. Goals are set for average length of stay and average admission rate and part of the payment to the hospital may be withheld, or, conversely, the plan may set aside a bonus pool. If the goals are met or exceeded, the hospital receives its withhold or bonus, and vice versa. One complication inherent in this method is the possibility that a hospital can make its statistics look good by simply sending patients to other hospitals, similar to problems encountered with physician capitation. If a service area is clearly defined, or the hospital is capitated, then it may be easier to apply a risk or reward program.

Outpatient Care

The shift from inpatient to outpatient care has not gone unnoticed by hospital administrators. As care has shifted, so have charges. In some cases, outpatient charges exceed inpatient charges. Most managed care plans will require this to be negotiated so as not to lead to an unexpected increase in costs as utilization shifts to the outpatient format. The most common reimbursement methods are discounts, flat charges, case rates, and capitation.

Professional Reimbursement

While there are few basic ways of reimbursing physicians and other professionals, there are many variations on the methods of paying them. The three basic methods of paying physicians are salary, capitation, and fee-for-service. Withholds, penalties, and incentive compensation may be applied to any method.

Salary

Salary is the predominant method in closed panel plans, as well as some group practices or situations in which physicians are employees (e.g., full-time faculty, government-employed physicians, or some full-time hospital-based physicians). Withholds may be applied to the base salary, and incentive plans are common.

Capitation

Although fee-for-service remains the most common form of reimbursement, capitation continues to be a powerful and popular option for managed care. The use of capitation is generally confined to HMOs. Capitation is most easily applied to PCPs in HMOs (well over half of open panel HMOs capitate PCPs), but may be used for high volume specialties as well.

Capitation payments are fixed payments made on a PMPM basis, regardless of the use of services. Payments are most often adjusted based on the age and sex of the member, since there is some correlation between those factors and utilization. Rarely, capitation may be adjusted based on other factors such as geographic location.

An important element to calculating a capitated rate is the number (and demographics) of the members for whom the provider is receiving capitation. That is why PCPs easily may be capitated in a model in which the member must select a single PCP to provide and coordinate care. For specialists, there must be some mechanism to ensure that all of the members for whom capitation is being paid will not seek or receive services from a noncapitated provider (except under special circumstances).

Capitation paid directly to providers may be subject to a withhold. A withhold is a portion of the payment (e.g., 20 percent) held back by the plan to pay for any excessive utilization. Withholds currently are somewhat less common, as many managed care plans have adopted programs based primarily on incentives, rather than penalties.

Incentive payments are common in managed care plans, at least for PCPs. The incentive is most commonly tied to utilization, although incentives based on quality are becoming more common. The incentive is usually tied to a capitated pool of money that the plan applies against expenses in a defined category, such as referral or hospital costs. Money left in the pool at the end of the year is paid (in part or in whole) to the physicians, based on the utilization of the entire panel of physicians, or each physician.

Fee-for-Service

Fee-for-service remains a significant form of reimbursement in HMOs, and nearly the only form of reimbursement in PPOs, service plans, and indemnity plans. While somewhat less conducive to managed care than capitation, fee-for-service is not grossly antithetical to managed care. Even in HMOs that capitate PCPs, referral specialists are usually fee-for-service. In those managed care plans in which POS is heavily represented, capitation presents problems as noted earlier, thus leading many of those HMOs to reimburse even PCPs on a fee-for-service basis.

Nevertheless, fee-for-service, if not managed properly, or if used in a plan where the provider's first priority is to make money, can lead to increased costs when compared to capitation. Therefore it is common for HMOs that use fee-for-service to place fees at some risk. A withhold on a percentage of the fee is the most common mechanism. If utilization exceeds budget, the withhold is used to cover the overage; if utilization is below budget, the withhold is paid out. Another form of risk is reductions in fees if utilization gets too high. Some plans have experi-mented with global fees (to avoid upcoding and unbundling) with some success. Other plans have tried adjusting physician fees on an individual basis according to each physician's utilization patterns.

UTILIZATION MANAGEMENT

Total health care costs may be thought of simplistically as the result of only two variables: price times volume. The preceding section briefly described issues germane to price; this section will briefly discuss volume, i.e., utilization. The management of utilization may be broadly divided into three categories: prospective, or before the event occurs; concurrent, or while the event is occurring; and retrospective, or after the event has occurred.

Prospective

Prospective management of utilization applies to two major categories: referral services and institutional services.

Referral Services

Management of referral services is principally confined to HMOs, and to those HMOs that use a PCP to coordinate care (the gatekeeper model). In this model, all care from any professional other than that rendered by the PCP must be authorized by the member's PCP. The only physician the member may see without authorization is the PCP, although many plans make exceptions for obstetrics and gynecology for women, and occasionally for mental health and substance abuse services. This authorization requirement allows the PCP to determine if the problem may be treated by the PCP, and if a referral is required the PCP utilizes a specialist under contract to the plan. The authorization is rarely open-ended, but rather, for a limited number of visits (e.g., one to three) except in certain circumstances.

It is exceedingly rare for the plan to become involved in this process other than to capture the authorization data in order to process the claim properly. The PCP is excepted to exercise proper clinical judgment without the plan's intervention. The plan should provide periodic reports to the PCP with data regarding referral rates and costs, and reports regarding the PCP's capitation pool or withhold if that is appropriate.

Institutional Services

Prospective management of institutional services, both inpatient and outpatient, is a staple of managed care in all types of plans. The procedure is simple: someone calls the plan to request authorization for an elective admission or outpatient procedure, the plan checks it against clinical criteria, and authorizes (or denies, though that is unusual) the procedure and a set amount of inpatient days as appropriate.

Who calls the plan for authorization depends on the type of plan. For indemnity plans or the out-of-network benefits in PPOs and POS, the member must call or face an economic penalty. For HMOs and the in-network benefits in PPOs and POS, the responsibility is on the provider, who must bear the economic penalty for failure to comply.

Clinical criteria for authorization are commercially available, or plans may develop their own. Likewise, maximum allowable length of stay guidelines are commercially available, and plans may modify those guidelines to suit the local area. Most managed care plans are now using computerized programs to provide this information quickly and to capture pertinent data.

Concurrent

This topic applies to inpatient care and large-case management (i.e., the management of major catastrophic illnesses).

Inpatient Care

This refers to the plan monitoring an active inpatient case. Some plans, such as indemnity or service plans or PPOs, will perform this activity from a remote site via telephone. The plan's utilization management (UM) nurse will call the hospital to determine the status of the case. If the case is conforming to guidelines, no further action is taken. If the case is going to exceed the previously authorized days in the hospital, the UM nurse will collect clinical data and either authorize continued days or deny them. Many HMOs send their UM nurses on-site to the hospital. This allows the nurse to obtain more detailed and timely information, and to more actively help manage the case.

In the event that there is any ambiguity or disagreement during this process, the UM nurse refers the case to a physician working with or for the health plan (either the medical director or a physician advisor). This physician may call the attending physician to discuss the case, and may then make a determination regarding authorization for further payments.

Large Case Management

This area has some of the greatest cost savings potential of any activity in managed care. Large-case management refers to those catastrophic or chronic cases that exceed routine costs by several orders of magnitude, and in which active intervention by trained nurses at the plan can have a significant effect. Examples of such cases include Acquired Immune Deficiency Syndrome (AIDS), transplants, serious trauma, brittle diabetes, and so forth. The nurses at the plan are able to coordinate many aspects of care such as rehabilitation, home care, and health education in order to better manage the case.

Retrospective

This refers to managing utilization after the utilization has actually occurred. It falls into two broad categories: case review and pattern analysis.

Case Review

This refers to the review of individual cases to look for appropriateness of care, billing errors, or other problems associated with an individual case. In some cases, a plan may place a provider on regular review if there is some suspicion of regular improprieties.

Pattern Analysis

This refers to synthesizing significant amounts of utilization data in order to determine if patterns exist. These patterns may be provider specific, such as looking for over- or under-utilization, or they may be planwide, such as an unanticipated increase in cardiac testing costs. After a pattern has been identified, the reasons for it must be investigated so that action may be taken if required.

Managed care plans are attempting to provide greater retrospective data to the providers in the network in order to allow the providers to compare themselves to their peers, and to modify their own practice patterns as appropriate. This form of feedback promises to be a useful adjunct in helping to control health care costs.

QUALITY MANAGEMENT

Managed care plans vary on the basis of model type in their approach to medical quality management. Indemnity and service plans, and even PPOs, generally are less aggressive in managing quality than are HMOs, although like all generalizations there are notable exceptions. As in UM, as model types progress through the continuum discussed earlier, greater attention is paid to the subject, and more resources are expended in managing quality. Almost all plans begin the quality management process through credentialing of the participating providers. In addition to credentialing, two general approaches to quality management exist, often in conjunction with each other: classic quality management, and new approaches such as total quality management (TQM) or continuous quality improvement (CQI). This section will provide a brief description of these approaches.

Credentialing

Credentialing refers to the activity of collating and reviewing the professional credentials of the participating providers. For hospitals and institutions, this generally is confined to accepting the accreditation of the Joint Commission on Accreditation of Healthcare Organizations (Joint Commission). For professionals, the plan does its own credentialing. Exhibit 34–2 pro-

vides an example of data elements that an HMO may require in a credentials review. HMOs, like hospitals, may also query the National Practitioner Data Bank.

Plans usually recredential every two years; basic data are reconfirmed, copies of current licenses and insurance face sheets are obtained, and changes are updated. Plans may also add data regarding member satisfaction, quality management, and administrative activities to the credentialing database.

Classic Quality Management

The classic approach to managing quality is based on the works of Avedis Donabedian of Ann Arbor, Michigan. The three key elements of this approach are structure, process, and outcome.

Structure

Structure looks at the infrastructure of the plan as it relates to quality. Examples include the makeup of the medical record (e.g., presence of a drug allergies list, laboratory notes, and so forth); immunization records; access to care (e.g., how long it takes to get routine and urgent appointments); waiting times in the office; and telephone responsiveness. Structure studies are usually done through on-site review by the plan's quality management nurses. A special form of structure study relates to the effect of the utilization system on access to care, where the plan performs studies to ensure that utilization is not inappropriately low, and that the authorization system is not forming a barrier to necessary care.

Process

Process refers to how care is actually rendered. One common method is through medical care evaluations (MCEs), in which plan nurses review a sample of outpatient medical records against practice parameters established by the quality management committee; these practice parameters are often specific to a particular disease or procedure. Degrees of compliance are

Exhibit 34–2 Basic Elements of Credentialing

1. Training (copy of certificates)
   - Location of training
   - Type of training
2. Specialty board eligibility or certification (copy of certificate)
3. Current state medical license (copy of certificate)
   - Restrictions
   - History of loss of license in any state
4. Drug Enforcement Agency (DEA) number (copy of certificate)
5. Hospital privileges
   - Name of hospitals
   - Scope of practice privileges
6. Malpractice insurance
   - Carrier name
   - Currency of coverage (copy of face sheet)
   - Scope of coverage (financial limits and procedures covered)
7. Malpractice history
   - Pending claims
   - Successful claims against the physician, either judged or settled
8. National Practitioner Data Bank status
9. Medicare, Medicaid, and federal tax ID numbers
10. Social Security number
11. Location and telephone numbers of all offices
12. Hours of operation
13. Yes/no questions regarding:
    - Limitations or suspensions of privileges
    - Suspension from government programs
    - Suspension or restriction of DEA license
    - Malpractice cancellation
    - Felony conviction
    - Drug or alcohol abuse
    - Chronic or debilitating illnesses
14. Provisions for emergency care and backup
15. Use of nonphysicians (i.e., midlevel) practitioners
16. In-office surgery capabilities
17. In-office testing capabilities
18. Areas of special medical interest
19. Record of continuing medical education

measured and reported back to the providers as well as to the plan. Similar reviews of inpatient care are also common.

Outcome

Outcome refers to the result of the care that is rendered. Plans generally look at outcome from two perspectives: planwide and adverse events. Adverse events refer to negative outcomes that could have been prevented, such as a hospital-acquired infection. Planwide outcomes refer to whether or not the medical care is beneficial; for example, successful treatment of designated conditions in outpatient care (e.g., control of hypertension without preventable side effects); good outcomes from hospitalized cases; and so forth. A special form of outcome is member satisfaction; the plan will regularly survey members, analyze complaints, and so forth to determine overall satisfaction levels and to act on identified problems.

Managed care has adopted many of the tenets of the recent approach to industrial quality improvement, often referred to as TQM or CQI.

These approaches lend themselves more to closed panel plans than to open panels or PPOs when applied to clinical care, but all types of plans can benefit from these techniques as applied to business practices.

OTHER OPERATIONAL ASPECTS OF MANAGED CARE

Managed care plans are fully operating companies that combine both the operational activities of medical management with those of an insurance company. Exhibit 34–3 provides a listing of some of these activities, and Exhibit 34–4 provides a listing of common management positions in a managed care plan.

MANAGEMENT AND FINANCIAL CRITERIA

Although the primary business of managed care is the financing and delivery of health care services, managed care plans cannot escape a reliance on ratios and financial criteria, similar to any business. These are used to calculate pre-

Exhibit 34–3 Other Operational Activities of a Managed Care Plan

1. Claims
   - Efficiency
   - Throughput
   - Accuracy
   - Timeliness
   - Link to authorization system
   - Review process for pended claims
   - Explanation of benefits statements
2. Management information systems (MIS)—computer and data support
   - Hardware
   - Software
   - Report generation
     - Medical utilization
     - Operational
     - Ad hoc versus routine
   - Support for reimbursement and utilization policies
3. Membership and billing
   - Enrollment and disenrollment processing
   - Eligibility checking
   - Evidence of coverage
   - Timely and accurate billing and reconciliations
4. Finance
5. Underwriting and pricing
6. Marketing
7. General administration
   - Coordination of all activities
   - Regulatory relations
   - Member services
   - Negotiations
   - Strategic planning
   - Office management
   - Public relations

mium rates, track expenses, track medical utilization, and to generally manage the business. The insurance industry, and the managed care industry in particular, use certain formats to track both cost and utilization, in addition to the more common methods such as net income, and return on investment. A few of these formats are described as follows.

Per Member Per Month (PMPM)

PMPM is an exceedingly common unit of measure. It refers to the number of "things" per applicable enrolled member (subscriber and dependents) per month. The things may be dollars, or units of utilization such as visits (although other measures of utilization are more common). Cost PMPM is the most common use of this unit of measure. For example, if the plan has 50,000 members and is spending $600,000 per month on primary care services, then the cost is $12.00 PMPM.

While cost is generally applied over all enrolled members, plans may restrict the measurement to only members to whom the measure applies. As an example, general medical costs for primary care services would apply to all members in the plan, while pharmacy services may

only apply to 75 percent of enrolled members. In that case, the plan would report PMPM pharmacy costs using only those members who had the benefits, otherwise a misleadingly low PMPM cost would be reported.

Per Member Per Year

Similar in concept to PMPM, per member per year (PMPY) simply uses a full 12 months rather than a single month. This measure is used not only for measuring dollar costs, but often for measuring utilization as well. For example, pharmacy costs may be reported as averaging 5.2 prescriptions PMPY, at a cost of $9.04 PMPM; simple arithmetic also yields two other common measures: $108.24 PMPY and $20.81 per prescription (this plan needs a pharmacy director!).

Per Thousand Members Per Year

This unit of measure applies almost solely to utilization. It is used to track units of utilization on an annualized basis. The most common example is bed days per thousand, per members per year, usually referred to simply as bed days per thousand (and often abbreviated as BD/K). This is the total number of days as hospital inpa-

Exhibit 34–4 Key Management Positions

1. Chief executive officer, executive director, or plan manager
2. Chief financial officer
3. Medical director
4. Other management positions critical for success:
   - Claims manager
   - Customer services manager
   - UM manager
   - Quality management manager
   - Data and systems manager
   - Provider relations manager
5. Other management positions required depending on plan configuration
   - Marketing director
   - Legal support
   - Facilities manager
   - Manager of medical support staff

tients used by an average 1,000 members in a year. For example, a typical HMO might report 300 bed days per thousand, meaning that for every 1,000 members in the HMO, 300 inpatient days will be incurred. Since most plans calculate this number every month, a formula must be applied to take 1 month's data and annualize it, both for the single month and for the month to date.

Related to bed days per thousand are admissions per thousand. For example, a typical HMO might incur 78 admissions per thousand. If that same plan also reports 300 bed days per thousand, that means the average length of stay is 3.8 days. Another example of this format includes outpatient visits per thousand, surgical procedures per thousand, and so forth.

Other Measurements

Financial measurements not only track utilization costs as described, as well as direct costs such as the cost of administration, but must also track costs for which no complete record yet exists. The reason for this is that a risk-bearing plan must accrue a liability each month for medical costs, even when the claims have not yet been submitted. These costs are referred to as Incurred But Not Reported (IBNR) costs. If a plan fails to accrue such expenses, it will seriously underestimate the true cost of health care, and not have enough money to pay claims. This quickly can lead to the fiscal demise of a plan. Calculating IBNRs is complex, and is a function of historical experience and assumptions based on actuarial information.

CONCLUSION

Managed care is in a rapidly evolving state, as is the health care system in the United States. Managed care, as broadly described in this chapter, is subject to the economic, regulatory, and creative forces that led to its creation. However, above all else, it is possible, through the intelligent application of management, to provide good access and high quality at an acceptable cost. This is the goal of managed health care.

SUGGESTED READINGS

Couch, J.B. 1991. *Health care quality management for the 21st century*. Tampa, Fla.: The American College of Physician Executives.

Donabedian, A. 1982. *Explorations in quality assessment and monitoring*. 3 vols. Ann Arbor, Mich.: Health Administration Press.

Doyle, R.L. 1990. *Healthcare management guidelines*. 3 vols. Milliman & Robertson, Inc.

Eisenberg, J.M. 1986. *Doctor's decisions and the cost of medical care*. Ann Arbor, Mich.: Health Administration Press.

Goldfield, N. et al. 1991. *Measuring and managing health care quality: Procedures, techniques, and protocols*. Gaithersburg, Md.: Aspen Publishers, Inc.

Kongstvedt, P.R. 1993. *The managed health care handbook*. 2nd ed. Gaithersburg, Md.: Aspen Publishers, Inc.

Pauly, M. et al. 1992. *Paying physicians: Options for controlling cost, volume, and intensity of services*. Ann Arbor, Mich.: Health Administration Press.

PETER R. KONGSTVEDT, MD, FACP, is a Partner at Ernst & Young in Washington, DC. He was previously Executive Vice President at Blue Cross and Blue Shield of the National Capital Area (BCBSNCA), a health plan in Washington, DC, with over 1,000,000 members, and was responsible for all operational aspects of the company. He was also responsible for overseeing the strategic development and implementation of managed care systems for BCBSNCA. Dr. Kongstvedt was also Executive Vice Chairman of CapitalCare, Inc., a 120,000-member IPA-model HMO and wholly owned subsidiary of BCBSNCA.

Dr. Kongstvedt has extensive experience in managed care. He has served primarily in operational and leadership roles, and has also worked as a consultant in managed care for a national consulting firm. In addition, Dr. Kongstvedt has served on a number of state and national level health care policy and strategy committees.

Chapter 35

International Health Care: A Comparison of the U.S., Canada, and Western Europe

Grant T. Savage and Elizabeth W. Michael

Changing the U.S. health care system is high on the national agenda of the 1990s. Underlying this agenda are concerns about the increasing number—more than 37 million—of uninsured Americans;[1] the rising portion of the U.S. gross domestic product—over 14 percent—devoted to health care;[2,3] and the public,[4] small business,[5] and legislative[6] dissatisfaction with health care costs and perceived benefits. These concerns reflect well-established trends that have been tracked by U.S. and international researchers and policy analysts during the past decade.[7] Hence, it is not surprising that the past several years have seen health care researchers and policy makers engaged in extended debates about the direction health care system reform should take in this country. Indeed, two leading health care journals—*Frontiers of Health Services Management* and *Health Affairs*—recently have devoted several issues to discussing various agendas for reform.[8,9,10,11] Proposed legislation ranges from national health care insurance subsidized by the federal government to minor changes in the present system, including caps on malpractice suits. Although a consensus has not clearly emerged from these debates, it is clear that the United States is moving away from the

1980s reliance on market competition to contain costs toward some additional form of governmental regulation in the 1990s.

This shift toward greater governmental regulation also reflects a shift in the values that are envisioned for a reformed U.S. health care system.[12] Equality of access to, and cost-effective coverage for, health care are perhaps the predominant values driving most ethical and political arguments for changing our health care system. Because of the U.S. system's shortcomings, researchers have been looking toward the health care systems in Canada[13,14,15,16] and in Western Europe[17,18,19,20] for solutions to providing health care in hospitals, in outpatient clinics, and in other ambulatory settings.

So that comparisons with the United States can be focused on countries with similar health care problems and socioeconomic conditions, Canada and seven western European countries are discussed in this chapter. Not only the United States, but also these industrialized countries, have considered, or are considering, the reform of health care delivery. These concerns are driven by the key issues of access, cost, and quality. As shown in Table 35–1, these national health care systems can be characterized and

Table 35–1 Selected Western European and North American Health Care Systems: Access, Cost, and Quality in 1991

	Access	Cost	Quality	
	Degree and Form of Coverage	Percentage of GDP	Life Expectancy at Birth	
Canada	Universal access via a centralized, single-payor system	10.0% 1.4 Δ avg	73.8 years 0.7 Δ avg	80.4 years 1.5 Δ avg
Denmark	Universal rights via a decentralized, single-payor system	6.5 −2.1 Δ avg	72.0 −1.1 Δ avg	77.7 −1.2 Δ avg
Finland	Universal rights via a decentralized, single-payor system	8.9 0.3 Δ avg	72.7 −0.4 Δ avg	78.9 0.0 Δ avg
Germany	Universal access within a two-tier system of compulsory insurance (90%) and private insurance	8.5 −0.1 Δ avg	72.6 −0.7 Δ avg	79.0 0.2 Δ avg
Netherlands	Universal access within a two-tier system of compulsory insurance (60%) and private insurance	8.3 −0.3 Δ avg	73.8 0.7 Δ avg	80.1 1.2 Δ avg
Norway	Universal rights via a decentralized, single-payor system, with minimal fee-for-service	7.6 −1.0 Δ avg	73.4 −0.7 Δ avg	76.9 −0.2 Δ avg
Sweden	Universal rights via a decentralized, single-payor system, with private insurance permitted	8.6 0.0 Δ avg	74.8 1.7 Δ avg	80.4 1.5 Δ avg
United Kingdom	Universal rights within a two-tier system of National Health Service and private insurance	6.6 −2.0 Δ avg	73.0 −0.1 Δ avg	78.5 −0.4 Δ avg
United States	Variable access within a multipayor system of private insurance (70%) and Medicare/Medicaid	13.2 4.6 Δ avg 8.6% Average % of GDP	72.6 −0.5 Δ avg 73.1 (male) Average Life Expectancy	78.8 −0.1 Δ avg 78.9 (female)

Source: Adapted from G.J. Schieber et al., Health Spending, Delivery, and Outcomes in OECB Countries, *Health Affairs*, Vol. 12, No. 4, pp. 120, 128, with permission of Project Hope, © 1993.

evaluated in terms of who may be treated, for how much money, and with what expected outcome.

Every system of health care must deal with trade-offs among these issues. For example, an emphasis on limiting costs influences both patient access and the quality of care. Underlying these trade-offs among these issues are three factors: the organization, financing, and outcomes from the provision of health care.

THE ORGANIZATION AND FINANCING OF HEALTH CARE

Consider how health care systems may be organized and financed. Table 35–1 indicates that national health care systems vary from highly centralized to highly decentralized. In Table 35–2, each country is ranked according to the degree of centralization. The centralized end is anchored by Canada's public health insurance plan and by the United Kingdom's National Health Service, while the decentralized end is anchored by the United States's mixture of fee-for-service, managed care, Medicare/Medicaid, Veterans Hospital Administration, and charity care. Following Abel-Smith's distinctions, Table 35–2 breaks out two aspects of this continuum, the direct versus indirect provision of health services by various national governments.[21] Direct financing of health services occurs if the main health insurer or government—whether national, regional, or local—owns health care facilities and employs health care professionals. Indirect financing, in contrast, occurs if the main insurer or government contracts for the provision of various health services. Because Medicare/Medicaid is funded by public health insurance in the United States, it is included under the indirect provision of health services. However, most of the health services provided in the United States are funded via private insurance and are not captured in Table 35–2.

Significantly, how national health care systems are organized and financed may have a large impact on access, cost, and quality. The decentralized nature of, as well as the mixture of social insurance and voluntary insurance within, the U.S. system effectively limits access to preventive and primary forms of health care[22] to anywhere from 35 to 60 million U.S. citizens at any given time.[23,24] Moreover, this restricted access raises the cost of health care because people without health insurance must be very ill before they can obtain treatment and often require more extensive and expensive interventions than if they had received preventive or timely primary care. Understandably, with increased morbidity also comes the problem of poorer outcomes; hence, the United States fares poorly on several measures of the quality of health care, especially infant mortality.[25]

In contrast, centralized health care systems such as the National Health Service (NHS) in the United Kingdom provide preventive and primary health care to every citizen. Nonetheless, such access within the NHS does not come without rationing and limiting the public's access to secondary and tertiary health care. And, as noted above, the current U.S. system of health care does provide the underfunded and indigent with access to secondary and tertiary care if they face life-threatening emergencies. Starfield argues that these limitations on access are a function of the way the United States and other nations finance the delivery of health care.[26] Specifically, she argues that financial access, at least to primary care, is the greatest in countries with national health services (e.g., the United Kingdom), is moderately high in countries having compulsory national insurance (e.g., Canada), is moderate in countries with mixtures of compulsory national and private insurance (e.g., Germany), and is low in countries relying primarily on voluntary insurance (e.g., the United States).

THE OUTCOMES ASSOCIATED WITH VARIOUS HEALTH CARE SYSTEMS

Across the national health care systems discussed in this chapter, there is a good amount of variance in terms of the outcomes from, and the money spent on, health care. Figure 35–1 shows both the level of gross domestic product (GDP) and the total amount of money devoted to health care by the United States, Canada, and seven European countries during 1991. As can be clearly seen, the United States spends much more than any other country on health care. Indeed, Schieber et al. argue that even when taking the influence of per capita GDP on health expenditures—i.e., wealthy nations typically spend more on health than poor nations—the United States spends far more than other nations of comparable wealth.[27]

Although the total cost of health care in the United States and other industrialized countries is certainly a focus of many reform efforts here and abroad, much of the focus of these efforts in the United States is on obtaining greater value for the money spent. While ideally one would like to compare national health care systems on the basis of clinical outcomes and quality of life and use some form of cost-benefit analysis to

Table 35–2 The Organization of Selected Western European and North American Health Care Systems in 1991

	Form of Coverage	Degree of Centralization	Provision of Services — Direct	Provision of Services — vs. Indirect
Canada	Universal access via a centralized, single-payor system of public health insurance	High	Community services and municipal/county (29%) and Provincial (14%) hospitals	All other health services; voluntary (46%) and religious hospitals (11%)
Denmark	Universal rights via a decentralized, single-payor system	Medium-High	Hospitals	GPs, specialists outside hospital, pharmacies, most dentists, and physiotherapists
Finland	Universal rights via a decentralized, single-payor system	Medium-High	Primary health centers, hospitals, doctors, and nurses	
Germany	Universal access within a two-tier system of compulsory insurance (90%) and private insurance	Medium-Low	—	All health services
Netherlands	Universal access within a two-tier system of compulsory insurance (60%) and private insurance	Medium-Low	—	All health services
Norway	Universal rights via a decentralized, single-payor system, with minimal fee-for-service	Medium-High	Public hospitals Specialists Public health nurses	Private hospitals
Sweden	Universal rights via a decentralized, single-payor system, with private insurance permitted	Medium-High	Public hospitals, health centers, clinics and nursing homes; doctors and dentists	Private hospitals and some doctors
United Kingdom	Universal rights within a two-tier system of National Health Service and private insurance	High	Hospitals and community services	GPs, pharmacies, most dentists, and opticians
United States	Variable access within a multipayor system of private insurance (70%) and Medicare/Medicaid	Low	Veterans Hospital Administration and some public health clinics	Medicare/Medicaid accepting hospitals (low income and elderly patients only)

Source: Adapted from B. Abel-Smith, Cost Containment and New Priorities in the European Community, *The Milbank Quarterly* Vol. 70, No. 3, pp. 393–416, with permission of the Milbank Memorial Fund, © 1992.

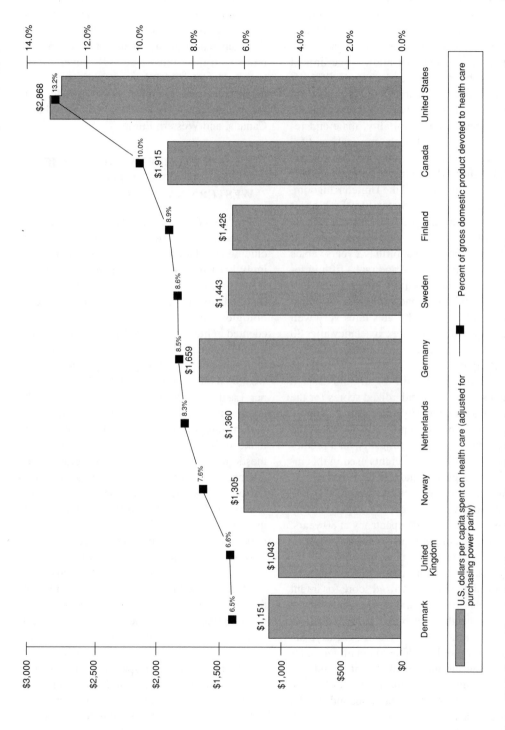

Figure 35–1 Selected International Comparisons of per Capita Expenditures and Gross Domestic Product Devoted to Health Care in 1991. *Source:* Reprinted from G.J. Schieber et al., Health Spending, Delivery, and Outcomes in OECD Countries, *Health Affairs* Vol. 12, No. 2, pp. 121–122, with permission of Project Hope, © 1993.

rank the system on these outcomes, national data for such comparisons are simply not available within the United States or elsewhere. What is available across industrialized nations are gross demographic statistics that allow some limited inferences about the outcomes from different health care systems. Figure 35–2 shows how the United States fares on five well-known health care outcomes—infant mortality, male and female life expectancy at birth, and male and female life expectancy at 80 years—in comparison with eight other industrialized countries, including Canada, Germany, and the United Kingdom.

Note that the United States has the highest rate of infant mortality per 1,000 births (9.1 versus a low of 5.6 in Finland), is tied second to last for male life expectancy at birth (72 years versus a high of 74.8 in Sweden), and ranks fifth in female life expectancy at birth (78.8 years versus a high of 80.4 in both Canada and Sweden). On a brighter note, the United States fares very well on both male and female life expectancy after 80 years, ranking first and second in these categories, respectively.

The outcome index in Figure 35–2 is a weighted sum of the standardized scores for the five outcomes previously discussed. Arguably, placing weights on the importance of each of the five outcomes is difficult to justify on a predictive basis. However, the weights used in this index reflect the general judgment of various experts such as Starfield, putting a weight of 2.5 on infant mortality, of 1.0 on life expectancy at birth, and of 0.25 on life expectancy at 80 years. Specifically, the algorithm for the outcome index sums the weighted, standardized scores for life expectancy and then subtracts from this subtotal the weighted, standardized score for infant mortality. Based on this index, the United States is ranked seventh, with only the United Kingdom and Germany faring worse. Clearly, the United States should be able to obtain far better value for the amount of money it spends on health care. Given that countries such as Canada and Sweden—ranked first and second on the outcome index—spend much less than the United States, but obtain much better health care

outcomes, some lessons might be learned from examining their health care systems, as well as those systems such as the United Kingdom and Germany that arguably obtain better cost-benefit ratios than the United States. However, before turning to an in-depth examination of these health care systems, it is important to understand the common problems facing the United States, Canada, and Western Europe.

COMMON PROBLEMS FACING THE UNITED STATES AND OTHER WESTERN NATIONS

The United States and other highly industrialized countries face some common problems, including populations that are and will be increasingly burdened with elderly people who suffer from chronic diseases. At the same time, Western medicine and science have developed technologies for extending life that are unprecedented in human history. This technical ability, however, is a double-edged sword: Medical technologies are costly and, even in very wealthy nations, much be rationed in some manner. Lastly, with the passing of the Cold War, the economies of the Western world, especially within Europe and North America, have had to make difficult realignments, both in terms of domestic industries and in terms of regional trade alliances. As a result, many of the countries discussed in this chapter have been or are facing severe budgetary difficulties sustaining the growth in health care expenditures that their elderly populations have come to expect.

Interestingly, many of the countries that will be examined have addressed the problems previously mentioned by resorting to one or more of three common solutions: cost containment, managed competition, and decentralization. Ironically, all but the third solution has also been touted in the United States. Hence, it should be enlightening to see what specific problems other comparable nations face and how well their health care systems handle these problems.

In the sections that follow, the health care systems in five countries will be examined—in-

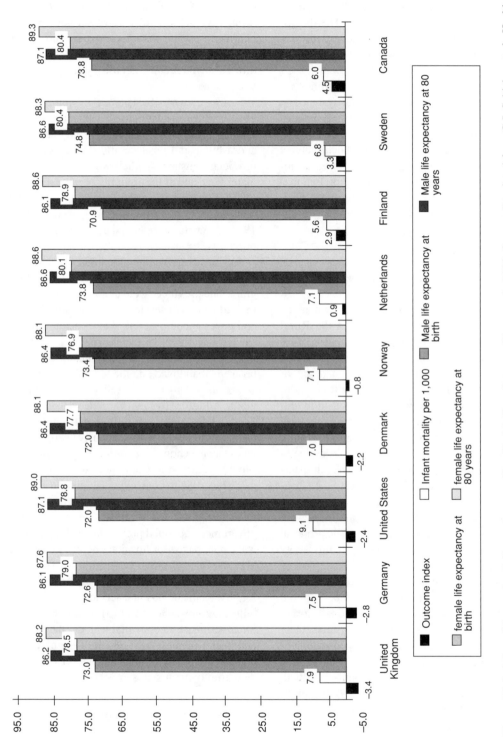

Figure 35–2 Selected International Comparisons on Five Health Care Outcome Measures in 1990. *Source:* Reprinted from G.J. Schieber et al., Health Spending, Delivery, and Outcomes in OECD Countries, *Health Affairs* Vol. 12, No. 2, p. 128, with permission of Project Hope, © 1993.

cluding Canada, Germany, the Netherlands, Sweden, and the United Kingdom. The discussion of each country's health care system provides background information about how the present system evolved, analyzes the system's structure and financing, and then examines the particular problems confronting the system and the steps being taken to address those problems. In addition, because each of the national health care systems is complex enough to be the subject for an extended monograph, this chapter addresses this complexity by focusing on two major aspects of any health care system: the management of hospitals and physicians.

HEALTH CARE IN CANADA

Background about the Canadian Health Act

Beginning as far back as 1909—when the province of Saskatchewan enacted the Rural Municipalities Act, leading to the creation of local medical care insurance schemes—providing medical care to its citizens has been of major concern for Canada.[28,29] Various initiatives to provide medical care were instituted individually by some of the provinces, but it was not until 1943, after examining about 40 plans from other countries, that proposals to provide federal subsidies to provincially administered health insurance programs were first presented to the Canadian House of Commons.[30] Despite much discussion and endorsement, the provinces were unable to reach agreement on a specific proposal and several provinces proceeded with university hospital insurance on their own.[31]

By the 1950s, provinces that provided insurance were being compared to provinces without such plans, as well as to early regionally organized capitation plans in the United States. Only the three provinces that had developed state-supported plans were judged to be adequately supplying medical care to their residents, and with costs comparable to—or less than—those provinces without such systems.[32] Moreover, during the 1950s, Canadian leaders and physicians began to actively support the premise that there should be reasonable access to quality health

care for all Canadians independent of financial means. By 1959, a fully universal government-operated hospital insurance system, providing 50 percent federal funding for provincial expenditures on medically necessary hospital care, was in place.[33,34]

However, when Saskatchewan implemented government-run insurance for physicians' services in 1962, physicians were strongly opposed and a bitter and unsuccessful 23-day strike by physicians ensued. As their worst fears failed to materialize and as they quickly became the highest-paid physicians in the country, professional opposition to the program decreased, and by 1971, all territories operated physician insurance programs.[35,36]

As Canada moved into the highly inflationary 1970s, problems began to develop with the program. The provinces were unable to control their individual health services priorities and the federal government lost control of its health budget, since it was forced to match whatever the provinces spent.[37] During 1977, the matching formulas were abandoned and the federal contribution was changed to an indexed per capita block grant. Additionally, the Extended Health Care Services Program was initiated to entice the provinces to develop less expensive support services, such as home and ambulatory health care. Most recently, the Canadian Health Act was passed in 1984 to consolidate all the earlier laws that authorized federal subsidies to the various insurance plans. As a result, there is a single, government-operated provincial health plan that is the sole payor for hospital and physician care in each of the 12 provinces/territories. The 1984 Health Act also eliminated (1) all user charges for physician and hospital services, (2) any extra billing by physicians, and (3) private insurance for covering services available under the provincial health plans; moreover, the Health Act increased eligibility to all residents regardless of their employment status.[38,39,40]

System Structure and Financing

Although all of the 12 provinces/territories have separate plans, the major differences among them involve the fee schedules used for physician payment and which additional services are covered. For example, six provinces offer dental services for children under age 16 (one is for low-income children only), and most offer some prescription drug benefit and reimbursement for physiotherapy services. User charges and co-payments are allowed for these types of added benefits, and supplemental private insurance (most often offered as an employee benefit) may be used for necessary services not covered by public plans. As a result, about 26 percent of Canada's total health expenditures are in the private sector, but it has not been determined how much private spending is insured and how much is paid out of pocket.[41]

The federal and provincial portions of health expenditures are paid for through taxes on personal and corporate incomes at both levels, as well as through payroll taxes, nonfederal sales and property taxes, and federal customs and excise taxes, which include a 13 percent national sales tax on (primarily) manufactured goods.[42] Hospitals account for a little over 39 percent of total health expenditures, and virtually all hospitals participate in the public insurance program.[43] Ninety-five percent of hospitals receive all their funding from provincial health plans and are called public hospitals; 57 percent of these hospitals are actually owned by voluntary organizations or religious orders. Only 5 percent of Canadian hospitals are private—the majority of them provide long-term care—and do not participate in the public insurance program.[44,45]

Participating hospitals must negotiate annually with the provincial health ministry to determine total operating budget (global budget), taking into account factors such as government determined bed/population and staff/patient ratios.[46,47] Periodic lump-sum payments are made, and hospital administrators, therefore, can be relatively flexible in deciding how to allocate resources. While provincial authorities were relatively generous in covering hospital deficits during the 1970s, recently they have been refusing to finance budget overruns.[48]

The authority to approve capital expansions and major renovations or acquisitions also rests with the provincial authorities, even should the necessary capital be raised by an institution. As a result, health care technology does not proliferate as extensively or as rapidly as it does in countries like the United States.[49,50,51] Moreover, with two exceptions, patients have the freedom to select their own physicians, and physicians are paid on a fee-for-service basis according to fee schedules negotiated periodically between provincial authorities and medical associations. First, a few medical group practices are paid by capitation. Second, some physicians do not participate in the insurance system at all, but nonparticipating physicians account for less than 1 percent of physicians nationwide.[52] Patients may pay privately for treatment if they wish, but physicians (and hospitals) are prohibited from treating both patients whose care is paid for under provincial plans *and* patients who pay out-of-pocket for their care.[53,54]

Community health centers (CHCs) and health services organizations (HSOs) are present in large numbers only in Ontario and Quebec, but such alternative arrangements are expected to increase in number as provinces try to deal effectively with health cost escalation. On one hand, CHCs are locally initiated and administered by a board of directors drawn from the communities they serve. The centers are intended to provide health care access for groups of people who have been identified as underserved, but also they may provide preventive and social services such as nutritional counseling, day care, and literacy programs. HSOs, on the other hand, are run by groups of physicians who have agreed to capitated arrangements with the provincial health plan. Similar to health maintenance organizations in the United States, HSOs provide only medical care and receive a monthly capitation payment for each patient who has signed with the organization, regardless of whether care has been requested. However, patients are under no obligation to utilize only those physicians belonging to the HSO; should they seek care elsewhere, the HSO loses the payment for that month.[55]

Physicians have an influential voice in health policy making, there is little questioning of clinical judgment, and they have the highest incomes among professional groups in Canada.[56] Recently, some provinces have begun experimenting with systems to reduce physician fees in subsequent years if there are excess increases in utilization in the monitored year, but only Quebec has gone so far as to set a yearly maximum amount payable for individual general practitioners (the majority of Canadian physicians are family or general practitioners).[57,58,59] Physician supply per capita in Canada is about the same as in the United States—210 versus 212 civilian physicians per 100,000 population—but the far north, other rural areas, and low-income, industrialized urban areas remain underserved, despite government attempts to increase physician supply.[60,61,62]

Present Problems and Reform Efforts

Despite the recent attention the Canadian health care system has received from countries interested in health care reform—most notably the United States[63,64,65,66]—the system is not without its problems. A number of researchers note that most of the current problems stem from what is often referred to as a basic policy conflict inherent in the system.[67,68,69,70,71] That is, while the federal and provincial governments remain adamant in their commitment to (1) public and universal funding of health care, (2) professional autonomy for physicians, (3) first-dollar coverage (no deductibles) and physician choice for citizens, and (4) budget control by provinces, each of these objectives cannot be met without having an impact on the others. For example, public funding requires public administration, which necessitates some loss of autonomy for physicians; at the same time, budgetary controls may require some modifications to both universal funding and first-dollar coverage for citizens. This latter point has taken on increasing urgency since, during the past few years, the federal government has decreased its support of the provincial health plans to try and cope with a large national budget deficit. Yet even within this recessionary economy, both patients and health care practitioners are demanding better access to

new medical technologies and remain generally opposed to higher taxes. Finally, the supply of physicians has increased faster than the population for every year since 1965, yet no definitive policy to control and direct this supply has been developed at either the federal or provincial level.[72,73,74]

Since the onus is on the provinces to control their budgets and national funding to support those budgets is diminishing, the provinces themselves have taken the lead in designing and implementing various experiments in cost containment. Several of these initiatives were mentioned earlier: caps on physician salaries and reduced fee payments following overutilization; CHCs; HSOs; and home health care. Other innovations, mentioned by various researchers, include: [75,76,77,78,79,80]

- increasing use of alternative providers such as physicians' assistants, nurse practitioners, and nurse midwives both to service those areas underserved by physicians—such as rural and low-income urban areas—and to aid and supplement physicians in HSOs and in home births

- closing hospital beds temporarily

- contracting with hospitals in some U.S. cities to provide patient care for certain conditions (mainly coronary bypass surgery and lithotripsy)

- promoting programs that emphasize prevention of disease and injury

- more strictly monitoring physician resource allocations, focusing mainly on patients receiving unnecessary treatments and procedures

- creating blue-ribbon working groups to seek solutions to identified problems

- subsidizing two years of intensive training for aspiring dental nurses who provide complete dental care to schoolchildren, countering the shortage of dentists

- providing incentives for using generic drugs

In spite of present difficulties, the Canadian health care system remains one of the most admired systems both at home—provincial health insurance plans are recognized as the country's most popular institutions—and in the world.[81,82,83,84,85] Indeed, a 1989 survey in *Health Management Quarterly* reported that when presented with descriptions of health care systems in the United States, Great Britain, and Canada, 61 percent of U.S. citizens surveyed said they preferred the Canadian system.[86]

Undoubtedly, the Canadian system will continue to change and evolve as medical knowledge and technology changes and as the world's and Canada's economy changes, but whether Canada will choose to turn, as other socialized health schemes have, to a pluralistic system with multiple-source funding, is unclear.[87,88] While there are proponents of private investment, especially among Canada's medical associations, both the provincial and federal governments seem content, for the moment at least, with developing innovative ways to constrain medical expenditures within the framework of the present system.

HEALTH CARE IN SWEDEN

Background on the Medical Care Act of 1982

In 1975, faced with growing concerns about rising costs, fragmented yet ever-increasing demands for care, and an inflexible, centralized system, the Swedish cabinet appointed a Commission of Inquiry to develop new legislation for medical care.[89] The commission was directed to specify overall goals and criteria for all aspects of health and sickness care under the guiding principle that everyone living in the country has an equal right to such care. The commission's recommendations were reviewed by the Parliament in 1981, and the legislation took effect in 1982. This act set general guidelines and parameters for the organization of medical care following four basic tenets:

1. Equality of care and the promotion of good health would be priorities.
2. Counties would have *total* responsibility and accountability for medical care.

3. Physicians were to direct all medical activity and delegate responsibility to others as much as possible.
4. The national government would be responsible for setting regulations to protect individuals and stating conditions for employment in medical care settings.

In accord with Swedish culture, details concerning planning and implementation were left to the county councils and local authorities.[90]

System Structure and Financing

Health services in Sweden are predominantly financed and produced within the public sector—90.6 percent to total health expenditures in 1987.[91] These health care expenditures are financed through a combination of taxes levied by the central government (6.5 percent) and county councils (65 percent), by health insurance drawn from the national social insurance fund's payroll tax (19 percent), and by consumer's out-of-pocket payments (9.5 percent).[92] General revenue at the national level is raised through progressive personal and corporate income taxes and by a 24 percent value-added tax. County council revenues are derived predominantly from a fixed percentage collected from the personal income earned by residents. (However, the national government limited the combined total of county and municipal taxes to 30 percent of earned income for the 1990–1991 tax years.) General social insurance taxes are paid by employers for each employee and part of this money goes to social health insurance funds, which finance ambulatory care—medical and dental—and prescriptions, and also reimburse patients for lost income due to illness (65 percent of social health insurance). In 1987, total social insurance, including pensions, amounted to about 46 percent of an employee's salary.[93,94]

Publicly operated health centers, together with maternity and child clinics, public dental facilities, and local nursing homes, provide primary care under the auspices of 26 county council/municipal provider agencies. Hospitals—with the exception of Sweden's two privately operated inpatient institutions—are financed through prospective annual budgets, which are set by their respective county councils, and all medical staff and support personnel are paid on a salaried basis. Payment to the private hospitals is tied to an initial bid to the county for a guaranteed number of procedures, and reimbursement is on a per episode basis.[95]

The majority of physicians in Sweden are publicly employed in primary-care or hospital settings and are paid on a 100 percent salary basis.[96] The small number who are privately employed or are in private or group practice—11 percent in 1985—are paid via their specific contracts with private- or public-sector purchasers of care. Recently, public-sector physicians have been allowed to treat private (usually fee-for-service) patients in their off-duty time, mainly at the private institutions mentioned earlier.[97]

Nominal personal charges are levied in connection with publicly provided health services and the purchase of certain health-related items such as eyeglasses. However, a wide range of indirect subsidies—including pensions, allowances for housing and children, unemployment insurance, etc.—permit nearly all Swedes to afford modest personal expenditures for health care. Several private insurance companies offer health insurance in Sweden, but since tax deductions for private health insurance premiums were disallowed in 1988, the small number of individuals covered by such policies has declined.

Present Problems and Reforms

Sweden continues to have one of the industrialized world's healthiest populations, with an infant morality rate of 5.8 per 1,000 live births and average life spans for males of 74.8 years and for females of 80.4 years (see Figure 35–2). However, the changes in medical care delivery under the 1982 law, as well as demographic and economic changes, are creating a crisis at the service delivery level. Some of the most pressing problems include the following:[98,99]

- a rapidly aging population, with the largest percentage of elderly (over 65 years) in the world—18 percent

- a need to reduce tax levels (among the highest in Europe) to remain industrially competitive

- demands from a population that, as it has become more affluent, has also become less willing to wait for procedures or to accept a health care system that is not responsive to patient influence

- pressures to keep abreast of new technology

- shortages of new professional personnel due to low salaries and a tight labor market

Proposed solutions have been many and varied, but most involve, to some degree, notions of competition and the inclusion of private-sector providers and/or insurers. Since 1990 most of Sweden's counties have been experimenting with various innovations in service delivery. Saltman discusses the two best-known efforts: the "Dalamodel" in Kopparberg County, and the ongoing sequence of experiments in Stockholm County.[100]

The Stockholm experiments center around attempts to shift to patient-choice-driven delivery systems with short-term budgets being influenced by provider performance. However, while rewarding those centers that are patient-preferred, the original experiments did not withhold funds from less successful facilities and did not allow for increases in salary for the personnel whose work levels increased in the good units. The newest round of experiments are attempting to address some of those shortcomings through competitive linkages between budgeting, productivity, and effectiveness, though all competing entities will be within the public sector.

The "Dalamodel" also involves a patient-driven component at the primary-care level, but adds a manager-driven, contract-based system for hospital services. In addition, private as well as publicly operated providers will be allowed to compete for the service contracts, which will provide a certain amount of direct financial competition.

These attempts to introduce market-style mechanisms into a public system are being closely watched by other European countries with similar systems facing like difficulties of increasing demographic and fiscal pressures. It is too early to tell, however, if the Swedish experiments will produce a viable model for Sweden, and certainly too early to determine if they can solve similar problems facing the industrialized nations of Western Europe and North America.

HEALTH CARE IN GERMANY

Background and Evolution of Sickness Funds

With the reunification in 1990, the Federal Republic of Germany (FRG) now encompasses both West and East Germany (the former German Democratic Republic) and consist of 16 states and city-states with a population of 80.3 million in 1992. The health care system in the FRG has its roots in cooperative organizations, called sickness funds, that were sponsored by guilds during medieval times. These sickness funds provided financial security to guild members and their families in the event of illnesses or injuries, usually by levying fixed fees two or three times a year on all guild members. Importantly, the sickness funds operated on the basis of maximizing social solidarity (group cohesion) rather than on the basis of minimizing individual losses. (Individualistic self-interest, by contrast, is the basis for the U.S. system of indemnity insurance, which attempts to spread risk across individuals and exclude those with exceptionally high risk potential.) As the German states became more mercantile between the sixteenth and mid-nineteenth centuries, the sickness funds were extended by various communities to include miners, foundry workers, and other artisans.[101]

However, the rapid industrialization of the newly unified Germany in the late nineteenth century created a large urban population of factory workers who were no longer adequately covered by the community-based and craft-centered sickness funds. By 1878, worker dissatisfaction with the monarchy and organized opposition from communists and labor unions so threatened the government that several laws were passed outlawing socialism, trade unions, and the Social Democratic Party. However, such legislation did little to obviate the causes of unrest. Under the urging of Chancellor Otto von Bismarck, the Parliament (Reichstag) in 1883 enacted compulsory national health insurance for all hourly laborers in order to secure social stability. The Health Insurance Act of 1883 and other acts to extend accident insurance for factory workers (1884) and agricultural workers (1886), as well as old-age and disability pensions (1899), established Europe's first social welfare state.[102]

However, these acts did not create the centrally administered, government-financed health service that Bismarck originally envisioned. Rather, opposition from business, agricultural, and other political and religious interests resulted in a health care system in which the national government set policy but the sickness funds retained their central role of financing and delivering health care. Two types of sickness funds were retained by the 1883 act—guild or craft-based funds called *Innungkassen,* and miners' funds called *Kappschftskassen*—while two other types of funds were established—local sickness funds called *Allgemeine Ortskrankensassen* or AOK, and company sickness funds called *Betriebskrankenkassen.* Although not provided for with the act, substitute funds called *Erstzkassen,* run as mutual aid societies for salaried employees, also prospered.[103]

During the ensuing years from 1883 to 1975, statutory health insurance was expanded to include not only blue-collar workers but also the following categories: transport and commercial workers (1901), agriculture and forestry workers and domestic servants (1911), civil service employees (1914), unemployed people (1918), seamen (1927), dependents of fund members

(1930), voluntary participants earning wages above the statutory limits (1941), pensioners (1941), farm workers and salesmen (1966), self-employed agricultural workers and dependents (1972), and students and disabled persons (1975).[104] The results of this expansion included exponential growth in sickness fund enrollment, steady consolidation of the sickness funds,[105] and a large increase in the number of physicians.[106]

During the first three decades of this expansion, the sickness funds exercised a great deal of power. Each fund was free to hire anyone to provide health care—often negotiating extremely low fees from doctors who had not passed their board exams—and typically restricted fund members from seeing physicians who did not hold a contract with a fund. However, during the first decade of the twentieth century, physicians both within and outside the sickness funds began to organize unions and to strike in order to better bargain with the funds. During 1911 and in 1913, the strife caused by the power imbalance was addressed, largely because of the pressure from two large physician groups, the *Hartmannbund* (representing office-based physicians) and the *Deutsche Ärztevereinsbund (DÄV*—the national umbrella group of medical associations). The Imperial Insurance Decree or *Reichsversicherungsordnung* (RVO) of 1911 required sickness funds to (1) give members a choice between at least two physicians, (2) pay physicians on a fee-for-service basis, and (3) pay only physicians with full certification. However, it also expanded the population covered by statutory insurance to include almost 30 percent of all Germans, while also permitting sickness funds to reimburse patients for medical services. After the *DÄV* threatened a nationwide strike of physicians, the government intervened, creating the Berlin Treaty of 1913, enabling doctors and sickness funds to negotiate differences and set standards on issues such as the physician/patient ratio.

During the hyperinflationary period following World War I, cost pressures and physician dissatisfaction with the worker-dominated sickness funds resulted in business joining physicians in calls for health care reform. The balance of power began to swing more to the physicians' side as the Weimar Republic issued a series of decrees to meet the demands of this stakeholder coalition, culminating in the Weimar Settlement of 1931. This decree increased the ratio of physicians to fund members, recognized medicine as a profession, and created sickness fund physicians' associations (*kassenärztliche Vereinigungen*–KVs). Significantly, each physician was now legally bound to join a KV in order to receive payments from a sickness fund. Most important, each KV established a bargaining monopoly for local physicians vis-a-vis the numerous sickness funds with whom physicians previously had to arrange separate contracts. From this point forward, the KVs have served as the primary mechanism through which physician charges flow to sickness funds and fund payments flow to physicians.

On the one hand, the power of the KVs was reinforced under the Nazi regime's policy of purging Jews and socialists from positions of power. These actions undermined both the representative governance of, and the calls for further health care reform from, the union-dominated sickness funds, particularly since the funds were placed under the dictatorial rule of Nazi sympathizers. On the other hand, Jewish physicians were excluded from the sickness funds, weakening the delivery of health care, especially in large urban areas where they were concentrated.[107]

The fall of the Third Reich divided Germany, creating two distinct health systems: (1) the Federal Republic of Germany, initially under Allied occupation, continued with the decentralized, sickness-fund-based system begun under Bismarck and (2) the German Democratic Republic, under Soviet oversight, developed a centralized, state-directed health system similar to the USSR's command-and-control model. These separate health care systems were conjoined after the 1990 reunification, with major reforms occurring in East Germany in order to make it similar to the West German system. (These reforms are discussed in a later section.)

In Western Germany, the period after the occupation through the 1960s was one of growth driven by the increasing prosperity of the newly reconstructed Germany. However, during the 1970s, the growth of health care expenditures began to exceed the growth in GDP to such a degree that a series of reforms were instituted to contain costs.[108] These various cost containment acts are summarized in Exhibit 35–1. One of the most notable elements of these acts was the establishment in 1987 of the Council for Concerted Action in Health Care—a panel of 70 representatives from the interested parties in health care—to set a ceiling on the rate of growth for ambulatory and dental care and pharmaceutical and other medical supplies.[109]

System Structure and Financing

During 1990, 99.8 percent of the population was covered by some form of health insurance. The greatest number of people are covered by statutory insurance (86.2 percent), with private insurance (11 percent), and other coverage (2.6 percent)—including social welfare, private charity, and the self-paying wealthy—accounting for the rest of the population in 1990.[110] Eight types of sickness funds are included within the statutory insurance category, with the six RVO (State Insurance Regulation) fund types encompassing about 60 percent of the population and the two substitute fund types accounting for another 28 percent.[111] During 1990, the RVO funds included (1) local (n=267, 42 percent); (2) company-based (n=692, 13 percent); (3) craft-affiliated (n=152, 5 percent); (4) agricultural workers (n=19, 2 percent); miners (n=1, 2 percent); and seamen (n=1, n.a.). Substitute funds, at that time, included blue-collar funds (n=8, 2 percent) and white-collar funds (n=7, 33 percent).[112]

The German health care system is dominated by a highly formalized system of ambulatory physician service and a large array of individual hospitals. Three types of hospitals provide most of the inpatient care: (1) public hospitals, (2) private voluntary hospitals, and (3) private proprietary hospitals. Public hospitals may be owned by federal, state, or local governments, and account for over 50 percent of the country's beds.

Religious institutions often own the private voluntary hospitals, which have about 35 percent of the beds, while doctors own most of the proprietary hospitals, with about 14 percent of the beds.[113] While operating costs for these hospitals are derived from the sickness funds and private insurers, the state governments provide almost all of the fund for capital investments, even for private hospitals. Both the public and the voluntary hospitals usually have salaried doctors; the per diem rates they negotiate with the sickness funds include the physicians' remuneration. In contrast, proprietary hospitals' per diem does not include the charges made by the physicians, who, as in the United States, are paid a separate fee. However, unlike their counterparts in the United States, hospital-based physicians in Germany seldom provide services on an outpatient basis, and ambulatory-based physicians rarely have admission privileges to hospitals.[114]

As indicated previously, the KVs and the sickness funds negotiate annually to establish a prospective lump sum for ambulatory physicians' services, typically adhering to the ceiling set forth by the Council for Concerted Action. These monies are then distributed by the KV to individual physicians based on their workload and fee schedule. At the same time, the KV monitors the quality and volume of each physician, disciplining those doctors whose practice patterns endanger patients or are too expensive. This "bilateral monopoly" between the KVs and the sickness funds, however, does not extend to control over patient volume. In other words, ambulatory physicians face the problem of the "commons," since any individual physician's increases in patient volume will depress the overall price for services rendered. Ambulatory physicians utilize a nationally negotiated fee schedule for about 2,500 types of service, based on a relative value scale that generates various points. These points, however, are reimbursed at different rates by private insurers (double that for RVO), substitute funds (often slightly higher than RVO), and RVO funds.[115]

During 1989, almost half—46 percent—of the funding for German health care came from statutory sickness funds, with premiums paid

Exhibit 35–1 The Cost Containment Acts of the Federal Republic of Germany: 1977–1989

Cost Containment Act of 1977
- The principle of an income-oriented expenditure policy is introduced.
- Concerted Action for Health Affairs is created.
- "Lump sum" prospective budgets for payments by sickness funds to physicians' associations are reintroduced.
- Utilization review of physicians is strengthened.
- Co-insurance of prescriptions: Payment of 20 percent of cost (maximum of 2.50 DM) is replaced by a co-payment of 1 DM for each drug.
- Reimbursement for dentures is limited to 80 percent of cost.
- Sickness funds are permitted to introduce co-insurance on orthodontics.
- Nursing care at home is obligatory under certain circumstances to reduce inpatient care.
- Costs for home help given by near relatives are no longer reimbursed.
- Family members with income above a certain level are no longer insured free of charge.
- Retired persons are accepted as members of sickness funds only if they were members during their working years (i.e., risk-sharing introduced).

Hospital Cost Containment Acts of 1981 and 1982
- Reduction of number of beds is to be accelerated by subsidies.
- Sickness funds must cooperate with the associations of hospitals in the hospital planning of the States.
- Sickness funds may bargain with hospitals over the level of reimbursement for daily health care rates.
- Regulation of hospital care is included in Concerted Action for Health Affairs.

Supplementary Cost Containment Acts of 1981 and 1982
- Fees for technical dental services are reduced for 1 year by 5 percent.
- Reimbursement for dentures is changed: Insurance pays 100 percent for dentists' services and up to 80 percent of material and laboratory costs.
- Co-payments for medical aids and appliances are introduced.
- New eyeglasses are reimbursable only once every 3 years if visual acuity does not change.
- Rehabilitation cures are granted only once every 3 years; a co-payment of 10 DM per day is required.
- Handicapped persons can become voluntary members of the sickness funds if they or their relatives have been members for at least 3 of the preceding 5 years.
- Length of stay after inpatient admission for childbirth is regularly limited to 6 (formerly 10) days.

- A co-payment of 5 DM is introduced for transportation costs.

Amended Budget Act of 1983
- Insured persons must pay 5 DM per day (for a maximum of 14 days) for inpatient care.
- The co-payment on drugs is raised to 2 DM per item.
- Expenses for home health care may be reimbursable if necessary to minimize inpatient care.
- Medicines for minor ailments are no longer covered after April 1, 1983.

Amended Budget Act of 1984
- Contributions to sickness funds must be applied on special wages, such as bonuses, tips, etc.
- Patients with sick benefits have to pay contributions to the social old-age and unemployment insurance; contributions are split between patients and sickness funds.

Hospitals Financing Act of 1985
- The present mixed financing of construction by the federal government and the states is shifted to the states.
- Sickness funds and hospitals may finance certain kinds of investments by per diem rates.

Federal Hospital Payment Regulation of 1986
- Prospective global budgets are introduced; these are to be negotiated by sickness funds and hospitals, based on inclusive costs and anticipated occupancy rates.
- Average per diem rates are to be set based on anticipated costs, with comparisons to similar efficient hospitals.
- Payments to be based on 75 percent of the agreed daily rate for shortfalls in actual days compared with expected days; only 25 percent of the agreed rate will be paid for surpluses in actual days compared with expected days.
- Hospitals are able to carry over surpluses into subsequent years.
- If the funds and hospitals do not agree on a budget, a neutral (nonstate) arbitration board decides.
- It is possible to arrange special daily rates for hospital departments and special payments for expensive types of care, e.g., heart operations.
- Patients receive detailed information about the care they receive; hospitals begin keeping statistics on the diagnosis, specialty, age, and length of stay of patients.

Need Planning Law of 1986
- Physicians' associations and sickness funds may lock out certain physician specialists in areas with more than a 50 percent excess of doctors in those specialties.

continues

Exhibit 35–1 continued

- Sickness funds and physicians' associations may provide incentives for early retirement of physicians.

Health Care Reform Act of 1989

- Blue-collar workers with incomes above the assessment ceiling may choose among insurance types, making legislation for these workers equal to that already applicable to white-collar workers.
- Sickness fund coverage for students is restricted.
- Compulsory insurance is extended to young adults in secondary educational programs.
- Compulsory insurance for certain categories of self-employed people is abolished.
- Requirements concerning prior insurance periods for retired persons are tightened.
- Qualifying conditions for voluntary membership in sickness funds are made stricter.
- Provisions are repealed under which retired persons, civil servants, and self-employed persons previously could join a health plan.
- The minimum contribution payable by voluntarily insured persons is doubled; also doubled are contributions for children insured in the public system by privately insured parents.
- The employer's share of contributions is set at 50 percent as a general rule.
- Compulsory and optional contribution-sharing arrangements are introduced.
- The system of revenue sharing of the sickness insurance for retired persons is reduced, with contributions set to the average for workers.
- Coverage for preventive care, e.g., preventive dental care and health check-ups, is expanded.
- Concept of "patient pays first, then is reimbursed" is introduced; coinsurance for dentures is increased; bonuses are payable if teeth are regularly attended to.
- Fixed reimbursement levels for pharmaceutical products and appliances are introduced; generic drugs are to be dispensed by pharmacists, following physician prescriptions.
- Family assistance is established as an autonomous insurance right.

- Provision of home care is expanded for long-term illnesses.
- Special services that require continuous attendance are made available.
- Certain provisions concerning death benefits are repealed, and certain transitional provisions are made.
- Severe restrictions are placed on reimbursement for travel or transportation costs.
- In all sickness fund and private insurance contracts, the principle of stability of contribution rates is to be prerequisite.
- Individual sickness funds are authorized to introduce new services temporarily on an experimental basis (for up to five years) and to test them scientifically under pilot conditions.
- Tighter procedures are introduced for monitoring the prescribing of sickness fund physicians.
- Hospitals must publish price lists; ambulatory physicians must consider the cost effectiveness of their referrals.
- Utilization review of medical services (both ambulatory and hospital-based) is to be conducted on a sample basis, pending negotiations among sickness funds, hospitals, and physicians' associations.
- General monitoring is to be done of costs and quality in hospitals, especially the coordination of inpatient and outpatient care; similarly, needs for major medical technologies are to be coordinated among sickness funds, hospitals, and physicians' associations; unresolved matters are to be referred to arbitration.
- Sickness funds may terminate contracts with inefficient hospitals.
- Tightening of conditions for physicians to be admitted to practice with sickness funds.
- Medical examiner service to be transformed into an independent medical advisory service for the sickness funds.
- State governments to restrict, through indirect means, the intake to medical schools.
- State governments to use financial incentives to reduce surplus hospital beds.

Source: Adapted from *Health Care Financing Review* Vol. 12, No. 3, pp. 79–81, 90–91, U.S. Department of Health and Human Services, 1991.

50/50 by employees and employers. Employers picked up an additional 17 percent of the total cost of health care, primarily in the form of sick pay during the first 6 weeks of employees' illnesses. Public social welfare and health programs accounted for another 14 percent of the total health care cost. Pensioners' insurance—jointly paid, at that time, by pensioners, pension funds, and sickness funds—and out-of-pocket payments by consumers each accounted for 7 percent, while private insurance paid for 6 percent of the health care costs. The remaining 3 percent of the health care costs were paid from statutory accident insurance funds.[116]

Present Problems and Reforms

One of the greatest problems facing the newly reunited Germany has been how to integrate and finance the provision of health care in eastern Germany, with its aged health care infrastructure, weak economy, and emphasis on preventive and primary health care. Health reforms within the former German Democratic Republic, begun in 1991, are modeled after the decentralized health care system in West Germany, with about 60 percent of the population obtaining compulsory insurance and served by local sickness funds (AOKs).[117] One holdover from the Soviet-style system is the retention of polyclinics and group practices, which were very popular among the eastern physicians, in contrast to the strong western tradition of ambulatory physicians settling into solo, office-based practices.[118] However, the polyclinics—"multispecialty groups of salaried physicians working in conjunction with public health workers, social workers, physical therapists, psychologists and other personnel"[119]—are, according to Knox, under a death warrant and their existence will be reviewed in 1995 to 1996 by a special commission composed of representatives from the polyclinics and the KVs.[120] Indeed, the proportion of physicians in private, ambulatory practice in eastern Germany has risen precipitously, from only 2 percent in 1989 to 91 percent by mid-1992.[121]

The other problems facing Germany's health care system are well known, and they include the following:

- The aging of the population is, and will continue to be, a strain on the existing way of financing social security and health care on a pay-as-you-go basis.[122]
- Because of the demarcation between ambulatory and hospital-based care, the fee-for-service tradition, and the fairly unfettered market for physician services, Germany spends more than most nations on medical technology and on secondary and tertiary care.[123] This overproduction is similar to that in the United States, and is conjoined with another similarity, as noted below.

- Like the United States, Germany has placed little emphasis on preventive care and psychiatric care.[124] In addition, it also faces a growing problem of providing adequate long-term care in either nursing homes or via home health care.[125]

- Unlike the United States, the average length of stay in hospitals is quite high in Germany. Hurst, among others, attributes this problem to the "role accorded per diem payments, from the sharp separation between ambulatory and hospital care, and from the dual hospital financing system, which means the State governments, which are responsible for planning and investment in capacity, are not responsible for running costs."[126]

- The projected growth of doctors—50 percent by the year 2000—is a two-sided issue. On one hand, it will place competitive pressure on the physicians' associations, lowering the cost of providing services. On the other hand, without any change in the fee-for-service system for ambulatory physicians, it is likely to generate supplier-induced increases in both services and procedures.[127]

- The inequity between sickness funds costs and premiums—i.e., between those available to white-collar versus blue-collar employees—has been, and is likely to continue to be, a problem, especially for those who have compulsory insurance and for the sickness funds that cover them. Given demographic and life style trends, the risk profiles of these two groups of employees will continue to diverge, with the poorer blue-collar employee contributing more proportionately for health services than the white-collar employee who can opt to join a fund with more affluent and lower risk members.[128] Such discrepancies have created deficits in the statutory sickness fund system, estimated at 11 billion DM ($5.3 billion) in 1992.[129]

In answer to the previous concerns, the Health Care Structural Reform Act was implemented on January 1, 1993. Although this act contains multiple and far-reaching provisions, two primary changes in funding are envisioned. First, an expert committee—appointed by Health Minister Hortst Seehofer—has been charged with determining a mandatory "basic benefits" package, with all other forms of benefits financed through voluntary private insurance. Second, a method to equalize the risk among sickness funds by transferring monies among them based on the risk profiles of their respective memberships is slated for implementation in 1994. This equalization is a precondition so that consumers can freely choose among the sickness funds and so that funds can compete for members by 1996. Knox argues that Germany may lack the political will to explicitly ration health care coverage via a basic benefits package; he is, however, more sanguine about the political feasibility of increasing the solidarity across sickness funds and introducing managed competition among the funds. Nonetheless, Knox also acknowledges that the equalization of risk within the sickness funds lays the groundwork for politicians to seek the equivalent of a single-payor system.[130]

HEALTH CARE IN THE UNITED KINGDOM

Background on the National Health Service

Although formally implemented in 1948, the British National Health Service (NHS) has its roots both in the laws for aiding the poor established in the 1600s and in the mutual aid societies that flourished in Great Britain during the 1840s. Well-to-do employers lent support to these societies in order to help sick but low-paid employees. While such measures in combination with the Poor Law system reduced the demand on general tax revenues, public outrage over the poor condition of recruits for the Boer War (nearly one-half of whom were considered unfit for service) led to the School Medical Service Act of 1907 and to an investigation by the Royal Commission on the Poor Laws and Relief of Distress. This commission issued two reports—a majority report, advocating better charity care, and a minority report, advocating a unified medical service—in 1909 that laid out the issues involved in establishing a national system of health care.[131]

Based on the Royal Commission's report, the National Health Insurance Act of 1911, introduced to Parliament by Lloyd George, and virtually unopposed except by physicians, established statutory insurance for all manual workers earning less than £160 (about $780) per year. (Interestingly, most physicians supported a mixture of voluntary health insurance and government-funded medical services for the poor, thus advocating a system similar to that in the United States today.) Contributions from both employees and employers were required, with the government funding the administration of the insurance and covering exceptionally low income and indigent persons' contributions. Benefits covered both visits to physicians who were general practitioners (GPs) and any prescribed medications. Although dental and other special services were not covered, the free outpatient services of a physician specialist associated with a public hospital were available through referral by the patient's GP. Hospitalization in public and some large voluntary hospitals, if necessary, was funded through local government support and charity contributions; hence, it was not included under the national insurance act.[132]

In some ways, national insurance in the United Kingdom paralleled the organization and structure of the sickness funds in Germany during this same time. Governmentally approved mutual aid societies received the contributions of employers and employees, but county/borough-based insurance committees—composed of representatives of the insured workers, local doctors, local government, and the Ministry of Health—controlled the payment of GPs and of pharmaceutical supplies. The societies enrolled employees and paid cash disability benefits. They also could fund supplemental benefits such as part of hospitalization costs, if they accumulated surplus funds. Moreover, approved societies—typically nonprofit subsidiaries of commercial insurance companies—could sell insurance for other benefits, including dental care and medical coverage for those not covered under the law, e.g., dependents or workers earning high incomes. For those making voluntary payments, these societies often offered expanded medical coverage, including fees for specialists at major hospitals and those of GPs in private, nursing/obstetric hospitals.[133]

Legally, the doctors on each insurance committee could decide how they were to receive payment for their services, whether on a fee-for-service basis, a capitated basis, or some mixture. As Roemer underscores, by 1927, practically all these GP representatives voluntarily had chosen to receive capitated payments, largely as a way to avoid bureaucratic hassles and to preclude competition among GPs in each insurance area. This voluntary pattern of capitated payment eventually became mandated under the National Health Service Act of 1946.[134] Here, of course, these British doctors diverged from the fee-for-service model that their German counterparts during this same time were striving to preserve and strengthen.

The period from World War I through 1938 established many of the values and the concepts on which the NHS would be based. Several significant documents emerged during this time, including the 1920 Dawson Report on health care policy, which advocated a hospital-centered integrated system of care; the 1920 Cave Report on saving voluntary hospitals; the 1926 Report of the Royal Commission on National Health Insurance; and the 1930 and 1938 Reports of the British Medical Association on national medical care policy that increased its public stature and enabled it to have considerable voice in health policy. Additionally, under the Labour government in 1938, the Ministry of Health initiated planning discussions for a national health care program.[135]

By the late 1930s, the number of people covered under mandatory (and voluntary) health insurance had steadily increased, especially as income thresholds for mandatory insurability were raised. Nonetheless, during the Depression, dissatisfaction with the national health insurance's "means-tested" coverage and limited benefits reached a level requiring major reforms.[136] Under Winston Churchill's Conservative government and the chairmanship of Sir William Beveridge, an Inter-Departmental Committee on Social Insurance and Allied Services was created and charged with surveying the existing national policies of social insurance, including health care insurance. The Beveridge Report, issued in 1942, made sweeping recommendations to expand all branches of social insurance, from old-age pensions to disability benefits. In particular, it set the stage of the NHS by recommending the establishment of a national health service to provide medical and rehabilitation treatment to all citizens. While sidestepping the issue of how to organize and administer a national service, the report did set a broad goal for the future:

> A comprehensive national health service will ensure that for every citizen there is available whatever medical treatment he requires, in whatever form he requires it, domiciliary or institutional, general, specialist, or consultant, and will ensure also the provision of dental, ophthalmic and surgical appliances, nursing and midwifery and rehabilitation after accidents.[137]

After World War II, the Labour Party won control of the government and sponsored the National Health Services Act of 1946. This draft legislation for creating a national health service was the target of fiery debates between the British Medical Association (BMA) and the Minister of Health, Aneurin Bevan, a Welshman and former coal miner. On the one hand, Bevan advocated paying GPs a salary with a capitation supplement, requiring private pay patients to use private hospitals, and establishing a network of health centers for both preventive and primary care. On the other hand, the BMA advocated an extension of the national health insurance to cover a higher level of income, the use of government grants to support voluntary hospitals' outreach to the poor and indigent, and the retention of a private health care market for those with high incomes.[138] Interestingly, based on an April 1948 plebiscite of the entire medical profession, continued opposition to the act within the BMA came from specialists rather than GPs:

> The plebiscite result, reported on 5 May 1948, still showed an overall majority of the profession against accepting service without further safeguards, but the number of opposing general practitioners had not reached the previously agreed majority. Thus did the NHS come into being on the duly appointed day.[139]

The final legislation for the NHS, implemented in July 1948, contained a number of compromises: (1) universal coverage was financed primarily by general revenues, with social insurance contributions limited to a small percentage of the total; (2) GPs were paid via capitation; (3) nearly all public and voluntary hospitals were put under the control of the national government; (4) public hospitals were permitted to maintain up to 5 percent of beds for private patients of consultants, i.e., senior hospital physician specialists; and (5) health centers were limited to a few experimental facilities.[140]

The basic structure of the NHS, as Roemer underscores, was balanced across the four primary stakeholders providing health care, including the general practitioners, the community hospitals and their staffs of specialists, the medical school-affiliated teaching hospitals, and the local public health authorities. Under the NHS,

the former insurance committees overseeing the remuneration of GPs were transformed into executive councils. These councils took up the task of administering not only primary medical care but also dental and optical services, as well as prescribed drugs, in their designated communities.[141]

To manage the community hospitals, the NHS set up a network of Regional Hospital Boards (RHBs), modeled upon the emergency committees that had coordinated hospital services during World War II. Because each RHB oversaw hospital services to 2 to 3 million people and about 30,000 beds, hospital management teams were appointed to manage the day-to-day operations of institutions operating between 1,000 to 2,000 beds. However, both capital and operating funds were centrally controlled, with each RHB receiving a budget from the national government. The RHB, in turn, controlled the budgets for each management committee. Unlike the GPs' remuneration through capitation, physician specialists and consultants were likely to be full-time salaried employees (60 percent), with even those specialists retaining a private practice (40 percent) often having salaried contracts requiring 70 to 80 percent of their activity to be hospital-based. As in the United States, physician specialists had and continue to have the most prestigious, and often the highest paying, positions in the medical community. This prestige is accentuated in the United Kingdom, however, since specialists must compete for appointments to NHS hospitals, and local GPs seldom have such appointments.[142]

The teaching hospitals for medical schools in England and Wales, arguing that their special missions and long tradition of highly qualified medical staffs would be undermined if included in the RHBs, were able to maintain a separate status with the NHS until the 1974 reforms. Prior to that time, the board of governors for the 36 hospitals (26 within London) reported to the Minister of Health and obtained funding directly from the national government.[143]

Local public health authorities, of course, predated the National Health Services Act. Although the local health authorities no longer were responsible for public hospitals under the NHS, they remained responsible for preventive care and their roles were expanded to include ambulance transport, visiting nurse services, and home-based and institutional services for the chronically ill and the aged. One important service provided by the local health authorities was preventive and maternal health care to children and pregnant women, provided through health department clinics and child welfare stations.[144]

This four-fold structure within the NHS was maintained until 1974, even though problems of coordinating care across the four branches and the increasing dominance of specialized hospital care led to calls for reform during the 1960s.[145] Also, throughout this period, there were ongoing clashes with both GPs and specialists over remuneration from the NHS. During the mid-1960s, dissatisfaction among GPs over capitation rates led to significant changes in their remuneration; by 1970, almost half of their incomes were derived from special fees and grants.[146] In 1962, the BMA's Porritt Committee advocated local coordination of all branches, and in 1968, the Labour government issued a green paper exploring the creation of area health authorities for this same purpose. By 1971, the Conservative government issued a second green paper, with a white paper following in the next year, and legislation to reform the NHS approved in 1973.[147]

To enhance local control, in April 1974, the NHS was reorganized to include 90 area health authorities (AHAs) and 14 Regional Health Authorities (RHAs). The RHAs took over the planning responsibilities of the former regional hospital boards, but also assumed planning oversight for preventive and ambulatory care. Similarly, each AHA became responsible for preventive, ambulatory, and hospital service, including the teaching hospitals. Moreover, the AHAs assumed the functions of the former hospital management committees. To match the scope of the AHAs' mission, the representation on their governing boards also was broadened to include nonmedical members with significant managerial experience, as well as community medicine specialists serving an important advi-

sory capacity. On the one hand, to represent the interests of GPs and provide advice to the AHAs, family practitioner committees were formed, replacing the role filled by the former executive councils. On the other hand, consumers' interests were represented to the AHAs through the formation of community health councils at the health district level. These councils provided advice to the district management team, i.e., the community medicine specialist, chief administrator, district nurse, and a peer-elected GP and specialist physician.[148]

By the late 1970s, the usefulness of the AHAs for coordinating and responding to local needs was brought into question. Rather than adding a fourth level of bureaucracy into the NHS, it was decided that the District Health Authorities (DHAs) would be consolidated into units serving populations of about 250,000. Thus, the former AHAs' responsibilities were devolved to DHAs.[149]

During the 1980s, the Thatcher-led Conservative government tried to control rising health care costs through cutbacks on the global budgets to the RHAs and the expansion of the private medical sector. Not only were physicians encouraged to devote part of their practice to private patients, but both employers and employees were allowed tax deductions for private insurance. Hence, the private market for health care expanded rapidly, from less than 2 percent of the population being covered by voluntary insurance in 1969[150] to about 6.3 percent in 1980[151] and to over 10 percent in 1990.[152] Even though only 6 percent of the total health care expenditures during 1987 occurred in the private sector, both the public and the medical professions became increasingly disenchanted with the NHS.[153]

Indeed, 1987 to 1988 was a time of crisis for the NHS, with hospitals closing down thousands of beds to meet budget constraints, long lines forming for all types of care, delays and cancellations for critical surgery, and DHAs running out of money.[154] In response to this turmoil, the Conservative government considered radical changes to the NHS, resulting in a white paper in

1989 that set out the reforms implemented between 1990 and 1991 and discussed in the next two sections.

System Structure and Financing under Reform

The NHS offers the entire U.K. population comprehensive health care largely through general taxation, with about 10 percent of the cost during 1989 derived from National Insurance contributions by employers, their employees, and the self-employed.[155] Although this basic formula has not changed, the role of the private sector was expanded by 1990 legislation that provided tax relief to people 60 or older paying voluntary health care premiums. Three major structural changes also have occurred to the NHS integrated system of public hospitals, ambulatory practices staffed by GPs, and health clinics: (1) purchasers—district and local health authorities—have been distinguished from providers—public and private hospitals, GPs, and home care providers; (2) providers are allowed to compete for contracts with purchasers; and (3) providers are accountable for the efficient and effective practice of medicine. The specific aspects of these changes on both public hospitals and their specialist physicians and on GPs are discussed below.

Public Hospitals

From its creation in 1948 through 1991, NHS hospitals were organized under a public integrated model, similar to the U.S. Department of Veterans Affairs, with global budgets and salaried physicians.[156] Thus, a global budget was allocated to the RHAs, who used a weighted population formula to allocate the budget to DHAs, who served as both purchasers and providers of health care. A great deal of physician autonomy occurred under this system because contracts with physicians were held by the RHAs, making it very difficult for DHAs and/or hospital managers to discipline or dismiss physicians.

Since April 1991, public hospitals have been subject to an internal market reform, by and large following the advice of Alain Enthoven.[157] These reforms are intended, among other purposes, to counteract the perverse economic incentives that existed under the public integrated model of rewarding inefficient hospital performance and of penalizing efficient hospital performance.[158,159] There are four major reforms for public hospitals: (1) DHAs serve solely as purchasers of health care services and administer physician contracts for the RHAs; (2) NHS public hospitals may seek to become NHS hospital trusts with their own board of directors and, thus, to operate as freestanding nonprofit hospitals, enabling them—like DHAs—to administer physician contracts and to have managerial discretion over capital, as well as operational, allocations; (3) NHS public hospitals, NHS trust hospitals, GP fundholders, and private hospitals compete for contracts from DHAs; and (4) clinical managers administer, with the help of a management team including a senior nurse and business manager, an operational budget for hospital departments.[160,161,162,163] This latter resource management initiative has meant that consultants (senior physicians) typically are now managing entire departments, not just serving as head of a medical staff.[164]

General Practitioners

The reform most directly affecting GPs is the ability to become NHS fundholders if a group practice has at least 11,000 patients (about 1,000 groups of this or greater size exist). GP fundholders are provided a budget for their patients, which includes a defined range of hospital services. These services include outpatient consultations and associated diagnostic and ancillary services and treatments, and inpatient procedures—limited to operations such as hip or cataract surgery. Also, GP fundholders are allowed to use their budgets on their diagnostic tests and X-rays, as well as their operating and administrative costs. As one of a diverse set of providers in the new NHS internal market, GP fundholders may negotiate with public or private hospitals for the services their patients need. However, even though fundholders may recoup up to a 5 percent budget overspend in their next fiscal year, they are subject to revocation of their budgets if they are overspent two years in a row.[165,166,167,168]

The Impact of Current Reforms

As a whole, these reforms represent a major trend to decentralize authority within the NHS and to encourage both efficiency in operations and greater responsiveness to patients. However, they are not without their critics, and their effectiveness has been mixed. For example, Pollock argues, based on several recent and major reports on the future direction of health care in the United Kingdom, that the outlook for equity, comprehensiveness, and equality of access in the NHS is threatened by the reforms. She points to two problems facing managers of public hospitals: (1) chronic underfunding and (2) tight governmental controls without a clear strategy. The latter leads to conflicts at the local level over preventive versus tertiary care. Additionally, and perhaps more significantly, the growth of the private health care sector means that the NHS has created a multitiered system "with different standards of care available to patient groups depending on their access to private care and ability to pay."[169]

Ham, in contrast, takes a more balanced view, noting that the reforms have placed a renewed emphasis on primary care, and more collaborative endeavors involving GPs and specialists, which should upgrade the quality of medical practice. He notes that the balance of power is thus swinging from hospitals to an alliance between health authorities and GPs. Nonetheless, he warns that the underfunding of the NHS may have dire consequences:

> Yet as constraints on funding begin to bite a new dynamic is becoming apparent. This involves combined action by hospital providers, who have fulfilled their contracts with a quarter of the year remaining, and general practi-

tioners, who as a consequence are unable to obtain hospital treatment for their patients, to put pressure on health authorities to increase the resources available to acute services...[E]quity is sacrificed as purchasing power rather than clinically diagnosed need determines which patients should be treated.[170]

HEALTH CARE IN THE NETHERLANDS

Background on the Dutch Multipayor System

Prior to World War II, health care in the Netherlands was provided largely through private enterprise and charity, with the government's role limited to monitoring the quality of care and ensuring the provision of preventive care. During the postwar years, however, the government took an increasingly more central role in the financing and regulation of primary through tertiary care, creating a complex mixture of private enterprise and government oversight.[171,172] Hence, the following acts of legislation were essential in establishing the modern Dutch health care system:

- The Sickness Funds Decree of 1941 and 1948 mandated that sickness funds must contract with all physicians in their region, simultaneously guaranteeing free choice of doctor by patients and eliminating competition among physicians.[173] The Decree of 1948 also created guidelines for social insurance to ensure financial access to health care among the poor while the Netherlands underwent a decade-long period of tightly planned reconstruction.[174]

- The Sickness Funds Insurance Act (*Ziekenfondswet*—ZFW) of 1964 replaced the Decree of 1948 and specifies the level of income under which social insurance is compulsory for acute and short-term illnesses.[175] It also establishes the eligible population for sickness funds and the territories set aside for them, and it continues to obligate sickness funds to contract with all providers in their regions. Premiums are paid into a central regulatory body, the Sickness Fund Council, which then reimburses the funds for the medical expenses of their members.[176] The premiums for social health insurance are based on a percentage of income, which varies for the employed, pensioners, and social security recipients. In 1987, the income threshold for ZFW was Dfl 49, 150 (about $25,000 U.S.); employees and employers each contributed 5.05 percent of gross wage income; pensioners contributed 3.05 percent and employers contributed 3.0 percent; and social security recipients contributed 5.05 percent.[177]

- The General Special Sickness Expenses Act (*Algemene Wet Bijzondere Ziektekosten*—AWBZ) of 1967 provides universal insurance for catastrophic and long-term illnesses, including physical and mental handicaps.[178] During 1987, AWBZ was funded through fixed percentage contributions (4.55 percent) from each employee (paid by employers) and the self-employed.[179]

- The Hospital Facilities Act (WZV) of 1971 and 1979 established central government licensing for the construction and for the size of hospitals. Its original goal was to lower the number of beds in acute care hospitals. (More comprehensive legislation, the Health Care Facilities Act of 1982, with implementation planned for 1984, was designed to regulate all institutional and ambulatory facilities. However, this act has been abandoned in light of the reforms discussed below.)[180] Under the WZV, a "new general hospital [must] have a minimum size of 175 beds, in order to guarantee the availability of two full-time medical specialists of each of the six so-called 'core specialties.'"[181]

- The Health Care Tariffs Act (WTG) of 1980, implemented in 1982, created "a specially appointed autonomous body, the Central Office on Health Care Tariffs (COTG) [which] sets out guidelines for the composition and calculation of tariffs," including both fees-for-service and capitation payments to physicians and hospitals.[182] Rather than directly setting prices, the COTG relies on setting the parameters for a bargaining process between providers—hospitals, physicians, and other medical professionals—and buyers, including both sickness funds and private insurers, for determining tariffs. The COTG then reviews these tariffs to ensure that they are within the guidelines.[183] This legislation has strengthened the power of the associations both for providers (especially GPs and specialists) and for insurers by institutionalizing a bilateral monopoly.[184]

- The Health Insurance Access Act (WTZ) of 1986 requires private insurers to provide "specified risk groups a comprehensive benefits package for a legally determined maximum premium."[185] The purpose of this legislation was to counteract the premium differentiation and market segmentation that—since the 1970s—had eroded the preservation of universal coverage for the elderly and other high-risk groups. In 1989, these benefits were extended to all people over 65; in 1991, they were mandated for all people who are privately insured who pay more than the maximum standard premium.

Currently, compulsory social health insurance (AWBZ) covers the entire Dutch population for chronic care and about 70 percent of the population for acute care (ZFW). The remaining population purchases voluntary insurance for acute care.[186] In 1987, health care was financed from five sources, comprising four categories: social insurance—AWBZ and ZFW (65.8 percent); private insurance (20.2 percent); out-of-pocket payments (7.5 percent); and general taxation

(6.6 percent).[187] In 1981, the percentage of gross family income spent on health insurance varied from less than 4 percent to more than 15 percent.[188] As in Germany, the mixture of public (ZFW) and private insurance for acute care has resulted in a regressive form of funding, with the poorest generally paying a greater percentage of their income for health care than the richest.[189]

Significantly, the Dutch system is characterized by a strict division between health care financing and delivery, with sickness funds "legally forbidden to employ providers or to run health care institutions" and private insurers not willing to interfere with medical practices.[190] As in the United Kingdom and Germany, primary care is provided by GPs who act as gatekeepers for ZFW and many privately insured patients, referring them to specialist physicians who provide secondary and tertiary care in hospitals. For these patients, GPs often receive a capitation fee.[191] However, for most privately insured patients, both GPs and specialists generally are paid fees for service.[192] To control physician supply, the government—since 1986—has regulated the location of GP practices, setting both upper and lower limits on the size of a practice. Moreover, it has restricted entry into medical schools and, in cooperation with the medical professions, which control medical training, it has supported the reduction of resident training capacity.[193]

Since 1984, Dutch hospitals, whether owned by local communities or—most typically—by private boards of trustees, have operated with prospective, global budgets that are negotiated annually with third-party payors (i.e., public sickness funds [ZFW] and private insurers) when setting per diem payments for patients.[194,195] Prior to that time, hospitals were reimbursed on a price per patient day, encouraging providers to admit patients for lengthy hospital stays.[196] In contrast to the United States, hospitals in the Netherlands are in highly concentrated markets, with more than 70 percent of the 25 regional markets in 1988 exceeding an Herfindahl-Hirschman Index of 1800. Moreover, Dutch hospitals during the 1980s underwent a wave of government supported consolidation, with the result that the market share of the two largest hospitals in each region increased an average of 10 percent from 1984 to 1988, while the total number of hospitals decreased from 169 in 1984 to 148 in 1988.[197]

Reflecting even greater market concentration than hospitals, 46 sickness funds (ZFW) offered compulsory coverage to residents in the 25 health care regions during 1987. In contrast, during 1986, the top 10 of the over 60 private insurers held a cumulative market share of 59.7 percent for all private premiums, and their Herfindahl-Hirschman Index measure of market concentration was a relatively low 545.[198] Importantly, the sickness funds, unlike the private insurers, were retrospectively reimbursed by the Sickness Fund Council up through 1990 for the medical expenses of their enrollees. Private insurers, however, were much more at risk since the regulation imposed in 1986 (WTZ) meant they incurred losses—35 percent of their total claims in 1991—on those high-risk groups they were legally mandated to cover at set premiums.[199]

Calls for major reforms of the Dutch system of health care were made during the 1970s and again in the 1980s. In 1974, the "Secretary of Health and Environmental Protection published a comprehensive study on the Dutch health care system, calling for more government controls on prices of medical care, decentralized governmental planning agencies for all health care facilities, and incorporation of the various health insurance Acts into an integrated social security system."[200] While price controls and government restrictions on hospital capacity and physician supply certainly had an impact during the 1980s, their total effect was disappointing.[201] Neither sickness funds nor physicians had any incentives to improve efficiency, while sickness funds and private insurers were unable to direct patients to the most cost-effective providers. At the same time, universal access to acute care was being threatened by the growing market segmentation and premium differentiation by private insurers. Within this context, the Dutch government set up an advisory Committee on the Structure and Financing of Health Care, chaired by Dr. W.

Dekker. The Dekker Report, published in March 1987, proposed major changes in the health care system that were subsequently endorsed by two coalition cabinets in 1988 and 1990.[202,203]

System Structure and Financing under Reform

Beginning in 1990, the Netherlands gradually has been introducing several reforms, largely based on the managed competition advice of Alain Enthoven.[204] The intent of these reforms is twofold: (1) to ensure universal coverage for acute care by gradually eliminating the distinction between sickness funds and private insurance and (2) to introduce efficiency and greater patient choice into a highly regulated market for third-party payors, hospitals, and physicians by creating managed competition.[205] The following brief description of the reforms and their planned effect on these three stakeholders draws upon the work of Enthoven;[206] Hurst;[207] Kirkman-Liff and van de Ven;[208] Schut;[209] and van der Gaag et al.[210]

Third-Party Payors

In January 1992, an amendment to the Sickness Fund Insurance Act (ZFW) removed both the regional boundary restrictions on the funds' subscribers pools and their obligation to contract with all health care providers. Hence, two important preconditions are now met for allowing sickness funds and private insurers (1) to compete for subscribers and (2) to contract selectively with health care providers, negotiating both the payments and the types of services to be supplied. Moreover, since 1990, sickness funds have been receiving prospective global budgets from the Sickness Fund Council rather than being reimbursed retrospectively for enrollees' medical costs.

To allow consumers to choose the best benefit-for-value insurer and to allow insurers to choose the most cost-efficient and quality-effective providers, the government is planning to set up a Central Fund for compulsory national health insurance and to mandate a basic benefit package that covers about 96 percent of all

medical expenses. The Central Fund will receive income-related contributions from the Dutch population and then pay out risk-related premiums to sickness funds and private insurers, based on the overall risk profile of each insurer's group of subscribers. However, the premiums third-party payors will receive will cover only about 85 percent of the cost of the basic benefit package. To make up this difference, the insurers will charge subscribers a flat premium (but no more than 15 percent of the government's risk-related premium). This premium should vary among insurers based on their ability to contain costs, allowing insurers to compete for subscribers. In short, the planned reforms assume that if there is sufficient competition within the markets for insurers and for health care providers, then consumers' choices should compel third-party payors to contract with cost-effective providers.

Hospitals

The planned reforms are intended to deregulate the hospital industry in two ways: (1) the Hospital Facilities Act (WZV) will be limited to apply only to the planning of large facilities and (2) the Health Care Tariffs Act's (WTG) detailed guidelines governing the negotiation of prices between hospitals and insurers gradually will be relaxed. Limitations on the impact of WZV regulations should enable hospitals to establish freestanding outpatient clinics for providing secondary and tertiary health care. Given the U.S. experience with outpatient and managed care during the past decade, ambulatory clinics should provide a robust substitute for many health care services provided by hospitals. Furthermore, relaxation of the WTG guidelines should—in the short term—encourage hospitals to contain costs and to differentiate their services in order to compete for contracts with insurers.

Physicians

Three aspects of the reforms that have been implemented should encourage competition among physicians: (1) as indicated previously, sickness funds no longer are obligated under ZFW to contract with all physicians in their respective regions; (2) WTG regulations on nego-tiating fees-for-service and capitation rates are gradually being relaxed, as noted above; and (3) as of 1992, practice location regulations for GPs are no longer regulated. Two assumptions, none-theless, must be fulfilled if competition within the physician market is to occur as anticipated. First, physicians must be willing to contract with insurers as individuals or groups rather than as a professional collective. Second, and perhaps most important, there must be a sufficient supply of physicians so that demand does not outstrip the ability to provide medical care.

The Impact and Status of Current Reforms

At the time of this writing, the reforms—other than those already implemented—are on hold pending resolution of electoral uncertainties in the Netherlands. At issue is the plan to establish a national comprehensive health insurance that incorporates both sickness funds and private in-surers. Both employers and employees are re-sisting paying higher premiums than they now do under risk-based private insurance. Physi-cians are equally resistant to this change; the Royal Dutch Medical Association argues that managed care will lower the quality of medical care by basing treatment decisions on econom-ics. And sickness funds, which insure the poor-est and the highest risk groups, are fearful that they will not receive their fair share of the health care budget.[211]

Nevertheless, both the reforms that have been implemented and those now on hold have had a noticeable impact on the actions of third-party payors and physicians. For example, sickness funds underwent a wave of mergers, reducing their number from 46 in 1988 to 26 in 1991. A dramatic increase in market concentration also occurred in the private sector. The average Herfindahl-Hirschman Index for private insurers increased from 545 in 1986 to 1,252 in 1992, with the top 10 insurers accounting for 91.8 percent of the market.[212] Similarly, the association of medi-cal professionals has made efforts to limit the supply of physicians by reducing the resident training capacity for both specialists and GPs.[213]

Moreover, because the Netherlands lacks an-titrust laws, the reforms may—in the long term—induce hospitals to merge and to seek vertical integration with other health care pro-viders in order to increase their bargaining lever-age, further consolidating not only the hospital industry but also all aspects of health care deliv-ery.[214] Summarizing the feasibility of managed competition in the Dutch health care system, Schut explains that

> On the one hand, the structural pre-conditions for a market-oriented health policy in the Netherlands may be relatively good as compared to other industrialized countries, because of the high population density and the large number of private institutions. On the other hand, the historically de-termined structure of the health care financing and delivery system, the long-standing tradition of anti-com-petitive self-regulation and of collec-tive bargaining by government pro-tected cartels of providers and insurers, put significant constraints on the possibility of workable competi-tion.[215]

LESSONS LEARNED AND FUTURE CONCERNS

At meetings with medical and other health care providers, one often hears the claim that comparisons of the United States with other countries are unfair because other countries do not face the United States's social, demographic, and logistical problems. However, although such an argument has some merit, the countries we have examined to this point share many simi-larities with the United States, with many of the differences arguably contributing to greater problems than those faced by the United States.

As Table 35–3 illustrates, the major demo-graphic characteristic of the United States is its large population—ranging from 32 times the size of Sweden to 3 times the size of Germany. Nonetheless, the United States is blessed both with a lower population density and a younger population than most of these other industrialized countries. Moreover, while the European nations' populations are growing more slowly, Canada's population is actually growing faster than the United States's.

Significantly, as displayed in Table 35–3, the United States is not alone in facing the social problem of assimilating foreign nationals, with both Germany and Canada having larger percentages of their population from foreign lands than the United States. Moreover, both Canada

Table 35–3 Sociodemographic Comparisons of Selected Western European and North American Countries[a]

	Canada	Germany[b]	Netherlands	Sweden	United Kingdom	United States
Land Area in Square Kilometers	9,976,139	357,410	40,844	449,964	244,100	9,372,614
1993 Population (thousands)	22,770	80,768	15,275	8,730	57,970	258,104
1993 Population (per square mile)	8	597	1,166	55	621	73
1985–1990 Population Natural Increase[c] (per thousand)	6.6	−1.1	4.0	0.8	1.8	6.3
1991 Urban Population (percent)	77	n.a.	89	84	89	75
1990 Population 65 or Older (percent)	11.5	15.0	12.7	18.0	15.7	12.5
2025 Population 65 or Older (percent)	20.7	24.4	23.7	23.7	21.5	18.7
Mid-1980s Single-year Poverty Rate (percent)	17.0	8.0	3.0	3.0	n.a.	20.0
Mid-1980s Poverty Escape Rate (percent)	23.0	24.0	23.0	45.0	n.a.	22.0
1990 Unemployment Rates for Labor Force (percent)	8.1	6.2	9.0	1.5	5.5	5.6
1990 Foreign or Foreign Born Population (percent)	14.7	8.2	4.6	5.6	3.3	7.9
1990 Largest Cultural or Language Minority Groups	Caribbean Vietnamese Yugoslav[d]	Turk Yugoslav	Moroccan Turk	Iranian Turk	Caribbean Guyanan Indian	Cuban Mexican

[a]*Sources:* Office of Technology Assessment (United States Congress), *International Health Statistics: What the Numbers Mean for the United States* (Washington, DC: U.S. Government Printing Office, 1993). United Nations, *Statistical Year Book, 38th Issue* (New York: United Nations, 1993). United States Bureau of the Census, *Statistical Abstract of the United States: 1993, 113th edition* (Washington, DC: U.S. Government Printing Office, 1993).

[b]Except for Land Area, all statistics are from data compiled by West Germany (former Federal Republic of Germany).

[c]The rate of natural population growth is the difference between the crude birth and death rates.

[d]Data from 1986.

and the United States—despite their wealth (see Figure 35–1)—face daunting social problems because of their level of poverty (defined as 50 percent below the median national income) during any single year. Nonetheless, except for Sweden, other European countries share similar problems with these North American countries in helping people escape from poverty (defined as earning 50 percent more income within a year's time). Additionally, the United States is about in the midrange for unemployment when compared with these five other countries.

While it is clear that none of the five countries discussed is identical to the United States, they are not so dissimilar that useful comparisons cannot be made, especially with regard to health care policy changes. Hence, as the United States seriously considers reform of its health care system, three key lessons may be drawn from our review of these five other health care systems: (1) the United States should create a national policy for health care; (3) this policy should provide universal access—both financial and physical—to health; and (3) the financing of health care should be on an equitable basis. Each of the systems we have reviewed have attempted to maintain universal financial and physical access to health care, with each achieving differential success in terms of the quality and cost of health care.

With regard to financing health care, Canada, Sweden, and the United Kingdom rely primarily on income as well as other taxes to fund health care, and a single payor—the government—disburses these funds. In contrast, Germany and the Netherlands rely largely on payroll taxes for funding health care, disbursing these funds via a multipayor mixture of public and private insurance.

As measured by indices of health care outcomes (see Figure 35–2), Sweden and Canada have attained the best health care quality, while having the most difficulty containing costs during the past decade. The United Kingdom, in comparison, has contained costs the most effectively, while attaining much poorer though arguably equitable outcomes. The multipayor sys-

tems—Germany and the Netherlands—also reflect this trade-off between cost and quality. While the Netherlands has attained better health care outcomes than Germany, it has been less successful in containing its costs. Nonetheless, both countries have been much more successful than the United States in controlling costs.[216] The problem facing each country, as Ham notes, is that it must determine "how to combine the control of expenditures at the macro level with real incentives for efficiency at the micro level. The country that is able to solve this puzzle will indeed be the envy of the world."[217] Within this context, it is significant that the Netherlands, the United Kingdom, and Germany are introducing various elements of managed competition in order to address similar issues, albeit caused by different problems, within their health care systems. In each of these countries, managed competition is viewed as a way to increase providers' efficiency when delivering health care, thus balancing the macromanagement of financing health care practiced in each country with a quasimarket mechanism for micromanaging expenditures.[218]

Toward U.S. Convergence with European Health Care Systems?

Interestingly, the planned changes in not only Germany and the Netherlands, but also in both the United Kingdom and Sweden are aimed at creating a mixture of regulation and market competition[219] that may converge with the regulatory reforms that seem likely to occur in the United States.[220] That is, the vision of a U.S. health care system to managed competition with a budgetary cap on total spending is similar to what is already occurring in several European countries.[221] Broadly speaking, these two approaches to financing and delivering health care rely on a public contract model, similar to the Medicare payments of HMOs in the United States.[222] While the economic efficiency and effectiveness of the public contract model in achieving health care policy objectives is touted by Hurst[223] and others,[224,225,226] researchers have just begun to explore its impact on the organizational structures[227] and management of hospitals and medical practices.[228,229]

European Lessons for Managing Competition

Arguably, of the five countries that have been reviewed, the German and Dutch health care systems are the most comparable to the U.S. system, especially given their mixture of private and public health insurance.[230,231,232] While both Cox and Weil indicate that several lessons for the United States can be gained from Germany, this is broadened herein to also encompass the Netherlands.[233,234] These lessons for the United States focus on how it might learn to manage competition within its public and private mixture of financing and delivering health care:

- The setting of global health care budgets—expenditure targets—at the system, sector, and provider levels has been the primary means by which Germany, and, to a lesser degree, the Netherlands have controlled costs. Presently the United States has no means to set such budgets for the private sector, but it could do so for Medicare and Medicaid. Certainly, this is an area of reform addressed by several plans under consideration.

- Three related principles have allowed both Germany and the Netherlands to reform and incrementally change their health care systems. One principle is to set health care policy by involving and negotiating with all major stakeholders, including insurers, hospitals, physicians, pharmaceutical companies, employers, labor unions, and other consumer representatives. The second principle is to involve provider stakeholders in all aspects of the regulation process. A third principle is ensuring that all stakeholders adhere to the same rules. For example, balancing the power of stakeholders—purchasers and providers—has been

the historical path in Germany that has made its health care policies work. Although one may argue about the efficacy of the policy-setting process being used in the United States in the 1990s, most stakeholders have had an opportunity to be involved. Hence, the second and third principles are ones that legislators and the executive branch should definitely consider once definitive health care reforms are set into motion in the United States.

- Central to both Germany's and the Netherlands's reliance on payroll taxes for health care is that they have created coherent mechanisms for connecting financing with health care delivery. The various reform plans that suggest that the United States should form Health Insurance Purchasing Cooperatives (HIPCs) point to this type of mechanism.

- Both Germany and the Netherlands have been fairly successful in protecting their private and public insurance funds from freeloading by consumers and cream-skimming by insurers. To ensure the integrity of the mixed financing system, both countries have levied high transaction costs on consumers who switch between public and private funds. In Germany, these same high costs are imposed by the private insurers, limiting switching from one fund to another. Within the U.S. system, these same sorts of mechanisms may need to be considered.

- Germany, in contrast to the Netherlands, has been more successful in cost containment because it limits expenditures to revenues raised for health care. The current reforms in the Netherlands are aimed, in part, at achieving this same "revenue-based expenditure" policy. Certainly the United States should also consider closing its open door to health care spending by setting up a similar mechanism, and several plans for health care reform attempt to address this point.

- Perhaps more controversial in the United States, with its reliance on market forces, would be the Dutch and German policies that restrict the supply of health care providers and their facilities. While certificate of need legislation has been attacked as just one more political pork barrel in the United States, it is a mechanism that should be reconsidered. Restrictions on physician training, of course, are already central to several health care proposals.

Clearly, the U.S. health care system can benefit from looking at the successes and failures within other systems. The insular focus of many of the health care reform discussions now underway misses the opportunity to gain perspective and insight from other health systems. Certainly, it is hoped that policy makers and all health care stakeholders will begin to take a look around the world in order to improve the financing, organizing, and delivery of health care in the United States.

NOTES

1. D.V. Himmelstein et al., The Vanishing Health Care Safety Net: New Data on Uninsured Americans, *International Journal of Health Services* 22, no. 3 (1992):381–396.

2. D.A. Rublee and M. Schneider, International Health Spending Comparisons, *Health Affairs* 10, no. 3 (1991):187–198.

3. G.J. Schieber et al., Health Care Systems in Twenty-Four Countries, *Health Affairs* 10, no. 3 (1991):22–38.

4. M.D. Smith et al., Taking the Public's Pulse on Health System Reform, *Health Affairs* 11, no. 2 (Summer 1992): 125–133.

5. J.N. Edwards et al., Small Business and the National Health Care Reform Debate, *Health Affairs* 11, no. 1 (1992):164–173.

6. M.A. Peterson, Momentum toward Health Care Reform in the U.S. Senate, *Journal of Health Politics, Policy and Law* 17, no. 3 (1992):553–573.

7. Organization for Economic Cooperation and Development, *Health Care Systems in Transition: The Search for Efficiency, Social Policy Studies No. 7* (Paris: OECD, 1990). (Also published as the 1989 Annual Supplement, *Health Care Financing Review*.)

8. An Agenda for Reform: The Health Care System at a Turning Point, *Frontiers of Health Services Management* 9, no. 1 (1992):1–47.

9. Managed Competition: Health Reform American Style? *Health Affairs* 12 (Supplement 1993):7–228.

10. Pursuit of Health Systems Reform, *Health Affairs* 10, no. 3 (1991):7–268.

11. State Models (Special Section), *Health Affairs* 12, no. 2 (1993):7–87.

12. R. Priester, A Values Framework for Health System Reform, *Health Affairs* 11, no. 1 (1992):84–107.

13. M.L. Barer and R.G. Evans, Interpreting Canada: Models, Mind-Sets, and Myths, *Health Affairs* 11, no. 1 (1992):44–61.

14. P.M. Danzon, Hidden Overhead Costs: Is Canada's System Less Expensive? *Health Affairs* 11, no. 1 (1992):21–43.

15. C.D. Naylor, A Different View of Queues in Ontario, *Health Affairs* 10, no. 3 (1991):44–61.

16. J.F. Sheils et al., O Canada: Do We Expect Too Much from Its Health System? *Health Affairs* 11, no. 1 (1992):7–20.

17. J.W. Hurst, Reform of Health Care in Germany, *Health Care Financing Review* 12, no. 3 (1991):73–86.

18. J.W. Hurst, Reforming Health Care in Seven European Nations, *Health Affairs* 10, no. 3 (1991):7–21.

19. B. Jönsson, What Can Americans Learn from Europeans? in *Health Care Systems in Transition: The Search for Efficiency, Social Policy Studies No. 7.* (Paris: OECD, 1990):87–101.

20. G.J. Schieber et al., Health Care Systems in Twenty-Four Countries.

21. B. Abel-Smith, Cost Containment and New Priorities in the European Community, *The Milbank Quarterly* 70, no. 3 (1992):393–416.

22. B. Starfield, Primary Care and Health: A Cross-National Comparison, *Journal of the American Medical Association* 266, no. 16 (1991):2268–2271.

23. D. V. Himmelstein et al., The Vanishing Health Care Safety Net, 381–396.

24. T.P. Weil, A Universal Access Plan: A Step toward National Health Insurance?, *Hospital & Health Services Administration* 37, no. 1 (1992):37–51.

25. Starfield, Primary Care and Health, 2268–2271.

26. Ibid.

27. G.J. Schieber et al., Health Spending, Delivery, and Outcomes in OECB Countries, *Health Affairs* 12, no. 2 (1993):120–129.

28. C. Sakala, The Development of National Medical Care Programs in the United Kingdom and Canada: Applicability to Current Conditions in the United States, *Jour-*

nal of Health Politics, Policy and Law 15, no. 4 (1990):709–753.

29. M. Taylor, *Health Insurance and Canadian Public Policy: The Seven Decisions That Created the Canadian Health Insurance System* (Montreal: McGill-Queen's University Press, 1978).

30. E. Neuscheler, *Canadian Health Care: The Implications of Public Health Insurance* (Washington, DC: Health Insurance Association of America, 1990).

31. M.I. Roemer, *National Strategies for Health Care Organization: A World Overview* (Ann Arbor, Mich.: Health Administration Press, 1985).

32. Sakala, The Development of National Medical Care Programs, 709–753.

33. T.J. Litman and L.S. Robins, *Health Politics and Policy* (New York: John Wiley & Sons, 1984).

34. H.E. Scully, Medicare: The Canadian Experience, *Annals Thoracic Surgery* 52 (1991):390–396.

35. D. Coburn, State Authority, Medical Dominance, and Trends in the Regulation of the Health Professions: The Ontario Case, *Social Science and Medicine* 37, no. 2 (1993):129–138.

36. Sakala, The Development of National Medical Care Programs, 709–753.

37. Litman and Robins, *Health Politics and Policy.*

38. Coburn, State Authority, 129–138.

39. Neuschler, *Canadian Health Care.*

40. Sakala, The Development of National Medical Care Programs, 709–753.

41. Neuschler, *Canadian Health Care.*

42. Ibid.

43. Health and Welfare Canada, *Notes on Hospital Financing in Canada* (Ottawa: Minister of Supply and Services, 1987).

44. Roemer, *National Strategies for Health Care Organization.*

45. Neuschler, *Canadian Health Care.*

46. Health and Welfare Canada, *Notes on Hospital Financing in Canada.*

47. Health and Welfare Canada, *Health Personnel in Canada in 1987* (Ottawa: Minister of Supply and Services, 1988).

48. M. Rachlis and C. Kushner, *Second Opinion: What's Wrong with Canada's Health Care System and How To Fix It* (Toronto: Harper & Collins, 1989).

49. J. David, Health Care a Major Topic for Canadian Public Policy Journal, *Canadian Medical Association Journal* 148, no. 10 (1993):1,806–1,808.

50. T.R. Marmor, Commentary on Canadian Health Insurance: Lessons for the United States, *International Journal of Health Services* 23, no. 1 (1993):45–62.

51. Scully, Medicare: The Canadian Experience, 390–396.

52. Health and Welfare Canada, *Notes on Hospital Financing in Canada.*

53. Coburn, State Authority, 129–138.

54. J.K. Iglehart, The United States Looks at Canadian Health Care, *The New England Journal of Medicine* 321, no. 25 (1989):1767–1772.

55. R.W. Sutherland and M.J. Fulton, *Health Care in Canada: A Description and Analysis of Canadian Health Services* (Ottawa: The Canadian Public Health Association, 1988).

56. Iglehart, The United States Looks at Canadian Health Care, 1767–1772.

57. M.M. Hagland, Looking Abroad for Changes to the U.S. Health Care System, *Hospitals* 65, no. 10 (1991): 30–35.

58. Iglehart, The United States Looks at Canadian Health Care, 1767–1772.

59. Scully, Medicare: The Canadian Experience, 390–396.

60. Coburn, State Authority, 129–138.

61. Roemer, *National Strategies for Health Care Organization.*

62. D. Swartz, The Politics of Reform: Public Health Insurance in Canada, *International Journal of Health Services* 23, no. 2 (1993):219–238.

63. Barer and Evans, Interpreting Canada, 44–61.

64. Danzon, Hidden Overhead Costs, 21–43.

65. Naylor, A Different View of Queues in Ontario, 44–61.

66. Sheils et al., O Canada, 7–20.

67. J.K. Iglehart, Canada's Health Care System Faces Its Problems, *The New England Journal of Medicine* 322, no. 8 (1990):562–568.

68. Marmor, Commentary on Canadian Health Insurance, 45–62.

69. Scully, Medicare: The Canadian Experience, 390–396.

70. Rachlis and Kushner, *Second Opinion.*

71. Weil, A Universal Access Plan, 37–51.

72. Iglehart, Canada's Health Care System Faces Its Problems, 562–568.

73. Marmor, Commentary on Canadian Health Insurance, 45–62.

74. Weil, A Universal Access Plan, 37–51.

75. Coburn, State Authority, 129–138.

76. David, Health Care a Major Topic for Canadian Public Policy Journal, 1806–1808.

77. Neuschler, *Canadian Health Care.*

78. A. Sepehri and R. Chernomas, Further Refinements of Canadian/U.S. Health Cost Containment Measures, *International Journal of Health Services* 23, no. 1 (1993):63–67.

79. Sutherland and Fulton, *Health Care in Canada.*

80. Swartz, The Politics of Reform, 219–238.

81. Iglehart, The United States Looks at Canadian Health Care, 1767–1772.

82. Iglehart, Canada's Health Care System Faces Its Problems, 562–568.

83. Marmor, Commentary on Canadian Health Insurance, 45–62.

84. Neuschler, *Canadian Health Care.*

85. Scully, Medicare: The Canadian Experience, 390–396.

86. R.J. Blendon, Three Systems: A Comparative Survey, *Health Management Quarterly* 11, no. 1 (1989):2–10.

87. Iglehart, Canada's Health Care System Faces Its Problems, 562–568.

88. Scully, Medicare: The Canadian Experience, 390–396.

89. R.M. Hessler and A.C. Twaddle, Sweden's Crises in Medical Care: Political and Legal Changes, *Journal of Health Politics, Policy and Law* 7, no. 2 (1982):440–459.

90. A.C. Twaddle and R.M. Hessler, Power and Change: The Case of the Swedish Commission of Inquiry on Health and Sickness Care, *Journal of Health Politics, Policy and Law* 11, no. 1 (1986):19–40.

91. R.B. Saltman, Competition and Reform in the Swedish Health System, *The Milbank Quarterly* 68, no. 4, (1990):597–618.

92. B. Lindgren, The Swedish Health Care System, in Organization for Economic Cooperation and Development, *Health Care Systems in Transition: The Search for Efficiency, Social Policy Studies No. 7* (Paris: OECD, 1990): 74–79.

93. Roemer, *National Strategies for Health Care Organization.*

94. Saltman, Competition and Reform in the Swedish Health System, 597–618.

95. A.J. Heidenheimer and L.N. Johansen, Organized Medicine and Scandinavian Professional Unionism: Hospital Policies and Exit Options in Denmark and Sweden, *Journal of Health Politics, Policy and Law* 10, no. 2 (1985):347–369.

96. Saltman, Competition and Reform in the Swedish Health System, 597–618.

97. Heidenheimer and Johansen, Organized Medicine and Scandinavian Professional Unionism, 347–369.

98. Saltman, Competition and Reform in the Swedish Health System, 597–618.

99. Twaddle and Hessler, Power and Change, 19–40.

100. Saltman, Competition and Reform in the Swedish Health System, 597–618.

101. R.A. Knox, *Germany: One Nation with Health Care for All* (New York: Faulkner & Gray, Inc., 1993), 23–24.

102. W. Carr, *A History of Germany, 1815–1990* (London: Edward Arnold/Hodder & Stoughton, 1991), 136–137.

103. Knox, *Germany,* 27–28.

104. D.A. Stone, *The Limits of Professional Power: National Health Care in the Federal Republic of Germany* (Cambridge, Mass.: The MIT Press, 1980), 78.

105. Knox, *Germany,* 30.

106. Stone, *The Limits of Professional Power,* 50.

107. S. Leibfried and F. Tennstedt, Health-Insurance Policy and *Berufsverbote* in the Nazi Takeover, in *Political Values and Health Care: The German Experience,* ed. D.W. Light and A. Schuller (Cambridge, Mass.: The MIT Press, 1985), 127–138.

108. Knox, *Germany,* 67.

109. J.W. Hurst, Reform of Health Care in Germany, *Health Care Financing Review* 12, no. 3 (1991):77–78.

110. Knox, *Germany,* 48.

111. Hurst, Reform of Health Care in Germany, 74.

112. Knox, *Germany,* 57.

113. Hurst, Reform of Health Care in Germany, 77.

114. Ibid., 78.

115. Ibid., 77.

116. Knox, *Germany,* 53.

117. Ibid., 263.

118. Hurst, Reform of Health Care in Germany, 75, 83.

119. Knox, *Germany,* 267.

120. Ibid., 269.

121. Ibid., 270.

122. Hurst, Reform of Health Care in Germany, 84.

123. Ibid.

124. Ibid.

125. M. Schneider, Health Care Cost Containment in the Federal Republic of Germany, *Health Care Financing Review* 12, no. 3 (1991):100.

126. Hurst, Reform of Health Care in Germany, 84.

127. Ibid.

128. Ibid.

129. Knox, *Germany,* 69.

130. Ibid., 69–71.

131. Sakala, The Development of National Medical Care Programs, 714, 718.

132. Roemer, *National Strategies for Health Care Organization,* 171.

133. Ibid., 171–172.

134. Roemer, *National Strategies for Health Care Organization,* 172–173.

135. Sakala, The Development of National Medical Care Programs, 715, 718, 731.

136. T.A. Madden, The Reform of the British National Health Services, *Journal of Public Health Policy* Autumn (1991):378–379.

137. W. Beveridge, *Social Insurance and Allied Services,* American edition (New York: Macmillan Co., 1942), 158.

138. Roemer, *National Strategies for Health Care Organization,* 173–174.

139. R. Murley, A Tale of Turbulent Times, *British Medical Journal* 289 December 22–29 (1984):1782–1783.

140. Roemer, *National Strategies for Health Care Organization,* 174.

141. Ibid., 174–175.

142. Ibid., 176–178.

143. Ibid., 178.

144. Ibid., 179.

145. Ibid., 188.

146. Ibid., 183–184.

147. Ibid., 187.

148. Ibid., 187–188.

149. Ibid.

150. Ibid., 186.

151. Ibid., 190.

152. J.K. Iglehart, Conference Report: Health Systems in Three Nations, *Health Affairs* 10, no. 3 (Fall 1991): 255.

153. Madden, The Reform of the British National Health Service, 380.

154. Ibid., 381.

155. Ibid., 379.

156. J.W. Hurst, Reforming Health Care in Seven European Nations, *Health Affairs* 10, no. 3 (1991):7–21.

157. A.C. Enthoven, Internal Market Reform of the British Health Service, *Health Affairs* 10, no. 3 (1991): 60–70.

158. A.C. Enthoven, What Can Europeans Learn from Americans, in Organizations for Economic Cooperation and Development, *Health Care Systems in Transition: The Search for Efficiency, Social Policy Studies No. 7* (Paris: OECD, 1990), 57–71.

159. Enthoven, Internal Market Reform of the British Health Service, 60–70.

160. P. Day and R. Klein, Britain's Health Care Experiment, *Health Affairs* 10, no. 3 (1991):22–38.

161. Enthoven, What Can Europeans Learn from Americans, 57–71.

162. Enthoven, Internal Market Reform of the British Health Service, 60–70.

163. B. Kirkman-Liff and E. Schneller, The Resource Management Initiative in the English National Health System, *Health Care Management Review* 17, no. 2 (1992):59–70.

164. Ibid.

165. Day and Klein, Britain's Health Care Experiment, 22–38.

166. Enthoven, What Can Europeans Learn from Americans, 57–71.

167. Enthoven, Internal Market Reform of the British Health Service, 60–70.

168. Kirkman-Liff and E. Schneller, The Resource Management Initiative in the English National Health System, 59–70.

169. A.M. Pollock, The Future of Health Care in the United Kingdom, *British Medical Journal,* 306, June 26 (1993):1703–1704.

170. C. Ham, How Go the NHS Reforms? *British Medical Journal* 306, January 9 (1993):77–78.

171. F.T. Schut, Workable Competition in Health Care: Prospects for the Dutch Design, *Social Science and Medicine* 35, no. 12 (1992):1445–1455.

172. J. van der Gaag et al., The Netherlands, in *Advances in Health Economics and Health Services Research, Supplement 1: Comparative Health Systems* (Greenwich, Conn.: JAI Press, 1990), 28–41.

173. Schut, Workable Competition in Health Care, 1450.

174. J. van der Gaag et al., The Netherlands, 28, 33.

175. Ibid., 28.

176. Schut, Workable Competition in Health Care, 1446.

177. E. Van Doorslaer et al., The Netherlands, in *Equity in the Finance and Delivery of Health Care: An International Perspective,* ed, E. Van Doorslaer, A. Wagstaff, and F. Rutten (Oxford: Oxford University Press, 1993), 168.

178. Van der Gaag et al., The Netherlands, 28.

179. Van Doorslaer et al., The Netherlands, 167–168.

180. Van der Gaag et al., The Netherlands, 28–29.

181. Schut, Workable Competition in Health Care, 1445–1455.

182. Ibid., 1447.

183. Van der Gaag et al., The Netherlands, 29.

184. Schut, Workable Competition in Health Care, 1447.

185. Ibid., 1445–1455.

186. J.W. Hurst, Reforming Health Care in Seven European Nations, *Health Affairs* 10, no. 3 (1991):11.

187. Van Doorslaer et al., The Netherlands, 168.

188. Van der Gaag et al., The Netherlands, 30.

189. Van Doorslaer et al., The Netherlands, 170–173.

190. Schut, Workable Competition in Health Care, 1445–1455.

191. Van Doorslaer et al., The Netherlands, 169.

192. Van der Gaag et al., The Netherlands, 28–29.

193. R.M. Lapré and A.A. de Roo, Medical Specialist Manpower Planning in the Netherlands, *Health Policy* 15 (1990):163–187.

194. Hurst, Reforming Health Care in Seven European Nations, 7–21.

195. B. Jönsson, What Can Americans Learn from Europeans?, in Organization for Economic Cooperation and Development, *Health Care Systems in Transition: The Search for Efficiency, Social Policy Studies No. 7.* (Paris: OECD, 1990), 87–101.

196. Van der Gaag et al., The Netherlands, 28.

197. Schut, Workable Competition in Health Care, 1452.

198. Ibid., 1449.

199. Ibid., 1446.

200. Van der Gaag et al., The Netherlands, 27–41.

201. F.F.H. Rutten, Market Strategies for Publicly Financed Health Care Systems, *Health Policy* 7 (1987):135–148.

202. Schut, Workable Competition in Health Care, 1447.

203. Enthoven, What Can Europeans Learn from Americans, 68.

204. A.C. Enthoven, The 1987 Professor Dr.F.de Vries lectures, in *Theory and Practice of Managed Competition in Health Care Finance* (New York: North Holland Publishing Company, 1988).

205. Schut, Workable Competition in Health Care, 1447–1448.

206. Enthoven, What Can Europeans Learn from Americans, 57–71.

207. Hurst, Reforming Health Care in Seven European Nations, 7–21.

208. B. Kirkman-Liff and W. van de Ven, Improving Efficiency in the Dutch Health Care System: Current Innovations and Future Options, *Health Policy* 13, no. 1 (1989).

209. Schut, Workable Competition in Health Care, 1447–1454.

210. Van der Gaag et al., The Netherlands, 37–39.

211. P. Dwyer and P. Oster, We'll Need Hillary Clinton in Holland, *Business Week* November 8 (1993):72–73.

212. Schut, Workable Competition in Health Care, 1449.

213. Ibid., 1451.

214. Ibid., 1453.

215. Ibid., 1445–1455.

216. Schieber et al., Health Spending, Delivery, and Outcomes in OECB Countries, 120–129.

217. C. Ham, Health Care Reform, *British Medical Journal* May 8 (1993):1223–1224.

218. U.E. Reinhardt, Response: What Can Americans Learn from Europeans, in Organization for Economic Cooperation and Development, *Health Care Systems in Transition: The Search for Efficiency, Social Policy Studies No. 7* (Paris: OECD, 1990), 105–112.

219. Jönsson, What Can Americans Learn from Europeans, 87–101.

220. Managed Competition: Health Reform American Style? *Health Affairs* 12 (Supplement 1993):7–228.

221. S.H. Altman and A.B. Cohen, The Need for a National Global Budget, *Health Affairs* 12 (Supplement 1993):194–203.

222. Hurst, Reforming Health Care in Seven European Nations, 7–21.

223. Ibid.

224. Enthoven, Internal Market Reform of the British Health Service, 60–70.

225. R.G. Evans and M.L. Barer, Response: The American Predicament, in Organization for Economic Cooperation and Development, *Health Care Systems in Transition: The Search for Efficiency, Social Policy Studies No. 7* (Paris: OECD, 1990), 80–85.

226. Jönsson, What Can Americans Learn from Europeans, 87–101.

227. Day and Klein, Britain's Health Care Experiment, 22–38.

228. A.I. Kabcenell et al., Importing a Model of Hospital Quality from the Netherlands, *Health Affairs* 10, no. 3 (1991):240–245.

229. Kirkman-Liff and Schneller, The Resource Management Initiative in the English National Health System, 59–70.

230. R.J. Blendon et al., Reform Lessons Learned from Physicians in Three Nations, *Health Affairs* 12, no. 3 (1993):194–203.

231. G.T. Savage, et al., An Exploratory Study of Hospital Manager–Physician–Nurse Relationships in the United Kingdom and the Netherlands, in *Proceedings of the Southern Management Association* (Valdosta, Ga.: Southern Management Association, 1993), 500–502.

232. U.E. Reinhardt, Reorganizing the Financial Flows in U.S. Health Care, *Health Affairs* 12 (Supplement 1993):172–193.

233. Cox, *Germany,* 292–294.

234. T.P. Weil, The German Health Care System: A Model for Hospital Reform in the United States, *Hospital & Health Services Administration* 37, no. 4 (1992):541–544.

GRANT T. SAVAGE, PhD, is Director of the MBA Program in Health Organization Management, Associate Professor of Management in the College of Business Administration, and Associate Professor of Health Organization Management in the School of Medicine at Texas Tech University. His research focuses primarily upon the health care industry. His disciplinary interests include communication and negotiation, as well as international, social issues, and strategic management. Professor Savage's current research in health care has a number of foci. One long-standing project is examining the relationships among hospital managers–physicians–nurses, linking these key stakeholder relationships to organizational change and development within and across national health care systems. This project involves collaboration with a number of colleagues from other U.S. foreign universities. Another major project—to conduct a national Delphi survey of the future of group practice and medical care—involves several colleagues and doctoral students at Texas Tech in a joint partnership with the Medical Group Management Association.

As a past Chair of the Health Care Administration Division within the Academy of Management, his research has been published in *Health Care Management Review, Hospital & Health Services Administration,* and the *Physician Executive Journal of Management,* as well as leading communication and management journals. He has also provided training and consultation for various health care organizations and businesses, as well as federal, state, and local government agencies. He received his PhD from Ohio State University.

ELIZABETH W. MICHAEL, MBA, is a registered nurse with certification in cardiac care, oncology/chemotherapy, and psychiatric nursing. She is a doctoral candidate in the College of Business Administration at Texas Tech University, concentrating in health organization management and strategic management. She teaches courses in management, business ethics, labor relations, and administrative policy. She also team-teaches biomedical ethics at the Texas Tech School of Medicine. Her writing and research interests include conflict management, international and domestic health care reform, total quality management, ethics and organizational change and relationships. She received her MBA from Texas Tech University.

Epilogue

The Future of an Industry in Transition

The following six essays represent the opinions of selected professionals from various segments of the industry, including university professors, consultants, hospital executives, and futurists. Some of the professionals are authors in this text, while others, such as Montague Brown and Russell Coile, Jr., were generous in making their independent contributions given their busy schedules. They are all to be thanked for contributing to this interesting and free-wheeling section of this text.

The essayists were asked to comment on where they think the industry will be by the year 2000, including achievements and failures. They could factor in their own areas of expertise, but that was not necessarily a goal. It is interesting to note that notwithstanding their areas of expertise, organizational affiliation, or the part of the United States in which they reside, most had similar visions, and shared common hopes and concerns about health care reform. The only apparent differences were more a matter of the degree of optimism versus pessimism, and of when outcomes of change would be observable.

Lawrence F. Wolper
Great Neck, New York

In many ways, the future of health care reform is predictable based on history both inside and outside the industry. First, major reform is not likely because incremental change is more characteristic of the U.S. government. Second, in the late 1970s through the mid-1980s there was a great deal of hospital corporate restructuring, merger, acquisition, and joint venturing. Many of these activities resulted in vertically integrated networks, and very few of them resulted in economies of scale. For-profit hospital chains, often more focused on price per share and profit, did not appear to achieve economies of scale in many of their activities. They grew through merger and acquisition, and years later, many proceeded through long periods of divestiture. The not-for-profits, by and large, did not achieve these economies either.

The answers to why these economies did not occur are complex, but much of the answer has to do with the fact that mergers/acquisitions and vertical integration in the health industry is markedly different from similar change in other industries. Mergers, acquisitions, and vertical integration in the health industry are too frequently only legal and structural in nature. Economies of scale begin with structural and organizational redesign, but will not fully occur without operational, clinical, and cultural mergers. True operational merger, with the concomitant reductions in and reassignment of personnel, as well as the downsizing of physical plant and services, did not occur often enough to affect overall expenditures, nor the success of many vertical networks in the past. It rarely affected the manner in which medical services were utilized and coordinated. Future merger, acquisition, and network development (whether horizontal or vertical) accomplished only for the purposes of market expansion and negotiating managed care contracts will not succeed in the long term. If executives from member hospitals in a large network cannot vote often enough for plans that are positive for the entire network, but may not be equally positive for their hospital (or may even be adverse to their hospital), networks will not have transitioned enough toward balancing stakeholder interests, and many will fail.

It can be speculated that in the next few years there will be a continuation in vertical integration efforts and the creation of provider networks in both the profit and nonprofit sectors. This will occur with or without government regulation. In the same period, there will be very aggressive attempts to design information systems and software that will provide management with the data that will be necessary to manage in a vertically integrated managed care environment. Hospitals and networks will need this information to succeed under managed care and capitation, but it is not likely that all provider networks will have the financial ability to purchase such substantial management information systems.

The profit and not-for-profit sectors will proceed through a similar growth and consolidation process over the next five years. The for-profits are more likely to expand quickly through acquisition because of their ability to access the capital markets. Those networks that effectively deal with the management issues of diverse stakeholders (many of whom involuntarily, or with resistance, will find themselves in a vertically integrated organization) will have greater success. Hospitals that through PHOs, MSOs or similar organizations provide management and billing services to their physicians, but underestimate the complexities of providing these services, thus further risking physician incomes, may alienate this large stakeholder group. Hospitals that choose low-cost low-quality hospital network "partners" because it makes them more competitive in managed care contracting, may find in the next few years that their network is not very marketable to the consumer. Why would a patient willingly be admitted to a neighborhood hospital that historically he or she never would have gone to, just because it is in a large network? Further, overly aggressive acquisition of physician practices and hospitals for the purpose of market expansion can result in overvalued acquired assets, and in the problems that often occur when managers attempt to operate businesses in which they have little experience. Both, while logical short-term measures, typically result in long-term problems. Health insurance companies, some through acquisition of physician practices, and others using alternative strategies, will dominate the industry more than they have historically. By becoming providers of care as well as insurers, they will fuel the long-standing debate over their dominance in the industry and their concern for large profits before patient care.

While all of this vertical integration is occurring in the next two to three years, health care expenditures will rise, but at a slower rate per year. This will happen because managed care contracting and industry consolidation will depress prices, not as a result of market forces and increased efficiency. After this period of time, the growth rate in health care expenditures will accelerate because many, but not enough, integrated provider networks, HMOs, and insurers will have created efficient systems, and some will begin to fail. Insurance company premiums are likely to increase because of their need to demonstrate profits. The impact of integrated systems, HMO, and insurance company failures will be compounded by a growth in HIV-related illnesses, drug-resistant organisms, and an aging population.

The key to what occurs at that point will be a function of the degree to which the American consumer is pleased with the system. If they are unhappy with rationing, loss of access to qualified specialists, loss of empowerment, and other factors, it may require a dramatic correction back to a more open delivery system, similar to that which is occurring in many other countries. It may be ironic that in trying to achieve a more integrated health care system, with the security of universal coverage, the consumer and local communities may be the least empowered stakeholders in the future.

At that time, after about a decade of balancing costs versus quality, and perhaps subordinating quality, there may be enough public discontent to cause a shift back in ownership from large provider networks and insurers to the community and patient.

Montague Brown
Washington, DC

It is a challenge to try and predict anything more than a few years from where we are today. Yet the urge to take a shot at thinking through where we might go is a challenge not easy to let pass. Before taking up the future, a look back is appropriate.

Twenty plus years ago, I spent some time at the University of North Carolina studying medical care organization, policy, and other related subjects. As a student of management with an abiding belief in the ability of people to make constructive change in organizations, I fully expected that within the next 20 years most hospitals in the United States would be in multihospital systems and that we would have achieved substantial integration of physicians, hospitals, and financing of health care. We have had substantial movement in this direction, but hospitals are still mainly merged with other hospitals; many communities still have substantial redundancy in capacity and remain without having merged assets and without having gotten on with the job of rationalizing capacity. I was dead right on direction of change and dead wrong on its speed.

Universal health coverage will be assured by 2010. Universal coverage will require a definition of just what is covered and this, in turn, will be greatly influenced by many special interests. The upshot will be a cost explosion requiring rationing in many forms.

Rationing of long-term-care beds coupled with guarantees for coverage will lead to a steadily increasing use of home care and more outpatient care. The geriatric industry will grow while cost pressures push providers in the direction of cheaper solutions to problems.

Capitated managed care, group practices, and other forms of vertical integration will continue to grow and dominate the field even if we have national health insurance, Canadian style. Managed care has the greatest potential for rationing services once the package of guarantees has been set. Managed care offers profit potential to insurers, physicians, and entrepreneurs. Much of the profit comes from greatly reduced utilization of high-cost services, especially hospitals and physicians. Thus managed care will prosper.

Communities will increasingly see themselves in a lose-lose situation when they continue to support duplicative, high-cost, and competing facilities. More mergers will take place, making reduction of capacity possible. However, before this happens many hospitals will fail financially, and many of these will sell out to entrepreneurs, managed care firms, and hospital chains. Those acquiring such financially failed institutions will be able to charge less for their services, thus placing more price pressure on surviving institutions.

Many of the institutions whose mission was more mercy than money will have dropped out of health care or turned their management over to managers who focus on the bottom line and make a business proposition out of health care.

All of these pressures and changes will drive the industry in the direction of greater orientation on profit. The ethic of medicine and hospitals that focused first and foremost on doing the best for the patient will increasingly focus on doing what payors (employers, government, and insurers) want to do, namely, focus on keeping costs down and profits up.

By 2010, this direction of the health care system will make it more likely that a public outcry will arise over ownership, motives, and uses of health care resources. Where has caring gone? This outcry will be for greater government oversight, community ownership, and participation.

By 2010, the entrepreneurs, insurers, and others who saw big profits to be made in managed care, hospital ownership, and the like will be seeing an industry that is increasingly threatened with public takeover. Profits will be going down, since cost pressures will not have abated. Owners will be looking for ways out.

How will the industry revert to its public and community ownership? First, the insurers and other owners will be looking to sell their assets back to the community at the point where the returns to be garnered from the industry drop below their investment criteria and long-range expectations. First the asset will be sold with the prior owner taking debt in return for a good interest rate return and the opportunity to continue to manage the operation. Thus the role of entrepreneurial firms may extend another 5 to 20 years, depending upon their ability to convince the new owners of their abilities.

When the baby boomers are entering retirement, Social Security and Medicare will be converted to welfare programs, and more and more private citizens will feel the heavy burden of high cost. Care will be tightly rationed, and may well by this time have been nationalized due to the inability of local communities and any investors still involved to raise capital for services that no longer offer sufficient profit potential to justify private investment.

Are there other alternatives? It might be possible for some communities to retake the high ground and make the changes in ownership, control, and use of resources that are necessary to become much more cost efficient without having to go through an entrepreneurial revolution in ownership. But anyone who expects that must confront the tenacity exhibited by local community boards, religious sponsors, government sponsors, their medical staffs, administrations, and others in maintaining the status quo decades after any reasoning persons would have safely concluded that the status quo is a major barrier to effective cost control.

Finally, if this prediction is as good as my earlier ones, what I think will happen by 2010 will probably not occur until 2030!

Roberta N. Clarke
Boston, Massachusetts

In 1976, when I was speaking to a national audience of not-for-profit home health care providers, I was asked: What is the key to keeping our organizations alive? They were at that time faced with retroactive denials of payment, difficulties in attracting and retaining high quality homemakers and home health aides, undercapitalization, physician disinterest in or lack of awareness of home health services, and the recent arrival of large for-profit professionally managed home health care competitors. In the face of all these challenges, I responded, the key is that size is power.

Since many of the home health agencies represented in the audience were relatively small, they were unable to afford to hire professional management, unable to invest heavily in training (which could have allowed some of them to expand into higher-tech, more profitable home health care such as parenteral nutrition or at-home chemotherapy), unable to promote aggressively due to lack of funds, and, had they somehow managed to dramatically increase demand for their services, unable to respond in a timely manner to that increased demand. A case could clearly be made for these organizations that they should seek to become larger in order to survive and thrive in the rapidly evolving competitive health care marketplace.

Almost 20 years later, most sectors of the health care industry have apparently also concluded that size is power. What had been characterized in the 1970s as a cottage industry was predicted in the 1980s to become a national oligopoly; some of the health care industry's leading experts forecast the development of a very small number of "supermeds," huge medical provider organizations which, like General Motors and Ford in the automobile industry, would cover the country with their services. The supermeds have not materialized, and some of the larger, better-known health care provider organizations have suffered setbacks or retrenchment; witness the ESOP of Hospital Corporation of America, which resulted in it spinning off roughly half of its hospitals.

Nonetheless, the health care world seems to be moving toward a bigger-is-better approach, a strategy that can be demonstrated and explained by the experience of hospitals and managed care organizations in Minneapolis. The high penetration rate of managed care in that city put managed care organizations in a strong position to negotiate deep discounts from hospitals afraid of losing significant business to other hospitals that might concede even more. As long as the managed care organizations could play off one hospital against another, individual hospitals had little basis on which to negotiate. To seek protection from their "customers" (the managed care organizations), Minneapolis hospitals banded together to form negotiating units of a larger size, giving them far greater power in the negotiating process. The managed care organizations did the same, leaving the greater Minneapolis area with a very few, very large hospital corporations and managed care organizations.

What this portends for the future of the health care industry in this country is unclear. Certainly, there are advantages to being large enough to do what the home health care agencies in the 1970s and other small organizations often couldn't do: hire professional management, invest in recruit-

ing and training, in equipment and facilities, and, particularly imperative today, in a wide-ranging and versatile information system that will need constant and costly upgrading. Without these capabilities, most health care organizations that have not already folded or been folded under someone else's wing will not survive.

However, the disadvantages of the size-is-power management philosophy may have not yet become apparent. In an effort to gain market power through size, health care organizations all over the country are buying or being bought by other health care organizations. They are engaging in a merger and acquisition frenzy reminiscent of the 1980s on Wall Street; it was a heady and exciting time back then for those involved in choosing corporate dance partners, much like it is now when, for example, two Harvard teaching hospitals, the Massachusetts General Hospital and Brigham and Women's Hospital, announced their intention to merge with each other. Front page news comes from such mergers. Group model HMOs are buying IPAs, managed care organizations and hospitals are buying medical group practices, acute care hospitals are buying specialty hospitals and subacute facilities, and so on, all with the objective of being bigger and more powerful in the marketplace.

Two questions arise from all this activity: (1) Will these organizations in fact become more powerful and better able to control their destiny in the marketplace? and (2) Will this result in the delivery of medical care that is better than what we have today, or even equal to our current level of care?

To answer the first question, we should look at the net results of the 1980s merger and acquisition activity, which fueled the rise of the stock market in that decade. A well-known book on the subject, *The Complete Guide to a Successful Leveraged Buyout,*[1] notes that vast numbers of mergers and acquisitions suffered from the winner's curse. The winner's curse arose when more than one company competed to acquire or merge with another unit of business; the greater the number of competing players, the higher the bidding for that unit of business would rise, most often resulting in the winner overpaying for the unit of business.

Once the initial excitement of winning the bid for the business wore off, the realization of the financial implications of the deal—of the winner's curse—took root and corporate disenchantment set in. The resulting volume of divestitures in the late 1980s and early 1990s speak to the dominance of optimism over realism in these decisions to merge or acquire.

In fact, the authors of *The Complete Guide* note that, almost always, sales, volume, and financial projections for these mergers were optimistic, reflecting neither past nor present performance but rather an expectation of improved performance. These projections did not take into account the volatility of gross margins and cash flow, nor the increasingly competitive nature of the industries in which many of these businesses competed, nor the recognition that, if the optimistic projections actually did occur, even greater cash demands would be placed on the merged organization because growth is costly in the short term.

Familiarity with the recent trend in health care mergers and acquisitions suggests that we had better look quite carefully at the experiences of nonhealth care mergers and acquisitions in the 1980s. Health care organizations appear to be following a remarkably similar path in the name of seeking greater vertical and horizontal integration, with the objective of achieving greater size and power.

Particularly notable is the risk involved with vertical integration. The book's authors point out that if an organization bought another organizational unit outside of its primary line of business, due to its lack of knowledge of that business's industry, it was far more likely to pay an unreasonably high premium to buy into an industry it didn't know merely because it wanted to get into this new business. This is a pretty good description of many health care organizations that are vertically extending themselves into businesses with which they are unfamiliar. Not only are they likely to have misled themselves with unreasonably optimistic projections

of future performance, thus overvaluing the worth of their new acquisition, but they also may have as a result negotiated away too much (from the standpoint of financial returns) for the acquisition. Only later when expected volume and cash flows do not materialize, when the realization of depressingly lower performance replaces the optimism that characterizes so many mergers and acquisitions, do they recognize the risk that such activities pose.

The author's description of the corporate mergers and acquisitions of the 1980s should be viewed as a mirror into which the health care industry is looking a decade later. The turbulent mergers and acquisitions recorded by Wall Street in the early 1980s gave way in the late 1980s and early 1990s to the tail-between-the-legs period of divestitures and fraudulent conveyances still being arbitrated in the courts. How wise health care organizations would be if they could learn from the mistakes of those who preceded them!

The most obvious lesson is that the equation of size with power is anything but guaranteed. In fact, the qualifications to this equation are so significant as to reflect negatively from a financial perspective on many of the health care mergers that have already taken place. If projections of future growth and cash flow requirements were more realistic and less optimistic, if acquiring organizations were not so eager to get into new businesses that they negotiate away more than they gain, if these same organizations understood better the nature of businesses with which they wish to merge so that they could more accurately predict the vast resources consumed by trying to merge different corporate cultures; different competitive players; different political, regulatory, and power structure concerns; and so on, then many organizations that are currently merged as one organization might still be independent and smaller. They might not, however, be less powerful because so many of the "merged" organizations have not really captured the benefits promised by size.

The answer to the above question, will larger organizations in fact become more powerful and better able to control their destiny in the market-place? therefore is at best a qualified yes and is dependent upon numerous financial and strategic variables, many of which have yet to be addressed wisely by many health care organizations.

The second question, will larger health care organizations result in the delivery of medical care that is better than what we have today, or even equal to our current level of care? has a less definitive answer because we have less data on which to base an answer. Certainly, there is clinical evidence that certain procedures are best done by hospitals and physicians who maintain enough volume to have developed an expertise in the procedure; a hospital that performs one cardiac surgery a year will not do as good a job as a hospital that performs 300 cardiac surgeries a year. Larger organizations will also be more likely to have the resources to afford the equipment, the support and professional staff, the information system, the overhead, and so on to carry out the required task.

However, there are indications that certain values will be lost in many organizations as they grow larger. The value of being able to choose one's medical providers has historically been at the root of the U.S. health care system; it is a manifestation of the free market system, which we so value in our economy that we are enthusiastically supporting its development in other (Eastern European) countries. Yet the basis on which many health care organizations justify internal growth as well as external growth, from merger with other organizations, is the anticipation of capturing patients from womb to tomb. Theoretically, consumers will stay within one health care plan voluntarily, seeking all their care over time from providers within that plan. However, the prospect of all providers in any one geographic area being divided up into a small number of very large managed care organizations suggests that our future choices may be very limited indeed.

If size equals power and only the largest managed care organizations will survive, then patients may find that, in order to keep their be-loved family doctor, they will have to accept the one hand specialist, the one breast cancer specialist, and so on, who is on the provider list of the managed care organization with which their family doctor contracts. With only a few managed care organizations surviving in each area, it is likely that primary care physicians will work exclusively for only one of these organizations. Does lessened freedom of choice equal better medical care? No one knows; however, it seems more than reasonable to conclude that less choice will result in less consumer satisfaction.

Another concern with size is depersonalization of medical care. Years of market research around the country show a pattern of consumers reporting that larger hospitals deliver depersonalized care while smaller ones provide more empathetic, warm, and friendly care. There may be host of reasons to explain why this distinction exists; what is important, however, is that many people indicate a willingness to bypass the expected better clinical care of the larger hospitals in order to receive the more personalized care they anticipate to be delivered from a smaller hospital. Given the increased productivity requirements being placed on health care providers, the high volume of patients who will need to be processed by these large providers, plus the reengineering processes to which health care providers (as well as many manufacturing and service organizations) are subjecting themselves—processes tend to stress technical and clinical process over human process because human process is less consistent, less measurable, and less definable—we can in fact expect that care delivered by larger health care organizations may be less personalized.

Truly well-managed organizations may be able to overcome the equation that size equals not only power but depersonalization. If consumers can develop and maintain relationships with not only their primary care physicians, but also with receptionists, nurse-practitioners, and others who are delivering peripheral but necessary service in the health care setting, then the organization will be functioning like a smaller health care organization, where the consumer is at least recognized as a familiar face. (Remember the television character Dr. Marcus Welby whose receptionist, Consuela, acknowledged every patient as soon as he or she walked in the door?) However, if the pressure to produce high volumes of service takes precedence over setting up organizational systems and structures whereby health care organization employees are expected to and are capable of recognizing and at least briefly socializing with the consumer, then our worst fears of depersonalized medicine can be expected to be realized.

This is particularly a problem as it applies to physicians. If physicians face continuing productivity adjustments, as they have through the mid-1990s, the time they will be allowed to spend with any one patient will decrease. In small organizations, this can be partially counteracted by seeing the same one, two, or three physicians whenever one has a medial encounter. However, many larger organizations have a sufficiently large physician panel to have instituted physician coverage systems, as well as patient-oriented after-hours services, which collectively increase the probability that patients will not see their own physicians. Under these conditions, a patient, whose time with a physician during a medical encounter is already extremely short, will be less likely to get to know his or her physician; similarly, the physician will be less familiar with his or her patient. While, with good information systems, health care organizations may be able to relay patient information from one medical encounter to the next, regardless of which physician is facing the patient at that moment, it seems inevitable that some knowledge of the patient that could be valuable in diagnosis or treatment—that this patient rarely complains of pain so that all complaints from this patient should be taken seriously or that another patient routinely is able to self-diagnose and should be listened to accordingly—will be lost in this scenario. It is difficult to believe, therefore, that the quality of medical care will at least occasionally, if not more often, suffer due to systems, structures, and management policies related to size.

The competitive advantages of size to health care organizations is clear, both absolute size and size relative to one's competitors and one's organizational customers. Our clarity diminishes, however, when it becomes necessary to identify the disadvantages that are concomitant with larger-sized health care provider organizations. With no industry history to guide us in this area, it becomes imperative that health care managers and policy makers stand on the lookout for the negative consequences that will accompany our unbridled enthusiasm for ever-larger health care provider systems.

Myron D. Fottler and Donna Malvey
Birmingham, Alabama

The future of health care organization and delivery may be reviewed from a short-term or a long-term perspective. We foresee a short-term period of great turbulence and change followed by a period of relative stability. We expect the short-term future (1995 to 2005) to be generally an acceleration of current trends. This means more managed care, more hospital and institutional restructuring, more assessment of technology, more pressure for health care organizations to document costs and clinical outcomes, and a greater emphasis on setting of priorities for health care expenditures.

Managed care will be the norm by the turn of the century. Most U.S. citizens in all areas of the country will be participating in some form of managed care (HMOs, PPOs, etc.) utilizing a "gatekeeper" concept. This will occur irrespective of which "health reform" (if any) passes Congress. Institutions will need to develop information systems to collect data on cost and quality by diagnostic category if they are to be competitive in bidding for managed care contracts. Pressure for documentation of costs and clinical outcomes is already occurring in many parts of the country as purchasers try to determine where they can get "the most bang for the buck."

Multi-institutional arrangements, vertical integration, diversification, and other restructuring efforts will accelerate as a means of improving efficiency and productivity while simultaneously assuring quality of care. However, since recent research indicates that many of the promised outcomes of these changes have not materialized, there will be a greater effort made to document the long-term results of these efforts. In the meantime, the health care system will continue to decentralize, outpatient care will continue to grow relative to inpatient care, and the role of the hospital as the central focus of health care delivery will continue to decline. Employment in health services will level off and grow more slowly in the immediate future as a result of various efforts to control costs.

One of the problems in the health services industry is that, unlike other industries, the cost of service does not appear to decline with the development of the technology. In the computer industry, for example, technological advances have created dramatic price reductions, and the technology has become more affordable with improvements in production processes and use of new materials. Cellular phones are another example of an industry where technology has led to affordability. However, in health care, technological advances appear to increase the cost of care dramatically. Magnetic resonance imaging (MRI) is a good example of this phenomenon. It has remained a high-cost item since its introduction over a decade ago.

Much of the new technology in health care has been cost-increasing rather than cost-reducing because the purpose has been to provide new treatments for previously untreatable health problems, rather than to develop less costly approaches for treatable problems. We believe that technology assessment in the immediate future will emphasize the cost-containment potential of new technology. Technology that is not cost-reducing will be increasingly difficult to justify and will be less available beyond a few tertiary care medical centers.

Finally, we will begin to see more efforts to develop priorities for the health care delivery system as a whole. We believe that the Oregon Plan, which prioritized illness categories eligible for Medicaid coverage, and similar plans will increase in number. In addition, many of the extremely sensitive issues of how we allocate money between children and the terminally ill will be addressed, as well as issues such as the right to die and the use of heroic measures to save lives. Since we cannot afford to do every procedure we are capable of doing, some group or organization will begin to take the lead in providing guidelines for establishing priorities.

Radical changes in the nature of health care will shape the health services industry from a longer-term perspective (2006+). In that period, we expect fewer organizational and system changes, but more scientific advances. Health services will be increasingly based on gene therapies, chromosomal manipulations, and drug interventions. Our future reality is being revealed daily with incredible scientific breakthroughs such as the cloning of a human embryo or the Human Genome Project's work in identifying chromosomes associated with particular diseases. All of these interventions suggest the future potential for eliminating the majority of invasive procedures that occupy activities, personnel, and beds in today's hospitals. We see a continuing reduced role for the hospital, but also for other providers, such as outpatient surgical centers, even though they will experience growth in the short-term.

Employment in health services may decline in the longer-term future as self-care in the home coupled with computer linkages to outside support services becomes the norm. Computers will play a significant role in transforming the way health care is organized and delivered. Assisted by a variety of in-home diagnostic tests, many of which are already available today, people will be able to transmit test results through their computers to their providers. Similarly, physicians and other health care workers will respond to patients by faxing prescriptions, or instructions for care through the computer. The nature of the interaction with the health care provider will change dramatically as computer technology will eliminate much of the need for office visits. Computer-assisted diagnosis exists today, but has not been integrated into the clinical process to the extent that is possible. Cardiologists can diagnose heart attack patients using a phone and a computer. Radiologists have access to radiographs located at a variety of sites because of computer archiving capabilities. Today, computers exist mainly in the business and adminis-

trative offices of most health care facilities, but as we move into tomorrow, integration of computer technology with clinical management processes will create possibilities for delivering care outside of the hospital or physician's office.

There will be hospitals in the future health services industry, but they will be far fewer in number, more geographically dispersed, and will be dedicated to treatment of exceptionally ill patients who require hospitalization. Today, decentralization in the health services industry means moving patient services out of the hospital and into other facilities. In the future, decentralization will mean patient care will be moved out of facilities and into the home.

Russell C. Coile, Jr.
Santa Clarita, California

Beyond the year 2000, the U.S. health care system will have been dramatically reshaped. In the postreform era, hospitals and physicians will be realigned into new partnerships with insurers/HMOs and purchasers. All parties will share a cooperative business strategy: to keep consumers healthy and minimize their dependency on the health care system.

These are the defining characteristics of tomorrow's health care system:

- Regional health care provider networks will have contractual responsibility for improving the health status of hundreds of thousands of "covered lives."
- "Report card" indicators will measure provider performance in terms of consumer health and quality of life—and the data will be public.
- Health insurers and HMOs will no longer represent the buyers; they will be integrators of care who own or partner with provider networks to represent the sellers.
- Cooperation—not competition—will become the dominant business strategy between buyers and sellers, physicians and

hospitals, and public and private health organizations.

- Stand-alone hospitals and solo physicians should almost disappear; virtually all (more than 95 percent) of health institutions and most (more than 75 percent) of doctors will be members of regional networks/systems and group medical practices.
- Capitation will become the dominant form of health care payment, with price competition between network health plans holding inflation to within one to two percentage points of the Consumer Price Index.
- Universal coverage will be close to completion by the year 2000, with employer mandates for all but the smallest firms, and tax incentives and subsidies for small businesses and the self-employed.
- Health levels of the population should begin to improve as the twenty-first century begins; the early effects of health promotion and disease prevention will start to show in the nation's health indicators.

The transition to a postreform U.S. health care system will be disruptive and painful for some.

Hospital use will decline more than 25 percent from mid-1990s levels, and at least 15 percent of U.S. hospitals are likely to close or be converted to nonacute health programs. Specialty physician incomes will not keep pace with inflation, and the days of seven-figure physician earnings will be gone. Primary care physicians should see their incomes jump by 50–100 percent in the same period, as the role of primary care moves center-stage to manage capitation. Fee-for-service medicine and indemnity insurance will be minimal (under 10 percent) factors in the health care market.

For some providers, the transformation to twenty-first century health care will be troublesome. Multihospital systems will have to adapt to the looser "network" model of organization. Doctors will choose a hospital on an exclusive basis. Religious facilities will be driven into regional health care organizations by the market, and will have to search for value-compatible partners. Academic medical centers will be forced to sharply cut medical costs and specialty teaching programs. Boston's merger of Massachusetts General Hospital with the Brigham & Women's Hospital was a wake-up call for teaching centers. A few medical schools can be expected to merge to share the shrinking funding for specialty medical education, as primary care and family practice specialties bloom with another 1,000 to 1,500 graduates per year.

Health care in the year 2000 should be both more accessible and more predictable. Phasing in universal coverage will start with an employer mandate for larger firms, and government subsidies for low-income women and children. Smaller firms and working adults will be phased in toward the end of the 1990s. Variation in medical practice should be dramatically reduced, with the widespread development of clinical pathways and standardized treatment protocols. Physicians and nurses will collaborate in standard-setting and care management.

"Health management" will be the most important business management strategy for regional provider networks and HMOs in the year 2000.

High-risk groups and individuals will be identified through computer analysis of their costs and use patterns. Chronically ill patients will be closely monitored and managed. The HMOs will know that only 15 percent of their patients may generate 60 to 75 percent of annual health costs. The costs of noncompliance will be brought under control. Borderline health risks like diabetics and hypertensives may wear biosensors to warn their health organizations of impending acuity. Consumers will be rewarded for healthy behaviors with incentives and rebates.

National health reform will be no panacea. There are likely to be many unresolved issues for health care in the year 2000. The restructuring of U.S. health care systems will leave urban public hospitals and some rural facilities in a backwater of declining patients and revenues. Maldistribution of physicians will continue, despite use of nurse practitioners and technology for remote rural areas and depressed inner cities. The rationing of high-cost technology will come through limiting employer health benefit coverage. Public officials will continue to waffle on this contentious issue.

As the dust begins to settle in the year 2000, hospitals and physicians will be able to take satisfaction in the fact that they will still be in charge of their patients and their future. Clinical autonomy and economic freedom will come with capitation payments, but the new provider networks will be absolutely at risk for the costs and quality of care. During the health reform debate, many health industry observers argued that there was enough money in the system to provide access to health care for all. Basically they were right, but it would take another $100 billion in annual costs to cover the 37 million uninsured, and improve benefits for the 30 to 40 million underinsured. Health care spending in the year 2000 may reach $1.5 trillion, but annual health care inflation will be low and stable at 3 to 5 percent. Coping with the aging of America and bringing genetic technology into mainstream medicine will be the leading challenges of twenty-first century health care.

Kevin W. Barr
Richmond, Virginia

Megamergers, acquisitions, network building, regional health care system formation, integrated delivery systems, physician–hospital organizations, hospital-affiliated group practices, dominant multispecialty group medical practices, lower reimbursement, capitation, thinner profit margins, re-engineering, downsizing, multiskilling, improved efficiency, clinical pathways, clinical protocols, quality report cards, economic profiling of physicians: Is this the future of health care? What's it all about? And will it ever end?

To answer such questions fully in the context of today's health care dialogue would require another text as long as this one. A simple answer to the first question is, yes, this is the current future of health care, a prospect well-documented in the popular writings of our industry. Regarding the second question, like most health care executives, I am asked almost daily to explain this outlook and, like most of my colleagues, I respond in a reasonably articulate manner using the jargon of the day. To be honest, I might add privately, I can't explain what it is all about, rather, I usually respond by saying that health care simply has become too costly for our society to accept in its current configuration.

About the last question: Will this future ever end? I hope not. For the health care executive, it is an exciting time to be in this industry that consumes an estimated 14 percent of our nation's gross national product. And, while onerous, whatever the particular industry in distress, it is times like these that kindle radical innovation and creative thinking. In the shadow of diversity and scarcity, creative and unprecedented solutions often result. Attribute it to the fear factor or plain adrenalin—it works. The threatening future of health care alone has caused historically disparate groups to act in more unified and integrated arrangements than ever before.

What of the future? Clearly, between now and the end of the century, cost effectiveness, consolidated and integrated health care entities, and the pursuit of market share will be significant forces with which to contend.

Controlling the cost of health care (price to the consumer) will dominate the cadre of strategies employed by providers and insurers throughout the late 1990s. Such strategies, designed to improve financial return through cost effectiveness and efficiencies, will remain central to provider behavior to manage costs within the context of financially constrained (distressed for some) systems. Providers will be on a seemingly endless quest for information-related technology as a means to:

- simplify administrative procedures in order to reduce overhead staff and paperwork
- standardize billing formats and accelerate the use of electronic billing and remittance procedures
- advance electronic benefits eligibility and clinical record keeping and charting capabilities
- support reduced labor costs through downsized staffs, wider spans of management, and elimination of non-value added work

With personnel-related expenses accounting for approximately 55 percent of hospital providers' costs, earnings pressure is likely to drive the use of automation to replace workers. This is particularly likely within the investor-owned health care chains, which are growing at an unprecedented pace through mergers, acquisitions, and consolidation. And physicians are awakening to the burden of labor-related expense overhead as well. It is a routine conclusion that those health care systems with lower overall patient costs will be the ones that will win managed care contracts and thereby command the size of market share required to remain viable in the approaching period of continuously reduced financial margins.

What about winning managed care contracts? Most industry analyses argue that providers must organize into integrated care networks in order to realize:

- the economies of scale benefits associated with shared overhead functions
- the market negotiating strength to capture large contracts or patient pools, particularly the expansive patient pools expected to result from health care reform

Such experts believe that integrated delivery systems, which include acute care, physician, insurance, and other medical support services under a common parent organization or structure, will dominate the industry after health care reform.

Without question, the trend toward the formation of integrated delivery systems will continue into the future and, most likely, will benefit consumers through reductions in health care provider costs and insurance premiums in addition to the illusive improvements of seamlessness (i.e., continuity) of care. However, one should be reminded of similar industry analysts who in the mid-to-late 1980s proclaimed that a small number of major megacorporations would dominate the hospital industry across the United States. Until recent years, most of the corporations anticipated evolving into one of these national health care contenders. For example, Hospital Corporation of America and Humana have followed a steady downward trend of divestitures and leveraged buyouts, reducing the number of facilities (and markets) under their direct control.

And what of the future significance of organizations historically viewed as health insurance companies? HMOs and managed care organizations are moving into the provider side of the health care industry at an unprecedented pace, building large employed-physician provider systems and acquiring hospitals in some markets. Consolidation, integration, and a continued blurring of the traditional lines of demarcation between providers and insurers is certain to continue throughout the late 1990s and until the turn of the century. There is simply too much energy behind such initiatives today for another conclusion to be pondered.

Most hospital executives are steadfast in their vision that the competitive position of their facility and the ability to retain sufficient market share will be dependent on their relationships with two key constituent groups—physicians and managed care organizations. The faithful pursuit of an increasingly larger market share seems inevitable in light of the economic and competitive future and declining inpatient admission use-rates.

This vision of the future embodies a market that one might describe as rather phobic—showing a significant element of fear, experiencing an obsession with economic conditions, affirming a state of excess capacity, and motivated by a radical repositioning for control. Such behavior supports the industry's frantic obsession with costs, integration, and intense price competition, the prevailing phase of the market life cycle. Ironically, less exchange is centered around the implications such reformation may have on the care rendered to the patient. With thinner profit margins, organizational reeengineering, and downsized staffing becoming the consequence of reduced payments, replacement of inpatient care by outpatient treatment choices, and reduced lengths of hospital stays, health care would appear to be evolving into an industry sustained by an increased emphasis on self-care, family participation in the care process, and home-based care options. Perhaps a similar obsession with quality and a commitment to the overall health care of a community is the next phase and will become the context of future dialogue by the year 2000.

There was a time when most health care was rendered in the home and hospitals were considered a place of last resort for the very sick and dying. Ironically, the past may look more similar to the future as we approach the turn of the century. Already, some physicians have returned to making house calls, an increased emphasis on primary care medicine is flourishing, and a 24-

hour inpatient stay for normal obstetrical cases is gaining wider acceptance. Several of the nation's largest companies are employing full-time medical groups to care for their employees at prenegotiated rates. Further yet, some mature integrated health care systems are scrutinizing the idea of providing capitated, guaranteed care for a defined population. The fundamental element of the health care reform proposal of the current administration in Washington is based upon a similar concept of guaranteed health care for every American. What will be the future of health care in the year 2000? It's hard to tell, there are simply too many alternatives—or are there?

NOTE

1. A. Michel and I. Shaked, *The Complete Guide to a Successful Leveraged Buyout* (Homewood, Ill.: Dow-Jones-Irwin, 1988). Also recommended reading on this subject is the same authors' earlier book, *Takeover Madness: Corporate America Fights Back*. (New York: John Wiley & Sons, 1986).

MONTAGUE BROWN, MBA, DrPH, JD, is Chairman of Strategic Management Services, Inc., a national management consulting firm in Washington, D.C. He is Of Counsel with the law firm of Calligaro and Mutryn, Washington, D.C. and is also Editor of *Health Care Management Review*.

Dr. Brown's practice focuses on strategic issues and policies including mergers, vision and strategy, active aging, and building comprehensive vertically integrated systems of health service.

Dr. Brown holds an AB and a MBA from the University of Chicago, a Doctor of Public Health and JD from the University of North Carolina. He has lectured at dozens of universities and participated in international workshops in Canada, Austria, Germany, and England. He continues to lecture, write, and participate actively in ongoing research and education programs.

RUSSELL C. COILE, JR., is President of the Health Forecasting Group of Santa Clarita, California. His latest books include *Revolution: The New Health Care System Takes Shape* (Grand Rounds Press/Whittle Books, 1993) and *The New Governance: Strategies for the Era of Health Reform* (Health Administration Press, 1994). He is the author/editor of the "Hospital Strategy Report" by Aspen Publishers, and his columns "Leading Edge" and "21st Century Physician" appear regularly in *Healthcare Forum Journal* and *California Physician*.

Index

Date Due
